The Complete

BIBLICAL

LIBRARY

The Complete
BIBLICAL
LIBRARY

THE NEW TESTAMENT
STUDY BIBLE

GALATIANS
through
PHILEMON

The Complete BIBLICAL LIBRARY

THE NEW TESTAMENT
Study Bible, Greek-English Dictionary,
Harmony of the Gospels

THE OLD TESTAMENT
Study Bible, Hebrew-English Dictionary

THE BIBLE ENCYCLOPEDIA

INTERNATIONAL EDITOR
THORALF GILBRANT

Executive Editor: Ralph W. Harris, M.A.
Computer Systems: Tor Inge Gilbrant

NATIONAL EDITORS

U.S.A.
Stanley M. Horton, Th.D.

NORWAY
Erling Utnem, Bishop
Arthur Berg, B.D.

DENMARK
Jorgen Glenthoj, Th.M.

SWEDEN
Hugo Odeberg, Ph.D., D.D.
Bertil E. Gartner, D.D.
Thorsten Kjall, M.A.
Stig Wikstrom, D.Th.M.

FINLAND
Aapelii Saarisalo, Ph.D.
Valter Luoto, Pastor
Matti Liljequist, B.D.

HOLLAND
Herman ter Welle, Pastor
Henk Courtz, Drs.

Project Coordinator: William G. Eastlake

INTERNATIONAL AND
INTERDENOMINATIONAL
BIBLE STUDY SYSTEM

THE NEW TESTAMENT STUDY BIBLE GALATIANS–PHILEMON

Executive Editor: Ralph W. Harris, M.A.

Editor: Stanley M. Horton, Th.D.

Managing Editor: Gayle Garrity Seaver, J.D.

WORLD LIBRARY PRESS, INC.
Springfield, Missouri, U.S.A.

Table of Contents

VERSE-BY-VERSE COMMENTARY
ERICH H. KIEHL, Th.D. **Galatians**
BERNARD ROSSIER, Ph.D. **Ephesians, Philippians, Colossians, Philemon**
GARY LEGGETT, M.A. **1, 2 Timothy, Titus**
STANLEY M. HORTON, Th.D. **1, 2 Thessalonians**

VARIOUS VERSIONS
GERARD J. FLOKSTRA, JR., D.Min.

BOARD OF REVIEW

Zenas Bicket, Ph.D.   Charles Harris, Ed.D.
Jesse Moon, D.Min.   Opal Reddin, D.Min.

STAFF

Production Coordinator: Cynthia Riemenschneider

Research Editor: Denis Vinyard, M.Div.

Senior Editors: Gary Leggett, M.A.; Dorothy B. Morris

Editorial Team: Lloyd Anderson; Ken Barney; Betty Bates; Norma Gott; Charlotte Gribben; Faith Horton, B.A.; Mary Jane Jaynes; Connie Leggett; Brenda Lochner; Marietta Vinyard

Art Director: Terry Van Someren, B.F.A.

Word Processing and Secretarial: Faye Faucett; Sonja Jensen; Don Williams, M.Div.; Rachel Wisehart, B.A.

Material written by Bernard Rossier adapted by him from his book *Praise from Prison: Ephesians, Philippians, Colossians and Philemon,* published by House of Bon Giovanni ©1968.

Introduction

This volume of the *Study Bible* is part of a 16-volume set titled *The Complete Biblical Library*. It is an ambitious plan to provide all the information one needs for a basic understanding of the New Testament—useful for scholars but also for students and lay people.

In addition to the Harmony, *The Complete Biblical Library* provides a 9-volume *Study Bible* and a 6-volume *Greek-English Dictionary*. They are closely linked. You will find information about the *Study Bible's* features later in the Introduction. The *Greek-English Dictionary* lists all the Greek words of the New Testament in their alphabetic order, provides a concordance showing each place the words appear in the New Testament, and includes an article explaining the background, significance, and meaning of the words.

FEATURES OF THE STUDY BIBLE

The *Study Bible* is a unique combination of study materials which will help both the scholar and the layman achieve a better understanding of the New Testament and the language in which it was written. All of these helps are available in various forms but bringing them together in combination will save many hours of research. Most scholars do not have in their personal libraries all the volumes necessary to provide the information so readily available here.

The editors of *The Complete Biblical Library* are attempting an unusual task: to help scholars in their research but also to make available to laymen the tools by which to acquire knowledge which up to this time has been available only to scholars.

Following are the major divisions of the *Study Bible*:

Overview

Each volume contains an encyclopedic survey of the New Testament book. It provides a general outline, discusses matters about which there may be a difference of opinion, and provides background information regarding the history, culture, literature, and philosophy of the era covered by the book.

Interlinear

Following the overall principle of providing help for both the scholar and the layman, we supply a unique *Interlinear*. Most interlinears, if not all, give merely the Greek text and the meanings of the words. Our *Interlinear* contains *five* parts:

1. *Greek Text.* Our Greek text is a comparative text which includes both the traditional text type and the text which is common in modern textual editions.

2. *Grammatical Forms.* These are shown above each Greek word, alongside its assigned number. This information is repeated, along with the Greek word, in the *Greek-English Dictionary* where more details may be found.

3. *Transliteration.* No other interlinears provide this. Its purpose is to familiarize laymen with the proper pronunciation of Greek words so they will feel comfortable when using them in teaching situations. Complete information on pronunciation is found on the page showing the Greek and Hebrew alphabets.

4. *Translation.* The basic meaning of each Greek word is found beneath it. Rather than merely accepting the work of past interlinears, we have assigned scholars to upgrade words to a more modern description. See a later section for the principles we have followed in translation of the Greek words in our *Interlinear*.

5. *Assigned Numbers.* The unique numbering system of *The Complete Biblical Library* makes cross-reference study between the *Study Bible* and the *Greek-English Dictionary* the ultimate in simplicity. Each Greek word has been assigned a number. *Alpha* is the first word in alphabetic order as well as the first letter of the Greek alphabet, so the number *1* has been assigned to it. The rest of the almost 5,000 words follow in numerical and alphabetic sequence.

The *Greek-English Dictionary* follows the same plan with each word listed in alphabetic sequence. If a student desires further study on a certain word, he can find its number above it and locate it in the dictionary. In moments he has access to all the valuable information he needs for a basic understanding of that word.

Textual Apparatus

As said above, our Greek text is a comparative text. A text based only upon the *Textus Receptus* is not adequate for today's needs. Also, an eclectic text—using the "best" from various text types—will not be satisfactory, because such an approach may be quite subjective, with decisions influenced by the personal viewpoint of the scholar. Our text is a combination of both the main types of the Greek New Testament text. We have the *Textus Receptus*, a Stephanus text, based on the Byzantine text type. When there are important variants which differ from the *Textus Receptus*, they are included within brackets in the text. In the narrow column to the left of the *Interlinear*, the sources of the variants are listed. This will provide a fascinating study for a scholar and student, and will save him innumerable hours of research.

Verse-by-Verse Commentary

Many Bible-loving scholars have combined their knowledge, study, and skills to provide this. It is not an exhaustive treatment (many other commentaries are available for that), but again it provides a basic understanding of every verse in the New Testament. It does not usually deal with textual criticism (that can be dealt with in another arena), but it opens up the nuances of the Greek New Testament as written by the inspired writers.

Various Versions

This offers a greatly amplified New Testament. Each verse is broken down into its phrases; the King James Version is shown in boldface type; then from more than 60 other versions we show various ways the Greek of that phrase may be translated. The Greek of the First Century was such a rich language that to obtain the full meaning of words, several synonyms may be needed.

TRANSLATION OF GREEK WORDS

No word-for-word translation can be fully "literal" in the sense of expressing all the nuances of the original language. Rather, our purpose is to help the student find the English word which most correctly expresses the original Greek word in that particular context. The Greek language is so rich in meaning that the same word may have a slightly different meaning in another context.

In any language idioms offer a special translation problem. According to the dictionary, this is an expression which has "a meaning which cannot be derived from the conjoined meanings of its elements." The Greek language abounds in such phrases which cannot be translated literally.

We have come to what we consider a splendid solution to the problem, whether the translation should be strictly literal or abound in a plethora of idiomatic expressions. From more than 60 translations, the *Various Versions* column presents the various ways phrases have been translated. Here the student will find the translations of the idioms. This enables us to make our English line in the *Interlinear* strictly literal. The student will have available both types of translation—and will have a fresh appreciation for the struggles through which translators go.

HOW THE NEW TESTAMENT CAME TO US

Volume 1 of *The Complete Biblical Library*, the *Harmony of the Gospels*, contains information on how the four Gospels came into being. The preponderance of proof points to the fact that the rest of the New Testament was written before A.D. 100. Like the Gospels, it was written in Greek, the universal language of that era. It was qualified in a special way for this purpose. Probably no other language is so expressive and able to provide such fine nuances of meaning.

Yet the New Testament Greek is not the perfectly structured form of the language from the old classical period. It is the more simple Koine Greek from the later Hellenistic age. This had become the lingua franca of the Hellenistic and Roman world. The Egyptian papyri have shown that the language which the New Testament writers used was the common language of the people. It seems as though God accomodated himself to a form of communication which would make His Word most readily accepted and easily understood.

7

At the same time we should recognize that the language of the Greek New Testament also is a *religious language*, with a tradition going back a couple of centuries to the Septuagint, the Greek translation of the Old Testament.

The Manuscripts

None of the original manuscripts (handwritten documents) still exist. Even in the First Century they must have often been copied so as to share their treasured truths with numerous congregations of believers. The original documents then soon became worn out through use. Evidently, only copies of the New Testament still exist.

Over 5,000 manuscripts of the New Testament have been discovered up to the present time. Most of them are small fragments of verses or chapters, a few books of the New Testament, some copies of the Gospels. Very few contain all or nearly all of the New Testament.

The manuscripts have come to us in various forms: (1) Egyptian papyri, (2) majuscules, (3) minuscules, (4) writings of the Early Church fathers, (5) lectionaries, and (6) early versions.

The Egyptian Papyri

These are the oldest copies of parts of the Greek New Testament. The earliest are dated about A.D. 200, a few even earlier, and the youngest are from the Seventh Century. Most of them date back to the Third, Fourth and Fifth Centuries of the Christian Era.

They were found in the late 1800s in Egypt. The dry climatic conditions of that country enabled them to be preserved. The largest fragments contain only a few dozen pages, while the smallest are the size of a postage stamp.

The papyri are listed in the back of this volume under the heading "Manuscripts."

The Majuscules

These are the second oldest kind of copies of New Testament manuscripts. They received this description because they were written in majuscules; that is, large letters (the uncials are a form of majuscules). Three major majuscules are the following:

1. Codex Aleph, also called Codex Sinaiticus, because it was discovered in the mid-1840s by the great scholar Tischendorf at St. Catharine's Monastery, located at the foot of Mount Sinai. Numbered 01, it contains all the New Testament and is dated in the Fourth Century.

2. Codex A, numbered 02, is named Alexandrinus, because it came from Alexandria in Egypt. In the Gospels, this manuscript is the foremost witness to the Byzantine text type.

3. Codex B, 03, is called Codex Vaticanus, because it is in the Vatican library. Along with the Sinaiticus, it is the main witness for the Egyptian text type. However, it is important to realize there are more than 3,000 differences between these 2 manuscripts in the Gospels alone (Hoskier).

See the list of majuscules in the back of this volume, under "Manuscripts."

The Minuscules

This is a kind of manuscript written in small letters. They are only a few hundred years old, beginning with the Ninth Century. Most come from the 12th to the 14th Century A.D. They form, by far, the greatest group of the New Testament manuscripts, numbering almost 2,800.

The minuscules represent the unbroken text tradition in the Greek Orthodox Church, and about 90 percent of them belong to the Byzantine text group. They are numbered 1, 2, 3, etc.

Lectionaries and Church Fathers

Lectionaries include manuscripts which were not Scripture themselves but contain Scripture quotations, used for the scheduled worship services of the annual church calendar. These are numbered consecutively and are identified by *lect.*

Practically all the New Testament could be retrieved from the writings of early Christian leaders, called church fathers. These lists are located in the back of this volume.

Early Versions

Translations of the New Testament from Greek are also of value. They are listed under "Manuscripts" in the back of this volume. The best known is the Latin Vulgate by Jerome.

Major Greek Texts

From the manuscripts which have just been described, various types of Greek texts have been formed:

The Western text can possibly be traced back to the Second Century. It was used mostly in Western Europe and North Africa. It tends to add to the text and makes long paraphrases of it. Today some scholars do not recognize it as a special text type.

The Caesarean text may have originated in Egypt and was brought, it is believed, to the city of Caesarea in Palestine. Later, it was carried to Jerusalem, then by Armenian missionaries into a province in the kingdom of Georgia, now a republic of the U.S.S.R. Some scholars consider it a mixture of other text types.

The two most prominent text types, however, are the Egyptian (also called the Alexandrian) and the Byzantine. These are the major ones considered in our *Interlinear* and *Textual Apparatus*. Except for the papyrus texts which are highly varied, these are the only text families which have any degree of support. References to numerous text groups which were so common a few decades ago must now probably be considered out of date. At any rate, out of practical considerations, we have kept the Byzantine and Egyptian (Alexandrian) as fixed text groups in our *Textual Apparatus*. Following is historical information about them.

The Byzantine Text

Many titles have been applied to this text type. It has been called the *K* (Koine), Syrian, Antiochian, and Traditional. It is generally believed to have been produced at Antioch in Syria, then taken to Byzantium, later known as Constantinople. For about 1,000 years, while the Byzantine Empire ruled the Middle East, this was the text used by the Greek Orthodox Church. It also influenced Europe.

Because of this background it became the basis for the first printed text editions, among others the famous *Textus Receptus*, called "the acknowledged text."

The Byzantine text form is also called the Majority text, since 80 to 90 percent of all existing manuscripts are represented in this text, though most of them are quite recent and evidently copies of earlier manuscripts. Like the Egyptian text, the Byzantine text can be traced back to the Fourth Century. It also contains some readings which seem to be the same as some papyri which can be traced back to a much earlier time. Among the oldest majuscules the Byzantine is, among others, represented by Codex Alexandrinus (02, A), 07, 08, 09, 010, 011, 012, 013, 015, and others.

The Egyptian Text

This text type originated in Egypt and is the one which gained the highest recognition and acceptance there in the Fourth Century. It was produced mainly by copyists in Alexandria, from which it received the name *Alexandrian*. This text form is represented mostly by two codices: Sinaiticus (01, Aleph) and Vaticanus (03, B) from the Fourth Century, also from Codex Ephraemi (04, C) from the Fifth Century. The use of this text type ceased about the year 450 but lived on in the Latin translation, the Vulgate version.

Printed Greek Texts

The invention of printing about 1450 opened the door for wider distribution of the Scriptures. In 1516 Erasmus, a Dutch scholar, produced the first *printed* Greek New Testament. It was based on the Byzantine text type, with most of the New Testament coming from manuscripts dated at about the 12th Century. He did his work very hurriedly, finishing his task in just a few months. His second edition, produced in 1519 with some of the mistakes corrected, became the basis for translations into German by Luther and into English by Tyndale.

A printed Greek New Testament was produced by a French printer, Stephanus, in 1550. His edition and those produced by Theodore Beza, of Geneva, between 1565 and 1604, based on the Byzantine text, have been entitled the *Textus Receptus*. That description, however, originated with the text produced by Elzevir. He described his second edition of 1633 by the Latin phrase *Textus Receptus*, or the "Received Text"; that is, the one accepted generally as the correct one.

A list of the printed editions of the Greek text is found in the section describing the relationship of the *Interlinear* and the *Textual Apparatus*.

Contribution of Westcott and Hort

Two British scholars, Westcott and Hort, have played a prominent role in deciding which text type should be used. They (especially Hort) called the Byzantine text "corrupt," because of the young age of its supporting manuscripts and proceeded to develop their own text (1881-86). It was really a restoration of the Egyptian text from the Fourth Century. It depended mainly on two codices, Sinaiticus and Vaticanus, but was also supported by numerous majuscules such as 02, 04, 019, 020, 025, 032, 033, 037, and 044.

Westcott and Hort opposed the *Textus Receptus* because it was based on the Byzantine text form. Most scholars agreed with their contention, and the *Textus Receptus* fell into disrepute. However, Westcott and Hort made their assumptions before the Greek papyri were discovered, and in recent years some scholars have come to the defense of the Byzantine text and the *Textus Receptus*. They have learned that some of the readings in the Byzantine text are the same as those found in the earliest papyri, dated about A.D. 200 and even earlier (p45, p46, p64 and p66, for example). This seems to take the Byzantine text back at least as far as the Egyptian.

Two important statements must be made: (1) We should always remember there are good men and scholars on both sides of the controversy, and their major concern is to obtain as pure a text as possible, to reassure Bible students that the New Testament we now possess conforms to that written in the First Century. (2) Since it was the original writings which were inspired by the Holy Spirit, it is important for us to ascertain as closely as possible how well our present-day text agrees with the original writings. It should alleviate the fears some may have as to whether we have the true gospel enunciated in the First Century to know that most of the differences in the Greek text (about 1 percent of the total) are minor in nature and do not affect the great Christian doctrines we hold dear. Significant differences may be found in only a very few cases.

We have consciously avoided polemics in the area of textual criticism. There is legitimacy for such discussion, but *The Complete Biblical Library* is not the arena for such a conflict. (1) Often the opposing views are conjectural. (2) There is insufficient space to treat subjects adequately and to raise questions without answering them fully leads to confusion.

LITERARY AND BIBLICAL STANDARDS

Several hundred people, highly qualified scholars and specialists in particular fields have participated in producing *The Complete Biblical Library*. Great care has been taken to maintain high standards of scholarship and ethics. By involving scholars in Boards of Review for the *Study Bible* and the *Greek-English Dictionary*, we added an extra step to the editorial process. We have been particularly concerned about giving proper credit for citations from other works and have instructed our writers to show care in this regard. Any deviation from this principle has been inadvertent and not intentional.

Obviously, with writers coming from widely differing backgrounds, there are differences of opinion as to how to interpret certain passages.

We have tried to be just. When there are strong differences on the meaning of a particular passage, we have felt it best to present the contrasting viewpoints.

STUDY HELPS

As you come to the Scripture section of this volume, you will find correlated pages for your study. The facing pages are designed to complement each other, so you will have a better understanding of the Word of God than ever before. Each two-page spread will deal with a group of verses.

On the left-hand page is the *Interlinear* with its fivefold helps: (1) the Greek text in which the New Testament was written; (2) the transliteration, showing how to pronounce each word; (3) the basic meaning of each word; (4) next to Greek words an assigned number (you will need this number to learn more about the word in the *Greek-English Dictionary*, companion to the *Study Bible*); and (5) the grammatical forms of each Greek word. The left-hand page also contains a column called the *Textual Apparatus*. This column is explained later.

The right-hand page contains two features. The *Verse-by-Verse Commentary* refers to each verse, except when occasionally it deals with some closely related verses. The *Various Versions* column provides an expanded understanding of the various ways Greek words or phrases can be translated. The phrase from the King James Version appears first in boldface print, then other meaningful ways the Greek language has been translated. This feature will bring to you the riches of the language in which the New Testament first appeared.

General Abbreviations

In a work of this nature it is necessary to use some abbreviations in order to conserve space. In deference to the Scriptures it is our custom not to abbreviate the titles of the books of the Bible, but abbreviations are used elsewhere. Becoming familiar with them will enable you to pursue in-depth study more effectively.

The following are general abbreviations which you will find used throughout the book:

cf.	compared to or see
ibid.	in the same place
id.	the same
idem	the same
i.e.	that is
e.g.	for example
f. ff.	and following page or pages
sic	intended as written
MS(S)	manuscript(s)
ET	editor's translation

Introduction Continued

Greek

A	α	alpha	a	(f<u>a</u>ther)
B	β	beta	b	
Γ	γ	gamma	g	(<u>g</u>ot)
Δ	δ	delta	d	
E	ε	epsilon	e	(g<u>e</u>t)
Z	ζ	zeta	z	dz (lea<u>ds</u>)
H	η	eta	ē	(<u>a</u>te)
Θ	θ	theta	th	(<u>th</u>in)
I	ι	iota	i	(s<u>i</u>n or mach<u>i</u>ne)
K	κ	kappa	k	
Λ	λ	lambda	l	
M	μ	mu	m	
N	ν	nu	n	
Ξ	ξ	xi	x	
O	ο	omicron	o	(l<u>o</u>t)
Π	π	pi	p	
P	ϱ	rho	r	
Σ	σ,ς[1]	sigma	s	
T	τ	tau	t	
Y	υ	upsilon	u	German ü
Φ	φ	phi	ph	(<u>ph</u>ilosophy)
X	χ	chi	ch	(<u>ch</u>aos)
Ψ	ψ	psi	ps	(li<u>ps</u>)
Ω	ω	omega	ō	(<u>o</u>cean)

Hebrew

א	aleph	ˀ [2]	
ב, בּ	beth	b, v	
ג, גּ	gimel	g, gh	
ד, דּ	daleth	d, dh	(<u>th</u>ey)[3]
ה	he	h	
ו	waw	w	
ז	zayin	z	
ח	heth	ch	(kh)
ט	teth	ṭ	
י	yodh	y	
כ, כּ ךּ	kaph	k, kh	
ל	lamedh	l	
מ ם	mem	m	
נ ן	nun	n	
ס	samekh	s̱	
ע	ayin	ˁ	
פּ, פ ף	pe	p, ph	
צ ץ	sadhe	ts	
ק	qoph	q	
ר	resh	r	
שׂ	sin	s	
שׁ	shin	sh	
ת, תּ	taw	t, th	(<u>th</u>ing)[3]

Hebrew Vowels

ā	father		u	rule		ê	they
a	dam		ō	role		âh	ah
e	men		û	tune		ă	hat
ē	they		ô	hole		ě	met
i	pin		î	machine		e	av<u>e</u>rage
o	roll		ê	they		ŏ	not

Greek Pronunciation Rules
Before another *g*, or before a *k* or a *ch*, *g* is pronounced and spelled with an *n*, in the transliteration of the Greek word.
In the Greek, *s* is written at the end of a word, elsewhere it appears as σ. The rough breathing mark (῾) indicates that an *h*-sound is to be pronounced before the initial vowel or diphthong. The smooth breathing mark (᾿) indicates that no such *h*-sound is to be pronounced.
There are three accents, the acute (—́), the circumflex (—̑) and the grave (—̀). These stand over a vowel and indicate that stress in pronunciation is to be placed on the syllable having any one of the accents.

Pronouncing Diphthongs
ai is pronounced like *ai* in aisle
ei is pronounced like *ei* in eight
oi is pronounced like *oi* in oil
au is pronounced like *ow* in cow

eu is pronounced like *eu* in feud
ou is pronounced like *oo* in food
ui is pronounced like *ui* in suite (sweet)

1. Where two forms of a letter are given, the one at the right is used at the end of a word.
2. Not represented in transliteration when the initial letter.
3. Letters underscored represent pronunciation of the second form only.

Old and New Testament Books and Apocrypha

As a service to you, we have listed the books of the Bible in their order. The Apocrypha is a series of books which were included in the Vulgate version (the Latin translation of the Bible endorsed by the Roman Catholic Church). Though not considered part of the canon by either the Jews or Protestants, they give interesting insights, on occasion, concerning the times with which they deal. They are not on the same level as the 66 books of our canon. These lists are located in the back of the book.

Bibliographic Citations

The Complete Biblical Library has adopted a system of coordinated citations in the text and bibliography material which accommodates every type of reader. For the sake of simplicity and space, information given in the text to document a source is minimal, often including only the last name of the writer, or a shortened title and a page number.

Those who would like to research the subject more deeply can easily do so by looking in the Bibliography in the back of the book under the last name or shortened title. The Bibliography lists complete information necessary to locate the source in a library, supplemented by the page number given in the citation in the text.

RELATIONSHIP OF THE INTERLINEAR AND THE TEXTUAL APPARATUS

The Greek text of the *Study Bible* provides a means of collating the traditional texts with modern text editions; that is, comparing them critically to discover their degree of similarity or divergence. The *Textual Apparatus* column provides information as to which manuscripts or groups of manuscripts support certain readings. Some scholarly works use an eclectic text, selecting from various sources the text they consider to be the best. In our view, our comparative text provides a better system for considering the relative merits of the major texts.

The *Textual Apparatus* refers to many different manuscripts but to just two text groups, the Byzantine and the Egyptian, also known as Alexandrian. Except for the papyri texts, which are highly varied, these two text families are the only ones which have a significant degree of support. Reference to many different text groups is now becoming passé. Using only the byz (Byzantine) and eg (Egyptian) text groups makes the work of the researcher less complicated and provides an adequate system of reference.

The *Interlinear* uses the Stephanus text as its basis but is not confined to it. Actually, most of the Greek text is the same in all the text types. For easy comparison variants are inserted in the text and are then considered in the *Textual Apparatus* column, which provides their background in the major and minor manuscripts.

Abbreviations and Signs Used in the Textual Apparatus

Using the information which follows you will be able to identify the variants and their sources and to compare them with the basic text and other variants.

Txt	The Greek text used, the TR
byz	Byzantine text form
eg	Egyptian text form
p 1, etc.	Papyrus manuscripts
01, etc.	Majuscule manuscripts
1, etc.	Minuscule manuscripts
lect	Lectionaries
org	Reading of original copier
corr 1, etc.	Change by another person
( )	Supports in principle
sa	Sahidic
bo	Bohairic

Printed Editions of the Greek Text (with abbreviations)

Steph	Stephanus, 1550
Beza	Beza, 1564-1604
Elzev	Elzevir, 1624
Gries	Griesbach, 1805
Lach	Lachmann, 1842-50
Treg	Tregelles, 1857-72
Alf	Alford, 1862-71
Tisc	Tischendorf, 1865-95
Word	Wordsworth, 1870
We/Ho	Westcott and Hort, 1881-86
Wey	Weymouth, 1885
Weis	Weiss, 1894-1900
Sod	von Soden, 1902-10
H/Far	Hodges and Farstad (Majority text)
☆	various modern text editions
UBS	United Bible Society

Understanding the Codes in the Greek Text and the Textual Apparatus

Definitions:

TR. The *Textus Receptus*, the basic text of this *Interlinear*.

Reading. A word or phrase from a Greek text.

Variant. A reading which differs from the TR.

The *Textual Apparatus* contains two divisions for analyzing the text when variants occur: *Txt*, meaning the TR (*Textus Receptus*); and *Var*, meaning variants, readings which differ from the TR. Under these two headings are listed the manuscripts which support either the TR or the variant.

Illustrations:

The following examples from Luke 10:19-21 show how to understand the relationship between the Greek text and the *Textual Apparatus*.

The half-parenthesis indicates that the next word begins a TR reading for which a variant is shown. See example A.

The variant itself is enclosed in brackets (note the example of this at the beginning of verse 19). The text (TR) reads, "I give . . . ," but the variant reads, "I have given . . . ." See example B.

The small *a* at the beginning of the bracket refers back to the *Textual Apparatus* column, showing it is the first variant in that particular verse. See example C. Only those variants identified by *a, b, c,* etc., are considered in the *Textual Apparatus*.

The star following the *a* means that the variant is used in some modern text editions, such as the UBS text. See example D.

Note that in variant *b* of verse 19 the star appears before the TR word. This means that in this case UBS and/or others do not follow the variant but read the same as the TR. See example E.

In verse 20, variant *a* appears between two half-parentheses, showing *mallon* ("rather") is not included in some texts. The TR reads, "Rejoice but rather that . . . ," while the variant (without *mallon*) reads, "Rejoice but that . . . ." See example F.

It is important to recognize that the star in the *Textual Apparatus* for verse 20 means that UBS and other modern texts support the variant reading. If the UBS supported the TR, the star would have appeared under the *Txt* heading. See example G.

Sometimes there is more than one variant reading, as in variant *b* of verse 20. In such cases they are numbered in order (see the *2* before the star in the second reading). This shows the difference and also provides an easy reference in the *Textual Apparatus*. See example H.

In verse 21, variant *a* presents a case where the word *en* ("in") is not a part of the TR but appears in other texts. The + sign indicates this. See example I.

Understanding the Codes in the Greek Text and the Textual Apparatus

Example A.

⌐

Example B.

[ ]

Example C.

abc

Example D.

☆

Example E.

Example F.

⌐ ⌐

Example G.

Example H.

123

Example I.

+

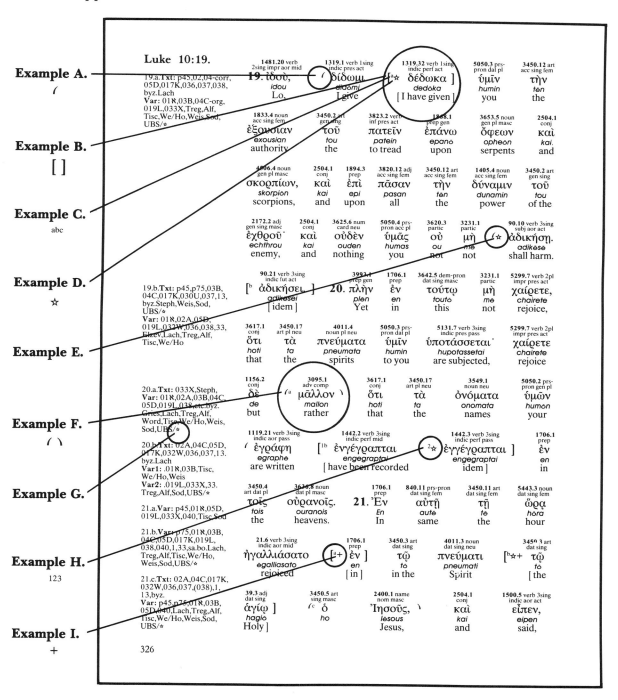

15

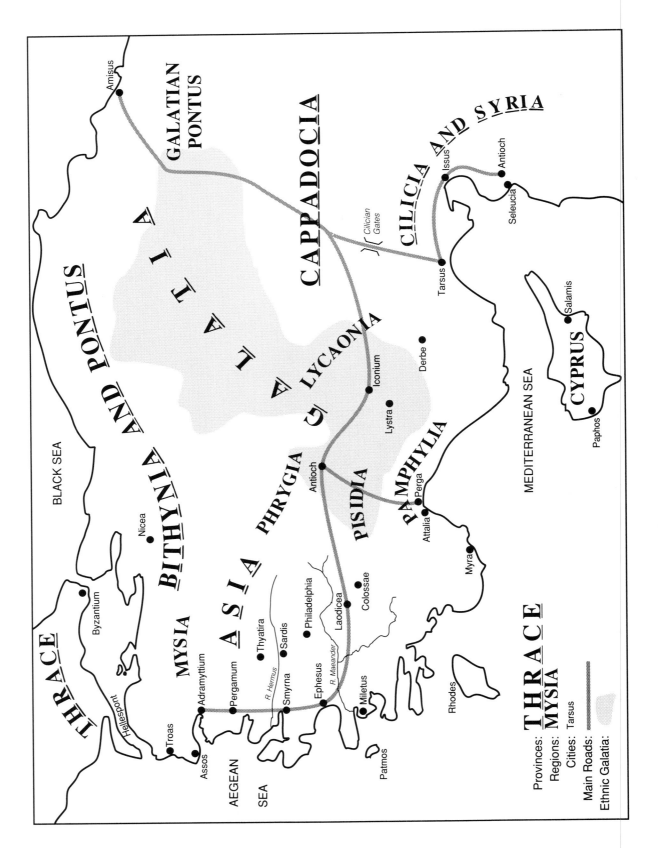

THRACE
MYSIA
Troas
Assos
Byzantium
Hellespont
AEGEAN
SEA
BITHYNIA AND PONTUS
Nicea
MYSIA
Adramyttium
Pergamum
R. Hermus
Thyatira
Sardis
Smyrna
ASIA
Ephesus
Philadelphia
Laodicea
Colossae
R. Maeander
Miletus
Patmos
Rhodes
BLACK SEA
Amisus
GALATIAN
PONTUS
GALATIA
PHRYGIA
Antioch
PISIDIA
Perga
Attalia
PAMPHYLIA
Myra
LYCAONIA
Iconium
Lystra
Derbe
CAPPADOCIA
Cilician
Gates
Tarsus
CILICIA AND SYRIA
Issus
Antioch
Seleucia
CYPRUS
Salamis
Paphos
MEDITERRANEAN SEA

Provinces: **THRACE**
Regions: MYSIA
Cities: Tarsus
Main Roads: ▬▬▬
Ethnic Galatia:

16

THE EPISTLE
OF PAUL TO THE
GALATIANS

Expanded Interlinear

Textual Critical Apparatus

Verse-by-Verse Commentary

Various Versions

4242.1
prep

1046.3
name gen fem

1976.1 noun
nom sing fem

3834.2 name
gen masc

Πρὸς Γαλάτας ἐπιστολὴ Παύλου

Pros   *Galatas*   *epistolē*   *Paulou*

To   Galatians   letter   of Paul

Textual Apparatus

3834.1 name nom masc	646.1 noun nom sing masc	3620.2 partic	570.2 prep	442.7 noun gen pl masc	3624.1 conj
1:1. Παῦλος	ἀπόστολος,	οὐκ	ἀπ'	ἀνθρώπων	οὐδὲ
Paulos	*apostolos*	*ouk*	*ap'*	*anthrōpōn*	*oude*
Paul	apostle,	not	from	men	nor

1217.1 prep	442.2 noun gen sing masc	233.2 conj	1217.2 prep	2400.2 name masc	5382.2 name gen masc	2504.1 conj
δι'	ἀνθρώπου,	ἀλλὰ	διὰ	Ἰησοῦ	Χριστοῦ,	καὶ
di'	*anthrōpou*	*alla*	*dia*	*Iēsou*	*Christou*	*kai*
through	man,	but	through	Jesus	Christ,	and

2296.2 noun gen sing masc	3824.2 noun gen sing masc	3450.2 art gen sing	1446.8 verb gen sing masc part aor act	840.6 prs-pron acc sing masc	1523.2 prep gen
θεοῦ	πατρὸς	τοῦ	ἐγείραντος	αὐτὸν	ἐκ
theou	*patros*	*tou*	*egeirantos*	*auton*	*ek*
God	Father,	the	having raised	him	from among

3361.2 adj gen pl	2504.1 conj	3450.7 art nom pl masc	4713.1 prep	1466.5 prs-pron dat 1sing	3820.7 adj nom pl masc	79.6 noun nom pl masc
νεκρῶν,	**2.** καὶ	οἱ	σὺν	ἐμοὶ	πάντες	ἀδελφοί,
nekrōn	*kai*	*hoi*	*sun*	*emoi*	*pantes*	*adelphoi*
dead,	and	the	with	me	all	brothers,

3450.14 art dat pl fem	1564.7 noun dat pl fem	3450.10 art gen sing fem	1046.1 name gen fem	5322.1 noun nom sing fem	5050.3 prs-pron dat 2pl
ταῖς	ἐκκλησίαις	τῆς	Γαλατίας·	**3.** χάρις	ὑμῖν
tais	*ekklēsiais*	*tēs*	*Galatias*	*charis*	*humin*
to the	assemblies	the	of Galatia.	Grace	to you

2504.1 conj	1503.1 noun nom sing fem	570.3 prep	2296.2 noun gen sing masc	3824.2 noun gen sing masc	2504.1 conj	2935.2 noun gen sing masc
καὶ	εἰρήνη	ἀπὸ	θεοῦ	πατρὸς	' καὶ	κυρίου
kai	*eirēnē*	*apo*	*theou*	*patros*	*kai*	*kuriou*
and	peace	from	God	Father	and	Lord

2231.2 prs-pron gen 1pl	2231.2 prs-pron gen 1pl	2504.1 conj	2935.2 noun gen sing masc	2400.2 name masc	5382.2 name gen masc
ἡμῶν	[☆ ἡμῶν	καὶ	κυρίου]	Ἰησοῦ	Χριστοῦ,
hēmōn	*hēmōn*	*kai*	*kuriou*	*Iēsou*	*Christou*
our	[our	and	Lord]	Jesus	Christ,

3450.2 art gen sing	1319.29 verb gen sing masc part aor act	1431.6 prs-pron acc sing masc	5065.1 prep	3875.1 prep
4. τοῦ	δόντος	ἑαυτὸν	'☆ ὑπὲρ	[ª περί]
tou	*dontos*	*heauton*	*huper*	*peri*
the	having given	himself	for	[on behalf of]

3450.1 art gen pl	264.6 noun gen pl fem	2231.2 prs-pron gen 1pl	3567.1 conj	1791.5 verb 3sing subj aor mid	2231.4 prs-pron acc 1pl
τῶν	ἁμαρτιῶν	ἡμῶν,	ὅπως	ἐξέληται	ἡμᾶς
tōn	*hamartiōn*	*hēmōn*	*hopōs*	*exelētai*	*hēmas*
the	sins	our,	so that	he might deliver	us

4.a.Txt: 01‭א‬-corr1,03B
015H,6,33,81,326,365
1175,1241,2464
Var: p46-vid,01‭א‬-org
02A,06D,010F,012G
044,byz.

18

THE EPISTLE OF PAUL TO THE
GALATIANS

1:1. In his letters Paul followed the usual ancient letter pattern: greetings, prayer for addressees, thanksgiving, the particular contents of the letter, special salutations and greetings. In Galatians, these divisions break down as follows: the greetings and prayer for the addressees, 1:1-5; the particular contents, 1:6 to 6:17; and the special salutations and greetings, 6:18. Paul has omitted the thanksgiving since the Galatian Christians were tempted to leave the way of grace for that of law, of works.

Some Jewish Christians in Jerusalem failed to understand the true meaning of salvation by grace alone; they thought that to believe in Jesus was only the beginning. Each believer was expected to live totally as a Jew in order to be saved. This included circumcision. Acts 15:1,2 informs us that these Jews from Jerusalem had come to Antioch and caused havoc in the church. Some went on to trouble the new churches in Galatia.

These Jewish Christians, often termed Judaizers, had told the Christians of Galatia Paul had not been faithful to his instruction, that he had failed to tell them the complete requirements for salvation. Because of this, in his opening statements Paul stressed that he had received his commission as an apostle not *from* men nor *through the agency of* man. Rather, he had been personally called "by Jesus Christ, and God the Father." Then he added an important phrase: "who raised him from the dead." Christ's resurrection guaranteed the certainty of salvation by grace alone (1 Corinthians 15; Colossians 1:13-23).

1:2-4. The Christians at Antioch, including Barnabas, joined Paul in greeting the churches which he and Barnabas had established during their first missionary journey (Acts chapters 13 and 14). "Grace" means God's unmerited love made possible through the atoning work of Jesus Christ. "Peace" with God is the blessed result of receiving God's unmerited grace. Peace is spiritual well-being (Romans 5:1,2). Paul added, "and from our Lord Jesus Christ." Because He has paid the ransom price for the believer's salvation, He is their Lord and King. Christians belong to Him completely as their spiritual King (Romans 6). "Jesus" means "Saviour" as the angel explained to Joseph (Matthew 1:21).

To stress the certainty of grace, Paul carefully explained the true role of Christ (verse 4), namely, as the One who gave himself freely for the salvation of the world. The Jews viewed the present age as the wicked age, the age of the Evil One. In contrast, the age to

Various Versions

1. Paul, an apostle, (not of men, neither by man, but by Jesus Christ, and God the Father, who raised him from the dead;): . . . a legate, *Murdock* . . . I, Paul, who am appointed and commissioned a messenger, *Phillips* . . . whose call to be an apostle did not come from man, *TEV* . . . not from man or through man, but appointed by, *Fenton* . . . not even through the intermediate agency of man, *Wuest* . . . not by human appointment or human commission, *NEB* . . . whose authority is not derived from men and is due, not to man, *TCNT* . . . I was not chosen by men, *SEB* . . . nor commissioned by any man, *Moffatt* . . . Who rouses Him from among the dead, *Concordant* . . . who made him come back from the dead, *BB*.

2. And all the brethren which are with me, unto the churches of Galatia: . . . and the group of friends now with me, *NEB* . . . all the Christians, *Beck* . . . who are beside me, *Moffatt* . . . to the assemblies, *Rotherham, Worrell, Fenton* . . . to the Communities of, *HistNT* . . . To the congregations in the Galatian area, *Fenton*.

3. Grace [be] to you and peace from God the Father, and [from] our Lord Jesus Christ: . . . be kind to you and give you peace, *Fenton* . . . will be good to you, *Everyday* . . . spiritual blessing, *Williams* . . . favor to you, *Wilson* . . . peace be granted to you from, *Weymouth*.

4. Who gave himself for our sins: . . . who according to the Father's plan, *Phillips* . . . Jesus sacrificed himself for, *Fenton* . . . who gave Himself to suffer for, *Weymouth*.

4.b.Txt: 01ℵ-corr,06D
018K,020L,025P,byz.it.
Var: 01ℵ-org,02A,03B
33,Lach,Treg,Alf,Tisc
We/Ho,Weis,Sod
UBS/✩

1523.2 prep gen	3450.2 art gen sing	1748.2 verb gen sing masc part perf act	163.1 noun gen sing masc	163.1 noun gen sing masc
ἐκ	τοῦ	⸉ ἐνεστῶτος	αἰῶνος	[b✩ αἰῶνος
ek	tou	enestotos	aionos	aionos
out of	the	having been present	age	[age

3450.2 art gen sing	1748.2 verb gen sing masc part perf act	4050.2 adj gen sing	2567.3 prep	3450.16 art sing neu
τοῦ	ἐνεστῶτος]	πονηροῦ,	κατὰ	τὸ
tou	enestotos	ponerou	kata	to
the	having been present]	evil,	according to	the

2284.1 noun sing neu	3450.2 art gen sing	2296.2 noun gen sing masc	2504.1 conj	3824.2 noun gen sing masc	2231.2 prs-pron gen 1pl
θέλημα	τοῦ	θεοῦ	καὶ	πατρὸς	ἡμῶν,
thelema	tou	theou	kai	patros	hemon
will	the	of God	and	Father	our;

3614.3 rel-pron dat sing	3450.9 art nom sing fem	1385.1 noun nom sing fem	1519.1 prep	3450.8 art acc pl masc	163.6 noun acc pl masc	3450.1 art gen pl
5. ᾧ	ἡ	δόξα	εἰς	τοὺς	αἰῶνας	τῶν
ho	he	doxa	eis	tous	aionas	ton
to whom	the	glory	to	the	ages	of the

163.4 noun gen pl masc	279.1 intrj	2273.2 verb 1sing indic pres act	3617.1 conj	3643.1 adv	4878.1 adv
αἰώνων.	ἀμήν.	6. Θαυμάζω	ὅτι	οὕτως	ταχέως
aionon	amen	Thaumazo	hoti	houtos	tacheos
ages.	Amen.	I marvel	that	thus	quickly

3216.3 verb 2pl indic pres mid	570.3 prep	3450.2 art gen sing	2535.15 verb gen sing masc part aor act	5050.4 prs-pron acc 2pl
μετατίθεσθε	ἀπὸ	τοῦ	καλέσαντος	ὑμᾶς
metatithesthe	apo	tou	kalesantos	humas
you are being changed	from	the	having called	you

1706.1 prep	5322.3 noun dat sing fem	5382.2 name gen masc	1519.1 prep	2066.1 adj sing	2077.1 noun sing neu
ἐν	χάριτι	Χριστοῦ,	εἰς	ἕτερον	εὐαγγέλιον·
en	chariti	Christou	eis	heteron	euangelion
in	grace	Christ's,	to	a different	gospel,

3614.16 rel-pron sing neu	3620.2 partic	1498.4 verb 3sing indic pres act	241.14 adj sing neu	1479.1 conj	3231.1 partic	4948.7 indef-pron nom pl masc
7. ὃ	οὐκ	ἔστιν	ἄλλο,	εἰ	μὴ	τινές
ho	ouk	estin	allo	ei	me	tines
which	not	is	another;	if	not	some

1498.7 verb 3pl indic pres act	3450.7 art nom pl masc	4866.2 verb nom pl masc part pres act	5050.4 prs-pron acc 2pl	2504.1 conj	2286.16 verb nom pl masc part pres act
εἰσιν	οἱ	ταράσσοντες	ὑμᾶς,	καὶ	θέλοντες
eisin	hoi	tarassontes	humas	kai	thelontes
there are	the	disturbing	you,	and	wanting

3214.1 verb inf aor act	3450.16 art sing neu	2077.1 noun sing neu	3450.2 art gen sing	5382.2 name gen masc
μεταστρέψαι	τὸ	εὐαγγέλιον	τοῦ	Χριστοῦ.
metastrepsai	to	euangelion	tou	Christou
to distort	to	good news	of the	Christ:

233.2 conj	2504.1 conj	1430.1 partic	2231.1 prs-pron nom 1pl	2211.1 conj	32.1 noun nom sing masc	1523.1 prep gen
8. ἀλλὰ	καὶ	ἐὰν	ἡμεῖς	ἢ	ἄγγελος	ἐξ
alla	kai	ean	hemeis	e	angelos	ex
but	even	if	we	or	an angel	out of

come was to be an age of peace and prosperity for those who were truly members of God's covenant people. Paul stressed that such deliverance is the will of God who is also the Father. This tremendous statement reminds the believer of God's promise that the woman's Seed would crush the power of the Evil One (Genesis 3:15) and the prophecy of Isaiah 53 that Jesus would become the obedient suffering and then victorious Servant for man's salvation. Through the Spirit's work, all believers in Christ now belong to Him, yet are still in the present evil age (2 Corinthians 5:17-21).

1:5. The beautiful doxology Paul added here is not found at the end of the greetings and prayers in his other letters. God's glory means the total radiance of His presence, all that God is. God is worthy of ongoing praise and adoration to the end of time into all eternity (Psalms 29:2; 96:8). Paul ended his doxology with "Amen," solemnly confirming what he had just said. In Hebrew *'amēn* had the same emphatic force; the hearer (or writer) was strongly affirming the truth of the preceding statement. Other New Testament doxologies also end with Amen (e.g., Romans 16:27; 2 Peter 3:18), as do the Old Testament doxologies at the end of the first four sections of Psalms (Psalms 41:13; 72:19; 89:52; 106:48).

1:6,7. Paul's style now became more terse. He went at once to the very heart of the Galatians' problem. Acts 14:21-23 records that Paul and Barnabas stopped at each of the new mission churches in Southern Galatia to strengthen, encourage, and organize them before returning to Antioch. Paul's use of the phrase "so soon" suggests that not much time had passed before he heard that the Galatians were being influenced by the message of the Judaizers. Paul expressed his utter amazement and astonishment.

The apostle used the verb "called." The Galatians had been called by the grace of Christ. The Holy Spirit, working through the gospel which Paul and Barnabas had shared, had worked faith in their hearts (Titus 3:4-8).

But now they were being tempted by the Judaizers who stressed that salvation was by works, by living as Jews. In Acts 15:10 Peter said that to live according to the Law was too heavy a yoke for even Jews to carry, let alone requiring Gentiles to live that way. History informs us that before A.D. 70, the Jewish rabbis had added 341 rules for daily life.

Paul emphatically stated that the so-called "gospel" with which the Galatians were being tempted was "another" gospel. The Greek word translated "another" (*heteron*, verse 6) means "different in kind." Paul used this word to emphasize that the gospel which the Judaizers said was the true gospel was a totally false gospel. Then he went on to describe it as not being in any way a gospel at all.

1:8,9. To emphasize that he and Barnabas had shared the *genuine* gospel with them, Paul used a decisive illustration. He stated

that he might deliver us from this present evil world, according to the will of God and our Father: . . . in order that he might rescue us, *Wilson* . . . to rescue us from this present wicked age, *TCNT* . . . take us for himself out of the present age, *Rotherham* . . . the present evil age, *Panin* . . . from the present evil world order, *Phillips* . . . the present wickid world, *Wyclif* . . . evil life, *Sawyer*.

5. To whom [be] glory for ever and ever. Amen: . . . to the ages, *Rotherham* . . . for the ages of the ages, *Wilson*.

6. I marvel that ye are so soon removed from him that called you into the grace of Christ unto another gospel: I wonder, *Douay* . . . I am astonished, *Wilson* . . . I am astonished...deserting him, *TCNT* . . . that thus quickly ye are making a change, *Rotherham* . . . so quickly deserting him, *Confraternity* . . . ye are so sone turned from him, *Tyndale* . . . you are transferred from him, *Rheims* . . . so soon turning from him, *Noyes* . . . so quickly turned away, *Sawyer* . . . so quickly removing from him, *Panin* . . . unto a different gospel, *Alford* . . . forsaking him that had called you, *Geneva*.

7. Which is not another: . . . which is nothynge els, *Cranmer*.

but there be some that trouble you, and would pervert the gospel of Christ: . . . except in this respect that, *Confraternity* . . . certain persons are disturbing you, *Scarlett* . . . people who are harassing you, *TCNT* . . . who disturb you, *Sawyer* . . . would subvert, *Wesley* . . . wishing to change the joyful message of, *Rotherham* . . . seeking to change entirely the gospel, *Noyes*.

8. But though we, or an angel from heaven:

Galatians 1:9

8.a.Txt: 03B,06D,015H
020L,byz.Weis,Sod
Var: 01א,02A,Tisc
We/Ho,UBS/∗

3636.2 noun gen sing masc	2076.8 verb 3sing subj pres mid	2076.29 verb 3sing subj aor mid
οὐρανοῦ	ʼ εὐαγγελίζηται	[ᵃ εὐαγγελίσηται]
ouranou	*euangelizētai*	*euangelisētai*
heaven	should announce good news	[idem]

5050.3 prs- pron dat 2pl	3706.1 prep	3614.16 rel- pron sing neu	2076.18 verb 1pl indic aor mid	5050.3 prs- pron dat 2pl
ὑμῖν	παρʼ	ὃ	εὐηγγελισάμεθα	ὑμῖν,
humin	*parʼ*	*ho*	*euēngelisametha*	*humin*
to you	contrary to	what	we announced	to you,

329.1 noun sing neu	1498.17 verb 3sing impr pres act	5453.1 conj	4136.3 verb 1pl indic perf act	2504.1 conj	732.1 adv
ἀνάθεμα	ἔστω.	**9.** ὡς	προειρήκαμεν,	καὶ	ἄρτι
anathema	*estō*	*hōs*	*proeirēkamen*	*kai*	*arti*
accursed	let him be.	As	we have said before,	also	now

3687.1 adv	2978.1 verb 1sing pres act	1479.1 conj	4948.3 indef- pron nom sing	5050.4 prs- pron acc 2pl	2076.4 verb 3sing indic pres mid
πάλιν	λέγω,	εἴ	τις	ὑμᾶς	εὐαγγελίζεται
palin	*legō*	*ei*	*tis*	*humas*	*euangelizetai*
again	I say,	If	anyone	you	announces the gospel

3706.1 prep	3614.16 rel- pron sing neu	3741.7 verb 2pl indic aor act	329.1 noun sing neu	1498.17 verb 3sing impr pres act
παρʼ	ὃ	παρελάβετε,	ἀνάθεμα	ἔστω.
parʼ	*ho*	*parelabete*	*anathema*	*estō*
contrary to	what	you received,	accursed	let him be.

732.1 adv	1056.1 conj	442.9 noun acc pl masc	3844.1 verb 1sing indic pres act	2211.1 conj	3450.6 art acc sing masc
10. Ἄρτι	γὰρ	ἀνθρώπους	πείθω	ἢ	τὸν
Arti	*gar*	*anthrōpous*	*peithō*	*ē*	*ton*
Now	for	men	do I persuade	or	

2296.4 noun acc sing masc	2211.1 conj	2195.3 verb 1sing indic pres act	442.8 noun dat pl masc	694.5 verb inf pres act	1479.1 conj
θεόν;	ἢ	ζητῶ	ἀνθρώποις	ἀρέσκειν;	εἰ
theon	*ē*	*zētō*	*anthrōpois*	*areskein*	*ei*
God?	or	do I seek	men	to please?	If

10.a.Txt: 06D-corr,018K
020L,025P,byz.
Var: 01א,02A,03B
06D-org,33,it.bo.Lach
Treg,Alf,Word,Tisc
We/Ho,Weis,Sod
UBS/∗

1056.1 conj	2068.1 adv	442.8 noun dat pl masc	694.11 verb indic imperf act	5382.2 name gen masc
ʼᵃ γὰρ ʼ	ἔτι	ἀνθρώποις	ἤρεσκον,	Χριστοῦ
gar	*eti*	*anthrōpois*	*ēreskon*	*Christou*
for	yet	men	I were pleasing,	Christ's

1395.1 noun nom sing masc	3620.2 partic	300.1 partic	1498.46 verb 1sing indic imperf act	1101.1 verb 1sing indic pres act	1156.2 conj
δοῦλος	οὐκ	ἂν	ἤμην.	**11.** Γνωρίζω	ʼ δὲ
doulos	*ouk*	*an*	*ēmēn*	*Gnōrizō*	*de*
slave	not		I should be.	I make known	but

11.a.Txt: 01א-org,02A
06D-corr,018K,020L
025P,byz.bo.Tisc
Var: 01א-corr,03B
06D-org,33,Treg,Alf
We/Ho,Weis,Sod
UBS/∗

1056.1 conj	5050.3 prs- pron dat 2pl	79.6 noun nom pl masc	3450.16 art sing neu	2077.1 noun sing neu	3450.16 art sing neu
[ᵃ γὰρ]	ὑμῖν,	ἀδελφοί,	τὸ	εὐαγγέλιον	τὸ
gar	*humin*	*adelphoi*	*to*	*euangelion*	*to*
[for]	to you,	brothers,	the	good news	the

2076.24 verb sing neu part aor pass	5097.2 prep	1466.3 prs- pron gen 1sing	3617.1 conj	3620.2 partic	1498.4 verb 3sing indic pres act
εὐαγγελισθὲν	ὑπʼ	ἐμοῦ,	ὅτι	οὐκ	ἔστιν
euangelisthen	*hupʼ*	*emou*	*hoti*	*ouk*	*estin*
having been announced	by	me,	that	not	it is

that even if an angel from heaven would bring a gospel different from what they had shared, God's eternal curse and condemnation would rest on him. He restated this fact in another way to emphasize most emphatically the fatal consequences of listening to the Judaizers and their false gospel. All who believed what these were promoting as the true gospel would experience God's wrath and His eternal damnation. What the Judaizers were promoting as the only way to salvation was in fact the certain path to damnation.

1:10. Paul went on to stress that his role as the called apostle of Jesus Christ was to be faithful to the true gospel. Seemingly the Judaizers had accused him of seeking to please the Galatians by not telling them they had to live as Jews in order to be saved. Paul carefully stressed that this accusation was totally untrue. The gospel which he preached was that which he had received from Jesus Christ himself. And this true gospel he had faithfully shared with them.

1:11,12. Next Paul provided decisive information on how he had received the gospel. In doing so, he used the term translated "brethren" (*adelphoi*), fellow members of God's family. He used this affectionate term a number of times in this letter, especially when he had to use harsh words to emphasize that the true way of salvation is grace, not works. In this way he stressed that, despite their spiritual wavering, he still had a deep love for them as the sheep of God's flock. He also frequently used this affectionate term in other letters in which he had to take his readers to task for unchristian behavior or had to encourage them in the light of difficulties they faced. This is especially true of 1 and 2 Corinthians and 1 and 2 Thessalonians.

Paul informed them that the origin of the gospel he shared with them went back directly to a revelation of Jesus Christ himself. The Book of Acts records what happened, once in Luke's account (Acts 9:3-19) and twice in what Paul himself told two different sets of hearers. In Acts 22:3-16 Paul spoke to the temple mob which had almost killed him. In Acts 26:12-18 he spoke especially to Agrippa II, a part-Jew. In each of these instances, his listeners would understand that Paul had experienced a heavenly appearance of God's glory.

Each of these accounts stresses that on the Damascus Road an exceedingly bright glory-light shone down from heaven on Saul (Paul) and his companions. From the heavenly light came the voice of the risen and ascended Christ. Saul's respectful reaction to that voice indicates that he understood it was the glorified Christ himself.

Acts 25:13ff. records that Herod Agrippa II made a state visit to the Roman governor Festus in Caesarea. He was reputed to be an expert in Jewish religious questions. He also had the right to appoint the high priest. In the words spoken to Agrippa II and Festus, Paul carefully informed them what Jesus had told him. He

preach any other gospel unto you than that which we have preached unto you, let him be accursed: ... should announce glad tidings, *Wilson* ... preach to you another Gospel, *Wesley* ... contrary to what we have preached, *Sawyer* ... than that which we delivered to you, *Worrell* ... any other gospel than the one you have heard, may he be damned! *Phillips* ... let him be anathema! *Confraternity.*

9. As we said before, so say I now again, If any [man] preach any other gospel unto you than that ye have received, let him be accursed: You have heard me say it before, and now I put it down in black and white, *Phillips* ... and I repeat it now, *TCNT* ... is delivering unto you, *Rotherham* ... preache vnto you otherwaies, *Geneva* ... contrary to what, *Scarlett* ... any other gospel than the one you have already heard be a damned soul! *Phillips.*

10. For do I now persuade men, or God? or do I seek to please men? for if I yet pleased men, I should not be the servant of Christ: Does that make you think now that I am serving man's interests or God's? *Phillips* ... do I now obey, *Wilson* ... am I now seeking the favor of men, *ASV* ... soliciting the favour of men, *Scarlett* ... men's favor, *Panin.*

11. But I certify you, brethren, that the gospel which was preached of me is not after man: But I assure you, *Noyes* ... For I give you to understand, *Douay, Confraternity* ... I make known to you, *Worrell* ... I would remind you...is not a human invention, *TCNT* ... not according to man, *Rotherham.*

23

2567.3 prep
κατὰ
kata
according to

442.4 noun acc sing masc
ἄνθρωπον·
anthrōpon
man.

3624.1 conj
12. οὐδὲ
oude
Neither

1056.1 conj
γὰρ
gar
for

1466.1 prs-pron nom 1sing
ἐγὼ
egō
I

3706.2 prep
παρὰ
para
from

442.2 noun gen sing masc
ἀνθρώπου
anthrōpou
man

3741.4 verb indic aor act
παρέλαβον
parelabon
received

840.15 prs-pron sing neu
αὐτό,
auto
it,

☆ οὔτε
3641.1 conj
oute
nor

3624.1 conj
[a οὐδέ]
oude
[and not]

12.a.**Txt:** p46,03B
06D-corr1,byz.
Var: 01ℵ,06D-org,010F
012G,025P,044,33,81
104,365,1175,1739
1881,2464

1315.22 verb 1sing indic aor pass
ἐδιδάχθην,
edidachthēn
was I taught,

233.2 conj
ἀλλὰ
alla
but

1217.1 prep
δι'
di'
by

597.2 noun gen sing fem
ἀποκαλύψεως
apokalupseōs
a revelation

2400.2 name masc
Ἰησοῦ
Iēsou
of Jesus

5382.2 name gen masc
Χριστοῦ.
Christou
Christ.

189.23 verb 2pl indic aor act
13. Ἠκούσατε
Ēkousate
You heard of

1056.1 conj
γὰρ
gar
for

3450.12 art acc sing fem
τὴν
tēn
the

1684.9 adj acc sing fem
ἐμὴν
emēn
my

389.3 noun acc sing fem
ἀναστροφήν
anastrophēn
conduct

4077.1 adv
ποτε
pote
once

1706.1 prep
ἐν
en
in

3450.3 art dat sing
τῷ
tō

2429.1 name dat sing masc
Ἰουδαϊσμῷ,
Ioudaismō
Judaism,

3617.1 conj
ὅτι
hoti
that

2567.2 prep
καθ'
kath'
according to

5073.3 noun acc sing fem
ὑπερβολὴν
huperbolēn
excess

1371.20 verb indic imperf act
ἐδίωκον
ediōkon
I was persecuting

3450.12 art acc sing fem
τὴν
tēn
the

1564.4 noun acc sing fem
ἐκκλησίαν
ekklēsian
assembly

3450.2 art gen sing
τοῦ
tou

2296.2 noun gen sing masc
θεοῦ
theou
of God

2504.1 conj
καὶ
kai
and

4058.2 verb 1sing indic imperf act
ἐπόρθουν
eporthoun
was ravaging

840.12 prs-pron acc sing fem
αὐτήν·
autēn
it;

2504.1 conj
14. καὶ
kai
and

4157.3 verb 1sing indic imperf act
προέκοπτον
proekopton
was advancing

1706.1 prep
ἐν
en
in

3450.3 art dat sing masc
τῷ
tō

2429.1 name dat sing masc
Ἰουδαϊσμῷ
Ioudaismō
Judaism

5065.1 prep
ὑπὲρ
huper
beyond

4044.8 adj acc pl masc
πολλοὺς
pollous
many

4765.1 noun acc pl masc
συνηλικιώτας
sunēlikiōtas
contemporaries

1706.1 prep
ἐν
en
in

3450.3 art dat sing
τῷ
tō

1079.3 noun dat sing neu
γένει
genei
race

1466.2 prs-pron gen 1sing
μου,
mou
my,

3917.2 adv comp
περισσοτέρως
perissoterōs
more abundantly

2190.1 noun nom sing masc
ζηλωτὴς
zēlōtēs
zealous

5062.6 verb nom sing masc part pres act
ὑπάρχων
huparchōn
being

3450.1 art gen pl
τῶν
tōn
of the

3829.1 adj gen pl fem
πατρικῶν
patrikōn
fathers

1466.2 prs-pron gen 1sing
μου
mou
my

3724.3 noun gen pl fem
παραδόσεων.
paradoseōn
for traditions.

15.a.**Txt:** 01ℵ,02A,06D
018K,020L,025P,byz.sa.
bo.We/Ho,Sod
Var: p46,03B,Alf,Tisc
Weis,UBS/☆

3616.1 conj
15. ὅτε
hote
When

1156.2 conj
δὲ
de
but

2085.7 verb 3sing indic aor act
εὐδόκησεν
eudokēsen
pleased

3450.5 art nom sing masc
a ὁ
ho

2296.1 noun nom sing masc
Θεὸς
Theos
God,

3450.5 art nom sing masc
ὁ
ho
the

was called to share Christ as the fulfillment of the prophecies of old. This message of salvation by grace alone was to bring men, through the work of the Holy Spirit, from darkness to light and free them from the control of the devil (Acts 26:15-18). As the servant of Christ, Paul had faithfully shared this message in Galatia.

The Greek term translated "servant" (*doulos*) in verse 10 actually means "slave," one who has been purchased and therefore totally belongs to the purchaser. Jesus had redeemed Paul with His precious blood from the power of the Evil One. Now Paul totally belonged to Christ, and this Paul never forgot. He remained faithful to Christ always.

1:13. Paul reminded the Galatians that they knew of his earlier way of life. He had probably shared this with them when he and Barnabas brought them the gospel. In describing his attitude recorded in Acts 26:11, Paul used a strong Greek word (*eporthoun*) to show his religious fury toward Christ's followers. He had regarded them as blasphemers for believing in One condemned by the Council as a blasphemer and executed at their behest.

This word *eporthoun* was also used of a wild animal which mauls and devours its prey. Wild animals were often used in the arenas in the cities and towns of Galatia to entertain people. Unarmed humans were forced to face such wild animals and, as a result, were mauled to death and devoured to the glee of the crowds present.

1:14,15. Paul reminded the Galatians that they knew of his life before Christ appeared and called him to be an apostle. He did this to emphasize that he knew the way of works and its implications far better than did the Judaizers. Paul had excelled his fellow Jews in his zeal for living totally as a Jew in accordance with the traditions of his fathers.

Paul's letter to the Philippians describes his former status as a Jew (Philippians 3:4-6). First of all, he noted that he was circumcised on the eighth day and thereby became a "son of the covenant." By descent he was an ethnically pure and true son of Israel, God's covenant people. As such, he was a descendant of Benjamin, the youngest son of Jacob and his beloved Rachel, who died soon after his birth. He was the only son of Jacob to be born in the land of Canaan, the covenant land. Because of the location of their small territory through which passed an important north-south road and several east-west roads, the Benjaminites were forced to be warlike. They were known to be first in battle. Psalm 68:24-27 states that they were also first in worship. Paul (Saul) was named after Saul of the tribe of Benjamin, the first king of Israel. The tribe of Benjamin remained faithful to David's dynasty.

Paul went on to say in Philippians that he was "a Hebrew of the Hebrews." The religious language of his pious home in Tarsus was Hebrew, the language of the inspired Scriptures. It was rather rare for this to be true of a Jewish family living in the Dispersion. In

12. For I neither received it of man, neither was I taught [it], but by the revelation of Jesus Christ: No man gave it...no man taught it...it came to me as a direct revelation, *Phillips*.

13. For ye have heard of my conversation in time past in the Jews' religion: . . . ye have heard of my behaviour, *Wesley* . . . of my former manner of life, *Confraternity* . . . my former course of life, *Murdock* . . . way of life, *Alford* . . . my former conduct, *Montgomery* . . . my past career, *Phillips* . . . as an adherent of the Jewish religion, *Williams* . . . as to my behaviour at one time in Judaism, *Rotherham* . . . when I was devoted to Judaism, *TCNT*.

how that beyond measure I persecuted the church of God, and wasted it: That I Exceedingly persecuted, *Wilson* . . . with fanatical zeal, and, in fact, did my best to destroy it, *Phillips* . . . I viciously persecuted, *Adams* . . . was persecuting the assembly of God, *Worrell* . . . how furiously I used to persecute the church, *Montgomery* . . . and made havoc of it, *TCNT* . . . and ravaged it, *Concordant* . . . tried to demolish it, *Adams*.

14. And profited in the Jews' religion above many my equals in mine own nation, being more exceedingly zealous of the traditions of my fathers: I progressed in Judaism, *Concordant* . . . and I advanced in the Jews' religion, *ASV* . . . I was far advanced in Judaism, *Norlie* . . . I outstripped many of my own, *Montgomery* . . . above many of my years among my countrymen, *Wesley* . . . above many contemporaries among my kindred, *Rotherham* . . . I was ahead of most of my contemporaries...and had a greater enthusiasm for the old traditions, *Phillips* . . . zealous for the doctrine, *Murdock* . . . being an extreme fanatic for my ancestral traditions, *Adams* . . . for my ancestral instructions, *Worrell*.

15. But when it pleased God: . . . when the time came for God, *Phillips*.

Galatians 1:16

866.5 verb nom sing masc part aor act	1466.6 prs-pron acc 1sing	1523.2 prep gen	2809.2 noun gen sing fem	3251.2 noun gen sing fem	1466.2 prs-pron gen 1sing
ἀφορίσας	με	ἐκ	κοιλίας	μητρός	μου,
aphorisas	me	ek	koilias	mētros	mou
having selected	me	from	womb	mother's	my,

2504.1 conj	2535.14 verb nom sing masc part aor act	1217.2 prep	3450.10 art gen sing fem	5322.2 noun gen sing fem	840.3 prs-pron gen sing
καὶ	καλέσας	διὰ	τῆς	χάριτος	αὐτοῦ,
kai	kalesas	dia	tēs	charitos	autou
and	having called	by	the	grace	his,

16.

596.3 verb inf aor act	3450.6 art acc sing masc	5048.4 noun acc sing masc	840.3 prs-pron gen sing	1706.1 prep	1466.5 prs-pron dat 1sing
ἀποκαλύψαι	τὸν	υἱὸν	αὐτοῦ	ἐν	ἐμοί,
apokalupsai	ton	huion	autou	en	emoi
to reveal	the	Son	his	in	me,

2419.1 conj	2076.7 verb 1sing subj pres mid		840.6 prs-pron acc sing masc	1706.1 prep	3450.4 art dat pl
ἵνα	εὐαγγελίζωμαι		αὐτὸν	ἐν	τοῖς
hina	euangelizōmai		auton	en	tois
that	I should announce the good news		him	among	the

1477.6 noun dat pl neu	2091.1 adv	3620.3 partic	4181.1 verb 1sing indic aor mid	4418.3 noun dat sing fem
ἔθνεσιν·	εὐθέως	οὐ	προσανεθέμην	σαρκὶ
ethnesin	eutheōs	ou	prosanethemēn	sarki
Gentiles,	immediately	not	I conferred	with flesh

2504.1 conj	129.3 noun dat sing neu	3624.1 conj	422.1 verb 1sing indic aor act	562.1 verb indic aor act	1519.1 prep
καὶ	αἵματι,	**17.** οὐδὲ	⸂✶ ἀνῆλθον	[ᵃ ἀπῆλθον]	εἰς
kai	haimati	oude	anēlthon	apēlthon	eis
and	blood,	nor	went I up	[departed]	to

2389.1 name	4242.1 prep	3450.8 art acc pl masc	4112.1 prep	1466.3 prs-pron gen 1sing	646.7 noun acc pl masc
Ἱεροσόλυμα	πρὸς	τοὺς	πρὸ	ἐμοῦ	ἀποστόλους,
Hierosoluma	pros	tous	pro	emou	apostolous
Jerusalem	to	the	before	me	apostles,

233.1 conj	233.2 conj	562.1 verb indic aor act	1519.1 prep	681.2 name acc fem	2504.1 conj
⸂ ἀλλ'	[✶ ἀλλὰ]	ἀπῆλθον	εἰς	Ἀραβίαν,	καὶ
all'	alla	apēlthon	eis	Arabian	kai
but	[idem]	I went away	into	Arabia,	and

3687.1 adv	5128.5 verb 1sing indic aor act	1519.1 prep	1149.2 name acc fem	1884.1 adv
πάλιν	ὑπέστρεψα	εἰς	Δαμασκόν.	**18.** Ἔπειτα
palin	hupestrepsa	eis	Damaskon	Epeita
again	returned	to	Damascus.	Then

3196.3 prep	2073.3 noun pl neu	4980.4 num card neu	4980.4 num card neu	2073.3 noun pl neu	422.1 verb 1sing indic aor act
μετὰ	⸂ ἔτη	τρία	[✶ τρία	ἔτη]	ἀνῆλθον
meta	etē	tria	tria	etē	anēlthon
after	years	three	[three	years]	I went up

1519.1 prep	2389.1 name	2450.1 verb inf aor act	3935.4 name acc masc
εἰς	Ἱεροσόλυμα	ἱστορῆσαι	⸂ Πέτρον,
eis	Hierosoluma	historēsai	Petron
to	Jerusalem	to make acquaintance with	Peter,

fact, in a synagogue service in the Dispersion, the Scriptures were first read in Hebrew if anyone present could read the Hebrew even if he did not understand what he was reading. This was then followed by a reading of the Scriptures in the Septuagint, in the Greek, the universal language of that day.

Paul was a Pharisee (see word study at number 5168 in *The Greek-English Dictionary*) trained by the illustrious Gamaliel, the successor of his famous grandfather Hillel who died about A.D. 20 (Acts 5:34-39; 22:3). In Philippians 3:6 Paul described himself as so excelling in righteousness that he was "blameless" from the Pharisaic viewpoint. A Jewish scholar has stated that before the year A.D. 70, 341 rules of the oral Law were added to what was already present in the written Law, the Torah (Pentateuch). These additional laws were to be followed by those zealous for living out their ancestral faith.

1:16,17. Like Jeremiah (Jeremiah 1:5) and John the Baptist (Luke 1:13-17), God had planned a special role for Paul before his birth. This included growing up in the cosmopolitan, international trade and cultural center of Tarsus. Historical references rank Tarsus after Athens and Alexandria as outstanding cultural centers.

All this was part of Paul's preparation for serving as a missionary to the Gentiles. Jesus' appearance to him on the Damascus Road totally changed his attitude and life, as he noted in Philippians 3:7-9. From the time of his call to the end of his life at the executioner's block, Paul lived in close association with the Gentiles as a humble servant of Jesus Christ. What he had cherished before as a dedicated and devout Pharisee, he now regarded as being sewage (*skubala*, Philippians 3:8).

Because of the false accusation of the Judaizers, Paul stressed that after his conversion he did not return at once to Jerusalem to receive further instruction and the approval of the apostles and the Church. Rather, as Luke informs us in Acts 9, he vigorously shared Christ in Damascus. This aroused the fury of the Jews. The one sent by the Council to arrest Christ's followers was now a forceful promoter of this blasphemous heresy. To save his life, Paul fled to Arabia, which can mean any place east of the Jordan and outside of Damascus. After 3 years he returned to Damascus and again very actively shared Christ with his fellow Jews. This resulted in their fierce anger against him.

1:18-20. Acts 9:22-25 and 2 Corinthians 11:32,33 tell us that the Jews, in league with the Nabataeans, planned to kill Paul. (Secular history does not provide information on the exact relationship between the Nabataeans [Arabs] and the Romans at this time.) Paul was let down from the walls at night to permit him to escape to Jerusalem. When the Christians avoided Paul, Barnabas vouched for him (Acts 9:26,27).

Paul explicitly stated that he went to Jerusalem to "see" Peter. The Greek term translated "see" (*historēsai*) means "to visit, to make someone's acquaintance." Although this term includes infor-

who separated me from my mother's womb, and called [me] by his grace: Who gave me birth from my mother, *Fenton* . . . who had chosen me from the moment of my birth, *Phillips* . . . who had set me apart, *Montgomery* . . . from my very birth, *Noyes* . . . reached me by his mercy, *TCNT* . . . by His unmerited favor, *Williams* . . . He had special plans for me, *SEB*.

16. To reveal his Son in me, that I might preach him among the heathen; immediately I conferred not with flesh and blood: He kindly decided to show me His Son, *Beck* . . . was pleased to reveal, *Adams* . . . that I might proclaim him to the non-Jewish world, *Phillips* . . . I did not confer, *Wesley* . . . I communed not of the matter, *Geneva* . . . I condescended not to, *Douay, Rheims* . . . consult with, *Wilson* . . . I didn't receive advice or get help from any human being, *SEB* . . . I did not at once consult some human authority, *Norlie* . . . I did not immediately submit it to flesh, *Concordant* . . . instead of consulting any human being, *TCNT* . . . without consulting a human being, *Montgomery* . . . any human creatures, *Williams*.

17. Neither went I up to Jerusalem to them which were apostles before me; but I went into Arabia, and returned again unto Damascus: I did not even go to Jerusalem to meet those who were God's messengers before me, *Phillips* . . . but at once I went, *Fenton* . . . rather, I went away to, *Adams* . . . I retired to Arabia, *Williams* . . . then came back to Damascus, *Beck*.

18. Then after three years I went up to Jerusalem to see Peter: . . . to get acquainted with, *Montgomery, Adams* . . . to get to know, *Beck* . . . to become acquainted with Cephas, *Rotherham* . . . to make the acquaintance of Peter, *Norlie* . . . to relate my story to Cephas, *Concordant* . . . to question Kephas, *Fenton*.

Galatians 1:19

18.a.Txt: 01ℵ-corr,06D
018K,020L,025P,byz.it.
Var: 01ℵ-org,02A,03B
33,bo.Lach,Treg,Alf
Word,Tisc,We/Ho,Weis
Sod,UBS/✱

2758.4 name acc masc	2504.1 conj	1946.5 verb 1sing indic aor act	4242.1 prep	840.6 prs-pron acc sing masc	2232.1 noun fem
[a✱ Κηφᾶν,]	καὶ	ἐπέμεινα	πρὸς	αὐτὸν	ἡμέρας
Kēphan	kai	epemeina	pros	auton	hēmeras
[Cephas,]	and	I remained	with	him	days

1173.1 num card		2066.1 adj sing	1156.2 conj	3450.1 art gen pl	646.5 noun gen pl masc	3620.2 partic
δεκαπέντε·	19.	ἕτερον	δὲ	τῶν	ἀποστόλων	οὐκ
dekapente		heteron	de	tōn	apostolōn	ouk
fifteen;		other	but	of the	apostles	not

1481.1 verb indic aor act	1479.1 conj	3231.1 partic	2362.4 name acc masc	3450.6 art acc sing masc	79.4 noun acc sing masc	3450.2 art gen sing
εἶδον,	εἰ	μὴ	Ἰάκωβον	τὸν	ἀδελφὸν	τοῦ
eidon	ei	mē	Iakōbon	ton	adelphon	tou
I saw,	if	not	James	the	brother	of the

2935.2 noun gen sing masc		3614.17 rel-pron pl neu	1156.2 conj	1119.1 verb 1sing indic pres act	5050.3 prs-pron dat 2pl	1481.20 verb 2sing impr aor mid
κυρίου.	20.	ἃ	δὲ	γράφω	ὑμῖν,	ἰδοὺ
kuriou		ha	de	graphō	humin	idou
Lord.		What	now	I write	to you,	lo

1783.1 prep	3450.2 art gen sing	2296.2 noun gen sing masc	3617.1 conj	3620.3 partic	5409.1 verb 1sing indic pres mid
ἐνώπιον	τοῦ	θεοῦ,	ὅτι	οὐ	ψεύδομαι.
enōpion	tou	theou	hoti	ou	pseudomai
before		God,		not	I lie.

1884.1 adv		2048.1 verb indic aor act	1519.1 prep	3450.17 art pl neu	2797.2 noun pl neu	3450.10 art gen sing fem
21.	Ἔπειτα	ἦλθον	εἰς	τὰ	κλίματα	τῆς
	Epeita	ēlthon	eis	ta	klimata	tēs
	Then	I came	into	the	regions	

4799.1 name gen fem	2504.1 conj	3450.10 art gen sing fem	2763.1 name gen fem	1498.46 verb 1sing indic imperf mid	1156.2 conj
Συρίας	καὶ	τῆς	Κιλικίας·	22. ἤμην	δὲ
Surias	kai	tēs	Kilikias	ēmēn	de
of Syria	and		Cilicia;	I was	but

49.12 verb nom sing masc part pres mid	3450.3 art dat sing	4241.3 noun dat sing neu	3450.14 art dat pl fem	1564.7 noun dat pl fem
ἀγνοούμενος	τῷ	προσώπῳ	ταῖς	ἐκκλησίαις
agnooumenos	tō	prosōpō	tais	ekklēsiais
being unknown	by the	face	to the	assemblies

3450.10 art gen sing fem	2424.2 name gen fem	3450.14 art dat pl fem	1706.1 prep	5382.3 name dat masc	3303.1 adv
τῆς	Ἰουδαίας	ταῖς	ἐν	Χριστῷ·	23. μόνον
tēs	Ioudaias	tais	en	Christō	monon
	of Judea	the	in	Christ,	only

1156.2 conj	189.14 verb nom pl masc part pres act	1498.37 verb 3pl indic imperf act	3617.1 conj	3450.5 art nom sing masc	1371.7 verb nom sing masc part pres act
δὲ	ἀκούοντες	ἦσαν,	Ὅτι	ὁ	διώκων
de	akouontes	ēsan	Hoti	ho	diōkōn
but	hearing	they were,	That	the	persecuting

2231.4 prs-pron acc 1pl	4077.1 adv	3431.1 adv	2076.4 verb 3sing indic pres mid	3450.12 art acc sing fem	3963.4 noun acc sing fem
ἡμᾶς	ποτε,	νῦν	εὐαγγελίζεται	τὴν	πίστιν
hēmas	pote	nun	euangelizetai	tēn	pistin
us	once,	now	announces the good news,	the	faith,

mal conversation, it does not permit any inference of formal training. Paul used this term to emphasize that he did not go to Jerusalem to be taught and formally certified for ministry by Peter and the leaders of the church in Jerusalem. He carefully made this point because the Judaizers said that he had been unfaithful to his training and certification.

While in Jerusalem, Paul also met James, the half brother of Jesus who served as the head of the mother church. Matthew 13:55 and Mark 6:3 give the names of four brothers of Jesus. They are also described as the sons of Mary. In actuality they were Jesus' half brothers.

While in Jerusalem Paul again vigorously shared the gospel for 15 days. Because of a plot against his life, he was taken by some Christians to the seaport of Caesarea and put on a ship bound for Tarsus in Cilicia (Acts 9:28-30). Paul closed this part of his account with an important legal phrase which included an oath: "Before God, I lie not." The Galatians understood the legal significance of this phrase. If used by someone in court to assure the correctness of his position, he won the case. But if the oath was thrown back by the other litigant, the swearer of the oath could lose his case. If used outside of court as a voluntary oath, it was a warning that the swearer was willing to proceed further.

Paul used this term to emphasize that the Judaizers had lied about him. He was truly an apostle, personally called by Jesus Christ. As he would emphasize again in Galatians 2, the gospel of salvation by grace alone, which he had faithfully shared with them, was the only true gospel.

1:21. Paul stated that he left Jerusalem to return to the regions of Syria and Cilicia. He did not provide further information on his activity there; neither did Luke do so directly. Acts 15:41 tells us that at the beginning of his second missionary journey, Paul (and by implication, Silas) went through Syria and Cilicia, confirming and strengthening the churches. At this time Syria, together with the eastern part of Cilicia in which Tarsus was located, formed one large province. It is possible that Paul was actively engaged in sharing the gospel in Cilicia as well as in the Syrian area north of Antioch.

1:22-24. In summarizing this part of his letter, Paul carefully stressed that the churches of Christ in Judea did not know him personally. Judea here probably means Palestine. In about A.D. 44 the various sections of the west bank of Palestine came under the rule of Herod Agrippa I. Paul wrote of "the churches of Judea which were in Christ" to stress that these assemblies were Christian churches. In the Septuagint the word translated "churches" (*ekklēsiais*) is used several times as a religious term for God's covenant people gathered for worship. These churches were praising God that the former ferocious persecutor of the Faith was now actively sharing the gospel.

and abode with him fifteen days: I only stayed with him just over, *Phillips* . . . I stayed a fortnight with him, *TCNT* . . . stayed in his company, *Berkeley* . . . and remained with him, *Wilson* . . . and tarried, *Panin* . . . and spent two weeks with him, *Montgomery, Williams*.

19. But other of the apostles saw I none, save James the Lord's brother: Yet I became acquainted with no one, *Concordant* . . . I did not meet any of the other messengers, *Phillips* . . . except James, *Confraternity* . . . the Master's brother, *TCNT*.

20. Now the things which I write unto you, behold, before God, I lie not: All this that I am telling you is...the plain truth, *Phillips* . . . I do not falsely affirm, *Wilson* . . . in presence of God, *Rotherham* . . . I call God to witness that I am telling the truth, *Montgomery* . . . I am not falsifying, *Berkeley*.

21. Afterwards I came into the regions of Syria and Cilicia: After that I went into the regions, *Norlie* . . . to the districts, *TCNT*.

22. And was unknown by face unto the churches of Judaea which were in Christ: I was not known by sight, *Adams* . . . they did not know me, *Beck* . . . did not know my face, *SEB* . . . but I was unknown personally, *Wilson*.

23. But they had heard only, That he which persecuted us in times past: They knew only by hearsay, *Norlie* . . . All they knew of me, in fact, was the saying, *Phillips* . . . our former persecutor, *Alford* . . . who persecuted us formerly, *Sawyer* . . . at one time, *Rotherham*.
now preacheth the faith which once he destroyed: . . . of which he once made havoc, *Panin* . . . he formerly made havoc, *PNT*.

3614.12 rel-pron acc sing fem
ἥν
hēn
which

4077.1 adv
ποτε
pote
once

4058.3 verb 3sing indic imperf act
ἐπόρθει,
eporthei
he was ravaging:

2504.1 conj
24. καὶ
kai
and

1386.18 verb 3pl indic imperf act
ἐδόξαζον
edoxazon
they were glorifying

1706.1 prep
ἐν
en
in

1466.5 prs-pron dat 1sing
ἐμοὶ
emoi
me

3450.6 art acc sing masc
τὸν
ton

2296.4 noun acc sing masc
θεόν.
theon
God.

1884.1 adv
2:1. Ἔπειτα
Epeita
Then

1217.2 prep
διὰ
dia
after

1175.2 num card gen
δεκατεσσάρων
dekatessarōn
fourteen

2073.4 noun gen pl neu
ἐτῶν
etōn
years

3687.1 adv
πάλιν
palin
again

303.12 verb 1sing indic aor act
ἀνέβην
anebēn
I went up

1519.1 prep
εἰς
eis
to

2389.1 name
Ἱεροσόλυμα
Hierosoluma
Jerusalem

3196.3 prep
μετὰ
meta
with

915.2 name masc
Βαρναβᾶ,
Barnaba
Barnabas,

4689.1 verb nom sing masc part aor act
συμπαραλαβὼν
sumparalabōn
having taken with

2504.1 conj
καὶ
kai
also

4951.4 name acc masc
Τίτον·
Titon
Titus;

303.12 verb 1sing indic aor act
2. ἀνέβην
anebēn
I went up

1156.2 conj
δὲ
de
but

2567.3 prep
κατὰ
kata
according to

597.4 noun acc sing fem
ἀποκάλυψιν,
apokalupsin
revelation,

2504.1 conj
καὶ
kai
and

392.1 verb 1sing indic aor mid
ἀνεθέμην
anethemēn
laid before

840.2 prs-pron dat pl
αὐτοῖς
autois
them

3450.16 art sing neu
τὸ
to
the

2077.1 noun sing neu
εὐαγγέλιον
euangelion
good news

3614.16 rel-pron sing neu
ὃ
ho
which

2756.1 verb 1sing indic pres act
κηρύσσω
kērussō
I proclaim

1706.1 prep
ἐν
en
among

3450.4 art dat pl
τοῖς
tois
the

1477.6 noun dat pl neu
ἔθνεσιν,
ethnesin
Gentiles,

2567.1 prep
κατ'
kat'
by

2375.11 adj acc sing fem
ἰδίαν
idian
one's own

1156.2 conj
δὲ
de
but

3450.4 art dat pl
τοῖς
tois
the

1374.2 verb dat pl masc part pres act
δοκοῦσιν,
dokousin
seeming,

3248.1 conj
' μήπως
mēpōs
lest somehow

3231.1 partic
[✶ μή
mē
[not

4315.1 adv
πως]
pōs
how]

1519.1 prep
εἰς
eis
in

2727.1 adj sing
κενὸν
kenon
vain

4983.1 verb 1sing pres act
τρέχω
trechō
I should be running

2211.1 conj
ἢ
ē
or

4983.10 verb indic aor act
ἔδραμον·
edramon
had run;

233.1 conj
3. ἀλλ'
all'
but

3624.1 conj
οὐδὲ
oude
not even

4951.1 name nom masc
Τίτος
Titos
Titus

3450.5 art nom sing masc
ὁ
ho
the

4713.1 prep
σὺν
sun
with

1466.5 prs-pron dat 1sing
ἐμοί,
emoi
me,

1659.1 name nom sing masc
Ἕλλην
Hellēn
a Greek

1498.21 verb nom sing masc part pres act
ὢν,
ōn
being,

313.8 verb 3sing indic aor pass
ἠναγκάσθη
ēnankasthē
was compelled

3919.11 verb inf aor pass
περιτμηθῆναι.
peritmēthēnai
to be circumcised;

1217.2 prep
4. διὰ
dia
on account of

1156.2 conj
δὲ
de
and

3450.8 art acc pl masc
τοὺς
tous
the

3782.1 adj acc pl masc
παρεισάκτους
pareisaktous
brought in secretly

2:1,2. Saul's persecution and Stephen's stoning caused some Greek-speaking Jews, who had come from the Dispersion to Palestine, to flee. They scattered to the island of Cyprus and along the eastern coastline up to Antioch, the cosmopolitan capital of the Roman province of Syria. Antioch was the third largest city in the Roman Empire, surpassed in population only by Rome and Alexandria. It was known for its moral laxity.

Luke noted that among these Jewish Christians were some who had come from Cyprus and from Cyrene in North Africa. These not only shared their faith in the synagogues of Antioch but also with the Gentiles. This was most unusual, but God richly blessed their witness. When the church in Jerusalem heard about it, they sent Barnabas, who had been born in Cyprus, to minister to them. Later, when God so richly blessed this outreach, he went to Tarsus to persuade Saul (Paul) to join him (Acts 4:36,37; 9:27; 11:19-26).

About A.D. 44, Agabus came to Antioch and foretold a great famine in various parts of the Roman Empire. The Antioch church resolved to gather an offering for the poor Christians in Palestine. The Jewish historian Josephus records that this famine hit Palestine in A.D. 46 (*Antiquities*, 20:2:5). (The 14 years seemingly refers back to Paul's conversion in A.D. 32.) According to secular history, various parts of the vast Roman Empire suffered famine at different times during this period.

Paul, Barnabas, and Titus were sent to Jerusalem with the offering. They also discussed the gospel privately with Peter, John, and James as the leaders of the church at Jerusalem to make sure that they totally shared the same gospel, namely, that salvation is by grace alone for both Jew and Gentile alike. They did this, Paul wrote, "lest by any means I should run, or had run, in vain." The Greek word for "run" (*trechō*) is a verb which to the Galatians meant all the energy and effort which was necessary in running to win in a race. Athletic events in the amphitheater were an intimate part of the life experience of Paul's readers. Paul meant that both the mother and daughter churches had to agree that there was no difference in requirements for salvation between Jew and Gentile.

2:3. The acid test came with Titus. Titus was a Greek, and therefore a Gentile Christian. As such, he had not been circumcised. In fact, circumcision for a Greek was considered unthinkable. To circumcise a man was thought to mutilate the body beautiful. Paul tersely stated that Titus was not compelled to be circumcised, despite the determined efforts of the "false brethren" (*pseudadelphous*, verse 4) to compel this.

Titus became one of Paul's stalwart helpers. When necessary for the sake of the gospel, he could be very firm. Later, perhaps in A.D. 55, Paul sent him to Corinth as his official representative to cope with the problems of that very difficult church. Titus was Paul's coworker in beginning the outreach on Crete; note what Paul says about the Cretians in Titus 1. Later Paul wrote the letter we know as the Epistle to Titus.

24. And they glorified God in me: . . . they praised God, *TCNT* . . . And they thanked God for what had happened to me, *Phillips* . . . on my account, *Wilson.*

1. Then fourteen years after I went up again to Jerusalem with Barnabas, and took Titus with [me] also:

2. And I went up by revelation: My visit on this occasion was by divine command, *Phillips* . . . in consequence of a revelation, *Confraternity.*

and communicated unto them that gospel which I preach among the Gentiles, but privately to them which were of reputation, lest by any means I should run, or had run, in vain: . . . and I conferred with them, *Confraternity* . . . and submitted to them, *Wilson* . . . I did this first in private conference with the Church leaders, to make sure that what I had done and proposed doing was acceptable to them, *Phillips* . . . laid before them...those of eminence, *Scarlett* . . . to persons of distinction, *Sawyer* . . . before those who are thought highly of, *TCNT* . . . particularly with them which were counted chiefe, *Geneva.*

3. But neither Titus, who was with me, being a Greek, was compelled to be circumcised: . . . my associate, *Wilson.*

4. And that because of false brethren unawares brought in: In fact, the suggestion would never have arisen but for the presence of some pseudo-Christians, *Phillips* . . . secretly introduced, *Wilson, Rotherham* . . . introduced unawares, *Wesley.*

5404.2 noun acc pl masc	3610.2 rel-pron nom pl masc	3784.2 verb 3pl indic aor act	2654.1 verb inf aor act
ψευδαδέλφους,	οἵτινες	παρεισῆλθον	κατασκοπῆσαι
pseudadelphous	hoitines	pareiselthon	kataskopēsai
false brothers,	who	infiltrated	to spy out

3450.12 art acc sing fem	1644.4 noun acc sing fem	2231.2 prs-pron gen 1pl	3614.12 rel-pron acc sing fem	2174.5 verb 1pl indic pres act	1706.1 prep
τὴν	ἐλευθερίαν	ἡμῶν	ἣν	ἔχομεν	ἐν
tēn	eleutherian	hēmōn	hēn	echomen	en
the	freedom	our	which	we have	in

5382.3 name dat masc	2400.2 name masc	2419.1 conj	2231.4 prs-pron acc 1pl	2585.2 verb 3pl subj aor mid
Χριστῷ	Ἰησοῦ,	ἵνα	ἡμᾶς	⸀ καταδουλώσωνται ·
Christō	Iēsou	hina	hēmas	katadoulōsōntai
Christ	Jesus,	that	us	they might bring into slavery;

4.a.Txt: 018K,(020L),byz.
Var: 01א,02A,03B-org
04C,06D,Lach,Treg,Alf
Word,Tisc,We/Ho,Weis
Sod,UBS/✠

2585.3 verb 3pl indic fut act	3614.4 rel-pron dat pl	3624.1 conj	4242.1 prep	5443.4 noun acc sing fem
[ᵃ✩ καταδουλώσουσιν ·]	5. οἷς	οὐδὲ	πρὸς	ὥραν
katadoulōsousin	hois	oude	pros	hōran
[they will enslave;]	to whom	not even	for	an hour

1493.1 verb 1pl indic aor act	3450.11 art dat sing fem	5130.1 noun dat sing fem	2419.1 conj	3450.9 art nom sing fem	223.1 noun nom sing fem
εἴξαμεν	τῇ	ὑποταγῇ,	ἵνα	ἡ	ἀλήθεια
eixamen	tē	hupotagē	hina	hē	alētheia
did we yield	in the	subjection,	that	the	truth

3450.2 art gen sing	2077.2 noun gen sing neu	1259.3 verb 3sing subj aor act	4242.1 prep	5050.4 prs-pron acc 2pl	570.3 prep
τοῦ	εὐαγγελίου	διαμείνη	πρὸς	ὑμᾶς.	6. Ἀπὸ
tou	euangeliou	diameinē	pros	humas	Apo
of the	good news	might continue	with	you.	From

1156.2 conj	3450.1 art gen pl	1374.10 verb gen pl masc part pres act	1498.32 verb inf pres act	4948.10 indef-pron sing neu	3560.4 intr-pron nom pl masc
δὲ	τῶν	δοκούντων	εἶναί	τι,	ὁποῖοί
de	tōn	dokounton	einai	ti	hopoioi
but	the	seeming	to be	something,	what

4077.1 adv	1498.37 verb 3pl indic imperf act	3625.6 num card neu	1466.4 prs-pron dat 1sing	1302.1 verb 3sing indic pres act
ποτε	ἦσαν	οὐδέν	μοι	διαφέρει ·
pote	ēsan	ouden	moi	diapherei
ever	they were	no	to me	makes difference:

6.a.Var: 01א,02A,025P
33,Tisc,We/Ho,Sod
UBS/✠

4241.1 noun sing neu	3450.5 art nom sing masc	2296.1 noun nom sing masc	442.2 noun gen sing masc	3620.3 partic
πρόσωπον	[ᵃ✩+ ὁ]	θεὸς	ἀνθρώπου	οὐ
prosōpon	ho	theos	anthrōpou	ou
face		God	of man	not

2956.4 verb 3sing indic pres act	1466.5 prs-pron dat 1sing	1056.1 conj	3450.7 art nom pl masc	1374.9 verb nom pl masc part pres act	3625.6 num card neu
λαμβάνει ·	ἐμοὶ	γὰρ	οἱ	δοκοῦντες	οὐδὲν
lambanei	emoi	gar	hoi	dokountes	ouden
does accept;	to me	for	the	seeming	nothing

4181.2 verb 3pl indic aor mid	233.2 conj	4967.1 noun sing neu	1481.17 verb nom pl masc part aor act
προσανέθεντο,	7. ἀλλὰ	τοὐναντίον,	ἰδόντες
prosanethento	alla	tounantion	idontes
conferred;	but	on the contrary,	having seen

2:4,5. Paul described how this event took place. While the six leaders were meeting in private session, some of the Judaizing Christians *pareisēlthon* ("came in by stealth") to demand that Titus be circumcised. In very vigorous language, Paul stated that they had sneaked in "to spy out our liberty" which Christians have in Christ and to attempt to bring them back into the slavery of the Law. This would result in eternal condemnation. By the phrase "liberty . . . in Christ," Paul meant freedom from the demands of the Law which believers in Christ have because of their faith in Him. Paul called these men "false brethren" because they did not understand the gospel of grace.

Not for a moment did the six leaders permit these false brethren to dictate to them. To have done so would have denied the cardinal truth of the gospel. It would have meant that salvation was strictly by works and not by grace. It is not wrong to make concessions for the sake of harmony but only if it does not violate basic principles.

Some have questioned why Paul refused to circumcise Titus but did circumcise Timothy. Acts 16:1-3 records that Timothy's father was a Greek but his mother was a Jewess. In fact, 2 Timothy reveals that both his mother and grandmother were very pious Jews and carefully trained Timothy in the Scriptures (2 Timothy 1:4,5; 3:15-17). Because his mother was a Jewess, Timothy was considered a Jew. So in good judgment, keeping in mind the work for which Timothy was to be trained, it was helpful to circumcise him. This did not in any way involve a compromise of the gospel. This was in line with Paul's principle to make himself "all things to all men."

2:6. Paul emphasized a very important point, namely, that God is not a respecter of persons, a truth found throughout the Scriptures. As God's faithful servant, Paul followed His example. And so, in verse 6, Paul suggested that the Judaizers may have sought to pit the Jerusalem leaders against him and Barnabas. Paul agreed that the three men—Peter, James, and John—were men of reputation. But these men in no way tried to impose their judgment on Paul and Barnabas. Rather, they agreed that Paul and Barnabas had been faithful to the gospel in not circumcising Titus. Thereby they had safeguarded the proper understanding of the gospel, that of salvation by grace alone.

2:7. In this whole episode, Paul demonstrated his keen mind, developed also during his training by Gamaliel. All of the Epistle to the Galatians has the character of a carefully written legal document, especially the first two chapters.

The Judaizers had accused Paul of being unfaithful to his instructions by the key men of the Church. Paul carefully docu-

who came in privily to spy out our liberty which we have in Christ Jesus, that they might bring us into bondage: . . . who wormed their way into our meeting...and then attempted to tie us up with rules and regulations, *Phillips* . . . came in surreptitiously, *PNT* . . . to spy upon our Christian liberty, *TCNT* . . . the freedom we enjoy, *Williams* . . . in order to enslave us again, *Montgomery* . . . into servitude, *Douay.*

5. To whom we gave place by subjection, no, not for an hour; that the truth of the gospel might continue with you: . . . to whom we did not yield, *Scarlett* . . . by submission, *Wilson* . . . But we did not yield to them even for a moment, *Norlie* . . . We did not give those men an inch, for the truth of the Gospel for you and all Gentiles was at stake, *Phillips* . . . might abide unshaken among you, *Montgomery* . . . might prevail for you, *Williams* . . . might always be yours! *TCNT* . . . might still abide with you, *Rotherham.*

6. But of these who seemed to be somewhat, (whatsoever they were, it maketh no matter to me: God accepteth no man's person:) for they who seemed [to be somewhat] in conference added nothing to me: . . . they who undoubtedly were something, *Wesley* . . . they which semed great, *Cranmer* . . . what rank they held, *Norlie* . . . is of no consequence, *Concordant* . . . as far as the leaders of the conference were concerned...God is not impressed with a man's office...they had nothing to add to my Gospel, *Phillips* . . . it makes no difference to me...God is partial to no man, *Sawyer* . . . God is no respecter of persons, *Montgomery* . . . God pays no attention to outward appearances, *Williams* . . . does not recognise human distinctions, *TCNT* . . . communicated nothing new, *Noyes* . . . laid no further burden on me, *Confraternity.*

7. But contrariwise: Rather, *Norlie.*

33

3617.1 conj	3961.61 verb 1sing indic perf mid	3450.16 art sing neu	2077.1 noun sing neu	3450.10 art gen sing fem
ὅτι	πεπίστευμαι	τὸ	εὐαγγέλιον	τῆς
hoti	*pepisteumai*	*to*	*euangelion*	*tēs*
that	I have been entrusted with	the	good news	of the

201.2 noun gen sing fem	2503.1 conj	3935.1 name nom masc	3450.10 art gen sing fem	3921.2 noun gen sing fem	3450.5 art nom sing masc
ἀκροβυστίας,	καθὼς	Πέτρος	τῆς	περιτομῆς·	**8.** ὁ
akrobustias	*kathōs*	*Petros*	*tēs*	*peritomēs*	*ho*
uncircumcision,	just as	Peter	of the	circumcision,	one

1056.1 conj	1738.7 verb nom sing masc part aor act	3935.3 name dat masc	1519.1 prep	645.2 noun acc sing fem	3450.10 art gen sing fem
γὰρ	ἐνεργήσας	Πέτρῳ	εἰς	ἀποστολὴν	τῆς
gar	*energēsas*	*Petrō*	*eis*	*apostolēn*	*tēs*
for	having operated	in Peter	for	apostleship	of the

3921.2 noun gen sing fem	1738.6 verb 3sing indic aor act	2504.1 conj	1466.5 prs-pron dat 1sing	1519.1 prep	3450.17 art pl neu
περιτομῆς,	ἐνήργησεν	καὶ	ἐμοὶ	εἰς	τὰ
peritomēs	*energēsen*	*kai*	*emoi*	*eis*	*ta*
circumcision,	worked	also	in me	towards	the

1477.4 noun pl neu	2504.1 conj	1091.28 verb nom pl masc part aor act	3450.12 art acc sing fem	5322.4 noun acc sing fem	3450.12 art acc sing fem
ἔθνη·	**9.** καὶ	γνόντες	τὴν	χάριν	τὴν
ethnē	*kai*	*gnontes*	*tēn*	*charin*	*tēn*
Gentiles,	and	having known	the	grace	the

1319.51 verb acc sing fem part aor pass	1466.4 prs-pron dat 1sing	2362.1 name nom masc	2504.1 conj	2758.1 name nom masc	2504.1 conj
δοθεῖσάν	μοι,	Ἰάκωβος	καὶ	Κηφᾶς	καὶ
dotheisan	*moi*	*Iakōbos*	*kai*	*Kēphas*	*kai*
having been given	to me,	James	and	Cephas	and

2464.1 name nom masc	3450.7 art nom masc	1374.9 verb nom pl masc part pres act	4620.3 noun nom pl masc	1498.32 verb inf pres act	1182.4 adj fem
Ἰωάννης,	οἱ	δοκοῦντες	στῦλοι	εἶναι,	δεξιὰς
Iōannēs	*hoi*	*dokountes*	*stuloi*	*einai*	*dexias*
John,	the	seeming	pillars	to be,	right hands

1319.17 verb 3pl indic aor act	1466.5 prs-pron dat 1sing	2504.1 conj	915.3 name dat masc	2815.2 noun gen sing fem	2419.1 conj
ἔδωκαν	ἐμοὶ	καὶ	Βαρναβᾷ	κοινωνίας,	ἵνα
edōkan	*emoi*	*kai*	*Barnaba*	*koinōnias*	*hina*
they gave	to me	and	Barnabas	of fellowship,	that

2231.1 prs-pron nom 1pl	1519.1 prep	3450.17 art pl neu	1477.4 noun pl neu	840.7 prs-pron nom pl masc	1156.2 conj	1519.1 prep
ἡμεῖς	εἰς	τὰ	ἔθνη,	αὐτοὶ	δὲ	εἰς
hēmeis	*eis*	*ta*	*ethnē*	*autoi*	*de*	*eis*
we	to	the	Gentiles,	they	and	to

3450.12 art acc sing fem	3921.4 noun acc sing fem	3303.1 adv	3450.1 art gen pl	4292.5 adj gen pl masc	2419.1 conj
τὴν	περιτομήν·	**10.** μόνον	τῶν	πτωχῶν	ἵνα
tēn	*peritomēn*	*monon*	*tōn*	*ptōchōn*	*hina*
the	circumcision:	only	the	poor	that

3285.3 verb 1pl subj pres act	3614.16 rel-pron sing neu	2504.1 conj	4557.2 verb 1sing indic aor act	840.15 prs-pron sing neu
μνημονεύωμεν,	ὃ	καὶ	ἐσπούδασα	αὐτὸ
mnēmoneuōmen	*ho*	*kai*	*espoudasa*	*auto*
we should remember,	which	also	I was eager	same

mented that his call and instruction came from Jesus Christ himself. He recorded that his special call as a missionary to the Gentiles was recognized by the leaders at Jerusalem. They recognized that Christ had entrusted the outreach to the Gentiles especially to Paul and the outreach to the Jews especially to Peter. It should be understood that in each case God's call was not categorical but each one was to concentrate his ministry on those to whom he had been called.

2:8. Paul restated the same truth in verse 8. The Greek word translated "wrought effectually" (*energēsas*) stresses that God was working equally in both Peter and Paul to enable them faithfully and effectively to carry out the mission for which God had chosen them.

2:9. Paul noted that Peter, James, and John were considered to be "pillars," the principal leaders of the mother church. These three men recognized the special role of Paul and Barnabas as given them by God and gave to them the right hand of fellowship (*koinōnia*). This important Greek word means Paul and Barnabas recognized that they were in total agreement with them on the cardinal doctrines of Scripture. In this instance, the focus was on salvation by grace alone through faith in Jesus Christ. This action again indicates that the Judaizers were wrong in their false accusations. Neither Jewish nor Gentile Christians had to be circumcised and live as Jews in order to be saved.

2:10. The leaders asked Paul and Barnabas to remember the urgent needs of the poor Christians, particularly those of Jerusalem. History informs us that Jerusalem, a city of around 35,000, was never economically independent. Its population was always underemployed. It did have a system of helping the poor. Once a week the poor residents received a basket of food and clothing: bread and beans for lentil stew without meat, and fruit in season. Special provisions were made for the poor to observe the Passover meal. It is unknown whether poor Jewish Christians were being excluded from such help because of their faith, but it might have happened.

Paul and Barnabas were most willing to ask the churches to gather such an offering. Doing so would also remind them of their ties with the mother church in Jerusalem. Paul and chosen representatives of churches founded by him brought such an offering to Jerusalem at the end of his third missionary journey (Acts 20:4; 21:15-19; 1 Corinthians 16:1-4; 2 Corinthians 8,9). This was also an opportunity for the delegates and believers in Jerusalem to understand more fully the unity of the Church.

when they saw that the gospel of the uncircumcision was committed unto me, as [the gospel] of the circumcision [was] unto Peter: . . . they recognized that I had been commissioned, *Norlie* . . . they saw that I had been entrusted with, *TCNT* . . . saw that I was entrusted with, *Scarlett* . . . seeing that I had been entrusted with, *Rotherham* . . . the Gospel for the uncircumcised was as much my commission as, *Phillips.*

8. (For he that wrought effectually in Peter to the apostleship of the circumcision, the same was mighty in me toward the Gentiles:): . . . who had done such great work in Peter's ministry...was plainly doing the same, *Phillips* . . . inwardly wrought in me, *Rotherham* . . . operated also in me for the gentiles, *Sawyer.*

9. And when James, Cephas, and John, who seemed to be pillars, perceived the grace that was given unto me, they gave to me and Barnabas the right hands of fellowship; that we [should go] unto the heathen, and they unto the circumcision: . . . who were reputed to be pillars, *Panin* . . . who were manifest pillars, *Sawyer* . . . and when they recognized, *Confraternity* . . . the right handes of societie, *Rheims* . . . Recognizing the charge...their hands in acknowledgement, *TCNT* . . . in full agreement that our mission was to, *Phillips.*

10. Only [they would] that we should remember the poor; the same which I also was forward to do: They make only one request of us...that very thing I have diligently tried to do, *Norlie* . . . I also gave diligence to do, *Panin* . . . warnynge only that, *Tyndale* . . . provided only that, *Confraternity* . . . only urging, *Wilson* . . . be mindful of the destitute, *Rotherham* . . . I was diligent to do, *Tyndale, Geneva* . . . I vvas careful to doe, *Rheims* . . . with this I was...only too ready to agree, *Phillips.*

Galatians 2:11

3642.17 dem-pron sing neu	4020.41 verb inf aor act	3616.1 conj	1156.2 conj	2048.3 verb 3sing indic aor act	3935.1 name nom masc
τοῦτο	ποιῆσαι.	11. Ὅτε	δὲ	ἦλθεν	ʿ Πέτρος
touto	poiēsai	Hote	de	ēlthen	Petros
thing	to do.	When	but	came	Peter

2758.1 name nom masc	1519.1 prep	487.3 name acc fem	2567.3 prep	4241.1 noun sing neu
[ᵃ✶ Κηφᾶς]	εἰς	Ἀντιόχειαν,	κατὰ	πρόσωπον
Kēphas	eis	Antiocheian	kata	prosōpon
[Cephas]	to	Antioch,	to	face

840.4 prs-pron dat sing	434.1 verb 1sing indic aor act	3617.1 conj	2578.2 verb nom sing masc part perf mid
αὐτῷ	ἀντέστην,	ὅτι	κατεγνωσμένος
autō	antestēn	hoti	kategnōsmenos
him	I withstood,	because	having been condemned

1498.34 verb sing indic imperf act	4112.1 prep	3450.2 art gen sing	1056.1 conj	2048.23 verb inf aor act	4948.9 indef-pron acc pl masc
ἦν.	12. πρὸ	τοῦ	γὰρ	ἐλθεῖν	τινας
ēn	pro	tou	gar	elthein	tinas
he was:	before	the	for	to come	some

570.3 prep	2362.2 name gen masc	3196.3 prep	3450.1 art gen pl	1477.5 noun gen pl neu	4756.5 verb 3sing indic imperf act
ἀπὸ	Ἰακώβου,	μετὰ	τῶν	ἐθνῶν	συνήσθιεν·
apo	Iakōbou	meta	tōn	ethnōn	sunēsthien
from	James,	with	the	Gentiles	he was eating;

3616.1 conj	1156.2 conj	2048.1 verb indic aor act	2048.3 verb 3sing indic aor act	5126.1 verb 3sing indic imperf act
ὅτε	δὲ	ʿ✶ ἦλθον,	[ᵃ ἦλθεν,]	ὑπέστελλεν
hote	de	ēlthon	ēlthen	hupestellen
when	but	they came,	[he came,]	he was drawing back

2504.1 conj	866.8 verb 3sing indic imperf act	1431.6 prs-pron acc sing masc	5236.7 verb nom sing masc part pres mid	3450.8 art acc pl masc	1523.2 prep gen
καὶ	ἀφώριζεν	ἑαυτόν,	φοβούμενος	τοὺς	ἐκ
kai	aphōrizen	heauton	phoboumenos	tous	ek
and	was separating	himself,	being afraid of	the	of

3921.2 noun gen sing fem	2504.1 conj	4794.1 verb 3pl indic aor pass	840.4 prs-pron dat sing	2504.1 conj
περιτομῆς·	13. καὶ	συνυπεκρίθησαν	αὐτῷ	ʿᵃ καὶ ʾ
peritomēs	kai	sunupekrithēsan	autō	kai
circumcision;	and	were joined in hypocrisy	with him	also

3450.7 art nom pl masc	3036.3 adj nom pl masc	2428.2 name-adj nom pl masc	5452.1 conj	2504.1 conj	915.1 name nom masc
οἱ	λοιποὶ	Ἰουδαῖοι,	ὥστε	καὶ	Βαρναβᾶς
hoi	loipoi	Ioudaioi	hōste	kai	Barnabas
the	rest	of Jews,	so that	even	Barnabas

4730.2 verb 3sing indic aor pass	840.1 prs-pron gen pl	3450.11 art dat sing fem	5110.3 noun dat sing fem	233.1 conj
συναπήχθη	αὐτῶν	τῇ	ὑποκρίσει.	14. Ἀλλ'
sunapēchthē	autōn	tē	hupokrisei	All'
was carried away	their	by the	hypocrisy.	But

3616.1 conj	1481.1 verb indic aor act	3617.1 conj	3620.2 partic	3579.1 verb 3pl indic pres act	4242.1 prep
ὅτε	εἶδον	ὅτι	οὐκ	ὀρθοποδοῦσιν	πρὸς
hote	eidon	hoti	ouk	orthopodousin	pros
when	I saw	that	not	they walk uprightly	according to

2:11. Some time after Paul, Barnabas, and Titus returned to Antioch, Peter came from Jerusalem to see for himself the vibrant life in this world missions church. He also joined in the fellowship meals of the church, at which Jewish and Gentile Christians ate together. This demonstrated the unity of their common faith in salvation by grace alone.

In practice Jews did not eat with Gentiles, whom they considered to be chronic sinners. In fact, of the 341 rules the rabbis had added for daily life (see note on 1:6,7), two-thirds dealt with table fellowship. Several times during His ministry Jesus was reproached for eating with people whom the Pharisees considered "sinners" (Matthew 9:9-13; Luke 19:1-9).

2:12,13. God had prepared Peter to understand that such a distinction was not part of His plan. From his experience with the Samaritan Christians (Acts 8:14-17) and especially through the special training God had given him prior to sharing the gospel with Cornelius and his Gentile friends (Acts 10:1 to 11:18), Peter had learned God makes no distinction between Jew and Gentile. Peter used God's action to refute the attack of "false brethren" in Jerusalem. Table fellowship of Jewish and Gentile Christians was in keeping with their common faith in Christ.

But then some of the "false brethren" of verse 4 came to Antioch. They are described as "certain (men) from James." As Acts 15 underlines, James (Jesus' half brother) was the head of the church at Jerusalem. Here James is a term for the Jerusalem church. The earlier verses of this chapter show that these men were not official representatives or that James shared their narrow views (see also Acts 15:1-32). They are described as "them which were of the circumcision." This description singles out their view that both Jews and Gentiles had to be circumcised in order to be saved.

When Peter saw them and learned how determined they were to enforce their narrow and unchristian views, he became very much afraid. Whereas earlier, during this visit in Antioch, Peter had freely eaten with Gentile Christians, he now avoided having table fellowship with them. The Jewish Christians at Antioch were prompted to follow Peter's example and did not eat with their fellow Gentile Christians. This practice of joyful table fellowship between Jewish and Gentile Christians had been going on for a number of years. This reveals the seriousness of the situation and the gross offense it gave.

In time, Barnabas also became afraid of what these hard-nosed, mistaken Jewish Christians from Jerusalem might do and also avoided eating with his Gentile members. This was a crushing experience especially for the Gentile Christians as well as a very disquieting development for all.

2:14. Called by the ascended Christ himself, Paul never forgot the great meaning of this call and its implications for his total life as Christ's apostle to the Gentiles. He never compromised the truth

11. But when Peter was come to Antioch, I withstood him to the face, because he was to be blamed: I rebuked him, *Murdock* . . . I opposed him to his face, because he stood convicted, *TCNT* . . . I resisted him in face, because he vvas reprehensible, *Rheims* . . . I had to oppose him publicly, for he was then plainly in the wrong, *Phillips* . . . Because he was blameable, *Wilson* . . . he had become worthy of blame, *Rotherham* . . . he had shown how wrong he was, *Beck* . . . because he was in the wrong, *Norlie* . . . he was obviously wrong, *Adams* . . . he stood condemned, *Williams*.

12. For before that certain came from James, he did eat with the Gentiles: It happened like this, *Phillips* . . . he used to eat, *Noyes* . . . he was in the habit of eating, *Williams* . . . with the converts from heathenism, *TCNT*. **but when they were come, he withdrew and separated himself, fearing them which were of the circumcision:** . . . and hold aloof, for fear of offending, *TCNT* . . . out of sheer fear of what the Jews might think, *Phillips*.

13. And the other Jews dissembled likewise with him; insomuch that Barnabas also was carried away with their dissimulation: Peter was two-faced, *SEB* . . . the remaining Jews, *Rotherham* . . . carried out a similar piece of deception, and the force of their bad example was so great that even Barnabas, *Phillips* . . . acted hypocritically, *Adams* . . . acted just as insincerely, *Beck* . . . joined him in this pretense...by their insincerity, *Norlie* . . . was carried away by, *Worrell* . . . led astray by their hypocrisy, *Wilson* . . . influenced to join them in their pretense, *Williams*.

14. But when I saw that they walked not uprightly according to the truth of the gospel: . . . walked not correctly, *Sawyer* . . . they were not keeping to the straight path, *TCNT*.

Galatians 2:15

3450.12 art acc sing fem	223.4 noun acc sing fem	3450.2 art gen sing	2077.2 noun gen sing neu	1500.3 verb indic aor act	3450.3 art dat sing
τὴν	ἀλήθειαν	τοῦ	εὐαγγελίου,	εἶπον	τῷ
tēn	alētheian	tou	euangeliou	eipon	tō
the	truth	of the	good news,	I said	

3935.3 name dat masc	2758.3 name dat masc	1699.1 prep	3820.4 adj gen pl	1479.1 conj
(Πέτρῳ	[ᵃ✶ Κηφᾷ]	ἔμπροσθεν	πάντων,	Εἰ
Petrō	Kēpha	emprosthen	pantōn	Ei
to Peter	[to Cephas]	before	all,	If

14.a.**Txt:** 06D,018K 020L,025P,byz. **Var:** 01‎א,02A,03B,04C 33,Lach,Treg,Alf,Word Tisc,We/Ho,Weis,Sod UBS/✭

4622.1 prs-pron nom 2sing	2428.6 name-adj nom sing masc	5062.6 verb nom sing masc part pres act	1476.1 adv	2180.6 verb 2sing indic pres act
σὺ,	Ἰουδαῖος	ὑπάρχων,	ἐθνικῶς	(ζῇς
su	Ioudaios	huparchōn	ethnikōs	zēs
you,	a Jew	being,	as a Gentile	live

2504.1 conj	3620.2 partic	2427.1 name-adv	2504.1 conj	3620.2 partic	2427.1 name-adv
καὶ	οὐκ	Ἰουδαϊκῶς,	[✩ καὶ	οὐκ	Ἰουδαϊκῶς
kai	ouk	Ioudaikōs	kai	ouk	Ioudaikōs
and	not	Jewishly,	[and	not	as a Jew

2180.6 verb 2sing indic pres act	4949.9 intr-pron nom sing neu	4316.1	3450.17 art pl neu	1477.4 noun pl neu	313.1 verb 2sing indic pres act
ζῇς,]	(τί	[ᵇ✶ πῶς]	τὰ	ἔθνη	ἀναγκάζεις
zēs	ti	pōs	ta	ethnē	anankazeis
live,]	why	[how]	the	Gentiles	do you compel

14.b.**Txt:** 018K,020L,byz. **Var:** 01‎א,02A,03B,04C 06D,025P,33,bo.Gries Lach,Treg,Alf,Word Tisc,We/Ho,Weis,Sod UBS/✭

2425.1 verb inf pres act	2231.1 prs-pron nom 1pl	5285.3 noun dat sing fem	2428.2 name-adj nom pl masc	2504.1 conj	3620.2 partic
Ἰουδαΐζειν;	15. Ἡμεῖς	φύσει	Ἰουδαῖοι,	καὶ	οὐκ
Ioudaizein	Hēmeis	phusei	Ioudaioi	kai	ouk
to judaize?	We,	by nature	Jews,	and	not

1523.1 prep gen	1477.5 noun gen pl neu	266.4 adj pl masc	3471.20 verb nom pl masc part perf act	1156.2 conj	3617.1 conj
ἐξ	ἐθνῶν	ἁμαρτωλοί,	16. εἰδότες	[ᵃ✶+ δὲ]	ὅτι
ex	ethnōn	hamartōloi	eidotes	de	hoti
of	Gentiles	sinners,	knowing	[and]	that

16.a.**Var:** 01‎א,03B,04C 06D,020L,it.Gries,Lach Treg,Alf,Word,Tisc We/Ho,Weis,Sod UBS/✭

3620.3 partic	1338.9 verb 3sing indic pres mid	442.1 noun nom sing masc	1523.1 prep gen	2024.5 noun gen pl neu	3414.2 noun gen sing masc
οὐ	δικαιοῦται	ἄνθρωπος	ἐξ	ἔργων	νόμου,
ou	dikaioutai	anthrōpos	ex	ergōn	nomou
not	is being justified	a man	by	works	of law,

1430.1 partic	3231.1 partic	1217.2 prep	3963.2 noun gen sing fem	2400.2 name masc	5382.2 name gen masc
ἐὰν	μὴ	διὰ	πίστεως	(Ἰησοῦ	Χριστοῦ,
ean	mē	dia	pisteōs	Iēsou	Christou
if	not	through	faith	of Jesus	Christ,

5382.2 name gen masc	2400.2 name masc	2504.1 conj	2231.1 prs-pron nom 1pl	1519.1 prep	5382.4 name acc masc
[Χριστοῦ,	Ἰησοῦ]	καὶ	ἡμεῖς	εἰς	Χριστὸν
Christou	Iēsou	kai	hēmeis	eis	Christon
[Christ,	of Jesus]	also	we	on	Christ

2400.3 name acc masc	3961.21 verb 1pl indic aor act	2419.1 conj	1338.16 verb 1pl subj aor pass	1523.2 prep gen
Ἰησοῦν	ἐπιστεύσαμεν,	ἵνα	δικαιωθῶμεν	ἐκ
Iēsoun	episteusamen	hina	dikaiōthōmen	ek
Jesus	believed,	that	we might be justified	by

of the gospel and its tremendous possibilities for faith and life. This becomes very apparent in working through his 13 letters.

Paul's greatness and his firm refusal to compromise the truth of God's Word can be seen in his reactions to this very disturbing situation. By their actions, Peter, Barnabas, who had been sent to lead the church at Antioch, and the Jewish Christians were denying the cardinal truth of the gospel: salvation by grace alone. It was through this message that the Spirit had brought the Gentiles to faith, and now by the actions of Peter and the other Jewish Christians it was being grossly and openly denied.

In this tense scene Paul publicly rebuked Peter. (He used the name "Cephas," his Aramaic name, which Paul normally used in his letters to refer to Peter.) He singled out Peter who, in the eyes of those present, represented the mother church in Jerusalem. By his actions Peter was denying the cardinal truth of the gospel. The Greek word translated "walk uprightly" (*orthopodousin*) literally means "walking in a straight line" according to the truth of the gospel. Technically, as a Jew, by eating with Gentiles the bread and other food which had been dedicated through prayer to God, Peter had been living as a Gentile. Paul questioned how he could insist (by now separating himself from the Gentiles) that they had to live as Jews?

2:15. Paul reminded Peter (and also all the Jewish Christians present) that by nature they were ethnically Jewish. By birth they were true descendants of Abraham, the father of God's covenant people (Genesis 12:1-3), and, as such, they were ethnically members of God's covenant people. The Gentiles were the exact opposite. Because of their ethnic origins, not being descended from Abraham, they were considered by the Jews to be habitual, chronic sinners. They were completely outside the covenant relationship with God. Therefore, they could not help but live in gross sin. They lived constantly under the eternal curse of God. This reflected the Jewish view of that day. Paul referred to this to demonstrate to the Jewish Christians the true meaning of their gross sinful act. Thereby they were denying that salvation is by grace alone.

2:16,17. Paul reminded all present that no one, Jew or Gentile, can be justified by the works of the Law, i.e., by seeking to earn salvation through works. In so doing, he echoed the truth of Psalm 143:2: "And enter not into judgment with thy servant: for in thy sight shall no man living be justified."

Paul used the verb *justify* three times in verse 16. He used it in the legal sense of "being declared just and righteous." This verb is passive in this verse. It is God alone who can declare one to be righteous, but only if the requirements of God's justice and righteousness have been fully met. Man's sinful nature causes him to commit sins, so he cannot consider himself righteous before God.

I said unto Peter before [them] all, If thou, being a Jew, livest after the manner of Gentiles, and not as do the Jews, why compellest thou the Gentiles to live as do the Jews?: . . . in the presence of all, *Wilson* . . . in such a way that all the other Jews could hear what I said, *SEB* . . . you, who are a Jew by nation, live like a foreigner and not like a Jew, how can you urge the foreigners to Judaize? *Fenton* . . . in front of everybody, *Adams* . . . why on earth do you try to make Gentiles live like Jews? *Phillips* . . . hou constreynest thou hethen men to bicome, *Wyclif* . . . adopt foreign ways of living...to adopt Jewish ways? *TCNT* . . . to live like Jews, *Adams* . . . follow Jewish customs, *Weymouth*.

15. We [who are] Jews by nature, and not sinners of the Gentiles: We are natural Jews, and not sinners from among the heathen, *Fenton* . . . We Jews were not born non-Jewish or sinners, *SEB* . . . by birth, *TCNT, Montgomery, Weymouth* . . . by race, *Sawyer* . . . sinners from among the gentiles, *Worrell*.

16. Knowing that a man is not justified by the works of the law, but by the faith of Jesus Christ, even we have believed in Jesus Christ: . . . being conscious that, *BB* . . . is not accepted as righteous, *Noyes* . . . not declared righteous, *Rotherham* . . . but we know that a man is not made righteous by ritualism, except through a faith of, *Fenton* . . . a man is justified not by performing what the Law commands but by faith in, *Phillips* . . . a person is not made right with God by following the law. Committing oneself to Jesus Christ is what makes a person right with God, *SEB* . . . as the result of actions done in obedience to Law, *TCNT* . . . through obedience to Law that a man can be declared free from guilt, *Weymouth* . . . but by simple trust in Christ, *Williams* . . . we ourselves also have put our faith in Christ, *Montgomery*.

Galatians 2:17

3963.2 noun gen sing fem	5382.2 name gen sing masc	2504.1 conj	3620.2 partic	1523.1 prep gen	2024.5 noun gen pl neu	3414.2 noun gen sing masc
πίστεως	Χριστοῦ,	καὶ	οὐκ	ἐξ	ἔργων	νόμου·
pisteōs	Christou	kai	ouk	ex	ergōn	nomou
faith	of Christ,	and	not	by	works	of law;

16.b.Txt: 04C,06D-corr
018K,020L,025P,byz.
Var: 01ℵ,02A,03B
06D-org,33,Lach,Treg
Alf,Tisc,We/Ho,Weis
Sod,UBS/⋆

1354.1 conj	3617.1 conj	3620.3 partic	1338.24 verb 3sing indic fut pass	1523.1 prep gen	2024.5 noun gen pl neu
⸌ διότι	[ᵇ⋆ ὅτι]	⸌ οὐ	δικαιωθήσεται	ἐξ	ἔργων
dioti	hoti	ou	dikaiōthēsetai	ex	ergōn
because	[idem]	not	shall be justified	by	works

3414.2 noun gen sing masc	1523.1 prep gen	2024.5 noun gen pl neu	3414.2 noun gen sing masc	3620.3 partic	1338.24 verb 3sing indic fut pass
νόμου	[⋆ ἐξ	ἔργων	νόμου	οὐ	δικαιωθήσεται]
nomou	ex	ergōn	nomou	ou	dikaiōthēsetai
of law	[from	works	of law	not	will be justified]

3820.9 adj nom sing fem	4418.1 noun nom sing fem		1479.1 conj	1156.2 conj	2195.10 verb nom pl masc part pres act
πᾶσα	σάρξ.	**17.**	εἰ	δὲ	ζητοῦντες
pasa	sarx		ei	de	zētountes
all	flesh.		If	now	seeking

1338.18 verb inf aor pass	1706.1 prep	5382.3 name dat masc	2128.33 verb 1pl indic aor pass	2504.1 conj	840.7 prs-pron nom pl masc
δικαιωθῆναι	ἐν	Χριστῷ	εὑρέθημεν	καὶ	αὐτοὶ
dikaiōthēnai	en	Christō	heurethēmen	kai	autoi
to be justified	in	Christ	we were found	also	ourselves

266.4 adj pl masc	680.1 partic	5382.1 name nom masc	264.1 noun fem	1243.1 noun nom sing masc	3231.1 partic
ἁμαρτωλοί,	ἆρα	Χριστὸς	ἁμαρτίας	διάκονος;	μὴ
hamartōloi	ara	Christos	hamartias	diakonos	mē
sinners,	then	Christ	of sin	minister?	Not

1090.44 verb 3sing opt aor mid		1479.1 conj	1056.1 conj	3614.17 rel-pron pl neu	2617.3 verb 1sing indic aor act	3642.18 dem-pron pl neu
γένοιτο.	**18.**	εἰ	γὰρ	ἃ	κατέλυσα	ταῦτα
genoito		ei	gar	ha	katelusa	tauta
may it be!		If	for	what	I threw down	these things

3687.1 adv	3481.1 verb 1sing pres act	3710.2 noun acc 1sing masc	1670.3 prs-pron acc 1sing masc	4771.1 verb 1sing indic pres act
πάλιν	οἰκοδομῶ,	παραβάτην	ἐμαυτὸν	⸌ συνίστημι.
palin	oikodomō	parabatēn	emauton	sunistēmi
again	I build,	a transgressor	myself	I constitute.

18.a.Txt: 06D-corr,018K
020L,byz.
Var: 01ℵ,02A,03B,04C
06D-org,025P,33,Gries
Lach,Treg,Alf,Word
Tisc,We/Ho,Weis,Sod
UBS/⋆

4771.13 verb 1sing indic pres act		1466.1 prs-pron nom 1sing	1056.1 conj	1217.2 prep	3414.2 noun gen sing masc
[ᵃ⋆ συνιστάνω.]	**19.**	Ἐγὼ	γὰρ	διὰ	νόμου
sunistanō		Egō	gar	dia	nomou
[idem]		I	for	through	law

3414.3 noun dat sing masc	594.9 verb indic aor act	2419.1 conj	2296.3 noun dat sing masc	2180.23 verb 1sing subj aor act	5382.3 name dat masc
νόμῳ	ἀπέθανον,	ἵνα	θεῷ	ζήσω.	**20.** Χριστῷ
nomō	apethanon	hina	theō	zēsō	Christō
to law	died,	that	to God	I may live.	Christ

4809.4 verb 1sing indic perf mid	2180.5 verb 1sing indic pres act	1156.2 conj	3629.1 adv	1466.1 prs-pron nom 1sing
συνεσταύρωμαι·	ζῶ	δὲ,	οὐκέτι	ἐγώ,
sunestaurōmai	zō	de	ouketi	egō
I have been crucified with,	I live	yet,	no longer	I,

By nature all, both Jews and Gentiles, are under God's righteous wrath.

To Peter and the Jewish Christians Paul emphatically stated that no one can justify himself by avoiding table fellowship with Gentiles and meeting other requirements of the Law. Both Jews and Gentiles are sinful, regardless of ethnic origins, and hence are under God's judgment. Only by faith in Christ and His atoning sacrifice can anyone be saved. This included also those who by birth considered themselves to be ethnically members of God's covenant people and descendants of Abraham. Paul stressed that regarding salvation there are no privileged (Jews) or underprivileged (Gentiles) people. All by nature are under God's wrath as Paul emphasized also in his other letters, for example, Romans 3:23-26 and Ephesians 2. He restated this fact again in the closing words of this verse to stress the decisive nature of grace alone for man's salvation.

Paul asked a very important question to emphasize what he had said. The actions of Peter, Barnabas, and the Jewish Christians implied that they wanted to be righteous by what they did. Paul in essence said that by their action of not eating with the Gentile Christians, they placed themselves again under the curse of the Law. *Hamartia* ("sin") is used here in its proper meaning of conduct which is in violation of true righteousness.

Paul answered with an emphatic "God forbid!" (*mē genoito*). In Galatians Paul used this emphatic expression twice, once here and again in 3:21. In this very dramatic manner, Paul forcefully demonstrated the true meaning and implication of their sinful action.

The expression "God forbid" in the New Testament is used almost exclusively by Paul. The single non-Pauline use is that of Luke 20:16 in the reaction of members of the Jewish Council to the meaning of Jesus' Parable of the Dishonest Lessees of the Vineyard (Luke 20:9-16; see also Isaiah 5). They understood that God would take the covenant relationship away from them and give it to the Gentiles.

2:18. To impress on his Jewish hearers the seriousness of what they had done, Paul made another telling statement. He reminded them that when they had come to faith, they had destroyed the basis of their former hope of salvation, namely, that of works. They had been led to see and confess that salvation is only by grace through faith in Christ. By their action in avoiding eating with the Gentile Christians, Peter, Barnabas, and the Jewish Christians had actually denied the way of grace and returned to that of works. That which they had declared invalid when they came to faith, they now by their action declared to be the only way of salvation. Hence, they had become transgressors. Transgression implies a law transgressed (Romans 4:15; 5:13). And no one can keep the Law.

2:19-21. Paul's words take on added meaning in view of the self-description he gave in Philippians 3:4-11. He, the proud Pharisee

that we might be justified by the faith of Christ, and not by the works of the law: ... that we might stand right with God through dependence upon faith, *TCNT* ... are justified by our faith and not by our obedience to the Law, *Phillips* ... not by doing what the law commands, *Williams*.

for by the works of the law shall no flesh be justified: Observance of the Law, *Norlie* ... for, by the deeds of the law, *Murdock* ... no one can achieve justification, *Phillips*.

17. But if, while we seek to be justified by Christ, we ourselves also are found sinners: ... as we grasp the real truth, *Phillips* ... to be declared righteous, *Rotherham*.

[is] therefore Christ the minister of sin? God forbid: ... does that mean that Christ makes us sinners? *Phillips* ... would that make Christ an agent of sin? Certainly not, *TCNT* ... does that make Christ a party to our sin? *Williams* ... By no means, *Confraternity* ... Absolutely not! *Norlie*.

18. For if I build again the things which I destroyed, I make myself a transgressor: ... if I reconstruct, *Confraternity* ... if I rebuild those...I constitute Myself, *Wilson* ... if, what things I pulled down, *Rotherham* ... the things I had demolished, *Murdock* ... I proved myself to have done wrong, *TCNT* ... a prevaricator, *Douay*.

19. For I through the law am dead to the law, that I might live unto God: I am dead to the Law's demands so that I may live for God, *Phillips*.

20. I am crucified with Christ: nevertheless I live; yet not I: I am nailed to the cross, *Douay* ... I died on the cross with Christ, *Phillips*.

2180.1 verb sing indic pres act	1156.2 conj	1706.1 prep	1466.5 prs-pron dat 1sing	5382.1 name nom masc	3614.16 rel-pron sing neu	1156.2 conj
ζῇ	δὲ	ἐν	ἐμοὶ	Χριστός·	ὃ	δὲ
zē	de	en	emoi	Christos	ho	de
lives	but	in	me	Christ;	which	but

3431.1 adv	2180.5 verb 1sing indic pres act	1706.1 prep	4418.3 noun dat sing fem	1706.1 prep	3963.3 noun dat sing fem	2180.5 verb 1sing indic pres act
νῦν	ζῶ	ἐν	σαρκί,	ἐν	πίστει	ζῶ
nun	zō	en	sarki	en	pistei	zō
now	I live	in	flesh,	in	faith	I live,

20.a.Txt: 01ℵ,02A,04C 06D-corr2,044,byz. **Var:** p46,03B,06D-org 010F,012G

3450.11 art dat sing fem	3450.2 art gen sing	5048.2 noun gen sing masc	3450.2 art gen sing	2296.2 noun gen sing masc	2296.2 noun gen sing masc
τῇ	τοῦ	⸆ υἱοῦ	τοῦ	θεοῦ,	[a θεοῦ
tē	tou	huiou	tou	theou	theou
the	of the	Son		of God,	[of God

2504.1 conj	5382.2 name gen masc	3450.2 art gen sing	25.21 verb gen sing masc part aor act	1466.6 prs-pron acc 1sing	2504.1 conj
καὶ	χριστοῦ,]	τοῦ	ἀγαπήσαντός	με	καὶ
kai	christou,]	tou	agapēsantos	me	kai
and	of Christ,]	the	having loved	me	and

3722.18 verb gen sing masc part aor act	1431.6 prs-pron acc sing masc	5065.1 prep	1466.3 prs-pron gen 1sing	3620.2 partic
παραδόντος	ἑαυτὸν	ὑπὲρ	ἐμοῦ.	21. οὐκ
paradontos	heauton	huper	emou.	ouk
having given up	himself	for	me.	Not

114.1 verb 1sing indic pres act	3450.12 art acc sing fem	5322.4 noun acc sing fem	3450.2 art gen sing	2296.2 noun gen sing masc	1479.1 conj	1056.1 conj
ἀθετῶ	τὴν	χάριν	τοῦ	θεοῦ·	εἰ	γὰρ
athetō	tēn	charin	tou	theou	ei	gar
I do set aside	the	grace		of God;	if	for

1217.2 prep	3414.2 noun gen sing masc	1336.1 noun nom sing fem	679.1 partic	5382.1 name nom masc	1425.1 adv
διὰ	νόμου	δικαιοσύνη,	ἄρα	Χριστὸς	δωρεὰν
dia	nomou	dikaiosunē	ara	Christos	dōrean
through	law	righteousness,	then	Christ	without cause

594.10 verb 3sing indic aor act	5434.1 intrj	451.1 adj nom pl masc	1045.1 name nom pl masc	4949.3 intr-pron nom sing	5050.4 prs-pron acc 2pl
ἀπέθανεν.	3:1. Ὦ	ἀνόητοι	Γαλάται,	τίς	ὑμᾶς
apethanen	Ō	anoētoi	Galatai	tis	humas
died.	O	senseless	Galatians,	who	you

1.a.Txt: 04C,06D-corr 018K,020L,025P,byz. **Var:** 01ℵ,02A,03B 06D-org,33-org,bo.Gries Lach,Treg,Alf,Word Tisc,We/Ho,Weis,Sod UBS/☆

933.1 verb 3sing indic aor act	3450.11 art dat sing fem	223.3 noun dat sing fem	3231.1 partic	3844.24 verb inf pres mid	3614.4 rel-pron dat pl
ἐβάσκανεν,	⸀a τῇ	ἀληθείᾳ	μὴ	πείθεσθαι; ⸃	οἷς
ebaskanen	tē	alētheia	mē	peithesthai	hois
bewitched,	the	truth	not	to obey?	whose

2567.1 prep	3652.8 noun acc pl masc	2400.1 name nom masc	5382.1 name nom masc	4129.2 verb 3sing indic aor pass
κατ'	ὀφθαλμοὺς	Ἰησοῦς	Χριστὸς	προεγράφη
kat'	ophthalmous	Iēsous	Christos	proegraphē
before	eyes	Jesus	Christ	was openly set forth

1.b.Txt: 06D,018K,020L 025P,byz. **Var:** 01ℵ,02A,03B,04C 33-org,sa.bo.Lach,Treg Alf,Tisc,We/Ho,Weis UBS/☆

1706.1 prep	5050.3 prs-pron dat 2pl	4568.17 verb nom sing masc part perf mid	3642.17 dem-pron sing neu	3303.1 adv
⸀b ἐν	ὑμῖν ⸃	ἐσταυρωμένος;	2. τοῦτο	μόνον
en	humin	estaurōmenos	touto	monon
among	you	having been crucified?	This	only

who considered himself to be totally blameless (*amemptos*) before God, realized when the exalted Christ appeared to him on the Damascus Road that his entire way of life and self-estimation was worthless. In fact, in Philippians 3:8 he used a very strong Greek word, *skubala*, properly translated "dung," "sewage." Through Christ's action, so beautifully and forcefully stated in Philippians 3:9-11, Paul died to the way of works of the Law, and empowered by the Spirit (Titus 3:4-8), began to live his life in grace to God.

Paul went on to say in one verse what he developed in much greater detail in Romans 3–8. In so doing he referred to a form of execution which was well known to his readers, namely, crucifixion. This was a very common form of execution in the Roman world, usually reserved for slaves and those of the lower classes of society. However, as history records, under certain circumstances a Roman citizen too could be, and was, crucified. Every larger town, such as the Galatian Antioch and Iconium, had its place of execution at a well-traveled place outside the town walls. The upright beam of the cross was always left in place, waiting for the next victim who would carry the crossbeam to the place of his execution.

Paul stressed that when Christ died on the cross, he was crucified with Him. When Christ rose from the dead, he rose with Him. Hence, it was not his life he lived, but that of Christ who lived in him—a truth which he so well restated in Romans 6:1-11. And so the life he now lived as a human being was lived by faith through the Spirit's work, a faith centered in Christ who gave himself for Paul and for all mankind (Romans 6 and 8).

In his notes on 2:20 the great expositor C.I. Scofield presented a basic truth: "Christianity is the outliving of an indwelling Christ" (*The Scofield Reference Bible*). Once a believer has captured this truth, he realizes that all he does must present a proper view of the Son of God reaching the world through him.

Paul closed with the words, "I do not frustrate the grace of God." The Greek word translated "frustrate" (*athetō*) actually means "make null and void." The action of Peter, Barnabas, and the other Jewish Christians had in fact nullified the true meaning of God's grace.

Paul had been accused of not sharing the full dimensions of the gospel by not carefully stressing that all had to live as Jews. And so Paul restated what this in actuality meant, namely, that if salvation is by works, then Christ had died in vain. Grace was non-existent.

3:1. Chapters 3 and 4 stress the certainty of salvation by grace alone. Paul now shifted the tone of his letter to exclaim, "O foolish Galatians!" The Greek word translated "foolish" (*anoētoi*) refers to those who knew better but failed to use what they knew.

Paul went on to ask, "Who hath bewitched you?" or, "Who has confused, hypnotized you?" In the second part of this verse, Paul reminded the Galatians that he and Barnabas had dramatically stressed the significance of Christ's crucifixion in God's plan of salvation by grace alone.

---

but Christ liveth in me: and the life which I now live in the flesh I live by the faith of the Son of God, who loved me, and gave himself for me: ... as for my present earthly life, *TCNT* ... The bodily life I now live, I live believing in...who loved me and sacrificed himself, *Phillips*.

21. I do not frustrate the grace of God: for if righteousness [come] by the law, then Christ is dead in vain: I cast not away, *Douay* ... I do not abrogate, *Geneva* ... I despyse not, *Cranmer* ... I do not cast away, *Confraternity* ... I refuse to stultify the grace, *Phillips* ... I refuse to ignore, *Norlie* ... I am not setting aside the favour of God...Christ needlessly died, *Rotherham* ... I refuse to set aside the mercy of God...then Christ died for nothing! *TCNT* ... died for nought, *Panin, ASV* ... died unnecessarily, *Wilson* ... died with out cause, *Wyclif* ... died needlessly! *Worrell*.

1. O foolish Galatians, who hath bewitched you, that ye should not obey the truth: O senseless, *Douay* ... O vnwitti galathianes, *Wyclif* ... O Thoughtless Galatians, *Wilson, Rotherham* ... you dear idiots...who has been casting a spell over you? *Phillips* ... You let someone trick you, *Everyday* ... who has been fascinating you, *TCNT*.

before whose eyes Jesus Christ hath been evidently set forth, crucified among you?: ... who saw Jesus Christ the crucified so plainly, *Phillips* ... were told very clearly about the death of Jesus, *Everyday* ... was previously represented as having been crucified, *Wilson* ... was openly set forth, *Panin, Rotherham, ASV, Worrell* ... was described before the eyes, *Tyndale* ... was described in your sight, *Geneva* ... was depicted as crucified? *TCNT* ... has been depicted crucified? *Confraternity* ... was portrayed among you, *PNT* ... clearly pictured before your eyes as the Crucified One? *Norlie*.

2286.1 verb 1 sing pres act	3101.13 verb inf aor act	570.1 prep	5050.2 prs- pron gen 2pl	1523.1 prep gen	2024.5 noun gen pl neu	3414.2 noun gen sing masc
θέλω	μαθεῖν	ἀφ᾽	ὑμῶν,	ἐξ	ἔργων	νόμου
thelō	mathein	aph᾽	humōn	ex	ergōn	nomou
I wish	to learn	from	you,	by	works	of law

3450.16 art sing neu	4011.1 noun sing neu	2956.16 verb 2pl indic aor act	2211.1 conj	1523.1 prep gen	187.2 noun gen sing fem	3963.2 noun gen sing fem
τὸ	πνεῦμα	ἐλάβετε,	ἢ	ἐξ	ἀκοῆς	πίστεως;
to	pneuma	elabete	ē	ex	akoēs	pisteōs
the	Spirit	receive you,	or	by	report	of faith?

	3643.1 adv	451.1 adj nom pl masc	1498.6 verb 2pl indic pres act	1712.2 verb nom pl masc part aor mid	4011.3 noun dat sing neu	3431.1 adv
3.	οὕτως	ἀνόητοί	ἐστε;	ἐναρξάμενοι	πνεύματι,	νῦν
	houtōs	anoētoi	este	enarxamenoi	pneumati	nun
	Thus	senseless	are you?	Having begun	in Spirit,	now

4418.3 noun dat sing fem	1989.9 verb 2pl indic pres mid		4965.9 dem- pron pl neu	3819.12 verb 2pl indic aor act
σαρκὶ	ἐπιτελεῖσθε;	**4.**	τοσαῦτα	ἐπάθετε
sarki	epiteleisthe		tosauta	epathete
in flesh	are you being perfected?		So many things	did you suffer

1488.1 adv	1480.1 conj	2504.1 conj	1488.1 adv	3450.5 art nom sing masc	3631.1 partic
εἰκῇ;	εἴγε	καὶ	εἰκῇ.	**5.** ὁ	οὖν
eikē	eige	kai	eikē	ho	oun
in vain?	if indeed	also	in vain.	The	therefore

2007.1 verb nom sing masc part pres act	5050.3 prs- pron dat 2pl	3450.16 art sing neu	4011.1 noun sing neu	2504.1 conj	1738.4 verb nom sing masc part pres act
ἐπιχορηγῶν	ὑμῖν	τὸ	πνεῦμα,	καὶ	ἐνεργῶν
epichorēgōn	humin	to	pneuma	kai	energōn
supplying	to you	the	Spirit,	and	working

1405.5 noun pl fem	1706.1 prep	5050.3 prs- pron dat 2pl	1523.1 prep gen	2024.5 noun gen pl neu	3414.2 noun gen sing masc
δυνάμεις	ἐν	ὑμῖν,	ἐξ	ἔργων	νόμου
dunameis	en	humin	ex	ergōn	nomou
works of power	among	you,	by	works	of law

2211.1 conj	1523.1 prep gen	187.2 noun gen sing fem	3963.2 noun gen sing fem	2503.1 conj	11.1 name masc
ἢ	ἐξ	ἀκοῆς	πίστεως;	**6.** καθὼς	Ἀβραὰμ
ē	ex	akoēs	pisteōs	kathōs	Abraam
or	by	report	of faith?	Even as	Abraham

3961.20 verb 3sing indic aor act	3450.3 art dat sing	2296.3 noun dat sing masc	2504.1 conj	3023.11 verb 3sing indic aor pass	840.4 prs- pron dat sing
ἐπίστευσεν	τῷ	θεῷ,	καὶ	ἐλογίσθη	αὐτῷ
episteusen	tō	theō	kai	elogisthē	autō
believed	to	God,	and	it was reckoned	to him

1519.1 prep	1336.4 noun acc sing fem		1091.5 verb 2pl indic pres act	679.1 partic	3617.1 conj	3450.7 art nom pl masc
εἰς	δικαιοσύνην.	**7.**	Γινώσκετε	ἄρα	ὅτι	οἱ
eis	dikaiosunēn		Ginōskete	ara	hoti	hoi
for	righteousness.		Know	then	that	the

1523.2 prep gen	3963.2 noun gen sing fem	3642.7 dem- pron nom pl masc	1498.7 verb 3pl indic pres act	5048.6 noun nom pl masc	5048.6 noun nom pl masc
ἐκ	πίστεως,	οὗτοι	ʼ εἰσιν	υἱοί	[✶ υἱοί
ek	pisteōs	houtoi	eisin	huioi	huioi
of	faith,	these	are	sons	[sons

3:2-5. Paul went on to ask in a dramatic manner (following the Greek sentence structure), "This only would I learn of you, received ye the Spirit by the works of the law, or by the hearing of faith?" Paul repeated the two phrases "works of the law" and "hearing of faith" again and again in this chapter to emphasize the certainty of salvation by grace through faith alone.

In Romans 10:17 Paul stated: "Faith cometh by hearing, and hearing by the word of God." Titus 3:4-8 carefully stresses the role of the Holy Spirit in bringing people to faith. And this fact Paul stressed again and again.

Again he asked, "Are ye so foolish?" And then continued, "Having begun in the Spirit, are ye now made perfect by (*epiteleisthe*, 'finishing in') the flesh?" Note the decisive tenses he used. He continued, "Have ye suffered so many things in vain?" Acts 13 and 14 shed some light on this question. Acts 14:2-5 indicates that Jews from Antioch stirred up people against the Christians in Iconium. Whether those in Antioch and Lystra suffered we are not specifically told.

Paul closed verse 4 with "if it be yet in vain." In other words, there was still hope! And then he restated in essence what he said earlier in verse 2. In verse 5 he again used a very strong word translated "worketh" (*energōn*). Acts 14:3 records that God used Paul and Barnabas to work "signs and wonders." Acts 14:8-10 records the healing of the man lame from birth, and verse 20 tells how Paul recovered after being stoned and left for dead.

3:6. This verse goes back to Genesis 15:6. Abraham had obeyed God's gracious call (Genesis 12:1) and had led his clan to Mamre, just north of Hebron, in the land of Canaan. Some years had gone by. God still had not given him and his aged wife Sarah a son as He had promised in Genesis 12:1-3. When God appeared to him in a vision, Abraham, in indirect Middle Eastern fashion, reminded God that He had failed to keep His promise (Genesis 15:2,3). God took him outside and asked him to count the stars in the heavens and told him, "So shall thy seed be!" (Genesis 15:5). Abraham's response was that he "believed God, and it was accounted to him for righteousness." Paul here quoted Genesis 15:6.

Humanly speaking, at the advanced age of Sarah, God's promise to give them a son seemed impossible. However, Abraham believed that God could and would keep His promise. This was fulfilled when Abraham was 100 and Sarah was 90 years old (Genesis 21).

The more important fulfillment of God's promises lay well in the future. The most important was that of sending the Seed, the Saviour. This Paul emphasized in the verses which follow. The Galatians had the privilege of living in the age when God's promises of the Saviour had been fulfilled.

3:7. Paul used a very strong imperative ("Know!") to remind the Galatians that all who believe in the certainty of God's promises are true descendants of Abraham, regardless of their ethnic origins.

2. This only would I learn of you, Received ye the Spirit by the works of the law, or by the hearing of faith?: . . . that I want to find out from you...or to your having listened with faith? *TCNT* . . . by the dedes of the lawe, or by the preachynge of the fayth? *Cranmer.*

3. Are ye so foolish? having begun in the Spirit, are ye now made perfect by the flesh?: Are ye so thoughtless? *Wesley* . . . so void of understanding? *Scarlett* . . . beginning with what is spiritual, *TCNT* . . . now you vvil be consummate vvith the flesh? *Rheims.*

4. Have ye suffered so many things in vain? if [it be] yet in vain: . . . if indeed it was really to no purpose! *TCNT* . . . it is for nothing, *Wilson.*

5. He therefore that ministereth to you the Spirit, and worketh miracles among you, [doeth he it] by the works of the law, or by the hearing of faith?: Who therefore supplieth you, *Panin* . . . and endows you with, *TCNT* . . . he then who imparteth, *Scarlett* . . . worketh mighty works in you, *Alford* . . . that imparts to you...and exercises miraculous powers...by the doctrine of faith? *Sawyer.*

6. Even as Abraham believed God, and it was accounted to him for righteousness: . . . and that was regarded by, *TCNT* . . . and it was credited to him, *Confraternity* . . . and it was ascribed to him, *Geneva.*

7. Know ye therefore that they which are of faith, the same are the children of Abraham: Know you, certainly, *Wilson* . . . Ye perceive, then, *Rotherham* . . . those whose lives are based on faith, *TCNT* . . . are the real sons of, *Confraternity.*

1498.7 verb 3pl indic pres act		11.1 name masc	4134.2 verb nom sing fem part aor act	1156.2 conj	3450.9 art nom sing fem	1118.1 noun nom sing fem
εἰσιν]		᾿Αβραάμ.	**8.** προϊδοῦσα	δὲ	ἡ	γραφὴ
eisin		Abraam	proidousa	de	hē	graphē
are]		of Abraham;	having foreseen	and	the	scripture

3617.1 conj	1523.2 prep gen	3963.2 noun gen sing fem	1338.1 verb 3sing indic pres act	3450.17 art pl neu	1477.4 noun pl neu	3450.5 art nom sing masc
ὅτι	ἐκ	πίστεως	δικαιοῖ	τὰ	ἔθνη	ὁ
hoti	ek	pisteōs	dikaioi	ta	ethnē	ho
that	by	faith	justifies	the	Gentiles	

2296.1 noun nom sing masc	4142.1 verb 3sing indic aor mid		3450.3 art dat sing	11.1 name masc
θεὸς,	προευηγγελίσατο		τῷ	᾿Αβραάμ,
theos,	proeuēngelisato		tō	Abraam
God,	before announced good news		to	to Abraham:

3617.1 conj	1741.1 verb 3pl indic fut pass	1706.1 prep	4622.3 prs-pron dat 2sing	3820.1 adj	3450.17 art pl neu
῞Οτι	᾿Ενευλογηθήσονται	ἐν	σοὶ	πάντα	τὰ
Hoti	Eneulogēthēsontai	en	soi	panta	ta
	Shall be blessed	in	you	all	the

1477.4 noun pl neu	5452.1 conj	3450.7 art nom pl masc	1523.2 prep gen	3963.2 noun gen sing fem	2108.14 verb 3pl indic pres mid
ἔθνη.	**9.** ὥστε	οἱ	ἐκ	πίστεως	εὐλογοῦνται
ethnē.	hoste	hoi	ek	pisteōs	eulogountai
nations.	So that	the	of	faith	are being blessed

4713.1 prep	3450.3 art dat sing	3964.4 adj dat sing masc	11.1 name masc	3607.2 rel-pron nom pl masc	1056.1 conj	1523.1 prep gen
σὺν	τῷ	πιστῷ	᾿Αβραάμ.	**10.** ὅσοι	γὰρ	ἐξ
sun	tō	pistō	Abraam	hosoi	gar	ex
with	the	believing	Abraham.	As many as	for	of

2024.5 noun gen pl neu	3414.2 noun gen sing masc	1498.7 verb 3pl indic pres act	5097.3 prep	2641.3 noun acc sing fem	1498.7 verb 3pl indic pres act
ἔργων	νόμου	εἰσὶν,	ὑπὸ	κατάραν	εἰσίν·
ergōn	nomou	eisin,	hupo	kataran	eisin
works	of law	are,	under	a curse	are.

1119.22 verb 3sing indic perf mid	1056.1 conj	3617.1 conj	1929.1 adj nom sing masc	3820.6 adj nom sing masc
γέγραπται	γὰρ,	[a☆+ ὅτι]	᾿Επικατάρατος	πᾶς
gegraptai	gar	hoti	Epikataratos	pas
It has been written	for,		Cursed	everyone

3614.5 rel-pron nom sing masc	3620.2 partic	1682.1 verb 3sing indic pres act	1706.1 prep	3820.5 adj dat pl	3450.4 art dat pl
῞Ος	οὐκ	ἐμμένει	⟨b ἐν ⟩	πᾶσιν	τοῖς
hos	ouk	emmenei	en	pasin	tois
who	not	does continue	in	all things	the

1119.30 verb dat pl neu part perf mid	1706.1 prep	3450.3 art dat sing	968.3 noun dat sing neu	3450.2 art gen sing	3414.2 noun gen sing masc
γεγραμμένοις	ἐν	τῷ	βιβλίῳ	τοῦ	νόμου,
gegrammenois	en	tō	bibliō	tou	nomou
having been written	in	the	book	of the	law

3450.2 art gen sing	4020.41 verb inf aor act	840.16 prs-pron pl neu	3617.1 conj	1156.2 conj	1706.1 prep	3414.3 noun dat sing masc
τοῦ	ποιῆσαι	αὐτά.	**11.** ῞Οτι	δὲ	ἐν	νόμῳ
tou	poiēsai	auta.	Hoti	de	en	nomō
the	to do	them.	That	but	by	law

10.a.**Var:** 01ℵ,02A,03B 04C,06D,025P,33,Gries Lach,Treg,Alf,Word Tisc,We/Ho,Weis,Sod UBS/☆

10.b.**Txt:** 01ℵ-corr,02A 04C,06D,018K,020L 025P,byz. **Var:** 01ℵ-org,03B,33 Treg,Tisc,We/Ho,Weis Sod,UBS/☆

The Greek uses the term *sons* (*huioi*) translated as "children." The term *son* had a special legal meaning in the thought pattern of that day. A son was legally an heir, and through him the family line continued. Paul used the term here in the nongender sense; this is reflected in the translation of "children." He did the same in Romans 8:14-17.

3:8,9. In verse 8 Paul made a very important statement. He said that Scripture foresaw God's plan of salvation. Second Timothy 3:16 and 2 Peter 1:20,21 carefully state that the Scriptures are the inspired Word of God. This Paul firmly believed. Hence, he emphasized that God in the Scriptures foretold His gracious plan of salvation.

God promised Abraham at the time of his call that in him would "all families of the earth be blessed" (Genesis 12:3). In Genesis 18:18 and 22:18 the phrase "all the nations of the earth" is used. And Paul added a very important statement. To experience such a spiritual blessing, it is necessary to believe in the certain promises of God, just as Abraham did. Physical ancestry from the line of Abraham means nothing spiritually. By the Spirit working through the Word, to believe as Abraham did is all important for salvation.

3:10. To emphasize what he had said, Paul restated it in the negative. In 2:16 he used the phrase "works of the law" three times. Here he used it again to stress that what the Judaizers were saying as necessary for salvation would result in being eternally under God's curse, resulting in eternal damnation.

To undergird what he said, he quoted from Deuteronomy 27:26. These words were spoken by Moses to Israel at Abel-Shittim east of the Jordan shortly before his death on Mount Nebo. They were carried out when Israel renewed its covenant with God at Mount Ebal and Mount Gerizim (Joshua 8:30-35).

Moses had been instructed that six tribes were to stand on Mount Gerizim, the Mount of Blessing, and six on Mount Ebal, the Mount of Cursing. The Levites were to recite the 12 curses found in Deuteronomy 27:15-26. After each curse the people were to respond with "Amen." The curses emphasized pagan idolatry and gross immorality which God's covenant people were to avoid. Whereas the first 11 curses placed a ban on specific acts of disobedience, the 12th was more comprehensive, especially as found in the Septuagint. To make sure there could be no misunderstanding, Paul changed the reading "of this law" to "which are written in the book of the law." The term "book of the law" refers to the five books of Moses, which in the Hebrew are known as *Torah*. *Torah* means "revelation, instruction." It is important to remember that sometimes this term should be understood this way rather than "law," also in the New Testament. Sometimes it has reference to the Pentateuch, and it is also sometimes used as a term for the entire Old Testament Scriptures.

8. And the scripture, foreseeing that God would justify the heathen through faith, preached before the gospel unto Abraham, [saying], In thee shall all nations be blessed: . . . because God knew beforehand, *Murdock* . . . anticipating God's justification, *Montgomery* . . . that God would make the heathen righteous by means of a faith promised from the first, *Fenton* . . . announced the good news beforehand, *Adams* . . . preached the gospel beforehand, *PNT* . . . really proclaimed the Gospel centuries ago in the words spoken to Abraham, *Phillips* . . . all the heathen shall be blessed, *TCNT*.

9. So then they which be of faith are blessed with faithful Abraham: All people who believe are blessed in the same way that Abraham was blessed for his faith, *Fenton* . . . All men of faith share the blessing of Abraham, *Phillips* . . . blessed as partners with trusting Abraham, *Williams* . . . with believing Abraham, *Murdock* . . . with the faith of Abraham, *Fenton* . . . Abraham who had faith, *Adams*.

10. For as many as are of the works of the law are under the curse: Now, all who depend on works, *Adams* . . . For whoever are dependent on a law of rituals, *Fenton* . . . but people who depend on following the law to make them right are under condemnation, *Fenton*.

for it is written, Cursed [is] every one that continueth not in all things which are written in the book of the law to do them: A person must do everything which is written in the book, *Fenton* . . . every one who does not abide by all, *TCNT* . . . who does not hold fast to, *Galatians* . . . all who do not continue in all the writings of the book, *Fenton* . . . in the scroll of the law, *Rotherham* . . . to perform them, *Confraternity* . . . to fulfyll them, *Cranmer* . . . Everyone, however, who is involved in trying to keep the Law's demands falls under a curse, *Phillips*.

3625.2 num card nom masc	1338.9 verb 3sing indic pres mid	3706.2 prep	3450.3 art dat sing	2296.3 noun dat sing masc	1206.1 adj sing
οὐδεὶς	δικαιοῦται	παρὰ	τῷ	θεῷ	δῆλον·
oudeis	dikaioutai	para	tō	theō	dēlon
no one	is being justified	with		God	clear;

3617.1 conj	3450.5 art nom sing masc	1337.3 adj nom sing masc	1523.2 prep gen	3963.2 noun gen sing fem	2180.29 verb 3sing indic fut mid
ὅτι	ὁ	δίκαιος	ἐκ	πίστεως	ζήσεται·
hoti	ho	dikaios	ek	pisteōs	zēsetai
because	the	just	by	faith	shall live;

3450.5 art nom sing masc	1156.2 conj	3414.1 noun nom sing masc	3620.2 partic	1498.4 verb 3sing indic pres act	1523.2 prep gen	3963.2 noun gen sing fem
12. ὁ	δὲ	νόμος	οὐκ	ἔστιν	ἐκ	πίστεως,
ho	de	nomos	ouk	estin	ek	pisteōs
the	but	law	not	is	of	faith;

12.a.**Txt:** 06D-corr,018K 020L,byz. **Var:** 01ℵ,02A,03B,04C 06D-org,025P,33,it.bo. Gries,Lach,Treg,Alf Word,Tisc,We/Ho,Weis Sod,UBS/☆

233.1 conj	3450.5 art nom sing masc	4020.37 verb nom sing masc part aor act	840.16 prs- pron pl neu	442.1 noun nom sing masc
ἀλλ'	ὁ	ποιήσας	αὐτὰ	⌜a ἄνθρωπος ⌝
all'	ho	poiēsas	auta	anthrōpos
but,	the	having done	these things	man

2180.29 verb 3sing indic fut mid	1706.1 prep	840.2 prs- pron dat pl	5382.1 name nom masc	2231.4 prs- pron acc 1pl
ζήσεται	ἐν	αὐτοῖς.	**13.** Χριστὸς	ἡμᾶς
zēsetai	en	autois	Christos	hēmas
shall live	by	them.	Christ	us

1789.1 verb 3sing indic aor act	1523.2 prep gen	3450.10 art gen sing fem	2641.2 noun gen sing fem	3450.2 art gen sing	3414.2 noun gen sing masc
ἐξηγόρασεν	ἐκ	τῆς	κατάρας	τοῦ	νόμου,
exēgorasen	ek	tēs	kataras	tou	nomou
ransomed	from	the	curse	of the	law,

1090.53 verb nom sing masc part aor mid	5065.1 prep	2231.2 prs- pron gen 1pl	2641.1 noun nom sing fem	1119.22 verb 3sing indic perf mid
γενόμενος	ὑπὲρ	ἡμῶν	κατάρα·	⌜ γέγραπται
genomenos	huper	hēmōn	katara	gegraptai
having become	for	us	a curse,	it has been written

13.a.**Txt:** 01ℵ,06D-corr 018K,020L,025P,byz.bo. **Var:** 02A,03B,04C 06D-org,33,Lach,Treg Alf,Word,Tisc,We/Ho Weis,Sod,UBS/☆

1056.1 conj	3617.1 conj	1119.22 verb 3sing indic perf mid	1929.1 adj nom sing masc	3820.6 adj nom sing masc
γὰρ	[a☆ ὅτι	γέγραπται,]	Ἐπικατάρατος	πᾶς
gar	hoti	gegraptai	Epikataratos	pas
for,	[because	it is written,]	Cursed	everyone

3450.5 art nom sing masc	2883.5 verb nom sing masc part aor mid	1894.3 prep	3448.2 noun gen sing neu	2419.1 conj	1519.1 prep	3450.17 art pl neu
ὁ	κρεμάμενος	ἐπὶ	ξύλου·	**14.** ἵνα	εἰς	τὰ
ho	kremamenos	epi	xulou	hina	eis	ta
the	having hung	on	a tree,	that	to	the

1477.4 noun pl neu	3450.9 art nom sing fem	2110.1 noun nom sing fem	3450.2 art gen sing	11.1 name masc	1090.40 verb 3sing subj aor mid
ἔθνη	ἡ	εὐλογία	τοῦ	Ἀβραὰμ	γένηται
ethnē	hē	eulogia	tou	Abraam	genētai
nations	the	blessing		of Abraham	might come

1706.1 prep	5382.3 name dat masc	2400.2 name masc	2400.2 name masc	5382.3 name dat masc	2419.1 conj
ἐν	⌜ Χριστῷ	Ἰησοῦ,	[Ἰησοῦ,	Χριστῷ]	ἵνα
en	Christō	Iēsou	Iēsou	Christō	hina
in	Christ	Jesus,	[Jesus,	Christ]	that

3:11-14. Everyone who seeks to earn salvation by his works is under God's curse, but those who believe in God's promises are declared righteous by Him. Paul quoted from Habakkuk 2:4: "The just shall live by his faith." Habakkuk served as God's prophet after the tragic death of King Josiah at Megiddo in the battle against Pharaoh-nechoh II of Egypt in 609 B.C., and the latter's defeat in 605 B.C. by Nebuchadnezzar of Babylonia. Judah then became a vassal state of Nebuchadnezzar (2 Kings 23 and 24). In 587 B.C. Jerusalem was destroyed and the people of Judah were taken into exile in Babylonia. Please note that even though there is some debate on this, possibly the better date for Jerusalem's destruction is 587 B.C.

In view of what the people of Judah viewed as stark tragedy, the emphasis of Habakkuk may be described as asking how God can permit evil so good may come out of it. God's answer is that this can only be understood from the vantage point of trusting in God and His righteous dealings. The key is to remember the crucial words: "The just shall live by faith," not by works.

Paul emphasized that believers can be just and righteous in God's sight only through the redemptive work of Christ. He quoted Deuteronomy 21:22,23 which speaks of the execution of one guilty of a capital offense. He was first executed and then his dead body was hung up for all to see. From two of the Dead Sea Scrolls, the Nahum Pesher (4QpHah, fragments 3 and 4, column 1, lines 5-8) and the Temple Scroll (column 64, lines 6-13), we know that by the Second Century B.C., anyone executed for certain religious crimes by crucifixion was understood to be under God's curse as found in Deuteronomy 21:22,23. Paul's words reflected this understanding.

Paul noted in 1 Corinthians 2:2 that he was determined "not to know any thing among you, save Jesus Christ, and him crucified." In 1 Corinthians 1:23 he stated that for Jews, as those who considered themselves to be the religious elite, Christ's crucifixion was a "stumblingblock" (*skandalon*). For Greeks, as the cultured elite, it was "foolishness" or nonsense (*mōrian*). But in the next verse Paul stated, to those who are called, both Jews and Gentiles, "Christ is the power of God, and the wisdom of God" (1 Corinthians 1:24).

In verse 14 Paul concluded this part of his decisive argument. It is totally through Christ's redemptive work as a fulfillment of God's promise to Abraham that Gentiles will also be saved through faith in His atoning merit.

Paul ended this verse with the words: "That we might receive the promise of the Spirit through faith." Luke 24:49 records some of Jesus' final words to His disciples, shortly before His ascension. He reminded His disciples that He would send them "the promise of my Father." In Acts 1:4 Jesus told His disciples to remain in Jerusalem and "wait for the promise of the Father."

These words also recall words Jesus spoke to His disciples (John 14—17) which reveal the role of the Holy Spirit as Christ's Spirit, whom the Father would send in Jesus' name (John 14:26). The verbs which Jesus used in His description of the ongoing work of the Spirit are very important: teach and remind (John 14:26); tell the truth about Him (John 15:26); convince (John 16:8); lead,

11. But that no man is justified by the law in the sight of God, [it is] evident: . . . none in law, *Fenton* . . . no one stands right with God, *TCNT* . . . is brought into right standing with God, *Williams* . . . It is made still plainer that no one is justified...by obeying the Law, *Phillips* . . . it is manifest, *Rheims* . . . is clear, *Adams*.

for, The just shall live by faith: The Scriptures say, The person who is right with God by faith will live forever, *SEB* . . . because the just person, *Adams* . . . The righteous, *Panin, Fenton, Phillips*.

12. And the law is not of faith: but, The man that doeth them shall live in them: . . . is not based on faith, *TCNT* . . . has nothing to do with faith, *Montgomery* . . . is not a matter of faith, *Phillips* . . . does not require faith, *Adams* . . . Instead, the law says, A person who wants to find life by following these things must do the things the law says, *SEB* . . . the ritual did not come from faith; on the contrary, the performer of them must live, *Fenton*.

13. Christ hath redeemed us from the curse of the law, being made a curse for us: for it is written, Cursed [is] every one that hangeth on a tree: . . . ransomed us, *TCNT* . . . purchased us...for is it written: cursed beyond measure, *Fenton* . . . The law put us under condemnation, but Christ took that condemnation away. He changed places with us, *SEB* . . . becoming in our behalf a curse, *Rotherham* . . . hanged on a beam of wood, *Noyes*.

14. That the blessing of Abraham might come on the Gentiles through Jesus Christ: Christ did this, so that God's promised blessing...could be given to all people, *SEB* . . . might come to, *Fenton* . . . might be realized by the Gentiles, *Adams* . . . might be extended to the heathen, *TCNT*.

Galatians 3:15

14.a.**Txt**: 01ℵ,02A,03B 04C,06D-corr2,044,byz. **Var**: p46,06D-org,010F 012G

3450.12 art acc sing fem	1845.4 noun acc sing fem	2110.4 noun acc sing fem	3450.2 art gen sing	4011.2 noun gen sing neu
τὴν tēn the	(✶ ἐπαγγελίαν epangelian promise	[ᵃ εὐλογίαν] eulogian [blessing]	τοῦ tou of the	πνεύματος pneumatos Spirit

2956.19 verb 1pl subj aor act	1217.2 prep	3450.10 art gen sing fem	3963.2 noun gen sing fem	79.6 noun nom pl masc
λάβωμεν labōmen we might receive	διὰ dia through	τῆς tēs the	πίστεως. pisteōs faith.	15. Ἀδελφοί, Adelphoi Brothers,

2567.3 prep	442.4 noun acc sing masc	2978.1 verb 1sing pres act	3539.1 adv	442.2 noun gen sing masc
κατὰ kata according to	ἄνθρωπον anthrōpon man	λέγω, legō I am speaking,	ὅμως homōs even	ἀνθρώπου anthrōpou of man

2937.2 verb acc sing fem part perf mid	1236.4 noun acc sing fem	3625.2 num card nom masc	114.2 verb 3sing indic pres act	2211.1 conj
κεκυρωμένην kekurōmenēn having been ratified	διαθήκην diathēkēn covenant	οὐδεὶς oudeis no one	ἀθετεῖ athetei nullifies,	ἢ ē or

1913.1 verb 3sing indic pres mid	3450.3 art dat sing	1156.2 conj	11.1 name masc	1500.24 verb 3pl indic aor pass
ἐπιδιατάσσεται. epidiatassetai makes additions.	16. τῷ tō But	δὲ de	Ἀβραὰμ Abraam to Abraham	(ἐρρήθησαν errhēthēsan were spoken

16.a.**Txt**: 03B-corr 06D-corr,018K,020L byz. **Var**: 01ℵ,02A,03B-org 04C,06D-org,025P,33 Lach,Treg,Alf,Tisc We/Ho,Weis,Sod UBS/✶

1500.31 verb 3pl indic aor pass	3450.13 art nom pl fem	1845.5 noun nom pl fem	2504.1 conj	3450.3 art dat sing	4543.3 noun dat sing neu
[ᵃ✶ ἐρρέθησαν] errhethēsan [idem]	αἱ hai the	ἐπαγγελίαι, epangeliai promises,	καὶ kai and	τῷ tō to the	σπέρματι spermati seed

840.3 prs- pron gen sing	3620.3 partic	2978.5 verb 3sing indic pres act	2504.1 conj	3450.4 art dat pl	4543.5 noun dat pl	5453.1 conj
αὐτοῦ· autou his:	οὐ ou not	λέγει, legei he does say,	Καὶ Kai And	τοῖς tois to the	σπέρμασιν, spermasin seeds,	ὡς hōs as

1894.3 prep	4044.1 adj gen pl	233.1 conj	5453.1 conj	1894.1 prep	1518.1 num card gen	2504.1 conj	3450.3 art dat sing
ἐπὶ epi of	πολλῶν, pollōn many;	ἀλλ' all' but	ὡς hōs as	ἐφ' eph' of	ἑνός, henos one,	Καὶ Kai And	τῷ tō to the

4543.3 noun dat sing neu	4622.2 prs- pron gen 2sing	3614.5 rel-pron nom sing masc	1498.4 verb 3sing indic pres act	5382.1 name nom sing masc	3642.17 dem- pron sing neu
σπέρματί spermati seed	σου, sou your;	ὅς hos which	ἐστιν estin is	Χριστός. Christos Christ.	17. τοῦτο touto This

1156.2 conj	2978.1 verb 1sing pres act	1236.4 noun acc sing fem	4159.1 verb acc sing fem part perf mid
δὲ de now	λέγω, legō I say,	διαθήκην diathēkēn covenant	προκεκυρωμένην prokekurōmenēn having been confirmed beforehand

17.a.**Txt**: 06D,018K 020L,byz. **Var**: p46,01ℵ,02A,03B 04C,025P,33,sa.bo.Lach Treg,Alf,Tisc,We/Ho Weis,Sod,UBS/✶

5097.3 prep	3450.2 art gen sing	2296.2 noun gen sing masc	1519.1 prep	5382.4 name acc masc	3450.5 art nom sing masc	3196.3 prep
ὑπὸ hupo by	τοῦ tou	θεοῦ theou God	(ᵃ εἰς eis to	Χριστον) Christon Christ,	ὁ ho the	μετὰ meta after

speak what He hears and tell what is coming, and glorify Christ (John 16:13,14).

Crucial in Paul's argument is the fact that through the Spirit's work, Gentiles also are led to believe in the certainty of salvation by grace alone.

3:15. To emphasize what he has said before, Paul used a variety of illustrations, with special reference to life and thought patterns so intimately a part of life in Galatia.

The first illustration is that of a last will and testament, using the Greek word *diathēkē*, in its secular meaning. This was an important word in the world of that time. It was as important then for one to properly draw up such a document as it is today, to make sure that the inheritance would be passed on as desired. Paul also used a number of other legal terms which at that time were also an intimate part of dealing with such a document. He said that "if it be confirmed" ("ratified") in the proper manner, "no man disannulleth," that is, sets it aside and annuls it, or "addeth thereto," that is, adds a codicil. Such a will could be activated only when the testator's death was registered as Hebrews 9:16,17 states. And the terms of the will had to be carried out exactly as stated in the document.

3:16. Paul used this illustration because a last will involves an inheritance as he now emphasized. God's promise was made to Abraham and his seed. To make certain there was no misunderstanding, "He saith not, And to seeds, as of many; but as of one, And to thy seed, which is Christ." The Greek word for "which" (*hos*) is exclusive; it can only refer to "seed" in the singular in this sentence. Paul's use of the term "seed" recalled God's words to Abraham in Genesis 22:18: "And in *thy seed* shall all the nations of the earth be blessed." This came through the redemptive work of Jesus Christ, the woman's Seed whose heel was bruised but who crushed the head of the Evil One by His crucifixion and His descent into hell (Genesis 3:15; 1 Peter 3:18,19).

3:17,18. The term *diathēkē* is used in the Greek secular meaning of "last will and testament" only three times in the New Testament (Galatians 3:15; Hebrews 9:16,17). Otherwise it is always used in the meaning of God's covenant of grace as a translation of the Old Testament Hebrew term *berîth*. In seeking to find a Greek word for the Hebrew *berîth*, the translators of the Hebrew Old Testament into Greek found this term to be the nearest in meaning to that of the Hebrew term.

Paul noted that God made His covenant of grace with Abraham 430 years before He formally received Abraham's descendants in covenant relationship at Mount Sinai (Exodus 19). God carefully emphasizes (especially in Exodus 19:4; 20:2; and Deuteronomy 7:6-10) that this was a tremendous grace event. Unfortunately as

that we might receive the promise of the Spirit through faith: . . . the Annunciation of the Spirit, *Wilson* . . . might become available to us all, *Phillips*.

15. Brethren, I speak after the manner of men: Let me take an illustration, Brothers, from daily life, *TCNT* . . . Let me give you an everyday illustration, *Phillips* . . . I speak humanly, *Fenton* . . . in human fashion, *Rotherham* . . . according to what is practised among men, *Noyes* . . . by an example from human relationships, *Adams*.

Though [it be] but a man's covenant, yet [if it be] confirmed, no man disannulleth, or addeth thereto: . . . a man has made his will, *Norlie* . . . even a testament made by a man, *Fenton* . . . Even a human contract, *Williams* . . . once it has been ratified, *Adams* . . . no one sets aside, *Rotherham* . . . no man doth abrogate it, *Geneva* . . . no one setteth aside, or changeth any thing in it, *Murdock* . . . or alters, *Confraternity* . . . or superadds conditions, *Wilson* . . . or adds conditions to it, *TCNT* . . . when it is established, *Sawyer*.

16. Now to Abraham and his seed were the promises made. He saith not, And to seeds, as of many; but as of one, And to thy seed, which is Christ: Note in passing that the scripture says not "seeds" but uses the singular "seed," meaning Christ, *Phillips* . . . and to his heir, *Fenton* . . . "and to your descendant," that is, Christ, *Williams*.

17. And this I say, [that] the covenant, that was confirmed before of God in Christ: Therefore, I argue, *Norlie* . . . And I assert this, *Fenton* . . . Now this is what I am trying to say, *Adams* . . . Now this I affirm...previously ratified by God, *Wilson* . . . My point is this: An agreement already confirmed, *TCNT* . . . already ratified by God, *Alford*.

2073.3 noun pl neu	4919.3 num card neu	2504.1 conj	4984.1 num card	4919.3 num card neu
ʽ ἔτη	τετρακόσια	καὶ	τριάκοντα	[✶ τετρακόσια
etē	tetrakosia	kai	triakonta	tetrakosia
years	four hundred	and	thirty	[four hundred

2504.1 conj	4984.1 num card	2073.3 noun pl neu	1090.7 verb nom sing masc part perf act	3414.1 noun nom sing masc
καὶ	τριάκοντα	ἔτη]	γεγονὼς	νόμος
kai	triakonta	etē	gegonōs	nomos
and	thirty	years]	having taken place	law

3620.2 partic	206.1 verb 3sing indic pres act	1519.1 prep	3450.16 art sing neu	2643.6 verb inf aor act	3450.12 art acc sing fem
οὐκ	ἀκυροῖ,	εἰς	τὸ	καταργῆσαι	τὴν
ouk	akuroi	eis	to	katargēsai	tēn
not	does nullify	to	the	to make of no effect	the

1845.4 noun acc sing fem	1479.1 conj	1056.1 conj	1523.2 prep gen	3414.2 noun gen sing masc	3450.9 art nom sing fem
ἐπαγγελίαν.	**18.** εἰ	γὰρ	ἐκ	νόμου	ἡ
epangelian	ei	gar	ek	nomou	hē
promise.	If	for	by	law	the

2790.1 noun nom sing fem	3629.1 adv	1523.1 prep gen	1845.1 noun fem	3450.3 art dat sing	1156.2 conj
κληρονομία,	οὐκέτι	ἐξ	ἐπαγγελίας·	τῷ	δὲ
klēronomia	ouketi	ex	epangelias	tō	de
inheritance,	no longer	by	promise;	to	but

11.1 name masc	1217.1 prep	1845.1 noun fem	5319.12 verb 3sing indic perf mid	3450.5 art nom sing masc
Ἀβραὰμ	δι'	ἐπαγγελίας	κεχάρισται	ὁ
Abraam	di'	epangelias	kecharistai	ho
to Abraham	through	promise	has granted	

2296.1 noun nom sing masc	4949.9 intr-pron sing neu	3631.1 partic	3450.5 art nom sing masc	3414.1 noun nom sing masc	3450.1 art gen pl
θεός.	**19.** Τί	οὖν	ὁ	νόμος;	τῶν
theos	Ti	oun	ho	nomos	tōn
God.	Why	then	the	law?	of the

3709.4 noun gen pl fem	5320.1 prep	4227.6 verb 3sing indic aor pass	884.1 conj	3614.2 rel-pron gen sing
παραβάσεων	χάριν	προσετέθη,	ἄχρις	ʽ οὗ
parabaseōn	charin	prosetethē	achris	hou
transgressions	for the sake of	it was added,	until	which

300.1 partic	2048.8 verb 3sing subj aor act	3450.16 art sing neu	4543.1 noun sing neu	3614.3 rel-pron dat sing
[ᵃ ἂν]	ἔλθῃ	τὸ	σπέρμα	ᾧ
an	elthē	to	sperma	hō
	should have come	the	seed	to whom

19.a.**Txt**: p46,01ℵ,02A 04C,06D,044,etc.byz. Tisc,Sod
Var: 03B,33,We/Ho Weis,UBS/✶

1846.7 verb 3sing indic perf mid	1293.8 verb nom sing masc part aor pass	1217.1 prep	32.6 noun gen pl masc
ἐπήγγελται,	διαταγεὶς	δι'	ἀγγέλων
epēngeltai	diatageis	di'	angelōn
promise has been made,	having been ordained	through	angels

1706.1 prep	5331.3 noun dat sing fem	3186.2 noun gen sing masc	3450.5 art nom sing masc	1156.2 conj	3186.1 noun nom sing masc
ἐν	χειρὶ	μεσίτου.	**20.** ὁ	δὲ	μεσίτης
en	cheiri	mesitou	ho	de	mesitēs
in	hand	a mediator's.	The	but	mediator

a result of their unfaithfulness before the Exile and the consequence of this traumatic experience, the Jews had made this grace event into a law event.

Important for Paul's argument is the fact that when God made His covenant of grace with Abraham, he was still an uncircumcised Gentile. In fact, it would be 24 years later that Abraham and all male members of his clan were circumcised (Genesis 17:23-27). This covenant was not annulled by the much later event at Sinai which the Jews had made into law.

In verse 18 Paul restated this important fact. They were the heirs of the promise of grace God had made to Abraham. As he had received the promise strictly in grace, the Galatians as his spiritual heirs had received it also in grace. The claim of the Judaizers that all had to be circumcised and live as Jews was totally without any scriptural basis. Their "gospel" was false. It had not come from God. The gospel Paul had shared with them was the *true* gospel, the eternal truth.

3:19,20. Paul then asked a very important question: "Why, then was the Law given? What purpose does it serve?" This question flows naturally from the argument of the preceding verses. And his answer: "Because (for the sake) of transgressions it was added" (Greek). The Greek word translated "transgressions" (*parabaseōn*) means that which happens when a law is made. Literally it means a law or a norm which is overstepped. So a sign reading "Keep off the grass" often results in the reaction of willfully walking on the grass. As Paul said in Romans 4:15, "Where no law is, there is no transgression." When a sinner meets the Law, he reacts by transgressing it, and this results in committing more sins.

To say this in another way: Prod a sleeping lion with a stick, and it at once reacts with anger. The stick does not make the lion a wild beast. That it already is. Prodding the lion merely results in *showing* what the lion truly is. So the Law exposes the innate sinfulness of man. Paul did not say "because of sin," since transgression is a violation of explicit law and results in the recognition of the sinfulness of such violation. In Romans 7:7 Paul said: "I had not known sin, but by the law: for I had not known lust, except the law had said, Thou shalt not covet." Transgression results in multiplying sin.

Paul continued: "Till the seed should come to whom the promise was made." The "seed" is patently the same as in verse 16, namely, *the Seed* of Abraham, who is Jesus Christ. This thought is further developed in verses 23-25.

The last part of verse 19 seems to reflect a Jewish thought pattern. A careful reading of the Sinai event as described in Exodus and reflected in other parts of the Old Testament does not shed direct light on this sentence. Deuteronomy 33:2 has been suggested as the source of the role of angels. A close translation of the Hebrew text results in: "He came from His holy myriads; from His right hand came a fiery law for them."

the law, which was four hundred and thirty years after, cannot disannul, that it should make the promise of none effect: ... which came into existence ...cannot render null...and thus rob the promise of its value, *Phillips* ... does not invalidate, *Worrell* ... to be set aside, *TCNT* ... so as to cancel, *Williams* ... to invalidate the promise, *Wilson* ... cannot abrogate the covenant previously established by God, *Sawyer* ... maketh not void to frustrate the promise, *Rheims* ... so as to cancel the promise in it, *Norlie*.

18. For if the inheritance [be] of the law, [it is] no more of promise: but God gave [it] to Abraham by promise: For if our inheritance depends on the law, *Williams* ... if the receiving of the promised blessing were not made...that would amount to a cancellation of the original, *Phillips* ... it ceaseth to be the consequence of the promise, *Noyes* ... so graciously bestowed, *Williams*.

19. Wherefore then [serveth] the law?: What...was the use of, *TCNT* ... To what end then was the Law? *Noyes* ... To what purpose, then, *Montgomery* ... What then was the design of the Law? *Scarlett* ... Why then the Law? *Wilson* ... Where then lies the point of the Law? *Phillips*.

It was added because of transgressions, till the seed should come to whom the promise was made: It was a later addition, *TCNT* ... It was enacted on account of, *Confraternity* ... It was to operate till, *Norlie* ... until the "Offspring" should come, *Montgomery* ... until the descendant to whom the promise was made should come, *Williams*.

[and it was] ordained by angels in the hand of a mediator: ... having been arranged through, *Worrell* ... having been instituted, *Wilson* ... was inaugurated in the presence of, *Phillips* ... being appointed by angels, *Sawyer*.

Galatians 3:21

1518.1 num card gen	3620.2 partic	1498.4 verb 3sing indic pres act	3450.5 art nom sing masc	1156.2 conj	2296.1 noun nom sing masc	1518.3 num card nom masc
ἑνὸς	οὐκ	ἔστιν,	ὁ	δὲ	θεὸς	εἷς
henos	ouk	estin	ho	de	theos	heis
of one	not	is,	ho	but	God	one

1498.4 verb 3sing indic pres act	3450.5 art nom sing masc	3631.1 partic	3414.1 noun nom sing masc	2567.3 prep	3450.1 art gen pl
ἔστιν.	**21.** Ὁ	οὖν	νόμος	κατὰ	τῶν
estin	Ho	oun	nomos	kata	tōn
is.	The	then	law	against	the

1845.6 noun gen pl fem	3450.2 art gen sing	2296.2 noun gen sing masc	3231.1 partic	1090.44 verb 3sing opt aor mid	1479.1 conj	1056.1 conj
ἐπαγγελιῶν	τοῦ	θεοῦ;	μὴ	γένοιτο·	εἰ	γὰρ
epangeliōn	tou	theou	mē	genoito	ei	gar
promises	tou	of God?	Not	may it be!	If	for

1319.44 verb 3sing indic aor pass	3414.1 noun nom sing masc	3450.5 art nom sing masc	1404.13 verb nom sing masc part pres mid	2210.4 verb inf aor act
ἐδόθη	νόμος	ὁ	δυνάμενος	ζωοποιῆσαι,
edothē	nomos	ho	dunamenos	zōopoiēsai
was given	a law	the	being able	to give life,

3552.1 adv	300.1 partic	1523.2 prep gen	3414.2 noun gen sing masc	1498.34 verb sing indic imperf act	1523.2 prep gen	3414.2 noun gen sing masc
ὄντως	ἂν	ἐκ	νόμου	ἦν	[☆ ἐκ	νόμου
ontōs	an	ek	nomou	ēn	ek	nomou
indeed	an	by	law	would have been	[by	law

300.1 partic	1498.34 verb sing indic imperf act	3450.9 art nom sing fem	1336.1 noun nom sing fem	233.2 conj
ἂν	ἦν]	ἡ	δικαιοσύνη·	**22.** ἀλλὰ
an	ēn	hē	dikaiosunē	alla
an	would have been]	the	righteousness;	but

4639.1 verb 3sing indic aor act	3450.9 art nom sing fem	1118.1 noun nom sing fem	3450.17 art pl neu	3820.1 adj	5097.3 prep
συνέκλεισεν	ἡ	γραφὴ	τὰ	πάντα	ὑπὸ
sunekleisen	hē	graphē	ta	panta	hupo
shut up	the	scripture	the	all things	under

264.4 noun acc sing fem	2419.1 conj	3450.9 art nom sing fem	1845.2 noun nom sing fem	1523.2 prep gen	3963.2 noun gen sing fem
ἁμαρτίαν,	ἵνα	ἡ	ἐπαγγελία	ἐκ	πίστεως
hamartian	hina	hē	epangelia	ek	pisteōs
sin,	that	the	promise	by	faith

2400.2 name masc	5382.2 name gen masc	1319.46 verb 3sing subj aor pass	3450.4 art dat pl	3961.3 verb dat pl masc part pres act
Ἰησοῦ	Χριστοῦ	δοθῇ	τοῖς	πιστεύουσιν.
Iēsou	Christou	dothē	tois	pisteuousin
of Jesus	Christ	might be given	the	believing.

4112.1 prep	3450.2 art gen sing	1156.2 conj	2048.23 verb inf aor act	3450.12 art acc sing fem	3963.4 noun acc sing fem
23. Πρὸ	τοῦ	δὲ	ἐλθεῖν	τὴν	πίστιν,
Pro	tou	de	elthein	tēn	pistin
Before	the	but	to come	the	faith,

5097.3 prep	3414.4 noun acc sing masc	5268.4 verb 1pl indic imperf pass	4639.3 verb nom pl masc part perf mid
ὑπὸ	νόμον	ἐφρουρούμεθα,	ʽ συγκεκλεισμένοι
hupo	nomon	ephrouroumetha	sunkekleismenoi
under	law	we were being guarded,	having been shut up

The Hebrew phrase for "a fiery law" is 'ēshdat; the meaning of this is uncertain. The Septuagint translates the Hebrew for "fiery law" as "at His right hand were angels with Him." This reading seems to be reflected in Stephen's comment: "Who have received the law by the disposition of angels" (Acts 7:53) and in Hebrews 2:2: "For if the word spoken by angels was steadfast . . . ." Josephus records Herod as saying: "We have learned the noblest of all our doctrines and the holiest of all laws through angels sent from God" (*Antiquities of the Jews*, 15:136).

The role of a mediator is clarified in verse 20. A mediator involves at least two parties. Paul emphatically said that God is *one*. God acted unilaterally for himself when He made His covenant of grace with Abraham, and this provides God's way of salvation for all, both Jew and Gentile alike.

3:21,22. Paul went on to state that the Law cannot give life; it merely results in exposing the inborn sinfulness of man and his transgressions, going back to man's fall into sin (Genesis 3; Romans 3:23; 5:12). The Scriptures record both man's sin and God's promise of the woman's Seed, whom He would send to secure salvation for all, whether Jew or Gentile. But only those who believe in this promise receive it as God's gift.

3:23-25. When Paul said "before faith came," he meant "before the Seed came" (by Christ). So from the time of Sinai until Christ's actual coming, Christ was the One promised to come sometime in the indefinite future. The faith of those living in the Old Testament era was in the certainty that God would keep His gracious promises. The Law, as it were, kept man in confinement until God's promises were fulfilled in Christ.

To drive home this point, Paul used an illustration well known to his readers. The Greek term *paidagōgos*, translated "schoolmaster" or "guardian-trainer," was a slave, one who was put in total charge of his owner's son. This began when the boy was old enough to leave the care of his nurse. The slave-attendant's duty was to teach the boy good manners and even punish him, if necessary. He walked him to school, carrying his satchel. A special place in the school was reserved for such slave-attendants, where they waited until the school day ended. Then the slave-attendant took the boy home, quizzed him on what he was to have learned, had him recite his memory work, and the like. The son was under the total care of such an attendant from about the age of 6 to 16. Crucial for the boy and his future was the character and previous training of the attendant since the boy would reflect in life the training the slave-attendant gave him.

Thus the Law's role was to bring us to Christ, to teach us that by the Law salvation is impossible. Keeping the Law perfectly in accordance with God's will is impossible for man. The history of

20. Now a mediator is not [a mediator] of one, but God is one: . . . an intermediary between a single individual cannot be, *Fenton* . . . isn't needed when there is only one party, *Adams* . . . The very fact that there was an intermediary is enough to show that this was not the fulfilling of the promise, *Phillips* . . . implies more than one person, *Montgomery* . . . but God is only one, *TCNT*.

21. [Is] the law then against the promises of God? God forbid: Does the Law, then, frustrate the promises, *Norlie* . . . Is the Law then to be looked upon as a contradiction of the promise? *Phillips* . . . then opposed to, *Montgomery* . . . contrary to, *Confraternity* . . . in opposition to, *TCNT* . . . Be it not so, *Panin* . . . Of course not! *Adams*.

for if there had been a law given which could have given life, verily righteousness should have been by the law: . . . was able to make alive, *Wilson* . . . was able to impart life, *Williams* . . . would have actually existed through Law, *TCNT* . . . then no doute ryghtewesnes, *Cranmer* . . . then surely justification would have been, *Adams*.

22. But the scripture hath concluded all under sin, that the promise by faith of Jesus Christ might be given to them that believe: . . . the Law makes all men guilty of sin, *Norlie* . . . pictures all mankind as prisoners of sin, *Williams* . . . locks up everybody under sins so that, *Adams* . . . to those having faith, *Rotherham*.

23. But before faith came, we were kept under the law: . . . were we being guarded, *Rotherham* . . . were kept in custody, *Scarlett* . . . under restraints, *TCNT* . . . we were guarded under Law, *Wilson*, *Adams* . . . we were perpetual prisoners under the Law, *Montgomery* . . . kept under the rule of the Law, *Norlie*.

Galatians 3:24

23.a.**Txt:** 04C,06D-corr
018K,020L,byz.Sod
Var: 03B-corr,025P
Lach,Treg,Alf,UBS/☆

4639.4 verb nom pl masc part pres mid	1519.1 prep	3450.12 art acc sing fem	3165.16 verb acc sing fem part pres act	3963.4 noun acc sing fem
[ª☆ συγκλειόμενοι]	εἰς	τὴν	μέλλουσαν	πίστιν
sunkleiomenoi	eis	tēn	mellousan	pistin
[idem]	to	the	being about	faith

596.10 verb inf aor pass	5452.1 conj	3450.5 art nom sing masc	3414.1 noun nom sing masc	3670.1 noun nom sing masc
ἀποκαλυφθῆναι·	**24.** ὥστε	ὁ	νόμος	παιδαγωγὸς
apokaluphthēnai	hōste	ho	nomos	paidagōgos
to be revealed.	So that	the	law	tutor

2231.2 prs-pron gen 1pl	1090.3 verb 3sing indic perf act	1519.1 prep	5382.4 name acc masc	2419.1 conj	1523.2 prep gen	3963.2 noun gen sing fem
ἡμῶν	γέγονεν	εἰς	Χριστόν,	ἵνα	ἐκ	πίστεως
hēmōn	gegonen	eis	Christon	hina	ek	pisteōs
our	has been	to	Christ,	that	by	faith

1338.16 verb 1pl subj aor pass	2048.20 verb gen sing fem part aor act	1156.2 conj	3450.10 art gen sing fem	3963.2 noun gen sing fem
δικαιωθῶμεν·	**25.** ἐλθούσης	δὲ	τῆς	πίστεως,
dikaiōthōmen	elthousēs	de	tēs	pisteōs
we might be justified.	Having come	but	the	faith,

3629.1 adv	5097.3 prep	3670.2 noun acc sing masc	1498.5 verb 1pl indic pres act	3820.7 adj nom pl masc
οὐκέτι	ὑπὸ	παιδαγωγόν	ἐσμεν.	**26.** Πάντες
ouketi	hupo	paidagōgon	esmen	Pantes
no longer	under	a tutor	we are;	all

1056.1 conj	5048.6 noun nom pl masc	2296.2 noun gen sing masc	1498.6 verb 2pl indic pres act	1217.2 prep	3450.10 art gen sing fem
γὰρ	υἱοὶ	θεοῦ	ἐστε	διὰ	τῆς
gar	huioi	theou	este	dia	tēs
for	sons	of God	you are	'hrough	the

3963.2 noun gen sing fem	1706.1 prep	5382.3 name dat masc	2400.2 name masc	3607.2 rel-pron nom pl masc	1056.1 conj
πίστεως	ἐν	Χριστῷ	Ἰησοῦ·	**27.** ὅσοι	γὰρ
pisteōs	en	Christō	Iēsou	hosoi	gar
faith	in	Christ	Jesus.	As many as	for

1519.1 prep	5382.4 name acc masc	901.16 verb 2pl indic aor pass	5382.4 name acc masc	1730.4 verb 2pl indic aor mid
εἰς	Χριστὸν	ἐβαπτίσθητε,	Χριστὸν	ἐνεδύσασθε.
eis	Christon	ebaptisthēte	Christon	enedusasthe
to	Christ	were baptized,	Christ	you did put on.

3620.2 partic	1746.1 verb 3sing indic pres act	2428.6 name-adj nom sing masc	3624.1 conj	1659.1 name nom sing masc	3620.2 partic
28. οὐκ	ἔνι	Ἰουδαῖος	οὐδὲ	Ἕλλην·	οὐκ
ouk	eni	Ioudaios	oude	Hellēn	ouk
Not	there is	Jew	nor	Greek;	not

1746.1 verb 3sing indic pres act	1395.1 noun nom sing masc	3624.1 conj	1645.1 adj nom sing masc	3620.2 partic	1746.1 verb 3sing indic pres act
ἔνι	δοῦλος	οὐδὲ	ἐλεύθερος·	οὐκ	ἔνι
eni	doulos	oude	eleutheros	ouk	eni
there is	servant	nor	free;	not	there is

728.3 adj sing neu	2504.1 conj	2315.3 adj sing neu	3820.7 adj nom pl masc	1056.1 conj	5050.1 prs-pron nom 2pl	1518.3 num card nom masc
ἄρσεν	καὶ	θῆλυ·	πάντες	γὰρ	ὑμεῖς	εἷς
arsen	kai	thēlu	pantes	gar	humeis	heis
male	and	female;	all	for	you	one

God's covenant people as recorded in the Old Testament tragically emphasizes this fact.

Already, before Sinai, they had demonstrated their sinfulness. When Pharaoh's military might came close to them at the Red Sea, they chided Moses. At Marah they grumbled because the water was bitter. They murmured bitterly against God in the Wilderness of Sin over food, and some ignored God's instructions with reference to the manna. During this time Moses also had to act as the mediator in disputes of which there were so many in Israel.

Soon after the solemn covenant event at Mount Sinai, Israel worshiped the golden calf and fell into gross immorality. At Kadesh-Barnea they believed the 10 spies who doubted they could defeat the peoples living in the land of Canaan, even though God had promised to give them the land. Many joined Korah, Dathan, and Abiram in their rebellion against God.

Israel failed to destroy all the inhabitants in the land of Canaan, and this resulted in unfaithfulness to God, as the Book of Judges faithfully records. Again and again God had to punish them to call them back to Him.

The history of the divided kingdoms shows their unfaithfulness. During the reigns of Omri and Ahab the Northern Kingdom fell into the immoral worship of the Canaanite fertility gods of Baal and Asherah. In time God took many of them into exile and later also the Southern Kingdom. After the return from exile, God's people again became unfaithful to Him. He had to send them men such as Nehemiah, Ezra, Haggai, Zechariah, and Malachi to seek to bring them back. The intertestamental history of the Jews reveals the same tragic fact.

3:26,27. But now Christ had come. In Him God's promises through the centuries were fulfilled. Through His redemptive work the fence (partition) between Jew and Gentile had been removed. Christ's role as the suffering, obedient, and then victorious Servant guaranteed the certainty of salvation by grace alone for all. This blessing is experienced by all who through the Spirit's work believe in Him.

To emphasize this very important fact, Paul used an example from the life experience of the Galatians. Only a Roman citizen had the right to wear the garment of his special status, the toga. This white woolen garment with its purple stripe(s) was a cherished symbol of his exalted status. When the son of a Roman citizen became of age, he could exercise his right and put on the toga which symbolized his high status. So, when a person comes to faith, "he puts on Christ."

3:28,29. Paul closed this part of his argument with a very important statement. When he said, "There is neither Jew nor Greek," he made a very telling point. In the Jewish view, they of all people were the religious elite. They and they alone knew the true God and were His covenant people. All others were under God's curse.

shut up unto the faith which should afterwards be revealed: ... being locked up, *Adams* ... we were all imprisoned under...with our only hope of deliverance the faith that was to be shown to us, *Phillips* ... in preparation for the Faith, *TCNT, Williams* ... which shuld afterwarde be declared, *Tyndale.*

24. Wherefore the law was our schoolmaster [to bring us] unto Christ, that we might be justified by faith: ... is become our tutor, *Panin* ... has become our child-conductor unto Christ, *Rotherham* ... was a monitor for us, *Murdock* ... was like a strict governess in charge of us until we went to the school of Christ and learned to be justified, *Phillips* ... has proved a guide to lead us...we may stand right with God, *TCNT.*

25. But after that faith is come, we are no longer under a schoolmaster: Once we had that faith we were completely free from the governess's authority, *Phillips* ... no longer under a guardian, *Adams* ... no longer under the leader of our childhood, *Fenton.*

26. For ye are all the children of God by faith in Christ Jesus: You are all God's sons through, *Adams* ... now that you have faith, *Phillips.*

27. For as many of you as have been baptized into Christ have put on Christ: For all ye that are baptised, *Tyndale* ... as were immersed...were clothed with, *Wilson* ... clothed yourselves with, *TCNT.*

28. There is neither Jew nor Greek, there is neither bond nor free, there is neither male nor female: ... there is neither servant, *Sawyer* ... neither slave, *Adams* ... nor one a slave, *Fenton.*

57

1498.6 verb 2pl indic pres act	1706.1 prep	5382.3 name dat masc	2400.2 name masc	**29.** 1479.1 conj	1156.2 conj
ἐστε	ἐν	Χριστῷ	Ἰησοῦ·	εἰ	δὲ
este	en	Christō	Iēsou	ei	de
are	in	Christ	Jesus:	if	but

5050.1 prs-pron nom 2pl	5382.2 name gen masc	679.1 partic	3450.2 art gen sing	11.1 name masc	4543.1 noun sing neu
ὑμεῖς	Χριστοῦ,	ἄρα	τοῦ	Ἀβραὰμ	σπέρμα
humeis	Christou	ara	tou	Abraam	sperma
you	Christ's,	then		Abraham's	seed

1498.6 verb 2pl indic pres act	2504.1 conj	2567.1 prep	1845.4 noun acc sing fem	2791.3 noun nom pl masc
ἐστέ,	⟨a καὶ ⟩	κατ'	ἐπαγγελίαν	κληρονόμοι.
este	kai	kat'	epangelian	klēronomoi
you are,	and	according to	promise	heirs.

29.a.Txt: 018K,020L 025P,byz.
Var: 01ℵ,02A,03B,04C 06D,33,bo.Lach,Treg Alf,Tisc,We/Ho,Weis Sod,UBS/✱

2978.1 verb 1sing pres act	1156.2 conj	1894.1 prep	3607.1 rel-pron sing	5385.4 noun acc sing masc	3450.5 art nom sing masc
4:1. Λέγω	δέ,	ἐφ'	ὅσον	χρόνον	ὁ
Legō	de	eph'	hoson	chronon	ho
I say	now,	for	as long as	time	the

2791.1 noun nom sing masc	3378.1 adj nom sing masc	1498.4 verb 3sing indic pres act	3625.6 num card neu	1302.1 verb 3sing indic pres act
κληρονόμος	νήπιός	ἐστιν,	οὐδὲν	διαφέρει
klēronomos	nēpios	estin	ouden	diapherei
heir	an infant	is,	nothing	he differs

1395.2 noun gen sing masc	2935.1 noun nom sing masc	3820.4 adj gen pl	1498.21 verb nom sing masc part pres act	233.2 conj
δούλου,	κύριος	πάντων	ὤν·	**2.** ἀλλὰ
doulou	kurios	pantōn	ōn	alla
from a slave,	lord	of all	being;	but

5097.3 prep	1996.3 noun acc pl masc	1498.4 verb 3sing indic pres act	2504.1 conj	3485.5 noun acc pl masc	884.2 conj
ὑπὸ	ἐπιτρόπους	ἐστὶν	καὶ	οἰκονόμους	ἄχρι
hupo	epitropous	estin	kai	oikonomous	achri
under	guardians	he is	and	stewards	until

3450.10 art gen sing fem	4146.1 noun gen sing fem	3450.2 art gen sing	3824.2 noun gen sing masc	3643.1 adv
τῆς	προθεσμίας	τοῦ	πατρός.	**3.** οὕτως
tēs	prothesmias	tou	patros	houtōs
the	time before appointed	of the	father.	So

2504.1 conj	2231.1 prs-pron nom 1pl	3616.1 conj	1498.36 verb 1pl indic imperf act	3378.3 adj nom pl masc	5097.3 prep	3450.17 art pl neu
καὶ	ἡμεῖς,	ὅτε	ἦμεν	νήπιοι,	ὑπὸ	τὰ
kai	hēmeis	hote	ēmen	nēpioi	hupo	ta
also	we,	when	we were	infants,	under	the

4598.1 noun pl neu	3450.2 art gen sing	2862.2 noun gen sing masc	1498.36 verb 1pl indic imperf act	1498.50 verb 1pl indic imperf act
στοιχεῖα	τοῦ	κόσμου	⟨ ἦμεν	[a✱ ἤμεθα]
stoicheia	tou	kosmou	ēmen	ēmetha
elements	of the	world	were	[idem]

3.a.Txt: 02A,03B,04C 06D-corr,018K,020L 025P,byz.
Var: p46,01ℵ,06D-org 33,Tisc,We/Ho,Weis Sod,UBS/✱

1396.6 verb nom pl masc part perf mid	3616.1 conj	1156.2 conj	2048.3 verb 3sing indic aor act	3450.16 art sing neu
δεδουλωμένοι·	**4.** ὅτε	δὲ	ἦλθεν	τὸ
dedoulōmenoi	hote	de	ēlthen	to
having been enslaved;	when	but	came	to the

From the viewpoint of the Greeks, only those who were ethnically Greeks were the culturally elite. The rest were barbarians.

Paul went on to say "neither bond (slave) nor free." The Galatians understood the great difference of both the social and legal status of those who were either slaves or free. Paul continued, "neither male nor female." The Septuagint in Genesis 1:27 uses the same words which Paul used, when it says, "male and female created he them." It is of crucial importance that Paul here speaks of the universality of salvation. By nature all, regardless of gender, are under the curse of sin. Through Christ's redemptive work all who believe enjoy the blessings of grace.

Verse 29 restates and summarizes what Paul has said in this chapter. All who are in Christ are spiritually Abraham's descendants and hence are heirs with him of the blessings God promised him, namely, salvation by grace alone, the gospel which Paul had faithfully shared with the Galatians.

4:1-3. In this chapter Paul used a number of other examples to reemphasize the certainty of salvation by grace alone. In verses 1-3 he used an illustration which was very much part of the life of the Galatians. As is true also today, a child whose parents had died was considered a minor even though he was the heir of the parental estate. According to Roman law, the heir as a minor was placed in the charge of a guardian (tutor) who had been nominated by the father, until he was 14 years old. The guardian was in total charge of the welfare of the minor, including also his education. The management of the estate was entrusted to an appointed manager(s) (governors) until the heir reached the age of 25. Only then could he take over his inheritance.

What was true of the minor was true of Paul and his fellow Jews. He used a strong Greek word translated "were in bondage" (*dedoulōmenoi*, "enslaved"). Paul referred back to the training period from the time of Sinai to Christ and His atoning work. The Jews were enslaved "under the elements of the world." The Greek word translated "elements" is *stoicheia*. This means primarily items placed side by side in a row, such as the ABCs, and hence the "first principles" or "rudiments" as in Hebrews 5:12. (See p.546 for further discussion.) Here Paul referred to the time from Sinai till Christ came. In this way, he said that God's covenant people were living under the Law, learning that salvation was not by or through the Law.

4:4,5. The phrase "fulness of the time" is a very inclusive term. It refers to all that God in His eternal wisdom had seen necessary to take place before the *right time* could come for His Son to be born and the fulfillment of His promise to Abraham.

God's people had to learn that salvation is by grace even though the Pharisees stressed the way of law and obedience as crucial in prompting God to send the Messianic Age. Many pagans recognized the bankruptcy of their ancestral religion and were looking for some meaning in life. Many of the more educated went through

for ye are all one in Christ Jesus: All distinctions between...have vanished, *TCNT* . . . for you all are united in Christ, *Fenton.*

29. And if ye [be] Christ's, then are ye Abraham's seed, and heirs according to the promise: . . . if you belong to, *Wilson* . . . ye are, consequently, Abraham's seed, *Worrell* . . . you are real descendants, *Williams* . . . then you are the descendants of Abraham, *Montgomery* . . . you are of Abraham's race, inheritors by the promise, *Fenton* . . . sharers in the inheritance, *TCNT* . . . in keeping with the promise, *Adams.*

1. Now I say, [That] the heir, as long as he is a child, differeth nothing from a servant, though he be lord of all: What I mean is this, *Montgomery* . . . Again, let me illustrate...become master of the whole estate, *Norlie* . . . is a babe, *Panin* . . . is a litle one, *Rheims* . . . is a minor he is no different from...though he is the owner of everything, *Adams* . . . though he be the owner of the whole inheritance, *Montgomery.*

2. But is under tutors and governors until the time appointed of the father: . . . is under guardians, *Panin* . . . and trustees, *Montgomery* . . . and stewards until the time that was set beforehand by, *Adams.*

3. Even so we, when we were children, were in bondage under the elements of the world: . . . when we were like infants, *TCNT* . . . So too we, when we were minors, were enslaved by the world's presuppositions, *Adams* . . . were held in servitude, *PNT* . . . were in subordination under the elements of the world, *Murdock* . . . were enslaved under the rudiments, *Wilson.*

4. But when the fulness of the time was come, God sent forth his Son, made of a woman, made under the law: . . . but when the time was ripe for it, *TCNT*

3998.1 noun sing neu	3450.2 art gen sing	5385.2 noun gen sing masc	1805.1 verb 3sing indic aor act	3450.5 art nom sing masc	2296.1 noun nom sing masc
πλήρωμα	τοῦ	χρόνου,	ἐξαπέστειλεν	ὁ	θεὸς
plērōma	tou	chronou,	exapesteilen	ho	theos
fullness	of the	time,	sent forth		God

3450.6 art acc sing masc	5048.4 noun acc sing masc	840.3 prs-pron gen sing	1090.51 verb sing part aor mid	1523.2 prep gen	1129.2 noun gen sing fem
τὸν	υἱὸν	αὐτοῦ,	γενόμενον	ἐκ	γυναικός,
ton	huion	autou,	genomenon	ek	gunaikos,
	Son	his,	come	of	woman,

1090.51 verb sing part aor mid	5097.3 prep	3414.4 noun acc sing masc	2419.1 conj	3450.8 art acc pl masc	5097.3 prep	3414.4 noun acc sing masc
γενόμενον	ὑπὸ	νόμον,	**5.** ἵνα	τοὺς	ὑπὸ	νόμον
genomenon	hupo	nomon,	hina	tous	hupo	nomon
having come	under	law,	that	the	under	law

1789.2 verb 3sing subj aor act	2419.1 conj	3450.12 art acc sing fem	5047.3 noun acc sing fem	612.7 verb 1pl subj aor act
ἐξαγοράσῃ,	ἵνα	τὴν	υἱοθεσίαν	ἀπολάβωμεν.
exagorasē,	hina	tēn	huiothesian	apolabōmen.
he might ransom,	that	the	adoption	we might receive.

3617.1 conj	1156.2 conj	1498.6 verb 2pl indic pres act	5048.6 noun nom pl masc	1805.1 verb 3sing indic aor act	3450.5 art nom sing masc
6. Ὅτι	δέ	ἐστε	υἱοί,	ἐξαπέστειλεν	ὁ
Hoti	de	este	huioi,	exapesteilen	ho
Because	but	you are	sons,	sent forth	

2296.1 noun nom sing masc	3450.16 art sing neu	4011.1 noun sing neu	3450.2 art gen sing	5048.2 noun gen sing masc	840.3 prs-pron gen sing
θεὸς	τὸ	πνεῦμα	τοῦ	υἱοῦ	αὐτοῦ
theos	to	pneuma	tou	huiou	autou
God	the	Spirit	of the	Son	his

1519.1 prep	3450.15 art acc pl fem	2559.1 noun fem	5050.2 prs-pron gen 2pl	2231.2 prs-pron gen 1pl	2869.7 verb sing neu part pres act
εἰς	τὰς	καρδίας	ὑμῶν,	[ᵃ✶ ἡμῶν,]	κρᾶζον,
eis	tas	kardias	humōn,	hēmōn,	krazon,
into	the	hearts	your,	[our,]	crying,

5.2 noun sing masc	3450.5 art nom sing masc	3824.1 noun nom sing masc	5452.1 conj	3629.1 adv	1498.3 verb 2sing indic pres act
Ἀββα	ὁ	πατήρ.	**7.** ὥστε	οὐκέτι	εἶ
Abba	ho	patēr.	hōste	ouketi	ei
Abba,		Father.	So	no longer	you are

1395.1 noun nom sing masc	233.1 conj	233.2 conj	5048.1 noun nom sing masc	1479.1 conj	1156.2 conj	5048.1 noun nom sing masc
δοῦλος	ἀλλ'	[✶ ἀλλὰ]	υἱός·	εἰ	δὲ	υἱός,
doulos	all'	alla	huios·	ei	de	huios,
a slave,	but	[idem]	son;	if	and	son,

2504.1 conj	2791.1 noun nom sing masc	2296.2 noun gen sing masc	1217.2 prep	5382.2 name gen masc	1217.2 prep
καὶ	κληρονόμος	θεοῦ	διὰ	Χριστοῦ.	[ᵃ✶ διὰ
kai	klēronomos	theou	dia	Christou.	dia
also	heir	of God	through	Christ.	[through

2296.2 noun gen sing masc	233.2 conj	4966.1 adv	3173.1 conj	3620.2 partic	3471.20 verb nom pl masc part perf act
θεοῦ.]	**8.** Ἀλλὰ	τότε	μὲν	οὐκ	εἰδότες
theou.]	Alla	tote	men	ouk	eidotes
God.]	But	then	indeed	not	having known

6.a.**Txt:** 06D-corr,018K 020L,byz. **Var:** p46,01ℵ,02A,03B 04C,06D-org,025P,it.sa. Gries,Lach,Treg,Alf Word,Tisc,We/Ho,Weis Sod,UBS/✶

7.a.**Txt:** 01ℵ-corr 04C-corr,06D,018K 020L,025P,byz. **Var:** p46,01ℵ-org,02A 03B,04C-org,33,bo.Lach Treg,Alf,Tisc,We/Ho Weis,Sod,UBS/✶

the motions of the religious rites which were an intimate part of civic functions. Others joined various mystery cults, thereby to experience union with the god(s) in the rite and with fellow worshipers, regardless of their status.

More Jews lived outside of Palestine in the Dispersion than in Palestine. Many of these continued to worship God. The relative simplicity of the Jewish religion attracted many pagans to visit and worship in the synagogue. Some of these became serious "God-fearers" or even proselytes, i.e., full Jews.

The conquests of Alexander the Great resulted in Greek becoming the common, international language and brought in a common Hellenistic culture. The conquests of Rome in time brought the Mediterranean world under its control. The reign of Emperor Augustus finally brought peace to this extensive area after centuries of warfare. For many the Greek word *euangelia*, "good news," was a fitting term for the Roman peace.

The Roman navy swept pirates off the seas, making maritime commerce and travel safe. Already in the Second Century B.C. the empire began establishing well-built, long-lasting roads. This continued into the early centuries A.D. In time over 50,000 miles of such roads were constructed. This facilitated not only governmental communications but also commerce. As a result of such activity in this glorious era of peace there came prosperity and high hopes of better things to come. The "fullness of time" was an era of great anticipation.

Isaiah 7:14 foretold the virgin birth of the Immanuel. Verses 15-25 in prophetic language speak of the sad events and turmoil which God's unfaithful covenant people would face before this prophecy would be fulfilled.

At the right time God sent His Son. Both Matthew and Luke carefully emphasize that Jesus was virgin born. In fact, Matthew 1:23 quotes Isaiah 7:14. Luke 2:21-24 records His circumcision and, as the firstborn, He was bought back through a sacrificial rite. The Synoptics record that He was tempted by Satan. Satan's direct confrontation failed, but he continued to try to entrap the woman's Seed through others. The agony in Gethsemane is an example of what Jesus faced in His role as the obedient and suffering Servant (Isaiah 53). His passion ended in that triumphant cry, "It is finished!" and His voluntary death (John 19:28-30). Hebrews 2:14-18 and 4:14-16 point out that Jesus faced genuine temptations but did not sin. All this was necessary "to redeem them that were under the law, that we might receive the adoption of sons." Adoption was also part of life at that time.

4:6,7. Paul dramatically emphasized the full meaning of being "sons" and all this term means. As sons, through the Spirit's work, we may call God "Father" with all its implications. In Romans 8 Paul so beautifully enlarged in great detail on its full significance. As sons, God, in grace, made us His heirs, heirs of eternal life. As sons, we have the privilege of saying "Abba," Aramaic for *Father*, but with the loving filial overtones of what is meant by *Daddy*.

. . . when the right time came, *SEB* . . . when the proper time came God sent his son, born of a human mother and born under the jurisdiction, *Phillips* . . . when the completion of the time came ...born under a ritual, *Fenton* . . . produced from, *Wilson* . . . born of a woman, *Adams* . . . born subject to law, *Williams.*

5. To redeem them that were under the law, that we might receive the adoption of sons: God did this, so that he could buy back the freedom of those, *SEB* . . . so that He might buy out those, *Fenton* . . . to redeem from captivity, *Montgomery* . . . to ransom those, *Norlie* . . . myght receaue the inheritaunce that belongeth vnto the natural sonnes, *Cranmer* . . . receive the privileges of sons, *TCNT.*

6. And because ye are sons, God hath sent forth the Spirit of his Son into your hearts, crying, Abba, Father: Who calls out, *Adams* . . . The Spirit cries out, *SEB* . . . exclaiming, *Wilson* . . . Dear, dear Father! *Montgomery.*

7. Wherefore thou art no more a servant, but a son; and if a son, then an heir of God through Christ: So that no one is now a slave, *Fenton* . . . you are no longer a slave...an heir by God's own act, *Williams* . . . God's child, God's heir, *SEB* . . . an heire also, *Rheims* . . . an heir as well, *Adams.*

8. Howbeit then, when ye knew not God: Formerly, *Norlie* . . . But at that former time, *Williams* . . . Once, however, *Adams* . . . at that time, *Wilson* . . . at formerly, in your ignorance of God, *TCNT* . . . In the past, you didn't know God, *SEB.*

2296.4 noun acc sing masc	1392.10 verb 2pl indic aor act	3450.4 art dat pl	3231.1 partic	5285.3 noun dat sing fem	5285.3 noun dat sing fem
θεὸν,	ἐδουλεύσατε	τοῖς	ʼ μὴ	φύσει	[✱ φύσει
theon	edouleusate	tois	mē	phusei	phusei
God,	you were enslaved	to the	not	by nature	[by nature

3231.1 partic	1498.24 verb dat pl masc part pres act	2296.7 noun dat pl masc	3431.1 adv	1156.2 conj	1091.28 verb nom pl masc part aor act
μὴ]	οὖσιν	θεοῖς·	9. νῦν	δὲ,	γνόντες
mē	ousin	theois	nun	de	gnontes
not]	being	gods;	now	but,	having known

2296.4 noun acc sing masc	3095.1 adv comp	1156.2 conj	1091.45 verb nom pl masc part aor pass	5097.3 prep	2296.2 noun gen sing masc
θεόν,	μᾶλλον	δὲ	γνωσθέντες	ὑπὸ	θεοῦ,
theon	mallon	de	gnōsthentes	hupo	theou
God,	rather	but	having been known	by	God,

4316.1 adv	1978.1 verb 2pl indic pres act	3687.1 adv	1894.3 prep	3450.17 art pl neu	766.2 adj	2504.1 conj
πῶς	ἐπιστρέφετε	πάλιν	ἐπὶ	τὰ	ἀσθενῆ	καὶ
pōs	epistrephete	palin	epi	ta	asthenē	kai
how	do you turn	again	to	the	weak	and

4292.9 adj pl neu	4598.1 noun pl neu	3614.4 rel-pron dat pl	3687.1 adv	505.1 adv	1392.8 verb inf pres act
πτωχὰ	στοιχεῖα	οἷς	πάλιν	ἄνωθεν	ʼ δουλεύειν
ptōcha	stoicheia	hois	palin	anōthen	douleuein
beggarly	elements	to which	again	anew	to serve

9.a.**Txt**: 02A,04C,06D 018K,020L,025P,etc.byz. Sod
Var: 01ℵ,03B,Treg,Tisc We/Ho,Weis,UBS/✱

1392.14 verb inf pres act	2286.5 verb 2pl indic pres act	2232.1 noun fem	3767.3 verb 2pl indic pres mid	2504.1 conj
[ᵃ δουλεῦσαι]	θέλετε;	10. ἡμέρας	παρατηρεῖσθε,	καὶ
douleusai	thelete	hēmeras	paratēreisthe	kai
[idem]	you desire?	Days	you observe,	and

3243.4 noun acc pl masc	2504.1 conj	2511.8 noun acc pl masc	2504.1 conj	1747.3 noun acc pl masc	5236.1 verb 1sing indic pres mid
μῆνας,	καὶ	καιροὺς,	καὶ	ἐνιαυτούς.	11. φοβοῦμαι
mēnas	kai	kairous	kai	eniautous	phoboumai
months,	and	times,	and	years.	I am afraid of

5050.4 prs-pron acc 2pl	3248.1 conj	1488.1 adv	2844.13 verb 1sing indic perf act	1519.1 prep	5050.4 prs-pron acc 2pl
ὑμᾶς,	μήπως	εἰκῆ	κεκοπίακα	εἰς	ὑμᾶς.
humas	mēpōs	eikē	kekopiaka	eis	humas
you,	lest somehow	in vain	I have labored	as to	you.

1090.19 verb 2pl impr pres mid	5453.1 conj	1466.1 prs-pron nom 1sing	3617.1 conj	2476.3 prs-pron nom	5453.1 conj
12. Γίνεσθε	ὡς	ἐγώ,	ὅτι	κἀγὼ	ὡς
Ginesthe	hōs	egō	hoti	kagō	hōs
Be	as	I,	for	I also	as

5050.1 prs-pron nom 2pl	79.6 noun nom pl masc	1183.1 verb 1sing indic pres mid	5050.2 prs-pron gen 2pl	3625.6 num card neu	1466.6 prs-pron acc 1sing
ὑμεῖς,	ἀδελφοί,	δέομαι	ὑμῶν·	οὐδέν	με
humeis	adelphoi	deomai	humōn	ouden	me
you,	brothers,	I urge	you:	in nothing	me

90.8 verb 2pl indic aor act	3471.6 verb 2pl indic perf act	1156.2 conj	3617.1 conj	1217.1 prep	763.4 noun acc sing fem
ἠδικήσατε.	13. οἴδατε	δὲ	ὅτι	δι'	ἀσθένειαν
ēdikēsate	oidate	de	hoti	di'	astheneian
you wronged.	You know	but	that	in	weakness

4:8,9. Paul specifically addressed those who were Gentiles. He reminded them that before their conversion they had worshiped gods which did not exist. Deuteronomy 32:21 uses a Hebrew term which means "no-god," a term echoed in Isaiah 37:19; Jeremiah 2:11; 5:7; and 16:20. In 1 Corinthians 12:2 Paul used the term "dumb idols." These had enslaved them. But now they were "known of God" as His redeemed children (Romans 8:29). Paul emphasized that what they had become in Christ was strictly God's doing, not theirs in any way. To emphasize his point Paul used a striking term—*slavery.* They knew well the meaning of slavery, since this was such an intimate part of life at that time. One could become a slave, a thing, as a result of war or through political or economic misfortune. And so Paul asked them if they wished again to become slaves, spiritual slaves. What was happening was so absurd, beyond all reason, if they would just stop to think what would happen to them. Once free through God's grace, they would again become enslaved to what Paul described as "weak and beggarly elements." He stressed these were completely devoid of any power whatsoever. In fact, they were nonexistent.

In this case, the Galatians were enamored with the legalism promoted by the Judaizers, namely, their insistence that whether a Jew or Gentile Christian, everyone had to be circumcised and live as a Jew in order to be saved. But, Paul stressed, the end result was the same: spiritual slavery and eternal condemnation. God's eternal curse would rest on them.

4:10,11. What is the meaning of verse 10? Each of these occasions is part of the Jewish worship calendar. "Days" refers to Sabbaths and other holy days. "Months" probably refers especially to the new moons, observed at the beginning of every month (Numbers 28:11-15). The Greek word *kairous,* translated "times," means "seasons." It is an indefinite period of time in either length or frequency of observance, and hence may best refer to the great festivals: Passover, Firstfruits, and Harvest ("Tabernacles"). "Years" probably refers to the sabbatical year (every seventh year) or the year of Jubilee, the 50th year. All of these were of utmost importance in the thinking of the Judaizers.

4:12. Again Paul used the loving term "brethren," brothers and sisters in Christ. For Paul this was an earnest term of endearment as he sought to persuade the Galatians that they were headed for condemnation. He wished to emphasize that he lovingly had their eternal welfare at heart. He was not concerned about himself or his own reputation. He basically said in summary form what he later wrote in 2 Corinthians 6: "My heart is wide open to you; let yours also be wide open to me!" He assured them that this was not in any way a personal matter with him.

ye did service unto them which by nature are no gods: . . . in bondage to them, *ASV* . . . under the authority of gods who had no real existence, *Phillips* . . . exist not, *Alford.*

9. But now, after that ye have known God, or rather are known of God, how turn ye again to the weak and beggarly elements, whereunto ye desire again to be in bondage?: . . . now that you have found God, *TCNT* . . . having acknowledged, *Wilson* . . . ye desyre afresshe, *Tyndale* . . . vnto impotent and beggerly ceremonies, *Geneva* . . . how can you revert to dead and sterile principles and consent to be under their power all over again? *Phillips* . . . poore elements, *Rheims* . . . weak and helpless elemental false gods, *Norlie.*

10. Ye observe days, and months, and times, and years: Your religion is beginning to be a matter of observing certain days, *Phillips* . . . scrupulously observing, *Worrell* . . . Seasons, *Wilson.*

11. I am afraid of you, lest I have bestowed upon you labour in vain: I am afraid, on your account, *Norlie* . . . Frankly, you stagger me, *Phillips* . . . lest I have expended, *Sawyer* . . . may have been wasted, *TCNT.*

12. Brethren, I beseech you, be as I [am]; for I [am] as ye [are]: ye have not injured me at all: I entreat you, *Wilson* . . . I also was as ye are, *Worrell* . . . become as I...Ye did me no wrong, *Panin* . . . Ye slighted me in no way, *PNT* . . . In nothing did ye wrong me, *Rotherham.*

3450.10 art gen sing fem	4418.2 noun gen sing fem	2076.15 verb 1sing indic aor mid	5050.3 prs-pron dat 2pl	3450.16 art sing neu
τῆς	σαρκὸς	εὐηγγελισάμην	ὑμῖν	τὸ
tēs	sarkos	euēngelisamēn	humin	to
of the	flesh	I announced the good news	to you	the

4245.2 adj comp sing neu	2504.1 conj	3450.6 art acc sing masc	3848.4 noun acc sing masc	1466.2 prs-pron gen 1sing
πρότερον,	14. καὶ	τὸν	πειρασμὸν	ʹ μου
proteron	kai	ton	peirasmon	mou
formerly;	and	the	temptation	my

3450.6 art acc sing masc	5050.2 prs-pron gen 2pl	1706.1 prep	3450.11 art dat sing fem	4418.3 noun dat sing fem	1466.2 prs-pron gen 1sing
τὸν	[ᵃ✶ ὑμῶν]	ἐν	τῇ	σαρκί	μου
ton	humōn	en	tē	sarki	mou
the	[your]	in	the	flesh	my

14.a.Txt: 06D-corr,018K 020L,025P,byz.sa. **Var:** 01ℵ-org,02A,03B 06D-org,33,it.bo.Lach Treg,Alf,Tisc,We/Ho Weis,Sod,UBS/✶

3620.2 partic	1832.5 verb 2pl indic aor act	3624.1 conj	1596.1 verb 2pl	233.1 conj
οὐκ	ἐξουθενήσατε	οὐδὲ	ἐξεπτύσατε,	ʹ ἀλλʹ
ouk	exouthenēsate	oude	exeptusate	all'
not	you despised	nor	rejected with contempt;	but

233.2 conj	5453.1 conj	32.4 noun acc sing masc	2296.2 noun gen sing masc	1203.7 verb 2pl indic aor mid	1466.6 prs-pron acc 1sing
[✶ ἀλλὰ]	ὡς	ἄγγελον	θεοῦ	ἐδέξασθέ	με,
alla	hōs	angelon	theou	edexasthe	me
[idem]	as	an angel	of God	you received	me,

15.a.Txt: 06D,018K 020L,byz. **Var:** 01ℵ,02A,03B,04C 025P,33,bo.Lach,Treg Alf,Word,Tisc,We/Ho Weis,Sod,UBS/✶

5453.1 conj	5382.4 name acc masc	2400.3 name acc masc	4949.3 intr-pron nom sing	4085.1 adv	3631.1 partic
ὡς	Χριστὸν	Ἰησοῦν.	15. ʹ τίς	[ᵃ✶ ποῦ]	οὖν
hōs	Christon	Iēsoun	tis	pou	oun
as	Christ	Jesus.	What	[where]	then

15.b.Txt: 06D,018K,byz. **Var:** 01ℵ,02A,03B,04C 020L,025P,Lach,Treg Alf,Word,Tisc,We/Ho Weis,Sod,UBS/✶

1498.34 verb sing indic imperf act	3450.5 art nom sing masc	3080.1 noun nom sing masc	5050.2 prs-pron gen 2pl	3113.1 verb 1sing pres act
ʹᵇ ἦν ʹ	ὁ	μακαρισμὸς	ὑμῶν;	μαρτυρῶ
ēn	ho	makarismos	humōn	marturō
was	the	blessedness	your?	I bear witness

1056.1 conj	5050.3 prs-pron dat 2pl	3617.1 conj	1479.1 conj	1409.3 adj sing neu	3450.8 art acc pl masc	3652.8 noun acc pl masc
γὰρ	ὑμῖν	ὅτι,	εἰ	δυνατὸν,	τοὺς	ὀφθαλμοὺς
gar	humin	hoti	ei	dunaton	tous	ophthalmous
for	you	that,	if	possible,	the	eyes

15.c.Txt: 01ℵ-corr 06D-corr,018K,020L 025P,byz. **Var:** 01ℵ-org,02A,03B 04C,06D-org,33,Lach Treg,Alf,Word,Tisc We/Ho,Weis,Sod UBS/✶

5050.2 prs-pron gen 2pl	1830.1 verb nom pl masc part aor act	300.1 partic	1319.16 verb 2pl indic aor act
ὑμῶν	ἐξορύξαντες	ʹᶜ ἄν ʹ	ἐδώκατέ
humōn	exoruxantes	an	edōkate
your	having plucked out		you would have given

1466.4 prs-pron dat 1sing	5452.1 conj	2172.1 adj nom sing masc	5050.2 prs-pron gen 2pl	1090.1 verb 1sing indic perf act
μοι.	16. ὥστε	ἐχθρὸς	ὑμῶν	γέγονα
moi	hōste	echthros	humōn	gegona
to me.	So	enemy	your	I became

224.1 verb nom sing masc part pres act	5050.3 prs-pron dat 2pl	2189.4 verb 3pl indic pres act	5050.4 prs-pron acc 2pl	3620.3 partic
ἀληθεύων	ὑμῖν;	17. Ζηλοῦσιν	ὑμᾶς	οὐ
alētheuōn	humin	Zēlousin	humas	ou
speaking truth	to you?	They are zealous after	you	not

4:13,14. Paul reminded them of the fine response they had shown when he shared the gospel with them. He deeply appreciated their loving reaction when he experienced an attack of what he described as an "infirmity of the flesh." In 2 Corinthians 12:7 he called it "a thorn in the flesh." It is impossible to be sure what this malady was. Fourteen different suggestions have been made as to what it might have been. Among the various possibilities are the following: pain in the head or ear; epilepsy; convulsive attacks; eye trouble; a speech impediment; malaria. This last one was proposed by the noted scholar William Ramsay. He suggested that Paul caught malaria in the mosquito-malaria ridden area of low-lying Pamphylia (pp.422-425). Acts 13:13-20 states that Paul and his companions arrived at Perga from Cyprus and immediately left to climb through the rugged Taurus Mountains to Antioch, lying 3,600 feet above sea level. This involved a distance of about 100 miles.

In Antioch Paul was struck by what may best be recognized as a malarial attack, which, for both the victim and those present, can be a very unpleasant experience. Paul carefully notes that, rather than despising or scorning him, they "received (him) as an angel of God, even as Christ Jesus" himself.

4:15-18. Paul contrasted the Galatian's reaction to him and the gospel message then and in their present uncertain state. The first part of verse 15 in this context is best translated, "Where is that sense of congratulation now? What has happened?" Paul asked. The Greek goes on to say, "I bear witness" (*marturō*), a strong legal phrase as Paul contrasted their loving reaction then and their subsequent puzzling behavior. He reminded them that formerly they would have shared their eyes, if this would have helped him in any way. He added that in telling them the truth he was their friend, even if they considered him an enemy. He had their welfare at heart.

The opening words in verse 17, following the Greek, may well be translated, "They are courting you but not for honorable intentions." The purpose of the Judaizers was to gain the Galatians as their followers. They wanted the Christians in Galatia to actively court their favor, to shut themselves off from fellowship with Paul and the belief in the certainty of salvation by grace alone. Their intentions were dishonorable and would result in their eternal damnation. Paul restated this positively in verse 18, following the Greek, "It is always good to be courted for honorable intentions, and not only when I am present with you."

Paul and Barnabas had gone to the Galatians with very honorable intentions, namely, to share with them the glad news of the fulfillment of God's promises of salvation by grace alone. To return to the illustration Paul used earlier in this chapter, the time of the guardians and the managers had come to an end. The time set by the Father had come.

Acts 13:16-41 tells us what Paul said when he was asked to speak in the synagogue at Antioch on the Sabbath. How carefully he stressed that in Jesus Christ the prophecies in the Old Testament

13. Ye know how through infirmity of the flesh: You remember that I was not well, *Norlie* . . . how handicapped I was, *Phillips* . . . illness was the cause, *TCNT.*

I preached the gospel unto you at the first: I euangelized to you heretofore, *Rheims.*

14. And my temptation which was in my flesh ye despised not, nor rejected; but received me as an angel of God, [even] as Christ Jesus: And ye did not slight or disdain my temptation, *Wesley* . . . You didn't shrink from me or let yourselves be revolted at the disease which was such a trial to me, *Phillips* . . . that trial of mine, *Wilson* . . . though I was a trial to you in my flesh, *Confraternity* . . . in my complaint, it did not inspire you with scorn or disgust, *TCNT.*

15. Where is then the blessedness ye spake of? for I bear you record, that, if [it had been] possible, ye would have plucked out your own eyes, and have given them to me: Where, then, [is] your happiness? *Rotherham* . . . What then [has become of] your high appreciation [of me]? *PNT* . . . is your self-congratulation? *Confraternity* . . . that if it might haue be don, *Wyclif* . . . you would have torn out, *TCNT* . . . you would have dug out, *Sawyer, Wilson.*

16. Am I therefore become your enemy, because I tell you the truth?: . . . the same truth, *Phillips.*

17. They zealously affect you, [but] not well: People are courting your favour, but not honourably, *TCNT* . . . They are zealous for you in no good way, *Panin* . . . thei louen (loveth) not you wel, *Wyclif* . . . They court you from no good motive, *Confraternity* . . . They love you ardently, not honorably, *Wilson* . . . but not in honesty, *Noyes* . . . but not rightly, *Scarlett* . . . not nobly, *Rotherham.*

2544.1 adv	233.2 conj	1563.1 verb inf aor act	5050.4 prs-pron acc 2pl	2286.6 verb 3pl indic pres act	2419.1 conj
καλῶς,	ἀλλὰ	ἐκκλεῖσαι	ὑμᾶς	θέλουσιν,	ἵνα
kalōs	alla	ekkleisai	humas	thelousin	hina
rightly,	but	to exclude	you	they desire,	that

18.a.Txt: 06D,018K
020L,025P,byz.
Var: 01א,02A,03B,04C
33,Lach,Treg,Alf,Tisc
We/Ho,Weis,Sod
UBS/✱

840.8 prs-pron acc pl masc	2189.1 verb 2pl pres act		2541.1 adj sing	1156.2 conj	3450.16 art sing neu
αὐτοὺς	ζηλοῦτε.	**18.**	καλὸν	δὲ	(a τὸ
autous	zēloute		kalon	de	to
them	you may be zealous after.	Right	but	the

2189.7 verb inf pres mid	1706.1 prep	2541.10 adj dat sing neu	3704.1 adv	2504.1 conj	3231.1 partic	3303.1 adv
ζηλοῦσθαι	ἐν	καλῷ	πάντοτε,	καὶ	μὴ	μόνον
zēlousthai	en	kalō	pantote	kai	mē	monon
to be zealous	in	a right	at all times,	and	not	only

1706.1 prep	3450.3 art dat sing	3780.12 verb inf pres act	1466.6 prs-pron acc 1sing	4242.1 prep	5050.4 prs-pron acc 2pl
ἐν	τῷ	παρεῖναί	με	πρὸς	ὑμᾶς,
en	tō	pareinai	me	pros	humas
in	the	to be present	my	with	you,

19.a.Txt: 01א-corr,02A
04C,06D-corr,018K
020L,025P,byz.We/Ho
Sod
Var: 01א-org,03B
06D-org,Lach,Treg,Tisc
Weis,UBS/✱

	4888.1 noun pl neu	4891.4 noun pl neu	1466.2 prs-pron gen 1sing	3614.8 rel-pron acc pl masc	3687.1 adv
19.	(τεκνία	[a τέκνα]	μου,	οὓς	πάλιν
	teknia	tekna	mou	hous	palin
	little children	[children]	my,	of whom	again

19.b.Txt: 01א-corr,02A
04C,06D,018K,020L
025P,byz.
Var: 01א-org,03B,Treg
Tisc,We/Ho,Weis,Sod
UBS/✱

5439.1 verb 1sing indic pres act	884.1 conj	3230.2 prep	3614.2 rel-pron gen sing	3308.1 verb 3sing subj aor pass
ὠδίνω	(ἄχρις	[b✱ μέχρις]	οὗ	μορφωθῇ
ōdinō	achris	mechris	hou	morphōthē
I travail	until	[idem]	which	shall have been formed

5382.1 name nom masc	1706.1 prep	5050.3 prs-pron dat 2pl	2286.30 verb indic imperf act	1156.2 conj	3780.12 verb inf pres act
Χριστὸς	ἐν	ὑμῖν·	**20.** ἤθελον	δὲ	παρεῖναι
Christos	en	humin	ēthelon	de	pareinai
Christ	in	you:	I was wishing	and	to be present

4242.1 prep	5050.4 prs-pron acc 2pl	732.1 adv	2504.1 conj	234.2 verb inf aor act	3450.12 art acc sing fem	5292.4 noun acc sing fem
πρὸς	ὑμᾶς	ἄρτι,	καὶ	ἀλλάξαι	τὴν	φωνήν
pros	humas	arti	kai	allaxai	tēn	phōnēn
with	you	now,	and	to change	the	voice

1466.2 prs-pron gen 1sing	3617.1 conj	633.1 verb 1sing indic pres mid	1706.1 prep	5050.3 prs-pron dat 2pl	2978.2 verb 2pl pres act
μου,	ὅτι	ἀπορούμαι	ἐν	ὑμῖν.	**21.** Λέγετέ
mou	hoti	aporoumai	en	humin	Legete
my,	for	I am perplexed	as to	you.	Tell

1466.4 prs-pron dat 1sing	3450.7 art nom pl masc	5097.3 prep	3414.4 noun acc sing masc	2286.16 verb nom pl masc part pres act	1498.32 verb inf pres act
μοι,	οἱ	ὑπὸ	νόμον	θέλοντες	εἶναι,
moi	hoi	hupo	nomon	thelontes	einai
me,	the	under	law	wishing	to be,

3450.6 art acc sing masc	3414.4 noun acc sing masc	3620.2 partic	189.2 verb 2pl pres act	1119.22 verb 3sing indic perf mid
τὸν	νόμον	οὐκ	ἀκούετε;	**22.** γέγραπται
ton	nomon	ouk	akouete	gegraptai
the	law	not	do you hear?	It has been written

of the coming Messiah had been fulfilled. One Bible scholar has computed that the Old Testament contains 333 prophecies about Christ which were fulfilled during his sojourn on earth.

Acts 13:42,43 records the response of the hearers. They heard the glad news of the fulfillment in Christ. They kept on pleading with Paul that on the next Sabbath he would speak to them again. Luke notes that many Jews and God-fearers (Gentiles) followed Paul and Barnabas, who instructed them and urged them to continue to believe in salvation by grace alone.

Acts 13:44-52 provides information on the reaction of the Jews to the presence of many Gentiles. Filled with envy, they vigorously contradicted and reviled Paul. Paul and Barnabas told them that they had brought the gospel of the fulfillment of the prophecies in Christ first to them as being ethnically God's covenant people. But now they would turn to the Gentiles. Working through devout Gentile women, the wives of the prominent men of Antioch, the Jews were able to force Paul and Barnabas to leave.

When Paul and Barnabas left at the end of the first missionary journey to return to Antioch, Syria, the Judaizers courted the Christians in Galatia with dishonorable intentions to seek to persuade them not to follow the way of grace but that of law.

4:19. Paul addressed them as "My little children!" in his fatherly affection for them. Then he used a dramatic word picture. When he and Barnabas first shared the gospel with the Galatians, they, as it were, went through the pains of giving birth to those who believed their message. Paul was asking if he had to do this again to be used of God in returning them to saving faith in Christ.

4:20. Paul faced the problem that as much as he would have liked, he could not return to Galatia to talk with the believers in person. The Judaizers had wreaked havoc also in Antioch. They claimed to speak for the leaders of the church in Jerusalem. As Acts 15 informs us, Paul, Barnabas, and others had to travel (probably walk) more than 300 miles from Antioch to Jerusalem to discuss this extremely serious problem.

Acts 15 records that after the Judaizers, followed by Peter, Barnabas, and Paul, had spoken, James stressed that God's plan of salvation by grace included also the Gentiles. Since the Judaizers had pretended to speak for the church (Acts 15:24), the official letter authorized by this meeting stated that they had *not* been official representatives. Their view of salvation was wrong. Salvation was by grace alone!

4:21-23. To reemphasize what he had said, Paul used an illustration from the life of Abraham. He introduced it just by the use of the term "law" in the legal sense; the second use means *Torah*, the Pentateuch. Paul asked, "Why don't you listen to Scripture, to the *Torah*!"

yea, they would exclude you, that ye might affect them: They want to isolate you, *TCNT* . . . What they desire is to exclude you from me, *Norlie* . . . They would like to see you and me separated altogether, and have you all to themselves, *Phillips*.

18. But [it is] good to be zealously affected always in [a] good [thing], and not only when I am present with you: Don't think I'm jealous—it is a grand thing that men should be keen to win you, whether I'm there or not, *Phillips* . . . But do you emulate the good in good, *Rheims* . . . it is good to be an object of zeal, *Noyes* . . . to loue earnestly, *Geneva* . . . in a good matter, *ASV*.

19. My little children, of whom I travail in birth again until Christ be formed in you: . . . in pains of childbirth, *Norlie* . . . vntill Christ be fassioned in you, *Tyndale* . . . be imprinted in you, *Geneva*.

20. I desire to be present with you now: How I wish I could be, *Norlie* . . . how I long to be with you now! *Phillips*.

and to change my voice; for I stand in doubt of you: . . . and speak in a different tone, *TCNT* . . . and to change my speech, *Scarlett* . . . and to change my tone; Because I am perplexed concerning you, *Wilson* . . . Perhaps I could then alter my tone to suit your mood. As it is, I honestly don't know how to deal with you, *Phillips* . . . for I am perplexed about you, *Panin* . . . I am ashamed for you, *Douay* . . . with you, *Rotherham*.

21. Tell me, ye that desire to be under the law, do ye not hear the law?: . . . ye who are wishing to be under law, *Worrell* . . . you who want the Law as your master, *Norlie* . . . do you not listen to the Law? *TCNT* . . . have you not read the Law? *Confraternity*.

1056.1 conj	3617.1 conj	11.1 name masc	1411.3 num card	5048.9 noun acc pl masc	2174.32 verb 3sing indic aor act
γὰρ,	ὅτι	Ἀβραὰμ	δύο	υἱούς	ἔσχεν·
gar	hoti	Abraam	duo	huious	eschen
for,	that	Abraham	two	sons	had;

1518.4 num card acc masc	1523.2 prep gen	3450.10 art gen sing fem	3677.2 noun gen sing fem	2504.1 conj	1518.4 num card acc masc
ἕνα	ἐκ	τῆς	παιδίσκης,	καὶ	ἕνα
hena	ek	tēs	paidiskēs	kai	hena
one	of	the	maid servant,	and	one

1523.2 prep gen	3450.10 art gen sing fem	1645.6 adj gen sing fem	233.1 conj	3450.5 art nom sing masc	3173.1 conj	1523.2 prep gen
ἐκ	τῆς	ἐλευθέρας·	**23.** ἀλλ'	ὁ	μὲν	ἐκ
ek	tēs	eleutheras	all'	ho	men	ek
of	the	free.	But	the	men	of

3450.10 art gen sing fem	3677.2 noun gen sing fem	2567.3 prep	4418.4 noun acc sing fem	1074.23 verb 3sing indic perf mid
τῆς	παιδίσκης,	κατὰ	σάρκα	γεγέννηται·
tēs	paidiskēs	kata	sarka	gegennētai
the	maid servant,	according to	flesh	has been born,

3450.5 art nom sing masc	1156.2 conj	1523.2 prep gen	3450.10 art gen sing fem	1645.6 adj gen sing fem	1217.2 prep
ὁ	δὲ	ἐκ	τῆς	ἐλευθέρας,	⌐ διὰ
ho	de	ek	tēs	eleutheras	dia
the	and	of	the	free,	through

3450.10 art gen sing fem	1217.1 prep	1845.1 noun fem	3610.6 rel-pron nom pl neu	1498.4 verb 3sing indic pres act
τῆς	[ᵃ δι']	ἐπαγγελίας.	**24.** ἅτινά	ἐστιν
tēs	di'	epangelias	hatina	estin
the	[through]	promise.	Which things	are

23.a.**Var:** p46,01ℵ,02A 04C,044,33,81,104 UBS/✰
Txt: 03B,06D,010F 012G,062,byz.Tisc,Sod

236.1 verb pl neu part pres mid	3642.13 dem-pron nom pl fem	1056.1 conj	1498.7 verb 3pl indic pres act	3450.13 art nom pl fem
ἀλληγορούμενα·	αὗται	γάρ	εἰσιν	⌐ᵃ αἱ ⌐
allēgoroumena	hautai	gar	eisin	hai
being allegorized;	these	for	are	the

24.a.**Txt:** 01ℵ-org,Steph **Var:** 01ℵ-corr,02A,03B 04C,06D,018K,020L 025P,byz.Gries,Lach Treg,Alf,Word,Tisc We/Ho,Weis,Sod UBS/✰

1411.3 num card	1236.5 noun nom pl fem	1518.5 num card nom fem	3173.1 conj	570.3 prep	3598.2 noun gen sing neu	4469.1 name neu
δύο	διαθῆκαι·	μία	μὲν	ἀπὸ	ὄρους	Σινᾶ,
duo	diathēkai	mia	men	apo	orous	Sina
two	covenants;	one	men	from	mount	Sinai,

1519.1 prep	1391.2 noun acc sing fem	1074.2 verb nom sing fem part pres act	3610.3 rel-pron nom sing fem	1498.4 verb 3sing indic pres act	28.1 name fem
εἰς	δουλείαν	γεννῶσα,	ἥτις	ἐστὶν	Ἄγάρ.
eis	douleian	gennōsa	hētis	estin	Agar
to	slavery	bringing forth,	which	is	Hagar.

25.a.**Txt:** 01ℵ,04C,018K 020L,025P,33-corr,byz. Tisc,Sod **Var:** 02A,03B,06D 33-org,bo.We/Ho,Weis UBS/✰

3450.16 art sing neu	1056.1 conj	1156.2 conj	28.1 name fem	4469.1 name neu	3598.1 noun sing neu
25. τὸ	⌐ γὰρ	[ᵃ✰ δὲ]	Ἄγάρ	Σινᾶ	ὄρος
to	gar	de	Agar	Sina	oros
to	For	[and]	Hagar	Sinai	mount

1498.4 verb 3sing indic pres act	1706.1 prep	3450.11 art dat sing fem	681.1 name dat fem	4812.1 verb 3sing indic pres act	1156.2 conj
ἐστὶν	ἐν	τῇ	Ἀραβίᾳ,	συστοιχεῖ	δὲ
estin	en	tē	Arabia	sustoichei	de
is	in	the	Arabia,	corresponds	and

In this letter Paul drew heavily on the life of Abraham, the father of God's covenant people. Abraham was 75 years old when God called him at Haran in Upper Mesopotamia (Genesis 12:1-3). His wife Sarah was 65 years old, beyond the childbearing age. Some time went by; how much we are not told.

In Genesis 15:1-3 Abraham reminded God that He had not as yet kept His promise. Since he was the head of a large clan (see Genesis 14:14), he had to provide a leader to take his place after his death. His proposal of adopting Eliezer as his legal son and heir reflects a Mesopotamian legal pattern. In an acted out reply, God told Abraham that he would have more descendants than the stars in the heavens. And Abraham reacted in firm belief that God would keep His promise.

Some years later Sarah's faith faltered. She persuaded Abraham to have intercourse with her Egyptian slavegirl, Hagar. In Mesopotamian law, the issue of such a union would be considered Sarah's legal son. Abraham's faith also faltered. He listened to Sarah, and in due time Ishmael was born. At that time Abraham was 86 years old (Genesis 16). Fourteen years later when Abraham was 100 years and Sarah 90 years old, the true covenant son Isaac was born to Abraham and Sarah as God had promised. When he was weaned, Ishmael ridiculed Isaac. Sarah told Abraham to send Hagar and Ishmael away. At first Abraham was unwilling, but at God's command, he did so (Genesis 21). Because his faith led to obedience, God has honored him: "Abraham believed God, and it was counted unto him for righteousness" (Romans 4:3).

Paul drew on this incident to emphasize the certainty of grace. Since Abraham was the father of God's covenant people, this illustration would have a special effect on the Jewish Christians in Galatia.

Sarah was a free woman and the wife of Abraham, and hence part of God's covenant promise. As Sarah's slave, Hagar was not part of God's covenant plan. Isaac was freeborn as the fulfillment of God's covenant promise (Genesis 12:2,3). Ishmael's conception was strictly due to a physical union and was not part of God's covenant plan. Isaac, not Ishmael, was the covenant son.

4:24-26. The Greek word sometimes translated "allegory" (*allēgoroumena*) is here better translated "illustration." In actuality, Paul's very effective but somewhat involved illustration is best identified as typology. Paul referred to an important Old Testament event to show its deeper meaning in God's overall covenant purpose.

Hagar and her son Ishmael were not part of God's covenant plan. Therefore, her descendants would be children "in bondage with her." She represents the covenant of the Law, given at Mount Sinai. Because the Jews misunderstood its purpose and expected to be justified by its works, they became in bondage to the Law. The "Jerusalem which now is" represents the present state of the Jews, still in bondage. The "Jerusalem which is above" represents

22. For it is written, that Abraham had two sons, the one by a bondmaid, the other by a freewoman: . . . where it is written, *Fenton* . . . by the slave, *Adams, Phillips.*

23. But he [who was] of the bondwoman was born after the flesh; but he of the freewoman [was] by promise: . . . the son of the slave, *Adams* . . . the child of the slave-girl, *Williams* . . . the child of the slave-woman was born in the ordinary course of nature, *TCNT* . . . was naturally produced, *Wilson* . . . was born in a natural way, *Norlie* . . . was born to fulfill, *Williams* . . . was born in fulfilment of a promise, *Montgomery* . . . in virtue of the promise, *Confraternity.*

24. Which things are an allegory: for these are the two covenants; the one from the mount Sinai, which gendereth to bondage, which is Agar: . . . for these represent, *Wilson* . . . these things may be allegorized...bearing children who will be slaves, *Adams* . . . Which thinges betoken mystery, *Tyndale* . . . have another meaning...bearing children unto bondage, *Alford* . . . one indeed, from Sinai Rock, born in slavery, *Fenton* . . . who beareth children into bondage, *Noyes* . . . which bringeth forth for bondage, *Murdock* . . . produces a race of slaves, *TCNT* . . . bearing children into slavery, typified by Hagar, *Phillips.*

25. For this Agar is mount Sinai in Arabia, and answereth to Jerusalem which now is: . . . and it corresponds to the present, *Wilson* . . . she resembles, however, *Rotherham* . . . Mount Sinai being in Arabia, the land of the descendants of Ishamael, *Phillips* . . . and bordreth vpon the citie, *Tyndale* . . . and represents the present Jerusalem, *Scarlett* . . . Jerusalem now existing, *Noyes.*

Galatians 4:26

25.b.Txt: 06D-corr,018K
020L,byz.
Var: 01‭א‬,02A,03B,04C
06D-org,025P,sa.bo.
Gries,Lach,Treg,Alf
Word,Tisc,We/Ho,Weis
Sod,UBS/☆

3450.11 art dat sing fem	3431.1 adv	2395.2 name fem	1392.3 verb 3sing indic pres act	1156.2 conj	1056.1 conj
τῇ	νῦν	Ἰερουσαλήμ,	δουλεύει	ʽ δὲ	[b☆ γὰρ]
tē	nun	Ierousalēm	douleuei	de	gar
to the	now	Jerusalem,	she is enslaved	and	[for]

3196.3 prep	3450.1 art gen pl	4891.5 noun gen pl neu	840.10 prs-pron gen sing fem	3450.9 art nom sing fem	1156.2 conj	504.1 adv
μετὰ	τῶν	τέκνων	αὐτῆς.	26. ἡ	δὲ	ἄνω
meta	tōn	teknōn	autēs	hē	de	anō
with	the	children	her;	the	but	above

2395.2 name fem	1645.5 adj nom sing fem	1498.4 verb 3sing indic pres act	3610.3 rel-pron nom sing fem	1498.4 verb 3sing indic pres act
Ἰερουσαλήμ,	ἐλευθέρα	ἐστίν,	ἥτις	ἐστὶν
Ierousalēm	eleuthera	estin	hētis	estin
Jerusalem,	free	is,	which	is

26.a.Txt: 01‭א‬-corr,02A
04C-corr,018K,020L
025P,byz.Sod
Var: p46,01‭א‬-org,03B
04C-org,06D,33,it.sa.bo.
Gries,Treg,Alf,Tisc
We/Ho,Weis,UBS/☆

3251.1 noun nom sing fem	3820.4 adj gen pl	2231.2 prs- pron gen 1 pl	1119.22 verb 3sing indic perf mid	1056.1 conj
μήτηρ	ʽa πάντων ʼ	ἡμῶν·	27. γέγραπται	γάρ,
mētēr	pantōn	hēmōn	gegraptai	gar
mother	of all	of us.	It has been written	for,

2146.9 verb 2sing impr aor pass	4574.1 adj nom sing fem	3450.9 art nom sing fem	3620.3 partic	4936.3 verb nom sing fem part pres act	4342.4 verb 2sing impr aor act
Εὐφράνθητι	στεῖρα	ἡ	οὐ	τίκτουσα·	ῥῆξον
Euphranthēti	steira	hē	ou	tiktousa	rhēxon
Rejoice,	O barren	the	not	bearing;	break forth

2504.1 conj	987.6 verb 2sing impr aor act	3450.9 art nom sing fem	3620.2 partic	5439.2 verb nom sing fem part pres act	3617.1 conj	4044.17 adj pl neu
καὶ	βόησον	ἡ	οὐκ	ὠδίνουσα·	ὅτι	πολλὰ
kai	boēson	hē	ouk	ōdinousa	hoti	polla
and	cry,	the	not	travailing;	because	many

3450.17 art pl neu	4891.4 noun pl neu	3450.10 art gen sing fem	2032.5 adj gen sing fem	3095.1 adv comp	2211.1 conj	3450.10 art gen sing fem
τὰ	τέκνα	τῆς	ἐρήμου	μᾶλλον	ἢ	τῆς
ta	tekna	tēs	erēmou	mallon	ē	tēs
the	children	of the	desolate	more	than	of the

28.a.Txt: 01‭א‬,02A,04C
byz.We/Ho
Var: p46,03B,06D-org
33,sa.Lach,Treg,Alf
Tisc,Weis,Sod,UBS/☆

2174.23 verb gen sing fem part pres act	3450.6 art acc sing masc	433.4 noun acc sing masc	2231.1 prs- pron nom 1pl	5050.1 prs- pron nom 2pl
ἐχούσης	τὸν	ἄνδρα.	28. ʽ Ἡμεῖς	[a☆ ὑμεῖς]
echousēs	ton	andra	Hēmeis	humeis
having	the	husband.	We	[You]

1156.2 conj	79.6 noun nom pl masc	2567.3 prep	2439.1 name masc	1845.1 noun fem	4891.4 noun pl neu
δέ,	ἀδελφοί,	κατὰ	Ἰσαὰκ,	ἐπαγγελίας	τέκνα
de	adelphoi	kata	Isaak	epangelias	tekna
but,	brothers,	according to	Isaac,	of promise	children

28.b.Txt: 01‭א‬,02A,04C
byz.We/Ho
Var: p46,03B,06D-org
33,sa.Lach,Treg,Alf
Tisc,Weis,Sod,UBS/☆

1498.5 verb 1pl indic pres act	1498.6 verb 2pl indic pres act	233.1 conj	5450.1 conj	4966.1 adv	3450.5 art nom sing masc
ʽ ἐσμέν·	[b☆ ἐστέ.]	29. ἀλλ'	ὥσπερ	τότε	ὁ
esmen	este	all'	hōsper	tote	ho
are.	[idem]	But	as	then	the

2567.3 prep	4418.4 noun acc sing fem	1074.17 verb nom sing masc part aor pass	1371.21 verb 3sing indic imperf act	3450.6 art acc sing masc
κατὰ	σάρκα	γεννηθεὶς	ἐδίωκεν	τὸν
kata	sarka	gennētheis	ediōken	ton
according to	flesh	having been born	was persecuting	the

the new covenant of grace.

Paul's readers would understand how this bondage was true of the Pharisees and their followers.

They brought their offerings and sacrifices to the temple in Jerusalem to fulfill the requirements of the Law. They, like the Judaizers, felt they could earn salvation by keeping the Law. But, Paul stressed, they would not experience salvation. They were and would continue to be in spiritual bondage.

Sarah, Abraham's wife, gave birth to Isaac, the son of the "free woman." He was the son of God's promise, part of His covenant plan of grace. Isaac's spiritual descendants are and will be "children of promise." The "Jerusalem which is above is free, which is the mother of us all," is the illustration Paul used for all who humbly and gratefully believe in God's promises of salvation by grace alone.

4:27,28. Paul continued with a quotation from Isaiah 54:1. Isaiah spoke of an event to take place in the future. In 587 B.C. the Babylonians took Jerusalem, destroyed it, and carried its inhabitants away. The Jews thought this could never happen. Because of their self-centered misinterpretation of their covenant status they thought God would not dare let the Babylonians destroy the city and especially the temple. If He did, the enemy would believe their great Babylonian gods, such as Marduk and Ishtar, were more powerful than the true God of Judah. But God did permit the great destruction and in so doing taught the Jews an important lesson: He would not allow anyone, even His beloved people, to sin and escape punishment.

Unfortunately the lesson which God sought to teach them through Jerusalem's destruction and the exile of the people did not last. The closing chapters of 2 Kings and 2 Chronicles as well as the books of Ezra and Nehemiah and the prophets of their day—Haggai, Zechariah, and Malachi—indicate that the full lesson had not been learned.

Israel had become spiritually barren. The Jews still counted too much on a special relationship with God, because they were of Abraham's ethnic line. But they did not have Abraham's faith. So the Jerusalem of Jesus and Paul's day was barren of spiritual life.

But the "barren" Jerusalem, in God's plan, would become a spiritual Jerusalem. There the Church would be born, and many spiritual children would be born, composed of those who put their trust in God's covenant of grace. So Paul could add: "Now we, brethren, as Isaac was, are the children of promise" (verse 28).

4:29,30. Paul states, "Even so it is now." The Judaizers were spiritual descendants of Ishmael, the son of the slavegirl Hagar. As Ishmael had mocked Isaac, the true son of promise as the son

and is in bondage with her children: . . . for the Jews are still, spiritually speaking, "slaves," *Phillips* . . . for she is in slavery with her children, *Adams* . . . she is enslaved with, *Fenton* . . . all of its people are slaves to the law, *SEB.*

26. But Jerusalem which is above is free, which is the mother of us all: But the free woman typifies, *Phillips* . . . the heavenly Jerusalem, *SEB* . . . the exalted Jerusalem, *Wilson* . . . the supreme Jerusalem is a free woman, *Fenton* . . . who is our mother, *Adams.*

27. For it is written, Rejoice, [thou] barren that bearest not; break forth and cry, thou that travailest not: for the desolate hath many more children than she which hath an husband: For the Scripture says, *Williams* . . . O childless woman, *Norlie* . . . break into shouts, thou who art never in labour, *TCNT* . . . into shouting, you who feel no birth pangs, *Williams* . . . who has not given birth to children, *Fenton* . . . the deserted one, *Rotherham* . . . the desolate woman has more children than the woman who has a husband! *Adams.*

28. Now we, brethren, as Isaac was, are the children of promise: Now you, brothers, like Isaac, *Adams* . . . are children according to the promise through Isaac, *Fenton* . . . was born in the normal way, *SEB* . . . we are children born "by promise," *Phillips.*

29. But as then he that was born after the flesh persecuted him [that was born] after the Spirit: . . . but just as in old times, *Montgomery* . . . born in the ordinary course of nature, *TCNT, Williams* . . . born according to, *Adams* . . . he who was born naturally despised him who was by the Spirit, *Fenton.*

2567.3 prep	4011.1 noun sing neu	3643.1 adv	2504.1 conj	3431.1 adv	233.2 conj
κατὰ	πνεῦμα,	οὕτως	καὶ	νῦν.	**30.** ἀλλὰ
kata	pneuma	houtōs	kai	nun	alla
according to	Spirit,	so	also	now.	But

4949.9 intr-pron sing neu	2978.5 verb 3sing indic pres act	3450.9 art nom sing fem	1118.1 noun nom sing fem	1531.17 verb 2sing impr aor act	3450.12 art acc sing fem
τί	λέγει	ἡ	γραφή;	Ἔκβαλε	τὴν
ti	legei	hē	graphē	Ekbale	tēn
what	says	the	scripture?	Cast out	the

3677.3 noun acc sing fem	2504.1 conj	3450.6 art acc sing masc	5048.4 noun acc sing masc	840.10 prs-pron gen sing fem	3620.3 partic
παιδίσκην	καὶ	τὸν	υἱὸν	αὐτῆς,	οὐ
paidiskēn	kai	ton	huion	autēs	ou
maid servant	and	the	son	her,	not

30.a.Txt: 02A,04C,018K 020L,byz.Sod
Var: 01א,03B,06D,025P 33,Lach,Treg,Tisc We/Ho,Weis,UBS/✶

1056.1 conj	3231.1 partic	2789.5 verb 3sing subj aor act	2789.10 verb 3sing indic fut act	3450.5 art nom sing masc
γὰρ	μὴ	ʿ κληρονομήσῃ	[a✶ κληρονομήσει]	ὁ
gar	mē	klēronomēsē	klēronomēsei	ho
for	not	may inherit	[will inherit]	the

5048.1 noun nom sing masc	3450.10 art gen sing fem	3677.2 noun gen sing fem	3196.3 prep	3450.2 art gen sing	5048.2 noun gen sing masc
υἱὸς	τῆς	παιδίσκης	μετὰ	τοῦ	υἱοῦ
huios	tēs	paidiskēs	meta	tou	huiou
son	of the	maid servant	with	the	son

31.a.Txt: p46,06D-corr 018K,020L,byz.
Var: 01א,03B,06D-org 33,Lach,Treg,Alf,Tisc We/Ho,Weis,Sod UBS/✶

3450.10 art gen sing fem	1645.6 adj gen sing fem	679.1 partic	1346.1 conj	79.6 noun nom pl masc
τῆς	ἐλευθέρας.	**31.** ʿ Ἄρα,	[a✶ διό,]	ἀδελφοί,
tēs	eleutheras	Ara	dio	adelphoi
of the	free.	So then,	[Wherefore,]	brothers,

3620.2 partic	1498.5 verb 1pl indic pres act	3677.2 noun gen sing fem	4891.4 noun pl neu	233.2 conj	3450.10 art gen sing fem
οὐκ	ἐσμὲν	παιδίσκης	τέκνα,	ἀλλὰ	τῆς
ouk	esmen	paidiskēs	tekna	alla	tēs
not	we are	of a maid servant	children,	but	of the

1.a.Txt: 018K,020L,byz.
Var: 01א,02A,03B 04C-org,06D-org,025P 33,Lach,Treg,Alf,Tisc We/Ho,Weis,Sod UBS/✶

1645.6 adj gen sing fem	3450.11 art dat sing fem	1644.3 noun dat sing fem	3631.1 partic	3614.11 rel-pron dat sing fem
ἐλευθέρας.	**5:1.** Τῇ	ἐλευθερίᾳ	ʿa οὖν	ᾗ ʾ
eleutheras	Tē	eleutheria	oun	hē
free.	In the	freedom	therefore	which

5382.1 name nom masc	2231.4 prs-pron acc 1pl	2231.4 prs-pron acc 1pl	5382.1 name nom masc	1646.1 verb 3sing indic aor act
ʿ Χριστὸς	ἡμᾶς	[✶ ἡμᾶς	Χριστὸς]	ἠλευθέρωσεν,
Christos	hēmas	hēmas	Christos	ēleutherōsen
Christ	us	[us	Christ]	made free,

1.b.Var: 01א,02A,03B 04C,025P,33,bo.Lach Treg,Alf,Word,Tisc We/Ho,Weis,Sod UBS/✶

4590.1 verb 2pl pres act	3631.1 partic	2504.1 conj	3231.1 partic	3687.1 adv	2201.2 noun dat sing masc
στήκετε	[b✶+ οὖν]	καὶ	μὴ	πάλιν	ζυγῷ
stēkete	oun	kai	mē	palin	zugō
stand fast,	[therefore]	and	not	again	in a yoke

1391.1 noun gen sing fem	1742.3 verb 2pl impr pres mid	1481.14 verb 2sing impr aor act	1466.1 prs-pron nom 1sing	3834.1 name nom masc	2978.1 verb 1sing pres act
δουλείας	ἐνέχεσθε.	**2.** Ἴδε	ἐγὼ	Παῦλος	λέγω
douleias	enechesthe	Ide	egō	Paulos	legō
of slavery	be held.	Lo,	I	Paul	say

of Abraham and Sarah, so Ishmael's true spiritual descendants were mocking the way of grace. They were slandering Paul by saying that he was not a true called apostle and that the gospel which he had shared was at best incomplete. They were persecuting the Galatian Christians, the true spiritual descendants of Isaac and the true heirs of God's promise of salvation by grace alone. They were telling the Galatians that salvation was one of works, of faithfully and totally living as a Jew to merit salvation. They were falsely claiming to be the official spokesmen for the Church, and any variation from what they said was wrong.

4:31. Paul once more emphasized the crucial significance of this passage for the Galatians. By their faith in salvation as God's gift of grace, like Isaac, they had become true children of Sarah, the free woman and wife of Abraham. He was summarizing what he had said, especially in verses 21-30. He wanted to be sure they understood that the message of the Judaizers was false. Salvation was not to be achieved by works, by living as a Jew and seeking to earn God's favor. The message of the Judaizers was one of damnation, not salvation. In the process of pointing out this truth Paul strongly demonstrated his deep concern about the salvation of these converts.

5:1. Paul dramatically restated in this verse what he had said in the preceding two verses. The order of the Greek words expresses greater emphasis: "In freedom Christ us has freed, stand therefore, and not again in a yoke of bondage be held fast!" In three verses Paul used a form of the word *free* four times (4:30,31; 5:1). He did this to state most emphatically that salvation is by grace, and not by works, as the Judaizers were teaching.

But Paul added another analogy to emphasize the grave danger confronting them in listening to the Judaizers. He wrote, following the Greek word order, "And not again in a yoke of slavery be held." Slavery was a basic part of life in the Roman Empire, including Galatia. Legally a slave belonged totally to his master who had complete control over him. Technically the slave was chattel: property that could be sold. His status was no greater than an animal. The Galatians were intimately acquainted with slavery and its implications. In fact, some among these Christians may well have been slaves or owners of slaves.

Paul's use of this analogy to express the real meaning of what would happen if the Galatians would listen to the Judaizers was very telling. There was no possibility they could misunderstand what he was saying, namely, that by heeding the Judaizers they would come into a far worse (spiritual) bondage.

5:2,3. Paul left nothing to chance. He showed how what the Judaizers had told them would affect their spiritual welfare. For the first time in this part of his argument he expressly mentioned

even so [it is] now: It is the same way now, *SEB* . . . so it is today, *Williams, Phillips.*

30. Nevertheless what saith the scripture? Cast out the bond-woman and her son: for the son of the bondwoman shall not be heir with the son of the free-woman: But what does the Scripture say? *SEB* . . . Yet what is the scriptural instruction? *Phillips* . . . Send away, *TCNT, Norlie, Montgomery* . . . the slave girl with her son; for the son of the slave girl shall not inherit, *Fenton* . . . Throw out the slave...for by no means shall the son of the slave share the inheritance, *Adams* . . . The son of the free woman will receive everything that his father has, *SEB* . . . shall not inherit with, *ASV* . . . shall in nowise inherit, *Worrell.*

31. So then, brethren, we are not children of the bondwoman, but of the free: . . . by that libertie, *Geneva* . . . we are not to look upon ourselves as the sons of the slave woman but of the free, not sons of slavery under the Law but sons of freedom under grace, *Phillips.*

1. Stand fast therefore in the liberty wherewith Christ hath made us free, and be not entangled again with the yoke of bondage: It was for freedom that Christ freed us; stand firm therefore, *Adams* . . . stand you firm, and do not again be held fast in a Yoke of Servitude, *Wilson* . . . on the freedom with which Christ has freed us, and submit not again to a yoke of slavery, *Fenton* . . . do not be caught again, *Confraternity* . . . and do not submit again, *Norlie* . . . be not again bound fast to, *Noyes* . . . Don't turn and go back into slavery, *SEB* . . . and wrappe not youre selves agayne in the yoke, *Tyndale* . . . stop letting your necks be fastened in the yoke of slavery again, *Williams* . . . be not again subject to a yoke of servitude, *Sawyer.*

5050.3 prs-pron dat 2pl	**3617.1** conj	**1430.1** partic	**3919.5** verb 2pl subj pres mid	**5382.1** name nom masc	**5050.4** prs-pron acc 2pl
ὑμῖν,	ὅτι	ἐὰν	περιτέμνησθε,	Χριστὸς	ὑμᾶς
humin	hoti	ean	peritemnēsthe	Christos	humas
to you,	that	if	you be circumcised,	Christ	you

3625.6 num card neu	**5456.5** verb 3sing indic fut act	**3113.31** verb 1sing indic pres mid	**1156.2** conj	**3687.1** adv	**3820.3** adj dat sing
οὐδὲν	ὠφελήσει·	**3.** μαρτύρομαι	δὲ	πάλιν	παντὶ
ouden	ōphelēsei	marturomai	de	palin	panti
nothing	shall profit.	I testify	and	again	to every

442.3 noun dat sing masc	**3919.7** verb dat sing masc part pres mid	**3617.1** conj	**3645.1** noun nom sing masc	**1498.4** verb 3sing indic pres act
ἀνθρώπῳ	περιτεμνομένῳ,	ὅτι	ὀφειλέτης	ἐστὶν
anthrōpō	peritemnomenō	hoti	opheiletēs	estin
man	being circumcised,	that	a debtor	he is

3513.1 adj sing	**3450.6** art acc sing masc	**3414.4** noun acc sing masc	**4020.41** verb inf aor act	**2643.15** verb 2pl indic aor pass
ὅλον	τὸν	νόμον	ποιῆσαι.	**4.** κατηργήθητε
holon	ton	nomon	poiēsai	katērgēthēte
whole	the	law	to do.	You have been cut off

570.3 prep	**3450.2** art gen sing	**5382.2** name gen masc	**3610.2** rel-pron nom pl masc	**1706.1** prep	**3414.3** noun dat sing masc
ἀπὸ	⌜ᵃ τοῦ ⌝	Χριστοῦ	οἵτινες	ἐν	νόμῳ
apo	tou	Christou	hoitines	en	nomō
from	the	Christ,	whosoever	in	law

1338.10 verb 2pl indic pres mid	**3450.10** art gen sing fem	**5322.2** noun gen sing fem	**1588.11** verb 2pl indic aor act	**2231.1** prs-pron nom 1pl
δικαιοῦσθε,	τῆς	χάριτος	ἐξεπέσατε·	**5.** ἡμεῖς
dikaiousthe	tēs	charitos	exepesate	hēmeis
are being justified;	the	grace	you fell from.	We

1056.1 conj	**4011.3** noun dat sing neu	**1523.2** prep gen	**3963.2** noun gen sing fem	**1667.4** noun acc sing fem	**1336.2** noun gen sing fem
γὰρ	πνεύματι	ἐκ	πίστεως	ἐλπίδα	δικαιοσύνης
gar	pneumati	ek	pisteōs	elpida	dikaiosunēs
for,	by Spirit	by	faith	hope	of righteousness

549.2 verb 1pl indic pres mid	**1706.1** prep	**1056.1** conj	**5382.3** name dat masc	**2400.2** name masc	**3641.1** conj
ἀπεκδεχόμεθα.	**6.** ἐν	γὰρ	Χριστῷ	Ἰησοῦ	οὔτε
apekdechometha	en	gar	Christō	Iēsou	oute
await.	In	for	Christ	Jesus	neither

3921.1 noun nom sing fem	**4948.10** indef-pron sing neu	**2453.2** verb 3sing indic pres act	**3641.1** conj	**201.1** noun nom sing fem	**233.2** conj
περιτομή	τι	ἰσχύει,	οὔτε	ἀκροβυστία,	ἀλλὰ
peritomē	ti	ischuei	oute	akrobustia	alla
circumcision	any	is of force,	nor	uncircumcision;	but

3963.1 noun nom sing fem	**1217.1** prep	**26.2** noun gen sing fem	**1738.9** verb nom sing fem part pres mid	**4983.13** verb 2pl indic imperf act
πίστις	δι'	ἀγάπης	ἐνεργουμένη.	**7.** Ἐτρέχετε
pistis	di'	agapēs	energoumenē	Etrechete
faith	by	love	working.	You were running

2544.1 adv	**4949.3** intr-pron nom sing	**5050.4** prs-pron acc 2pl	**346.1** verb 3sing indic aor act	**1458.2** verb 3sing indic aor act
καλῶς	τίς	ὑμᾶς	⌜ ἀνέκοψεν	[ᵃ✶ ἐνέκοψεν]
kalōs	tis	humas	anekopsen	enekopsen
well:	who	you	hindered	[idem]

4.a.**Txt:** 02A,06D-corr 018K,020L,byz. **Var:** 01א,03B,04C 06D-org,025P,Lach Treg,Tisc,We/Ho,Weis Sod,UBS/✶

7.a.**Txt:** Steph **Var:** 01א,02A,03B,04C 06D,018K,020L,025P byz.Gries,Lach,Treg,Alf Word,Tisc,We/Ho,Weis Sod,UBS/✶

circumcision. From the viewpoint of a Jew circumcision was absolutely necessary for salvation. Only through circumcision could one become a true son of Abraham, a son of the covenant. The Galatians knew that for one who was a Greek and for many who were part of the Hellenistic culture of that day, circumcision meant a mutilation of the body and brought a heavy negative stigma. In the men's section of the public baths circumcision became immediately apparent to all present.

Paul drew on his apostolic authority as Christ's chosen apostle when he said, "I Paul say unto you." He expressly addressed this to the uncircumcised Gentile Christians that if they allowed themselves to be circumcised, they would have to keep the Law completely. Then they would have no claim on Christ. There is no middle ground. Salvation is strictly by grace.

5:4-6. Paul stressed again the full implications of what he had said. The Judaizers taught that only by keeping the Law was it possible to be justified before God. Paul used a very strong Greek verb, prefaced by a preposition, to stress that all who wished to be justified by the Law were totally cut off from Christ; they had "fallen out of" (*exepesate*) grace. They had absolutely no hope of salvation.

Now Paul restated in the positive what he had said so emphatically in the negative. He described the way of grace: "For we *through the Spirit* wait for the hope of righteousness by faith" (verse 5; cf. Titus 3:4-8; Romans 5:1,2; 6:1-12,23; 2 Corinthians 5:16-21). Then he stated that in God's sight circumcision, or lack of it, makes no difference *as long as it is not considered necessary* for salvation. Acts 16:3 informs us that Paul circumcised Timothy as an act of good judgment since his mother was a Jewess and hence, he would be considered a Jew. But Paul refused to circumcise Titus, a Greek; this would have been a gross denial of salvation by grace alone (2:3-5).

Both Jews and Gentiles were numbered among the Galatian Christians. Their salvation, regardless of ethnic origins, came about because of true faith which "became effective" (*energoumenē*) by love. Through the Spirit's work, Christ's self-giving love (*agapē*) fills those who believe (Romans 5:5). And such love again expresses itself in the ongoing daily life of the Christian (see verses 22-26). In all his letters Paul always stressed that the faith that is alive is the faith that is lived in daily life (for example, Romans 12-15).

5:7,8. When Paul wrote, "Ye did run well," the imagery of the athletic events would flash before the eyes of the Galatians. As ruins and archaeological excavations reveal, larger towns had an amphitheater and other facilities for athletic events. These events played a very important role in both the community and individual lives of people. The Galatians knew well the tremendous physical exertion required for competitive running events.

2. Behold, I Paul say unto you, that if ye be circumcised, Christ shall profit you nothing: Listen, *Phillips* . . . will be of no advantage to you, *TCNT, Confraternity* . . . will be of no benefit to you, *Wilson* . . . will avail you nothing, *Scarlett* . . . will not be of any help to you, *Norlie.*

3. For I testify again to every man that is circumcised, that he is a debtor to do the whole law: . . . to every one who becometh circumcised, *Noyes* . . . that he binds himself to obey, *TCNT* . . . That he is bound to perform, *Wilson* . . . to obey all the rest of the Law! *Phillips.*

4. Christ is become of no effect unto you, whosoever of you are justified by the law; ye are fallen from grace: Ye are severed from, *PNT* . . . ye are fallen away from, *Panin, Noyes* . . . You have severed yourselves from Christ...you have become outcasts from mercy, *TCNT* . . . you put yourself outside the range of his grace, *Phillips.*

5. For we through the Spirit wait for the hope of righteousness by faith: . . . are ardently waiting, *Rotherham* . . . the righteousness we hope to see, *Phillips.*

6. For in Jesus Christ neither circumcision availeth any thing, nor uncircumcision; but faith which worketh by love: . . . there is no validity in either...faith which expresses itself in love, *Phillips* . . . which by love is mighty in operacion, *Tyndale* . . . is all important, *TCNT* . . . Faith operating in us by Love, *Wilson* . . . strongly operating by love, *Scarlett.*

7. Ye did run well: You were once making good progress! *TCNT* . . . You were making progress, *Norlie* . . . splendid progress, *Phillips.*

Galatians 5:8

7.b.Txt: 01ℵ-corr,04C 06D,018K,020L,byz.Sod
Var: 01ℵ-org,02A,03B Treg,Tisc,We/Ho,Weis UBS/✶

3450.11 art dat sing fem
⌐b τῇ ⌐
tē
the

223.3 noun dat sing fem
ἀληθείᾳ
alētheia
truth

3231.1 partic
μὴ
mē
not

3844.24 verb inf pres mid
πείθεσθαι;
peithesthai
to obey?

3450.9 art nom sing fem
8. ἡ
hē
The

3850.1 noun nom sing fem
πεισμονὴ
peismonē
persuasion

3620.2 partic
οὐκ
ouk
not

1523.2 prep gen
ἐκ
ek
of

3450.2 art gen sing
τοῦ
tou
the

2535.5 verb gen sing masc part pres act
καλοῦντος
kalountos
calling

5050.4 prs-pron acc 2pl
ὑμᾶς.
humas
you.

3262.9 adj nom sing fem
9. Μικρὰ
Mikra
A little

2202.1 noun nom sing fem
ζύμη
zumē
leaven

3513.1 adj sing
ὅλον
holon
whole

3450.16 art sing neu
τὸ
to
to the

5281.1 noun sing neu
φύραμα
phurama
lump

2203.1 verb 3sing indic pres act
ζυμοῖ.
zumoi
leavens.

1466.1 prs-pron nom 1sing
10. ἐγὼ
egō
I

3844.8 verb 1sing indic perf act
πέποιθα
pepoitha
am persuaded

1519.1 prep
εἰς
eis
as to

5050.4 prs-pron acc 2pl
ὑμᾶς
humas
you

1706.1 prep
ἐν
en
in

2935.3 noun dat sing masc
κυρίῳ,
kuriō
Lord,

3617.1 conj
ὅτι
hoti
that

3625.6 num card neu
οὐδὲν
ouden
nothing

241.14 adj sing neu
ἄλλο
allo
other

5262.10 verb 2pl indic fut act
φρονήσετε,
phronēsete
you will think

3450.5 art nom sing masc
ὁ
ho
the

1156.2 conj
δὲ
de
and

4866.1 verb nom sing masc part pres act
ταράσσων
tarassōn
disturbing

5050.4 prs-pron acc 2pl
ὑμᾶς
humas
you

934.15 verb 3sing indic fut act
βαστάσει
bastasei
shall bear

3450.16 art sing neu
τὸ
to
to the

2890.1 noun sing neu
κρίμα,
krima
judgment,

3610.1 rel-pron nom sing masc
ὅστις
hostis
whosoever

300.1 partic
⌐ ἂν
an
an

1430.1 partic
[a✶ ἐὰν]
ean

1498.10 verb 3sing subj pres act
ᾖ.
ē
he may be.

1466.1 prs-pron nom 1sing
11. Ἐγὼ
Egō
I

1156.2 conj
δέ,
de
but,

79.6 noun nom pl masc
ἀδελφοί,
adelphoi
brothers,

1479.1 conj
εἰ
ei
if

3921.4 noun acc sing fem
περιτομὴν
peritomēn
circumcision

10.a.Txt: 04C,06D,018K 020L,byz.
Var: 01ℵ,02A,03B,025P 33,Treg,Alf,Tisc,We/Ho Weis,Sod,UBS/✶

2068.1 adv
ἔτι
eti
still

2756.1 verb 1sing indic pres act
κηρύσσω,
kērussō
I proclaim,

4949.9 intr-pron sing neu
τί
ti
why

2068.1 adv
ἔτι
eti
still

1371.22 verb 1sing indic pres mid
διώκομαι;
diōkomai
am I persecuted?

679.1 partic
ἄρα
ara
Then

2643.17 verb 3sing indic perf mid
κατήργηται
katērgētai
has been nullified

3450.16 art sing neu
τὸ
to
to the

4480.1 noun sing neu
σκάνδαλον
skandalon
offense

3450.2 art gen sing
τοῦ
tou
of the

4567.2 noun gen sing masc
σταυροῦ.
staurou
cross.

3649.1 partic
12. ὄφελον
ophelon
I would

2504.1 conj
καὶ
kai
even

604.4 verb 3pl indic fut mid
ἀποκόψονται
apokopsontai
they would cut themselves off

3450.7 art nom pl masc
οἱ
hoi
the

385.1 verb nom pl masc part pres act
ἀναστατοῦντες
anastatountes
throwing into confusion

5050.4 prs-pron acc 2pl
ὑμᾶς.
humas
you.

5050.1 prs-pron nom 2pl
13. Ὑμεῖς
Humeis
You

1056.1 conj
γὰρ
gar
for

1894.2 prep
ἐπ'
ep'
for

Paul followed this with another athletic term translated "hinder" but better translated in this context as "cut you off," as often happens in such athletic events. Runners then as today tried to cut off a competitor and thereby seek to win the race.

Paul asked the Galatians a very striking and attention-getting question: "Who has cut you off from the way of grace?" To cut someone off in an athletic event was always for personal advantage. In verse 8 Paul stated emphatically that this was not the work of Christ, who *is calling* (*kalountos*) you. (The tense of the verb is important.) Through the ongoing work of the Holy Spirit, and also through Paul's letter, Christ was continuing to call them to stay on the way of grace. Those who were seeking to cut them off from grace for their own gain were the Judaizers (see 6:13).

5:9,10. Paul used a well-known illustration from their daily life to emphasize what he had said. The use of yeast in the bread baking process was an intimate part of their daily life experience. In promoting their false doctrine (leaven, yeast), the Judaizers had not told the Galatians the full story. Paul warned them that what these enemies of Christ had said would in the process destroy their hope of salvation. And the Judaizers would experience God's eternal wrath and suffer the consequences of eternal damnation.

In verse 10 Paul contrasted himself with those who were disturbing the Galatians. On his part he had been and still *is* confident (following the Greek perfect tense, *pepoitha*) that they will listen and in the end not accept the false doctrine of the Judaizers.

After the Jerusalem meeting which stressed grace as the only way of salvation, Silas (Roman name: Silvanus) joined Paul on his second missionary journey. As the official representative of the Jerusalem meeting (Acts 15:22), Silas could speak for the church to the Galatian Christians to stress that salvation was by grace alone. It seems certain that the Galatians were persuaded of this important truth (Acts 15:41 to 16:5). Paul also revisited these churches at the beginning of their third missionary journey (see Acts 18:22,23; 19:1). The "upper coasts" (Greek: regions) is the area between Antioch in Galatia and Ephesus.

5:11,12. Seemingly it had been said that Paul was stressing the importance of circumcision. Paul took note of this. He again affectionately said, "Brethren." If this was true, he asked, why was he still being attacked, slandered, and persecuted? Then the Jews and Judaizers would have no reason to be offended at the Cross. For then salvation would be through works and not grace.

Paul's reference here to the offense (scandal) of the Cross was probably meant more in the sense of the Cross as a symbol of grace earned by Christ through His suffering and death. In 1 Corinthians 1:23 the same Greek word (*skandalon*) is used to mean "a cause for stumbling." God's curse was seen to rest on all who had been executed for a religious crime and hung up for all to see (Deuteronomy 21:22,23).

who did hinder you that ye should not obey the truth?: ... who put you off the course you had set for the truth? *Phillips.*

8. This persuasion [cometh] not of him that calleth you: Him inviting you, *Wilson.*

9. A little leaven leaveneth the whole lump: Alas, it takes only a little leaven to affect, *Phillips* ... ferments the whole mass, *Confraternity* ... corrupteth the vvhole paste, *Rheims* ... all the dough, *TCNT* ... the Whole Mass, *Wilson.*

10. I have confidence in you through the Lord, that ye will be none otherwise minded: but he that troubleth you shall bear his judgment, whosoever he be: Still, I have faith in you...will receive his condemnation, *Norlie* ... I have become persuaded, *Rotherham* ... you will not take any fatal step. But whoever it is who is worrying you will have a serious charge to answer one day, *Phillips* ... the man who is disturbing your minds, *TCNT.*

11. And I, brethren, if I yet preach circumcision, why do I yet suffer persecution? then is the offence of the cross ceased: ... then the hostility due to the cross, *Norlie* ... the scandal of the cross, *Wilson, Douay* ... Then is the stumbling-block of the cross removed! *Confraternity* ... been done away, *PNT, ASV.*

12. I would they were even cut off which trouble you: I wish those who are so eager to cut your bodies, *Phillips* ... would go the length of mutilating themselves, *TCNT* ... would even cut themselves off! *Alford* ... who unsettle you, *Clementson.*

1644.3 noun dat sing fem	2535.38 verb 2pl indic aor pass	79.6 noun nom pl masc	3303.1 adv	3231.1 partic	3450.12 art acc sing fem
ἐλευθερίᾳ	ἐκλήθητε,	ἀδελφοί·	μόνον	μὴ	τὴν
eleutheria	eklēthēte	adelphoi	monon	mē	tēn
freedom	were called,	brothers;	only	not	the

1644.4 noun acc sing fem	1519.1 prep	867.1 noun acc sing fem	3450.11 art dat sing fem	4418.3 noun dat sing fem	233.2 conj	1217.2 prep
ἐλευθερίαν	εἰς	ἀφορμὴν	τῇ	σαρκί,	ἀλλὰ	διὰ
eleutherian	eis	aphormēn	tē	sarki	alla	dia
freedom	for	an occasion	to the	flesh,	but	by

3450.10 art gen sing fem	26.2 noun gen sing fem	1392.1 verb 2pl pres act	238.2 prs-pron dat pl	3450.5 art nom sing masc	1056.1 conj
τῆς	ἀγάπης	δουλεύετε	ἀλλήλοις.	**14.** ὁ	γὰρ
tēs	agapēs	douleuete	allēlois	ho	gar
the	love	serve you	one another.	The	for

3820.6 adj nom sing masc	3414.1 noun nom sing masc	1706.1 prep	1518.2 num card dat	3030.3 noun dat sing masc	3997.16 verb 3sing indic pres mid
πᾶς	νόμος	ἐν	ἑνὶ	λόγῳ	ʿ πληροῦται,
pas	nomos	en	heni	logō	plēroutai
all	law	in	one	word	is being fulfilled,

3997.29 verb 3sing indic perf mid	1706.1 prep	3450.3 art dat sing	25.24 verb 2sing indic fut act	3450.6 art acc sing masc
[a☆ πεπλήρωται,]	ἐν	τῷ,	Ἀγαπήσεις	τὸν
peplērōtai	en	tō	Agapēseis	ton
[has been fulfilled,]	in	the	You shall love	the

3999.1 adv	4622.2 prs-pron gen 2sing	5453.1 conj	1431.6 prs-pron acc sing masc	4427.4 prs-pron acc sing masc
πλησίον	σου	ὡς	ʿ ἑαυτόν.	[b☆ σεαυτόν.]
plēsion	sou	hōs	heauton	seauton
neighbor	your	as	yourself;	[idem]

14.a.Txt: 06D,018K 020L,025P,byz. Var: 01א,02A,03B,04C 33,Lach,Treg,Alf,Word Tisc,We/Ho,Weis,Sod UBS/☆

14.b.Txt: 020L,025P,byz. Var: 01א,02A,03B,04C 06D,018K,33,Gries Lach,Treg,Alf,Word Tisc,We/Ho,Weis,Sod UBS/☆

1479.1 conj	1156.2 conj	238.3 prs-pron acc pl masc	1137.1 verb 2pl indic pres act	2504.1 conj	2688.2 verb 2pl indic pres act
15. εἰ	δὲ	ἀλλήλους	δάκνετε	καὶ	κατεσθίετε,
ei	de	allēlous	daknete	kai	katesthiete
if	but	one another	you bite	and	devour,

984.1 verb 2pl pres act	3231.1 partic	5097.3 prep	5097.2 prep	238.1 prs-pron gen pl	353.3 verb 2pl subj aor pass
βλέπετε	μὴ	ʿ ὑπὸ	[☆ ὑπ']	ἀλλήλων	ἀναλωθῆτε.
blepete	mē	hupo	hup'	allēlōn	analōthēte
take heed	not	by	[idem]	one another	you be consumed.

2978.1 verb 1sing pres act	1156.2 conj	4011.3 noun dat sing neu	3906.1 verb 2pl pres act	2504.1 conj
16. Λέγω	δέ,	Πνεύματι	περιπατεῖτε,	καὶ
Legō	de	Pneumati	peripateite	kai
I say	but,	By Spirit	walk you,	and

1924.4 noun acc sing fem	4418.2 noun gen sing fem	3620.3 partic	3231.1 partic	4903.6 verb 2pl subj aor act	3450.9 art nom sing fem
ἐπιθυμίαν	σαρκὸς	οὐ	μὴ	τελέσητε.	**17.** ἡ
epithumian	sarkos	ou	mē	telesēte	hē
desire	flesh's	not	not	should you fulfill.	The

1056.1 conj	4418.1 noun nom sing fem	1922.1 verb 3sing indic pres act	2567.3 prep	3450.2 art gen sing	4011.2 noun gen sing neu
γὰρ	σὰρξ	ἐπιθυμεῖ	κατὰ	τοῦ	πνεύματος,
gar	sarx	epithumei	kata	tou	pneumatos
for	flesh	desires	against	the	Spirit,

5:13,14. Paul next began to write about what it means to live the freedom which is the believer's through Christ. Christians have been called to be free. The Greek word *eklēthēte*, translated "called," is used here as a term for God's effort through the gospel to call them to the way of grace. But Paul warned the Galatian Christians that freedom in Christ does not mean license. A central facet of the Christian life is serving one another in self-giving love (*agapē*; see verse 6). By quoting Leviticus 19:18, Paul reemphasizes one of the central messages of Jesus (Matthew 19:19; 22:39; Mark 12:31; cf. Luke 10:25-37).

Paul's encouragement to "serve one another" calls to mind one of the great words of the New Testament—*doulos*. It is usually translated "servant" or "bondservant," but more precisely it means "slave." It is the word Paul used in Philippians 2:7 when he said Jesus took on himself the "form of a servant." It calls to remembrance the concept of the love slave of Exodus 21:1-6. The man had the right to become free, but because of his love for his master, he chose to become a slave forever. The man had his ear lobe pierced with an awl and became a marked man from that time on, for the scar would remain. Those who now serve Christ through love instead of duty are marked men and women. They are different!

5:15. The stress on salvation by works tended to promote controversy. Paul used very vigorous language to counter this. The strong verbs translated "bite" and "devour" suggest the imagery of wild animals preying on each other and engaging in deadly struggle. This too was part of the life experience of the Galatians. Each major town had its amphitheater which, among other entertainments, would feature the activities of wild animals. Sometimes condemned criminals would be executed by being forced to fight such animals and, in the process, be mangled and devoured by them. Paul warned the Galatian believers to be on guard, lest, in the process of senseless controversy brought on by the Judaizers, they would be devoured by such sinful activity.

5:16-18. To emphasize what he now added, Paul used the expression, "I say!" Grammatically the Greek is best translated, "Keep on walking by the Spirit." The Greek preposition translated "by" (expressed by the dative case, cf. *pneumati*) stresses that only through the Spirit's work is this possible. In this letter Paul emphasized the ongoing role of the Spirit in the lives of believers. It is only through His work in their hearts that they will not carry out and fulfill the lusts of their sinful nature, the flesh (the self-life), which seeks to satisfy its own sinful and destructive desires and reactions.

In verse 17 Paul contrasted the sinful flesh and its desires with the Spirit and His work. These are constantly clashing with each other. The Greek word translated "lusteth" (*epithumei*) perhaps is better understood as "strongly desires." What the sinful flesh, man

13. For, brethren, ye have been called unto liberty; only [use] not liberty for an occasion to the flesh, but by love serve one another: . . . invited to Freedom...be you subservient to each other, *Wilson* . . . for freedom, *Clementson* . . . be careful that this freedom does not become an excuse for sinful gratifications, *Norlie* . . . be careful that freedom does not become mere opportunity for your lower nature, *Phillips* . . . for self-indulgence, *TCNT* . . . for sensuality, *Confraternity* . . . as an indulgence to the flesh, *Scarlett*.

14. For all the law is fulfilled in one word, [even] in this; Thou shalt love thy neighbour as thyself: . . . the entire law, *Rotherham* . . . can be summarized...in one command, *Norlie* . . . is comprised in one precept, *Scarlett* . . . is summed up by this one command, *Phillips* . . . fulfilled in one saying, *Alford*.

15. But if ye bite and devour one another, take heed that ye be not consumed one of another: . . . continually wounding and preying upon one another, *TCNT* . . . lest you destroy one another altogether! *Norlie* . . . by each other, *Wilson*.

16. [This] I say then, Walk in the Spirit, and ye shall not fulfil the lust of the flesh: Heed my advice, *Norlie* . . . Let your steps be guided by the Spirit...will not gratify the cravings of your earthly nature, *TCNT* . . . you shal not accomplish, *Rheims*.

17. For the flesh lusteth against the Spirit: . . . hath desires opposite to the Spirit, *Scarlett* . . . lusteth contrary to the sprete, *Cranmer* . . . are contrary to those of the Spirit, *Norlie*.

3450.16 art sing neu	1156.2 conj	4011.1 noun sing neu	2567.3 prep	3450.10 art gen sing fem	4418.2 noun gen sing fem
τὸ	δὲ	πνεῦμα	κατὰ	τῆς	σαρκός·
to	de	pneuma	kata	tēs	sarkos
the	and	Spirit	against	the	flesh;

17.a.Txt: 01ℵ-corr,02A 04C,06D-corr,018K 020L,025P,byz.Sod **Var:** 01ℵ-org,03B 06D-org,33,it.bo.Lach Treg,Alf,Word,Tisc We/Ho,Weis,UBS/☆

3642.18 dem-pron pl neu	1156.2 conj	1056.1 conj	477.1 verb 3sing indic pres mid	238.2 prs-pron dat pl
ταῦτα	΄ δὲ	[ᵃ☆ γὰρ]	΄ ἀντίκειται	ἀλλήλοις,
tauta	de	gar	antikeitai	allēlois
these things	and	[for]	are opposing	to one another,

238.2 prs-pron dat pl	477.1 verb 3sing indic pres mid	2419.1 conj	3231.1 partic	3614.17 rel-pron pl neu	300.1 partic
[☆ ἀλλήλοις	ἀντίκειται,]	ἵνα	μὴ	ἃ	΄ ἂν
allēlois	antikeitai	hina	mē	ha	an
[one another	opposing,]	that	not	whatsoever	an

17.b.Txt: 03B-org 04C-corr,06D,018K 020L,025P,byz. **Var:** 01ℵ,02A,03B-corr Lach,Treg,Alf,Tisc We/Ho,Weis,Sod UBS/☆

1430.1 partic	2286.9 verb 2pl subj pres act	3642.18 dem-pron pl neu	4020.9 verb 2pl subj pres act	1479.1 conj
[ᵇ☆ ἐὰν]	θέλητε	ταῦτα	ποιῆτε.	**18.** εἰ
ean	thelēte	tauta	poiēte	ei
	you may wish	these things	you should do;	if

1156.2 conj	4011.3 noun dat sing neu	70.19 verb 2pl indic pres mid	3620.2 partic	1498.6 verb 2pl indic pres act	5097.3 prep
δὲ	πνεύματι	ἄγεσθε,	οὐκ	ἐστὲ	ὑπὸ
de	pneumati	agesthe	ouk	este	hupo
but	by Spirit	you are led,	not	you are	under

3414.4 noun acc sing masc	5156.4 adj	1156.2 conj	1498.4 verb 3sing indic pres act	3450.17 art pl neu	2024.4 noun pl neu
νόμον.	**19.** φανερὰ	δέ	ἐστιν	τὰ	ἔργα
nomon	phanera	de	estin	ta	erga
law.	Obvious	now	are	the	works

19.a.Txt: 01ℵ-corr,06D 018K,020L,byz. **Var:** 01ℵ-org,02A,03B 04C,025P,33,bo.Gries Lach,Treg,Alf,Word Tisc,We/Ho,Weis,Sod UBS/☆

3450.10 art gen sing fem	4418.2 noun gen sing fem	3610.6 rel-pron nom pl neu	1498.4 verb 3sing indic pres act	3293.1 noun nom sing fem
τῆς	σαρκός,	ἅτινά	ἐστιν	΄ᵃ μοιχεία, ΄
tēs	sarkos	hatina	estin	moicheia
of the	flesh,	which	are	adultery,

4061.2 noun nom sing fem	165.1 noun nom sing fem	760.1 noun nom sing fem	1485.1 noun nom sing fem
πορνεία,	ἀκαθαρσία,	ἀσέλγεια,	**20.** ΄ εἰδωλολατρεία,
porneia	akatharsia	aselgeia	eidōlolatreia
fornication,	uncleanness,	licentiousness,	idolatry,

1485.4 noun nom sing fem	5169.1 noun nom sing fem	2171.4 noun nom pl fem	2038.5 noun pl fem
[☆ εἰδωλολατρία,]	φαρμακεία,	΄ ἔχθραι,	΄ ἔρεις,
eidōlolatria	pharmakeia	echthrai	ereis
[idem]	sorcery,	enmities,	rivalries,

20.a.Txt: 04C,06D-corr 018K,020L,byz.Sod **Var:** 03B,06D-org,Lach Treg,Alf,Word,Tisc We/Ho,Weis,UBS/☆

2188.5 noun pl	2038.1 noun nom sing fem	2188.1 noun nom sing	2349.4 noun nom pl masc	2036.4 noun nom pl fem
ζῆλοι,	[ᵃ☆ ἔρις,	ζῆλος,]	θυμοί,	ἐριθείαι,
zēloi	eris	zēlos	thumoi	eritheiai
jealousies,	[rivalry,	jealousy,]	indignations,	contentions,

21.a.Txt: 02A,04C,06D 018K,020L,025P,byz.it. bo.Weis,Sod **Var:** p46,01ℵ,03B,33,sa. Tisc,We/Ho,UBS/☆

1364.1 noun nom pl fem	138.4 noun pl fem	5192.5 noun nom pl masc	5245.4 noun nom pl masc
διχοστασίαι,	αἱρέσεις,	**21.** φθόνοι,	΄ᵃ φόνοι, ΄
dichostasiai	haireseis	phthonoi	phonoi
divisions,	sects,	envyings,	murders,

in his sinfulness, desires is the opposite of what the Spirit, working in the believer's heart, desires. If a man chooses to do what is evil, the Spirit opposes this. If he chooses to do what is good, the sinful flesh seeks to hinder this. Some view Romans 7:18-25 as a description of this ongoing conflict: "O wretched man that I am! who shall deliver me from the body of this death?" (Romans 7:24).

Paul closed this part of his argument with the comforting statement of verse 18. To "be led of the Spirit" means "to walk by the Spirit," to be empowered by Him. To walk by the Spirit means freedom from the power of sin. "For sin shall not have dominion over you: for ye are not under the law, but under grace" (Romans 6:14). Sin and the devil have lost their power over the believer.

5:19. Paul went on to give a list of vices. These fall into four categories. The *first* category is that of varying degrees of sexual immorality. The first vice mentioned is *porneia*, translated as "adultery" or "fornication." Although it primarily refers to immoral relations with harlots, it is also used of all kinds of immoral sexual relations. Our English word *pornography* comes from the root of this word. The second term, *akatharsia*, means "impurity" and has a wider meaning: the misuse of sex and indulging in other forms of immorality. It is used to show the tendency of vice to be contagious. The next term is *aselgeia*, "wantonness," flaunting of self without any restraint whatsoever. Immorality of all kinds, also as part of idol worship, was for many an intimate way of life in the time of Paul, and this was very true also of Galatia.

5:20,21. The *second* category is that of sinful worship of idols or any substitute for true worship. In some pagan religions of that time this also involved sexual immorality. The term "witchcraft" (*pharmakeia*) is literally translated "sorcery." This term can refer to the use of magic arts of any kind, which was very popular at that time. Acts 19:11-20 speaks of Sceva's sons and the magical documents. It can also refer to witchcraft which involved the use of drugs to harm others. This was a serious offense in Roman law and resulted in severe punishment.

The *third* category of vices involves interpersonal relations. The first is "hatred," normally translated "enmities." This term provides the keynote for the various expressions of negative interpersonal relationships in this category, such as, ill feeling or hatred against others, resulting in hostile acts. The next vice ("variance") is a Greek word best translated as "strife" or "quarrelsomeness."

The next vice is translated "emulations." In our idiom this word is best translated as "jealousy" or "envy," depending on the context of its use (Acts 5:17; 13:45; Romans 13:13; 1 Corinthians 3:3; James 3:14-16). Its expression easily results in "wrath," the next term Paul used. In its negative meaning, the Greek word stresses the outburst of rage.

and the Spirit against the flesh: and these are contrary the one to the other: so that ye cannot do the things that ye would: . . . while the whole power of the Spirit is contrary to the lower nature. Here is the conflict, *Phillips* . . . in opposition to those of our earthly nature, *TCNT* . . . for these are opposed to each other, *Confraternity* . . . for they two are antagonistic, *Montgomery* . . . these oppose one another, *Noyes* . . . for these ben aduersaries to gidre, *Wyclif* . . . you cannot always do what you would or should, *Norlie* . . . do not perform the things which you wish, *Wilson* . . . you cannot do anything you please, *Williams*.

18. But if ye be led of the Spirit, ye are not under the law: . . . if you are habitually led by, *Montgomery* . . . if you are guided by, *Williams* . . . if you are following the guidance of the Spirit, *TCNT* . . . if you follow the leading of the Spirit, you stand clear of the Law, *Phillips*.

19. Now the works of the flesh are manifest, which are [these]; Adultery, fornication, uncleanness, lasciviousness: The activities of the lower nature are obvious, *Phillips* . . . are evident, *Norlie* . . . whoredom, *Murdock* . . . Impurity, *Wilson* . . . unchastity, *TCNT* . . . immodesty, luxury, *Douay* . . . indecency, *Montgomery* . . . wantonness, *Rotherham, Noyes*.

20. Idolatry, witchcraft, hatred, variance, emulations, wrath, strife, seditions, heresies: . . . sorcery, quarrels, *TCNT* . . . magic...discords, *Murdock* . . . Resentments, Altercations, *Wilson* . . . outbursts of wrath, *Noyes* . . . ill-temper...divisions, *Norlie* . . . party-spirit, *Montgomery* . . . enchantment, enmities, strife, jealousy...factions, divisions, *Rotherham* . . . contentions, *Sawyer* . . . sects, *Douay*.

3149.2 noun nom pl fem	2943.1 noun nom pl masc	2504.1 conj	3450.17 art pl neu	3527.7 adj pl neu	3642.3 dem-pron dat pl
μέθαι,	κῶμοι,	καὶ	τὰ	ὅμοια	τούτοις·
methai	kōmoi	kai	ta	homoia	toutois
drunkennesses,	revels,	and	the things	like	these;

3614.17 rel-pron pl neu	4161.1 verb 1sing indic pres act	5050.3 prs-pron dat 2pl	2503.1 conj	2504.1 conj
ἃ	προλέγω	ὑμῖν,	καθὼς	(b καὶ)
ha	prolegō	humin	kathōs	kai
which	I tell beforehand	you,	even as	also

21.b.Txt: 01ℵ-corr,02A 04C,06D,018K,020L 025P,byz.bo.Sod **Var:** 01ℵ-org,03B,Treg Tisc,We/Ho,Weis UBS/✸

4135.1 verb 1sing indic aor act	3617.1 conj	3450.7 art nom pl masc	3450.17 art pl neu	4955.14 dem-pron acc pl neu	4097.9 verb nom pl masc part pres act
προεῖπον,	ὅτι	οἱ	τὰ	τοιαῦτα	πράσσοντες
proeipon	hoti	hoi	ta	toiauta	prassontes
I said before,	that	the	the	such things	doing

926.4 noun acc sing fem	2296.2 noun gen sing masc	3620.3 partic	2789.11 verb 3pl indic fut act	3450.5 art nom sing masc
βασιλείαν	θεοῦ	οὐ	κληρονομήσουσιν.	**22.** Ὁ
basileian	theou	ou	klēronomēsousin	Ho
kingdom	God's	not	shall inherit.	The

1156.2 conj	2561.1 noun nom sing masc	3450.2 art gen sing	4011.2 noun gen sing neu	1498.4 verb 3sing indic pres act	26.1 noun nom sing fem
δὲ	καρπὸς	τοῦ	πνεύματός	ἐστιν	ἀγάπη,
de	karpos	tou	pneumatos	estin	agapē
but	fruit	of the	Spirit	is	love,

5315.1 noun nom sing fem	1503.1 noun nom sing fem	3087.1 noun nom sing fem	5379.1 noun nom sing fem	19.1 noun nom sing fem
χαρά,	εἰρήνη,	μακροθυμία,	χρηστότης,	ἀγαθωσύνη,
chara	eirēnē	makrothumia	chrēstotēs	agathōsunē
joy,	peace,	patience,	kindness,	goodness,

3963.1 noun nom sing fem	4095.1 noun nom sing fem	4095.8 noun nom sing fem	1459.1 noun nom sing fem	2567.3 prep
πίστις,	**23.** (πραότης,	[✸ πραΰτης,]	ἐγκράτεια·	κατὰ
pistis	praotēs	prautēs	enkrateia	kata
faith,	gentleness,	[idem]	self control:	against

3450.1 art gen pl	4955.1 dem-pron gen pl	3620.2 partic	1498.4 verb 3sing indic pres act	3414.1 noun nom sing masc	3450.7 art nom pl masc
τῶν	τοιούτων	οὐκ	ἔστιν	νόμος.	**24.** οἱ
tōn	toioutōn	ouk	estin	nomos	hoi
the	such things	no	there is	law.	The

24.a.Var: 01ℵ,02A,03B 04C,025P,33,sa.bo.Lach Treg,Alf,Tisc,We/Ho Weis,Sod,UBS/✸

1156.2 conj	3450.2 art gen sing	5382.2 name gen masc	2400.2 name masc	3450.12 art acc sing fem	4418.4 noun acc sing fem
δὲ	τοῦ	Χριστοῦ	[a✰+ Ἰησοῦ]	τὴν	σάρκα
de	tou	Christou	Iēsou	tēn	sarka
but	of the	Christ	[Jesus]	the	flesh

4568.3 verb 3pl indic aor act	4713.1 prep	3450.4 art dat pl	3667.4 noun dat pl neu	2504.1 conj	3450.14 art dat pl fem
ἐσταύρωσαν	σὺν	τοῖς	παθήμασιν	καὶ	ταῖς
estaurōsan	sun	tois	pathēmasin	kai	tais
crucified	with	the	passions	and	the

1924.7 noun dat pl fem	1479.1 conj	2180.3 verb 1pl pres act	4011.3 noun dat sing neu	4011.3 noun dat sing neu
ἐπιθυμίαις.	**25.** εἰ	ζῶμεν	πνεύματι,	πνεύματι
epithumiais	ei	zōmen	pneumati	pneumati
desires.	If	we live	by Spirit,	by Spirit

The next three vices have a close relationship with each other. The first is translated "strife," and in New Testament usage is the result of a selfish ambition, giving rise to rivalry and a party spirit. From this come "seditions" (dissensions or "divisions") which result from a party spirit. This again describes those who hold set views and opinions. The term "heresies" is better translated today as "cliques." The final vices in this category—"envyings, murders"—are specific acts of an envying spirit, due to a grudging spirit which cannot bear someone else's prosperity.

The *fourth* category begins with "drunkenness," excessive drinking resulting in drunken orgies. The next term, "revelings," involves what accompanies such orgies. Paul stressed that the vices listed in verses 17-21 result in a loss of salvation.

5:22,23. Paul next spoke of the *fruit* of the Spirit. Note that he said "fruit"; this is the result of the Spirit's work. The first fruit is that of love (*agape*), self-giving, self-sacrificing love which has its source in Christ's self-giving love resulting in man's salvation (1 Corinthians 13:13). The result of love is "joy" and "peace," grounded in the believer's grace relationship with God (Romans 14:17; 15:13). These form a triad.

From this triad flow "long-suffering" or patience, the quality of being long-tempered, especially when others may seek to provoke the Christian. "Gentleness" in the original has the meaning of "kindness." Next is "goodness" with special reference to generosity. This is followed by the Greek word *pistis*, "faith," which in Paul's usage may be translated as "faithfulness," especially referring to one's relationship with others. In modern English the quality of "meekness" is best expressed with "gentleness" in dealings with others. The Greek meaning of "temperance" is best expressed as "self-control" of human desires. All of these virtues are the result of the Spirit's work.

5:24-26. All of the above are the fruits of Christ's redemptive work. Paul wrote that all who belong to Christ "have crucified the flesh with the affections (*pathemasin*, 'sinful desires') and lusts (*epithumais*, 'passions')." Christ kept the Law for sinful mankind. The writer of Hebrews stressed that Jesus was tested as believers are, but He did not sin (Hebrews 2:18; 4:15). Through His crucifixion and death on the cross He paid the awesome penalty for man's sin. Toward the close of the 3 hours of darkness, He cried out, "My God, my God, why hast thou forsaken me?" (Matthew 27:46; Psalm 22:1). (The essence of eternal punishment consists in being forever separated from God.) And just before voluntarily giving up His life He cried out, "It is finished!" (John 19:30). The Greek word for "finished" (*tetelestai*) is in the perfect tense, which emphasizes that except for dying and rising again, Jesus' role as Redeemer was completed. Paul beautifully stressed Christ's redemption and its significance in Romans 6:1-13.

21. Envyings, murders, drunkenness, revellings, and such like: Inebrieties, Revellings, *Wilson* . . . outbursts of passion, *TCNT* . . . carousings, *Confraternity* . . . glottony, *Geneva* . . . and things like these, *Noyes*.

of the which I tell you before, as I have also told [you] in time past, that they which do such things shall not inherit the kingdom of God: . . . as I did forewarn you, *ASV* . . . which I forewarn you, *Panin, Clementson* . . . I solemnly assure you...that those who indulge in such things, *Phillips* . . . that those practicing such things, *Worrell*.

22. But the fruit of the Spirit is love, joy, peace, longsuffering, gentleness, goodness, faith: . . . produces in human life fruits such as these, *Phillips* . . . graciousness, *Rotherham* . . . forbearance...trustfulness, *TCNT* . . . kindness, *Panin* . . . fidelity, *Wesley, Wilson*.

23. Meekness, temperance: against such there is no law: . . . modesty, continency, *Confraternity* . . . Mildness, *Douay, Rheims* . . . self-control, *Panin*.

24. And they that are Christ's have crucified the flesh with the affections and lusts: Note that it is those who belong to, *Norlie* . . . they who belong to Christ, *Scarlett* . . . have already crucified their earthly nature, with its passions and its cravings, *TCNT* . . . with the vices and concupiscences, *Douay, Rheims* . . . passions and desires, *Wilson*.

25. If we live in the Spirit: . . . if we live by the Spirit, *Norlie* . . . If our lives are centered in the Spirit, *Phillips* . . . is due to the Spirit, *TCNT*.

2504.1 conj	4599.2 verb 1pl subj pres act	3231.1 partic	1090.16 verb 1pl subj pres mid	2726.1 adj nom pl masc
καὶ	στοιχῶμεν.	26. μὴ	γινώμεθα	κενόδοξοι,
kai	stoichōmen	mē	ginōmetha	kenodoxoi
also	we should walk.	Not	we should become	conceited,

238.3 prs-pron acc pl masc	4151.1 verb nom pl masc part pres mid	238.2 prs-pron dat pl	5191.1 verb nom pl masc part pres act
ἀλλήλους	προκαλούμενοι,	ἀλλήλοις	φθονοῦντες.
allēlous	prokaloumenoi	allēlois	phthonountes
one another	provoking,	one another	envying.

79.6 noun nom pl masc	1430.1 partic	2504.1 conj	4160.3 verb 3sing subj aor pass	4160.4 verb 3sing subj aor pass
6:1. Ἀδελφοί,	ἐὰν	καὶ	ʹ προληφθῇ	[☆ προλημφθῇ]
Adelphoi	ean	kai	prolēphthē	prolēmphthē
Brothers,	if	even	be taken	[idem]

442.1 noun nom sing masc	1706.1 prep	4948.2 indef-pron dat sing	3761.3 noun dat sing neu	5050.1 prs-pron nom 2pl	3450.7 art nom pl masc
ἄνθρωπος	ἕν	τινι	παραπτώματι,	ὑμεῖς	οἱ
anthrōpos	en	tini	paraptōmati	humeis	hoi
a man	in	some	offense,	you,	the

4012.3 adj nom pl masc	2645.1 verb 2pl impr pres act	3450.6 art acc sing masc	4955.2 dem-pron sing	1706.1 prep
πνευματικοὶ	καταρτίζετε	τὸν	τοιοῦτον	ἐν
pneumatikoi	katartizete	ton	toiouton	en
spiritual,	restore	the	such a one	in

4011.3 noun dat sing neu	4095.2 noun gen sing fem	4095.7 noun gen sing fem	4503.3 verb nom sing masc part pres act
πνεύματι	ʹ πραότητος,	[☆ πραΰτητος,]	σκοπῶν
pneumati	praotētos	prautētos	skopōn
a spirit	of gentleness,	[idem]	considering

4427.4 prs-pron acc sing masc	3231.1 partic	2504.1 conj	4622.1 prs-pron nom 2sing	3847.16 verb 2sing subj aor pass	238.1 prs-pron gen pl
σεαυτόν	μὴ	καὶ	σὺ	πειρασθῇς.	2. Ἀλλήλων
seauton	mē	kai	su	peirasthēs	Allēlōn
yourself	not	also	you	be tempted.	One another's

3450.17 art pl neu	916.3 noun pl neu	934.4 verb 2pl impr pres act	2504.1 conj	3643.1 adv	376.2 verb 2pl indic aor act
τὰ	βάρη	βαστάζετε,	καὶ	οὕτως	ʹ ἀναπληρώσατε
ta	barē	bastazete	kai	houtōs	anaplērōsate
the	burdens	bear you,	and	thus	you fulfilled

376.7 verb 2pl indic fut act	3450.6 art acc sing masc	3414.4 noun acc sing masc	3450.2 art gen sing	5382.2 name gen masc
[a☆ ἀναπληρώσετε]	τὸν	νόμον	τοῦ	Χριστοῦ.
anaplērōsete	ton	nomon	tou	Christou
[you will fulfill]	the	law	of the	Christ.

2.a.Txt: 01א,02A,04C 06D,018K,020L,025P byz.We/Ho,Sod Var: 03B,it.sa.bo.Lach Tisc,Weis,UBS/☆

1479.1 conj	1056.1 conj	1374.5 verb 3sing indic pres act	4948.3 indef-pron nom sing	1498.32 verb inf pres act	4948.10 indef-pron sing neu
3. εἰ	γὰρ	δοκεῖ	τις	εἶναί	τι,
ei	gar	dokei	tis	einai	ti
If	for	thinks	anyone	to be	something,

3235.6 num card neu	1498.21 verb nom sing masc part pres act	1431.6 prs-pron acc sing masc	5258.1 verb 3sing indic pres act	5258.1 verb 3sing indic pres act
μηδὲν	ὤν,	ʹ ἑαυτόν	φρεναπατᾷ·	[☆ φρεναπατᾷ
mēden	ōn	heauton	phrenapata	phrenapata
nothing	being,	himself	he deceives:	[he deceives

In verse 25 Paul reminded the Galatians what it means to live in the Spirit. Through the Spirit's work Christians are to "walk in a straight line" (*stoichōmen*) with the Spirit. In verses 22 and 23, Paul had carefully sketched what this means.

In verse 26 Paul warned his readers against the opposite of what it means to walk in the Spirit. The Greek term *kenodoxoi*, "vainglory," means to boast when there is nothing to boast about, to have a false estimate of self. "Provoking one another" was used for challenging one another in an athletic event or combat. Paul used it to refer to challenging others to do what they may hesitate to do or to envying others for what we dare not do. Against such temptations of the Evil One, Christians must always be on guard.

6:1,2. Paul began his final words with the endearing term "Brethren," brothers and sisters in Christ! He used this term 10 times in Galatians. Lovingly he reminded them that those who walk in the Spirit also need to express a loving concern for others. If a fellow Christian inadvertently becomes involved in a fault (the Greek word *paraptōmati* means "a false step"), those who walk in the Spirit will in a gentle, loving way, seek to restore him. They are to remember, Paul warned, that they too are equally as vulnerable to temptation (1 Corinthians 10:12). Believers are to treat their fellowman as lovingly as they would wish to be treated if they had fallen into sin. Paul reminded the Galatians, as do other passages in Scripture, that the Evil One keeps on tempting those who are in Christ, seeking to lead them to destruction. In 1 Peter 5:8,9 Peter graphically describes him roaming about as a roaring lion, "seeking whom he may devour."

The Greek word *bastazete*, translated "bear," is a term which is often used for carrying a heavy burden. Paul used it to emphasize the responsibility of those who seek to walk in the Spirit to bear the burden of those who appear to be weak in the Faith (Romans 15:1). His words recall Jesus' loving invitation (Matthew 11:28-30). At the Last Supper Jesus told His disciples: "A new commandment I give unto you, That ye love one another; as I have loved you, that ye also love one another" (John 13:34). The "law of Christ" means the law of God as spoken and lived out by Jesus Christ.

6:3. Paul warned against the Christian comparing himself to fellow Christians. This is the result of spiritual pride. The tendency is to imagine that he himself is something and pride himself in what he thinks he is. In the Greek Paul used the strong verb *phrenapata* which is used only here in the New Testament. It means "to deceive" or "delude" oneself. Such false estimation easily results in having no positive understanding and sympathy with others in their shortcomings and, as a result, failing to be loving and gentle.

let us also walk in the Spirit: . . . let us press on after, *Murdock* . . . let us also keep step in, *Montgomery* . . . let us be guided by, *Phillips* . . . by the Spirit, *Norlie*.

26. Let us not be desirous of vain glory, provoking one another, envying one another: . . . not become conceited, nor should we provoke, *Norlie* . . . Let us not be ambitious for our own reputations, for that only means making one another jealous, *Phillips*.

1. Brethren, if a man be overtaken in a fault, ye which are spiritual, restore such an one in the spirit of meekness; considering thyself, lest thou also be tempted: . . . should be surprised by, *Wilson* . . . be preoccupied in any fault, *Rheims* . . . be overtaken in any trespass, *Panin* . . . be caught in any trespass, *Worrell* . . . is caught in some wrongdoing, you who are spiritual should set him right, *Norlie* . . . should be caught in a guilty act...put the man right, *TCNT* . . . helpe to amende him, *Geneva* . . . instruct such a one in the spirit of, *Douay* . . . enfoorme ye such oon in spirit of softnesse, *Wyclif*.

2. Bear ye one another's burdens, and so fulfil the law of Christ: Carry...and so live out, *Phillips* . . . and so render full obedience, *TCNT* . . . of the Anointed one, *Wilson*.

3. For if a man think himself to be something, when he is nothing, he deceiveth himself: . . . fancies himself to be somebody, when he is really nobody, *TCNT* . . . deceaueth hys awne mynde, *Cranmer* . . . he is mentally deceiving himself, *Rotherham* . . . he seduceth him self, *Rheims* . . . he is fooling himself, *Norlie* . . . in his ymaginacion, *Tyndale*.

4. τὸ δὲ ἔργον ἑαυτοῦ δοκιμαζέτω

1431.6 prs-pron acc sing masc — ἑαυτόν] — heauton — himself;]

3450.16 art sing neu — τὸ — to — the

1156.2 conj — δὲ — de — but

2024.1 noun sing neu — ἔργον — ergon — work

1431.4 prs-pron gen sing — ἑαυτοῦ — heautou — of himself

1375.4 verb 3sing impr pres act — δοκιμαζέτω — dokimazetō — let prove

1524.3 adj nom sing masc — ἕκαστος, — hekastos — each,

2504.1 conj — καὶ — kai — and

4966.1 adv — τότε — tote — then

1519.1 prep — εἰς — eis — to

1431.6 prs-pron acc sing masc — ἑαυτὸν — heauton — himself

3304.1 adj sing neu — μόνον — monon — alone

3450.16 art sing neu — τὸ — to — the

2715.1 noun sing neu — καύχημα — kauchēma — boasting

2174.39 verb 3sing indic fut act — ἕξει, — hexei — he will have,

2504.1 conj — καὶ — kai — and

3620.2 partic — οὐκ — ouk — not

1519.1 prep — εἰς — eis — to

3450.6 art acc sing masc — τὸν — ton — the

2066.1 adj sing — ἕτερον — heteron — another.

5. ἕκαστος γὰρ τὸ ἴδιον φορτίον βαστάσει.

1524.3 adj nom sing masc — ἕκαστος — hekastos — Each

1056.1 conj — γὰρ — gar — for

3450.16 art sing neu — τὸ — to — the

2375.4 adj sing — ἴδιον — idion — his own

5249.1 noun sing neu — φορτίον — phortion — load

934.15 verb 3sing indic fut act — βαστάσει. — bastasei — shall bear.

6. Κοινωνείτω δὲ ὁ κατηχούμενος τὸν

2814.4 verb 3sing impr pres act — Κοινωνείτω — Koinōneitō — Let share

1156.2 conj — δὲ — de — but

3450.5 art nom sing masc — ὁ — ho — the

2697.3 verb nom sing masc part pres mid — κατηχούμενος — katēchoumenos — being taught in

3450.6 art acc sing masc — τὸν — ton — the

3030.4 noun acc sing masc — λόγον — logon — word

3450.3 art dat sing — τῷ — tō — with the

2697.1 verb dat sing masc part pres act — κατηχοῦντι — katēchounti — teaching

1706.1 prep — ἐν — en — in

3820.5 adj dat pl — πᾶσιν — pasin — all

18.5 adj dat pl — ἀγαθοῖς. — agathois — good things.

7. Μὴ πλανᾶσθε, θεὸς οὐ μυκτηρίζεται·

3231.1 partic — Μὴ — Mē — Not

3966.11 verb 2pl pres mid — πλανᾶσθε, — planasthe — be misled;

2296.1 noun nom sing masc — θεὸς — theos — God

3620.3 partic — οὐ — ou — not

3318.1 verb 3sing indic pres mid — μυκτηρίζεται· — muktērizetai — is being mocked;

3614.16 rel-pron sing neu — ὃ — ho — whatsoever

1056.1 conj — γὰρ — gar — for

1430.1 partic — ἐὰν — ean — ean

4540.1 verb 3sing subj act — σπείρῃ — speirē — may sow

442.1 noun nom sing masc — ἄνθρωπος, — anthrōpos — a man,

3642.17 dem-pron sing neu — τοῦτο — touto — that

2504.1 conj — καὶ — kai — also

2302.9 verb 3sing indic fut act — θερίσει· — therisei — he shall reap.

8. ὅτι ὁ σπείρων εἰς

3617.1 conj — ὅτι — hoti — For

3450.5 art nom sing masc — ὁ — ho — the

4540.5 verb nom sing masc part pres act — σπείρων — speirōn — sowing

1519.1 prep — εἰς — eis — to

3450.12 art acc sing fem — τὴν — tēn — the

4418.4 noun acc sing fem — σάρκα — sarka — flesh

1431.4 prs-pron gen sing — ἑαυτοῦ — heautou — of himself,

1523.2 prep gen — ἐκ — ek — from

3450.10 art gen sing fem — τῆς — tēs — the

4418.2 noun gen sing fem — σαρκὸς — sarkos — flesh

2302.9 verb 3sing indic fut act — θερίσει — therisei — shall reap

5193.4 noun acc sing fem — φθοράν· — phthoran — corruption;

3450.5 art nom sing masc — ὁ — ho — the

1156.2 conj — δὲ — de — but

4540.5 verb nom sing masc part pres act — σπείρων — speirōn — sowing

1519.1 prep — εἰς — eis — to

6:4,5. In verse 4 Paul used the Greek verb *dokimazetō* which means to "test or examine" (KJV: "prove"). This involves careful, discerning self-examination in the light of how God views the believer. Doing this will keep a Christian from assuming or even boasting about himself without honestly recognizing the true condition of his own spiritual state. He will recognize that all that he is in the sight of God is solely God's work, not his, and hence, he has nothing to boast about. Not to do so will result in that of which the Pharisee was guilty in Luke 18:9-14. Paul stressed that everyone is answerable to God for himself. In 1 Corinthians 4:4 he told the criticizing Corinthians: "He that judgeth me is the Lord."

The Greek term for "rejoicing," *kauchēma*, means "ground for boasting," "achievement." Any such ground for boasting is strictly the work of the Holy Spirit. Doing this through the Spirit's guidance keeps us from comparing ourself with "another." Note what Paul says in Romans 15:17-19 and 2 Corinthians 10:13-18. In the latter passage troublemakers were part of the context. It is possible that this was true also of the Judaizers and their troubling activity in Galatia.

Paul then quoted a common saying and in so doing used a strong Greek word for "burden" (*phortion*) which can mean the cargo of a ship (Acts 27:10). Everyone is responsible to God for what he is: that is his burden. The seriousness of this is emphasized in Philippians 2:12,13 where Paul said, "Work out your own salvation with fear and trembling," and then he stressed that "it is God which worketh in you both to will and to do of his good pleasure."

6:6. At first glance the immediate connection between this verse and the preceding is somewhat puzzling. The Greek verb (*koinōneitō*) translated "communicate" ("share") may refer to the material or the spiritual. Many take it to mean that those who are taught the Word are to contribute toward the teacher's material support. However, it may also mean, because of the context, that Christians should share, take part in all good things, that is, the Word which is taught. Acts 14:23 records that Paul and Barnabas appointed elders to be in charge of each church in Galatia and its spiritual growth. These may or may not have served without remuneration.

6:7,8. Paul's vigorous comment is very much in order. The Galatians were to share in the "good things" which they were taught, namely, the message of salvation by grace alone. But the Judaizers were promoting a false gospel. Paul emphatically warned against listening to them. Do not be misled, he said; God is not mocked! The Greek word for "mocked," *muktērizetai*, means "to turn up one's nose." Both the Judaizers and those who were listening to them as well as also being boastful about themselves would receive God's judgment. To sow refers back to 5:16 and its expression of walking in the Spirit. To sow to the flesh means to do those sins

4. But let every man prove his own work, and then shall he have rejoicing in himself alone, and not in another: . . . examine his own conduct, *Murdock* . . . learn to assess properly the value of his own work and he can then be glad when he has done something worth doing without depending on the approval of others, *Phillips* . . . test his own work...rather than comparing himself with another, *Adams* . . . will have boasting, *Wilson* . . . and not in comparison with another, *Noyes*.

5. For every man shall bear his own burden: . . . must carry his own load, *TCNT, Williams* . . . must carry his own pack load, *Montgomery* . . . bear his own load, *Worrell, Adams* . . . shoulder his own pack, *Phillips*.

6. Let him that is taught in the word communicate unto him that teacheth in all good things: . . . him who is instructed, *Scarlett* . . . him that is catechized, *Rheims* . . . him that is being orally-instructed, *Rotherham* . . . minister vnto him, *Geneva* . . . should share with his teacher, *Norlie* . . . share in all good things, *Panin* . . . share everything good that he has with the one who instructs him, *Adams*.

7. Be not deceived; God is not mocked: for whatsoever a man soweth, that shall he also reap: Do not mistake, *Murdock* . . . God is not to be derided, *Wilson* . . . is not to be trifled with, *TCNT* . . . is not to be scoffed at, *Williams* . . . is not scorned, *Wyclif*.

8. For he that soweth to his flesh shall of the flesh reap corruption: . . . who sows for, *Adams* . . . to gratify his own flesh, *Norlie* . . . of their earthly nature will reap decay, *TCNT* . . . will reap destruction, *Williams*.

3450.16 art sing neu	4011.1 noun sing neu	1523.2 prep gen	3450.2 art gen sing	4011.2 noun gen sing neu	2302.9 verb 3sing indic fut act
τὸ	πνεῦμα	ἐκ	τοῦ	πνεύματος	θερίσει
to	pneuma	ek	tou	pneumatos	therisei
the	Spirit,	from	the	Spirit	shall reap

2205.4 noun acc sing fem	164.1 adj sing	3450.16 art sing neu	1156.2 conj	2541.1 adj sing	4020.17 verb nom pl masc part pres act
ζωὴν	αἰώνιον.	**9.** τὸ	δὲ	καλὸν	ποιοῦντες
zōēn	aiōnion.	to	de	kalon	poiountes
life	eternal:	the	but	well	doing

9.a.**Txt:** 04C,06D-corr
018K,020L,025P,byz.
Sod
Var: 01א,02A,03B-corr
33,Lach,Treg,Alf,Word
Weis,UBS/⋆

3231.1 partic	1560.2 verb 1pl subj pres act		1450.1 verb 1pl subj pres act	2511.3 noun dat sing masc	1056.1 conj
μὴ	⸀ ἐκκακῶμεν·		[ᵃ⋆ ἐγκακῶμεν,]	καιρῷ	γὰρ
mē	ekkakōmen		enkakōmen	kairō	gar
not	we should lose heart;		[idem]	in time	for

2375.3 adj dat sing	2302.10 verb 1pl indic fut act	3231.1 partic	1577.2 verb nom pl masc part pres mid	679.1 partic	3631.1 partic
ἰδίῳ	θερίσομεν,	μὴ	ἐκλυόμενοι.	**10.** ἄρα	οὖν
idiō	therisomen,	mē	ekluomenoi.	ara	oun
its own	we shall reap	not	fainting.	So	then

10.a.**Txt:** p46,02A,04C
06D,010F,012G,044,byz.
Var: 01א,03B-org,6,33
104,326,614

5453.1 conj	2511.4 noun acc sing masc	2174.5 verb 1pl indic pres act	2174.8 verb 1pl subj pres act	2021.6 verb 1pl subj pres mid
ὡς	καιρὸν	⸀⋆ ἔχομεν	[ᵃ ἔχωμεν]	ἐργαζώμεθα
hōs	kairon	echomen	echōmen	ergazōmetha
as	time	we have	[we may have]	we should work

3450.16 art sing neu	18.3 adj sing	4242.1 prep	3820.8 adj acc pl masc	3094.1 adv sup	1156.2 conj	4242.1 prep
τὸ	ἀγαθὸν	πρὸς	πάντας,	μάλιστα	δὲ	πρὸς
to	agathon	pros	pantas,	malista	de	pros
the	good	towards	all,	especially	and	towards

3450.8 art acc pl masc	3472.3 adj acc pl masc	3450.10 art gen sing fem	3963.2 noun gen sing fem	1481.15 verb 2pl impr aor act	3941.2 intr-pron dat pl neu
τοὺς	οἰκείους	τῆς	πίστεως.	**11.** Ἴδετε	πηλίκοις
tous	oikeious	tēs	pisteōs.	Idete	pēlikois
the	household	of the	faith.	See	in how large

5050.3 prs-pron dat 2pl	1115.5 noun dat pl neu	1119.7 verb 1sing indic aor act	3450.11 art dat sing fem	1684.8 adj dat sing fem	5331.3 noun dat sing fem
ὑμῖν	γράμμασιν	ἔγραψα	τῇ	ἐμῇ	χειρί.
humin	grammasin	egrapsa	tē	emē	cheiri.
to you	letters	I wrote	with the	my	hand.

3607.2 rel-pron nom pl masc	2286.6 verb 3pl indic pres act	2126.1 verb inf aor act	1706.1 prep	4418.3 noun dat sing fem
12. ὅσοι	θέλουσιν	εὐπροσωπῆσαι	ἐν	σαρκί,
hosoi	thelousin	euprosōpēsai	en	sarki,
As many as	wish	to have a fair appearance	in	flesh,

3642.7 dem-pron nom pl masc	313.2 verb 3pl indic pres act	5050.4 prs-pron acc 2pl	3919.9 verb inf pres mid
οὗτοι	ἀναγκάζουσιν	ὑμᾶς	περιτέμνεσθαι,
houtoi	anankazousin	humas	peritemnesthai,
these	compel	you	to be circumcised,

3303.1 adv	2419.1 conj	3231.1 partic	3450.3 art dat sing	4567.3 noun dat sing masc	3450.2 art gen sing	5382.2 name gen masc
μόνον	ἵνα	⸀ μὴ	τῷ	σταυρῷ	τοῦ	Χριστοῦ
monon	hina	mē	tō	staurō	tou	Christou
only	that	not	for the	cross	of the	Christ

which are listed in 5:19-21. To sow to the Spirit refers to the fruit of His work as listed in 5:22-26. Again Paul stressed the role of the Spirit and the blessed result of His work. (Paul's analogy of sowing and reaping was part of the annual experience of the Galatians.)

but he that soweth to the Spirit shall of the Spirit reap life everlasting: . . . for the Spirit will reap eternal life, *Adams* . . . enduring Life, *TCNT.*

6:9,10. The verb *to reap* provides the connection with the preceding. Paul reminded believers that, through the Spirit's work, to keep on walking in the Spirit is an ongoing process. To slow down or even to stop is never in order for a Christian. This temptation was and is a common one. Paul in his other letters stressed this ongoing need (1 Corinthians 15:58; 16:13; Philippians 1:27-30; 2:14,15; 4:1,4-9; 1 Thessalonians 3:12,13; 2 Thessalonians 3:13). Paul added, "For in due season we shall reap, if we faint not." It is essential to remember that such reaping is again an expression of God's grace.

Paul restated in the positive what he had just said in the negative. The Galatians were reminded to do that which was beneficial, and especially spiritually beneficial to all men, "especially unto them who are of the household of faith." The word "household" was an important legal and social term at that time. All who were part of a given household (family, servants, and slaves) were part of this inclusive unit. For example, when Lydia came to faith, she and her whole house (household) were baptized. The same metaphor is used in Ephesians 2:19, 1 Timothy 3:15, and 1 Peter 4:17. All who share faith in Christ form religiously a single unit, a household. Paul stressed an important principle of the Christian life. If believers ignore the spiritual welfare of their fellow Christians, less thought will be given to the spiritual welfare of the unbeliever.

9. And let us not be weary in well doing: for in due season we shall reap, if we faint not: . . . let us not lose heart, *PNT* . . . let us not be faint-hearted, *Noyes* . . . Let us stop getting tired of doing good, *Williams* . . . for, unless we throw in our hand, the ultimate harvest is assured, *Phillips* . . . at the proper season, *Wilson* . . . if we do not grow weary, *TCNT* . . . if we do not give up, *Williams* . . . if we do not lose courage, *Norlie* . . . if we don't slacken, *Adams.*

10. As we have therefore opportunity, let us do good unto all [men], especially unto them who are of the household of faith: . . . let us treat every one with kindness, *TCNT* . . . especially to the members of the family, *Sawyer* . . . especially those who belong to the Christian household, *Phillips* . . . to those who are of one family with us in the faith, *Norlie* . . . the family of faith, *Williams.*

6:11. Paul customarily dictated his letters. His purpose for the Galatians was to warn that they would fall from grace if they listened to the Judaizers. Now he himself took up the pen and graphically called their attention to it. He did this also at the close of several other crucial letters to churches facing grave problems (1 Corinthians 16:21; Colossians 4:18; 2 Thessalonians 3:17). His letter was to be read to all the churches in Southern Galatia.

11. Ye see how large a letter I have written unto you with mine own hand: Notice the large letters, *Adams* . . . Look at these huge letters I am making, *Phillips* . . . in how large letters, *Scarlett* . . . in my own handwriting! *Montgomery.*

6:12,13. In the verses which follow, Paul quickly summarized the basic points he had made previously. He began by noting the selfish motives of the Judaizers. Their concern was to "make a good showing" (*euprosōpēsai*) for themselves. They differed from their fellow Jews only in that they had accepted Jesus as the promised Messiah, but failed to understand His true mission and its saving significance. Seemingly they wished to remain in good standing with the main-

12. As many as desire to make a fair show in the flesh, they constrain you to be circumcised: . . . who are disposed to glory, *Murdock* . . . who wish to appear to advantage in regard to outward things, *TCNT* . . . to make a fair appearance, *Sawyer, PNT* . . . They want to present a pleasing front to the world, *Phillips* . . . a fine outward show, *Williams* . . . compel you, *Panin, Clementson.*

Galatians 6:13

12.a.Txt: 018K,020L,byz.
Var: 03B,We/Ho,Weis
UBS/⋆

3450.3 art dat sing	4567.3 noun dat sing masc	3450.2 art gen sing	5382.2 name gen masc	3231.1 partic
[ᵃ☆ τῷ	σταυρῷ	τοῦ	Χριστοῦ	μὴ]
tō	staurō	tou	Christou	mē
[for the	cross	of the	Christ	not]

12.b.Txt: 01ℵ,03B,06D
018K,044,33,365,614
630,1739,2495
Var: p46,02A,04C,010F
012G,020L,025P,6,81
104,326,629,1175

1371.23 verb 3pl subj pres pass	1371.28 verb 3pl indic pres pass	3624.1 conj
(☆ διώκωνται.	[ᵇ διώκονται.]	13. οὐδὲ
diōkōntai	diōkontai	oude
they may be persecuted.	[they are being persecuted.]	Neither

13.a.Txt: 01ℵ,02A,04C
06D,018K,025P,33,81
104,1739,2464
Var: p46,03B,010F
020L,044,6,365,614
630,1175,2495

1056.1 conj	3450.7 art nom pl masc	3919.8 verb nom pl masc part pres mid	3919.14 verb nom pl masc part perf mid
γὰρ	οἱ	(☆ περιτεμνόμενοι	[ᵃ περιτετμημένοι]
gar	hoi	peritemnomenoi	peritetmēmenoi
for	the	being circumcised	[having been circumcised]

840.7 prs-pron nom pl masc	3414.4 noun acc sing masc	5278.1 verb 3pl indic pres act	233.2 conj	2286.6 verb 3pl indic pres act
αὐτοὶ	νόμον	φυλάσσουσιν·	ἀλλὰ	θέλουσιν
autoi	nomon	phulassousin	alla	thelousin
themselves	law	keep;	but	they wish

5050.4 prs-pron acc 2pl	3919.9 verb inf pres mid	2419.1 conj	1706.1 prep	3450.11 art dat sing fem	5052.6 adj dat 2sing fem
ὑμᾶς	περιτέμνεσθαι,	ἵνα	ἐν	τῇ	ὑμετέρᾳ
humas	peritemnesthai	hina	en	tē	humetera
you	to be circumcised,	that	in	the	your

4418.3 noun dat sing fem	2714.13 verb 3pl subj aor mid	1466.5 prs-pron dat 1sing	1156.2 conj	3231.1 partic	1090.44 verb 3sing opt aor mid
σαρκὶ	καυχήσωνται.	14. ἐμοὶ	δὲ	μὴ	γένοιτο
sarki	kauchēsōntai	emoi	de	mē	genoito
flesh	they might boast.	For me	but	not	may it be

2714.10 verb inf pres mid	1479.1 conj	3231.1 partic	1706.1 prep	3450.3 art dat sing	4567.3 noun dat sing masc	3450.2 art gen sing
καυχᾶσθαι	εἰ	μὴ	ἐν	τῷ	σταυρῷ	τοῦ
kauchasthai	ei	mē	en	tō	staurō	tou
to boast	if	not	in	the	cross	of the

14.a.Txt: 04C-corr
06D-corr,018K,020L
byz.
Var: 01ℵ,02A,03B
04C-org,06D-org,025P
33,Lach,Treg,Alf,Tisc
We/Ho,Weis,Sod
UBS/⋆

2935.2 noun gen sing masc	2231.2 prs-pron gen 1pl	2400.2 name masc	5382.2 name gen masc	1217.1 prep	3614.2 rel-pron gen sing
κυρίου	ἡμῶν	Ἰησοῦ	Χριστοῦ·	δι'	οὗ
kuriou	hēmōn	Iēsou	Christou	di'	hou
Lord	our	Jesus	Christ;	through	whom

15.a.Txt: 01ℵ,02A,04C
06D,018K,020L,025P
etc.byz.
Var: 03B,33,Treg,Alf
Tisc,We/Ho,Weis,Sod
UBS/⋆

1466.5 prs-pron dat 1sing	2862.1 noun nom sing masc	4568.16 verb 3sing indic perf mid	2476.3 prs-pron nom	3450.3 art dat sing	2862.3 noun dat sing masc
ἐμοὶ	κόσμος	ἐσταύρωται,	κἀγὼ	(ᵃ τῷ \	κόσμῳ.
emoi	kosmos	estaurōtai	kagō	tō	kosmō
to me	world	has been crucified,	and I	to the	world.

15.b.Txt: 01ℵ-corr
06D-corr,018K,020L
025P,byz.
Var: 01ℵ-org,02A,03B
04C,06D-org,33,sa.bo.
Gries,Lach,Treg,Alf
Word,Tisc,We/Ho,Weis
Sod,UBS/⋆

1706.1 prep	1056.1 conj	5382.3 name dat masc	2400.2 name masc	3641.1 conj	3641.1 conj
15. ἐν	γὰρ	Χριστῷ	Ἰησοῦ	(οὔτε	[ᵃ☆ οὔτε
en	gar	Christō	Iēsou	oute	oute
In	for	Christ	Jesus	neither	[neither

1056.1 conj	3921.1 noun nom sing fem	4949.9 indef-pron sing neu	2453.2 verb 3sing indic pres act	1498.4 verb 3sing indic pres act
γὰρ]	περιτομή	τί	(ἰσχύει,	[ᵇ☆ ἐστιν]
gar	peritomē	ti	ischuei	estin
for]	circumcision	any	is of effect,	[is]

90

line Jewish community. For them to be able to boast that they had persuaded Jewish and Gentile Christians to return to the way of the Law would give them a favorable reputation in Jerusalem. Then they would not face the disfavor and wrath of the Jewish opposition.

Paul stressed that the Judaizers desired to persuade the Galatian Christians to be circumcised so they could boast to Jerusalem about their zeal for the Law. In other words, the Judaizers were not concerned about the spiritual welfare of the Galatians, but rather about their own standing in the Jewish community. Their concern was to avoid persecution for the cross of Christ.

The value of a believer's actions are not marked by how much is done so much as it is by his reason for acting. What motivates him? Why does he act in a certain way? That is what counts.

6:14,15. In sharp contrast to the attitude of the Judaizers, Paul carefully set forth his own basis for boasting. His only basis was, and always would be, not self but strictly God's grace expressed in the cross of Christ. It must be remembered that even to speak of the cross in polite Roman society of that time was unthinkable. The cross in that culture was the symbol of the greatest ignominy and disgrace, normally used only as the form of execution for slaves and the lower levels of society. It was considered such a horrible, unthinkable form of execution that no cartoonist would even think of doing a cartoon of crucifixion. And thus far, no cartoon of crucifixion dating back to the First Century has been found.

Paul added: "By (through) whom the world is crucified unto me, and I unto the world." When the risen and ascended Christ appeared to him on the Damascus Road, it had a decisive effect on him. All that he had valued in the past was now seen to be mere sewage, the meaning of the Greek word *skubala* Paul used in Philippians 3:8. In direct contrast is "the world," which stands for the world at enmity against God. It includes also the desire to be justified by works. In the analogy Paul used, the Cross was the permanent barrier between him and the world, also between what he once had been as Saul the self-righteous Pharisee, and Paul, the humble and grateful missionary, personally called by the glorified Christ. This must always be true of all believers in Christ.

In Paul's past, circumcision made an effective distinction between Jew and Gentile. Only the circumcised could be true sons of Abraham, and therefore true members of God's covenant people. But now, through the cross of Christ, this physical distinction was no longer valid. Whether one was circumcised or not made no difference at all. Through the Cross, all who are led by the Spirit to believe in Christ have become a new creation (Titus 3:4-6; 2 Corinthians 5:17). No longer are they under the curse of the Law, but they have the great privilege and joy of living under grace with the certain hope of eternal life. In this way, Paul stressed again his faithfulness to the commission which he had received from Christ himself. And for this he paid the supreme penalty (2 Timothy 4:6-8).

only lest they should suffer persecution for the cross of Christ: . . . for the simple reason, *Berkeley* . . . solely that, *Fenton* . . . they want to avoid being persecuted, *Phillips* . . . only that they may not be persecuted, *ASV* . . . fearing they will be persecuted, *SEB* . . . that they may escape persecution, *Adams*.

13. For neither they themselves who are circumcised keep the law; but desire to have you circumcised, that they may glory in your flesh: For the circumcisers themselves never observe the ritual; but they wish you to be circumcised, so that they may boast about your body, *Fenton* . . . These men who are circumcised do not obey the law themselves, *SEB* . . . so that they can boast of your submission, *Norlie* . . . about your submission to their ruling, *Phillips* . . . so that they may boast of your observance of the rite, *TCNT* . . . boast of you as members of their party, *Williams*.

14. But God forbid that I should glory, save in the cross of our Lord Jesus Christ, by whom the world is crucified unto me, and I unto the world: But for me, perish the thought, *Berkeley* . . . But, may I never boast, *Scarlett* . . . But I myself will not become boastful, *Fenton* . . . but fer be it fro me to haue glorie, *Wyclif* . . . I hope that I will never brag about something like that! *SEB* . . . that I should glory in anything except in, *Montgomery* . . . that I should boast about anything or anybody...which means that the world is a dead thing to me, *Phillips* . . . except about the cross, *Adams* . . . is dead to me, *TCNT*.

15. For in Christ Jesus neither circumcision availeth any thing: It doesn't matter whether a person is, *SEB* . . . is of any account, *Adams* . . . has any value, *Williams* . . . is of any importance, *TCNT* . . . that counts, *Phillips*.

3641.1 conj
οὔτε
oute
nor

201.1 noun nom sing fem
ἀκροβυστία,
akrobustia
uncircumcision;

233.2 conj
ἀλλὰ
alla
but

2508.3 adj nom sing fem
καινὴ
kainē
a new

2909.1 noun nom sing fem
κτίσις.
ktisis
creation.

2504.1 conj
16. καὶ
kai
And

3607.2 rel-pron nom pl masc
ὅσοι
hosoi
as many as

3450.3 art dat sing
τῷ
tō
by the

2554.2 noun dat sing masc
κανόνι
kanoni
rule

3642.5 dem-pron dat sing masc
τούτῳ
toutō
this

4599.5 verb 3pl indic fut act
⟨☆ στοιχήσουσιν,
stoichēsousin
shall walk,

16.a.Txt: 01ℵ,03B
04C-corr2,044,byz.
Var: 02A,04C-org,06D
010F,012G,1739,1881

4599.3 verb 3pl indic pres act
[ᵃ στοιχοῦσιν,]
stoichousin
[walk,]

1503.1 noun nom sing fem
εἰρήνη
eirēnē
peace

1894.2 prep
ἐπ'
ep'
upon

840.8 prs-pron acc pl masc
αὐτοὺς
autous
them

2504.1 conj
καὶ
kai
and

1643.2 noun sing neu
ἔλεος,
eleos
mercy,

2504.1 conj
καὶ
kai
and

1894.3 prep
ἐπὶ
epi
upon

3450.6 art acc sing masc
τὸν
ton
the

2447.1 name masc
Ἰσραὴλ
Israēl
Israel

3450.2 art gen sing
τοῦ
tou
of

2296.2 noun gen sing masc
θεοῦ.
theou
of God.

3450.2 art gen sing
17. Τοῦ
Tou
For

3036.7 adj gen sing neu
λοιποῦ,
loipou
the rest,

2845.7 noun acc pl masc
κόπους
kopous
troubles

1466.4 prs-pron dat 1sing
μοι
moi
to me

3235.3 num card nom masc
μηδεὶς
mēdeis
no one

3792.4 verb 3sing impr pres act
παρεχέτω·
parechetō
let give,

1466.1 prs-pron nom 1sing
ἐγὼ
egō
I

1056.1 conj
γὰρ
gar
for

3450.17 art pl neu
τὰ
ta
the

4593.1 noun pl neu
στίγματα
stigmata
marks

3450.2 art gen sing
τοῦ
tou
of the

2935.2 noun gen sing masc
⟨ᵃ κυρίου ⟩
kuriou
Lord

2400.2 name masc
Ἰησοῦ
Iēsou
Jesus

1706.1 prep
ἐν
en
in

17.a.Txt: 04C-corr
06D-corr,018K,020L
byz.Sod
Var: 02A,03B,04C-org
33,Lach,Treg,Alf,Word
Tisc,We/Ho,Weis
UBS/☆

3450.3 art dat sing
τῷ
tō
the

4835.3 noun dat sing neu
σώματί
sōmati
body

1466.2 prs-pron gen 1sing
μου
mou
my

934.1 verb 1sing indic pres act
βαστάζω.
bastazō
bear.

3450.9 art nom sing fem
18. Ἡ
Hē
The

5322.1 noun nom sing fem
χάρις
charis
grace

3450.2 art gen sing
τοῦ
tou
of the

2935.2 noun gen sing masc
κυρίου
kuriou
Lord

2231.2 prs-pron gen 1pl
ἡμῶν
hēmōn
our

2400.2 name masc
Ἰησοῦ
Iēsou
Jesus

5382.2 name gen masc
Χριστοῦ
Christou
Christ

3196.3 prep
μετὰ
meta
with

3450.2 art gen sing
τοῦ
tou
the

4011.2 noun gen sing neu
πνεύματος
pneumatos
spirit

5050.2 prs-pron gen 2pl
ὑμῶν,
humōn
your,

79.6 noun nom pl masc
ἀδελφοί.
adelphoi
brothers.

279.1 intrj
ἀμήν.
amēn
Amen.

4242.1 prep
⟨ᵃ Πρὸς
Pros
To

18.a.Txt: 03B-corr,018K
025P,Steph
Var: Gries,Lach,Word
Tisc,We/Ho,Weis,Sod
UBS/☆

1046.3 name gen fem
Γαλάτας
Galatas
Galatians

1119.21 verb 3sing indic aor pass
ἐγράφη
egraphē
written

570.3 prep
ἀπὸ
apo
from

4373.1 name gen fem
Ῥώμης. ⟩
Rhōmēs
Rome.

6:16. The Greek word *kanon* translated "rule" has the meaning in classical Greek of the straight edge of a ruler used by masons and carpenters. It is used here metaphorically in the sense of that which sets a standard or principle. It is in keeping with this meaning that Paul used a verb which means "walking in a straight line" according to a rule. The Galatians understood this illustration from the use of a ruler in daily life. Paul thereby sought to impress on them that circumcision promoted by the Judaizers as necessary for salvation is meaningless to all who understand who they are through Christ; also, that to be led by the Spirit in their faith and life is imperative.

All who are led by the Spirit to live in grace are the true Israel of God. The term "Israel" is another title for those who through the Spirit's work are members of God's covenant people, regardless of ethnic origins. As such they experience spiritual peace and well-being and also His ongoing mercy as a gift. They are the *new* Israel through faith; they and they alone will experience God's gracious gift of eternal life. This verse concludes the paragraph begun in verse 11.

6:17. Before his final benediction, Paul introduced a strong closing remark. The Judaizers in their attempt to enslave the Christians in "work-righteousness" had caused Paul much concern. In his closing appeal, he stressed that he carried on his body the "brand-marks" (*stigmata*) of Jesus Christ. This was language that the Galatians understood. Slaves were sometimes branded to identify them as slaves. This was especially true of a runaway slave, who upon being caught, could be branded as such for the rest of his life. He could also be branded by having to wear an inscribed metal band welded around his neck.

What were the marks (*stigmata*) of Christ? No specific answer can be given. Acts 14:19 records that Paul was stoned at Lystra and dragged out of the town. Second Corinthians, perhaps written in late summer of A.D. 55, records other painful experiences of Paul (2 Corinthians 11:23-27). However, he did not in each case say when he suffered them. His body bore scars from the ill treatment he had received.

6:18. Paul closed with a benediction which is almost the same as in Philippians 4:23 and Philemon 25. His closing words, "the grace of our Lord Jesus Christ" restate the emphasis of Paul in this letter, namely, grace alone! Paul went on to say "be with your spirit." Those who through the Spirit's work live in grace also enjoy spiritual peace. Paul closed with "Amen" as he did in the opening greeting in 1:5. "So let it be!"

nor uncircumcision, but a new creature: All that is important is, *SEB* . . . What counts is a new birth, *Norlie* . . . but a new creation, *Panin, Wilson, Fenton* . . . but a new nature, *TCNT* . . . but the power of new birth, *Phillips.*

16. And as many as walk according to this rule, peace [be] on them, and mercy, and upon the Israel of God: Peace and mercy to, *SEB* . . . And whoever follow, *Confraternity* . . . all who will govern their lives by this rule, *Montgomery* . . . on all who are in line with this rule, *Adams* . . . they who press forward in this path, *Murdock* . . . And as many as discipline themselves by this rule, *Fenton* . . . To all who live by this principle, to the true Israel, *Phillips* . . . they are God's Israel, *TCNT* . . . upon God's true Israel! *Norlie* . . . the true Israel of God, *Williams.*

17. From henceforth let no man trouble me: for I bear in my body the marks of the Lord Jesus: Finally, *Wilson* . . . But from now let none of them trouble me; for I carry in my body, *Fenton* . . . interfere with me after this. I carry on my scarred body the marks of my owner, *Phillips* . . . let no one cause me trouble, since I bear on my body the brand-marks, *Adams* . . . From this time forth...of Jesus, my Master, *Montgomery* . . . For the future...branded on my body, *TCNT* . . . let no man be troublesome to me, *Douay* . . . the brandmarks, *Rotherham* . . . the tokenes of, *Wyclif* . . . I carry scars on my body which show that I belong to Jesus, *SEB* . . . the scars that mark me as Jesus' slave, *Williams.*

18. Brethren, the grace of our Lord Jesus Christ [be] with your spirit. Amen: Brothers, may the gracious love of, *SEB* . . . May the blessing, *TCNT* . . . The spiritual blessing, *Williams.*

THE EPISTLE
OF PAUL TO THE
EPHESIANS

Expanded Interlinear

Textual Critical Apparatus

Verse-by-Verse Commentary

Various Versions

4242.1 prep	2162.2 name-adj acc pl masc	1976.1 noun nom sing fem	3834.2 name gen masc
Πρὸς	Ἐφεσίους	ἐπιστολὴ	Παύλου
Pros	Ephesious	epistolē	Paulou
To	Ephesians	letter	of Paul

Textual Apparatus

3834.1 name nom masc	646.1 noun nom sing masc	2400.2 name masc	5382.2 name gen masc	5382.2 name gen masc
1:1. Παῦλος	ἀπόστολος	ʼ Ἰησοῦ	Χριστοῦ	[✶ Χριστοῦ
Paulos	apostolos	Iēsou	Christou	Christou
Paul,	apostle	of Jesus	Christ	[of Christ

2400.2 name masc	1217.2 prep	2284.2 noun gen sing neu	2296.2 noun gen sing masc	3450.4 art dat pl	39.8 adj dat pl masc
Ἰησοῦ]	διὰ	θελήματος	θεοῦ,	τοῖς	ἁγίοις
Iēsou	dia	thelēmatos	theou	tois	hagiois
Jesus]	by	will	of God,	to the	saints

3450.4 art dat pl	1498.24 verb dat pl masc part pres act	1706.1 prep	2163.2 name dat fem	2504.1 conj	3964.8 adj dat pl masc
τοῖς	οὖσιν	[a ἐν	Ἐφέσῳ \	καὶ	πιστοῖς
tois	ousin	en	Ephesō	kai	pistois
the	being	at	Ephesus	and	faithful

1.a.**Txt:** 01ℵ-corr,02A 03B-corr,06D,018K 020L,025P,byz.it.sa.bo. Tisc,We/Ho,Weis,Sod UBS/✶
Var: p46,01ℵ-org 03B-org,Weis

1706.1 prep	5382.3 name dat masc	2400.2 name masc	5322.1 noun nom sing fem	5050.3 prs-pron dat 2pl	2504.1 conj	1503.1 noun nom sing fem
ἐν	Χριστῷ	Ἰησοῦ·	**2.** χάρις	ὑμῖν	καὶ	εἰρήνη
en	Christō	Iēsou	charis	humin	kai	eirēnē
in	Christ	Jesus.	Grace	to you	and	peace

570.3 prep	2296.2 noun gen sing masc	3824.2 noun gen sing masc	2231.2 prs-pron gen 1pl	2504.1 conj	2935.2 noun gen sing masc	2400.2 name masc
ἀπὸ	θεοῦ	πατρὸς	ἡμῶν	καὶ	κυρίου	Ἰησοῦ
apo	theou	patros	hēmōn	kai	kuriou	Iēsou
from	God	Father	our	and	Lord	Jesus

5382.2 name gen masc	2109.1 adj nom sing masc	3450.5 art nom sing masc	2296.1 noun nom sing masc	2504.1 conj	3824.1 noun nom sing masc
Χριστοῦ.	**3.** Εὐλογητὸς	ὁ	θεὸς	καὶ	πατὴρ
Christou	Eulogētos	ho	theos	kai	patēr
Christ.	Blessed	the	God	and	Father

3450.2 art gen sing	2935.2 noun gen sing masc	2231.2 prs-pron gen 1pl	2400.2 name masc	5382.2 name gen masc	3450.5 art nom sing masc
τοῦ	κυρίου	ἡμῶν	Ἰησοῦ	Χριστοῦ,	ὁ
tou	kuriou	hēmōn	Iēsou	Christou	ho
of the	Lord	our	Jesus	Christ,	the

2108.9 verb nom sing masc part aor act	2231.4 prs-pron acc 1pl	1706.1 prep	3820.11 adj dat sing fem	2110.3 noun dat sing fem	4012.5 adj dat sing fem
εὐλογήσας	ἡμᾶς	ἐν	πάσῃ	εὐλογίᾳ	πνευματικῇ
eulogēsas	hēmas	en	pasē	eulogia	pneumatikē
having blessed	us	with	every	blessing	spiritual

3.a.**Var:** 01ℵ,02A,03B 06D,018K,020L,025P Elzev,Gries,Lach,Treg Alf,Word,Tisc,We/Ho Weis,Sod,UBS/✶

1706.1 prep	3450.4 art dat pl	2016.8 adj dat pl neu	1706.1 prep	5382.3 name dat masc	2503.1 conj
ἐν	τοῖς	ἐπουρανίοις	[a✶+ ἐν]	Χριστῷ,	**4.** καθὼς
en	tois	epouraniois	en	Christō	kathōs
in	the	heavenlies	[in]	with Christ;	according as

THE EPISTLE OF PAUL TO THE
EPHESIANS

1:1. The name "Paul" comes from the Latin and means "small." Hebrew parents often gave their sons Gentile names in addition to Jewish ones. Because of the nature of this epistle, the Holy Spirit inspired Paul to introduce himself as an apostle. Much debate exists relative to the exact recipients of this letter. Three of the oldest manuscripts, the Chester Beatty Papyrus (dated circa 200); the Codex Sinaiticus; and the Codex Vaticanus (usually dated in the Fourth Century), do not contain the words "at Ephesus." The earliest extant manuscript containing the words "at Ephesus" is at least two centuries later than the last two manuscripts referred to above. This fact and others have led some scholars to believe the epistle actually was written as a cyclical letter to be read in all the churches of Asia Minor.

1:2. Paul greeted his readers in the normal fashion of the day. It was conventional first to mention the author's name, then refer to the recipients of the letter, and lastly to greet them in a pleasant way. What is different about Paul's approach is that, in addition to the fact that the Holy Spirit very definitely inspired him to do so, he constantly used the Greek idea of "grace" (*charis*) and the Hebrew idea of "peace" which was translated into Greek and became a very common word of that day (*eirēnē*). "Grace" contains the meaning of receiving something completely undeserved, and "peace" contains the idea of enjoying inner tranquility, undisturbed by external circumstances.

1:3. In many of his epistles Paul gradually built up to his major thesis, but in this letter he began with one of the most important of all theological truths: God's purpose for the New Testament Church. The position of the believer is "in the heavenlies in Christ"; this describes the sphere and the nature of our spiritual experiences. "In Christ" or its equivalent can be found 10 times from verses 3 through 13 of the first chapter, and the preposition "in" (*en*) is used approximately 120 times in the 6 chapters of Ephesians. Because verses 3 through 14 are one complete sentence in the Greek, it is obvious the passage should be treated as one complete thought. Some Bible scholars believe this passage was used as a hymn sung in the Early Church in praise to God.

Various Versions

1. Paul, an apostle of Jesus Christ by the will of God: ... messenger...by God's choice, *Phillips* ... by the pleasure of God, *Murdock* ... because that is what God wanted, *Everyday.*

to the saints which are at Ephesus, and to the faithful in Christ Jesus: God's holy people, *Everyday* ... even to Believers in, *Wilson* ... sanctified, and believing, *Murdock* ... faithful followers of, *Norlie* ... To the holy people who live in the city of, *SEB* ... to them which believe on Iesus, *Tyndale* ... to all faithful Christians...and other places where this letter is read, *Phillips.*

2. Grace [be] to you, and peace: Favour to you, *Rotherham* ... May gracious love and peace come to you, *SEB* ... spiritual blessing, *Williams.*

from God our Father, and [from] the Lord Jesus Christ:

3. Blessed [be] the God and Father of our Lord Jesus Christ: Praise be to, *TCNT* ... Praise God! He is the Father, *SEB* ... Let the God and Father...be blessed, *Fenton.*

who hath blessed us with all spiritual blessings in heavenly [places] in Christ: ... who, through our union with Christ, *TCNT* ... for giving us through Christ every possible spiritual benefit as citizens of Heaven! *Phillips* ... has given us every spiritual blessing in heaven, *Everyday* ... in heuenly thynges, *Cranmer* ... among the celestials, *Concordant* ... in the heavenly spheres, *Berkeley* ... that heaven itself enjoys, *Norlie* ... in the heavenly regions in Christ, *Noyes* ... on high in Christ, *Confraternity.*

97

1573.3 verb 3sing indic aor mid	2231.4 prs-pron acc 1pl	1706.1 prep	840.4 prs-pron dat sing	4112.1 prep	2573.1 noun gen sing fem
ἐξελέξατο	ἡμᾶς	ἐν	αὐτῷ	πρὸ	καταβολῆς
exelexato	hēmas	en	autō	pro	katabolēs
he chose	us	in	him	before	foundation

2862.2 noun gen sing masc	1498.32 verb inf pres act	2231.4 prs-pron acc 1pl	39.9 adj acc pl masc	2504.1 conj	297.4 adj acc pl masc
κόσμου,	εἶναι	ἡμᾶς	ἁγίους	καὶ	ἀμώμους
kosmou	einai	hēmas	hagious	kai	amōmous
of world,	to be	for us	holy	and	blameless

2684.1 prep	840.3 prs-pron gen sing	1706.1 prep	26.3 noun dat sing fem	840.3 prs-pron gen sing	1706.1 prep
κατενώπιον	' αὐτοῦ	ἐν	ἀγάπῃ,	[☆ αὐτοῦ,	ἐν
katenōpion	autou	en	agapē	autou	en
before	him	in	love;	[him,	in

26.3 noun dat sing fem	4168.2 verb nom sing masc part aor act	2231.4 prs-pron acc 1pl	1519.1 prep	5047.3 noun acc sing fem	1217.2 prep
ἀγάπῃ]	5. προορίσας	ἡμᾶς	εἰς	υἱοθεσίαν	διὰ
agapē	proorisas	hēmas	eis	huiothesian	dia
love]	having predestined	us	for	adoption	through

2400.2 name masc	5382.2 name gen masc	1519.1 prep	840.6 prs-pron acc sing masc	2567.3 prep	3450.12 art acc sing fem
Ἰησοῦ	Χριστοῦ	εἰς	αὐτόν,	κατὰ	τὴν
Iēsou	Christou	eis	auton	kata	tēn
Jesus	Christ	to	him,	according to	the

2086.3 noun acc sing fem	3450.2 art gen sing	2284.2 noun gen sing neu	840.3 prs-pron gen sing	1519.1 prep	1853.2 noun acc sing masc
εὐδοκίαν	τοῦ	θελήματος	αὐτοῦ,	6. εἰς	ἔπαινον
eudokian	tou	thelēmatos	autou	eis	epainon
good pleasure	of the	will	his,	to	praise

1385.2 noun gen sing fem	3450.10 art gen sing fem	5322.2 noun gen sing fem	840.3 prs-pron gen sing	1706.1 prep	3614.11 rel-pron dat sing fem
δόξης	τῆς	χάριτος	αὐτοῦ,	' ἐν	ᾗ
doxēs	tēs	charitos	autou	en	hē
of glory	of the	grace	his,	in	which

3614.10 rel-pron gen sing fem	5323.1 verb 3sing indic aor act	2231.4 prs-pron acc 1pl	1706.1 prep	3450.3 art dat sing
[a☆ ἧς]	ἐχαρίτωσεν	ἡμᾶς	ἐν	τῷ
hēs	echaritōsen	hēmas	en	tō
[idem]	he made objects of grace	us	in	the

25.29 verb dat sing masc part perf mid	1706.1 prep	3614.3 rel-pron dat sing	2174.5 verb 1pl indic pres act	2174.52 verb 1pl indic aor act
ἠγαπημένῳ·	7. ἐν	ᾧ	'☆ ἔχομεν	[a ἔσχομεν]
ēgapēmenō	en	hō	echomen	eschomen
having been loved:	in	whom	we have	[we had]

3450.12 art acc sing fem	623.3 noun acc sing fem	1217.2 prep	3450.2 art gen sing	129.2 noun gen sing neu	840.3 prs-pron gen sing
τὴν	ἀπολύτρωσιν	διὰ	τοῦ	αἵματος	αὐτοῦ,
tēn	apolutrōsin	dia	tou	haimatos	autou
the	redemption	through	the	blood	his,

3450.12 art acc sing fem	852.3 noun acc sing fem	3450.1 art gen pl	3761.4 noun gen pl neu	2567.3 prep
τὴν	ἄφεσιν	τῶν	παραπτωμάτων,	κατὰ
tēn	aphesin	tōn	paraptōmatōn	kata
the	remission	of the	offenses,	according to

6.a.Txt: 01ℵ-corr,06D 018K,020L,byz.
Var: 01ℵ-org,02A,03B 025P,33,Lach,Treg,Alf Tisc,We/Ho,Weis,Sod UBS/☆

7.a.Var: 01ℵ-org 06D-org,044,104,2495

1:4. Now we come to the extremely important question, "How can God be sovereign and man be free at the same time?" Many take this verse, as well as verse 5, to teach the election by God of some to salvation and some to damnation. They understand the word "chosen" (*exelexato*) to mean God chooses some individuals to be spared to the exclusion of all others. An alternative to this position states that what God determined before the creation of the world was not who would be saved and who would be lost, but the institution of the New Testament Church.

The verb "chose" is a middle voice verb meaning "He chose us for himself." The "in him" in this verse, as well as the statement in verse 3, indicates that all God's blessings come to people "in Christ" (literally "in the sphere of Christ").

One of the main ideas behind the term *election* is that God has taken the initiative to provide salvation. This passage places more emphasis on the method of election than on the persons involved. Election is a choosing based upon God's grace, not upon man's merit. In addition the verse focuses not as much upon *whom* God has chosen (i.e., individuals or a Body), but upon *why:* that we should be holy and blameless ("without blemish") before Him.

Again, there are differing views of what the latter part of the verse means. Some say it teaches that holiness and blamelessness are imputed to the individual at the time of his election. Others believe it is a reference to progressive sanctification.

1:5. This verse further describes why God has chosen believers: that through His Mediator, Jesus Christ, we may stand before Him as children. Whereas "election" looks back to discover whom God has chosen, "predestination" points forward to what God has determined shall be the destiny of those who are His. Because it pleased Him to do so, He predetermined that He would adopt us as His own children based on the merits of Christ alone. It is "not by works of righteousness which we have done, but according to his mercy he has saved us" (Titus 3:5).

Some interpret these passages to say that after God predestined believers to adoption, He elected them to be holy, etc. Others insist that election and adoption are accomplished simultaneously. Meyer points out that elsewhere in the New Testament predestination is not distinguished from election "as something preceding it; it rather substantially coincides with it" (*Meyer's Commentary*, 7:315). Only "foreknowledge" seems to be a prior activity on God's part (cf. Romans 8:29).

1:6. Salvation and all its benefits are the results of God's glorious grace (His unmerited favor). As such it deserves our praise. "Accepted in the beloved" introduces a transition to Christ who is the subject of the following verses.

1:7. If this total passage from verse 3 through verse 14 was used as a hymn by the Early Church, the second stanza focused on the

4. According as he hath chosen us in him before the foundation of the world: . . . consider what he has done, *Phillips* . . . before a foundation, *Rotherham* . . . before the constitution, *Rheims* . . . before the casting down of the world, *Clementson* . . . bifor the makynge of the world, *Wyclif* . . . were layd, *Geneva*.

that we should be holy and without blame before him in love: . . . intending that we, *TCNT* . . . and unspotted, *Douay* . . . and immaculate, *Rheims* . . . blameless in his presence, *Wilson, Rotherham* . . . living within his constant care, *Phillips*.

5. Having predestinated us unto the adoption of children by Jesus Christ to himself: . . . having before appointed us, *Scarlett* . . . having foreordained us, *ASV* . . . having in Love previously marked us out for Sonship, *Wilson* . . . for the privileges of his sons, *TCNT*.

according to the good pleasure of his will: . . . in fulfilment of his loving purposes, *TCNT* . . . to the purpose of his will, *Douay*.

6. To the praise of the glory of his grace: . . . to the praise of his glorious grace, *Sawyer, Scarlett* . . . and so we praise His glorious mercy, *Norlie* . . . that we might learn to praise that glorious generosity of his, *Phillips*.

wherein he hath made us accepted in the beloved: . . . he hath graced us in his beloved son, *Douay* . . . by which He has made us the objects of His favor through His beloved, *Norlie* . . . which He freely bestowed on us in the Beloved, *Clementson* . . . which has made us welcome in the everlasting love he bears toward the Son, *Phillips*.

7. In whom we have redemption through his blood: For by union with Christ, *TCNT* . . . at the cost of, *Phillips*.

the forgiveness of sins: . . . freely forgiven, *Phillips* . . . in the pardon of our offences, *TCNT*.

Ephesians 1:8

7.b.Txt: 01ℵ-corr
06D-corr,018K,020L
byz.
Var: 01ℵ-org,02A,03B
06D-org,025P,Lach
Treg,Alf,Word,Tisc
We/Ho,Weis,Sod
UBS/✩

3450.6 art acc sing masc	4009.3 noun acc sing masc	3450.16 art sing neu	4009.1 noun sing masc	3450.10 art gen sing fem	5322.2 noun gen sing fem
ʽ τὸν	πλοῦτον	[ᵇ✩ τὸ	πλοῦτος]	τῆς	χάριτος
ton	plouton	to	ploutos	tēs	charitos
the	riches	[the	riches]	of the	grace

840.3 prs-pron gen sing	3614.10 rel-pron gen sing fem	3915.13 verb 3sing indic aor act	1519.1 prep	2231.4 prs-pron acc 1pl
αὐτοῦ·	8. ἧς	ἐπερίσσευσεν	εἰς	ἡμᾶς
autou	hēs	eperisseusen	eis	hēmas
his;	which	he caused to abound	toward	us

1706.1 prep	3820.11 adj dat sing fem	4531.3 noun dat sing fem	2504.1 conj	5264.1 noun dat sing fem	1101.8 verb nom sing masc part aor act
ἐν	πάσῃ	σοφίᾳ	καὶ	φρονήσει,	9. γνωρίσας
en	pasē	sophia	kai	phronēsei	gnōrisas
in	all	wisdom	and	understanding,	having made known

2231.3 prs-pron dat 1pl	3450.16 art sing neu	3328.1 noun sing neu	3450.2 art gen sing	2284.2 noun gen sing neu	840.3 prs-pron gen sing
ἡμῖν	τὸ	μυστήριον	τοῦ	θελήματος	αὐτοῦ,
hēmin	to	mustērion	tou	thelēmatos	autou
to us	the	mystery	of the	will	his,

2567.3 prep	3450.12 art acc sing fem	2086.3 noun acc sing fem	840.3 prs-pron gen sing	3614.12 rel-pron acc sing fem
κατὰ	τὴν	εὐδοκίαν	αὐτοῦ,	ἣν
kata	tēn	eudokian	autou	hēn
according to	the	good pleasure	his,	which

4246.2 verb 3sing indic aor mid	1706.1 prep	840.4 prs-pron dat sing	1519.1 prep	3484.2 noun acc sing fem	3450.2 art gen sing
προέθετο	ἐν	αὐτῷ	10. εἰς	οἰκονομίαν	τοῦ
proetheto	en	autō	eis	oikonomian	tou
he purposed	in	him	for	administration	of the

3998.2 noun gen sing neu	3450.1 art gen pl	2511.6 noun gen pl masc	344.2 verb inf aor mid	3450.17 art pl neu
πληρώματος	τῶν	καιρῶν,	ἀνακεφαλαιώσασθαι	τὰ
plērōmatos	tōn	kairōn	anakephalaiōsasthai	ta
fullness	of the	times;	to head up	the

3820.1 adj	1706.1 prep	3450.3 art dat sing	5382.3 name dat masc	3450.17 art pl neu	4885.1 conj
πάντα	ἐν	τῷ	Χριστῷ,	τὰ	ʽᵃ τε ʼ
panta	en	tō	Christō	ta	te
all things	in	the	Christ,	the things	both

10.a.Txt: Steph
Var: 01ℵ-org,02A,03B
06D,018K,020L,025P
Lach,Treg,Alf,Word
Tisc,We/Ho,Weis,Sod
UBS/✩

10.b.Txt: 01ℵ-corr,02A
018K,025P,byz.bo.
Var: 01ℵ-org,03B,06D
020L,Lach,Treg,Alf
Tisc,We/Ho,Weis,Sod
UBS/✩

1706.1 prep	1894.3 prep	3450.4 art dat pl	3636.8 noun dat pl masc	2504.1 conj	3450.17 art pl neu	1894.3 prep
ʽ ἐν	[ᵇ✩ ἐπὶ]	τοῖς	οὐρανοῖς	καὶ	τὰ	ἐπὶ
en	epi	tois	ouranois	kai	ta	epi
in	[upon]	the	heavens	and	the things	upon

3450.10 art gen sing fem	1087.2 noun gen sing fem	1706.1 prep	840.4 prs-pron dat sing	1706.1 prep	3614.3 rel-pron dat sing	2504.1 conj
τῆς	γῆς·	11. ἐν	αὐτῷ,	ἐν	ᾧ	καὶ
tēs	gēs	en	autō	en	hō	kai
the	earth;	in	him,	in	whom	also

2793.1 verb 1pl indic aor pass	4168.3 verb nom pl masc part aor pass	2567.3 prep
ἐκληρώθημεν,	προορισθέντες	κατὰ
eklērōthēmen	prooristhentes	kata
we obtained an inheritance,	having been predestined	according to

redemptive work of Christ. The word "redemption" actually has a definite article before it in the original language, so it specifies "the redemption," indicating the one and only way of salvation. The language used here was very familiar to a person of that day to whom the slave market was a common sight, a place where human beings were offered for sale to the highest bidders. The mention of Christ's blood (*tou haimatos autou*) refuted the docetic Gnostic notion that Christ did not have a real body but only seemed to have one. The "riches of his grace" caused Christ to redeem us by the payment of a price (Greek, *lutron*; cf. *apolutrōsin*), the giving of himself as a sacrifice for our sins.

1:8. What God did He performed "in all wisdom and prudence," or with wisdom and intelligence. Because He is omniscient, God never is without knowledge of what is transpiring, and He is able to apply that knowledge to make prudent decisions. The term "lavished" used by the NIV translators very appropriately expresses the idea contained in the Greek term Paul used here (*eperisseusen*) to refer to the way God's grace "abounded" toward us.

1:9. The term "mystery" (*mustērion*) refers to something kept hidden until a certain time, something only God could reveal. It does not describe something mysterious, but something that remains hidden until God chooses to reveal it. Paul used it mainly in Ephesians to describe the fact that in the New Testament Church no distinction exists between Gentiles and Jews.

1:10. The language used continues to express the purpose which God had in mind, that in this day in which we are privileged to live, all those people "in Christ" would be part of the same Body, with no distinctions. The scope of this verse, however, cannot be limited just to the present age. The work of subjecting this universe totally to Christ will continue in the Millennium. The word translated "dispensation" (*oikonomian*) comes from two Greek words placed together, one meaning "law" (*nomos*) and the other meaning "house" (*oikos*). It literally becomes "house-law" and often is translated "stewardship." Because the word can be used in different ways, the Bible student must look at it within the context where it is used. Here it obviously relates to the overall purpose of God to subject everything to Christ in an ultimate sense.

1:11. It is almost beyond the human mind to fathom that God allows us to share the glory that belongs to Christ, the One to whom this total universe will be subjected ultimately. His will not only includes the exaltation of Christ, it also includes our participation in His blessings because we are part of those who are "in Christ." This verse reminds us again that all this happens because of God's design. In fact, in this verse Paul used three words that have the

according to the riches of his grace: . . . through that full and generous grace, *Phillips*.

8. Wherein he hath abounded toward us: . . . so abundantly did he lavish upon us, *Montgomery* . . . heaped upon us, *TCNT* . . . moste plentifully, *Geneva* . . . which has overflowed into our lives and opened our eyes to the truth, *Phillips*.

in all wisdom and prudence: . . . by countless gifts of wisdom, *TCNT* . . . and all spiritual understanding, *Murdock* . . . and Intelligence, *Wilson*.

9. Having made known unto us the mystery of his will: . . . the sacrament of his vvill, *Rheims* . . . the secret purpose of his will, *Montgomery* . . . the secret of his plan, *Phillips*.

according to his good pleasure which he hath purposed in himself: . . . according to his fre beneuolence, *Geneva*.

10. That in the dispensation of the fulness of times he might gather together in one all things in Christ: . . . when the tyme were full come, *Tyndale* . . . for the government of the fulness of the ages, *Montgomery* . . . as regards the administration of, *PNT* . . . the fulness of the seasons, *Panin* . . . to reunite for himself, *Rotherham* . . . to re-establish all things, *Confraternity* . . . to re-unite under one head, *Scarlett* . . . the establishment of a New Order, *TCNT*.

both which are in heaven, and which are on earth; [even] in him: . . . everything that exists in Heaven or earth shall find its perfection and fulfillment in him, *Phillips*.

11. In whom also we have obtained an inheritance: . . . vve also are called by lot, *Rheims* . . . that in all which will one day belong to him we have been promised a share, *Phillips*.

4145.4 noun acc sing fem **πρόθεσιν** *prothesin* purpose	3450.2 art gen sing **τοῦ** *tou* the	3450.17 art pl neu **τὰ** *ta* the	3820.1 adj **πάντα** *panta* all things	1738.3 verb gen sing part pres act **ἐνεργοῦντος** *energountos* working	2567.3 prep **κατὰ** *kata* according to
3450.12 art acc sing fem **τὴν** *tēn* the	1005.4 noun acc sing fem **βουλὴν** *boulēn* counsel	3450.2 art gen sing **τοῦ** *tou* of the	2284.2 noun gen sing neu **θελήματος** *thelēmatos* will	840.3 prs-pron gen sing **αὐτοῦ,** *autou* his,	1519.1 prep **12. εἰς** *eis* for
3450.16 art sing neu **τὸ** *to* the	1498.32 verb inf pres act **εἶναι** *einai* to be	2231.4 prs-pron acc 1pl **ἡμᾶς** *hēmas* us	1519.1 prep **εἰς** *eis* to	1853.2 noun acc sing masc **ἔπαινον** *epainon* praise	3450.10 art gen sing fem ⌜a **τῆς** ⌝ *tēs* of the
1385.2 noun gen sing fem **δόξης** *doxēs* glory	840.3 prs-pron gen sing **αὐτοῦ,** *autou* his;	3450.8 art acc pl masc **τοὺς** *tous* the	4137.1 verb acc pl masc part perf act **προηλπικότας** *proēlpikotas* having first put hope	1706.1 prep **ἐν** *en* in	3450.3 art dat sing **τῷ** *tō* the
5382.3 name dat masc **Χριστῷ·** *Christō* Christ:	1706.1 prep **13. ἐν** *en* in	3614.3 rel-pron dat sing **ᾧ** *hō* whom	2504.1 conj **καὶ** *kai* also	5050.1 prs-pron nom 2pl ⌜✶ **ὑμεῖς,** *humeis* you,	2231.1 prs-pron nom 1pl [a **ἡμεῖς,**] *hēmeis* [we,]
189.32 verb nom pl masc part aor act **ἀκούσαντες** *akousantes* having heard	3450.6 art acc sing masc **τὸν** *ton* the	3030.4 noun acc sing masc **λόγον** *logon* word	3450.10 art gen sing fem **τῆς** *tēs* of the	223.2 noun gen sing fem **ἀληθείας,** *alētheias* truth,	3450.16 art sing neu **τὸ** *to* the
2077.1 noun sing neu **εὐαγγέλιον** *euangelion* good news	3450.10 art gen sing fem **τῆς** *tēs* of the	4843.2 noun gen sing fem **σωτηρίας** *sōtērias* salvation	5050.2 prs-pron gen 2pl **ὑμῶν,** *humōn* your	1706.1 prep **ἐν** *en* in	3614.3 rel-pron dat sing **ᾧ** *hō* whom
2504.1 conj **καὶ** *kai* also,	3961.31 verb nom pl masc part aor act **πιστεύσαντες** *pisteusantes* having believed,	4824.6 verb 2pl indic aor pass **ἐσφραγίσθητε** *esphragisthēte* you were sealed	3450.3 art dat sing **τῷ** *tō* with the	4011.3 noun dat sing neu **πνεύματι** *pneumati* Spirit	
3450.10 art gen sing fem **τῆς** *tēs* of the	1845.1 noun fem **ἐπαγγελίας** *epangelias* promise	3450.3 art dat sing **τῷ** *tō* the	39.3 adj dat sing **ἁγίῳ,** *hagiō* Holy,	3614.5 rel-pron nom sing masc **14.** ⌜ **ὅς** *hos* who	3614.16 rel-pron sing neu [a✶ **ὅ**] *ho* [idem]
1498.4 verb 3sing indic pres act **ἐστιν** *estin* is	722.1 noun nom sing masc **ἀρραβὼν** *arrhabōn* pledge	3450.10 art gen sing fem **τῆς** *tēs* of the	2790.2 noun gen sing fem **κληρονομίας** *klēronomias* inheritance	2231.2 prs-pron gen 1pl **ἡμῶν,** *hēmōn* our,	1519.1 prep **εἰς** *eis* to
623.3 noun acc sing fem **ἀπολύτρωσιν** *apolutrōsin* redemption	3450.10 art gen sing fem **τῆς** *tēs* of the	3910.1 noun gen sing fem **περιποιήσεως,** *peripoiēseōs* acquired possession,	1519.1 prep **εἰς** *eis* to	1853.2 noun acc sing masc **ἔπαινον** *epainon* praise	

12.a.Txt: 02A,Steph **Var:** 01א,03B,06D 018K,020L,025P,byz. Lach,Treg,Alf,Word Tisc,We/Ho,Weis,Sod UBS/✶

13.a.Txt: p46,01א-org 03B,06D,010F,012G byz. **Var:** 01א-corr1,02A 018K,020L,044,326,629 630,1241

14.a.Txt: 01א,06D,044 byz. **Var:** p46,02A,03B,010F 012G,020L,025P,6,81 104,365,1175,1739 1881,2495

idea of "will" expressed in them. *Prothesin* normally contains the idea of "purpose." *Boulēn* sometimes expresses the idea of "counsel," but usually relates to "purpose" or "will." The third term or last noun in the verse (*thelēmatos*) is a general Greek term for "will." This approach is very typical of Paul's epistles when he multiplied synonyms to amplify an idea.

1:12. The phrase "praise of his glory" occurs in relation to each member of the Trinity: of God (verse 6), of Christ (verse 12), and the Holy Spirit (verse 14).

1:13. The finishing touches on this beautiful portrait show the work of the Holy Spirit in redemption. Verse 12 says "we" (Jews) and verse 13, "ye" (Gentiles). The Holy Spirit is the One who, after we hear and believe the truth of the gospel, actually places a seal of ownership upon us. Seals were in common use in those days. A person often stamped his letters with a seal or a sign to prove they were sent by him. Pagan cults often stamped their devotees with seals in the form of tattoos. A seal indicated a document was genuine and authentic. We do much the same thing today when we brand steers, sheep, etc., or when we use the corporate seal of an organization to certify some statement or authenticate a document.

A person who is "in Christ" has been sealed as God's property. This does not happen until a person hears and believes the gospel message. This does not mean that God does the sealing first, and then the person hears the gospel message. "After that ye believed" actually comes from a Greek aorist participle (*pisteusantes*) which is used in an adverbial sense here and normally would be translated "after believing."

The original term for "heard" (*akousantes*) is also an aorist active participle and means "after hearing." According to the order used in the verse, "after hearing" comes first, followed by "after believing," and the whole process culminates with an aorist passive verb (*esphragisthēte*) meaning "you were sealed." This verb indicates that God performed the act of sealing, as well as indicating that it was a decisive act. To understand what is being said, it is absolutely crucial to look at this passage in its entirety from verse 3 through verse 14.

1:14. This becomes even more obvious when one realizes the "in Christ" person has been given an *arrhabōn* ("earnest, down payment, deposit") as a pledge that the full payment will be given when Jesus returns to this earth. The down payment we have received is the Holy Spirit himself (Romans 8:9,16). His indwelling presence is a guarantee that God will consummate all His promises to us when the proper time arrives.

The noun "redemption" (*apolutrōsin*) refers to the culmination of the process which will become a reality when Jesus returns to this earth and believers are resurrected.

being predestinated according to the purpose of him: . . . previously marked out, *Wilson* . . . being marked out beforehand, *Rotherham* . . . chosen beforehand, *Montgomery* . . . according to the plan of Him, *Norlie* . . . foreordained, *Panin*.

who worketh all things after the counsel of his own will: . . . is executing his own fixed purpose, *TCNT* . . . who achieves his purposes by his sovereign will, *Phillips* . . . agreeably to the counsel, *Wilson* . . . the counsel of his pleasure, *Murdock*.

12. That we should be to the praise of his glory: . . . that we should win praise for his glorious Name, *TCNT* . . . bring praise to his glory! *Phillips*.

who first trusted in Christ: . . . we who had first put our hope in, *Williams* . . . before placed our hope in the Messiah, *Noyes* . . . had before hoped in Christ, *ASV*.

13. In whom ye also [trusted], after that ye heard the word of truth, the gospel of your salvation: And you too trusted him, *Phillips*.

in whom also after that ye believed, ye were sealed with that holy Spirit of promise: . . . you were signed with, *Douay* . . . have been stamped with the seal of, *Williams* . . . in him were marked as his by receiving the holy Spirit, *TCNT* . . . even the holy [Spirit], *Alford*.

14. Which is the earnest of our inheritance: . . . the pledge of our common heritage, *Montgomery* . . . as a guarantee of purchase, *Phillips*.

until the redemption of the purchased possession: . . . that we might be fully restored to libertie, *Geneva* . . . for the recouering of the purchased possession, *Cranmer* . . . unto the complete redemption of his purchased property, *Montgomery* . . . until the redemption of them that are alive, *Murdock*.

3450.10 art gen sing fem	1385.2 noun gen sing fem	840.3 prs-pron gen sing	1217.2 prep	3642.17 dem-pron sing neu	2476.3 prs-pron nom
τῆς	δόξης	αὐτοῦ.	**15.** Διὰ	τοῦτο	κἀγώ
tēs	doxēs	autou.	Dia	touto	kagō
of the	glory	his.	Because of	this	I also

189.31 verb nom sing masc part aor act	3450.12 art acc sing fem	2567.2 prep	5050.4 prs-pron acc 2pl	3963.4 noun acc sing fem	1706.1 prep	3450.3 art dat sing
ἀκούσας	τὴν	καθ'	ὑμᾶς	πίστιν	ἐν	τῷ
akousas	tēn	kath'	humas	pistin	en	tō
having heard of	the	among	you	faith	in	the

15.a.**Txt:** 01ℵ-corr
06D-corr2,044,byz.
Var: p46,01ℵ-org,03B
025P,33,1739

2935.3 noun dat sing masc	2400.2 name masc	2504.1 conj	3450.12 art acc sing fem	26.4 noun acc sing fem	3450.12 art acc sing fem	1519.1 prep
κυρίῳ	Ἰησοῦ,	καὶ	⌐a τὴν	ἀγάπην ⌐	τὴν	εἰς
kuriō	Iēsou,	kai	tēn	agapēn	tēn	eis
Lord	Jesus,	and	the	love	the	toward

3820.8 adj acc pl masc	3450.8 art acc pl masc	39.9 adj acc pl masc	3620.3 partic	3835.2 verb 1sing indic pres mid	2149.6 verb nom sing masc part pres act
πάντας	τοὺς	ἁγίους,	**16.** οὐ	παύομαι	εὐχαριστῶν
pantas	tous	hagious,	ou	pauomai	eucharistōn
all	the	saints,	not	do cease	giving thanks

16.a.**Txt:** 06D-corr,018K
020L,025P,byz.bo.
Var: 01ℵ,02A,03B
06D-org,33,Lach,Treg
Alf,Tisc,We/Ho,Weis
Sod,UBS/☆

5065.1 prep	5050.2 prs-pron gen 2pl	3281.2 noun acc sing fem	5050.2 prs-pron gen 2pl	4020.64 verb nom sing masc part pres mid	1894.3 prep
ὑπὲρ	ὑμῶν,	μνείαν	⌐a ὑμῶν ⌐	ποιούμενος	ἐπὶ
huper	humōn,	mneian	humōn	poioumenos	epi
for	you,	mention	of you	making	in

3450.1 art gen pl	4194.6 noun gen pl fem	1466.2 prs-pron gen 1sing	2419.1 conj	3450.5 art nom sing masc	2296.1 noun nom sing masc
τῶν	προσευχῶν	μου·	**17.** ἵνα	ὁ	θεὸς
tōn	proseuchōn	mou	hina	ho	theos
the	prayers	my,	that	the	God

3450.2 art gen sing	2935.2 noun gen sing masc	2231.2 prs-pron gen 1pl	2400.2 name masc	5382.2 name gen masc	3450.5 art nom sing masc
τοῦ	κυρίου	ἡμῶν	Ἰησοῦ	Χριστοῦ,	ὁ
tou	kuriou	hēmōn	Iēsou	Christou,	ho
of the	Lord	our	Jesus	Christ,	the

3824.1 noun nom sing masc	3450.10 art gen sing fem	1385.2 noun gen sing fem	1319.62 verb 3sing subj aor act	5050.3 prs-pron dat 2pl	4011.1 noun sing neu
πατὴρ	τῆς	δόξης,	δώῃ	ὑμῖν	πνεῦμα
patēr	tēs	doxēs,	dōē	humin	pneuma
Father	of the	glory,	may give	to you	spirit

4531.2 noun gen sing fem	2504.1 conj	597.2 noun gen sing fem	1706.1 prep	1907.3 noun dat sing fem	840.3 prs-pron gen sing
σοφίας	καὶ	ἀποκαλύψεως	ἐν	ἐπιγνώσει	αὐτοῦ,
sophias	kai	apokalupseōs	en	epignōsei	autou,
of wisdom	and	revelation	in	knowledge	of him,

18.a.**Txt:** Steph
Var: 01ℵ,02A,03B,06D
018K,020L,025P,byz.it.
bo.Gries,Lach,Treg,Alf
Tisc,We/Ho,Weis,Sod
UBS/☆

18.b.**Txt:** 01ℵ,02A,06D
010F,012G,044,byz.
Var: p46,03B,6,33,1175
1739,1881

5297.10 verb acc pl masc part perf mid	3450.8 art acc pl masc	3652.8 noun acc pl masc	3450.10 art gen sing fem
18. πεφωτισμένους	τοὺς	ὀφθαλμοὺς	τῆς
pephōtismenous	tous	ophthalmous	tēs
having been enlightened	the	eyes	the

1265.1 noun gen sing fem	2559.1 noun fem	5050.2 prs-pron gen 2pl	1519.1 prep	3450.16 art sing neu	3471.25 verb inf perf act
⌐ διανοίας	[a☆ καρδίας]	⌐b ὑμῶν, ⌐	εἰς	τὸ	εἰδέναι
dianoias	kardias	humōn,	eis	to	eidenai
mind	[heart]	of your,	for	the	to know

All these promises should make us burst into praise as they did the apostle Paul. Now we can see a little more clearly why it is a mistake to take only a few statements out of this complete sentence from verse 3 through verse 14. God does not give us only part of the total picture and leave us confused. He has informed us clearly about the function of each member of the Trinity in the work of redemption. The Father planned, the Son provided, and the Holy Spirit protects the ones who accept God's provision!

1:15. The normal custom in writing letters was to include thanksgiving and prayer somewhere near the beginning of an epistle. This verse speaks of the believers' "faith in the Lord Jesus" and their "love unto all the saints." The word "heard" suggests that the apostle did not know personally many of the recipients.

Just as we saw one complete sentence in the Greek in verses 3-14, we again see one complete sentence in verses 15-23. "Wherefore" (*dia touto*) literally means "on account of this" and refers back to 3-14. It is as if Paul were saying, "Now that you are part of God's predestined elect, what is next?"

1:16. Therefore, Paul prayed constantly that believers would be recipients of the lasting benefits of salvation, or that they would mature in their spiritual experiences.

1:17. Verse 17 begins with the Greek word *hina*, a very strong way of expressing purpose that normally is translated "in order that." It is followed by a verb (*dōē*) which is in the optative mood. According to some grammarians, the optative mood is found only 67 times in the New Testament, most often to express a wish. It denotes the blessing Paul desired for believers: that they would comprehend fully what they had received in Christ. Paul's earnest prayer was that God would continue to bestow upon believers the gift of His Holy Spirit already imparted to them, with the result of making them wise in understanding the bestowments of His grace.

It should not be taken for granted that this would happen automatically. Even though they already knew God in a special way, he wanted them to know Him better. He emphasized a full knowledge, or a complete understanding of God's redemptive work in Christ. This could take place only with the help of the Holy Spirit. Even though the word for "spirit" here (*pneuma*) lacks a definite article in the Greek text, it likely refers to the Holy Spirit, the One who helps Christians grow spiritually. "Wisdom" probably refers to a continued condition of proper application of knowledge; while "revelation" most likely relates to the single glances afforded believers into the will of God in special circumstances.

1:18. Paul prayed that the "heart" (see variant) would have eyes (*opthalmous*) with which to look out toward Christ. After making

unto the praise of his glory: ... vnto the laude of his glory, *Tyndale.*

15. Wherefore I also: On this account, *Wilson* ... For this reason, *Adams* ... Since, then, *Phillips.*

after I heard of your faith in the Lord Jesus: ... hearing about, *Adams* ... that prevails among you, *TCNT.*

and love unto all the saints: ... and about your love, *Adams* ... and the practical way in which you are expressing it toward fellow Christians, *Phillips.*

16. Cease not to give thanks for you: ... do not omit giving thanks, *Wilson* ... thank God continually, *Phillips.*

making mention of you in my prayers: ... making constant mention, *TCNT* ... making a memorie of you, *Rheims* ... I never give up praying for you, *Phillips.*

17. That the God of our Lord Jesus Christ, the Father of glory: ... the Father most glorious, *Montgomery* ... the Glorious Father, *Wilson* ... who is the all-glorious Father, *Norlie.*

may give unto you the spirit of wisdom and revelation: ... may grant you, *Williams* ... to inspire you with, *TCNT* ... give you spiritual wisdom and the insight, *Phillips.*

in the knowledge of him: ... in the full Knowledge of him, *Wilson* ... in the recognition of him, *Murdock* ... through an intimate knowledge, *Montgomery* ... through a growing knowledge of Him, *Williams* ... to know more of him, *Phillips.*

18. The eyes of your understanding being enlightened: And that your mind, *Norlie* ... eyes of your heart, *Worrell* ... that your mental vision may be made so clear, *TCNT* ... may be flooded with light, *Montgomery.*

Ephesians 1:19

5050.4 prs-pron acc 2pl	**4949.3** intr-pron nom sing	**1498.4** verb 3sing indic pres act	**3450.9** art nom sing fem	**1667.1** noun nom sing fem	**3450.10** art gen sing fem
ὑμᾶς	τίς	ἐστιν	ἡ	ἐλπὶς	τῆς
humas	tis	estin	hē	elpis	tēs
you	what	is	the	hope	of the

18.c.Txt: 01ℵ-corr
06D-corr,018K,020L
025P,byz.
Var: 01ℵ-org,02A,03B
06D-org,33,Lach,Treg
Alf,Tisc,We/Ho,Weis
Sod,UBS/∗

2794.2 noun gen sing fem	**840.3** prs-pron gen sing	**2504.1** conj	**4949.3** intr-pron nom sing	**3450.5** art nom sing masc	**4009.1** noun sing masc
κλήσεως	αὐτοῦ,	⸆ καὶ ⸆	τίς	ὁ	πλοῦτος
klēseōs	autou	kai	tis	ho	ploutos
calling	his,	and	what	the	riches

3450.10 art gen sing fem	**1385.2** noun gen sing fem	**3450.10** art gen sing fem	**2790.2** noun gen sing fem	**840.3** prs-pron gen sing	**1706.1** prep
τῆς	δόξης	τῆς	κληρονομίας	αὐτοῦ	ἐν
tēs	doxēs	tēs	klēronomias	autou	en
of the	glory	of the	inheritance	his	in

3450.4 art dat pl	**39.8** adj dat pl masc	**2504.1** conj	**4949.9** intr-pron nom sing neu	**3450.16** art sing neu	**5072.4** verb sing neu part pres act
τοῖς	ἁγίοις,	**19.** καὶ	τί	τὸ	ὑπερβάλλον
tois	hagiois,	kai	ti	to	huperballon
the	saints,	and	what	to	surpassing

3145.1 noun sing neu	**3450.10** art gen sing fem	**1405.2** noun gen sing fem	**840.3** prs-pron gen sing	**1519.1** prep	**2231.4** prs-pron acc 1pl
μέγεθος	τῆς	δυνάμεως	αὐτοῦ	εἰς	ἡμᾶς
megethos	tēs	dunameōs	autou	eis	hēmas
greatness	of the	power	his	toward	us

3450.8 art acc pl masc	**3961.15** verb acc pl masc part pres act	**2567.3** prep	**3450.12** art acc sing fem	**1737.2** noun acc sing fem	
τοὺς	πιστεύοντας	κατὰ	τὴν	ἐνέργειαν	
tous	pisteuontas	kata	tēn	energeian	
the	believing	according to	the	working	

3450.2 art gen sing	**2877.2** noun gen sing neu	**3450.10** art gen sing fem	**2452.2** noun gen sing fem	**840.3** prs-pron gen sing	**3614.12** rel-pron acc sing fem
τοῦ	κράτους	τῆς	ἰσχύος	αὐτοῦ,	**20.** ἣν
tou	kratous	tēs	ischuos	autou,	hēn
of the	might	of the	strength	his,	which

20.a.Txt: 01ℵ,06D,018K
020L,025P,byz.
Var: 02A,03B,Lach,Alf
Tisc,We/Ho,Weis,Sod
UBS/∗

1738.6 verb 3sing indic aor act	**1738.13** verb 3sing indic perf act	**1706.1** prep	**3450.3** art dat sing	**5382.3** name dat masc	
⸂ ἐνήργησεν	[ᵃ✲ ἐνήργηκεν]	ἐν	τῷ	Χριστῷ	
enērgēsen	enērgēken	en	tō	Christō	
he exerted	[he has operated]	in	the	Christ,	

1446.7 verb nom sing masc part aor act	**840.6** prs-pron acc sing masc	**1523.2** prep gen	**3361.2** adj gen pl	**2504.1** conj	
ἐγείρας	αὐτὸν	ἐκ	νεκρῶν,	καὶ	
egeiras	auton	ek	nekrōn,	kai	
having raised	him	from among	dead,	and	

20.b.Txt: 06D,018K
020L,025P,byz.
Var: 01ℵ,02A,03B,33
Lach,Treg,Alf,Tisc
We/Ho,Weis,Sod
UBS/∗

2495.3 verb 3sing indic aor act	**2495.9** verb nom sing masc part aor act	**1706.1** prep	**1182.5** adj dat sing fem	**840.3** prs-pron gen sing	**1706.1** prep
⸂ ἐκάθισεν	[ᵇ✲ καθίσας]	ἐν	δεξιᾷ	αὐτοῦ	ἐν
ekathisen	kathisas	en	dexia	autou	en
seated	[having seated]	at	right hand	his	in

3450.4 art dat pl	**2016.8** adj dat pl neu	**5068.1** prep	**3820.10** adj gen sing fem	**741.2** noun gen sing fem	
τοῖς	ἐπουρανίοις,	**21.** ὑπεράνω	πάσης	ἀρχῆς	
tois	epouraniois,	huperanō	pasēs	archēs	
the	heavenlies,	above	every	principality	

the purpose of his prayer clear, Paul pinpointed three very important matters essential to Christian maturity, as if to say, "If you really want to grow spiritually, you must understand these matters."

Paul prefaced each of the three items with "what" (*tis, ti*). First, if believers are to grow properly in the Lord, they must understand "the hope of his calling." "Hope" (*elpis*) was a term Paul often used and refers to an "expectant attitude." The apostle had just explained in verse 14 that Christians receive at salvation only a down payment of all that God has promised them. A proper attitude of hope longs for and expects God to consummate all His promises to His people. This tremendous hope serves as a strong incentive to spur believers on to spiritual maturity.

Secondly, understanding "God's inheritance in the saints" will lead to growth in the Lord. The Bible speaks in many places about the inheritance God has promised His people, but in this verse there is a locative case expression in the Greek which literally means "in the sphere of the saints." Obviously, God does not "need" anything from us. However, He does "want" our praise (verses 6,12,14). When Christians truly realize they are the only part of God's creation that can praise God willingly because they have experienced salvation (Revelation 5:9,10), it should give tremendous motivation toward spiritual maturity.

1:19. Thirdly, understanding "the exceeding greatness of his power to us-ward who believe" will make possible growth in the Lord. The apostle explained this idea throughout the remainder of the chapter. To explain just how much power is available to believers, Paul used four different Greek terms in this verse. "Power" (*dunamis*) means "inherent ability, capability, potential." "Working" comes from the Greek word from which we get *energy* (*energeia*) and denotes "operative power." "Mighty" (*kratos*) refers to "manifested strength." The last word in the verse ("power," *ischus*) is "power as an endowment" or "the possession of power."

1:20. This power always operates "in Christ." In other words, believers cannot do with this power what they choose, but its use must conform to the direction given by Christ, the head of the Church. The proper exercise of this power requires continuous faith in Christ, just as we believed in Him at conversion. The resurrection of Christ was the greatest possible manifestation of God's power. "Set him at his own right hand" relates to the position of authority which He has. Notice the beautiful progression in Paul's description of the power of God available to help believers grow in Christ. First, he made a strong appeal about realizing the necessity. He continued by saying that the power must operate through Christ. Lastly, he used the greatest example of the power of God— the resurrection of Christ.

that ye may know what is the hope of his calling: . . . that you may receive that inner illumination of the spirit which will make you realize how great is the hope to which he is calling you, *Phillips* . . . of his invitation, *Wilson* . . . of his vocation, *Rheims* . . . to which He calls you, *Williams*.

and what the riches of the glory of his inheritance in the saints: . . . the magnificence and splendor of the inheritance promised to, *Phillips* . . . of His glorious inheritance for the saints are, *Adams*.

19. And what [is] the exceeding greatness of his power to us-ward who believe: . . . and what is the excellence of the majesty of his power, *Murdock* . . . how tremendous is the power available to us, *Phillips* . . . the immeasurable greatness, *Adams* . . . the surpassing Greatness, *Wilson, Rotherham* . . . and how surpassingly great is the power, *TCNT* . . . of his might in us who believe, *Montgomery* . . . available to us who believe, *Norlie*.

according to the working of his mighty power: . . . measured by His tremendously mighty power, *Williams* . . . according to the operation, *Sawyer* . . . as seen in the energy of that resistless might, *Montgomery* . . . It is in keeping with the force of His mighty strength, *Adams* . . . according to the efficiency of the strength of his power, *Murdock* . . . the strength of his might, *Panin, Worrell* . . . the energy of his mighty strength, *Wilson* . . . the inward working of the strength, *Rotherham* . . . to the energy of his mighty power, *Scarlett*.

20. Which he wrought in Christ, when he raised him from the dead: Which he exerted, *Wesley* . . . which he performed, *Sawyer* . . . demonstrated, *Phillips* . . . exerted for Christ, *Adams*.

and set [him] at his own right hand in the heavenly [places]: . . . seated him, *Adams* . . . gave him the place of supreme honor, *Phillips* . . . in the highest heaven, *Norlie*.

2504.1 conj	1833.1 noun fem	2504.1 conj	1405.2 noun gen sing fem	2504.1 conj	2936.1 noun gen sing fem
καὶ	ἐξουσίας	καὶ	δυνάμεως	καὶ	κυριότητος,
kai	exousias	kai	dunameōs	kai	kuriotētos
and	authority	and	power	and	lordship,

2504.1 conj	3820.2 adj gen sing	3549.3 noun gen sing neu	3550.7 verb gen sing neu part pres mid	3620.3 partic	3303.1 adv
καὶ	παντὸς	ὀνόματος	ὀνομαζομένου	οὐ	μόνον
kai	pantos	onomatos	onomazomenou	ou	monon
and	every	name	being named,	not	only

1706.1 prep	3450.3 art dat sing	163.2 noun dat sing masc	3642.5 dem-pron dat sing masc	233.2 conj	2504.1 conj	1706.1 prep
ἐν	τῷ	αἰῶνι	τούτῳ,	ἀλλὰ	καὶ	ἐν
en	tō	aiōni	toutō	alla	kai	en
in	the	age	this,	but	also	in

3450.3 art dat sing	3165.10 verb dat sing part pres act	2504.1 conj	3820.1 adj	5131.2 verb 3sing indic aor act	5097.3 prep
τῷ	μέλλοντι·	22. καὶ	πάντα	ὑπέταξεν	ὑπὸ
tō	mellonti	kai	panta	hupetaxen	hupo
the	coming;	and	all things	he put	under

3450.8 art acc pl masc	4087.7 noun acc pl masc	840.3 prs-pron gen sing	2504.1 conj	840.6 prs-pron acc sing masc	1319.14 verb 3sing indic aor act
τοὺς	πόδας	αὐτοῦ·	καὶ	αὐτὸν	ἔδωκεν
tous	podas	autou	kai	auton	edōken
the	feet	his,	and	him	gave

2747.4 noun acc sing fem	5065.1 prep	3820.1 adj	3450.11 art dat sing fem	1564.3 noun dat sing fem	3610.3 rel-pron nom sing fem
κεφαλὴν	ὑπὲρ	πάντα	τῇ	ἐκκλησίᾳ,	23. ἥτις
kephalēn	huper	panta	tē	ekklēsia	hētis
head	over	all things	to the	assembly,	which

1498.4 verb 3sing indic pres act	3450.16 art sing neu	4835.1 noun sing neu	840.3 prs-pron gen sing	3450.16 art sing neu	3998.1 noun sing neu
ἐστὶν	τὸ	σῶμα	αὐτοῦ,	τὸ	πλήρωμα
estin	to	sōma	autou	to	plērōma
is	the	body	his,	the	fullness

3450.2 art gen sing	3450.17 art pl neu	3820.1 adj	1706.1 prep	3820.5 adj dat pl	3997.18 verb gen sing masc part pres mid
τοῦ	[a☆+ τὰ]	πάντα	ἐν	πᾶσιν	πληρουμένου.
tou	ta	panta	en	pasin	plēroumenou
the	[the]	all things	in	all	filling,

23.a.Var: 01א,02A,03B 06D,018K,020L,025P Gries,Lach,Treg,Alf Word,Tisc,We/Ho,Weis Sod,UBS/☆

2504.1 conj	5050.4 prs-pron acc 2pl	1498.25 verb acc pl masc part pres act	3361.7 adj acc pl masc	3450.4 art dat pl
2:1. Καὶ	ὑμᾶς	ὄντας	νεκροὺς	τοῖς
Kai	humas	ontas	nekrous	tois
and	you	being	dead	in the

3761.5 noun dat pl neu	2504.1 conj	3450.14 art dat pl fem	264.7 noun dat pl fem	5050.2 prs-pron gen 2pl
παραπτώμασιν	καὶ	ταῖς	ἁμαρτίαις,	[a☆+ ὑμῶν,]
paraptōmasin	kai	tais	hamartiais	humōn
in offenses	and	the	sins,	[your,]

1.a.Var: 01א,03B,06D 025P,bo.Lach,Treg,Alf Tisc,We/Ho,Weis,Sod UBS/☆

1706.1 prep	3614.14 rel-pron dat pl fem	4077.1 adv	3906.20 verb 2pl indic aor act	2567.3 prep
2. ἐν	αἷς	ποτε	περιεπατήσατε	κατὰ
en	hais	pote	periepatēsate	kata
in	which	once	you walked	according to

1:21. This verse continues to exalt Christ and indicates His position of superiority over all creatures, both in heaven and earth. Jews of Paul's day generally believed that angels controlled human destiny, so Paul used the normal Jewish hierarchy of terms to indicate that Christ is in control. He has absolute authority because He is infinitely superior. Gnostics also conceived of angels as being intermediary beings between the so-called "unknowable God" and mankind. Paul, of course, did not agree with any type of Jewish or Gnostic angelic hierarchy. Much to the contrary, this verse serves as a good example of the way the apostle used the very teachings of antibiblical groups to expose the heresy inherent in them. This verse is also an example of Paul's method of piling up expressions in order to prove the point that Christ is superior to all these beings, and He will be superior also to whatever authorities will exist in the coming age.

1:22. This statement comes from Psalm 8:6 with special emphasis on the perfect man, Jesus Christ. The fact that God's plan included the incarnation of Christ still continues to be one of the most outstanding doctrines of the New Testament Church.

1:23. Paul's emphasis on the necessity of understanding the power of God available to believers comes to a conclusion with a classic reminder that the Church is the beneficiary of that power. Because the Church is a living organism with Christ as its head, God manifests His power through it. "Fullness" (*plērōma*) was a favorite term of the Gnostics who used the word to refer to the so-called intermediary beings between God and people. Paul used the verb form here in a passive sense It contains the idea of the Church being not only Christ's body, but of its being filled by Him.

2:1. The first 10 verses in this chapter are among the most evangelistic in the Scriptures, explaining beautifully the actual steps which occur in salvation. Paul began by reminding believers of their wretched condition before God performed the miracle of redemption. "Were dead" comes from a combination of a participle and an adjective (*ontas nekrous*), so it literally means "being dead" and refers to spiritual death which is the state of separation from God. While some Bible scholars say it is impossible to make a distinction between the words "trespasses" and "sins," others claim "trespasses" refers to outward manifestations of sin and "sins" relates to the sinful nature of a fallen human being.

2:2. This verse further depicts the lost condition of mankind by specifying the forces working against them. First, unbelievers walk

21. Far above all principality, and power, and might, and dominion: ... infinitely superior to any conceivable command, *Phillips* ... exalting him above all angelic Beings, *TCNT* ... far above all hierarchies, *Montgomery* ... far above every government, authority, *Williams* ... and authority...and lordship, *Sawyer* ... all rule, and authority, and power, and lordship, *Alford*.

and every name that is named: ... above every name, *Confraternity* ... yea, far above every other title that can be conferred, *Williams* ... that can be mentioned, *TCNT* ... that could ever be used, *Phillips*.

not only in this world, but also in that which is to come: ... in the future age, *Wilson*.

22. And hath put all [things] under his feet: ... subjected All things, *Wilson, Murdock* ... under the power of Christ, *Phillips*.
and gave him [to be] the head over all [things] to the church: ... and constituted Him, *Wilson* ... set him up as head of everything, *Phillips* ... as its supreme Head, *TCNT* ... the heed of the congregacion, *Tyndale*.

23. Which is his body: For the Church is, *Phillips*.
the fulness of him that filleth all in all: ... the full development of Him, *Wilson* ... who is wholly fulfilled in all, *Confraternity* ... who in every respect and everywhere is perfect, *Norlie* ... who fills the universe, *Montgomery* ... who fills everything everywhere, *Williams*.

1. And you [hath he quickened]: And he filleth you, *Scarlett* ... did he make alive, *ASV*.
who were dead in trespasses and sins: ... at one time spiritually dead, *Norlie* ... by reason of your offenses, *Confraternity*.

2. Wherein in time past ye walked according to the course of this world: For at one time you lived in sin, *TCNT* ... in which you passed your lives after the way

3450.6 art acc sing masc	163.3 noun acc sing masc	3450.2 art gen sing	2862.2 noun gen sing masc	3642.1 dem- pron gen sing	2567.3 prep
τὸν ton the	αἰῶνα aiōna age	τοῦ tou of the	κόσμου kosmou world	τούτου, toutou, this,	κατὰ kata according to

3450.6 art acc sing masc	752.4 noun acc sing masc	3450.10 art gen sing fem	1833.1 noun fem	3450.2 art gen sing	108.2 noun gen sing masc
τὸν ton the	ἄρχοντα archonta ruler	τῆς tēs of the	ἐξουσίας exousias authority	τοῦ tou of the	ἀέρος, aeros, air,

3450.2 art gen sing	4011.2 noun gen sing neu	3450.2 art gen sing	3431.1 adv	1738.3 verb gen sing part pres act	1706.1 prep
τοῦ tou the	πνεύματος pneumatos spirit	τοῦ tou the	νῦν nun now	ἐνεργοῦντος energountos working	ἐν en in

3450.4 art dat pl	5048.8 noun dat pl masc	3450.10 art gen sing fem	539.1 noun gen sing fem	1706.1 prep	3614.4 rel- pron dat pl	2504.1 conj
τοῖς tois the	υἱοῖς huiois sons	τῆς tēs of the	ἀπειθείας· apeitheias disobedience:	**3.** ἐν en among	οἷς hois whom	καὶ kai also

2231.1 prs- pron nom 1pl	3820.7 adj nom pl masc	388.7 verb 1pl indic aor pass	4077.1 adv	1706.1 prep	3450.14 art dat pl fem
ἡμεῖς hēmeis we	πάντες pantes all	ἀνεστράφημέν anestraphēmen had our conduct	ποτε pote once	ἐν en in	ταῖς tais the

1924.7 noun dat pl fem	3450.10 art gen sing fem	4418.2 noun gen sing fem	2231.2 prs- pron gen 1pl	4020.17 verb nom pl masc part pres act	3450.17 art pl neu
ἐπιθυμίαις epithumiais desires	τῆς tēs of the	σαρκὸς sarkos flesh	ἡμῶν, hēmōn, our,	ποιοῦντες poiountes doing	τὰ ta the

2284.4 noun pl neu	3450.10 art gen sing fem	4418.2 noun gen sing fem	2504.1 conj	3450.1 art gen pl	1265.4 noun gen pl fem	2504.1 conj
θελήματα thelēmata wishes	τῆς tēs of the	σαρκὸς sarkos flesh	καὶ kai and	τῶν tōn of the	διανοιῶν, dianoiōn, thoughts,	καὶ kai and

1498.36 verb 1pl indic imperf act	1498.50 verb 1pl indic imperf mid	4891.4 noun pl neu	5285.3 noun dat sing fem	3572.2 noun gen sing fem	5453.1 conj
⸆ ἦμεν ēmen were	[ᵃ☆ ἤμεθα] ēmetha [idem]	τέκνα tekna children,	φύσει phusei by nature,	ὀργῆς, orgēs, of wrath,	ὡς hōs as

2504.1 conj	3450.7 art nom pl masc	3036.3 adj nom pl masc	3450.5 art nom sing masc	1156.2 conj	2296.1 noun nom sing masc	4004.1 adj nom sing masc
καὶ kai even	οἱ hoi the	λοιποί· loipoi rest:	**4.** ὁ ho	δὲ de but	θεὸς, theos God,	πλούσιος plousios rich

1498.21 verb nom sing masc part pres act	1706.1 prep	1643.4 noun dat sing neu	1217.2 prep	3450.12 art acc sing fem	4044.12 adj acc sing fem
ὢν ōn being	ἐν en in	ἐλέει, eleei, mercy,	διὰ dia because of	τὴν tēn the	πολλὴν pollēn great

26.4 noun acc sing fem	840.3 prs- pron gen sing	3614.12 rel- pron acc sing fem	25.14 verb 3sing indic aor act	2231.4 prs- pron acc 1pl	2504.1 conj
ἀγάπην agapēn love	⸆ᵃ☆ αὐτοῦ ⸃ autou his	ἣν hēn wherewith	ἠγάπησεν ēgapēsen he loved	ἡμᾶς, hēmas, us,	**5.** καὶ kai also

3.a.**Txt:** 02A,06D,018K
020L,025P,byz.
Var: 01א,03B,33,Treg
Alf,Tisc,We/Ho,Weis
Sod,UBS/☆

4.a.**Txt:** 01א,03B,04C
06D-corr2,044,byz.
Var: p46,06D-org,010F
012G

"according to the course of this world." This is a way of saying that fallen creatures manifest their state of spiritual death by living lives of enslavement to the world's standard of values, values that are human-centered, not God-centered.

Secondly, the rest of the verse informs us of the power that works behind this "spirit" of the age, or the ways of this world. Satan takes advantage of man's lost condition. He is at work "in the children of disobedience" or he is "operating in the sons of disobedience."

Here the writer of this epistle depicts the forces which war against believers as they seek to live godly lives: the world, the flesh, and the devil. The world is an external foe, its evil influences surrounding the believer. The flesh (the self-life) is an internal enemy, its weaknesses making it susceptible to temptation. Satan is an infernal foe, going about like a roaring lion, seeking whom he may devour. He uses the influences of the world to seduce believers, and he takes advantage of believers by attacking them at their weakest points. But God has not left believers at the mercy of these enemies of the soul. He is the eternal Friend and Deliverer who will bring victory.

2:3. Here Paul uses the pronoun "we" (*hēmeis*) to show that the sinful condition he had just described applied to Jews as well as to Gentiles. In verse 1 he refers to "you," the Gentile believers to whom he was writing. Next, Paul specified the third force that works against unbelievers—their fallen sinful nature. The word for "lusts" (*epithumiais*) may be used in a good sense (Luke 22:15) or in an evil sense, depending on its use in the specific context. Paul's use here obviously refers to evil desires. Unbelievers habitually yield to the cravings of the sinful nature with which they were born (Romans 5:12). As a result, they "were by nature the children of wrath." The word "wrath" speaks of God's abiding opposition to evil (Matthew 3:7; Romans 1:18), and it is a reminder that those individuals who continue to practice sin are facing the wrath of God.

2:4. After describing what believers were in the past, the apostle began his picture of the present condition of Christians with "but God" (*de theos*). Man does not have to continue to live on the lower plain described in the first three verses of this chapter; God made a higher level of life possible for those who would accept it. God intervened because of His great love (*tēn pollēn agapēn autou*), the motivating force behind all that He does. In 1 Corinthians 13, the great classic in which he described this marvelous love, Paul detailed very specifically many of the important aspects of love. At the same time, he reminded believers that this same love must be the motivating force behind all their deeds as Christians.

This love caused God to act in mercy (*eleeō*), which can be defined as love in action. Because He loves so much, God performs specific acts of mercy.

of, *Montgomery* . . . you drifted along on the stream of this world's ideas of living, *Phillips* . . . to the worldliness of this world, *Murdock*.

according to the prince of the power of the air: . . . and obeyed its unseen ruler, *Phillips* . . . according to the pleasure of the prince potentate, *Murdock* . . . the governer that ruleth in the ayer, *Tyndale*.

the spirit that now worketh in the children of disobedience: . . . now operating in, *Wilson* . . . which now operates, *Sawyer* . . . who is still operating in those who do not respond to the truth of God, *Phillips* . . . inwardly working in the sons of obstinacy, *Rotherham* . . . children of unbelief, *Douay*.

3. Among whom also we all had our conversation in times past in the lusts of our flesh: . . . we all once passed our lives, indulging the passions of, *Montgomery* . . . once lived while gratifying the cravings of our lower nature, *Williams*.

fulfilling the desires of the flesh and of the mind: . . . doing the promptings, *Confraternity* . . . the will of, *Douay* . . . and followed the impulses and imaginations of our evil nature, *Phillips* . . . and of the thoughts, *Panin, Wilson*.

and were by nature the children of wrath, even as others: . . . children, by nature, of anger, *Rotherham* . . . and by nature we were exposed to God's wrath, as the rest of mankind, *Williams* . . . being in fact under the wrath of God by nature, like everyone else, *Phillips* . . . we were exposed to the divine judgement, like the rest of mankind, *TCNT* . . . like all the rest, *Montgomery*.

4. But God, who is rich in mercy:
for his great love wherewith he loved us: . . . gave Life to us in, *TCNT*.

Ephesians 2:6

1498.25 verb acc pl masc part pres act	2231.4 prs-pron acc 1pl	3361.7 adj	3450.4 art dat pl	3761.5 noun dat pl neu
ὄντας	ἡμᾶς	νεκρούς	τοῖς	παραπτώμασιν,
ontas	hēmas	nekrous	tois	paraptōmasin
being	we	dead	in the	in offenses,

5.a.Var: p46,03B,33

4657.1 verb 3sing indic aor act	1706.1 prep	3450.3 art dat sing	5382.3 name dat masc	5322.3 noun dat sing fem
συνεζωοποίησεν	[a+ ἐν]	τῷ	Χριστῷ·	χάριτί
sunezōopoiēsen	en	tō	Christō	chariti
made alive with	[in]	the	Christ,	by grace

1498.6 verb 2pl indic pres act	4834.30 verb nom pl masc part perf mid	2504.1 conj	4741.1 verb 3sing indic aor act	2504.1 conj
ἐστε	σεσωσμένοι·	6. καὶ	συνήγειρεν,	καὶ
este	sesōsmenoi	kai	sunēgeiren	kai
you are	having been saved,	and	raised up together,	and

4627.1 verb 3sing indic aor act	1706.1 prep	3450.4 art dat pl	2016.8 adj dat pl neu	1706.1 prep	5382.3 name dat masc
συνεκάθισεν	ἐν	τοῖς	ἐπουρανίοις	ἐν	Χριστῷ
sunekathisen	en	tois	epouraniois	en	Christō
seated together	in	the	heavenlies	in	Christ

2400.2 name masc	2419.1 conj	1715.7 verb 3sing subj aor mid	1706.1 prep	3450.4 art dat pl	163.5 noun dat pl masc	3450.4 art dat pl
Ἰησοῦ·	7. ἵνα	ἐνδείξηται	ἐν	τοῖς	αἰῶσιν	τοῖς
Iēsou	hina	endeixētai	en	tois	aiōsin	tois
Jesus,	that	he might shew	in	the	ages	the

7.a.Txt: 06D-corr,018K 020L,025P,byz.
Var: 01א-corr,02A,03B 06D-org,33,Lach,Treg Alf,Word,Tisc,We/Ho Weis,Sod,UBS/✶

1889.5 verb dat pl masc part pres mid	3450.6 art acc sing masc	5072.1 verb acc sing masc part pres act	4009.3 noun acc sing masc	3450.16 art sing neu
ἐπερχομένοις	⌐ τὸν	ὑπερβάλλοντα	πλοῦτον	[a✶ τὸ
eperchomenois	ton	huperballonta	plouton	to
coming	the	surpassing	riches	[the

5072.4 verb sing neu part pres act	4009.1 noun sing masc	3450.10 art gen sing fem	5322.2 noun gen sing fem	840.3 prs-pron gen sing	1706.1 prep
ὑπερβάλλον	πλοῦτος]	τῆς	χάριτος	αὐτοῦ	ἐν
huperballon	ploutos	tēs	charitos	autou	en
excelling	riches]	of the	grace	his	in

5379.3 noun dat sing fem	1894.1 prep	2231.4 prs-pron acc 1pl	1706.1 prep	5382.3 name dat masc	2400.2 name masc
χρηστότητι	ἐφ'	ἡμᾶς	ἐν	Χριστῷ	Ἰησοῦ.
chrēstotēti	eph'	hēmas	en	Christō	Iēsou
kindness	toward	us	in	Christ	Jesus.

3450.11 art dat sing fem	1056.1 conj	5322.3 noun dat sing fem	1498.6 verb 2pl indic pres act	4834.30 verb nom pl masc part perf mid	1217.2 prep
8. τῇ	γὰρ	χάριτί	ἐστε	σεσωσμένοι	διὰ
tē	gar	chariti	este	sesōsmenoi	dia
By the	for	grace	you are	having been saved	through

3450.10 art gen sing fem	3963.2 noun gen sing fem	2504.1 conj	3642.17 dem-pron sing neu	3620.2 partic	1523.1 prep gen	5050.2 prs-pron gen 2pl
⌐a τῆς ⌐	πίστεως·	καὶ	τοῦτο	οὐκ	ἐξ	ὑμῶν,
tēs	pisteōs	kai	touto	ouk	ex	humōn
the	faith;	and	this	not	of	yourselves;

8.a.Txt: 06D-corr,018K 020L,byz.
Var: 01א,03B,06D-org 025P,33,Lach,Treg,Tisc We/Ho,Weis,Sod UBS/✶

2296.2 noun gen sing masc	3450.16 art sing neu	1428.1 noun sing neu	3620.2 partic	1523.1 prep gen	2024.5 noun gen pl neu	2419.1 conj
θεοῦ	τὸ	δῶρον·	9. οὐκ	ἐξ	ἔργων,	ἵνα
theou	to	dōron	ouk	ex	ergōn	hina
God's	to the	gift:	not	of	works,	that

2:5. God's greatest act of mercy is explained in this verse. Even though we were dead spiritually, He "quickened us together with Christ" (*sunezōopoiēsen tō Christō*). This verb is the first of three in the context that has the prefix *sun-* ("with"). The second (*sunēgeiren*) was translated by the NIV "raised us *with* Christ," and the third (*sunekathisen*), "seated us *with* him." These verbs beautifully summarize what God does for believers in the Lord Jesus Christ. First, He implants spiritual life within; then He elevates them to a new level of life; and thirdly, He permits them to enjoy a continuous relationship with Christ in this present earthly life. He accomplishes all this "by grace," *chariti*, an instrumental case construction in the Greek language which expresses the means by which something is accomplished.

"Grace" explains how God operates. It refers to "undeserved favor" and is a constant reminder that God does not manifest acts of mercy toward people because they deserve them. "Ye are saved" in this verse actually comes from a perfect tense participle ("having been saved," *sesōsmenoi*), showing a completed action with continuous results. Salvation is probably expressed this way because of the necessity of an initial act of conversion. However, God does not cease working in believers' lives after conversion.

2:6. The last verse in this section shows the marked contrast between the believers' former lost condition and their present situation in Christ. While believers still live in mortal bodies on earth, they also participate in the resurrection life of Christ. The emphasis in this context is the believer's identification with Christ in His death (verse 5), His resurrection (verse 6), and His ascension (verse 6).

2:7. However, the story is not yet complete. Verse 7 shows why God has done all that verses 4-6 describe. This verse begins with a strong statement of purpose, "that" or "in order that" (*hina*). Throughout all eternity the Church will be a demonstration to all creation of God's grace. Believers will truly be "trophies" of God's grace forever. "He might show" (*endeixētai*) is a middle voice verb meaning "to show for one's self" or for His own glory. So, for eternity believers will be glorifying God.

2:8. Verses 8-10 remind believers that they need to accept what God has provided them in Christ Jesus. We see an amplification of the statement in verse 5, "by grace ye are saved." In the original language this verse begins with the definite article "the" before "grace" (*tē . . . chariti*). Also, the verse begins in the Greek with a postpositive "for" (*gar*) which could be translated "because." Grace is the "cause" for the total plan of God. On the one hand, grace is the objective, instrumental cause of salvation. On the other hand, faith is the subjective medium for the process of salvation, so it is a necessary condition. "It is the gift of God" refers to the whole process of salvation, not just to the granting of faith to believe.

5. Even when we were dead in sins: . . . when we were spiritually dead because of our sins, *Norlie*.

hath quickened us together with Christ: . . . gave us life together, *Phillips* . . . made us live together, *Montgomery* . . . he made alive together, *Wilson*.

(by grace ye are saved;): It is by God's mercy, *TCNT* . . . remember, by grace and not by achievement, *Phillips* . . . and rescued us by his grace, *Murdock*.

6. And hath raised [us] up together, and made [us] sit together in heavenly [places] in Christ Jesus: . . . has lifted us right out of the old life, *Phillips* . . . and reserved a seat for us near Him in the heavenly home, *Norlie* . . . in the celestials, *Rheims* . . . in the heavenly realm, *Montgomery*.

7. That in the ages to come he might show the exceeding riches of his grace: . . . he might exhibit, *Wilson* . . . the overflowing riches, *Confraternity* . . . the amazing riches, *Montgomery* . . . the boundless wealth of his mercy, *TCNT* . . . the magnitude of the riches of his grace, *Murdock* . . . the immeasurable wealth of His mercy, *Norlie*.

in [his] kindness toward us through Christ Jesus: . . . in his bounty, *Douay* . . . he has expressed toward us, *Phillips*.

8. For by grace are ye saved through faith: . . . are ye made safe through fayth, *Geneva* . . . through your faith, *TCNT*.

and that not of yourselves: It is not due to yourselves, *TCNT* . . . this is not from you, *Wilson* . . . this is not your own doing, *Norlie*.

[it is] the gift of God:

9. Not of works: . . . and cometh not of workes, *Cranmer* . . . earning, *Phillips*.

Ephesians 2:10

3231.1 partic	4948.3 indef-pron nom sing	2714.12 verb 3sing subj aor mid	840.3 prs-pron gen sing	1056.1 conj	1498.5 verb 1pl indic pres act
μή	τις	καυχήσηται.	**10.** αὐτοῦ	γάρ	ἐσμεν
mē	tis	kauchēsētai	autou	gar	esmen
not	anyone	might boast.	His	for	we are

4021.1 noun sing neu	2908.10 verb nom pl masc part aor pass	1706.1 prep	5382.3 name dat masc	2400.2 name masc
ποίημα,	κτισθέντες	ἐν	Χριστῷ	Ἰησοῦ
poiēma	ktisthentes	en	Christō	Iēsou
workmanship,	having been created	in	Christ	Jesus

1894.3 prep	2024.6 noun dat pl neu	18.5 adj dat pl	3614.4 rel-pron dat pl	4141.1 verb 3sing indic aor act	3450.5 art nom sing masc
ἐπὶ	ἔργοις	ἀγαθοῖς,	οἷς	προητοίμασεν	ὁ
epi	ergois	agathois	hois	proētoimasen	ho
for	works	good,	which	before prepared	ho

2296.1 noun nom sing masc	2419.1 conj	1706.1 prep	840.2 prs-pron dat pl	3906.21 verb 1pl subj aor act	1346.1 conj
θεὸς	ἵνα	ἐν	αὐτοῖς	περιπατήσωμεν.	**11.** Διὸ
theos	hina	en	autois	peripatēsōmen	Dio
God	that	in	them	we should walk.	Wherefore

3285.1 verb 2pl pres act	3617.1 conj	5050.1 prs-pron nom 2pl	4077.1 adv	4077.1 adv	5050.1 prs-pron nom 2pl
μνημονεύετε	ὅτι	ʽ ὑμεῖς	ποτὲ	[✶ ποτὲ	ὑμεῖς]
mnēmoneuete	hoti	humeis	pote	pote	humeis
remember	that	you	once	[once	you]

3450.17 art pl neu	1477.4 noun pl neu	1706.1 prep	4418.3 noun dat sing fem	3450.7 art nom pl masc	2978.32 verb nom pl masc part pres mid
τὰ	ἔθνη	ἐν	σαρκί,	οἱ	λεγόμενοι
ta	ethnē	en	sarki	hoi	legomenoi
the	Gentiles	in	flesh,	the	being called

201.1 noun nom sing fem	5097.3 prep	3450.10 art gen sing fem	2978.34 verb gen sing fem part pres mid	3921.2 noun gen sing fem
ἀκροβυστία	ὑπὸ	τῆς	λεγομένης	περιτομῆς
akrobustia	hupo	tēs	legomenēs	peritomēs
uncircumcision	by	the	being called	circumcision

12.a.**Txt:** 06D-corr,018K 020L,025P,byz.bo. **Var:** 01א,02A,03B 06D-org,33,Lach,Treg Alf,Word,Tisc,We/Ho Weis,Sod,UBS/✶

1706.1 prep	4418.3 noun dat sing fem	5335.3 adj gen sing fem	3617.1 conj	1498.1 verb 2pl act	1706.1 prep
ἐν	σαρκὶ	χειροποιήτου,	**12.** ὅτι	ἦτε	ʽa ἐν ʼ
en	sarki	cheiropoiētou	hoti	ēte	en
in	flesh	made by hand,	that	you were	at

3450.3 art dat sing	2511.3 noun dat sing masc	1552.4 dem-pron dat sing masc	5400.1 prep	5382.2 name gen masc
τῷ	καιρῷ	ἐκείνῳ	χωρὶς	Χριστοῦ,
tō	kairō	ekeinō	chōris	Christou
the	time	that	apart from	Christ,

522.1 verb nom pl masc part perf mid	3450.10 art gen sing fem	4034.1 noun gen sing fem	3450.2 art gen sing
ἀπηλλοτριωμένοι	τῆς	πολιτείας	τοῦ
apēllotriōmenoi	tēs	politeias	tou
having been alienated from	the	commonwealth	tou

2447.1 name masc	2504.1 conj	3443.3 adj nom pl masc	3450.1 art gen pl	1236.6 noun gen pl fem	3450.10 art gen sing fem
Ἰσραὴλ,	καὶ	ξένοι	τῶν	διαθηκῶν	τῆς
Israēl	kai	xenoi	tōn	diathēkōn	tēs
of Israel,	and	strangers	from the	covenants	of the

2:9. This is probably the reason Paul reminds us in the previous verse that salvation cannot be earned in any way. There is no possibility of self-achieved salvation, and no reason for boasting.

2:10. Even though it is not possible to earn salvation, this verse reminds us that work indeed is involved in the total process, that is, God's work. We are the result of that work. The total passage has come "full circle." Verse 2 reminds us that those in a lost state "walked" (*periepatēsate*) a certain way. The last word in verse 10 in the Greek language is the word "walk" (*peripatēsōmen*) again. Only here the walking as believers is as His "workmanship," as products of what God's grace can do in people. Christians are God's "work of art," His "masterpiece," so they may "walk about" in good works. In fact, believers were "created in Christ Jesus" for that very purpose. Good works do not bring salvation to a person; they are the result of salvation.

2:11. These words were written to Gentile Christians who had been brought out of the darkness of paganism and into the light of God's love. "Remember" comes from a present imperative Greek verb (*mnēmoneuete*) and could be translated "keep on remembering." Notice the exclusiveness and contempt that most Jews ("the Circumcision") held for Gentiles ("Uncircumcision"). Circumcision was instituted by God himself (Genesis 17:10-14) as an external sign of the covenant He made with Abraham. This important rite signified externally what had happened to Abraham internally. However, by Paul's time this physical sign had become more of a sign of the difference between Jew and Gentile than of a person's relationship to God. Paul reminds people that internal—not external—circumcision is what really matters (Galatians 5:6; Colossians 2:11). The apostle certainly did not share the contempt most Jews held for Gentiles. Incidentally, most Gentiles at that time also looked at Jews with contempt.

2:12. Paul reminds his Gentile readers of a far more important matter, their actual condition before they became united with Christ. Their former condition is summarized by a series of five descriptive statements. First, they previously "were without Christ." In the original language this consists of an ablative case construction which in itself normally indicates separation.

Secondly, they were "aliens from the commonwealth of Israel." The word translated "commonwealth" or "citizenship" (*politeias*) is used also in Acts 22:28 where it refers to Paul's Roman citizenship. These Gentiles had no rights of citizenship in "spiritual Israel" (Romans 9:6,7; 11:1-5).

Thirdly, these Gentiles were "strangers from the covenants of promise." "Covenants" refers to God's promises to Abraham (Genesis 12:2,3; 13:14-17; 15:1-5; 17:1-22; 22:15-18). "Promise," or literally "the promise," is a reminder that all the promises of God

lest any man should boast: No one can pride himself upon, *Phillips* . . . in order that, *Alford* . . . that no man may glory, *Douay* . . . lest any one glory, *Murdock*.

10. For we are his workmanship: . . . what we are we owe to the hand of God upon us, *Phillips* . . . for we are his creation, *Sawyer, Murdock* . . . his handiwork, *Montgomery*.

created in Christ Jesus unto good works: . . . having been formed in, *Wilson*.

which God hath before ordained that we should walk in them: . . . to do those good deeds which God planned for us to do, *Phillips* . . . which God before prepared, *Rotherham* . . . afore prepared, *Clementson, ASV* . . . made ready beforehand, *Confraternity* . . . predestined us to make our daily way of life, *Montgomery* . . . that we should devote our lives to them, *TCNT*.

11. Wherefore remember, that ye [being] in time past Gentiles in the flesh: . . . you were at one time heathen, *Norlie* . . . that ye formerly were carnal, *Murdock* . . . formerly gentiles by birth, *Sawyer*.

who are called Uncircumcision by that which is called the Circumcision in the flesh made by hands: . . . performed by hand, *Noyes* . . . performed upon the body by the hand of man, *TCNT*.

12. That at that time ye were without Christ: . . . at that time you were separated from Christ, *Norlie* . . . in that season, separate from Christ, *Rotherham*.

being aliens from the commonwealth of Israel: . . . alienated from the polity of, *Sawyer* . . . from the regulations of, *Murdock*.

and strangers from the covenants of promise: . . . you were outsiders, *TCNT* . . . you knew nothing about the covenant that God had promised to make, *Norlie*.

Ephesians 2:13

1845.1 noun fem	1667.4 noun acc sing fem	3231.1 partic	2174.19 verb nom pl masc part pres act	2504.1 conj	112.1 adj nom pl masc
ἐπαγγελίας,	ἐλπίδα	μὴ	ἔχοντες,	καὶ	ἄθεοι
epangelias	elpida	mē	echontes	kai	atheoi
promise,	hope	not	having,	and	without God

1706.1 prep	3450.3 art dat sing	2862.3 noun dat sing masc		3432.1 adv	1156.2 conj	1706.1 prep	5382.3 name dat masc
ἐν	τῷ	κόσμῳ·	**13.**	νυνὶ	δὲ	ἐν	Χριστῷ
en	tō	kosmō		nuni	de	en	Christō
in	the	world:		now	but	in	Christ

2400.2 name masc	5050.1 prs-pron nom 2pl	3450.7 art nom pl masc	4077.1 adv	1498.23 verb nom pl masc part pres act	3084.1 adv
Ἰησοῦ,	ὑμεῖς	οἱ	ποτε	ὄντες	μακρὰν
Iēsou	humeis	hoi	pote	ontes	makran
Jesus,	you	the	once	being	afar off

1445.1 adv	1090.35 verb 2pl indic aor pass	1090.35 verb 2pl indic aor pass	1445.1 adv	1706.1 prep	3450.3 art dat sing
῾ ἐγγὺς	ἐγενήθητε	[✶ ἐγενήθητε	ἐγγὺς]	ἐν	τῷ
engus	egenēthēte	egenēthēte	engus	en	tō
near	became	[became	near]	by	the

129.3 noun dat sing neu	3450.2 art gen sing	5382.2 name gen masc	840.5 prs-pron nom sing masc	1056.1 conj	1498.4 verb 3sing indic pres act
αἵματι	τοῦ	Χριστοῦ.	**14.** Αὐτὸς	γὰρ	ἐστιν
haimati	tou	Christou	Autos	gar	estin
blood	of the	Christ.	He	for	is

3450.9 art nom sing fem	1503.1 noun nom sing fem	2231.2 prs-pron gen 1pl	3450.5 art nom sing masc	4020.37 verb nom sing masc part aor act	3450.17 art pl neu
ἡ	εἰρήνη	ἡμῶν,	ὁ	ποιήσας	τὰ
hē	eirēnē	hēmōn	ho	poiēsas	ta
the	peace	our,	the	having made	the

295.4 adj pl neu	1518.9 num card neu	2504.1 conj	3450.16 art sing neu	3190.1 noun sing neu	3450.2 art gen sing
ἀμφότερα	ἓν,	καὶ	τὸ	μεσότοιχον	τοῦ
amphotera	hen	kai	to	mesotoichon	tou
both	one,	and	to the	middle wall	of the

5254.1 noun gen sing masc	3061.13 verb nom sing masc part aor act	3450.12 art acc sing fem	2171.3 noun acc sing fem	1706.1 prep
φραγμοῦ	λύσας·	**15.** τὴν	ἔχθραν	ἐν
phragmou	lusas	tēn	echthran	en
partition	having broken down,	the	enmity	in

3450.11 art dat sing fem	4418.3 noun dat sing fem	840.3 prs-pron gen sing	3450.6 art acc sing masc	3414.4 noun acc sing masc	3450.1 art gen pl
τῇ	σαρκὶ	αὐτοῦ,	τὸν	νόμον	τῶν
tē	sarki	autou	ton	nomon	tōn
the	flesh	his,	the	law	of the

1769.5 noun gen pl fem	1706.1 prep	1372.3 noun dat pl neu	2643.4 verb nom sing masc part aor act	2419.1 conj
ἐντολῶν	ἐν	δόγμασιν	καταργήσας·	ἵνα
entolōn	en	dogmasin	katargēsas	hina
commandments	in	decrees	having annulled,	that

15.a.**Txt:** 01א-corr,06D 018K,020L,byz.
Var: 01א-org,02A,03B 025P,33,Lach,Treg,Alf Tisc,We/Ho,Weis,Sod UBS/✶

3450.8 art acc pl masc	1411.3 num card	2908.3 verb 3sing subj aor act	1706.1 prep	1431.5 prs-pron dat sing masc	840.4 prs-pron dat sing
τοὺς	δύο	κτίσῃ	ἐν	῾ ἑαυτῷ	[ᵃ✶ αὐτῷ]
tous	duo	ktisē	en	heautō	autō
the	two	he might create	in	himself	[idem]

116

to Abraham, Isaac, and Jacob stemmed from that one great promise of the coming Messiah (Genesis 3:15).

Fourthly, the Gentiles to whom Paul was writing had been in a state of "having no hope," which is the natural consequence of being without Christ (1 Thessalonians 4:13). Lastly, they had been "without God."

2:13. What a definite contrast verses 13-22 show when compared with verses 11 and 12. In verse 12 these Gentiles were "in the world," but in verse 13 they were "in Christ Jesus." In verse 12 the words "at that time" are contrasted in verse 13 with "now." They once were "far off," but "are made nigh." All this took place, of course, "by the blood of Christ." Because the docetic Gnostics denied the humanity of Christ, Paul was very careful to specify that He was a real human with genuine blood. Redemption came through the death of Christ, and the means of cleansing was His shed blood. It was not an ordinary death. Those who opt for a "bloodless religion" do so outside the parameters of Scripture and manifest a modern form of gnosticism.

2:14. Notice the shift here to "our," denoting that Jesus has brought both Gentiles and Jews into a body that is characterized by peace. The apostle used the term "peace" as the basis of unity in the body of Christ. The temple itself was divided into various courts: Holy of Holies, Holy Place, priests, Israel, women, Gentiles. A wall, about 3 or 4 feet high, ran through the temple area separating the Court of the Gentiles from the inner court into which Jews only were permitted. This wall contained an inscription which read: "No foreigner may enter within the barricade which surrounds the sanctuary and enclosure. Any(one) who is caught doing so will have himself to blame for his ensuing death." Paul himself nearly got into serious trouble because some people falsely accused him of taking an Asian Gentile, Trophimus, beyond this point (Acts 21:27-29).

2:15. Much of the language of this section, verses 13-18, is language that relates to a body. Comparing the Church to a human body was one of the New Testament's favorite metaphors. How did Jesus accomplish this unity of Gentiles and Jews into one body? This verse says He did so by "having abolished in his flesh the enmity" which was the "law of commandments."

Jesus "abolished" the Mosaic law in the sense that He fulfilled all its requirements. He himself said He had not come to destroy the Law or the Prophets, but to fulfill them (Matthew 5:17,18).

having no hope, and without God in the world: . . . not possessing, *Wilson* . . . had nothing to look forward to and no God to whom you could turn, *Phillips* . . . and godless, in the world, *Rotherham*.

13. But now in Christ Jesus ye who: . . . through the blood, *Phillips* . . . But now you are in union with Christ, *Norlie*.

sometimes were far off: . . . who formerly were, *Wilson* . . . who were formerly far off, *PNT* . . . were once outside the pale, *Phillips*.

are made nigh by the blood of Christ: . . . have been brought near by, *Murdock* . . . are with us inside the circle of God's love and purpose, *Phillips*.

14. For he is our peace: He Himself is, *Williams* . . . living peace, *Phillips*.

who hath made both one: . . . made the two divisions of mankind one, *TCNT* . . . He is the one who has made us both into one body, *Williams* . . . made a unity of the conflicting elements, *Phillips*.

and hath broken down the middle wall of partition [between us]: . . . and hath demolished, *Murdock* . . . and having removed the enmity, *Wilson* . . . and dissoluing the middle vvall, *Rheims* . . . has broken down the party-wall, *Montgomery* . . . broke down the barrier which separated them, *TCNT* . . . broken down the dividing wall that separated us, *Norlie* . . . broken down the barrier that kept us apart, *Williams* . . . the middle wall of separation, *Scarlett* . . . wall of the enclosure broke down, *Rotherham*.

15. Having abolished in his flesh the enmity, [even] the law of commandments [contained] in ordinances: He has put a stop to the hostility, *Williams* . . . annulled the Law, *Wilson* . . . contained in decrees, *Scarlett* . . . In abrogating through his flesshe the hatred, *Geneva* . . . the cause of hatred, *Cranmer*.

Ephesians 2:16

1519.1 prep	1518.4 num card acc masc	2508.1 adj sing	442.4 noun acc sing masc	4020.15 verb nom sing masc part pres act
εἰς	ἕνα	καινὸν	ἄνθρωπον,	ποιῶν
eis	*hena*	*kainon*	*anthrōpon*	*poiōn*
into	one	new	man,	making

1503.4 noun acc sing fem	2504.1 conj	599.2 verb 3sing subj aor act	3450.8 art acc pl masc	295.3 adj acc pl masc
εἰρήνην·	**16.** καὶ	ἀποκαταλλάξῃ	τοὺς	ἀμφοτέρους
eirēnēn	*kai*	*apokatallaxē*	*tous*	*amphoterous*
peace;	and	might reconcile	the	both

1706.1 prep	1518.2 num card dat	4835.3 noun dat sing neu	3450.3 art dat sing	2296.3 noun dat sing masc	1217.2 prep	3450.2 art gen sing
ἐν	ἑνὶ	σώματι	τῷ	θεῷ	διὰ	τοῦ
en	*heni*	*sōmati*	*tō*	*theō*	*dia*	*tou*
in	one	body		to God	through	the

4567.2 noun gen sing masc	609.10 verb nom sing masc part aor act	3450.12 art acc sing fem	2171.3 noun acc sing fem	1706.1 prep	840.4 prs-pron dat sing
σταυροῦ,	ἀποκτείνας	τὴν	ἔχθραν	ἐν	αὐτῷ·
staurou	*apokteinas*	*tēn*	*echthran*	*en*	*autō*
cross,	having slain	the	enmity	by	it;

2504.1 conj	2048.13 verb nom sing masc part aor act	2076.17 verb 3sing indic aor mid	1503.4 noun acc sing fem
17. καὶ	ἐλθὼν	εὐηγγελίσατο	εἰρήνην
kai	*elthōn*	*euēngelisato*	*eirēnēn*
and	having come	he announced the good news,	peace

17.a.Var: 01א,02A,03B
06D,025P,33,Lach,Treg
Alf,Word,Tisc,We/Ho
Weis,Sod,UBS/✻

5050.3 prs-pron dat 2pl	3450.4 art dat pl	3084.1 adv	2504.1 conj	1503.4 noun acc sing fem	3450.4 art dat pl
ὑμῖν	τοῖς	μακρὰν	καὶ	[a✻+ εἰρήνην]	τοῖς
humin	*tois*	*makran*	*kai*	*eirēnēn*	*tois*
to you	the	afar off	and	[peace]	to the

1445.1 adv	3617.1 conj	1217.1 prep	840.3 prs-pron gen sing	2174.5 verb 1pl indic pres act	3450.12 art acc sing fem
ἐγγύς,	**18.** ὅτι	δι'	αὐτοῦ	ἔχομεν	τὴν
engus	*hoti*	*di'*	*autou*	*echomen*	*tēn*
near.	Because	through	him	we have	the

4176.1 noun acc sing fem	3450.7 art nom pl masc	295.1 adj nom pl masc	1706.1 prep	1518.2 num card dat	4011.3 noun dat sing neu
προσαγωγὴν	οἱ	ἀμφότεροι	ἐν	ἑνὶ	πνεύματι
prosagōgēn	*hoi*	*amphoteroi*	*en*	*heni*	*pneumati*
access	the	both	by	one	Spirit

4242.1 prep	3450.6 art acc sing masc	3824.4 noun acc sing masc	679.1 partic	3631.1 partic	3629.1 adv
πρὸς	τὸν	πατέρα.	**19.** ἄρα	οὖν	οὐκέτι
pros	*ton*	*patera*	*ara*	*oun*	*ouketi*
to	the	Father.	So	then	no longer

19.a.Var: 01א,02A,03B
04C,06D-org,33,Lach
Treg,Alf,Tisc,We/Ho
Weis,Sod,UBS/✻

1498.6 verb 2pl indic pres act	3443.3 adj nom pl masc	2504.1 conj	3803.2 adj nom pl masc	233.2 conj	1498.6 verb 2pl indic pres act
ἐστὲ	ξένοι	καὶ	πάροικοι,	ἀλλὰ	[a✻+ ἐστὲ]
este	*xenoi*	*kai*	*paroikoi*	*alla*	*este*
are you	strangers	and	sojourners,	but	[you are]

4698.1 noun nom pl masc	3450.1 art gen pl	39.4 adj gen pl	2504.1 conj	3472.1 adj nom pl masc	3450.2 art gen sing
συμπολῖται	τῶν	ἁγίων	καὶ	οἰκεῖοι	τοῦ
sumpolitai	*tōn*	*hagiōn*	*kai*	*oikeioi*	*tou*
fellow citizens	of the	saints	and	of the household	

Therefore, Jesus was the only one qualified to remove all previous distinctions between Jews and Gentiles and "to make in himself . . . one new man," a definite reference to the New Testament Church in which no distinctions exist.

2:16. Just as verse 15 indicates that Christ is the point of convergence for all people, so verse 16 shows that the Cross is the place of convergence. God is the great Reconciler. Even though it was man who had separated himself from God by his sins, God initiated the act of reconciliation by sending His Son. Now we are reconciled to Him and to one another because He has "broken down the middle wall of partition between us" (verse 14).

2:17. This verse is a clear statement of the reason for Christ's coming to this earth. He "preached peace" (*euēngelisato eirēnēn*) to the ones "which were afar off," the Gentiles to whom Paul wrote this important epistle, and "to them that were nigh," the Jews.

2:18. As a result of the peace that Jesus' death on the cross provides for both Jews and Gentiles, both groups have access to the Father through Christ by the Holy Spirit. The term "access" comes from a Greek word (*prosagōgues*) which was the title used for the official in an oriental court who introduced visitors to the potentate. The word does not refer just to liberty of approach, but to an actual introduction.

Notice the involvement of the Trinity. Through Christ, or because of His sacrifice on the cross (Romans 5:2), the Holy Spirit introduces believers to the Father. The Bible is marvelously consistent about the total involvement of the Trinity in all that God does for us and through us as His people. All of God's blessings have always come to mankind through Jesus Christ, and the Holy Spirit has always been the member of the Trinity who performs the specific acts. This pattern can be seen in the Bible even from creation itself (Genesis 1:1,2; John 1:1-3). The emphasis in this verse relates to the fact that access to the Father does not depend upon any value inherent in the believer, but is dependent upon the sacrifice of Christ on his behalf.

2:19. Up to this point in this total passage which began in verse 11, we have seen the New Testament Church mainly has been compared to the unity of a human body, but now this verse begins a comparison of the New Testament Church to a beautiful temple with each stone occupying an important position in the total structure. Believers are no longer "strangers and foreigners" but members of this temple with all the rights and privileges of membership. The first term (*xenoi*) relates to short-term transients and the second (*paroikoi*) to aliens who have settled in a particular country but have no intrinsic rights because they are not citizens.

for to make in himself of twain one new man: . . . that he might create of the two one new man, *Noyes* . . . and made in himself out of the two, *Phillips* . . . by uniting both to himself, *TCNT*.
[so] making peace: . . . thus producing peace, *Phillips*.

16. And that he might reconcile both unto God in one body by the cross: . . . united in one Body, *TCNT* . . . by the sacrifice of one body on the cross, *Phillips*.
having slain the enmity thereby: . . . destroyed the enmity, *Wilson* . . . and put an end to their antagonism, *Norlie* . . . had killed the hostility through it, *Williams* . . . made utterly irrelevant the antagonism between them, *Phillips*.

17. And came and preached peace to you which were afar off, and to them that were nigh: . . . told both you who were far from God...that the war was over, *Phillips*.

18. For through him we both have access by one Spirit unto the Father: . . . united in spirit, are now able to approach the Father, *TCNT* . . . we both have the introduction, *Wilson* . . . we both haue an open way, *Geneva*.

19. Now therefore: Take notice then, *Montgomery* . . . So, *Williams*.
ye are no more strangers and foreigners: . . . outsiders and aliens, *TCNT, Phillips* . . . sojourners, *Panin, Wilson, Clementson, Murdock*.
but fellowcitizens with the saints: . . . with every other Christian, *Phillips*.
and of the household of God: . . . you belong now to, *Phillips* . . . You are members of God's own family, *Norlie* . . . the domestics, *Douay* . . . and members of God's Household, *TCNT*.

2296.2 noun gen sing masc	2010.6 verb nom pl masc part aor pass	1894.3 prep	3450.3 art dat sing	2287.2 noun dat sing
θεοῦ,	20. ἐποικοδομηθέντες	ἐπὶ	τῷ	θεμελίῳ
theou	epoikodomēthentes	epi	tō	themeliō
of God,	having been built up	on	the	foundation

3450.1 art gen pl	646.5 noun gen pl masc	2504.1 conj	4254.5 noun gen pl masc	1498.19 verb gen sing part pres act
τῶν	ἀποστόλων	καὶ	προφητῶν,	ὄντος
tōn	apostolōn	kai	prophētōn	ontos
of the	apostles	and	prophets,	being

202.1 noun gen sing masc	840.3 prs-pron gen sing	2400.2 name masc	5382.2 name gen masc	5382.2 name gen masc
ἀκρογωνιαίου	αὐτοῦ	᾿Ιησοῦ	Χριστοῦ,	[✶ Χριστοῦ
akrogōniaiou	autou	Iēsou	Christou	Christou
cornerstone	himself	Jesus	Christ,	[Christ

21.a.Txt: 01‭א‬-corr,02A 04C,025P,sa.bo.Steph Var: 01‭א‬-org,03B,06D 018K,020L,33,byz.Lach Treg,Alf,Word,Tisc We/Ho,Weis,Sod UBS/✶

2400.2 name masc	1706.1 prep	3614.3 rel-pron dat sing	3820.9 adj nom sing fem	3450.9 art nom sing fem	3482.1 noun nom sing fem
᾿Ιησοῦ,]	21. ἐν	ᾧ	πᾶσα	(ᾱ ἡ)	οἰκοδομὴ
Iēsou	en	hō	pasa	hē	oikodomē
Jesus,]	in	whom	all	the	building

4734.1 verb nom sing fem part pres mid	831.1 verb 3sing indic pres act	1519.1 prep	3348.4 noun acc sing masc	39.1 adj sing	1706.1 prep
συναρμολογουμένη	αὔξει	εἰς	ναὸν	ἅγιον	ἐν
sunarmologoumenē	auxei	eis	naon	hagion	en
being fitted together	increases	to	a temple	holy	in

2935.3 noun dat sing masc	1706.1 prep	3614.3 rel-pron dat sing	2504.1 conj	5050.1 prs-pron nom 2pl	4776.1 verb 2pl indic pres mid
κυρίῳ,	22. ἐν	ᾧ	καὶ	ὑμεῖς	συνοικοδομεῖσθε
kuriō	en	hō	kai	humeis	sunoikodomeisthe
Lord;	in	whom	also	you	are being built together

1519.1 prep	2702.1 noun sing neu	3450.2 art gen sing	2296.2 noun gen sing masc	1706.1 prep	4011.3 noun dat sing neu
εἰς	κατοικητήριον	τοῦ	θεοῦ	ἐν	πνεύματι.
eis	katoikētērion	tou	theou	en	pneumati
for	a habitation	of the	of God	in	Spirit.

3642.1 dem-pron gen sing	5320.1 prep	1466.1 prs-pron nom 1sing	3834.1 name nom masc	3450.5 art nom sing masc	1192.1 noun nom sing masc
3:1. Τούτου	χάριν	ἐγὼ	Παῦλος	ὁ	δέσμιος
Toutou	charin	egō	Paulos	ho	desmios
Of this	cause	I	Paul	the	prisoner

1.a.Txt: p46,01‭א‬-corr2 06D-corr2,044,byz.bo. Var: 01‭א‬-org,06D-org 010F,012G

3450.2 art gen sing	5382.2 name gen masc	2400.2 name masc	5065.1 prep	5050.2 prs-pron gen 2pl	3450.1 art gen pl
τοῦ	Χριστοῦ	(ᾱ ᾿Ιησοῦ)	ὑπὲρ	ὑμῶν	τῶν
tou	Christou	Iēsou	huper	humōn	tōn
of the	Christ	Jesus	for	you	the

1477.5 noun gen pl neu	1480.1 conj	1479.1 conj	1058.1 partic	189.23 verb 2pl indic aor act	3450.12 art acc sing fem
ἐθνῶν	2. (εἴγε	[✶ εἴ	γε]	ἠκούσατε	τὴν
ethnōn	eige	ei	ge	ēkousate	tēn
Gentiles,	if indeed	[if	indeed]	you heard of	the

3484.2 noun acc sing fem	3450.10 art gen sing fem	5322.2 noun gen sing fem	3450.2 art gen sing	2296.2 noun gen sing masc	3450.10 art gen sing fem
οἰκονομίαν	τῆς	χάριτος	τοῦ	θεοῦ	τῆς
oikonomian	tēs	charitos	tou	theou	tēs
administration	of the	grace	of the	of God	the

2:20. God is constructing a beautiful temple, the Church. Paul refers to "the foundation of the apostles and prophets." The Old Testament prophetic word and the New Testament apostolic word form the basis of our Christian faith and teaching. Through the preaching of the gospel, the apostolic ministry brought the New Testament Church into existence. The reference to "the chief corner stone" comes from Psalm 118:22,23, a passage which Jesus related to himself (Mark 12:10,11) and Peter ascribed to Christ (Acts 4:11; 1 Peter 2:7). It sometimes meant the stone placed at the extreme corner, so it could bind together the other stones in the structure. It was the most important stone in a building because the stability of all the others depended upon it. It also provided the standard to follow for straight lines both horizontal and vertical.

2:21. This is another important reminder that Jesus is the One who holds the New Testament Church together and in a state of unity. "Framed together" comes from a present participle in the Greek language (*sunarmologoumenē*) which literally means "being joined together" and shows that the work is continuous and progressive.

2:22. This verse contains Paul's personal note to the Ephesian believers. Perhaps some of them felt like second-class citizens because they did not live in Jerusalem and were not part of that important local body. The apostle reminded them that they were just as important to God as any other group of Christians.

3:1. "For this cause" probably refers back to Paul's statements in chapter 2 comparing the New Testament Church first to a human body and secondly to a temple. The apostle did not admit he was a prisoner of the Roman emperor, Nero. The genitive case used here in the Greek language does not signify merely a prisoner who belonged to Christ; rather, it refers to the fact that Christ, not Nero, had imprisoned him. In other words, Paul knew his stay in prison was part of God's will for his life.

This confinement resulted in benefit for the Gentiles. Had he never been imprisoned in Rome, Paul probably would not have had such a tremendous impact upon the believers in Rome (Philippians 1:14), an impact that touched the entire Roman Empire.

3:2. Paul felt compelled by the Holy Spirit to explain more thoroughly what he had mentioned only briefly about Jews and Gentiles being incorporated into the "one body" with no distinctions and

20. And are built upon the foundation of the apostles and prophets:
Jesus Christ himself being the chief corner [stone]: . . . being the highest corner stone, *Rheims* . . . the actual foundation-stone being, *Phillips.*

21. In whom all the building fitly framed together: . . . an entire building, in process of being fitly conjoined together, *Rotherham* . . . all the edifice is framed, *Murdock* . . . the whole structure is closely fitted together, *Confraternity* . . . United in him, *TCNT* . . . is harmoniously fitted together, *Williams* . . . being harmoniously cemented together, *Scarlett* . . . fitly compacted together, *Wilson.*
groweth unto an holy temple in the Lord: . . . increases into, *Wilson* . . . sacred through its union with the Lord, *Williams* . . . grows together into a temple consecrated to God, *Phillips.*

22. In whom ye also are builded together: You are all part of this building, *Phillips* . . . are continuously built together, *Montgomery* . . you yourselves, in union with Him, in fellowship with one another, are being built up, *Williams.*
for an habitation of God through the Spirit: . . . for a dwelling-place, *Montgomery* . . . for God through the Spirit, *Williams* . . . so that God can find in you a dwelling-place for His Spirit, *Norlie* . . . for a spiritual habitation, *Sawyer, Wilson.*

1. For this cause I Paul: This, then, is the reason why I, *TCNT.*
the prisoner of Jesus Christ for you Gentiles: . . . in behalf of you nations, *Panin.*

2. If ye have heard of the dispensation of the grace of God: . . . the responsible charge with which God entrusted me, *TCNT* . . . a steward of His grace, *Norlie.*

Ephesians 3:3

3.a.**Txt:** 01א,02A,04C 06D,044,bo.byz.
Var: p46,03B,010F 012G

1319.49 verb gen sing fem part aor pass	1466.4 prs-pron dat 1sing	1519.1 prep	5050.4 prs-pron acc 2pl	3617.1 conj	2567.3 prep
δοθείσης	μοι	εἰς	ὑμᾶς,	3. ⟨a ὅτι ⟩	κατὰ
dotheisēs	moi	eis	humas	hoti	kata
having been given	to me	towards	you,	that	by

3.b.**Txt:** 06D-corr,018K 020L,byz.
Var: 01א,02A,03B,04C 06D-org,025P,33,Gries Lach,Treg,Alf,Word Tisc,We/Ho,Weis,Sod UBS/✻

597.4 noun acc sing fem	1101.5 verb 3sing indic aor act	1101.14 verb 3sing indic aor pass	1466.4 prs-pron dat 1sing
ἀποκάλυψιν	⟨ ἐγνώρισέν	[b✫ ἐγνωρίσθη]	μοι
apokalupsin	egnōrisen	egnōristhē	moi
revelation	he made known	[was made known]	to me

3450.16 art sing neu	3328.1 noun sing neu	2503.1 conj	4129.1 verb 1sing indic aor act	1706.1 prep	3504.2 adj dat sing
τὸ	μυστήριον,	καθὼς	προέγραψα	ἐν	ὀλίγῳ,
to	mustērion	kathōs	proegrapsa	en	oligō
the	mystery,	just as	I wrote before	in	brief,

4242.1 prep	3614.16 rel-pron sing neu	1404.6 verb 2pl masc part indic pres mid	312.5 verb nom pl masc part pres act	3401.7 verb inf aor act
4. πρὸς	ὃ	δύνασθε	ἀναγινώσκοντες	νοῆσαι
pros	ho	dunasthe	anaginōskontes	noēsai
by	which	you are able,	reading	to preceive

3450.12 art acc sing fem	4757.3 noun acc sing fem	1466.2 prs-pron gen 1sing	1706.1 prep	3450.3 art dat sing	3328.3 noun dat sing neu
τὴν	σύνεσίν	μου	ἐν	τῷ	μυστηρίῳ
tēn	sunesin	mou	en	tō	mustēriō
the	understanding	my	in	the	mystery

5.a.**Txt:** bo.Steph
Var: 01א,02A,03B,04C 06D,018K,020L,025P,it. Gries,Lach,Treg,Alf Word,Tisc,We/Ho,Weis Sod,UBS/✻

3450.2 art gen sing	5382.2 name gen masc	3614.16 rel-pron sing neu	1706.1 prep	2066.14 adj dat pl fem	1067.7 noun dat pl fem
τοῦ	Χριστοῦˑ	5. ὃ	⟨a ἐν ⟩	ἑτέραις	γενεαῖς
tou	Christou	ho	en	heterais	geneais
of the	Christ,	which	in	other	generations

3620.2 partic	1101.14 verb 3sing indic aor pass	3450.4 art dat pl	5048.8 noun dat pl masc	3450.1 art gen pl	442.7 noun gen pl masc
οὐκ	ἐγνωρίσθη	τοῖς	υἱοῖς	τῶν	ἀνθρώπων,
ouk	egnōristhē	tois	huiois	tōn	anthrōpōn
not	was made known	to the	sons	of the	men,

5453.1 conj	3431.1 adv	596.7 verb 3sing indic aor pass	3450.4 art dat pl	39.8 adj dat pl masc	646.6 noun dat pl masc
ὡς	νῦν	ἀπεκαλύφθη	τοῖς	ἁγίοις	ἀποστόλοις
hōs	nun	apekaluphthē	tois	hagiois	apostolois
as	now	it was revealed	to the	holy	apostles

840.3 prs-pron gen sing	2504.1 conj	4254.6 noun dat pl masc	1706.1 prep	4011.3 noun dat sing neu	1498.32 verb inf pres act
αὐτοῦ	καὶ	προφήταις	ἐν	πνεύματιˑ	6. εἶναι
autou	kai	prophētais	en	pneumati	einai
his	and	prophets	by	Spirit,	to be

3450.17 art pl neu	1477.4 noun pl neu	4640.3 adj pl neu	2504.1 conj	4806.1 adj pl neu
τὰ	ἔθνη	συγκληρονόμα	καὶ	σύσσωμα
ta	ethnē	sunklēronoma	kai	sussōma
the	Gentiles	joint heirs	and	a joint body

6.a.**Txt:** 06D-corr,018K 020L,byz.Sod
Var: 01א,02A,03B,04C 06D-org,025P,33,bo. Lach,Treg,Alf,Tisc We/Ho,Weis,UBS/✻

2504.1 conj	4681.2 adj pl neu	3450.10 art gen sing fem	1845.1 noun fem	840.3 prs-pron gen sing
καὶ	συμμέτοχα	τῆς	ἐπαγγελίας	⟨a αὐτοῦ ⟩
kai	summetocha	tēs	epangelias	autou
and	joint partakers	of the	promise	his

with equal privileges and responsibilities (2:16). Paul had been given "the dispensation of the grace of God" or an "administration of God's grace." "Dispensation" (*oikonomia*) literally means "house manager" and could be translated "stewardship, economy, administration, arrangement, plan, task." In other words, God had given him the responsibility of making known to the world the meaning of the mystery God had revealed to him: the amazing unity of the New Testament Church, with no distinction between Gentiles and Jews.

3:3. According to this verse, he had already mentioned this mystery. Perhaps he was referring to two previous statements in this epistle (1:9; 2:16). "Mystery" (*musterion*) does not mean something mystical but something that is incomprehensible until God chooses to reveal it. The term for the "revelation" (*apokalupsis*) is the same word from which we derive the title of the last book in the Bible. In the New Testament it means something undiscoverable by humans unless God makes it known to them. It was a very common term to people of that day. For example, it was used of the unveiling of a statue the public had not seen until that time.

3:4. Some people minimize the written Word of God and emphasize the spoken word more than they should. While the spoken word certainly is important, it cannot supersede the written Scriptures. Paul apparently intended that the recipients of this letter spend time reading the Scriptures.

3:5. We do not know why God had not revealed this "mystery" before this time. Peter also made it clear in his first epistle that God did not choose to manifest certain things to people nor even to angels (1 Peter 1:1-12). The Old Testament is full of examples of what is known in the science of hermeneutics as a "progressive revelation." God revealed certain matters to mankind in stages. Paul explained to the Galatians that Christ did not come to this world until "the fulness of time was come" (Galatians 4:4).

3:6. In this verse we see a clear example of Paul's use of the term "mystery" (the word may not have the same meaning in every context). The mystery was not that a Gentile finally could be saved. Paul himself quoted several Old Testament passages indicating God's redemptive work among Gentiles (Romans 9:24-33; 10:19-21; 15:9-12). Three terms are used in verse 6 which are prefixed by adding the preposition *sun-* ("with"). "Fellow heirs" (*sunkleronoma*), "same body" (*sussoma*), and "partakers" (*summetocha*) serve as excellent examples of Paul's common practice of reinforcement by compounding synonyms or phrases that are very close in meaning. Therefore, the mystery was that Gentiles and Jews would belong equally to the same body.

which is given me to you-ward: . . . appointed me to be...intended for you, *Norlie* . . . entrusted to me for you? *Montgomery* . . . with respect to you, *PNT*.

3. How that by revelation he made known unto me the mystery: . . . by direct revelation, *Montgomery* . . . the secret, *Wilson*.

(as I wrote afore in few words: . . . as I have already briefly told you, *TCNT* . . . as I have briefly written before, *Williams* . . . written briefly of this above, *Phillips* . . . wrote briefly before, *Wilson*.

4. Whereby, when ye read: ye may understand my knowledge in the mystery of Christ): . . . ye may perceive my insight into, *Noyes* . . . will explain to you, *Phillips* . . . you can judge of my insight into that secret truth, *Montgomery*.

5. Which in other ages was not made known unto the sons of men: . . . was hidden to past generations of mankind, *Phillips* . . . In former generations, *TCNT* . . . in other generations, *Panin, Wilson*.

as it is now revealed unto his holy apostles and prophets by the Spirit: . . . been made plain to God's consecrated messengers, *Phillips*.

6. That the Gentiles should be fellowheirs, and of the same body: . . . the heathen are jointheirs, *TCNT* . . . the Gentiles form one body with us, *Montgomery* . . . be co-heirs, *Scarlett* . . . should be sharers of his inheritance, *Murdock* . . . and a Joint-body, *Wilson* . . . and jointpartners, *Rotherham* . . . equal heirs, *Phillips*.

and partakers of his promise: . . . and Co-partners, *Wilson* . . . and are coheirs and copartners, *Montgomery* . . . and partners with us, *Worrell*.

6.b.Txt: 06D,018K,020L byz.
Var: 01א,02A,03B,04C 025P,33,bo.Lach,Treg Alf,Tisc,We/Ho,Weis Sod,UBS/☆

6.c.Var: 01א,02A,03B 04C,025P,33,bo.Lach Treg,Alf,Tisc,We/Ho Weis,Sod,UBS/☆

7.a.Txt: 04C,06D-corr 018K,020L,byz.01א 02A,03B,06D-org,025P 33,Lach,Treg,Alf,Word Tisc,We/Ho,Weis,Sod UBS/☆

7.b.Txt: 06D-corr,018K 020L,byz.
Var: 01א,02A,03B,04C 06D-org,025P,33,Gries Lach,Treg,Alf,Tisc We/Ho,Weis,Sod UBS/☆

8.a.Txt: 025P,Steph
Var: 01א,02A,03B,04C 06D,018K,020L,byz. Gries,Lach,Treg,Alf Word,Tisc,We/Ho,Weis Sod,UBS/☆

8.b.Txt: 06D,018K,020L byz.it.
Var: 01א,02A,03B,04C 025P,Lach,Treg,Alf Tisc,We/Ho,Weis,Sod UBS/☆

8.c.Txt: 01א-corr 06D-corr,018K,020L 025P,byz.
Var: 01א-org,02A,03B 04C,06D-org,33,Lach Treg,Alf,Word,Tisc We/Ho,Weis,Sod UBS/☆

8.d.Txt: 01א-corr 06D-corr,018K,020L 025P,byz.
Var: 01א-org,02A,03B 04C,06D-org,33,Lach Treg,Alf,Word,Tisc We/Ho,Weis,Sod UBS/☆

9.a.Txt: p46,01א-corr 03B,04C,06D,018K 020L,025P,byz.it.sa.bo. Weis,Sod
Var: 01א-org,02A,1739 Tisc,We/Ho,UBS/☆

1706.1 prep — ἐν — *en* — in
3450.3 art / dat sing — (b τῷ) — *tō* — the
5382.3 name / dat masc — Χριστῷ, — *Christō* — Christ
2400.2 name masc — [c☆+ Ἰησοῦ] — *Iēsou* — [Jesus]
1217.2 prep — διὰ — *dia* — through
3450.2 art / gen sing — τοῦ — *tou* — the

2077.2 noun / gen sing neu — εὐαγγελίου, — *euangeliou* — good news;
3614.2 rel-pron gen sing — 7. οὗ — *hou* — of which
1090.30 verb 1sing indic aor mid — ἐγενόμην — *egenomēn* — I became
1090.78 verb 1sing indic aor pass — [a☆ ἐγενήθην] — *egenēthēn* — [idem]

1243.1 noun / nom sing masc — διάκονος — *diakonos* — servant
2567.3 prep — κατὰ — *kata* — according to
3450.12 art / acc sing fem — τὴν — *tēn* — the
1424.4 noun / acc sing fem — δωρεὰν — *dōrean* — gift
3450.10 art / gen sing fem — τῆς — *tēs* — of the

5322.2 noun / gen sing fem — χάριτος — *charitos* — grace
3450.2 art / gen sing — τοῦ — *tou*
2296.2 noun / gen sing masc — θεοῦ — *theou* — of God
3450.12 art / acc sing fem — (τὴν — *tēn* — the
1319.51 verb acc sing fem part aor pass — δοθεῖσάν — *dotheisan* — having been given

3450.10 art / gen sing fem — [b☆ τῆς — *tēs* — [the
1319.49 verb gen sing fem part aor pass — δοθείσης] — *dotheisēs* — having been given]
1466.4 prs-pron dat 1sing — μοι — *moi* — to me,
2567.3 prep — κατὰ — *kata* — according to
3450.12 art / acc sing fem — τὴν — *tēn* — the

1737.2 noun / acc sing fem — ἐνέργειαν — *energeian* — working
3450.10 art / gen sing fem — τῆς — *tēs* — of the
1405.2 noun / gen sing fem — δυνάμεως — *dunameōs* — power
840.3 prs-pron gen sing — αὐτοῦ· — *autou* — his.
1466.5 prs-pron dat 1sing — 8. ἐμοὶ — *emoi* — To me,
3450.3 art / dat sing — τῷ — *tō* — the

1634.1 adj comp dat sing masc — ἐλαχιστοτέρῳ — *elachistoterō* — less than the least
3820.4 adj gen pl — πάντων — *pantōn* — of all
3450.1 art gen pl — (a τῶν) — *tōn* — the
39.4 adj gen pl — ἁγίων — *hagiōn* — saints,
1319.44 verb 3sing indic aor pass — ἐδόθη — *edothē* — was given

3450.9 art / nom sing fem — ἡ — *hē* — the
5322.1 noun / nom sing fem — χάρις — *charis* — grace
3642.9 dem-pron nom sing fem — αὕτη, — *hautē* — this,
1706.1 prep — (b ἐν) — *en* — among
3450.4 art dat pl — τοῖς — *tois* — the
1477.6 noun dat pl neu — ἔθνεσιν — *ethnesin* — Gentiles

2076.25 verb inf aor mid — εὐαγγελίσασθαι — *euangelisasthai* — to announce the good news,
3450.6 art / acc sing masc — (τὸν — *ton* — the
3450.16 art sing neu — [c☆ τὸ] — *to* — [idem]
419.2 adj sing neu — ἀνεξιχνίαστον — *anexichniaston* — unsearchable

4009.3 noun / acc sing masc — (πλοῦτον — *plouton* — riches
4009.1 noun / sing masc — [d☆ πλοῦτος] — *ploutos* — [idem]
3450.2 art / gen sing — τοῦ — *tou* — of the
5382.2 name / gen masc — Χριστοῦ, — *Christou* — Christ,
2504.1 conj — 9. καὶ — *kai* — and

5297.5 verb inf aor act — φωτίσαι — *phōtisai* — to enlighten
3820.8 adj / acc pl masc — (a πάντας) — *pantas* — all
4949.3 intr-pron nom sing — τίς — *tis* — what
3450.9 art / nom sing fem — ἡ — *hē* — the
2815.1 noun nom sing fem — (κοινωνία — *koinōnia* — fellowship

During the Old Testament period Gentiles had been allowed to become Jewish proselytes and to share in God's blessings, but a distinction always existed between them and those who were Jews by birth. Why did not Paul give this definition in chapter 2 when he started expounding the subject of Gentiles being "fellow heirs" with Israel? It often was his style to lead up to his theme.

3:7. Verses 7-13 show clearly the attitude Paul had concerning the great responsibility God had given him to publish this mystery to the world. First, he realized that to be a servant (*diakonos*) of God is "the gift of the grace of God." His grace puts people into ministries in His church, and His power makes it possible for them to fulfill these ministries. Paul used two Greek terms to describe this ability. "Effectual working" comes from the word from which we get *energy* (*energeia*), and "power" comes from the familiar word *dunamis*. Unfortunately, many connect this second term only with the concept of power. Perhaps the noun *ability* would better indicate its meaning in most contexts. The same God who gave Paul the tremendous responsibility to reveal God's plan to the world also performed this act purely out of His grace and promised to give the ability or the power necessary to carry out the responsibility.

3:8. Instead of boasting about his own abilities and the fact that God had given him such an important task, the apostle considered himself an unworthy servant, mainly because previous to his conversion he had persecuted Christ by persecuting His church (Acts 9:5; 1 Corinthians 15:9; Philippians 3:6; 1 Timothy 1:13). In spite of his previous position of violently opposing the New Testament Church, God gave Paul the privilege and responsibility of proclaiming to the world the mystery of that Church.

One should not get the impression from Paul's terminology about himself that he was putting himself down. That would have been false humility, which really is just another form of pride. People sometimes become "proud of their humility" by trying to manifest it to other people. No one can read Paul's writings and think he was like that. He did not boast about his abilities, even though he had many of them. Exceptional abilities and positions of prominence in themselves do not corrupt individuals, but the temptation to allow one's self to become proud definitely increases in such situations. The antidote to the danger is a very simple but effective one: allow God to keep you humble. He certainly did it for Paul (2 Corinthians 12:1-10).

3:9. "To make all men see" actually means "to bring to light" or "to turn on the light." This Greek infinitive comes from the word

in Christ by the gospel: . . . through the good news, *Williams.*

7. Whereof I was made a minister: . . . for which I was called to serve, *Williams.*
according to the gift of the grace of God: . . . according to the free-gift, *Rotherham* . . . God's unmerited favor, *Williams.*
given unto me by the effectual working of his power: . . . which was imparted to me by the energy of, *Wilson* . . . by the operation of, *Murdock* . . . the exercise of his power, *TCNT, Williams* . . . by the power with which he equipped me, *Phillips.*

8. Unto me, who am less than the least of all saints: . . . the very lowest, *Wilson* . . . less than the least, *Phillips* . . . the least deserving, *TCNT* . . . of all His people, *Williams.*
is this grace given: . . . this unmerited favor was bestowed, *Williams.*
that I should preach among the Gentiles: . . . to enable me to proclaim, *Phillips* . . . that I might preach as good news to the heathen, *Williams.*
the unsearchable riches of Christ: . . . the unfathomable riches, *Norlie* . . . the incalculable riches, *Phillips* . . . the boundless riches of Christ, *Williams* . . . of the undreamt-of wealth that exists in the Christ, *TCNT.*

9. And to make all [men] see what [is] the fellowship of the mystery: . . . and to enlighten all, *Sawyer, Rotherham, Alford* . . . and to illuminate al men, *Rheims* . . . should show to all men what is the dispensation, *Murdock* . . . and to bring to light what is the dispensation, *Panin* . . . and to make clear how is to be carried out the trusteeship of this secret, *Williams* . . . the new dispensa-

Ephesians 3:10

9.b.Txt: Steph
Var: 01א,02A,03B,04C
06D,018K,020L,025P
byz.it.bo.Gries,Lach
Treg,Alf,Word,Tisc
We/Ho,Weis,Sod
UBS/☆

3484.3 noun nom sing fem	3450.2 art gen sing	3328.2 noun gen sing neu	3450.2 art gen sing	607.4 verb gen sing neu part perf mid
[b☆ οἰκονομία]	τοῦ	μυστηρίου	τοῦ	ἀποκεκρυμμένου
oikonomia	tou	mustēriou	tou	apokekrummenou
[stewardship]	of the	mystery	the	having been hidden

570.3 prep	3450.1 art gen pl	163.4 noun gen pl masc	1706.1 prep	3450.3 art dat sing	2296.3 noun dat sing masc	3450.3 art dat sing
ἀπὸ	τῶν	αἰώνων	ἐν	τῷ	θεῷ,	τῷ
apo	tōn	aiōnōn	en	tō	theō	tō
from	the	ages	in	the	God,	the

9.c.Txt: 06D-corr,018K
020L,byz.
Var: 01א,02A,03B,04C
06D-org,025P,33,bo.
Gries,Lach,Treg,Alf
Word,Tisc,We/Ho,Weis
Sod,UBS/☆

3450.17 art pl neu	3820.1 adj	2908.5 verb dat sing masc part aor act	1217.2 prep	2400.2 name masc	5382.2 name gen masc
τὰ	πάντα	κτίσαντι	[c διὰ	Ἰησοῦ	Χριστοῦ,]
ta	panta	ktisanti	dia	Iēsou	Christou,
the	all things	having created	by	Jesus	Christ,

2419.1 conj	1101.15 verb 3sing subj aor pass	3431.1 adv	3450.14 art dat pl fem	741.6 noun dat pl fem	2504.1 conj
10. ἵνα	γνωρισθῇ	νῦν	ταῖς	ἀρχαῖς	καὶ
hina	gnōristhē	nun	tais	archais	kai
that	might be known	now	to the	principalities	and

3450.14 art dat pl fem	1833.7 noun dat pl fem	1706.1 prep	3450.4 art dat pl	2016.8 adj dat pl neu	1217.2 prep
ταῖς	ἐξουσίαις	ἐν	τοῖς	ἐπουρανίοις	διὰ
tais	exousiais	en	tois	epouraniois	dia
the	authorities	in	the	heavenlies	through

3450.10 art gen sing fem	1564.1 noun fem	3450.9 art nom sing fem	4042.1 adj nom sing fem	4531.1 noun nom sing fem
τῆς	ἐκκλησίας	ἡ	πολυποίκιλος	σοφία
tēs	ekklēsias	hē	polupoikilos	sophia
the	assembly	the	diversified	wisdom

3450.2 art gen sing	2296.2 noun gen sing masc	2567.3 prep	4145.4 noun acc sing fem	3450.1 art gen pl	163.4 noun gen pl masc
τοῦ	θεοῦ,	**11.** κατὰ	πρόθεσιν	τῶν	αἰώνων,
tou	theou,	kata	prothesin	tōn	aiōnōn,
of the	of God,	according to	purpose	of the	ages,

11.a.Var: 01א-corr,02A
03B,04C-org,33,Lach
Treg,Alf,Tisc,We/Ho
Weis,Sod,UBS/☆

3614.12 rel-pron acc sing fem	4020.24 verb 3sing indic aor act	1706.1 prep	3450.3 art dat sing	5382.3 name dat masc	2400.2 name masc
ἣν	ἐποίησεν	ἐν	[a☆+ τῷ]	Χριστῷ	Ἰησοῦ
hēn	epoiēsen	en	tō	Christō	Iēsou
which	he made	in	[the]	Christ	Jesus

3450.3 art dat sing	2935.3 noun dat sing masc	2231.2 prs-pron gen 1pl	1706.1 prep	3614.3 rel-pron dat sing	2174.5 verb 1pl indic pres act
τῷ	κυρίῳ	ἡμῶν,	**12.** ἐν	ᾧ	ἔχομεν
tō	kuriō	hēmōn,	en	hō	echomen
the	Lord	our,	in	whom	we have

12.a.Txt: 04C,06D-corr
018K,020L,025P,byz.
Var: 01א-org,02A,03B
33,Lach,Treg,Tisc
We/Ho,Weis,Sod
UBS/☆

3450.12 art acc sing fem	3816.4 noun acc sing fem	2504.1 conj	3450.12 art acc sing fem	4176.1 noun acc sing fem	1706.1 prep
τὴν	παρρησίαν	καὶ	[a τὴν]	προσαγωγὴν	ἐν
tēn	parrhēsian	kai	tēn	prosagōgēn	en
the	boldness	and	the	access	in

3870.1 noun dat sing fem	1217.2 prep	3450.10 art gen sing fem	3963.2 noun gen sing fem	840.3 prs-pron gen sing	1346.1 conj
πεποιθήσει	διὰ	τῆς	πίστεως	αὐτοῦ.	**13.** διὸ
pepoithēsei	dia	tēs	pisteōs	autou	dio
confidence	by	the	faith	of him.	Wherefore

which translates into English as *photo* and serves as the prefix for many English terms. Paul did not picture himself in some small room turning on a light. His vision went far beyond that limited idea. The apostle pictured himself in the center of the earth, exposing to the entire world the revelation that God had made known to him.

The Lord made it very clear to His disciples in His commission to them (Matthew 28:19,20) that believers have two main responsibilities relative to people in this world. One is to evangelize them. The apostle Paul took this challenge seriously.

The second responsibility Jesus gave His disciples was to help other believers to mature in their faith. Again, Paul took this matter seriously, and much of his ministry was involved in training people to minister to others.

3:10. This verse should be compared with 1 Peter 1:12 which explains that even angels did not previously know what God had planned for the Church Age. Some people elevate angels to positions far beyond what the Bible gives them. God, on the other hand, elevates people to positions of importance in His kingdom, and He uses angels to help them (Hebrews 1:7). The Gnostics of Paul's day made the mistake of completely reversing the matter. Apparently even heavenly beings, described in this verse as "the principalities and powers," did not understand the "mystery" of the New Testament Church until God chose to reveal it through the apostle Paul.

3:11. Even though God purposed from before the creation of the world (1:4,5) that the New Testament Church would be brought into being in "the fulness of time," He did not reveal the fact until He allowed Paul the glorious privilege of making that truth known to the world.

3:12. In fact, even the ability to know God comes to us through Christ. The NIV renders "access" (*prosagōgēn*) as "approach." The previous use of the term (2:18) is in a different context, that of comparing the New Testament Church to a human body.

The second use of the term tells believers they have access to God "by the faith of him" or "through faith in him (NIV)," that is, through faith in Christ, not faith in some angel or other creature. Believers can enter the Father's presence with "boldness" and "confidence" because they are covered with the righteousness of Christ. Those who have placed their faith in Him have done so because they realize He is the only One who met the requirements of God laid down in the Old Testament law. Therefore, when God looks at those people who live by faith in the Lord Jesus Christ, He sees the righteousness of Christ.

tion of that secret purpose, *Montgomery* . . . the meaning of that secret, *Phillips*.

which from the beginning of the world hath been hid in God, who created all things by Jesus Christ: . . . which has been concealed from the ages, *Wilson* . . . which has for ages been hidden away, *Williams* . . . has been hidden from eternity, *Confraternity* . . . has kept hidden from the creation until now, *Phillips*.

10. To the intent that now unto the principalities and powers in heavenly [places]: And the object of this is, *TCNT* . . . The purpose is that all the angelic powers, *Phillips* . . . in order that now may be made known to the Governments, *Wilson* . . . to the rulers and authorities in heaven, *Williams* . . . that now his manifold wisdom, *Montgomery* . . . in the heavenly regions, *Scarlett*.

might be known by the church the manifold wisdom of God: . . . in order that now his manifold wisdom should, *Montgomery* . . . should now see the complex wisdom of God's plan, *Phillips* . . . many-sided wisdom, *TCNT* . . . so that the many phases of God's wisdom, *Williams* . . . the much diversified Wisdom, *Wilson*.

11. According to the eternal purpose which he purposed in Christ Jesus our Lord: . . . to a plan of the ages, *Panin* . . . in conformity to that timeless purpose which he centered in, *Phillips* . . . which he accomplished in, *Confraternity* . . . executed in the gift of Christ, *Williams* . . . our Master, *TCNT*.

12. In whom we have boldness and access with confidence by the faith of him: . . . this freedom of speech, *Wilson* . . . By union with Him and through faith in Him we have a free and confidential introduction to God, *Williams* . . . we dare...to approach God, *Phillips* . . . this fearless confidence, *Montgomery* . . . and entrance with confidence, *Geneva*.

Ephesians 3:14

13.a.Txt: 04C,06D-corr
018K,020L,025P,byz.
Var: 01א,03B-corr,Lach
Treg,Alf,Word,Weis
Sod,UBS/⋆

153.22 verb 1sing indic pres mid	3231.1 partic	1560.3 verb inf pres act	1450.3 verb inf pres act	1706.1 prep	3450.14 art dat pl fem
αἰτοῦμαι	μὴ	ʽ ἐκκακεῖν	[ᵃ⋆ ἐγκακεῖν]	ἐν	ταῖς
aitoumai	mē	ekkakein	enkakein	en	tais
I ask	not	to faint	[idem]	at	the

2324.7 noun dat pl fem	1466.2 prs-pron gen 1sing	5065.1 prep	5050.2 prs-pron gen 2pl	3610.3 rel-pron nom sing fem	1498.4 verb 3sing indic pres act
θλίψεσίν	μου	ὑπὲρ	ὑμῶν,	ἥτις	ἐστὶν
thlipsesin	mou	huper	humōn	hētis	estin
tribulations	my	for	you,	which	is

1385.1 noun nom sing fem	5050.2 prs-pron gen 2pl	3642.1 dem-pron gen sing	5320.1 prep	2549.1 verb 1sing indic pres act	3450.17 art pl neu
δόξα	ὑμῶν.	**14.** Τούτου	χάριν	κάμπτω	τὰ
doxa	humōn	Toutou	charin	kamptō	ta
glory	your.	For this	cause	I bow	the

14.a.Txt: 01א-corr,06D
018K,020L,byz.it.
Var: p46,01א-org,02A
03B,04C,025P,33,sa.bo.
Lach,Treg,Alf,Word
Tisc,We/Ho,Weis,Sod
UBS/⋆

1113.3 noun pl neu	1466.2 prs-pron gen 1sing	4242.1 prep	3450.6 art acc sing masc	3824.4 noun acc sing masc	3450.2 art gen sing
γόνατά	μου	πρὸς	τὸν	πατέρα	ʽᵃ τοῦ
gonata	mou	pros	ton	patera	tou
knees	my	to	the	Father	the

2935.2 noun gen sing masc	2231.2 prs-pron gen 1pl	2400.2 name masc	5382.2 name gen masc	1523.1 prep gen	3614.2 rel-pron gen sing
κυρίου	ἡμῶν	Ἰησοῦ	Χριστοῦ, ʽ	**15.** ἐξ	οὗ
kuriou	hēmōn	Iēsou	Christou	ex	hou
Lord	our	Jesus	Christ,	of	whom

3820.9 adj nom sing fem	3827.1 noun nom sing fem	1706.1 prep	3636.8 noun dat pl masc	2504.1 conj	1894.3 prep	1087.2 noun gen sing fem
πᾶσα	πατριὰ	ἐν	οὐρανοῖς	καὶ	ἐπὶ	γῆς
pasa	patria	en	ouranois	kai	epi	gēs
every	family	in	heavens	and	on	earth

16.a.Txt: 06D,018K
020L,025P,byz.
Var: 01א,02A,03B,04C
33,Lach,Treg,Alf,Tisc
We/Ho,Weis,Sod
UBS/⋆

3550.4 verb 3sing indic pres mid	2419.1 conj	1319.24 verb 3sing opt aor act	1319.19 verb 3sing subj aor act	5050.3 prs-pron dat 2pl
ὀνομάζεται,	**16.** ἵνα	ʽ δώῃ	[ᵃ⋆ δῷ]	ὑμῖν
onomazetai	hina	dōē	dō	humin
is being named,	that	he may give	[idem]	you

16.b.Txt: 06D-corr,018K
020L,byz.
Var: 01א,02A,03B,04C
06D-org,025P,Lach
Treg,Alf,Word,Tisc
We/Ho,Weis,Sod
UBS/⋆

2567.3 prep	3450.6 art acc sing masc	4009.3 noun acc sing masc	3450.16 art sing neu	4009.1 noun sing masc
κατὰ	ʽ τὸν	πλοῦτον	[ᵇ⋆ τὸ	πλοῦτος]
kata	ton	plouton	to	ploutos
according to	the	riches	[the	riches]

3450.10 art gen sing fem	1385.2 noun gen sing fem	840.3 prs-pron gen sing	1405.3 noun dat sing fem	2874.2 verb inf aor pass
τῆς	δόξης	αὐτοῦ,	δυνάμει	κραταιωθῆναι
tēs	doxēs	autou	dunamei	krataiōthēnai
of the	glory	his,	with power	to be strengthened

1217.2 prep	3450.2 art gen sing	4011.2 noun gen sing neu	840.3 prs-pron gen sing	1519.1 prep	3450.6 art acc sing masc	2059.1 prep
διὰ	τοῦ	πνεύματος	αὐτοῦ	εἰς	τὸν	ἔσω
dia	tou	pneumatos	autou	eis	ton	esō
by	the	Spirit	his	in	the	inner

442.4 noun acc sing masc	2700.13 verb inf aor act	3450.6 art acc sing masc	5382.4 name acc masc	1217.2 prep
ἄνθρωπον,	**17.** κατοικῆσαι	τὸν	Χριστὸν	διὰ
anthrōpon	katoikēsai	ton	Christon	dia
man;	to dwell	the	Christ,	through

3:13. A person in prison, as Paul was, might have a tendency to pity himself and to want other people to feel sorry for him. However, Paul asked his readers not to be discouraged because of his suffering for them. The word he used for "tribulations" normally refers to that narrow set of circumstances the person finds himself in at the moment. It could be compared to a person climbing a steep path that is very narrow. On the one side the path is bordered by mammoth rocks that would be impossible to scale. The other side of the path is bordered by a steep cliff. Therefore, the person traveling this path cannot swerve to the left, nor to the right. He has no choice but to press ahead or to turn around and go back. Of course, the idea of going back was not an acceptable option to Paul.

3:14,15. Here begins another of Paul's Spirit-inspired prayers. He is about to express his desires for the believers as he prays to the God who has a Father relationship with them.

Paul's first prayer (1:15-23) was concerned with the necessity of Christian growth, and this second prayer concerns the necessity of Christian service. This verse contains a statement about the fatherhood of God that confuses some people. They take this verse and others like it to mean that everyone is a child of God by virtue of being part of His creation. But there is a definite distinction between the fatherhood of God relative to creation and the fatherhood of God relative to conversion. Only those who have accepted Jesus Christ as Lord and Saviour are the children of God (John 8:44). It seems that in this verse Paul was referring to the fatherhood of God relative to creation.

3:16. Paul's actual prayer consists of five petitions. The first two are introduced in verse 16 in the original language by *hina* ("in order that"). The third and fourth are introduced by another *hina* in verse 18. The fifth petition is introduced by the third *hina* in the latter part of verse 19. It is as if the apostle was saying, "If you really want to serve God properly, these five items must be considered important matters."

First, he prayed that God would strengthen the believers or give them the power of the Holy Spirit. "To be strengthened with might" comes from two Greek words put together to state that no one can serve God adequately without the ability the Holy Spirit gives. *Dunamis* relates to "inherent ability" (as in Acts 1:8) to be witnesses unto Christ, and *kratos* relates to "manifested strength" and shows that power in action.

3:17. Secondly, Paul prayed that "Christ may dwell in your hearts by faith." This does not mean the believers were not already Chris-

13. Wherefore I desire that ye faint not at my tribulations for you: Do not, then, lose courage, *Norlie* . . . I beg you not to lose heart, *Montgomery* . . . beg you not to be dismayed at the sufferings, *TCNT* . . . I entreat you not to be disheartened, *Noyes* . . . pray, that I may not be discouraged by my afflictions, *Murdock* . . . over the sorrows that I am suffering for your sake, *Williams* . . . on account of my afflictions, *Sawyer*.

which is your glory: . . . they bring you honor, *Williams* . . . for they are an honour to you, *TCNT* . . . Indeed, you should be honored, *Phillips*.

14. For this cause I bow my knees unto the Father of our Lord Jesus Christ: For this reason I kneel before, *Williams* . . . fall on my knees, *Phillips*.

15. Of whom the whole family in heaven and earth: . . . all fatherhood, earthly or heavenly, *Phillips* . . . from whom every family, *Williams*.

is named: . . . derives its name, *Williams, Phillips*.

16. That he would grant you, according to the riches of his glory: . . . the riches of His perfect character, *Williams* . . . the glorious richness of his resources, *Phillips*.

to be strengthened with might by his Spirit in the inner man: . . . to be Powerfully strengthened, *Wilson* . . . to be fortified by his Spirit, *Rheims* . . . to be made mighty through his Spirit, *Panin* . . . by breathing his Spirit into your very souls, *TCNT* . . . in the inward man, *ASV* . . . in your inmost being, *Montgomery*.

17. That Christ may dwell in your hearts by faith: . . . may make His permanent home, *Williams* . . . actually live in your hearts, *Phillips*.

3450.10 art gen sing fem	3963.2 noun gen sing fem	1706.1 prep	3450.14 art dat pl fem	2559.7 noun dat pl fem	5050.2 prs- pron gen 2pl
τῆς	πίστεως	ἐν	ταῖς	καρδίαις	ὑμῶν·
tēs	pisteōs	en	tais	kardiais	humōn
the	faith,	in	the	hearts	your,

1706.1 prep	26.3 noun dat sing fem	4348.1 verb nom pl masc part perf mid	2504.1 conj	2288.4 verb nom pl masc part perf mid
18. ἐν	ἀγάπῃ	ἐῤῥιζωμένοι	καὶ	τεθεμελιωμένοι,
en	agapē	errhizōmenoi	kai	tethemeliōmenoi,
in	love	being rooted	and	having been founded,

2419.1 conj	1823.1 verb 2pl subj aor act	2608.11 verb inf aor mid	4713.1 prep	3820.5 adj dat pl
ἵνα	ἐξισχύσητε	καταλαβέσθαι	σὺν	πᾶσιν
hina	exischusēte	katalabesthai	sun	pasin
that	you may be fully able	to apprehend	with	all

3450.4 art dat pl	39.8 adj dat pl masc	4949.9 intr- pron sing neu	3450.16 art sing neu	3974.1 noun sing neu	2504.1 conj	3240.1 noun sing neu
τοῖς	ἁγίοις	τί	τὸ	πλάτος	καὶ	μῆκος
tois	hagiois	ti	to	platos	kai	mēkos
the	saints	what	the	width	and	length

2504.1 conj	893.1 noun sing neu	2504.1 conj	5149.1 noun sing neu	5149.1 noun sing neu	2504.1 conj
καὶ	ʹ βάθος	καὶ	ὕψος,	[✶ ὕψος	καὶ
kai	bathos	kai	hupsos,	hupsos	kai
and	depth	and	height;	[height	and

893.1 noun sing neu	1091.29 verb inf aor act	4885.1 conj	3450.12 art acc sing fem	5072.3 verb acc sing fem part pres act
βάθος,]	**19.** γνῶναί	τε	τὴν	ὑπερβάλλουσαν
bathos,]	gnōnai	te	tēn	huperballousan
depth,]	to know	and	the	surpassing

3450.10 art gen sing fem	1102.2 noun gen sing fem	26.4 noun acc sing fem	3450.2 art gen sing	5382.2 name gen masc	2419.1 conj
τῆς	γνώσεως	ἀγάπην	τοῦ	Χριστοῦ,	ἵνα
tēs	gnōseōs	agapēn	tou	Christou,	hina
the	knowledge	love	of the	Christ;	that

3997.23 verb 2pl subj aor pass	1519.1 prep	3820.17 adj sing neu	3450.16 art sing neu	3998.1 noun sing neu	3450.2 art gen sing
πληρωθῆτε	εἰς	πᾶν	τὸ	πλήρωμα	τοῦ
plērōthēte	eis	pan	to	plērōma	tou
you may be filled	unto	all	the	fullness	of the

2296.2 noun gen sing masc	3450.3 art dat sing	1156.2 conj	1404.14 verb dat sing masc part pres mid	5065.1 prep	3820.1 adj
θεοῦ.	**20.** Τῷ	δὲ	δυναμένῳ	ὑπὲρ	πάντα
theou.	Tō	de	dunamenō	huper	panta
of God.	To the	but	being able	above	all things

4020.41 verb inf aor act	5065.1 prep	1523.2 prep gen	3916.2 adj gen sing neu	5076.1 adv
ποιῆσαι	ʹ ὑπὲρ	ἐκ	περισσοῦ	[✶ ὑπερεκπερισσοῦ]
poiēsai	huper	ek	perissou	huperekperissou
to do	beyond	from	above	[superabundantly]

3614.1 rel- pron gen pl	153.23 verb 1pl indic pres mid	2211.1 conj	3401.1 verb 1pl indic pres act	2567.3 prep	3450.12 art acc sing fem
ὧν	αἰτούμεθα	ἢ	νοοῦμεν	κατὰ	τὴν
hōn	aitoumetha	ē	nooumen	kata	tēn
what	we ask	or	think,	according to	the

tians and that Christ did not already dwell in them. The idea expressed is that of a permanent dwelling as opposed to a temporary experience. Paul wanted the believers to maintain a consistent experience so that Christ would indeed "feel at home" on a permanent basis. When He can "settle down and be at home," the Christian's witness for Him will be a consistent one.

Paul was also concerned that the believers should be "rooted and grounded in love." Both of these first two terms come from perfect passive participles in the Greek language, showing the necessity of the initial work of salvation being accomplished by God, and indicating the necessity of continued results.

3:18. Thirdly, Paul prayed that the believers would be able to comprehend "what is the breadth, and length, and depth, and height," the overwhelming richness of the gospel and of the love of Christ. As long as we are here on earth, this knowledge can be only in part (1 Corinthians 13:9). We can know it and learn about it by experience as we share with other believers the spiritual insights and experiences God brings to us.

It is like exploring a diamond mine. The farther and deeper we go, the more treasures we discover and the more desire we have to acquire all that God desires to provide for us.

3:19. Fourthly, Paul prayed for believers "to know the love of Christ, which passeth knowledge." This is not a repetition of the thought in verse 18, but is an appeal to experience personally this vast love of God. We shall not only have a theoretical and intellectual knowledge of this love, but also a real, personal experience of it. The Greek word used here (*gnōnai*) is often used in the New Testament for experiential knowledge.

Lastly, Paul prayed that Christians "might be filled with all the fulness of God." Christ was "full of grace and truth" (John 1:14), descriptive of the glory of God, His character. Further, "Of his fulness have all we received" (John 1:16). Believers have various levels of capacity (which can be increased), but they can be recipients of those qualities which constitute the "fulness of God."

3:20. The possibility of always reaching out for more of the ability the Holy Spirit gives caused Paul to break forth into a doxology, expressing the fact that God does "exceeding" or "superabundantly" (*huperekperissou*) more than we can request or even imagine, according to His power (*dumamis*) that works (*energeia*) within us. This great promise is conditional. The degree that we allow God's power to work *in* us determines the extent of what He can do *for* us.

that ye, being rooted and grounded in love: . . . when firmly rooted and established, *TCNT* . . . so deeply rooted and so firmly grounded, *Montgomery* . . . You must be deeply rooted, your foundations must be strong, *Williams* . . . and well-established, *Wilson* . . . firmly fixed, *Phillips.*

18. May be able to comprehend with all saints: . . . that ye may be full mighty to grasp firmly, *Rotherham* . . . that ye may be able to explore, *Murdock* . . . may receive power to grasp the dimensions, *Norlie* . . . may be strong enough to grasp the idea, *Williams.*

what [is] the breadth, and length, and depth, and height: . . . how wide and deep and long and high, *Phillips* . . . and the depnesse, *Wyclif.*

19. And to know the love of Christ, which passeth knowledge: . . . yes to come at last to know...although it far surpasses human understanding, *Williams* . . . the knowledge-surpassing love of Christ, *Worrell* . . . though it is beyond all understanding, *TCNT* . . . so far beyond our comprehension, *Phillips* . . . which transcends all knowing, *Montgomery* . . . which exceeds knowledge, *Sawyer.* . . more excellent thanne science, *Wyclif.*

that ye might be filled with all the fulness of God: . . . may be filled to the full with God himself, *TCNT* . . . filled through all your being, *Phillips* . . . with all the "plenitude" of, *Montgomery* . . . with the perfect fullness of, *Williams.*

20. Now unto him that is able to do exceeding abundantly above: . . . able to accomplish, *Confraternity* . . . to do infinitely more, *Montgomery* . . . by his almighty power, *Murdock.*

all that we ask or think: . . . than we ever dare to ask, *Phillips* . . . or conceiving, *Rotherham* . . . or imagine, *Williams.*

according to the power that worketh in us: . . . by his power within us, *Phillips* . . . operating in us, *Wilson.*

1405.4 noun acc sing fem	3450.12 art acc sing fem	1738.11 verb acc sing fem part pres mid	1706.1 prep	2231.3 prs- pron dat 1pl	840.4 prs- pron dat sing
δύναμιν	τὴν	ἐνεργουμένην	ἐν	ἡμῖν,	21. αὐτῷ
dunamin	tēn	energoumenēn	en	hēmin	autō
power	the	working	in	us,	to him

21.a.Var: 01א,02A,03B
04C,33,bo.Lach,Treg
Alf,Tisc,We/Ho,Weis
Sod,UBS/★

3450.9 art nom sing fem	1385.1 noun nom sing fem	1706.1 prep	3450.11 art dat sing fem	1564.3 noun dat sing fem	2504.1 conj
ἡ	δόξα	ἐν	τῇ	ἐκκλησίᾳ	[ᵃ★+ καὶ]
hē	doxa	en	tē	ekklēsia	kai
the	glory	in	the	assembly	[and]

1706.1 prep	5382.3 name dat masc	2400.2 name masc	1519.1 prep	3820.16 adj acc pl fem	3450.15 art acc pl fem	1067.1 noun fem
ἐν	Χριστῷ	Ἰησοῦ,	εἰς	πάσας	τὰς	γενεὰς
en	Christō	Iēsou	eis	pasas	tas	geneas
in	Christ	Jesus,	to	all	the	generations

3450.2 art gen sing	163.1 noun gen sing masc	3450.1 art gen pl	163.4 noun gen pl masc	279.1 intrj	3731.1 verb 1sing indic pres act
τοῦ	αἰῶνος	τῶν	αἰώνων.	ἀμήν.	4:1. Παρακαλῶ
tou	aiōnos	tōn	aiōnōn	amēn	Parakalō
of the	age	of the	ages.	Amen.	I urge

3631.1 partic	5050.4 prs- pron acc 2pl	1466.1 prs- pron nom 1sing	3450.5 art nom sing masc	1192.1 noun nom sing masc	1706.1 prep	2935.3 noun dat sing masc
οὖν	ὑμᾶς	ἐγὼ	ὁ	δέσμιος	ἐν	κυρίῳ
oun	humas	egō	ho	desmios	en	kuriō
therefore	you,	I	the	prisoner	in	Lord,

512.1 adv	3906.23 verb inf aor act	3450.10 art gen sing fem	2794.2 noun gen sing fem	3614.10 rel- pron gen sing fem
ἀξίως	περιπατῆσαι	τῆς	κλήσεως	ἧς
axiōs	peripatēsai	tēs	klēseōs	hēs
worthily	to walk	of the	calling	which

2535.38 verb 2pl indic aor pass	3196.3 prep	3820.10 adj gen sing fem	4863.1 noun gen sing fem	2504.1 conj
ἐκλήθητε,	2. μετὰ	πάσης	ταπεινοφροσύνης	καὶ
eklēthēte	meta	pasēs	tapeinophrosunēs	kai
you were called,	with	all	humility	and

4095.2 noun gen sing fem	4095.7 noun gen sing fem	3196.3 prep	3087.2 noun gen sing fem
ʼ πραότητος,	[★ πραΰτητος,]	μετὰ	μακροθυμίας,
praotētos	prautētos	meta	makrothumias
meekness,	[idem]	with	patience,

428.3 verb nom pl masc part pres mid	238.1 prs- pron gen pl	1706.1 prep	26.3 noun dat sing fem	4557.1 verb nom pl masc part pres act
ἀνεχόμενοι	ἀλλήλων	ἐν	ἀγάπῃ,	3. σπουδάζοντες
anechomenoi	allēlōn	en	agapē	spoudazontes
bearing with	one another	in	love;	being diligent

4931.11 verb inf pres act	3450.12 art acc sing fem	1759.1 noun acc sing fem	3450.2 art gen sing	4011.2 noun gen sing neu	1706.1 prep
τηρεῖν	τὴν	ἑνότητα	τοῦ	πνεύματος	ἐν
tērein	tēn	henotēta	tou	pneumatos	en
to keep	the	unity	of the	Spirit	in

3450.3 art dat sing	4736.2 noun dat sing masc	3450.10 art gen sing fem	1503.2 noun gen sing fem	1518.9 num card neu	4835.1 noun sing neu
τῷ	συνδέσμῳ	τῆς	εἰρήνης.	4. Ἕν	σῶμα
tō	sundesmō	tēs	eirēnēs.	Hen	sōma
the	bond	of the	peace.	One	body

3:21. Because the ability and energy to accomplish the work of the New Testament Church really come from God, the glory must go to Him for what is accomplished. Even though he was in captivity, Paul's ability to praise God was not chained. Many of his most exuberant outbursts of praise are found in the Prison Epistles and came out of very trying circumstances.

The word "glory" in this verse comes from the Greek noun from which we derive *doxology (doxa)*. According to Paul's instruction, this praise should come forth from the Church, a reminder of the main purpose for which the Church exists. The chapter ends with the truth that this praise will continue forever, an excellent reminder of our eternal vocation, praising God through Jesus Christ.

4:1. This chapter begins the practical section of Ephesians. Paul normally balanced his epistles with a theological portion and a practical portion. The "therefore" of verse 1 serves as a bridge connecting all the apostle had written up to this point with what follows.

In the Greek text "beseech" (*parakalō*) is first in the sentence for emphasis. Paul was concerned that believers should cross the bridge from analysis to action, from theology to morality, from Christian faith to Christian life, from the revelation of doctrine to the development of practice. He made this very strong appeal as "the prisoner of the Lord."

Verses 1-16 describe the unity and diversity of the New Testament Church. Paul began his exhortation by appealing to the Ephesians to live lives worthy of the calling God had given them. "Worthy" (*axiōs*) is an adverb of manner used with scales. Basically it means "bringing up the other beam of the scales" or "bringing into equilibrium." It carries the idea of one thing being the equivalent of another thing. In other words, a Christian's practice should "weigh as much as" or "be equivalent to" his profession. If it truly does "weigh as much as," that person will be doing what the whole Book of Ephesians tells him to do.

4:2. Furthermore, it will be reflected in the three qualities mentioned in verse 2. The first two, "lowliness and meekness," refer to a person's attitude toward self. A person with a proper balance between profession and practice will be humble, will not be full of haughty pride. A truly humble individual will be in balance, not thinking too highly of himself, nor, at the other extreme, putting himself down. Such a person will also be meek, which is the opposite of self-assertion. The third quality, forbearance, is a social virtue, expressing the ability to be patient with the weaknesses of other people.

4:3. The absence of these three qualities will definitely jeopardize Christian unity. Unity does not just happen. Because this is a present tense idea, we must constantly work at it.

21. Unto him [be] glory in the church by Christ Jesus: . . . through Christ, *Phillips.*
throughout all ages, world without end: . . . for all generations, age after age, *TCNT* . . . down through all the ages of time without end, *Confraternity* . . . to all the generations of eternal ages, *Alford* . . . from tyme to tyme, *Cranmer* . . . for ever and ever, *Phillips.*
Amen:

1. I therefore, the prisoner of the Lord, beseech you: I urge you, then, *TCNT* . . . I summon you then, *Montgomery* . . . therefore plead with you, *Norlie* . . . entreat you, *Williams* . . . I am in prison because I belong to the Lord, *Everyday.*
that ye walk worthy of the vocation wherewith ye are called: . . . live lives...of your high calling, *Phillips.*

2. With all lowliness: Accept life with, *Phillips* . . . vvith al humilitie, *Rheims* . . . with perfect humility, *Williams* . . . lowliness of mind, *Rotherham.*
and meekness: . . . and mildenes, *Rheims* . . . and gentleness, *Montgomery.*
with longsuffering, forbearing one another in love: . . . sustaining each other in Love, *Wilson* . . . put up with one another in love, *Norlie* . . . making allowances for one another, *Phillips.*

3. Endeavouring to keep: Make it your aim, *Phillips* . . . to preserve, *Montgomery.*
the unity of the Spirit in the bond of peace: . . . to be at one in the Spirit, *Phillips.*

2504.1 conj	1518.9 num card neu	4011.1 noun sing neu	2503.1 conj	2504.1 conj	2535.38 verb 2pl indic aor pass	1706.1 prep
καὶ	ἓν	πνεῦμα,	καθὼς	καὶ	ἐκλήθητε	ἐν
kai	hen	pneuma	kathōs	kai	eklēthēte	en
and	one	Spirit,	even as	also	you were called	in

1518.7 num card dat fem	1667.3 noun dat sing fem	3450.10 art gen sing fem	2794.2 noun gen sing fem	5050.2 prs-pron gen 2pl	1518.3 num card nom masc
μιᾷ	ἐλπίδι	τῆς	κλήσεως	ὑμῶν·	5. εἷς
mia	elpidi	tēs	klēseōs	humōn	heis
one	hope	of the	calling	your;	one

2935.1 noun nom sing masc	1518.5 num card nom fem	3963.1 noun nom sing fem	1518.9 num card neu	902.1 noun sing neu	1518.3 num card nom masc
κύριος,	μία	πίστις,	ἓν	βάπτισμα·	6. εἷς
kurios	mia	pistis	hen	baptisma	heis
Lord,	one	faith,	one	baptism;	one

2296.1 noun nom sing masc	2504.1 conj	3824.1 noun nom sing masc	3820.4 adj gen pl	3450.5 art nom sing masc	1894.3 prep	3820.4 adj gen pl
θεὸς	καὶ	πατὴρ	πάντων,	ὁ	ἐπὶ	πάντων,
theos	kai	patēr	pantōn	ho	epi	pantōn
God	and	Father	of all,	the	over	all,

2504.1 conj	1217.2 prep	3820.4 adj gen pl	2504.1 conj	1706.1 prep	3820.5 adj dat pl	5050.3 prs-pron dat 2pl
καὶ	διὰ	πάντων,	καὶ	ἐν	πᾶσιν	(a ὑμῖν.)
kai	dia	pantōn	kai	en	pasin	humin
and	through	all,	and	in	all	you.

1518.2 num card dat	1156.2 conj	1524.4 adj dat sing masc	2231.2 prs-pron gen 1pl	1319.44 verb 3sing indic aor pass	3450.9 art nom sing fem
7. Ἑνὶ	δὲ	ἑκάστῳ	ἡμῶν	ἐδόθη	(a ἡ)
Heni	de	hekastō	hēmōn	edothē	hē
To one	but	each	of us	was given	the

5322.1 noun nom sing fem	2567.3 prep	3450.16 art sing neu	3228.3 noun sing neu	3450.10 art gen sing fem	1424.2 noun gen sing fem
χάρις	κατὰ	τὸ	μέτρον	τῆς	δωρεᾶς
charis	kata	to	metron	tēs	dōreas
grace	according to	the	measure	of the	gift

3450.2 art gen sing	5382.2 name gen masc	1346.1 conj	2978.5 verb 3sing indic pres act	303.17 verb nom sing masc part aor act
τοῦ	Χριστοῦ.	8. διὸ	λέγει,	Ἀναβὰς
tou	Christou	dio	legei	Anabas
of the	Christ.	Wherefore	he says,	Having ascended up

1519.1 prep	5149.1 noun sing neu	160.2 verb 3sing indic aor act	159.1 noun acc sing fem	2504.1 conj
εἰς	ὕψος	ᾐχμαλώτευσεν	αἰχμαλωσίαν,	(a καὶ)
eis	hupsos	ēchmalōteusen	aichmalōsian	kai
on	high	he led captive	captivity,	and

1319.14 verb 3sing indic aor act	1384.2 noun pl neu	3450.4 art dat pl	442.8 noun dat pl masc	3450.16 art sing neu	1156.2 conj
ἔδωκεν	δόματα	τοῖς	ἀνθρώποις.	9. Τὸ	δὲ
edōken	domata	tois	anthrōpois	To	de
gave	gifts	to the	men.	The	but

303.13 verb 3sing indic aor act	4949.9 intr-pron sing neu	1498.4 verb 3sing indic pres act	1479.1 conj	3231.1 partic	3617.1 conj	2504.1 conj
Ἀνέβη,	τί	ἐστιν	εἰ	μὴ	ὅτι	καὶ
Anebē	ti	estin	ei	mē	hoti	kai
he ascended,	what	is it	if	not	that	also

6.a.Txt: Steph
Var: 01א,02A,03B,04C 025P,33,bo.Lach,Treg Alf,Tisc,We/Ho,Weis Sod,UBS/☆

7.a.Txt: p46,01א,02A 04C,06D-corr3,08E 018K,025P-corr3,We/Ho byz.
Var: 03B,06D-org,010F 012G,020L,025P-org,1 209-org

8.a.Txt: 01א-corr,03B 04C-org,06D-corr,018K 020L,025P,byz.We/Ho Sod
Var: p46,01א-org,02A 04C-corr,06D-org,33,it. sa.bo.Lach,Word,Tisc Weis,UBS/☆

4:4. The apostle then gave the perfect example of unity—that which is exhibited among the members of the Trinity. They never disagree. Verse 4 describes the work of the Holy Spirit. There is one Body, and the Holy Spirit is the One who makes us members of it. As a result, we share "one hope," an expectant attitude concerning the second coming of Christ and all the benefits related to it.

4:5. Verse 5 reminds us that there is only one Lord. When Paul wrote these words, nearly every cult of mystery religion had its own lord. However, the New Testament has only one Head, the Lord Jesus Christ, and He is the only means of access into His church.

The term "faith" is used several different ways in the Scriptures. Sometimes it relates to the subjective placing of confidence in God; sometimes it refers to the body of doctrine that believers accept; sometimes it refers to a means of access. The last is the use in this context.

The statement concerning "one baptism" does not deny the reality of other types of baptism (in water, in the Holy Spirit, in suffering) but refers to the one baptism without which the others would not be possible—the baptism into the body of Christ (1 Corinthians 12:13).

4:6. The Father is described as the One who originated all that verses 4 and 5 describe. The Father is sovereign ("above all"), the sustainer ("through all"), and the One who gives the energy for all that happens ("in . . . all").

4:7. Suddenly Paul moved from discussing the Church as a whole to the individuals comprising the Church in order to show that unity is not uniformity. In His work of developing unity among God's people the Holy Spirit does not obliterate their individuality. In fact, He uses their differences. Christ gives "unto every one of us" a function or ministry in His body, and these functions are diverse. It is inconsistent to say, "I am a Christian, but I do not have a ministry." Christ gives to every Christian a ministry.

4:8. In verse 8 Paul paraphrased Psalm 68:18 to show the qualifications of Christ to grant these "gifts" or ministries to His disciples. This psalm gives a description of what probably was a return of King David after a military conquest. At the same time it is a messianic psalm of victory describing the completed work of Christ in accomplishing the plan of salvation.

4:9. Three major possibilities exist about the meaning of this verse. A few commentators think these statements refer to the

4. [There is] one body, and one Spirit: You all belong to one body, *Phillips.*

even as ye are called i.. one hope of your calling: . . . as you all experienced one calling to one hope, *Phillips* . . . just as there is but one hope resulting from the call you have received, *Williams.*

5. One Lord, one faith, one baptism: One Immersion, *Wilson, Scarlett.*

6. One God and Father of all: who [is] above all, and through all, and in you all: . . . who is the one over all...and the one living in all, *Phillips* . . . works through all, *TCNT* . . . who pervades us all, *Williams.*

7. But unto every one of us is given grace: . . . individually grace is given to us in different ways, *Phillips* . . . to each one of us, *Wilson* . . . has been entrusted with some charge, *TCNT.*
according to the measure of the gift of Christ: . . . measured out as a gift from Christ, *Norlie* . . . donation of Christ, *Rheims.*

8. Wherefore he saith: Concerning this the Scripture says, *Williams.*
When he ascended up on high: he led captivity captive: . . . led a multitude of Captives, *Wilson* . . . He led a host of captives, *Williams.*
and gave gifts unto men: . . . gave gifts to mankind, *TCNT.*

9. (Now that he ascended: what is it but that he also descended first: . . . implies that he also descended, *Montgomery* . . . except that He had first gone down into the lower regions, *Williams.*

Ephesians 4:10

9.a.Txt: 01ℵ-corr,03B
04C-corr,018K,020L
025P,byz.Weis,Sod
Var: p46,01ℵ-org,02A
04C-org,06D,33,bo.
Gries,Lach,Treg,Alf
Word,Tisc,We/Ho
UBS/✶

9.b.Txt: 01ℵ,02A,03B
04C,06D-corr2,016I,044
byz.
Var: p46,06D-org,010F
012G

2568.14 verb 3sing indic aor act κατέβη katebē he descended	⌐a **4270.1** adv πρῶτον ⌐ prōton first	**1519.1** prep εἰς eis into	**3450.17** art pl neu τὰ ta the	**2707.1** adj comp pl neu κατώτερα katōtera lower	⌐b **3183.4** noun pl neu μέρη merē parts
3450.10 art gen sing fem τῆς tēs of the	**1087.2** noun gen sing fem γῆς; gēs earth?	**3450.5** art sing masc **10.** ὁ ho The	**2568.20** verb nom sing masc part aor act καταβὰς katabas having descended	**840.5** prs-pron nom sing masc αὐτός autos the same	**1498.4** verb 3sing indic pres act ἐστιν estin is
2504.1 conj καὶ kai also	**3450.5** art nom sing masc ὁ ho the	**303.17** verb nom sing masc part aor act ἀναβὰς anabas having ascended	**5068.1** prep ὑπεράνω huperanō above	**3820.4** adj gen pl πάντων pantōn all	**3450.1** art gen pl τῶν tōn the
3636.7 noun gen pl masc οὐρανῶν, ouranōn heavens,	**2419.1** conj ἵνα hina that	**3997.5** verb 3sing subj aor act πληρώσῃ plērōsē he might fill	**3450.17** art pl neu τὰ ta the	**3820.1** adj πάντα. panta all things;	**2504.1** conj **11.** καὶ kai and
840.5 prs-pron nom sing masc αὐτὸς autos he	**1319.14** verb 3sing indic aor act ἔδωκεν edōken gave	**3450.8** art acc pl masc τοὺς tous the	**3173.1** conj μὲν men men	**646.7** noun acc pl masc ἀποστόλους, apostolous apostles,	**3450.8** art acc pl masc τοὺς tous the
1156.2 conj δὲ de and	**4254.7** noun acc pl masc προφήτας, prophētas prophets,	**3450.8** art acc pl masc τοὺς tous the	**1156.2** conj δὲ de and	**2078.2** noun acc pl masc εὐαγγελιστάς, euangelistas evangelists,	**3450.8** art acc pl masc τοὺς tous the
1156.2 conj δὲ de and	**4026.5** noun acc pl masc ποιμένας poimenas shepherds	**2504.1** conj καὶ kai and	**1314.6** noun acc pl masc διδασκάλους, didaskalous teachers,	**4242.1** prep **12.** πρὸς pros to	**3450.6** art acc sing masc τὸν ton the
2647.1 noun acc sing masc καταρτισμὸν katartismon equipping	**3450.1** art gen pl τῶν tōn of the	**39.4** adj gen pl ἁγίων, hagiōn saints;	**1519.1** prep εἰς eis for	**2024.1** noun sing neu ἔργον ergon work	**1242.2** noun gen sing fem διακονίας, diakonias of service,
1519.1 prep εἰς eis for	**3482.3** noun acc sing fem οἰκοδομὴν oikodomēn building up	**3450.2** art gen sing τοῦ tou of the	**4835.2** noun gen sing neu σώματος sōmatos body	**3450.2** art gen sing τοῦ tou of the	**5382.2** name gen masc Χριστοῦ· Christou Christ;
3230.1 prep **13.** μέχρι mechri until	**2628.5** verb 1pl subj aor act καταντήσωμεν katantēsōmen we may arrive	**3450.7** art nom pl masc οἱ hoi the	**3820.7** adj nom pl masc πάντες pantes all	**1519.1** prep εἰς eis at	**3450.12** art acc sing fem τὴν tēn the
1759.1 noun acc sing fem ἑνότητα henotēta unity	**3450.10** art gen sing fem τῆς tēs of the	**3963.2** noun gen sing fem πίστεως pisteōs faith	**2504.1** conj καὶ kai and	**3450.10** art gen sing fem τῆς tēs of the	**1907.2** noun gen sing fem ἐπιγνώσεως epignōseōs knowledge

136

coming of the Holy Spirit on the Day of Pentecost (Acts 2), but this interpretation is not very plausible. Others believe they are a reference to the incarnation and subsequent ascension of Christ after He accomplished what He came to earth to do. Still others believe Jesus actually descended into Hades to proclaim that His work of redemption was complete.

4:10. While there may be disagreement concerning what Paul meant, it is clear that he was explaining Christ's right to give specific ministries to the Church. Here Paul used a word often found in his writings which usually is translated "fullness" (*plērōma*) but here is a verb that translates "might fill." This same word was used often by the Gnostics to refer to angelic beings they considered as intermediary beings between God and human beings. The apostle made it clear, however, that Christ is all in all. He is the One who fills the whole universe because He is omnipresent; angels are not.

4:11. Paul lists here various types of ministries. The apostolic ministry is carried on by leaders who take the gospel where it has not gone before. Sometimes missionaries have this type of ministry. The prophetic ministry is to forthtell (for the present) and sometimes foretell God's will and plans. Evangelists are individuals who constantly present the message of salvation through redemption accomplished at Calvary. Because the Greek text shows only one definite article (*tous*) before "pastors . . . teachers," the two words may be referring to the same office. However, because the definite article here is plural, Paul may have been writing of two different offices. The pastor is the individual leader who shepherds God's people, while the teacher systematizes and teaches sound doctrine to believers. Yet the pastor might easily have a teaching function, as he surely needs in our present time. This list is not in order of importance, but in order of necessity. Each ministry is important for the proper functioning of the Church.

4:12. The remainder of the passage through verse 16 describes clearly the two basic reasons why God places some people into full-time ministry. Christ has given every Christian a ministry, but not every Christian is a full-time minister in the sense of it being an occupation. First, these occupational ministers exist "for the perfecting of the saints" or to equip the saints so they in turn can minister for Christ. Some scholars believe the comma after the word "saints" does not belong there and stress that every believer has a ministry to fulfill. The word used here comes from *katartismos* and normally refers to furnishing something. The body of Christ will be built up as all Christians are involved in ministry.

4:13. Secondly, God has called full-time, occupational ministers to help believers mature in the Lord, or to become more and more

into the lower parts of the earth?: . . . into the inferiour partes, *Rheims* . . . to the under-regions of the earth? *Norlie* . . . to the depth of this world, *Phillips*.

10. He that descended is the same also that ascended up far above all heavens: . . . is identically the same person, *Phillips* . . . up beyond the highest Heaven, *TCNT*.
that he might fill all things.): . . . that he might fulfill, *Murdock* . . . that the whole universe from lowest to highest might know his presence, *Phillips* . . . to fill the whole universe with his presence, *TCNT*.

11. And he gave some, apostles; and some, prophets: He appointed some men, *Montgomery* . . . His "gifts unto men" were varied, *Phillips*.
and some, evangelists; and some, pastors and teachers: Missionaries, *TCNT* . . . preachers of the Gospel, *Phillips* . . . shepherds, *Panin, Wilson* . . . and doctors, *Douay*.

12. For the perfecting of the saints, for the work of the ministry: . . . in order to equip, *Montgomery* . . . to the consummation of the sainctes, *Rheims* . . . might have all thinges necessarie to worke, *Tyndale* . . . with a view to, *Clementson* . . . to the fitting of, *Rotherham* . . . for the complete qualification, *Wilson* . . . with a view to fitting his People, *TCNT* . . . for the immediate equipment of God's people, *Williams*.
for the edifying of the body of Christ: . . . for the building up of, *Worrell*.

13. Till we all come in the unity of the faith: Until we all meet into, *Douay* . . . until we all attain to that unity, *TCNT* . . . until we all advance into the oneness, *Rotherham*.

Ephesians 4:14

3450.2 art gen sing	5048.2 noun gen sing masc	3450.2 art gen sing	2296.2 noun gen sing masc	1519.1 prep	433.4 noun acc sing masc
τοῦ	υἱοῦ	τοῦ	θεοῦ,	εἰς	ἄνδρα
tou	huiou	tou	theou	eis	andra
of the	Son	of the	of God,	at	a man

4894.1 adj sing neu	1519.1 prep	3228.3 noun sing neu	2227.1 noun gen sing fem	3450.2 art gen sing	3998.2 noun gen sing neu
τέλειον,	εἰς	μέτρον	ἡλικίας	τοῦ	πληρώματος
teleion	eis	metron	hēlikias	tou	plērōmatos
complete,	at	measure	of stature	of the	fullness

3450.2 art gen sing	5382.2 name gen masc	2419.1 conj	3239.1 adv	1498.11 verb 1pl subj pres act	3378.3 adj nom pl masc
τοῦ	Χριστοῦ·	**14.** ἵνα	μηκέτι	ὦμεν	νήπιοι,
tou	Christou	hina	mēketi	ōmen	nēpioi
of the	Christ;	that	no longer	we may be	infants,

2804.1 verb nom pl masc part pres mid	2504.1 conj	3924.4 verb nom pl masc part pres mid	3820.3 adj dat sing	415.3 noun dat sing masc
κλυδωνιζόμενοι	καὶ	περιφερόμενοι	παντὶ	ἀνέμῳ
kludōnizomenoi	kai	peripheromenoi	panti	anemō
being tossed	and	being carried about	by every	wind

3450.10 art gen sing fem	1313.1 noun fem	1706.1 prep	3450.11 art dat sing fem	2912.1 noun dat sing fem	3450.1 art gen pl
τῆς	διδασκαλίας	ἐν	τῇ	κυβείᾳ	τῶν
tēs	didaskalias	en	tē	kubeia	tōn
of the	teaching	in	the	trickery	of the

442.7 noun gen pl masc	1706.1 prep	3696.1 noun dat sing fem	4242.1 prep	3450.12 art acc sing fem	3151.1 noun acc sing fem
ἀνθρώπων,	ἐν	πανουργίᾳ	πρὸς	τὴν	μεθοδείαν
anthrōpōn	en	panourgia	pros	tēn	methodeian
men,	in	craftiness	to	the	systematizing

3450.10 art gen sing fem	3967.2 noun gen sing fem	224.2 verb nom pl masc part pres act	1156.2 conj	1706.1 prep	26.3 noun dat sing fem
τῆς	πλάνης·	**15.** ἀληθεύοντες	δὲ	ἐν	ἀγάπῃ
tēs	planēs	alētheuontes	de	en	agapē
of the	error;	holding the truth	but	in	love

831.8 verb 1pl subj aor act	1519.1 prep	840.6 prs-pron acc sing masc	3450.17 art pl neu	3820.1 adj	3614.5 rel-pron nom sing masc
αὐξήσωμεν	εἰς	αὐτὸν	τὰ	πάντα,	ὅς
auxēsōmen	eis	auton	ta	panta,	hos
we may grow up	into	him	the	all things,	who

1498.4 verb 3sing indic pres act	3450.9 art nom sing fem	2747.1 noun nom sing fem	3450.5 art nom sing masc	5382.1 name nom masc	1523.1 prep gen
ἐστιν	ἡ	κεφαλή,	⟨a ὁ ⟩	Χριστός,	**16.** ἐξ
estin	hē	kephalē	ho	Christos	ex
is	the	head,	the	Christ:	from

3614.2 rel-pron gen sing	3820.17 adj sing neu	3450.16 art sing neu	4835.1 noun sing neu	4734.2 verb sing neu part pres mid
οὗ	πᾶν	τὸ	σῶμα	συναρμολογούμενον
hou	pan	to	sōma	sunarmologoumenon
whom	all	the	body,	being fitted together

2504.1 conj	4673.4 verb sing neu part pres mid	1217.2 prep	3820.10 adj gen sing fem	853.1 noun gen sing fem	3450.10 art gen sing fem
καὶ	συμβιβαζόμενον	διὰ	πάσης	ἁφῆς	τῆς
kai	sumbibazomenon	dia	pasēs	haphēs	tēs
and	being joined together	by	every	joint	of the

15.a.**Txt:** 01ℵ-corr,06D
018K,020L,025P,byz.
Var: 01ℵ-org,02A,03B
04C,33,Lach,Treg,Alf
Word,Tisc,We/Ho,Weis
Sod,UBS/☆

like Christ himself. As believers mature they will advance from the infancy state into full-grown adults. Some theologians enjoy emphasizing the similarities between natural birth and spiritual birth and natural growth and spiritual growth. They fail sometimes, however, to describe the differences between them. For example, in natural birth a person has no choice as to which family he will be part of in life. In spiritual birth an individual does make a choice to become part of the family of God. In natural life growth is nearly automatic, unless something is wrong organically with the child. However, spiritual growth is never automatic.

4:14. Instability is one definite sign of immaturity. Paul himself upbraided some Corinthians who were still "babes in Christ" after apparently being Christians for about 5 years (1 Corinthians 3:1-4). The writer of Hebrews dealt with the same basic problem in his letter (Hebrews 5:11 to 6:12).

"Cunning" comes from an interesting Greek word (*kubeia*, "cube") which was used literally of dice throwing. A clever trickster actually could hold two sets of dice in his hand and throw whichever set he desired. Tricksters who use crafty methods appeal to immature Christians who do not grow spiritually. These "babes in Christ" seem always to be looking for something a little more sensational than the last thing that appealed to them. Unfortunately, these individuals help many religious hucksters to build their own kingdom, rather than concentrating on building God's kingdom.

4:15. Instead of falling for trickery Christians should be obedient to Christ. Obedience to Christ and the ability to recognize religious charlatans are definite signs of Christian maturity. Christ is the source from which the ability to grow comes, and He is the object or goal of that growth. Immature Christians have a tendency to overly revere Christian leaders. Obviously, leaders should be respected. Sometimes, however, respect can turn into worship. Paul dealt with this tendency to exalt leaders when he wrote his first letter to the Corinthians (1 Corinthians 1:10-17). While Christian leaders do help us grow spiritually, we need to keep our concentration on Christ, the perfect example.

4:16. In addition to the fact that a mature Christian will be stable and obedient, the last verse of the section shows this will result in a coordinated "body" with each member fulfilling his function. Just as the human body grows as a total organism with each part being involved, so the body of Christ grows as believers allow Christ His rightful place and as they do their part in the total process.

Unfortunately, many modern congregations have adopted the unscriptural philosophy of "hiring" a pastor to perform all the ministry for the congregation. These congregations can grow only

and of the knowledge of the Son of God: . . . and common knowledge of, *Phillips*.

unto a perfect man, unto the measure of the stature of the fulness of Christ: . . . we arrive at real maturity—that measure of development which is meant by, *Phillips* . . . a full grown Man, *Wilson*.

14. That we [henceforth] be no more children: We are not to remain as, *Phillips* . . . that we may no longer be, *Noyes* . . . be Infants no longer, *Wilson*.

tossed to and fro, and carried about with every wind of doctrine: . . . billow-tossed and shifted round, *Rotherham* . . . fluctuating to and fro, *Wesley* . . . and whirled about, *Scarlett* . . . backward and forward and blown about by every breath of human teaching, *TCNT* . . . not borun aboute with eche wynde of techynge, *Wyclif* . . . wind of teaching, *Panin*.

by the sleight of men, [and] cunning craftiness, whereby they lie in wait to deceive: . . . devised in the wickedness...according to the wiles of error, *Confraternity* . . . in the weywardnesse of men, *Wyclif* . . . by the wickedness of men, *Douay* . . . through the dishonest tricks of men, and their cunning in the wily arts of error, *Noyes* . . . which is in the trickery of men...in systematic deception, *Wilson* . . . that leadeth to the system of error, *Alford*.

15. But speaking the truth in love: But being followers of truth, *Alford* . . . to hold firmly to the truth, *Phillips*.

may grow up into him in all things, which is the head, [even] Christ: . . . we shall grow into complete union, *TCNT* . . . to grow up in every way, *Phillips*.

16. From whom the whole body fitly joined together and compacted by that which every joint supplieth: . . . and united, *Wilson* . . . yf all the body be coupled and knet, *Cranmer* . . . a harmonious structure knit together by the joints, *Phillips*.

Ephesians 4:17

2008.1 noun gen sing fem	2567.1 prep	1737.2 noun acc sing fem	1706.1 prep	3228.2 noun dat sing neu	1518.1 num card gen
ἐπιχορηγίας	κατ᾿	ἐνέργειαν	ἐν	μέτρῳ	ἑνὸς
epichorēgias	kat'	energeian	en	metrō	henos
supply	according to	working	in	measure	of each

1524.2 adj gen sing	3183.2 noun gen sing neu	3450.12 art acc sing fem	832.1 noun acc sing fem	3450.2 art gen sing	4835.2 noun gen sing neu
ἑκάστου	μέρους,	τὴν	αὔξησιν	τοῦ	σώματος
hekastou	merous,	tēn	auxēsin	tou	sōmatos
one	part,	the	increase	of the	body

4020.61 verb 3sing indic pres mid	1519.1 prep	3482.3 noun acc sing fem	1431.4 prs-pron gen sing	1706.1 prep	26.3 noun dat sing fem
ποιεῖται	εἰς	οἰκοδομὴν	ἑαυτοῦ	ἐν	ἀγάπῃ.
poieitai	eis	oikodomēn	heautou	en	agapē
makes for itself	to	building up	of itself	in	love.

3642.17 dem-pron sing neu	3631.1 partic	2978.1 verb 1sing pres act	2504.1 conj	3113.31 verb 1sing indic pres mid	1706.1 prep
17. Τοῦτο	οὖν	λέγω	καὶ	μαρτύρομαι	ἐν
Touto	oun	legō	kai	marturomai	en
This	therefore	I say,	and	testify	in

2935.3 noun dat sing masc	3239.1 adv	5050.4 prs-pron acc 2pl	3906.17 verb inf pres act	2503.1 conj	2504.1 conj	3450.17 art pl neu
κυρίῳ,	μηκέτι	ὑμᾶς	περιπατεῖν	καθὼς	καὶ	τὰ
kuriō,	mēketi	humas	peripatein	kathōs	kai	ta
Lord,	no longer	you	to walk	even as	also	the

3036.9 adj pl neu	1477.4 noun pl neu	3906.4 verb 3sing indic pres act	1706.1 prep	3125.2 noun dat sing fem	3450.2 art gen sing
⸃ λοιπὰ ⸃	ἔθνη	περιπατεῖ	ἐν	ματαιότητι	τοῦ
loipa	ethnē	peripatei	en	mataiotēti	tou
rest,	Gentiles,	are walking	in	vanity	of the

3426.2 noun gen sing masc	840.1 prs-pron gen pl		4509.4 verb nom pl masc part perf mid		4511.3 verb nom pl masc part perf mid
νοὸς	αὐτῶν,	**18.** ⸃	ἐσκοτισμένοι	[ᵃ✰	ἐσκοτωμένοι]
noos	autōn,		eskotismenoi		eskotōmenoi
mind	their,		having been darkened		[idem]

3450.11 art dat sing fem	1265.2 noun dat sing fem	1498.23 verb nom pl masc part pres act		522.1 verb nom pl masc part perf mid	
τῇ	διανοίᾳ,	ὄντες		ἀπηλλοτριωμένοι	
tē	dianoia,	ontes		apēllotriōmenoi	
in the	understanding,	being		having been alienated from	

3450.10 art gen sing fem	2205.2 noun gen sing fem	3450.2 art gen sing	2296.2 noun gen sing masc	1217.2 prep	3450.12 art acc sing fem
τῆς	ζωῆς	τοῦ	θεοῦ,	διὰ	τὴν
tēs	zōēs	tou	theou,	dia	tēn
the	life	of the	of God,	on account of	the

51.3 noun acc sing fem	3450.12 art acc sing fem	1498.29 verb acc sing fem part pres act	1706.1 prep	840.2 prs-pron dat pl	1217.2 prep
ἄγνοιαν	τὴν	οὖσαν	ἐν	αὐτοῖς,	διὰ
agnoian	tēn	ousan	en	autois,	dia
ignorance	the	being	in	them,	on account of

3450.12 art acc sing fem	4314.3 noun acc sing fem	3450.10 art gen sing fem	2559.1 noun fem	840.1 prs-pron gen pl	3610.2 rel-pron nom pl masc
τὴν	πώρωσιν	τῆς	καρδίας	αὐτῶν·	**19.** οἵτινες
tēn	pōrōsin	tēs	kardias	autōn	hoitines
the	hardness	of the	heart	their,	who

to a certain point because one person can accomplish only so much. How refreshing it is, though, to see a local assembly where most of the members are involved in some kind of ministry. That church will be a growing assembly, meeting the needs of people in the area and reaching the lost for Christ.

Believers need to be taught that full-time ministers are placed in the Church by Christ to help equip the saints so they in turn can minister and help others mature in the Lord. Even the first New Testament apostles were concerned about being able to give themselves to prayer and the ministry of the Word (Acts 6:4). A careful study of Acts chapter 6 will show that the apostles considered themselves "in the service of the Word" or "the deacon of the Word" (*tē diakonia tou logou*). The first obligation of occupational ministers must be to pray and to expound God's Word.

4:17. There is a long-standing debate about what happens to the fallen, sinful nature of a person who becomes a Christian. For example, some individuals think it is completely eradicated at conversion. Others take a "group encounter" approach in which through a "self-discovery" or "catharsis" method they attempt to bring the sinful nature under control. The Bible clearly expresses the fact that God does not remove the sinful nature at salvation, but its power is broken so a Christian need no longer be governed by it, though he still must grapple with it. Instead of removing the Adamic nature when a person becomes a believer, God places a new nature within the person, the indwelling Holy Spirit (Romans 8:9). Romans, chapter 7, Galatians 2:20; 5:13-26; Colossians 3:1-17, as well as many other passages, describe the constant internal warfare within the Christian between the "new nature of Christ" and the Adamic nature. Ephesians 4:17-32 is one of these passages.

Paul approached the matter by first explaining the negative aspect of the process and further showing how God broke the power of the sinful nature at the person's conversion. The apostle first encouraged the Gentile believers not to live as they had before their conversion to Christ. They formerly lived "in the vanity of their mind," the way pagans were living. They had lived in the sphere of the emptiness of their minds, denoting an ignorance of divine things, a lack of knowledge that involved moral blindness.

4:18. They were ignorant because they had hardened their hearts against God. The "blindness of their heart" or hardening of their hearts led to a condition of callousness that made it impossible for them to experience true spiritual life that comes only from God. The apostle made these Gentiles personally responsible for what had happened to them. He certainly did not teach some fatalistic kind of approach that they had no responsibility for their actions. While Paul definitely believed in the sovereignty of God and constantly emphasized His grace, he balanced that view by stressing man's freedom of choice and the necessity for exercising faith.

according to the effectual working in the measure of every part, maketh increase of the body unto the edifying of itself in love: . . . gets each part to work properly, develops each part accordingly, *Norlie* . . . to the proportionate Energy of Each single Part, *Wilson* . . . according to the functioning in due measure of each single part, *Confraternity* . . . in proportion to the activity of each individual part, *TCNT* . . . makes continual growth, *Montgomery* . . . for its building up in love, *Williams.*

17. This I say therefore, and testify in the Lord: This is my instruction, then, which I give you from God, *Phillips* . . . and attesting in, *Rotherham* . . . and give witness, *BB.*

that ye henceforth walk not as other Gentiles walk, in the vanity of their mind: Do not live any longer as, *Phillips* . . . that you are to go no longer in the way of the Gentiles, *BB* . . . that you no longer walk, *Wilson* . . . as the heathen usually do, in the frivolity of, *Williams* . . . in the perverseness, *Montgomery* . . . in aimlessness of, *Rotherham.*

18. Having the understanding darkened: . . . they live blindfold in a world of illusion, *Phillips* . . . their cogitation darkened, *Geneva* . . . their vnderstanding obscured, *Rheims.*

being alienated from the life of God: . . . they are cut off from the Life of God, *TCNT* . . . beynge farre from a godly lyfe, *Cranmer* . . . estranged from the life of God, *Williams* . . . the life of God is strange, *BB.*

through the ignorance that is in them: . . . of the stupidity, *Wilson* . . . that exists among them, *Williams.*

because of the blindness of their heart: . . . because of the hardening, *Clementson, Montgomery* . . . because of the stubbornness of their hearts, *Williams* . . . and insensitiveness, *Phillips.*

141

520.1 verb nom pl
masc part perf act
ἀπηλγηκότες
apēlgēkotes
having cast off all feeling,

1431.8 prs-
pron acc pl masc
ἑαυτοὺς
heautous
themselves

3722.14 verb 3pl
indic aor act
παρέδωκαν
paredōkan
gave up

3450.11 art
dat sing fem
τῇ
tē
to the

760.2 noun
dat sing fem
ἀσελγείᾳ
aselgeia
licentiousness,

1519.1
prep
εἰς
eis
for

2022.2 noun
acc sing fem
ἐργασίαν
ergasian
working

165.2 noun
gen sing fem
ἀκαθαρσίας
akatharsias
of uncleanness

3820.10 adj
gen sing fem
πάσης
pasēs
all

1706.1
prep
ἐν
en
with

3984.3 noun
dat sing fem
πλεονεξίᾳ·
pleonexia
craving.

5050.1 prs-
pron nom 2pl
20. ὑμεῖς
humeis
You

1156.2
conj
δὲ
de
but

3620.1
partic
οὐχ
ouch
not

3643.1
adv
οὕτως
houtōs
thus

3101.9 verb 2pl
indic aor act
ἐμάθετε
emathete
learned

3450.6 art
acc sing masc
τὸν
ton
the

5382.4 name
acc masc
Χριστόν,
Christon
Christ,

1480.1
conj
21. ⸂ εἴγε
eige
if indeed

1479.1
conj
[✱ εἴ
ei
[if

1058.1
partic
γε]
ge
indeed]

840.6 prs-pron
acc sing masc
αὐτὸν
auton
him

189.23 verb 2pl
indic aor act
ἠκούσατε
ēkousate
you heard

2504.1
conj
καὶ
kai
and

1706.1
prep
ἐν
en
in

840.4 prs-
pron dat sing
αὐτῷ
autō
him

1315.23 verb 2pl
indic aor pass
ἐδιδάχθητε,
edidachthēte
were taught,

2503.1
conj
καθὼς
kathōs
according as

1498.4 verb 3sing
indic pres act
ἐστιν
estin
is

223.1 noun
nom sing fem
ἀλήθεια
alētheia
truth

1706.1
prep
ἐν
en
in

3450.3 art
dat sing
τῷ
tō

2400.2
name masc
Ἰησοῦ·
Iēsou
Jesus;

653.5 verb
inf aor mid
22. ἀποθέσθαι
apothesthai
to have put off

5050.4 prs-
pron acc 2pl
ὑμᾶς
humas
you

2567.3
prep
κατὰ
kata
according to

3450.12 art
acc sing fem
τὴν
tēn
the

4245.1 adj comp
acc sing fem
προτέραν
proteran
former

389.3 noun
acc sing fem
ἀναστροφὴν
anastrophēn
conduct

3450.6 art
acc sing masc
τὸν
ton
the

3683.1
adj sing
παλαιὸν
palaion
old

442.4 noun
acc sing masc
ἄνθρωπον,
anthrōpon
man,

3450.6 art
acc sing masc
τὸν
ton
the

5188.7 verb acc sing
masc part pres mid
φθειρόμενον
phtheiromenon
being corrupt

2567.3
prep
κατὰ
kata
according to

3450.15 art
acc pl fem
τὰς
tas
the

1924.1
noun fem
ἐπιθυμίας
epithumias
desires

3450.10 art
gen sing fem
τῆς
tēs
of the

535.2 noun
gen sing fem
ἀπάτης·
apatēs
deceit;

364.1 verb
inf pres mid
23. ἀνανεοῦσθαι
ananeousthai
to be renewed

1156.2
conj
δὲ
de
and

3450.3 art
dat sing
τῷ
tō
in the

4011.3 noun
dat sing neu
πνεύματι
pneumati
spirit

3450.2 art
gen sing
τοῦ
tou
of the

3426.2 noun
gen sing masc
νοὸς
noos
mind

5050.2 prs-
pron gen 2pl
ὑμῶν·
humōn
your;

2504.1
conj
24. καὶ
kai
and

1730.11 verb
inf aor mid
⸂✱ ἐνδύσασθαι
endusasthai
to have put on

4:19. This hardening of their hearts led to a condition of "being past feeling." This latter term relates to losing all sensitivity to pain. This calloused condition prevented them from experiencing any moral consciousness. Just as thick callouses prevent people from feeling physical pain, willful rebellion against the work of the conscience eventually makes the conscience completely ineffective.

The description of a constant falling more deeply into sin is reminiscent of Romans 1:18-32 where Paul again characterized the Gentile world away from God. A careful search of that passage, especially verse 20, will show the same general emphasis on human responsibility, so it is impossible for a person to justify his lost condition.

"Lasciviousness" refers to "sensuality" which leads to all types of impurity or uncleanness that goes deeper and deeper into sin because it never is satisfied. In Romans chapter 1 the apostle Paul also dealt with the subject of homosexuality that is described here in verse 19. Three times he said that God gave them over to something. First, "God gave them over in the sinful desires of their hearts to sexual impurity for the degrading of their bodies with one another" (Romans 1:24, NIV). Secondly, "God gave them over to shameful lusts" (Romans 1:26, NIV). Thirdly, "He gave them over to a depraved mind, to do what ought not to be done" (Romans 1:28, NIV).

4:20,21. This verse begins with a very important "But." Because God had performed a miracle in the Ephesians, they no longer existed in this state of ignorance and separation from God. He said, "Ye have not so learned Christ."

Paul could write these words with assurance because he and the members of his evangelistic team had much to do with teaching the Ephesian Christians what they knew about Christ.

4:22. Even though the legal work of salvation had taken place in these lives, it was necessary for them to discard completely the old way of life. This passage contains one of the great paradoxes of Scripture because, after explaining the legal work of salvation God had performed in their lives, Paul went on to appeal for an experiential casting off of sin. The same verb appears in Colossians 3:8 with the same basic idea of putting off a former way of life. A person does this by denying the cravings of the sinful nature (Romans 6:13; Galatians 2:20; 5:13).

4:23. Now we come to the positive aspect of the process. Because the Christian life is not a void, people need to "be renewed." This phrase comes from a present passive infinitive (*ananeousthai*). It is present because it is a continuous process. It is passive because God accomplishes the work only as believers yield to the Holy Spirit. It takes place "in the spirit of your mind," a probable reference to the fact that the will is involved in causing the process to continue.

19. Who being past feeling have given themselves over unto lasciviousness: For lost to all sense of shame, *TCNT* . . . They have stifled their consciences and then surrendered themselves, *Phillips* . . . who being without feeling have given themselves up to lewdness, *Sawyer* . . . They have become callous, have abandoned themselves to sensuality, *Norlie.*

to work all uncleanness with greediness: . . . and greedily practice any form of vice that lust can crave, *Norlie* . . . practicing any form of impurity which lust can suggest, *Phillips* . . . with covetousness, *Panin* . . . unto covetousness, *Douay.*

20. But ye have not so learned Christ: . . . you have learned nothing like that, *Phillips.*

21. If so be that ye have heard him, and have been taught by him: . . . you really listened to him, *TCNT* . . . if you have really heard his voice and . . . that he has taught you, *Phillips.*

as the truth is in Jesus: . . . understood the truth, *Phillips.*

22. That ye put off concerning the former conversation the old man: . . . you should lay aside your former mode of life, *Sawyer* . . . respecting your former conduct, *Scarlett* . . . the former Course of life, *Wilson* . . . and your former habits, *Norlie.*

which is corrupt according to the deceitful lusts: . . . who perisheth, *Noyes* . . . owing to the passions fostered by Error, *TCNT* . . . according to the desire of error, *Douay.*

23. And be renewed in the spirit of your mind: . . . undergo a mental and spiritual transformation, *TCNT* . . . in the spirit of youre soule, *Wyclif* . . . must be renewed continually, *Norlie.*

Ephesians 4:25

24.a.Txt: p49-vid,02A
06D-org,010F,012G,044
byz.
Var: p46,01א,03B-org
06D-corr2,018K,104
323,1881

1730.8 verb 2pl impr aor mid	**3450.6** art acc sing masc	**2508.1** adj sing	**442.4** noun acc sing masc	**3450.6** art acc sing masc
[ᵃ ἐνδύσασθε]	τὸν	καινὸν	ἄνθρωπον,	τὸν
endusasthe	*ton*	*kainon*	*anthrōpon*	*ton*
[put on]	the	new	man,	the

2567.3 prep	**2296.4** noun acc sing masc	**2908.9** verb acc sing masc part aor pass	**1706.1** prep	**1336.3** noun dat sing fem
κατὰ	θεὸν	κτισθέντα	ἐν	δικαιοσύνῃ
kata	*theon*	*ktisthenta*	*en*	*dikaiosunē*
according to	God	having been created	in	righteousness

2504.1 conj	**3604.1** noun dat sing fem	**3450.10** art gen sing fem	**223.2** noun gen sing fem	**1346.1** conj	**653.4** verb nom pl masc part aor mid
καὶ	ὁσιότητι	τῆς	ἀληθείας.	**25.** Διὸ	ἀποθέμενοι
kai	*hosiotēti*	*tēs*	*alētheias*	*Dio*	*apothemenoi*
and	holiness	of the	truth.	Wherefore	having put off

3450.16 art sing neu	**5414.1** noun sing neu	**2953.10** verb 2pl impr pres act	**223.4** noun acc sing fem	**1524.3** adj nom sing masc	**3196.3** prep
τὸ	ψεῦδος,	λαλεῖτε	ἀλήθειαν	ἕκαστος	μετὰ
to	*pseudos*	*laleite*	*alētheian*	*hekastos*	*meta*
the	falsehood,	speak	truth	each	with

3450.2 art gen sing	**3999.1** adv	**840.3** prs-pron gen sing	**3617.1** conj	**1498.5** verb 1pl indic pres act	**238.1** prs-pron gen pl
τοῦ	πλησίον	αὐτοῦ·	ὅτι	ἐσμὲν	ἀλλήλων
tou	*plēsion*	*autou*	*hoti*	*esmen*	*allēlōn*
the	neighbor	his,	because	we are	of one another

3166.2 noun pl neu	**3573.1** verb 2pl impr pres mid	**2504.1** conj	**3231.1** partic	**262.1** verb 2pl pres act	**3450.5** art nom sing masc
μέλη.	**26.** Ὀργίζεσθε	καὶ	μὴ	ἁμαρτάνετε·	ὁ
melē	*Orgizesthe*	*kai*	*mē*	*hamartanete*	*ho*
members.	Be angry,	and	not	sin;	the

26.a.Txt: 01א-corr,06D
018K,020L,025P,etc.byz.
Sod
Var: 01א-org,02A,03B
Lach,Treg,Tisc,We/Ho
Weis,UBS/★

2229.1 noun nom sing masc	**3231.1** partic	**1916.1** verb 3sing impr pres act	**1894.3** prep	**3450.3** art dat sing	**3812.1** noun dat sing masc
ἥλιος	μὴ	ἐπιδυέτω	ἐπὶ	⌐ᵃ τῷ ⌐	παροργισμῷ
hēlios	*mē*	*epiduetō*	*epi*	*tō*	*parorgismō*
sun	not	let set	upon	the	provocation

27.a.Txt: Steph
Var: 01א,02A,03B,06D
018K,020L,025P,byz.
Lach,Treg,Alf,Word
Tisc,We/Ho,Weis,Sod
UBS/★

5050.2 prs-pron gen 2pl	**3250.1** conj	**3234.1** adv	**1319.4** verb 2pl impr pres act	**4964.4** noun acc sing masc	**3450.3** art dat sing
ὑμῶν,	**27.** ⌐ μήτε	[ᵃ★ μηδὲ]	δίδοτε	τόπον	τῷ
humōn	*mēte*	*mēde*	*didote*	*topon*	*tō*
your,	neither	[idem]	give	place	to the

1222.3 adj dat sing masc	**3450.5** art nom sing masc	**2786.4** verb nom sing masc part pres act	**3239.1** adv	**2786.3** verb 3sing impr pres act	
διαβόλῳ.	**28.** ὁ	κλέπτων	μηκέτι	κλεπτέτω,	
diabolō	*ho*	*kleptōn*	*mēketi*	*kleptetō*	
devil.	The	stealing	no more	let him steal,	

3095.1 adv comp	**1156.2** conj	**2844.4** verb 3sing impr pres act	**2021.8** verb nom sing masc part pres mid	**3450.16** art sing neu	**18.3** adj sing
μᾶλλον	δὲ	κοπιάτω,	ἐργαζόμενος	⌐ τὸ	ἀγαθόν
mallon	*de*	*kopiatō*	*ergazomenos*	*to*	*agathon*
rather	but	let him labor,	working	to	good

28.a.Txt: 020L,044,byz.
Var: 01א-org,02A,06D
Lach,Treg,Word,Tisc
Weis,Sod,UBS/★

3450.14 art dat pl fem	**5331.7** noun dat pl fem	**3450.14** art dat pl fem	**2375.12** adj dat pl fem	**5331.7** noun dat pl fem	**3450.16** art sing neu
ταῖς	χερσὶν,	[ᵃ★ ταῖς	ἰδίαις	χερσὶν	τὸ
tais	*chersin*	*tais*	*idiais*	*chersin*	*to*
with the	hands,	[with the	his own	hands	to the

4:24. At the same time Christians must also "put on the new man," a reference to allowing the Holy Spirit to be the controlling force in their lives. If they are doing this it will manifest itself in "righteousness and true holiness." The Greek word for "new" (*kainos*) here refers to newness in quality. God is not only the pattern but also the author of this new life.

4:25. The fruit that comes from a person's life—his actions—proves whether the person is yielding to the sinful nature or to the Holy Spirit. To illustrate his point Paul used four representative examples of problems that were very important in his day and still are today. Verse 25 deals with lying, an obvious manifestation of the fallen nature. By way of contrast, Paul encouraged Christians to "speak every man truth with his neighbor," because they are members of the same Body.

4:26. In the second example there is also a negative and a positive. This admonition relates to the improper use of anger which results from yielding to the Adamic nature, and the proper use of anger which results from yielding to the Holy Spirit. "Be ye angry, and sin not" comes from the imperative verbs "be angry" and "do not sin" and is a quotation of Psalm 4:4.

The same word for anger (*orgē*) is used of God (Matthew 3:7; Mark 3:5; Romans 1:18; 12:19), so anger in itself is not sinful. Jesus certainly was angry when He cleansed the temple in Jerusalem (John 2:13-16). There are times when righteous anger should be manifested against injustice and other forms of sin.

"Let not the sun go down upon your wrath" also comes from a present imperative prohibition so it could be rendered, "Stop letting the sun go down on your wrath." Anger easily can lead to resentment or bitterness, the meaning of the second word (*parorgismos*) which is translated "wrath" in this verse. If a person becomes angry for some legitimate reason, whatever triggered the anger should be settled before the day is past, a way of saying it should be taken care of immediately.

4:27. The devil will use anything he can to hinder God's people, and the improper use of anger is one of his greatest tools. Never give Satan an opportunity to take advantage of them.

4:28. Stealing is another manifestation of yielding to the Adamic nature. Pilfering was a way of life for many of the Ephesian Chris-

24. And that ye put on the new man: . . . put on the clean fresh clothes of the new life, *Phillips* . . . the man of new mould, *Rotherham.*

which after God is created in righteousness and true holiness: . . . who, according to God, *Wilson* . . . created after God's likeness, *Montgomery* . . . is shapen in ryghtewesnes, *Cranmer* . . . and sacredness of the truth, *Rotherham.*

25. Wherefore putting away lying: Finish, *Phillips* . . . put away falseness, *Montgomery* . . . leaving off falsehood, *Wilson* . . . stripping off what is false, *Rotherham* . . . let falsehood be abandoned, *Norlie.*

speak every man truth with his neighbour: . . . tell your neighbor the truth, *Phillips.*

for we are members one of another: . . . for we are all parts of the same body, *Norlie.*

26. Be ye angry, and sin not: . . . be sure that it is not out of wounded pride or bad temper, *Phillips.*

let not the sun go down upon your wrath: Never go to bed angry, *Phillips* . . . upon your angrymood, *Rotherham.*

27. Neither give place to the devil: . . . don't give the devil that sort of foothold, *Phillips* . . . and do not give any opportunity, *TCNT* . . . give no case to, *Murdock* . . . give occasion to, *Alford* . . . nor give an Opportunity for the Accuser, *Wilson* . . . the backbyter, *Cranmer* . . . the adversary, *Rotherham.*

28. Let him that stole steal no more:
but rather let him labour, working with [his] hands the thing which is good: . . . in honest industry, *Montgomery* . . . rather let him toil, *Wilson* . . . find employment, and do good work with his hands, *Norlie.*

18.3 adj sing	2419.1 conj	2174.7 verb 3sing subj pres act	3200.2 verb inf pres act	3450.3 art dat sing	5367.3 noun acc sing fem
ἀγαθόν,]	ἵνα	ἔχῃ	μεταδιδόναι	τῷ	χρείαν
agathon	hina	echē	metadidonai	tō	chreian
good,]	that	he may have	to impart	the	need

2174.18 verb dat sing masc part pres act	3820.6 adj nom sing masc	3030.1 noun nom sing masc	4407.2 adj nom sing masc	1523.2 prep gen	3450.2 art gen sing
ἔχοντι.	**29.** πᾶς	λόγος	σαπρὸς	ἐκ	τοῦ
echonti	pas	logos	sapros	ek	tou
having.	Every	word	corrupt	out of	the

4601.2 noun gen sing neu	5050.2 prs-pron gen 2pl	3231.1 partic	1594.3 verb 3sing impr pres mid	233.1 conj	233.2 conj
στόματος	ὑμῶν	μὴ	ἐκπορευέσθω,	‘ ἀλλ’	[✶ ἀλλὰ]
stomatos	humōn	mē	ekporeuesthō	all'	alla
mouth	your	not	let go forth,	but	[idem]

1479.1 conj	4948.3 indef-pron nom sing	18.6 adj nom sing masc	4242.1 prep	3482.3 noun acc sing fem	3450.10 art gen sing fem
εἴ	τις	ἀγαθὸς	πρὸς	οἰκοδομὴν	τῆς
ei	tis	agathos	pros	oikodomēn	tēs
if	any	good	for	building up	in the

5367.1 noun fem	2419.1 conj	1319.19 verb 3sing subj aor act	5320.1 prep	3450.4 art dat pl	189.3 verb dat pl part pres act
χρείας,	ἵνα	δῷ	χάριν	τοῖς	ἀκούουσιν.
chreias	hina	dō	charin	tois	akouousin
need,	that	it may give	grace	the	hearing.

2504.1 conj	3231.1 partic	3048.2 verb 2pl impr pres act	3450.16 art sing neu	4011.1 noun sing neu	3450.16 art sing neu
30. καὶ	μὴ	λυπεῖτε	τὸ	πνεῦμα	τὸ
kai	mē	lupeite	to	pneuma	to
And	not	grieve	the	Spirit	to

39.1 adj sing	3450.2 art gen sing	2296.2 noun gen sing masc	1706.1 prep	3614.3 rel-pron dat sing	4824.6 verb 2pl indic aor pass
ἅγιον	τοῦ	θεοῦ,	ἐν	ᾧ	ἐσφραγίσθητε
hagion	tou	theou	en	hō	esphragisthēte
Holy	tou	of God,	by	which	you were sealed

1519.1 prep	2232.4 noun acc sing fem	623.2 noun gen sing fem	3820.9 adj nom sing fem	3949.1 noun nom sing fem
εἰς	ἡμέραν	ἀπολυτρώσεως.	**31.** πᾶσα	πικρία
eis	hēmeran	apolutrōseōs	pasa	pikria
for	day	of redemption.	All	bitterness,

2504.1 conj	2349.1 noun nom sing masc	2504.1 conj	3572.1 noun nom sing fem	2504.1 conj	2879.1 noun nom sing fem	2504.1 conj
καὶ	θυμὸς	καὶ	ὀργὴ	καὶ	κραυγὴ	καὶ
kai	thumos	kai	orgē	kai	kraugē	kai
and	indignation,	and	wrath,	and	shouting,	and

981.2 noun nom sing fem	142.27 verb 3sing impr aor pass	570.1 prep	5050.2 prs-pron gen 2pl	4713.1 prep	3820.11 adj dat sing fem
βλασφημία	ἀρθήτω	ἀφ’	ὑμῶν,	σὺν	πάσῃ
blasphēmia	arthētō	aph'	humōn	sun	pasē
slander	let be removed	from	you,	with	all

2520.3 noun dat sing fem	1090.19 verb 2pl impr pres mid	1156.2 conj	1519.1 prep	238.3 prs-pron acc pl masc	5378.2 adj nom pl masc
κακίᾳ·	**32.** γίνεσθε	δὲ	εἰς	ἀλλήλους	χρηστοί,
kakia	ginesthe	de	eis	allēlous	chrēstoi
malice;	be	and	to	one another	kind,

tians before their conversion. Apparently some of them continued to practice it even after becoming Christians because Paul literally told them to "stop stealing." Working is the best practical antidote to stealing. Furthermore, the person who works hard will have something to share with others who are in need.

that he may have to give to him that needeth: . . . he may have something to share, *TCNT* . . . to distribute to the indigent, *Scarlett* . . . that you may be able to give to those in need, *Phillips.*

4:29. The fourth issue, "corrupt communication," really deals with "putrid, rotten, corrupt, filthy, rancid" speech. When Christians constantly work and live with other people who are not believers, they are often subjected to such ungodly language. However, they must not use that fact as an excuse for succumbing to that which is a normal way of life for the unsaved people around them.

29. Let no corrupt communication proceed out of your mouth: Let no evil speech, *Douay* . . . no evil word, *Sawyer* . . . corrupt discourse, *Wesley* . . . no putrid discourse, *Rotherham* . . . corrupt Word proceed, *Wilson* . . . Al naughtie speache let it not proceede out, *Rheims.*

but that which is good to the use of edifying: . . . good words instead, *Phillips.*

that it may minister grace unto the hearers: . . . that it may afford benefit, *Sawyer* . . . it may confer a Benefit, *Wilson* . . . which God can use to help other people, *Phillips.*

4:30. In addition to the four specific items mentioned, Paul warned the Ephesians literally to "stop grieving the Holy Spirit." His presence in a person's life is one of the most important proofs that he belongs to God. Because of this serious matter believers must be careful not to do anything that would grieve Him.

Sins of attitude are referred to in the closing verses of the chapter. Apparently these grieve the Holy Spirit as much as the four sins the apostle warned against. Among other things, this verse portrays the Holy Spirit as a Person with the ability to be grieved.

30. And grieve not the holy Spirit of God: . . . be not making sorrowful, *Rotherham* . . . Never hurt, *Phillips.*

whereby ye are sealed unto the day of redemption: He is...the personal pledge of your eventual full redemption, *Phillips* . . . in whom ye were sealed, *Panin, ASV* . . . in whiche ye ben markid, *Wyclif.*

4:31. Therefore, we need to "put away" all "bitterness" (*pikria,* resentfulness), "wrath" (*thumos,* a violent outburst of anger), "anger" (*orgē,* a settled feeling of anger), "clamor" (*kraugē,* shouting), "evil speaking" (*blasphēmia,* blasphemy), and "malice" (*kakia,* ill feeling).

31. Let all bitterness, and wrath, and anger, and clamour, and evil speaking: . . . indignation, *Douay, Confraternity* . . . passion...brawling, and abusive language, as well as all spitefulness, *TCNT* . . . and outcry and defamation, *Rotherham* . . . and cursed speaking, *Geneva.*

be put away from you: Banish from among you, *TCNT* . . . be banished from, *Sawyer.*

with all malice: . . . with all baseness, *Rotherham.*

4:32. This verse begins in the Greek language with an appeal to "keep on becoming kind to one another." The idea expressed is that of abandoning one attitude completely and replacing it with another attitude. Forgiving other people is not always easy, but Christians have the greatest of all incentives for doing so, the fact that Christ forgave them.

This total passage, along with many others, shows that the apostle Paul certainly did not believe the fallen, sinful nature was removed completely at salvation. Instead, at conversion the power of the Adamic nature is broken so a person is no longer a slave to it. At the same time God places within the person His Holy Spirit, so in a real sense he then has two natures. This results in a struggle that

32. And be ye kind one to another: You must practice, *Williams.*

Ephesians 5:1

2136.1 adj nom pl masc	5319.2 verb nom pl masc part pres mid	1431.7 prs-pron dat pl masc	2503.1 conj	2504.1 conj
εὔσπλαγχνοι,	χαριζόμενοι	ἑαυτοῖς,	καθὼς	καὶ
eusplanchnoi	charizomenoi	heautois	kathōs	kai
tender hearted,	forgiving	each other,	according as	also

3450.5 art nom sing masc	2296.1 noun nom sing masc	1706.1 prep	5382.3 name dat masc	5319.5 verb 3sing indic aor mid	5050.3 prs-pron dat 2pl
ὁ	θεὸς	ἐν	Χριστῷ	ἐχαρίσατο	ὑμῖν.
ho	theos	en	Christō	echarisato	humin
	God	in	Christ	forgave	you.

32.a.Var: 03B,06D 018K,020L,33,byz.Lach Weis

2231.3 prs-pron dat 1pl	1090.19 verb 2pl impr pres mid	3631.1 partic	3266.1 noun nom pl masc	3450.2 art gen sing
[a ἡμῖν.]	5:1. Γίνεσθε	οὖν	μιμηταὶ	τοῦ
hēmin	Ginesthe	oun	mimētai	tou
[us.]	Be you	therefore	imitators	

2296.2 noun gen sing masc	5453.1 conj	4891.4 noun pl neu	27.10 adj pl neu	2504.1 conj	3906.1 verb 2pl pres act
θεοῦ,	ὡς	τέκνα	ἀγαπητά·	2. καὶ	περιπατεῖτε
theou	hōs	tekna	agapēta	kai	peripateite
of God,	as	children	beloved,	and	walk

1706.1 prep	26.3 noun dat sing fem	2503.1 conj	2504.1 conj	3450.5 art nom sing masc	5382.1 name nom masc	25.14 verb 3sing indic aor act
ἐν	ἀγάπῃ,	καθὼς	καὶ	ὁ	Χριστὸς	ἠγάπησεν
en	agapē	kathōs	kai	ho	Christos	ēgapēsen
in	love,	even as	also	the	Christ	loved

2.a.Txt: p46,01א-corr 06D,018K,020L,byz.it. **Var:** 01א-org,02A,03B 025P,sa.bo.Treg,Alf Tisc,We/Ho,Weis,Sod UBS/✷

2231.4 prs-pron acc 1pl	5050.4 prs-pron acc 2pl	2504.1 conj	3722.10 verb 3sing indic aor act	1431.6 prs-pron acc sing masc	5065.1 prep
ἡμᾶς,	[a ὑμᾶς]	καὶ	παρέδωκεν	ἑαυτὸν	ὑπὲρ
hēmas	humas	kai	paredōken	heauton	huper
us,	[you]	and	gave up	himself	for

2231.2 prs-pron gen 1pl	4234.4 noun acc sing fem	2504.1 conj	2355.4 noun acc sing fem	3450.3 art dat sing	2296.3 noun dat sing masc	1519.1 prep
ἡμῶν	προσφορὰν	καὶ	θυσίαν	τῷ	θεῷ	εἰς
hēmōn	prosphoran	kai	thusian	tō	theō	eis
us,	an offering	and	a sacrifice	to	to God	for

3606.3 noun acc sing fem	2156.2 noun gen sing fem	4061.2 noun nom sing fem	1156.2 conj	2504.1 conj	3820.9 adj nom sing fem
ὀσμὴν	εὐωδίας.	3. Πορνεία	δὲ	καὶ	πᾶσα
osmēn	euōdias	Porneia	de	kai	pasa
an odor	of a sweet smell.	Fornication	but	and	all

165.1 noun nom sing fem	165.1 noun nom sing fem	3820.9 adj nom sing fem	2211.1 conj	3984.1 noun nom sing fem
ἀκαθαρσία	[✷ ἀκαθαρσία	πᾶσα]	ἢ	πλεονεξία
akatharsia	akatharsia	pasa	ē	pleonexia
uncleanness	[uncleanness	all]	or	covetousness

3234.1 adv	3550.5 verb 3sing impr pres mid	1706.1 prep	5050.3 prs-pron dat 2pl	2503.1 conj	4100.1 verb 3sing indic pres act
μηδὲ	ὀνομαζέσθω	ἐν	ὑμῖν,	καθὼς	πρέπει
mēde	onomazesthō	en	humin	kathōs	prepei
not even	let it be named	among	you,	even as	is becoming

39.8 adj dat pl masc	2504.1 conj	150.1 noun nom sing fem	2504.1 conj	3335.1 noun nom sing fem	2211.1 conj
ἁγίοις·	4. καὶ	αἰσχρότης	καὶ	μωρολογία	ἢ
hagiois	kai	aischrotēs	kai	mōrologia	ē
to saints;	and	filthiness	and	foolish talking	or

continues throughout this earthly life. But the more the Christian yields to the Holy Spirit, the easier it becomes. Also, the more a person resists the cravings of the Adamic nature, the easier it will be for his spiritual nature to dominate his way of life.

5:1. Verses 1-20 serve as one of the most beautiful descriptions of the Christian life that can be found in the Bible. Paul first instructed Christians to be "followers of God" or "imitators of God." The English word *mimic* comes from the Greek term for "followers" (*mimētai*). This word normally is used of imitating people (1 Corinthians 4:16; 11:1; 1 Thessalonians 1:6; Hebrews 6:12) and churches (1 Thessalonians 2:14). Here, however, it is used of the imitation of God, which is the loftiest endeavor that could ever be placed before a person.

The appeal sounds very reminiscent of Jesus' appeal to His disciples in the Sermon on the Mount (Matthew 5:48). It is another way of saying, "Allow Christ to be your prototype." Just as growing from an infant into an adult consists of a long, gradual process, so the apostle told believers literally to "keep on becoming." There is no point in this earthly life when a person can afford to let up his effort in this matter. God's great love for His children makes it possible for them to constantly become more like Christ.

5:2. As believers do this, they will be constantly ordering their behavior in the sphere of love (*agapē*). Because "God is love" (1 John 4:8,16), as believers imitate Him they will be living in a manner that manifests that same love (1 Corinthians 13). In the light of all that Christ did on the cross, that should not be too much to ask. That is what makes it possible for Christians to live lives of love. He acted not only as a priest but also as the very sacrifice himself. The Greek word for "sacrifice" (*thusia*) describes one who is innocent of crime shielding with his body the one who deserves the punishment. The expiatory character of Christ's death includes giving himself in our place as a sacrifice.

5:3. In the light of the wonderful sacrifice of Christ, Paul warned believers in verses 3-7 to sever themselves completely from their former way of life. Obviously, he listed only some representative sins of people who were not walking in the sphere of the love of God. "Fornication" (sexual immorality) and "uncleanness" (any kind of impurity) were serious external sins in that day. However, the apostle considered "covetousness" (greed) just as improper for God's holy people. Any kind of sin is inconsistent with a life of love. God's love does not motivate us to sin!

5:4. "Filthiness" (obscenity) literally means "filthy language." "Foolish talking" is talk that is characteristic of fools, people literally with "empty heads." The first type of verbal sin mentioned here

tenderhearted: . . . compassionate, *Wilson* . . . and merciful, *Confraternity* . . . be understanding, *Phillips*.

forgiving one another, even as God for Christ's sake hath forgiven you: Be as ready to forgive others as, *Phillips* . . . pardoning one another, *Rheims* . . . has generously forgiven you, *Confraternity* . . . has graciously forgiven you, *Williams* . . . freely forgave you, *Clementson*.

1. Be ye therefore followers of God, as dear children: Become therefore, *Wilson* . . . Learn then to imitate, *Montgomery* . . . as moost dereworthe sones, *Wyclif* . . . try to be like God, *Everyday*.

2. And walk in love, as Christ also hath loved us: Live your lives in, *Phillips* . . . Let love guide your footsteps, *Norlie* . . . and practice living in love, *Williams*.

and hath given himself for us an offering and a sacrifice to God for a sweetsmelling savour: . . . and which he perfectly expressed when, *Phillips* . . . and delivered himself up, *Wilson* . . . as a fragrant offering, *Williams* . . . an oblation, *Rheims*.

3. But fornication, and all uncleanness: As for sexual vice, *Montgomery* . . . and every kind of impurity, *TCNT* . . . All impurity, *Wilson* . . . or sensual greed, *Williams*.

or covetousness: . . . and avarice, *Murdock* . . . or unbridled Lust, *Wilson* . . . inordinate desire, *Scarlett* . . . the itch to get your hands on what belongs to other people, *Phillips*.

let it not be once named among you: . . . don't even talk about such things, *Phillips* . . . these should not even be mentioned, *Norlie*.

as becometh saints: . . . they are no fit subjects for Christians to talk about, *Phillips* . . . as Christ's People, *TCNT* . . . as becomes Holy persons, *Wilson*.

4. Neither filthiness, nor foolish talking, nor jesting: The keynote of your conversation should

Ephesians 5:5

4.a.Txt: 06D,018K,020L byz.
Var: 01ℵ,02A,03B,025P (33),Lach,Treg,Alf,Tisc We/Ho,Weis,Sod UBS/✱

2141.1 noun nom sing fem	3450.17 art pl neu	3620.2 partic	431.2 verb pl neu part pres act	3614.17 rel-pron pl neu	3620.2 partic
εὐτραπελία,	ʿ τὰ	οὐκ	ἀνήκοντα,	[ᵃ✱ ἃ	οὐκ
eutrapelia	ta	ouk	anēkonta	ha	ouk
jesting,	the	not	becoming;	[which	not

431.3 verb 3sing indic imperf act	233.2 conj	3095.1 adv comp	2150.2 noun nom sing fem	3642.17 dem-pron sing neu
ἀνῆκεν,]	ἀλλὰ	μᾶλλον	εὐχαριστία.	5. τοῦτο
anēken	alla	mallon	eucharistia	touto
was becoming,]	but	rather	thanksgiving.	This

5.a.Txt: 06D-corr,018K 020L,byz.
Var: 01ℵ,02A,03B 06D-org,025P,it.sa.bo. Gries,Lach,Treg,Alf Word,Tisc,We/Ho,Weis Sod,UBS/✱

1056.1 conj	1498.6 verb 2pl indic pres act	3471.1 verb 2pl perf act	1091.12 verb nom pl masc part pres act	3617.1 conj	3820.6 adj nom sing masc
γὰρ	ʿ ἐστε	[ᵃ✱ ἴστε]	γινώσκοντες	ὅτι	πᾶς
gar	este	iste	ginōskontes	hoti	pas
for	you are	[have known]	knowing	that	every

4064.1 noun nom sing masc	2211.1 conj	167.2 adj nom sing masc	2211.1 conj	3983.1 noun nom sing masc	3614.5 rel-pron nom sing masc
πόρνος,	ἢ	ἀκάθαρτος,	ἢ	πλεονέκτης,	ʿ ὅς
pornos	ē	akathartos	ē	pleonektēs	hos
fornicator,	or	unclean person,	or	covetous,	who

5.b.Txt: 02A,06D,018K 020L,025P,byz.bo.Weis
Var: 01ℵ,03B,33,Lach Treg,Alf,Tisc,We/Ho Sod,UBS/✱

3614.16 rel-pron sing neu	1498.4 verb 3sing indic pres act	1486.1 noun nom sing masc	3620.2 partic	2174.4 verb 3sing indic pres act
[ᵇ✱ ὅ]	ἐστιν	εἰδωλολάτρης,	οὐκ	ἔχει
ho	estin	eidōlolatrēs	ouk	echei
[idem]	is	an idolater,	not	has

2790.3 noun acc sing fem	1706.1 prep	3450.11 art dat sing fem	926.3 noun dat sing fem	3450.2 art gen sing	5382.2 name gen masc
κληρονομίαν	ἐν	τῇ	βασιλείᾳ	τοῦ	Χριστοῦ
klēronomian	en	tē	basileia	tou	Christou
inheritance	in	the	kingdom	of the	Christ

2504.1 conj	2296.2 noun gen sing masc	3235.3 num card nom masc	5050.4 prs-pron acc 2pl	534.1 verb 3sing impr pres act	2727.4 adj dat pl masc
καὶ	θεοῦ.	6. Μηδεὶς	ὑμᾶς	ἀπατάτω	κενοῖς
kai	theou	Mēdeis	humas	apatatō	kenois
and	of God.	No one	you	let deceive	with empty

3030.7 noun dat pl masc	1217.2 prep	3642.18 dem-pron pl neu	1056.1 conj	2048.34 verb 3sing indic pres mid	3450.9 art nom sing fem
λόγοις·	διὰ	ταῦτα	γὰρ	ἔρχεται	ἡ
logois	dia	tauta	gar	erchetai	hē
words;	on account of	these things	for	comes	the

3572.1 noun nom sing fem	3450.2 art gen sing	2296.2 noun gen sing masc	1894.3 prep	3450.8 art acc pl masc	5048.9 noun acc pl masc	3450.10 art gen sing fem
ὀργὴ	τοῦ	θεοῦ	ἐπὶ	τοὺς	υἱοὺς	τῆς
orgē	tou	theou	epi	tous	huious	tēs
wrath	of the	of God	upon	the	sons	of the

539.1 noun gen sing fem	3231.1 partic	3631.1 partic	1090.19 verb 2pl impr pres mid	4681.1 adj nom pl masc
ἀπειθείας.	7. μὴ	οὖν	γίνεσθε	συμμέτοχοι
apeitheias	mē	oun	ginesthe	summetochoi
disobedience.	Not	therefore	be	joint partakers with

840.1 prs-pron gen pl	1498.1 verb 2pl act	1056.1 conj	4077.1 adv	4510.1 noun sing	3431.1 adv	1156.2 conj	5295.1 noun sing neu
αὐτῶν.	8. ἦτε	γὰρ	ποτε	σκότος,	νῦν	δὲ	φῶς
autōn	ēte	gar	pote	skotos	nun	de	phōs
them;	you were	for	once	darkness,	but	now	light

needs very little explanation, except to emphasize that it takes a concentrated effort to avoid it, especially if a person lives in a non-Christian family or works in an environment where this type of language is a way of life. Good, clean jokes certainly have their place, even among God's people. But there is a difference between a joke that merely helps to lighten the atmosphere with good laughter and one that borders on that which is coarse or base.

"Foolish talking" probably is the most difficult of the three verbal sins mentioned here to define. The apostle did not imply that people always have to be serious in order to please God. "Foolish talking" is empty or vain conversation which does not contribute to the spiritual maturity of individuals. Such "talking," as well as obscenities and coarse joking, are out of place for believers. Instead, Christians should constantly verbalize thanksgiving.

5:5. This verse could be misinterpreted very easily to mean that a person who commits a single sin suddenly loses his relationship to God. The emphasis here is the same as in many other scriptural passages; that is, if a person can consistently practice sin without repentance, it is obvious the person does not know God any longer. People who can constantly practice immorality, impurity, greed, or similar sins, are giving priority to these sins rather than to God. That is probably why Paul called such a person "an idolater." Anything that becomes more important than God himself has become a "god."

5:6. Verse 6 probably contains a warning against some kind of gnosticism which held that such practices as the apostle Paul condemned here were irrelevant to spiritual life, because they related to the body only and not to the spiritual nature of a person. Many of the Gnostics believed all matter was evil. Because the human body is matter, according to them, it also is evil. Some of them practiced extreme asceticism in order to control the "evil" body, while others went to the opposite extreme and practiced extreme licentiousness. Because the body supposedly was evil, whatever a person did with it would not influence him spiritually.

Paul warned against being deceived with such empty words. The term for "vain words" (*kenois logois*) literally relates to words without reality or substance. Listening and succumbing to this kind of suggestion is not only dangerous, it also brings the wrath of God upon those who practice this kind of life-style.

5:7. Paul's advice was not to partake with them. Because the construction here is a present imperative prohibition, it literally means "stop becoming partakers with them."

5:8. Again we see a definite contrast between the past and the present. Because these believers had been delivered from their

not be, *Phillips* . . . Neither obscenity, *Wesley* . . . and shamelessness, *Rotherham* . . . nor double meanings, *Scarlett* . . . with anything dishonourable, *TCNT* . . . nor indecent jesting, *Noyes.*

which are not convenient: . . . which is to no purpose, *Douay* . . . which are beneath [you], *Rotherham* . . . for these are not becoming to Christians, *Norlie.*

but rather giving of thanks: Substitute for them thanksgiving, *TCNT* . . . but a sense of all that we owe to God, *Phillips.*

5. For this ye know, that no whoremonger, nor unclean person, nor covetous man, who is an idolater: . . . this ye know, assuredly, *Worrell* . . . no Fornicator, *Wilson* . . . (which makes him an idolator), *Norlie.*

hath any inheritance in the kingdom of Christ and of God: . . . can have any share in the kingdom, *Norlie.*

6. Let no man deceive you with vain words: . . . seduce you, *Rheims* . . . with meaningless phrases, *TCNT* . . . with empty words, *Panin, Wilson, Worrell* . . . with worthless arguments, *Norlie.*

for because of these things cometh the wrath of God upon the children of disobedience: It is these very things which bring down, *Phillips.*

7. Be not ye therefore partakers with them: Have nothing to do with men like that, *Phillips* . . . do not become their Associates, *Wilson* . . . Be not ye therfore companyons of them, *Cranmer* . . . become co-partners, *Rotherham.*

8. For ye were sometimes darkness: . . . once you were, *Phillips* . . . you were formerly, *Sawyer.*

Ephesians 5:9

9.a.Txt: p46,06D-corr
018K,020L,byz.
Var: p49,01ℵ,02A,03B
06D-org,025P,33,it.sa.
bo.Gries,Lach,Treg,Alf
Word,Tisc,We/Ho,Weis
Sod,UBS/✶

1706.1 prep	2935.3 noun dat sing masc	5453.1 conj	4891.4 noun pl neu	5295.2 noun gen sing neu	3906.1 verb 2pl pres act	3450.5 art nom sing masc
ἐν	κυρίῳ·	ὡς	τέκνα	φωτὸς	περιπατεῖτε·	9. ὁ
en	kuriō	hōs	tekna	phōtos	peripateite	ho
in	Lord;	as	children	of light	walk,	the

1056.1 conj	2561.1 noun nom sing masc	3450.2 art gen sing	4011.2 noun gen sing neu	5295.2 noun gen sing neu	1706.1 prep
γὰρ	καρπὸς	τοῦ	πνεύματος	[a✶ φωτὸς]	ἐν
gar	karpos	tou	pneumatos	phōtos	en
for	fruit	of the	Spirit	[light]	in

3820.11 adj dat sing fem	19.3 noun dat sing fem	2504.1 conj	1336.3 noun dat sing fem	2504.1 conj	223.3 noun dat sing fem
πάσῃ	ἀγαθωσύνῃ	καὶ	δικαιοσύνῃ	καὶ	ἀληθείᾳ·
pasē	agathōsunē	kai	dikaiosunē	kai	alētheia
all	goodness	and	righteousness	and	truth,

1375.7 verb nom pl masc part pres act	4949.9 intr-pron sing neu	1498.4 verb 3sing indic pres act	2080.4 adj sing	3450.3 art dat sing
10. δοκιμάζοντες	τί	ἐστιν	εὐάρεστον	τῷ
dokimazontes	ti	estin	euareston	tō
proving	what	is	well pleasing	to the

2935.3 noun dat sing masc	2504.1 conj	3231.1 partic	4641.1 verb 2pl impr pres act	3450.4 art dat pl	2024.6 noun dat pl neu
κυρίῳ.	11. καὶ	μὴ	συγκοινωνεῖτε	τοῖς	ἔργοις
kuriō	kai	mē	sunkoinōneite	tois	ergois
Lord;	and	no	have fellowship with	the	works

3450.4 art dat pl	173.5 adj dat pl neu	3450.2 art gen sing	4510.3 noun gen sing neu	3095.1 adv comp	1156.2 conj	2504.1 conj
τοῖς	ἀκάρποις	τοῦ	σκότους,	μᾶλλον	δὲ	καὶ
tois	akarpois	tou	skotous	mallon	de	kai
the	unfruitful	of the	darkness,	rather	but	even

1638.4 verb 2pl impr pres act	3450.17 art pl neu	1056.1 conj	2903.1 adv	1090.27 verb pl neu part pres mid	5097.2 prep	840.1 prs-pron gen pl
ἐλέγχετε·	12. τὰ	γὰρ	κρυφῇ	γινόμενα	ὑπ'	αὐτῶν
elenchete	ta	gar	kruphē	ginomena	hup'	autōn
expose;	the things	for	in secret	being done	by	them

149.1 adj sing neu	1498.4 verb 3sing indic pres act	2504.1 conj	2978.24 verb inf pres act	3450.17 art pl neu	1156.2 conj	3820.1 adj
αἰσχρόν	ἐστιν	καὶ	λέγειν.	13. τὰ	δὲ	πάντα
aischron	estin	kai	legein	ta	de	panta
shameful	it is	even	to say.	The	but	all

1638.11 verb pl neu part pres mid	5097.3 prep	3450.2 art gen sing	5295.2 noun gen sing neu	5157.7 verb 3sing indic pres mid
ἐλεγχόμενα	ὑπὸ	τοῦ	φωτὸς	φανεροῦται·
elenchomena	hupo	tou	phōtos	phaneroutai
being exposed	by	the	light	are being made manifest;

3820.17 adj sing neu	1056.1 conj	3450.16 art sing neu	5157.9 verb sing neu part pres mid	5295.1 noun sing neu
πᾶν	γὰρ	τὸ	φανερούμενον	φῶς
pan	gar	to	phaneroumenon	phōs
everything	for	the	being made manifest	light

1498.4 verb 3sing indic pres act	1346.1 conj	2978.5 verb 3sing indic pres act	1446.28 verb 2sing impr aor mid	1446.34 verb 2sing impr pres act
ἐστιν·	14. διὸ	λέγει,	Ἔγειραι	[✶ Ἔγειρε,]
estin	dio	legei	Egeirai	Egeire
is.	Wherefore	he says,	Arouse,	[Rise,]

former spiritual darkness, they were not to be content with living in some ambiguous twilight. Probably much of this section, from verse 8 through verse 14 is based upon Jesus' statement about himself (John 8:12) and His followers (Matthew 5:14) being the "light of the world."

5:9. Just as the rays of the sun help cause plants and flowers to grow, so the light of the Lord should bring to life in believers the qualities mentioned in this verse. Because God is good in the ultimate sense of the word, if a person allows His will to become important in his life, God's goodness will be reflected in him as well. "Righteousness" or "justice" basically means to do that which is right. The light of God should cause believers to treat other people fairly or with justice.

"Truth" normally is defined as "that which conforms to reality." Of course, the problem is determining what is reality. The Bible makes it clear that Christ is the personification of truth (John 14:6), and the Bible is the written expression of that truth (John 17:17).

5:10. "Light" comes from the Greek term *phōtos* from which we get *photography* and several other terms. It is a very common expression in the Bible, normally depicting the drastic difference between "what is acceptable unto the Lord" and what is characteristic of a life of practicing sin.

5:11. According to this verse, Christians have two basic obligations with respect to sin: have nothing to do with it and "reprove" it. The idea contained in the first obligation is literally "stop participating with people who practice sin." The second obligation is even more drastic, because sinners usually do not like the light turned on when they are practicing evil in darkness.

5:12. The writings of Paul always emphasize the exceeding sinfulness of sin, but never more evidently than here. Some of the sins committed by people under cover of darkness were so abhorrent to Paul that he hesitated even to mention them.

5:13. Societies may change, and methods of committing sin may change, but one truth does not change. When sin is exposed to the light of God's truth, something drastic happens. People who allow the Bible to have access to their lives will become very uncomfortable if they are practicing sin. The Holy Spirit is extremely faithful in reproving the world of sin (John 16:8). In other words, He proves the world, or nonbelievers, wrong about their attitudes toward sin, righteousness, and judgment. He seeks to bring them to the realization that the sacrifice of Jesus is the only sacrifice given for the sins of mankind.

but now [are ye] light in the Lord:
walk as children of light: Live then as, *Phillips.*

9. (For the fruit of the Spirit [is] in all goodness and righteousness and truth;): . . . for the fruit of the light, *Confraternity* . . . consysteth in all goodnes, *Cranmer.*

10. Proving what is acceptable unto the Lord: . . . always be trying to find out, *TCNT* . . . searching out, *Wilson* . . . Accept that which is pleasinge, *Tyndale* . . . You must learn to do what is pleasing to the Lord, *Norlie.*

11. And have no fellowship with the unfruitful works of darkness: . . . be not partakers, *Sawyer* . . . Steer clear of the activities of darkness, *Phillips.*
but rather reprove [them]: . . . let your lives show by contrast how dreary and futile these things are, *Phillips.*

12. For it is a shame even to speak of those things which are done of them in secret: It is degrading, *TCNT* . . . it is indecent ever to mention, *Wilson.*

13. But all things that are reproved are made manifest by the light: . . . light is capable of "showing up" everything for what it really is, *Phillips* . . . their true character made manifest, *TCNT.*
for whatsoever doth make manifest is light: . . . for it is light that discouereth all things, *Geneva.*

14. Wherefore he saith: The Scripture therefore says, *Norlie* . . . Thus God speaks through the scriptures, *Phillips.*

3450.5 art nom sing masc	2490.7 verb nom sing masc part pres act	2504.1 conj	448.7 verb 2sing impr aor act	1523.2 prep gen	3450.1 art gen pl
ὁ	καθεύδων,	καὶ	ἀνάστα	ἐκ	τῶν
ho	katheudōn	kai	anasta	ek	tōn
the	sleeping,	and	rise up	from among	the

3361.2 adj gen pl	2504.1 conj	2001.1 verb 3sing indic fut act	4622.3 prs-pron dat 2sing	3450.5 art nom sing masc	5382.1 name nom masc
νεκρῶν,	καὶ	ἐπιφαύσει	σοι	ὁ	Χριστός.
nekrōn	kai	epiphausei	soi	ho	Christos
dead,	and	shall shine upon	you	the	Christ.

984.1 verb 2pl pres act	3631.1 partic	4316.1 adv	197.1 adv	197.1 adv	4316.1 adv
15. Βλέπετε	οὖν	ʹ πῶς	ἀκριβῶς	[✶ ἀκριβῶς	πῶς]
Blepete	oun	pōs	akribōs	akribōs	pōs
Watch out	therefore	how	accurately	[carefully	how]

3906.1 verb 2pl pres act	3231.1 partic	5453.1 conj	775.1 adj nom pl masc	233.1 conj	5453.1 conj	4533.3 adj nom pl masc
περιπατεῖτε,	μὴ	ὡς	ἄσοφοι,	ἀλλ'	ὡς	σοφοί,
peripateite	mē	hōs	asophoi	all'	hōs	sophoi
you walk,	not	as	unwise,	but	as	wise,

1789.3 verb nom pl masc part pres mid	3450.6 art acc sing masc	2511.4 noun acc sing masc	3617.1 conj	3450.13 art nom pl fem
16. ἐξαγοραζόμενοι	τὸν	καιρόν,	ὅτι	αἱ
exagorazomenoi	ton	kairon	hoti	hai
ransoming	the	time,	because	the

2232.5 noun nom pl fem	4050.13 adj nom pl fem	1498.7 verb 3pl indic pres act	1217.2 prep	3642.17 dem-pron sing neu	3231.1 partic
ἡμέραι	πονηραί	εἰσιν.	17. διὰ	τοῦτο	μὴ
hēmerai	ponērai	eisin	dia	touto	mē
days	evil	are.	Because of	this	not

17.a.Txt: 06D-corr,018K 020L,byz.
Var: 01א,02A,03B,025P 33,Lach,Treg,Alf,Tisc We/Ho,Weis,Sod UBS/✶

1090.19 verb 2pl impr pres mid	871.4 adj nom pl masc	233.2 conj	4770.6 verb nom pl masc part pres act	4770.1 verb 2pl pres act
γίνεσθε	ἄφρονες,	ἀλλὰ	ʹ συνιέντες	[ᵃ✶ συνίετε]
ginesthe	aphrones	alla	sunientes	suniete
be	foolish,	but	understanding	[understand]

4949.9 intr-pron sing neu	3450.16 art sing neu	2284.1 noun sing neu	3450.2 art gen sing	2935.2 noun gen sing masc	2504.1 conj	3231.1 partic
τί	τὸ	θέλημα	τοῦ	κυρίου.	18. καὶ	μὴ
ti	to	thelēma	tou	kuriou	kai	mē
what	the	will	of the	Lord.	And	not

3153.1 verb 2pl impr pres mid	3494.3 noun dat sing masc	1706.1 prep	3614.3 rel-pron dat sing	1498.4 verb 3sing indic pres act	804.1 noun nom sing fem
μεθύσκεσθε	οἴνῳ,	ἐν	ᾧ	ἐστιν	ἀσωτία·
methuskesthe	oinō	en	hō	estin	asōtia
be drunk	with wine,	in	which	is	foolish;

233.2 conj	3997.17 verb 2pl impr pres mid	1706.1 prep	4011.3 noun dat sing neu	2953.16 verb nom pl masc part pres act	1431.7 prs-pron dat pl masc
ἀλλὰ	πληροῦσθε	ἐν	πνεύματι,	19. λαλοῦντες	ἑαυτοῖς
alla	plērousthe	en	pneumati	lalountes	heautois
but	be filled	with	Spirit,	speaking	yourselves

5403.4 noun dat pl masc	2504.1 conj	5054.1 noun dat pl masc	2504.1 conj	5437.2 noun dat pl fem	4012.6 adj dat pl fem
ψαλμοῖς	καὶ	ὕμνοις	καὶ	ᾠδαῖς	πνευματικαῖς,
psalmois	kai	humnois	kai	ōdais	pneumatikais
in psalms	and	hymns	and	songs	spiritual,

5:14. This verse could be a loose paraphrase of Isaiah 26:19 and 60:1, or Paul could have been quoting an early baptismal hymn or some poem familiar to his readers. The metaphor is that of the morning, when the darkness of night is dispelled by the rising of the sun. The idea expressed in the Greek language literally is to "stand up out of the dead ones."

5:15. "See" (*blepete*) is another way of saying "watch out" or "take heed" or "be very careful." The old term "circumspectly" (literally "looking around") contains the idea of walking "strictly."

5:16. The present participle in this verse is in the middle voice and refers to purchasing for one's self or for one's personal benefit on a continuous basis. "The days are *evil*" (*poneros*) speaks of evil "in active opposition to that which is good." If Christians are not careful, the evil nature of this age will rob them of the opportunities to do God's will.

5:17. Doing God's will cannot become a reality in a person's life unless that person understands what God's will is. Actually, "be ye not unwise" in this verse comes from another present imperative prohibition, so it literally means "stop becoming those who are foolish."

5:18. Above all else, that which makes the Christian life successful and pleasing to God is living in the power of the Holy Spirit. Quoting Proverbs 23:30, Paul warned against the folly of indulging in wine. Bacchus, the wine god, was one of the "gods" worshiped by pagans. Therefore, drunkenness was a normal part of pagan life. Apparently some of the Gentile Christians continued to follow their former practice, even though to them Bacchus was no longer a "god." The command comes from another present imperative prohibition, and it could be translated "stop being drunk with wine." Drunkenness only leads to "excess" or debauchery.

Instead of being filled physically, Paul encouraged Christians to be filled spiritually. The command here is from a present passive imperative verb, literally, "be being filled with the Spirit"; it is not optional. It is passive, denoting that God has to accomplish it. Thirdly, it is present, meaning it is an ongoing process.

5:19. This verse gives some excellent advice about staying full of the Holy Spirit. A person does so by worshiping God. Paul here mentioned only two of the many ways to worship God. We worship God through singing psalms set to music, through hymns which are songs of praise to God, and through spiritual songs. It is difficult to know exactly what is meant by this last type. Some Bible scholars think it refers to songs of testimony which are based upon spiritual

Awake thou that sleepest: and arise from the dead, and Christ shall give thee light: . . . stande vp from death, *Geneva* . . . will enlighten thee, *Confraternity* . . . vvil illuminate thee, *Rheims* . . . shine upon thee, *Phillips.*

15. See then that ye walk circumspectly: Be extremely careful, then, *TCNT* . . . Take hede therefore, *Tyndale, Cranmer* . . . Look therefore carefully how ye walk, *PNT.*
not as fools, but as wise: . . . not as men who do not know the meaning and purpose of life, *Phillips.*

16. Redeeming the time, because the days are evil: . . . avoydyng occasyon, *Cranmer* . . . making the most of every opportunity, *TCNT* . . . Make the best use of your time, *Phillips.*

17. Wherefore be ye not unwise: . . . be not thoughtless, *Scarlett* . . . inconsiderate, *Wilson* . . . vague, *Phillips.*
but understanding what the will of the Lord [is]: . . . but firmly grasp what you know to be the will of God, *Phillips.*

18. And be not drunk with wine, wherein is excess: Do not drink wine to excess, for that leads to profligacy, *TCNT* . . . wherein is riot, *Panin, ASV* . . . luxury, *Douay* . . . for in that is debauchery, *Confraternity* . . . by which comes Debauchery, *Wilson* . . . rioteousnes, *Rheims.*
but be filled with the Spirit: . . . let the Spirit stimulate your souls, *Phillips.*

19. Speaking to yourselves in psalms and hymns and spiritual songs: Express your joy, *Phillips* . . . speaking to one another, *Confraternity* . . . canticles, *Douay.*

Ephesians 5:20

19.a.**Txt:** 01א-corr,02A
06D,018K,020L,025P
etc.byz.it.bo.Sod
Var: 01א-org,03B,Tisc
We/Ho,Weis,UBS/⋆

102.2 verb nom pl masc part pres act	2504.1 conj	5402.2 verb nom pl masc part pres act	1706.1 prep	3450.11 art dat sing fem	2559.3 noun dat sing fem
ἄδοντες	καὶ	ψάλλοντες	[a ἐν ⟩	τῇ	καρδίᾳ
adontes	kai	psallontes	en	tē	kardia
singing	and	praising	with	the	heart

5050.2 prs-pron gen 2pl	3450.3 art dat sing	2935.3 noun dat sing masc	2149.7 verb nom pl masc part pres act	3704.1 adv
ὑμῶν	τῷ	κυρίῳ,	**20.** εὐχαριστοῦντες	πάντοτε
humōn	tō	kuriō	eucharistountes	pantote
your	to the	Lord;	giving thanks	at all times

5065.1 prep	3820.4 adj gen pl	1706.1 prep	3549.4 noun dat sing neu	3450.2 art gen sing	2935.2 noun gen sing masc	2231.2 prs-pron gen 1pl
ὑπὲρ	πάντων	ἐν	ὀνόματι	τοῦ	κυρίου	ἡμῶν
huper	pantōn	en	onomati	tou	kuriou	hēmōn
for	all things	in	name	of the	Lord	our

2400.2 name masc	5382.2 name gen masc	3450.3 art dat sing	2296.3 noun dat sing masc	2504.1 conj	3824.3 noun dat sing masc
Ἰησοῦ	Χριστοῦ	τῷ	θεῷ	καὶ	πατρί·
Iēsou	Christou	tō	theō	kai	patri
Jesus	Christ	the	God	and	Father,

	5131.12 verb nom pl masc part pres mid	238.2 prs-pron dat pl	1706.1 prep	5238.3 noun dat sing masc	2296.2 noun gen sing masc
21.	ὑποτασσόμενοι	ἀλλήλοις	ἐν	φόβῳ	⟨ Θεοῦ.
	hupotassomenoi	allēlois	en	phobō	Theou
	submitting yourselves	to one another	in	fear	of God.

21.a.**Txt:** byz.
Var: 01א,02A,03B,020L
025P,bo.Gries,Lach
Treg,Alf,Word,Tisc
We/Ho,Weis,Sod
UBS/⋆

22.a.**Txt:** (01א),(02A)
018K,020L,byz.
Var: p46,03B,Alf,Tisc
We/Ho,UBS/⋆

23.a.**Txt:** Steph
Var: 01א,02A,03B,06D
018K,020L,025P,byz.
Gries,Lach,Treg,Alf
Word,Tisc,We/Ho,Weis
Sod,UBS/⋆

23.b.**Txt:** 01א-corr
06D-corr,018K,020L
025P,byz.
Var: 01א-org,02A,03B
06D-org,Gries,Lach
Treg,Alf,Word,Tisc
We/Ho,Weis,Sod
UBS/⋆

23.c.**Txt:** 01א-corr
06D-corr,018K,020L
025P,byz.bo.
Var: 01א-org,02A,03B
06D-org,33,Lach,Treg
Alf,Word,Tisc,We/Ho
Weis,Sod,UBS/⋆

24.a.**Txt:** 06D-corr,018K
020L,byz.
Var: 01א,02A,06D-org
025P,33,Lach,Treg,Alf
Tisc,We/Ho,Weis,Sod
UBS/⋆

5382.2 name gen masc	3450.13 art nom pl fem	1129.6 noun nom pl fem	3450.4 art dat pl	2375.5 adj dat pl
[a⋆ Χριστοῦ.]	**22.** Αἱ	γυναῖκες,	τοῖς	ἰδίοις
Christou	Hai	gunaikes	tois	idiois
[of Christ]	The	wives,	to the	your own

433.8 noun dat pl masc	5131.10 verb 2pl impr pres mid	5453.1 conj	3450.3 art dat sing	2935.3 noun dat sing masc
ἀνδράσιν	⟨a ὑποτάσσεσθε, ⟩	ὡς	τῷ	κυρίῳ·
andrasin	hupotassesthe	hōs	tō	kuriō
husbands	submit yourselves,	as	to the	Lord,

3617.1 conj	3450.5 art nom sing masc	433.1 noun nom sing masc	1498.4 verb 3sing indic pres act	2747.1 noun nom sing fem	3450.10 art gen sing fem
23. ὅτι	⟨a ὁ ⟩	ἀνήρ	ἐστιν	κεφαλὴ	τῆς
hoti	ho	anēr	estin	kephalē	tēs
for	the	husband	is	head	of the

1129.2 noun gen sing fem	5453.1 conj	2504.1 conj	3450.5 art nom sing masc	5382.1 name nom masc	2747.1 noun nom sing fem	3450.10 art gen sing fem
γυναικὸς,	ὡς	καὶ	ὁ	Χριστὸς	κεφαλὴ	τῆς
gunaikos	hōs	kai	ho	Christos	kephalē	tēs
wife,	as	also	the	Christ	head	of the

1564.1 noun fem	2504.1 conj	840.5 prs-pron nom sing masc	1498.4 verb 3sing indic pres act	4842.1 noun nom sing masc	3450.2 art gen sing
ἐκκλησίας,	⟨b καὶ ⟩	αὐτὸς	⟨c ἐστιν ⟩	σωτὴρ	τοῦ
ekklēsias	kai	autos	estin	sōtēr	tou
assembly,	and	he	is	Saviour	of the

4835.2 noun gen sing neu		233.1 conj	233.2 conj	5450.1 conj	5453.1 conj	3450.9 art nom sing fem
σώματος·	**24.**	⟨ ἀλλ'	[⋆ ἀλλὰ]	⟨ ὥσπερ	[a⋆ ὡς]	ἡ
sōmatos		all'	alla	hōsper	hōs	hē
body.		But	[idem]	even as	[as]	the

experiences, while others think it refers to singing in other tongues (cf. 1 Corinthians 14:15). Our worship in song certainly should contain a balance among these three types of singing.

5:20. Believers also worship God by constant thanksgiving. The Greek term from which we get the word *thanksgiving* comes from the word that translates into English as *eucharist* (*eucharisteō*), a term for the Communion service.

5:21. In the Greek language this important section of Ephesians begins with the statement, "subjecting yourselves to one another out of reverence for Christ" or "out of regard for His will and His glory." Paul reveals the most conspicuous of areas in which Christians should submit to one another. Marriage, family, and work are three areas in life where a person needs to have a peaceful relationship.

The structure of the entire passage from 5:21 through 6:9 stems from the participle *hupotassomenoi* which begins verse 21, occupying the emphatic position. Because it is a present participle it refers to an activity that must be continuous. Because it is middle voice (the middle and passive voices have identical endings in present tense verb forms) it indicates it must be voluntary. In Colossians 3:18 Paul used the verb form of the word, but the same participle occurs in Titus 2:5, and also 1 Peter 3:1,5. In all these instances the middle voice is used, showing the necessity of voluntary submission.

5:22. These statements about wives and husbands were very radical in an age that definitely belonged to men. This passage of Scripture clearly establishes the fact there should be no sense of inequality among God's people.

In the ideal Christian family, the wife should voluntarily submit to the leadership role of her husband as "priest" of the family. He is responsible for the spiritual welfare of the family. He should not force his wife to submit to him, nor should she take a passive approach in submitting. A woman who voluntarily submits to the leadership of her husband will be the main recipient of benefits derived from the action.

5:23. This verse should be considered in light of the phrase "as unto the Lord" in verse 22. God certainly does not expect a Christian wife to do unscriptural things out of obedience to her unsaved husband. The term "head" here again relates to the function of the husband as the spiritual leader of the family. In a family where the husband is not a Christian the wife may have to accept the position of spiritual leadership while she is doing what the Bible instructs her so that her husband will also become a Christian (1 Corinthians 7:10,11).

singing and making melody in your heart to the Lord: Keep on praying and praising, *Williams* . . . using your voice in songs, *BB* . . . chaunting, *Rheims* . . . and making music, *Wilson, Adams* . . . and dancing in your hearts, *Fenton* . . . for the ears of God! *Phillips.*

20. Giving thanks always for all things: Thank God at all times, *Phillips* . . . continue giving thanks for everything, *Williams* . . . at all times, *Rotherham.*
unto God and the Father in the name of our Lord Jesus Christ:

21. Submitting yourselves one to another in the fear of God: And "fit in with" one another, because of your common reverence, *Phillips* . . . keep on living in subordination, *Williams* . . . being subordinate to each other, *Scarlett* . . . be ruled by one another, *BB* . . . subjecting yourselves, *Panin* . . . out of reverence, *TCNT* . . . out of respect, *Adams* . . . reverence for Christ, *Montgomery.*

22. Wives, submit yourselves unto your own husbands, as unto the Lord: . . . must learn to adapt yourselves to, *Phillips* . . . live in subordination to, *Williams* . . . be under the authority of, *BB.*

23. For the husband is the head of the wife: . . . since a husband, *Adams.*
even as Christ is the head of the church: . . . just as, *Williams* . . . in the same way as, *TCNT, Phillips* . . . heed of the congregacion, *Tyndale, Cranmer* . . . Head of the assembly, *Worrell.*
and he is the saviour of the body: He Himself is, *Adams* . . . a Preserver, *Wilson* . . . the same is he that minystreth saluacyon vnto the body, *Cranmer.*

Ephesians 5:25

1564.2 noun nom sing fem	5131.7 verb 3sing indic pres mid	3450.3 art dat sing	5382.3 name dat masc	3643.1 adv	2504.1 conj
ἐκκλησία	ὑποτάσσεται	τῷ	Χριστῷ,	οὕτως	καὶ
ekklēsia	hupotassetai	tō	Christō	houtōs	kai
assembly	is being subjected	to the	Christ,	so	also

24.b.Txt: 02A,06D-corr 018K,020L,025P,byz.bo. **Var:** 01א,03B,06D-org 33,Lach,Treg,Alf,Tisc We/Ho,Weis,Sod UBS/✶

3450.13 art nom pl fem	1129.6 noun nom pl fem	3450.4 art dat pl	2375.5 adj dat pl	433.8 noun dat pl masc	1706.1 prep
αἱ	γυναῖκες	τοῖς	⌐ᵇ ἰδίοις ⌐	ἀνδράσιν	ἐν
hai	gunaikes	tois	idiois	andrasin	en
the	wives	to the	their own	husbands	in

3820.3 adj dat sing	3450.7 art nom pl masc	433.6 noun nom pl masc	25.1 verb 2pl pres act	3450.15 art acc pl fem	1129.9 noun acc pl fem
παντί.	**25.** Οἱ	ἄνδρες,	ἀγαπᾶτε	τὰς	γυναῖκας
panti	Hoi	andres	agapate	tas	gunaikas
everything.	The	husbands,	love	the	wives

25.a.Txt: 06D,018K 020L,byz.Sod **Var:** 01א,02A,03B,33 Lach,Treg,Alf,Tisc We/Ho,Weis,UBS/✶

1431.2 prs-pron gen pl	2503.1 conj	2504.1 conj	3450.5 art nom sing masc	5382.1 name nom masc	25.14 verb 3sing indic aor act
⌐ᵃ ἑαυτῶν, ⌐	καθὼς	καὶ	ὁ	Χριστὸς	ἠγάπησεν
heautōn	kathōs	kai	ho	Christos	ēgapēsen
your own,	even as	also	the	Christ	loved

3450.12 art acc sing fem	1564.4 noun acc sing fem	2504.1 conj	1431.6 prs-pron acc sing masc	3722.10 verb 3sing indic aor act	5065.1 prep
τὴν	ἐκκλησίαν,	καὶ	ἑαυτὸν	παρέδωκεν	ὑπὲρ
tēn	ekklēsian	kai	heauton	paredōken	huper
the	assembly,	and	himself	gave up	for

840.10 prs-pron gen sing fem	2419.1 conj	840.12 prs-pron acc sing fem	37.6 verb 3sing subj aor act	2483.9 verb nom sing masc part aor act
αὐτῆς·	**26.** ἵνα	αὐτὴν	ἁγιάσῃ,	καθαρίσας
autēs	hina	autēn	hagiasē	katharisas
it,	that	it	he might sanctify,	having cleansed

3450.3 art dat sing	3039.2 noun dat sing neu	3450.2 art gen sing	5045.2 noun gen sing neu	1706.1 prep	4343.3 noun dat sing neu	2419.1 conj
τῷ	λουτρῷ	τοῦ	ὕδατος	ἐν	ῥήματι,	**27.** ἵνα
tō	loutrō	tou	hudatos	en	rhēmati	hina
by the	washing	of the	water	by	word,	that

27.a.Txt: 06D-corr,018K byz. **Var:** 01א,02A,03B 06D-org,020L,025P,33 Gries,Lach,Treg,Alf Word,Tisc,We/Ho,Weis Sod,UBS/✶

3798.7 verb 3sing subj aor act	840.12 prs-pron acc sing fem	840.5 prs-pron nom sing masc	1431.5 prs-pron dat sing masc	1725.3 adj acc sing fem
παραστήσῃ	⌐ αὐτὴν	[ᵃ✶ αὐτὸς]	ἑαυτῷ	ἔνδοξον
parastēsē	autēn	autos	heautō	endoxon
he might present	it	[idem]	to himself	glorious

3450.12 art acc sing fem	1564.4 noun acc sing fem	3231.1 partic	2174.25 verb acc sing fem part pres act	4548.1 noun acc sing masc	2211.1 conj
τὴν	ἐκκλησίαν	μὴ	ἔχουσαν	σπίλον	ἢ
tēn	ekklēsian	mē	echousan	spilon	ē
the	assembly,	not	having	spot,	or

4369.1 noun acc sing fem	2211.1 conj	4948.10 indef-pron sing neu	3450.1 art gen pl	4955.1 dem-pron gen pl	233.1 conj	2419.1 conj
ῥυτίδα	ἢ	τι	τῶν	τοιούτων,	ἀλλ᾽	ἵνα
rhutida	ē	ti	tōn	toioutōn	all'	hina
wrinkle,	or	any	of the	such things;	but	that

1498.10 verb 3sing subj pres act	39.10 adj nom sing fem	2504.1 conj	297.5 adj nom sing fem		3643.1 adv
ᾖ	ἁγία	καὶ	ἄμωμος.		**28.** οὕτως
ē	hagia	kai	amōmos		houtōs
it might be	holy	and	blameless.		So

5:24. Again, this submission must be voluntary or it will not work. The term "every thing" also must be considered in the light of the qualifier in verse 22, "as unto the Lord." The wife has a supportive role, something like soldiers under the leadership of an officer. They need each other.

5:25. The rest of the chapter describes the husband's responsibility. Just as the wife's primary responsibility can be summarized in "voluntary submission," so the husband's special duty is "love" (*agapaō*). Just as the submission of the Church to Christ serves as the wife's model, the love of Christ for the Church reflects the husband's attitude toward his wife. Christ loved His church enough to die for it. If the genuine love of the husband (like that of Christ for the Church) balances the loving, voluntary submission of the wife, she will find it easy to fulfill her role. Real love will not take advantage of the partner.

If a man truly loves his wife, he will want to share with her in every possible way. The arrangement God established between a wife and a husband does not imply that he is to make all the decisions. If he truly loves her, he will share the decision-making responsibilities with her, as long as he does not abdicate his position as the spiritual leader of the family.

5:26. Individuals are cleansed from their sins and become members of the body of Christ as they respond to the Word (*rhēma*, Romans 10:8; 1 Peter 1:25). Other passages describe the process of cleansing that occurs at conversion (John 3:5; Titus 3:5; Hebrews 10:22). Paul is here speaking of the cleansing power of the Word of God. The Scriptures often use water in a metaphoric sense, in relation to the work of regeneration. But the Word also continues to have a cleansing ministry throughout our Christian life.

5:27. Not only does Christ perform the initial work of cleansing at salvation, but He continues to work in believers to remove every stain and wrinkle. "Spot" or "stain" refers to impurity, and "wrinkle" is a sign of age or decay. Therefore Christ, through the work of the Holy Spirit, continues to purify those who are His, thereby removing from them the stains left by their former lives.

Furthermore, in a real sense, even though the body may be deteriorating, the work of Christ in the continuous sanctification process is making the soul "younger." It is difficult to know exactly why the word "wrinkle" is used in the context, but perhaps it carries the idea of reversing the inward process of deterioration that was occurring before conversion.

24. Therefore as the church is subject unto Christ: The willing subjection of, *Phillips.*

so [let] the wives [be] to their own husbands in every thing: . . . so the married women, *Williams* . . . should be reproduced in the submission of wives, *Phillips.*

25. Husbands, love your wives, even as Christ also loved the church, and gave himself for it: But, remember, this means that the husband must give his wife the same sort of love, *Phillips* . . . and delivered Himself up for it, *Worrell, Murdock* . . . delivered Himself up for her sake, *Fenton.*

26. That he might sanctify and cleanse it: . . . to consecrate her, *Williams* . . . having purified her, *Wilson* . . . that after cleansing her, *Montgomery* . . . so as to consecrate it, *Norlie.*

with the washing of water by the word: . . . by the laver of water, *Douay* . . . in the fountayne of water, *Tyndale* . . . by the bath of the water in the word, *Noyes* . . . with the water of His message, *Fenton* . . . according to his promise, *TCNT* . . . in the word of liif? *Wyclif.*

27. That he might present it to himself a glorious church: . . . and might constitute it, *Murdock* . . . the rectified church, *Fenton* . . . a Church full of splendor, *Norlie* . . . gloriously arrayed, *Adams.*

not having spot, or wrinkle, or any such thing; but that it should be holy and without blemish: . . . free from spots, wrinkles or any other disfigurements...perfect, *Phillips* . . . or Blemish, *Wilson* . . . or any such blemish; but on the contrary holy and faultless, *Montgomery* . . . and vndefoulid, *Wyclif* . . . but holy and faultless in every respect, *Norlie* . . . but to be consecrated and faultless, *Williams* . . . nor anything like them, *Fenton.*

Ephesians 5:29

28.a.Var: 03B,33,Treg
Alf,We/Ho,Weis,Sod
UBS/⋆

3648.5 verb 3pl indic pres act	2504.1 conj	3450.7 art nom pl masc	433.6 noun nom pl masc	25.11 verb inf pres act	3450.15 art acc pl fem
ὀφείλουσιν	[ᵃ⋆+ καὶ]	οἱ	ἄνδρες	ἀγαπᾶν	τὰς
opheilousin	kai	hoi	andres	agapan	tas
ought	[and]	the	husbands	to love	the

1431.2 prs- pron gen pl	1129.9 noun acc pl fem	5453.1 conj	3450.17 art pl neu	1431.2 prs- pron gen pl	4835.4 noun pl neu
ἑαυτῶν	γυναῖκας	ὡς	τὰ	ἑαυτῶν	σώματα·
heautōn	gunaikas	hōs	ta	heautōn	sōmata
their own	wives	as	the	their own	bodies:

3450.5 art nom sing masc	25.8 verb nom sing masc part pres act	3450.12 art acc sing fem	1431.4 prs- pron gen sing	1129.4 noun acc sing fem	1431.6 prs-pron acc sing masc
ὁ	ἀγαπῶν	τὴν	ἑαυτοῦ	γυναῖκα	ἑαυτὸν
ho	agapōn	tēn	heautou	gunaika	heauton
the	loving	the	his own	wife	himself

25.2 verb 3sing pres act	3625.2 num card nom masc	1056.1 conj	4077.1 adv	3450.12 art acc sing fem	1431.4 prs- pron gen sing
ἀγαπᾷ·	29. οὐδεὶς	γὰρ	ποτε	τὴν	ἑαυτοῦ
agapa	oudeis	gar	pote	tēn	heautou
loves.	No one	for	at any time	the	his own

4418.4 noun acc sing fem	3268.13 verb 3sing indic aor act	233.1 conj	233.2 conj	1611.1 verb 3sing indic pres act	2504.1 conj
σάρκα	ἐμίσησεν,	ᶜ ἀλλ᾽	[⋆ ἀλλὰ]	ἐκτρέφει	καὶ
sarka	emisēsen	all'	alla	ektrephei	kai
flesh	hated,	but	[idem]	nourishes	and

2259.1 verb 3sing indic pres act	840.12 prs-pron acc sing fem	2503.1 conj	2504.1 conj	3450.5 art nom sing masc	2935.1 noun nom sing masc
θάλπει	αὐτήν,	καθὼς	καὶ	ὁ	ᶜ Κύριος
thalpei	autēn	kathōs	kai	ho	Kurios
cherishes	it,	even as	also	the	Lord

29.a.Txt: 06D-corr,018K
020L,byz.Sod
Var: 01א,02A,03B
06D-org,025P,33,it.sa.
bo.Gries,Lach,Treg,Alf
Word,Tisc,We/Ho,Weis
UBS/⋆

5382.1 name nom masc	3450.12 art acc sing fem	1564.4 noun acc sing fem	3617.1 conj	3166.2 noun pl neu
[ᵃ⋆ Χριστὸς]	τὴν	ἐκκλησίαν.	30. ὅτι	μέλη
Christos	tēn	ekklēsian	hoti	melē
[Christ]	the	assembly:	for	members

30.a.Txt: 01א-corr,06D
020L,025P,byz.it.Sod
Var: p46,01א-org,02A
03B,33,sa.bo.Lach,Treg
Tisc,We/Ho,Weis
UBS/⋆

1498.5 verb 1pl indic pres act	3450.2 art gen sing	4835.2 noun gen sing neu	840.3 prs- pron gen sing	1523.2 prep gen	3450.10 art gen sing fem
ἐσμὲν	τοῦ	σώματος	αὐτοῦ,	ᶜ ἐκ	τῆς
esmen	tou	sōmatos	autou	ek	tēs
we are	of the	body	his,	of	the

4418.2 noun gen sing fem	840.3 prs- pron gen sing	2504.1 conj	1523.2 prep gen	3450.1 art gen pl	3609.2 noun gen pl neu	840.3 prs- pron gen sing
σαρκὸς	αὐτοῦ,	καὶ	ἐκ	τῶν	ὀστέων	αὐτοῦ. ᶜ
sarkos	autou	kai	ek	tōn	osteōn	autou
flesh	his,	and	of	the	bones	his.

470.2 prep	3642.1 dem- pron gen sing	2611.8 verb 3sing indic fut act	442.1 noun nom sing masc	3450.6 art acc sing masc
31. Ἀντὶ	τούτου	καταλείψει	ἄνθρωπος	τὸν
Anti	toutou	kataleipsei	anthrōpos	ton
Because of	this	shall leave	a man	the

31.a.Txt: 01א-corr,02A
06D-corr,018K,020L
025P,byz.
Var: 01א-org,03B
06D-org,33,Lach,Treg
Alf,Tisc,We/Ho,Weis
Sod,UBS/⋆

3824.4 noun acc sing masc	840.3 prs- pron gen sing	2504.1 conj	3450.12 art acc sing fem	3251.4 noun acc sing fem	2504.1 conj
πατέρα	ᶜ αὐτοῦ ᶜ	καὶ	τὴν	μητέρα,	καὶ
patera	autou	kai	tēn	mētera	kai
father	his	and	the	mother,	and

5:28. This verse describes another reason for a husband to love his wife—the fact they are one flesh. No sane person destroys his own body, so for a husband to treat his wife merely as property means he is damaging himself in the process. The apostle already had used Christ's love for the Church as the model for the husband. Just as Christ never bullies His church, so the husband should not be guilty of that error.

The mystical union between a wife and a husband is one of the most marvelous relationships known to humans. Next to the spiritual relationship a Christian has with Jesus himself, the marital bond is no doubt the strongest tie any one person could have with another person. This is one reason the act of sexual intercourse is so sacred. It is the ultimate expression of two companions showing their love to each other. It should not be cheapened! Again, of course, the matter of voluntary submission comes into focus. Christians who truly follow Paul's instructions in verse 21 are people who will enjoy their marital relationship.

5:29. The fact that Christ "nourisheth and cherisheth" or "feeds and cares for" His church is one of the most prominent truths taught in Scripture. As its organic Head, He gives the orders in a manner that expresses true concern. He alone truly knows the needs of His people, and He operates in them through the Holy Spirit in the light of those needs. He gave the written Word of God so that Christians would have answers to the pressing problems of life. A person who consistently studies the Bible will gain an understanding of Jesus that is not possible in any other way.

5:30. This verse encapsulates what the Bible teaches in detail in many other places. Notice how the institution of marriage is elevated throughout this passage by comparing it to the relationship between Christ and His body, the Church. Jesus is not just a figurehead; He truly is the operating Head of His church. As the "Vine," He is the One who possesses eternal life, but He shares it with the "branches" (John 15:5). Branches do not possess life in themselves, but draw upon the life that exists in the vine. In the same way the members of a body do not give orders to the head, just as the members of Christ's church should not presume to give orders to Him.

5:31. The Scriptures reinforce the truth that husbands must love their wives as Christ loves the Church by referring to Genesis 2:24. This probably constitutes the most profound and fundamental statement in all Scripture relative to God's plan concerning marriage. It describes beautifully the leaving, cleaving, and weaving process through which people go as they leave their childhood homes and establish homes of their own (Mark 10:7-9).

First, there must be a definite leaving behind of the childhood family. While it may work in some cases, it probably would be much

---

28. So ought men to love their wives as their own bodies: In like manner, *Noyes* . . . In similar way, *Berkeley* . . . In the same way, *Adams* . . . married men ought to, *Weymouth* . . . ought to give their wives the love they naturally have for, *Phillips* . . . as being their own, *HistNT*.

He that loveth his wife loveth himself: The man who loves, *SEB* . . . The lover of, *Fenton* . . . his own wife, *HistNT* . . . is the extending of his love for himself to enfold her, *Phillips* . . . does but love himself, *Conybeare* . . . is thereby loving himself, *Way*.

29. For no man ever yet hated his own flesh: . . . his own body, *Weymouth* . . . ever hated his own person, *Way* . . . neglects, *Phillips*.

but nourisheth and cherisheth it: . . . nay, it is nourished, *HistNT* . . . on the contrary, he feeds and warms it, *Fenton* . . . He feeds it and cares for it, *Norlie* . . . feeds his body and takes care of it, *TCNT* . . . and looks after it, *Phillips* . . . and cherishes it, *Weymouth* . . . carefully protects it, *Berkeley* . . . and provideth for it, *Murdock*.

even as the Lord the church: . . . even as is the Community also by, *HistNT* . . . as Christ treats, *Berkeley* . . . as Christ does for the church, *Adams* . . . Christ does the same thing for his community, *SEB* . . . for his body, *Phillips*.

30. For we are members of his body, of his flesh, and of his bones: . . . because we are, as it were, *Weymouth* . . . because we are parts of His body, *Fenton* . . . we are his flesh and blood! *Phillips*.

31. For this cause shall a man leave his father and mother: On this account, *Wilson, Berkeley* . . . For this reason, *Adams* . . . This is why, *SEB* . . . Instead, *HistNT* . . . Therefore shall, *Moffatt* . . . a man is to leave, *Weymouth* . . . shall a man forsake father and mother, and shall be knit to his wife, *Way*.

4205.2 verb 3sing indic fut pass
προσκολληθήσεται
proskollēthēsetai
shall be joined

4242.1 prep
πρὸς
pros
to

3450.12 art acc sing fem
τὴν
tēn
the

1129.4 noun acc sing fem
γυναῖκα
gunaika
wife

840.3 prs-pron gen sing
αὐτοῦ,
autou
his,

2504.1 conj
καὶ
kai
and

1498.43 verb 3pl indic fut mid
ἔσονται
esontai
shall be

3450.7 art nom pl masc
οἱ
hoi
the

1411.3 num card
δύο
duo
two

1519.1 prep
εἰς
eis
for

4418.4 noun acc sing fem
σάρκα
sarka
flesh

1518.8 num card acc fem
μίαν.
mian
one.

3450.16 art sing neu
32. Τὸ
To
The

3328.1 noun sing neu
μυστήριον
mustērion
mystery

3642.17 dem-pron sing neu
τοῦτο
touto
this

3144.16 adj sing neu
μέγα
mega
great

1498.4 verb 3sing indic pres act
ἐστίν·
estin
is,

1466.1 prs-pron nom 1sing
ἐγὼ
egō
I

1156.2 conj
δὲ
de
but

2978.1 verb 1sing pres act
λέγω
legō
speak

1519.1 prep
εἰς
eis
as to

5382.4 name acc masc
Χριστὸν
Christon
Christ

2504.1 conj
καὶ
kai
and

1519.1 prep
εἰς
eis
as to

3450.12 art acc sing fem
τὴν
tēn
the

1564.4 noun acc sing fem
ἐκκλησίαν.
ekklēsian
assembly.

3993.1 conj
33. πλὴν
plēn
However

2504.1 conj
καὶ
kai
also

5050.1 prs-pron nom 2pl
ὑμεῖς
humeis
you

3450.7 art nom pl masc
οἱ
hoi
the

2567.2 prep
καθ᾽
kath᾽
according to,

1518.4 num card acc masc
ἕνα,
hena
one

1524.3 adj nom sing masc
ἕκαστος
hekastos
each

3450.12 art acc sing fem
τὴν
tēn
the

1431.4 prs-pron gen sing
ἑαυτοῦ
heautou
his own

1129.4 noun acc sing fem
γυναῖκα
gunaika
wife

3643.1 adv
οὕτως
houtōs
so

25.7 verb 3sing impr pres act
ἀγαπάτω
agapatō
let love

5453.1 conj
ὡς
hōs
as

1431.6 prs-pron acc sing masc
ἑαυτόν·
heauton
himself;

3450.9 art nom sing fem
ἡ
hē
the

1156.2 conj
δὲ
de
and

1129.1 noun nom sing fem
γυνὴ
gunē
wife

2419.1 conj
ἵνα
hina
that

5236.4 verb 3sing subj pres mid
φοβῆται
phobētai
she may fear

3450.6 art acc sing masc
τὸν
ton
the

433.4 noun acc sing masc
ἄνδρα.
andra
husband.

3450.17 art pl neu
6:1. Τὰ
Ta
The

4891.4 noun pl neu
τέκνα,
tekna
children,

5057.1 verb 2pl pres act
ὑπακούετε
hupakouete
obey

3450.4 art dat pl
τοῖς
tois
the

1112.3 noun dat pl masc
γονεῦσιν
goneusin
parents

5050.2 prs-pron gen 2pl
ὑμῶν
humōn
your

1706.1 prep
⌐a ἐν
en
in

2935.3 noun dat sing masc
κυρίῳ· ⌐
kuriō
Lord,

3642.17 dem-pron sing neu
τοῦτο
touto
this

1056.1 conj
γὰρ
gar
for

1498.4 verb 3sing indic pres act
ἐστιν
estin
is

1337.1 adj sing
δίκαιον.
dikaion
just.

4939.4 verb 2sing impr pres act
2. Τίμα
Tima
Honor

3450.6 art acc sing masc
τὸν
ton
the

3824.4 noun acc sing masc
πατέρα
patera
father

4622.2 prs-pron gen 2sing
σου
sou
your

2504.1 conj
καὶ
kai
and

3450.12 art acc sing fem
τὴν
tēn
the

3251.4 noun acc sing fem
μητέρα·
mētera
mother,

3610.3 rel-pron nom sing fem
ἥτις
hētis
which

1498.4 verb 3sing indic pres act
ἐστὶν
estin
is

1.a.**Txt:** p46,01אּ,02A
06D-corr1,044,byz.
Var: 03B,06D-org,010F
012G

better for newly wedded couples not to live with their families, nor even extremely close to them. Secondly, they need to cleave to each other in every sense of the word. This means accepting the other person completely and not trying to reform each other. Thirdly, as they allow the process to work, the two will be experientially woven into one fabric. Legally this takes place when they are united in marriage, but experientially it takes an entire lifetime.

5:32. Paul's reflection on Genesis 2:24 probably caused the apostle to exclaim, "This is a great mystery." The fact that people could become one with Christ as members of His body was almost too much to comprehend. The same wonder applies to the wife-husband relationship. Paul's own experience illustrated this truth. All of his life until he reached approximately 30 years of age, religion had been uppermost. He was so zealous for what he thought pleased God that he persecuted the Early Church severely. Suddenly, because of the manifestation of Christ to him, all this changed, and for the first time in his life he was able to enjoy an intimate relationship with Christ.

5:33. The entire passage concludes by again reminding the Ephesians of the total emphasis throughout, that husbands should love their wives, and wives should respect their husbands.

6:1. The fact that children are addressed directly indicates they must have been a part of local churches and attended public worship services. Children are told to "obey" their "parents." The qualifier "in the Lord" shows that God does not want children to do wrong just because their parents command them to do so. Paul was describing the ideal Christian family where parents had dedicated themselves to the Lord, and were bringing up their children "in the nurture and admonition of the Lord" (verse 4). Both Old and New Testaments condemn disobedience to parents (Proverbs 30:17; Romans 1:30; 2 Timothy 3:2).

6:2. The apostle reinforced his imperative by quoting the fifth commandment of the Decalogue (Exodus 20:12; Deuteronomy 5:16). A puzzling statement is added calling it "the first commandment with promise." Some commentators take this to mean the first commandment of the second table of the Decalogue, if indeed there were two tables. The Jews, however, normally divided the Ten Commandments into two groups of five each. Other Bible scholars take the adjective "first" (*prōtē*) to mean "primary" or "chief." Still others understand the term "commandment" to refer to all the divine commandments, not just the ones recorded in the Decalogue. The third idea seems more consistent with the manner in which Jesus prioritized commandments (Matthew 22:37-40; Mark 12:28-31).

and shall be joined unto his wife: ... and adhere to, *Murdock* ... and be closely united, *TCNT* ... and shall cleave to, *Panin, Douay, Adams* ... and so perfectly unite himself, *Williams* ... united to his wife, *Wilson, Rotherham, Fenton.*

and they two shall be one flesh: ... shall become one body, *Fenton.*

32. This is a great mystery: There is a deep truth here, *TCNT* ... The marriage relationship is doubtless, *Phillips* ... a great secret, *Wilson* ... a great sacrament, *Douay, Rheims.*

but I speak concerning Christ and the church: I mean in reference to, *Confraternity* ... now with reference to, *TCNT* ... but I give it as a picture of Christ and the Church, *Norlie* ... with respect to, *Rotherham* ... in regard to, *Fenton* ... of something deeper still, *Phillips.*

33. Nevertheless let every one of you in particular so love his wife even as himself: And especially you, every individual, *Fenton* ... each one of you, individually, *Wilson* ... love his wyfe truely, *Tyndale* ... in the same way that, *Adams.*

and the wife [see] that she reverence [her] husband: ... must respect, *Williams, Adams* ... show respect for, *TCNT* ... have proper respect for, *Norlie* ... let the wife reverence her husband in the same way, *Fenton.*

1. Children, obey your parents in the Lord: ... be obedient to your parents, *Fenton* ... as those whom God has set over you, *Phillips.*

for this is right: ... the right thing for you to do, *Phillips* ... this is a just precept, *Wilson.*

2. Honour thy father and mother: You must honor, *Williams.*

which is the first commandment with promise: The first commandment to contain a promise, *Phillips* ... promise attached, *Montgomery.*

1769.1 noun nom sing fem	4272.9 num ord nom sing fem	1706.1 prep	1845.3 noun dat sing fem	2419.1 conj	2074.1 adv
ἐντολὴ	πρώτη	ἐν	ἐπαγγελίᾳ·	3. ἵνα	εὖ
entolē	prōtē	en	epangelia	hina	eu
commandment	the first	with	a promise,	that	well

4622.3 prs-pron dat 2sing	1090.40 verb 3sing subj aor mid	2504.1 conj	1498.39 verb 2sing indic fut mid	3090.1 adj nom sing masc	
σοι	γένηται,	καὶ	ἔσῃ	μακροχρόνιος	
soi	genētai	kai	esē	makrochronios	
with you	it may be,	and	you may be	long lived	

1894.3 prep	3450.10 art gen sing fem	1087.2 noun gen sing fem	2504.1 conj	3450.7 art nom pl masc	3824.6 noun nom pl masc	3231.1 partic
ἐπὶ	τῆς	γῆς.	4. Καὶ	οἱ	πατέρες,	μὴ
epi	tēs	gēs	Kai	hoi	pateres	mē
on	the	earth.	And	the	fathers,	not

3811.1 verb 2pl impr pres act	3450.17 art pl neu	4891.4 noun pl neu	5050.2 prs-pron gen 2pl	233.1 conj	233.2 conj
παροργίζετε	τὰ	τέκνα	ὑμῶν,	‛ ἀλλ’	[✻ ἀλλὰ]
parorgizete	ta	tekna	humōn	all’	alla
do provoke	the	children	your,	but	[idem]

1611.2 verb 2pl impr pres act	840.16 prs-pron pl neu	1706.1 prep	3672.3 noun dat sing fem	2504.1 conj	3422.1 noun dat sing fem	2935.2 noun gen sing masc
ἐκτρέφετε	αὐτὰ	ἐν	παιδείᾳ	καὶ	νουθεσίᾳ	κυρίου.
ektrephete	auta	en	paideia	kai	nouthesia	kuriou
bring up	them	in	discipline	and	admonition	of Lord.

3450.7 art nom pl masc	1395.6 noun nom pl masc	5057.1 verb 2pl pres act	3450.4 art dat pl	2935.8 noun dat pl masc	2567.3 prep
5. Οἱ	δοῦλοι,	ὑπακούετε	τοῖς	‛ κυρίοις	κατὰ
Hoi	douloi	hupakouete	tois	kuriois	kata
The	slaves,	obey	the	masters	according to

4418.4 noun acc sing fem	2567.3 prep	4418.4 noun acc sing fem	2935.8 noun dat pl masc	3196.3 prep	5238.2 noun gen sing masc
σάρκα	[✻ κατὰ	σάρκα	κυρίοις]	μετὰ	φόβου
sarka	kata	sarka	kuriois	meta	phobou
flesh	[according to	flesh	masters]	with	fear

2504.1 conj	4997.2 noun gen sing masc	1706.1 prep	567.2 noun dat sing fem	3450.10 art gen sing fem	2559.1 noun fem	5050.2 prs-pron gen 2pl
καὶ	τρόμου,	ἐν	ἁπλότητι	τῆς	καρδίας	ὑμῶν,
kai	tromou	en	haplotēti	tēs	kardias	humōn
and	trembling,	in	simplicity	of the	heart	your,

5453.1 conj	3450.3 art dat sing	5382.3 name dat masc	3231.1 partic	2567.1 prep	3651.1 noun acc sing fem
ὡς	τῷ	Χριστῷ·	6. μὴ	κατ’	‛ ὀφθαλμοδουλείαν
hōs	tō	Christō	mē	kat’	ophthalmodouleian
as	to the	Christ;	not	with	eye service

	3651.4 noun acc sing fem		5453.1 conj	439.1 adj nom pl masc	233.1 conj
	[✻ ὀφθαλμοδουλίαν]		ὡς	ἀνθρωπάρεσκοι,	ἀλλ’
	ophthalmodoulian		hōs	anthrōpareskoi	all’
	[idem]		as	men pleasers;	but

5453.1 conj	1395.6 noun nom pl masc	3450.2 art gen sing	5382.2 name gen masc	4020.17 verb nom pl masc part pres act	3450.16 art sing neu
ὡς	δοῦλοι	‛a τοῦ ‛	Χριστοῦ,	ποιοῦντες	τὸ
hōs	douloi	tou	Christou	poiountes	to
as	slaves	of the	Christ,	doing	the

6.a.**Txt:** 06D-corr,018K 020L,byz.
Var: 01‭א‬,02A,03B 06D-org,025P,Lach Treg,Alf,Word,Tisc We/Ho,Weis,Sod UBS/✻

6:3. This verse contains the promise. It is a quotation of Deuteronomy 5:16 and expresses the fact that obedience to God's laws will bring God's blessings. In the context of the statement in Deuteronomy, many commandments were given to Israel. Obedience to these commandments would benefit in many ways, including the matter of enjoying longer life. Although many of the specific commandments given to Israel were not transferred into the New Testament, the basic philosophy behind them was.

6:4. Verse 4 warns fathers against nagging their children to the point where they feel helpless to achieve parental expectations. This certainly was a revolutionary concept in a society where the father's authority was absolute. Actually the Greek term for "father" (*patera*) sometimes was used to mean "parent" (Hebrews 11:23), so Paul may have been addressing both parents. Parents who constantly goad their children may cause them to fall into a state of perpetual resentment. Instead, parents should train and instruct their children.

The first term, "nurture" (*paideia*), is the word from which we derive *pedagogy*. It can refer to discipline but normally contains a broad meaning of "education," the entire training and instruction of the young. The second term, "admonition" (*nouthesia*), is a narrower term, referring to training by word or instruction.

6:5. Most writers estimate that approximately 60 million people, or one-third of the population of the Roman Empire, were slaves at that time. Paul carefully encouraged these slaves who had become followers of Christ to obey their masters (*kurioi*) as they would obey Christ. In other words, they should not use their Christian freedom for an excuse not to render faithful service. While it may be stretching the passage too far, it is easy to make some comparisons between these statements about slave-master relationships and employee-employer relationships today. Christians should feel more obligated to do a good job.

6:6. Whatever Christians do, they should do for the glory of God. While it may be important to want to impress the ones for whom they work, it is much more important to realize that Jesus is always cognizant of what they are doing. There is a definite connection between the responsibility to do a good day's work and the will of God. Paul had defined the Christian work ethic in 2 Thessalonians 3:6-15. Christians can bring reproach on the name of Christ by stealing time; some witness for the Lord when they are being paid to work. Paul made it clear to these Christian slaves that faithful service would be a testimony to their masters. Some of their masters were also Christians, but no doubt many of them were not.

3. That it may be well with thee: ... so that thou mayest prosper, *TCNT* ... That thou mayst be in good estate, *Geneva*.

and thou mayest live long on the earth: ... shalt be long-lived upon the land, *Rotherham*.

4. And, ye fathers:
provoke not your children to wrath: ... fret not your children to anger, *Alford* ... do not irritate, *Wilson* ... do not exasperate your children, *Scarlett* ... don't overcorrect your children or make it difficult for them to obey the commandment, *Phillips*.

but bring them up in the nurture and admonition of the Lord: ... but educate them, *Scarlett* ... but rear them in the discipline, *Confraternity* ... with Christian training and advice, *TCNT* ... with Christian teaching in Christian doctrine, *Phillips* ... in the techynge and chastisynge, *Wyclif* ... in the instruction and discipline, *Wesley* ... and correction of the Lord, *Douay* ... and informacion of the Lorde, *Tyndale*.

5. Servants, be obedient to them that are [your] masters according to the flesh: ... be subject to, *Sawyer* ... vnto your carnal masters, *Geneva* ... to your lordes, *Rheims*.

with fear and trembling, in singleness of your heart, as unto Christ: ... giving them undivided service, *TCNT* ... in the sincerity of, *Sawyer* ... in the Integrity of, *Wilson* ... in the simplicity, *Douay*.

6. Not with eyeservice, as menpleasers; but as the servants of Christ:
doing the will of God from the heart: ... doing what you believe to be the will of God for you, *Phillips* ... trying to carry out, *Williams* ... from the Soul, *Wilson, Scarlett, Adams* ... out of [the] soul, *Rotherham*.

2284.1 noun sing neu	3450.2 art gen sing	2296.2 noun gen sing masc	1523.2 prep gen	5425.2 noun gen sing fem	3196.2	2114.1 noun sing fem
θέλημα	τοῦ	θεοῦ	ἐκ	ψυχῆς,	7. μετ'	εὐνοίας
thelēma	tou	theou	ek	psuchēs,	met'	eunoias
will		of God	from	soul,	with	good will

7.a.Var: 01ℵ,02A,03B 06D-org,025P,Gries Lach,Treg,Alf,Word Tisc,We/Ho,Weis,Sod UBS/☆

1392.7 verb nom pl masc part pres act	5453.1 conj	3450.3 art dat sing	2935.3 noun dat sing masc	2504.1 conj	3620.2 partic
δουλεύοντες	[a+ ὡς]	τῷ	κυρίῳ	καὶ	οὐκ
douleuontes	hōs	tō	kuriō	kai	ouk
doing service	[as]	to the	Lord	and	not

442.8 noun dat pl masc	3471.20 verb nom pl masc part perf act	3617.1 conj	3614.16 rel-pron sing neu	1430.1 partic	4948.10 indef-pron sing neu
ἀνθρώποις·	8. εἰδότες	ὅτι	ὅ	ἐάν	τι
anthrōpois	eidotes	hoti	ho	ean	ti
to men;	knowing	that	what		whatever

8.a.Txt: (018K),020L,byz. **Var:** 03B,Alf,Tisc We/Ho,Weis,UBS/☆

1524.3 adj nom sing masc	1524.3 adj nom sing masc	1430.1 partic	4948.10 indef-pron sing neu	4020.29 verb 3sing subj aor act
ἕκαστος	[a☆ ἕκαστος,	ἐάν	τι]	ποιήσῃ
hekastos	hekastos	ean	ti	poiēsē
each	[each		whatever]	may have done

8.b.Txt: 01ℵ-corr 06D-corr,018K,020L byz.Sod **Var:** 01ℵ-org,02A,03B 06D-org,025P,Lach Treg,Alf,Tisc,We/Ho Weis,UBS/☆

18.3 adj sing	3642.17 dem-pron sing neu	2837.8 verb 3sing indic fut mid	2837.12 verb 3sing indic fut mid	3706.2 prep
ἀγαθόν,	τοῦτο	κομιεῖται	[b☆ κομίσεται]	παρὰ
agathon	touto	komieitai	komisetai	para
good,	this	he shall receive	[idem]	from

8.c.Txt: 018K,020L,byz. **Var:** 01ℵ,02A,03B,06D 025P,Gries,Lach,Treg Alf,Word,Tisc,We/Ho Weis,Sod,UBS/☆

3450.2 art gen sing	2935.2 noun gen sing masc	1521.1 conj	1395.1 noun nom sing masc	1521.1 conj	1645.1 adj nom sing masc
τοῦ	κυρίου,	εἴτε	δοῦλος	εἴτε	ἐλεύθερος.
tou	kuriou,	eite	doulos	eite	eleutheros.
the	Lord,	whether	slave	or	free.

2504.1 conj	3450.7 art nom pl masc	2935.6 noun nom pl masc	3450.17 art pl neu	840.16 prs-pron pl neu	4020.2 verb 2pl pres act	4242.1 prep
9. Καὶ	οἱ	κύριοι,	τὰ	αὐτὰ	ποιεῖτε	πρὸς
Kai	hoi	kurioi,	ta	auta	poieite	pros
And	the	masters,	the	same things	do	towards

840.8 prs-pron acc pl masc	445.1 verb nom pl masc part pres act	3450.12 art acc sing fem	543.3 noun acc sing fem	3471.20 verb nom pl masc part perf act
αὐτούς,	ἀνιέντες	τὴν	ἀπειλήν·	εἰδότες
autous,	anientes	tēn	apeilēn	eidotes
them,	giving up	the	threatening,	knowing

9.a.Txt: 018K,byz. **Var:** 02A,03B,06D-org 025P,33,Lach,Treg,Alf Word,Tisc,We/Ho,Weis Sod,UBS/☆

3617.1 conj	2504.1 conj	5050.2 prs-pron gen 2pl	840.1 prs-pron gen pl	840.1 prs-pron gen pl	2504.1 conj	5050.2 prs-pron gen 2pl
ὅτι	καὶ	ὑμῶν	αὐτῶν	[a☆ αὐτῶν	καὶ	ὑμῶν]
hoti	kai	humōn	autōn	autōn	kai	humōn
that	also	your	self	[of them	and	of you]

3450.5 art nom sing masc	2935.1 noun nom sing masc	1498.4 verb 3sing indic pres act	1706.1 prep	3636.8 noun dat pl masc	2504.1 conj
ὁ	κύριός	ἐστιν	ἐν	οὐρανοῖς,	καὶ
ho	kurios	estin	en	ouranois,	kai
the	master	is	in	heavens,	and

4240.1 noun nom sing fem	4240.3 noun	3620.2 partic	1498.4 verb 3sing indic pres act
προσωπολημψία	[☆ προσωπολημψία]	οὐκ	ἔστιν
prosōpolēpsia	prosōpolēmpsia	ouk	estin
respect of persons	[idem]	not	there is

6:7. These words may seem almost unfair when one considers that Paul was addressing people who were owned by other people. Slaves had no real rights of their own, which from a purely human viewpoint might seem justification enough to encourage them to shirk their responsibilities or at least not to put too much effort into them. Instead, they are advised to serve "with good will" or "wholeheartedly." While it is not certain why the inspired writer kept emphasizing the matter of serving as "to the Lord," it may have been because some of these slaves were having trouble with their own attitudes and therefore not being good Christian examples to their masters.

6:8. The bottom line is the fact that a Christian's ultimate reward will come from the Lord, so service must be rendered as unto Him. At the judgment seat of Christ (1 Corinthians 3) all believers will stand on the same level. There will be no slave-master, employee-employer distinctions when we stand in His presence. Christians should realize that He is the only One who knows whether what a person does is truly a "good thing." A master or an employer may have the wrong attitude about certain things and may not credit the slave or employee properly because of that improper attitude. There need be no fear of that happening with Christ. His motives are always good and right. More than that, He knows exactly what each believer's motives are, and He will judge rightly.

6:9. Masters are warned to treat their slaves fairly, realizing their own ultimate responsibility and accountability to their own Master in heaven. Obviously, some of the Ephesian Christians were slave owners. In the light of the fact that slaves of that day normally had no rights, Paul's language was very revolutionary. The brief letter to Philemon shows how concerned Paul was for Christian slaves of the day. Even though neither he, nor the Early Church in general, spoke out forcefully against slavery, one should not get the impression that they favored it. In 1 Timothy 1:9,10 Paul placed "men-stealers" or "slave traders" (NIV) in some very bad company. He wrote, "We also know that law is made not for good men, but for lawbreakers and rebels, the ungodly and sinful, the unholy and irreligious; for those who kill their fathers or mothers, for murderers, for adulterers and perverts, for slave traders and liars and perjurers—and for whatever else is contrary to the sound doctrine" (NIV).

While this teaching about slavery may not seem very radical to the modern individual, it certainly was for Paul's day. No doubt this teaching helped mankind eventually to see the unscripturalness of slavery. It was not until later that Christianity made a concerted effort against this evil, but New Testament teachings laid much of the groundwork for later actions. Certainly no one can charge the apostle Paul with being in favor of slavery. Thank God for the progress we have made in this matter. There is still a long way to go.

7. With good will doing service: . . . performing service kindly, *Sawyer* . . . Give your service heartily and cheerfully, *TCNT* . . . serving as slaves with good will, *Adams* . . . keep on working as slaves, *Williams*.

as to the Lord, and not to men: . . . not for people, *Adams*.

8. Knowing that whatsoever good thing any man doeth, the same shall he receive of the Lord: You may be sure that God will reward a man for good work, *Phillips* . . . will get his reward from the Lord, *Williams*.

whether [he be] bond or free: . . . irrespectively of whether the man be, *Phillips*.

9. And, ye masters, do the same things unto them, forbearing threatening: You slaveowners, too must maintain the same attitude, *Williams* . . . show the same spirit to your slaves, and stop threatening them, *Montgomery* . . . Don't threaten, *Adams* . . . be conscientious and responsible, *Phillips*.

knowing that your Master also is in heaven: . . . nor forgetting that you are responsible yourselves to a Heavenly employer, *Phillips* . . . knowing that in the heavens is One Who is both Lord of them and of you, *Adams* . . . for you know that their real Lord and yours is, *Williams*.

neither is there respect of persons with him: . . . he recognizes no distinctions between, *TCNT* . . . and that He never shows, *Williams* . . . there is no favoritism, *Adams* . . . there is no Partiality, *Wilson* . . . makes no distinction between master and man, *Norlie, Phillips*.

Ephesians 6:10

10.a.Txt: 01א-corr,06D
018K,020L,025P,byz.
Var: 01א-org,02A,03B
33,Lach,Treg,Alf,Tisc
We/Ho,Weis,Sod
UBS/⋆

10.b.Txt: 01א-corr,018K
020L,025P,byz.bo.
Var: 01א-org,03B,06D
33,Lach,Treg,Alf,Tisc
We/Ho,Weis,Sod
UBS/⋆

3706.1 prep	840.4 prs-pron dat sing	3450.16 art sing neu	3036.8 adj sing neu	3450.2 art gen sing	3036.7 adj gen sing neu
παρ'	αὐτῷ.	10. ʽ Τὸ	λοιπόν,	[a⋆ Τοῦ	λοιποῦ]
par'	autō	To	loipon	Tou	loipou
with	him.	The	remaining	[The	remaining]

79.6 noun nom pl masc	1466.2 prs-pron gen 1sing	1727.5 verb 2pl impr pres mid	1706.1 prep	2935.3 noun dat sing masc
ʽb ἀδελφοί	μου, ʼ	ἐνδυναμοῦσθε	ἐν	κυρίῳ,
adelphoi	mou	endunamousthe	en	kuriō
brothers	my,	be empowered	in	Lord,

2504.1 conj	1706.1 prep	3450.3 art dat sing	2877.3 noun dat sing neu	3450.10 art gen sing fem	2452.2 noun gen sing fem	840.3 prs-pron gen sing
καὶ	ἐν	τῷ	κράτει	τῆς	ἰσχύος	αὐτοῦ.
kai	en	tō	kratei	tēs	ischuos	autou
and	in	the	might	of the	strength	his.

1730.8 verb 2pl impr aor mid	3450.12 art acc sing fem	3695.1 noun acc sing fem	3450.2 art gen sing	2296.2 noun gen sing neu
11. ἐνδύσασθε	τὴν	πανοπλίαν	τοῦ	θεοῦ,
endusasthe	tēn	panoplian	tou	theou
Put on	the	whole armor		of God,

4242.1 prep	3450.16 art sing neu	1404.22 verb inf pres mid	5050.4 prs-pron acc 2pl	2449.14 verb inf aor act	4242.1 prep
πρὸς	τὸ	δύνασθαι	ὑμᾶς	στῆναι	πρὸς
pros	to	dunasthai	humas	stēnai	pros
for	the	to be able	you	to stand	against

3450.15 art acc pl fem	3151.2 noun acc pl fem	3450.2 art gen sing	1222.2 adj gen sing masc	3617.1 conj	3620.2 partic
τὰς	μεθοδείας	τοῦ	διαβόλου·	12. ὅτι	οὐκ
tas	methodeias	tou	diabolou	hoti	ouk
the	schemings	of the	devil:	because	not

12.a.Txt: 01א,02A
06D-corr2,016I,023O
byz.
Var: p46,03B,06D-org
010F,012G,044,81,1175

1498.4 verb 3sing indic pres act	2231.3 prs-pron dat 1pl	5050.3 prs-pron dat 2pl	3450.9 art nom sing fem	3685.1 noun nom sing fem
ἔστιν	ʽ⋆ ἡμῖν	[a ὑμῖν]	ἡ	πάλη
estin	hēmin	humin	hē	palē
is	to us	[to you]	the	wrestling

4242.1 prep	129.1 noun sing neu	2504.1 conj	4418.4 noun acc sing fem	233.2 conj	4242.1 prep	3450.15 art acc pl fem
πρὸς	αἷμα	καὶ	σάρκα,	ἀλλὰ	πρὸς	τὰς
pros	haima	kai	sarka	alla	pros	tas
against	blood	and	flesh,	but	against	the

741.7 noun acc pl fem	4242.1 prep	3450.15 art acc pl fem	1833.1 noun fem	4242.1 prep	3450.8 art acc pl masc
ἀρχάς,	πρὸς	τὰς	ἐξουσίας,	πρὸς	τοὺς
archas	pros	tas	exousias	pros	tous
principalities,	against	the	authorities,	against	the

12.b.Txt: 01א-corr
06D-corr,018K,020L
025P,byz.Sod
Var: 01א-org,02A,03B
06D-org,33,bo.Gries
Lach,Treg,Alf,Word
Tisc,We/Ho,Weis
UBS/⋆

2861.1 noun acc pl masc	3450.2 art gen sing	4510.3 noun gen sing neu	3450.2 art gen sing	163.1 noun gen sing masc
κοσμοκράτορας	τοῦ	σκότους	ʽb τοῦ ·	αἰῶνος ʼ
kosmokratoras	tou	skotous	tou	aiōnos
world rulers	of the	darkness	of the	age

3642.1 dem-pron gen sing	4242.1 prep	3450.17 art pl neu	4012.10 adj pl neu	3450.10 art gen sing fem	4049.1 noun gen sing fem
τούτου,	πρὸς	τὰ	πνευματικὰ	τῆς	πονηρίας
toutou	pros	ta	pneumatika	tēs	ponērias
this,	against	the	spirituals	of the	wickedness

6:10. Verses 10-20 deal with the counterpart of the Christian's internal warfare described earlier (4:17-32). "Finally" literally means "for the rest" (*to loipon*). From a description of the ideal home the focus suddenly shifted to the battlefield. Paul's writings frequently speak of the Christian life in military terms. The language here, however, describes something that is more than just a figure of speech. This battle is real, difficult, and dangerous. Although salvation may be free to the person who receives it, it is not culminated ultimately without great effort. No true soldier of Jesus Christ can expect to be immune from the assaults of the enemy, and no Christian can afford to be neutral in the conflict.

In the light of the seriousness of this warfare, the Christian cannot be self-reliant. "Be strong" comes from a present passive verb, indicating a command to be strong "in the Lord" or "in the sphere of the Lord" or "to participate in the strength that is inherent in Him." It is present, indicating the necessity of continuous dependence upon Him. It is also passive, showing that strength must come from outside the believer, for without God's help he would never make it.

6:11. Therefore, the inspired writer advised putting on the whole armor (*panoplia*) God has provided for Christians so they may stand victoriously in this battle. The emphasis on "to stand" can be found again in verses 13 and 14. It contains the idea of being successful in this spiritual battle.

Because "put on" comes from a middle voice verb, it contains the idea of "putting on for one's self." Christians must do this in order to counter the "wiles" or "schemes" or "strategies" of the devil. The original word here (*methodeias*) is transliterated into English as *method* and would be an appropriate rendering of the idea expressed. The word for "devil" (*diabolos*) in this context literally means "slanderer."

The order in this passage about spiritual warfare cannot be overemphasized. While it is not wise to overemphasize the devil, neither is it wise to go to the other extreme and ignore him.

6:12. The conflict is serious because the battle is not against natural forces, but spiritual. Paul referred to "principalities" (*archas*), "powers" (*exousias*), "rulers" (*kosmokratoras*), and "spiritual wickedness." The language shows that these beings are spiritual and not like people whose bodies consist of blood and flesh, etc. "High places" or "heavenly realms" merely denotes the unseen realm in general and not the atmosphere.

Christians are not just shadowboxing in this spiritual warfare. The enemies are real, but thank God they can be overcome by His grace. When describing the reality of these enemies, some commentators add that sometimes in those days the loser in a Greek wrestling contest had his eyes gouged out with resulting blindness for the remainder of his life. That should give a little idea of the reality of these enemies.

10. Finally, my brethren, be strong in the Lord: In conclusion, *Phillips* . . . For the rest: Be getting empowered in, *Rotherham* . . . get empowered in, *PNT*.

and in the power of his might: . . . of his boundless resource, *Phillips.*

11. Put on the whole armour of God: . . . the complete-armour, *Rotherham.*

that ye may be able to stand against the wiles of the devil: . . . you can successfully resist, *Phillips* . . . be able to stand your ground, *TCNT* . . . that ye may stande stedfast against the craftie assaultes, *Geneva* . . . against the subtle ways, *PNT* . . . against the deceites of the Deuil, *Rheims* . . . against the spiritual [forces] of evil in the heavenlies, *Rotherham* . . . so that you may be able to resist the devil's cunning tactics, *Norlie.*

12. For we wrestle not against flesh and blood: . . . for our conflict, *Sawyer* . . . the struggle is not against, *Worrell* . . . is not only with flesh, *Scarlett* . . . is not against any physical enemy, *Phillips.*

but against principalities, against powers, against the rulers of the darkness of this world: . . . with the governments, with the authorities, *Wilson* . . . against the authorities, *Panin* . . . against the potentates of the darkness of this world, *Sawyer.*

against spiritual wickedness in high [places]: . . . against wicked spirits in heavenly places, *Wesley* . . . agaynst spretuall craftynes in heauenly thynges, *Cranmer* . . . against the spiritual [hosts] of evil in the heavenly [worlds], *Sawyer* . . . the spiritual forces of wickedness on high, *Confraternity* . . . spiritual wickednesses, which are aboue, *Geneva* . . . against the wicked spiritual forces of the underworld itself, *Norlie* . . . in the aerial regions, *Scarlett* . . . in the celestials, *Rheims.*

Ephesians 6:13

1706.1 prep	3450.4 art dat pl	2016.8 adj dat pl neu	1217.2 prep	3642.17 dem-pron sing neu	351.3 verb 2pl impr aor act
ἐν	τοῖς	ἐπουρανίοις.	**13.** διὰ	τοῦτο	ἀναλάβετε
en	tois	epouraniois	dia	touto	analabete
in	the	heavenlies.	Because of	this	take up

3450.12 art acc sing fem	3695.1 noun acc sing fem	3450.2 art gen sing	2296.2 noun gen sing masc	2419.1 conj	1404.28 verb 2pl subj aor pass
τὴν	πανοπλίαν	τοῦ	θεοῦ,	ἵνα	δυνηθῆτε
tēn	panoplian	tou	theou	hina	dunēthēte
the	whole armor		of God,	that	you may be able

434.4 verb inf aor act	1706.1 prep	3450.11 art dat sing fem	2232.3 noun dat sing fem	3450.11 art dat sing fem	4050.12 adj dat sing fem
ἀντιστῆναι	ἐν	τῇ	ἡμέρᾳ	τῇ	πονηρᾷ
antistēnai	en	tē	hēmera	tē	ponēra
to withstand	in	the	day	the	evil,

2504.1 conj	533.1 adj	2686.12 verb nom pl masc part aor mid	2449.14 verb inf aor act	2449.6 verb 2pl aor act
καὶ	ἅπαντα	κατεργασάμενοι	στῆναι.	**14.** στῆτε
kai	hapanta	katergasamenoi	stēnai	stēte
and	all things	having worked out	to stand.	Stand

3631.1 partic	3887.2 verb nom pl masc part aor mid	3450.12 art acc sing fem	3613.3 noun acc sing fem	5050.2 prs-pron gen 2pl	1706.1 prep
οὖν	περιζωσάμενοι	τὴν	ὀσφὺν	ὑμῶν	ἐν
oun	perizōsamenoi	tēn	osphun	humōn	en
therefore,	having girded about	the	loins	your	with

223.3 noun dat sing fem	2504.1 conj	1730.10 verb nom pl masc part aor mid	3450.6 art acc sing masc	2359.1 noun acc sing masc	3450.10 art gen sing fem
ἀληθείᾳ,	καὶ	ἐνδυσάμενοι	τὸν	θώρακα	τῆς
alētheia	kai	endusamenoi	ton	thōraka	tēs
truth,	and	having put on	the	breastplate	of the

1336.2 noun gen sing fem	2504.1 conj	5102.2 verb nom pl masc part aor mid	3450.8 art acc pl masc	4087.7 noun acc pl masc
δικαιοσύνης,	**15.** καὶ	ὑποδησάμενοι	τοὺς	πόδας
dikaiosunēs	kai	hupodēsamenoi	tous	podas
righteousness,	and	having shod	the	feet

1706.1 prep	2070.1 noun dat sing fem	3450.2 art gen sing	2077.2 noun gen sing neu	3450.10 art gen sing fem	1503.2 noun gen sing fem
ἐν	ἑτοιμασίᾳ	τοῦ	εὐαγγελίου	τῆς	εἰρήνης·
en	hetoimasia	tou	euangeliou	tēs	eirēnēs
with	preparation	of the	good news	of the	peace:

16.a.**Txt:** 02A,06D,018K 020L,byz.Weis
Var: 01ℵ,03B,025P,33 Lach,Treg,Tisc,We/Ho Sod,UBS/☆

1894.3 prep	1706.1 prep	3820.5 adj dat pl	351.5 verb nom pl masc part aor act	3450.6 art acc sing masc	2352.1 noun acc sing masc
16. ⸉ ἐπὶ	[ᵃ☆ ἐν]	πᾶσιν	ἀναλαβόντες	τὸν	θυρεὸν
epi	en	pasin	analabontes	ton	thureon
besides	[in]	all	having taken up	the	shield

3450.10 art gen sing fem	3963.2 noun gen sing fem	1706.1 prep	3614.3 rel-pron dat sing	1404.32 verb 2pl indic fut mid	3820.1 adj
τῆς	πίστεως,	ἐν	ᾧ	δυνήσεσθε	πάντα
tēs	pisteōs	en	hō	dunēsesthe	panta
of the	faith,	with	which	you will be able	all

16.b.**Txt:** 01ℵ,02A 06D-corr2,044,byz.
Var: p46,03B,06D-org 010F,012G

3450.17 art pl neu	949.1 noun pl neu	3450.2 art gen sing	4050.2 adj gen sing	3450.17 art pl neu	4306.6 verb pl neu part perf mid
⸉ᵇ τὰ ⸊	βέλη	τοῦ	πονηροῦ	τὰ	πεπυρωμένα
ta	belē	tou	ponērou	ta	pepurōmena
the	darts	of the	wicked one	the	having been burning

6:13. The word "wherefore" literally means "on account of this" (*dia touto*) and relates back to the earlier description of the conflict and the enemies. "Take unto you" refers to the decisive act of taking all the armor God has supplied so that a person can stand his ground when the evil days come, a probable reference to the time when the conflict becomes most severe. As a result, "having done all" or "after you have won the battle," the Christian can stand victoriously.

6:14. Before the armor could be put on, the soldier had to bind the loose, flowing garments worn by people of that day, so he could enjoy freedom of movement. To tighten the belt meant a soldier was ready for duty, and to loosen it meant he was going off duty. In the Scriptures "loins" (*osphun*) were used often to signify strength. Girded loins meant the opposite of self-indulgence, ease, or carelessness. Paul compared the wide leather belt of the soldier to the belt of truth worn by the Christian who stands literally "in the realm of truth." The person who operates in the realm of the truth of God's Word will not be defeated in battle.

"The breastplate" usually was composed of metallic scales, but sometimes it was made of leather or bronze. It covered the torso, and so protected the vital organs of the body—the heart, the lungs, etc. The breastplate often saved the Roman soldier from being mortally wounded. Similarly, the person who is just or righteous, because he has accepted the righteousness of Christ, will not be mortally wounded in the spiritual warfare in which he is engaged. Putting on the breastplate of righteousness means an individual has come to grips with the basic tenets of the gospel.

6:15. Thirdly, the soldier needed sure footing to enable him to march and to move quickly when necessary. The Roman sandal or military shoe was bound by a thong over the instep and around the ankle, and the sole was studded with nails to permit surefootedness. "The preparation of the gospel of peace" is a fitting way of stating that a Christian must be prepared with the gospel which has peace as its message.

6:16. "Above all" literally means "besides all." Believers should never be without the shield of faith. The large body-shield usually measured about 4 feet high by 2½ feet wide. It normally was constructed of alternating layers of bronze and oxhide. Many of Rome's enemies used arrows dipped in pitch which would be set aflame and propelled toward the Roman soldiers. The shield would break the arrow's force and cause them to fall harmlessly to the ground. Just as the soldier could not afford to be without this protective shield at any time, the follower of Christ cannot for one moment afford to be without faith.

13. Wherefore take unto you the whole armour of God: On this account, take up, *Worrell* . . . On account of this take up the complete, *Wilson* . . . you must wear, *Phillips*.

that ye may be able to withstand in the evil day: . . . be able to resist, *Wilson, Scarlett* . . . resist evil in its day of power, *Phillips*.

and having done all, to stand: . . . having done all thoroughly, *Panin* . . . having accomplished all, *Alford* . . . when you have fought to a standstill, *Phillips* . . . to stonde perfect in all thinges, *Tyndale* . . . and, when it is all over, you will still be holding your own, *Norlie*.

14. Stand therefore, having your loins girt about with truth: Stand firm, then, girt about with the belt of, *Montgomery* . . . Take your stand then with truth as your belt, *Phillips*.

and having on the breastplate of righteousness: . . . and wearing, *Montgomery*.

15. And your feet shod with the preparation of the gospel of peace: . . . with the firm foothold of the Good News of Peace, *TCNT* . . . shod with the stability of, *Montgomery* . . . firmly on your feet, *Phillips*.

16. Above all, taking the shield of faith: . . . in addition to all, *Noyes* . . . take to you the confidence of faith, *Murdock*.

wherewith ye shall be able to quench all the fiery darts of the wicked: . . . able to extinguish, *TCNT, Douay* . . . it can quench every burning missile the enemy hurls at you, *Phillips* . . . the firie dartes of the most vvicked one, *Rheims* . . . the flaming darts of the Evil One, *Montgomery* . . . all the fire-tipped arrows shot by the evil one, *Williams*.

4426.3 verb inf aor act	2504.1 conj	3450.12 art acc sing fem	3893.1 noun acc sing fem	3450.2 art gen sing	4844.3 adj gen sing neu
σβέσαι˙	**17.** καὶ	τὴν	περικεφαλαίαν	τοῦ	σωτηρίου
sbesai	kai	tēn	perikephalaian	tou	sōtēriou
to quench.	Also	the	helmet	of the	salvation

1203.12 verb 2pl impr aor mid	2504.1 conj	3450.12 art acc sing fem	3134.4 noun acc sing fem	3450.2 art gen sing	4011.2 noun gen sing neu
δέξασθε,	καὶ	τὴν	μάχαιραν	τοῦ	πνεύματος,
dexasthe	kai	tēn	machairan	tou	pneumatos
receive,	and	the	sword	of the	Spirit,

3614.16 rel- pron sing neu	1498.4 verb 3sing sing indic pres act	4343.1 noun sing neu	2296.2 noun gen sing masc	1217.2 prep	3820.10 adj gen sing fem
ὅ	ἐστιν	ῥῆμα	θεοῦ˙	**18.** διὰ	πάσης
ho	estin	rhēma	theou	dia	pasēs
which	is	word	God's;	by	all

4194.2 noun gen sing fem	2504.1 conj	1157.2 noun gen sing fem	4195.13 verb nom pl masc part pres mid	1706.1 prep
προσευχῆς	καὶ	δεήσεως	προσευχόμενοι	ἐν
proseuchēs	kai	deēseōs	proseuchomenoi	en
prayer	and	supplication	praying	in

3820.3 adj dat sing	2511.3 noun dat sing masc	1706.1 prep	4011.3 noun dat sing neu	2504.1 conj	1519.1 prep	840.15 prs- pron sing neu
παντὶ	καιρῷ	ἐν	πνεύματι,	καὶ	εἰς	αὐτὸ
panti	kairō	en	pneumati	kai	eis	auto
every	season	in	Spirit,	and	unto	same

18.a.Txt: 06D-corr,018K
020L,025P,byz.
Var: 01א,02A,03B
06D-org,33,bo.Lach
Treg,Alf,Tisc,We/Ho
Weis,Sod,UBS/★

3642.17 dem- pron sing neu	68.3 verb nom pl masc part pres act	1706.1 prep	3820.11 adj dat sing fem	4202.1 noun dat sing fem
⸂a τοῦτο ⸃	ἀγρυπνοῦντες	ἐν	πάσῃ	προσκαρτερήσει
touto	agrupnountes	en	pasē	proskarterēsei
this thing	watching	with	all	perseverance

2504.1 conj	1157.3 noun dat sing fem	3875.1 prep	3820.4 adj gen pl	3450.1 art gen pl	39.4 adj gen pl	2504.1 conj
καὶ	δεήσει	περὶ	πάντων	τῶν	ἁγίων,	**19.** καὶ
kai	deēsei	peri	pantōn	tōn	hagiōn	kai
and	supplication	for	all	the	saints;	and

19.a.Txt: Steph
Var: 01א,02A,03B,06D
018K,020L,025P,byz.
Gries,Lach,Treg,Alf
Word,Tisc,We/Ho,Weis
Sod,UBS/★

5065.1 prep	1466.3 prs- pron gen 1sing	2419.1 conj	1466.4 prs- pron dat 1sing	1319.47 verb 3sing opt aor pass	1319.46 verb 3sing subj aor pass
ὑπὲρ	ἐμοῦ	ἵνα	μοι	⸂ δοθείη	[a★ δοθῇ]
huper	emou	hina	moi	dotheiē	dothē
for	me	that	to me	may be given	[idem]

3030.1 noun nom sing masc	1706.1 prep	454.1 noun dat sing fem	3450.2 art gen sing	4601.2 noun gen sing neu	1466.2 prs- pron gen 1sing
λόγος	ἐν	ἀνοίξει	τοῦ	στόματός	μου
logos	en	anoixei	tou	stomatos	mou
utterance	in	opening	of the	mouth	my

1706.1 prep	3816.3 noun dat sing fem	1101.9 verb inf aor act	3450.16 art sing neu	3328.1 noun sing neu
ἐν	παρρησίᾳ,	γνωρίσαι	τὸ	μυστήριον
en	parrhēsia	gnōrisai	to	mustērion
with	boldness	to make known	to the	mystery

3450.2 art gen sing	2077.2 noun gen sing neu	5065.1 prep	3614.2 rel- pron gen sing	4102.1 verb 1sing indic pres act
τοῦ	εὐαγγελίου,	**20.** ὑπὲρ	οὗ	πρεσβεύω
tou	euangeliou	huper	hou	presbeuō
of the	good news,	for	which	I am an ambassador

6:17. The fifth item, the helmet, was made of bronze with leather attachments, or of leather strengthened with metallic plates. It protected the head of the individual. First Thessalonians 5:8 makes another reference to this piece of equipment, calling it "the hope of salvation." It seems to refer to the fact that a person's will, a very important part of his intellectual process, is involved in the hope of full salvation. Christians must continue to will to serve God if they expect the ultimate consummation of all His promises. The head may also symbolize the mind which needs protection. Finally, Paul spoke of the offensive weapon, the "sword of the Spirit, which is the word of God."

6:18. Because the proper attitude in battle is just as important as the proper equipment, Paul reminded the Ephesians of the need for prayer and watchfulness in this spiritual conflict. Prayer must be "in the Spirit" or "in the sphere of the Holy Spirit" in order to be effective. "Praying" comes from a more general word for prayer. It speaks of the necessity of always being in an attitude of prayer, of having a consistent prayer life. "Supplication" comes from a Greek term which relates to special times of need. If Christians truly practice prayer as a way of life, when the special times of need come they will be prepared for them.

"Watching" (*agrupnountes*) translated literally means "to be awake or alert." Having the proper attitude in this spiritual warfare cannot be overemphasized. It is dangerous to take a flippant attitude about something this serious. The conflict is a real one, the enemies are spiritual forces that are not limited to the physical realm, but God has provided sufficient necessary equipment for believers to be victorious in the battle.

6:19. Because Paul practiced what he preached, he asked the Ephesians to pray that God would help him proclaim the gospel, even though he was in chains. The apostle's request teaches an important lesson about the purpose of prayer. While there is no doubt that Paul also prayed for his own needs, the main emphasis of this prayer request was that God would give him the enablement to present the gospel message with boldness. This is consistent with Jesus' words to His disciples that His children should seek His kingdom and His righteousness first, and depend upon Him to supply their needs (Matthew 6:33). Perhaps Christians would receive more answers to prayer if they followed Paul's example and prayed more for the power to proclaim the gospel, rather than always asking God for things for self.

6:20. From the time of his conversion (Acts 9), Paul was consumed with one chief aim in life—proclaiming the gospel to the world. He considered himself a special appointee of Jesus Christ himself, much as a president of a country appoints an ambassador to represent him personally in another country. An ambassador

17. And take the helmet of salvation: And receive, *Worrell* . . . take the helmet salvation provides, *Williams.*

and the sword of the Spirit: . . . and in your hand, *Phillips* . . . the sword the Spirit wields, *Williams.*

which is the word of God: . . . which is God's Truth, *TCNT.*

18. Praying always with all prayer and supplication in the Spirit: Continue to pray, *Montgomery* . . . Do all of this with prayer and petition, *Adams* . . . Keep on praying in the Spirit, *Williams* . . . praying at all seasons, *Clementson* . . . at every Season, *Wilson* . . . at all times, *Scarlett* . . . praying at every opportunity in [the] Spirit, *PNT* . . . Pray much, and at every opportunity, *Norlie* . . . with every kind of spiritual prayer, *Phillips.*

and watching thereunto with all perseverance and supplication for all saints: . . . keeping alert and persistent, *Phillips* . . . and to that end stay alert...concerning all of the saints, *Adams* . . . be vigilant in all perseverance, *Confraternity* . . . and Entreaty, *Wilson* . . . and interceding for all the saints, *Murdock.*

19. And for me, that utterance may be given unto me, that I may open my mouth boldly: . . . and on my behalf, *ASV* . . . particularly for me, *Scarlett* . . . on my behalf, that Eloquence, *Wilson* . . . that I may be given the right words to say, *Adams.* . . . that I may be able to speak freely here, *Phillips.*

to make known the mystery of the gospel: . . . that I may courageously make known the secret truths, *TCNT* . . . the secret of the good news, *Adams.*

20. For which I am an ambassador in bonds: . . . of which I am an envoy in prison, *Williams* . . . a messenger in chains, *Murdock* . . . an ambassador with a chain, *Adams.*

1706.1 prep	252.1 noun dat sing fem	2419.1 conj	1706.1 prep	840.4 prs-pron dat sing	3817.6 verb 1sing subj aor mid
ἐν	ἁλύσει,	ἵνα	ἐν	αὐτῷ	παρρησιάσωμαι
en	halusei	hina	en	autō	parrhēsiasōmai
in	a chain,	that	in	it	I may be bold

5453.1 conj	1158.1 verb 3sing indic pres act	1466.6 prs-pron acc 1sing	2953.37 verb inf aor act	2419.1 conj	1156.2 conj
ὡς	δεῖ	με	λαλῆσαι.	21. Ἵνα	δὲ
hōs	dei	me	lalēsai	Hina	de
as	it is necessary for	me	to speak.	That	but

3471.17 verb 2pl subj perf act	2504.1 conj	5050.1 prs-pron nom 2pl	3450.17 art pl neu	2567.1 prep	1466.7 prs-pron acc 1sing
εἰδῆτε	καὶ	ὑμεῖς	τὰ,	κατ'	ἐμέ,
eidēte	kai	humeis	ta	kat'	eme
may know	also	you	the things	concerning	me,

4949.9 intr-pron sing neu	4097.1 verb 1sing indic pres act	3820.1 adj	5050.3 prs-pron dat 2pl	1101.11 verb 3sing indic fut act
τί	πράσσω,	πάντα	ὑμῖν	γνωρίσει
ti	prassō	panta	humin	gnōrisei
what	I am doing,	all things	to you	will make known

1101.11 verb 3sing indic fut act	5050.3 prs-pron dat 2pl	5031.1 name nom masc	3450.5 art nom sing masc	27.3 adj nom sing masc
[✶ γνωρίσει	ὑμῖν]	Τυχικὸς	ὁ	ἀγαπητὸς
gnōrisei	humin	Tuchikos	ho	agapētos
[will make known	to you]	Tychicus	the	beloved

79.1 noun nom sing masc	2504.1 conj	3964.2 adj nom sing masc	1243.1 noun nom sing masc	1706.1 prep	2935.3 noun dat sing masc
ἀδελφὸς	καὶ	πιστὸς	διάκονος	ἐν	κυρίῳ·
adelphos	kai	pistos	diakonos	en	kuriō
brother	and	faithful	servant	in	Lord;

3614.6 rel-pron acc sing masc	3854.5 verb 1sing indic aor act	4242.1 prep	5050.4 prs-pron acc 2pl	1519.1 prep	840.15 prs-pron acc sing neu	3642.17 dem-pron sing neu
22. ὃν	ἔπεμψα	πρὸς	ὑμᾶς	εἰς	αὐτὸ	τοῦτο,
hon	epempsa	pros	humas	eis	auto	touto
whom	I sent	to	you	for	same	this thing,

2419.1 conj	1091.19 verb 2pl aor act	3450.17 art pl neu	3875.1 prep	2231.2 prs-pron gen 1pl	2504.1 conj
ἵνα	γνῶτε	τὰ	περὶ	ἡμῶν	καὶ
hina	gnōte	ta	peri	hēmōn	kai
that	you might know	the things	concerning	us	and

3731.4 verb 3sing subj pres act	3450.15 art acc pl fem	2559.1 noun fem	5050.2 prs-pron gen 2pl	1503.1 noun nom sing fem
παρακαλέσῃ	τὰς	καρδίας	ὑμῶν.	23. Εἰρήνη
parakalesē	tas	kardias	humōn	Eirēnē
he might encourage	the	hearts	your.	Peace

3450.4 art dat pl	79.8 noun dat pl masc	2504.1 conj	26.1 noun nom sing fem	3196.3 prep	3963.2 noun gen sing fem	570.3 prep
τοῖς	ἀδελφοῖς	καὶ	ἀγάπη	μετὰ	πίστεως	ἀπὸ
tois	adelphois	kai	agapē	meta	pisteōs	apo
to the	brothers,	and	love	with	faith	from

2296.2 noun gen sing masc	3824.2 noun gen sing masc	2504.1 conj	2935.2 noun gen sing masc	2400.2 name masc	5382.2 name gen masc
θεοῦ	πατρὸς	καὶ	κυρίου	Ἰησοῦ	Χριστοῦ.
theou	patros	kai	kuriou	Iēsou	Christou
God	Father	and	Lord	Jesus	Christ.

does not speak for himself, but for the prominent person he represents. This gives a certain amount of boldness to the ambassador. How much more this should be true of a representative of Jesus Christ.

6:21,22. Verses 21 and 22 are almost identical with Colossians 4:7-9. Tychicus was the "beloved brother" who took this letter to the Ephesians. The word for "brother" (*adelphos*) contains the idea of "coming from the same womb," and "minister" comes from the word *diakonos* from which we get *deacon*.

In our contemporary society where speedy travel from one part of the world to another is commonplace, it is hard to appreciate the importance of this comment. Tychicus traveled with Onesimus (Colossians 4:9) on this journey. Onesimus was a slave who had run away from his master, Philemon. Many slaves were killed for doing much less than Onesimus had done. By being with this slave, Tychicus was endangering his own life as well. Traveling the great distance from Rome to Asia Minor and placing his life in danger paled into insignificance when compared with his mission of reporting the welfare of Paul and his team and of encouraging the believers of Ephesus and the surrounding communites. The word "comfort" or "encourage" comes from the same Greek term (*parakaleō*) from which we get one of the names for the Holy Spirit—Paraclete.

The word "our" in the verse may refer to some or all of the people Paul listed in the closing statements of his epistle to the Colossians (Aristarchus, Mark, Jesus called Justus, Epaphras, Luke, and Demas). The Prison Epistles indicate that the apostle Paul normally had a sizable retinue of helpers with him or at least assisting him in some ways. He was a very secure man who was not threatened by other people. In fact, he seemed to enjoy elevating other people by referring to them at various times. Many of these younger and lesser-known associates received important recognition in the Christian world by the references of the apostle. The people of that day did not have an elaborate means of recommending people to congregations and to fellow Christians, so comments like Paul's concerning Tychicus and others were very important.

6:23. In his closing benediction there are some of the same terms Paul used to begin this classic letter. He wanted the Ephesians to enjoy the peace of God, that inner tranquility that is not disturbed by external circumstances. Furthermore, he emphasized the love of God that operates in a person through faith. In the Scriptures this word *agapē* consistently relates to the motivating force behind all that God does. As it operates in believers, whatever they do will have the same motivation (1 Corinthians 13). There is a relationship between faith and love. What many people call "love" really is not related to Biblical love. Unfortunately, an erotic substitute for Biblical love has become very prominent.

that therein I may speak boldly, as I ought to speak: . . . have the courage, *TCNT* . . . speak as courageously as, *Williams* . . . as it is necessary for me to speak, *PNT* . . . that I may speak out about it, *Phillips* . . . as is my duty, *Norlie*.

21. But that ye also may know my affairs: . . . to know all that concerns me, *TCNT* . . . how I am faring, *Noyes* . . . what condicion I am in, *Tyndale*.
[and] how I do: . . . and what I do, *Tyndale* . . . and how I am getting on, *Phillips*.
Tychicus, a beloved brother and faithful minister in the Lord: . . . faithful Christian minister, *Phillips*.
shall make known to you all things: . . . will inform you, *Sawyer, Noyes* . . . will acquaint you, *Murdock* . . . will give you all the information, *Williams* . . . will tell you personally, *Phillips*.

22. Whom I have sent unto you for the same purpose: I am sending him to you bringing this letter, *Phillips* . . . that is the very reason I am sending him, *Williams* . . . for this very thing, *Wesley* . . . for this very purpose, *Confraternity, Montgomery*.
that ye might know our affairs: . . . to let you know how I am, *Williams* . . . you may learn all about us, *TCNT* . . . that ye may know our state, *Panin* . . . know about us, *Montgomery*.
and [that] he might comfort your hearts: . . . he might console, *Rotherham* . . . and that he may cheer your hearts, *Montgomery* . . . may take fresh heart, *Phillips*.

23. Peace [be] to the brethren: . . . to the brothers, *Williams* . . . to all Christian brothers, *Phillips*.
and love with faith:
from God the Father and the Lord Jesus Christ: . . . our Father, *Williams*.

3450.9 art nom sing fem	5322.1 noun nom sing fem	3196.3 prep	3820.4 adj gen pl	3450.1 art gen pl	25.9 verb gen pl masc part pres act
24. Ἡ	χάρις	μετὰ	πάντων	τῶν	ἀγαπώντων
Hē	charis	meta	pantōn	tōn	agapōntōn
The	grace	with	all	the	loving

3450.6 art acc sing masc	2935.4 noun acc sing masc	2231.2 prs- pron gen 1pl	2400.3 name acc masc	5382.4 name acc masc	1706.1 prep
τὸν	κύριον	ἡμῶν	Ἰησοῦν	Χριστὸν	ἐν
ton	kurion	hēmōn	Iēsoun	Christon	en
the	Lord	our	Jesus	Christ	in

854.1 noun dat sing fem	279.1 intrj	4242.1 prep	2162.2 name- adj acc pl masc	1119.21 verb 3sing indic aor pass
ἀφθαρσίᾳ.	⟨a ἀμήν. ⟩	⟨b Πρὸς	Ἐφεσίους	ἐγράφη
aphtharsia	amēn	Pros	Ephesious	egraphē
incorruption.	Amen.	To	Ephesians	written

570.3 prep	4373.1 name gen fem	1217.2 prep	5031.2 name gen masc
ἀπὸ	Ῥώμης,	διὰ	Τυχικοῦ. ⟩
apo	Rhōmēs	dia	Tuchikou
from	Rome,	by	Tychicus.

24.a.**Txt:** 01ℵ-corr,06D
018K,020L,025P,byz.
Var: 01ℵ-org,02A,03B
33,Gries,Lach,Treg,Alf
Tisc,We/Ho,Weis,Sod
UBS/⋆

24.b.**Txt:** Steph
Var: Gries,Lach,Word
Tisc,We/Ho,Weis,Sod
UBS/⋆

6:24. Paul's Prison Epistles place great emphasis upon the term "grace." The apostle was a "gracious" man because he was a recipient of God's grace, and one of his main desires was that other people would also receive this grace. Grace truly does come to "all them that love our Lord Jesus Christ in sincerity." When a person truly responds to the unmerited favor bestowed by God, how can he help but respond in sincere love?

The twin of "grace" is "gratitude." The two should be coupled in an inseparable manner in a Christian's life. They certainly were in Paul's. His constant praise from prison was an explicit manifestation of an important truth taught throughout the Bible: God's grace is not limited to our circumstances. When reading Ephesians, believers should not forget that Paul was in prison when he wrote it.

24. Grace [be] with all them that love our Lord Jesus Christ in sincerity. Amen: May God's blessing be with all, *TCNT* . . . Help be with all...with an incorruptible love, *Adams* . . . whose love to our Lord Jesus Christ is love imperishable, *HistNT* . . . who love our Lord Jesus, *TEV* . . . who have true love for, *BB* . . . who have a love unfailing for, *Confraternity, Goodspeed* . . . with all who have an undying love for, *Williams, Beck, Moffatt* . . . with all those people who love our Lord Jesus Christ with a love that never dies, *SEB* . . . to their immortalitie, *Geneva* . . . who sincerely love our Lord, *Phillips* . . . in incorruption, *Panin, Douay, Rotherham, Rheims* . . . with constancy, *Sawyer* . . . without corruptness, *Murdock* . . . with perfect sincerity, *Weymouth* . . . with a love which will never die, *Barclay.*

THE EPISTLE
OF PAUL TO THE
PHILIPPIANS

Expanded Interlinear

Textual Critical Apparatus

Verse-by-Verse Commentary

Various Versions

4242.1 prep	5211.2 name- adj acc pl masc	1976.1 noun nom sing fem	3834.2 name gen masc
Πρὸς	Φιλιππησίους	ἐπιστολὴ	Παύλου
Pros	Philippēsious	epistolē	Paulou
To	Philippians	letter	of Paul

**Textual
Apparatus**

3834.1 name nom masc	2504.1 conj	4943.1 name nom masc	1395.6 noun nom pl masc	2400.2 name masc	5382.2 name gen masc
1:1. Παῦλος	καὶ	Τιμόθεος	δοῦλοι	ʼ Ἰησοῦ	Χριστοῦ,
Paulos	kai	Timotheos	douloi	Iēsou	Christou,
Paul	and	Timothy,	slaves	of Jesus	Christ,

5382.2 name gen masc	2400.2 name masc	3820.5 adj dat pl	3450.4 art dat pl	39.8 adj dat pl masc	1706.1 prep	5382.3 name dat masc
[☆ Χριστοῦ	Ἰησοῦ]	πᾶσιν	τοῖς	ἁγίοις	ἐν	Χριστῷ
Christou	Iēsou	pasin	tois	hagiois	en	Christō
[of Christ	Jesus]	to all	the	saints	in	Christ

2400.2 name masc	3450.4 art dat pl	1498.24 verb dat pl masc part pres act	1706.1 prep	5212.2 name dat masc	4713.1 prep
Ἰησοῦ	τοῖς	οὖσιν	ἐν	Φιλίπποις,	σὺν
Iēsou	tois	ousin	en	Philippois	sun
Jesus	the	being	in	Philippi,	with

1969.2 noun dat pl masc	2504.1 conj	1243.4 noun dat pl masc	5322.1 noun nom sing fem	5050.3 prs- pron dat 2pl	2504.1 conj
ἐπισκόποις	καὶ	διακόνοις	2. χάρις	ὑμῖν	καὶ
episkopois	kai	diakonois	charis	humin	kai
overseers	and	deacons.	Grace	to you	and

1503.1 noun nom sing fem	570.3 prep	2296.2 noun gen sing masc	3824.2 noun gen sing masc	2231.2 prs- pron gen 1pl	2504.1 conj	2935.2 noun gen sing masc
εἰρήνη	ἀπὸ	θεοῦ	πατρὸς	ἡμῶν	καὶ	κυρίου
eirēnē	apo	theou	patros	hēmōn	kai	kuriou
peace	from	God	Father	our	and	Lord

2400.2 name masc	5382.2 name gen masc	2149.1 verb 1sing indic pres act	3450.3 art dat sing	2296.3 noun dat sing masc	1466.2 prs- pron gen 1sing
Ἰησοῦ	Χριστοῦ.	3. Εὐχαριστῶ	τῷ	θεῷ	μου
Iēsou	Christou.	Eucharistō	tō	theō	mou
Jesus	Christ.	I thank	God	God	my

1894.3 prep	3820.11 adj dat sing fem	3450.11 art dat sing fem	3281.1 noun dat sing fem	5050.2 prs- pron gen 2pl	3704.1 adv
ἐπὶ	πάσῃ	τῇ	μνείᾳ	ὑμῶν,	4. πάντοτε
epi	pasē	tē	mneia	humōn,	pantote
on	all	the	remembrance	of you,	always

1706.1 prep	3820.11 adj dat sing fem	1157.3 noun dat sing fem	1466.2 prs- pron gen 1sing	5065.1 prep	3820.4 adj gen pl	5050.2 prs- pron gen 2pl
ἐν	πάσῃ	δεήσει	μου	ὑπὲρ	πάντων	ὑμῶν
en	pasē	deēsei	mou	huper	pantōn	humōn
in	every	prayer	my	for	all	you

3196.3 prep	5315.2 noun gen sing fem	3450.12 art acc sing fem	1157.4 noun acc sing fem	4020.64 verb nom sing masc part pres mid	1894.3 prep
μετὰ	χαρᾶς	τὴν	δέησιν	ποιούμενος,	5. ἐπὶ
meta	charas	tēn	deēsin	poioumenos,	epi
with	joy	the	prayer	making,	for

THE EPISTLE OF PAUL TO THE
PHILIPPIANS

1:1. In the Epistle to the Philippians Paul followed the usual manner in his introduction, according to the pattern of letter writing which we discover from surviving papyri. Sometimes the apostle used an amanuensis (a person who writes what another dictates) (cf. Romans 16:22). However, there is no clear indication of an amanuensis here.

"Servants" (*douloi*) suggests submission without servility, slavery that is motivated by love, and service of a willing spirit. "Saints" (*hagioi*) means "set apart ones" who have confessed Christ as Saviour. Paul made no sharp distinction between clergy and laity. Rather, he emphasized the bond between them. Further, he did not use the title *bishop* in the sense Ignatius did in the Second Century in reference to a threefold ministry of bishops, presbyters, and deacons. Evangelicals generally recognize the same New Testament leader being addressed as "bishop, overseer, superintendent" (*episkopos*—Acts 20:28; Titus 1:7); "elder, presbyter" (*presbuteros*—Acts 20:17; Titus 1:5; 1 Peter 5:1); and "pastor, shepherd" (*poimēn*—Acts 20:28; 1 Peter 5:2).

1:2. The apostle often coupled the terms "grace" and "peace" in his greetings. The term "grace" comes from the Greek word *charis* and generally refers to a favor done out of the pure generosity of the heart, expecting nothing in return. "Peace" (*eirēnē*) is a Hebrew concept (*shalōm*) which denotes the harmony and well-being of a life that has been reconciled to God through Jesus Christ.

1:3. It was common for Paul to pray for the people to whom he wrote, and his prayers of thanksgiving and supplication usually go together. The basis of his thanksgiving was his overall remembrance of the believers in Philippi.

1:4. As he contemplated all that God had done for them and through them, Paul was filled with joy. Joy is the keynote of the entire epistle. Because joy is the by-product of something else, the apostle was not referring to some superficial happiness when he made this statement.

Various Versions

1. Paul and Timotheus: the servants of Jesus Christ: ...true servants, *Phillips* ...bondmen, *Panin, Wilson* ...slaves, *Williams*.

to all the saints in Christ Jesus which are at Philippi: To all Christ's People, *TCNT* ...to alle the holi men, *Wyclif* ...to all God's people in union with, *Williams* ...all true Christians, *Phillips* ...who live in Philippi, *Everyday*.

with the bishops and deacons: ...including the pastors, *Norlie* ...with overseers, *Panin, Wilson* ...with the elders, *Murdock* ...and ministers, *Rotherham, PNT* ...with the Presidents and Assistant-Officers, *TCNT* ...and assistants, *Williams*.

2. Grace [be] unto you, and peace, from God our Father, and [from] the Lord Jesus Christ: ...spiritual blessing, *Williams*.

3. I thank my God upon every remembrance of you: I thank God every time I remember you, *Everyday* ...in al memorie of you, *Rheims* ...in every entreaty, *Williams* ...for all my memories of you, *Norlie* ...at the constant recollection of you, *Murdock* ...whenever I think of you, *Phillips*.

4. Always in every prayer of mine for you all: I always pray for all of you, *Everyday* ...My constant prayers for you, *Phillips* ...always making supplication, *Scarlett* ...in every petition, *Montgomery*.

making request with joy: ...making supplication on behalf of you, *Wilson* ...are full of joy, *TCNT* ...are a real joy, *Phillips*.

Philippians 1:6

3450.11 art
dat sing fem
τῇ
tē
the

2815.3 noun
dat sing fem
κοινωνίᾳ
koinōnia
fellowship

5050.2 prs-
pron gen 2pl
ὑμῶν
humōn
your

1519.1
prep
εἰς
eis
in

3450.16 art
sing neu
τὸ
to
the

2077.1 noun
sing neu
εὐαγγέλιον,
euangelion
good news,

570.3
prep
ἀπὸ
apo
from

3450.10 art
gen sing fem
[ᵃ✶+ τῆς]
tēs
[the]

4272.10 num ord
gen sing fem
πρώτης
prōtēs
first

2232.1
noun fem
ἡμέρας
hēmeras
day

884.2
conj
ἄχρι
achri
until

3450.2 art
gen sing
τοῦ
tou
the

3431.1
adv
νῦν·
nun
now;

3844.13 verb nom sing
masc part perf act
6. πεποιθὼς
pepoithōs
having been persuaded of

840.15 prs-
pron sing neu
αὐτὸ
auto
same thing

3642.17 dem-
pron sing neu
τοῦτο,
touto
this,

3617.1
conj
ὅτι
hoti
that

3450.5 art
nom sing masc
ὁ
ho
the

1712.1 verb nom sing
masc part aor mid
ἐναρξάμενος
enarxamenos
having begun

1706.1
prep
ἐν
en
in

5050.3 prs-
pron dat 2pl
ὑμῖν
humin
you

2024.1 noun
sing neu
ἔργον
ergon
a work

18.3
adj sing
ἀγαθὸν
agathon
good

1989.8 verb 3sing
indic fut act
ἐπιτελέσει
epitelesei
will complete

884.1
conj
ʿ ἄχρις
achris
until

884.2
conj
[✶ ἄχρι]
achri
[idem]

2232.1
noun fem
ἡμέρας
hēmeras
day

2400.2
name masc
ʿ Ἰησοῦ
Iēsou
of Jesus

5382.2 name
gen masc
Χριστοῦ
Christou
Christ:

5382.2 name
gen masc
[✶ Χριστοῦ
Christou
[of Christ

2400.2
name masc
Ἰησοῦ·]
Iēsou
Jesus.]

2503.1
conj
7. καθώς
kathōs
as

1498.4 verb 3sing
indic pres act
ἐστιν
estin
it is

1337.1
adj sing
δίκαιον
dikaion
righteous

1466.5 prs-
pron dat 1sing
ἐμοὶ
emoi
for me

3642.17 dem-
pron sing neu
τοῦτο
touto
this

5262.9 verb
inf pres act
φρονεῖν
phronein
to think

5065.1
prep
ὑπὲρ
huper
as to

3820.4
adj gen pl
πάντων
pantōn
all

5050.2 prs-
pron gen 2pl
ὑμῶν,
humōn
you,

1217.2
prep
διὰ
dia
because

3450.16 art
sing neu
τὸ
to
the

2174.29 verb
inf pres act
ἔχειν
echein
to have

1466.6 prs-
pron acc 1sing
με
me
me

1706.1
prep
ἐν
en
in

3450.11 art
dat sing fem
τῇ
tē
the

2559.3 noun
dat sing fem
καρδίᾳ
kardia
heart

5050.4 prs-
pron acc 2pl
ὑμᾶς,
humas
you,

1706.1
prep
ἔν
en
in

4885.1
conj
τε
te
both

3450.4
art dat pl
τοῖς
tois
the

1193.5
noun dat pl
δεσμοῖς
desmois
bonds

1466.2 prs-
pron gen 1sing
μου
mou
my

2504.1
conj
καὶ
kai
and

1706.1
prep
[ᵃ✶+ ἐν]
en
[in]

3450.11 art
dat sing fem
τῇ
tē
in the

621.3 noun
dat sing fem
ἀπολογίᾳ
apologia
defense

2504.1
conj
καὶ
kai
and

944.1 noun
dat sing fem
βεβαιώσει
bebaiōsei
confirmation

3450.2 art
gen sing
τοῦ
tou
of the

2077.2 noun
gen sing neu
εὐαγγελίου
euangeliou
good news,

4642.2 noun
acc pl masc
συγκοινωνούς
sunkoinōnous
fellow partakers

1466.2 prs-
pron gen 1sing
μου
mou
my

3450.10 art
gen sing fem
τῆς
tēs
of the

1:5. This joy resulted from their fellowship (*koinōnia*) with him in the gospel. People who refer to fellowship as "two people in a ship" certainly cheapen the idea expressed in the original term. It meant far more than just enjoying someone else's company. In the original sense it expressed a joint participation in a common ministry or interest. *Partnership* is a very appropriate contemporary term to express the idea. (See the word study on *koinōnia* in the *Greek-English Dictionary.*) The Philippians had participated in Paul's ministry with their prayers and finances for approximately 10 years, from the beginning of the assembly until the writing of this epistle. In fact, there is a definite article before the adverb "now" (literally, "the now"), so Paul probably was pointing to the gift they just had extended to him through Epaphroditus.

The Philippians seem to have found a very special place in the heart of the apostle. His mind raced back to "the first day," when he became acquainted with them. The warm relationship between a true pastor and his people continues even after he has moved away.

1:6. Conversely, even though he had much cause for thanksgiving as he remembered the Philippian saints, Paul was not entirely satisfied with their spiritual state. His desire for them was that God would continue the work He had begun in them.

Deists teach that God merely wound up the universe and withdrew from it, allowing it to operate by itself. Just as the Bible counters this kind of theory relative to creation, it also stresses that God is interested not only in the spiritual birth of His people, but also in their continued growth and maturity. A person certainly does not receive all of God's benefits at the conversion experience. That is only the starting point, the gateway to many benefits from God. Paul was "confident" that God would keep believers in this process until the day Jesus returns to receive His people unto himself.

1:7. The apostle's confidence in the Philippians was based upon the fact that they had shared God's grace with him for approximately 10 years. Even though he was in prison, God's grace was not imprisoned. Some of the greatest fruits of his ministry came while Paul was in prison. At least five of the Epistles the Holy Spirit inspired him to write were written while he was in prison. There the apostle's influence reached many, even in Nero's palace.

The term "defense" comes from the Greek word from which we derive *apologetics* (*apologia*). However, Paul used the word in connection with the "confirmation of the gospel." Too often we think of the term "defense" in a negative sense, as if we had to keep unbelievers from taking something from the gospel. Paul realized the process of defending would result in the confirmation of the gospel.

5. For your fellowship in the gospel: . . . for they bring back to my mind how we have worked together, *Phillips* . . . your communication, *Douay* . . . your communicating, *Rheims* . . . because of your association with me in spreading the gospel, *Confraternity* . . . in furtherance of the gospel, *ASV* . . . in forwarding the gospel, *Montgomery.*

from the first day until now: . . . until the present, *Rotherham.*

6. Being confident of this very thing: For of this I am quite sure, *TCNT* . . . I am convinced of this, *Confraternity* . . . Of this I am fully persuaded, *Montgomery* . . . having become persuaded of, *Worrell* . . . being persuaded of this very thing, *PNT.*

that he which hath begun a good work in you: . . . he who commenced, *Wilson.*

will perform [it] until the day of Jesus Christ: . . . you will perfect it, *Panin, Alford* . . . will keep on perfecting it, *Norlie* . . . will accomplish them, *Murdock* . . . will go on completing it, *Montgomery* . . . will bring it to perfection, *Confraternity* . . . will carry it on till, *Sawyer* . . . will continue to complete it, *Wilson* . . . will be completing it, *Scarlett* . . . will fully complete [it], *Rotherham* . . . will go on developing it, *Phillips.*

7. Even as it is meet for me to think this of you all: It is only natural, *Phillips.*

because I have you in my heart: I have an affectionate remembrance of you, *TCNT* . . . because I hold you in heart, *PNT* . . . you are very dear to me, *Phillips.*

inasmuch as both in my bonds: . . . during the time I was in prison, *Phillips* . . . in these fetters of mine, *Montgomery.*

and in the defence and confirmation of the gospel: . . . when I have been free to defend and vindicate the Gospel, *Norlie* . . . in the work of defending and establishing the Good News, *TCNT.*

ye all are partakers of my grace: . . . being joint-contributors, *Wilson* . . . as sharers in my joy, *Confraternity.*

Philippians 1:8

5322.2 noun gen sing fem	3820.8 adj acc pl masc	5050.4 prs-pron acc 2pl	1498.25 verb acc pl masc part pres act	3116.1 noun nom sing masc	1056.1 conj
χάριτος	πάντας	ὑμᾶς	ὄντας.	8. μάρτυς	γάρ
charitos	*pantas*	*humas*	*ontas*	*martus*	*gar*
grace	all	you	being.	Witness	for

8.a.Txt: 01א-corr,02A
06D,018K,020L,025P
byz.
Var: 01א-org,03B,33
Treg,Alf,Tisc,We/Ho
Weis,Sod,UBS/⋆

1466.2 prs-pron gen 1sing	1498.4 verb 3sing indic pres act	3450.5 art nom sing masc	2296.1 noun nom sing masc	5453.1 conj	1955.1 verb 1sing indic pres act
μου	(ᵃ ἐστὶν)	ὁ	θεός,	ὡς	ἐπιποθῶ
mou	*estin*	*ho*	*theos*	*hōs*	*epipothō*
my	is	the	God,	how	I long for

3820.8 adj acc pl masc	5050.4 prs-pron acc 2pl	1706.1 prep	4551.2 noun dat pl neu	2400.2 name masc	5382.2 name gen masc
πάντας	ὑμᾶς	ἐν	σπλάγχνοις	(Ἰησοῦ	Χριστοῦ.
pantas	*humas*	*en*	*splanchnois*	*Iēsou*	*Christou*
all	you	in	inner affections	of Jesus	Christ.

5382.2 name gen masc	2400.2 name masc	2504.1 conj	3642.17 dem-pron sing neu	4195.2 verb 1sing indic pres mid
[⋆ Χριστοῦ	Ἰησοῦ.]	9. καὶ	τοῦτο	προσεύχομαι,
Christou	*Iēsou*	*kai*	*touto*	*proseuchomai*
[of Christ	Jesus.]	And	this	I pray,

2419.1 conj	3450.9 art nom sing fem	26.1 noun nom sing fem	5050.2 prs-pron gen 2pl	2068.1 adv	3095.1 adv comp	2504.1 conj	3095.1 adv comp
ἵνα	ἡ	ἀγάπη	ὑμῶν	ἔτι	μᾶλλον	καὶ	μᾶλλον
hina	*hē*	*agapē*	*humōn*	*eti*	*mallon*	*kai*	*mallon*
that	the	love	your	yet	more	and	more

9.a.Txt: p46,01א,02A
018K-corr2,020L,We/Ho
byz.
Var: 03B,06D,08E,044
69,81,2464,2495

3915.6 verb 3sing subj pres act	3915.14 verb 3sing subj aor act	1706.1 prep	1907.3 noun dat sing fem	2504.1 conj
(⋆ περισσεύῃ	[ᵃ περισσεύσῃ]	ἐν	ἐπιγνώσει	καὶ
perisseuē	*perisseusē*	*en*	*epignōsei*	*kai*
may increase	[idem]	in	knowledge	and

3820.11 adj dat sing fem	144.1 noun dat sing fem	1519.1 prep	3450.16 art sing neu	1375.8 verb inf pres act	5050.4 prs-pron acc 2pl
πάσῃ	αἰσθήσει,	10. εἰς	τὸ	δοκιμάζειν	ὑμᾶς
pasē	*aisthēsei*	*eis*	*to*	*dokimazein*	*humas*
all	intelligence,	for	the	to approve	you

3450.17 art pl neu	1302.3 verb pl neu part pres act	2419.1 conj	1498.1 verb 2pl act	1496.1 adj nom pl masc	2504.1 conj
τὰ	διαφέροντα,	ἵνα	ἦτε	εἰλικρινεῖς	καὶ
ta	*diapheronta*	*hina*	*ēte*	*eilikrineis*	*kai*
the things	excelling,	that	you may be	pure	and

671.2 adj nom pl	1519.1 prep	2232.4 noun acc sing fem	5382.2 name gen masc	3997.30 verb nom pl masc part perf mid
ἀπρόσκοποι	εἰς	ἡμέραν	Χριστοῦ,	11. πεπληρωμένοι
aproskopoi	*eis*	*hēmeran*	*Christou*	*peplērōmenoi*
without offense	for	day	of Christ,	having been filled

11.a.Txt: 025P,byz.bo.
Var: 01א,02A,(03B)
06D,018K,020L,it.sa.
Gries,Lach,Treg,Alf
Word,Tisc,We/Ho,Weis
Sod,UBS/⋆

11.b.Txt: 025P,byz.bo.
Var: 01א,02A,(03B)
06D,018K,020L,it.sa.
Gries,Lach,Treg,Alf
Word,Tisc,We/Ho,Weis
Sod,UBS/⋆

2561.4 noun gen pl masc	2561.3 noun acc sing masc	1336.2 noun gen sing fem	3450.1 art gen pl	3450.6 art acc sing masc
(καρπῶν	[ᵃ⋆ καρπὸν]	δικαιοσύνης	(τῶν	[ᵇ⋆ τὸν
karpōn	*karpon*	*dikaiosunēs*	*tōn*	*ton*
with fruits	[fruit]	of righteousness	the	[idem]

1217.2 prep	2400.2 name masc	5382.2 name gen masc	1519.1 prep	1385.4 noun acc sing fem	2504.1 conj	1853.2 noun acc sing masc
διὰ	Ἰησοῦ	Χριστοῦ,	εἰς	δόξαν	καὶ	ἔπαινον
dia	*Iēsou*	*Christou*	*eis*	*doxan*	*kai*	*epainon*
by	Jesus	Christ,	to	glory	and	praise

1:8. Paul compared his longing for the Philippians to the straining of an athlete reaching forward to the goal set for him. This longing was motivated by the love Jesus has for His own people, an affection so great that He died for His people. In King James' day "bowels" referred to the seat of the emotions.

1:9. Paul's actual prayer for the Philippians begins in this verse and includes two specific requests. His supplication for them was prefaced with one of the Greek terms expressing purpose (*hina*, "in order that"). He prayed that their love would abound more and more in knowledge and in perception. Thus it is possible for a believer's love (*agapē*) to increase. In like manner, "knowledge" (*epignōsis*) here denotes full or ever-increasing understanding.

"Judgment" or "perception" or "depth of insight," on the other hand, is concerned with practical application of love. Scriptural love is not indiscriminate love that is manifested in any manner a person chooses. The Christian experiences increasing love in his life and the ability to discern the proper application of it.

1:10. According to this verse, this combination will enable Christians to discern what is best for them. A gullible love accepts anything, but a love manifested in full knowledge and in practical application distinguishes the genuine from the spurious.

The root word translated "approve" here was used of the assaying of metals, as well as of the approval of candidates for the degree of medicine. Therefore, it refers to the act of testing something for the purpose of approving it. God does not want Christians to accept everything, but He wants them to approve only what is "best" or "excellent." Some things may be "good" in the normal sense of the word but may not be "best." Paul wanted the Philippians to accept the approved things that would help them "be sincere and without offense."

The second request in Paul's prayers for the Philippians relates to the level of personal character and demeanor. This sincere and unoffending attitude will be manifested ultimately at the judgment of believers by Christ himself.

1:11. Such an attitude also will yield a harvest of righteousness through Jesus Christ. In a real sense God is working in believers to make them more and more like the Lord Jesus Christ. When a person becomes a Christian and chooses to follow Jesus, that person accepts the righteousness of Christ as the only righteousness sufficient to satisfy the requirements of God. At the same time, a process begins in that life so that the righteousness of Christ becomes gradually imparted to that individual. Initially the righteousness of Christ is imputed at the time the person becomes a Christian, but the righteousness of Christ is imparted by the Holy Spirit throughout the believer's entire lifetime.

8. For God is my record: God knows, *Phillips* . . . is my witness, *Panin*.

how greatly I long after you all:

in the bowels of Jesus Christ: . . . with the tenderness of, *TCNT* . . . with the tender Sympathies, *Wilson* . . . in tender affections, *Rotherham* . . . in tender mercies of, *Panin* . . . in the tender heart of, *Alford* . . . with the deepest Christian love and affection, *Phillips*.

9. And this I pray: My prayer for you, *Phillips*.

that your love may abound yet more and more: . . . may grow yet stronger and stronger, *TCNT* . . . may have still more love, *Phillips*.

in knowledge and [in] all judgment: . . . and with perfect discernment, *TCNT* . . . and all discernment, *Panin* . . . and in all spiritual sense, *Wesley* . . . all Perception, *Wilson, Rotherham, Alford* . . . and in all understanding, *Douay*.

10. That ye may approve things that are excellent: . . . examine the differences of things, *Wilson* . . . approve the better things, *Confraternity*.

that ye may be sincere and without offence: . . . you may be without fault, *Sawyer* . . . that ye may be incorrupt, *Rotherham* . . . that ye may be pure, *Noyes*.

till the day of Christ:

11. Being filled with the fruits of righteousness, which are by Jesus Christ: . . . that you may bear a rich harvest, *TCNT* . . . produced by the power that Jesus Christ gives you, *Phillips*.

unto the glory and praise of God:

2296.2 noun
gen sing masc
θεοῦ.
theou
of God.

12. 1091.14 verb
inf pres act
Γινώσκειν
Ginōskein
To know

1156.2
conj
δὲ
de
but

5050.4 prs-
pron acc 2pl
ὑμᾶς
humas
you

1007.1 verb 1sing
indic pres mid
βούλομαι,
boulomai
I wish,

79.6 noun
nom pl masc
ἀδελφοί,
adelphoi
brothers,

3617.1
conj
ὅτι
hoti
that

3450.17
art pl neu
τὰ
ta
the things

2567.1
prep
κατ'
kat'
concerning

1466.7 prs-
pron acc 1sing
ἐμὲ
eme
me

3095.1
adv comp
μᾶλλον
mallon
rather

1519.1
prep
εἰς
eis
to

4156.2 noun
acc sing fem
προκοπὴν
prokopēn
advancement

3450.2 art
gen sing
τοῦ
tou
of the

2077.2 noun
gen sing neu
εὐαγγελίου
euangeliou
good news

2048.26 verb 3sing
indic perf act
ἐλήλυθεν·
elēluthen
have turned out,

13. 5452.1
conj
ὥστε
hōste
so as

3450.8 art
acc pl masc
τοὺς
tous
the

1193.6
noun pl
δεσμούς
desmous
bonds

1466.2 prs-
pron gen 1sing
μου
mou
my

5156.3 adj
acc pl masc
φανεροὺς
phanerous
manifest

1706.1
prep
ἐν
en
in

5382.3 name
dat masc
Χριστῷ
Christō
Christ

1090.63 verb
inf aor mid
γενέσθαι
genesthai
to have become

1706.1
prep
ἐν
en
in

3513.3 adj
dat sing
ὅλῳ
holō
whole

3450.3 art
dat sing
τῷ
tō
the

4091.2 noun
dat sing neu
πραιτωρίῳ
praitōriō
praetorium

2504.1
conj
καὶ
kai
and

3450.4
art dat pl
τοῖς
tois
to the

3036.2
adj dat pl
λοιποῖς
loipois
rest

3820.5
adj dat pl
πάσιν·
pasin
all;

14. 2504.1
conj
καὶ
kai
and

3450.8 art
acc pl masc
τοὺς
tous
the

3979.4 adj
comp acc pl
πλείονας
pleionas
most

3450.1
art gen pl
τῶν
tōn
of the

79.7 noun
gen pl masc
ἀδελφῶν
adelphōn
brothers

1706.1
prep
ἐν
en
in

2935.3 noun
dat sing masc
κυρίῳ
kuriō
Lord

3844.15 verb acc pl
masc part perf act
πεποιθότας
pepoithotas
having been persuaded

3450.4
art dat pl
τοῖς
tois
by the

1193.5
noun dat pl
δεσμοῖς
desmois
bonds

1466.2 prs-
pron gen 1sing
μου
mou
my

3917.2
adv comp
περισσοτέρως
perissoterōs
more abundantly

4958.4 verb
inf pres act
τολμᾶν
tolman
to dare

863.1
adv
ἀφόβως
aphobōs
fearlessly

3450.6 art
acc sing masc
τὸν
ton
the

3030.4 noun
acc sing masc
λόγον
logon
word

[a+ 3450.2 art
gen sing
τοῦ
tou

2296.2 noun
gen sing masc
θεοῦ]
theou
[of God]

2953.24 verb
inf pres act
λαλεῖν.
lalein
to speak.

15. 4948.7 indef-
pron nom pl masc
Τινὲς
Tines
Some

3173.1
conj
μὲν
men
indeed

14.a.**Var**: 01**א**,02A,03B
06D-org,025P,33,it.sa.
bo.Lach,Treg,Alf,Tisc
We/Ho,Weis,Sod
UBS/★

2504.1
conj
καὶ
kai
even

1217.2
prep
διὰ
dia
from

5192.4 noun
acc sing masc
φθόνον
phthonon
envy

2504.1
conj
καὶ
kai
and

2038.4 noun
acc sing fem
ἔριν,
erin
strife,

4948.7 indef-
pron nom pl masc
τινὲς
tines
some

1156.2
conj
δὲ
de
but

2504.1
conj
καὶ
kai
also

1217.1
prep
δι'
di'
from

2086.3 noun
acc sing fem
εὐδοκίαν
eudokian
good will

3450.6 art
acc sing masc
τὸν
ton
the

5382.4 name
acc masc
Χριστὸν
Christon
Christ

2756.4 verb 3pl
indic pres act
κηρύσσουσιν.
kērussousin
are proclaiming.

1:12. In verses 12-26 the apostle described his ambition more clearly than in any other place in his writings. Further, the passage expresses what the ambition of every Christian should be. It is summarized best in verse 20 with the statement, "Christ shall be magnified in my body, whether it be by life, or by death."

The apostle initially introduced the subject in verse 12 by indicating two factors which did not serve as the basis for his purpose in life. First, he said his ambition was not based upon circumstances. Literally, he was "not under the circumstances." He controlled them, not vice versa.

1:13. Paul then proceeded to give examples which proved that his being in prison had not curtailed his work for the Lord, but rather, had advanced the cause of Christ. First, his circumstances had enabled him to witness to the palace guard (*praitōriō*). The term for "palace" could refer to at least four different things: (1) those forming the praetorian guard, (2) the emperor's palace, (3) the barracks of the praetorian guard, or (4) the judicial authorities. The context seems to support the first option. Emperor Tiberius concentrated 10,000 soldiers in Rome with the express purpose of guarding him and his court. They were handpicked soldiers with special qualifications and special privileges. To reach men of this caliber for Christ was a remarkable achievement for the gospel.

1:14. While serving as "chaplain" to this group, Paul also encouraged the Christians in Rome. "Many of the brethren" in Rome had been encouraged "to speak the word" because of Paul's circumstances. Perhaps the joy and contentment he manifested while in prison had a strong impact upon them. This example and the one expressed in verse 13 clearly show that Paul was not "under the circumstances." Too many times Christians allow opposing forces to discourage them from doing what God has called them to do. Circumstances sometimes can be changed, but sometimes they cannot be. If God does not see fit to change them, He must have some purpose for them.

1:15. Paul knew opposition from false preachers even in prison. He had experienced it from the beginning of his ministry for Christ (Acts 9), and it continued until his earthly life was complete. Paul recognized that some people preached Christ out of pure motives and some others preached Christ out of impure motives. The latter group consisted of people who envied Paul's authority, position, and ministry. Perhaps while he was able to move freely in his proclamation of the gospel, they hesitated to move against him. However, when Paul was placed in prison, these jealous individuals probably felt unhindered in their activities. They preached Christ, but their real objective was to gain adherents for themselves.

12. But I would ye should understand: I want you to know, *Phillips.*

brethren, that the things [which happened] unto me: . . . that my experiences, *Confraternity.*

have fallen out rather unto the furtherance of the gospel: . . . have resulted in the advancement, *Sawyer* . . . turned out to the advantage of, *Phillips* . . . chaunced vnto the greate furtheraunce of, *Cranmer* . . . to the great furtheryng, *Geneva* . . . unto the progress of, *ASV* . . . rather unto an advancement, *Rotherham* . . . Advancement of the Glad Tidings, *Wilson* . . . unto the progress of the gospel, *Clementson.*

13. So that my bonds in Christ are manifest in all the palace and in all other [places]: My imprisonment has been plainly seen, *TCNT* . . . my imprisonment means a personal witness, *Phillips* . . . are famous throughout all the, *Geneva* . . . in the whole praetorium, *Panin* . . . in the whole of the praetorian camp, *Rotherham.*

14. And many of the brethren in the Lord, waxing confident by my bonds: . . . gaining courage from my chains, *Confraternity* . . . beynge encoraged thorow my bandes, *Cranmer* . . . somehow taking fresh heart in the Lord from the very fact that I am a prisoner, *Phillips.*

are much more bold to speak the word without fear: . . . now venture with far greater freedom, *TCNT* . . . should be much more abundantly bold, *Rotherham* . . . more abundant courage, *Sawyer, Wilson* . . . in boldly proclaiming, *Phillips.*

15. Some indeed preach Christ even of envy and strife: . . . some actually proclaim the Christ out of jealousy and opposition, *TCNT* . . . and contentiousness, *Confraternity.*

and some also of good will: . . . in good faith, *Phillips.*

16.a.Txt: 06D-corr,018K byz.
Var: 01ℵ,02A,03B 06D-org,025P,33,sa.bo. Gries,Lach,Treg,Alf Word,Tisc,We/Ho,Weis Sod,UBS/✶

16.b.Txt: 06D-corr,018K 020L,byz.
Var: 01ℵ,02A,03B 06D-org,33,Lach,Treg Alf,Word,Tisc,We/Ho Weis,Sod,UBS/✶

16/17 in reverse order:
Txt: 06D-corr1,044,byz.
Var: p46,01ℵ,02A,03B 06D-org,010F,012G,025P 33,81,365,1739,1881 UBS/✶

17.a.Txt: 06D-corr,018K byz.
Var: 01ℵ,02A,03B 06D-org,025P,33,sa.bo. Gries,Lach,Treg,Alf Word,Tisc,We/Ho,Weis Sod,UBS/✶

18.a.Var: 01ℵ,02A,025P 33,sa.Lach,Treg,Alf Tisc,We/Ho,Weis,Sod UBS/✶

3450.7 art nom pl masc	3173.1 conj	1523.1 prep gen	2036.2 noun gen sing fem	3450.6 art acc sing masc	5382.4 name acc masc
16. οἱ	μὲν	[a ἐξ	ἐριθείας	τὸν	Χριστὸν
hoi	men	ex	eritheias	ton	Christon
The	indeed	out of	contention	the	Christ

2576.1 verb 3pl indic pres act	3620.1 partic	56.1 adv	3496.2 verb nom pl masc part pres mid	2324.4 noun acc sing fem
καταγγέλλουσιν,	οὐχ	ἁγνῶς,	οἰόμενοι	θλῖψιν
katangellousin	ouch	hagnōs	oiomenoi	thlipsin
are announcing.	not	purely,	supposing	tribulation

2002.2 verb inf pres act	1446.4 verb inf pres act	3450.4 art dat pl	1193.5 noun dat pl	1466.2 prs-pron gen 1sing
[ἐπιφέρειν	[b✶ ἐγείρειν]	τοῖς	δεσμοῖς	μου ·]
epipherein	egeirein	tois	desmois	mou
to add	[to raise]	to the	bonds	my,

3450.7 art nom pl masc	1156.2 conj	1523.1 prep gen	26.2 noun gen sing fem	3471.20 verb nom pl masc part perf act	3617.1 conj
17. οἱ	δὲ	[a ἐξ	ἀγάπης,	εἰδότες	ὅτι
hoi	de	ex	agapēs	eidotes	hoti
the	but	out of	love,	knowing	that

1519.1 prep	621.4 noun acc sing fem	3450.2 art gen sing	2077.2 noun gen sing neu	2719.1 verb 1sing indic pres mid	4949.9 intr-pron sing neu
εἰς	ἀπολογίαν	τοῦ	εὐαγγελίου	κεῖμαι,]	**18.** τί
eis	apologian	tou	euangeliou	keimai	ti
for	defense	of the	good news	I am set.	What

1056.1 conj	3993.1 conj	3617.1 conj	3820.3 adj dat sing	4999.2 noun dat sing masc	1521.1 conj
γάρ;	πλὴν	[a✶+ ὅτι]	παντὶ	τρόπῳ,	εἴτε
gar	plēn	hoti	panti	tropō	eite
for?	nevertheless	[that]	in every	way,	whether

4250.1 noun dat sing fem	1521.1 conj	223.3 noun dat sing fem	5382.1 name nom masc	2576.9 verb 3sing indic pres mid
προφάσει	εἴτε	ἀληθείᾳ,	Χριστὸς	καταγγέλλεται ·
prophasei	eite	alētheia	Christos	katangelletai
in pretext	or	in truth,	Christ	is being announced;

2504.1 conj	1706.1 prep	3642.5 dem-pron dat sing masc	5299.1 verb 1sing indic pres act	233.2 conj	2504.1 conj
καὶ	ἐν	τούτῳ	χαίρω,	ἀλλὰ	καὶ
kai	en	toutō	chairō	alla	kai
and	in	this	I rejoice,	but,	also

5299.22 verb 1sing indic fut mid	3471.2 verb 1sing indic perf act	1056.1 conj	3617.1 conj	3642.17 dem-pron sing neu	1466.4 prs-pron dat 1sing
χαρήσομαι.	**19.** οἶδα	γὰρ	ὅτι	τοῦτό	μοι
charēsomai	oida	gar	hoti	touto	moi
I will rejoice:	I know	for	that	this	for me

571.3 verb 3sing indic fut mid	1519.1 prep	4843.3 noun acc sing fem	1217.2 prep	3450.10 art gen sing fem	5050.2 prs-pron gen 2pl
ἀποβήσεται	εἰς	σωτηρίαν	διὰ	τῆς	ὑμῶν
apobēsetai	eis	sōtērian	dia	tēs	humōn
shall turn out	to	salvation	through	the	your

1157.2 noun gen sing fem	2504.1 conj	2008.1 noun gen sing fem	3450.2 art gen sing	4011.2 noun gen sing neu	2400.2 name masc
δεήσεως,	καὶ	ἐπιχορηγίας	τοῦ	πνεύματος	Ἰησοῦ
deēseōs	kai	epichorēgias	tou	pneumatos	Iēsou
prayer,	and	support	of the	Spirit	of Jesus

1:16. This verse begins the apostle's own commentary on the statement he made in the previous verse. The motive behind a person's actions may not always be known to other people, but God knows what it is. People who preach Christ "out of good will" do so out of love (*agapē*). However, another group preached Christ out of "contention." These individuals apparently thought they could enhance their own positions by degrading the apostle.

The term "affliction" (*thlipsis*) means "trouble involving direct suffering" (Louw and Nida, *Lexicon*, 1:243). One pictures the painful rubbing of iron chains on Paul's hands and legs.

Notice the marks of hypocrisy manifested by these individuals: (1) envy, which makes a person want what belongs to someone else; (2) strife, or an attitude of competitiveness; (3) contention, which causes a person to resort to all kinds of intrigue in order to elevate self; (4) insincerity, or the opposite of doing something out of good will; and (5) pretense, which leads a person to cloak ulterior motives.

1:17. However, the worthy group manifested the following marks of honesty: good will, love, and truth. They did this because they knew Paul was defending the gospel in a scriptural manner.

1:18. To summarize, Paul responded, "What does it matter?" He, of course, did not condone preaching from false motives, but he knew the hearers could be saved when Christ is preached regardless. False ministerial motives cannot cancel the truth of the gospel as the power of God unto salvation.

1:19. Paul's ambition was not based upon his circumstances, nor upon the opinions of other people. He made it clear that his ambition to magnify Christ in his body was possible only because of his relationship to Christ. The chief priority in any believer's life is to keep Christ first in his life (Matthew 6:33).

The apostle was confident that he could count on two kinds of aid: human and divine. "Your prayer" shows how much Paul desired and depended upon the prayers of God's people. "The supply of the Spirit of Jesus Christ" indicates the divine aid that always comes to the person whose total trust rests in God. "Supply" or "help" comes from the term *epichorēgia* which means "help which undergirds and strengthens the object." This results from a proper relationship with Christ, where everything else will fall into place.

It is difficult to know exactly what Paul meant by the word "salvation" or "deliverance" (NIV) in this verse, but it certainly seems to indicate he expected to be released soon from prison. It could, of course, refer to "deliverance" from this earthly life, when he would have the privilege of being with Christ. His Master meant everything to him.

16. The one preach Christ of contention: . . . in a spirit of rivalry, *TCNT* . . . out of rivalry, *Montgomery* . . . of a factious spirit preach Christ with no pure intent, *Noyes*.

not sincerely: . . . and not purely, *Geneva*.

supposing to add affliction to my bonds: . . . to superadd Affliction to, *Wilson* . . . adding bitterness to, *Montgomery* . . . hoping to make my chains even more galling than they would otherwise, *Phillips*.

17. But the other of love: . . . out of their love for me, *Phillips*.

knowing that I am set for the defence of the gospel: God has set me here in prison to defend our right to preach, *Phillips* . . . for the vindication of, *Murdock*.

18. What then?: But what does it matter? *Phillips*.

notwithstanding, every way: However they may look at it, *Phillips* . . . nevertheless, *Sawyer* . . . In one way or another, *Norlie*.

whether in pretence, or in truth: . . . or syncerely, *Geneva*.

Christ is preached: . . . is being made known, *TCNT* . . . is proclaimed, *Panin*.

and I therein do rejoice, yea, and will rejoice: . . . that fact makes me very happy, *Phillips*.

19. For I know that this shall turn to my salvation: . . . this will result in, *Sawyer* . . . My Deliverance, *Wilson* . . . will be for the good of my own soul, *Phillips*.

through your prayer: . . . thanks to, *Phillips* . . . through your intercession, *Scarlett*.

and the supply of the Spirit of Jesus Christ: . . . and the assistance of, *Confraternity* . . . and the subministration of, *Rheims* . . . and because of the bountiful resources, *Norlie* . . . and a rich supply of the Spirit of Jesus, *Montgomery*.

5382.2 name gen masc	2567.3 prep	3450.12 art acc sing fem	598.2 noun acc sing fem	2504.1 conj
Χριστοῦ, *Christou* Christ:	**20.** κατὰ *kata* according to	τὴν *tēn* the	ἀποκαραδοκίαν *apokaradokian* earnest expectation	καὶ *kai* and

1667.4 noun acc sing fem	1466.2 prs- pron gen 1sing	3617.1 conj	1706.1 prep	3625.7 num card dat neu	152.4 verb 1sing indic fut pass
ἐλπίδα *elpida* hope	μου, *mou* my,	ὅτι *hoti* that	ἐν *en* in	οὐδενὶ *oudeni* nothing	αἰσχυνθήσομαι, *aischunthēsomai* I shall be ashamed,

233.1 conj	1706.1 prep	3820.11 adj dat sing fem	3816.3 noun dat sing fem	5453.1 conj	3704.1 adv	2504.1 conj
ἀλλ' *all'* but	ἐν *en* in	πάσῃ *pasē* all	παῤῥησίᾳ, *parrhēsia* boldness,	ὡς *hōs* as	πάντοτε, *pantote* always,	καὶ *kai* also

3431.1 adv	3141.6 verb 3sing indic fut pass	5382.1 name nom masc	1706.1 prep	3450.3 art dat sing	4835.3 noun dat sing neu
νῦν *nun* now	μεγαλυνθήσεται *megalunthēsetai* shall be magnified	Χριστὸς *Christos* Christ	ἐν *en* in	τῷ *tō* the	σώματί *sōmati* body

1466.2 prs- pron gen 1sing	1521.1 conj	1217.2 prep	2205.2 noun gen sing fem	1521.1 conj	1217.2 prep	2265.2 noun gen sing masc
μου *mou* my	εἴτε *eite* whether	διὰ *dia* by	ζωῆς *zōēs* life	εἴτε *eite* or	διὰ *dia* by	θανάτου. *thanatou* death.

1466.5 prs- pron dat 1sing	1056.1 conj	3450.16 art sing neu	2180.19 verb inf pres act	5382.1 name nom masc	2504.1 conj	3450.16 art sing neu
21. Ἐμοὶ *Emoi* To me	γὰρ *gar* for	τὸ *to* the	ζῆν *zēn* to live	Χριστὸς, *Christos* Christ,	καὶ *kai* and	τὸ *to* the

594.20 verb inf aor act	2742.1 noun sing neu	1479.1 conj	1156.2 conj	3450.16 art sing neu	2180.19 verb inf pres act
ἀποθανεῖν *apothanein* to die	κέρδος. *kerdos* gain;	**22.** εἰ *ei* If	δὲ *de* but	τὸ *to* the	ζῆν *zēn* to live

1706.1 prep	4418.3 noun dat sing fem	3642.17 dem- pron sing neu	1466.4 prs- pron dat 1sing	2561.1 noun nom sing masc	2024.2 noun gen sing neu	2504.1 conj
ἐν *en* in	σαρκί, *sarki* flesh,	τοῦτό *touto* this	μοι *moi* for me	καρπὸς *karpos* fruit	ἔργου· *ergou* of labor:	καὶ *kai* and

4949.9 intr- pron sing neu	141.3 verb 1sing indic fut mid	3620.3 partic	1101.1 verb 1sing indic pres act	4762.6 verb 1sing indic pres mid
τί *ti* what	αἱρήσομαι *hairēsomai* I shall choose	οὐ *ou* not	γνωρίζω· *gnōrizō* I know.	**23.** συνέχομαι *sunechomai* I am being caught

1056.1 conj	1156.2 conj	1523.2 prep gen	3450.1 art gen pl	1411.3 num card	3450.12 art acc sing fem	1924.4 noun acc sing fem
(γὰρ *gar* for	[a☆ δὲ] *de* [but]	ἐκ *ek* by	τῶν *tōn* the	δύο, *duo* two,	τὴν *tēn* the	ἐπιθυμίαν *epithumian* desire

2174.17 verb nom sing masc part pres act	1519.1 prep	3450.16 art sing neu	358.1 verb inf aor act	2504.1 conj	4713.1 prep
ἔχων *echōn* having	εἰς *eis* for	τὸ *to* the	ἀναλῦσαι, *analusai* to depart,	καὶ *kai* and	σὺν *sun* with

23.a.Txt: Steph
Var: 01ℵ,02A,03B,06D
018K,020L,025P,byz.it.
sa.Gries,Lach,Treg,Alf
Word,Tisc,We/Ho,Weis
Sod,UBS/☆

1:20. Paul stated his purpose in life with the term *apokaradokian*, which usually is translated "eager expectation," "earnest expectation," "deepest desire," "undivided and intense expectation." It consists of three Greek words combined into one, indicating the craning of a person's neck in order to catch a glimpse of what is ahead. The word was used in classical Greek of a watchman in the bow of a ship peering into the darkness, eagerly looking for a beacon of light.

Clearly the apostle's ambition was to glorify Christ in his body. He knew that whatever happened, God would not let him fall into a situation of hopelessness or abandon him in any way. Because Paul was one with the Lord he knew that nothing, even death, could break that union. In fact, death would only make the union more complete. If a person's life consists primarily in the acquisition of things, then death would mean a cessation of the chief reason for being. Such a person would have to leave behind everything of importance to him.

1:21. Here Paul clearly describes his concept of life. The personal pronoun "me" occupies the emphatic position in the original language, expressing more than just an opinion about life, but indicating Paul's actual situation. He knew he was ready for life or for death. Death would only give him more of Christ.

The word for "gain" (*kerdos*) was used in Paul's time to mean "interest, gains, profits." Death would be like cashing in the principal and the interest. Paul sounded like a bird in a cage; death would be liberation from that captivity, or the limitations of the flesh. Eternal life begins when one believes on Christ; however, he does not possess it in the sense of being able to do with it as he wills. Still, he maintains it as long as he is in vital relationship to Jesus. Jesus attempted to impress upon Martha that Lazarus really had not died in an eternal sense because the person who believes upon Him as Lord will never die.

1:22. However, if Paul lived longer, he would be afforded more opportunity to work for God and harvest more fruit. While dying physically meant gain for him, continuing on this earth meant gain for those people who would hear the gospel message through him.

1:23. Paul was torn between two alternatives. A definite article in the Greek makes the statement read "the two." The idea is that of strong pressure bearing upon him "from" or "by" (*ek*) two sources: his desire to be with Christ and his desire to work longer for Him. "To depart" is a euphemism for physical death and comes from a

20. According to my earnest expectation and [my] hope: As I hartely loke for, *Geneva* . . . It all accords with my own earnest wishes, *Phillips.*

that in nothing I shall be ashamed: . . . that I shall never feel, *Montgomery* . . . hope that I shall never disgrace myself, *Williams.*

but [that] with all boldness, as always: . . . but with All Confidence, *Wilson* . . . but that with fearless courage, *Montgomery* . . . with the utmost boldness, *Phillips.*

[so] now also Christ shall be magnified in my body: . . . will be honoured, *TCNT.*

whether [it be] by life, or by death: . . . whether that means I am to face death or to go on living, *Phillips.*

21. For to me to live [is] Christ: . . . living means Christ, *Williams.*
and to die [is] gain: . . . and deeth is to me a vauntage, *Tyndale* . . . and dying brings gain, *Williams.*

22. But if I live in the flesh, this [is] the fruit of my labour: But if to keep on living here means fruit from my labor, *Williams* . . . my labours bear fruit? *TCNT.*
yet what I shall choose I wot not: I do not exactly know, *Wilson* . . . I cannot say, *Noyes* . . . I cannot tell which to choose, *Williams.*

23. For I am in a strait betwixt two: . . . but am in a quandary, *Montgomery* . . . held in constraint, *Rotherham* . . . I am hesitating between two desires, *Williams* . . . I am hard pressed from both sides, *Confraternity* . . . For I am constrayned of these two thinges, *Cranmer.*
having a desire to depart, and to be with Christ: I have a strong desire to break camp, *Montgomery* . . . to be dissolved, *Douay.*

23.b.**Var:** 01ℵ-corr,02A
03B,04C,33,bo.Elzev
Gries,Lach,Treg,Alf
Word,Tisc,We/Ho,Weis
Sod,UBS/✶

5382.3 name dat masc	1498.32 verb inf pres act	4044.3 adj dat sing	1056.1 conj	3095.1 adv comp	2882.6 adj comp sing neu
Χριστῷ	εἶναι,	πολλῷ	[b✶+ γὰρ]	μᾶλλον	κρεῖσσον
Christō	einai,	pollō	gar	mallon	kreisson
Christ	to be,	much	[for]	more	better;

24.a.**Txt:** 03B,06D,018K
020L,byz.Weis
Var: 01ℵ,02A,04C,025P
Tisc,We/Ho,Sod,UBS/✶

3450.16 art sing neu	1156.2 conj	1946.4 verb inf pres act	1706.1 prep	3450.11 art dat sing fem	4418.3 noun dat sing fem
24. τὸ	δὲ	ἐπιμένειν	(a ἐν)	τῇ	σαρκὶ
to	de	epimenein	en	tē	sarki
the	but	to remain	in	the	flesh

314.5 adj comp sing neu	1217.1 prep	5050.4 prs- pron acc 2pl	2504.1 conj	3642.17 dem- pron sing neu
ἀναγκαιότερον	δι'	ὑμᾶς·	25. καὶ	τοῦτο
anankaioteron	di'	humas	kai	touto
more necessary	for the sake of	you;	and	this

3844.13 verb nom sing masc part perf act	3471.2 verb 1sing indic perf act	3617.1 conj	3176.27 verb 1sing indic fut act	2504.1 conj
πεποιθὼς	οἶδα	ὅτι	μενῶ	καὶ
pepoithōs	oida	hoti	menō	kai
having been persuaded of,	I know	that	I shall stay	and

25.a.**Txt:** 06D-corr,018K
020L,025P,byz.
Var: 01ℵ,02A,03B,04C
06D-org,33,Lach,Treg
Alf,Tisc,We/Ho,Weis
Sod,UBS/✶

4690.1 verb 1sing indic pres act	3748.3 verb 1sing indic fut act	3820.5 adj dat pl	5050.3 prs- pron dat 2pl	1519.1 prep
(συμπαραμενῶ	[a✶ παραμενῶ]	πᾶσιν	ὑμῖν	εἰς
sumparamenō	paramenō	pasin	humin	eis
continue with	[I shall remain with]	all	you;	for

3450.12 art acc sing fem	5050.2 prs- pron gen 2pl	4156.2 noun acc sing fem	2504.1 conj	5315.4 noun acc sing fem	3450.10 art gen sing fem	3963.2 noun gen sing fem
τὴν	ὑμῶν	προκοπὴν	καὶ	χαρὰν	τῆς	πίστεως,
tēn	humōn	prokopēn	kai	charan	tēs	pisteōs,
the	your	progress	and	joy	of the	faith;

2419.1 conj	3450.16 art sing neu	2715.1 noun sing neu	5050.2 prs- pron gen 2pl	3450.10 art gen sing fem	3915.6 verb 3sing subj pres act	1706.1 prep
26. ἵνα	τὸ	καύχημα	ὑμῶν		περισσεύῃ	ἐν
hina	to	kauchēma	humōn		perisseuē	en
that	the	boasting	your		may increase	in

5382.3 name dat masc	2400.2 name masc	1706.1 prep	1466.5 prs- pron dat 1sing	1217.2 prep	3450.10 art gen sing fem	1684.7 adj gen sing fem
Χριστῷ	Ἰησοῦ	ἐν	ἐμοὶ	διὰ	τῆς	ἐμῆς
Christō	Iēsou	en	emoi	dia	tēs	emēs
Christ	Jesus	in	me	through	the	my

3814.2 noun gen sing fem	3687.1 adv	4242.1 prep	5050.4 prs- pron acc 2pl	3303.1 adv	512.1 adv
παρουσίας	πάλιν	πρὸς	ὑμᾶς.	27. Μόνον	ἀξίως
parousias	palin	pros	humas.	Monon	axiōs
presence	again	with	you.	Only	worthily

3450.2 art gen sing	2077.2 noun gen sing neu	3450.2 art gen sing	5382.2 name gen masc	4036.1 verb 2pl impr pres mid
τοῦ	εὐαγγελίου	τοῦ	Χριστοῦ	πολιτεύεσθε,
tou	euangeliou	tou	Christou	politeuesthe,
of the	good news	of the	Christ	conduct yourselves,

2419.1 conj	1521.1 conj	2048.13 verb nom sing masc part aor act	2504.1 conj	1481.16 verb nom sing masc part aor act	5050.4 prs- pron acc 2pl
ἵνα	εἴτε	ἐλθὼν	καὶ	ἰδὼν	ὑμᾶς,
hina	eite	elthōn	kai	idōn	humas,
that	whether	having come	and	having seen	you,

military term meaning "to strike camp" and from a nautical expression meaning "to release a vessel from its moorings."

1:24. This verse clearly expresses Paul's unselfishness. It reminds one of an elderly person who should be able to sit back in retirement and allow someone else to do the work. Instead, that person takes a position that entails much responsibility and works harder than ever. Many times older people have reached the zenith of their knowledge and experience, and their knowledge and experience can be of great assistance in God's kingdom. Apparently Paul felt that way. There was proper balance in his life. He knew the Church would continue to grow and expand without him, but he also realized his own value to the members of that church.

1:25. Even though Paul had a great desire to be with the Lord, he knew his ministry on earth was not yet complete. The word for "confidence" (*pepoithōs*) is a perfect participle which indicates Paul's confidence in the matter was one which resulted from the past action of turning the matter over to the Lord, and it indicates he still maintained this confidence while he wrote this epistle. The apostle emphasized the "furtherance and joy" or "progress and exaltation" the Philippians would experience as the result of his release.

1:26. So, Paul's ultimate goal of glorifying Christ in his body would be realized, whether in life or in death. He was confident of that fact because he determined to maintain his relationship with Christ as the basis for everything else in life. In his negative approach to the matter of a person's ambition in the beginning of this passage, Paul uncovered the two issues in life that probably give people the most problems—circumstances and the opinions of others. While God does at times use circumstances to show us His will, we cannot afford to be dominated by them. Sometimes we can change our circumstances, and sometimes we should. On the other hand, we should not rule out the providence of God in our circumstances.

It also is possible to go to two extremes with reference to the opinions of other people. Christians should not ignore the advice of godly people. Still, they must be careful not to be overly disturbed by the criticism of others who are not totally committed to God.

1:27. The bulk of Paul's epistle consists of a series of exhortations to these believers who meant so much to him. Some of the exhortations are especially local in their application, but all of them relate to all of Christianity in all ages and to all local churches. His first exhortation is an appeal for Christians to follow Christ's example. "Only" or "whatever happens" (NIV), from the Greek *monon*, appears first in the sentence and is in the emphatic position; it

which is far better: . . . obviously the best thing for me, *Phillips* . . . far, far better, *Rotherham.*

24. Nevertheless to abide in the flesh [is] more needful for you: . . . that I should stay here still, *TCNT* . . . is more necessary, *Alford* . . . is necessary for your sake, *Confraternity* . . . that I should stay here on earth, *Phillips.*

25. And having this confidence: That is why I feel pretty well convinced, *Phillips* . . . having become assured of this, *Worrell* . . . with this conviction, *Confraternity* . . . fully believing this, *Wilson.*

I know that I shall abide and continue with you all: . . . and stay behind, *Rotherham.*

for your furtherance and joy of faith: . . . for your progress, *Panin, Wilson, Montgomery* . . . for your advancement, *Noyes* . . . to help you forward in Christian living, *Phillips.*

26. That your rejoicing may be more abundant in Jesus Christ for me: . . . that your boasting respecting me may abound, *PNT.*

by my coming to you again: . . . when I come to see you, *Phillips.*

27. Only let your conversation be: No matter what happens, you must live lives, *Norlie* . . . do lead lives, *Montgomery* . . . let your lives be, *TCNT, Confraternity* . . . Let your conduct be, *Murdock* . . . let your behavior be, *Wesley* . . . Only conduct yourselves, *Alford* . . . behave yourselves, *Wilson* . . . let your manner of life, *ASV* . . . lyue ye worthili, *Wyclif.*

as it becometh the gospel of Christ: . . . in a manner worthy of, *Noyes* . . . worthily, *Wilson* . . . be worthy of, *ASV* . . . worthy of the Good News, *TCNT.*

that whether I come and see you, or else be absent, I may hear of your affairs: . . . or remain absent, *Confraternity* . . . I may hear

Philippians 1:28

27.a.Txt: 01ℵ-corr,02A
04C,06D-corr,018K
020L,byz.Sod
Var: 01ℵ-org,03B
06D-org,025P,Lach
Treg,Tisc,We/Ho,Weis
UBS/☆

1521.1 conj	544.2 verb nom sing masc part pres act	189.25 verb 1sing subj aor act	189.1 verb 1sing pres act	3450.17 art pl neu
εἴτε	ἀπὼν	ʼ ἀκούσω	[ᵃ☆ ἀκούω]	τὰ
eite	apōn	akousō	akouō	ta
or	being absent	I might hear	[I hear]	the things

3875.1 prep	5050.2 prs-pron gen 2pl	3617.1 conj	4590.1 verb 2pl pres act	1706.1 prep	1518.2 num card dat
περὶ	ὑμῶν,	ὅτι	στήκετε	ἐν	ἑνὶ
peri	humōn	hoti	stēkete	en	heni
concerning	you,	that	you stand fast	in	one

4011.3 noun dat sing neu	1518.7 num card dat fem	5425.3 noun dat sing fem	4717.1 verb nom pl masc part pres act	3450.11 art dat sing fem	3963.3 noun dat sing fem
πνεύματι,	μιᾷ	ψυχῇ	συναθλοῦντες	τῇ	πίστει
pneumati	mia	psuchē	sunathlountes	tē	pistei
spirit,	with one	soul	striving together	for the	faith

3450.2 art gen sing	2077.2 noun gen sing neu	2504.1 conj	3231.1 partic	4284.1 verb nom pl masc part pres mid	1706.1 prep
τοῦ	εὐαγγελίου,	**28.** καὶ	μὴ	πτυρόμενοι	ἐν
tou	euangeliou,	kai	mē	pturomenoi	en
of the	good news;	and	not	being frightened	in

3235.2 num card dat	5097.3 prep	3450.1 art gen pl	477.5 verb gen pl masc part pres mid	3610.3 rel-pron nom sing fem	840.2 prs-pron dat pl
μηδενὶ	ὑπὸ	τῶν	ἀντικειμένων·	ἥτις	ʼ αὐτοῖς
mēdeni	hupo	tōn	antikeimenōn	hētis	autois
nothing	by	the	opposing;	which	to them

28.a.Txt: 018K,020L,byz.
Var: 01ℵ,02A,03B,04C
06D-org,33,Gries,Lach
Treg,Alf,Word,Tisc
We/Ho,Weis,Sod
UBS/☆

3173.1 conj	1498.4 verb 3sing indic pres act	1498.4 verb 3sing indic pres act	840.2 prs-pron dat pl	1716.1 noun nom sing fem
μέν	ἐστὶν	[ᵃ☆ ἐστὶν	αὐτοῖς	ἔνδειξις
men	estin	estin	autois	endeixis
	is	[is	to them]	a demonstration

28.b.Txt: 06D-corr,018K
020L,byz.
Var: 01ℵ,02A,03B
04C-corr,025P,33,Lach
Treg,Alf,Word,Tisc
We/Ho,Weis,Sod
UBS/☆

677.2 noun gen sing fem	5050.3 prs-pron dat 2pl	5050.2 prs-pron gen 2pl	1156.2 conj	4843.2 noun gen sing fem	2504.1 conj
ἀπωλείας,	ʼ ὑμῖν	[ᵇ☆ ὑμῶν]	δὲ	σωτηρίας,	καὶ
apōleias,	humin	humōn	de	sōtērias,	kai
of destruction,	to you	[your]	but	of salvation,	and

3642.17 dem-pron sing neu	570.3 prep	2296.2 noun gen sing masc	3617.1 conj	5050.3 prs-pron dat 2pl	5319.4 verb 3sing indic aor pass
τοῦτο	ἀπὸ	θεοῦ·	**29.** ὅτι	ὑμῖν	ἐχαρίσθη
touto	apo	theou	hoti	humin	echaristhē
this	from	God;	because	to you	it was granted

3450.16 art sing neu	5065.1 prep	5382.2 name gen masc	3620.3 partic	3303.1 adv	3450.16 art sing neu	1519.1 prep
τὸ	ὑπὲρ	Χριστοῦ,	οὐ	μόνον	τὸ	εἰς
to	huper	Christou,	ou	monon	to	eis
the	concerning	Christ,	not	only	the	on

840.6 prs-pron acc sing masc	3961.16 verb inf pres act	233.2 conj	2504.1 conj	3450.16 art sing neu	5065.1 prep
αὐτὸν	πιστεύειν,	ἀλλὰ	καὶ	τὸ	ὑπὲρ
auton	pisteuein,	alla	kai	to	huper
him	to believe,	but	also	the	concerning

840.3 prs-pron gen sing	3819.9 verb inf pres act	3450.6 art acc sing masc	840.6 prs-pron acc sing masc	72.2 noun acc sing masc	2174.19 verb nom pl masc part pres act
αὐτοῦ	πάσχειν·	**30.** τὸν	αὐτὸν	ἀγῶνα	ἔχοντες
autou	paschein	ton	auton	agōna	echontes
him	to suffer,	the	same	conflict	having

means "above all else," "whatever may happen," "at all costs." The matter of chief importance in Paul's mind was for God's people to use Christ as the model for the process in which they found themselves. If a believer's ambition truly is to magnify Christ in his body (1:20), that person will not only live for Christ (1:21), but will become more and more like the Son of God.

"Conversation" or "conduct yourselves" (*politeuesthe*) bears a relationship to two Greek terms (*polis*, "city"; *politēs*, "citizen"). The total idea then is to live as a citizen of God's kingdom, to have a deportment worthy of the gospel of Christ, to perform the duties of a citizen.

"Becometh" means to "weigh as much," to "have a value equal to," to "be worth as much." The word "spirit" here refers to the unity of spirit that a local body of believers will have if they have blended and fused themselves together to accomplish God's plan for them.

1:28. When believers strive together for the gospel, there will be opposition. When Christ lives His life in them, there will be freedom from cowardice. This was beautifully illustrated in the early disciples (Acts 4:18-20; 5:40-42). The fact that the Philippians also were suffering persecution was like a two-edged sword. On the one hand, it served as a sign or pointer or proof that their persecutors were enemies of the gospel and were headed for eternal destruction. On the other hand, it confirmed the salvation of the Philippian saints. People reflect what they are by their actions. Those who oppose the simple message of the gospel indicate by their actions that they do not know the Author of the gospel message.

1:29. It is not new for Christians who are proclaiming the message of salvation to attract the antagonism of the world. Jesus warned about it in John 15:18-25. Anyone who attacks evil will face opposition. The apostle connected believing on Christ with suffering for Him. Believers should not get the impression that somehow by suffering for the cause of Christ they can add to Jesus' sacrificial work on the cross. There is no way believers can add to the infinite sacrifice of Christ in their behalf, but they can share in the same kind of rejection that Jesus faced from people who did not want to accept Him. Because servants are not greater than their master, the followers of the Lord should expect the same kind of treatment He received.

1:30. In his closing statement of this section, Paul referred to his experience as a struggle, and he reminded the Philippians that they were experiencing the same kind of struggle. He used the term *agōna* from which we get the word *agony*. It certainly expresses very well the nature of the battle in which believers find themselves.

concerning you, *Scarlett* . . . I maye yet heare of your condicyon, *Cranmer* . . . hear about you from a distance, *Phillips*.

that ye stand fast in one spirit: . . . that you are standing firm, animated by one spirit, *TCNT* . . . that ye continue in, *Geneva* . . . in a united spirit, *Phillips*.

with one mind striving together for the faith of the gospel: . . . having one purpose, *Norlie* . . . battling with a single mind, *Phillips* . . . with one soul striving together, *Noyes* . . . and in one soule, labouringe, *Tyndale* . . . and that with one purpose you are continuing to co-operate in the fight for faith in the good news, *Williams*.

28. And in nothing terrified by your adversaries: . . . and in nothynge fearinge youre adversaries, *Tyndale* . . . in no way terrorized by its enemies, *Montgomery* . . . not caring two straws for your enemies, *Phillips* . . . frightened by your opponents, *Williams* . . . by the opposers, *Wilson*.

which is to them an evident token of perdition: . . . vhich to them is cause of, *Rheims* . . . this will be an indication of coming Ruin, *TCNT* . . . Your fearlessness will then be to them a sign of their own coming defeat, *Norlie*.

but to you of salvation, and that of God: . . . but to you cause of helthe, *Wyclif* . . . you yourselves are being saved, *Phillips*.

29. For unto you it is given in the behalf of Christ: . . . it has been graciously granted to you, *Williams* . . . the privilege, *Phillips*.

not only to believe on him: . . . not merely of believing, *Phillips* . . . of trusting in him, *TCNT*.

but also to suffer for his sake:

30. Having the same conflict which ye saw in me: . . . having the same contest, *Rotherham*

195

Philippians 2:1

30.a.Txt: 03B-corr
06D-corr,018K,020L
025P,byz.
Var: 01א,02A,03B-org
04C,06D-org,33,Lach
Treg,Alf,Word,Tisc
We/Ho,Weis,Sod
UBS/✱

3497.1 rel-pron sing	1481.15 verb 2pl impr aor act	1481.6 verb 2pl indic aor act	1706.1 prep	1466.5 prs-pron dat 1sing	2504.1 conj
οἷον	ἴδετε	[ᵃ✱ εἴδετε]	ἐν	ἐμοὶ,	καὶ
hoion	idete	eidete	en	emoi,	kai
which	you saw	[idem]	in	me,	and

3431.1 adv	189.2 verb 2pl pres act	1706.1 prep	1466.5 prs-pron dat 1sing	2:1. 1479.1 conj	4948.3 indef-pron nom sing	3631.1 partic
νῦν	ἀκούετε	ἐν	ἐμοί.	2:1. Εἴ	τις	οὖν
nun	akouete	en	emoi.	Ei	tis	oun
now	hear	in	me.	If	any	then

3735.1 noun nom sing fem	1706.1 prep	5382.3 name dat masc	1479.1 conj	4948.10 indef-pron sing neu	3751.1 noun sing neu
παράκλησις	ἐν	Χριστῷ,	εἴ	τι	παραμύθιον
paraklēsis	en	Christō,	ei	ti	paramuthion
encouragement	in	Christ,	if	any	consolation

26.2 noun gen sing fem	1479.1 conj	4948.3 indef-pron nom sing	2815.1 noun nom sing fem	4011.2 noun gen sing neu	1479.1 conj
ἀγάπης,	εἴ	τις	κοινωνία	πνεύματος,	εἴ
agapēs,	ei	tis	koinōnia	pneumatos,	ei
of love,	if	any	fellowship	of Spirit,	if

1.a.Txt: byz.Weis
Var: 01א,02A,03B,04C
06D,018K,020L,025P
Gries,Lach,Treg,Alf
Tisc,We/Ho,Sod,UBS/✱

4948.5 indef-pron	4948.3 indef-pron nom sing	4551.1 noun pl neu	2504.1 conj	3490.1 noun nom pl masc
τινα	[ᵃ✱ τις]	σπλάγχνα	καὶ	οἰκτιρμοί,
tina	tis	splanchna	kai	oiktirmoi
any	[idem]	inside affections	and	mercies,

3997.7 verb 2pl impr aor act	1466.2 prs-pron gen 1sing	3450.12 art acc sing fem	5315.4 noun acc sing fem	2419.1 conj	3450.16 art sing neu
2. πληρώσατέ	μου	τὴν	χαρὰν,	ἵνα	τὸ
plērōsate	mou	tēn	charan,	hina	to
fulfill	my	the	joy,	that	the

840.15 prs-pron sing neu	5262.6 verb 2pl subj pres act	3450.12 art acc sing fem	840.12 prs-pron acc sing fem	26.4 noun acc sing fem
αὐτὸ	φρονῆτε,	τὴν	αὐτὴν	ἀγάπην
auto	phronēte,	tēn	autēn	agapēn
same thing	you may think,	the	same	love

2.a.Txt: p46,01א-corr2
03B,06D,010F,012G
We/Ho,byz.
Var: 01א-org,02A,04C
016I,044,33,81,441
2464

2174.19 verb nom pl masc part pres act	4712.1 adj nom pl masc	3450.16 art sing neu	1518.9 num card neu	840.15 prs-pron sing neu
ἔχοντες,	σύμψυχοι,	τὸ	ἓν	[ᵃ αὐτὸ]
echontes,	sumpsuchoi,	to	hen	auto
having,	joined in soul,	the	one thing	[same thing]

5262.8 verb nom pl masc part pres act	3235.6 num card neu	2567.3 prep	2567.1 prep	2036.3 noun acc sing fem
φρονοῦντες·	3. μηδὲν	κατὰ	[✱ κατ']	ἐριθείαν
phronountes	mēden	kata	kat'	eritheian
thinking,	nothing	according to	[idem]	contention

3.a.Txt: 06D,018K,020L
025P,byz.
Var: 01א-org,02A,03B
04C,33,Lach,Treg,Alf
Tisc,We/Ho,Weis,Sod
UBS/✱

2211.1 conj	3234.1 adv	2567.3 prep	2725.1 noun acc sing fem	233.2 conj	3450.11 art dat sing fem
ἢ	[ᵃ✱ μηδὲ	κατὰ]	κενοδοξίαν,	ἀλλὰ	τῇ
ē	mēde	kata	kenodoxian,	alla	tē
or	[and not	according to]	vain glory,	but	in the

4863.2 noun dat sing fem	238.3 prs-pron acc pl masc	2216.7 verb nom pl masc part pres mid	5080.2 verb acc pl masc part pres act
ταπεινοφροσύνῃ	ἀλλήλους	ἡγούμενοι	ὑπερέχοντας
tapeinophrosunē	allēlous	hēgoumenoi	huperechontas
humility	one another	esteeming	surpassing

The apostle did not say he had experienced this struggle only before his imprisonment. He was still facing it. The agony of the spiritual battle was not lessened in captivity. It is difficult to know exactly what Paul meant by this statement, but no doubt agonizing in prayer must have been an integral part of the total matter.

2:1. Christians are not only to be imitators of Christ in conduct, but also in humility. Paul's "therefore" here indicates a definite connection with his appeal for unity in 1:27-33. Humility is a very important requisite for unity, and without unity God's people cannot experience the joy of the Lord.

In the Greek grammar Paul's "if" here does not question the existence of what he is about to mention. Rather, it carries the meaning "since" or "in view of the fact." His first statement indicates that encouragement or consolation does exist. Secondly, God's love brings comfort as it flows among His people. Christians also enjoy fellowship, or joint participation, in the Holy Spirit. Lastly, "bowels and mercies" or tenderness and compassion do exist in God's church. By using this form of address the apostle not only was affirming the reality of these qualities, but he was also appealing for them to be exercised in the assembly.

2:2. The fourfold appeal listed in verse 1 immediately precedes a fourfold declaration of results in verse 2. The statement "fulfil ye my joy" shows that the Philippians fell somewhat short of Paul's expectations. Here we see a slight glimpse into the apostle's philosophy about spiritual progress in the believer's life. He probably commended the Philippian church as much or more than any other group to whom he wrote, but he realized they still had room for growth. "Be like-minded, having the same love, being of one accord, of one mind" are all terms that show an same love, being of one accord, of one mind" are all terms that show an intentional piling up of expression to emphasize the necessity of unity.

2:3. Verse 3 seems to imply that some egotism and boastfulness existed in the Philippian assembly. Each exalted self and his own group. Humility serves as an antidote to such a sinful spirit. Paul's statements about it indicate a humble person refuses to do anything for selfish ambition or vain conceit.

"Strife" (*eritheian*) contains the idea not only of strife but of rivalry, so a person who practices this approach does things at the expense of other people in order to elevate self. "Vainglory" (*kenodoxian*) contains the word for *glory*, but Paul amplified it by adding the word for *empty* or *vain*, implying that this kind of activity brings a kind of glory that has no substance and therefore is meaningless. "Let each esteem other better than themselves" does not mean putting down self, but refers to being concerned about the needs of others before the needs of self.

. . . that I am still having, *Williams.*

and now hear [to be] in me: . . . and which you hear that I am maintaining still, *TCNT* . . . concerning me, *Wilson.*

1. If [there be] therefore any consolation in Christ: . . . any exhortation, *Panin* . . . Any Comfort, *Wilson* . . . any encouragement comes through Christ, *TCNT.*

if any comfort of love: . . . any solace, *Rotherham* . . . Any Soothing of Love, *Wilson* . . . any persuasive power in love, *TCNT.*

if any fellowship of the Spirit: . . . if any participation of, *Sawyer* . . . if any society, *Douay* . . . if any communion, *Scarlett* . . . if any partaking of, *Noyes.*

if any bowels and mercies: . . . if any tender mercies, *Panin* . . . any tender-affections, *Rotherham.*

2. Fulfil ye my joy: . . . make my happiness complete, *TCNT* . . . complete My Joy, *Wilson.*

that ye be likeminded:

having the same love: . . . maintaining the same love, *Scarlett.*

[being] of one accord, of one mind: . . . sympathizing with each other, having one opinion, *Sawyer* . . . joined-in-soul, *Rotherham* . . . united in soul, *Wilson.*

3. [Let] nothing [be done] through strife or vainglory: . . . in a spirit of rivalry or from vanity, *TCNT* . . . from Party-spirit, *Wilson* . . . out of contentiousness, *Confraternity* . . . by way of factiousness, nor yet by way of empty-glory, *Rotherham.*

but in lowliness of mind: . . . but in humility, *Noyes.*

let each esteem other better than themselves: . . . regard the others as his superiors, *Confraternity.*

Philippians 2:4

4.a.Txt: p46,01ℵ,04C
06D,018K,020L,025P
byz.sa.bo.Sod
Var: 02A,03B,33,Lach
Treg,Alf,Tisc,We/Ho
Weis,UBS/✻

4.b.Txt: 020L,byz.
Var: 01ℵ,02A,03B,04C
06D,025P,Gries,Lach
Treg,Alf,Word,Tisc
We/Ho,Weis,Sod
UBS/✻

4.c.Txt: 04C,018K,020L
byz.
Var: p46,01ℵ,02A,03B
06D,025P,33,Gries
Lach,Treg,Alf,Word
Tisc,We/Ho,Weis,Sod
UBS/✻

5.a.Txt: 018K,020L
025P,byz.
Var: 01ℵ-org,02A,03B
04C-org,(06D),33,Lach
Treg,Alf,Tisc,We/Ho
Weis,UBS/✻

1431.2 prs-pron gen pl	3231.1 partic	3450.17 art pl neu	1431.2 prs-pron gen pl	1524.3 adj nom sing masc
ἑαυτῶν,	**4.** μὴ	τὰ	ἑαυτῶν	⸌ ἕκαστος
heautōn	mē	ta	heautōn	hekastos
themselves,	not	the things	of themselves	each

1524.8 adj nom pl masc	4503.2 verb 2pl impr pres act	4503.6 verb nom pl masc part pres act	233.2 conj	2504.1 conj
[ᵃ✭ ἕκαστοι]	⸌ σκοπεῖτε,	[ᵇ✭ σκοποῦντες,]	ἀλλὰ	καὶ
hekastoi	skopeite	skopountes	alla	kai
[idem]	consider,	[considering,]	but	also

3450.17 art pl neu	2066.3 adj gen pl	1524.3 adj nom sing masc	1524.8 adj nom pl masc	3642.17 dem-pron sing neu
τὰ	ἑτέρων	⸌ ἕκαστος.	[ᶜ✭ ἕκαστοι.]	**5.** Τοῦτο
ta	heterōn	hekastos	hekastoi	Touto
the things	of others	each.	[idem]	This

1056.1 conj	5262.13 verb 3sing impr pres mid	5262.1 verb 2pl pres act	1706.1 prep	5050.3 prs-pron dat 2pl	3614.16 rel-pron sing neu
⸌ γὰρ	φρονείσθω	[ᵃ✭ φρονεῖτε]	ἐν	ὑμῖν	ὃ
gar	phroneisthō	phroneite	en	humin	ho
for	let mind be	[think you]	in	you	which

2504.1 conj	1706.1 prep	5382.3 name dat masc	2400.2 name masc	3614.5 rel-pron nom sing masc	1706.1 prep	3307.1 noun dat sing fem
καὶ	ἐν	Χριστῷ	Ἰησοῦ,	**6.** ὃς	ἐν	μορφῇ
kai	en	Christō	Iēsou	hos	en	morphē
also	in	Christ	Jesus;	who,	in	form

2296.2 noun gen sing masc	5062.6 verb nom sing masc part pres act	3620.1 partic	719.1 noun acc sing masc	2216.13 verb 3sing indic aor mid
θεοῦ	ὑπάρχων,	οὐχ	ἁρπαγμὸν	ἡγήσατο
theou	huparchōn	ouch	harpagmon	hēgēsato
of God	being,	not	robbery	considered it

3450.16 art sing neu	1498.32 verb inf pres act	2443.6 adj pl neu	2296.3 noun dat sing masc	233.1 conj	233.2 conj
τὸ	εἶναι	ἴσα	θεῷ,	**7.** ⸌ ἀλλ'	[✭ ἀλλὰ]
to	einai	isa	theō	all'	alla
the	to be	equal	with God;	but	[idem]

1431.6 prs-pron acc sing masc	2729.1 verb 3sing indic aor act	3307.2 noun acc sing fem	1395.2 noun gen sing masc	2956.25 verb nom sing masc part aor act	1706.1 prep
ἑαυτὸν	ἐκένωσεν,	μορφὴν	δούλου	λαβών,	ἐν
heauton	ekenōsen	morphēn	doulou	labōn	en
himself	emptied,	form	a slave's	having taken,	in

3530.1 noun dat sing neu	442.7 noun gen pl masc	1090.53 verb nom sing masc part aor mid	2504.1 conj	4828.2 noun dat sing neu
ὁμοιώματι	ἀνθρώπων	γενόμενος·	**8.** καὶ	σχήματι
homoiōmati	anthrōpōn	genomenos	kai	schēmati
likeness	of men	having become;	and	in figure

2128.39 verb nom sing masc part aor pass	5453.1 conj	442.1 noun nom sing masc	4864.2 verb 3sing indic aor act	1431.6 prs-pron acc sing masc
εὑρεθεὶς	ὡς	ἄνθρωπος,	ἐταπείνωσεν	ἑαυτὸν,
heuretheis	hōs	anthrōpos	etapeinōsen	heauton
having been found	as	a man,	he humbled	himself,

1090.53 verb nom sing masc part aor mid	5093.1 adj nom sing masc	3230.1 prep	2265.2 noun gen sing masc	2265.2 noun gen sing masc	1156.2 conj
γενόμενος	ὑπήκοος	μέχρι	θανάτου,	θανάτου	δὲ
genomenos	hupēkoos	mechri	thanatou	thanatou	de
having become	obedient	unto	death,	death	even

2:4. So, instead of following party spirit and promotion of self, Paul enjoined Christians to put the interests of other people first. A truly humble person encourages and helps others.

2:5. Paul used the perfect example of humility to illustrate his point and appealed to believers to share the attitude of Christ. While verses 5-11 contain some of the most important Christological truths in the Bible, they were written in a context which should encourage Christians to emulate the example of Christ in humility. Thus, having the mind of Christ means "to think as Christ thought."

2:6. Many Bible scholars think verses 6-11 comprise the substance of a hymn early Christians sang in worship of Christ. This verse makes it clear that even though He possessed equality with the Father, Jesus did not cling to it. The term "form" or "nature" (NIV), from the Greek *morphē*, refers to possessing the essential attributes which belong to the essence or nature (*ousia*) of God. Jesus could not have possessed the essential attributes of God without being God. However, He did not hang onto what was rightfully His. (See *Overview*, p.538, for further discussion.)

2:7. Instead of clinging to what was rightfully His, Christ emptied himself (*heauton ekenōsen*). Pondering this, theologians pose several questions. Did He empty himself of His divine nature? Did He cease to be deity for a short period of time? That would have been impossible. How could God cease to be God? How could a human cease to be a human? Therefore, He divested himself not of the nature nor attributes of deity, but of the prerogatives that belonged to Him. In other words, He emptied himself of the expression of deity, not the possession of deity.

It is important to note that His emptying was voluntary. He had to do this in order to take upon himself the essential attributes (*morphē*) of a servant. Perhaps scholars argue so much about what Jesus laid aside that they fail to see that He actually took something upon himself. Becoming a human, of course, necessitated that He lay aside the prerogatives of deity, so it was a true self-emptying. The term for "likeness" (*homoiōmati*) implies a true human likeness and not a mere phantom, as the docetic Gnostics suggested.

2:8. Jesus also took the "fashion" (*schēma*) or "appearance" (NIV) of a man, which means His outward appearance was definitely that of a man. Further, He died as a criminal, therefore taking the curse (Deuteronomy 21:23) of the cross upon himself.

4. Look not every man on his own things: None of you should think only of his own affairs, *Phillips*.

but every man also on the things of others: ... but each should learn to see things from other people's point of view, *Phillips*.

5. Let this mind be in you, which was also in Christ Jesus: Let the spirit of, *TCNT* ... Let Christ himself be your example as to what your attitude should be, *Phillips* ... this disposition, *Wilson*.

6. Who, being in the form of God: ... had the divine nature, *TCNT* ... had always been God by nature, *Phillips* ... beyng in the shape of God, *Geneva*.

thought it not robbery to be equal with God: ... counted it no act of robbery, *Wesley* ... deemed not his equality with God a thing to grasp at, *Alford* ... did not cling to his prerogatives as God's equal, *Phillips* ... something to be clung to, *TCNT*.

7. But made himself of no reputation: ... emptied himself, *Wesley, Confraternity* ... but impoverished himself, *TCNT* ... but he abased himself, *Sawyer* ... but divested Himself, *Wilson* ... of no consideration, *Noyes*.

and took upon him the form of a servant: ... by consenting to be a slave, *Phillips* ... by taking the nature of, *TCNT*.

and was made in the likeness of men: ... became lyke vnto men, *Cranmer* ... made into the similitude of men, *Rheims* ... as mortal man, *Phillips*.

8. And being found in fashion as a man: ... founde in his aparell, *Tyndale* ... in condition, *Wilson*.

he humbled himself, and became obedient unto death: ... by submitting even to death, *TCNT*.

even the death of the cross:

4567.2 noun gen sing masc	1346.1 conj	2504.1 conj	3450.5 art nom sing masc	2296.1 noun nom sing masc	840.6 prs-pron acc sing masc
σταυροῦ.	9. διὸ	καὶ	ὁ	θεὸς	αὐτὸν
staurou	dio	kai	ho	theos	auton
of cross.	Wherefore	also		God	him

9.a.Var: 01‫א‬,02A,03B 04C,33,Lach,Treg,Alf Word,Tisc,We/Ho,Weis Sod,UBS/✫

5089.1 verb 3sing indic aor act	2504.1 conj	5319.5 verb 3sing indic aor mid	840.4 prs-pron dat sing	3450.16 art sing neu	3549.2 noun sing neu
ὑπερύψωσεν	καὶ	ἐχαρίσατο	αὐτῷ	[a✫+ τὸ]	ὄνομα
huperupsōsen	kai	echarisato	autō	to	onoma
highly exalted	and	granted	to him	[the]	a name

3450.16 art sing neu	5065.1 prep	3820.17 adj sing neu	3549.2 noun sing neu	2419.1 conj	1706.1 prep	3450.3 art dat sing
τὸ	ὑπὲρ	πᾶν	ὄνομα·	10. ἵνα	ἐν	τῷ
to	huper	pan	onoma	hina	en	tō
the	above	every	name,	that	at	the

3549.4 noun dat sing neu	2400.2 name masc	3820.17 adj sing neu	1113.1 noun sing neu	2549.3 verb 3sing subj aor act	2016.2 adj gen pl
ὀνόματι	Ἰησοῦ	πᾶν	γόνυ	κάμψῃ	ἐπουρανίων
onomati	Iēsou	pan	gonu	kampsē	epouraniōn
name	of Jesus	every	knee	should bow	of in heaven

2504.1 conj	1904.1 adj gen pl	2504.1 conj	2678.1 adj gen pl masc	2504.1 conj	3820.9 adj nom sing fem
καὶ	ἐπιγείων	καὶ	καταχθονίων·	11. καὶ	πᾶσα
kai	epigeiōn	kai	katachthoniōn	kai	pasa
and	on earth	and	under the earth,	and	every

11.a.Txt: p46,01‫א‬,03B 044,104,23,2495 **Var:** 02A,04C,06D,010F 012G,018K,020L,025P 6,33,81,365,1175,1739 1881,2464

1094.1 noun nom sing fem	1827.5 verb 3sing subj aor mid	1827.7 verb 3sing indic fut mid	3617.1 conj
γλῶσσα	⟨✫ ἐξομολογήσηται	[a ἐξομολογήσεται]	ὅτι
glōssa	exomologēsētai	exomologēsetai	hoti
tongue	should confess	[will confess]	that

2935.1 noun nom sing masc	2400.1 name nom masc	5382.1 name nom masc	1519.1 prep	1385.4 noun acc sing fem	2296.2 noun gen sing masc
κύριος	Ἰησοῦς	Χριστὸς	εἰς	δόξαν	θεοῦ
kurios	Iēsous	Christos	eis	doxan	theou
Lord	Jesus	Christ	to	glory	of God

3824.2 noun gen sing masc	5452.1 conj	27.6 adj pl masc	1466.2 prs-pron gen 1sing	2503.1 conj	3704.1 adv
πατρός.	12. Ὥστε,	ἀγαπητοί	μου,	καθὼς	πάντοτε
patros	Hōste	agapētoi	mou	kathōs	pantote
Father.	So that,	beloved	my,	just as	always

5057.6 verb 2pl indic aor act	3231.1 partic	5453.1 conj	1706.1 prep	3450.11 art dat sing fem	3814.3 noun dat sing fem
ὑπηκούσατε,	μὴ	ὡς	ἐν	τῇ	παρουσίᾳ
hupēkousate	mē	hōs	en	tē	parousia
you obeyed,	not	as	in	the	presence

1466.2 prs-pron gen 1sing	3303.1 adv	233.2 conj	3431.1 adv	4044.3 adj dat sing	3095.1 adv comp	1706.1 prep
μου	μόνον,	ἀλλὰ	νῦν	πολλῷ	μᾶλλον	ἐν
mou	monon	alla	nun	pollō	mallon	en
my	only,	but	now	much	more	in

3450.11 art dat sing fem	660.1 noun dat sing fem	1466.2 prs-pron gen 1sing	3196.3 prep	5238.2 noun gen sing masc	2504.1 conj
τῇ	ἀπουσίᾳ	μου,	μετὰ	φόβου	καὶ
tē	apousia	mou	meta	phobou	kai
the	absence	my,	with	fear	and

2:9. As a result of this obedience to the plan of the Father, the Son possessed something He did not have before His incarnation. What did Jesus have after His crucifixion, resurrection, and ascension that He did not have before all this transpired? What did He take back to heaven that He did not have previously? His humanity has to be the only answer to these questions. He always was the Son of God, but He was not a human until His incarnation.

Because there is a definite article before "name" in verse 10, some scholars believe the reference must be to a specific name for God. Verse 11 ascribes to Jesus Christ the term "Lord" (*kurios*), the word used by the Septuagint translators when they translated the Old Testament into Greek. They consistently used this title for the Old Testament name Yahweh or Jehovah. This was the ineffable Name that Jews hesitated to write or say.

2:10. So Jesus has been freely given all the attributes of deity ascribed to the Father in the Old Testament by the Hebrew name *Jehovah*. All creation will ultimately acknowledge the man Jesus as fully God (Lord), with a position equal to that of the Father.

2:11. "Lord" was the characteristic confession of the Early Church, and it should be the characteristic confession of all contemporary believers. The Greek word for "Lord" (*kurios*) is one of the terms meaning "master."

2:12. Paul followed his profound description of the self-humbling of Christ with a practical application to the situation in the Philippian church. The apostle was just as practical as he was profound. Furthermore, he did not divorce learning from living. The "wherefore" in verse 12 seems to be a return to the exhortation in 1:27-30 to emulate Christ's example in conduct. It sounds as if Paul was saying, "Because you have the example of Christ's humility to imitate, the example of His exaltation to encourage you, you need to obey Him and continue steadfastly in your faith." The example of Christ served as a much stronger incentive to good works than Paul's own physical presence with them.

The apostle carefully informed the Philippians that they were responsible before God for their own salvation. They could not lean upon him, so his absence should not make a difference in whether or not they were faithful to God. Paul, of course, did not tell the Philippians they should work *for* their salvation. A person cannot "work out" what he does not have. Nowhere in Scripture is the paradox of divine sovereignty and human responsibility more clearly shown than here. "Work out" contains the idea of carrying out to an ultimate conclusion. In this process, which obviously is a reference to the work of sanctification, the attitude must be one of serious caution.

9. Wherefore God also hath highly exalted him: This is why, *Williams* . . . for which thing god enhauncid him, *Wyclif* . . . raised him to the very highest place, *TCNT* . . . has now lifted him so high, *Phillips* . . . uplifted him far on high, *Rotherham* . . . supremely exalted Him, *Wilson*.

and given him a name which is above every name: . . . and freely granted to him, *Wilson* . . . and graciously bestowed upon him, *Montgomery* . . . which ranks above all others, *TCNT* . . . which is more excellent than all names, *Murdock*.

10. That at the name of Jesus every knee should bow: . . . so that in the name of Jesus everyone should kneel, *Williams*.

of [things] in heaven, and [things] in earth: . . . whether in, *Phillips* . . . of beings, *Sawyer* . . . of the celestials, terrestrials, *Rheims*.

and [things] under the earth: . . . and of hellis, *Wyclif* . . . and infernals, *Rheims* . . . in the underworld, *Williams*.

11. And [that] every tongue should confess: And that is why, in the end, *Phillips* . . . everyone, *Williams* . . . every tongue should acknowledge, *TCNT*.

that Jesus Christ [is] Lord, to the glory of God the Father: . . . vnto the prayse of, *Tyndale*.

12. Wherefore, my beloved: . . . my moost dereworthe britheren, *Wyclif* . . . my dearly loved friends, *Williams* . . . my dearest friends, *Phillips*.

as ye have always obeyed: . . . as you have always been obedient, *Williams* . . . as you have always followed my advice, *Phillips*.

not as in my presence only, but now much more in my absence: . . . not only when I was present to give it, *Phillips* . . . not only as though I were with you but much more because I am away, *Williams*.

4997.2 noun gen sing masc
τρόμου
tromou
trembling

3450.12 art acc sing fem
τὴν
tēn
the

1431.2 prs-pron gen pl
ἑαυτῶν
heautōn
of yourselves

4843.3 noun acc sing fem
σωτηρίαν
sōtērian
salvation

2686.3 verb 2pl impr pres mid
κατεργάζεσθε·
katergazesthe
work out,

13. [a ὁ ⟩
3450.5 art nom sing masc
ho

2296.1 noun nom sing masc
θεὸς
theos
God

1056.1 conj
γάρ
gar
for

1498.4 verb 3sing indic pres act
ἐστιν
estin
it is

3450.5 art nom sing masc
ὁ
ho
the

1738.4 verb nom sing masc part pres act
ἐνεργῶν
energōn
working

1706.1 prep
ἐν
en
in

5050.3 prs-pron dat 2pl
ὑμῖν
humin
you

2504.1 conj
καὶ
kai
both

3450.16 art sing neu
τὸ
to
the

2286.19 verb inf pres act
θέλειν
thelein
to will

2504.1 conj
καὶ
kai
and

3450.16 art sing neu
τὸ
to
the

1738.5 verb inf pres act
ἐνεργεῖν
energein
to work

5065.1 prep
ὑπὲρ
huper
according to

3450.10 art gen sing fem
τῆς
tēs
the

2086.2 noun gen sing fem
εὐδοκίας.
eudokias
good pleasure.

14. πάντα
3820.1 adj
panta
All things

4020.2 verb 2pl pres act
ποιεῖτε
poieite
do

5400.1 prep
χωρὶς
chōris
without

1106.2 noun gen pl masc
γογγυσμῶν
gongusmōn
grumblings

2504.1 conj
καὶ
kai
and

1255.5 noun gen pl masc
διαλογισμῶν,
dialogismōn
reasonings,

15. ἵνα
2419.1 conj
hina
that

1090.42 verb 2pl subj aor mid
γένησθε
genēsthe
you may be

271.2 adj nom pl masc
ἄμεμπτοι
amemptoi
blameless

2504.1 conj
καὶ
kai
and

183.1 adj nom pl masc
ἀκέραιοι,
akeraioi
simple,

4891.4 noun pl neu
τέκνα
tekna
children

2296.2 noun gen sing masc
θεοῦ
theou
of God

296.2 adj pl neu
⟨ ἀμώμητα
amōmēta
unblemished

297.6 adj pl neu
[a☆ ἄμωμα]
amōma
[faultless]

1706.1 prep
⟨ ἐν
en
in

3189.1 adj dat sing
μέσῳ
mesō
midst

3189.5 adj
[b☆ μέσον]
meson
[idem]

1067.1 noun fem
γενεᾶς
geneas
of a generation

4501.2 adj gen sing fem
σκολιᾶς
skolias
crooked

2504.1 conj
καὶ
kai
and

1288.4 verb gen sing fem part perf mid
διεστραμμένης,
diestrammenēs
having been perverted;

1706.1 prep
ἐν
en
among

3614.4 rel-pron dat pl
οἷς
hois
whom

5154.7 verb 2pl pres mid
φαίνεσθε
phainesthe
you appear

5453.1 conj
ὡς
hōs
as

5293.2 noun nom pl masc
φωστῆρες
phōstēres
luminaries

1706.1 prep
ἐν
en
in

2862.3 noun dat sing masc
κόσμῳ,
kosmō
world,

16. λόγον
3030.4 noun acc sing masc
logon
word

2205.2 noun gen sing fem
ζωῆς
zōēs
of life

1892.3 verb nom pl masc part pres act
ἐπέχοντες,
epechontes
holding forth,

1519.1 prep
εἰς
eis
for

2715.1 noun acc sing neu
καύχημα
kauchēma
a boast

1466.5 prs-pron dat 1sing
ἐμοὶ
emoi
to me

1519.1 prep
εἰς
eis
in

2232.4 noun acc sing fem
ἡμέραν
hēmeran
day

5382.2 name gen masc
Χριστοῦ,
Christou
Christ's,

3617.1 conj
ὅτι
hoti
that

3620.2 partic
οὐκ
ouk
not

1519.1 prep
εἰς
eis
in

2727.1 adj sing
κενὸν
kenon
vain

4983.10 verb indic aor act
ἔδραμον
edramon
I ran

13.a.Txt: 06D-corr,020L byz.
Var: 01א,02A,03B,04C 06D-org,018K,025P,33 Lach,Treg,Alf,Word Tisc,We/Ho,Weis,Sod UBS/☆

15.a.Txt: 06D,018K 020L,025P,byz.Sod
Var: 01א,02A,03B,04C 33,Lach,Treg,Alf,Tisc We/Ho,Weis,UBS/☆

15.b.Txt: 06D-corr,018K 020L,byz.
Var: 01א,02A,03B,04C 06D-org,025P,33,Lach Treg,Alf,Word,Tisc We/Ho,Weis,Sod UBS/☆

2:13. God, of course, not only gives the *will* to please Him, but also the *ability.* So, verse 12 delineates human responsibility and verse 13 divine responsibility. It is never "either/or." The scriptural approach is not "let go and let God," but "get in there with God." Paul exhorted the followers of Christ as if he were an Arminian. At the same time he prayed as if he were a Calvinist. Both approaches contain truth. In a sense Christians "were saved" the moment they believed; they "are being saved" as the Holy Spirit applies the sanctification process to their lives; and they "will be saved" at the resurrection.

2:14. After carefully instructing the Philippians about the necessity of allowing the sanctification process to work, Paul added that they should do so without "murmurings" and "disputings." "Murmurings" is an onomatopoetic word (*gongusmōn*), a word in which the sound resembles its meaning. It refers to undertone mumbling and is constantly used in the Septuagint for the prolific murmuring of the Israelites in the wilderness when they journeyed from Egypt to Canaan. "Disputings" relates to ill-natured controversies.

2:15. Instead of murmuring and disputing about the process through which the Holy Spirit takes us, Christians should become "blameless and harmless." "Become" (NIV) shows the progressive nature of the experience. "Blameless" literally means "free from defect," and "harmless" has the sense of "unadulterated." The latter term often was used in that day to distinguish wine that had been watered down. All this beautiful process takes place in a "crooked" or "wicked" and "perverse" generation. Christians live in a real world rather than growing in a "greenhouse" setting.

2:16. In verse 15 Paul expressed a twofold purpose for the Philippians: their own spiritual development or maturity, and their witness to unbelievers. In verse 16 Christians are instructed to shine as "luminaries" in this sin-darkened age. It could be compared to two travelers proceeding in the darkness, one with a light and the other without a light. The one extends his light to the other person to help guide him on his journey. The "word of life," of course, is the gospel message.

The apostle connected the continuance of the Philippian believers with his own accountability on the Day of Judgment when all Christians will give account to Christ of the deeds performed in their earthly lives after becoming Christians. Paul was not concerned only with beginning a church in the city of Philippi; he wanted to see those believers stand faithfully in the Lord until their earthly life ended. As a result, "in the day of Christ," the judgment day for Christians (1 Corinthians 3:10-23), Paul would be able to glory in the fact that his labors in Philippi had not been wasted.

work out your own salvation with fear and trembling: . . . be keener than ever to work out the salvation...with a proper sense of awe and responsibility, *Phillips* . . . with reverence and awe, *TCNT.*

13. For it is God which worketh in you both to will and to do of [his] good pleasure: . . . for God is he who is working effectually among you, *Wilson* . . . and the performance, *Confraternity* . . . to accomplish according to his good will, *Douay* . . . and also the dede, euen of his fre beneuolence, *Geneva.*

14. Do all things without murmurings and disputings: . . . avoid discontent and dissension, *TCNT* . . . and hesitations, *Douay* . . . and without questioning, *Confraternity* . . . without grucchingis and doutingis, *Wyclif* . . . and staggerings, *Rheims.*

15. That ye may be blameless and harmless: . . . that ye may become faultless, *Rotherham* . . . that ye maye be faute lesse and pure, *Tyndale* . . . that ye maye be soch as no man can complayne on, *Cranmer* . . . and sincere, *Sawyer.*

the sons of God, without rebuke: . . . the simple children, *Rheims* . . . without blemish, *Panin, ASV* . . . unrebukable, *Wesley* . . . and inoffensive, irreproachable, *Wilson.*

in the midst of a crooked and perverse nation: . . . in the middes of a naughtie and wicked, *Geneva* . . . of a depraved and, *Confraternity* . . . of an evil-disposed, *TCNT.*

among whom ye shine as lights in the world: . . . appear as Luminaries, *Wilson* . . . shining like stars in a dark world, *TCNT.*

16. Holding forth the word of life: . . . exhibiting, *Wilson.*
that I may rejoice in the day of Christ:
that I have not run in vain, neither laboured in vain: . . . that I did not live my life for nothing, nor toil for nothing, *TCNT.*

Philippians 2:17

3624.1 conj	1519.1 prep	2727.1 adj sing	2844.10 verb 1sing indic aor act		233.1 conj	233.2 conj
οὐδὲ	εἰς	κενὸν	ἐκοπίασα.	**17.** ʽ	ἀλλ᾽	[☆ ἀλλὰ]
oude	*eis*	*kenon*	*ekopiasa.*		*all'*	*alla*
nor	in	vain	labored.		But	[idem]

1479.1 conj	2504.1 conj	4542.1 verb 1sing indic pres mid		1894.3 prep	3450.11 art dat sing fem	2355.3 noun dat sing fem
εἰ	καὶ	σπένδομαι		ἐπὶ	τῇ	θυσίᾳ
ei	*kai*	*spendomai*		*epi*	*tē*	*thusia*
if	also	I am being poured out		on	the	sacrifice

2504.1 conj	2983.2 noun dat sing fem	3450.10 art gen sing fem	3963.2 noun gen sing fem	5050.2 prs-pron gen 2pl	5299.1 verb 1sing indic pres act
καὶ	λειτουργίᾳ	τῆς	πίστεως	ὑμῶν,	χαίρω
kai	*leitourgia*	*tēs*	*pisteōs*	*humōn*	*chairō*
and	ministration	of the	faith	your,	I rejoice,

2504.1 conj	4647.1 verb 1sing indic pres act	3820.5 adj dat pl	5050.3 prs-pron dat 2pl	3450.16 art sing neu	1156.1 conj	1156.2 conj
καὶ	συγχαίρω	πᾶσιν	ὑμῖν·	**18.** τὸ	ʽ δ᾽	[☆ δὲ]
kai	*sunchairō*	*pasin*	*humin*	*to*	*d'*	*de*
and	rejoice with	all	you.	The	and	[idem]

840.15 prs-pron sing neu	2504.1 conj	5050.1 prs-pron nom 2pl	5299.7 verb 2pl impr pres act	2504.1 conj	4647.3 verb 2pl impr pres act	1466.4 prs-pron dat 1sing
αὐτὸ	καὶ	ὑμεῖς	χαίρετε	καὶ	συγχαίρετέ	μοι.
auto	*kai*	*humeis*	*chairete*	*kai*	*sunchairete*	*moi.*
same	also	you	rejoice	and	rejoice with	me.

	1666.1 verb 1sing indic pres act	1156.2 conj	1706.1 prep	2935.3 noun dat sing masc	2400.2 name masc	4943.4 name acc masc
19.	Ἐλπίζω	δὲ	ἐν	κυρίῳ	Ἰησοῦ	Τιμόθεον
	Elpizō	*de*	*en*	*kuriō*	*Iēsou*	*Timotheon*
	I hope	but	in	Lord	Jesus	Timothy

4878.1 adv	3854.17 verb inf aor act	5050.3 prs-pron dat 2pl	2419.1 conj	2476.3 prs-pron nom	2155.1 verb 1sing subj pres act
ταχέως	πέμψαι	ὑμῖν,	ἵνα	κἀγὼ	εὐψυχῶ
tacheōs	*pempsai*	*humin*	*hina*	*kagō*	*eupsuchō*
soon	to send	to you,	that	I also	may be of good courage,

1091.26 verb nom sing masc part aor act	3450.17 art pl neu	3875.1 prep	5050.2 prs-pron gen 2pl		3625.3 num card acc masc
γνοὺς	τὰ	περὶ	ὑμῶν·	**20.**	οὐδένα
gnous	*ta*	*peri*	*humōn*		*oudena*
having known	the things	concerning	you.		No one

1056.1 conj	2174.1 verb 1sing pres act	2446.1 adj acc sing masc	3610.1 rel-pron nom sing masc	1098.1 adv	3450.17 art pl neu
γὰρ	ἔχω	ἰσόψυχον,	ὅστις	γνησίως	τὰ
gar	*echō*	*isopsuchon*	*hostis*	*gnēsiōs*	*ta*
for	have I	like minded,	who	genuinely	the things

3875.1 prep	5050.2 prs-pron gen 2pl	3179.7 verb 3sing indic fut act		3450.7 art nom pl masc	3820.7 adj nom pl masc
περὶ	ὑμῶν	μεριμνήσει·	**21.**	οἱ	πάντες
peri	*humōn*	*merimnēsei*		*hoi*	*pantes*
concerning to	you	will care for.		The	all

1056.1 conj	3450.17 art pl neu	1431.2 prs-pron gen pl	2195.2 verb 3pl indic pres act	3620.3 partic	3450.17 art pl neu
γὰρ	τὰ	ἑαυτῶν	ζητοῦσιν,	οὐ	τὰ
gar	*ta*	*heautōn*	*zētousin*	*ou*	*ta*
for	the things	of themselves	are seeking,	not	the things

2:17,18. In the earlier part of the chapter Paul spoke of the perfect example of self-abnegation of Christ himself. In these verses there is another example of the same attitude, his own. Paul expressed his unselfish willingness to give his life as a martyr for the Lord. Several years later he used nearly the same terminology just before he actually did suffer martyrdom (2 Timothy 4:6). He used the metaphor of a cup of wine being poured upon a burnt offering. He wrote about the pouring out of his blood upon the sacrifice which was the Philippians' testimony and service for God. The Philippians understood very well this type of language. They often saw public ceremonies where animals would be sacrificed and wine would be poured on top of the sacrifice.

Just as the Philippians and Paul both had a part in the sacrifice, so they would all rejoice. In this there is a good reminder of the present blessing that comes from performing good deeds. Even though the ultimate reward will come at the judgment seat of Christ, a certain satisfaction comes to the individual at the time the deed is performed.

There is another reference to the main theme of this epistle, the joy of the Lord that believers experience. If Christians truly are to experience this joy on a continuous basis, they must be concerned about good deeds coming from their lives. While believers do not come to an experience of salvation because of their good works, good works should be the natural outgrowth of the conversion experience. James referred to this, stating, "Faith without works is dead" (James 2:26).

Verses 12-18 depict progression in the Christian life. No believer is satisfied just being saved. He works with God in the process of sanctification. Good works result. The unconverted take notice, believe, and rejoice.

2:19. The reader encounters Paul's love for people here as elsewhere in his writings. In a study of his works, one frequently comes across associates whom Paul trusted and tried to help in the ministry. Timothy was one of the most outstanding. He certainly lived up to his name which means "good comfort."

2:20. After stating that he was sending Timothy to the Philippians to help guide them and to cheer him by advising him of their situation, Paul made a puzzling statement. Timothy was the only one who was "likeminded," or the only one who had the same kind of genuine interest in the Philippians that Paul had. This complaint should not be taken to mean Paul had no genuine Christian friends in Rome, but apparently Timothy was the only one Paul felt comfortable to send as his representative to Philippi.

2:21. However, the words "for all seek their own" must be taken seriously. Sometimes even well-meaning believers put their own interests before those interests that belong to the work of God.

17. Yea, and if I be offered upon the sacrifice and service of your faith: . . . if I am even to be poured out, *Rotherham* . . . if I am even poured out on, *Noyes.*
I joy, and rejoice with you all:

18. For the same cause also do ye joy, and rejoice with me: . . . for the selfsame thing, *Douay.*

19. But I trust in the Lord Jesus to send Timotheus shortly unto you:
that I also may be of good comfort: . . . that I may be refreshed, *Sawyer.*
when I know your state: . . . when I knowe what case ye stonde in, *Tyndale* . . . I know your circumstances, *Confraternity* . . . I knovv the things pertaining to you, *Rheims.*

20. For I have no man likeminded: No one like disposed, *Wilson.*
who will naturally care for your state: . . . who will care truly, *ASV* . . . who is so genuinely solicitous for you, *Confraternity* . . . who would take a genuine interest, *TCNT* . . . who will genuinely care, *Panin* . . . will be genuinely anxious as to, *Rotherham* . . . wyth so pure affection careth for your matters, *Geneva* . . . who really will care for your interests, *Sawyer.*

21. For all seek their own: . . . seeking their own interests, *Montgomery.*

Philippians 2:22

21.a.Txt: Steph
Var: 01ℵ,02A,03B,04C
06D,018K,020L,025P
byz.Gries,Lach,Treg,Alf
Word,Tisc,We/Ho,Weis
Sod,UBS/∗

21.b.Txt: 03B,byz.
Var: p46,01ℵ,02A,04C
06D,010F,012G,025P
044,33,81,326,1739
1881,2464,2495

3450.2 art gen sing	5382.2 name gen masc	2400.2 name masc	2400.2 name masc	5382.2 name gen masc
[a τοῦ]	(Χριστοῦ	Ἰησοῦ	[b☆ Ἰησοῦ	Χριστοῦ]
tou	Christou	Iēsou	Iēsou	Christou
tou	of Christ	Jesus.	[Jesus	of Christ.]

3450.12 art acc sing fem	1156.2 conj	1376.4 noun acc sing fem	840.3 prs-pron gen sing	1091.5 verb 2pl indic pres act	3617.1 conj
22. τὴν	δὲ	δοκιμὴν	αὐτοῦ	γινώσκετε,	ὅτι
tēn	de	dokimēn	autou	ginōskete	hoti
The	but	proof	of him	you know,	that,

5453.1 conj	3824.3 noun dat sing masc	4891.1 noun sing neu	4713.1 prep	1466.5 prs-pron dat 1sing	1392.9 verb 3sing indic aor act
ὡς	πατρὶ	τέκνον,	σὺν	ἐμοὶ	ἐδούλευσεν
hōs	patri	teknon	sun	emoi	edouleusen
as	to a father	a child,	with	me	he served

1519.1 prep	3450.16 art sing neu	2077.1 noun sing neu	3642.6 dem-pron acc sing masc	3173.1 conj	3631.1 partic
εἰς	τὸ	εὐαγγέλιον.	**23.** τοῦτον	μὲν	οὖν
eis	to	euangelion	touton	men	oun
for	to	the	good news.	This	men	therefore

23.a.Txt: 03B-corr,04C
06D-corr,018K,020L
025P,byz.Weis,Sod
Var: 01ℵ,02A,03B-org
06D-org,33,Lach,Treg
Alf,Tisc,We/Ho,UBS/∗

1666.1 verb 1sing indic pres act	3854.17 verb inf aor act	5453.1 conj	300.1 partic	538.1 verb 1sing subj aor act	538.2 verb 1sing subj aor act
ἐλπίζω	πέμψαι	ὡς	ἂν	(ἀπίδω	[a☆ ἀφίδω]
elpizō	pempsai	hōs	an	apidō	aphidō
I hope	to send	when		I shall have seen	[idem]

3450.17 art pl neu	3875.1 prep	1466.7 prs-pron acc 1sing	1808.1 adv	3844.8 verb 1sing indic perf act
τὰ	περὶ	ἐμὲ,	ἐξαυτῆς·	**24.** πέποιθα
ta	peri	eme	exautēs	pepoitha
the things	concerning	me	at once:	I am persuaded

1156.2 conj	1706.1 prep	2935.3 noun dat sing masc	3617.1 conj	2504.1 conj	840.5 prs-pron nom sing masc	4878.1 adv
δὲ	ἐν	κυρίῳ	ὅτι	καὶ	αὐτὸς	ταχέως
de	en	kuriō	hoti	kai	autos	tacheōs
but	in	Lord	that	also	myself	soon

24.a.Txt: p46,01ℵ-corr2
03B,06D,010F,012G
044,byz.
Var: 01ℵ-org,02A,04C
025P,326,629,2464,bo.

2048.54 verb 1sing indic fut mid	4242.1 prep	5050.4 prs-pron acc 2pl	314.3 adj sing neu	1156.2 conj
ἐλεύσομαι.	[a+ πρὸς	ὑμᾶς]	**25.** Ἀναγκαῖον	δὲ
eleusomai	pros	humas	Anankaion	de
I shall come:	[to	you:]	necessary	but

2216.12 verb 1sing indic aor mid	1876.2 name acc masc	3450.6 art acc sing masc	79.4 noun acc sing masc	2504.1 conj
ἡγησάμην	Ἐπαφρόδιτον	τὸν	ἀδελφὸν	καὶ
hēgēsamēn	Epaphroditon	ton	adelphon	kai
I esteemed	Epaphroditus,	the	brother	and

4754.3 adj acc sing masc	2504.1 conj	4813.2 noun acc sing masc	1466.2 prs-pron gen 1sing	5050.2 prs-pron gen 2pl	1156.2 conj
συνεργὸν	καὶ	συστρατιώτην	μου,	ὑμῶν	δὲ
sunergon	kai	sustratiōtēn	mou	humōn	de
fellow worker	and	fellow soldier	my,	your	but

646.3 noun acc sing masc	2504.1 conj	2985.2 noun acc sing masc	3450.10 art gen sing fem	5367.1 noun fem	1466.2 prs-pron gen 1sing
ἀπόστολον	καὶ	λειτουργὸν	τῆς	χρείας	μου,
apostolon	kai	leitourgon	tēs	chreias	mou
messenger	and	minister	of the	need	my,

Where were Aristarchus, Mark, Jesus Justus, and Demas whom Paul mentioned in his closing remarks in his letter to the Colossians? Although this may be conjecture, perhaps Demas' problem began at this time. We know from the apostle's comment in his second letter to Timothy that Demas ultimately forsook him (2 Timothy 4:10). Apparently Timothy was so dedicated to the work of the Lord that Paul could depend upon him to lay aside his own interests and make time to visit Philippi.

2:22. Paul was so concerned about the Philippians that he was willing to give up Timothy's companionship and dispatch him to them. Timothy had proved himself over a period of time. The Greek word for "proof" (*dokimēn*) refers to putting someone or something to the test for the purpose of obtaining approval. The apostle had observed Timothy very carefully before making this statement concerning him. No one received Paul's approval without "having the goods."

2:23. Comments like "so soon as I shall see how it will go with me" cause some Bible scholars to think Paul sensed he was about to be released from prison. Several other comments in Philippians seem to suggest the same possibility though the apostle always made it clear he committed his future to the Lord regardless of what it held. Even so, reliable tradition indicates Paul was released from prison and experienced several more years of ministry.

2:24. In this verse we see the other side of the coin. While he was not positive what would happen in the future, Paul had placed his confidence in the Lord who is omniscient. The idea expressed in this verse is probably close to what a person would mean when saying, "I trust I will be able to do so and so." It indicates a goal orientation which is essential if a person ever is to accomplish anything worthwhile in life, but at the same time it expresses a realization that God may have other plans. Paul was a goal-oriented person. He normally made careful plans relative to what he wanted to do next, but at the same time he allowed for God to change the plans if He so desired.

2:25. The man the Philippians had sent as their messenger to Paul was about to return home, and the apostle desired that they honor Epaphroditus in the Lord. His name means "charming," and he certainly lived up to his name. Even though the shorter form of Epaphroditus is Epaphras, this is not the same person referred to in Colossians 4:12. Paul used some very complimentary titles for this man. In addition to calling him a "messenger," he also was a "brother," a "companion" or "fellow worker" (NIV), and a "fellow soldier," a person in active combat against the enemy.

not the things which are Jesus Christ's: . . . not for the interests of, *Williams* . . . do not really care for the business of, *Phillips*.

22. But ye know the proof of him: . . . you have had proof of his worth, *Norlie* . . . you know his tested character, *Williams* . . . his worth, *Confraternity* . . . an experiment of him, *Rheims*.

that, as a son with the father: . . . like a son helping his father, *Montgomery* . . . in fellowship with his father, *Williams*.

he hath served with me in the gospel: . . . working with me, *Phillips* . . . toiled with me like a slave in preaching the good news, *Williams*.

23. Him therefore I hope to send presently: . . . to send immediately, *Wilson*.

so soon as I shall see how it will go with me: . . . just as soon as I can see how my case is going to turn out, *Williams* . . . as soon as I can tell how things will work out for me, *Phillips*.

24. But I trust in the Lord: God gives me some hope, *Phillips* . . . having confidence, *Wilson*.

that I also myself shall come shortly: I myself shall follow, *TCNT* . . . that it will not be long before I am able to come, *Phillips*.

25. Yet I supposed it necessary to send to you Epaphroditus: I esteemed, *Wilson*, *Rotherham* . . . I have considered it desirable, *Phillips* . . . But I counted it necessary to, *Clementson* . . . and I gessid it nedeful, *Wyclif*.

my brother, and companion in labour, and fellowsoldier: . . . fellow worker and comrade-in-arms, *Phillips*.

but your messenger, and he that ministered to my wants: . . . your apostle, *Douay* . . . and minister to my need, *Clementson*.

3854.17 verb inf aor act	4242.1 prep	5050.4 prs-pron acc 2pl		1879.1 conj	1955.3 verb nom sing masc part pres act	1498.34 verb sing indic imperf act
πέμψαι	πρὸς	ὑμᾶς·	**26.** ἐπειδὴ		ἐπιποθῶν	ἦν
pempsai	pros	humas	epeidē		epipothōn	ēn
to send	to	you,	since		longing after	he was

3820.8 adj acc pl masc	5050.4 prs-pron acc 2pl	1481.19 verb inf aor act	2504.1 conj	84.1 verb nom sing masc part pres act	1354.1 conj
πάντας	ὑμᾶς,	[a+ ἰδεῖν,]	καὶ	ἀδημονῶν	διότι
pantas	humas	idein	kai	adēmonōn	dioti
all	you,	[to see,]	and	deeply depressed	because

26.a.Txt: p46,01א-corr2
010F,012G,018K,020L
025P,044,sa.byz.
Var: 01א-org,02A,04C
06D,08E,33,81,104,326
365,1175,2495,bo.

189.23 verb 2pl indic aor act	3617.1 conj	764.12 verb 3sing indic aor act	2504.1 conj	1056.1 conj	764.12 verb 3sing indic aor act
ἠκούσατε	ὅτι	ἠσθένησεν.	**27.** καὶ	γὰρ	ἠσθένησεν
ēkousate	hoti	ēsthenēsen	kai	gar	ēsthenēsen
you heard	that	he was sick;	indeed	for	he was sick

3758.1 adj sing neu	2265.3 noun dat sing masc	233.1 conj	233.2 conj	3450.5 art nom sing masc	2296.1 noun nom sing masc
παραπλήσιον	θανάτῳ·	ἀλλ'	[☆ ἀλλὰ]	ὁ	θεὸς
paraplēsion	thanatō	all'	alla	ho	theos
coming near	to death,	but	[idem]	ho	God

840.6 prs-pron acc sing masc	1640.7 verb 3sing indic aor act	1640.7 verb 3sing indic aor act	840.6 prs-pron acc sing masc	3620.2 partic
⌐ αὐτόν	ἠλέησεν,	[☆ ἠλέησεν	αὐτόν,]	οὐκ
auton	eleēsen	eleēsen	auton	ouk
him	had mercy on,	[had mercy on	him,]	not

840.6 prs-pron acc sing masc	1156.2 conj	3303.1 adv	233.2 conj	2504.1 conj	1466.7 prs-pron acc 1sing	2419.1 conj
αὐτὸν	δὲ	μόνον,	ἀλλὰ	καὶ	ἐμέ,	ἵνα
auton	de	monon	alla	kai	eme	hina
him	and	alone,	but	also	me,	that

3231.1 partic	3049.4 noun acc sing fem	1894.3 prep	3049.3 noun dat sing fem	3049.4 noun acc sing fem	2174.33 verb 1sing subj aor act
μὴ	λύπην	ἐπὶ	⌐ λύπῃ	[a☆ λύπην]	σχῶ.
mē	lupēn	epi	lupē	lupēn	schō
not	sorrow	upon	sorrow	[idem]	I might have.

27.a.Txt: Steph
Var: 01א,02A,03B,04C
06D,020L,025P,byz.
Gries,Lach,Treg,Alf
Word,Tisc,We/Ho,Weis
Sod,UBS/☆

4560.2 adv comp	3631.1 partic	3854.5 verb 1sing indic aor act	840.6 prs-pron acc sing masc	2419.1 conj
28. σπουδαιοτέρως	οὖν	ἔπεμψα	αὐτὸν,	ἵνα
spoudaioterōs	oun	epempsa	auton	hina
The more diligently	therefore	I sent	him,	that

1481.17 verb nom pl masc part aor act	840.6 prs-pron acc sing masc	3687.1 adv	5299.20 verb 2pl aor pass	2476.3 prs-pron nom
ἰδόντες	αὐτὸν	πάλιν	χαρῆτε,	κἀγὼ
idontes	auton	palin	charēte	kagō
having seen	him	again	you might rejoice,	and I

251.1 adj comp nom sing masc	1498.8 verb 1sing subj pres act	4185.3 verb 2pl impr pres mid	3631.1 partic	840.6 prs-pron acc sing masc
ἀλυπότερος	ὦ.	**29.** προσδέχεσθε	οὖν	αὐτὸν
alupoteros	ō	prosdechesthe	oun	auton
less sorrowful	might be.	Receive	therefore	him

1706.1 prep	2935.3 noun dat sing masc	3196.3 prep	3820.10 adj gen sing fem	5315.2 noun gen sing fem	2504.1 conj	3450.8 art acc pl masc
ἐν	κυρίῳ	μετὰ	πάσης	χαρᾶς,	καὶ	τοὺς
en	kuriō	meta	pasēs	charas	kai	tous
in	Lord	with	all	joy,	and	the

2:26. While in Rome, Epaphroditus suffered the very common malady of homesickness, and the apostle did not try to cover up the fact. This seems to indicate to a certain degree what a strong tie Epaphroditus had with the Philippian church. Some Bible scholars conjecture that he was the pastor of the assembly and had left Archippus in charge during his absence (Colossians 4:17). In addition to being homesick, he actually contracted some serious physical illness while with Paul in Rome. Some writers think that he contracted the "Roman fever," an especially dangerous disease to unacclimated strangers. If he arrived at Rome during the hot season, this would have been even more likely. His condition must have been a protracted one, because enough time had elapsed for word of his condition to reach Philippi and for a return message to get back to Rome.

2:27. Even though his main mission seems to have been to take the financial gift to Paul, Epaphroditus himself became a gift of comfort and strength to the apostle who was awaiting trial. Whatever malady struck his life nearly killed him, but God healed him. In describing the healing of his friend on this occasion, the apostle used a common Greek word (*eleeō*) for "mercy." It stems from God's love (*agapē*) for people. In this miracle of healing the Lord showed mercy not only to Epaphroditus but to Paul as well. His explanation of it showed how tenderhearted he was.

2:28. Having gone through this experience certainly made Epaphroditus more capable of glorifying the Lord. Whether or not a Christian receives lasting spiritual benefits from the trials of life depends to a great extent on the person's own attitude. No doubt Paul was able to help Epaphroditus maintain a proper attitude through this total experience. As a result both lives benefited spiritually.

Evidently Paul also wanted the entire assembly in Philippi to benefit from the experience. Therefore, the fact that God had healed Epaphroditus brought joy to himself, to Paul, and ultimately to the entire assembly at Philippi. The Bible makes it clear that physical healing is not an end in itself. God performs these acts of mercy so that as a result people will turn to Him. God was glorified through the healing of Epaphroditus.

2:29. This verse contains another example of the way Paul loved to honor other people who deserved it. He certainly was an unselfish man who felt no compulsion to put down other people in order to elevate himself. He encouraged the Philippian assembly to welcome this man with open arms and honor him for his work for Christ. The honor Christians bestow upon other people needs to be "in the Lord" or "in the realm of the Lord" so that God receives the ultimate glory for all that is accomplished in His kingdom. He receives this ultimate glory if we truly honor Christian

26. For he longed after you all, and was full of heaviness, because that ye had heard that he had been sick: He has been homesick for all of you, *Norlie* . . . and was sore troubled, *Panin, ASV* . . . and was much troubled, *Noyes* . . . and was much depressed, *Wilson* . . . and in great distress, *Rotherham* . . . and has been distressed, *Adams* . . . and was anxious, *Murdock.*

27. For indeed he was sick nigh unto death: And I can assure you that his illness very nearly proved fatal, *TCNT* . . . and came near to death, *Adams* . . . so sick that he was on the point of dying, *Williams.*

but God had mercy on him: . . . took pity on, *Williams* . . . pitied him, *Wilson.*

and not on him only, but on me also, lest I should have sorrow upon sorrow: . . . to keep me from having one sorrow after another, *Williams* . . . leest I hadde heuynesse on heuynes, *Wyclif* . . . have grief upon grief! *Adams* . . . added to my other troubles, *Norlie.*

28. I sent him therefore the more carefully: I am particularly anxious, *Phillips* . . . I am all the more eager to send him, *Adams* . . . therfor more haistli I sente him, *Wyclif* . . . the more diligently, *Panin* . . . the more speedily, *Noyes.*

that, when ye see him again, ye may rejoice: . . . you may be glad of it, *Williams.*

and that I may be the less sorrowful: . . . and to know of your joy will lighten my own sorrows, *Phillips* . . . and my own sorrow may be lightened, *TCNT* . . . I may have less anxiety, *Norlie* . . . my grief may be lessened, *Adams.*

29. Receive him therefore in the Lord with all gladness: So give him a hearty Christian welcome, *Williams* . . . Welcome him in the Lord, *Phillips* . . . with all joy, *Montgomery.*

Philippians 2:30

4955.8 dem-pron acc pl masc	1768.3 adj acc pl masc	2174.2 verb 2pl pres act	3617.1 conj	1217.2 prep	3450.16 art sing neu
τοιούτους	ἐντίμους	ἔχετε·	**30.** ὅτι	διὰ	τὸ
toioutous	entimous	echete	hoti	dia	to
such	in honor	hold;	because	for the sake of	the

2024.1 noun sing neu	3450.2 art gen sing	5382.2 name gen masc	3230.1 prep	2265.2 noun gen sing masc	1443.9 verb 3sing indic aor act
ἔργον	(a τοῦ)	Χριστοῦ	μέχρι	θανάτου	ἤγγισεν,
ergon	tou	Christou	mechri	thanatou	ēngisen
work	of the	Christ	unto	death	he went near,

	3713.1 verb nom sing masc part aor mid		3711.1 verb nom sing masc part aor mid		3450.11 art dat sing fem
	(παραβουλευσάμενος		[b☆ παραβολευσάμενος]		τῇ
	parabouleusamenos		paraboleusamenos		tē
	having disregarded		[idem]		the

5425.3 noun dat sing fem	2419.1 conj	376.4 verb 3sing subj aor act	3450.16 art sing neu	5050.2 prs-pron gen 2pl	5140.2 noun sing neu
ψυχῇ,	ἵνα	ἀναπληρώσῃ	τὸ	ὑμῶν	ὑστέρημα
psuchē	hina	anaplērōsē	to	humōn	husterēma
life,	that	he might fill up	the	your	deficiency

3450.10 art gen sing fem	4242.1 prep	1466.6 prs-pron acc 1sing	2983.1 noun gen sing fem		3450.16 art sing neu
τῆς	πρός	με	λειτουργίας.	**3:1.** Τὸ	
tēs	pros	me	leitourgias	To	
of the	towards	me	service.	The	

3036.8 adj sing neu	79.6 noun nom pl masc	1466.2 prs-pron gen 1sing	5299.7 verb 2pl impr pres act	1706.1 prep	2935.3 noun dat sing masc
λοιπόν,	ἀδελφοί	μου,	χαίρετε	ἐν	κυρίῳ
loipon	adelphoi	mou	chairete	en	kuriō
remaining,	brothers	my,	rejoice	in	Lord:

3450.17 art pl neu	840.16 prs-pron pl neu	1119.5 verb inf pres act	5050.3 prs-pron dat 2pl	1466.5 prs-pron dat 1sing	3173.1 conj	3620.2 partic
τὰ	αὐτὰ	γράφειν	ὑμῖν,	ἐμοὶ	μὲν	οὐκ
ta	auta	graphein	humin	emoi	men	ouk
the	same things	to write	to you,	to me	men	not

3499.3 adj sing neu	5050.3 prs-pron dat 2pl	1156.2 conj	798.2 adj sing neu	984.1 verb 2pl pres act	3450.8 art acc pl masc
ὀκνηρόν,	ὑμῖν	δὲ	ἀσφαλές.	**2.** Βλέπετε	τοὺς
oknēron	humin	de	asphales	Blepete	tous
irksome,	for you	and	safe.	Watch out for	the

2938.4 noun acc pl masc	984.1 verb 2pl pres act	3450.8 art acc pl masc	2527.4 adj acc pl masc	2023.5 noun acc pl masc	984.1 verb 2pl pres act
κύνας,	βλέπετε	τοὺς	κακοὺς	ἐργάτας,	βλέπετε
kunas	blepete	tous	kakous	ergatas	blepete
dogs,	beware of	the	evil	workers,	watch out for

3450.12 art acc sing fem	2668.1 noun acc sing fem	2231.1 prs-pron nom 1pl	1056.1 conj	1498.5 verb 1pl indic pres act	3450.9 art nom sing fem
τὴν	κατατομήν·	**3.** ἡμεῖς	γὰρ	ἐσμεν	ἡ
tēn	katatomēn	hēmeis	gar	esmen	hē
the	concision.	We	for	are	the

3921.1 noun nom sing fem	3450.7 art nom pl masc	4011.3 noun dat sing neu	2296.3 noun dat sing masc	2296.2 noun gen sing masc	
περιτομή,	οἱ	πνεύματι	(θεῷ	[a☆ θεοῦ]	
peritomē	hoi	pneumati	theō	theou	
circumcision,	the	in spirit	God	[of God]	

30.a.**Txt:** 06D,018K 020L,byz. **Var:** p46,03B,Lach,Treg Alf,Tisc,We/Ho,Weis Sod,UBS/☆

30.b.**Txt:** 04C,018K 020L,025P,byz. **Var:** 01ℵ,02A,03B,06D Gries,Lach,Treg,Alf Word,Tisc,We/Ho,Weis Sod,UBS/☆

3.a.**Txt:** 01ℵ-corr 06D-org,025P,it.Steph **Var:** 01ℵ-org,02A,03B 04C,06D-corr,018K 020L,33,byz.sa.bo.Lach Treg,Alf,Word,Tisc We/Ho,Weis,Sod UBS/☆

leaders in a scriptural fashion. Because the danger of self-elevation always is present, Paul's practice here can serve as a good example for all Christians to follow.

2:30. It is highly possible Epaphroditus' sickness had resulted from overexertion. Perhaps his body was so weakened by all the work involved in helping at this time that he was sick and "nigh unto death."

3:1. "Finally" does not imply the apostle was about to close the epistle. Although the Greek term *to loipon* sometimes does mean "finally," it more likely means "for the rest" in this context.

At first glance, verse 1 may not seem to be connected to the verses that follow, but Paul's encouragement to "rejoice in the Lord" should be considered as a positive preventative to becoming entangled in the false teaching that he was about to expose and condemn. People who are constantly rejoicing in the Lord probably have less chance of succumbing to false teaching than those who do not seem to consider worshiping God very important. The Philippians stood in danger of being led astray by two types of false teachings: legalism, and its opposite, antinomianism.

3:2. Verse 2 contains a threefold warning showing the gravity of the situation. Three times Paul wrote "beware" or "watch out for" to emphasize what he was about to say. In addition to a threefold "beware," Paul also had a threefold epithet for these false teachers. He first called them "dogs." He labeled them such because their characteristics resembled those of the wild packs of scavengers roaming the streets at the time, causing havoc wherever they went, in addition to attacking people. Secondly, Paul called them "evil workers," which implies they actively opposed the gospel of God's grace. Thirdly, he designated them "the concision." While they claimed to be "the circumcision," Paul said they were really only "mutilated." In other words, their mechanical, unscriptural approach to the important rite of circumcision reduced it to mere laceration of the body. Mutilation of the body was practiced regularly in pagan religious rites, but this practice was forbidden in the Old Testament (Leviticus 21:5; 1 Kings 18:28).

3:3. Paul used the true term for circumcision (*peritomē*) which is used in the New Testament for "circumcision of the heart" (Romans 2:25-29) and refers to the breaking of the power of the fallen nature (Colossians 2:11). The three characteristics listed in this verse describe the people who truly have been circumcised: (1) they "worship God in the spirit"; (2) they "rejoice" or "glory" in Christ

and hold such in reputation: You should hold men like him in highest honor, *Phillips* . . . and such intreate vvith honour, *Rheims* . . . show honor to men like him, *Confraternity* . . . make muche of such, *Geneva* . . . have such in estimation, *Sawyer* . . . such like persons, *Wilson* . . . in honor, *Panin* . . . in esteem, *Scarlett*.

30. Because for the work of Christ he was nigh unto death: . . . his loyalty to Christ brought him very near death, *Phillips* . . . at the point of death, *TCNT*.
not regarding his life: . . . he risked his life, *Phillips* . . . yelding his life, *Rheims* . . . hazarding his life, *Alford* . . . imperiling his soul, *Worrell*.
to supply your lack of service toward me: . . . what distance prevented you all from doing, *Phillips* . . . your deficiency of service, *Wesley*.

1. Finally, my brethren: As to what remains, *Rotherham, Scarlett*.
rejoice in the Lord:
To write the same things to you, to me indeed [is] not grievous: To repeat what I have already written, *TCNT* . . . to me surely it is not tedious, *Rheims* . . . is not irksome, *Panin, Wilson, Rotherham*.
but for you [it is] safe: . . . and to you it is necessarie, *Rheims*.

2. Beware of dogs: Look out for the, *Panin*.
beware of evil workers: . . . evildoers, *Norlie*.
beware of the concision: Beware of dissensyon, *Cranmer* . . . of the men who mutilate themselves, *TCNT*.

3. For we are the circumcision: . . . we are truly circumcised, *Norlie*.
which worship God in the spirit: . . . we who are serving, *Wilson*.

Philippians 3:4

2973.5 verb nom pl masc part pres act
λατρεύοντες,
latreuontes
serving,

2504.1 conj
καὶ
kai
and

2714.8 verb nom pl masc part pres mid
καυχώμενοι
kauchōmenoi
boasting

1706.1 prep
ἐν
en
in

5382.3 name dat masc
Χριστῷ
Christō
Christ

2400.2 name masc
Ἰησοῦ,
Iēsou
Jesus,

2504.1 conj
καὶ
kai
and

3620.2 partic
οὐκ
ouk
not

1706.1 prep
ἐν
en
in

4418.3 noun dat sing fem
σαρκὶ
sarki
flesh

3844.14 verb nom pl masc part perf act
πεποιθότες,
pepoithotes
having trusted.

2510.1 conj
4. καίπερ
kaiper
Though

1466.1 prs-pron nom 1sing
ἐγὼ
egō
I

2174.17 verb nom sing masc part pres act
ἔχων
echōn
having

3870.2 noun acc sing fem
πεποίθησιν
pepoithēsin
trust

2504.1 conj
καὶ
kai
even

1706.1 prep
ἐν
en
in

4418.3 noun dat sing fem
σαρκί·
sarki
flesh;

1479.1 conj
εἴ
ei
if

4948.3 indef-pron nom sing
τις
tis
any

1374.5 verb 3sing indic pres act
δοκεῖ
dokei
thinks

241.4 adj nom sing masc
ἄλλος
allos
other

3844.16 verb inf perf act
πεποιθέναι
pepoithenai
to trust

1706.1 prep
ἐν
en
in

5.a.Txt: Steph
Var: Elzev,Gries,Lach
Treg,Alf,Word,Tisc
We/Ho,Weis,Sod
UBS/✶

4418.3 noun dat sing fem
σαρκί,
sarki
flesh,

1466.1 prs-pron nom 1sing
ἐγὼ
egō
I

3095.1 adv comp
μᾶλλον·
mallon
more:

3921.1 noun nom sing fem
5. ⸆ περιτομὴ
peritomē
circumcision

3921.3 noun dat sing fem
[ᵃ✶ περιτομῇ]
peritomē
[idem]

3500.1 adj nom sing masc
ὀκταήμερος,
oktaēmeros
on eighth day;

1523.2 prep gen
ἐκ
ek
from

1079.2 noun gen sing neu
γένους
genous
race

2447.1 name masc
Ἰσραήλ,
Israēl
of Israel,

5279.1 noun gen sing fem
φυλῆς
phulēs
of tribe

951.1 name masc
Βενιαμίν,
Beniamin
of Benjamin,

1439.1 name nom sing masc
Ἑβραῖος
Hebraios
Hebrew

1523.1 prep gen
ἐξ
ex
of

1439.3 name gen pl masc
Ἑβραίων,
Hebraiōn
Hebrews;

2567.3 prep
κατὰ
kata
according to

6.a.Txt: 01ℵ-corr
06D-corr,018K,020L
025P,byz.Sod
Var: 01ℵ-org,02A,03B
06D-org,Lach,Treg,Alf
Word,Tisc,We/Ho,Weis
UBS/✶

3414.4 noun acc sing masc
νόμον
nomon
law

5168.1 name nom sing masc
Φαρισαῖος,
Pharisaios
a Pharisee;

2567.3 prep
6. κατὰ
kata
according to

2188.4 noun sing
⸆ ζῆλον
zēlon
zeal,

2188.1 noun sing
[ᵃ✶ ζῆλος]
zēlos
[idem]

1371.7 verb nom sing masc part pres act
διώκων
diōkōn
persecuting

3450.12 art acc sing fem
τὴν
tēn
the

1564.4 noun acc sing fem
ἐκκλησίαν,
ekklēsian
assembly;

2567.3 prep
κατὰ
kata
according to

1336.4 noun acc sing fem
δικαιοσύνην
dikaiosunēn
righteousness

3450.12 art acc sing fem
τὴν
tēn
the

1706.1 prep
ἐν
en
in

3414.3 noun dat sing masc
νόμῳ
nomō
law,

1090.53 verb nom sing masc part aor mid
γενόμενος
genomenos
having become

271.1 adj nom sing
ἄμεμπτος.
amemptos
blameless;

233.1 conj
7. ⸆ ἀλλ'
all'
but

233.2 conj
[✶ ἀλλὰ]
alla
[idem]

3610.6 rel-pron nom pl neu
ἅτινα
hatina
what things

1498.34 verb sing indic imperf act
ἦν
ēn
were

1466.4 prs-pron dat 1sing
μοι
moi
to me

2742.3 noun pl neu
κέρδη,
kerdē
gain,

Jesus (not in personal attainments); and, (3) they do not trust in the "flesh." The term for "flesh" here does not refer to the body, but to the unregenerate human nature. Paul, of course, was not being egotistical by using the pronoun "we" in this statement. Instead he was expressing the certainty of the personal relationship he had with Christ. This is a good definition of true circumcision.

3:4. In verses 4-6 we see a catalog of Paul's own attainments before his conversion. His purpose in giving this list of merits was certainly not to boast. In fact, the opposite is true. He did it deliberately to show the folly of trusting in human merits. His inventory of attainments includes seven items which can be divided into two categories. The first category includes four involuntary privileges that belonged to him because of heredity and environment.

3:5. First, he was circumcised when 8 days old as required by the Law (Leviticus 12:3). By contrast, proselytes were circumcised as adults. Ishmael was 13 years old when he experienced this rite (Genesis 17:24-26).

Secondly, Paul was an Israelite. The term designates God's chosen nation which He selected to represent Him and be His witnesses on earth (Isaiah 43:1-10; Romans 11:1; 2 Corinthians 11:22).

Paul also claimed he was a member of a special tribe, that of Benjamin. This tribe alone was faithful to Judah when the other 10 tribes left to form their own kingdom (1 Kings 12:21), and after the Babylonian Exile it actually merged with Judah (Ezra 4:1).

Lastly, Paul was "a Hebrew of the Hebrews," which informs us that he was raised in a home where Hebrew and Aramaic were used (Acts 21:40; 22:2). Many Jews of the day spoke only the Greek language and followed Greek customs, and therefore they were designated "Hellenists."

The last three items in Paul's catalog of human merits belonged to him by choice. He chose to be a Pharisee, the strictest of the religious groups of the day.

3:6. He also chose to be extremely zealous for what he believed to be true. In fact, he was so zealous that he persecuted the followers of Jesus (Acts 9:1,2), a practice for which he was sorry the rest of his earthly life. Thirdly, judged by legalistic righteousness, he was "blameless."

3:7. However, what things were gain to Paul, or that he considered as profit, he suddenly reckoned as nothing when compared to knowing Christ. The Greek verb for "counted" (*hēgēmai*) is a perfect tense verb which could be rendered "I have counted" and speaks of an action with continuing results. The action part has to

and rejoice in Christ Jesus: . . . we find our joy in Christ Jesus, *Phillips.*

and have no confidence in the flesh: . . . and trust not, *Alford* . . . in such mutilation of the flesh, *Norlie.*

4. Though I might also have confidence in the flesh: . . . although I have ground of confidence, *Sawyer.*

If any other man thinketh that he hath whereof he might trust in the flesh, I more: . . . can rely upon external privileges, *TCNT* . . . thinketh that he hath reason for confidence, *Noyes* . . . I rather! *Rotherham.*

5. Circumcised the eighth day: of the stock of Israel: . . . of the kinred of, *Geneva* . . . from Israel's race, *Rotherham* . . . a true Jew, *Phillips.*

[of] the tribe of Benjamin, an Hebrew of the Hebrews: . . . of Hebrew parentage, *Norlie* . . . a full-blooded Jew, *Phillips.*

as touching the law, a Pharisee: As far as keeping the Law is concerned, *Phillips.*

6. Concerning zeal, persecuting the church: . . . you can judge my enthusiasm, *Phillips* . . . the congregacion, *Tyndale.*

touching the righteousness which is in the law, blameless: . . . respecting the righteousnes, *Scarlett* . . . as regards the, *TCNT* . . . I don't think anyone could have found fault with me, *Phillips* . . . I was irreproachable, *Wilson* . . . having become faultless, *Rotherham* . . . I was vnrebukable, *Geneva.*

7. But what things were gain to me: . . . every advantage that I had gained, *Phillips* . . . which once stood to my credit, *TCNT* . . . the thynges that were vauntage vnto me, *Cranmer.*

Philippians 3:8

3642.18 dem-pron pl neu	2216.16 verb 1sing indic perf mid	1217.2 prep	3450.6 art acc sing masc	5382.4 name acc masc
ταῦτα	ἥγημαι	διὰ	τὸν	Χριστὸν
tauta	hēgēmai	dia	ton	Christon
these	I have esteemed,	on account of	the	Christ,

2192.2 noun acc sing fem	233.2 conj	3174.1 partic	3173.1 partic	1058.1 partic	2504.1 conj
ζημίαν.	8. ἀλλὰ	ʽ μενοῦνγε	[μενοῦν	γε]	καὶ
zēmian	alla	menounge	menoun	ge	kai
loss.	But	yes rather,	[rather	indeed]	also

2216.1 verb 1sing indic pres mid	3820.1 adj	2192.2 noun acc sing fem	1498.32 verb inf pres act	1217.2 prep
ἡγοῦμαι	πάντα	ζημίαν	εἶναι	διὰ
hēgoumai	panta	zēmian	einai	dia
I am esteeming	all things	loss	to be	on account of

3450.16 art sing neu	5080.5 verb sing neu part pres act	3450.10 art gen sing fem	1102.2 noun gen sing fem	5382.2 name gen masc	2400.2 name masc
τὸ	ὑπερέχον	τῆς	γνώσεως	Χριστοῦ	Ἰησοῦ
to	huperechon	tēs	gnōseōs	Christou	Iēsou
to	excellency	of the	knowledge	of Christ	Jesus

3450.2 art gen sing	2935.2 noun gen sing masc	1466.2 prs-pron gen 1sing	1217.1 prep	3614.6 rel-pron acc sing masc	3450.17 art pl neu
τοῦ	κυρίου	μου,	δι’	ὃν	τὰ
tou	kuriou	mou	di’	hon	ta
of the	Lord	my,	on account of	whom	the

3820.1 adj	2193.1 verb 1sing indic aor pass	2504.1 conj	2216.1 verb 1sing indic pres mid	4512.1 noun pl neu
πάντα	ἐζημιώθην,	καὶ	ἡγοῦμαι	σκύβαλα
panta	ezēmiōthēn	kai	hēgoumai	skubala
all things	I suffered loss of,	and	esteem	refuse

1498.32 verb inf pres act	2419.1 conj	5382.4 name acc masc	2741.4 verb 1sing subj aor act	2504.1 conj	2128.35 verb 1sing subj aor pass
ʽ a εἶναι ʼ	ἵνα	Χριστὸν	κερδήσω	9. καὶ	εὑρεθῶ
einai	hina	Christon	kerdēsō	kai	heurethō
to be,	that	Christ	I may gain;	and	be found

1706.1 prep	840.4 prs-pron dat sing	3231.1 partic	2174.17 verb nom sing masc part pres act	1684.9 adj acc sing fem	1336.4 noun acc sing fem
ἐν	αὐτῷ,	μὴ	ἔχων	ἐμὴν	δικαιοσύνην
en	autō	mē	echōn	emēn	dikaiosunēn
in	him,	not	having	my	righteousness

3450.12 art acc sing fem	1523.2 prep gen	3414.2 noun gen sing masc	233.2 conj	3450.12 art acc sing fem	1217.2 prep	3963.2 noun gen sing fem
τὴν	ἐκ	νόμου,	ἀλλὰ	τὴν	διὰ	πίστεως
tēn	ek	nomou	alla	tēn	dia	pisteōs
the	of	law,	but	the	by	faith

5382.2 name gen masc	3450.12 art acc sing fem	1523.2 prep gen	2296.2 noun gen sing masc	1336.4 noun acc sing fem	1894.3 prep
Χριστοῦ,	τὴν	ἐκ	θεοῦ	δικαιοσύνην	ἐπὶ
Christou	tēn	ek	theou	dikaiosunēn	epi
of Christ,	the	of	God	righteousness	on

3450.11 art dat sing fem	3963.3 noun dat sing fem	3450.2 art gen sing	1091.29 verb inf aor act	840.6 prs-pron acc sing masc	2504.1 conj
τῇ	πίστει,	10. τοῦ	γνῶναι	αὐτὸν	καὶ
tē	pistei	tou	gnōnai	auton	kai
the	faith,	the	to know	him	and

8.a.Txt: 01ℵ-corr,02A
06D-corr,018K,020L
025P,byz.Sod
Var: 01ℵ-org,03B
06D-org,33,Lach,Treg
Tisc,We/Ho,Weis
UBS/⋆

be a reference to his conversion recorded in Acts chapter 9. The progression implied in the verb relates to the fact that from the time of his conversion until the time of writing this statement, Paul continued to consider all that gain as nothing compared to knowing Christ in a personal way. The language here is very similar to a bookkeeper's ledger in which the accountant would erase the word "gains" or "credit" and write the term "loss" or "debit."

those I counted loss for Christ: . . . esteemed as a Loss, *Wilson* . . . esteemed for Christ, detriments, *Rheims* . . . accounted a detriment, *Murdock*.

3:8. Here Paul repeated his declaration for emphasis and added a few more details. He used the same word "count" twice, but this time in the present tense in the Greek language, mainly referring to something being progressive. Time relates only to this type of verb in a secondary sense; progression is the primary factor emphasized. "Dung" or "rubbish" (NIV) refers to something thrown out as worthless. The apostle considered an intimate and continuous knowledge of Christ as his personal Saviour more important than all his former attainments mentioned in the context. It would be difficult to study Paul's writings in very much detail without seeing his constant emphasis upon the personal relationship between two persons, God and a human being. Christianity is more than just religion; it is relationship.

8. Yea doubtless, and I count all things [but] loss: Yes, indeed, I certainly do count everything as loss, *Williams*.

for the excellency of the knowledge of Christ Jesus my Lord: . . . compared with the priceless privilege, *Williams* . . . because of the superiority of the knowledge, *Rotherham* . . . as compared to the priceless worth of knowing Jesus, *Norlie*.

for whom I have suffered the loss of all things: For his sake I have suffered, *Montgomery* . . . I have lost everything, *Williams*.

and do count them [but] dung: . . . and esteem them, *Montgomery* . . . and value it all as mere refuse, *Williams* . . . reckon it all the merest refuse, *TCNT* . . . account them as filth, *Scarlett* . . . and do iudge them but vyle, *Cranmer* . . . to be vile refuse, *Wilson*.

that I may win Christ: . . . in order to, *Williams* . . . gain Christ, *Douay*.

3:9. In his beautiful description of all God had accomplished in his life, Paul suddenly took his readers to the future judgment seat of Christ. He realized that every believer will stand before the Lord to be judged for his works after his conversion. The apostle did not want to stand in Christ's presence depending upon his own righteousness because he knew it would not suffice. Instead of his own righteousness that previously had meant so much to him, he wanted to be covered with the righteousness of Christ. He reminded the Philippian believers that this righteousness of Christ comes only from God as a gift, and faith is the medium through which it comes.

9. And be found in him: . . . and be actually in union with Him, *Williams*.

not having mine own righteousness, which is of the law:

but that which is through the faith of Christ: . . . that which spryngeth of the fayth, *Tyndale*.

the righteousness which is of God by faith: . . . the real right standing...which originates from Him and rests on faith, *Williams* . . . which is derived from God and is founded on faith, *TCNT* . . . on the ground of faith, *PNT*.

3:10. Next the apostle returned to the present in his thoughts. He realized his earthly life had not ended, so he still had to live with present realities. He wanted to enjoy four realities in his earthly life: (1) to know Christ, or to have a richer experience in Him; (2) to know the power of His resurrection, or to experience constantly the same power that raised Christ from the dead; (3) to participate in the sufferings of Christ for the sake of righteousness; and (4) to be conformed to the death of Christ, or to experience the same self-emptying described of Jesus (2:7).

Verse 10 gives an excellent catalog of items that a Christian should want to be present realities on a continuous basis. Even

10. That I may know him: My aim is to get to know, *TCNT* . . . I long to come to know Him, *Williams*.

10.a.**Txt:** 06D,018K
020L,025P,etc.byz.Sod
Var: 01א-org,02A,03B
Lach,Treg,Tisc,We/Ho
Weis,UBS/☆

10.b.**Txt:** 01א-corr,02A
06D,018K,020L,025P
etc.byz.Sod
Var: 01א-org,03B,Treg
Tisc,We/Ho,Weis
UBS/☆

10.c.**Txt:** 01א-corr
06D-corr,018K,020L
byz.
Var: (01א-org),02A,03B
(06D-org),025P,33,Lach
Treg,Alf,Word,Tisc
We/Ho,Weis,Sod
UBS/☆

3450.12 art acc sing fem	1405.4 noun acc sing fem	3450.10 art gen sing fem	384.2 noun gen sing fem	840.3 prs-pron gen sing	2504.1 conj
τὴν	δύναμιν	τῆς	ἀναστάσεως	αὐτοῦ,	καὶ
tēn	dunamin	tēs	anastaseōs	autou	kai
the	power	of the	resurrection	his,	and

3450.12 art acc sing fem	2815.4 noun acc sing fem	3450.1 art gen pl	3667.3 noun gen pl neu	840.3 prs-pron gen sing
⟨a τὴν ⟩	κοινωνίαν	⟨b τῶν ⟩	παθημάτων	αὐτοῦ,
tēn	koinōnian	tōn	pathēmatōn	autou
the	fellowship	of the	sufferings	his,

4684.1 verb nom sing masc part pres mid	4682.1 verb nom sing masc part pres mid	3450.3 art dat sing	2265.3 noun dat sing masc
⟨ συμμορφούμενος	[c☆ συμμορφιζόμενος]	τῷ	θανάτῳ
summorphoumenos	summorphizomenos	tō	thanatō
being conformed	[idem]	to the	death

840.3 prs-pron gen sing	1479.1 conj	4315.1 adv	2628.4 verb 1sing subj aor act	1519.1 prep	3450.12 art acc sing fem
αὐτοῦ,	**11.** εἴ	πως	καταντήσω	εἰς	τὴν
autou	ei	pōs	katantēsō	eis	tēn
his,	if	how	I may arrive	at	the

11.a.**Txt:** 018K,020L,byz.
Var: 01א,02A,03B,06D
025P,33,Lach,Treg,Alf
Word,Tisc,We/Ho,Weis
Sod,UBS/☆

1799.1 noun acc sing fem	3450.1 art gen pl	3450.12 art acc sing fem	1523.2 prep gen	3361.2 adj gen pl	3620.1 partic
ἐξανάστασιν	⟨ τῶν	[a☆ τὴν	ἐκ]	νεκρῶν.	**12.** Οὐχ
exanastasin	tōn	tēn	ek	nekrōn	Ouch
resurrection	of the	[the	of]	dead.	Not

3617.1 conj	2218.1 adv	2956.12 verb indic aor act	2211.1 conj	2218.1 adv	4896.13 verb 1sing indic perf mid
ὅτι	ἤδη	ἔλαβον,	ἢ	ἤδη	τετελείωμαι·
hoti	ēdē	elabon	ē	ēdē	teteleiōmai
that	already	I received,	or	already	have been perfected;

1371.1 verb 1sing indic pres act	1156.2 conj	1479.1 conj	2504.1 conj	2608.2 verb 1sing subj aor act	1894.1 prep	3614.3 rel-pron dat sing
διώκω	δὲ	εἰ	καὶ	καταλάβω	ἐφ'	ᾧ
diōkō	de	ei	kai	katalabō	eph'	hō
I am pursuing	but,	if	also	I may lay hold,	for	that

12.a.**Txt:** 018K,020L,byz.
Var: 01א,02A,03B
06D-org,025P,33,Gries
Lach,Treg,Alf,Word
Tisc,We/Ho,Weis,Sod
UBS/☆

2504.1 conj	2608.7 verb 1sing indic aor pass	2608.13 verb 1sing indic aor pass	5097.3 prep	3450.2 art gen sing
καὶ	⟨ κατελήφθην	[☆ κατελήμφθην]	ὑπὸ	⟨a τοῦ ⟩
kai	katelēphthēn	katelēmphthēn	hupo	tou
also	I was laid hold of	[idem]	by	the

12.b.**Txt:** p46,p61,01א
02A,044,byz.
Var: 03B,06D-corr2
010F,012G,33

5382.2 name gen masc	2400.2 name masc	79.6 noun nom pl masc	1466.1 prs-pron nom 1sing	1670.3 prs-pron acc 1sing masc
Χριστοῦ	⟨b Ἰησοῦ. ⟩	**13.** ἀδελφοί,	ἐγὼ	ἐμαυτὸν
Christou	Iēsou	adelphoi	egō	emauton
Christ	Jesus.	Brothers,	I	myself

13.a.**Txt:** p46,03B
06D-corr,018K,020L
byz.it.sa.Weis
Var: 01א,02A,06D-org
025P,33,bo.Tisc,We/Ho
Sod,UBS/☆

3620.3 partic	3632.1 adv	3023.2 verb 1sing indic pres mid	2608.5 verb inf perf act	1518.9 num card neu
⟨ οὐ	[a☆ οὔπω]	λογίζομαι	κατειληφέναι·	ἓν
ou	oupō	logizomai	kateilēphenai	hen
not	[not yet]	do reckon	to have laid hold;	one thing

1156.2 conj	3450.17 art pl neu	3173.1 conj	3557.1 adv	1935.2 verb nom sing masc part pres mid	3450.4 art dat pl
δέ,	τὰ	μὲν	ὀπίσω	ἐπιλανθανόμενος,	τοῖς
de	ta	men	opisō	epilanthanomenos	tois
but,	the things	men	behind	forgetting,	to the things

though a Christian obviously knows Christ, that knowledge can increase and become more intimate as the person experiences spiritual growth. Paul related the power (*dunamis*) of the Resurrection to the necessity of experiencing spiritual strength to live an overcoming Christian life on a continuous basis. Many people quote this marvelous verse but leave out the segment relating to suffering and conforming to the death of Christ.

3:11. Paul next expressed his ultimate desire to be part of the physical resurrection of believers (Revelation 20:6). His comment in the previous verse about spiritual resurrection would only have shown half the picture had he not made this reference to the physical resurrection that Christians will enjoy one day. The Greek term here literally refers to "the out-resurrection from the dead" and vividly depicts the fact that some people will be snatched from among the dead long before the remainder are resurrected.

The term "attain" does not imply Paul viewed being part of the first resurrection a matter of works. However, he did emphasize the necessity of constantly maintaining an integral relationship with Christ, because only people definitely related to Jesus via conversion will be included in the first resurrection.

3:12. Paul again returned to the present and expressed the realization that he had not arrived at any pinnacle of perfection. Apparently some of the Philippians were making such a claim for themselves. First, he approached the matter with an aorist verb (*elabon*) which was translated "attained," indicating that at the time of his conversion he did not receive everything God had for him. In addition, his statement "either were already perfect" indicates that from the moment of conversion until the writing of the epistle he still had not been perfected. This second verb is a perfect tense so it refers to an initial act followed by continuous action or results. In this case it probably refers to continuous action.

Thus Paul's two verbs both stress he did not claim to have yet reached perfection. Instead of feeling he had arrived, he said, "I follow after" or "press on" (NIV).

3:13. Verse 13 contains even stronger language than verse 12. After carefully repeating the fact that he had not yet arrived at the goal set for him by God himself, Paul emphasized that what he did constantly was to stretch forward toward it. In order to keep pressing toward the goal, he had to forget what was behind. "Forgetting" in this context does not imply obliterating something from the mind, but refers to the constant necessity of pushing something out of the mind. It speaks of a continuous process rather than a momentary occurrence. Again, the language is that of a runner completely forgetting his opponents who are following him in a race. Even the slightest looking back will slow down his progress.

Philippians 3:13

and the power of his resurrection: . . . and the efficacy of, *Murdock* . . . the power shown by, *Phillips* . . . and experience the power of His resurrection, *Norlie.*

and the fellowship of his sufferings: . . . now I long to share, *Phillips* . . . and the participation, *Sawyer* . . . and the societie of his passions, *Rheims.*

being made conformable unto his death: . . . even to die as he died, *Phillips.*

11. If by any means I might attain: . . . if possibly, *Wilson* . . . I may advance into, *Rotherham.*

unto the resurrection of the dead: . . . that lifts me out from among the dead, *Williams.*

12. Not as though I had already attained: . . . nor do I consider myself, *Phillips* . . . No, I have not yet reached that goal, *Norlie* . . . I do not say that I have already won, *Montgomery* . . . secured it, *TCNT.*

either were already perfect: . . . or already have reached perfection, *Rotherham, Williams.*

but I follow after, if that I may apprehend that for which also I am apprehended of Christ Jesus: But I am pressing on, *TCNT* . . . but I pursue...I was laid hold on, *Wilson* . . . I keep going on, grasping ever more firmly, *Phillips* . . . I am pressing on to see if I can capture it, *Williams* . . . that I may attain that for which also I was arrested by, *Sawyer* . . . also I was laid hold on by Christ, *Alford* . . . I am also comprehended of Christ, *Rheims.*

13. Brethren, I count not myself to have apprehended: . . . to have laid hold, *Rotherham, ASV, Worrell* . . . that I haue gotten it as yet, *Cranmer* . . . to have fully grasped it even now, *Phillips.*

but [this] one thing [I do]: I do concentrate on this, *Phillips.*

forgetting those things which are behind: . . . leave the past behind, *Phillips* . . . what is behind me, *Montgomery.*

Philippians 3:14

1156.2 conj
δὲ
de
and

1699.1 prep
ἔμπροσθεν
emprosthen
before

1886.1 verb nom sing masc part pres mid
ἐπεκτεινόμενος,
epekteinomenos
stretching out,

2567.3 prep
14. κατὰ
kata
towards

4504.1 noun acc sing masc
σκοπὸν
skopon
goal

14.a.Txt: 06D,018K
020L,025P,byz.
Var: 01ℵ,02A,03B,33
Lach,Treg,Alf,Tisc
We/Ho,Weis,Sod
UBS/✶

1371.1 verb 1sing indic pres act
διώκω
diōkō
I pursue

1894.3 prep
⌐ ἐπὶ
epi
for

1519.1 prep
[ᵃ✶ εἰς]
eis
[idem]

3450.16 art sing neu
τὸ
to
the

1010.1 noun sing neu
βραβεῖον
brabeion
prize

3450.10 art gen sing fem
τῆς
tēs
of the

504.1 adv
ἄνω
anō
on high

2794.2 noun gen sing fem
κλήσεως
klēseōs
calling

3450.2 art gen sing
τοῦ
tou

2296.2 noun gen sing masc
θεοῦ
theou
of God

1706.1 prep
ἐν
en
in

5382.3 name dat masc
Χριστῷ
Christō
Christ

2400.2 name masc
Ἰησοῦ.
Iēsou
Jesus.

3607.2 rel-pron nom pl masc
15. Ὅσοι
Hosoi
As many as

3631.1 partic
οὖν
oun
therefore

4894.3 adj nom pl masc
τέλειοι
teleioi
mature

3642.17 dem-pron sing neu
τοῦτο
touto
this

5262.5 verb 1pl subj pres act
φρονῶμεν·
phronōmen
let us think;

2504.1 conj
καὶ
kai
and

1479.1 conj
εἴ
ei
if

4948.10 indef-pron sing neu
τι
ti
anything

2067.1 adv
ἑτέρως
heterōs
differently

5262.1 verb 2pl pres act
φρονεῖτε,
phroneite
you are thinking,

2504.1 conj
καὶ
kai
also

3642.17 dem-pron sing neu
τοῦτο
touto
this

3450.5 art nom sing masc
ὁ
ho

2296.1 noun nom sing masc
θεὸς
theos
God

5050.3 prs-pron dat 2pl
ὑμῖν
humin
to you

596.4 verb 3sing indic fut act
ἀποκαλύψει.
apokalupsei
will reveal.

3993.1 prep
16. πλὴν
plēn
But

1519.1 prep
εἰς
eis
to

16.a.Txt: 01ℵ-corr,018K
020L,025P,byz.
Var: p16,p46,01ℵ-org
02A,03B,33,sa.bo.Gries
Lach,Treg,Alf,Tisc
We/Ho,Weis,Sod
UBS/✶

3614.16 rel-pron sing neu
ὃ
ho
what

5185.2 verb 1pl indic aor act
ἐφθάσαμεν,
ephthasamen
we attained,

3450.3 art dat sing
τῷ
tō
by the

840.4 prs-pron dat sing
αὐτῷ
autō
same

4599.4 verb inf pres act
στοιχεῖν.
stoichein
to continue

2554.2 noun dat sing masc
⌐ᵃ κανόνι,
kanoni
rule,

3450.16 art sing neu
τὸ
to
to

840.15 prs-pron sing neu
αὐτὸ
auto
same

5262.9 verb inf pres act
φρονεῖν. ⌐
phronein
to think.

4682.1 noun nom pl masc
17. Συμμιμηταί
Summimētai
Imitators together

1466.2 prs-pron gen 1sing
μου
mou
of me

1090.19 verb 2pl impr pres mid
γίνεσθε,
ginesthe
be,

79.6 noun nom pl masc
ἀδελφοί,
adelphoi
brothers,

2504.1 conj
καὶ
kai
and

4503.2 verb 2pl impr pres act
σκοπεῖτε
skopeite
consider

3450.8 art acc pl masc
τοὺς
tous
the

3643.1 adv
οὕτως
houtōs
thus

3906.16 verb acc pl masc part pres act
περιπατοῦντας
peripatountas
walking

2503.1 conj
καθὼς
kathōs
as

2174.2 verb 2pl pres act
ἔχετε
echete
you have

5020.2 noun acc sing masc
τύπον
tupon
a pattern

2231.4 prs-pron acc 1pl
ἡμᾶς.
hēmas
us;

4044.7 adj nom pl masc
18. πολλοὶ
polloi
many

1056.1 conj
γὰρ
gar
for

3906.2 verb 3pl indic pres act
περιπατοῦσιν
peripatousin
are walking

3614.8 rel-pron acc pl masc
οὓς
hous
whom

4038.1 adv
πολλάκις
pollakis
often

3:14. The culmination of Paul's testimony in verse 14 contains a statement about the goal and the prize God placed before him. To him Christ was both the goal and the prize. This is one of the amazing marvels of Scripture. In a human contest the goal and the prize could not, at least normally, be the same.

The Bible speaks often of the process of maturing through which God takes His followers. However, it does not take place automatically. Christians have a part, and God has a part (2:12,13). Even so, full maturity will not be attained until the resurrection. Therefore, the glorified life in heaven is both the goal and the prize.

3:15. At first verse 15 may seem to contradict verses 12 and 13. Paul had renounced the false idea that it is possible in this earthly life to reach a level of absolute sinless perfection. The language of the previous section might lead a person to say, "Since I cannot arrive at a level of absolute sinless perfection, why should I constantly put forth effort to become like Christ?" Paul immediately countered that tendency by making it clear that although it is impossible to reach a place of absolute sinless perfection in this life, it is possible to reach a certain level of Christian perfection.

The same idea expressed in the Greek term for "perfect" or "mature" (*teleios*) is also emphasized in 1 Corinthians 2:6; 14:20; Ephesians 4:13,14; Colossians 1:28; 4:12; Hebrews 5:14; and 6:1. It does not contain the implication of being perfect in the sense of flawlessness; rather, it refers to having reached a level of completeness or maturity. In verse 12 Paul was speaking of a finished product, whereas in verse 15 he was referring to a relative spiritual maturity where there is room for development and growth. An apple serves as a good illustration of this matter. In June it is a perfect apple, but it is far from mature. In September it is far more mature, perfect, or complete.

3:16. This verse shows the meaning of Christian perfection, or a state of Christian maturity. When we live up to what God has already shown us, He is able to lead us further on the route to perfection. However, if believers balk at the instructions written in the Scriptures, they hinder the process. We may never fully understand all of Scripture; God illuminates it to us by degrees. Still, we can learn to act like Christ, the Perfect One.

3:17. Paul encouraged the Philippians to follow his example in this matter. "Us" probably refers to Timothy, Silas, and Luke who assisted the apostle in his initial ministry in Philippi. The Greek word for "ensample" or "example" (*tupos*) sometimes refers to the impression left by a stroke, and it is the same word used for the nail prints left in Jesus' hands (John 20:25). It also can be used to mean "a pattern" (1 Corinthians 10:6,11; 1 Thessalonians 1:7), and this is the meaning here. The Philippians were warned to mark the ones who did not follow that pattern.

and reaching forth unto those things which are before: I strain forward, *Confraternity* . . . and straining every nerve, *TCNT* . . . and stretching forth, *Wilson, Douay.*

14. I press toward the mark: I go straight for, *Phillips* . . . to press on to the winning-post, *TCNT* . . . toward the goal, *Scarlett, ASV.*

for the prize of the high calling of God in Christ Jesus: . . . my reward the honor of being called by God, *Phillips* . . . of the heavenly calling, *Alford* . . . of the upward calling, *Panin* . . . the supernal vocation, *Douay.*

15. Let us therefore, as many as be perfect, be thus minded: . . . as [are] of full growth, let this be our resolve, *Rotherham* . . . attend to this, *Scarlett.*

and if in any thing ye be otherwise minded: . . . but if ye should think differently, *Scarlett* . . . if ye have a different mind, *Noyes* . . . if at present you cannot see this, *Phillips.*

God shall reveal even this unto you: . . . this is the attitude which God is leading you to adopt, *Phillips* . . . will make that also plain to you, *TCNT.*

16. Nevertheless, whereto we have already attained, let us walk by the same rule, let us mind the same thing: . . . walk on by the same path, *Alford.*

17. Brethren, be followers together of me: . . . join one another in copying my example, *TCNT.*

and mark them which walk so as ye have us for an ensample: . . . as you have us for a Pattern, *Wilson* . . . you have our model, *Douay.*

18. (For many walk, of whom I have told you often:

2978.25 verb indic imperf act	5050.3 prs-pron dat 2pl	3431.1 adv	1156.2 conj	2504.1 conj	2772.5 verb nom sing masc part pres act	2978.1 verb 1sing pres act
ἔλεγον	ὑμῖν,	νῦν	δὲ	καὶ	κλαίων	λέγω,
elegon	humin	nun	de	kai	klaiōn	legō
I was telling	you,	now	and	even	weeping	I tell

3450.8 art acc pl masc	2172.7 adj acc pl masc	3450.2 art gen sing	4567.2 noun gen sing masc	3450.2 art gen sing	5382.2 name gen masc
τοὺς	ἐχθροὺς	τοῦ	σταυροῦ	τοῦ	Χριστοῦ·
tous	echthrous	tou	staurou	tou	Christou
the	enemies	of the	cross	of the	Christ:

	3614.1 rel-pron gen pl	3450.16 art sing neu	4904.1 noun sing neu	677.1 noun nom sing fem	3614.1 rel-pron gen pl	3450.5 art nom sing masc
19.	ὧν	τὸ	τέλος	ἀπώλεια,	ὧν	ὁ
	hōn	to	telos	apōleia	hōn	ho
	whose	the	end	destruction,	whose	

2296.1 noun nom sing masc	3450.9 art nom sing fem	2809.1 noun nom sing fem	2504.1 conj	3450.9 art nom sing fem	1385.1 noun nom sing fem	1706.1 prep
θεὸς	ἡ	κοιλία,	καὶ	ἡ	δόξα	ἐν
theos	hē	koilia	kai	hē	doxa	en
God	the	belly,	and	the	glory	in

3450.11 art dat sing fem	151.3 noun dat sing fem	840.1 prs-pron gen pl	3450.7 art nom pl masc	3450.17 art pl neu	1904.3 adj pl neu
τῇ	αἰσχύνῃ	αὐτῶν,	οἱ	τὰ	ἐπίγεια
tē	aischunē	autōn	hoi	ta	epigeia
the	shame	their,	the	the	earthly things

5262.8 verb nom pl masc part pres act		2231.2 prs-pron gen 1pl	1056.1 conj	3450.16 art sing neu	4035.1 noun sing neu	1706.1 prep
φρονοῦντες.	**20.**	ἡμῶν	γὰρ	τὸ	πολίτευμα	ἐν
phronountes		hēmōn	gar	to	politeuma	en
thinking:		our	for	the	citizenship	in

3636.8 noun dat pl masc	5062.2 verb 3sing indic pres act	1523.1 prep gen	3614.2 rel-pron gen sing	2504.1 conj	4842.4 noun acc sing masc
οὐρανοῖς	ὑπάρχει,	ἐξ	οὗ	καὶ	σωτῆρα
ouranois	huparchei	ex	hou	kai	sōtēra
heavens	exists,	from	which	also	Saviour

549.2 verb 1pl indic pres mid	2935.4 noun acc sing masc	2400.3 name acc masc	5382.4 name acc masc		3614.5 rel-pron nom sing masc
ἀπεκδεχόμεθα	κύριον	Ἰησοῦν	Χριστόν,	**21.**	ὃς
apekdechometha	kurion	Iēsoun	Christon		hos
we are awaiting	Lord	Jesus	Christ,		who

3215.2 verb 3sing indic fut act	3450.16 art sing neu	4835.1 noun sing neu	3450.10 art gen sing fem	4865.1 noun gen sing fem
μετασχηματίσει	τὸ	σῶμα	τῆς	ταπεινώσεως
metaschēmatisei	to	sōma	tēs	tapeinōseōs
will transform	the	body	of the	humiliation

2231.2 prs-pron gen 1pl	1519.1 prep	3450.16 art sing neu	1090.63 verb inf aor mid	840.15 prs-pron sing neu	4683.2 adj sing neu
ἡμῶν,	⌜a εἰς	τὸ	γενέσθαι	αὐτὸ ⌝	σύμμορφον
hēmōn	eis	to	genesthai	auto	summorphon
our,	for	the	to become	it	conformed

3450.3 art dat sing	4835.3 noun dat sing neu	3450.10 art gen sing fem	1385.2 noun gen sing fem	840.3 prs-pron gen sing	2567.3 prep	3450.12 art acc sing fem
τῷ	σώματι	τῆς	δόξης	αὐτοῦ,	κατὰ	τὴν
tō	sōmati	tēs	doxēs	autou	kata	tēn
to the	body	of the	glory	his,	according to	the

21.a.**Txt:** 06D-corr,018K 020L,025P,byz. **Var:** 01ℵ,02A,03B 06D-org,bo.Gries,Lach Treg,Alf,Word,Tisc We/Ho,Weis,Sod UBS/✶

3:18. After warning the Philippians to mark certain people, Paul here described them as enemies of the cross of Christ. One cannot be sure whether he referred to false teachers within the Philippian church or to outsiders. Perhaps both groups existed. These were not the legalistic people described at the outset of the chapter. They no doubt were professing Christians who allowed their liberty to degenerate into license (Galatians 5:13). They could be called antinomians. They believed in no laws, no regulations. However, the extreme legalists and the antinomians Paul described in this chapter had one thing in common: they lived as enemies of the gospel of Christ.

3:19. The people Paul described here were probably Gentiles with Epicurean tendencies. The Epicureans constituted a Greek school of philosophy with the basic views that satisfaction of the physical appetites was the highest purpose of mankind. In addition to describing these people as enemies of the Cross, Paul designated their end as destruction, a reference to eternal separation from God. A person's god is that to which he gives himself. These people had made their own unbridled lusts their gods. Although they gloried in their "freedom" to live as they pleased, their perverted actions only brought them shame. Paul's closing description of these false teachers is a very straightforward one—"who mind earthly things."

3:20. In contrast to false teachers, those people who choose to follow Christ recognize a standard based upon something far more important than earthly pursuits. Paul used the same word for "conversation" or "citizenship" that he used in 1:27, but there he used the verb *politeuomai*, and here the noun *politeuma*. The Christian is a citizen of heaven and he longs for the kingdom of heaven to become a present reality (Matthew 6:10; Ephesians 2:19). In a sense the Church is a "colony of heaven" much as Philippi was a Roman colony. The realization that the Saviour of believers one day will return for those citizens of heaven constitutes a powerful incentive for correct living.

3:21. When He returns for His church believers' bodies will be changed like His own (1 John 3:2). The term translated "change" (*metaschēmatisei*) refers to the outward change of these "vile" or "lowly" (NIV) bodies. Redeemed souls will occupy redeemed bodies such as Christ's after His resurrection. Then since doctrine determines conduct and destiny, Christians must avoid the extremes of both legalism and antinomianism.

and now tell you even weeping, [that they are] the enemies of the cross of Christ: . . . even with tears, *Phillips* . . . who behave as though they hated the cross of, *Norlie.*

19. Whose end [is] destruction, whose God [is their] belly: Their end is ruin, *Confraternity* . . . whose ende is dampnacion, *Tyndale* . . . end is perdition, *Alford* . . . whos god is the wombe, *Wyclif* . . . their stomach, *Sawyer.*
and [whose] glory [is] in their shame: They take pride in their shame, *Norlie* . . . their glorie in their confusion, *Rheims* . . . their pride is in what they should be ashamed of, *Phillips.*
who mind earthly things.): . . . who regard, *Sawyer* . . . who are engrossed with earthly things, *Wilson* . . . which are worldely mynded, *Geneva* . . . this world is the limit of their horizon, *Phillips.*

20. For our conversation is in heaven: For our enrollment as citizens, *Rotherham* . . . For our place of administration, *Clementson* . . . our citizenship, *Panin* . . . our country is in the heavens, *Alford.*
from whence also we look for the Saviour, the Lord Jesus Christ: . . . we expect the, *Sawyer* . . . are we ardently awaiting, *Rotherham* . . . we are waiting with longing expectation, *Clementson* . . . we await [the] Saviour, *PNT* . . . we also are awaiting the return of, *Norlie.*

21. Who shall change our vile body: . . . who will refashion, *Confraternity* . . . who shall fashion anew, *Panin* . . . who will transform, *Wilson, Worrell* . . . our humble body, *Sawyer* . . . the body of our humiliation, *Alford.*
that it may be fashioned like unto his glorious body: . . . that it may be conformed, *ASV* . . . to resemble, *Phillips.*

Philippians 4:1

1737.2 noun acc sing fem	3450.2 art gen sing	1404.22 verb inf pres mid	840.6 prs-pron acc sing masc	2504.1 conj	5131.6 verb inf aor act
ἐνέργειαν *energeian* working	τοῦ *tou* of the	δύνασθαι *dunasthai* to be able	αὐτὸν *auton* his	καὶ *kai* even	ὑποτάξαι *hupotaxai* to subdue

1431.5 prs-pron dat sing masc	840.4 prs- pron dat sing	3450.17 art pl neu	3820.1 adj	5452.1 conj
ʿ ἑαυτῷ *heautō* to himself	[b✶ αὐτῷ] *autō* [to him]	τὰ *ta* the	πάντα. *panta.* all things.	**4:1.** Ὥστε, *Hōste,* So that,

79.6 noun nom pl masc	1466.2 prs- pron gen 1sing	27.6 adj pl masc	2504.1 conj	1957.1 adj nom pl masc	5315.1 noun nom sing fem
ἀδελφοί *adelphoi* brothers	μου *mou* my	ἀγαπητοὶ *agapētoi* beloved	καὶ *kai* and	ἐπιπόθητοι, *epipothētoi* longed for,	χαρὰ *chara* joy

2504.1 conj	4586.1 noun nom sing masc	1466.2 prs- pron gen 1sing	3643.1 adv	4590.1 verb 2pl pres act	1706.1 prep	2935.3 noun dat sing masc
καὶ *kai* and	στέφανός *stephanos* crown	μου, *mou* my,	οὕτως *houtōs* thus	στήκετε *stēkete* stand fast	ἐν *en* in	κυρίῳ, *kuriō* Lord,

27.6 adj pl masc	2157.1 name acc fem	2157.2 name acc fem	3731.1 verb 1sing indic pres act	2504.1 conj
ἀγαπητοί. *agapētoi* beloved.	**2.** ʿ Εὐωδίαν *Euōdian* Euodias	[✶ Εὐοδίαν] *Euodian* [idem]	παρακαλῶ, *parakalō* I encourage,	καὶ *kai* and

4793.1 name acc fem	3731.1 verb 1sing indic pres act	3450.16 art sing neu	840.15 prs- pron sing neu	5262.9 verb inf pres act	1706.1 prep
Συντύχην *Suntuchēn* Syntyche	παρακαλῶ, *parakalō* I encourage,	τὸ *to* to	αὐτὸ *auto* same thing	φρονεῖν *phronein* to think	ἐν *en* in

2935.3 noun dat sing masc	2504.1 conj	3346.1 intrj	2049.2 verb 1sing indic pres act	2504.1 conj	4622.4 prs- pron acc 2sing
κυρίῳ· *kuriō* Lord.	**3.** ʿ καὶ *kai* And	[a✶ ναὶ] *nai* [Yes]	ἐρωτῶ *erōtō* I ask	καὶ *kai* also	σέ, *se* you,

4656.1 adj voc sing masc	1097.1 adj voc sing masc	1097.1 adj voc sing masc	4656.1 adj voc sing masc	4666.8 verb 2sing impr pres mid
ʿ σύζυγε *suzuge* yokefellow	γνήσιε, *gnēsie* true,	[✶ γνήσιε *gnēsie* [true	σύζυγε,] *suzuge* yokefellow,]	συλλαμβάνου *sullambanou* assist

840.14 prs- pron dat pl fem	3610.4 rel- pron nom pl fem	1706.1 prep	3450.3 art dat sing	2077.3 noun dat sing neu	4717.2 verb 3pl indic aor act
αὐταῖς, *autais* them,	αἵτινες *haitines* who	ἐν *en* in	τῷ *tō* the	εὐαγγελίῳ *euangeliō* good news	συνήθλησάν *sunēthlēsan* strove together

1466.4 prs- pron dat 1sing	3196.3 prep	2504.1 conj	2788.1 name gen masc	2504.1 conj	3450.1 art gen pl	3036.1 adj gen pl
μοι, *moi* with me;	μετὰ *meta* with	καὶ *kai* also	Κλήμεντος, *Klēmentos* Clement,	καὶ *kai* and	τῶν *tōn* the	λοιπῶν *loipōn* rest

4754.5 adj gen pl masc	1466.2 prs- pron gen 1sing	3614.1 rel- pron gen pl	3450.17 art pl neu	3549.1 noun pl neu	1706.1 prep
συνεργῶν *sunergōn* of fellow workers	μου, *mou* my,	ὧν *hōn* whose	τὰ *ta* the	ὀνόματα *onomata* names	ἐν *en* in

21.b.Txt: 01ℵ-corr
06D-corr,020L,it.Steph
Var: 01ℵ-org,02A,03B
06D-org,025P,Lach
Treg,Alf,Tisc,We/Ho
Weis,Sod,UBS/✶

3.a.Txt: Steph
Var: 01ℵ,02A,03B,06D
018K,020L,025P,byz.
Gries,Lach,Treg,Alf
Word,Tisc,We/Ho,Weis
Sod,UBS/✶

4:1. The first four verses of this chapter may seem unrelated to each other; however, if one remembers Paul's stress on joy, the association becomes clear. Verse 1 begins with another "therefore," which in this case comes from a Greek term literally meaning "so as" (*hōste*). This "so as" refers back to the entire first three chapters of the letter, to which Paul gives an excellent climax in this fourth chapter.

The term for "crown" (*stephanos*) is the word from which we derive the name *Stephen*. It relates to the laurel wreath placed around the neck or upon the head of the victor in an athletic contest. It was not at all like a diadem (*diadēma*) worn by a ruler or priest of the day. The laurel began to wilt shortly after it was picked from a tree, so it was only transitory. On the other hand, the Philippian saints consisted of Paul's permanent joy and crown, or his reward for his labors in Philippi.

4:2. Perhaps the problem he pinpointed in verse 2 represented many such differences in the assembly. People cannot constantly experience joy if they are always bickering over minor matters. Paul therefore appealed to Euodias and Syntyche to settle their differences. While he could have *ordered* them to solve their problem, he instead *begged* them to do so. The Greek word behind the term "beseech" (*parakalō*) is the same word from which we derive *Paraclete*, one of the prominent New Testament names for the Holy Spirit, the One who is the master pleader.

It is unfortunate that the only thing we know about these two ladies, in addition to the fact that they labored with Paul when he ministered in Philippi, is that they could not get along and could not reconcile their differences. When Paul told them to "be of the same mind in the Lord," he used the same word as in 2:5 (*phronein*) where he instructed the Philippians to have the attitude of Christ.

These ladies certainly did not live up to their names. *Euodias* means "prosperous journey" and *Syntyche* means "pleasant acquaintance." Paul did not insist they think alike in everything, but if each had the selfless attitude of Christ, each would respect the other's viewpoint, and neither would be contentious.

4:3. According to verse 3, these two women definitely had assisted Paul in his ministry in Philippi. From the very genesis of the assembly, women filled prominent places in the Philippian church (Acts 16:13ff.). It is a well-known historical fact that women held more prominent positions in the province of Macedonia, the province in which Philippi was located, than they did in most other parts of the Roman world. The apostle asked a third party to assist Euodias and Syntyche to settle their differences. Commentators disagree as to whether "true yokefellow" merely describes the person addressed or whether his actual name was Suzugos, the literal Greek noun from which "yokefellow" comes. Clement and other individuals not only helped Paul in his ministry in Philippi, but their names were known to God.

according to the working whereby he is able even to subdue all things unto himself: . . . by the exertion of the power, *Williams* . . . by the power that enables Him, *Adams* . . . by the energy with which he is able even to subject all things to himself, *Montgomery* . . . which makes him the master of everything that is, *Phillips*.

1. Therefore, my brethren, dearly beloved and longed for: So, my brothers whom I hold dear and greatly desire to see, *Adams*.

my joy and crown: . . . and winner's wreath, *Adams*.

so stand fast in the Lord, [my] dearly beloved: . . . by the help of the Lord keep on standing firm, dearly loved friends, *Williams* . . . who are very dear to me, *TCNT* . . . my deerest, *Rheims* . . . dear friends, *Adams* . . . and remember how much I love you, *Phillips*.

2. I beseech Euodias, and beseech Syntyche: I exhort, *Panin* . . . I beg you by name, *Phillips* . . . I urge, *Adams*.

that they be of the same mind in the Lord: . . . to live in harmony as fellow-Christians, *TCNT* . . . to think alike in the Lord, *Adams* . . . by the help of the Lord, *Williams*.

3. And I entreat thee also, true yokefellow: I request you also, *Worrell* . . . Yes, I also ask you, who have shown yourself to be genuine in bearing the yoke together with me, *Adams* . . . genuine yokefellow, *Rotherham* . . . my true comrade, *Williams*.

help those women which laboured with me in the gospel: . . . assist those, *Wilson* . . . give them aid, *Noyes* . . . keep on co-operating with, *Williams* . . . who struggled together with me for the good news, *Adams*.

with Clement also, and [with] other my fellowlabourers, whose names [are] in the book of life: . . . the rest of my fellow-workers, *Williams*.

969.3 noun dat sing fem	2205.2 noun gen sing fem	5299.7 verb 2pl impr pres act	1706.1 prep	2935.3 noun dat sing masc	3704.1 adv
βίβλῳ	ζωῆς.	4. Χαίρετε	ἐν	κυρίῳ	πάντοτε·
biblō	zōēs	Chairete	en	kuriō	pantote
book	of life.	Rejoice	in	Lord	always:

3687.1 adv	2029.9 verb 1sing indic fut act	5299.7 verb 2pl impr pres act	3450.16 art sing neu	1918.5 adj sing neu	5050.2 prs-pron gen 2pl
πάλιν	ἐρῶ,	χαίρετε.	5. τὸ	ἐπιεικὲς	ὑμῶν
palin	erō	chairete	to	epieikes	humōn
again	I will say,	rejoice.	The	gentleness	your

1091.44 verb 3sing impr aor pass	3820.5 adj dat pl	442.8 noun dat pl masc	3450.5 art nom sing masc	2935.1 noun nom sing masc	1445.1 adv
γνωσθήτω	πᾶσιν	ἀνθρώποις.	ὁ	κύριος	ἐγγύς.
gnōsthētō	pasin	anthrōpois	ho	kurios	engus
let be known	to all	men.	The	Lord	near.

3235.6 num card neu	3179.1 verb 2pl pres act	233.1 conj	1706.1 prep	3820.3 adj dat sing	3450.11 art dat sing fem
6. Μηδὲν	μεριμνᾶτε,	ἀλλ'	ἐν	παντὶ	τῇ
Mēden	merimnate	all'	en	panti	tē
Nothing	be anxious about,	but	in	everything	by the

4194.3 noun dat sing fem	2504.1 conj	3450.11 art dat sing fem	1157.3 noun dat sing fem	3196.3 prep	2150.1 noun fem
προσευχῇ	καὶ	τῇ	δεήσει	μετὰ	εὐχαριστίας
proseuchē	kai	tē	deēsei	meta	eucharistias
prayer	and	by the	entreaty	with	thanksgiving

3450.17 art pl neu	154.2 noun pl neu	5050.2 prs-pron gen 2pl	1101.13 verb 3sing impr pres mid	4242.1 prep	3450.6 art acc sing masc
τὰ	αἰτήματα	ὑμῶν	γνωριζέσθω	πρὸς	τὸν
ta	aitēmata	humōn	gnōrizesthō	pros	ton
the	requests	your	let be made known	to	

2296.4 noun acc sing masc	2504.1 conj	3450.9 art nom sing fem	1503.1 noun nom sing fem	3450.2 art gen sing	2296.2 noun gen sing masc	3450.9 art nom sing fem
θεόν·	7. καὶ	ἡ	εἰρήνη	τοῦ	θεοῦ	ἡ
theon	kai	hē	eirēnē	tou	theou	hē
God;	and	the	peace		of God	the

5080.3 verb nom sing fem part pres act	3820.1 adj	3426.4 noun acc sing masc	5268.1 verb 3sing indic fut act	3450.15 art acc pl fem
ὑπερέχουσα	πάντα	νοῦν	φρουρήσει	τὰς
huperechousa	panta	noun	phrourēsei	tas
surpassing	every	understanding	shall guard	the

2559.1 noun fem	5050.2 prs-pron gen 2pl	2504.1 conj	3450.17 art pl neu	3402.2 noun pl neu	5050.2 prs-pron gen 2pl	1706.1 prep
καρδίας	ὑμῶν	καὶ	τὰ	νοήματα	ὑμῶν	ἐν
kardias	humōn	kai	ta	noēmata	humōn	en
hearts	your	and	the	thoughts	your	in

5382.3 name dat masc	2400.2 name masc	3450.16 art sing neu	3036.8 adj sing neu	79.6 noun nom pl masc	3607.8 rel-pron pl neu
Χριστῷ	Ἰησοῦ.	8. Τὸ	λοιπόν,	ἀδελφοί,	ὅσα
Christō	Iēsou	To	loipon	adelphoi	hosa
Christ	Jesus.	The	rest,	brothers,	whatever

1498.4 verb 3sing indic pres act	225.4 adj	3607.8 rel-pron pl neu	4441.3 adj pl neu	3607.8 rel-pron pl neu	1337.14 adj pl neu
ἐστὶν	ἀληθῆ,	ὅσα	σεμνά,	ὅσα	δίκαια,
estin	alēthē	hosa	semna	hosa	dikaia
are	true,	whatever	honorable,	whatsoever	just,

4:4. People who actively serve God generally reflect the joy of the Lord, and this may explain Paul's sudden outburst in verse 4. Bible commentators generally agree that this verse reflects most clearly the theme of the letter.

4:5. Because joy is the outward expression of some inward cause, Paul quickly moved from external matters to internal matters. If the peace of God truly abides within a person, it will reflect itself in outward joy. Joy is a wonderful by-product of the peace described in verse 7 which contains the central theme from verses 5-9. The rest of the passage describes what we must do in order to constantly experience this peace.

Verse 5 gives the first condition as "moderation" or "forbearance" (RSV). In other words, a person cannot enjoy the peace of God unless he can forbear other people. Paul buttressed his command by adding a solemn warning about the Lord's nearness. He may have had Psalm 145:18 in mind, or he may have been referring to the Aramaic expression *Maran atha* ("O Lord, Come"—1 Corinthians 16:22). In the light of Paul's constant references to the imminency of the Lord's return, the latter probably is what he meant.

4:6. Secondly, to know God's peace we must not worry, since that betrays a lack of trust in God. Paul's words can be translated, "Stop being anxious." Then the apostle offered prayer as the solution to worry.

Paul gave a complete picture of the process by using four different Greek terms. (1) "Prayer" (*proseuchē*) is used constantly in the New Testament of prayer in general. (2) "Supplication" (*deēsis*) concerns special times of need. (3) "Thanksgiving" (*eucharistia*) looks back to previous answers to prayer in which God helped in similar situations. (4) "Requests" (*aitēmata*) refers to specific requests for specific needs.

4:7. Then if anyone does the above things, God's peace will keep him. The apostle used a military term here: "keep" here literally means "to garrison, to guard, to keep, to arbitrate, to umpire" our hearts and minds. Because Philippi was a Roman colony and a military outpost, the garrisoning of the city by Roman soldiers was a very familiar sight. Since "hearts" (*kardias*) and "minds" (*noun*) suffer most at the lack of inner tranquility, God promises to guard both.

4:8. The third condition to enjoying the peace of God relates to a person's thought life. Christians cannot enjoy God's peace if they are always allowing unwholesome thoughts to fill their minds. Paul gave a representative list of six types of things on which believers should concentrate, but no doubt he could have continued the list.

4. Rejoice in the Lord alway: Delight yourselves in God, *Phillips*.

[and] again I say, Rejoice: . . . yes, find your joy in him at all times, *Phillips*.

5. Let your moderation be known unto all men: Let your gentleness, *Panin, Wilson* . . . Let your considerateness, *Rotherham* . . . Let your yieldedness, *Clementson* . . . Let your forbearing spirit be plain to every one, *TCNT* . . . Let your modesty be known to all men, *Douay* . . . Have a reputation for gentleness, *Phillips*.

The Lord [is] at hand: . . . never forget the nearness of, *Phillips* . . . is near, *Wilson* . . . is nigh, *Douay*.

6. Be careful for nothing: Do not be anxious about anything, *TCNT* . . . In nothing be anxious, *Panin* . . . For nothing be anxious, *Rotherham* . . . Have no anxiety, *Confraternity*.

but in every thing by prayer and supplication with thanksgiving let your requests be made known unto God: . . . let your petitions, *Confraternity*.

7. And the peace of God, which passeth all understanding: . . . which surpasses every human conception, *TCNT* . . . which surpasses all Conception, *Wilson* . . . which rises above every mind, *Rotherham*.

shall keep your hearts and minds through Christ Jesus:

8. Finally, brethren: In conclusion, *TCNT*.

whatsoever things are true:

whatsoever things [are] honest: . . . as many as [are] dignified, *Rotherham* . . . are honorable, *Wilson* . . . modest, *Douay* . . . chast, *Wyclif* . . . are venerable, *PNT*.

whatsoever things [are] just:

Philippians 4:9

3607.8 rel- pron pl neu ὅσα *hosa* whatsoever	52.7 adj pl neu ἁγνά, *hagna* pure,	3607.8 rel- pron pl neu ὅσα *hosa* whatsoever	4233.1 adj pl neu προσφιλῆ, *prosphilē* lovely,	3607.8 rel- pron pl neu ὅσα *hosa* whatsoever

2144.1 adj pl neu εὔφημα, *euphēma* of good report;	1479.1 conj εἴ *ei* if	4948.3 indef- pron nom sing τις *tis* any	697.1 noun nom sing fem ἀρετὴ *aretē* virtue	2504.1 conj καὶ *kai* and	1479.1 conj εἴ *ei* if	4948.3 indef- pron nom sing τις *tis* any

1853.1 noun nom sing masc ἔπαινος, *epainos* praise,	3642.18 dem- pron pl neu ταῦτα *tauta* these things	3023.1 verb 2pl pres mid λογίζεσθε· *logizesthe* consider.	3614.17 rel- pron pl neu **9.** ἃ *ha* What	2504.1 conj καὶ *kai* also	3101.9 verb 2pl indic aor act ἐμάθετε *emathete* you learned

2504.1 conj καὶ *kai* and	3741.7 verb 2pl indic aor act παρελάβετε *parelabete* received	2504.1 conj καὶ *kai* and	189.23 verb 2pl indic aor act ἠκούσατε *ēkousate* heard	2504.1 conj καὶ *kai* and	1481.6 verb 2pl indic aor act εἴδετε *eidete* saw	1706.1 prep ἐν *en* in

1466.5 prs- pron dat 1sing ἐμοί, *emoi* me,	3642.18 dem- pron pl neu ταῦτα *tauta* these things	4097.6 verb 2pl impr pres act πράσσετε· *prassete* do;	2504.1 conj καὶ *kai* and	3450.5 art nom sing masc ὁ *ho* the	2296.1 noun nom sing masc θεὸς *theos* God

3450.10 art gen sing fem τῆς *tēs* of the	1503.2 noun gen sing fem εἰρήνης *eirēnēs* peace	1498.40 verb 3sing indic fut mid ἔσται *estai* shall be	3196.1 prep μεθ᾽ *meth'* with	5050.2 prs- pron gen 2pl ὑμῶν. *humōn* you.	5299.15 verb 1sing indic aor pass **10.** Ἐχάρην *Echarēn* I rejoiced

1156.2 conj δὲ *de* but	1706.1 prep ἐν *en* in	2935.3 noun dat sing masc κυρίῳ *kuriō* Lord	3143.1 adv μεγάλως, *megalōs* greatly,	3617.1 conj ὅτι *hoti* that	2218.1 adv ἤδη *ēdē* now	4077.1 adv ποτὲ *pote* at length

328.1 verb 2pl indic aor act ἀνεθάλετε *anethalete* you revived	3450.16 art sing neu τὸ *to* the	5065.1 prep ὑπὲρ *huper* on behalf of	1466.3 prs- pron gen 1sing ἐμοῦ *emou* me	5262.9 verb inf pres act φρονεῖν· *phronein* to think;	1894.1 prep ἐφ᾽ *eph'* on

3614.3 rel- pron dat sing ᾧ *hō* which	2504.1 conj καὶ *kai* also	5262.12 verb 2pl indic imperf act ἐφρονεῖτε *ephroneite* you were thinking,	168.1 verb 2pl indic imperf mid ἠκαιρεῖσθε *ēkaireisthe* you were lacking opportunity

1156.2 conj δέ. *de* but.	3620.1 partic **11.** οὐχ *ouch* Not	3617.1 conj ὅτι *hoti* that	2567.2 prep καθ᾽ *kath'* as to	5141.2 noun acc sing fem ὑστέρησιν *husterēsin* lack	2978.1 verb 1sing pres act λέγω· *legō* I speak;	1466.1 prs- pron nom 1sing ἐγὼ *egō* I

1056.1 conj γὰρ *gar* for	3101.6 verb 1sing indic aor act ἔμαθον *emathon* learned	1706.1 prep ἐν *en* in	3614.4 rel- pron dat pl οἷς *hois* what	1498.2 verb 1sing indic pres act εἰμι, *eimi* I am,	836.1 adj nom sing masc αὐτάρκης *autarkēs* content

"True" (*alēthē*) refers to truth in the widest sense. Jesus called himself "the way, the truth, and the life" (John 14:6), and He designated God's Word as truth (John 17:17). "Honest" (*semna*) relates to things worthy of honor, or things worthy of reverence, as opposed to a flippancy that lacks seriousness. "Just" (*dikaia*) has to do with what is right according to God's standard which is spelled out in the Scriptures; we have no excuse for not knowing what is right. "Pure" (*hagna*) means "stainless" or "chaste" and relates to things that encourage purity. "Lovely" (*prosphilē*) refers to things that incite true love, rather than erotic behavior. "Good report" (*euphēma*) relates to things attractive in character.

The "if" here is an indicative mood "if" (*ei*) in the Greek language and often is called "a condition of the first class." It often is translated "since." In other words, these attributes, and many similar ones, do exist and should be considered virtuous and worthy of praise.

4:9. The last and perhaps most important condition for enjoying God's peace is to practice (*prassete*) what we have heard and seen. The emphasis shifts from right thinking to right doing. The former verse enumerated the proper subjects of meditation; this verse encourages the proper course of action which naturally should follow right thinking. If a person will take seriously the four conditions given by the apostle Paul and put them into practice, God will prove himself faithful to His promise.

4:10. In his application to the Philippian saints, Paul had one more topic to treat. He used the immediate occasion, which was his sincere expression of appreciation for their financial support, to teach them an extremely important lesson. The phrase "your care of me hath flourished again" may indicate a suspension of their financial support for a time due to the influence of false teachers.

4:11. Paul had learned the true secret of life, and he desired to share it with them. The verb "learned" here is an aorist verb and is a good example of what grammarians call a *resultative* or *culminative* aorist. "The culminative aorist views the act as having occurred but emphasizes the end of the action or the state of being resulting from the action" (Summers, p.67). At some particular point in his life, Paul made a commitment to serve the Lord faithfully no matter what circumstances he had to face. The results of that decision still were evident in his life when he wrote this short letter to the Philippians. We know from Acts chapter 9 that shortly after Paul's conversion, he faced persecution, and certain enemies of the gospel attempted to kill him. God protected him though, and some believers lowered the apostle to the ground in a basket (Acts 9:25). Perhaps it was then that he determined to serve God faithfully no matter what happened.

whatsoever things [are] pure: . . . holy, *Phillips.*

whatsoever things [are] lovely: . . . are amiable, *Wilson* . . . whatever benevolent, *Scarlett* . . . whatever lovable, *Confraternity.*

whatsoever things [are] of good report: . . . are reputable, *Sawyer* . . . or anything attractive, *TCNT.*

if [there be] any virtue, and if [there be] any praise:
think on these things: . . . the same be taking into account, *Rotherham* . . . attentively consider, *Wilson* . . . there let your thoughts dwell, *TCNT* . . . consider these things, *Sawyer.*

9. Those things, which ye have both learned, and received, and heard, and seen in me, do: . . . you should continually put into practice, *TCNT* . . . these things practice, *Wilson.*

and the God of peace shall be with you: . . . and you will find, *Phillips.*

10. But I rejoiced in the Lord greatly: I was exceedingly glad, *TCNT* . . . It has been a great joy to me, *Phillips.*

that now at the last your care of me hath flourished again: . . . now at length, *Douay* . . . has revived, *Confraternity* . . . ye have revived your thoughtfulness for me, *PNT* . . . your thought for me, *ASV* . . . in your care for my welfare, *Noyes.*

wherein ye were also careful, but ye lacked opportunity: I don't mean that you had forgotten me, *Phillips.*

11. Not that I speak in respect of want: . . . under the pressure of want, *TCNT.*

for I have learned, in whatsoever state I am, [therewith] to be content: . . . in whatever circumstances, *Sawyer* . . . in whatever condition, *Wilson* . . . learnt to be independent of circumstances, *TCNT* . . . to be self-sufficing, *Confraternity.*

227

Philippians 4:12

12.a.Txt: Steph
Var: 01א,02A,03B,06D
018K,020L,025P,byz.
Gries,Lach,Treg,Alf
Word,Tisc,We/Ho,Weis
Sod,UBS/*

1498.32 verb inf pres act	3471.2 verb 1sing indic pres act	1156.2 conj	2504.1	4864.5 verb inf pres mid
εἶναι. einai to be.	12. οἶδα oida I know	ʿ δὲ de and	[ᵃ☆ καὶ] kai [idem]	ταπεινοῦσθαι, tapeinousthai to be humbled,

3471.2 verb 1sing indic perf act	2504.1 conj	3915.12 verb inf pres act	1706.1 prep	3820.3 adj dat sing	2504.1 conj
οἶδα oida I know	καὶ kai and	περισσεύειν· perisseuein to abound.	ἐν en In	παντὶ panti everything	καὶ kai and

1706.1 prep	3820.5 adj dat pl	3315.1 verb 1sing indic perf mid	2504.1 conj	5361.3 verb inf pres mid
ἐν en in	πᾶσιν pasin all things	μεμύημαι memuēmai I have been initiated	καὶ kai both	χορτάζεσθαι chortazesthai to be full

2504.1 conj	3845.6 verb inf pres act	2504.1 conj	3915.12 verb inf pres act	2504.1 conj	5139.12 verb inf pres mid
καὶ kai and	πεινᾶν, peinan to hunger,	καὶ kai both	περισσεύειν perisseuein to abound	καὶ kai and	ὑστερεῖσθαι· hustereisthai to be deficient.

3820.1 adj	2453.1 verb 1sing indic pres act	1706.1 prep	3450.3 art dat sing	1727.1 verb dat sing masc part pres act
13. πάντα panta All things	ἰσχύω ischuō I am strong for	ἐν en in	τῷ tō the	ἐνδυναμοῦντί endunamounti empowering

13.a.Txt: 01א-corr
06D-corr,018K,020L
025P,byz.
Var: 01א-org,02A,03B
06D-org,33,bo.Gries
Lach,Treg,Alf,Word
Tisc,We/Ho,Weis,Sod
UBS/*

1466.6 prs- pron acc 1sing	5382.3 name dat masc	3993.1 prep	2544.1 adv	4020.26 verb 2pl indic aor act
με me me	ʿᵃ Χριστῷ. ʾ Christō Christ.	14. πλὴν plēn But	καλῶς kalōs well	ἐποιήσατε, epoiēsate you did,

4641.3 verb nom pl masc part aor act	1466.2 prs- pron gen 1sing	3450.11 art dat sing fem	2324.3 noun dat sing fem	3471.6 verb 2pl indic perf act
συγκοινωνήσαντές sunkoinōnēsantes having fellowship in	μου mou my	τῇ tē the	θλίψει. thlipsei tribulation.	15. Οἴδατε Oidate Know

1156.2 conj	2504.1 conj	5050.1 prs- pron nom 2pl	5211.1 name- adj nom pl masc	3617.1 conj	1706.1 prep	741.3 noun dat sing fem
δὲ de and	καὶ kai also	ὑμεῖς, humeis you,	Φιλιππήσιοι, Philippēsioi O Philippians,	ὅτι hoti that	ἐν en in	ἀρχῇ archē beginning

3450.2 art gen sing	2077.2 noun gen sing neu	3616.1 conj	1814.1 verb indic aor act	570.3 prep	3081.2 name gen fem
τοῦ tou of the	εὐαγγελίου, euangeliou good news,	ὅτε hote when	ἐξῆλθον exēlthon I came out	ἀπὸ apo from	Μακεδονίας, Makedonias Macedonia,

3625.4 num card nom fem	1466.4 prs- pron dat 1sing	1564.2 noun nom sing fem	2814.6 verb 3sing indic aor act	1519.1 prep
οὐδεμία oudemia not any	μοι moi with me	ἐκκλησία ekklēsia assembly	ἐκοινώνησεν ekoinōnēsen had fellowship	εἰς eis with regard to

3030.4 noun acc sing masc	1388.2 noun gen sing fem	2504.1 conj	3002.1 noun gen sing fem	3002.2 noun gen sing fem	1479.1 conj
λόγον logon an account	δόσεως doseōs of giving	καὶ kai and	ʿ λήψεως lēpseōs receiving,	[☆ λήμψεως] lēmpseōs [idem]	εἰ ei if

228

4:12. The idea expressed at the end of verse 11 and in verse 12 literally means "I have learned the secret" or "I have been initiated." It is the translation of a Greek word (*memuēmai*) used by the Stoic school of philosophy to mean a man should be self-sufficient for all things, or independent of external circumstances. The word also was used for the feeding of animals, so a fattened or satisfied animal was described this way.

Even though Paul used the very word Stoics used to boast about their self-sufficiency, his sufficiency was based upon his relationship to Christ. His sufficiency came not through the kind of mechanical self-discipline practiced by the Stoics, but because of his union with a personal God. In addition, verse 12 also clarifies the fact that his sufficiency was not based upon material possessions.

4:13. Paul's sufficiency did not come from circumstances, but from Christ. Since the Greek text here contains the title "Christ," He obviously was the One empowering Paul so that he could accomplish "all things," or whatever God wanted him to do.

4:14. One could get the impression from the writer's statements in verses 10-13 that he did not appreciate the Philippians' help as much as he should have. To counter this possible impression, verse 14 begins with the preposition *plēn* ("notwithstanding" [KJV]; "yet" [NIV]; "nevertheless" [NASB]). He truly did appreciate their faithful help from the early stages of his ministry in Macedonia (Acts chapters 16 and 17), about 10 years before the writing of this letter.

Even though his dependence rested in God, Paul was wise enough to know that God works through His people. In fact, in this verse he used a term related to the normal word for "partnership" (*koinōnia*). God used the Philippians to *share* in the problems the apostle faced at that time. Paul described these problems by using the Greek term *thlipsis* which normally means "tribulation." It was not an easy period of time for him, and he wanted them to know they had done well to share with him. In fact, their assembly seems to have been the only one that faithfully supported him over an extended period of time.

4:15. The terminology here, and again in verse 17, suggests the Philippians actually kept records and had an account of their giving to Paul. "Giving and receiving" comes from a general expression used in that day of "debits and credits" and can be found in many references to business transactions of that period. They had shared with him in his affliction or troubles. The example of the Philippian church should serve as an incentive for contemporary assemblies to share in the ministries of ministers like the apostle Paul. He normally did not settle down in one place, so was dependent upon the Holy Spirit speaking to people in local churches to help support him, a practice that is still followed.

12. I know both how to be abased: I am initiated both to be, *PNT* . . . how to be brought low, *Rotherham* . . . how to live humbly, *Confraternity* . . . how to be in low estate, *Alford* . . . when things are difficult, *Phillips*.

and I know how to abound: . . . how to have more than enough, *Rotherham* . . . when things are prosperous, *Phillips*.

every where and in all things I am instructed both to be full and to be hungry: I have been schooled, *Confraternity* . . . I have been well taught, *Noyes* . . . have I learned the secret both, *Clementson*.

both to abound and to suffer need: I have learned the secret of facing either poverty or plenty, *Phillips* . . . into prosperity and want, *TCNT* . . . and to be in want, *Panin* . . . and to be destitute, *Wilson*.

13. I can do all things through Christ which strengtheneth me: I endure all things with him that strengthens me, *Sawyer* . . . I have strength for all things in him, *Alford* . . . I have strength for all circumstances, *PNT* . . . of him who makes me strong! *TCNT* . . . in him who empowers me, *Rotherham*.

14. Notwithstanding ye have well done: . . . ye did well, *Noyes*.

that ye did communicate with my affliction: . . . ye had fellowship with my tribulation, *Clementson* . . . in sharing with me, *Noyes* . . . in sympathizing with, *Wilson* . . . my tribulation, *Douay*.

15. Now ye Philippians know also, that in the beginning of the gospel: . . . that in the early days of the Good News, *TCNT*.

when I departed from Macedonia:

no church communicated with me as concerning giving and receiving, but ye only: . . . you were the only Church who shared with me the fellowship of, *Phillips*.

Philippians 4:16

3231.1 partic	5050.1 prs-pron nom 2pl	3304.5 adj nom pl masc		3617.1 conj	2504.1 conj	1706.1 prep	2309.2 name dat fem
μὴ	ὑμεῖς	μόνοι·	**16.**	ὅτι	καὶ	ἐν	Θεσσαλονίκῃ
mē	humeis	monoi		hoti	kai	en	Thessalonikē
not	you	alone;		because	also	in	Thessalonica

2504.1 conj	526.1 adv	2504.1 conj	1361.1 adv	1519.1 prep	3450.12 art acc sing fem	5367.3 noun acc sing fem	1466.4 prs-pron dat 1sing
καὶ	ἅπαξ	καὶ	δὶς	εἰς	τὴν	χρείαν	μοι
kai	hapax	kai	dis	eis	tēn	chreian	moi
both	once	and	twice	for	the	need	my

3854.8 verb 2pl indic aor act		3620.1 partic	3617.1 conj	1919.1 verb 1sing indic pres act	3450.16 art sing neu	1384.1 noun sing neu
ἐπέμψατε.	**17.**	οὐχ	ὅτι	ἐπιζητῶ	τὸ	δόμα,
epempsate		ouch	hoti	epizētō	to	doma
you sent.		Not	that	I seek after	to	gift,

233.1 conj	233.2 conj	1919.1 verb 1sing indic pres act	3450.6 art acc sing masc	2561.3 noun acc sing masc	3450.6 art acc sing masc
' ἀλλ'	[✶ ἀλλὰ]	ἐπιζητῶ	τὸν	καρπὸν	τὸν
all'	alla	epizētō	ton	karpon	ton
but	[idem]	I seek after	the	fruit	the

3981.2 verb part pres act	1519.1 prep	3030.4 noun acc sing masc	5050.2 prs-pron gen 2pl		563.1 verb 1sing indic pres act	1156.2 conj
πλεονάζοντα	εἰς	λόγον	ὑμῶν·	**18.**	ἀπέχω	δὲ
pleonazonta	eis	logon	humōn		apechō	de
abounding	to	account	your.		I have	but

3820.1 adj	2504.1 conj	3915.1 verb 1sing indic pres act	3997.28 verb 1sing indic perf mid	1203.13 verb nom sing masc part aor mid
πάντα	καὶ	περισσεύω·	πεπλήρωμαι,	δεξάμενος
panta	kai	perisseuō	peplērōmai	dexamenos
all things	and	abound;	I am full,	having received

3706.2 prep	1876.1 name gen masc	3450.17 art pl neu	3706.1 prep	5050.2 prs-pron gen 2pl	3606.3 noun acc sing fem
παρὰ	Ἐπαφροδίτου	τὰ	παρ'	ὑμῶν,	ὀσμὴν
para	Epaphroditou	ta	par'	humōn	osmēn
from	Epaphroditus	the things	from	you,	an odor

2156.2 noun gen sing fem	2355.4 noun acc sing fem	1178.4 adj acc sing fem	2080.4 adj sing	3450.3 art dat sing
εὐωδίας,	θυσίαν	δεκτήν,	εὐάρεστον	τῷ
euōdias	thusian	dektēn	euareston	tō
of a sweet smell,	a sacrifice	acceptable,	well pleasing	to

2296.3 noun dat sing masc	3450.5 art nom sing masc	1156.2 conj	2296.1 noun nom sing masc	1466.2 prs-pron gen 1sing	3997.14 verb 3sing indic fut act
θεῷ.	**19.** ὁ	δὲ	θεός	μου	πληρώσει
theō	ho	de	theos	mou	plērōsei
to God.		But	God	my	will fill up

3820.12 adj acc sing fem	5367.3 noun acc sing fem	5050.2 prs-pron gen 2pl	2567.3 prep	3450.6 art acc sing masc	4009.3 noun acc sing masc
πᾶσαν	χρείαν	ὑμῶν	κατὰ	' τὸν	πλοῦτον
pasan	chreian	humōn	kata	ton	plouton
all	need	your	according to	the	riches

19.a.Txt: 06D-corr,018K 020L,byz.
Var: 01ℵ-org,02A,03B 06D-org,025P,33,Lach Treg,Alf,Word,Tisc We/Ho,Weis,Sod UBS/✶

3450.16 art sing neu	4009.1 noun sing masc	840.3 prs-pron gen sing	1706.1 prep	1385.3 noun dat sing fem	1706.1 prep
[ᵃ✶ τὸ	πλοῦτος]	αὐτοῦ	ἐν	δόξῃ	ἐν
to	ploutos	autou	en	doxē	en
[the	riches]	his	in	glory	in

4:16. Generally, local churches that are truly evangelistic will also be strong missionary churches. Philippi must have been that kind of church. Even while Paul ministered in Thessalonica (Acts 17:1-9), the Philippian believers allowed their ministry to advance beyond their own geographic borders and assisted the apostle in his activities among the Thessalonians. During that period of ministry in Thessalonica Paul faced very trying circumstances. No doubt being able to depend upon the Lord using the Philippians to help him must have meant a lot to him.

4:17. Paul was quick to add in this verse, however, that he was not writing in this way because he was asking for another offering. In these statements Christians see the attitude they should have with respect to financial help from other people. On the one hand, they must be grateful. On the other hand, they must always remember, as well as remind other people, that God is the One who meets their needs. The apostle considered their offerings to him as really "unto the Lord." Verse 17 indicates that the fruit which resulted from their joint participation with him would be added to their account. By investing in Paul's ministry they could expect to receive rich dividends from God.

4:18. At the same time that the Philippians benefited spiritually from their acts of kindness to Paul, he was reaping the benefit as well. Paul considered the gift they sent via Epaphroditus as enough to make him "abound," and he assured them he was "full." Because these people certainly were not obligated to give to assist Paul, he looked at their gifts as if they had been given to God. The Philippians understood the kind of language Paul used here, because they often viewed public sacrifices of animals. Paul assured them their sacrifice was accepted by God in the same manner a fragrant aroma would be accepted by a human.

4:19. The apostle went on to assure the Philippians that the same God who met all his needs also would meet all their needs. Many times people quote this verse by changing the "your" to "our" or "my." Paul wanted his friends in Philippi to enjoy God's divine supply just as he was. In a sense, God's treatment of the Philippians would correspond to their treatment of Paul. Paul wrote "my God" probably because he had tested and tried Him as his own provider. Some people interpret the King James' language here to mean riches in a specific place (heaven), but the statement refers to the glorious bounty of God's riches. God would recompense the Philippians because His resources are limitless. He does everything "in glory" (*en doxē*) or "in a glorious way" because of His limitless resources, and He manifests them "by Christ Jesus."

16. For even in Thessalonica ye sent once and again unto my necessity: ... you twice sent me help, *Phillips* ... you sent money, *Williams* ... you sent more than once to relieve my wants, *TCNT* ... for my need, *Wilson.*

17. Not because I desire a gift: It is really not the gifts that I crave, *Norlie* ... It isn't the value of the gift that I am keen on, *Phillips.*

but I desire fruit that may abound to your account: ... but I do want the profits to pile up to your credit, *Williams* ... the profit accumulating to your account, *Confraternity* ... the abundant profit that accrues, *Montgomery* ... that increaseth, *Panin* ... I wish fruits may multiply unto you, *Murdock.*

18. But I have all, and abound: I have received your payment in full, and more too, *Williams* ... and to spare, *TCNT* ... in fact I am rich, *Phillips.*

I am full: I am amply supplied, *Williams* ... quite content, *Phillips.*

having received of Epaphroditus the things [which were sent] from you: ... thanks to your gifts, *Phillips* ... the gifts which you sent me, *TCNT.*

an odour of a sweet smell, a sacrifice acceptable, wellpleasing to God: ... they are like sweet incense, *Williams* ... a Fragrant Odor, *Wilson* ... lovely fragrance, *Phillips.*

19. But my God shall supply all your need: ... will fully supply, *Wilson* ... will liberally supply, *Worrell* ... will fill up your every need, *Rotherham* ... will amply supply your every need, *Williams* ... all your necessity, *Murdock.*

according to his riches in glory by Christ Jesus: ... according to his Glorious wealth, *Wilson* ... so great is his wealth, *TCNT* ... from his glorious resources, *Phillips.*

5382.3 name dat masc	2400.2 name masc	3450.3 art dat sing	1156.2 conj	2296.3 noun dat sing masc	2504.1 conj	3824.3 noun dat sing masc
Χριστῷ	Ἰησοῦ.	20. τῷ	δὲ	θεῷ	καὶ	πατρὶ
Christō	Iēsou.	tō	de	theō	kai	patri
Christ	Jesus.	To the	but	God	and	Father

2231.2 prs-pron gen 1pl	3450.9 art nom sing fem	1385.1 noun nom sing fem	1519.1 prep	3450.8 art acc pl masc	163.6 noun acc pl masc	3450.1 art gen pl
ἡμῶν	ἡ	δόξα	εἰς	τοὺς	αἰῶνας	τῶν
hēmōn	hē	doxa	eis	tous	aiōnas	tōn
our	the	glory	to	the	ages	of the

163.4 noun gen pl masc	279.1 intrj	776.9 verb 2pl impr aor mid	3820.1 adj	39.1 adj sing	1706.1 prep
αἰώνων·	ἀμήν.	21. Ἀσπάσασθε	πάντα	ἅγιον	ἐν
aiōnōn	amēn.	Aspasasthe	panta	hagion	en
ages.	Amen.	Greet	every	saint	in

5382.3 name dat masc	2400.2 name masc	776.3 verb 3pl indic pres mid	5050.4 prs-pron acc 2pl	3450.7 art nom pl masc	4713.1 prep
Χριστῷ	Ἰησοῦ.	ἀσπάζονται	ὑμᾶς	οἱ	σὺν
Christō	Iēsou.	aspazontai	humas	hoi	sun
Christ	Jesus.	Greet	you	the	with

1466.5 prs-pron dat 1sing	79.6 noun nom pl masc	776.3 verb 3pl indic pres mid	5050.4 prs-pron acc 2pl	3820.7 adj nom pl masc	3450.7 art nom pl masc
ἐμοὶ	ἀδελφοί.	22. ἀσπάζονται	ὑμᾶς	πάντες	οἱ
emoi	adelphoi.	aspazontai	humas	pantes	hoi
me	brothers.	Greet	you	all	the

39.7 adj nom pl masc	3094.1 adv sup	1156.2 conj	3450.7 art nom pl masc	1523.2 prep gen	3450.10 art gen sing fem	2512.1 name gen masc
ἅγιοι,	μάλιστα	δὲ	οἱ	ἐκ	τῆς	Καίσαρος
hagioi	malista	de	hoi	ek	tēs	Kaisaros
saints,	especially	and	the	of	the	of Caesar

3477.1 noun fem	3450.9 art nom sing fem	5322.1 noun nom sing fem	3450.2 art gen sing	2935.2 noun gen sing masc	2231.2 prs-pron gen 1pl
οἰκίας.	23. Ἡ	χάρις	τοῦ	κυρίου	⌐a ἡμῶν ⌐
oikias	Hē	charis	tou	kuriou	hēmōn
household.	The	grace	of the	Lord	our

2400.2 name masc	5382.2 name gen masc	3196.3 prep	3820.4 adj gen pl	5050.2 prs-pron gen 2pl	3450.2 art gen sing
Ἰησοῦ	Χριστοῦ	μετὰ	⌐ πάντων	ὑμῶν.	[b ✶ τοῦ
Iēsou	Christou	meta	pantōn	humōn.	tou
Jesus	Christ	with	all	you.	[the

4011.2 noun gen sing neu	5050.2 prs-pron gen 2pl	279.1 intrj	4242.1 prep	5211.2 name-adj acc pl masc
πνεύματος	ὑμῶν.]	⌐c ἀμήν. ⌐	⌐d Πρὸς	Φιλιππησίους
pneumatos	humōn.	amēn.	Pros	Philippēsious
spirit	your]	Amen.	To	Philippians

1119.21 verb 3sing indic aor pass	570.3 prep	4373.1 name gen fem	1217.1 prep	1876.1 name gen masc
ἐγράφη	ἀπὸ	Ῥώμης,	δι'	Ἐπαφροδίτου. ⌐
egraphē	apo	Rhōmēs,	di'	Epaphroditou.
written	from	Rome,	by	Epaphroditus.

23.a.Txt: 06D,025P,bo. Steph
Var: 01א,02A,03B 018K,020L,byz.Lach Treg,Alf,Word,Tisc We/Ho,Weis,Sod UBS/✫

23.b.Txt: 01א-corr,018K 020L,044,byz.
Var: p46,01א-org,02A 03B,06D,025P,33,sa.bo. Lach,Treg,Alf,Word Tisc,We/Ho,Weis,Sod UBS/✫

23.c.Txt: p46,01א,02A 06D,018K,020L,025P byz.bo.Sod
Var: 03B,sa.Treg,Tisc We/Ho,Weis,UBS/✫

23.d.Txt: 018K,Steph
Var: Gries,Lach,Word Tisc,We/Ho,Weis,Sod UBS/✫

4:20. In the light of the insights Paul shared above and the wonderful promise specified in the previous verse, one can understand Paul's sudden outburst in verse 20. Contemplating all this, he broke forth in a beautiful doxology.

4:21. The New Testament term *saints* relates to all Christians. In this verse the term literally reads "every saint" (*panta hagion*). The Greek word for the term normally is an adjective and indicates a quality of a person. It relates to being "holy" or "sanctified" and basically describes a person set apart for God's service. The word also can be used of objects dedicated to the service of the Lord, much like the furnishings of the Old Testament tabernacle or temple. Several "brethren" were with Paul at the time he wrote this epistle, and the apostle used the words *saints* and *brothers* interchangeably.

4:22. In this verse Paul switched his terminology to "all the saints" (*pantes hoi hagioi*). He must have been referring to all the believers in Rome, many of whom he had met during his 2-year imprisonment.

Paul's brief note about the saints within the household of Caesar in itself speaks volumes to the world. Nero, one of the most infamous of the Caesars, was ruling at that time. It is very doubtful that Nero had heard very much about Paul at the time Paul wrote these words. While we cannot be sure exactly what happened, Paul's case may have been dismissed because of the expiration of the statute of limitations. Apparently, if a case was not settled within 2 years, it was dismissed. Ironically, Paul who may have been obscure to Nero has won far more fame down though the centuries than all the Caesars combined.

4:23. After exchanging greetings, Paul spelled out the reason it is possible for a person to cope with life and still possess the joy of the Lord. One word in the apostle's last statement serves as the answer—"grace." Invariably, Paul seemed to feel compelled to summarize his writings with some reference to God's grace. Perhaps the personal miracle God performed for him was the main reason for that practice. If anyone deserved the judgment of God, he knew he did, but instead God had manifested His grace to him.

20. Now unto God and our Father [be] glory for ever and ever. Amen: Give glory to our God, *SEB* . . . be the honour for ever and ever, *Fenton, HistNT* . . . be prayse for euer more, *Geneva* . . . be glorie vvorld vvithout end, *Rheims* . . . the ages of the ages, *Panin, Wilson, Weymouth.*

21. Salute every saint in Christ Jesus: Remember me to, *Williams* . . . Greet, *Adams* . . . Give my greetings, in the fellowship of Christ Jesus, *NEB* . . . Greetings to every true Christian, *Phillips* . . . Greet each believer who is in union with Messiah Jesus, *Way* . . . My Christian greetings to every one of God's people, *Weymouth* . . . everyone who is holy, *Beck* . . . euery holi man, *Wyclif* . . . to all our fellow-Christians, *TCNT* . . . to every one of God's dedicated people, *Barclay.*

The brethren which are with me greet you: The brothers beside me salute you, *Moffatt* . . . send you their good wishes, *TCNT* . . . send their greetings, *Weymouth* . . . wish to be remembered to you, *Williams* . . . would like to send their best wishes, *Phillips.*

22. All the saints salute you: All the holy, *Fenton* . . . All God's people, *Weymouth* . . . people here greet you, *SEB* . . . wish to be remembered to you, *Norlie, Williams.*

chiefly they that are of Caesar's household: . . . but especially, *Rotherham* . . . especially the Imperial slaves, *Moffatt* . . . those who belong to, *HistNT* . . . the members of the Emperor's household, *Williams* . . . those who belong to the imperial establishment, *NEB* . . . of Caesar's court, *Berkeley* . . . of Caesar's family, *Sawyer.*

23. The grace of our Lord Jesus Christ [be] with you all. Amen: The spiritual blessing of, *Williams* . . . May the gracious love of, *SEB* . . . be with your spirit, *Clementson, Adams, HistNT.*

THE EPISTLE OF PAUL TO THE
COLOSSIANS

Expanded Interlinear
Textual Critical Apparatus
Verse-by-Verse Commentary
Various Versions

4242.1 prep	2825.3 name dat fem	1976.1 noun nom sing fem	3834.2 name gen masc
Πρὸς	Κολασσαεῖς	ἐπιστολὴ	Παύλου
Pros	Kolassaeis	epistolē	Paulou
To	Colossians	letter	of Paul

Textual Apparatus

3834.1 name nom masc	646.1 noun nom sing masc	2400.2 name masc	5382.2 name gen masc	5382.2 name gen masc
1:1. Παῦλος	ἀπόστολος	ʻ Ἰησοῦ	Χριστοῦ	[✶ Χριστοῦ
Paulos	apostolos	Iēsou	Christou	Christou
Paul	apostle	of Jesus	Christ	[of Christ

2400.2 name masc	1217.2 prep	2284.2 noun gen sing neu	2296.2 noun gen sing masc	2504.1 conj	4943.1 name nom masc	3450.5 art nom sing masc
Ἰησοῦ]	διὰ	θελήματος	θεοῦ,	καὶ	Τιμόθεος	ὁ
Iēsou	dia	thelēmatos	theou	kai	Timotheos	ho
Jesus]	by	will	God's,	and	Timothy	the

2.a.**Txt:** 018K,025P,33
Steph
Var: 01א,03B,06D-corr
020L,Elzev,Tisc,We/Ho
Weis,Sod,UBS/✶

79.1 noun nom sing masc	3450.4 art dat pl	1706.1 prep	2825.1 name dat fem	2825.2 name dat fem
ἀδελφός	**2.** τοῖς	ἐν	ʻ Κολασσαῖς	[ᵃ✶ Κολοσσαῖς]
adelphos	tois	en	Kolassais	Kolossais
brother,	to the	in	Colosse	[idem]

39.8 adj dat pl masc	2504.1 conj	3964.8 adj dat pl masc	79.8 noun dat pl masc	1706.1 prep	5382.3 name dat sing	5322.1 noun nom sing fem
ἁγίοις	καὶ	πιστοῖς	ἀδελφοῖς	ἐν	Χριστῷ·	χάρις
hagiois	kai	pistois	adelphois	en	Christō	charis
saints	and	faithful	brothers	in	Christ.	Grace

5050.3 prs-pron dat 2pl	2504.1 conj	1503.1 noun nom sing fem	570.3 prep	2296.2 noun gen sing masc	3824.2 noun gen sing masc	2231.2 prs-pron gen 1pl
ὑμῖν	καὶ	εἰρήνη	ἀπὸ	θεοῦ	πατρὸς	ἡμῶν
humin	kai	eirēnē	apo	theou	patros	hēmōn
to you	and	peace	from	God	Father	our

2.b.**Txt:** 01א,02A,04C
byz.bo.
Var: 03B,06D,018K
020L,33,it.sa.Gries
Treg,Alf,Word,Tisc
We/Ho,Weis,Sod
UBS/✶

2504.1 conj	2935.2 noun gen sing masc	2400.2 name masc	5382.2 name gen masc	2149.4 verb 1pl indic pres act
ʻᵇ καὶ	κυρίου	Ἰησοῦ	Χριστοῦ. ʼ	**3.** Εὐχαριστοῦμεν
kai	kuriou	Iēsou	Christou	Eucharistoumen
and	Lord	Jesus	Christ.	We give thanks

3.a.**Txt:** 01א,02A
04C-corr,06D-corr,018K
020L,025P,33,byz.Tisc
Sod
Var: 03B,04C-org,17,39
Lach,Alf,We/Ho,Weis
UBS/✶

3450.3 art dat sing	2296.3 noun dat sing masc	2504.1 conj	3824.3 noun dat sing masc	3450.2 art gen sing	2935.2 noun gen sing masc
τῷ	θεῷ	ʻᵃ καὶ ʼ	πατρὶ	τοῦ	κυρίου
tō	theō	kai	patri	tou	kuriou
to the	God	and	Father	of the	Lord

2231.2 prs-pron gen 1pl	2400.2 name masc	5382.2 name gen masc	3704.1 adv	3875.1 prep	5050.2 prs-pron gen 2pl
ἡμῶν	Ἰησοῦ	Χριστοῦ,	πάντοτε	περὶ	ὑμῶν
hēmōn	Iēsou	Christou	pantote	peri	humōn
our	Jesus	Christ,	continually	for	you

4195.13 verb nom pl masc part pres mid	189.32 verb nom pl masc part aor act	3450.12 art acc sing fem	3963.4 noun acc sing fem	5050.2 prs-pron gen 2pl
προσευχόμενοι·	**4.** ἀκούσαντες	τὴν	πίστιν	ὑμῶν
proseuchomenoi	akousantes	tēn	pistin	humōn
praying,	having heard	the	faith	your

THE EPISTLE OF PAUL TO THE
COLOSSIANS

1:1. Colossians begins with the typical salutation of the day: the name of the writer or writers, the name of the recipient or recipients of the letter, and a few words of greeting. In the opening statement, Paul probably had at least two reasons for designating himself an apostle. Unlike the Philippians, the Colossians did not know him personally. Furthermore, he was writing to refute the serious unscriptural gnosticism that had crept into the assembly. As an apostle he was an official representative of the Saviour himself and was clothed with His authority.

At the very outset of this epistle Paul linked his office and call to the will of God. He had certainly not chosen this position for himself. Note also the manner in which he connected himself with Christ Jesus. He literally belonged to Christ as His representative.

The use of the term "Jesus Christ" at the very outset may have been a deliberate attempt to emphasize the exalted position of Jesus. The Gnostics constantly endeavored to denigrate the deity of Christ by seeking to rob Him of His full majesty. It is interesting to note that Paul did not use the name of Jesus by itself in the entire epistle. He would have nothing to do with the mentality that relegated Jesus to anything less than true God and true man. Although Paul mentioned Timothy as being with him, it is not certain that Timothy served as secretary on this occasion.

1:2. "To the saints" refers to the status of the recipients of this letter, rather than to a degree of holiness attained. The second half of the title could be translated either "faithful brothers" or "believing brothers," although the first makes more sense because the second would be redundant. The most important fact expressed is that they were "in Christ," or "lived in the realm of Christ," as people related to Him through the new birth. As he normally did, Paul combined the Greek greeting "grace" and the Hebrew greeting "peace."

1:3. Also, according to his normal custom, the apostle followed his greeting with a sincere thanksgiving to God for the believers to whom he was writing. He and his associates thanked God for the Colossians relative to four matters. This verse gives a good pattern for people to follow when they pray. It should be preceded by thanksgiving.

Various Versions

1. Paul, an apostle of Jesus Christ by the will of God: Paul—appointed through God's will, *Way* . . . messenger of, *Phillips* . . . by the pleasure of, *Murdock* . . . through the will of, *Weymouth* . . . God wanted me to be an apostle of Christ, *SEB*.

and Timotheus [our] brother: . . . brother Timothy, *Phillips*.

2. To the saints and faithful brethren in Christ which are at Colosse: To Christ's People, *TCNT* . . . to all faithful Christians, *Phillips* . . . To the people of God, *Weymouth* . . . to God's consecrated ones in . . . to the brothers who are still true to their union with Messiah, *Way* . . . to the consecrated . . . who are in union with, *Williams* . . . holi and feithful britheren, *Wyclif* . . . to the holy and faithful fellow believers, *Beck* . . . to the holy and believing brothers, *Montgomery* . . . believing brethren, *Concordant*.

Grace [be] unto you, and peace, from God our Father and the Lord Jesus Christ: Favor and Peace, *Wilson* . . . Blessing, *Fenton* . . . May gracious love and peace come to you from, *SEB* . . . be granted to you from, *Weymouth*.

3. We give thanks to God and the Father of our Lord Jesus Christ: I want you to know by this letter, *Phillips* . . . We constantly give thanks, *Berkeley* . . . I am continually thanking God, *Montgomery*.

praying always for you: Every time we pray, *Williams* . . . We are always praying, *SEB* . . . when we pray for you, *Adams, Moffatt* . . . constantly praying for you, *Weymouth, Phillips* . . . at all times in your behalf praying, *Rotherham*.

Colossians 1:5

1706.1 prep	5382.3 name dat masc	2400.2 name masc	2504.1 conj	3450.12 art acc sing fem	26.4 noun acc sing fem	3450.12 art acc sing fem
ἐν	Χριστῷ	Ἰησοῦ,	καὶ	τὴν	ἀγάπην	⌐ τὴν
en	Christō	Iēsou	kai	tēn	agapēn	tēn
in	Christ	Jesus,	and	the	love	the

4.a.Txt: 06D-corr,018K
020L,byz.Weis
Var: 01‭א‬,02A,04C
06D-org,025P,bo.Lach
Treg,Alf,Word,Tisc
We/Ho,Sod,UBS/✱

3614.12 rel-pron acc sing fem	2174.2 verb 2pl pres act	1519.1 prep	3820.8 adj acc pl masc	3450.8 art acc pl masc	39.9 adj acc pl masc
[a✶ ἣν	ἔχετε]	εἰς	πάντας	τοὺς	ἁγίους,
hēn	echete	eis	pantas	tous	hagious
[which	you have]	toward	all	the	saints,

1217.2 prep	3450.12 art acc sing fem	1667.4 noun acc sing fem	3450.12 art acc sing fem	601.2 verb acc sing fem part pres mid
5. διὰ	τὴν	ἐλπίδα	τὴν	ἀποκειμένην
dia	tēn	elpida	tēn	apokeimenēn
on account of	the	hope	the	laying up

5050.3 prs-pron dat 2pl	1706.1 prep	3450.4 art dat pl	3636.8 noun dat pl masc	3614.12 rel-pron acc sing fem	4116.1 verb 2pl indic aor act
ὑμῖν	ἐν	τοῖς	οὐρανοῖς,	ἣν	προηκούσατε
humin	en	tois	ouranois	hēn	proēkousate
for you	in	the	heavens;	which	you heard of before

1706.1 prep	3450.3 art dat sing	3030.3 noun dat sing masc	3450.10 art gen sing fem	223.2 noun gen sing fem	3450.2 art gen sing
ἐν	τῷ	λόγῳ	τῆς	ἀληθείας	τοῦ
en	tō	logō	tēs	alētheias	tou
in	the	word	of the	truth	of the

2077.2 noun gen sing neu	3450.2 art gen sing	3780.9 verb gen sing neu part pres act	1519.1 prep	5050.4 prs-pron acc 2pl	2503.1 conj
εὐαγγελίου,	6. τοῦ	παρόντος	εἰς	ὑμᾶς,	καθὼς
euangeliou	tou	parontos	eis	humas	kathōs
good news,	the	coming	to	you,	even as

6.a.Txt: 06D-corr,018K
020L,byz.
Var: p46,01‭א‬,02A,03B
04C,06D-org,025P,33,sa.
bo.Lach,Treg,Alf,Word
Tisc,We/Ho,Weis,Sod
UBS/✱

2504.1 conj	1706.1 prep	3820.3 adj dat sing	3450.3 art dat sing	2862.3 noun dat sing masc	2504.1 conj	1498.4 verb 3sing indic pres act
καὶ	ἐν	παντὶ	τῷ	κόσμῳ,	⌐a καὶ ⌐	ἐστὶν
kai	en	panti	tō	kosmō	kai	estin
also	in	all	the	world,	and	are

6.b.Var: 01‭א‬,02A,03B
04C,06D-org,020L,025P
bo.Gries,Lach,Treg,Alf
Word,Tisc,We/Ho,Weis
Sod,UBS/✱

2563.6 verb sing neu part pres mid	2504.1 conj	831.17 verb sing neu part pres mid	2503.1 conj
καρποφορούμενον,	[b✶+ καὶ	αὐξανόμενον]	καθὼς
karpophoroumenon	kai	auxanomenon	kathōs
bringing forth fruit,	[and	growing]	even as

2504.1 conj	1706.1 prep	5050.3 prs-pron dat 2pl	570.1 prep	3614.10 rel-pron gen sing fem	2232.1 noun fem	189.23 verb 2pl indic aor act
καὶ	ἐν	ὑμῖν,	ἀφ᾽	ἧς	ἡμέρας	ἠκούσατε
kai	en	humin	aph'	hēs	hēmeras	ēkousate
also	among	you,	from	which	day	you heard

2504.1 conj	1906.5 verb 2pl indic aor act	3450.12 art acc sing fem	5322.4 noun acc sing fem	3450.2 art gen sing	2296.2 noun gen sing masc	1706.1 prep
καὶ	ἐπέγνωτε	τὴν	χάριν	τοῦ	θεοῦ	ἐν
kai	epegnōte	tēn	charin	tou	theou	en
and	knew	the	grace	of God	in

7.a.Txt: 06D-corr,018K
020L,byz.
Var: 01‭א‬,02A,03B,04C
06D-org,025P,33,bo.
Lach,Treg,Alf,Word
Tisc,We/Ho,Weis,Sod
UBS/✱

223.3 noun dat sing fem	2503.1 conj	2504.1 conj	3101.9 verb 2pl indic aor act	570.3 prep	1874.2 name gen masc
ἀληθείᾳ·	7. καθὼς	⌐a καὶ ⌐	ἐμάθετε	ἀπὸ	Ἐπαφρᾶ
alētheia	kathōs	kai	emathete	apo	Epaphra
truth:	even as	also	you learned	from	Epaphras

1:4. This verse introduces the specific items for which Paul thanked God when he thought of the Colossian Christians. First, he was grateful to God because they had placed their faith in Christ Jesus. Although there are many things for which Christians should thank God, none is more important than the one Paul listed first: faith in the Lord Jesus Christ. If a person does not have that, nothing else really counts for much. The apostle knew the Colossians had taken the first step, the step that definitely is the all-important one.

It is the Holy Spirit that makes faith in Christ possible. A person does not just decide to place his faith in the Lord. The Holy Spirit must first give the impetus. Even Jesus made it clear that a person cannot come to Him without this divine initiative (John 6:44). The whole process of salvation happens as a result of God's grace (Ephesians 2:8).

Secondly, the apostle and his associates thanked God always for the love the Colossians extended to all the saints. Their faith did not consist merely of verbal profession. They translated their confession of Jesus Christ into action, and this action was prompted by the love (*agapē*) that God alone is able to infuse into a person.

1:5. Thirdly, this faith and love results from hope which is based upon the gospel message received. "Hope" can either be subjective or objective, depending upon the context. As the word is used here, it is obviously objective. In other words, the salvation the Colossians already enjoyed also had a future aspect when God would consummate His promises to them. In a sense, they had received a down payment of God's blessings, but the remainder would be given in heaven.

Notice the manner in which Paul connected this hope with the gospel. From the very beginning (Genesis 3:15), people have cherished the hope that one day the Messiah would come to earth and remedy the sinful condition of mankind. Truly the simple gospel message that Jesus died, was buried, and rose again according to the Scriptures constitutes the greatest impetus to hope that mankind has ever known.

1:6. Fourthly, the Colossians were producing fruit because they were permitting the gospel to work in them. Notice the beautiful progression in the four items for which the apostle and his associates always thanked God when they remembered the Colossians. Faith, love, and hope naturally should lead to fruit. Just as surely as a seed planted in soil will produce fruit if it is given the proper care, so the gospel will produce fruit where people allow it to do so. Paul made it clear in this verse that God's grace or unmerited favor is manifested to people as they accept the gospel and allow it to grow in their lives. Because all the benefits God bestows upon people come to them by grace through faith, continuous belief in the truth of the gospel is absolutely essential to the total process.

4. Since we heard of your faith in Christ Jesus: . . . whenever we do we thank God...because you believe, *Phillips*.

and of the love [which ye have] to all the saints: . . . and of your love for all God's people, *Williams* . . . you are showing true Christian love toward other Christians, *Phillips* . . . for all the fellow-Christians, *Norlie* . . . for all of the holy people, *SEB*.

5. For the hope which is laid up for you in heaven: We know that you are showing these qualities because you have grasped the hope, *Phillips* . . . because of your hope of what is, *Williams* . . . being preserved for you, *Wilson* . . . that is hidden away, *SEB* . . . which awaits fulfilment in Heaven, *TCNT*.

whereof ye heard before in the word of the truth of the gospel: Long ago you heard of this hope through the message of, *Williams* . . . that hope which first became yours when the truth was brought to you, *Phillips* . . . of which you previously heard in the plea for the truth of, *Fenton* . . . the truth of the joyful message, *Rotherham* . . . in the Word of truth concerning the good news, *Adams*.

6. Which is come unto you, as [it is] in all the world; and bringeth forth fruit, as [it doth] also in you: . . . which is present among you, *Scarlett* . . . which reached you, and since it is bearing fruit and is growing among you, just as it is all over the world, *Williams* . . . as also in the whole world it is bearing fruit and growing in the same way, *Adams* . . . it produces Christian character, *Phillips* . . . It is producing fruit and increasing its influence, *SEB*.

since the day ye heard [of it], and knew the grace of God in truth: . . . from the day you first heard of God's favor and...came to know it, *Williams* . . . from the day you heard and truly recognised the Divine gift, *Fenton* . . . from the time you first heard and realized the amazing fact of God's grace, *Phillips* . . . and acknowledged the favor, *Wilson* . . . and truly knew, *Adams* . . . and understood what that mercy really is, *TCNT*.

Colossians 1:8

3450.2 art gen sing	27.4 adj gen sing	4739.2 noun gen sing masc	2231.2 prs- pron gen 1pl	3614.5 rel-pron nom sing masc	1498.4 verb 3sing indic pres act
τοῦ	ἀγαπητοῦ	συνδούλου	ἡμῶν,	ὅς	ἐστιν
tou	*agapētou*	*sundoulou*	*hēmōn*	*hos*	*estin*
the	beloved	fellow slave	our,	who	is

7.b.**Var:** p46,01ℵ-org
02A,03B,06D-org,Lach
Treg,Alf,We/Ho,Sod

3964.2 adj nom sing masc	5065.1 prep	5050.2 prs- pron gen 2pl	2231.2 prs- pron gen 1pl	1243.1 noun nom sing masc	3450.2 art gen sing
πιστὸς	ὑπὲρ	ʿ ὑμῶν	[ᵇ ἡμῶν]	διάκονος	τοῦ
pistos	*huper*	*humōn*	*hēmōn*	*diakonos*	*tou*
faithful	for	you	[us]	a servant	of the

5382.2 name gen masc	3450.5 art nom sing masc	2504.1 conj	1207.4 verb nom sing masc part aor act	2231.3 prs- pron dat 1pl	3450.12 art acc sing fem
Χριστοῦ,	8. ὁ	καὶ	δηλώσας	ἡμῖν	τὴν
Christou	*ho*	*kai*	*dēlōsas*	*hēmin*	*tēn*
Christ,	the	also	having signified	to us	the

5050.2 prs- pron gen 2pl	26.4 noun acc sing fem	1706.1 prep	4011.3 noun dat sing neu	1217.2 prep	3642.17 dem- pron sing neu
ὑμῶν	ἀγάπην	ἐν	πνεύματι.	9. Διὰ	τοῦτο
humōn	*agapēn*	*en*	*pneumati*	*Dia*	*touto*
your	love	in	Spirit.	On account of	this

2504.1 conj	2231.1 prs- pron nom 1pl	570.1 prep	3614.10 rel- pron gen sing fem	2232.1 noun fem	189.22 verb 1pl indic aor act
καὶ	ἡμεῖς	ἀφ'	ἧς	ἡμέρας	ἠκούσαμεν,
kai	*hēmeis*	*aph'*	*hēs*	*hēmeras*	*ēkousamen*
also	we	from	which	day	we heard,

3620.3 partic	3835.4 verb 1pl indic pres mid	5065.1 prep	5050.2 prs- pron gen 2pl	4195.13 verb nom pl masc part pres mid	2504.1 conj
οὐ	παυόμεθα	ὑπὲρ	ὑμῶν	προσευχόμενοι	καὶ
ou	*pauometha*	*huper*	*humōn*	*proseuchomenoi*	*kai*
not	do cease	for	you	praying	and

153.26 verb nom pl masc part pres mid	2419.1 conj	3997.23 verb 2pl subj aor pass	3450.12 art acc sing fem	1907.4 noun acc sing fem
αἰτούμενοι	ἵνα	πληρωθῆτε	τὴν	ἐπίγνωσιν
aitoumenoi	*hina*	*plērōthēte*	*tēn*	*epignōsin*
asking	that	you may be filled with	the	knowledge

3450.2 art gen sing	2284.2 noun gen sing neu	840.3 prs- pron gen sing	1706.1 prep	3820.11 adj dat sing fem	4531.3 noun dat sing fem	2504.1 conj
τοῦ	θελήματος	αὐτοῦ	ἐν	πάσῃ	σοφίᾳ	καὶ
tou	*thelēmatos*	*autou*	*en*	*pasē*	*sophia*	*kai*
of the	will	his	in	all	wisdom	and

10.a.**Txt:** 01ℵ-corr
06D-corr,018K,020L
025P,byz.
Var: 01ℵ-org,02A,03B
04C,06D-org,33,Gries
Lach,Treg,Alf,Tisc
We/Ho,Weis,Sod
UBS/✶

4757.2 noun dat sing fem	4012.5 adj dat sing fem	3906.23 verb inf aor act	5050.4 prs- pron acc 2pl
συνέσει	πνευματικῇ,	10. περιπατῆσαι	ʿᵃ ὑμᾶς ʾ
sunesei	*pneumatikē*	*peripatēsai*	*humas*
understanding	spiritual,	to walk	you

512.1 adv	3450.2 art gen sing	2935.2 noun gen sing masc	1519.1 prep	3820.12 adj acc sing fem	693.1 noun acc sing fem
ἀξίως	τοῦ	κυρίου	εἰς	πᾶσαν	ἀρεσκείαν·
axiōs	*tou*	*kuriou*	*eis*	*pasan*	*areskeian*
worthily	of the	Lord	to	all	pleasing,

1706.1 prep	3820.3 adj dat sing	2024.3 noun dat sing neu	18.4 adj dat sing	2563.3 verb nom pl masc part pres act	2504.1 conj
ἐν	παντὶ	ἔργῳ	ἀγαθῷ	καρποφοροῦντες	καὶ
en	*panti*	*ergō*	*agathō*	*karpophorountes*	*kai*
in	every	work	good	bringing forth fruit	and

1:7. This verse is the first reference in this lovely epistle to the individual known as "Epaphras." The apostle designated him "our dear fellow servant" or "our beloved (*agapētou*) fellow slave." "Servant" or "slave" comes from the common New Testament word *doulos* which could denote a love-slave relationship. In other words, a person willingly dedicates himself to the Lord somewhat as a person would become a willing slave to another person. The term *bondslave* probably best expresses the idea. It is similar to the love-slave concept described in Exodus 21:1-6. Paul added the Greek preposition *sun* to the word "servant" that indicates being with someone, or being together in the sense of close relationship.

Epaphras also was a "faithful minister." "Minister" comes from the Greek term *diakonos* normally translated "deacon." Epaphras most likely was converted during the approximately 3 years Paul ministered in Ephesus (Acts 20:31), was trained in Paul's school, and returned to his hometown to begin a New Testament church.

1:8. There is a good possibility that Epaphras became the pastor of the assembly in Colossae. Epaphras was so in touch with the pulse of the assembly in Colossae that he was able to relate to the apostle what the latter called "your love in the Spirit." In the original language the term "Spirit" (*pneumati*) is not preceded by a definite article, but it still obviously refers to the Holy Spirit and not just to the human spirit.

1:9. Having expressed his gratitude to God for all these facts relayed to him by Epaphras, Paul then earnestly prayed for the Colossian saints. Paul's 218-word sentence in the original language begins at verse 9 and continues through verse 20. First, he prayed they would receive a greater knowledge of God's will. The term "filled" suggests the idea of filling to completeness. He wanted them to have a thorough or full knowledge (*epignōsis*) or an ever-increasing knowledge. Paul described a thorough knowledge which involved a deep, accurate, and comprehensive acquaintance with the way God expressed himself in the Bible.

Apparently the Colossians did not lack knowledge, but they were in need of help in the area of spiritual perception, without which they could be easily victimized by a system of thought that could undermine their whole experience with God. The Colossians already had some knowledge of God's will, but they needed more or a fuller development.

This full knowledge would consist of spiritual wisdom and understanding. The first of these two terms is a general word embracing the whole range of mental faculties, and the second term refers to insight which discriminates between the true and the false.

1:10. Paul's second petition is a consequence of the first. The knowledge of God is not imparted to be an end in itself, but is given to enable believers to live in a manner worthy of the Lord.

7. As ye also learned of Epaphras our dear fellowservant: You learned these things, we understand, *Phillips* . . . our dearly loved fellow-slave, *Williams*.

who is for you a faithful minister of Christ: . . . who faithfully represents us as a minister, *TCNT* . . . who is in the same service as we are, *Phillips*.

8. Who also declared unto us your love in the Spirit: It is he who has told us about, *Norlie* . . . who also related to us, *Wilson* . . . who also made evident to us, *Rotherham* . . . it was from him that we heard about your growth in Christian love, *Phillips* . . . which is inspired by the Spirit, *TCNT* . . . who told me of the love awakened in you by, *Williams* . . . hath manifested to us...in the spirit, *Douay*.

9. For this cause we also, since the day we heard [it], do not cease to pray for you: This is why, *Williams* . . . so you will understand that since we heard, *Phillips* . . . For this reason from the day I heard of it, *Montgomery*.

and to desire that ye might be filled with the knowledge of his will: . . . and making request that, *Alford* . . . and to ask that, *Noyes* . . . that ye myght be fulfylled, *Cranmer* . . . and to ask that ye may be filled, *Noyes* . . . that ye may be filled up to the full-knowledge of, *Rotherham* . . . as to the exact knowledge, *Wilson*.

in all wisdom and spiritual understanding: . . . with spiritual wisdom, *TCNT* . . . and spiritual insight, *Montgomery*.

10. That ye might walk worthy of the Lord unto all pleasing: . . . so that your manner of life may be, *Montgomery* . . . that ye myght be fulfylled, *Cranmer* . . . so as to please him, *Noyes*.

being fruitful in every good work: . . . by perennially bearing fruit, *Williams* . . . by good actions of every kind, *TCNT*.

Colossians 1:11

10.b.**Txt:** 06D-corr,018K
020L,byz.
Var: 01‭א‬,02A,03B,04C
06D-org,025P,33,Gries
Lach,Treg,Alf,Word
Tisc,We/Ho,Weis,Sod
UBS/✶

831.11 verb nom pl masc part pres mid	1519.1 prep	3450.12 art acc sing fem	1907.4 noun acc sing fem	1706.1 prep	3450.11 art dat sing fem
αὐξανόμενοι	ʹ εἰς	τὴν	ἐπίγνωσιν	[b✶ ἐν	τῇ
auxanomenoi	eis	tēn	epignōsin	en	tē
growing	into	the	knowledge	[in	the

1907.3 noun dat sing fem	3450.2 art gen sing	2296.2 noun gen sing masc	1706.1 prep	3820.11 adj dat sing fem	1405.3 noun dat sing fem
ἐπιγνώσει]	τοῦ	θεοῦ,	**11.** ἐν	πάσῃ	δυνάμει
epignōsei	tou	theou,	en	pasē	dunamei
knowledge]	tou	of God;	with	all	power

1406.1 verb nom pl masc part pres mid	2567.3 prep	3450.16 art sing neu	2877.1 noun sing neu	3450.10 art gen sing fem	1385.2 noun gen sing fem
δυναμούμενοι	κατὰ	τὸ	κράτος	τῆς	δόξης
dunamoumenoi	kata	to	kratos	tēs	doxēs
being strengthened	according to	the	might	of the	glory

840.3 prs-pron gen sing	1519.1 prep	3820.12 adj acc sing fem	5119.4 noun acc sing fem	2504.1 conj	3087.4 noun acc sing fem
αὐτοῦ	εἰς	πᾶσαν	ὑπομονὴν	καὶ	μακροθυμίαν
autou	eis	pasan	hupomonēn	kai	makrothumian
his	to	all	endurance	and	patience

12.a.**Var:** p46,03B

3196.3 prep	5315.2 noun gen sing fem	2149.7 verb nom pl masc part pres act	258.1 adv	3450.3 art dat sing
μετὰ	χαρᾶς·	**12.** εὐχαριστοῦντες	[a+ ἅμα]	τῷ
meta	charas	eucharistountes	hama	tō
with	joy;	giving thanks	[together with]	to the

12.b.**Txt:** 02A,04C,06D
018K,020L,025P,byz.it.
bo.Sod
Var: 01‭א‬,03B,sa.Tisc
We/Ho,Weis,UBS/✶

3824.3 noun dat sing masc	3450.3 art dat sing	2403.2 verb dat sing masc part aor act	2231.4 prs-pron acc 1pl	5050.4 prs-pron acc 2pl
πατρὶ	τῷ	ἱκανώσαντι	ʹ ἡμᾶς	[b✶ ὑμᾶς]
patri	tō	hikanōsanti	hēmas	humas
Father,	the	having made competent	us	[you]

1519.1 prep	3450.12 art acc sing fem	3182.3 noun acc sing fem	3450.2 art gen sing	2792.2 noun gen sing masc	3450.1 art gen pl	39.4 adj gen pl
εἰς	τὴν	μερίδα	τοῦ	κλήρου	τῶν	ἁγίων
eis	tēn	merida	tou	klērou	tōn	hagiōn
for	the	share	of the	inheritance	of the	saints

1706.1 prep	3450.3 art dat sing	5295.3 noun dat sing neu	3614.5 rel-pron nom sing masc	4363.6 verb 3sing indic aor mid	2231.4 prs-pron acc 1pl	1523.2 prep gen
ἐν	τῷ	φωτί,	**13.** ὃς	ἐρρύσατο	ἡμᾶς	ἐκ
en	tō	phōti,	hos	errhusato	hēmas	ek
in	the	light,	who	delivered	us	from

3450.10 art gen sing fem	1833.1 noun fem	3450.2 art gen sing	4510.3 noun gen sing neu	2504.1 conj	3150.2 verb 3sing indic aor act
τῆς	ἐξουσίας	τοῦ	σκότους,	καὶ	μετέστησεν
tēs	exousias	tou	skotous,	kai	metestēsen
the	authority	of the	darkness,	and	transferred

1519.1 prep	3450.12 art acc sing fem	926.4 noun acc sing fem	3450.2 art gen sing	5048.2 noun gen sing masc	3450.10 art gen sing fem	26.2 noun gen sing fem
εἰς	τὴν	βασιλείαν	τοῦ	υἱοῦ	τῆς	ἀγάπης
eis	tēn	basileian	tou	huiou	tēs	agapēs
into	the	kingdom	of the	Son	of the	love

840.3 prs-pron gen sing	1706.1 prep	3614.3 rel-pron dat sing	2174.5 verb 1pl indic pres act	3450.12 art acc sing fem	623.3 noun acc sing fem
αὐτοῦ,	**14.** ἐν	ᾧ	ἔχομεν	τὴν	ἀπολύτρωσιν
autou,	en	hō	echomen	tēn	apolutrōsin
his:	in	whom	we have	the	redemption

To "walk worthy of the Lord" means in general to live a life commensurate with what the Lord has done for a person. Doctrine and ethics were inseparable to Paul. Right knowledge should lead to right behavior. The Greek word translated "worthy" (axiōs) often was used in connection with a pair of scales in which the item on one side should weigh as much as the item on the other side.

Paul did not imply that believers can ever repay the Lord for what He has done for them. On the other hand, it would be a real affront to Him if Christians did not live in a worthy manner. Paul used four parallel participles in this passage to define precisely the ways a worthy life will be manifested. First, the believer who is walking properly will be "fruitful." Secondly, that person will be "increasing in the knowledge of God."

1:11. Thirdly, a person who is living a worthy life will experience being "strengthened with all might." In making this statement Paul purposely piled up expressions for emphasis. Both "strengthened" and "might" come from one of the common Greek words for power or "inherent ability" (dunamis), while the word "power" in the next part of the statement comes from a word basically meaning "manifested strength" (kratos).

This mighty power in turn will manifest itself in "patience," "long-suffering," and "joyfulness." The first term relates to perseverance in spite of all kinds of obstacles. The Greek word actually means more than "patience"; it especially contains the idea of holding to a course of action with steadfast determination. This kind of perseverance seems most difficult when affliction is present. "Long-suffering" basically means to forbear other people. It more closely denotes the idea of patience than does hupomonē. "Joyfulness" is self-explanatory, but is an ingredient not always present along with patience and long-suffering.

1:12. The remainder of the passage through verse 14 contains the basis for wanting to live the right kind of life. God has qualified believers, or made them fit, to share in the inheritance of His saints by delivering them from the realm of spiritual darkness and placing them in His Son's kingdom through His wonderful sacrifice.

1:13. This verse makes the drastic nature of the experience of regeneration even more evident. The language is quite typical of the way Paul pictured the life of a person before accepting Jesus Christ as Lord. He constantly described the lost condition of people outside of Christ. He wrote about God's delivering believers from "the power of darkness." "Power" actually comes from a common Greek term (exousia) normally translated "authority." The language depicts a very drastic experience, being snatched out of one condition and placed in another condition. This second condition occurs when a person becomes part of Christ's kingdom or comes under His rulership.

and increasing in the knowledge of God: . . . and growing in, *Worrell* . . . may grow yet deeper, *Phillips.*

11. Strengthened with all might, according to his glorious power: May you be completely strengthened, *Confraternity* . . . with a strength proportionate to the power displayed in God's majesty, *TCNT* . . . by the might of his glory, *Montgomery* . . . from God's boundless resources, *Phillips.*

unto all patience and longsuffering with joyfulness: . . . so that you will find yourselves able to pass through an experience and endure it with courage, *Phillips* . . . with patience and good cheer, *Norlie.*

12. Giving thanks unto the Father, which hath made us meet: . . . who has made us fit, *Sawyer* . . . who enabled us to share in, *Noyes* . . . made us worthy, *Confraternity* . . . and qualified us, *Wilson* . . . who is qualifying us, *Scarlett* . . . who enabled us to share, *Montgomery.*

to be partakers of the inheritance of the saints in light: . . . to share the lot of, *Confraternity* . . . for a portion in the inheritance, *Sawyer* . . . the lot of His people in the realm of light, *Williams* . . . those who are living in, *Phillips.*

13. Who hath delivered us from the power of darkness: . . . rescued us from the tyranny of Darkness, *TCNT* . . . rescued us from the empire of darkness, *Noyes* . . . delivered us out of the dominion of darkness, *Worrell, Montgomery, Williams.*

and hath translated [us] into the kingdom of his dear Son: . . . and transferred us, *Confraternity* . . . and reestablished us, *Phillips* . . . and transplanted us, *Montgomery* . . . and has removed us, *TCNT* . . . of the Son of his love, *Sawyer, Rotherham.*

14.a.Txt: Steph
Var: 01א,02A,03B,04C
06D,018K,020L,025P
byz.Gries,Lach,Treg,Alf
Word,Tisc,We/Ho,Weis
Sod,UBS/⋆

1217.2 prep	3450.2 art gen sing	129.2 noun gen sing neu	840.3 prs-pron gen sing	3450.12 art acc sing fem	852.3 noun acc sing fem
διὰ	τοῦ	αἵματος	αὐτοῦ,	τὴν	ἄφεσιν
dia	tou	haimatos	autou	tēn	aphesin
through	the	blood	his,	the	forgiveness

3450.1 art gen pl	264.6 noun gen pl fem	3614.5 rel-pron nom sing masc	1498.4 verb 3sing indic pres act	1494.1 noun nom sing fem	3450.2 art gen sing
τῶν	ἁμαρτιῶν·	15. ὅς	ἐστιν	εἰκὼν	τοῦ
tōn	hamartiōn	hos	estin	eikōn	tou
of the	sins;	who	is	image	the

2296.2 noun gen sing masc	3450.2 art gen sing	513.1 adj gen sing masc	4274.1 adj nom sing masc	3820.10 adj gen sing fem	2909.2 noun gen sing fem
θεοῦ	τοῦ	ἀοράτου,	πρωτότοκος	πάσης	κτίσεως·
theou	tou	aoratou	prōtotokos	pasēs	ktiseōs
of God	the	invisible,	firstborn	of all	creation;

16.a.Txt: 01א-corr,02A
06D-corr,018K,020L
byz.Weis,Sod
Var: 01א-org,03B
06D-org,025P,33,Lach
Treg,Tisc,We/Ho
UBS/⋆

16.b.Txt: 01א-corr,02A
04C,06D,018K,020L
025P,etc.byz.Sod
Var: 01א-org,03B,Tisc
We/Ho,Weis,UBS/⋆

3617.1 conj	1706.1 prep	840.4 prs-pron dat sing	2908.7 verb 3sing indic aor pass	3450.17 art pl neu	3820.1 adj
16. ὅτι	ἐν	αὐτῷ	ἐκτίσθη	τὰ	πάντα,
hoti	en	autō	ektisthē	ta	panta
because	by	him	were created	the	all things,

3450.17 art pl neu	1706.1 prep	3450.4 art dat pl	3636.8 noun dat pl masc	2504.1 conj	3450.17 art pl neu	1894.3 prep
τὰ	ἐν	τοῖς	οὐρανοῖς	καὶ	τὰ	ἐπὶ
ta	en	tois	ouranois	kai	ta	epi
the things	in	the	heavens	and	the things	upon

3450.10 art gen sing fem	1087.2 noun gen sing fem	3450.17 art pl neu	3570.1 adj pl neu	2504.1 conj	3450.17 art pl neu	513.4 adj pl neu
τῆς	γῆς,	τὰ	ὁρατὰ	καὶ	τὰ	ἀόρατα,
tēs	gēs	ta	horata	kai	ta	aorata
the	earth,	the	visible	and	the	invisible,

1521.1 conj	2339.5 noun nom pl masc	1521.1 conj	2936.3 noun nom pl fem	1521.1 conj	741.5 noun nom pl fem	1521.1 conj
εἴτε	θρόνοι	εἴτε	κυριότητες	εἴτε	ἀρχαὶ	εἴτε
eite	thronoi	eite	kuriotētes	eite	archai	eite
whether	thrones,	or	lordships,	or	rulers,	or

1833.5 noun nom pl fem	3450.17 art pl neu	3820.1 adj	1217.1 prep	840.3 prs-pron gen sing	2504.1 conj	1519.1 prep
ἐξουσίαι·	τὰ	πάντα	δι'	αὐτοῦ	καὶ	εἰς
exousiai	ta	panta	di'	autou	kai	eis
authorities:	the	all things	by	him	and	for

840.6 prs-pron acc sing masc	2908.11 verb 3sing indic perf mid	2504.1 conj	840.5 prs-pron nom sing masc	1498.4 verb 3sing indic pres act
αὐτὸν	ἔκτισται·	17. καὶ	αὐτός	ἐστιν
auton	ektistai	kai	autos	estin
him	have been created.	And	he	is

4112.1 prep	3820.4 adj gen pl	2504.1 conj	3450.17 art pl neu	3820.1 adj	1706.1 prep	840.4 prs-pron dat sing
πρὸ	πάντων,	καὶ	τὰ	πάντα	ἐν	αὐτῷ
pro	pantōn	kai	ta	panta	en	autō
before	all,	and	the	all things	in	him

4771.9 verb 3sing indic perf act	2504.1 conj	840.5 prs-pron nom sing masc	1498.4 verb 3sing indic pres act	3450.9 art nom sing fem
συνέστηκεν·	18. καὶ	αὐτός	ἐστιν	ἡ
sunestēken	kai	autos	estin	hē
has subsisted.	And	he	is	the

1:14. Paul could not have closed his prayer in a more fitting manner than by reminding the Colossians of the redemptive work of the Messiah, the most important work of all history. In the original language the term "redemption" contains a definite article, literally meaning "the redemption." *Redeem* carries the idea of "buying back" something that had been sold. Possibly Paul was thinking of his own experience when he referred to "the forgiveness of sins." The entire prayer from verse 9 through verse 14 serves as an excellent reminder of the necessity of a proper balance between knowledge and experience. A person needs proper knowledge, it must be translated into experience.

1:15. This verse begins the main theme of the letter: the preeminence or supremacy of Christ. The Gnostic heresy which apparently had infected the Colossian assembly contained many unscriptural doctrines, but its main error was its depreciation of the person and work of Christ. Many Bible scholars believe this section of Scripture consisted of a hymn sung by the Early Church.

Paul first described Christ as "the image of the invisible God." The Bible states in several locations that the essence or substance of God is invisible to human beings (Romans 1:20; 1 Timothy 1:17; Hebrews 11:27). It also states that no man can ever see God, an obvious reference to the Father, but that Christ has made the Father known (John 1:18; 14:9).

"Image" expresses two crucial points. First, it suggests "representation, likeness." Hebrews 1:3 reflects the same idea through another Greek term that was translated "exact representation" in the New International Version. "Manifestation" is the second idea reflected in the term "image" (John 1:18; 14:9). Paul also described Christ as "the firstborn of every creature." "Firstborn" (*prōtotokos*) does not imply that Jesus is part of creation, but rather indicates His priority and sovereignty over all creation.

1:16. This verse reinforces this interpretation by emphasizing that Christ's relationship to creation is not that of being part of it but that of bringing all things into existence. Notice the progression in this passage. First, Paul showed Christ's relationship to deity, and then His relationship to creation. The words "by him" in this verse would be translated better as "in Him" because they express the fact that He was the agent through which everything was created (John 1:3). The tense of the verb "were created" is aorist in the first instance and perfect tense in the second, referring to the continuous result. (See *Overview*, pp.548f.)

1:17. Here Paul summarizes the previous affirmations of the supremacy of Jesus in creation. Not only did Jesus always exist (John 1:1; 8:58), but He holds all creation together. Thus, the Gnostic philosophy that matter is evil and was created by some being other than Christ is completely unscriptural.

14. In whom we have redemption through his blood: For it is by his Son alone that we have been redeemed, *Phillips*.

[even] the forgiveness of sins: . . . the remission of our sins, *Confraternity*.

15. Who is the image of the invisible God: . . . who is the likeness, *Murdock* . . . He is a visible image of, *Montgomery* . . . is the very incarnation of the unseen God, *TCNT*.

the firstborn of every creature: . . . and Head of all creation, *TCNT* . . . He existed before creation began, *Phillips*.

16. For by him were all things created: . . . for it was through him that everything was made, *Phillips*.

that are in heaven, and that are in earth, visible and invisible: . . . all that is seen and all that is unseen, *Murdock*.

whether [they be] thrones, or dominions, or principalities, or powers: . . . whether they be Maiestie or Lordeship, *Geneva* . . . or Lordships, or Governments, or authorities, *Wilson* . . . or sovereignties, *Murdock* . . . angelic Beings whatever their power or rank, *TCNT*.

all things were created by him, and for him: Through him, *Phillips*.

17. And he is before all things: He is both the first principle, *Phillips* . . . and he precedes, *Wilson* . . . he was prior to all, *Murdock*.

and by him all things consist: . . . and the upholding principle of the whole scheme of creation, *Phillips* . . . and all things depend upon him for their existence, *TCNT* . . . they all in him hold together, *Rotherham* . . . all things have been permanently placed, *Wilson* . . . alle thingis ben made of nought bi him, *Wyclif* . . . all things have held together, *Worrell* . . . all things subsist, *Montgomery*.

2747.1 noun nom sing fem	3450.2 art gen sing	4835.2 noun gen sing neu	3450.10 art gen sing fem	1564.1 noun fem	3614.5 rel-pron nom sing masc
κεφαλὴ	τοῦ	σώματος	τῆς	ἐκκλησίας·	ὅς
kephalē	tou	sōmatos	tēs	ekklēsias	hos
head	of the	body,	the	assembly;	who

18.a.Var: p46,03B,6,104 1175,1739

1498.4 verb 3sing indic pres act	3450.9 art nom sing fem	741.1 noun nom sing fem	4274.1 adj nom sing masc	1523.2 prep gen
ἐστιν	[a+ ἡ]	ἀρχή,	πρωτότοκος	ἐκ
estin	hē	archē	prōtotokos	ek
is	[the]	beginning,	firstborn	from among

3450.1 art gen pl	3361.2 adj gen pl	2419.1 conj	1090.40 verb 3sing subj aor mid	1706.1 prep	3820.5 adj dat pl	840.5 prs-pron nom sing masc
τῶν	νεκρῶν,	ἵνα	γένηται	ἐν	πᾶσιν	αὐτὸς
tōn	nekrōn	hina	genētai	en	pasin	autos
the	dead,	that	might be	in	all things	he

4267.1 verb nom sing masc part pres act	3617.1 conj	1706.1 prep	840.4 prs-pron dat sing	2085.7 verb 3sing indic aor act
πρωτεύων·	19. ὅτι	ἐν	αὐτῷ	εὐδόκησεν
prōteuōn	hoti	en	autō	eudokēsen
holding the first place;	because	in	him	was pleased

3820.17 adj sing neu	3450.16 art sing neu	3998.1 noun sing neu	2700.13 verb inf aor act	2504.1 conj	1217.1 prep
πᾶν	τὸ	πλήρωμα	κατοικῆσαι,	20. καὶ	δι'
pan	to	plērōma	katoikēsai	kai	di'
all	the	fullness	to dwell,	and	by

840.3 prs-pron gen sing	599.3 verb inf aor act	3450.17 art pl neu	3820.1 adj	1519.1 prep	840.6 prs-pron acc sing masc
αὐτοῦ	ἀποκαταλλάξαι	τὰ	πάντα	εἰς	αὐτόν,
autou	apokatallaxai	ta	panta	eis	auton
him	to reconcile	the	all things	to	himself,

1505.1 verb nom sing masc part aor act	1217.2 prep	3450.2 art gen sing	129.2 noun gen sing neu	3450.2 art gen sing	4567.2 noun gen sing masc
εἰρηνοποιήσας	διὰ	τοῦ	αἵματος	τοῦ	σταυροῦ
eirēnopoiēsas	dia	tou	haimatos	tou	staurou
having made peace	by	the	blood	of the	cross

20.a.Txt: p46,01א,02A 04C,06D-corr1 06D-corr2,08E,018K 025P,bo.byz. Var: 03B,06D-org,010F 012G,020L,81,104,1175 1739,1881,2464,sa.

840.3 prs-pron gen sing	1217.1 prep	840.3 prs-pron gen sing	1521.1 conj	3450.17 art pl neu	1894.3 prep
αὐτοῦ,	⌈a δι'	αὐτοῦ, ⌉	εἴτε	τὰ	ἐπὶ
autou	di'	autou	eite	ta	epi
his,	by	him,	whether	the things	on

3450.10 art gen sing fem	1087.2 noun gen sing fem	1521.1 conj	3450.17 art pl neu	1706.1 prep	3450.4 art dat pl	3636.8 noun dat pl masc
τῆς	γῆς	εἴτε	τὰ	ἐν	τοῖς	οὐρανοῖς.
tēs	gēs	eite	ta	en	tois	ouranois
the	earth,	or	the things	in	the	heavens.

2504.1 conj	5050.4 prs-pron acc 2pl	4077.1 adv	1498.25 verb acc pl masc part pres act	522.2 verb acc pl masc part perf mid
21. Καὶ	ὑμᾶς	ποτε	ὄντας	ἀπηλλοτριωμένους
Kai	humas	pote	ontas	apēllotriōmenous
And	you	once	being	having been alienated

2504.1 conj	2172.7 adj acc pl masc	3450.11 art dat sing fem	1265.2 noun dat sing fem	1706.1 prep	3450.4 art dat pl	2024.6 noun dat pl neu
καὶ	ἐχθροὺς	τῇ	διανοίᾳ	ἐν	τοῖς	ἔργοις
kai	echthrous	tē	dianoia	en	tois	ergois
and	enemies	in the	mind	by	the	works

1:18. Just as Christ is supreme over the natural creation, so is He sovereign over the new creation, the New Testament Church of which He is the Head. He is supreme in the spiritual realm as well as in the material realm.

The constant use of the term "body" for the Church suggests several important facts. First, it designates the Church as a living organism, composed of members vitally connected to one another. Secondly, it points to the Church as the means through which Christ accomplishes His purposes and performs His work in the world. Thirdly, it shows that the union between Christ and His church constitutes a very vital and intimate one.

Verse 18 establishes the ground for Christ's vital headship of the Church. He is the "beginning" (*archē*) or "source" or "origin." He is the "firstborn" (*prōtotokos*), the first to rise from the realm of the dead in a permanent fashion (Revelation 1:5). This implies the idea of opening the way for others to follow. Because of these achievements, Christ deserves recognition as the Preeminent One.

1:19. God planned that His "fulness" (*plērōma*) would reside in Christ. *Fullness* was the very term used by the Gnostics for the totality of so-called divine emanations, or intermediary beings, which they believed controlled people's lives.

The Gnostic teachers parceled out deity among the many spirit beings, called "aeons," which they envisioned as filling the space between God and the world. According to them, any communication between God and the world and between the world and God had to pass through the spheres in which these intermediary beings exercised rule. They included Christ as one of many such "divine beings," but the apostle made it clear that Christ is the only mediator between God and men (1 Timothy 2:5).

1:20. God willed that through Christ all reconciliation would occur. "Reconcile" literally means bringing back into proper relationship. Because God was not the offender, the Bible uses the term relative to men being brought back into the proper relationship with God.

Reconciliation has both an objective and a subjective side. Objectively, God removed the barrier between himself and sinful man by the death of Christ on the cross, so sinners may experience a living relationship with God. Subjectively, people must accept the possibility for reconciliation that God has provided.

1:21. Paul reminded the Colossians in a very straightforward manner of their condition before their reconciliation to God. The language is very reminiscent of Romans 1:18-32 and gives a vivid picture of heathenism at its worst. The apostle probably carefully pinpointed the Colossians' former evil behavior because many Gnostics taught that it mattered little how a person lived in the body, as long as he cultivated the spirit.

18. And he is the head of the body, the church: . . . which is composed of all Christian people, *Phillips.*

who is the beginning, the firstborn from the dead: Life from nothing began through him, and life from the dead began through him, *Phillips.*

that in all [things] he might have the preeminence: . . . so that He alone should stand first in everything, *Williams* . . . he is the source of its Life, that he in all things may stand first, *TCNT* . . . he might be prefident, *Scarlett* . . . in al things holding the primacie, *Rheims.*

19. For it pleased [the Father] that in him should all fulness dwell: . . . it was the divine choice that all the divine fullness should dwell, *Williams* . . . that the divine nature in all its fulness should dwell in Christ, *TCNT.*

20. And, having made peace through the blood of his cross: . . . pacifying by the bloud, *Rheims* . . . through the blood He shed on His cross, *Williams.*

by him to reconcile all things unto himself: . . . that through Him, *Williams.*

by him, [I say], whether [they be] things in earth, or things in heaven:

21. And you, that were sometime alienated and enemies in [your] mind by wicked works: . . . because youre myndes were set in euyll worckes, *Cranmer* . . . were once estranged, *TCNT* . . . that were once alienated, *Noyes* . . . formerly being Aliens, *Wilson* . . . and hostile in [your] intention, *Rotherham* . . . hostile at heart in your evil deeds, *Montgomery* . . . and hostile in disposition as shown by your wrong-doings, *Williams* . . . because of your evil deeds, *Murdock* . . . in evil works, *Worrell.*

3450.4 art dat pl	4050.5 adj dat pl	3432.1 adv	1156.2 conj	599.1 verb 3sing indic aor act	1706.1 prep
τοῖς	πονηροῖς,	νυνὶ	δὲ	ἀποκατήλλαξεν	22. ἐν
tois	ponērois	nuni	de	apokatēllaxen	en
the	wicked,	now	yet	he reconciled	in

3450.3 art dat sing	4835.3 noun dat sing neu	3450.10 art gen sing fem	4418.2 noun gen sing fem	840.3 prs-pron gen sing	1217.2 prep	3450.2 art gen sing
τῷ	σώματι	τῆς	σαρκὸς	αὐτοῦ	διὰ	τοῦ
tō	sōmati	tēs	sarkos	autou	dia	tou
the	body	of the	flesh	his	through	the

22.a.Txt: p46-vid,03B
04C,06D,010F,012G
044,byz.
Var: 01א,02A,025P,81
326,614,630,2464

2265.2 noun gen sing masc	840.3 prs-pron gen sing	3798.12 verb inf aor act	5050.4 prs-pron acc 2pl	39.9 adj acc pl masc
θανάτου,	[a+ αὐτοῦ,]	παραστῆσαι	ὑμᾶς	ἁγίους
thanatou	autou	parastēsai	humas	hagious
death,	[his,]	to present	you	holy

2504.1 conj	297.4 adj acc pl masc	2504.1 conj	408.4 adj acc pl masc	2684.1 prep
καὶ	ἀμώμους	καὶ	ἀνεγκλήτους	κατενώπιον
kai	amōmous	kai	anenklētous	katenōpion
and	unblemished	and	irreproachable	before

840.3 prs-pron gen sing	1480.1 conj	1479.1 conj	1058.1 partic	1946.1 verb 2pl indic pres act
αὐτοῦ·	23. ⸂ εἴγε	[✶ εἴ	γε]	ἐπιμένετε
autou	eige	ei	ge	epimenete
him,	if indeed	[if	indeed]	you continue

3450.11 art dat sing fem	3963.3 noun dat sing fem	2288.4 verb nom pl masc part perf mid	2504.1 conj	1469.2 adj nom pl masc	2504.1 conj
τῇ	πίστει	τεθεμελιωμένοι	καὶ	ἑδραῖοι,	καὶ
tē	pistei	tethemeliōmenoi	kai	hedraioi	kai
in the	faith	having been founded	and	firm,	and

3231.1 partic	3204.1 verb nom pl masc part pres mid	570.3 prep	3450.10 art gen sing fem	1667.2 noun gen sing fem	3450.2 art gen sing
μὴ	μετακινούμενοι	ἀπὸ	τῆς	ἐλπίδος	τοῦ
mē	metakinoumenoi	apo	tēs	elpidos	tou
not	being moved away	from	the	hope	of the

2077.2 noun gen sing neu	3614.2 rel-pron gen sing	189.23 verb 2pl indic aor act	3450.2 art gen sing	2756.26 verb gen sing neu part aor pass
εὐαγγελίου	οὗ	ἠκούσατε,	τοῦ	κηρυχθέντος
euangeliou	hou	ēkousate	tou	kēruchthentos
good news,	which	you heard,	the	having been proclaimed

1706.1 prep	3820.11 adj dat sing fem	3450.11 art dat sing fem	2909.3 noun dat sing fem	3450.11 art dat sing fem	5097.3 prep	3450.6 art acc sing masc
ἐν	πάσῃ	⸂a τῇ ⸃	κτίσει	τῇ	ὑπὸ	τὸν
en	pasē	tē	ktisei	tē	hupo	ton
in	all	the	creation	the	under	the

23.a.Txt: 01א-corr
06D-corr,018K,020L
025P,byz.
Var: 01א-org,02A,03B
04C,06D-org,33,Lach
Treg,Alf,Word,Tisc
We/Ho,Weis,Sod
UBS/✶

3636.4 noun acc sing masc	3614.2 rel-pron gen sing	1090.30 verb 1sing indic aor mid	1466.1 prs-pron nom 1sing	3834.1 name nom masc	1243.1 noun nom sing masc
οὐρανόν,	οὗ	ἐγενόμην	ἐγὼ	Παῦλος	διάκονος.
ouranon	hou	egenomēn	egō	Paulos	diakonos
heaven,	of which	became	I	Paul	servant.

24.a.Txt: 01א-corr,Steph
Var: 01א-org,02A,03B
04C,06D,018K,020L
025P,byz.Gries,Lach
Treg,Alf,Word,Tisc
We/Ho,Weis,Sod
UBS/✶

3431.1 adv	5299.1 verb 1sing indic pres act	1706.1 prep	3450.4 art dat pl	3667.4 noun dat pl neu	1466.2 prs-pron gen 1sing
24. Νῦν	χαίρω	ἐν	τοῖς	παθήμασιν	⸂a μου ⸃
Nun	chairō	en	tois	pathēmasin	mou
Now,	I am rejoicing	in	the	sufferings	my

This approach serves as a very convenient justification for practicing sin. Paul connected the word "mind" with "wicked works." "Yet now" in this verse indicates God's intervention. Notice the obvious contrast between the frank statements "were sometime alienated and enemies" and "yet now hath he reconciled."

1:22. Paul very carefully combined two Greek words in this verse (*sōma*, "body," and *sarx*, "flesh") to specify the actual humanity and genuine body of Jesus. The Gnostics generally taught that reconciliation could be accomplished only by spiritual beings, but Paul emphasized that it happened by the putting to death of Jesus' physical body. "In the body of his flesh" indicates the sphere in which reconciliation took place, and "through death" specifies the instrument by which it happened.

Christ's ultimate purpose in this glorious process of reconciliation is to present believers before God at His second coming as those who have become Christlike through the sanctification process. This statement, as well as the following verse, should be enough to show that Christians are not perfected at conversion. Even though positionally believers are perfect because the perfection of Christ has been imputed to them, experientially they must go through the process of progressive sanctification in which the Holy Spirit works in them to make them actually like the Lord Jesus Christ.

1:23. The last verse in this section about the supremacy of Christ in redemption contains a warning to the Colossians against relapsing into their former condition and an encouragement to continue to recognize Jesus as their all-sufficient Saviour.

The "if" here is the focal point of much controversy because it is an indicative mood "if" (*ei*) in the Greek language. Because of the mood involved, it often is translated "since," so it is used by some people to deny any element of condition in the context. Although certainly not all grammarians agree concerning this point, in the indicative mood "if" may denote the fact that the actor in a situation knows what decision he will make, but other people do not know. Therefore, "if ye continue" would mean the Colossians knew their own intentions, but other people may not have.

Obviously, just making the decision is not all that is involved in the matter. The Holy Spirit gives us the ability to continue in "the faith," but He cannot help us unless we permit Him to do so. The language of the entire verse seems to lend support to the conditional element involved in continuing to allow Christ to accomplish His work in our lives. He is not satisfied just to bring us to an initial experience with himself. He obviously wants that relationship to continue. The passage closes with a lovely statement showing the universality of the gospel which God manifested to mankind.

1:24. In his description of the supremacy or preeminence of Christ, Paul went from creation (1:15-17) to redemption (1:18-23)

yet now hath he reconciled: ... to you, he hath now given peace, *Murdock.*

22. In the body of his flesh through death: ... by His death in His human body, *Williams* ... through the death of his body on the cross, *Phillips.*

to present you holy and unblameable and unreproveable in his sight: ... that he might welcome you to his presence, *Phillips* ... and without blemish, *Panin* ... without sin, *Norlie* ... and without offence, *Murdock* ... and undefiled and irreproachable, *Confraternity* ... to present you consecrated, faultless, and blameless, *Williams* ... and unaccusable in his presence, *Rotherham* ... and unaccusable before Him, *Clementson* ... irreproachable before his presence, *PNT.*

23. If ye continue in the faith grounded and settled: Only you must remain firmly founded, *Confraternity* ... and established, *Sawyer* ... if, that is, you remain true to your Faith, *TCNT* ... if indeed you continue well grounded and firm in faith, *Williams* ... and steadfast, *Worrell.*

and [be] not moved away from the hope of the gospel, which ye have heard: ... and that you do not shift away from, *Norlie* ... and immoveable from the hope, *Douay* ... the hope inspired by the good news, *Williams.*

[and] which was preached to every creature which is under heaven: ... which has been preached all over the world, *Williams* ... indeed, the whole world is now having an opportunity of hearing, *Phillips.*

whereof I Paul am made a minister:

24. Who now rejoice in my sufferings for you: I am now glad to be suffering, *Williams* ... on your behalf, *TCNT* ... on your account, *Wilson.*

5065.1 prep	5050.2 prs-pron gen 2pl	2504.1 conj	463.1 verb 1sing indic pres act	3450.17 art pl neu	5140.3 noun pl neu
ὑπὲρ	ὑμῶν,	καὶ	ἀνταναπληρῶ	τὰ	ὑστερήματα
huper	humōn	kai	antanaplērō	ta	husterēmata
for	you,	and	I am filling up	the	lacking

3450.1 art gen pl	2324.6 noun gen pl fem	3450.2 art gen sing	5382.2 name gen masc	1706.1 prep	3450.11 art dat sing fem	4418.3 noun dat sing fem
τῶν	θλίψεων	τοῦ	Χριστοῦ	ἐν	τῇ	σαρκί
tōn	thlipseōn	tou	Christou	en	tē	sarki
of the	tribulations	of the	Christ	in	the	flesh

1466.2 prs-pron gen 1sing	5065.1 prep	3450.2 art gen sing	4835.2 noun sing neu	840.3 prs-pron gen sing	3614.16 rel-pron sing neu
μου	ὑπὲρ	τοῦ	σώματος	αὐτοῦ,	ὅ
mou	huper	tou	sōmatos	autou	ho
my	for	the	body	his,	which

1498.4 verb 3sing indic pres act	3450.9 art nom sing fem	1564.2 noun nom sing fem	3614.10 rel-pron gen sing fem	1090.30 verb 1sing indic aor mid
ἐστιν	ἡ	ἐκκλησία·	25. ἧς	ἐγενόμην
estin	hē	ekklēsia	hēs	egenomēn
is	the	assembly;	of which	became

1466.1 prs-pron nom 1sing	1243.1 noun nom sing masc	2567.3 prep	3450.12 art acc sing fem	3484.2 noun acc sing fem
ἐγὼ	διάκονος	κατὰ	τὴν	οἰκονομίαν
egō	diakonos	kata	tēn	oikonomian
I	servant,	according to	the	administration

3450.2 art gen sing	2296.2 noun gen sing masc	3450.12 art acc sing fem	1319.51 verb acc sing fem part aor pass	1466.4 prs-pron dat 1sing	1519.1 prep
τοῦ	θεοῦ	τὴν	δοθεῖσάν	μοι	εἰς
tou	theou	tēn	dotheisan	moi	eis
	of God	the	having given	me	towards

5050.4 prs-pron acc 2pl	3997.9 verb inf aor act	3450.6 art acc sing masc	3030.4 noun acc sing masc	3450.2 art gen sing	2296.2 noun gen sing masc
ὑμᾶς	πληρῶσαι	τὸν	λόγον	τοῦ	θεοῦ,
humas	plērōsai	ton	logon	tou	theou
you	to complete	the	word		of God,

3450.16 art sing neu	3328.1 noun sing neu	3450.16 art sing neu	607.5 verb sing neu part perf mid	570.3 prep
26. τὸ	μυστήριον	τὸ	ἀποκεκρυμμένον	ἀπὸ
to	mustērion	to	apokekrummenon	apo
the	mystery	to	having been hidden	from

3450.1 art gen pl	163.4 noun gen pl masc	2504.1 conj	570.3 prep	3450.1 art gen pl	1067.6 noun gen pl fem	3432.1 adv
τῶν	αἰώνων	καὶ	ἀπὸ	τῶν	γενεῶν,	(νυνὶ
tōn	aiōnōn	kai	apo	tōn	geneōn	nuni
the	ages	and	from	the	generations,	now

3431.1 adv	1156.2 conj	5157.10 verb 3sing indic aor pass	3450.4 art dat pl masc	39.8 adj dat pl masc	840.3 prs-pron gen sing
[☆ νῦν]	δὲ	ἐφανερώθη	τοῖς	ἁγίοις	αὐτοῦ·
nun	de	ephanerōthē	tois	hagiois	autou
[idem]	but	was made manifest	to the	saints	his;

3614.4 rel-pron dat pl	2286.22 verb 3sing indic aor act	3450.5 art nom sing masc	2296.1 noun nom sing masc	1101.9 verb inf aor act
27. οἷς	ἠθέλησεν	ὁ	θεὸς	γνωρίσαι
hois	ethelēsen	ho	theos	gnōrisai
to whom	did will		God	to make known

and then to his own ministry in the present passage through verse 29. Some people take the statement in verse 24 to mean that something is lacking in the atoning value of Christ's sacrifice and Paul was able to supplement the saving work of Christ through his own sufferings. The whole system of a treasury of merit consisting of the sufferings of Christ plus the afflictions of "the saints," and dispensed in the form of indulgences, comes from a false interpretation of this verse and from other statements.

While we cannot be positive about exactly what Paul had in mind, he probably was referring to the thought that the union between Christ and His church is so intimate that He suffers when they suffer. His personal sufferings may be over, but His people cannot suffer without its having an impact on Him as well.

The apostle surely did not believe Christians are exempt from suffering. A philosophy that teaches God exempts Christians from any form of suffering is dangerous because people who believe it will not be prepared when the difficulties of life arise.

1:25. The word translated "dispensation" (*oikonomia*) literally means "house-manager" and could be rendered "stewardship, administration, economy." The apostle was keenly aware that God had given him a divine commission to preach the Word. Furthermore, he was always concerned about giving out the Word of God.

While Paul may have had something else in mind, it is possible he was referring to the necessity of people receiving the Word of God and practicing it. In other words, he was not pleased just to dispense the truth of the Scriptures in a manner similar to scattering seeds in a field. He was concerned that the seed of the Word of God would take root and produce fruit in people's lives.

Apparently the translators of the New International Version believed Paul was referring to presenting the totality of the Word of God. That idea is very consistent with the statement by the apostle to the Ephesian elders (Acts 20:27) in his farewell address to them. His constant intention always involved informing people of all the will of God, not just certain segments of it. Either interpretation seems consistent with the total teachings of the apostle. Whatever he meant, the verse obviously shows the apostle's intense determination to present the Word of God to other people.

Paul's chief concern in regard to his personal ministry was very clear. He wanted Christ to be supreme in it. He did not want to become sidetracked on some minor issue that did not emphasize the centrality of the gospel. A person who truly declares the gospel message as central is a person who will make Christ supreme in his ministry. This is the kind of ministry that truly touches and changes lives for Christ.

1:26,27. Paul was faithful to the divine commission God had entrusted to him (Acts 9:15), but he made it clear in this passage that the revelation of this mystery was disclosed to the saints in general and not just to him. Paul had more to say about God's

and fill up that which is behind of the afflictions of Christ in my flesh: I supplement the afflictions endured by the Christ, *TCNT* . . . and supply the deficiencies, *Sawyer* . . . and am filling up the deficiencies, *Rotherham* . . . that vvant of the passions of Christ, *Rheims.*

for his body's sake, which is the church: . . . in behalf of, *Montgomery.*

25. Whereof I am made a minister: . . . have been made, *Williams.*

according to the dispensation of God which is given to me for you: It was God who appointed me to this office, *Norlie* . . . according to the administration, *Rotherham* . . . according to the ordinance of God, *Geneva* . . . the stewardship entrusted to me, *Montgomery* . . . that stewardship of God, *Wilson* . . . a commission granted to me for your benefit, *Phillips.*

to fulfil the word of God: . . . to complete the word of God, *Sawyer* . . . fully to declare God's message, *Montgomery* . . . that I might prove among you the universal message of God, *Williams.*

26. [Even] the mystery which hath been hid from ages and from generations: . . . that sacred mystery which up till now, *Phillips* . . . the secret which was concealed, *Wilson* . . . the mystery concealed from ages, *Sawyer* . . . from former ages, *TCNT.*

but now is made manifest to his saints: . . . but now is opened to his saynctes, *Tyndale* . . . but is now revealed to his saints, *Murdock* . . . but now uncovered to God's people, *Williams* . . . but which is now as clear as daylight to those who love God, *Phillips.*

27. To whom God would make known: They are those to whom God has planned to give a vision, *Phillips.*

Colossians 1:28

4949.3 intr-pron nom sing	3450.5 art nom sing masc	4949.9 intr-pron nom sing neu	3450.16 art sing neu	4009.1 noun sing masc	3450.10 art gen sing fem
ʹ τίς	ὁ	[ᵃ☆ τί	τὸ]	πλοῦτος	τῆς
tis	ho	ti	to	ploutos	tēs
what	the	[what	the]	wealth	of the

1385.2 noun gen sing fem	3450.2 art gen sing	3328.2 noun gen sing neu	3642.1 dem-pron gen sing	1706.1 prep	3450.4 art dat pl	1477.6 noun dat pl neu
δόξης	τοῦ	μυστηρίου	τούτου	ἐν	τοῖς	ἔθνεσιν,
doxēs	tou	mustēriou	toutou	en	tois	ethnesin,
glory	of the	mystery	this	among	the	nations,

3614.5 rel-pron nom sing masc	3614.16 rel-pron sing neu	1498.4 verb 3sing indic pres act	5382.1 name nom masc	1706.1 prep	5050.3 prs-pron dat 2pl
ʹ ὅς	[ᵇ☆ ὅ]	ἐστιν	Χριστὸς	ἐν	ὑμῖν,
hos	ho	estin	Christos	en	humin
which	[who]	is	Christ	in	you

3450.9 art nom sing fem	1667.1 noun nom sing fem	3450.10 art gen sing fem	1385.2 noun gen sing fem	3614.6 rel-pron acc sing masc	2231.1 prs-pron nom 1pl
ἡ	ἐλπὶς	τῆς	δόξης·	**28.** ὃν	ἡμεῖς
hē	elpis	tēs	doxēs	hon	hēmeis
the	hope	of the	glory:	whom	we

2576.3 verb 1pl indic pres act	3423.4 verb nom pl masc part pres act	3820.1 adj	442.4 noun acc sing masc	2504.1 conj
καταγγέλλομεν,	νουθετοῦντες	πάντα	ἄνθρωπον,	καὶ
katangellomen,	nouthetountes	panta	anthrōpon,	kai
announce,	admonishing	every	man,	and

1315.9 verb nom pl masc part pres act	3820.1 adj	442.4 noun acc sing masc	1706.1 prep	3820.11 adj dat sing fem	4531.3 noun dat sing fem
διδάσκοντες	πάντα	ἄνθρωπον	ἐν	πάσῃ	σοφίᾳ,
didaskontes	panta	anthrōpon	en	pasē	sophia,
teaching	every	man	in	all	wisdom,

2419.1 conj	3798.8 verb 1pl subj aor act	3820.1 adj	442.4 noun acc sing masc	4894.1 adj sing	1706.1 prep
ἵνα	παραστήσωμεν	πάντα	ἄνθρωπον	τέλειον	ἐν
hina	parastēsōmen	panta	anthrōpon	teleion	en
that	we may present	every	man	perfect	in

5382.3 name dat masc	2400.2 name masc	1519.1 prep	3614.16 rel-pron sing neu	2504.1 conj	2844.1 verb 1sing indic pres act
Χριστῷ	ʹᵃ Ἰησοῦ. ˋ	**29.** εἰς	ὃ	καὶ	κοπιῶ,
Christō	Iēsou.	eis	ho	kai	kopiō,
Christ	Jesus.	Unto	which	also	I labor,

74.3 verb nom sing masc part pres mid	2567.3 prep	3450.12 art acc sing fem	1737.2 noun acc sing fem	840.3 prs-pron gen sing
ἀγωνιζόμενος	κατὰ	τὴν	ἐνέργειαν	αὐτοῦ
agōnizomenos	kata	tēn	energeian	autou
striving	according to	the	working	his

3450.12 art acc sing fem	1738.11 verb acc sing fem part pres mid	1706.1 prep	1466.5 prs-pron dat 1sing	1706.1 prep	1405.3 noun dat sing fem
τὴν	ἐνεργουμένην	ἐν	ἐμοὶ	ἐν	δυνάμει.
tēn	energoumenēn	en	emoi	en	dunamei.
the	working	in	me	in	power.

2286.1 verb 1sing pres act	1056.1 conj	5050.4 prs-pron acc 2pl	3471.25 verb inf perf act	2228.1 intr-pron acc sing masc	72.2 noun acc sing masc
2:1. Θέλω	γὰρ	ὑμᾶς	εἰδέναι	ἡλίκον	ἀγῶνα
Thelō	gar	humas	eidenai	hēlikon	agōna
I wish	for	you	to know	how great	struggle

purpose for Christians in general in the first seven verses of chapter 2, but his brief reference here indicates the way he constantly reminded other people of their responsibility to proclaim the gospel. A careful search of the apostle's writings will reveal several passages where Paul first described his own responsibility to carry out the commission God gave to him, only then in turn reminded Christians of their responsibility to do the same. God will use anyone to propagate His message to the world. The obligation belongs to all believers. Truly the fact that Christ actually indwells believers constitutes one of the greatest mysteries the human race has ever known. He, of course, does so in the person of the Holy Spirit who indwells every believer (Romans 8:9).

1:28. This statement reflects beautifully the fact that Paul was not satisfied just to enjoy fellowship with the Lord personally. He wanted everyone else to enjoy this same experience. For that reason he proclaimed Christ, and his associates did the same. This proclamation consisted of "warning" unbelievers and "teaching" believers so the latter would mature in Christ. His ultimate goal was to present spiritually mature people to Christ at His second coming. He used the term "every man" three times in this verse, showing that he was not an exclusionist. This verse also shows that Christ always was central in his ministry.

One can see the proper balance Paul and his associates practiced in their ministries. First, they were concerned about the unconverted and warned them with the Word of God with the express purpose of helping them to turn to the Lord Jesus in order to find forgiveness for their sins. However, that concern did not end when people became Christians. It only changed to a different type of concern, that of helping individual believers become more and more Christlike. This is God's ultimate purpose for believers.

1:29. This verse serves as an excellent culmination of Paul's comments about his own ministry. His ministry did not cease just because of his incarceration, but even while in prison he was able to "labor." "Striving" or "struggling" (NIV) comes from a Greek participle which has the word from which we get *agony* (*agōna*) as its basis. How could he agonize in prison? He must have been referring mainly to prayer. He also purposely used two Greek words relating to power. The first was translated "working" and comes from a Greek term which gives us our word *energy* (*energeia*). The second was translated "mightily" and comes from the word for *inherent ability* or *power* (*dunamis*). In this first chapter of Colossians, the apostle set forth Christ as supreme in every sense of the word, in creation, in redemption, in an individual's own ministry, and in his practical Christian living.

2:1. After carefully stating the supremacy of Christ in his own ministry, Paul made it clear that the Lord should be preeminent

what [is] the riches of the glory of this mystery among the Gentiles: . . . the riches of this glorious mystery, *Wesley* . . . the glorious wealth of this secret, *Wilson* . . . of his secret plan for the sons of men, *Phillips* . . . when exhibited among the heathen, *TCNT*.

which is Christ in you, the hope of glory: And the secret is simply this...bringing with him the hope of all the glorious things to come, *Phillips* . . . Christ in union with you, your Hope of glory! *TCNT*.

28. Whom we preach: . . . whom we announce, *Wilson* . . . We are proclaiming Him, *Williams*.

warning every man: . . . admonishing, *Wilson, Douay, Confraternity*.

and teaching every man in all wisdom: . . . we teach everyone we can, all that we know about him, *Phillips* . . . with ample wisdom, *Williams*.

that we may present every man perfect in Christ Jesus: . . . into God's presence perfected by union with Christ, *TCNT* . . . every man complete in Christ, *Rotherham* . . . everyone mature through union with Christ, *Williams*.

29. Whereunto I also labour: . . . to which end I also am laboring, *Noyes* . . . whereunto I am also toiling, *Rotherham*.

striving according to his working, which worketh in me mightily: . . . ardently contending, *Wilson* . . . with all the strength that God gives me, *Phillips* . . . which operates in me with power, *Sawyer*.

1. For I would that ye knew what great conflict I have for you: I would ye knewe what fyghtyng, *Geneva* . . . what a struggle I have, *Murdock* . . . how great a contest I am waging for you, *Montgomery* . . . how great a struggle I have entered upon for you, *TCNT* . . . how Great a Struggle I have about you, *Wilson* . . . that I have struggled inwardly a great deal,

Colossians 2:2

1.a.Txt: 06D-org,018K 020L,byz.
Var: 01א,02A,03B,04C 06D-corr,025P,33,Lach Treg,Alf,Tisc,We/Ho Weis,Sod,UBS/☆

1.b.Txt: 01א-corr 06D-corr,018K,020L byz.Sod
Var: 01א-org,02A,03B 04C,06D-org,025P,Tisc We/Ho,Weis,UBS/☆

2.a.Txt: 01א-corr 06D-corr,018K,020L byz.
Var: 01א-org,02A,03B 025P,33,Gries,Lach Treg,Alf,Word,Tisc,Sod UBS/☆

2.b.Txt: 01א-corr,06D 018K,020L,025P,byz.
Var: 01א-org,03B,Alf Tisc,We/Ho,Weis,Sod UBS/☆

2.c.Txt: 06D-corr,018K 020L,byz.
Var: p46,03B,Gries Lach,Treg,Alf,Word Tisc,We/Ho,Weis UBS/☆

3.a.Txt: 01א-corr,02A 06D-corr,018K,020L 025P,byz.
Var: 01א-org,03B,04C 06D-org,33,Lach,Treg Alf,Tisc,We/Ho,Weis Sod,UBS/☆

2174.1 verb 1sing pres act	3875.1 prep	5065.1 prep	5050.2 prs-pron gen 2pl	2504.1 conj	3450.1 art gen pl
ἔχω	ʹ περὶ	[ᵃ☆ ὑπὲρ]	ὑμῶν	καὶ	τῶν
echō	peri	huper	humōn	kai	tōn
I have	for	[on behalf of]	you,	and	the
1706.1 prep	2965.2 name dat fem	2504.1 conj	3607.2 rel-pron nom pl masc	3620.1 partic	3571.14 verb 3pl indic perf act
ἐν	Λαοδικείᾳ,	καὶ	ὅσοι	οὐχ	ʹ ἑωράκασιν
en	Laodikeia	kai	hosoi	ouch	heōrakasin
in	Laodicea,	and	as many as	not	have seen
3571.37 verb 3pl indic perf act	3450.16 art sing neu	4241.1 noun sing neu	1466.2 prs-pron gen 1sing	1706.1 prep	
[ᵇ☆ ἑόρακαν]	τὸ	πρόσωπόν	μου	ἐν	
heorakan	to	prosōpon	mou	en	
[idem]	the	face	my	in	
4418.3 noun dat sing fem	2419.1 conj	3731.28 verb 3pl subj aor pass	3450.13 art nom pl fem	2559.5 noun nom pl fem	
σαρκί,	**2.** ἵνα	παρακληθῶσιν	αἱ	καρδίαι	
sarki	hina	paraklēthōsin	hai	kardiai	
flesh;	that	may be encouraged	the	hearts	
840.1 prs-pron gen pl	4673.5 verb gen pl masc part aor pass	4673.7 verb nom pl masc part aor pass	1706.1 prep		
αὐτῶν,	ʹ συμβιβασθέντων	[ᵃ☆ συμβιβασθέντες]	ἐν		
autōn	sumbibasthentōn	sumbibasthentes	en		
their,	having been united	[idem]	in		
26.3 noun dat sing fem	2504.1 conj	1519.1 prep	3820.1 adj	4009.3 noun acc sing masc	3820.17 adj sing neu
ἀγάπῃ,	καὶ	εἰς	ʹ πάντα	πλοῦτον	[ᵇ☆ πᾶν
agapē	kai	eis	panta	plouton	pan
love,	and	to	all	wealth	[all
4009.1 noun sing masc	3450.10 art gen sing fem	3996.1 noun sing fem	3450.10 art gen sing fem	4757.1 noun gen sing fem	
πλοῦτος]	τῆς	πληροφορίας	τῆς	συνέσεως,	
ploutos	tēs	plērophorias	tēs	suneseōs	
riches]	of the	full assurance	of the	understanding;	
1519.1 prep	1907.4 noun acc sing fem	3450.2 art gen sing	3328.2 noun gen sing neu	3450.2 art gen sing	2296.2 noun gen sing masc
εἰς	ἐπίγνωσιν	τοῦ	μυστηρίου	τοῦ	θεοῦ
eis	epignōsin	tou	mustēriou	tou	theou
to	knowledge	of the	mystery	of the	of God
2504.1 conj	3824.2 noun gen sing masc	2504.1 conj	3450.2 art gen sing	5382.2 name gen masc	1706.1 prep
ʹᶜ καὶ	πατρὸς	καὶ	τοῦ ʹ	Χριστοῦ,	**3.** ἐν
kai	patros	kai	tou	Christou	en
and	of Father	and	of the	Christ;	in
3614.3 rel-pron dat sing	1498.7 verb 3pl indic pres act	3820.7 adj nom pl masc	3450.7 art nom pl masc	2321.5 noun nom pl masc	3450.10 art gen sing fem
ᾧ	εἰσιν	πάντες	οἱ	θησαυροὶ	τῆς
hō	eisin	pantes	hoi	thēsauroi	tēs
whom	are	all	the	treasures	of the
4531.2 noun gen sing fem	2504.1 conj	3450.10 art gen sing fem	1102.2 noun gen sing fem	608.1 adj nom pl masc	3642.17 dem-pron sing neu
σοφίας	καὶ	ʹᵃ τῆς ʹ	γνώσεως	ἀπόκρυφοι.	**4.** Τοῦτο
sophias	kai	tēs	gnōseōs	apokruphoi	Touto
wisdom	and	of the	knowledge	hid.	This

in every Christian's life. In fact, he struggled for them in prayer that God's purpose would be realized in their lives. The English word *agony* comes from the Greek term translated "conflict" in this verse. The language sounds as if he was in perpetual distress over them, and the possibility of their relapse into their former sinful ways brought him dismay and sorrow. Paul's statement also clearly demonstrates his loving concern for believers. He did not want them to stagnate, but to mature in their faith. Many commentators use this verse to prove that Paul did not start the churches in Colossae and Laodicea. Yet Paul had a concern for both churches. Notice that he asked the Colossian believers to pass the epistle along to the Laodicean church.

2:2. Paul began in verse 2 to express the purpose for this struggle in prayer for them. He prefaced his comments with a very strong Greek term (*hina*) often used to preface statements of purpose and usually translated "in order that." First, Paul coveted for them encouragement, comfort, or inner strength. Second, he desired that they be united or "knit together" in love (*agapē*). While error is divisive, true love that emanates from God himself is the motivating force that binds God's people together. Thirdly, he wanted them to have a full knowledge, or constantly increasing knowledge of what it meant to have Christ indwelling them, what Paul labeled here "the mystery of God." It is a marvelous mystery that Christ does indwell His people, but the more we understand God's work in the believers, the clearer this "mystery" becomes. This is an excellent reminder that our knowledge of Christ improves progressively throughout the Christian life. While all Christians "know" Christ because of the living relationship that exists between the Lord and His people, Christian maturity enables them to know Christ in an ever-increasing manner.

2:3. This verse continues the idea and shows why it is so important for believers to progress in their knowledge of Christ as a result of their relationship with Him. The verse contains an obvious reply to the Gnostics who taught a limited and perverted kind of knowledge. It is absolutely necessary for Christians to have a proper knowledge of Christ, because in Him "are hid all the treasures of wisdom and knowledge." The Gnostics taught that knowledge was an end in itself and had to be parceled out through intermediary beings. Paul vehemently rejected this mentality, insisting that a full knowledge of God comes only through Christ. As well as countering Gnostic thought, this statement militates against any religious philosophy that claims people can come to salvation without Christ. As Peter said to the religious hierarchy in Jerusalem, "There is none other name under heaven given among men, whereby we must be saved" (Acts 4:12).

Norlie . . . what great concern, *Confraternity* . . . what great wrestling, *PNT* . . . what bisynesse I haue for you, *Wyclif*.

and [for] them at Laodicea:
and [for] as many as have not seen my face in the flesh: . . . and on behalf of those, *Adams* . . . yes, for all who have never known me personally, *Williams* . . . and whoever have not seen my bodily presence, *Fenton* . . . for all who have never met me, *Phillips*.

2. That their hearts might be comforted: . . . may be consoled, *Rotherham*, *Fenton* . . . may be confirmed, *Alford* . . . may be encouraged, *Williams*, *Adams*, *Phillips*.

being knit together in love: . . . find out more and more how strong are the bonds of Christian love, *Phillips* . . . We want you welded together, *Berkeley* . . . as they are joined together in love, *Adams* . . . and bound together with love, *SEB* . . . being closely united, *Scarlett* . . . united in love, *Sawyer*.

and unto all riches of the full assurance of understanding: . . . leading to, *Adams* . . . and by having attained to the full assurance, *Williams* . . . be ever so richly convinced, *Beck* . . . and all the wealth of the full conviction of reason, *Fenton* . . . for you to grow more certain in your knowledge, *Phillips*.

to the acknowledgment of the mystery of God, and of the Father, and of Christ: . . . that in turn results in, *Adams* . . . in comprehending the secret of God, *Fenton* . . . May they come to a perfect knowledge, *Montgomery* . . . so that they may finally reach the fullest knowledge of the open secret, *Williams* . . . more sure in your grasp of God himself, *Phillips* . . . knowing God's secret—Christ, *SEB*.

3. In whom are hid all the treasures of wisdom and knowledge: . . . secret knowledge, *Fenton* . . . and hidden wisdom are found in Christ, *SEB* . . . in which are stored, *Wilson* . . . are to be found stored up, *TCNT* . . . are concealed, *Concordant*.

4.a.**Txt:** 01ℵ-corr
02A-corr,04C,06D,018K
020L,025P,byz.Weis
Sod
Var: 01ℵ-org,02A-org
03B,Tisc,We/Ho,UBS/✶

4.b.**Txt:** 01ℵ-corr,018K
020L,byz.
Var: 01ℵ-org,02A,03B
04C,06D,025P,33,Lach
Treg,Alf,Word,Tisc
We/Ho,Weis,Sod
UBS/✶

1156.2 conj	2978.1 verb 1sing pres act	2419.1 conj	3231.1 partic	4948.3 indef-pron nom sing	3235.3 num card nom masc
⌜a δὲ ⌝	λέγω,	ἵνα	⌜ μὴ	τις	[b✶ μηδεὶς]
de	legō	hina	mē	tis	mēdeis
and	I say,	that	not	anyone	[no one]

5050.4 prs-pron acc 2pl	3745.1 verb 3sing subj pres mid	1706.1 prep	3947.1 noun dat sing fem	1479.1 conj
ὑμᾶς	παραλογίζηται	ἐν	πιθανολογίᾳ·	5. εἰ
humas	paralogizētai	en	pithanologia	ei
you	may delude	by	persuasive speech.	If

1056.1 conj	2504.1 conj	3450.11 art dat sing fem	4418.3 noun dat sing fem	544.1 verb 1sing indic pres act	233.2 conj	3450.3 art dat sing
γὰρ	καὶ	τῇ	σαρκὶ	ἄπειμι,	ἀλλὰ	τῷ
gar	kai	tē	sarki	apeimi	alla	tō
for	indeed	in the	flesh	I am absent,	yet	in the

4011.3 noun dat sing neu	4713.1 prep	5050.3 prs-pron dat 2pl	1498.2 verb 1sing indic pres act	5299.8 verb nom sing masc part pres act	2504.1 conj
πνεύματι	σὺν	ὑμῖν	εἰμι,	χαίρων	καὶ
pneumati	sun	humin	eimi	chairōn	kai
spirit	with	you	I am,	rejoicing	and

984.12 verb nom sing masc part pres act	5050.2 prs-pron gen 2pl	3450.12 art acc sing fem	4861.2 noun acc sing fem	2504.1 conj	3450.16 art sing neu
βλέπων	ὑμῶν	τὴν	τάξιν,	καὶ	τὸ
blepōn	humōn	tēn	taxin	kai	to
seeing	your	the	order,	and	to the

4584.1 noun sing neu	3450.10 art gen sing fem	1519.1 prep	5382.4 name acc masc	3963.2 noun gen sing fem	5050.2 prs-pron gen 2pl
στερέωμα	τῆς	εἰς	Χριστὸν	πίστεως	ὑμῶν.
stereōma	tēs	eis	Christon	pisteōs	humōn
firmness	the	in	Christ	of faith	your.

5453.1 conj	3631.1 partic	3741.7 verb 2pl indic aor act	3450.6 art acc sing masc	5382.4 name acc masc
6. Ὡς	οὖν	παρελάβετε	τὸν	Χριστὸν
Hōs	oun	parelabete	ton	Christon
As	therefore	you received	the	Christ,

2400.3 name acc masc	3450.6 art acc sing masc	2935.4 noun acc sing masc	1706.1 prep	840.4 prs-pron dat sing	3906.1 verb 2pl pres act
Ἰησοῦν	τὸν	κύριον,	ἐν	αὐτῷ	περιπατεῖτε,
Iēsoun	ton	kurion	en	autō	peripateite
Jesus	the	Lord,	in	him	walk,

4348.1 verb nom pl masc part perf mid	2504.1 conj	2010.5 verb nom pl masc part pres mid	1706.1 prep	840.4 prs-pron dat sing
7. ἐρῥιζωμένοι	καὶ	ἐποικοδομούμενοι	ἐν	αὐτῷ,
errhizōmenoi	kai	epoikodomoumenoi	en	autō
having been rooted	and	being built up	in	him,

7.a.**Txt:** 01ℵ,06D-corr
018K,020L,025P,byz.
Sod
Var: 03B,06D-org,33
Lach,Treg,Tisc,We/Ho
Weis,UBS/✶

7.b.**Txt:** 03B,06D-corr
015H,018K,020L,byz.
We/Ho,Sod
Var: 01ℵ-org,02A,04C
33,sa.Treg,Tisc,Weis
UBS/✶

2504.1 conj	943.5 verb nom pl masc part pres mid	1706.1 prep	3450.11 art dat sing fem	3963.3 noun dat sing fem	2503.1 conj
καὶ	βεβαιούμενοι	⌜a ἐν ⌝	τῇ	πίστει,	καθὼς
kai	bebaioumenoi	en	tē	pistei	kathōs
and	being confirmed	in	the	faith,	even as

1315.23 verb 2pl indic aor pass	3915.8 verb nom pl masc part pres act	1706.1 prep	840.11 prs-pron dat sing fem	1706.1 prep
ἐδιδάχθητε,	περισσεύοντες	⌜b ἐν ⌝	αὐτῇ ⌝	ἐν
edidachthēte	perisseuontes	en	autē	en
you were taught,	abounding	in	it	with

2:4. Fourthly, the apostle was concerned that the Colossians not be deceived with "enticing words" or "fine-sounding arguments" (NIV) or "persuasive speech." Apparently the Gnostics (as are most false teachers) were very adept at deluding people because they majored in persuasive speech. Their "fast talk" was a proof that the art of persuasion, although the height of oratory, can degenerate into trickery.

Paul sincerely hoped the Colossians would remain faithful to the truth of God's Word. They lived in an age when rhetoric was emphasized as a sign of an educated person. Obviously, both the ability to relate a message and having the proper message are extremely important to our effectiveness as Christian workers. One can tell quickly from the writings of the apostle that he not only was a profound writer, but he also knew well the art and science of proper rhetoric. However, he was always careful to depend upon the power of the Holy Spirit. He knew mere human ability could not meet the need of a lost soul (1 Corinthians 2:1-5).

2:5. Paul's desire for the Colossian saints relative to the four items he mentioned in his letter was not dependent upon his physically being with them. In this verse he used two words in a military sense to express his desire that they stand in "order" and in "steadfastness," comparing them to the orderly array of a well-disciplined army. A certain beauty exists in an orderly array whether in a military unit or in something else. A military commander must experience a certain satisfaction from observing his unit at attention.

2:6. Actually, this verse and verse 7 serve both as a conclusion to verses 1-5 and as an introduction to the rest of the chapter. The Colossians and their neighbors had begun their life in Christ, and Paul encouraged them to continue to live in Him. It is not enough to be converted. God wants His children to continue to grow until they reach maturity. This verse beautifully summarizes the total Christian life. It begins when a person accepts the provision God made through the sacrifice of Christ on the cross, and it continues by depending upon that same work of grace. Both occur through faith.

2:7. Paul summarized the manner in which Christians should live by using four Greek participles: (1) "Rooted" comes from a perfect tense participle (*errhizōmenoi*) which normally would be translated "having been rooted" and expresses the initial experience of being connected to Christ, as well as the continuing result of that initial relationship. (2) "Built up" (*epoikodomoumenoi*) shows Paul's change from an agricultural metaphor to one of construction, expressing the idea of allowing God to continue His work of construction in the believer's life. It is very encouraging to know God is not finished with the believer yet, but He patiently continues

4. And this I say, lest any man should beguile you with enticing words: . . . that no one may impose on you, *Noyes* . . . I write like this to prevent you from being led astray by someone or other's attractive arguments, *Phillips* . . . may deceive You with Persuasive speech, *Wilson* . . . that no one may reason you aside with plausible discourse, *Rotherham* . . . may delude you with persuasive speech, *Worrell* . . . deceiue you in loftines of vvordes, *Rheims* . . . by loftiness of words, *Douay* . . . with persuasiveness of speech, *Clementson*.

5. For though I be absent in the flesh, yet am I with you in the spirit: I am not with you in person, *TCNT* . . . though I am a long way away from you in body, in spirit I am by your side, *Phillips* . . . in body, *Douay.*

joying and beholding your order: . . . watching like a proud father, *Phillips.*

and the stedfastness of your faith in Christ: . . . the stability of your faith, *Wilson* . . . and the firm foundation, *Alford* . . . of the solid front which you present through your faith, *TCNT* . . . and the solid structure of your faith towards Christ, *Rotherham.*

6. As ye have therefore received Christ Jesus the Lord, [so] walk ye in him: Now, therefore, just as you have accepted Christ Jesus as your Lord, *Norlie* . . . live your lives in union with him, *TCNT* . . . so go on living in him, *Phillips.*

7. Rooted and built up in him, and stablished in the faith: . . . founded, *Sawyer* . . . May you become stronger and yet stronger in, *Norlie.*

as ye have been taught:

abounding therein with thanksgiving: . . . overflowing with, *Rotherham* . . . may your lives overflow with gratitude! *Norlie* . . . with joy and thankfulness, *Phillips.*

Colossians 2:8

2150.3 noun dat sing fem	984.1 verb 2pl pres act	3231.1 partic	4948.3 indef-pron nom sing	5050.4 prs-pron acc 2pl	1498.40 verb 3sing indic fut act
εὐχαριστίᾳ.	8. βλέπετε	μή	τις	ὑμᾶς	ἔσται
eucharistia	blepete	mē	tis	humas	estai
thanksgiving.	Take heed	not	anyone	you	there shall be

3450.5 art nom sing masc	4663.1 verb nom sing masc part pres act	1217.2 prep	3450.10 art gen sing fem	5221.1 noun gen sing fem
ὁ	συλαγωγῶν	διὰ	τῆς	φιλοσοφίας
ho	sulagōgōn	dia	tēs	philosophias
the	making a prey of	through	the	philosophy

2504.1 conj	2727.7 adj gen sing fem	535.2 noun gen sing fem	2567.3 prep	3450.12 art acc sing fem	3724.2 noun acc sing fem
καὶ	κενῆς	ἀπάτης,	κατὰ	τὴν	παράδοσιν
kai	kenēs	apatēs	kata	tēn	paradosin
and	empty	deceit,	according to	the	tradition

3450.1 art gen pl	442.7 noun gen pl masc	2567.3 prep	3450.17 art pl neu	4598.1 noun pl neu	3450.2 art gen sing
τῶν	ἀνθρώπων,	κατὰ	τὰ	στοιχεῖα	τοῦ
tōn	anthrōpōn	kata	ta	stoicheia	tou
of the	men,	according to	the	elements	of the

2862.2 noun gen sing masc	2504.1 conj	3620.3 partic	2567.3 prep	5382.4 name acc masc	3617.1 conj	1706.1 prep
κόσμου,	καὶ	οὐ	κατὰ	Χριστόν·	9. ὅτι	ἐν
kosmou	kai	ou	kata	Christon	hoti	en
world,	and	not	according to	Christ.	For	in

840.4 prs-pron dat sing	2700.2 verb 3sing indic pres act	3820.17 adj sing neu	3450.16 art sing neu	3998.1 noun sing neu	3450.10 art gen sing fem
αὐτῷ	κατοικεῖ	πᾶν	τὸ	πλήρωμα	τῆς
autō	katoikei	pan	to	plērōma	tēs
him	dwells	all	the	fullness	of the

2297.1 noun gen sing fem	4837.1 adv	2504.1 conj	1498.6 verb 2pl indic pres act	1706.1 prep	840.4 prs-pron dat sing
θεότητος	σωματικῶς,	10. καὶ	ἐστὲ	ἐν	αὐτῷ
theotētos	sōmatikōs	kai	este	en	autō
Godhead	bodily;	and	you are	in	him

3997.30 verb nom pl masc part perf mid	3614.5 rel-pron nom sing masc	1498.4 verb 3sing indic pres act	3450.9 art nom sing fem	2747.1 noun nom sing fem
πεπληρωμένοι·	ὅς	ἐστιν	ἡ	κεφαλὴ
peplērōmenoi	hos	estin	hē	kephalē
having been complete,	who	is	the	head

3820.10 adj gen sing fem	741.2 noun gen sing fem	2504.1 conj	1833.1 noun fem	1706.1 prep	3614.3 rel-pron dat sing
πάσης	ἀρχῆς	καὶ	ἐξουσίας·	11. ἐν	ᾧ
pasēs	archēs	kai	exousias	en	hō
of all	rule	and	authority,	in	whom

2504.1 conj	3919.10 verb 2pl indic aor pass	3921.3 noun dat sing fem	879.2 adj dat sing fem
καὶ	περιετμήθητε	περιτομῇ	ἀχειροποιήτῳ
kai	perietmēthēte	peritomē	acheiropoiētō
also	you were circumcised	with circumcision	not made by hand,

11.a.Txt: 01ℵ-corr 06D-corr,018K,020L byz.
Var: 01ℵ-org,02A,03B 04C,06D-org,025P,33 Gries,Lach,Treg,Alf Word,Tisc,We/Ho,Weis Sod,UBS/☆

1706.1 prep	3450.11 art dat sing fem	551.1 noun dat sing fem	3450.2 art gen sing	4835.2 noun gen sing neu	3450.1 art gen pl
ἐν	τῇ	ἀπεκδύσει	τοῦ	σώματος	⌈ᵃ τῶν
en	tē	apekdusei	tou	sōmatos	tōn
in	the	putting off	of the	body	of the

His work of construction in them. (3) "Stablished" (*bebaioumenoi*), or "being strengthened," refers to making firm or stable, expressing the ultimate purpose God has for working in our lives. (4) "Abounding" (*perisseuontes*) completes the cycle, because everything a Christian does should be permeated with thanksgiving.

Perhaps Paul emphasized the necessity of beginning in Christ and continuing in Christ just before his next message to the Colossians because if they did these two things they would not drift into false doctrine. Continuing to make Christ the central or focal point of the Christian life will serve as a positive preventive from drifting into false teachings.

2:8. This verse begins the main doctrinal section of this epistle. Paul made it very clear to the Colossians that Christ is always central in scriptural doctrine. Verse 8 contains a negative warning to Christians not to allow themselves to be taken captive by a philosophy that does not allow Christ the preeminence.

The term "spoil" in the King James Version sometimes contains the idea of kidnapping. In the original language "philosophy" (*philosophias*) is preceded by a definite article. Thus the reference seems to relate to a particular false teaching, probably gnosticism. In this verse *stoicheia* likely refers to elementary religious teachings (cf. 2:20). (For further discussion of *stoicheia*, see *Overview*, pp.546f.)

2:9. This verse begins the positive side of the matter. While the Gnostics' view represented the fullness of deity as distributed among the angels, Paul was adamant about the fact that all physical manifestation of deity comes only through Christ. In fact, the Greek term for "dwelleth" (*katoikei*) is the same word used in 1:19 and means "permanently dwell." In several places the Bible emphatically states that the essence or nature of God is invisible to humans (John 1:18; Romans 1:20; Colossians 1:15; 1 Timothy 1:17).

2:10. Because of that important fact, believers have all they need in Christ. "Complete" or "fullness" (NIV) comes from a perfect passive participle and literally refers to "having been filled." Because of their relationship to Christ through regeneration, believers have all the completeness they need in Christ.

2:11. The rest of the passage continues a masterful description of just what we do enjoy of this "completeness" or "fullness" in Christ. First, we have received true circumcision, defined here as "putting off of the sinful nature" (NIV). External circumcision occupied a very prominent position under the Old Testament economy (Genesis 17:9-14), but even under it God required that it be accompanied by circumcision of heart (Jeremiah 4:4). Apparently God instituted the rite of circumcision with Abraham as the out-

8. Beware lest any man spoil you through philosophy and vain deceit: Take care, *Wilson* . . . that nobody spoils your faith through intellectualism or high-sounding nonsense, *Phillips* . . . See that no one leads you off as a prey, *Sawyer* . . . some one who will capture you, *TCNT* . . . make you naked by philosophy, *Murdock* . . . drag you away captive, *Montgomery* . . . captures you by the idle fancies of his so-called philosophy, *Williams* . . . make a prey of you...and empty deceit, *Scarlett* . . . and disceatfull vanitie, *Cranmer.*

after the tradition of men, after the rudiments of the world, and not after Christ: . . . according to the instruction of men, *Rotherham* . . . following human tradition, *Williams* . . . and the world's crude notions, *Montgomery* . . . on men's ideas of the nature of the world, and disregards Christ! *Phillips* . . . not according to Christ, *Wilson.*

9. For in him dwelleth all the fulness of the Godhead bodily: For it is in Him that all the fullness of Deity continues to live embodied, *Williams* . . . the Deity bodily, *Wilson* . . . resided substantially in Him, *Scarlett* . . . in a bodily form, *TCNT* . . . corporally, *Rheims.*

10. And ye are complete in him: . . . and ye are filled full in him, *PNT* . . . ye are made full, *ASV* . . . you are in him replenished, *Rheims* . . . through union with Him you too are filled with it, *Williams.*

which is the head of all principality and power: . . . who is the fountainhead of all authority, *Norlie* . . . He is the Head of all principalities and dominions, *Williams.*

11. In whom also ye are circumcised with the circumcision made without hands: . . . through your union with Him you once received, not a hand-performed circumcision, *Williams.*

in putting off the body of the sins of the flesh by the circumcision of Christ: . . . even in putting off your sensual nature,

Colossians 2:12

264.6 noun gen pl fem	3450.10 art gen sing fem	4418.2 noun gen sing fem	1706.1 prep	3450.11 art dat sing fem	3921.3 noun dat sing fem
ἁμαρτιῶν	τῆς	σαρκός,	ἐν	τῇ	περιτομῇ
hamartiōn	tēs	sarkos	en	tē	peritomē
sins	of the	flesh,	in	the	circumcision

3450.2 art gen sing	5382.2 name gen masc	4766.2 verb nom pl masc part aor pass		840.4 prs-pron dat sing	1706.1 prep
τοῦ	Χριστοῦ,	**12.** συνταφέντες		αὐτῷ	ἐν
tou	Christou	suntaphentes		autō	en
of the	Christ;	having been buried with		him	in

12.a.**Txt:** 01ℵ-org,02A 04C,06D-corr2,044,byz. **Var:** p46,01ℵ-corr2,03B 06D-org,010F,012G,6 365,1739,1881

3450.3 art dat sing	902.3 noun dat sing neu	903.4 noun dat sing masc	1706.1 prep	3614.3 rel-pron dat sing
τῷ	βαπτίσματι·	[ᵃ☆ βαπτισμῷ,]	ἐν	ᾧ
tō	baptismati	baptismō	en	hō
the	baptism,	[idem]	in	which

2504.1 conj	4741.2 verb 2pl indic aor pass	1217.2 prep	3450.10 art gen sing fem	3963.2 noun gen sing fem
καὶ	συνηγέρθητε	διὰ	τῆς	πίστεως
kai	sunēgerthēte	dia	tēs	pisteōs
also	you were raised with	through	the	faith

3450.10 art gen sing fem	1737.1 noun gen sing fem	3450.2 art gen sing	2296.2 noun gen sing masc	3450.2 art gen sing	1446.8 verb gen sing masc part aor act
τῆς	ἐνεργείας	τοῦ	θεοῦ	τοῦ	ἐγείραντος
tēs	energeias	tou	theou	tou	egeirantos
of the	working	of	God	the	having raised

12.b.**Txt:** 03B,06D,33 byz.Weis **Var:** 01ℵ,02A,04C 018K,020L,025P,Gries Tisc,We/Ho,Sod,UBS/☆

840.6 prs-pron acc sing masc	1523.2 prep gen	3450.1 art gen pl	3361.2 adj gen pl	2504.1 conj	5050.4 prs-pron acc 2pl
αὐτὸν	ἐκ	ᵇ τῶν	νεκρῶν·	**13.** καὶ	ὑμᾶς
auton	ek	tōn	nekrōn	kai	humas
him	from among	the	dead.	And	you,

13.a.**Txt:** 01ℵ-corr,02A 04C,06D,018K,025P byz.Sod **Var:** 01ℵ-org,03B,020L 33,Treg,Tisc,We/Ho Weis,UBS/☆

3361.7 adj acc pl masc	1498.25 verb acc pl masc part pres act	1706.1 prep	3450.4 art dat pl	3761.5 noun dat pl neu
νεκροὺς	ὄντας	ᵃ ἐν	τοῖς	παραπτώμασιν
nekrous	ontas	en	tois	paraptōmasin
dead	being	in	the	offenses

2504.1 conj	3450.11 art dat sing fem	201.3 noun dat sing fem	3450.10 art gen sing fem	4418.2 noun gen sing fem	5050.2 prs-pron gen 2pl
καὶ	τῇ	ἀκροβυστίᾳ	τῆς	σαρκὸς	ὑμῶν,
kai	tē	akrobustia	tēs	sarkos	humōn
and	in the	uncircumcision	of	flesh	your,

13.b.**Var:** 01ℵ-org,02A 04C,06D,018K,020L,sa.bo. Lach,Treg,Alf,Word Tisc,We/Ho,Weis,Sod UBS/☆

4657.2 verb 3sing indic aor act		4657.1 verb 3sing indic aor act		5050.4 prs-pron acc 2pl
συνεζωοποίησεν		[☆ συνεζωοποίησεν]		[ᵇ☆+ ὑμᾶς]
sunezōopoiēsen		sunezōopoiēsen		humas
he made alive together		[idem]		[you]

4713.1 prep	840.4 prs-pron dat sing	5319.7 verb nom sing masc part aor mid	2231.3 prs-pron dat 1pl	3820.1 adj	3450.17 art pl neu
σὺν	αὐτῷ,	χαρισάμενος	ἡμῖν	πάντα	τὰ
sun	autō	charisamenos	hēmin	panta	ta
with	him,	having forgiven	us	all	the

3761.6 noun pl neu	1797.1 verb nom sing masc part aor act	3450.16 art sing neu	2567.2 prep	2231.2 prs-pron gen 1pl
παραπτώματα·	**14.** ἐξαλείψας	τὸ	καθ᾽	ἡμῶν
paraptōmata	exaleipsas	to	kath'	hēmōn
offenses;	having wiped away	the	against	us

ward manifestation of what God had done inwardly for Abraham. Here Paul labeled circumcision as the breaking of the power of the Adamic nature of a person that takes place at conversion. No longer is the regenerated person a slave to that fallen nature which he possesses from natural birth.

2:12. This verse provides truth very similar to that found in Romans 6, where Paul likened the experience of water baptism to a spiritual death, burial, and resurrection. The water is a symbol of a grave, and the immersion of a believer represents burial. When he is brought out of the water again, it represents his "resurrection" to the new life. It is a picture of dying to the old life of sin, taking a public stand that he is dead to the old life. He has received a new nature, he is a child of God. He will live a different kind of life. It should mean something more than a mere ritual. The Holy Spirit has baptized the new believer into the body of Christ (1 Corinthians 12:13). Water baptism is an outward sign of an inward work. Dead to the old life and alive unto God, the believer is to walk in "newness of life" (Romans 6:4).

2:13. Paul here gave one of the best definitions of death that a person can discover anywhere in the Scriptures or elsewhere. Death basically relates to separation. Paul reminded the Colossians of their state of spiritual death or separation from God previous to their conversion to Christ. He explained it as being dead in their sinful practices, because the circumcision of which he wrote in verse 11 had not taken place in their lives. But God had raised them from the dead spiritually, so they were enjoying true resurrection, or spiritual resurrection, as well as true forgiveness. They had been separated from God because of sin, but now, through Jesus' death, there was no longer any separation. They were close to Him.

2:14. Not only does God forgive, but He also forgets the charges against the one forgiven. Because of His omniscience God does not "forget" in the same way humans often speak of forgetting. Rather, He removes the charges and does not hold them against the one forgiven any longer. The entire Mosaic law, which Paul described as "the handwriting of ordinances," presents a condemnation of the entire human race. The law of Moses points out how God expects people to live, but Christ is the only one who fulfilled all the requirements of the Old Testament law. Because He fulfilled the requirement by taking the penalty of sin upon himself, God accepts the righteousness of Christ in the believer's behalf.

Ephesians 2:15 contains a statement very similar to the one in this verse. "Nailing it to the cross" (NIV) shows how truly Jesus identified with sinners, being made sin for us (2 Corinthians 5:21). It was customary under Roman law to write out a copy of the law

Montgomery . . . in stripping you of your lower nature, *Williams* . . . the getting rid of the tyranny of the earthly body, *TCNT* . . . you were set free from your sinful nature, *Norlie* . . . being set free from the sins of the flesh by virtue of, *Phillips*.

12. Buried with him in baptism: . . . for you were buried, *Williams* . . . being jointly-buried, *Rotherham* . . . just as in baptism you shared in his death, *Phillips*.

wherein also ye are risen with [him] through the faith of the operation of God: . . . sharing the miracle of rising again to new life—and all this because you have faith in, *Phillips* . . . and raised to life with Him through your faith in the power of God, *Williams* . . . in the working of God, *Confraternity* . . . through a belief of the energy of God, *Scarlett* . . . in the energy of that God, *Montgomery*.

who hath raised him from the dead:

13. And you, being dead in your sins and the uncircumcision of your flesh: . . . dead in the offenses, *Rheims* . . . of your sensual nature, *Montgomery* . . . who were spiritually dead because of, *Phillips* . . . although you were dead through your shortcomings and were physically uncircumcised, *Williams* . . . and your uncircumcised nature, *TCNT*.

hath he quickened together with him, having forgiven you all trespasses: . . . hath he given life, *Noyes* . . . God made you live again through fellowship with Christ. He graciously forgave us all our shortcomings, *Williams* . . . He pardoned all our sins! *TCNT* . . . having freely pardoned All our offences, *Wilson* . . . pardoning you al offenses, *Rheims* . . . forgiven us all our sins, *Murdock*.

14. Blotting out the handwriting of ordinances that was against us, which was contrary to us: He cancelled the bond (consisting of

5334.1 noun sing neu	3450.4 art dat pl	1372.3 noun dat pl neu	3614.16 rel-pron sing neu	1498.34 verb sing indic imperf act
χειρόγραφον	τοῖς	δόγμασιν,	ὃ	ἦν
cheirographon	tois	dogmasin	ho	ēn
handwriting	in the	decrees,	which	was

5064.2 adj sing neu	2231.3 prs-pron dat 1pl	2504.1 conj	840.15 prs-pron sing neu	142.19 verb 3sing indic perf act	1523.2 prep gen
ὑπεναντίον	ἡμῖν,	καὶ	αὐτὸ	ἦρκεν	ἐκ
hupenantion	hēmin	kai	auto	ērken	ek
against	us,	also	it	he has taken	out of

3450.2 art gen sing	3189.4 adj gen sing neu	4197.1 verb nom sing masc part aor act	840.15 prs-pron sing neu	3450.3 art dat sing	4567.3 noun dat sing masc
τοῦ	μέσου,	προσηλώσας	αὐτὸ	τῷ	σταυρῷ,
tou	mesou	prosēlōsas	auto	tō	staurō
the	midst,	having nailed	it	to the	cross;

550.1 verb nom sing masc part aor mid	3450.15 art acc pl fem	741.7 noun acc pl fem	2504.1 conj	3450.15 art acc pl fem
15. ἀπεκδυσάμενος	τὰς	ἀρχὰς	καὶ	τὰς
apekdusamenos	tas	archas	kai	tas
having stripped	the	rulers	and	the

1833.1 noun fem	1160.1 verb 3sing indic aor act	1706.1 prep	3816.3 noun dat sing fem	2335.2 verb nom sing masc part aor act
ἐξουσίας	ἐδειγμάτισεν	ἐν	παῤῥησίᾳ,	θριαμβεύσας
exousias	edeigmatisen	en	parrhēsia	thriambeusas
authorities,	he made a show	with	openness,	having led in triumph

840.8 prs-pron acc pl masc	1706.1 prep	840.4 prs-pron dat sing	3231.1 partic	3631.1 partic	4948.3 indef-pron nom sing
αὐτοὺς	ἐν	αὐτῷ.	16. Μὴ	οὖν	τις
autous	en	autō	Mē	oun	tis
them	in	it.	Not	therefore	anyone

16.a.Txt: 01ℵ,02A,04C 06D,018K,020L,025P etc.byz.Tisc **Var:** 03B,bo.Alf,We/Ho Weis,Sod,UBS/✛

5050.4 prs-pron acc 2pl	2892.7 verb 3sing impr pres act	1706.1 prep	1028.3 noun dat sing fem	2211.1 conj	2504.1 conj	1706.1 prep
ὑμᾶς	κρινέτω	ἐν	βρώσει	⌐ ἢ	[ᵃ✛ καὶ]	ἐν
humas	krinetō	en	brōsei	ē	kai	en
you	let judge	in	food	or	[and]	in

4072.2 noun dat sing fem	2211.1 conj	1706.1 prep	3183.3 noun dat sing fem	1844.2 noun gen sing fem	2211.1 conj	3424.1 noun gen sing fem
πόσει,	ἢ	ἐν	μέρει	ἑορτῆς	ἢ	⌐ νουμηνίας
posei	ē	en	merei	heortēs	ē	noumēnias
drink,	or	in	respect	of feast,	or	new moon,

16.b.Txt: 01ℵ,02A,04C 06D,018K,020L,025P byz.Tisc,Sod **Var:** 03B,Lach,Treg We/Ho,Weis,UBS/✛

3363.1 noun gen sing fem	2211.1 conj	4378.4 noun gen pl neu	3614.17 rel-pron pl neu	1498.4 verb 3sing indic pres act
[ᵇ✛ νεομηνίας]	ἢ	σαββάτων·	17. ἃ	ἐστιν
neomēnias	ē	sabbatōn	ha	estin
[idem]	or	sabbaths,	which	are

4494.1 noun nom sing fem	3450.1 art gen pl	3165.11 verb gen pl part pres act	3450.16 art sing neu	1156.2 conj	4835.1 noun sing neu
σκιὰ	τῶν	μελλόντων,	τὸ	δὲ	σῶμα
skia	tōn	mellontōn	to	de	sōma
a shadow	of the	coming;	the	but	body

3450.2 art gen sing	5382.2 name gen masc	3235.3 num card nom masc	5050.4 prs-pron acc 2pl	2574.1 verb 3sing impr pres act
τοῦ	Χριστοῦ.	18. μηδεὶς	ὑμᾶς	καταβραβευέτω
tou	Christou	mēdeis	humas	katabrabeuetō
of the	Christ.	No one	you	let defraud of the prize,

that a criminal had broken and nail that inscription above the person's head on the cross on which he was impaled. Sometimes the placard also contained a description of the offense of the person being crucified.

2:15. This verse carries further the explanation of the believer's completeness in Christ by describing the true freedom Christians enjoy as a result of being in Christ. Satan took advantage of mankind's helpless condition. Therefore, the drama of the Cross involves spiritual beings as well as human beings. By His wonderful sacrifice, Christ not only released His people from the guilt of sin and also its dominion.

The language used here suggests the homecoming parade called a triumph that was accorded a victorious Roman general who had conquered a foreign land (2 Corinthians 2:14). Just as the Roman general made a public spectacle of his enemies, Christ made a public spectacle of Satan and all his forces.

2:16. Not only do people become complete in Christ, but they also stay complete in Christ. The prohibition here, because it is a present active imperative form of the verb, probably prohibits the continuation of an action, so it could be translated: "Stop letting anyone judge you." The Colossians apparently were listening to false ideas and as a result were straying from their completeness in Christ. Because Christ had freed them from their former bondage to the requirements of the Mosaic law, they were to resist any attempt to ensnare them in a new bondage to legalistic requirements. They were told to stop allowing the use of the list of ceremonial matters that followed Paul's warning as a basis for judging their standing before God.

Commentators vary as to whether the regulations listed in verse 16 refer to the dietetic injunctions of the Mosaic law or to a form of asceticism taught and practiced by the Colossian Gnostics. Probably both are true. Jesus taught that foods themselves are neither moral nor immoral (Mark 7:18,19). "Holyday" no doubt refers to the annual Jewish feasts, and "new moon" to the monthly Jewish celebration held in connection with their lunar calendar. The "sabbath" was a weekly festival held from sundown Friday until sundown Saturday.

2:17. Paul clarified the reason for not allowing such matters to be a basis for judgment concerning their standing in Christ. Such things were only a shadow (Hebrews 10:1) of what was to come. The transitory items should be discarded in favor of the "body" or reality they now knew in Christ.

2:18. For the believer to allow anyone to lead him away from his completeness in Christ could "beguile" or rob him of his reward.

rules and regulations), *TCNT* . . . He freely wiped out our law-breaking and left out the unreasoning complaints written against us, *Klingensmith.*

and took it out of the way, nailing it to his cross: . . . and took it away out of the midst, *Rotherham* . . . and has removed it from the midst, having nailed it, *Wilson* . . . fastening it to the cross, *Douay.*

15. [And] having spoiled principalities and powers: Disarming, *Confraternity* . . . having disarmed, *Noyes.*

he made a show of them openly, triumphing over them in it: He made an example of them openly, *Clementson* . . . made a public exhibition of them, *Wilson* . . . held them up to open contempt when he celebrated his triumph over them on the cross! *TCNT* . . . and led them captive in triumph, *Noyes* . . . celebrating a triumph over them thereby, *Rotherham.*

16. Let no man therefore judge you in meat, or in drink: . . . judge you in eating, *Alford* . . . therefore rule you as regards eating, *PNT.*

or in respect of an holyday, or of the new moon, or of the sabbath [days]: . . . of a Festival, *Wilson.*

17. Which are a shadow of things to come: . . . of the future things, *Wilson.*

but the body [is] of Christ: . . . the substance is in the Christ, *TCNT.*

18. Let no man beguile you of your reward: . . . seduce you, *Douay* . . . cheat you, *Confraternity* . . . defraud you of your prize, *Alford* . . . rob you of your prize, *Clementson.*

Colossians 2:19

2286.12 verb nom sing masc part pres act	1706.1 prep	4863.2 noun dat sing fem	2504.1 conj	2333.3 noun dat sing fem	3450.1 art gen pl
θέλων	ἐν	ταπεινοφροσύνῃ	καὶ	θρησκείᾳ	τῶν
thelōn	en	tapeinophrosunē	kai	thrēskeia	tōn
doing will	in	humility	and	worship	of the

32.6 noun gen pl masc	3614.17 rel-pron pl neu	3231.1 partic	3571.11 verb 3sing indic perf act	3571.36 verb 3sing indic perf act
ἀγγέλων,	ἃ	⌐a μὴ ⌐	⌐ ἑώρακεν ⌐	[✱ ἑώρακεν]
angelōn,	ha	mē	heōraken	heōraken
angels,	things which	not	he has seen	[idem]

1674.1 verb nom sing masc part pres act	1488.1 adv	5284.4 verb nom sing masc part pres mid	5097.3 prep	3450.2 art gen sing	3426.2 noun gen sing masc
ἐμβατεύων,	εἰκῇ	φυσιούμενος	ὑπὸ	τοῦ	νοὸς
embateuōn	eikē	phusioumenos	hupo	tou	noos
inquiring into,	vainly	being puffed up	by	the	mind

3450.10 art gen sing fem	4418.2 noun gen sing fem	840.3 prs-pron gen sing		2504.1 conj	3620.3 partic	2875.7 verb nom sing masc part pres act
τῆς	σαρκὸς	αὐτοῦ,	19. καὶ	οὐ	κρατῶν
tēs	sarkos	autou,	kai	ou	kratōn
of the	flesh	his,	and	not	holding fast

3450.12 art acc sing fem	2747.4 noun acc sing fem	1523.1 prep gen	3614.2 rel-pron gen sing	3820.17 adj sing neu	3450.16 art sing neu	4835.1 noun sing neu
τὴν	κεφαλήν,	ἐξ	οὗ	πᾶν	τὸ	σῶμα
tēn	kephalēn,	ex	hou	pan	to	sōma
the	head,	from	whom	all	to	body,

1217.2 prep	3450.1 art gen pl	853.2 noun gen pl fem	2504.1 conj	4736.4 noun gen pl masc	2007.3 verb sing neu part pres mid
διὰ	τῶν	ἁφῶν	καὶ	συνδέσμων	ἐπιχορηγούμενον
dia	tōn	haphōn	kai	sundesmōn	epichorēgoumenon
by	the	joints	and	bands	being supplied

2504.1 conj	4673.4 verb sing neu part pres mid	831.1 verb 3sing indic pres act	3450.12 art acc sing fem	832.1 noun acc sing fem
καὶ	συμβιβαζόμενον,	αὔξει	τὴν	αὔξησιν
kai	sumbibazomenon,	auxei	tēn	auxēsin
and	being joined together,	increases	with the	increase

3450.2 art gen sing	2296.2 noun gen sing masc	1479.1 conj	3631.1 partic	594.12 verb 2pl indic aor act	4713.1 prep
τοῦ	θεοῦ.	20. Εἰ	⌐a οὖν ⌐	ἀπεθάνετε	σὺν
tou	theou.	Ei	oun	apethanete	sun
of God.		If	then	you died	with

3450.3 art dat sing	5382.3 name dat masc	570.3 prep	3450.1 art gen pl	4598.2 noun gen pl neu	3450.2 art gen sing
⌐b τῷ ⌐	Χριστῷ	ἀπὸ	τῶν	στοιχείων	τοῦ
tō	Christō	apo	tōn	stoicheiōn	tou
the	Christ	from	the	elements	of the

2862.2 noun gen sing masc	4949.9 intr-pron sing neu	5453.1 conj	2180.13 verb nom pl masc part pres act	1706.1 prep	2862.3 noun dat sing masc
κόσμου,	τί	ὡς	ζῶντες	ἐν	κόσμῳ
kosmou,	ti	hōs	zōntes	en	kosmō
world,	why	as if	living	in	world

1373.1 verb 2pl indic pres mid		3231.1 partic	674.12 verb 2sing subj aor mid	3234.1 adv
δογματίζεσθε·		21. Μὴ	ἅψῃ	μηδὲ
dogmatizesthe		Mē	hapsē	mēde
do you subject yourselves to decrees?		Not	touch,	Not

18.a.Txt: 01ℵ-corr,04C
06D-corr,018K,020L
025P,byz.
Var: p46,01ℵ-org,02A
03B,06D-org,016I,33,sa.
bo.Treg,Alf,Tisc,We/Ho
Weis,Sod,UBS/✱

20.a.Txt: 01ℵ-org,byz.
Var: 01ℵ-corr,02A,03B
04C,06D,018K,020L
025P,Gries,Lach,Treg
Alf,Word,Tisc,We/Ho
Weis,Sod,UBS/✱

20.b.Txt: Steph
Var: 01ℵ,02A,03B,04C
06D,018K,020L,025P
byz.Gries,Lach,Treg,Alf
Word,Tisc,We/Ho,Weis
Sod,UBS/✱

The imperative verb used in this verse ((*katabrabeuetō*) is translated best in the New American Standard Bible as "Let no one keep defrauding you of your prize." Seemingly, Paul was encouraging the Colossians not to allow anyone to divert them with false teachings, because doing so would cause them to waste precious time that should be used in making spiritual progress, progress which ultimately would bring them reward at the judgment of believers.

Normally Paul described humility as a virtue; consequently, here it must be a reference to false humility. Just what is the connection between false humility and the worship of angels? Perhaps this can best be answered by looking at the approach some people take toward the Lord. They feel they are too sinful and too unworthy to go directly to the Lord, therefore they must go through some intermediary being. This attitude may be very pious and may represent humility, but it often expresses a subtle kind of pride. (Cf. *Overview*, pp.544-546 for a discussion of angel worship.)

2:19. According to Paul's continued emphasis, the basic problem of that person related to "not holding the Head," or to losing "connection with the Head" (NIV), an obvious reference to Christ. This phrase stresses the necessity of a continuous relationship with Jesus, the One who will cause every part of the Body to function properly as it remains connected to Him (Ephesians 4:15,16).

2:20. In concluding the matter, the apostle Paul summarized the issue of completeness in Christ by warning the Colossians against being led back into the basic principles of the world; he used the same term (*stoicheia*) in verse 8. It is used in 2 Peter 3:10 of the basic elements of the physical universe and in Hebrews 5:12 of the elementary truths of the Scriptures. It refers to anything in a row or series, like the letters of an alphabet.

The "if" in verse 20 could be translated "since." In other words, since they had rejected the way of the world in which they had lived before their conversion to Christ, why after being *in Christ* would they want to live by the world's standards? The world's rules or dogmas are based on the false idea that salvation can be obtained by "doing something" and often amounts to a list of negatives. Strangely enough, many times non-Christians accuse Christians of being negative, when actually the opposite is true.

Christianity does not consist of a list of "do's and don'ts." It begins with the positive step of committing one's life to Jesus Christ and gaining a relationship with Him. From the moment of conversion the Holy Spirit indwells the believer. Becoming a follower of Christ makes the grace and mercy of God available to that person. A plethora of spiritual benefits, including the fullness of the Holy Spirit, become available to the believer. In the process of giving these benefits to the Christian, God also removes undesirable habits from him. Salvation certainly does not come to an individual merely by "giving up" something.

in a voluntary humility and worshipping of angels: . . . by persuading you to make yourselves "humble" and fall down and worship angels, *Phillips* . . . and religion of Angels, *Rheims.*

intruding into those things which he hath not seen, vainly puffed up by his fleshly mind: . . . defraud you as an umpire, *Williams* . . . speculating about the things, *Worrell* . . . prying into things, *Wilson* . . . dwelling in the things which he hath seen, *ASV* . . . inflated by an unspiritual imagination, *Phillips* . . . speculates about visions he has had, and is proud in his sensual mind, *Norlie* . . . is vainly inflated in his fleshly mind, *Murdock* . . . by their merely human intellect, *TCNT* . . . by his mere human mind, *Confraternity* . . . by his material mind, *Montgomery.*

19. And not holding the Head: It is from the head alone, *Phillips.*

from which all the body by joints and bands having nourishment ministered, and knit together: . . . by means of the arteries, *PNT* . . . and compacted together, *Wilson.*

increaseth with the increase of God: . . . grows with a divine growth, *TCNT, Montgomery* . . . with a growth that God produces, *Williams* . . . is nourished and built up and grows according to God's laws of growth, *Phillips* . . . wrought by God, *Noyes.*

20. Wherefore if ye be dead with Christ from the rudiments of the world: . . . you are dead to the principles of this world's life, *Phillips* . . . from the elements, *Panin* . . . to worldly ways of looking at things, *Norlie.*

why, as though living in the world, are ye subject to ordinances: . . . why do you now ...submit to its rules, *Norlie* . . . to such rules as, *TCNT* . . . are ye submitting to decrees, *Rotherham* . . . submit yourselves to dogmatisms founded on teachings and doctrines of men, *Montgomery.*

Colossians 2:22

1083.3 verb 2sing subj aor mid	3234.1 adv	2322.1 verb 2sing subj aor act	3614.17 rel-pron pl neu	1498.4 verb 3sing indic pres act
γεύσῃ	μηδὲ	θίγῃς·	22. ἅ	ἔστιν
geusē	mēde	thigēs	ha	estin
taste,	Neither	handle,	which things	are

3820.1 adj	1519.1 prep	5193.4 noun acc sing fem	3450.11 art dat sing fem	665.1 noun dat sing fem	2567.3 prep
πάντα	εἰς	φθορὰν	τῇ	ἀποχρήσει·	κατὰ
panta	eis	phthoran	tē	apochrēsei	kata
all	unto	corruption	in the	using,	according to

3450.17 art pl neu	1762.1 noun pl neu	2504.1 conj	1313.1 noun fem	3450.1 art gen pl	442.7 noun gen pl masc
τὰ	ἐντάλματα	καὶ	διδασκαλίας	τῶν	ἀνθρώπων·
ta	entalmata	kai	didaskalias	tōn	anthrōpōn
the	injunctions	and	teachings	of the	men,

3610.6 rel-pron nom pl neu	1498.4 verb 3sing indic pres act	3030.4 noun acc sing masc	3173.1 conj	2174.15 verb part pres act
23. ἅτινά	ἔστιν	λόγον	μὲν	ἔχοντα
hatina	estin	logon	men	echonta
which	are	an appearance	indeed	having

4531.2 noun gen sing fem	1706.1 prep	1472.1 noun dat sing fem	1472.2 noun dat sing fem	2504.1 conj
σοφίας	ἐν	⸀ ἐθελοθρησκείᾳ	[☆ ἐθελοθρησκίᾳ]	καὶ
sophias	en	ethelothrēskeia	ethelothrēskia	kai
of wisdom	in	voluntary worship	[idem]	and

4863.2 noun dat sing fem	2504.1 conj	850.1 noun dat sing fem	4835.2 noun gen sing neu
ταπεινοφροσύνῃ	⸀a καὶ ⸀	ἀφειδίᾳ	σώματος,
tapeinophrosunē	kai	apheidia	sōmatos,
humility	and	unsparing treatment	of body,

23.a.**Txt**: 01א,02A,04C 06D-org,010F,012G 015H,044,byz. **Var**: p46,03B,1739

3620.2 partic	1706.1 prep	4940.3 noun dat sing fem	4948.2 indef-pron dat sing	4242.1 prep	4000.1 noun acc sing fem	3450.10 art gen sing fem
οὐκ	ἐν	τιμῇ	τινι	πρὸς	πλησμονὴν	τῆς
ouk	en	timē	tini	pros	plēsmonēn	tēs
not	in	honor	a certain	for	satisfaction	of the

4418.2 noun gen sing fem	1479.1 conj	3631.1 partic	4741.2 verb 2pl indic aor pass	3450.3 art dat sing
σαρκός.	3:1. Εἰ	οὖν	συνηγέρθητε	τῷ
sarkos	Ei	oun	sunēgerthēte	tō
flesh.	If	therefore	you were raised with	the

5382.3 name dat masc	3450.17 art pl neu	504.1 adv	2195.1 verb 2pl pres act	3619.1 adv	3450.5 art nom sing masc
Χριστῷ,	τὰ	ἄνω	ζητεῖτε,	οὗ	ὁ
Christō	ta	anō	zēteite	hou	ho
Christ,	the things	above	seek,	where	the

5382.1 name nom masc	1498.4 verb 3sing indic pres act	1706.1 prep	1182.5 adj dat sing fem	3450.2 art gen sing	2296.2 noun gen sing masc
Χριστός	ἔστιν	ἐν	δεξιᾷ	τοῦ	θεοῦ
Christos	estin	en	dexia	tou	theou
Christ	is	at	right hand	of the	of God

2493.6 verb nom sing masc part pres mid	3450.17 art pl neu	504.1 adv	5262.1 verb 2pl pres act	3231.1 partic	3450.17 art pl neu
καθήμενος·	2. τὰ	ἄνω	φρονεῖτε,	μὴ	τὰ
kathēmenos	ta	anō	phroneite	mē	ta
sitting:	the things	above	mind,	not	the things

2:21. Paul made it clear that nonbelievers are the negative ones. Non-Christians are the ones who mistakenly think salvation comes to an individual who does not do certain things or supposedly "gives up" certain habits. Paul summarized this kind of religious approach very accurately when he wrote, "Touch not; taste not; handle not." Asceticism is not true holiness.

2:22. Besides, these things perish with use. Everything finally wears out. Furthermore, these dogmas are purely of human invention. Before drawing a conclusion that the apostle Paul was a very liberal man, the first 17 verses of chapter 3 of this letter need to be studied. He definitely believed in proper Christian standards, but standards that come from God, not standards that originate in the human mind. So, Paul's final appraisal of asceticism was that it is a dismal failure. One may punish the human body to the limit and still have a soul filled with ungodly lusts. Paul believed in the necessity of controlling the human body, but he warned that the real danger of asceticism is its avoidance of the real problem: that of dealing with the sinful, Adamic nature.

2:23. If a person keeps his body under subjection and gloats over the fact, thinking he is superior to other Christians, he has become the modern counterpart of a Pharisee. In this verse the apostle summarized the activities of people who fail to accept Jesus as their Head, and instead attempt to satisfy God through their own efforts. First, he emphasized that their approach may seem to be a wise one. As a result, they probably will receive commendation from many people for the good moral lives they live. Secondly, they practice "will-worship" or "self-imposed worship" (NIV) rather than accepting the pattern God has given in the Scriptures. Thirdly, Paul accused these individuals of a "false humility" (NIV). So, instead of developing a scriptural humility, these people substituted a self-manufactured one that glorified self, not God. Fourthly, Paul castigated these false teachers "neglecting of the body" as being ineffective relative to controlling the "satisfying of the flesh" or relative to "restraining sensual indulgence" (NIV). Genuine humility brings glory to God.

3:1. The Bible teaches true holiness and very clearly tells how to obtain it. It begins with the believer continuously centering his interest in Christ. If a person has truly been converted he is enjoying the resurrection life of Christ. Christ not only is the Author of his new life, but the constant source of it. The phrase "the right hand of God" indicates the position of supreme authority; so Christ, not some angel, must be the focal point for a proper system of ethics.

3:2. "Set your affection" refers to a continuous experience and definitely denotes the place a person's will has relative to true ho-

21. (Touch not; taste not; handle not: Don't touch this, Don't taste that and Don't handle the other? *Phillips.*

22. Which all are to perish with the using;): . . . referred to cease to exist, *TCNT* . . . are consumed, *Wilson* . . . all perysshe thorow the very abuse, *Cranmer* . . . will all pass away after use! *Phillips.*
after the commandments and doctrines of men?: . . . the precepts and teachings of men? *Clementson* . . . these purely human prohibitions, *Phillips.*

23. Which things have indeed a show of wisdom in will worship: Which have an appearance of, *Sawyer* . . . shevv of vvisedom in superstition, *Rheims* . . . in Self-devised worship, *Wilson* . . . in a self-devised religious observance, *Clementson.*
and humility, and neglecting of the body: . . . self-abasement and self-control of the body, *Norlie* . . . and humblenes, *Geneva* . . . and harsh treatment of the body, *TCNT* . . . and severe treatment of, *Worrell* . . . and severity to the body, *Noyes.*
not in any honour to the satisfying of the flesh: . . . in no respect for the surfeiting, *Sawyer* . . . but are of no real value against the indulgence of our earthly nature, *TCNT* . . . not of any value for perfecting of the flesh, *PNT* . . . lead to the full gratification of, *Confraternity* . . . for a Gratification of the flesh, *Wilson.*

1. If ye then be risen with Christ:
seek those things which are above: . . . reach out for the highest gifts of Heaven, *Phillips.*
where Christ sitteth on the right hand of God: . . . where your master reigns in power, *Phillips.*

2. Set your affection on things above: Fix your thoughts, *TCNT* . . . Set your mind, *ASV* . . . Mind the things, *Wilson* . . . employ your minds, *Sawyer* . . . Keep thinking of the things, *Worrell.*

1894.3 prep	3450.10 art gen sing fem	1087.2 noun gen sing fem	594.12 verb 2pl indic aor act	1056.1 conj	2504.1 conj	3450.9 art nom sing fem
ἐπὶ	τῆς	γῆς·	**3.** ἀπεθάνετε	γάρ,	καὶ	ἡ
epi	tēs	gēs	apethanete	gar	kai	hē
on	the	earth;	you died	for,	and	the

2205.1 noun nom sing fem	5050.2 prs-pron gen 2pl	2900.7 verb 3sing indic perf mid	4713.1 prep	3450.3 art dat sing	5382.3 name dat masc
ζωὴ	ὑμῶν	κέκρυπται	σὺν	τῷ	Χριστῷ
zōē	humōn	kekruptai	sun	tō	Christō
life	your	has been hid	with	the	Christ

1706.1 prep	3450.3 art dat sing	2296.3 noun dat sing masc	3615.1 conj	3450.5 art nom sing masc	5382.1 name nom masc
ἐν	τῷ	θεῷ·	**4.** ὅταν	ὁ	Χριστὸς
en	tō	theō	hotan	ho	Christos
in	to	God.	When	the	Christ

4.a.Txt: 03B,06D-corr1 015H,sa.byz. **Var:** p46,01ℵ,04C 06D-org,010F,012G 025P,044,33,81,104 365,945,1881,bo.

5157.12 verb 3sing subj aor pass	3450.9 art nom sing fem	2205.1 noun nom sing fem	2231.2 prs-pron gen 1pl	5050.2 prs-pron gen 2pl
φανερωθῇ,	ἡ	ζωὴ	⌐ ἡμῶν,	[a✶ ὑμῶν,]
phanerōthē	hē	zōē	hēmōn	humōn
may be manifested	the	life	our,	[your,]

4966.1 adv	2504.1 conj	5050.1 prs-pron nom 2pl	4713.1 prep	840.4 prs-pron dat sing	5157.21 verb 2pl indic fut pass	1706.1 prep
τότε	καὶ	ὑμεῖς	σὺν	αὐτῷ	φανερωθήσεσθε	ἐν
tote	kai	humeis	sun	autō	phanerōthēsesthe	en
then	also	you	with	him	shall be manifested	in

5.a.Txt: 01ℵ-corr,02A 04C-corr,06D,018K 020L,025P,byz.it.bo. **Var:** 01ℵ-org,03B 04C-org,33,Treg,Alf Tisc,We/Ho,Weis,Sod UBS/✶

1385.3 noun dat sing fem	3362.1 verb 2pl impr aor act	3631.1 partic	3450.17 art pl neu	3166.2 noun pl neu	5050.2 prs-pron gen 2pl
δόξῃ.	**5.** Νεκρώσατε	οὖν	τὰ	μέλη	⌐a ὑμῶν ⌐
doxē	Nekrōsate	oun	ta	melē	humōn
glory.	Put to death	therefore	the	members	your

3450.17 art pl neu	1894.3 prep	3450.10 art gen sing fem	1087.2 noun gen sing fem	4061.4 noun acc sing fem	165.4 noun acc sing fem
τὰ	ἐπὶ	τῆς	γῆς,	πορνείαν,	ἀκαθαρσίαν,
ta	epi	tēs	gēs	porneian	akatharsian
the	on	the	earth,	fornication,	uncleanness,

3669.2 noun sing neu	1924.4 noun acc sing fem	2527.5 adj acc sing fem	2504.1 conj	3450.12 art acc sing fem	3984.4 noun acc sing fem
πάθος,	ἐπιθυμίαν	κακήν,	καὶ	τὴν	πλεονεξίαν,
pathos	epithumian	kakēn	kai	tēn	pleonexian
passion,	desire	evil,	and	the	covetousness,

3610.3 rel-pron nom sing fem	1498.4 verb 3sing indic pres act	1485.1 noun nom sing fem	1485.4 noun nom sing fem
ἥτις	ἐστὶν	⌐ εἰδωλολατρεία,	[✶ εἰδωλολατρία,]
hētis	estin	eidōlolatreia	eidōlolatria
which	is	idolatry.	[idem]

1217.1 prep	3614.17 rel-pron pl neu	2048.34 verb 3sing indic pres mid	3450.9 art nom sing fem	3572.1 noun nom sing fem	3450.2 art gen sing
6. δι'	ἃ	ἔρχεται	ἡ	ὀργὴ	τοῦ
di'	ha	erchetai	hē	orgē	tou
On account of	which things	comes	the	wrath	

6.a.Txt: 01ℵ,02A,04C 06D,015H,016I,018K 020L,025P,33,byz.it.bo. Sod **Var:** p46,03B,sa.Treg Alf,Tisc,We/Ho,Weis UBS/✶

2296.2 noun gen sing masc	1894.3 prep	3450.8 art acc pl masc	5048.9 noun acc pl masc	3450.10 art gen sing fem	539.1 noun gen sing fem
θεοῦ	⌐a ἐπὶ	τοὺς	υἱοὺς	τῆς	ἀπειθείας· ⌐
theou	epi	tous	huious	tēs	apeitheias
of God	upon	the	sons	of the	disobedience.

liness. God does not force His will upon people to make them conduct their lives in complete accordance with His plan. The basis for this new style of life comes from heaven itself, the same place from which the new birth originated (John 3:3). The same One who makes this new birth possible also makes a new standard of life possible. Christians are obligated to judge everything by the standards of this new life.

3:3. This is possible because they have died to the old order, to the world's way of thinking and doing. "Dead" comes from the Greek word *apethanete* that relates to a definite act, so believers are "hid with Christ in God" or live by God's power.

3:4. Verse 4 contains another very important reason for the Christian to constantly center his interests on Christ. One day He will return to receive His people unto himself. The Greek word used here for "appear" (*phanerōthē*) contains the idea of *manifestation*. At that time Christ will display to the world that there is only one way of salvation, through His sacrifice on the cross. Furthermore, there is only one way of true holiness: for the believer to allow the life of Christ to be manifested through him.

3:5. This verse gives another of the paradoxes, or seeming contradictions, in Paul's writings. He had just told the Colossians (verse 3) that they had "died," but in verse 5 he tells them to "mortify" or "put to death" (NIV) their "members which are upon the earth" or "whatever belongs to your earthly nature" (NIV).

Because Christ is the focal point or center of the Christian's life, he can depend upon His power to help him overcome the sinful nature with which he was born. Although believers died to the world's way of thinking when they became Christians, their fallen Adamic nature was not completely removed. While the power of the sinful nature was broken, they still have to contend with it.

Because Paul was not content to treat sin in an abstract way, he enumerated representative sins to be laid aside. "Fornication" relates to all illicit sexual activities, and in this context, "uncleanness, inordinate affection," and "evil concupiscence" probably also refer to sexual matters. "Covetousness" or "greed" (NIV) is idolatry because it means placing the affections on earthly rather than heavenly things.

3:6. This verse warns that such yielding to sin brings the wrath of God. Some people mistakenly have the idea that God dislikes sin only in the unbeliever, but He excuses sin in the Christian. God certainly does forgives sins (1 John 1:9), but that does not mean He condones it.

not on things on the earth: . . . not on earthly things, *Montgomery* . . . not to the passing things of earth, *Phillips.*

3. For ye are dead:
and your life is hid with Christ in God: . . . and your true life is a hidden one, *Phillips.*

4. When Christ, [who is] our life, shall appear: . . . the secret center of our lives, *Phillips* . . . shall be manifested, *Panin, Wilson, Worrell.*
then shall ye also appear with him in glory: . . . shall you also be made manifest in, *Sawyer* . . . shall be manifested, *Murdock* . . . manifested in glory, *Alford* . . . and you will all share in that magnificent denouement, *Phillips.*

5. Mortify therefore: . . . kill, *TCNT* . . . Put to death, *Panin, Wilson* . . . slay, *Montgomery.*
your members which are upon the earth: . . . all your animal appetites, *TCNT* . . . your baser inclinations, *Montgomery.*
fornication, uncleanness, inordinate affection: Impurity, *Wilson* . . . passion, *Panin, Sawyer, Worrell* . . . base coveting, *Rotherham* . . . unnatural desires, *Montgomery* . . . vnnaturall lust, *Cranmer* . . . lustful passion, *Alford.*
evil concupiscence, and covetousness: . . . evil desires, and especially greed, *TCNT* . . . inordinate lust, *Wilson* . . . and the greed, *Montgomery.*
which is idolatry: . . . is as serious a sin as idolatry, *Phillips.*

6. For which things' sake the wrath of God cometh on the children of disobedience: . . . of incredulitie, *Rheims.*

Colossians 3:7

7.a.**Txt:** 06D-corr,018K
020L,byz.
Var: 018א,02A,03B,04C
06D-org,025P,33,Lach
Treg,Alf,Word,Tisc
We/Ho,Weis,Sod
UBS/✱

1706.1 prep	3614.4 rel-pron dat pl	2504.1 conj	5050.1 prs-pron nom 2pl	3906.20 verb 2pl indic aor act	4077.1 adv
7. ἐν	οἷς	καὶ	ὑμεῖς	περιεπατήσατέ	ποτε
en	hois	kai	humeis	periepatēsate	pote
Among	whom	also	you	walked	once

3616.1 conj	2180.28 verb 2pl indic imperf act	1706.1 prep	840.2 prs-pron dat pl	3642.3 dem-pron dat pl
ὅτε	ἐζῆτε	ἐν	ʿαὐτοῖς·	[ᵃ✩ τούτοις.]
hote	ezēte	en	autois	toutois
when	you were living	in	them.	[these.]

3432.1 adv	1156.2 conj	653.3 verb 2pl impr aor mid	2504.1 conj	5050.1 prs-pron nom 2pl	3450.17 art pl neu	3820.1 adj
8. νυνὶ	δὲ	ἀπόθεσθε	καὶ	ὑμεῖς	τὰ	πάντα,
nuni	de	apothesthe	kai	humeis	ta	panta,
Now	but,	put off	also	you,	the	all things,

3572.4 noun acc sing fem	2349.3 noun acc sing masc	2520.4 noun acc sing fem	981.3 noun acc sing fem	148.1 noun acc sing fem
ὀργήν,	θυμόν,	κακίαν,	βλασφημίαν,	αἰσχρολογίαν
orgēn,	thumon,	kakian,	blasphēmian,	aischrologian
wrath,	indignation,	malice,	blasphemy,	foul language

1523.2 prep gen	3450.2 art gen sing	4601.2 noun gen sing neu	5050.2 prs-pron gen 2pl	3231.1 partic	5409.4 verb 2pl impr pres mid
ἐκ	τοῦ	στόματος	ὑμῶν·	**9.** Μὴ	ψεύδεσθε
ek	tou	stomatos	humōn	Mē	pseudesthe
out of	the	mouth	your.	Not	do lie

1519.1 prep	238.3 prs-pron acc pl masc	550.2 verb nom pl masc part aor mid	3450.6 art acc sing masc	3683.1 adj sing
εἰς	ἀλλήλους,	ἀπεκδυσάμενοι	τὸν	παλαιὸν
eis	allēlous,	apekdusamenoi	ton	palaion
to	one another,	having put off	the	old

442.4 noun acc sing masc	4713.1 prep	3450.14 art dat pl fem	4093.3 noun dat pl fem	840.3 prs-pron gen sing	2504.1 conj
ἄνθρωπον	σὺν	ταῖς	πράξεσιν	αὐτοῦ,	**10.** καὶ
anthrōpon	sun	tais	praxesin	autou,	kai
man	with	the	deeds	his,	and

1730.10 verb nom pl masc part aor mid	3450.6 art acc sing masc	3365.1 adj sing	3450.6 art acc sing masc	339.2 verb acc sing masc part pres mid
ἐνδυσάμενοι	τὸν	νέον	τὸν	ἀνακαινούμενον
endusamenoi	ton	neon	ton	anakainoumenon
having put on	the	new	the	being renewed

1519.1 prep	1907.4 noun acc sing fem	2567.1 prep	1494.4 noun acc sing fem	3450.2 art gen sing	2908.4 verb gen sing masc part aor act
εἰς	ἐπίγνωσιν	κατ'	εἰκόνα	τοῦ	κτίσαντος
eis	epignōsin	kat'	eikona	tou	ktisantos
into	knowledge	according to	image	of the	having created

840.6 prs-pron acc sing masc	3562.1 adv	3620.2 partic	1746.1 verb 3sing indic pres act	1659.1 name nom sing masc	2504.1 conj
αὐτόν·	**11.** ὅπου	οὐκ	ἔνι	Ἕλλην	καὶ
auton	hopou	ouk	eni	Hellēn	kai
him;	where	not	there is	Greek	and

2428.6 name-adj nom sing masc	3921.1 noun nom sing fem	2504.1 conj	201.1 noun nom sing fem	910.1 adj nom sing masc
Ἰουδαῖος,	περιτομὴ	καὶ	ἀκροβυστία,	βάρβαρος,
Ioudaios	peritomē	kai	akrobustia,	barbaros,
Jew,	circumcision	and	uncircumcision,	barbarian,

3:7. Paul reminded the Colossians that the sins he had just listed were representative of their lives before becoming Christians. Then he listed other sins that must be resisted so they would not question in their minds exactly what he meant. This reminder also served to counter the false teaching of many licentious Gnostics who taught that what was done with the physical body had no influence upon the spiritual nature of the individual because they considered the body, as well as all other matter, to be evil.

3:8. "Put off" contains the idea of laying aside, as a person would lay aside old worn-out clothing. They were to rid themselves of "anger" (*orgēn*), or "a settled attitude of anger." "Wrath" (*thumon*) refers to "a violent outburst of wrath." "Malice" (*kakian*) means "a tendency of mind that wants to harm other people." "Blasphemy" (*blasphēmian*) relates to "injuring other people with words." "Filthy communication" (*aischrologian*) or "abusive language" completes Paul's enumeration of terms descriptive of the Colossians before they became Christians, but the list certainly does not comprise an exhaustive one.

3:9. Because the prohibition here consists of a present imperative one, it literally means "stop lying to each other." This type of activity, though a regular part of the old life, is not consistent with the new life in Christ. Paul included lying with a list of some very unsavory habits, apparently indicating that lying is just as terrible in the sight of God as the other matters.

Paul's basis for making this prohibitive statement about lying should be considered carefully. He used a Greek participle (*apekdusamenoi*) which literally means "after putting off" or "having put off." Therefore, the Colossians had rejected "the old man," or the old sinful nature, when they became Christians. Why then would they want to pick it up again and allow it to manifest itself in actions such as lying?

3:10. God encourages His people to actions that will help them progress in the sanctification process, the purifying process through which God is taking all Christians so He can make them more like Christ. The believer's new nature resembles a growing plant that grows stronger and stronger in a continuous, advancing process. Yielding to the fallen Adamic nature does not help the process. This verse serves as a marvelous reminder that God has reversed the process of degeneration that the Scriptures speak about. God knows how to recycle people.

3:11. All types of bigotry are actually part of the old life. "Greek nor Jew" refers to racial prejudice; "circumcision nor uncircumcision" to religious bias; "Barbarian, Scythian" to cultural distinctions; and "bond nor free" to social barriers. Initially, the term

7. In the which ye also walked some time: And never forget that you had your part in those dreadful things, *Phillips*.

when ye lived in them: . . . when you lived that old life, *Phillips*.

8. But now ye also put off all these: . . . you also must renounce them all, *Montgomery* . . . But now, put all these things behind you, *Phillips*.

anger, wrath, malice, blasphemy, filthy communication out of your mouth: . . . no more evil temper or furious rage, *Phillips* . . . passion, spite, slandering, and bad language, *TCNT* . . . and foul talk, *Norlie* . . . shameful speaking, *Panin* . . . shameful-talk, *Rotherham* . . . vile conversation, *Sawyer* . . . Evil speaking, *Wilson* . . . abusive language and foul-mouthed utterances, *Confraternity* . . . foul language, *Alford* . . . obscene discourse out of your mouth, *Scarlett*.

9. Lie not one to another: Do not speak falsely, *Wilson* . . . Stop these practices, *Norlie*.

seeing that ye have put off the old man with his deeds: Get rid of your old self and its habits, *TCNT* . . . but strip off the old self with its doings, *Montgomery* . . . with his practices, *Wilson, Rotherham, Murdock*.

10. And have put on the new [man]: . . . and have begun life as the new man, *Phillips*.

which is renewed in knowledge after the image of him that created him: . . . which is in the process of being made new, *Williams* . . . who is being moulded afresh, *Rotherham* . . . in the likeness of the Creator, *Norlie*.

11. Where there is neither Greek nor Jew, circumcision nor uncircumcision: In which state, *Wilson*.

11.a.**Txt:** 01ℵ-corr,03B 06D,018K,020L,025P byz.Tisc,Weis,Sod
Var: 01ℵ-org,02A,04C 33,We/Ho,UBS/☆

4513.1 name nom sing masc	1395.1 noun nom sing masc	1645.1 adj nom sing masc	233.2 conj	3450.17 art pl neu	3820.1 adj	2504.1 conj
Σκύθης,	δοῦλος,	ἐλεύθερος·	ἀλλὰ	[a τὰ]	πάντα	καὶ
Skuthēs	doulos	eleutheros	alla	ta	panta	kai
Scythian,	servant,	free;	but	the	all things	and

1706.1 prep	3820.5 adj dat pl	5382.1 name nom masc		1730.8 verb 2pl impr aor mid	3631.1 partic	5453.1 conj
ἐν	πᾶσιν	Χριστός.	**12.** Ἐνδύσασθε		οὖν,	ὡς
en	pasin	Christos	Endusasthe		oun	hōs
in	all	Christ.	Put on		therefore,	as

1575.3 adj nom pl masc	3450.2 art gen sing	2296.2 noun gen sing masc	39.7 adj nom pl masc	2504.1 conj	25.30 verb nom pl masc part perf mid
ἐκλεκτοὶ	τοῦ	θεοῦ,	ἅγιοι	καὶ	ἠγαπημένοι,
eklektoi	tou	theou	hagioi	kai	ēgapēmenoi
elect		of God,	holy	and	having been loved,

12.a.**Txt:** 018K,Steph
Var: 01ℵ,02A,03B,04C 06D-corr,020L,025P,byz. Gries,Lach,Treg,Alf Word,Tisc,We/Ho,Weis Sod,UBS/☆

4551.1 noun pl neu	3490.2 noun gen pl masc	3490.3 noun gen sing masc	5379.4 noun acc sing fem
σπλάγχνα	[οἰκτιρμῶν,	[a☆ οἰκτιρμοῦ,]	χρηστότητα,
splanchna	oiktirmōn	oiktirmou	chrēstotēta
bowels	of compassions,	[of compassion]	kindness,

4863.3 noun acc sing fem	4095.4 noun acc sing fem	4095.5 noun acc sing fem
ταπεινοφροσύνην,	[πραότητα,	[☆ πραϋτητα,]
tapeinophrosunēn	praotēta	prautēta
humility,	meekness,	[idem]

3087.4 noun acc sing fem	428.3 verb nom pl masc part pres mid	238.1 prs-pron gen pl	2504.1 conj
μακροθυμίαν·	**13.** ἀνεχόμενοι	ἀλλήλων,	καὶ
makrothumian	anechomenoi	allēlōn	kai
patience;	bearing with	one another,	and

5319.2 verb nom pl masc part pres mid	1431.7 prs-pron dat pl masc	1430.1 partic	4948.3 indef-pron nom sing	4242.1 prep	4948.5 indef-pron
χαριζόμενοι	ἑαυτοῖς,	ἐάν	τις	πρός	τινα
charizomenoi	heautois	ean	tis	pros	tina
forgiving	each other,	if	any	against	any

2174.7 verb 3sing subj pres act	3300.1 noun acc sing fem	2503.1 conj	2504.1 conj	3450.5 art nom sing masc	5382.1 name nom masc
ἔχῃ	μομφήν·	καθὼς	καὶ	ὁ	[Χριστὸς
echē	momphēn	kathōs	kai	ho	Christos
should have	a complaint;	even as	also	the	Christ

13.a.**Txt:** 01ℵ-corr,04C 06D-corr,018K,020L 025P,byz.sa.bo.Tisc,Sod
Var: p46,02A,03B 06D-org.it.Lach,Treg Alf,We/Ho,Weis,UBS/☆

2935.1 noun nom sing masc	5319.5 verb 3sing indic aor mid	5050.3 prs-pron dat 2pl	3643.1 adv	2504.1 conj	5050.1 prs-pron nom 2pl
[a☆ κύριος]	ἐχαρίσατο	ὑμῖν,	οὕτως	καὶ	ὑμεῖς·
kurios	echarisato	humin	houtōs	kai	humeis
[Lord]	forgave	you,	so	also	you.

14.a.**Txt:** 01ℵ-corr 06D-corr,018K,020L byz.Sod
Var: 02A,03B,04C,025P 33,Lach,Treg,Alf,Word Tisc,We/Ho,Weis UBS/☆

1894.3 prep	3820.5 adj dat pl	1156.2 conj	3642.3 dem-pron dat pl	3450.12 art acc sing fem	26.4 noun acc sing fem	3610.3 rel-pron nom sing fem
14. ἐπὶ	πᾶσιν	δὲ	τούτοις	τὴν	ἀγάπην,	[ἥτις
epi	pasin	de	toutois	tēn	agapēn	hētis
To	all	and	these	the	love,	which

3614.16 rel-pron sing neu	1498.4 verb 3sing indic pres act	4736.1 noun nom sing masc	3450.10 art gen sing fem	4895.1 noun gen sing fem
[a☆ ὅ]	ἐστιν	σύνδεσμος	τῆς	τελειότητος
ho	estin	sundesmos	tēs	teleiotētos
[idem]	is	bond	of the	perfectness.

"Barbarian" denoted a person who could not speak Greek, but by New Testament times it had come to mean anyone who did not participate in the Greco-Roman civilization, a so-called "uncivilized person." Scythians were considered the lowest class of barbarians. As far as God is concerned all these distinctions are man-made and result from our fallen sinful condition. Christ abolishes all these sinful distinctions.

3:12. Paul next turned from the negative to the positive. God's people should not yield to the kinds of sins enumerated in verses 5-11. Instead, as they would replace old worn-out garments with new ones, they should "put on" the items he was about to mention. "Bowels of mercies" is an Old English way of saying "deeply felt affection" or "sensitivity to people in need." "Kindness" refers to "sweetness of disposition." "Humbleness" means "a proper estimate of one's self." "Meekness" is the opposite of being harsh, and "long-suffering" means to "forbear other people." "Put on" is located first in the sentence in the Greek and indicates the position of most emphasis. These are the "garments" of the new life.

3:13. The "garments" of the new life also include the ability to forgive one another as the Lord forgives the believer. As a result of the wonderful work of Christ on the cross, believers have experienced true forgiveness (2:13), and God has canceled the multitudinous charges that stood against them (2:14). In the light of this glorious fact, how can Christians harbor grievances against fellow Christians? Because every person in the world is different from every other person to some degree, each is bound to find characteristics in others that grate against his own characteristics. This does not change when individuals become Christians. Sometimes the differences among people seemingly become more than they can bear, and they say things they should not say to one another. In these cases the only recourse is to ask for forgiveness and to be quick to grant forgiveness to one another.

3:14. "Charity" or "love" (NIV) (*agapē*) is the belt which keeps all the other virtues in place. It could also be compared to a lubricant that enables the parts of a complicated machine to function smoothly. It is the motivating force for a believer, uniting all the other qualities into a state of completeness.

The language of the verse comes from the type of garments worn by people in the day in which this statement was written. Because people normally wore loose-flowing outer garments, it often became necessary to "gird the loins" before moving into action. Having the "loins girded" indicated a state of readiness. For instance, a soldier could not move quickly against the enemy unless he tied his garments with his belt or girdle. Without a sincere love for other people it would be impossible to overlook the faults they manifest.

Barbarian, Scythian, bond [nor] free: . . . foreigner, *Rotherham* . . . or savage, *Phillips.*

but Christ [is] all, and in all: Christ is all that matters, for Christ lives in them all, *Phillips.*

12. Put on therefore, as the elect of God, holy and beloved: Clothe yourselves, *Clementson* . . . picked representatives of the new humanity, purified and beloved of God himself, *Phillips.*

bowels of mercies, kindness, humbleness of mind: . . . with the entrails of mercie, *Wyclif* . . . hearts of compassion, *Sawyer* . . . with tender affections of compassion, *Clementson* . . . tenderness of heart, *TCNT* . . . an heart of pity, *Alford* . . . lowliness of mind, *Rotherham, Noyes.*

meekness, longsuffering: . . . modestie, *Rheims* . . . Patient endurance, *Wilson.*

13. Forbearing one another, and forgiving one another: Bear with one another, *Confraternity* . . . you must be tolerant with one another, *Norlie* . . . supporting one an other: and pardoning one an other, *Rheims* . . . and freely forgiving, *Wilson, Worrell.*

if any man have a quarrel against any: . . . if any one has a charge, *Sawyer* . . . may have a Cause of complaint, *Wilson* . . . if any of you have grounds for complaint against others, *TCNT* . . . if you have a difference with anyone, *Phillips.*

even as Christ forgave you, so also [do] ye: . . . forgive one another freely, *TCNT* . . . as freely as the Lord has forgiven you, *Phillips.*

14. And above all these things [put on] charity: . . . and in addition to all these, *Sawyer* . . . put on the robe of love, *Noyes* . . . be truly loving, *Phillips.*

which is the bond of perfectness: . . . the bond of the completeness, *Wilson* . . . the golden chain of all the virtues, *Phillips.*

Colossians 3:15

15.a.Txt: 01ℵ-corr
04C-corr,06D-corr,018K
020L,33,byz.
Var: 01ℵ-org,02A,03B
04C-org,06D-org,025P
sa.bo.Gries,Lach,Treg
Alf,Word,Tisc,We/Ho
Weis,Sod,UBS/✱

2504.1 conj	3450.9 art nom sing fem	1503.1 noun nom sing fem	3450.2 art gen sing	2296.2 noun gen sing masc	3450.2 art gen sing
15. καὶ	ἡ	εἰρήνη	⸂τοῦ	Θεοῦ	[ᵃ✱ τοῦ
kai	*hē*	*eirēnē*	*tou*	*Theou*	*tou*
And	the	peace	of God	[of the

5382.2 name gen masc	1011.1 verb 3sing impr pres act	1706.1 prep	3450.14 art dat pl fem	2559.7 noun dat pl fem	5050.2 prs-pron gen 2pl
Χριστοῦ]	βραβευέτω	ἐν	ταῖς	καρδίαις	ὑμῶν,
Christou	*brabeuetō*	*en*	*tais*	*kardiais*	*humōn*
Christ]	let preside	in	in the	hearts	your,

15.b.Var: p46,03B,6
1739,1881

1519.1 prep	3614.12 rel-pron acc sing fem	2504.1 conj	2535.38 verb 2pl indic aor pass	1706.1 prep	1518.2 num card dat
εἰς	ἣν	καὶ	ἐκλήθητε	ἐν	⸂ᵇ ἑνὶ ⸃
eis	*hēn*	*kai*	*eklēthēte*	*en*	*heni*
to	which	also	you were called	in	one

4835.3 noun dat sing neu	2504.1 conj	2151.1 adj nom pl masc	1090.19 verb 2pl impr pres mid	3450.5 art nom sing masc	3030.1 noun nom sing masc
σώματι·	καὶ	εὐχάριστοι	γίνεσθε.	**16.** ὁ	λόγος
sōmati	*kai*	*eucharistoi*	*ginesthe*	*ho*	*logos*
body,	and	thankful	be.	The	word

3450.2 art gen sing	5382.2 name gen masc	1758.1 verb 3sing impr pres act	1706.1 prep	5050.3 prs-pron dat 2pl	4005.1 adv
τοῦ	Χριστοῦ	ἐνοικείτω	ἐν	ὑμῖν	πλουσίως,
tou	*Christou*	*enoikeitō*	*en*	*humin*	*plousiōs*
of the	Christ	let dwell	in	you	richly,

16.a.Txt: 04C-corr
06D-corr,018K,020L
byz.sa.bo.
Var: 01ℵ,03B,04C-org
06D-org,Lach,Treg,Alf
Word,Tisc,We/Ho,Weis
Sod,UBS/✱

1706.1 prep	3820.11 adj dat sing fem	4531.3 noun dat sing fem	1315.9 verb nom pl masc part pres act	2504.1 conj	3423.4 verb nom pl masc part pres act
ἐν	πάσῃ	σοφίᾳ	διδάσκοντες	καὶ	νουθετοῦντες
en	*pasē*	*sophia*	*didaskontes*	*kai*	*nouthetountes*
in	all	wisdom;	teaching	and	admonishing

16.b.Txt: 04C-corr
06D-corr,018K,020L
byz.sa.bo.
Var: 01ℵ,03B,04C-org
06D-org,Lach,Treg,Alf
Word,Tisc,We/Ho,Weis
Sod,UBS/✱

1431.8 prs-pron acc pl masc	5403.4 noun dat pl masc	2504.1 conj	5054.1 noun dat pl masc	2504.1 conj	5437.2 noun dat pl fem
ἑαυτοὺς	ψαλμοῖς	⸂ᵃ καὶ ⸃	ὕμνοις	⸂ᵇ καὶ ⸃	ᾠδαῖς
heautous	*psalmois*	*kai*	*humnois*	*kai*	*ōdais*
each other	in psalms	and	hymns	and	songs

16.c.Var: 01ℵ-corr,03B
06D-org,Lach,Treg,Alf
Word,Tisc,Weis,UBS/✱

4012.6 adj dat pl fem	1706.1 prep	3450.11 art dat sing fem	5322.3 noun dat sing fem	102.2 verb nom pl masc part pres act	1706.1 prep
πνευματικαῖς	ἐν	[ᶜ+ τῇ]	χάριτι	ᾄδοντες	ἐν
pneumatikais	*en*	*tē*	*chariti*	*adontes*	*en*
spiritual	with	[the]	grace	singing	in

16.d.Txt: 06D-corr,018K
020L,byz.
Var: 01ℵ,02A,03B,04C
06D-org,sa.bo.Gries
Lach,Treg,Alf,Word
Tisc,We/Ho,Weis,Sod
UBS/✱

3450.11 art dat sing fem	2559.3 noun dat sing fem	3450.14 art dat pl fem	2559.7 noun dat pl fem	5050.2 prs-pron gen 2pl	3450.3 art dat sing
⸂ τῇ	καρδίᾳ	[ᵈ✱ ταῖς	καρδίαις]	ὑμῶν	⸂ τῷ
tē	*kardia*	*tais*	*kardiais*	*humōn*	*tō*
the	heart	[the	hearts]	your	to the

16.e.Txt: 04C-corr
06D-corr,018K,020L
byz.bo.
Var: 01ℵ,02A,03B
04C-org,06D-org,33,it.
sa.bo.Gries,Lach,Treg
Alf,Word,Tisc,We/Ho
Weis,Sod,UBS/✱

2935.3 noun dat sing masc	3450.3 art dat sing	2296.3 noun dat sing masc	2504.1 conj	3820.17 adj sing neu	3614.16 rel-pron sing neu
κυρίῳ·	[ᵉ✱ τῷ	θεῷ·]	**17.** καὶ	πᾶν	ὃ
kuriō	*tō*	*theō*	*kai*	*pan*	*ho*
Lord.	[to	[God.]	And	everything,	what

17.a.Txt: 01ℵ,02A,04C
06D,018K,byz.Tisc,Sod
Var: 03B,020L,Lach
Treg,We/Ho,Weis
UBS/✱

4948.10 indef-pron sing neu	300.1 partic	1430.1 partic	4020.9 verb 2pl subj pres act	1706.1 prep	3030.3 noun dat sing masc	2211.1 conj
τι	⸂ ἂν	[ᵃ✱ ἐὰν]	ποιῆτε	ἐν	λόγῳ	ἢ
ti	*an*	*ean*	*poiēte*	*en*	*logō*	*ē*
anything	an	ean	you may do	in	word	or

3:15. As the Christian allows these virtues to abide within him and as he permits God's love to hold all these "garments" in place, the "peace of God" will serve as an umpire. This refers to the peace Christ gives to His people (John 14:27). Situations often arise in which a person must choose among various options. A wise Christian is one who does not allow any course of action to ruffle the peace within him.

This principle also could apply to a local congregation of believers. Some assemblies seem always to be at odds over some matters, usually very minor ones. On the other hand, some local churches do not allow such matters to upset the balance of peace that exists among them. "Peace" (*eirēnē*), or "inner tranquility," will reign supremely if given a chance to do so.

On the other hand, peace seems to be very delicate and can be frustrated very easily. This peace needs to be accompanied by thankfulness. If thankfulness becomes a way of life, it will make it much easier to maintain a state of peace. It helps us look on the bright side instead of focusing upon the events which can disturb our calm.

3:16. This verse contains another imperative about allowing the "word of Christ" to dwell within us. This probably has reference to the gospel message that should be central in all our teachings. If that is true, it will be "wise teaching" (*didaskontes*) and "admonishing" or "counseling" (*nouthetountes*).

Furthermore, the gospel message should be central in our singing, which here is described ideally as a balance among the Old Testament Psalms put to music, "hymns," which are songs addressing praise to God, and "spiritual songs," which probably are songs of testimony addressed to God. The last term also could mean singing in other languages as people worship God.

3:17. The total passage closes in this verse with a summary of the fundamental principle of Christian ethics. While the New Testament does contain many negatives such as the ones listed in verses 5-11, it is not just a list of do's and don'ts. Rather, the main guiding principle for word and action is that we should not bring reproach on the name of the Lord Jesus. If we say and do everything in harmony with His revealed will and because we are His followers, it truly will be said and done by His authority.

The last part of verse 17 shows that this kind of life-style does not come out of a sense of duty, but out of gratitude to God the Father for all that Christ has done for us. It is very fitting that Christians should respond to God out of gratitude for His marvelous grace extended to them. The apostle Paul definitely believed in Christian standards, but standards that are Christ-centered and that emanate from the Scriptures.

15. And let the peace of God rule in your hearts: . . . the peace that Christ can give keep on acting as umpire, *Williams* . . . arbitrate in, *Panin* . . . rejoice in your hearts, *Douay* . . . reign in your hearts, *Confraternity* . . . preside in your hearts, *Scarlett* . . . control your thinking, *Everyday* . . . exult in your hartes, *Rheims*.

to the which also ye are called in one body: . . . for you were called to this state as members of, *Williams* . . . You were all called together in one body, *Everyday* . . . as members of the same body you are called to live in harmony, *Phillips*.

and be ye thankful: And practice being thankful, *Williams* . . . and never forget to be thankful, *Phillips*.

16. Let the word of Christ dwell in you richly in all wisdom: Let the teaching of Christ, *Everyday* . . . have its home in you, *Montgomery* . . . dwell in you abundantly, *Confraternity, Scarlett* . . . dwel in you plenteously, *Geneva* . . . aboundantly, *Rheims* . . . continue to live in you in all its wealth of wisdom, *Williams*.

teaching and admonishing one another in psalms and hymns and spiritual songs: . . . keep on teaching it to one another and training one another in it with thankfulness, *Williams* . . . and help one another along the right road with your psalms and hymns and Christian songs, *Phillips* . . . and spiritual canticles, *Rheims*.

singing with grace in your hearts to the Lord: . . . in [your] gratitude singing, *Rotherham* . . . in your hearts singing praise, *Williams* . . . with thankfulness, *Everyday* . . . with gratitude in your hearts, *Wilson* . . . singing God's praises with joyful hearts, *Phillips*.

17. And whatsoever ye do in word or deed: Everything you say and everything you do, *Everyday* . . . whatever you say or do, *Williams* . . . or in work, *Sawyer, Rheims* . . . or action, *Scarlett*.

Colossians 3:18

1706.1 prep	2024.3 noun dat sing neu	3820.1 adj	1706.1 prep	3549.4 noun dat sing neu	2935.2 noun gen sing masc	2400.2 name masc
ἐν	ἔργῳ,	πάντα	ἐν	ὀνόματι	κυρίου	Ἰησοῦ,
en	ergō	panta	en	onomati	kuriou	Iēsou
in	work,	all	in	name	of Lord	Jesus,

	2149.7 verb nom pl masc part pres act	3450.3 art dat sing	2296.3 noun dat sing masc	2504.1 conj	3824.3 noun dat sing masc	1217.1 prep
	εὐχαριστοῦντες	τῷ	θεῷ	‹b καὶ ›	πατρὶ	δι'
	eucharistountes	tō	theō	kai	patri	di'
	giving thanks	to	God	and	Father	by

840.3 prs-pron gen sing		5131.10 verb 2pl impr pres mid	3450.4 art dat pl
αὐτοῦ.	**18.** Αἱ	γυναῖκες,	ὑποτάσσεσθε	τοῖς
autou	Hai	gunaikes,	hupotassesthe	tois
him.	The	wives,	subject yourselves	to the

2375.5 adj dat pl	433.8 noun dat pl masc	5453.1 conj	431.3 verb 3sing indic imperf act	1706.1 prep	2935.3 noun dat sing masc
‹a ἰδίοις ›	ἀνδράσιν,	ὡς	ἀνῆκεν	ἐν	κυρίῳ.
idiois	andrasin	hōs	anēken	en	kuriō
your own	husbands,	as	was becoming	in	Lord.

3450.7 art nom pl masc	433.6 noun nom pl masc	25.1 verb 2pl pres act	3450.15 art acc pl fem	1129.9 noun acc pl fem	2504.1 conj
19. Οἱ	ἄνδρες,	ἀγαπᾶτε	τὰς	γυναῖκας	καὶ
Hoi	andres,	agapate	tas	gunaikas	kai
The	husbands,	love	the	wives,	and

3231.1 partic	3948.2 verb 2pl impr pres mid	4242.1 prep	840.13 prs-pron acc pl fem	3450.17 art pl neu	4891.4 noun pl neu
μὴ	πικραίνεσθε	πρὸς	αὐτάς.	**20.** Τὰ	τέκνα,
mē	pikrainesthe	pros	autas.	Ta	tekna,
not	be bitter	against	them.	The	children,

5057.1 verb 2pl pres act	3450.4 art dat pl	1112.3 noun dat pl masc	2567.3 prep	3820.1 adj	3642.17 dem-pron sing neu	1056.1 conj
ὑπακούετε	τοῖς	γονεῦσιν	κατὰ	πάντα·	τοῦτο	γὰρ
hupakouete	tois	goneusin	kata	panta	touto	gar
obey	the	parents	in	all things;	this	for

1498.4 verb 3sing indic pres act	2080.4 adj sing	2080.4 adj sing	1498.4 verb 3sing indic pres act	3450.3 art dat sing
‹ ἐστιν	εὐάρεστόν	[✱ εὐάρεστόν	ἐστιν]	‹ τῷ
estin	euareston	euareston	estin	tō
is	well pleasing	[well pleasing	is]	to the

1706.1 prep	2935.3 noun dat sing masc	3450.7 art nom pl masc	3824.6 noun nom pl masc	3231.1 partic	2025.1 verb 2pl impr pres act
[a✱ ἐν]	κυρίῳ.	**21.** Οἱ	πατέρες,	μὴ	‹✱ ἐρεθίζετε
en	kuriō	Hoi	pateres,	mē	erethizete
[in]	Lord.	The	fathers,	not	do provoke

3811.1 verb 2pl impr pres act	3450.17 art pl neu	4891.4 noun pl neu	5050.2 prs-pron gen 2pl	2419.1 conj	3231.1 partic
[a παρογίζετε]	τὰ	τέκνα	ὑμῶν,	ἵνα	μὴ
parorgizete	ta	tekna	humōn,	hina	mē
[provoke to anger]	the	children	your,	that	not

120.1 verb 3pl subj pres act	3450.7 art nom pl masc	1395.6 noun nom pl masc	5057.1 verb 2pl pres act	2567.3 prep
ἀθυμῶσιν.	**22.** Οἱ	δοῦλοι,	ὑπακούετε	κατὰ
athumōsin.	Hoi	douloi,	hupakouete	kata
they be disheartened.	The	slaves,	obey	in

17.b.Txt: 06D,018K 020L,33,byz.it. **Var:** 01ℵ,02A,03B,04C sa.bo.Lach,Treg,Alf Word,Tisc,We/Ho,Weis Sod,UBS/✱

18.a.Txt: 020L,byz. **Var:** 01ℵ,02A,03B,04C 06D-corr,018K,33,Gries Lach,Treg,Alf,Word Tisc,We/Ho,Weis,Sod UBS/✱

20.a.Txt: Steph **Var:** 01ℵ,02A,03B,04C 06D,018K,020L,byz. Gries,Lach,Treg,Alf Word,Tisc,We/Ho,Weis Sod,UBS/✱

21.a.Txt: p46-vid,01ℵ 03B,06D-corr2,044,byz. **Var:** 02A,04C,06D-org 010F,012G,020L,0198 33,81,104,365,1175

3:18. After describing Christ as the only all-sufficient Saviour for mankind and the source of the Christian's life, Paul applied the supremacy of Christ to particular groups of people. A correct understanding of the word "submit" (*hupotassō*) here can come only by realizing the verb is in the middle voice.

Because the verb is not active the husband cannot say, "You must submit to me," and because it is not passive, the wife cannot say, "I am forced to submit to you." The middle voice represents the actor in a sentence somehow participating in the results of the action. Here the verb is middle voice to show the necessity of this submission being voluntary. This does not imply he is any more important than she, nor that she is on any lower level (Galatians 3:28).

The Bible makes it clear that not every person fills the same function (Romans 12:3-8; 1 Corinthians 12:27-31; Ephesians 4:11). The same is true in the family that is true in the Church in general. The husband's role is to be the spiritual leader of the family, and the wife's is to support him in that role. The supportive role is just as important as the leadership role. Paul added, "as it is fit in the Lord," or "this is in harmony with His will."

3:19. Husbands, on the other hand, are obligated to love their wives and not to treat them harshly. The fact that Paul wrote such terse statements in Colossians relative to the relationship between husbands and wives serves as one reason some think he wrote this letter first, then followed it with Ephesians.

3:20. Christ also should be supreme in the relationship between children and parents. Children are instructed to obey their parents in everything. One should realize again that this is referring to a Christian family where the parents and children are believers. God, of course, does not expect a Christian child to sin just to obey the whim of an unbelieving parent. Paul added the qualifier "in the Lord" (Ephesians 6:1).

3:21. The term "fathers" here may actually refer to parents as it does in Hebrews 11:23. It is not clear whether Paul intended to give this instruction to both parents, but the apostle considered fathers the spiritual leaders of their homes. As such they ultimately were accountable for what happened in the home.

Paul warned fathers against becoming too severe with their children, lest the latter become discouraged because of the severity of the demands placed upon them. Sincere parents, of course, want their children to surrender their lives to Christ and do His will. Because of this they have a strong tendency to pressure their children to do right, and if they are not very careful, this pressure can take the form of constant nagging. While the Scriptures definitely instruct children to obey their parents, parents should not depend on force but administer discipline in love, justice, and moderation.

[do] all in the name of the Lord Jesus: . . . let it all be done with reference to, *Williams*.

giving thanks to God and the Father by him: . . . and through Him continue to give thanks to God the Father, *Williams*.

18. Wives, submit yourselves unto your own husbands: . . . continue to live in subordination to, *Williams* . . . adapt yourselves to, *Phillips*.

as it is fit in the Lord: . . . as is becoming, *Rotherham* . . . for that is your duty as Christians, *TCNT*.

19. Husbands, love [your] wives: . . . be sure you give your wives much love and sympathy, *Phillips*.

and be not bitter against them: . . . and never treat them harshly, *TCNT* . . . and do not behave harshly to them, *Wilson* . . . and be not cross or surly with them, *Montgomery* . . . don't let bitterness or resentment spoil your marriage, *Phillips*.

20. Children, obey [your] parents in all things: . . . your duty is to obey your parents, *Phillips*.

for this is well pleasing unto the Lord: . . . for at your age this is one of the best things you can do to show your love for God, *Phillips*.

21. Fathers, provoke not your children [to anger]: . . . be not fault-finding, *Sawyer* . . . be not irritating, *Rotherham* . . . do not exasperate, *Scarlett* . . . do not harass, *Montgomery* . . . do not provoke your children to resentment, *Norlie* . . . to indignation, *Rheims*.

lest they be discouraged: . . . or they may become disheartened, *TCNT* . . . lest they be of a desperate mynde, *Cranmer* . . . lest you make them spiritless, *Montgomery*.

3820.1 adj	3450.4 art dat pl	2567.3 prep	4418.4 noun acc sing fem	2935.8 noun dat pl masc	3231.1 partic
πάντα	τοῖς	κατὰ	σάρκα	κυρίοις,	μὴ
panta	tois	kata	sarka	kuriois	mē
all things	the	according to	flesh	masters,	not

1706.1 prep	3651.2 noun dat pl fem	3651.3 noun dat sing fem	5453.1 conj
ἐν	ʿ ὀφθαλμοδουλείαις	[✶ ὀφθαλμοδουλίᾳ]	ὡς
en	ophthalmodouleiais	ophthalmodoulia	hōs
with	eye services,	[eye service]	as

439.1 adj nom pl masc	233.1 conj	1706.1 prep	567.2 noun dat sing fem	2559.1 noun fem
ἀνθρωπάρεσκοι,	ἀλλ'	ἐν	ἁπλότητι	καρδίας,
anthrōpareskoi	all'	en	haplotēti	kardias
men pleasers,	but	in	simplicity	of heart,

22.a.Txt: 01ℵ-corr 06D-corr,018K,byz.bo. **Var:** 01ℵ-org,02A,03B 04C,06D-org,020L Gries,Lach,Treg,Alf Word,Tisc,We/Ho,Weis Sod,UBS/✶

5236.8 verb nom pl masc part pres mid	3450.6 art acc sing masc	2296.4 noun acc sing masc	3450.6 art acc sing masc	2935.4 noun acc sing masc
φοβούμενοι	ʿ τὸν	Θεόν·	[ᵃ✶ τὸν	κύριον.]
phoboumenoi	ton	Theon	ton	kurion
fearing		God.	[the	Lord.]

23.a.Txt: 06D-corr,018K 020L,byz. **Var:** 01ℵ-org,02A,03B 04C,33,it.bo.Lach,Treg Alf,Word,Tisc,We/Ho Weis,Sod,UBS/✶

2504.1 conj	3820.17 adj sing neu	3614.16 rel-pron sing neu	4948.10 indef-pron sing neu	3614.16 rel-pron sing neu	1430.1 partic
23. ʿ καὶ	πᾶν	ὃ	τι	[ᵃ✶ ὃ]	ἐὰν
kai	pan	ho	ti	ho	ean
And	all	what	anything	[what]	

4020.9 verb 2pl subj pres act	1523.2 prep gen	5425.2 noun gen sing fem	2021.1 verb 2pl pres mid	5453.1 conj	3450.3 art dat sing	2935.3 noun dat sing masc
ποιῆτε,	ἐκ	ψυχῆς	ἐργάζεσθε,	ὡς	τῷ	κυρίῳ
poiēte	ek	psuchēs	ergazesthe	hōs	tō	kuriō
you may do,	from	soul	work,	as	to the	Lord

2504.1 conj	3620.2 partic	442.8 noun dat pl masc	3471.20 verb nom pl masc part perf act	3617.1 conj	570.3 prep	2935.2 noun gen sing masc
καὶ	οὐκ	ἀνθρώποις·	**24.** εἰδότες	ὅτι	ἀπὸ	κυρίου
kai	ouk	anthrōpois	eidotes	hoti	apo	kuriou
and	not	to men;	knowing	that	from	Lord

24.a.Txt: 06D-corr,018K 020L,byz.Sod **Var:** 01ℵ,02A,03B,04C 06D-org,33,it.bo.Lach Treg,Alf,Word,Tisc We/Ho,Weis,UBS/✶

612.11 verb 2pl indic fut mid	612.13 verb 2pl indic fut mid	3450.12 art acc sing fem	466.1 noun acc sing fem
ʿ ἀπολήψεσθε	[✶ ἀπολήμψεσθε]	τὴν	ἀνταπόδοσιν
apolēpsesthe	apolēmpsesthe	tēn	antapodosin
you shall receive	[idem]	the	recompense

25.a.Txt: 06D-corr,018K 020L,byz. **Var:** 01ℵ,02A,03B,04C 06D-org,33,it.bo.Lach Treg,Alf,Word,Tisc We/Ho,Weis,Sod UBS/✶

3450.10 art gen sing fem	2790.2 noun gen sing fem	3450.3 art dat sing	1056.1 conj	2935.3 noun dat sing masc	5382.3 name dat masc
τῆς	κληρονομίας·	τῷ	ʿᵃ γὰρ ʾ	κυρίῳ	Χριστῷ
tēs	klēronomias	tō	gar	kuriō	Christō
of the	inheritance,	the	for	Lord	Christ

25.b.Txt: 01ℵ-org,02A 04C,06D-org,33,byz. Tisc **Var:** 01ℵ-corr,03B 06D-corr,018K,020L Lach,We/Ho,Weis,Sod UBS/✶

1392.1 verb 2pl pres act	3450.5 art nom sing masc	1156.2 conj	1056.1 conj	90.4 verb nom sing masc part pres act
δουλεύετε.	**25.** ὁ	ʿ δὲ	[ᵃ✶ γὰρ]	ἀδικῶν
douleuete	ho	de	gar	adikōn
you serve.	The	but	[for]	doing wrong

2837.8 verb 3sing indic fut mid	2837.12 verb 3sing indic fut mid	3614.16 rel-pron sing neu	90.6 verb 3sing indic aor act	2504.1 conj
ʿ κομιεῖται.	[ᵇ✶ κομίσεται]	ὃ	ἠδίκησεν,	καὶ
komieitai	komisetai	ho	ēdikēsen	kai
shall receive	[idem]	what	he did wrong,	and

3:22. One should not assume from these comments that the apostle Paul favored slavery. Nowhere in his writings does he endorse this system. In fact, in 1 Timothy 1:10 "menstealers" or "slave traders" are classed with "whoremongers," "liars," and other evildoers. The Roman world at that time was full of slaves. Some Bible commentators estimate that approximately one-third of the population of the Roman world consisted of slaves. Paul did not recommend outright revolt by slaves against their masters but rather advocated faithful service, as unto the Lord.

3:23. "Do it heartily" actually comes from a Greek phrase containing the word for *soul* (*psuchē*). The statement serves as good proof that more than the body is involved. The terminology used shows that attitude is just as important as physical condition.

The attitude expressed in this verse certainly militates against the selfish approach often fostered by some people. Sometimes individual employees have become so selfish they keep seeking more and more from employers until eventually companies are forced to close. In other cases, employees have been willing to make wage concessions in order to save their company and their jobs. Whether slaves or employees, when a person looks at labor as working for the Lord, their total mental outlook changes.

3:24. Paul could have encouraged the slaves to rebel against their owners. Instead he reminded them of the permanent reward they would receive from the Lord, providing they were laboring for His glory. The Bible promises God's people an eternal reward that will far outweigh the difficulties experienced in these few years upon this earth.

3:25. Interestingly enough, the apostle Paul included failure to fulfill our responsibilities in our vocations in the category of items considered wrong or unrighteous. The principle of sowing and reaping is emphasized in many places in the Scriptures. Just as a person who sows corn can expect to reap a harvest of corn, so a person who sows righteous acts can expect to reap righteousness. No one is foolish enough to think he can sow one type of seed and reap some other type of fruit, but many people seem to think they can sow unrighteousness without reaping the results. The reaping is just as sure as the sowing.

Paul reminded the Colossians that God does not show favoritism. The Greek term from which we derive "respect of persons" actually comes from the word for *face* (*prosōpon*). Therefore, Paul is saying that what a person's face looks like does not make any difference with God. Because of attractive physical features, some people are able to get away with things other people might not be able to get away with in their human relationships. God, however, does not make His decisions based upon the facial features of a person. He will reward according to the inner motives of the individual.

22. Servants, obey in all things [your] masters according to the flesh: Slaves, practice obedience to your earthly masters in everything, *Williams.*

not with eyeservice, as menpleasers; but in singleness of heart, fearing God: . . . not as though they were watching you and as though you were merely pleasing men, *Williams* . . . giving them undivided service, in reverent awe of the Master, *TCNT* . . . with a sincere heart, *Sawyer* . . . in Sincerity of Heart, *Wilson* . . . out of reverence for your Lord, *Montgomery* . . . in simplicity of heart, fearing the Lord, *PNT.*

23. And whatsoever ye do, do [it] heartily: . . . whatever ye are employed in, work from the heart, *Scarlett* . . . So no matter what the task, do your work heartily, *Norlie* . . . do it with all your heart, *Williams* . . . work it from the soul, *Wilson* . . . put your whole heart and soul into it, *Phillips.*

as to the Lord, and not unto men: . . . as doing it for the Lord, *Norlie* . . . as work for the Lord and not for men, *Williams* . . . as into work done for God, and not merely for, *Phillips.*

24. Knowing that of the Lord ye shall receive the reward of the inheritance: . . . the recompense of the inheritance, *Clementson* . . . for you know that it is from the Lord that you are going to get your pay in the form of an inheritance, *Williams.*

for ye serve the Lord Christ: . . . so keep on serving, *Williams* . . . since you are actually employed by, *Phillips.*

25. But he that doeth wrong shall receive for the wrong which he hath done: . . . but the delinquent will receive, *Murdock* . . . he who acts unjustly, *Wilson, Scarlett* . . . will be paid back, *Montgomery* . . . the wrong he has done, *Williams.*

3620.2 partic	1498.4 verb 3sing indic pres act		4240.1 noun nom sing fem		4240.3 noun nom sing fem
ΟὐΚ	ἔστιν	⸀	προσωποληψία.	[✸	προσωπολημψία.]
ouk	estin		prosōpolēpsia		prosōpolēmpsia
no	there is		respect of persons.		[idem]

3450.7 art nom pl masc	2935.6 noun nom pl masc	3450.16 art sing neu	1337.1 adj sing	2504.1 conj	3450.12 art acc sing fem	2444.3 noun acc sing fem
4:1. Οἱ	κύριοι,	τὸ	δίκαιον	καὶ	τὴν	ἰσότητα
Hoi	kurioi	to	dikaion	kai	tēn	isotēta
The	masters,	the	just	and	the	equal

3450.4 art dat pl	1395.8 noun dat pl masc	3792.12 verb 2pl impr pres mid	3471.20 verb nom pl masc part perf act	3617.1 conj	2504.1 conj
τοῖς	δούλοις	παρέχεσθε,	εἰδότες	ὅτι	καὶ
tois	doulois	parechesthe	eidotes	hoti	kai
to the	slaves	give,	knowing	that	also

5050.1 prs-pron nom 2pl	2174.2 verb 2pl pres act	2935.4 noun acc sing masc	1706.1 prep	3636.8 noun dat pl masc	3636.3 noun dat sing masc
ὑμεῖς	ἔχετε	κύριον	ἐν	⸀ οὐρανοῖς.	[ᵃ✸ οὐρανῷ.]
humeis	echete	kurion	en	ouranois	ouranō
you	have	a Master	in	heavens.	[heaven.]

3450.11 art dat sing fem	4194.3 noun dat sing fem	4201.2 verb 2pl impr pres act	1121.5 verb nom pl masc part pres act	1706.1 prep
2. Τῇ	προσευχῇ	προσκαρτερεῖτε,	γρηγοροῦντες	ἐν
Tē	proseuchē	proskartereite	grēgorountes	en
In the	prayer	steadfastly continue,	watching	in

840.11 prs-pron dat sing fem	1706.1 prep	2150.3 noun dat sing fem	4195.13 verb nom pl masc part pres mid	258.1 adv
αὐτῇ	ἐν	εὐχαριστίᾳ·	3. προσευχόμενοι	ἅμα
autē	en	eucharistia	proseuchomenoi	hama
it	with	thanksgiving;	praying	together

2504.1 conj	3875.1 prep	2231.2 prs-pron gen 1pl	2419.1 conj	3450.5 art nom sing masc	2296.1 noun nom sing masc	453.6 verb 3sing subj aor act
καὶ	περὶ	ἡμῶν,	ἵνα	ὁ	θεὸς	ἀνοίξῃ
kai	peri	hēmōn	hina	ho	theos	anoixē
also	for	us,	that		God	may open

2231.3 prs-pron dat 1pl	2351.4 noun acc sing fem	3450.2 art gen sing	3030.2 noun gen sing masc	2953.37 verb inf aor act	3450.16 art sing neu
ἡμῖν	θύραν	τοῦ	λόγου	λαλῆσαι	τὸ
hēmin	thuran	tou	logou	lalēsai	to
to us	a door	of the	word	to speak	the

3328.1 noun sing neu	3450.2 art gen sing	5382.2 name gen masc	1217.1 prep	3614.16 rel-pron sing neu
μυστήριον	τοῦ	Χριστοῦ,	δι'	ὃ
mustērion	tou	Christou	di'	ho
mystery	of the	Christ,	on account of	which

2504.1 conj	1204.13 verb 1sing indic perf mid	2419.1 conj	5157.4 verb 1sing subj aor act	840.15 prs-pron sing neu
καὶ	δέδεμαι,	4. ἵνα	φανερώσω	αὐτὸ
kai	dedemai	hina	phanerōsō	auto
also	I have been bound,	that	I may make manifest	it

5453.1 conj	1158.1 verb 3sing indic pres act	1466.6 prs-pron acc 1sing	2953.37 verb inf aor act	1706.1 prep	4531.3 noun dat sing fem
ὡς	δεῖ	με	λαλῆσαι.	5. Ἐν	σοφίᾳ
hōs	dei	me	lalēsai	En	sophia
as	it compels	me	to speak.	In	wisdom

1.a.Txt: 01ℵ-corr,06D
018K,020L,byz.
Var: 01ℵ-org,02A,03B
04C,33,Lach,Treg,Alf
Word,Tisc,We/Ho,Weis
Sod,UBS/✸

4:1. Paul's comments in this section seem to be rather one-sided, but he did not leave the subject without a stern warning that masters should treat their slaves properly, because they also had a Lord or Master. "Just" in this verse refers to providing justice, and "equal" relates to the necessity of being equitable in all transactions with slaves. Apparently these masters worshiped God in the local assembly alongside their own slaves. A tendency might develop to give preference to the masters.

4:2. After showing in detail that Christ must be supreme in everything, from creation even to our actions at home, Paul exhorted the Colossians with respect to two very important matters: prayer and their conduct toward unbelievers. With respect to the first exhortation concerning prayer, the apostle first clarified the fact that God's will concerning prayer is that we devote ourselves to it, or that we continue in it. Although prayer is to be maintained as a regular habit, it should not become just a routine matter. It is to be accompanied with watchfulness, which denotes diligence and persistence. The term "watch" literally means "to be awake." Paul emphasized thankfulness as needed to accompany prayer.

4:3. The apostle certainly was not above asking other people to pray for him. However, this verse indicates his request was not for selfish ends. His statement reveals one of the most important purposes for prayer, liberty to proclaim the gospel message. No one can doubt that Paul's consuming desire was for the advancement of the gospel. The pronoun "us" no doubt includes his coworkers mentioned later in the chapter. He literally requested the Colossians to pray that God would "open . . . a door" for the Word. He may have been expressing his desire that the obstacles standing in the way of the preaching of the gospel be removed (1 Corinthians 16:9; 2 Corinthians 2:12), or he may have been asking for the Holy Spirit's help (Ephesians 6:19,20).

4:4. This verse seems to indicate that Paul had in mind the necessity of having the Holy Spirit's assistance in proclaiming the gospel. He knew his efforts would be futile without that divine aid. The "it" comes from a personal pronoun (*auto*) that is neuter in gender, referring back to the phrase in verse 3, "the mystery of Christ," which also is neuter. The term probably means the same as it does in 2:2, that Christ does indeed indwell His people, and it is possible for a person to have a living relationship with Him. Helping people know this glorious fact was one of the most prominent passions of Paul's life.

For many years he lived a religious life. He was extremely zealous for what he thought was right (Galatians 1:14), but he exchanged all that for the privilege of knowing Christ, or having a personal relationship with Him through being born from above (Philippians 3:7). From the time of his personal conversion to Christ (Acts 9)

and there is no respect of persons: . . . and human distinctions will not be recognised, *TCNT* . . . and there will be no favoritism, *Montgomery* . . . and there are no exceptions, *Williams* . . . naturally no distinction will be made between master and man, *Phillips*.

1. Masters, give unto [your] servants that which is just and equal: . . . you must practice doing the right and square things by your slaves, *Williams* . . . do equity, *Murdock* . . . render justice and equity to, *Worrell* . . . and equitable, *PNT* . . . deal justly and fairly with, *Montgomery*.
knowing that ye also have a Master in heaven: . . . have a heavenly employer, *Phillips*.

2. Continue in prayer: Always maintain the habit, *Phillips* . . . Attend constantly, *Wilson* . . . Persevere in prayer, *Murdock* . . . Devote yourselves to prayer, *TCNT*.
and watch in the same with thanksgiving: . . . be both alert and thankful, *Phillips* . . . and by this means stay wide awake when you give thanks, *Williams*.

3. Withal praying also for us: At the same time keep on praying for me too, *Williams*.
that God would open unto us a door of utterance: . . . for the entrance of, *Phillips*.
to speak the mystery of Christ: . . . to announce, *Confraternity* . . . to declare, *Sawyer* . . . talk freely of, *Phillips* . . . that I may tell the open secret about Christ, *Williams*.
for which I am also in bonds: . . . for which I am even confined, *Scarlett*.

4. That I may make it manifest, as I ought to speak: . . . that I may declare it plainly, *Sawyer* . . . that I may unfold it, *Murdock*.

3906.1 verb 2pl pres act	4242.1 prep	3450.8 art acc pl masc	1838.1 adv	3450.6 art acc sing masc	2511.4 noun acc sing masc
περιπατεῖτε	πρὸς	τοὺς	ἔξω,	τὸν	καιρὸν
peripateite	pros	tous	exō	ton	kairon
walk	towards	the	outside,	the	time

1789.3 verb nom pl masc part pres mid		3450.5 art nom sing masc	3030.1 noun nom sing masc	5050.2 prs- pron gen 2pl	3704.1 adv
ἐξαγοραζόμενοι.	**6.** ὁ	λόγος	ὑμῶν	πάντοτε
exagorazomenoi	ho	logos	humōn	pantote
redeeming.	The	word	your	always

1706.1 prep	5322.3 noun dat sing fem	215.2 noun dat sing neu	736.2 verb nom sing masc part perf mid	3471.25 verb inf perf act	4316.1 adv
ἐν	χάριτι,	ἅλατι	ἠρτυμένος,	εἰδέναι	πῶς
en	chariti	halati	ērtumenos	eidenai	pōs
with	grace,	with salt	having been seasoned,	to know	how

1158.1 verb 3sing indic pres act	5050.4 prs- pron acc 2pl	1518.2 num card dat	1524.4 adj dat sing masc	552.3 verb inf pres mid
δεῖ	ὑμᾶς	ἑνὶ	ἑκάστῳ	ἀποκρίνεσθαι.
dei	humas	heni	hekastō	apokrinesthai
it is necessary	you	one	each	to answer.

3450.17 art pl neu	2567.1 prep	1466.7 prs- pron acc 1sing	3820.1 adj	1101.11 verb 3sing indic fut act
7. Τὰ	κατ'	ἐμὲ	πάντα	γνωρίσει
Ta	kat'	eme	panta	gnōrisei
The things	concerning	me	all	will make known

5050.3 prs- pron dat 2pl	5031.1 name nom masc	3450.5 art nom sing masc	27.3 adj nom sing masc	79.1 noun nom sing masc	2504.1 conj
ὑμῖν	Τυχικὸς	ὁ	ἀγαπητὸς	ἀδελφὸς	καὶ
humin	Tuchikos	ho	agapētos	adelphos	kai
to you	Tychicus	the	beloved	brother	and

3964.2 adj nom sing masc	1243.1 noun nom sing masc	2504.1 conj	4739.1 noun nom sing masc	1706.1 prep	2935.3 noun dat sing masc
πιστὸς	διάκονος	καὶ	σύνδουλος	ἐν	κυρίῳ,
pistos	diakonos	kai	sundoulos	en	kuriō
faithful	minister	and	fellow servant	in	Lord;

3614.6 rel-pron acc sing masc	3854.5 verb 1sing indic aor act	4242.1 prep	5050.4 prs- pron acc 2pl	1519.1 prep	840.15 prs- pron sing neu	3642.17 dem- pron sing neu
8. ὃν	ἔπεμψα	πρὸς	ὑμᾶς	εἰς	αὐτὸ	τοῦτο,
hon	epempsa	pros	humas	eis	auto	touto
whom	I sent	to	you	for	same	this thing,

8.a.**Txt**: p46,01ℵ-corr
04C,06D-corr,018K
020L,byz.it.bo.Sod
Var: 02A,03B,06D-org
025P,048,33,sa.Lach
Treg,Tisc,We/Ho,Weis
UBS/✶

8.b.**Txt**: p46,01ℵ-corr
04C,06D-corr,018K
020L,byz.it.bo.Sod
Var: 02A,03B,06D-org
025P,048,33,sa.Lach
Treg,Tisc,We/Ho,Weis
UBS/✶

2419.1 conj	1091.22 verb 3sing subj aor act	1091.19 verb 2pl aor act	3450.17 art pl neu	3875.1 prep
ἵνα	γνῷ	[ᵃ✶ γνῶτε]	τὰ	περὶ
hina	gnō	gnōte	ta	peri
that	he might know	[you might know]	the things	concerning

5050.2 prs- pron gen 2pl	2231.2 prs- pron gen 1pl	2504.1 conj	3731.4 verb 3sing subj pres act	3450.15 art acc pl fem	2559.1 noun fem
ὑμῶν	[ᵇ✶ ἡμῶν]	καὶ	παρακαλέσῃ	τὰς	καρδίας
humōn	hēmōn	kai	parakalesē	tas	kardias
you,	[us]	and	might encourage	the	hearts

5050.2 prs- pron gen 2pl	4713.1 prep	3545.2 name dat masc	3450.3 art dat sing	3964.4 adj dat sing masc	2504.1 conj
ὑμῶν,	**9.** σὺν	Ὀνησίμῳ	τῷ	πιστῷ	καὶ
humōn	sun	Onēsimō	tō	pistō	kai
your;	with	Onesimus,	the	faithful	and

until the time of his death, the apostle's consuming desire was to help other people know this same kind of experience.

4:5. New Testament Christians used the term "them that are without" or "outsiders" (*tous exō*) for those people who were unbelievers (1 Corinthians 5:12,13; 1 Thessalonians 4:12; 1 Timothy 3:7), but they did not use the term in a derogatory manner. Paul's instruction to "walk in wisdom toward them" shows his first reason for stating Christians should be "redeeming the time." They were to "buy up" every opportunity to be guided by wisdom, or to take every opportunity to live up to the light of God's will (1:9).

5. Walk in wisdom toward them that are without: Be wise in your behavior toward non-Christians, *Phillips*.

redeeming the time: ... and lose no oportunite, *Cranmer* ... buying up your opportunities, *Montgomery* ... make the best possible use of, *Phillips*.

4:6. Paul's second area of concern was related to the speech of the Colossian saints. He encouraged them to have speech "with grace," or "gracious" (RSV) speech. The person who manifests gracious speech can do so because he has experienced the grace of God in a personal way. Having experienced this marvelous grace should make a person want to see other people also enjoy it. Therefore, gracious speech comes as a result of God's grace being manifested in a Christian.

"Seasoned with salt" comes from a perfect participle (*ērtumenos*) and literally means "having been seasoned," indicating something previously appropriated that continues to operate. The term could refer to the attractiveness of one's speech as salt enhances flavor, or to the idea that salt prevents corruption, from the common use of salt as a preservative. Paul probably had the latter idea in view.

6. Let your speech [be] alway with grace, seasoned with salt: Speak pleasantly to them, but never sentimentally, *Phillips* ... be all wayes well favoured, *Tyndale*.

that ye may know how ye ought to answer every man: ... that ye may know how it is necessary for you to answer each other, *Clementson* ... how to give every man a fitting answer, *Montgomery* ... each one in a proper way, *Norlie*.

4:7. Paul's rather lengthy conclusion to the epistle gives a beautiful portrait of his fellow laborers in the gospel, in addition to referring casually to Barnabas. Paul was not a loner; he apparently enjoyed being with other people. More importantly, he was a very secure man who was not afraid to share his ministry with other people. He normally seemed to have several associates assisting him. He definitely had learned the important lesson of reproducing himself through other people. Paul called Tychicus a "beloved brother," a "faithful minister and fellow servant" (Acts 20:4; Ephesians 6:21; 2 Timothy 4:12; Titus 3:12).

7. All my state shall Tychicus declare unto you: All my circumstances, *PNT* ... All my affairs, *ASV* ... will inform you of all things relating to me, *Sawyer*.

[who is] a beloved brother, and a faithful minister and fellow-servant in the Lord: ... and Faithful Assistant, *Wilson* ... in the Master's work, *TCNT*.

4:8. Tychicus proved himself to be such a faithful associate of Paul that the latter was able to send him all the way from Rome to visit the Colossians. Paul knew these saints were concerned about his welfare, and he was concerned about their state of affairs. So, he sent a personal emissary at least 1,000 miles.

8. Whom I have sent unto you for the same purpose: This is partly why, *Phillips* ... for this very purpose, *Montgomery*.

that he might know your estate, and comfort your hearts: The other reasons are...that he may put new heart into you, *Phillips* ... the things that concern you, *Douay* ... that he might know your affairs, *Murdock* ... that he may know your condition, *Noyes* ... that he may give your hearts renewed courage, *Norlie* ... to cheer your hearts, *Montgomery*.

27.2 adj dat sing	79.3 noun dat sing masc	3614.5 rel-pron nom sing masc	1498.4 verb 3sing indic pres act	1523.1 prep gen	5050.2 prs- pron gen 2pl
ἀγαπητῷ	ἀδελφῷ,	ὅς	ἐστιν	ἐξ	ὑμῶν
agapētō	adelphō	hos	estin	ex	humōn
beloved	brother,	who	is	of	you.

9.a.Txt: 01ℵ-org,02A
04C,06D-corr,018K
020L,33,byz.Tisc,Sod
Var: 01ℵ-corr,03B,025P
Lach,We/Ho,Weis
UBS/✩

3820.1 adj	5050.3 prs- pron dat 2pl	1101.12 verb 3pl indic fut act	1101.18 verb 3pl indic fut act
πάντα	ὑμῖν	⸂ γνωριοῦσιν	[a☆ γνωρίσουσιν]
panta	humin	gnōriousin	gnōrisousin
All things	to you	they will make known	[idem]

3450.17 art pl neu	5436.1 adv	776.2 verb 3sing indic pres mid	5050.4 prs- pron acc 2pl	702.1 name nom masc
τὰ	ὧδε.	**10.** Ἀσπάζεται	ὑμᾶς	Ἀρίσταρχος
ta	hōde	Aspazetai	humas	Aristarchos
the things	here.	Greets	you	Aristarchus

3450.5 art nom sing masc	4720.1 noun nom sing masc	1466.2 prs- pron gen 1sing	2504.1 conj	3111.1 name nom masc	3450.5 art nom sing masc
ὁ	συναιχμάλωτός	μου,	καὶ	Μᾶρκος	ὁ
ho	sunaichmalōtos	mou	kai	Markos	ho
the	fellow prisoner	my,	and	Mark,	the

429.1 noun nom sing masc	915.2 name masc	3875.1 prep	3614.2 rel- pron gen sing	2956.16 verb 2pl indic aor act
ἀνεψιὸς	Βαρναβᾶ,	περὶ	οὗ	ἐλάβετε
anepsios	Barnaba	peri	hou	elabete
cousin	of Barnabas,	concerning	whom	you received

1769.7 noun acc pl fem	1430.1 partic	2048.8 verb 3sing subj aor act	4242.1 prep	5050.4 prs- pron acc 2pl	1203.12 verb 2pl impr aor mid
ἐντολάς·	ἐὰν	ἔλθῃ	πρὸς	ὑμᾶς	δέξασθε
entolas	ean	elthē	pros	humas	dexasthe
orders,	if	he come	to	you,	receive

840.6 prs-pron acc sing masc	2504.1 conj	2400.1 name nom masc	3450.5 art nom sing masc	2978.30 verb nom sing masc part pres mid	2434.1 name nom masc
αὐτόν·	**11.** καὶ	Ἰησοῦς	ὁ	λεγόμενος	Ἰοῦστος,
auton	kai	Iēsous	ho	legomenos	Ioustos
him,	and	Jesus	the	being called	Justus,

3450.7 art nom pl masc	1498.23 verb nom pl masc part pres act	1523.2 prep gen	3921.2 noun gen sing fem	3642.7 dem- pron nom pl masc
οἱ	ὄντες	ἐκ	περιτομῆς	οὗτοι
hoi	ontes	ek	peritomēs	houtoi
the	being	of	circumcision.	These

3304.5 adj nom pl masc	4754.4 adj nom pl masc	1519.1 prep	3450.12 art acc sing fem	926.4 noun acc sing fem	3450.2 art gen sing
μόνοι	συνεργοὶ	εἰς	τὴν	βασιλείαν	τοῦ
monoi	sunergoi	eis	tēn	basileian	tou
only	fellow workers	for	the	kingdom	tou

2296.2 noun gen sing masc	3610.2 rel- pron nom pl masc	1090.37 verb 3pl indic aor pass	1466.4 prs- pron dat 1sing	3793.1 noun nom sing fem
θεοῦ,	οἵτινες	ἐγενήθησάν	μοι	παρηγορία.
theou	hoitines	egenēthēsan	moi	parēgoria
of God,	who	were	to me	a consolation.

776.2 verb 3sing indic pres mid	5050.4 prs- pron acc 2pl	1874.1 name nom masc	3450.5 art nom sing masc	1523.1 prep gen
12. ἀσπάζεται	ὑμᾶς	Ἐπαφρᾶς	ὁ	ἐξ
aspazetai	humas	Epaphras	ho	ex
Greets	you	Epaphras	the	of

4:9. Onesimus, Philemon's runaway slave who had been converted under Paul's ministry in Rome, was a native of Colossae and is described in detail in the apostle's letter to Philemon. Onesimus and Tychicus took the letter to the Colossian church. By the time Paul wrote his epistle to the Colossians Onesimus had become "a faithful and beloved brother."

4:10. Next, Paul mentioned three Jews who were assisting him at that time. Aristarchus (Acts 19:29; 20:4; 27:2) was a Macedonian from Thessalonica. While it is possible that this man voluntarily became a prisoner in order to assist Paul, the title "fellow prisoner" may be used in a metaphorical sense to denote a person's voluntary submission to Christ.

John Mark was Barnabas' cousin who had abandoned Paul and Barnabas during Paul's first missionary journey (Acts 13:5,13). (Although the King James' translators referred to Mark as Barnabas' nephew, most commentators render the Greek term *ho anepsios* as "cousin." The word actually could mean either.)

When Barnabas wanted to take Mark on the second journey, a serious rift developed between him and Paul (Acts 15:37-39). The apostle eventually was reconciled to both men (1 Corinthians 9:6; 2 Timothy 4:11; Philemon 24). As far as we know, Paul's reference to Mark here is the first mention made of the latter since that separation. The apostle's attitude toward Mark had made a complete about-face. This same Mark was a companion to Peter (1 Peter 5:13) and wrote the second Gospel. The parentheses in verse 10 may indicate Paul had written previously to the Colossian church.

4:11. Jesus Justus completed the trio of Jews who were a comfort to Paul at that time. "Jesus," the Greek form of *Joshua* or *Jeshua*, was a common Jewish name, but in this case it was coupled with the Latin surname *Justus*, meaning "the just" or "the righteous." This is the only reference to him in the Scriptures. Paul's comment in this verse does not imply these men were the only Jews to accept the gospel message. It just means that at that time they were the only Jews assisting him in his ministry. The statement probably relates only to Jews who were connected with Paul's ministry while he was in prison.

4:12. Paul also mentioned three Gentiles who were supporting him for the gospel at that time. Epaphras, who probably started the churches in Colossae, Laodicea, and Hierapolis, had been sent by the Colossians to visit the apostle. He must have been converted during the 3 years Paul ministered in Ephesus (Acts 20:31), spent some time under Paul's tutelage, and returned to his home area to publish the good news about Jesus Christ to his family, friends, and others. In this verse Paul commended Epaphras for being a servant of Christ Jesus and for earnestly praying for the saints in

9. With Onesimus, a faithful and beloved brother: . . . our dear trustworthy Brother, *TCNT* . . . well loved, *Phillips.*

who is [one] of you: . . . who is one of your own number, *Williams* . . . of your own congregations, *Phillips.*

They shall make known unto you all things which [are done] here: They will tell You, *Wilson* . . . will inform you of every thing here, *Noyes* . . . of conditions and activities here, *Phillips* . . . that is going on here, *TCNT.*

10. Aristarchus my fellow-prisoner saluteth you: . . . my fellow-captive, *Wilson, Murdock* . . . sends you his good wishes, *TCNT* . . . wishes to be remembered to you, *Williams.*

and Marcus, sister's son to Barnabas: . . . the first-cousin, *Rotherham* . . . the cousin of, *Panin, Montgomery.*

(touching whom ye received commandments: I believe I told you before about him, *Phillips* . . . about whom you received, *Montgomery* . . . received instructions, *Confraternity* . . . received directions, *Noyes.*

if he come unto you, receive him;): . . . give him welcome, *Rotherham* . . . give him a hearty welcome, *Williams.*

11. And Jesus, which is called Justus: So does Jesus who is called, *Williams* . . . Joshua, *TCNT.*

who are of the circumcision. These only [are my] fellowworkers unto the kingdom of God, which have been a comfort unto me: Of the Jewish Christians, *Norlie* . . . another Hebrew Christian, *Phillips* . . . though still holding to circumcision, *TCNT* . . . These are the only converts from Judaism that are fellowworkers with me here for the kingdom of God, who have proved a real comfort to me, *Williams* . . . became to me an encouragement, *Rotherham* . . . which were vnto my consolacion, *Tyndale.*

12. Epaphras, who is [one] of you: . . . one of your own number, *Williams* . . . another member of your Church, *Phillips.*

12.a.Var: 01א,02A,03B
04C,020L,33,bo.Lach
Treg,Alf,Tisc,We/Ho
Weis,Sod,UBS/✶

5050.2 prs-pron gen 2pl	1395.1 noun nom sing masc	5382.2 name gen masc	2400.2 name masc	3704.1 adv
ὑμῶν	δοῦλος	Χριστοῦ,	[a✶+ Ἰησοῦ,]	πάντοτε
humōn	doulos	Christou	lēsou	pantote
you,	a slave	of Christ,	[Jesus,]	always

74.3 verb nom sing masc part pres mid	5065.1 prep	5050.2 prs-pron gen 2pl	1706.1 prep	3450.14 art dat pl fem
ἀγωνιζόμενος	ὑπὲρ	ὑμῶν	ἐν	ταῖς
agōnizomenos	huper	humōn	en	tais
striving	for	you	in	the

12.b.Txt: 01א-corr,02A
04C,06D,018K,020L
025P,etc.byz.
Var: 01א-org,03B,Treg
Tisc,We/Ho,Weis,Sod
UBS/✶

4194.7 noun dat pl fem	2419.1 conj	2449.6 verb 2pl aor act	2449.55 verb 2pl subj aor pass	4894.3 adj nom pl masc
προσευχαῖς,	ἵνα	στῆτε	[b✶ σταθῆτε]	τέλειοι
proseuchais	hina	stēte	stathēte	teleioi
prayers,	that	you may stand	[idem]	perfect

12.c.Txt: 06D-corr,018K
020L,025P,byz.
Var: 01א,02A,03B,04C
06D-org,33,Lach,Treg
Alf,Word,Tisc,We/Ho
Weis,Sod,UBS/✶

2504.1 conj	3997.30 verb nom pl masc part perf mid	3995.6 verb nom pl masc part perf mid	1706.1 prep
καὶ	πεπληρωμένοι	[c✶ πεπληροφορημένοι]	ἐν
kai	peplērōmenoi	peplērophorēmenoi	en
and	having been complete	[having been fully convinced]	in

3820.3 adj dat sing	2284.3 noun dat sing neu	3450.2 art gen sing	2296.2 noun gen sing masc	3113.1 verb 1sing pres act	1056.1 conj
παντὶ	θελήματι	τοῦ	θεοῦ.	13. μαρτυρῶ	γὰρ
panti	thelēmati	tou	theou	marturō	gar
every	will	the	of God.	I bear witness	for

13.a.Txt: 018K,020L
044,byz.
Var: 01א,02A,03B,04C
025P,Gries,Lach,Treg
Alf,Tisc,We/Ho,Weis
Sod,UBS/✶

840.4 prs-pron dat sing	3617.1 conj	2174.4 verb 3sing indic pres act	2188.4 noun sing	4044.6 adj acc sing masc	4044.6 adj acc sing masc
αὐτῷ	ὅτι	ἔχει	ζῆλον	πολὺν	[a✶ πολὺν
autō	hoti	echei	zēlon	polun	polun
to him	that	he has	zeal	much	[much

4051.4 noun acc sing masc	5065.1 prep	5050.2 prs-pron gen 2pl	2504.1 conj	3450.1 art gen pl	1706.1 prep	2965.2 name dat fem
πόνον]	ὑπὲρ	ὑμῶν	καὶ	τῶν	ἐν	Λαοδικείᾳ
ponon	huper	humōn	kai	tōn	en	Laodikeia
anguish]	for	you	and	the	in	Laodicea

2504.1 conj	3450.1 art gen pl	1706.1 prep	2380.1 name dat fem	776.2 verb 3sing indic pres mid	5050.4 prs-pron acc 2pl
καὶ	τῶν	ἐν	Ἱεραπόλει.	14. ἀσπάζεται	ὑμᾶς
kai	tōn	en	Hierapolei	aspazetai	humas
and	them	in	Hierapolis.	Greets	you

3037.1 name nom masc	3450.5 art nom sing masc	2372.1 noun nom sing masc	3450.5 art nom sing masc	27.3 adj nom sing masc	2504.1 conj
Λουκᾶς	ὁ	ἰατρὸς	ὁ	ἀγαπητὸς,	καὶ
Loukas	ho	iatros	ho	agapētos	kai
Luke	the	physician	the	beloved,	and

1208.1 name nom masc	776.9 verb 2pl impr aor mid	3450.8 art acc pl masc	1706.1 prep	2965.2 name dat fem
Δημᾶς.	15. Ἀσπάσασθε	τοὺς	ἐν	Λαοδικείᾳ
Dēmas	Aspasasthe	tous	en	Laodikeia
Demas.	Greet	the	in	Laodicea

79.9 noun acc pl masc	2504.1 conj	3427.1 name acc masc	2504.1 conj	3450.12 art acc sing fem	2567.1 prep	3486.4 noun acc sing masc
ἀδελφοὺς,	καὶ	Νυμφᾶν	καὶ	τὴν	κατ’	οἶκον
adelphous	kai	Numphan	kai	tēn	kat’	oikon
brothers,	and	Nymphas,	and	the	in	house

Colossae, Laodicea, and Hierapolis because he wanted them to mature in Christ.

4:13. This verse continues to emphasize how concerned Epaphras was that these three churches should be delivered from the Gnostic heresy. The fact that he traveled all the way from Colossae to Rome to seek Paul's advice and help certainly indicates the severity of the situation. Too often believers allow false doctrines to infiltrate church congregations without taking the matter seriously.

Much gnosticism under different names has infiltrated into some contemporary churches. Perhaps if more people were wrestling in prayer as Epaphras did, there would be less trouble with such heresy. People who are in constant communion with God in prayer certainly are more capable of detecting false doctrine when the devil tries to introduce it into an assembly. If he cannot keep people from believing the gospel, he will try to get them off track with false doctrine. Many modern assemblies seem to be troubled with some of the same false doctrines that Paul exposed in this epistle, especially in the second chapter where he specifically pinpointed certain views that were inconsistent with the completeness of believers in Christ.

a servant of Christ, saluteth you: ... wishes to be remembered to you, *Williams* ... sends his greeting, *Phillips.*

always labouring fervently for you in prayers: ... always striving, *Sawyer* ... who is ever solicitous for you, *Confraternity* ... He works hard for you, *Phillips* ... always earnestly pleading for you in his prayers, *Williams* ... always agonizing for you, *Montgomery* ... striving for you, *Panin* ... contending in your behalf, *Rotherham.*

that ye may stand perfect and complete in all the will of God: ... that you may become mature, *Phillips* ... that you may hold out and perfectly carry out God's will in everything, *Norlie* ... that you may stand fast as men mature and of firm convictions in everything required by the will of God, *Williams* ... fully assured in, *Panin, Rotherham, Alford, Noyes* ... in the Whole Will of God, *Wilson* ... in all the good pleasure of God, *Murdock.*

4:14. Luke, the author of the third Gospel and Acts, was a physician who accompanied Paul on parts of his second and third missionary journeys, as well as on his voyage to Rome. He may have used his healing skills to help the apostle, but we know for certain he faithfully assisted Paul in the gospel ministry (2 Timothy 4:10,11; Philemon 24).

Anyone who knows much about the Greek language will agree that Luke's writings reflect the knowledge of a highly educated person. That, of course, would have meant nothing without the help of the Holy Spirit. The way the Acts of the Apostles was written should be ample proof of Luke's dependence upon the Spirit. Incidentally, Luke wrote a larger part of the New Testament than even Paul did, although the latter wrote a greater number of books. Some people give the impression that education helps very little when a person dedicates himself to Christian ministry. They stress that inspiration is far more important than education. Obviously, education will not suffice by itself. However, when inspiration, or the help of the Holy Spirit, is coupled with education, a person often has a wider sphere of ministry.

13. For I bear him record: For I can testify, *Williams* ... From my own observation I can tell you, *Phillips.*

that he hath a great zeal for you: ... to his deep interest in you, *Montgomery* ... he has a real passion for your welfare, *Phillips* ... how great his toiling for you is, *Williams* ... much labour for you, *Douay, ASV.*

and them [that are] in Laodicea and them in Hierapolis: ... and for the brothers, *Williams* ... and for that of the Churches at, *Phillips.*

14. Luke, the beloved physician, and Demas, greet you: ... our much-loved doctor, *TCNT* ... the most deere, *Rheims* ... Our dearly loved ...wish to be remembered to you, *Williams.*

4:15. During the first centuries of the Early Church, local bodies of believers normally met for worship in houses like this one. Many of them contained large upper rooms which lent themselves to large gatherings of people. Normally only people who were fairly wealthy

15. Salute the brethren which are in Laodicea, and Nymphas: ... greetings, *Phillips* ... Remember me to the brothers, *Williams.*

Colossians 4:16

15.a.**Txt:** 06D,018K
020L,byz.bo.Sod
Var1: 03B,1739,sa.Lach
We/Ho,Weis,UBS/★
Var2: 01ℵ,02A,04C
025P,33,bo.Treg,Alf
Tisc

840.3 prs-pron gen sing	840.10 prs-pron gen sing fem	840.1 prs-pron gen pl	1564.4 noun acc sing fem	2504.1 conj
῾ αὐτοῦ	[1a★ αὐτῆς	2 αὐτῶν]	ἐκκλησίαν·	16. καὶ
autou	autēs	autōn	ekklēsian	kai
his	[her	their]	assembly.	And

3615.1 conj	312.17 verb 3sing subj aor pass	3706.1 prep	5050.3 prs-pron dat 2pl	3450.9 art nom sing fem	1976.1 noun nom sing fem
ὅταν	ἀναγνωσθῇ	παρ'	ὑμῖν	ἡ	ἐπιστολή,
hotan	anagnōsthē	par'	humin	hē	epistolē
when	may be read	among	you	the	epistle,

4020.36 verb 2pl impr aor act	2419.1 conj	2504.1 conj	1706.1 prep	3450.11 art dat sing fem	2966.1 name-adj gen pl masc
ποιήσατε	ἵνα	καὶ	ἐν	τῇ	Λαοδικέων
poiēsate	hina	kai	en	tē	Laodikeōn
cause	that	also	in	the	of Laodiceans

1564.3 noun dat sing fem	312.17 verb 3sing subj aor pass	2504.1 conj	3450.12 art acc sing fem	1523.2 prep gen	2965.1 name gen fem
ἐκκλησίᾳ	ἀναγνωσθῇ,	καὶ	τὴν	ἐκ	Λαοδικείας
ekklēsia	anagnōsthē	kai	tēn	ek	Laodikeias
assembly	it may be read,	and	the	from	Laodicea

2419.1 conj	2504.1 conj	5050.1 prs-pron nom 2pl	312.8 verb 2pl subj aor act	2504.1 conj	1500.1 verb 2pl aor act
ἵνα	καὶ	ὑμεῖς	ἀναγνῶτε·	17. καὶ	εἴπατε
hina	kai	humeis	anagnōte	kai	eipate
that	also	you	may read.	And	say

746.1 name dat masc	984.10 verb 2sing impr pres act	3450.12 art acc sing fem	1242.4 noun acc sing fem	3614.12 rel-pron acc sing fem
Ἀρχίππῳ,	Βλέπε	τὴν	διακονίαν	ἣν
Archippō	Blepe	tēn	diakonian	hēn
to Archippus,	Take heed to	the	service	which

3741.5 verb 2sing indic aor act	1706.1 prep	2935.3 noun dat sing masc	2419.1 conj	840.12 prs-pron acc sing fem	3997.1 verb 2sing subj pres act
παρέλαβες	ἐν	κυρίῳ,	ἵνα	αὐτὴν	πληροῖς.
parelabes	en	kuriō	hina	autēn	plērois
you did receive	in	Lord,	that	it	you fulfill.

3450.5 art nom sing masc	777.1 noun nom sing masc	3450.11 art dat sing fem	1684.8 adj dat sing fem	5331.3 noun dat sing fem	3834.2 name gen masc
18. Ὁ	ἀσπασμὸς	τῇ	ἐμῇ	χειρὶ	Παύλου.
Ho	aspasmos	tē	emē	cheiri	Paulou
The	greeting	by the	my	hand	of Paul.

18.a.**Txt:** 01ℵ-corr,06D
018K,020L,025P,byz.bo.
Var: 01ℵ-org,02A,03B
04C,33,Gries,Lach,Treg
Alf,Word,Tisc,We/Ho
Weis,Sod,UBS/★

3285.1 verb 2pl pres act	1466.2 prs-pron gen 1sing	3450.1 art gen pl	1193.4 noun gen pl	3450.9 art nom sing fem	5322.1 noun nom sing fem
μνημονεύετέ	μου	τῶν	δεσμῶν.	ἡ	χάρις
mnēmoneuete	mou	tōn	desmōn	hē	charis
Remember	my	the	bonds.	The	grace

18.b.**Txt:** 018K,Steph
Var: Gries,Lach,Word
Tisc,We/Ho,Weis,Sod
UBS/★

3196.1 prep	5050.2 prs-pron gen 2pl	279.1 intrj	4242.1 prep	2825.3 name dat fem	1119.21 verb 3sing indic aor pass
μεθ'	ὑμῶν.	῾a ἀμήν. ῾	῾b Πρὸς	Κολασσαεῖς	ἐγράφη
meth'	humōn	amēn	Pros	Kolassaeis	egraphē
with	you.	Amen.	To	Colossians	written

570.3 prep	4373.1 name gen fem	1217.2 prep	5031.2 name gen masc	2504.1 conj	3545.1 name gen masc
ἀπὸ	Ῥώμης,	διὰ	Τυχικοῦ	καὶ	Ὀνησίμου. ῾
apo	Rhōmēs	dia	Tuchikou	kai	Onēsimou
from	Rome,	by	Tychicus	and	Onesimus.

could afford such houses, so Nymphas must have been relatively affluent. Later in church history, the crowds became too large to meet in individual homes, so buildings were constructed for worship. Of course, Jesus himself made it clear that true worship does not depend upon the physical location (John 4:21-24).

and the church which is in his house: . . . and the assembly, *PNT* . . . the congregation, *Phillips* . . . the church that meets at her house, *Williams* . . . which meets at her home, *Montgomery.*

4:16. The "epistle from Laodicea" is a mystery. Some commentators think the statement is a reference to the letter we know as Ephesians. Ephesians probably was written as a cyclical letter to be circulated throughout the churches in Asia Minor, but it is very unlikely the author of the letter would call it the "letter from Laodicea" (NIV). A spurious letter that claims to be this "letter from Laodicea" does exist, but even a novice can detect that it consists of plagiarism of some of Paul's writings. The most likely and simplest explanation of this problem is that Paul did indeed write a letter to the Laodiceans which was lost for some reason. The fact that Paul told the Colossians to have this epistle read also in the Loaodicean church seems proof enough of this latter theory.

16. And when this epistle is read among you: When this letter has been read to you, *Williams* . . . in your Church, *Phillips.*

cause that it be read also in the church of the Laodiceans: . . . have it read to, *Williams.*

and that ye likewise read the [epistle] from Laodicea: . . . and see to it that you too read the one that is coming from, *Williams* . . . see that you read the letter I have written to them, *Phillips.*

4:17. Although we cannot be positive, Archippus probably was the son of Philemon and Apphia (Philemon 2) and may have been selected by the church as interim pastor during the absence of the pastor, Epaphras. The language of this verse does seem to indicate that some ministerial responsibility had been assigned to Archippus. "Take heed" literally comes from a Greek word (*blepe*) usually translated "look to" in this type of construction, and "ministry" is derived from the term from which we normally get *deacon* (*diakonian*), often meaning "ministry." Paul seemed convinced that Archippus had received this ministry "in the Lord," so it was not assigned to him through the will of man alone.

17. And say to Archippus: A brief message to, *Phillips* . . . tell Archippus, *Williams.*

Take heed to the ministry which thou hast received in the Lord, that thou fulfil it: Be attentive, *Murdock* . . . Attend to...to perform it fully, *Sawyer* . . . Attend on the service, *Wilson* . . . See to it that you continue until you fill full your ministry which you received in the Lord's work, *Williams* . . . be careful to discharge to the best of his ability the office to which he was appointed, *TCNT* . . . God called you into his service—Oh, do not fail Him! *Norlie.*

4:18. Apparently an amanuensis, a person who writes what someone else dictates, had written the epistle up to this point. Most of Paul's epistles seem to indicate this normal pattern. Some people argue that Paul's use of this procedure proves his sight had deteriorated to the point that he was forced to use a secretary. It also could stem from the possibility that he had very poor handwriting, so used someone whose handwriting would be more readable. It was customary for Paul to write a few words of greeting with his own hand to mark the autographed letter as genuine and to discourage the spread of spurious letters.

Finally, he reminded the Colossians of his physical chains, a fact he referred to several times throughout the Prison Epistles. He did not state this to elicit sympathy, but perhaps to remind believers that his circumstances had been sifted through the grace of God. Perhaps that is why he included his final benediction, "Grace be with you." He knew God did not show special favor to him, but would manifest His grace to all individuals who would depend upon it. That fact has never changed.

18. The salutation by the hand of me Paul: This farewell greeting is, *Williams* . . . add this farewell in my own hand-writing, *TCNT, Montgomery* . . . My personal greeting to you written by myself, *Phillips.*

Remember my bonds: Be mindful of my bonds, *Wesley* . . . be ye myndeful of my boondis, *Wyclif* . . . Keep in mind, *Rotherham* . . . My chains! *Wilson* . . . Remember that I am still a prisoner, *Williams* . . . Don't forget I'm in prison, *Phillips.*

Grace [be] with you. Amen: Spiritual blessing, *Williams* . . . God's blessing be with you, *TCNT.*

THE FIRST EPISTLE
OF PAUL TO THE
THESSALONIANS

Expanded Interlinear

Textual Critical Apparatus

Verse-by-Verse Commentary

Various Versions

4242.1 prep
Πρὸς
Pros
To

2309.4 name dat fem
Θεσσαλονικεῖς
Thessalonikeis
Thessalonians

1976.1 noun nom sing fem
ἐπιστολὴ
epistolē
letter

3834.2 name gen masc
Παύλου
Paulou
of Paul

4272.9 num ord nom sing fem
πρώτη
prōtē
first

3834.1 name nom masc
1:1. Παῦλος
Paulos
Paul

2504.1 conj
καὶ
kai
and

4465.1 name nom masc
Σιλουανὸς
Silouanos
Silvanus

2504.1 conj
καὶ
kai
and

4943.1 name nom masc
Τιμόθεος,
Timotheos
Timothy,

3450.11 art dat sing fem
τῇ
tē
to the

1564.3 noun dat sing fem
ἐκκλησίᾳ
ekklēsia
assembly

2308.2 name-adj gen pl masc
Θεσσαλονικέων
Thessalonikeōn
of Thessalonians

1706.1 prep
ἐν
en
in

2296.3 noun dat sing masc
θεῷ
theō
God

3824.3 noun dat sing masc
πατρὶ
patri
Father

2504.1 conj
καὶ
kai
and

2935.3 noun dat sing masc
κυρίῳ
kuriō
Lord

2400.2 name masc
Ἰησοῦ
Iēsou
Jesus

5382.3 name dat masc
Χριστῷ·
Christō
Christ.

5322.1 noun nom sing fem
χάρις
charis
Grace

5050.3 prs-pron dat 2pl
ὑμῖν
humin
to you

2504.1 conj
καὶ
kai
and

1503.1 noun nom sing fem
εἰρήνη
eirēnē
peace

⌐a **570.3** prep
ἀπὸ
apo
from

2296.2 noun gen sing masc
Θεοῦ
Theou
God

3824.2 noun gen sing masc
πατρὸς
patros
Father

2231.2 prs-pron gen 1pl
ἡμῶν
hēmōn
our

2504.1 conj
καὶ
kai
and

2935.2 noun gen sing masc
κυρίου
kuriou
Lord

2400.2 name masc
Ἰησοῦ
Iēsou
Jesus

5382.2 name gen masc
Χριστοῦ. ⌐
Christou
Christ.

2149.4 verb 1pl indic pres act
2. Εὐχαριστοῦμεν
Eucharistoumen
We give thanks

3450.3 art dat sing
τῷ
tō
to the

2296.3 noun dat sing masc
θεῷ
theō
to God

3704.1 adv
πάντοτε
pantote
always

3875.1 prep
περὶ
peri
concerning

3820.4 adj gen pl
πάντων
pantōn
all

5050.2 prs-pron gen 2pl
ὑμῶν,
humōn
you,

3281.2 noun acc sing fem
μνείαν
mneian
mention

⌐a **5050.2** prs-pron gen 2pl
ὑμῶν ⌐
humōn
of you

4020.65 verb nom pl masc part pres mid
ποιούμενοι
poioumenoi
making

1894.3 prep
ἐπὶ
epi
at

3450.1 art gen pl
τῶν
tōn
the

4194.6 noun gen pl fem
προσευχῶν
proseuchōn
prayers

2231.2 prs-pron gen 1pl
ἡμῶν,
hēmōn
our,

88.1 adv
3. ἀδιαλείπτως
adialeiptōs
unceasingly

3285.6 verb nom pl masc part pres act
μνημονεύοντες
mnēmoneuontes
remembering

5050.2 prs-pron gen 2pl
ὑμῶν
humōn
your

3450.2 art gen sing
τοῦ
tou
the

2024.2 noun gen sing neu
ἔργου
ergou
work

3450.10 art gen sing fem
τῆς
tēs
of the

3963.2 noun gen sing fem
πίστεως
pisteōs
faith

2504.1 conj
καὶ
kai
and

3450.2 art gen sing
τοῦ
tou
the

2845.2 noun gen sing masc
κόπου
kopou
labor

3450.10 art gen sing fem
τῆς
tēs
of the

26.2 noun gen sing fem
ἀγάπης
agapēs
love

1.a.**Txt:** 01א,02A,04C (06D),018K,020L,025P 33,etc.byz.
Var: 03B,044,1739,it.sa. Treg,Alf,Tisc,We/Ho Weis,Sod,UBS/∗

2.a.**Txt:** 01א-corr,04C 06D,018K,020L,025P byz.
Var: 01א-org,02A,03B 33,Lach,Treg,Tisc We/Ho,Weis,Sod UBS/∗

THE FIRST EPISTLE OF PAUL TO THE
THESSALONIANS

1:1. Silas and Timothy joined Paul in greeting the church at Thessalonica. Silas, a leader of the Jerusalem church (Acts 15:22), traveled with Paul on his second missionary journey. Both spread the news of the Spirit's word of wisdom that Gentile Christians were not required to become Jewish proselytes or to be circumcised. Like Paul, Silas was a Roman citizen, and he proved to be an ideal companion in their travels (Acts 16:20,37).

Timothy, on the other hand, was a young man who had a Greek father but a godly Jewish mother and grandmother. The believers in his home church told Paul what an outstanding young believer he was. This led Paul to take Timothy along as a helper and student. Thus the churches sent both younger and older leaders who were well qualified into the work of missions. Both Silas and Timothy were with Paul when the church at Thessalonica was founded.

In saluting the church (the assembly of free citizens of heaven who are under Christ's rule), Paul combined the two greetings, grace (commonly used by the Greeks) and peace (used by the Jews). Many used these words casually, like our "hello," but Paul used them with deep meaning. Grace is given first place. All we have, are, and hope for as Christians comes through the grace ("unmerited favor") of God, shown us by the death of His Son in our place. Then, with our sins taken care of at Calvary, we become recipients of the peace (health, well-being, wholeness, spiritual prosperity) that is our heritage in Christ (John 14:27).

1:2. Though the Thessalonians had needs, Paul did not begin immediately to counsel or exhort the believers. His first thought was to express genuine thanksgiving for them, reminding them of his faithful prayers for them.

1:3. It was never Paul's habit to look on the dark side. His prayers for the Thessalonian Christians were full of the memory of the work which was inspired by their faith, the labor (unremitting toil) that flowed from their love, and the patience (steadfastness, endurance) based on their hope. Though Paul was with them only a short time, the preaching of the Word in the power of the Spirit had established in them the central and most abiding principles of Christian life. As Paul later told the Corinthians, faith, hope, and love will remain when all other gifts and blessings have fulfilled their function and have faded into the past (1 Corinthians 13:13).

Various Versions

1. Paul, and Silvanus, and Timotheus:
unto the church of the Thessalonians: . . . to the ecclesia, *Concordant* . . . to the congregation, *Campbell* . . . to the [local] assembly, *Wuest.*
[which is] in God the Father and [in] the Lord Jesus Christ: . . . assembled in God, *Lilly* . . . in union with God, *TCNT.*
Grace [be] unto you, and peace, from God our Father, and the Lord Jesus Christ: May you have His loving favor, *NLT* . . . Blessing and, *Fenton* . . . Gracious love, *SEB* . . . Favor to you, *Klingensmith* . . . [Sanctifying] grace to you and [tranquilizing] peace, *Wuest.*

2. We give thanks to God always for you all: We offer thanks, *Berkeley* . . . We always thank God, *SEB* . . . I am continually thanking God, *Montgomery.*
making mention of you in our prayers: . . . regularly mentioning you, *Adams* . . . incessantly remembering, *Campbell* . . . constantly mentioning you, *RSV* . . . continually making a remembrance of you, *Confraternity.*

3. Remembering without ceasing your work of faith: We cannot forget, *Norlie* . . . as I call to mind, *Montgomery* . . . we never fail to recall the efforts, *TCNT* . . . and without intermission recall your active faith, *Berkeley* . . . remembering your work that comes from faith, *Adams* . . . produced and characterized by the faith, *Wuest.*
and labour of love: . . . and labor that comes from love, *Adams* . . . and your toil motivated and characterized by your divine and self-sacrificial love, *Wuest* . . . your loving labour, *Fenton.*

1 Thess. 1:4

2504.1 conj	3450.10 art gen sing fem	5119.2 noun gen sing fem	3450.10 art gen sing fem	1667.2 noun gen sing	3450.2 art gen sing
καὶ	τῆς	ὑπομονῆς	τῆς	ἐλπίδος	τοῦ
kai	tēs	hupomonēs	tēs	elpidos	tou
and	the	endurance	of the	hope	of the

2935.2 noun gen sing masc	2231.2 prs-pron gen 1pl	2400.2 name masc	5382.2 name gen masc	1699.1 prep	3450.2 art gen sing
κυρίου	ἡμῶν	Ἰησοῦ	Χριστοῦ,	ἔμπροσθεν	τοῦ
kuriou	hēmōn	Iēsou	Christou	emprosthen	tou
Lord	our	Jesus	Christ,	before	

2296.2 noun gen sing masc	2504.1 conj	3824.2 noun gen sing masc	2231.2 prs-pron gen 1pl	3471.20 verb nom pl masc part perf act	79.6 noun nom pl masc
θεοῦ	καὶ	πατρὸς	ἡμῶν·	**4.** εἰδότες,	ἀδελφοὶ
theou	kai	patros	hēmōn	eidotes	adelphoi
God	and	Father	our;	knowing,	brothers

4.a.Var: 01א,02A,04C 018K,025P,sa.Tisc We/Ho,Sod,UBS/☆

25.30 verb nom pl masc part perf mid	5097.3 prep	3450.2 art gen sing	2296.2 noun gen sing masc	3450.12 art acc sing fem
ἠγαπημένοι	ὑπὸ	[ᵃ☆+ τοῦ]	θεοῦ,	τὴν
ēgapēmenoi	hupo	tou	theou	tēn
having been loved	by		God,	the

1576.3 noun acc sing fem	5050.2 prs-pron gen 2pl	3617.1 conj	3450.16 art sing neu	2077.1 noun sing neu	2231.2 prs-pron gen 1pl
ἐκλογὴν	ὑμῶν	**5.** ὅτι	τὸ	εὐαγγέλιον	ἡμῶν
eklogēn	humōn	hoti	to	euangelion	hēmōn
election	your.	Because	to	good news	our

3620.2 partic	1090.32 verb 3sing indic aor pass	1519.1 prep	5050.4 prs-pron acc 2pl	1706.1 prep	3030.3 noun dat sing masc	3303.1 adv
οὐκ	ἐγενήθη	εἰς	ὑμᾶς	ἐν	λόγῳ	μόνον,
ouk	egenēthē	eis	humas	en	logō	monon,
not	came	to	you	in	word	only,

233.2 conj	2504.1 conj	1706.1 prep	1405.3 noun dat sing fem	2504.1 conj	1706.1 prep	4011.3 noun dat sing masc	39.3 adj dat sing
ἀλλὰ	καὶ	ἐν	δυνάμει	καὶ	ἐν	πνεύματι	ἁγίῳ,
alla	kai	en	dunamei	kai	en	pneumati	hagiō,
but	also	in	power	and	in	Spirit	Holy,

5.a.Txt: p65,02A,04C 06D,018K,020L,025P byz.Sod **Var:** 01א,03B,33,sa.bo. Tisc,We/Ho,Weis UBS/☆

2504.1 conj	1706.1 prep	3996.2 noun dat sing fem	4044.11 adj dat sing fem	2503.1 conj	3471.6 verb 2pl indic perf act
καὶ	⌐ᵃ ἐν ⌐	πληροφορίᾳ	πολλῇ,	καθὼς	οἴδατε
kai	en	plērophoria	pollē,	kathōs	oidate
and	in	full assurance	much,	even as	you know

5.b.Txt: 03B,06D,010F 012G,044,byz. **Var:** 01א,02A,04C,025P 048,33,81,104,945 1739,1881

3497.3 rel-pron nom pl masc	1090.34 verb 1pl indic aor pass	1706.1 prep	5050.3 prs-pron dat 2pl	1217.1 prep
οἷοι	ἐγενήθημεν	⌐ᵇ ἐν ⌐	ὑμῖν	δι'
hoioi	egenēthēmen	en	humin	di'
what	we were	among	you	for the sake of

5050.4 prs-pron acc 2pl	2504.1 conj	5050.1 prs-pron nom 2pl	3266.1 noun nom pl masc	2231.2 prs-pron gen 1pl	1090.35 verb 2pl indic aor pass
ὑμᾶς.	**6.** καὶ	ὑμεῖς	μιμηταὶ	ἡμῶν	ἐγενήθητε
humas.	kai	humeis	mimētai	hēmōn	egenēthēte
you:	and	you	imitators	of us	became

2504.1 conj	3450.2 art gen sing	2935.2 noun gen sing masc	1203.14 verb nom pl masc part aor mid	3450.6 art acc sing masc	3030.4 noun acc sing masc
καὶ	τοῦ	κυρίου,	δεξάμενοι	τὸν	λόγον
kai	tou	kuriou,	dexamenoi	ton	logon
and	of the	Lord,	having accepted	the	word

The order is different here from that in First Corinthians, however. Faith, love, and hope is the order of experience rather than of importance. The preaching of the gospel first becomes effective when it is received in faith. The truth of Christ then gives a confidence in God and brings us to a commitment that is expressed in obedient work. The word *pisteōs* carries the idea of "faith-obedience."

1:4. Paul's thanksgiving for the Thessalonians was tied not only to their faith, love, and hope but also to their "election." The Greek word *eklogēn,* from which comes the English word "election," means a choosing out, the manner of choosing, and the way in which the choice is made. Ephesians 1:4 states that believers are elected in Jesus Christ and that this election was from before the foundation of the world. It was not an arbitrary election but an election "according to the foreknowledge of God the Father" (1 Peter 1:2). The Bible speaks much of God's election and is equally clear concerning man's responsibility to make his calling and election sure by faith and faithfulness.

1:5. Verses 5 and 6 give two reasons Paul knew their faith was real and why he could recognize them as brothers loved by God (loved with a continuing, abiding, faithful, holy love).

First, Paul knew their faith was real because of the way the gospel was presented. It was not just a matter of reasoning or eloquence. Paul had not come with the ranting of a deranged leader, nor with the persuasion of some modern philosopher, nor with the high pressure methods of some of the modern cults. He presented the gospel in word. It had content and meaning. But it came also in mighty power (*dunamei*), and in the Holy Spirit, and in much assurance. (See Acts 1:8; John 15:26,27.) The message clearly was not from men but from God. (See 1 Corinthians 2:4,5.)

Paul was not like those promoters of products and ideas who know that much of what they say is pure fabrication. When he preached the necessity of Jesus' death and resurrection in order to satisfy God's justice and show His love, he did so with full confidence in the truth of his message (Acts 17:2,3). The Thessalonians recognized also that Paul and Silas backed up the message by the kind of lives they lived. They knew the character of these men by their kindness toward them, in that all they did was for the sake of the believers. They saw how unselfish the messengers were. They also saw them growing and developing in the power of the Spirit, just as they expected the believers to do.

1:6. Secondly, Paul knew their choice was real because of their response to the gospel. They became followers (imitators) of Paul and of Christ. This was seen in the way they received (welcomed)

and patience of hope: . . . and your enduring hope, *Confraternity* . . . and endurance of hope, *Klingensmith* . . . and steadfastness of hope, *RSV* . . . your hope that never gives up, *NLT*.
in our Lord Jesus Christ:
in the sight of God and our Father: . . . in front of, *Concordant* . . . in the presence of, *Montgomery*.

4. Knowing, brethren beloved, your election of God: I know, O brothers, beloved of God, *Montgomery* . . . we know His choice of you, *Berkeley* . . . that He has chosen you, *Norlie*, *Williams*.

5. For our gospel came not unto you in word only: . . . for the evangel of our God, *Concordant* . . . not merely reach you in talk, *Berkeley* . . . not in mere words, *Norlie* . . . not merely as so many words, *TCNT*.
but also in power, and in the Holy Ghost, and in much assurance: . . . and in much fullness, *Confraternity* . . . and it carried with it full conviction, *TCNT* . . . and with sound conviction, *Berkeley* . . . with full conviction, *RSV* . . . and with deep conviction, *Montgomery* . . . and in much confidence, *Klingensmith* . . . and with absolute certainty, *Williams*.
as ye know what manner of men we were among you for your sake: It was for your good, *Norlie* . . . the manner in which I behaved myself among you, *Montgomery*.

6. And ye became followers of us, and of the Lord: You copied us, *SEB* . . . followed our example, *Norlie* . . . And you imitated us, *Klingensmith* . . . you began to follow the pattern, *Montgomery* . . . followed the example set by us, *Williams*.
having received the word in much affliction: . . . having embraced the word, *Campbell* . . . in spite of great affliction, *Lilly* . . . in great tribulation, *Confraternity*.

1706.1 prep
ἐν
en
in

2324.3 noun dat sing fem
θλίψει
thlipsei
tribulation

4044.11 adj dat sing fem
πολλῇ
pollē
much

3196.3 prep
μετὰ
meta
with

5315.2 noun gen sing fem
χαρᾶς
charas
joy

4011.2 noun gen sing neu
πνεύματος
pneumatos
of Spirit

39.2 adj gen sing
ἁγίου,
hagiou
Holy,

5452.1 conj
7. ὥστε
hōste
so that

1090.63 verb inf aor mid
γενέσθαι
genesthai
to become

5050.4 prs-pron acc 2pl
ὑμᾶς
humas
you

5020.4 noun acc pl masc
⸀ τύπους
tupous
patterns

5020.2 noun acc sing masc
[ᵃ☆ τύπον]
tupon
[a pattern]

3820.5 adj dat pl
πᾶσιν
pasin
to all

3450.4 art dat pl
τοῖς
tois
the

3961.3 verb dat pl masc part pres act
πιστεύουσιν
pisteuousin
believing

1706.1 prep
ἐν
en
in

3450.11 art dat sing fem
τῇ
tē

3081.3 name dat fem
Μακεδονίᾳ
Makedonia
Macedonia

2504.1 conj
καὶ
kai
and

1706.1 prep
[ᵇ☆+ ἐν]
en
[in]

3450.11 art dat sing fem
τῇ
tē

875.3 name dat fem
Ἀχαίᾳ.
Achaia
Achaia:

570.1 prep
8. ἀφ'
aph'
from

5050.2 prs-pron gen 2pl
ὑμῶν
humōn
you

1056.1 conj
γὰρ
gar
for

1820.1 verb 3sing indic perf mid
ἐξήχηται
exēchētai
has sounded out

3450.5 art nom sing masc
ὁ
ho
the

3030.1 noun nom sing masc
λόγος
logos
word

3450.2 art gen sing
τοῦ
tou
of the

2935.2 noun gen sing masc
κυρίου
kuriou
Lord

3620.3 partic
οὐ
ou
not

3303.1 adv
μόνον
monon
only

1706.1 prep
ἐν
en
in

3450.11 art dat sing fem
τῇ
tē

3081.3 name dat fem
Μακεδονίᾳ
Makedonia
Macedonia

2504.1 conj
καὶ
kai
and

1706.1 prep
[ᵃ+ ἐν
en
[in]

3450.11 art dat sing fem
τῇ]
tē

875.3 name dat fem
Ἀχαίᾳ,
Achaia
Achaia,

233.2 conj
⸀ ἀλλὰ
alla
but

233.1 conj
[☆ ἀλλ']
all'
[idem]

2504.1 conj
⸀ᵇ καὶ
kai
also

1706.1 prep
ἐν
en
in

3820.3 adj dat sing
παντὶ
panti
every

4964.3 noun dat sing masc
τόπῳ
topō
place

3450.9 art nom sing fem
ἡ
hē
the

3963.1 noun nom sing fem
πίστις
pistis
faith

5050.2 prs-pron gen 2pl
ὑμῶν
humōn
your

3450.9 art nom sing fem
ἡ
hē
the

4242.1 prep
πρὸς
pros
towards

3450.6 art acc sing masc
τὸν
ton

2296.4 noun acc sing masc
θεὸν
theon
God

1814.22 verb 3sing indic perf act
ἐξελήλυθεν,
exelēluthen
has gone abroad,

5452.1 conj
ὥστε
hōste
so as

3231.1 partic
μὴ
mē
no

5367.3 noun acc sing fem
χρείαν
chreian
need

2231.4 prs-pron acc 1pl
⸀ ἡμᾶς
hēmas
for us

2174.29 verb inf pres act
ἔχειν
echein
to have

2174.29 verb inf pres act
[☆ ἔχειν
echein
[to have

2231.4 prs-pron acc 1pl
ἡμᾶς]
hēmas
us]

2953.24 verb inf pres act
λαλεῖν
lalein
to say

4948.10 indef-pron nom sing neu
τι
ti
anything;

840.7 prs-pron nom pl masc
9. αὐτοὶ
autoi
themselves

1056.1 conj
γὰρ
gar
for

3875.1 prep
περὶ
peri
concerning

2231.2 prs-pron gen 1pl
ἡμῶν
hēmōn
us

514.2 verb 3pl indic pres act
ἀπαγγέλλουσιν
apangellousin
relate

the Word and in the way they continued to welcome it with Spirit-given joy even when severe affliction (persecution) arose.

1:7. The word *hōste* introduces a result clause and links together verses 6 and 7. Because they had received and continued welcoming the Word joyfully in the midst of tribulation (verse 6), the believers in Thessalonica had become "patterns" (*tupous*) for Christians not only in their own province of Macedonia but in Achaia (Greece) as well. Originally the word *tupon* described the impression left by a blow. Here the word carries an ethical meaning; that is, they served as "patterns" for Christian conduct and "examples" others could follow (see Morris, *New International Commentary on the New Testament, 1&2 Thessalonians*, p.60). In other words, the entire church became a model for what a Christian church or assembly of the citizens of the kingdom of God ought to be.

Even today the Christian is under careful observation, and his life serves as an example to others, for good or for bad. This is especially true when the believer is in the midst of tribulations. If he remains steadfast in the Faith and loyal to the Lord, his message and his Master are wonderfully proclaimed. If, however, he departs from the Faith and deserts the Saviour, the credibility of the gospel suffers. To the unbeliever in particular, one's actions speak louder than one's words.

1:8. By pointing to them as an example Paul did not mean the church was without problems. That which made them a pattern for others was the fact that from them the Word of the Lord (the message concerning Christ) rang out and *continued* to ring out (expressed by the perfect tense verb *exēchētai*). The picturesque word translated "sounded out" in the KJV occurs but once in the New Testament. From the time of Chrysostom (ca. A.D. 347–407) it has been thought to symbolize the brilliant tone and dynamic resonance of a sustained trumpet blast (see "Homilies on Thessalonians" in *Nicence and Post-Nicene Fathers*, 13:327ff.). Chrysostom also makes this observation about the virtuous character of a true Christian: "As a sweet-smelling ointment keeps not its fragrance shut up in itself, but diffuses it afar, . . . so too illustrious and admirable men do not shut up their virtue within themselves, but by their good report benefit many and render them better" (ibid., 13:327). Their message was clear and loud, like the crashing of thunder or like the continuous, clear call of a trumpeter leading an army attacking an enemy.

Not only was their witness effective in Macedonia and Achaia, but their location on the Egnatian Way, a major Roman trade route, brought them in contact with travelers from all over the Roman Empire. The believers took advantage of their opportunities and won many to Christ. The report of the extraordinary faith they expressed to God was spreading in all directions.

with joy of the Holy Ghost: . . . with the delight of, *Fenton* . . . with such joy in, *Beck* . . . joy from, *Adams* . . . with joy inspired by, *RSV* . . . with a gladness inspired by, *TCNT* . . . joy that had its source in, *Wuest*.

7. So that ye were ensamples to all that believe: . . . with the result that you became a model for all those, *Adams* . . . so that you become models to all, *Concordant* . . . you became a pattern to, *Montgomery, Wuest*.
in Macedonia and Achaia: . . . and Greece, *Beck*.

8. For from you sounded out the word of the Lord: . . . it was from you that the Lord's Message resounded, *TCNT* . . . there has been caused to sound forth in a loud, unmistakable proclamation the word, *Wuest* . . . Not only has the Lord's Word spread from you through, *Beck* . . . The Lord's message rang out from you, *SEB* . . . has rung out from you, *Williams* . . . ring out loud and clear throughout, *Norlie* . . . has been echoed abroad, *Fenton*.
not only in Macedonia and Achaia, but also in every place your faith to God-ward is spread abroad: . . . the echo of which still rolls on...in every place your faith which is directed toward God has gone forth, *Wuest* . . . and its sound has been heard...in every place where the tidings of your faith toward God, *Montgomery* . . . but everywhere people have heard of your faith in God, *Beck* . . . but in every place where your faith in God has become known, *Adams* . . . has gone forth, *Lilly* . . . has been broadcast everywhere, *Berkeley* . . . has spread far and wide, *TCNT*.
so that we need not to speak any thing: . . . so that we are not under any necessity to be saying a thing, *Wuest* . . . we need not say another word, *Norlie* . . . so that we don't need to say anything about it, *Adams* . . . so that we need never mention it, *Williams*.

1 Thess. 1:10

9.a.**Txt:** Steph
Var: 01א,02A,03B,04C
06D,018K,020L,25,byz.
Gries,Lach,Treg,Alf
Word,Tisc,We/Ho,Weis
Sod,UBS/☆

3560.2 intr-pron acc sing fem	1513.3 noun acc sing fem	2174.5 verb 1pl indic pres act	2174.52 verb 1pl indic aor act	4242.1 prep
ὁποίαν	εἴσοδον	ʽ ἔχομεν	[a☆ ἔσχομεν]	πρὸς
hopoian	eisodon	echomen	eschomen	pros
what	entrance in	we have	[we had]	to

5050.4 prs-pron acc 2pl	2504.1 conj	4316.1 adv	1978.5 verb 2pl indic aor act	4242.1 prep	3450.6 art acc sing masc	2296.4 noun acc sing masc
ὑμᾶς,	καὶ	πῶς	ἐπεστρέψατε	πρὸς	τὸν	θεὸν
humas	kai	pōs	epestrepsate	pros	ton	theon
you,	and	how	you turned	to	the	God

570.3 prep	3450.1 art gen pl	1487.4 noun gen pl neu	1392.8 verb inf pres act	2296.3 noun dat sing masc	2180.12 verb dat sing masc part pres act
ἀπὸ	τῶν	εἰδώλων,	δουλεύειν	θεῷ	ζῶντι
apo	tōn	eidōlōn	douleuein	theō	zōnti
from	the	idols,	to serve	a God	living

2504.1 conj	226.3 adj dat sing masc	2504.1 conj	360.1 verb inf pres act	3450.6 art acc sing masc	5048.4 noun acc sing masc
καὶ	ἀληθινῷ,	10. καὶ	ἀναμένειν	τὸν	υἱὸν
kai	alēthinō	kai	anamenein	ton	huion
and	true,	and	to await	the	Son

840.3 prs-pron gen sing	1523.2 prep gen	3636.7 noun gen pl masc	3614.6 rel-pron acc sing masc	1446.5 verb 3sing indic aor act	1523.2 prep gen
αὐτοῦ	ἐκ	οὐρανῶν,	ὃν	ἤγειρεν	ἐκ
autou	ek	ouranōn	hon	ēgeiren	ek
his	from	heavens,	whom	he raised	from

10.a.**Var:** 01א,03B,06D
020L,025P,Gries,Lach
Treg,Alf,Tisc,We/Ho
Weis,Sod,UBS/☆

3450.1 art gen pl	3361.2 adj gen pl	2400.3 name acc masc	3450.6 art acc sing masc	4363.3 verb acc sing masc part pres mid	2231.4 prs-pron acc 1pl
[a☆+ τῶν]	νεκρῶν,	Ἰησοῦν	τὸν	ῥυόμενον	ἡμᾶς
tōn	nekrōn	Iēsoun	ton	rhuomenon	hēmas
[the]	dead,	Jesus,	the	delivering	us

10.b.**Txt:** 04C,06D,018K
020L,byz.
Var: 01א,02A,03B,025P
33,Treg,Tisc,We/Ho
Weis,Sod,UBS/☆

570.3 prep	1523.2 prep gen	3450.10 art gen sing fem	3572.2 noun gen sing fem	3450.10 art gen sing fem	2048.50 verb sing fem part pres mid
ʽ ἀπὸ	[b☆ ἐκ]	τῆς	ὀργῆς	τῆς	ἐρχομένης.
apo	ek	tēs	orgēs	tēs	erchomenēs
from	[idem]	the	wrath	the	coming.

840.7 prs-pron nom pl masc	1056.1 conj	3471.6 verb 2pl indic perf act	79.6 noun nom pl masc	3450.12 art acc sing fem	1513.3 noun acc sing fem
2:1. Αὐτοὶ	γὰρ	οἴδατε,	ἀδελφοί,	τὴν	εἴσοδον
Autoi	gar	oidate	adelphoi	tēn	eisodon
Yourselves	for	you know,	brothers,	the	entrance in

2231.2 prs-pron gen 1pl	3450.12 art acc sing fem	4242.1 prep	5050.4 prs-pron acc 2pl	3617.1 conj	3620.3 partic	2727.6 adj nom sing fem
ἡμῶν	τὴν	πρὸς	ὑμᾶς,	ὅτι	οὐ	κενὴ
hēmōn	tēn	pros	humas	hoti	ou	kenē
our	the	to	you,	that	not	void

2.a.**Txt:** Steph
Var: 01א,02A,03B,04C
06D,018K,020L,025P
byz.sa.bo.Gries,Lach
Treg,Alf,Word,Tisc
We/Ho,Weis,Sod
UBS/☆

1090.3 verb 3sing indic perf act	233.2 conj	2504.1 conj	4169.1 verb nom pl masc part aor act	2504.1 conj
γέγονεν,	2. ἀλλὰ	ʽa καὶ ʼ	προπαθόντες	καὶ
gegonen	alla	kai	propathontes	kai
it has been;	but	also	having before suffered	and

5036.4 verb nom pl masc part aor pass	2503.1 conj	3471.6 verb 2pl indic perf act	1706.1 prep	5212.2 name dat masc
ὑβρισθέντες,	καθὼς	οἴδατε,	ἐν	Φιλίπποις,
hubristhentes	kathōs	oidate	en	Philippois
having been insulted,	even as	you know,	at	Philippi,

1:9. Thus it was that when travelers from various parts of the Roman Empire met Paul in Corinth they would immediately begin to tell what they had heard in Thessalonica. They knew that Paul had entered the city and established a church. They told how the Thessalonians had turned to God from idols. This was no mere switching of religious affiliation or changing of philosophies such as the heathen might do. The Thessalonian believers had made a complete and total change in their lives and worship. They were now serving (as love slaves) the living and true (real, genuine) God. By this, they made it clear that the gods they once worshiped were not real. (Compare Isaiah 40:19; 41:7; 44:15-19.)

1:10. As soon as the Thessalonians responded to the truth of the gospel preached in the power of the Holy Spirit, they knew God to be real, and they came to know and love Him. Thus they did not find it hard to serve Him and wait for His Son to come from heaven.

Central to the faith of the Thessalonians was the fact that God had raised Jesus from the dead. His resurrection guarantees the resurrection of the believer (1 Corinthians 15:20; John 11:25,26; 14:19). It also gives the assurance that what Jesus did by His sacrificial death on Calvary makes Him the believer's Deliverer (Rescuer, Preserver) from the wrath which is sure to come on a sinful world.

Paul's preaching to the Gentiles in Thessalonica must have been similar to his preaching to Gentiles in Athens (Acts 17:22-31). Paul taught that God is holy. He cannot go against His own nature. Thus, He cannot bring in Christ's holy kingdom without dealing with sin. He made provision for removing sin at the Cross. But His wrath (which is against sin, not against people) must come. The present world order must be destroyed before Christ can introduce the promised new order (Daniel 2:34,35,44; 7:26,27; John 3:36; Romans 1:18; 9:22; Ephesians 5:6; Colossians 3:6; Revelation 1:18; 14:10,19; 15:7; 16:1; 19:15). In view of this, the believers were always working, always ready, always prepared to meet the Lord.

2:1. What travelers were saying (1:9) about Paul's effective presentation of the gospel, the Thessalonians themselves knew to be true. His ministry was not "in vain" (empty). His preaching was neither foolish, worthless, nor ineffective. More important, the manner of his preaching and the nature of his ministry were not empty in the sense of being hollow, unreal, false, or pretentious.

2:2. These evangelists were not seeking comfort, ease, or the praise of men. The Thessalonians knew what had happened at Philippi (Act 16:19-24) where Paul and Silas were shamefully insulted and treated outrageously. Though they were Roman citizens, they were beaten and thrown into a dank, inner dungeon where they were placed in stocks.

9. For they themselves show of us what manner of entering in we had unto you: For they voluntarily tell about us, *Berkeley* . . . For others, of their own accord, *Montgomery* . . . what a welcome we had among you, *RSV* . . . tell about our coming to you, *Klingensmith* . . . what sort of entrance, *Campbell*.

and how ye turned to God from idols to serve the living and true God: . . . from false gods, *SEB* . . . to be slaves of a true, *Montgomery* . . . the God who lives on and is real, *Williams*.

10. And to wait for his Son from heaven, whom he raised from the dead:

[even] Jesus, which delivered us from the wrath to come: Jesus, our deliverer from the punishment which is impending, *TCNT* . . . our Deliverer from the terror of the future, *Fenton* . . . will rescue us from the punishment that is coming from God, *SEB* . . . who keeps us from the coming wrath, *Klingensmith* . . . from the coming retribution, *Berkeley* . . . out of the coming indignation, *Concordant* . . . from the anger of God that is coming, *NLT*.

1. For yourselves, brethren, know our entrance in unto you, that it was not in vain: You yourselves can testify, *Norlie* . . . did not fail of its purpose, *Montgomery* . . . was not futile, *Berkeley* . . . was by no means a failure, *Williams* . . . was not a failure, *NIV* . . . was not wasted, *NLT* . . . was not without results, *TCNT* . . . was not ineffectual, *Fenton*.

2. But even after that we had suffered before, and were shamefully entreated, as ye know, at Philippi: . . . although I had already borne, *Montgomery* . . . having been injuriously treated, *Young* . . . and being outraged in, *Concordant* . . . and had been insulted, *SEB* . . . shamefully handled, *Campbell* . . . had been ill-treated and insulted, *Norlie*.

3817.5 verb 1pl indic aor mid	1706.1 prep	3450.3 art dat sing	2296.3 noun dat sing masc	2231.2 prs-pron gen 1pl	2953.37 verb inf aor act
ἐπαρρησιασάμεθα	ἐν	τῷ	θεῷ	ἡμῶν	λαλῆσαι
eparrhēsiasametha	en	tō	theō	hēmōn	lalēsai
we were bold	in		God	our	to speak

4242.1 prep	5050.4 prs-pron acc 2pl	3450.16 art sing neu	2077.1 noun sing neu	3450.2 art gen sing	2296.2 noun gen sing masc	1706.1 prep
πρὸς	ὑμᾶς	τὸ	εὐαγγέλιον	τοῦ	θεοῦ	ἐν
pros	humas	to	euangelion	tou	theou	en
to	you	the	good news		of God	in

4044.3 adj dat sing	72.1 noun dat sing masc	3450.9 art nom sing fem	1056.1 conj	3735.1 noun nom sing fem	2231.2 prs-pron gen 1pl	3620.2 partic
πολλῷ	ἀγῶνι.	3. Ἡ	γὰρ	παράκλησις	ἡμῶν	οὐκ
pollō	agōni	Hē	gar	paraklēsis	hēmōn	ouk
much	conflict.	The	for	exhortation	our	not

3.a.Txt: 06D-corr,018K
020L,byz.Sod
Var: 01א,02A,03B,04C
06D-org,025P,33,Lach
Treg,Alf,Word,Tisc
We/Ho,Weis,UBS/☆

1523.2 prep gen	3967.2 noun gen sing fem	3624.1 conj	1523.1 prep gen	165.2 noun gen sing fem	3641.1 conj	3624.1 conj
ἐκ	πλάνης,	οὐδὲ	ἐξ	ἀκαθαρσίας	ʻοὔτε	[a☆ οὐδὲ]
ek	planēs	oude	ex	akatharsias	oute	oude
of	error,	nor	of	uncleanness,	nor	[idem]

1706.1 prep	1382.3 noun dat sing masc	233.2 conj	2503.1 conj	1375.16 verb 1pl indic perf mid	5097.3 prep
ἐν	δόλῳ,	4. ἀλλὰ	καθὼς	δεδοκιμάσμεθα	ὑπὸ
en	dolō	alla	kathōs	dedokimasmetha	hupo
in	deceit;	but	even as	we have been approved	by

3450.2 art gen sing	2296.2 noun gen sing masc	3961.60 verb inf aor pass	3450.16 art sing neu	2077.1 noun sing neu
τοῦ	θεοῦ	πιστευθῆναι	τὸ	εὐαγγέλιον,
tou	theou	pisteuthēnai	to	euangelion
	God	to be entrusted with	the	good news,

3643.1 adv	2953.4 verb 1pl indic pres act	3620.1 partic	5453.1 conj	442.8 noun dat pl masc	694.3 verb nom pl masc part pres act
οὕτως	λαλοῦμεν,	οὐχ	ὡς	ἀνθρώποις	ἀρέσκοντες,
houtōs	laloumen	ouch	hōs	anthrōpois	areskontes
so	we speak;	not	as	men	pleasing,

4.a.Txt: 01א-corr,02A
06D-corr,018K,020L
byz.Sod
Var: 01א-org,03B,04C
06D-org,025P,Treg,Alf
Tisc,We/Ho,Weis
UBS/☆

233.2 conj	3450.3 art dat sing	2296.3 noun dat sing masc	1375.6 verb dat sing masc part pres act	3450.15 art acc pl fem	2559.1 noun fem
ἀλλὰ	ʻa τῷ ʼ	θεῷ,	δοκιμάζοντι	τὰς	καρδίας
alla	tō	theō	dokimazonti	tas	kardias
but	the	God,	proving	the	hearts

2231.2 prs-pron gen 1pl	3641.1 conj	1056.1 conj	4077.1 adv	1706.1 prep	3030.3 noun dat sing masc	2823.1 noun gen sing fem
ἡμῶν.	5. Οὔτε	γὰρ	ποτε	ἐν	λόγῳ	κολακείας
hēmōn	Oute	gar	pote	en	logō	kolakeias
our.	Neither	for	at any time	with	word	of flattery

1090.34 verb 1pl indic aor pass	2503.1 conj	3471.6 verb 2pl indic perf act	3641.1 conj	1706.1 prep	4250.1 noun dat sing fem
ἐγενήθημεν,	καθὼς	οἴδατε,	οὔτε	ἐν	προφάσει
egenēthēmen	kathōs	oidate	oute	en	prophasei
were we,	even as	you know,	nor	with	a pretext

3984.2 noun gen sing fem	2296.1 noun nom sing masc	3116.1 noun nom sing masc	3641.1 conj	2195.10 verb nom pl masc part pres act
πλεονεξίας,	θεὸς	μάρτυς,	6. οὔτε	ζητοῦντες
pleonexias	theos	martus	oute	zētountes
of covetousness,	God	witness;	nor	seeking

But their suffering and abuse at Philippi had not caused Paul and Silas to be timid or wary in presenting the gospel when they came to Thessalonica. The message they preached was the gospel, the good news of God. God gave it, and Paul and Silas were bold, free, open, and fearless in presenting it. Even in the face of great opposition, with enemies contesting every move, they could not keep still. (Compare Jeremiah 20:9.) The greater the conflict, the more intense the struggle, the more courageous the apostles became.

we were bold in our God: . . . we had confidence in, *Confraternity* . . . we took great courage, *Berkeley* . . . we dared to tell you, *NIV*.

to speak unto you the gospel of God with much contention: . . . in much conflict, *Young* . . . amidst a great combat, *Campbell* . . . in spite of great opposition, *TCNT* . . . in spite of the terrific strain, *Williams*.

2:3. There was nothing of pretense about Paul and Silas. However, a strong defense of their ministry was needed, comments F.F. Bruce, because there were so many "wandering charlatans" peddling their religious and philosophical wares for profit (*Word Biblical Commentary*, 45:26). But Paul was not motivated by personal ambition, pride, or prestige. Instead, it was the "love of Christ" that constrained him (see 2 Corinthians 5:14). As a result, their preaching or exhorting did not have its source in deceit (error, delusion, a wandering from the path of truth). Nor did it come from uncleanness (impurity, immorality, vicious or unnatural motives). Paul's methods were also free from guile (cunning, craftiness, and falsity).

3. For our exhortation [was] not of deceit, nor of uncleanness, nor in guile: For our entreaty, *Concordant* . . . For our appeal did not originate from, *Williams* . . . our appeal to you was not based on a delusion, *TCNT* . . . we did not make our appeal by advocating false doctrines, *Norlie* . . . our appeal springs neither from delusion, nor from impure motives, *Berkeley* . . . was not from error, nor from impure motives, *Confraternity* . . . or tricky motives, *SEB*.

2:4. Paul and Silas knew in their own hearts that they were approved of God, no matter what people might say about them. God, in fact, showed His approval by the very tests He put them through. By approving them in testing and finding them worthy He allowed them to be entrusted with the gospel.

This God-given trust was their only reason for speaking to the people. Nothing they said in their preaching or in their attempts to persuade men to accept Christ came from any desire to please or accommodate men. Their only desire was to please God, knowing they could not deceive Him or "pull the wool" over His eyes. He tries (examines, tests) the heart. (See 1 Samuel 16:7; 1 Chronicles 28:9; 29:17; Psalm 11:4; Jeremiah 11:20; 17:10; Romans 8:27.) Thus Paul had to be true to the full gospel (1 Corinthians 9:16).

4. But as we were allowed of God: . . . for since we have been so approved by God, *Williams*.

to be put in trust with the gospel, even so we speak: . . . as to be entrusted with...we are now telling it, *Williams*.

not as pleasing men, but God, which trieth our hearts: . . . not to ingratiate ourselves with men, *Berkeley* . . . who looks at our hearts, *Norlie* . . . God tests and proves our hearts, *NLT*.

2:5. The preaching of Paul and Silas was free also from the flattery and covetousness so common among those who seek to persuade. Flattering words usually cover up ulterior motives. Those who flatter usually want something for themselves or they want to use another person for their own benefit. God himself, who sees all, was a witness that Paul's preaching was not a cloak for covetousness. The Bible warns us against false teachers who may seem very good, very pious, but whose religion is only a cover-up for avarice. Their real god is their belly (Romans 16:18; Philippians 3:19). They pay lip service to Christ, but their real concern is to satisfy their greed.

5. For neither at any time used we flattering words, as ye know: . . . we never used smooth-sounding words, *NLT*.

nor a cloak of covetousness; God [is] witness: . . . neither were we under some pretext after money, *Berkeley* . . . or a pretext for, *Campbell* . . . or make false professions in order to hide selfish aims, *TCNT* . . . nor any pretext for avarice, *Confraternity* . . . with a pretense for greed, *Concordant*.

1523.1 prep gen
ἐξ
ex
from

442.7 noun gen pl masc
ἀνθρώπων
anthrōpōn
men

1385.4 noun acc sing fem
δόξαν,
doxan
glory,

3641.1 conj
οὔτε
oute
neither

570.1 prep
ἀφ'
aph'
from

5050.2 prs-pron gen 2pl
ὑμῶν
humōn
you

3641.1 conj
οὔτε
oute
nor

570.2 prep
ἀπ'
ap'
from

241.1 adj gen pl
ἄλλων,
allōn
others,

1404.16 verb nom pl masc part pres mid
δυνάμενοι
dunamenoi
having power

1706.1 prep
ἐν
en
with

916.1 noun dat sing neu
βάρει
barei
weight

1498.32 verb inf pres act
εἶναι
einai
to be

5453.1 conj
ὡς
hōs
as

5382.2 name gen masc
Χριστοῦ
Christou
Christ's

646.4 noun nom pl masc
ἀπόστολοι.
apostoloi
apostles;

7. ⟨ **233.1** conj
ἀλλ'
all'
but

[✶ **233.2** conj
ἀλλὰ]
alla
[idem]

1090.34 verb 1pl indic aor pass
ἐγενήθημεν
egenēthēmen
we were

7.a.Var: p65,01ℵ-org 03B,04C-org,06D-org 016I,it.bo.Lach,We/Ho

⟨ **2239.2** adj nom pl masc
ἤπιοι
ēpioi
gentle

[a **3378.3** adj nom pl masc
νήπιοι]
nēpioi
[infants]

1706.1 prep
ἐν
en
in

3189.1 adj dat sing
μέσῳ
mesō
midst

5050.2 prs-pron gen 2pl
ὑμῶν,
humōn
your,

5453.1 conj
ὡς
hōs
as

⟨ **300.1** partic
ἂν
an
an

7.b.Txt: 01ℵ-org,02A 06D-corr,018K,020L byz.01ℵ-corr,03B,04C 06D-org,025P,Lach Treg,Alf,Tisc,We/Ho Weis,Sod,UBS/✶

[b✶ **1430.1** partic
ἐὰν]
ean
ean

5003.1 noun nom sing fem
τροφὸς
trophos
a nurse

2259.2 verb 3sing subj pres act
θάλπῃ
thalpē
would cherish

3450.17 art pl neu
τὰ
ta
the

1431.9 prs-pron gen sing fem
ἑαυτῆς
heautēs
her own

4891.4 noun pl neu
τέκνα.
tekna
children.

8.a.Txt: Steph **Var**: 01ℵ,02A,03B,04C 06D,018K,020L,025P Gries,Lach,Treg,Alf Word,Tisc,We/Ho,Weis Sod,UBS/✶

8. **3643.1** adv
οὕτως
houtōs
Thus

⟨ **2418.1** verb nom pl masc part pres mid
ἱμειρόμενοι
himeiromenoi
yearning over

[a✶ **3518.1** verb nom pl masc part pres mid
ὁμειρόμενοι]
homeiromenoi
[longing for]

5050.2 prs-pron gen 2pl
ὑμῶν,
humōn
you,

8.b.Txt: 01ℵ,02A,04C 06D,018K,020L,025P etc.byz.Tisc,Sod **Var**: 03B,We/Ho,Weis UBS/✶

⟨ **2085.3** verb 1pl indic pres act
εὐδοκοῦμεν
eudokoumen
we are pleased

[b **2085.12** verb 1pl indic imperf act
ηὐδοκοῦμεν]
ēudokoumen
[we were pleased]

3200.5 verb inf aor act
μεταδοῦναι
metadounai
to have imparted

5050.3 prs-pron dat 2pl
ὑμῖν
humin
to you

3620.3 partic
οὐ
ou
not

3303.1 adv
μόνον
monon
only

3450.16 art sing neu
τὸ
to
to the

2077.1 noun sing neu
εὐαγγέλιον
euangelion
good news

3450.2 art gen sing
τοῦ
tou
of

2296.2 noun gen sing masc
θεοῦ,
theou
God,

233.2 conj
ἀλλὰ
alla
but

2504.1 conj
καὶ
kai
also

3450.15 art acc pl fem
τὰς
tas
the

1431.2 prs-pron gen pl
ἑαυτῶν
heautōn
our own

5425.8 noun acc pl fem
ψυχάς,
psuchas
lives,

1354.1 conj
διότι
dioti
because

27.6 adj pl masc
ἀγαπητοὶ
agapētoi
beloved

8.c.Txt: 018K,byz. **Var**: 01ℵ,02A,03B,04C 06D,020L,025P,Lach Treg,Word,Tisc We/Ho,Weis,Sod UBS/✶

2231.3 prs-pron dat 1pl
ἡμῖν
hēmin
to us

⟨ **1090.64** verb 2pl indic perf mid
γεγένησθε.
gegenēsthe
you have become.

[c✶ **1090.35** verb 2pl indic aor pass
ἐγενήθητε.]
egenēthēte
[you became.]

9. **3285.1** verb 2pl pres act
μνημονεύετε
mnēmoneuete
You remember

1056.1 conj
γάρ,
gar
for,

79.6 noun nom pl masc
ἀδελφοί,
adelphoi
brothers,

3450.6 art acc sing masc
τὸν
ton
the

2845.4 noun acc sing masc
κόπον
kopon
labor

2231.2 prs-pron gen 1pl
ἡμῶν
hēmōn
our

2504.1 conj
καὶ
kai
and

3450.6 art acc sing masc
τὸν
ton
the

2:6. For others, religion is just an act by which they try to get glory, honor, praise, and approval from men. Paul and his companions were not like that. At no time did any of them try to build up their personal prestige or exalt themselves. Never did they say things just to get the "amens" of the people.

Most often, Paul delighted to call himself a servant (literally, *doulos*, "a slave") of the Lord Jesus. A slave did not spend his time contending for his rights or exalting his own dignity. He had none. He was completely at his master's disposal. This is in line with the very word *apostolos* ("apostle") which means "sent one," a person sent with an obligation to carry out the commission given by his superior. Jesus was sent by the Father, sent to serve, not to be waited on. He gave His life (Mark 10:45). He told His apostles, "So send I you" (John 20:21).

6. Nor of men sought we glory, neither of you, nor [yet] of others: . . . neither did we seek plaudations from, *Berkeley*.

when we might have been burdensome, as the apostles of Christ: We might have acted with authority, *Campbell* . . . we could have made heavy demands, *Norlie* . . . we could have claimed a position of honor among you, *Confraternity* . . . I might have exercised authority as Christ's apostle, *Montgomery* . . . as apostles we could have stood on our official dignity, *Williams*.

2:7. Nor did Paul and Silas try to throw their weight around. They did not wield apostolic authority in a haughty way or insist on their own importance as apostles. Instead of declaring who they were, they declared who Christ is. They saw their apostleship as a burden on their own hearts, not as a burden to be placed on the people. Thus they were never dictatorial. Instead of being burdensome, they were gentle. This was more than an occasional act of kindness. Their kindness was like that of a nursing mother who cherishes her own children, suckling them, keeping them warm, comforting them with all kinds of tender, loving care.

7. But we were gentle among you: On the contrary, *Montgomery* . . . mild-mannered in your circle, *Berkeley* . . . in your midst, *Young* . . . with a childlike simplicity, *TCNT*.

even as a nurse cherisheth her children: . . . like a nursing mother tenderly fostering her own, *Berkeley* . . . like a mother caring for, *NLT* . . . who fondles her own children, *Norlie* . . . when she tenderly nurses her own children, *Montgomery*.

2:8. The apostles were not cold, harsh announcers of doom, and the "gospel" is not simply a homily preached from a pulpit or a street corner. It also involves the testimony, character, and lifestyle of the one who calls himself a Christian. Best remarks, "The missionary is not someone specialized in the delivery of a message but someone whose whole being, completely committed to a message which demands all, is communicated to his hearers" (*Black's New Testament Commentaries*, 10:102,103). They approached the Thessalonians with affectionate desire, with warm, kindly feelings. Though as Gentiles the Thessalonians were ungodly and undoubtedly had many bad habits, the apostles did not withdraw from them or look down on them but were well pleased to share the gospel of God. They continued to share with the same attitudes when the Thessalonians began to accept the gospel. Then the people became even more beloved, and Paul, Silas, and Timothy were pleased to pour out their very souls for them. They shared their innermost selves, their whole personalities, even to the point of being willing to give their lives for the believers. This was no pretense. They really cared.

8. So being affectionately desirous of you: We loved you very much, *SEB* . . . We liked you so much, *Klingensmith* . . . being ardently attached to you, *Concordant* . . . in my fine affection, *Montgomery*.

we were willing to have imparted unto you, not the gospel of God only, but also our own souls, because ye were dear unto us: . . . it was my joy to give you, *Montgomery* . . . to lay down our very lives too for you, *Williams* . . . because you came to be beloved by us, *Concordant* . . . but also our lives...You had become precious to us, *SEB*.

2:9. Paul and Silas proved they cared. Some people might declare they would die for another, but when put to the test they would not cross the street to give help. But the Thessalonians would well

9. For ye remember, brethren, our labour and travail: You recall, *Montgomery* . . . our toil and hardship, *NIV* . . . We were exhausted, *SEB* . . . you remember our hard work and sweat, *Klingensmith*.

1 Thess. 2:10

9.a.**Txt:** 06D-corr,018K
020L,byz.
Var: 01א,02A,03B
06D-org,015H,025P,sa.
bo.Gries,Lach,Treg,Alf
Word,Tisc,We/Ho,Weis
Sod,UBS/⋆

3313.2 noun acc sing masc	3433.2 noun gen sing fem	1056.1 conj	2504.1 conj	2232.1 noun fem	2021.10 verb nom pl masc part pres mid
μόχθον·	νυκτὸς	⸂a γὰρ ⸃	καὶ	ἡμέρας	ἐργαζόμενοι,
mochthon	nuktos	gar	kai	hēmeras	ergazomenoi
toil,	night	for	and	day	working,

4242.1 prep	3450.16 art sing neu	3231.1 partic	1897.2 verb inf aor act	4948.5 indef-pron	5050.2 prs-pron gen 2pl
πρὸς	τὸ	μὴ	ἐπιβαρῆσαί	τινα	ὑμῶν,
pros	to	mē	epibarēsai	tina	humōn
for	the	not	to burden	anyone	of you,

2756.12 verb 1pl indic aor act	1519.1 prep	5050.4 prs-pron acc 2pl	3450.16 art sing neu	2077.1 noun sing neu	3450.2 art gen sing
ἐκηρύξαμεν	εἰς	ὑμᾶς	τὸ	εὐαγγέλιον	τοῦ
ekēruxamen	eis	humas	to	euangelion	tou
we proclaimed	to	you	the	good news	

2296.2 noun gen sing masc	5050.1 prs-pron nom 2pl	3116.4 noun nom pl masc	2504.1 conj	3450.5 art nom sing masc	2296.1 noun nom sing masc
θεοῦ.	**10.** ὑμεῖς	μάρτυρες	καὶ	ὁ	θεός,
theou	humeis	martures	kai	ho	theos
of God.	You	witnesses,	and	ho	God,

5453.1 conj	3605.1 adv	2504.1 conj	1341.1 adv	2504.1 conj	272.1 adv	5050.3 prs-pron dat 2pl
ὡς	ὁσίως	καὶ	δικαίως	καὶ	ἀμέμπτως	ὑμῖν
hōs	hosiōs	kai	dikaiōs	kai	amemptōs	humin
how	holily	and	righteously	and	blamelessly	with you

3450.4 art dat pl	3961.3 verb dat pl masc part pres act	1090.34 verb 1pl indic aor pass	2481.1 conj	3471.6 verb 2pl indic perf act
τοῖς	πιστεύουσιν	ἐγενήθημεν,	**11.** καθάπερ	οἴδατε,
tois	pisteuousin	egenēthēmen	kathaper	oidate
the	believing	we were:	even as	you know,

5453.1 conj	1518.4 num card acc masc	1524.1 adj sing	5050.2 prs-pron gen 2pl	5453.1 conj	3824.1 noun nom sing masc	4891.4 noun pl neu
ὡς	ἕνα	ἕκαστον	ὑμῶν	ὡς	πατὴρ	τέκνα
hōs	hena	hekaston	humōn	hōs	patēr	tekna
how	one	each	of you,	as	a father	children

1431.4 prs-pron gen sing	3731.9 verb nom pl masc part pres act	5050.4 prs-pron acc 2pl	2504.1 conj	3749.2 verb nom pl masc part pres mid
ἑαυτοῦ,	παρακαλοῦντες	ὑμᾶς	καὶ	παραμυθούμενοι
heautou	parakalountes	humas	kai	paramuthoumenoi
his own,	exhorting	you	and	consoling

12.a.**Txt:** 06D-org,Steph
Var: 01א,03B,06D-corr
015H,018K,020L,33
Treg,Alf,Word,Tisc
We/Ho,Weis,Sod
UBS/⋆

12.b.**Txt:** 06D-corr,018K
020L,byz.
Var: 01א,02A,03B
06D-org,025P,33,Lach
Treg,Alf,Word,Tisc
We/Ho,Weis,Sod
UBS/⋆

2504.1 conj	3113.33 verb nom pl masc part pres mid	3113.43 verb nom pl masc part pres mid	1519.1 prep
12. καὶ	⸂ μαρτυρούμενοι,	[a⋆ μαρτυρόμενοι]	εἰς
kai	marturoumenoi	marturomenoi	eis
and	testifying,	[idem]	for

3450.16 art sing neu	3906.23 verb inf aor act	3906.17 verb inf pres act	5050.4 prs-pron acc 2pl	512.1 adv
τὸ	⸂ περιπατῆσαι	[b⋆ περιπατεῖν]	ὑμᾶς	ἀξίως
to	peripatēsai	peripatein	humas	axiōs
to	to walk	[idem]	you	worthily

12.c.**Txt:** 03B,06D,010F
012G,015H,018K,020L
025P
Var: 01א,02A,104,326
606,1611,1831,1906
1912,2005

3450.2 art gen sing	2296.2 noun gen sing masc	3450.2 art gen sing	2535.5 verb gen sing masc part pres act	2535.15 verb gen sing masc part aor act
τοῦ	θεοῦ	τοῦ	⸂⋆ καλοῦντος	[c καλέσαντος]
tou	theou	tou	kalountos	kalesantos
	of God,	the	calling	[having called]

remember the apostle's toil (hard work and exertion) in the midst of hardship. Night and day they worked hard and struggled to overcome difficulties so they would not be a burden to any. By his tentmaking, Paul supported the whole evangelistic party (Acts 20:34). The general picture seems to be that he worked from dawn until noon or a little after at his trade. Then he spent the rest of the day preaching, teaching, and going from house to house exhorting and encouraging the people (Acts 18:3,4; 19:9; 20:20,31).

Paul did not have to work so hard at his tentmaking. Even Jesus recognized that the worker who is spreading the gospel should receive wages for that work (Luke 10:7). Paul told the Corinthians that the command of the Law not to muzzle an ox while it is treading out the grain (Deuteronomy 25:4) was written for believers. Those who sow spiritual seed by the preaching of the gospel have a right to reap a material harvest from those who receive the benefits of the gospel. Paul, however, did not use this right (1 Corinthians 9:3-18). He did not want to burden the new churches he was founding. He wanted to do everything possible to establish them in the Lord. He was not preaching the gospel for money but because of a divine commission that he could not escape. Yet he taught the churches to support their elders who directed the affairs of the church and were faithful in teaching and preaching (1 Timothy 5:17,18).

2:10. Not only were the apostles gentle, kind, and considerate, they were also men of integrity both in their actions and in their inner thoughts and purposes. The Thessalonians were witnesses to their behavior, as was God also. They knew what a holy (God-pleasing), just (right, upright), and blameless way of life the apostles showed in all their relationships with the believers. None of them could point a finger of reproach or accusation against any of Paul's company. Every one of them were men and women of unimpeachable honesty and sincere devotion. What a contrast they were to the false teachers who were making accusations against them.

2:11. To the gentleness of a mother, then, they added the continuous care, concern, and firm guidance of a father, treating the believers with the same faithful love that a good father shows toward his own children. In this they felt a responsibility to be the loving guardians of their spiritual children. They did not bring people to the Lord and then leave them to drift along or follow their own devices. They knew it would be all too easy in that environment for the new converts to be enslaved again by the sin and false religions around them. Like a good father, the apostles could not neglect their children.

2:12. With fatherly concern, then, they exhorted and challenged, comforted and encouraged believers, in order to warn, instruct, and confirm each one of them. In this their whole purpose was to help the believers walk worthy of God.

for labouring night and day: . . . we worked at our trades, *TCNT* . . . working at manual labor, *Wuest*.

because we would not be chargeable unto any of you: . . . so as not to be burdensome, *Concordant* . . . that we might not become a burden, *Adams*.

we preached unto you the gospel of God: . . . while we proclaimed, *Wuest* . . . we heralded to you, *Berkeley* . . . I proclaimed to you, *Montgomery*.

10. Ye [are] witnesses, and God [also], how holily and justly and unblameably we behaved ourselves among you that believe: You can testify...with what pure, upright, and irreproachable motives, *Williams* . . . you are those who bear testimony...how blamelessly we ordered our lives among you, *Wuest* . . . and so is God, *Montgomery* . . . how purely, righteously, and blamelessly, we were with you believers, *Fenton* . . . and righteous and irreproachable we were in our relationships to you, *Adams* . . . was our conduct towards you, *Confraternity* . . . and beyond reproach, *TCNT*.

11. As ye know how we exhorted and comforted and charged every one of you, as a father [doth] his children: . . . even as you know how as a father exhorts and encourages his own children, *Wuest* . . . we urged and encouraged, *Adams* . . . appealed to each of you and cheered you on, *Berkeley* . . . how I was wont to treat each of you...exhorting and imploring and adjuring each one, *Montgomery* . . . as a father deals with his own children, *NIV* . . . treats his own children, *SEB*.

12. That ye would walk worthy of God: . . . that you should be habitually ordering your behavior in a manner worthy, *Wuest* . . . to walk in a manner that is, *Adams* . . . you should live to please God, *NLT*.

5050.4 prs-pron acc 2pl	1519.1 prep	3450.12 art acc sing fem	1431.4 prs-pron gen sing	926.4 noun acc sing fem	2504.1 conj
ὑμᾶς	εἰς	τὴν	ἑαυτοῦ	βασιλείαν	καὶ
humas	eis	tēn	heautou	basileian	kai
you	to	the	his own	kingdom	and

1385.4 noun acc sing fem		2504.1 conj	1217.2 prep	3642.17 dem-pron sing neu	2504.1 conj
δόξαν.	**13.** [ᵃ☆+ Καὶ]	Διὰ	τοῦτο	καὶ
doxan	Kai	Dia	touto	kai
glory.	[And]	Because of	this	also

13.a.**Var:** 01א,02A,03B 025P,bo,Lach,Tisc Steph,Alf,Tisc,We/Ho Weis,Sod,UBS/☆

2231.1 prs-pron nom 1pl	2149.4 verb 1pl indic pres act	3450.3 art dat sing	2296.3 noun dat sing masc	88.1 adv
ἡμεῖς	εὐχαριστοῦμεν	τῷ	θεῷ	ἀδιαλείπτως,
hēmeis	eucharistoumen	tō	theō	adialeiptōs
we	give thanks	to	to God	unceasingly,

3617.1 conj	3741.11 verb nom pl masc part aor act	3030.4 noun acc sing masc	187.2 noun gen sing fem	3706.1 prep	2231.2 prs-pron gen 1pl
ὅτι	παραλαβόντες	λόγον	ἀκοῆς	παρ'	ἡμῶν
hoti	paralabontes	logon	akoēs	par'	hēmōn
that,	having received	word	of report	by	us

3450.2 art gen sing	2296.2 noun gen sing masc	1203.7 verb 2pl indic aor mid	3620.3 partic	3030.4 noun acc sing masc	442.7 noun gen pl masc
τοῦ	θεοῦ	ἐδέξασθε	οὐ	λόγον	ἀνθρώπων,
tou	theou	edexasthe	ou	logon	anthrōpōn
of God,	you accepted	not	word	men's,

233.2 conj	2503.1 conj	1498.4 verb 3sing indic pres act	228.1 adv	228.1 adv	1498.4 verb 3sing indic pres act
ἀλλὰ	καθὼς	ʼ ἐστιν	ἀληθῶς,	[ἀληθῶς	ἐστιν]
alla	kathōs	estin	alēthōs	alēthōs	estin
but	even as	it is	truly,	[truly	is]

3030.4 noun acc sing masc	2296.2 noun gen sing masc	3614.5 rel-pron nom sing masc	2504.1 conj	1738.8 verb 3sing indic pres mid	1706.1 prep
λόγον	θεοῦ,	ὃς	καὶ	ἐνεργεῖται	ἐν
logon	theou	hos	kai	energeitai	en
word	God's,	which	also	works	in

5050.3 prs-pron dat 2pl	3450.4 art dat pl	3961.3 verb dat pl masc part pres act	5050.1 prs-pron nom 2pl	1056.1 conj	3266.1 noun nom pl masc
ὑμῖν	τοῖς	πιστεύουσιν.	**14.** ὑμεῖς	γὰρ	μιμηταὶ
humin	tois	pisteuousin	humeis	gar	mimētai
you	the	believing.	You	for	imitators

1090.35 verb 2pl indic aor pass	79.6 noun nom pl masc	3450.1 art gen pl	1564.6 noun gen pl fem	3450.2 art gen sing	2296.2 noun gen sing masc
ἐγενήθητε,	ἀδελφοί,	τῶν	ἐκκλησιῶν	τοῦ	θεοῦ
egenēthēte	adelphoi	tōn	ekklēsiōn	tou	theou
became,	brothers,	of the	assemblies	of God

3450.1 art gen pl	1498.31 verb gen pl fem part pres act	1706.1 prep	3450.11 art dat sing fem	2424.3 name dat fem	1706.1 prep	5382.3 name dat masc
τῶν	οὐσῶν	ἐν	τῇ	Ἰουδαίᾳ	ἐν	Χριστῷ
tōn	ousōn	en	tē	Ioudaia	en	Christō
the	being	in	in	Judea	in	Christ

14.a.**Txt:** 02A,Steph **Var:** 01א,03B,06D 018K,020L,025P,byz. Gries,Lach,Treg,Alf Word,Tisc,We/Ho,Weis Sod,UBS/☆

2400.2 name masc	3617.1 conj	4874.1 dem-pron pl neu	3450.17 art pl neu	840.16 prs-pron pl neu
Ἰησοῦ,	ὅτι	ʼ ταῦτὰ	[ᵃ☆ τὰ	αὐτὰ]
Iēsou	hoti	tauta	ta	auta
Jesus;	because	the same things	[the	same things]

God's kingdom and glory are closely intertwined here. The "kingdom" is not a topic discussed in great detail by Paul, although it is strongly emphasized in the Gospels. The New Testament teaches that the kingdom of God has both present (Matthew 13:38; Mark 1:15; 9:1) and future (James 2:5; Revelation 11:15) aspects. Some say that we must be working now to establish the kingdom of God on earth before the return of Christ. This teaching is not Biblical. Morris states, "In the Scriptures, it is clear that God and no other establishes the kingdom" (*New International Commentary on the New Testament, 1&2 Thessalonians*, p.85).

God's kingdom has to do with His royal power and rule rather than with territory. His glory has to do with the revelation of His holy nature, not only in majesty and might but also in goodness, righteousness, love, and mercy. This is the same glory John says was revealed in Christ, a glory "full of grace and truth" (John 1:14). It includes gracious help that is the outflow of the divine nature, the practical effect of God's life and love as it is ministered to believers by the Holy Spirit. As Christians receive of this grace and glory they come to know the truth of God in all His faithfulness and reality. This makes it possible for believers to show they are in the Kingdom or under the rule of God by manifesting His rule in righteousness, peace, and joy in the Holy Spirit (Romans 14:17).

2:13. The remainder of this passage (2:13-16) expresses Paul's continuous and increasing thanksgiving for the way the Thessalonians received the Word and continued in it.

In this verse two different Greeks words are used for the reception of the gospel. When the apostles came preaching their God-given message, the people accepted it, taking it into their hearts (*paralabontes*, "having received, accepted"). Why? Because they welcomed it (*edexasthe*, "welcomed, accepted") not as the clever or beautiful product of human thinking or human genius, but as the Word of God, which it truly is. (See Romans 10:13-17.) The Word thus accepted and welcomed could not help but work in them in an effective way, especially since they not only began to believe (expressed an initial faith) but kept on believing.

Notice that though Paul and Silas proclaimed the Word as God's agents, the Word itself was the instrument God used to do His work. The Word is God's hammer, the Holy Spirit's sword (Jeremiah 23:29; Ephesians 6:17). It is God's best tool by which He builds the Church, His best weapon for winning victories that glorify His name. However, the Word must be mixed with faith if it is to be effective (Hebrews 4:2). Even Jesus was hindered by an atmosphere of unbelief (Matthew 13:58).

2:14. Part of the effective working of God in Thessalonica was seen in the way the new believers became imitators of the assemblies in Judea, the Jewish believers whose sphere of life was in Christ Jesus.

who hath called you unto his kingdom and glory: Who is calling you into His empire, *Adams* . . . who summons you, *Wuest* . . . to share in his Glory, *TCNT*.

13. For this cause also thank we God without ceasing: On this account, *Campbell* . . . I am giving continual thanks, *Montgomery* . . . we also thank God regularly, *Adams* . . . constantly giving thanks...unceasingly, *Wuest*.

because, when ye received the word of God which ye heard of us: . . . when you heard from me, *Montgomery* . . . because you welcomed the word, *Klingensmith* . . . when you took hold of the divine message, *Berkeley* . . . having received a reason for listening to us concerning God, *Fenton* . . . because when you appropriated to yourselves the word, *Wuest*.

ye received [it] not [as] the word of men: . . . you accepted it, *SEB, Fenton* . . . you did not accept it as a human message, *Berkeley* . . . not as a word finding its source in men, *Wuest* . . . as a human Word, *Adams* . . . not a human message, *SEB*.

but as it is in truth, the word of God: . . . but rather, for what it truly is, *Adams* . . . but as it actually is, *NIV* . . . which in truth it is, *Montgomery* . . . as it truly is, a Divine reason, *Fenton*.

which effectually worketh also in you that believe: . . . who himself is effectually at work in you, *Montgomery* . . . And it is still working in you, *Klingensmith* . . . which is being constantly set in operation in you who believe, *Wuest* . . . which is at work in you, *Adams* . . . who have accepted the Faith, *TCNT*.

14. For ye, brethren, became followers of the churches of God which in Judaea are in Christ Jesus: . . . became imitators of God's churches, *Adams* . . . began to follow the example of, *Montgomery* . . . of the assemblies of God, *Young*.

1 Thess. 2:15

3819.12 verb 2pl indic aor act	2504.1 conj	5050.1 prs-pron nom 2pl	5097.3 prep	3450.1 art gen pl	2375.1 adj gen pl	4704.1 noun gen pl masc
ἐπάθετε	καὶ	ὑμεῖς	ὑπὸ	τῶν	ἰδίων	συμφυλετῶν
epathete	kai	humeis	hupo	tōn	idiōn	sumphuletōn
suffered	also	you	from	the	your own	countrymen

2503.1 conj	2504.1 conj	840.7 prs-pron nom pl masc	5097.3 prep	3450.1 art gen pl	2428.3 name-adj gen pl masc	3450.1 art gen pl
καθὼς	καὶ	αὐτοὶ	ὑπὸ	τῶν	Ἰουδαίων,	15. τῶν
kathōs	kai	autoi	hupo	tōn	Ioudaiōn	tōn
as	also	they	from	the	Jews,	the

2504.1 conj	3450.6 art acc sing masc	2935.4 noun acc sing masc	609.11 verb gen pl masc part aor act	2400.3 name acc masc	2504.1 conj
καὶ	τὸν	κύριον	ἀποκτεινάντων	Ἰησοῦν	καὶ
kai	ton	kurion	apokteinantōn	Iēsoun	kai
both	the	Lord	having killed	Jesus	and

3450.8 art acc pl masc	2375.8 adj acc pl masc	4254.7 noun acc pl masc	2504.1 conj	5050.4 prs-pron acc 2pl	2231.4 prs-pron acc 1pl
τοὺς	⌐a ἰδίους ¬	προφήτας,	καὶ	⌐ ὑμᾶς	[b☆ ἡμᾶς]
tous	idious	prophētas	kai	humas	hēmas
the	their own	prophets,	and	you	[us]

1546.1 verb gen pl masc part aor act	2504.1 conj	2296.3 noun dat sing masc	3231.1 partic	694.4 verb gen pl masc part pres act	2504.1 conj
ἐκδιωξάντων,	καὶ	θεῷ	μὴ	ἀρεσκόντων,	καὶ
ekdiōxantōn	kai	theō	mē	areskontōn	kai
drove out,	and	God	not	pleasing,	and

3820.5 adj dat pl	442.8 noun dat pl masc	1711.2 adj gen pl masc	2940.4 verb gen pl masc part pres act	2231.4 prs-pron acc 1pl
πᾶσιν	ἀνθρώποις	ἐναντίων,	16. κωλυόντων	ἡμᾶς
pasin	anthrōpois	enantiōn,	kōluontōn	hēmas
all	to men	contrary,	forbidding	us

3450.4 art dat pl	1477.6 noun dat pl neu	2953.37 verb inf aor act	2419.1 conj	4834.27 verb 3pl subj aor pass	1519.1 prep
τοῖς	ἔθνεσιν	λαλῆσαι	ἵνα	σωθῶσιν,	εἰς
tois	ethnesin	lalēsai	hina	sōthōsin	eis
to the	Gentiles	to speak	that	they may be saved,	for

3450.16 art sing neu	376.5 verb inf aor act	840.1 prs-pron gen pl	3450.15 art acc pl fem	264.1 noun acc pl fem	3704.1 adv
τὸ	ἀναπληρῶσαι	αὐτῶν	τὰς	ἁμαρτίας	πάντοτε·
to	anaplērōsai	autōn	tas	hamartias	pantote
the	to fill up	their	the	sins	always:

5185.1 verb 3sing indic aor act	5185.4 verb 3sing indic perf act	1156.2 conj	1894.2 prep	840.8 prs-pron acc pl masc	3450.9 art nom sing fem
⌐ ἔφθασεν	[a ἔφθακεν]	δὲ	ἐπ'	αὐτοὺς	ἡ
ephthasen	ephthaken	de	ep'	autous	hē
came	[has come]	but	upon	them	the

3572.1 noun nom sing fem	1519.1 prep	4904.1 noun sing neu	2231.1 prs-pron nom 1pl	1156.2 conj	79.6 noun nom pl masc
ὀργὴ	εἰς	τέλος.	17. Ἡμεῖς	δέ,	ἀδελφοί,
orgē	eis	telos.	Hēmeis	de	adelphoi
wrath	to	uttermost.	We	but,	brothers,

636.1 verb nom pl masc part aor pass	570.1 prep	5050.2 prs-pron gen 2pl	4242.1 prep	2511.4 noun acc sing masc	5443.1 noun nom fem
ἀπορφανισθέντες	ἀφ'	ὑμῶν	πρὸς	καιρὸν	ὥρας
aporphanisthentes	aph'	humōn	pros	kairon	hōras
having been bereaved	of	you	for	time	of an hour

15.a.Txt: 06D-corr,018K 020L,1241,byz. Var: 01א,02A,03B 06D-org,025P,33,it.sa. bo.Gries,Lach,Treg,Alf Word,Tisc,We/Ho,Weis Sod,UBS/✰

15.b.Txt: Steph Var: 01א,02A,03B,06D 018K,020L,025P,etc.byz. Elzev,Gries,Lach,Treg Alf,Word,Tisc,We/Ho Weis,Sod,UBS/✰

16.a.Txt: 01א,02A 06D-corr1,010F,012G byz. Var: 03B,06D-org,044 104

Paul reminded the believers of the way jealous synagogue leaders had stirred up mob violence against the new Thessalonian disciples, taking evil, malicious men from among the marketplace loafers and inciting them to cause a riot (Acts 17:5). Thus the Thessalonian believers suffered at the hand of their own countrymen, just as the believers in Judea had.

2:15. Verses 15 and 16 may sound anti-Semitic on the surface. However, they refer not to Jews in general but to those Jews who were rebels against God. These were the Jews who killed the Lord Jesus and also their own prophets (Matthew 5:12; 23:29-37; Luke 13:33,34; Acts 3:15). They do not include the mass of the Jewish people, nor even all of their leaders. Men like Nicodemus, Joseph of Arimathea, and even Gamaliel, certainly did not have any part in the killing of Jesus. The Jews in Judea as a whole respected the apostles at first and held the Church in high honor (Acts 2:47; 5:13). Even when the Sanhedrin stoned Stephen, devout Jews (who were not Christians) buried him and wept over him (Acts 8:2). The persecution was carried out by leaders like Paul himself who created an atmosphere of threats and murder (Acts 8:1; 9:1).

After his conversion, Paul also was persecuted by his former compatriots. They thought they were pleasing God and doing Him a service by persecuting Paul and hounding him from place to place. But the jealousy that made them do this did not please God. It only showed they were opposed and hostile to all men. They had built up such a prejudice against others because they knew nothing of the love of God.

2:16. The unbelieving Jews in Thessalonica even went so far as to forbid (hinder, try to prevent) Paul and his friends from speaking or even talking to the Gentiles with a view to their salvation. The present participle (*areskontōn*, verse 15) emphasizes that this was a continual, ongoing activity of these Jews. They wanted to keep God, His love, and His promises to themselves! Instead, they were only filling up the measure of their own sins. Like the Canaanites who were driven out before Israel, the cup of their iniquity was finally full. (See Genesis 15:16.) The wrath of God would come on them "to the uttermost," that is, in the end, and forever.

2:17. Paul used a strong word to show how he and Silas felt when they were forced to leave their new brothers in Christ. They were taken from them, made orphans as it were, by separation from them. The apostles felt bereaved (torn, desolate) when separated from them even for a brief time (more literally, a season of an hour). Yet, they wanted the people to know that the separation was only outward, only in person, not in heart.

Paul tried to help the believers realize how much it hurt him to leave them when he knew they needed teaching and encourage-

for ye also have suffered like things of your own countrymen: . . . the same sort of ill-treatment, *Williams* . . . by your own fellow-tribesmen, *Concordant* . . . of your fellow-citizens, *TCNT.*
even as they [have] of the Jews:

15. Who both killed the Lord Jesus, and their own prophets: . . . who put to death, *Berkeley* . . . and the early preachers, *NLT.*
and have persecuted us: . . . and also drove us out, *NIV.*
and they please not God: They still continue to displease God, *Norlie.*
and are contrary to all men: They hinder everybody, *Klingensmith* . . . and opponents of all people, *Berkeley* . . . and are hostile to, *Confraternity, NIV.*

16. Forbidding us to speak to the Gentiles: . . . by trying to keep us from, *Williams* . . . they try to prohibit us, *Norlie* . . . they try to prevent us, *TCNT* . . . They try to stop us, *SEB.*
that they might be saved:
to fill up their sins alway: All their sins have piled up upon them, *Klingensmith* . . . they are always piling up their sins, *Norlie* . . . to fill to the brim the cup of their sins, *Williams* . . . they always heap up their sins to the limit, *JB* . . . their iniquities, *Campbell.*
for the wrath is come upon them to the uttermost: . . . divine indignation has at last overtaken them, *Berkeley* . . . is coming upon them at length, *Campbell* . . . God's judgment has overtaken them at last! *TCNT.*

17. But we, brethren, being taken from you for a short time: . . . being bereaved of you, *Confraternity* . . . our having been absent from you, *TCNT* . . . we were forced to leave you, *SEB.*

4241.3 noun dat sing neu
προσώπῳ
prosōpō
in face,

3620.3 partic
οὐ
ou
not

2559.3 noun dat sing fem
καρδία,
kardia
in heart,

3917.2 adv comp
περισσοτέρως
perissoterōs
more abundantly

4557.3 verb 1pl indic aor act
ἐσπουδάσαμεν
espoudasamen
were diligent

3450.16 art sing neu
τὸ
to
the

4241.1 noun sing neu
πρόσωπον
prosōpon
face

5050.2 prs-pron gen 2pl
ὑμῶν
humōn
your

1481.19 verb inf aor act
ἰδεῖν
idein
to see

1706.1 prep
ἐν
en
with

4044.11 adj dat sing fem
πολλῇ
pollē
much

1924.3 noun dat sing fem
ἐπιθυμίᾳ·
epithumia
desire;

1346.1 conj
18. ʽ διὸ
dio
wherefore

1354.1 conj
[a☆ διότι]
dioti
[idem]

2286.23 verb 1pl indic aor act
ἠθελήσαμεν
ēthelēsamen
we wished

2048.23 verb inf aor act
ἐλθεῖν
elthein
to come

18.a.Txt: 06D-corr,018K 020L,byz.
Var: 01א,02A,03B 06D-org,025P,33,Lach Treg,Alf,Word,Tisc We/Ho,Weis,Sod UBS/☆

4242.1 prep
πρὸς
pros
to

5050.4 prs-pron acc 2pl
ὑμᾶς,
humas
you,

1466.1 prs-pron nom 1sing
ἐγὼ
egō
I

3173.1 conj
μὲν
men
indeed

3834.1 name nom masc
Παῦλος
Paulos
Paul,

2504.1 conj
καὶ
kai
both

526.1 adv
ἅπαξ
hapax
once

2504.1 conj
καὶ
kai
and

1361.1 adv
δίς,
dis
twice,

2504.1 conj
καὶ
kai
and

1458.2 verb 3sing indic aor act
ἐνέκοψεν
enekopsen
hindered

2231.4 prs-pron acc 1pl
ἡμᾶς
hēmas
us

3450.5 art nom sing masc
ὁ
ho

4423.1 noun nom sing masc
Σατανᾶς.
Satanas
Satan;

4949.3 intr-pron nom sing
19. τίς
tis
what

1056.1 conj
γὰρ
gar
for

2231.2 prs-pron gen 1pl
ἡμῶν
hēmōn
our

1667.1 noun nom sing fem
ἐλπὶς
elpis
hope

2211.1 conj
ἢ
ē
or

5315.1 noun nom sing fem
χαρὰ
chara
joy

2211.1 conj
ἢ
ē
or

4586.1 noun nom sing masc
στέφανος
stephanos
crown

2716.2 noun gen sing fem
καυχήσεως;
kauchēseōs
of boasting?

2211.1 conj
ἢ
ē
or

3644.1 adv
οὐχὶ
ouchi
not

2504.1 conj
καὶ
kai
even

5050.1 prs-pron nom 2pl
ὑμεῖς
humeis
you

1699.1 prep
ἔμπροσθεν
emprosthen
before

19.a.Txt: 020L,byz.sa.bo.
Var: 01א,02A,03B,06D 018K,025P,Lach,Treg Alf,Tisc,We/Ho,Weis Sod,UBS/☆

3450.2 art gen sing
τοῦ
tou
the

2935.2 noun gen sing masc
κυρίου
kuriou
Lord

2231.2 prs-pron gen 1pl
ἡμῶν
hēmōn
our

2400.2 name masc
Ἰησοῦ
Iēsou
Jesus

5382.2 name gen masc
ʽa Χριστοῦ ʼ
Christou
Christ

1706.1 prep
ἐν
en
at

3450.11 art dat sing fem
τῇ
tē
the

840.3 prs-pron gen sing
αὐτοῦ
autou
his

3814.3 noun dat sing fem
παρουσίᾳ;
parousia
coming?

5050.1 prs-pron nom 2pl
20. ὑμεῖς
humeis
you

1056.1 conj
γάρ
gar
for

1498.6 verb 2pl indic pres act
ἐστε
este
are

3450.9 art nom sing fem
ἡ
hē
the

1385.1 noun nom sing fem
δόξα
doxa
glory

2231.2 prs-pron gen 1pl
ἡμῶν
hēmōn
our

2504.1 conj
καὶ
kai
and

3450.9 art nom sing fem
ἡ
hē
the

5315.1 noun nom sing fem
χαρά.
chara
joy.

1346.1 conj
3:1. Διὸ
Dio
Wherefore

1.a.Txt: 06D,018K,020L byz.Weis,Sod
Var: 01א,03B,025P Treg,Tisc,We/Ho UBS/☆

3239.1 adv
μηκέτι
mēketi
no longer

4573.4 verb nom pl masc part pres act
στέγοντες,
stegontes
enduring,

2085.8 verb 1pl indic aor act
ʽ εὐδοκήσαμεν
eudokēsamen
we thought good

2085.11 verb 1pl indic aor act
[a ηὐδοκήσαμεν]
ēudokēsamen
[idem]

ment. He certainly had no desire or intention to stay away. In fact, ever since he left them he had been making tremendous efforts to see their faces again "with great desire." It was not a case of "out of sight, out of mind" with him. To Paul, nothing took the place of personal contact with those converted under his ministry. The love of Christ that made him reach out to lost sinners made him reach out even more to them once they had believed.

2:18. On two specific occasions Paul wanted to come. In each case he would have come except that Satan hindered or thwarted him. Paul recognized that Satan (the adversary) is the real enemy behind all opposition to the gospel. As the adversary, Satan's purpose is to hinder the work of God and stop the forward march of the Church. As the god of this world, he blinds the minds of unbelievers, trying to keep out the light of the glorious gospel of Christ (2 Corinthians 4:4). As the prince or ruler of the power or domain of the air, he is the spirit who works in those who are disobedient to God (Ephesians 2:2). Believers are warned not to give any chance or opportunity to the devil to exert his influence (Ephesians 4:27). Though the shield of faith is sufficient to quench all the fiery darts he throws at them (Ephesians 6:16), he can still hinder. In spite of their intention, purpose, and desire, Satan can sometimes cause a setback for God's people. Apparently God permitted this hindrance without telling Paul why.

2:19. Paul's delay in returning to Thessalonica, then, was due to Satan, not to any lack of loving care on his part. The Thessalonian believers meant everything to Paul. They were his hope, his joy, his victor's crown of rejoicing. This was a crown to be proud of when Paul and his fellow workers would stand before the Lord Jesus Christ at His coming, that is, when He returns in royal power and glory to judge the earth and bring in His kingdom.

2:20. Very emphatically Paul repeated that the believers were indeed the glory and joy of those who led them to Christ.

Paul was not saying here that he was looking for some reward for winning the Thessalonians to the Lord. The very fact that they had accepted Christ filled Paul and his companions with joy. Just to see these believers stand in the presence of the Lord at His coming would fulfill the apostles' hope and would be all the glory and joy they wanted. They were like parents who rejoice to see their children have good success. They were like teachers who feel rewarded when their students go on to live a worthwhile life.

3:1. Paul's concern for the Thessalonians weighed heavily upon him. Even though he had no news from Thessalonica, he knew very well that the unbelievers who had pursued him to Beroea (Acts 17:13) would not cease putting pressure on the Christians in

in presence, not in heart: . . . in person, *Fenton* . . . but not in spirit, *Norlie.*

endeavoured the more abundantly to see your face with great desire: . . . out of great desire, *Adams* . . . have striven very eagerly, *Fenton* . . . made eager efforts to behold you face to face, with strong longing, *Montgomery* . . . longing to see you personally, *Berkeley* . . . we made every effort to see you, *JB.*

18. Wherefore we would have come unto you, even I Paul, once and again: Accordingly, we wanted to, *Adams* . . . for that reason I would fain have visited you, *Montgomery* . . . we wished on two occasions, *Fenton* . . . did more than once, *TCNT.*

but Satan hindered us: . . . but the adversary, *Campbell* . . . but Satan got in the way, *Klingensmith* . . . interfered with us, *Berkeley* . . . blocked our way, *Adams* . . . prevented it, *Williams.*

19. For what [is] our hope, or joy, or crown of rejoicing?: . . . or winner's wreath about which I boast? *Adams* . . . the victor's wreath in which I exult? *Montgomery.*

[Are] not even ye in the presence of our Lord Jesus Christ at his coming?: Isn't it you? *Adams* . . . What but your own selves, *Montgomery* . . . in his presence? *Klingensmith* . . . when He will appear? *Fenton.*

20. For ye are our glory and joy: Yes, you are, *Adams* . . . are already our pride and our delight! *TCNT* . . . our boast, *Fenton* . . . my pride and delight, *Montgomery.*

1. Wherefore when we could no longer forbear: . . . when we could not stand it any longer, *Berkeley* . . . enduring it no longer, *Fenton* . . . when I could no longer stand it, *Klingensmith* . . . when I could no longer bear it, *Montgomery* . . . we could wait no longer, *NLT.*

2611.11 verb
inf aor pass
καταλειφθῆναι
kataleiphthēnai
to be left

1706.1 prep
ἐν
en
in

116.2 name
dat fem
Ἀθήναις
Athēnais
Athens

3304.5 adj
nom pl masc
μόνοι,
monoi
alone,

2504.1 conj
2. καὶ
kai
and

3854.7 verb 1pl
indic aor act
ἐπέμψαμεν
epempsamen
sent

4943.4 name
acc masc
Τιμόθεον
Timotheon
Timothy

3450.6 art
acc sing masc
τὸν
ton
the

79.4 noun
acc sing masc
ἀδελφὸν
adelphon
brother

2231.2 prs-
pron gen 1pl
ἡμῶν
hēmōn
our

2504.1 conj
καὶ
kai
and

1243.2 noun
acc sing masc
⌐ διάκονον
diakonon
servant

4754.3 adj
acc sing masc
[a✱ συνεργὸν]
sunergon
[fellow worker]

3450.2 art
gen sing
τοῦ
tou

2296.2 noun
gen sing masc
Θεοῦ
Theou
of God

2504.1 conj
⌐b καὶ
kai
and

4754.3 adj
acc sing masc
συνεργὸν
sunergon
fellow worker

2231.2 prs-
pron gen 1pl
ἡμῶν ⌐
hēmōn
our

1706.1 prep
ἐν
en
in

3450.3 art
dat sing
τῷ
tō
the

2077.3 noun
dat sing neu
εὐαγγελίῳ
euangeliō
good news

3450.2 art
gen sing
τοῦ
tou
of the

5382.2 name
gen masc
Χριστοῦ,
Christou
Christ,

1519.1 prep
εἰς
eis
for

3450.16 art
sing neu
τὸ
to
to

4592.2 verb
inf aor act
στηρίξαι
stērixai
to establish

5050.4 prs-
pron acc 2pl
ὑμᾶς
humas
you

2504.1 conj
καὶ
kai
and

3731.15 verb
inf aor act
παρακαλέσαι
parakalesai
to encourage

5050.4 prs-
pron acc 2pl
⌐c ὑμᾶς ⌐
humas
you

3875.1 prep
⌐ περὶ
peri
concerning

5065.1 prep
[d✱ ὑπὲρ]
huper
[on behalf of]

3450.10 art
gen sing fem
τῆς
tēs
the

3963.2 noun
gen sing fem
πίστεως
pisteōs
faith

5050.2 prs-
pron gen 2pl
ὑμῶν
humōn
your

3450.3 art
dat sing
3. ⌐ τῷ
tō
the

3450.16 art
sing neu
[a✱ τὸ]
to
[idem]

3235.4 num
card acc masc
μηδένα
mēdena
no one

4382.1 verb
inf pres mid
σαίνεσθαι
sainesthai
to be moved

1706.1 prep
ἐν
en
by

3450.14 art
dat pl fem
ταῖς
tais
the

2324.7 noun
dat pl fem
θλίψεσιν
thlipsesin
tribulations

3642.14 dem-
pron dat pl fem
ταύταις·
tautais
these.

840.7 prs-pron
nom pl masc
αὐτοὶ
autoi
Yourselves

1056.1 conj
γὰρ
gar
for

3471.6 verb 2pl
indic perf act
οἴδατε
oidate
know

3617.1 conj
ὅτι
hoti
that

1519.1 prep
εἰς
eis
for

3642.17 dem-
pron sing neu
τοῦτο
touto
this

2719.3 verb 1pl
indic pres mid
κείμεθα·
keimetha
we are set;

2504.1 conj
4. καὶ
kai
also

1056.1 conj
γὰρ
gar
for,

3616.1 conj
ὅτε
hote
when

4242.1 prep
πρὸς
pros
with

5050.4 prs-
pron acc 2pl
ὑμᾶς
humas
you

1498.36 verb 1pl
indic imperf act
ἦμεν,
ēmen
we were,

4161.2 verb 1pl
indic imperf act
προελέγομεν
proelegomen
we were telling beforehand

5050.3 prs-
pron dat 2pl
ὑμῖν
humin
you

3617.1 conj
ὅτι
hoti
that

3165.4 verb 1pl
indic pres act
μέλλομεν
mellomen
we are about

2323.6 verb
inf pres mid
θλίβεσθαι,
thlibesthai
to suffer tribulation,

2503.1 conj
καθὼς
kathōs
even as

2504.1 conj
καὶ
kai
also

1090.33 verb 3sing
indic aor mid
ἐγένετο
egeneto
it came to pass

their own city. In those days there was no question about it. Those who became believers were sure to suffer; they were persecuted; they were attacked by Satan and by the people who were his willing agents. Satan has usurped authority that really belongs to God and claims the whole world as his territory. The Thessalonians were suffering, and Paul's concern caused him to stay in Athens alone.

3:2. Paul therefore sent Timothy to establish, confirm, and strengthen them by thoroughly grounding them in the Word of God. He was also to comfort, encourage, and challenge them to strengthen their faith. Notice how Paul encouraged them to accept Timothy and his ministry. Paul did not talk about Timothy as a novice or apprentice but as a true brother (in the Lord) to the apostles, a minister (servant and love-slave of God), and a fellow worker with the apostles in the gospel of Christ. The Thessalonian Christians could have confidence in the teaching and encouragement he would give them.

3:3. Timothy's purpose was to strengthen them so none of them would be moved (shaken, disturbed) by those afflictions (troubles, tribulation, persecution) Paul knew they were enduring. In fact, the Thessalonian believers themselves already well knew that followers of Christ are appointed (destined, set) to suffer for the Lord's sake. (See Matthew 5:10-12.)

3:4. When they were first converted, Paul warned them in advance that they were about to suffer tribulation (trouble, persecution, affliction) because of their loyalty to Christ. Even before Paul left this actually began to take place.

Again and again the Bible foretells that suffering, testing, and persecution will become the lot of true believers. A hostile world says that real Christianity is perverse and unwholesome. The enemy still tempts believers to turn aside from the plain path of holiness and total dedication to Christ that God has set before them and seek an easier road.

In the light of what the Bible as a whole says about the end of the age, we should prepare ourselves to prosper in spite of suffering and persecution. We need to understand the real teaching of Scripture concerning prosperity and aim at entering the Kingdom through much tribulation (Acts 14:22). *Prosper* in the Bible means "to go well" or "do wisely" and usually refers to our final success. Joshua 1:7,8 uses "prosper" in this sense and explains it by a word for success that really means "to do wisely" (as in 1 Samuel 18:5,14). It is translated "deal prudently" (KJV) of the suffering Servant of the Lord (Isaiah 52:13). Yet His greatest success came when God "prospered" His purposes in Him by taking Him by the way of Gethsemane and the Cross (Isaiah 53:4-10). Paul knew what this meant and found God's grace sufficient (2 Corinthians 11:23-27; 12:9,10).

we thought it good to be left at Athens alone: . . . we thought it best, *Norlie* . . . we decided to remain at, *Confraternity* . . . I made up my mind to be left behind...all alone, *Montgomery* . . . to stay behind alone in Athens, *SEB*.

2. And sent Timotheus, our brother, and minister of God, and our fellowlabourer in the gospel of Christ:

to establish you, and to comfort you concerning your faith: . . . to give strength, *NLT* . . . to hearten you, *Montgomery* . . . to strengthen and encourage you, *NASB, Fenton* . . . to give you advice on matters of your faith, *Berkeley* . . . to console you for the sake of, *Concordant*.

3. That no man should be moved by these afflictions: . . . so that no one should be shaken, *Montgomery* . . . may be disturbed, *NASB* . . . didn't want anyone to be shaken by these troubles, *SEB* . . . might be deceived amid these difficulties, *Williams* . . . by these sufferings, *Fenton* . . . by these distresses, *Berkeley*.

for yourselves know that we are appointed thereunto: . . . to which you are aware that we are exposed, *Fenton* . . . appointed for this, *KJII* . . . that we are appointed to troubles, *Montgomery*.

4. For verily, when we were with you, we told you before that we should suffer tribulation: We, too, had warned you of this, *Norlie* . . . we told you in advance, *Berkeley* . . . we predicted to you, *Concordant* . . . For even when I was with you I used to tell you beforehand that I was to suffer affliction, *Montgomery* . . . we were certain to encounter trouble, *TCNT* . . . we were going to be pressed with difficulties, *Williams*.

even as it came to pass, and ye know: And so it proved, *TCNT, Montgomery* . . . and so it came to pass, *NASB* . . . exactly as you know it happened, *Berkeley*.

| 2504.1 conj **καὶ** *kai* and | 3471.6 verb 2pl indic perf act **οἴδατε·** *oidate* you know. | 1217.2 prep **5. διὰ** *dia* Because of | 3642.17 dem-pron sing neu **τοῦτο** *touto* this | 2476.3 prs-pron nom **κἀγὼ** *kagō* I also | 3239.1 adv **μηκέτι** *mēketi* no longer |

| 4573.3 verb nom sing masc part pres act **στέγων,** *stegōn* enduring, | 3854.5 verb 1sing indic aor act **ἔπεμψα** *epempsa* sent | 1519.1 prep **εἰς** *eis* for | 3450.16 art sing neu **τὸ** *to* the | 1091.29 verb inf aor act **γνῶναι** *gnōnai* to know | 3450.12 art acc sing fem **τὴν** *tēn* the |

| 3963.4 noun acc sing fem **πίστιν** *pistin* faith | 5050.2 prs-pron gen 2pl **ὑμῶν,** *humōn* your, | 3248.1 conj **μήπως** *mēpōs* lest perhaps | 3231.1 partic [☆ **μή** *mē* [not | 4315.1 adv **πως**] *pōs* how] | 3847.6 verb 3sing indic aor act **ἐπείρασεν** *epeirasen* did tempt |

| 5050.4 prs-pron acc 2pl **ὑμᾶς** *humas* you | 3450.5 art nom sing masc **ὁ** *ho* the | 3847.4 verb nom sing masc part pres act **πειράζων,** *peirazōn* tempting, | 2504.1 conj **καὶ** *kai* and | 1519.1 prep **εἰς** *eis* to | 2727.1 adj sing **κενὸν** *kenon* void |

| 1090.40 verb 3sing subj aor mid **γένηται** *genētai* should become | 3450.5 art nom sing masc **ὁ** *ho* the | 2845.1 noun nom sing masc **κόπος** *kopos* labor | 2231.2 prs-pron gen 1pl **ἡμῶν.** *hēmōn* our. | 732.1 adv **6. Ἄρτι** *Arti* Now | 1156.2 conj **δὲ** *de* but |

| 2048.14 verb gen sing masc part aor act **ἐλθόντος** *elthontos* having come | 4943.2 name gen masc **Τιμοθέου** *Timotheou* Timothy | 4242.1 prep **πρὸς** *pros* to | 2231.4 prs-pron acc 1pl **ἡμᾶς** *hēmas* us | 570.1 prep **ἀφ'** *aph'* from | 5050.2 prs-pron gen 2pl **ὑμῶν,** *humōn* you, |

| 2504.1 conj **καὶ** *kai* and | 2076.20 verb gen sing masc part aor mid **εὐαγγελισαμένου** *euangelisamenou* having announced good reports | | 2231.3 prs-pron dat 1pl **ἡμῖν** *hēmin* to us | 3450.12 art acc sing fem **τὴν** *tēn* the | 3963.4 noun acc sing fem **πίστιν** *pistin* faith |

| 2504.1 conj **καὶ** *kai* and | 3450.12 art acc sing fem **τὴν** *tēn* the | 26.4 noun acc sing fem **ἀγάπην** *agapēn* love | 5050.2 prs-pron gen 2pl **ὑμῶν,** *humōn* your, | 2504.1 conj **καὶ** *kai* and | 3617.1 conj **ὅτι** *hoti* that | 2174.2 verb 2pl pres act **ἔχετε** *echete* you have |

| 3281.2 noun acc sing fem **μνείαν** *mneian* remembrance | 2231.2 prs-pron gen 1pl **ἡμῶν** *hēmōn* of us | 18.12 adj acc sing fem **ἀγαθὴν** *agathēn* good | 3704.1 adv **πάντοτε,** *pantote* always, | 1955.4 verb nom pl masc part pres act **ἐπιποθοῦντες** *epipothountes* longing | |

| 2231.4 prs-pron acc 1pl **ἡμᾶς** *hēmas* us | 1481.19 verb inf aor act **ἰδεῖν,** *idein* to see, | 2481.1 conj **καθάπερ** *kathaper* even as | 2504.1 conj **καὶ** *kai* also | 2231.1 prs-pron nom 1pl **ἡμεῖς** *hēmeis* we | 5050.4 prs-pron acc 2pl **ὑμᾶς,** *humas* you: |

| 1217.2 prep **7. διὰ** *dia* because of | 3642.17 dem-pron sing neu **τοῦτο** *touto* this | 3731.26 verb 1pl indic aor pass **παρεκλήθημεν,** *pareklēthēmen* we were encouraged, | | 79.6 noun nom pl masc **ἀδελφοί,** *adelphoi* brothers, | 1894.1 prep **ἐφ'** *eph'* as to |

3:5. Paul was not sure, however, that the Thessalonians had learned the lessons he had learned. (See Philippians 4:12.) The word *mēpōs* is often used with a verb in the subjunctive mood (see *genētia*, "should become") to express a feared result. Combined with the subjunctive it can also indicate anxiety "directed toward warding off something still dependent on the will" (Rienecker, p.594). Paul recognized that while a peril existed, apostasy was not inevitable. The will of the believer was the determining factor. He knew, however, there was a definite danger that the tempter (Satan) might use their persecutions and troubles to tempt them to fall away. Should the tempter succeed, all the work Paul and his company had done in Thessalonica would go for nothing. Paul did not really expect this, yet he could not bear the thought. For this cause he sent Timothy to find out the state of their faith.

3:6. Before Timothy returned, Paul left Athens and went on to Corinth, where more opposition and difficulty awaited him (Acts 18:6,12). What joy it was, then, when Timothy returned and brought good news, first of the Thessalonians' faith and love, then of their good remembrance (including warm, kindly feelings) of Paul, and their desire, longing, and yearning to see him.

The verb used here of bringing good news (*euangelisamenou*) is the one used almost everywhere else in the New Testament of proclaiming good news concerning Jesus. Except for the angelic announcements of the birth of Jesus, it is used everywhere for the proclaiming or preaching of the gospel. But calling Timothy's report good news was appropriate in that it confirmed to Paul that the gospel was still being received and was still effective in the Thessalonian believers' lives. Their faith was the result of the gospel. The very word for faith used here (*pistin*) indicates a faith expressed by obedience to God and His Word. It was a faith that works or operates and is made effective by love (Galatians 5:6). Their love was also the result of the gospel, for it was the outflow of the love God revealed in Christ at the Cross. Their acceptance of and continuance in the gospel was the cause of their regard for Paul and their desire to see him, a desire as strong as his was to see them.

3:7. Thus, after months of apprehensive concern, after all Paul's fears about what Satan might do to the Thessalonians through persecution and temptation, Timothy's report brought comfort and encouragement to Paul. The enemies of the gospel had not been able to turn the believers from the Lord or from Paul. Paul, now rejoined by Silas also (Acts 18:5), was in the midst of much affliction, with painful circumstances involving physical privation and distress caused by persecution, pressure, and crushing trouble. The report of the continuing faith of the Thessalonian believers

5. For this cause, when I could no longer forbear: Consequently when, *Confraternity* . . . without delay, *Fenton* . . . That was why, *Williams* . . . so, it was for this reason, *Adams* . . . when I could no longer bear the suspense, *Norlie* . . . no longer endure the uncertainty, *TCNT* . . . no longer concealing my anxiety, *Campbell*.

I sent to know your faith: . . . to learn about, *Adams* . . . to find out about your faith, *Montgomery*.

lest by some means the tempter have tempted you: . . . fearing that, *Montgomery* . . . the Tempter had over-tried you, *Fenton*.

and our labour be in vain: . . . our toil might prove of no avail, *TCNT* . . . come to naught, *Confraternity* . . . would be wasted, *NLT* . . . and our labor might be lost, *Williams* . . . and our work had been for nothing, *Fenton*.

6. But now when Timotheus came from you unto us: . . . now that Timothy has returned, *Montgomery* . . . now returned to us from you, *Norlie*.

and brought us good tidings of your faith and charity: . . . has brought good news, *Montgomery*.

and that ye have good remembrance of us always: . . . you always think kindly of us, *NASB* . . . that you are still holding me in affectionate remembrance, *Montgomery* . . . how you retain us constantly in loving remembrance, *Berkeley* . . . that you always have good memories of us, *SEB, Adams*.

desiring greatly to see us, as we also [to see] you: . . . always longing to see me as I also am longing, *Montgomery* . . . just as we are longing to see you, *TCNT*.

7. Therefore, brethren, we were comforted over you: For this reason, *Adams* . . . These things have cheered us, *Norlie* . . . I have been comforted...in regard to you, *Montgomery* . . . I have been encouraged about you, *Williams*.

1 Thess. 3:8

5050.3 prs-pron dat 2pl	1894.3 prep	3820.11 adj dat sing fem	3450.11 art dat sing fem	2324.3 noun dat sing fem	2504.1 conj	316.3 noun dat sing fem
ὑμῖν,	ἐπὶ	πάσῃ	τῇ	ʹ θλίψει	καὶ	ἀνάγκῃ
humin	epi	pasē	tē	thlipsei	kai	anankē
you,	in	all	the	tribulation	and	necessity

316.3 noun dat sing fem	2504.1 conj	2324.3 noun dat sing fem	2231.2 prs-pron gen 1pl	1217.2 prep	3450.10 art gen sing fem
[✩ ἀνάγκῃ	καὶ	θλίψει]	ἡμῶν,	διὰ	τῆς
anankē	kai	thlipsei	hēmōn	dia	tēs
[necessity	and	tribulation]	our,	through	the

5050.2 prs-pron gen 2pl	3963.2 noun gen sing fem	3617.1 conj	3431.1 adv	2180.3 verb 1pl pres act	1430.1 partic
ὑμῶν	πίστεως·	8. ὅτι	νῦν	ζῶμεν	ἐὰν
humōn	pisteōs	hoti	nun	zōmen	ean
your	faith,	because	now	we live	if

8.a.Txt: 01ℵ-org,06D byz.
Var: 01ℵ-corr,02A,03B 018K,020L,Treg,Alf Tisc,We/Ho,Weis,Sod UBS/✩

5050.1 prs-pron nom 2pl	4590.3 verb 2pl subj pres act	4590.1 verb 2pl pres act	1706.1 prep	2935.3 noun dat sing masc
ὑμεῖς	ʹ στήκητε	[ᵃ✩ στήκετε]	ἐν	κυρίῳ.
humeis	stēkēte	stēkete	en	kuriō
you	should stand fast	[are standing]	in	Lord.

4949.1 intr-pron	1056.1 conj	2150.4 noun acc sing fem	1404.5 verb 1pl indic pres mid	3450.3 art dat sing
9. τίνα	γὰρ	εὐχαριστίαν	δυνάμεθα	τῷ
tina	gar	eucharistian	dunametha	tō
What	for	thanksgiving	are we able	

9.a.Txt: 01ℵ-corr2,02A 03B,06D-corr2,044,byz.
Var: 01ℵ-org,06D-org 010F,012G

2296.3 noun dat sing masc	2935.3 noun dat sing masc	464.1 verb inf aor act	3875.1 prep	5050.2 prs-pron gen 2pl
ʹ✩ θεῷ	[ᵃ κυρίῳ]	ἀνταποδοῦναι	περὶ	ὑμῶν,
theō	kuriō	antapodounai	peri	humōn
to God	[Lord]	to render	concerning	you,

1894.3 prep	3820.11 adj dat sing fem	3450.11 art dat sing fem	5315.3 noun dat sing fem	3614.11 rel-pron dat sing fem	5299.3 verb 1pl indic pres act
ἐπὶ	πάσῃ	τῇ	χαρᾷ	ᾗ	χαίρομεν
epi	pasē	tē	chara	hē	chairomen
for	all	the	joy	in which	we rejoice

1217.1 prep	5050.4 prs-pron acc 2pl	1699.1 prep	3450.2 art gen sing	2296.2 noun gen sing masc
δι'	ὑμᾶς	ἔμπροσθεν	τοῦ	θεοῦ
di'	humas	emprosthen	tou	theou
on account of	you	before		God

2231.2 prs-pron gen 1pl	3433.2 noun gen sing fem	2504.1 conj	2232.1 noun fem	5065.1 prep	1586.1 adv
ἡμῶν,	10. νυκτὸς	καὶ	ἡμέρας	ʹ ὑπὲρ	ἐκπερισσοῦ
hēmōn	nuktos	kai	hēmeras	huper	ekperissou
our,	night	and	day	above	exceedingly

5076.1 adv	1183.4 verb nom pl masc part pres mid	1519.1 prep	3450.16 art sing neu	1481.19 verb inf aor act
[✩ ὑπερεκπερισσοῦ]	δεόμενοι	εἰς	τὸ	ἰδεῖν
huperekperissou	deomenoi	eis	to	idein
[idem]	beseeching	for	the	to see

5050.2 prs-pron gen 2pl	3450.16 art sing neu	4241.1 noun sing neu	2504.1 conj	2645.3 verb inf aor act	3450.17 art pl neu
ὑμῶν	τὸ	πρόσωπον,	καὶ	καταρτίσαι	τὰ
humōn	to	prosōpon	kai	katartisai	ta
your	the	face,	and	to perfect	the

not only cheered him and relieved the pressure of his passionate concern, it gave him new courage to go on.

3:8. The word *stēkēte* emphasizes the idea of standing firmly. The anxiety expressed in verses 5 through 7 seems to fade as Paul recognized that it was their faith "in the Lord" that produced this firm stand. Notice also that the common but important Pauline theme of a believer's position "in Christ" is seen in the phrase "in the Lord." This verse, therefore, does not imply any further doubt about their condition. "If" here has almost the idea of *when* or *whenever.* What Paul meant was that the assurance they were standing firm in the Lord gave him a new burst of life. Paul could now throw himself into the work at Corinth with new energy. Life to Paul meant spreading the gospel. His consuming passion was to turn men to Christ and see them established in the truth.

3:9. Paul's troubles and sufferings for the gospel's sake were not even worth considering in comparison to the joy the good news of the Thessalonians' faith brought to him. His rejoicing in God's presence was pure and unselfish. Joyfully, he recognized what God had done and cried out, "What thanks can we render to God?" In other words, any thanks believers give Him is totally inadequate to express what is really due Him.

3:10. The joy and good news did not lessen Paul's concern for these new converts, however. It only increased it. Now that he knew how well they were getting along, he wanted all the more to see them in order to perfect or complete what was lacking in their faith, that is, in what they still needed to add to their knowledge and understanding of the gospel.

There is, of course, no insinuation here that there was any deficiency in their personal faith in the Lord. Paul simply recognized that the new converts needed further teaching. While rejoicing in what God had done, he knew God had much more for them. "Perfect that which is lacking" was a phrase often used in those days for the supplying of an army with provisions. Paul wanted to provide these new believers with spiritual food that would help them march on to greater and greater victories. The good food of God's Word would bring further spiritual growth.

As an apostle Paul had the responsibility to train the new believers who had turned their backs on the world to follow Jesus. It was God's purpose that all of them would come to the place where they could do the work of ministry and edify or build up the body of Christ both spiritually and in numbers. Then the whole Body, united to Christ, the Head, and to their fellow members in love, would be able to grow by what each individual believer received from Christ (Ephesians 4:11-16).

in all our affliction and distress by your faith: . . . in your every distress and crushing affliction, this encouragement finding its source in your faith, *Wuest* . . . for all our hardship and suffering, *Fenton* . . . over your faith, *Montgomery.*

8. For now we live, if ye stand fast in the Lord: . . . now I am really living, *Montgomery* . . . we enjoy living, *Berkeley* . . . It brings to us renewed life, *Norlie.*

9. For what thanks can we render to God again for you: How can we ever thank God adequately, *Adams* . . . give back to God in return concerning you, *Wuest* . . . in your behalf, *Montgomery.*

for all the joy wherewith we joy for your sakes before our God: . . . for all of the joy that we have experienced because of you, *Adams* . . . for all the delight with which we rejoice, *Fenton* . . . in return for all the joy which you cause me in the presence of, *Montgomery* . . . with which we are rejoicing on account of you, *Wuest* . . . the joy you give us? *NLT.*

10. Night and day praying exceedingly: . . . we pray early and late, *Norlie* . . . most earnestly, *NASB, TCNT* . . . earnestly wishing, *Fenton* . . . earnestly requesting, *Campbell* . . . asking in prayer quite beyond measure and as earnestly as possible, *Wuest* . . . to pray with deepest earnestness and keenest eagerness, *Williams.*

that we might see your face, and might perfect: . . . to see you personally, *Berkeley* . . . that I may see you face to face, *Montgomery* . . . may supply, *Confraternity* . . . and complete the things, *Wuest* . . . We want to help your faith to be complete, *NLT.*

1 Thess. 3:11

5140.3 noun pl neu ὑστερήματα husterēmata things lacking	**3450.10** art gen sing fem τῆς tēs in the	**3963.2** noun gen sing fem πίστεως pisteōs faith	**5050.2** prs-pron gen 2pl ὑμῶν; humōn your?	**840.5** prs-pron nom sing masc **11.** Αὐτὸς Autos Himself	**1156.2** conj δὲ de but

3450.5 art nom sing masc ὁ ho	**2296.1** noun nom sing masc θεὸς theos God	**2504.1** conj καὶ kai and	**3824.1** noun nom sing masc πατὴρ patēr Father	**2231.2** prs-pron gen 1pl ἡμῶν hēmōn our	**2504.1** conj καὶ kai and	**3450.5** art nom sing masc ὁ ho the

11.a.**Txt**: 06D-corr,018K 020L,byz.
Var: 01ℵ,02A,03B 06D-org,33,Lach,Treg Alf,Tisc,We/Ho,Weis Sod,UBS/⋆

2935.1 noun nom sing masc κύριος kurios Lord	**2231.2** prs-pron gen 1pl ἡμῶν hēmōn our	**2400.1** name nom masc Ἰησοῦς Iēsous Jesus	**5382.1** name nom masc ⌐a Χριστὸς ⌐ Christos Christ	**2690.1** verb 3sing opt aor act κατευθύναι kateuthunai may direct	

3450.12 art acc sing fem τὴν tēn the	**3461.4** noun acc sing fem ὁδὸν hodon way	**2231.2** prs-pron gen 1pl ἡμῶν hēmōn our	**4242.1** prep πρὸς pros to	**5050.4** prs-pron acc 2pl ὑμᾶς· humas you.	**5050.4** prs-pron acc 2pl **12.** ὑμᾶς humas You	**1156.2** conj δὲ de but

3450.5 art nom sing masc ὁ ho the	**2935.1** noun nom sing masc κύριος kurios Lord	**3981.5** verb 3sing opt aor act πλεονάσαι pleonasai may make to exceed	**2504.1** conj καὶ kai and	**3915.15** verb 3sing opt aor act περισσεύσαι perisseusai to abound

3450.11 art dat sing fem τῇ tē in the	**26.3** noun dat sing fem ἀγάπῃ agapē love	**1519.1** prep εἰς eis toward	**238.3** prs-pron acc pl masc ἀλλήλους allēlous one another	**2504.1** conj καὶ kai and	**1519.1** prep εἰς eis toward	**3820.8** adj acc pl masc πάντας, pantas, all,

2481.1 conj καθάπερ kathaper even as	**2504.1** conj καὶ kai also	**2231.1** prs-pron nom 1pl ἡμεῖς hēmeis we	**1519.1** prep εἰς eis toward	**5050.4** prs-pron acc 2pl ὑμᾶς, humas, you,	**1519.1** prep **13.** εἰς eis for	**3450.16** art sing neu τὸ to the

4592.2 verb inf aor act στηρίξαι stērixai to establish	**5050.2** prs-pron gen 2pl ὑμῶν humōn your	**3450.15** art acc pl fem τὰς tas the	**2559.1** noun fem καρδίας kardias hearts	**271.3** adj acc pl fem ἀμέμπτους amemptous blameless	**1706.1** prep ἐν en in

41.2 noun dat sing fem ἁγιωσύνῃ hagiōsunē holiness	**1699.1** prep ἔμπροσθεν emprosthen before	**3450.2** art gen sing τοῦ tou	**2296.2** noun gen sing masc θεοῦ theou God	**2504.1** conj καὶ kai and	**3824.2** noun gen sing masc πατρὸς patros Father

2231.2 prs-pron gen 1pl ἡμῶν hēmōn our,	**1706.1** prep ἐν en in	**3450.11** art dat sing fem τῇ tē the	**3814.3** noun dat sing fem παρουσίᾳ parousia coming	**3450.2** art gen sing τοῦ tou of the	**2935.2** noun gen sing masc κυρίου kuriou Lord	**2231.2** prs-pron gen 1pl ἡμῶν hēmōn our

13.a.**Txt**: 020L,byz.bo.
Var: 01ℵ,02A,03B,06D 018K,Lach,Treg,Alf Word,Tisc,We/Ho,Weis Sod,UBS/⋆

2400.2 name masc Ἰησοῦ Iēsou Jesus	**5382.2** name gen masc ⌐a Χριστοῦ ⌐ Christou Christ	**3196.3** prep μετὰ meta with	**3820.4** adj gen pl πάντων pantōn all	**3450.1** art gen pl τῶν tōn the	**39.4** adj gen pl ἁγίων hagiōn saints

So intense was Paul's desire to do this that day and night he was praying (literally, begging) exceedingly (beyond all measure, with utmost earnestness) for God to permit him to minister to the Thessalonians again in person.

3:11. With the mention of prayer Paul actually broke out into a prayer: "Now God himself and our Father, and our Lord Jesus Christ, direct our way unto you." "Direct" includes the idea of making a straight path and removing obstacles. Satan had twice hindered Paul from coming. God alone could clear the way.

3:12. Paul's prayer was primarily for the believers. He could teach them, but only God through Christ could cause them to increase and abound (excel and overflow) in love. "Love" here is *the* love," Calvary love, not just brotherly love. God would make this kind of love overflow toward each other and toward all people.

God had caused that kind of love to pour out of the apostles' hearts toward the Thessalonians. It was the same love God showed "toward us, in that, while we were yet sinners" and really His enemies, "Christ died for us" (Romans 5:8,10). No one can work up this kind of love by his own efforts or reasoning. It comes only as Christ fills believers' hearts, and His love in them overflows. This too is the work of the Holy Spirit as He strengthens His children with mighty power in their inner being so Christ may continue to dwell in their hearts by faith, and they, being rooted and grounded in love, may be strong enough to grasp and make their own the love of Christ (Ephesians 4:16-19).

3:13. The overflow of love is also the key to spiritual advancement and holiness. Creeds, doctrines, and rules may have a place and may be good in themselves, just as the law of Moses was holy, just, and good (Romans 7:12). Yet, they become deadly without superabundant love. Only as Christians love one another with Calvary love and reach out in that love to unlovely, rebellious sinners does the Lord establish their hearts (strengthening and confirming the purposes of their hearts) so they will stand blameless "in holiness before God, even our Father, at the coming of our Lord Jesus Christ with all his saints." "Holiness" here is holy dedication to the will and service of the Lord.

There is some controversy about whether "his saints" (holy ones) refers to angels, to believers, or both. In some cases *saints* does refer to angels. (See Zechariah 14:5 as interpreted by Jesus in Mark 8:38. See also Matthew 25:31.) Yet "the saints" in Paul's epistles are usually the believers who have turned their backs on the world to follow Jesus and who stand in His righteousness, not their own. Most take it that the word "all" removes restrictions and thus includes both angels and believers. The important thing is that the expression of Christ's love in and through believers prepares them to be part of the company who are in Christ at His coming.

that which is lacking in your faith?: . . . whatever is yet lacking in your faith, *Montgomery* . . . anything that is missing, *SEB* . . . to adjust the deficiencies, *Concordant.*

11. Now God himself and our Father:
and our Lord Jesus Christ, direct our way unto you: . . . facilitate our journey to you! *Fenton* . . . prepare our way, *Berkeley* . . . guide my way to you! *Williams* . . . guide our steps to you! *Norlie* . . . lead us to you, *Beck* . . . my path to you, *Montgomery.*

12. And the Lord make you to increase and abound in love one toward another, and toward all [men]: And as for you, *Wuest* . . . Meanwhile, may the Lord cause you, *Montgomery* . . . make you grow in love and overflow with it for one another and for everybody, *Beck* . . . make your love for one another and for all people, *Adams* . . . fill you to overflowing with love, *Fenton* . . . and multiply in, *KJII.*
even as we [do] toward you: . . . as my love for you does, *Williams* . . . even as also we have this divine...love for you, *Wuest* . . . just as ours does for you, *Adams* . . . just as we love you, *Beck.*

13. To the end he may stablish your hearts unblameable in holiness: . . . that He might stabilize, *Wuest* . . . and so may He give you inward strength to be holy and without a fault, *Beck* . . . so that He may strengthen your hearts to be faultless in purity, *Williams* . . . you will be spotlessly holy, *Berkeley* . . . in spotless holiness, *Fenton* . . . make your spirits strong, *SEB* . . . irreproachable in holiness, *Adams.*
before God, even our Father: . . . in the presence of, *Wuest* . . . in the sight of, *Williams.*
at the coming of our Lord Jesus Christ with all his saints: . . . at the appearance of our Lord, *Fenton* . . . when our Lord Jesus comes, *Beck* . . . with all the holy ones, *Klingensmith* . . . when our Lord Jesus comes back with all His consecrated ones, *Williams.*

1 Thess. 4:1

13.b.**Txt:** 01ℵ-corr1,03B
06D-corr2,010F,012G
044,sa.byz.
Var: 01ℵ-org,01ℵ-corr2
02A,06D-org,81,629,bo.

1.a.**Txt:** 03B-corr,Steph
Var: 01ℵ,02A,03B-org
06D,018K,020L,33
Gries,Lach,Treg,Alf
Word,Tisc,We/Ho,Weis
Sod,UBS/⋆

1.b.**Var:** 03B,06D-org,33
it.bo.Lach,Treg,Alf,Tisc
We/Ho,Weis,Sod
UBS/⋆

1.c.**Var:** 01ℵ,02A,03B
06D-org,33,sa.bo.Lach
Treg,Alf,Word,Tisc
We/Ho,Weis,Sod
UBS/⋆

840.3 prs-pron gen sing	279.1 intrj	3450.16 art sing neu	3036.8 adj sing neu	3631.1 partic	79.6 noun nom pl masc
αὐτοῦ.	[b+ ἀμήν.]	4:1. (a Τὸ)	λοιπὸν	οὖν,	ἀδελφοί,
autou	*amēn*	*To*	*loipon*	*oun*	*adelphoi*
his.	[Amen.]	The	rest	then,	brothers,

2049.3 verb 1pl indic pres act	5050.4 prs-pron acc 2pl	2504.1 conj	3731.2 verb 1pl indic pres act	1706.1 prep	2935.3 noun dat sing masc
ἐρωτῶμεν	ὑμᾶς	καὶ	παρακαλοῦμεν	ἐν	κυρίῳ
erōtōmen	*humas*	*kai*	*parakaloumen*	*en*	*kuriō*
we beseech	you	and	we exhort	in	Lord

2400.2 name masc	2419.1 conj	2503.1 conj	3741.7 verb 2pl indic aor act	3706.1 prep	2231.2 prs-pron gen 1pl
Ἰησοῦ,	[b⋆+ ἵνα]	καθὼς	παρελάβετε	παρ'	ἡμῶν
Iēsou	*hina*	*kathōs*	*parelabete*	*par'*	*hēmōn*
Jesus,	[that]	even as	you received	from	us

3450.16 art sing neu	4316.1 adv	1158.1 verb 3sing indic pres act	5050.4 prs-pron acc 2pl	3906.17 verb inf pres act	2504.1 conj
τὸ	πῶς	δεῖ	ὑμᾶς	περιπατεῖν	καὶ
to	*pōs*	*dei*	*humas*	*peripatein*	*kai*
the	how	it is necessary for	you	to walk	and

694.5 verb inf pres act	2296.3 noun dat sing masc	2503.1 conj	2504.1 conj	3906.1 verb 2pl pres act	2419.1 conj
ἀρέσκειν	θεῷ,	[c⋆+ καθὼς	καὶ	περιπατεῖτε,]	ἵνα
areskein	*theō*	*kathōs*	*kai*	*peripateite*	*hina*
to please	God,	[as	even	you do walk,]	that

3915.7 verb 2pl subj pres act	3095.1 adv comp	3471.6 verb 2pl indic perf act	1056.1 conj	4949.8 intr-pron acc pl fem	
περισσεύητε	μᾶλλον.	2. οἴδατε	γὰρ	τίνας	
perisseuēte	*mallon*	*oidate*	*gar*	*tinas*	
you should abound	more.	You know	for	what	

3714.1 noun fem	1319.15 verb 1pl indic aor act	5050.3 prs-pron dat 2pl	1217.2 prep	3450.2 art gen sing	2935.2 noun gen sing masc
παραγγελίας	ἐδώκαμεν	ὑμῖν	διὰ	τοῦ	κυρίου
parangelias	*edōkamen*	*humin*	*dia*	*tou*	*kuriou*
injunctions	we gave	you	through	the	Lord

2400.2 name masc	3642.17 dem-pron sing neu	1056.1 conj	1498.4 verb 3sing indic pres act	2284.1 noun sing neu	3450.2 art gen sing
Ἰησοῦ.	3. τοῦτο	γάρ	ἐστιν	θέλημα	τοῦ
Iēsou	*touto*	*gar*	*estin*	*thelēma*	*tou*
Jesus.	This	for	is	will	

2296.2 noun gen sing masc	3450.5 art nom sing masc	38.1 noun nom sing masc	5050.2 prs-pron gen 2pl	563.9 verb inf pres mid	5050.4 prs-pron acc 2pl
θεοῦ,	ὁ	ἁγιασμὸς	ὑμῶν,	ἀπέχεσθαι	ὑμᾶς
theou	*ho*	*hagiasmos*	*humōn*	*apechesthai*	*humas*
God's,	the	sanctification	your,	to abstain	you

570.3 prep	3450.10 art gen sing fem	4061.1 noun fem	3471.25 verb inf perf act	1524.1 adj sing	5050.2 prs-pron gen 2pl
ἀπὸ	τῆς	πορνείας,	4. εἰδέναι	ἕκαστον	ὑμῶν
apo	*tēs*	*porneias*	*eidenai*	*hekaston*	*humōn*
from	the	fornication,	to know	each	of you

3450.16 art sing neu	1431.4 prs-pron gen sing	4487.1 noun sing neu	2904.2 verb inf pres mid	1706.1 prep	38.2 noun dat sing masc
τὸ	ἑαυτοῦ	σκεῦος	κτᾶσθαι	ἐν	ἁγιασμῷ
to	*heautou*	*skeuos*	*ktasthai*	*en*	*hagiasmō*
the	his own	vessel	to possess	in	sanctification

4:1. The practical section of this epistle now begins. What is said here was not new to the Thessalonians. Nor did Paul give them harsh or arbitrary commands. He knew the kind of society in which they lived, so he wanted to encourage them.

Those to whom Paul so tenderly addressed these exhortations were brethren. (*Adelphoi* often includes both brothers and sisters.) They had already received and accepted Paul's answer to the questions "How must we live?" and "How are we to please God?" They were indeed striving to please God. In fact, the assurance that it is possible to please God, and that God takes pleasure in His people, was a strong incentive to holy living. But no believer can rest on his laurels. So Paul urged the Thessalonian Christians to abound more and more.

4:2. The secret of this progress in excellence was to continue to follow the loving instructions already made known to them by Paul. These precepts were not Paul's, however. They came from God through Jesus.

4:3. The reason Jesus gave instructions instead of letting believers go their own way is that sanctification (holiness, consecration, dedication to God's plan and purposes) is God's will for every believer. Sanctification also means a separation from all that is unclean, specifically from fornication (immorality, sexual freedom).

4:4. Paul went on to say that for believers, keeping away from immorality involves knowing how to possess their vessels in sanctification (consecration, dedication to God) and honor (respecting its value).

Many take "possess his vessel" to mean "acquire a wife." They appeal to such passages as 1 Peter 3:7 which speaks of the wife as "the weaker vessel" and 1 Corinthians 7:2 which says that to avoid immorality each man should have his own wife and each woman her own husband. This view emphasizes that the purpose of marriage is greater than sexual indulgence. Unbridled lustful passion that treated the wife as a mere sex object characterized many heathen marriages. Marriage that does not show respect and honor to the wife is not likely to help a person avoid immorality.

Others point out that 1 Peter 3:7 looks at both man and wife as vessels. The body is spoken of as an earthen vessel (2 Corinthians 4:7). Moreover, in dealing with this same subject of immorality, Paul spoke of the body as the temple of the Holy Spirit (1 Corinthians 6:18,19; see also Romans 6:12).

The Greek in this verse (4:4) is not conclusive. "Possess" is often used of acquiring land, or gold, or gifts, and could be used of acquiring a wife. However, the Biblical declaration is that in fornication or any sexual immorality the sin is against one's own body (1 Corinthians 6:18). This would seem to favor taking "vessel" as "body" here.

1. Furthermore then we beseech you, brethren: Finally then...I continue to, *Montgomery* . . . Therefore, for the rest, *Fenton.*

and exhort [you] by the Lord Jesus: . . . and strongly advise you, *Berkeley* . . . and appeal to you, *JB.*

that as ye have received of us how ye ought to walk and to please God: . . . as you learned of me, *Montgomery* . . . we gave you instructions, *SEB* . . . as to what your daily life must be, *TCNT.*

[so] ye would abound more and more: So let it increase more, *Klingensmith* . . . to keep on doing still better, *Berkeley.*

2. For ye know what commandments we gave you by the Lord Jesus: You have not forgotten the instructions, *JB* . . . what charges I laid upon you, *Montgomery* . . . the directions that we gave you, *TCNT* . . . by authority of, *Berkeley.*

3. For this is the will of God: What God wants, *JB.*

[even] your sanctification: . . . is for you all to be holy, *JB* . . . that you be holy, *Norlie* . . . that you grow in holiness, *NAB.*

that ye should abstain from fornication: . . . keep yourselves away from lewdness, *Berkeley* . . . that you should practice abstinence from sexual immorality, *Williams* . . . Stay away from sexual sin, *SEB* . . . from all prostitution, *Concordant* . . . from whoredom, *Campbell* . . . from sex sins, *NLT.*

4. That every one of you should know how to possess his vessel: . . . should see the duty of making one woman his wife, *TCNT* . . . how to control his own body, *SEB* . . . to win his own wife, *Berkeley* . . . should learn to take his own wife out of pure and honorable motives, *Williams* . . . see to it that he chooses for himself a wife to be held, *Norlie.*

in sanctification and honour: . . . in holiness, *Confraternity* . . . in purity, *Berkeley.*

2504.1 conj	4940.3 noun dat sing fem	3231.1 partic	1706.1 prep	3669.1 noun dat sing neu	1924.1 noun fem	2481.1 conj
καὶ	τιμῇ,	5. μὴ	ἐν	πάθει	ἐπιθυμίας	καθάπερ
kai	timē	mē	en	pathei	epithumias	kathaper
and	honor,	not	in	passion	of lust	even as

2504.1 conj	3450.17 art pl neu	1477.4 noun pl neu	3450.17 art pl neu	3231.1 partic	3471.24 verb pl neu part perf act	3450.6 art acc sing masc
καὶ	τὰ	ἔθνη	τὰ	μὴ	εἰδότα	τὸν
kai	ta	ethnē	ta	mē	eidota	ton
also	the	nations	the	not	knowing	

2296.4 noun acc sing masc	3450.16 art sing neu	3231.1 partic	5070.1 verb inf pres act	2504.1 conj	3982.1 verb inf pres act
θεόν·	6. τὸ	μὴ	ὑπερβαίνειν	καὶ	πλεονεκτεῖν
theon	to	mē	huperbainein	kai	pleonektein
God,	the	not	to go beyond	and	to overreach

1706.1 prep	3450.3 art dat sing	4088.3 noun dat sing neu	3450.6 art acc sing masc	79.4 noun acc sing masc	840.3 prs-pron gen sing
ἐν	τῷ	πράγματι	τὸν	ἀδελφὸν	αὐτοῦ,
en	tō	pragmati	ton	adelphon	autou
in	the	matter	the	brother	his;

6.a.Txt: 01ℵ-corr 06D-corr,018K,020L byz.
Var: 01ℵ-org,02A,03B 06D-org,33,Lach,Treg Alf,Tisc,We/Ho,Weis Sod,UBS/☆

1354.1 conj	1545.1 adj nom sing masc	3450.5 art nom sing masc	2935.1 noun nom sing masc	3875.1 prep	3820.4 adj gen pl
διότι	ἔκδικος	(a ὁ)	κύριος	περὶ	πάντων
dioti	ekdikos	ho	kurios	peri	pantōn
because	avenger	the	Lord	concerning	all

3642.2 dem-pron gen pl	2503.1 conj	2504.1 conj	4135.3 verb 1pl indic aor act	5050.3 prs-pron dat 2pl	2504.1 conj
τούτων,	καθὼς	καὶ	προείπαμεν	ὑμῖν	καὶ
toutōn	kathōs	kai	proeipamen	humin	kai
these things,	even as	also	we told before	you	and

1257.7 verb 1pl indic aor mid	3620.3 partic	1056.1 conj	2535.9 verb 3sing indic aor act	2231.4 prs-pron acc 1pl	3450.5 art nom sing masc
διεμαρτυράμεθα.	7. οὐ	γὰρ	ἐκάλεσεν	ἡμᾶς	ὁ
diemarturametha	ou	gar	ekalesen	hēmas	ho
fully testified.	Not	for	called	us	

2296.1 noun nom sing masc	1894.3 prep	165.3 noun dat sing fem	233.1 conj	1706.1 prep	38.2 noun dat sing masc
θεὸς	ἐπὶ	ἀκαθαρσίᾳ	ἀλλ'	ἐν	ἁγιασμῷ.
theos	epi	akatharsia	all'	en	hagiasmō
God	to	uncleanness,	but	in	sanctification.

4952.1 partic	3450.5 art nom sing masc	114.5 verb nom sing masc part pres act	3620.2 partic	442.4 noun acc sing masc
8. τοιγαροῦν	ὁ	ἀθετῶν,	οὐκ	ἄνθρωπον
toigaroun	ho	athetōn	ouk	anthrōpon
So then	the	setting aside,	not	man

8.a.Txt: 01ℵ,06D-org 06D-corr2,010F,012G 044,byz.
Var: 02A,03B,06D-corr1 016I,33,365,614,2464 bo.

114.2 verb 3sing indic pres act	233.2 conj	3450.6 art acc sing masc	2296.4 noun acc sing masc	3450.6 art acc sing masc	2504.1 conj
ἀθετεῖ,	ἀλλὰ	τὸν	θεὸν,	τὸν	(a καὶ)
athetei	alla	ton	theon	ton	kai
sets aside,	but	the	God,	the	also

8.b.Txt: 01ℵ-corr,02A 018K,020L,byz.Sod
Var: 01ℵ-org,03B,06D Lach,Treg,Tisc,We/Ho Weis,UBS/☆

1319.30 verb acc sing masc part aor act	1319.8 verb acc sing masc part pres act	3450.16 art sing neu	4011.1 noun sing neu	840.3 prs-pron gen sing
(δόντα	[b☆ διδόντα]	τὸ	πνεῦμα	αὐτοῦ
donta	didonta	to	pneuma	autou
having given	[idem]	the	Spirit	his

4:5. Our "vessel," then, must be kept in honor, not in lustful passion in the manner of the Gentile pagans who did not know God. In other words, if one really knows God he will learn to gain control of his vessel in such a way as to maintain its dedication to God and its honor. However, if "vessel" does refer to a wife, a comparison between the Christian and the pagan is in view. (Although the term *ethnē* often refers to Gentiles or non-Jews versus Jews, here the term is used to contrast believers and nonbelievers.) Reflecting upon ideas conveyed in verses 4 and 5, Frame points out that "pagan marriage was marked by the absence of holiness and respect for the wife and by the presence of passionate lust" (*International Critical Commentary*, 38:151). On the other hand, the Christian marriage should demonstrate qualities which are an outgrowth of consecration to the Lord, i.e., "sanctification and honor" (verse 4).

The word *epithumias* by itself can simply mean a desire or a longing without a negative connotation (see Luke 22:15, for example, where Jesus said, "With *desire* I have desired to eat this passover with you before I suffer"). *Pathos*, however, always expresses a negative sense in Pauline writings (see Romans 1:26 and Colossians 3:5). The phrase *pathei epithumias*, therefore, describes someone who is "caught in the grip of lustful passions he is quite unable to control" (Morris, *New International Commentary on the New Testament, 1&2 Thessalonians*, p.124).

4:6. Another reason for keeping away from immorality is that what it does to our brother calls for divine punishment. Immorality will always "go beyond" or overstep and transgress proper limits in disregard of the rights of others. It defrauds a brother, cheating and taking advantage, not only of him but also the neighbor whom Christians are supposed to love as themselves (Luke 10:27). All sins cheat. Premarital sex cheats one out of virginity. Adultery cheats the true marriage partner. Homosexuality cheats one out of the kind of relationship between a man and a woman that God intended from the beginning (Matthew 19:4,5).

4:7. God offers more than a fire escape from hell. His call is into a way of life that brings glory to the One who has called the individual out of darkness into His marvelous light (1 Peter 2:9). Not immorality but holiness brings a person into conformity with the will of God.

4:8. Those who reject the call to holiness and the warning against immorality, setting them aside as if null and void, are rejecting not man but God who is the giver of the Holy Spirit. They forget that the Spirit is supremely holy, and a believer's body is His temple.

5. Not in the lust of concupiscence: . . . not in lack of self-control, *Klingensmith* . . . not in passionate desire, *NAB* . . . not in lustful passion, *Berkeley* . . . not in the passion of lust, *Confraternity*.

even as the Gentiles which know not God: . . . like the heathen, *Fenton*.

6. That no [man] go beyond and defraud his brother in [any] matter: Let no one cheat or trick, *Klingensmith* . . . that no one transgress and overreach his brother, *Confraternity* . . . take advantage of, *Berkeley* . . . by taking advantage of a brother, *JB*.

because that the Lord [is] the avenger of all such: . . . is a punisher, *Berkeley*.

as we also have forewarned you and testified: . . . as we said to you before also, and certify, *Concordant*.

7. For God hath not called us unto uncleanness, but unto holiness: . . . to a life of immorality, but to one of personal purity, *Williams* . . . but to a holy life, *Berkeley*.

8. He therefore that despiseth, despiseth not man, but God: . . . he who rejects these things, *Confraternity* . . . whoever rejects this teaching, *Williams* . . . he who is repudiating is not repudiating man, *Concordant* . . . is not objecting to a human authority, *JB* . . . the slighter of it does not slight man but God, *Berkeley*.

who hath also given unto us his holy Spirit: . . . who continues to put His Spirit in you, *Williams*.

1 Thess. 4:9

8.c.Txt: 02A,Steph
Var: 01ℵ,03B,06D
015H,018K,020L,byz.
Lach,Treg,Alf,Word
Tisc,We/Ho,Weis,Sod
UBS/✶

3450.16 art sing neu	39.1 adj sing	1519.1 prep	2231.4 prs-pron acc 1pl	5050.4 prs-pron acc 2pl	3875.1 prep
τὸ	ἅγιον	εἰς	ʼ ἡμᾶς.	[c✶ ὑμᾶς.]	9. Περὶ
to	hagion	eis	hēmas	humas	Peri
the	holy	to	us.	[you.]	Concerning

1156.2 conj	3450.10 art gen sing fem	5197.2 noun gen sing fem	3620.3 partic	5367.3 noun acc sing fem	2174.2 verb 2pl pres act
δὲ	τῆς	φιλαδελφίας	οὐ	χρείαν	ʼ ἔχετε
de	tēs	philadelphias	ou	chreian	echete
now	the	brotherly love	no	need	you have

9.a.Txt: 01ℵ-org,02A
06D-corr1,015H,byz.
Var: 01ℵ-corr2,06D-org
010F,012G,044,6,104
365,1739,1881,2464

2174.5 verb 1pl indic pres act	1119.5 verb inf pres act	5050.3 prs-pron dat 2pl	840.7 prs-pron nom pl masc	1056.1 conj	5050.1 prs-pron nom 2pl
[a ἔχομεν]	γράφειν	ὑμῖν,	αὐτοὶ	γὰρ	ὑμεῖς
echomen	graphein	humin	autoi	gar	humeis
[we have]	to write	to you,	yourselves	for	you

2289.1 adj nom pl masc	1498.6 verb 2pl indic pres act	1519.1 prep	3450.16 art sing neu	25.11 verb inf pres act	238.3 prs-pron acc pl masc
θεοδίδακτοί	ἐστε	εἰς	τὸ	ἀγαπᾶν	ἀλλήλους
theodidaktoi	este	eis	to	agapan	allēlous
taught of God	are	for	the	to love	one another.

2504.1 conj	1056.1 conj	4020.2 verb 2pl pres act	840.15 prs-pron sing neu	1519.1 prep	3820.8 adj acc pl masc	3450.8 art acc pl masc
10. καὶ	γὰρ	ποιεῖτε	αὐτὸ	εἰς	πάντας	τοὺς
kai	gar	poieite	auto	eis	pantas	tous
Also	for	you do	this	towards	all	the

79.9 noun acc pl masc	3450.8 art acc pl masc	1706.1 prep	3513.8 adj dat sing fem	3450.11 art dat sing fem	3081.3 name dat fem
ἀδελφοὺς	τοὺς	ἐν	ὅλῃ	τῇ	Μακεδονίᾳ.
adelphous	tous	en	holē	tē	Makedonia
brothers	the	in	whole		of Macedonia;

3731.2 verb 1pl indic pres act	1156.2 conj	5050.4 prs-pron acc 2pl	79.6 noun nom pl masc	3915.12 verb inf pres act
παρακαλοῦμεν	δὲ	ὑμᾶς,	ἀδελφοί,	περισσεύειν
parakaloumen	de	humas	adelphoi	perisseuein
we urge	but	you,	brothers,	to abound

3095.1 adv comp	2504.1 conj	5226.3 verb inf pres mid	2248.1 verb inf pres act	2504.1 conj
μᾶλλον,	11. καὶ	φιλοτιμεῖσθαι	ἡσυχάζειν	καὶ
mallon	kai	philotimeisthai	hēsuchazein	kai
more,	and	to endeavour earnestly	to be quiet	and

4097.13 verb inf pres act	3450.17 art pl neu	2375.13 adj pl neu	2504.1 conj	2021.12 verb inf pres mid	3450.14 art dat pl fem
πράσσειν	τὰ	ἴδια,	καὶ	ἐργάζεσθαι	ταῖς
prassein	ta	idia	kai	ergazesthai	tais
to do	the	your own things,	and	to work	with the

11.a.Txt: 01ℵ-org,02A
06D-corr,018K,020L
byz.Sod
Var: 01ℵ-corr,03B
06D-org,Lach,Treg,Alf
Word,Tisc,We/Ho,Weis
UBS/✶

2375.12 adj dat pl fem	5331.7 noun dat pl fem	5050.2 prs-pron gen 2pl	2503.1 conj	5050.3 prs-pron dat 2pl	3715.8 verb 1pl indic aor act
ʼa ἰδίαις ʼ	χερσὶν	ὑμῶν,	καθὼς	ὑμῖν	παρηγγείλαμεν,
idiais	chersin	humōn	kathōs	humin	parēngeilamen
own	hands	your,	even as	on you	we enjoined,

2419.1 conj	3906.8 verb 2pl subj pres act	2137.1 adv	4242.1 prep	3450.8 art acc pl masc	1838.1 adv
12. ἵνα	περιπατῆτε	εὐσχημόνως	πρὸς	τοὺς	ἔξω,
hina	peripatēte	euschēmonōs	pros	tous	exō
that	you may walk	properly	towards	the	without,

4:9. Brotherly love will help Christians in their battle against immorality. Such love in that day was used by the Greeks and Romans to refer almost exclusively to love between blood brothers and sisters. It implied affection, kindness, and consideration for one another (Romans 12:10). But from the beginning believers felt a kinship with one another stronger than any natural blood tie. They were truly in one family with God as their Father in a very personal way. (See Romans 8:14-17.)

Paul did not want the Thessalonians to think his mention of brotherly love suggested any lack on their part, however. He did not really need to remind them. They were "taught of God" to love one another (John 6:45). The love that God teaches is something greater even than brotherly love. It is *agapē*, a love that usually refers to a high, holy, faithful, self-giving love. God taught it by demonstrating His love in sending His Son to die on Calvary (Romans 5:8). God wants to make believers channels of His love toward all by their love toward their brothers and sisters in Christ. He wants them to demonstrate this love in very practical ways. (See 1 Corinthians 13:4-8.)

4:10. The Thessalonians did not discriminate in their love. It was expressed to all throughout the whole country. They did not pick out only those who were nice to them, who agreed with them, or who were like them. God shows no partiality, no respect of persons in His love. Neither did they. But Paul still urged them to increase more and more in their love. God is still pouring out His love. He wants all believers to be ever-increasing channels for that love.

4:11. Christians must be careful, however, lest love and concern for others turn them into spiritual busybodies, always poking their noses into other people's business. Paul asked the believers to do three things to balance their outgoing love.

First, they were to make it their aim to live a quiet life. Christians are not to try to be spectacular or flamboyant. They are not to seek to be the center of attention, demanding that the spotlight be focused on them.

Second, they are to busy themselves with their own affairs, minding their own business, their own concerns, taking care of their own homes. This will give them enough to do without meddling and trying to run other believers' lives.

Third, believers are to work with their own hands. Paul set an example in this (1 Corinthians 4:12). He instructed Christians to follow that example. Manual labor is good for all.

4:12. Another reason for working with their own hands (including all productive work) was so they could walk honestly (behave decently) toward outsiders (nonbelievers). The able-bodied Christian is not to depend on others to support him and his family. Nor

9. But as touching brotherly love ye need not that I write unto you: . . . there is really no reason, *Norlie* . . . you have no need of, *Williams.*

for ye yourselves are taught of God to love one another: . . . are Divinely instructed, *Fenton.*

10. And indeed ye do it toward all the brethren which are in all Macedonia: . . . you practise it, *Confraternity.*

but we beseech you, brethren, that ye increase more and more: But I exhort you...to abound in this yet more, *Montgomery* . . . we beg you, love them even more! *SEB* . . . to make even greater progress, *Confraternity.*

11. And that ye study to be quiet: . . . and that you be ambitious, *Concordant* . . . to keep advancing in it, *Berkeley* . . . make your ambition to be quiet, *Klingensmith* . . . to make a point of living quietly, *JB.*

and to do your own business: . . . and practice your own trade, *Klingensmith* . . . and attend to your own affairs, *NAB* . . . Mind your own business, *SEB* . . . to mind your own affairs, *Berkeley, Campbell.*

and to work with your own hands:

as we commanded you: . . . as we recommended to you, *Berkeley* . . . as I charged you, *Montgomery* . . . as we directed you, *TCNT.*

12. That ye may walk honestly toward them that are without: Then outsiders will respect the way you live, *SEB* . . . that you may be well conducted before the outsiders, *Fenton* . . . that you are seen to be respectable, *JB* . . . that you may be walking respectably, *Concordant* . . . that you may live influentially with the outsiders, *Williams* . . . may win respect from outsiders, *TCNT.*

1 Thess. 4:13

2504.1 conj	3235.1 num card gen	5367.3 noun acc sing fem	2174.9 verb 2pl subj pres act	3620.3 partic	2286.1 verb 1sing pres act
καὶ	μηδενὸς	χρείαν	ἔχητε.	13. Οὐ	΄ θέλω
kai	mēdenos	chreian	echēte	Ou	thelō
and	nothing	need	may have.	Not	I do wish

2286.4 verb 1pl indic pres act	1156.2 conj	5050.4 prs-pron acc 2pl	49.9 verb inf pres act	79.6 noun nom pl masc
[ᵃ☆ θέλομεν]	δὲ	ὑμᾶς	ἀγνοεῖν,	ἀδελφοί,
thelomen	de	humas	agnoein	adelphoi
[we do wish]	but	you	to be ignorant,	brothers,

3875.1 prep	3450.1 art gen pl	2810.11 verb gen pl masc part perf mid	2810.3 verb gen pl masc part pres mid
περὶ	τῶν	΄ κεκοιμημένων,	[ᵇ☆ κοιμωμένων,]
peri	tōn	kekoimēmenōn	koimōmenōn
concerning	the	having fallen asleep,	[sleeping,]

2419.1 conj	3231.1 partic	3048.7 verb 2pl subj pres mid	2503.1 conj	2504.1 conj	3450.7 art nom pl masc	3036.3 adj nom pl masc
ἵνα	μὴ	λυπῆσθε,	καθὼς	καὶ	οἱ	λοιποὶ
hina	mē	lupēsthe	kathōs	kai	hoi	loipoi
that	not	you be grieved,	even as	also	the	rest

3450.7 art nom pl masc	3231.1 partic	2174.19 verb nom pl masc part pres act	1667.4 noun acc sing fem	1479.1 conj	1056.1 conj
οἱ	μὴ	ἔχοντες	ἐλπίδα.	14. εἰ	γὰρ
hoi	mē	echontes	elpida	ei	gar
the	not	having	hope.	If	for

3961.7 verb 1pl indic pres act	3617.1 conj	2400.1 name nom masc	594.10 verb 3sing indic aor act	2504.1 conj	448.2 verb 3sing indic aor act
πιστεύομεν	ὅτι	Ἰησοῦς	ἀπέθανεν	καὶ	ἀνέστη,
pisteuomen	hoti	Iēsous	apethanen	kai	anestē
we believe	that	Jesus	died	and	rose again,

3643.1 adv	2504.1 conj	3450.5 art nom sing masc	2296.1 noun nom sing masc	3450.8 art acc pl masc	2810.9 verb acc pl masc part aor pass
οὕτως	καὶ	ὁ	θεὸς	τοὺς	κοιμηθέντας
houtōs	kai	ho	theos	tous	koimēthentas
so	also		God	the	having fallen asleep

1217.2 prep	3450.2 art gen sing	2400.2 name masc	70.16 verb 3sing indic fut act	4713.1 prep	840.4 prs-pron dat sing	3642.17 dem-pron sing neu
διὰ	τοῦ	Ἰησοῦ	ἄξει	σὺν	αὐτῷ.	15. Τοῦτο
dia	tou	Iēsou	axei	sun	autō	Touto
through		Jesus	will bring	with	him.	This

1056.1 conj	5050.3 prs-pron dat 2pl	2978.6 verb 1pl indic pres act	1706.1 prep	3030.3 noun dat sing masc	2935.2 noun gen sing masc	3617.1 conj
γὰρ	ὑμῖν	λέγομεν	ἐν	λόγῳ	κυρίου,	ὅτι
gar	humin	legomen	en	logō	kuriou	hoti
for	to you	we say	in	word	of Lord,	that

2231.1 prs-pron nom 1pl	3450.7 art nom pl masc	2180.13 verb nom pl masc part pres act	3450.7 art nom pl masc	3898.1 verb nom pl masc part pres mid
ἡμεῖς	οἱ	ζῶντες,	οἱ	περιλειπόμενοι
hēmeis	hoi	zōntes	hoi	perileipomenoi
we	the	living	the	remaining

1519.1 prep	3450.12 art acc sing fem	3814.4 noun acc sing fem	3450.2 art gen sing	2935.2 noun gen sing masc	3620.3 partic	3231.1 partic
εἰς	τὴν	παρουσίαν	τοῦ	κυρίου,	οὐ	μὴ
eis	tēn	parousian	tou	kuriou	ou	mē
to	the	coming	of the	Lord,	not	not

is he to expect continual supernatural supply. By his own labors he is to have no lack of anything he really needs.

4:13. In Paul's concern for morals and behavior in this life, he did not forget the life to come. The Bible always looks ahead. It sees our behavior in this life in the light of God's great plan that will climax when Jesus returns.

At this point in this letter, Paul turned to answer a question which arose because some believers had already died. The Thessalonians were from a Greek background where they formerly supposed the dead went down into a dark underworld from which there was no return. Some of the new believers apparently felt that those who died before the return of Christ would miss that glory and joy.

This false impression or false teaching needed to be corrected. False teachers arose very quickly in the Early Church. But instead of destroying the truth, they only succeeded in causing it to be brought out more clearly and more powerfully by the apostles. Possibly the false teachers here suggested those who died would not share in the benefits of Jesus' coming. If so, this would bring sorrow to the believers who remained alive.

"Sorrow" here has the idea of distress, hurt feelings, and mental anguish. In this kind of sorrow they were coming very close to the black despair and empty hopelessness reflected on the tombstones of the heathen of the time. The present participle *echontes* denotes ongoing activity—in this instance, the unrelenting hopelessness experienced by a nonbeliever with respect to death. Paul wanted them to know the truth that would keep them from that kind of grief. Christians are not like the heathen who have no hope.

4:14. The key to a Christian's hope is his belief in the fact that Jesus died and rose again. The word "if" does not imply any question of that belief. It introduces a "first class" conditional clause (a clause with *ei* and an indicative mood verb in the "protasis" or "if" side of an "if-then" statement) and is properly translated "since." It simply indicates that as surely as they believed, so surely will the dead believers be with Jesus when He returns. Their belief in Christ's death and resurrection was not a mere mental acceptance of the facts, however. It involved a personal identification with Jesus in His death and resurrection, as pictured in water baptism.

4:15. Paul had a clear word from the Lord about this. Of course, all he wrote in his epistles was by inspiration of the Holy Spirit. But in this case Paul also had a definite saying of Jesus. Jesus himself, in giving Paul the gospel, made it clear that those who are alive and remain till the coming of the Lord will not precede, get ahead of, or have any advantage over those who died with their faith in Jesus. The fact Paul used "we" in this verse does not mean

and [that] ye may have lack of nothing: . . . won't need to be dependent, *Adams* . . . you need not depend on anyone, *Berkeley* . . . that you may not need help from any man, *Montgomery* . . . and will not be on relief, *Klingensmith.*

13. But I would not have you to be ignorant, brethren: We desire you not to be, *Fenton* . . . we don't want you to be, *Adams* . . . to have any misunderstanding, *Williams.*

concerning them which are asleep: . . . those who have died, *NLT* . . . who have already died, *SEB* . . . about those who sleep, *Adams* . . . who are falling asleep, *Montgomery.*

that ye sorrow not, even as others which have no hope: . . . that you may not be grieved, *Campbell* . . . You must not sorrow like other men, *Montgomery* . . . You have no reason to grieve like the rest, *Norlie* . . . so you may not grieve as others do, *Berkeley* . . . otherwise you might yield to grief, *NAB* . . . lest you grieve as others who haven't any hope, *Adams* . . . who have no expectation, *Concordant* . . . who are without a hope, *Fenton.*

14. For if we believe that Jesus died and rose again, even so them also which sleep in Jesus will God bring with him: . . . in the same way, through Jesus, *Adams* . . . God will, by means of Jesus, restore with Him those, *Fenton.*

15. For this we say unto you by the word of the Lord: I tell you, *Montgomery* . . . by the Lord's Word, *Adams* . . . as a message from the Lord, *Fenton.*

that we which are alive [and] remain unto the coming of the Lord: . . . we who live, who survive until, *Confraternity* . . . we who may be still living when, *Norlie* . . . we who are left behind living, *Klingensmith.*

5185.3 verb 1pl subj aor act	3450.8 art acc pl masc	2810.9 verb acc pl masc part aor pass	3617.1 conj	840.5 prs-pron nom sing masc
φθάσωμεν	τοὺς	κοιμηθέντας·	**16.** ὅτι	αὐτὸς
phthasōmen	tous	koimēthentas	hoti	autos
may precede	the	having fallen asleep;	because	himself

3450.5 art nom sing masc	2935.1 noun nom sing masc	1706.1 prep	2723.1 noun dat sing neu	1706.1 prep	5292.3 noun dat sing fem
ὁ	κύριος	ἐν	κελεύσματι,	ἐν	φωνῇ
ho	kurios	en	keleusmati	en	phōnē
the	Lord	with	a shout of command,	with	voice

738.2 noun gen sing masc	2504.1 conj	1706.1 prep	4393.3 noun dat sing fem	2296.2 noun gen sing masc	2568.28 verb 3sing indic fut mid
ἀρχαγγέλου	καὶ	ἐν	σάλπιγγι	θεοῦ	καταβήσεται
archangelou	kai	en	salpingi	theou	katabēsetai
archangel's	and	with	trumpet	of God	shall descend

570.2 prep	3636.2 noun gen sing masc	2504.1 conj	3450.7 art nom pl masc	3361.5 adj nom pl masc	1706.1 prep	5382.3 name dat masc
ἀπ'	οὐρανοῦ,	καὶ	οἱ	νεκροὶ	ἐν	Χριστῷ
ap'	ouranou	kai	hoi	nekroi	en	Christō
from	heaven,	and	the	dead	in	Christ

448.21 verb 3pl indic fut mid	4270.1 adv	1884.1 adv	2231.1 prs-pron nom 1pl	3450.7 art nom pl masc
ἀναστήσονται	πρῶτον·	**17.** ἔπειτα	ἡμεῖς	οἱ
anastēsontai	prōton	epeita	hēmeis	hoi
shall rise	first;	then	we	the

2180.13 verb nom pl masc part pres act	3450.7 art nom pl masc	3898.1 verb nom pl masc part pres mid	258.1 adv	4713.1 prep	840.2 prs-pron dat pl
ζῶντες	οἱ	περιλειπόμενοι	ἅμα	σὺν	αὐτοῖς
zōntes	hoi	perileipomenoi	hama	sun	autois
living	the	remaining,	together	with	them

720.11 verb 1pl indic fut pass	1706.1 prep	3369.7 noun dat pl fem	1519.1 prep	525.1 noun acc sing fem	3450.2 art gen sing
ἁρπαγησόμεθα	ἐν	νεφέλαις	εἰς	ἀπάντησιν	τοῦ
harpagēsometha	en	nephelais	eis	apantēsin	tou
shall be caught away	in	clouds	for	meeting	of the

2935.2 noun gen sing masc	1519.1 prep	108.3 noun acc sing masc	2504.1 conj	3643.1 adv	3704.1 adv	4713.1 prep
κυρίου	εἰς	ἀέρα,	καὶ	οὕτως	πάντοτε	σὺν
kuriou	eis	aera	kai	houtōs	pantote	sun
Lord	in	air;	and	thus	always	with

2935.3 noun dat sing masc	1498.41 verb 1pl indic fut mid	5452.1 conj	3731.6 verb 2pl impr pres act	238.3 prs-pron acc pl masc
κυρίῳ	ἐσόμεθα.	**18.** Ὥστε	παρακαλεῖτε	ἀλλήλους
kuriō	esometha	Hōste	parakaleite	allēlous
Lord	we shall be.	So	encourage	one another

1706.1 prep	3450.4 art dat pl	3030.7 noun dat pl masc	3642.3 dem-pron dat pl	3875.1 prep	1156.2 conj
ἐν	τοῖς	λόγοις	τούτοις.	**5:1.** Περὶ	δὲ
en	tois	logois	toutois	Peri	de
with	the	words	these.	Concerning	but

3450.1 art gen pl	5385.5 noun gen pl masc	2504.1 conj	3450.1 art gen pl	2511.6 noun gen pl masc	79.6 noun nom pl masc	3620.3 partic
τῶν	χρόνων	καὶ	τῶν	καιρῶν,	ἀδελφοί,	οὐ
tōn	chronōn	kai	tōn	kairōn	adelphoi	ou
the	times	and	the	seasons,	brothers,	no

he was sure he would be alive. He simply meant whoever is alive at Christ's return.

4:16. Those who die before the return of Christ will not miss a thing. The Lord will descend from heaven with a shout or command, with the voice of the archangel, and with the trumpet of God. Then the dead in Christ will immediately rise in response to His command. (See *Overview*, pp.553-555.)

4:17. The moment after the dead arise, those who are alive and remain will join with them to form one great body. Together we will all be caught up (snatched up in a powerful manner, carried up suddenly in great power) to meet the Lord (for a meeting with the Lord) in the air.

This sudden snatching away to meet the Lord is often referred to as the "rapture." Some try to belittle this word and say we should not use it because it is not in the Bible. In-depth study shows, however, there is justification for using it. The Greek word used here meant "to seize." Then, it came to mean "to snatch up forcibly." It was used of robbers snatching up whatever they wanted to steal, or of an eagle snatching up its prey. Paul used it of being caught up to the third heaven (2 Corinthians 12:2).

The Greek word was translated into the Latin by *raptus*. From this comes our English words *rapt* and *rapture*. Today these words usually speak of being carried away emotionally or spiritually. But one meaning of *rapt* in current dictionaries is "lifted up and carried away." Thus it is perfectly good English to translate this verse, "Then we which are alive and remain shall be rapt (or raptured) together with them in the clouds." A force far beyond gravity, a supernatural power far greater than the rockets that lift astronauts into space, will suddenly snatch us into the air for a meeting with Jesus. *Meeting* is a word often used in connection with the coming (*parousia*) of a king, emperor, or governor to visit a city. The people would go out to welcome the dignitary.

Paul said nothing here about the events of the meeting (which include the judgment seat of Christ and the Marriage Supper of the Lamb). Nor did he say anything of our return with Christ to destroy the armies of the Antichrist and set up His millennial kingdom. Paul concluded simply by saying that believers will always, forever, be with the Lord.

4:18. There is no greater comfort, encouragement, or exhortation that can be given to another than the fact that whether Christians live or die they will be caught up to be with Christ when He comes.

5:1. The fear that they might miss something if they died before the Rapture made the Thessalonian believers want to know how

shall not prevent them which are asleep: . . . shall not at all take precedence over those asleep, *Berkeley* . . . will not get ahead of the sleepers, *Klingensmith* . . . will not go ahead of those who have died, *NLT* . . . will have no advantage over those who have passed to their rest, *TCNT*.

16. For the Lord himself shall descend from heaven with a shout, with the voice of the archangel, and with the trump of God: . . . shall personally descend, *Berkeley* . . . with a loud summons, *TCNT* . . . with a command, with the voice of the angel leader, *SEB* . . . at a call from the archangel, *Norlie* . . . the voice of the archangel will call out the command, *JB*.

and the dead in Christ shall rise first: . . . those who died in union with Christ, *TCNT* . . . will rise again, *Fenton*.

17. Then we which are alive [and] remain shall be caught up together with them in the clouds: . . . afterward we, the living...be instantly taken up in clouds, *Campbell* . . . the survivors, *NAB* . . . the living remnant, shall at the same time be carried up in clouds, *Fenton* . . . at the same time be snatched away together, *Concordant*.

to meet the Lord in the air: and so shall we ever be with the Lord: . . . in the sky! *Norlie*, *NLT* . . . for an introduction by the Lord into the eternal condition, *Fenton*.

18. Wherefore comfort one another with these words: Because of this, *NLT* . . . Encourage and console one another, *Norlie* . . . with this truth, *Williams*.

1. But of the times and the seasons, brethren: Relative to periods, *Berkeley* . . . with regard to the exact time and date, *TCNT* . . . about dates and times, *SEB* . . . and dates, *Lilly* . . . and the eras, *Concordant* . . . when and at what kind of times these things will happen, *NLT*.

1 Thess. 5:2

5367.3 noun acc sing fem	2174.2 verb 2pl pres act	5050.3 prs- pron dat 2pl	1119.20 verb inf pres mid	840.7 prs-pron nom pl masc	1056.1 conj
χρείαν	ἔχετε	ὑμῖν	γράφεσθαι	2. αὐτοὶ	γὰρ
chreian	*echete*	*humin*	*graphesthai*	*autoi*	*gar*
need	you have	for you	to be written,	yourselves	for

2.a.Txt: 02A,018K,020L
byz.Sod
Var: 01א,03B,06D,025P
33,Lach,Treg,Word,Tisc
We/Ho,Weis,UBS/☆

197.1 adv	3471.6 verb 2pl indic perf act	3617.1 conj	3450.9 art nom sing fem	2232.2 noun nom sing fem	2935.2 noun gen sing masc
ἀκριβῶς	οἴδατε	ὅτι	⌈a ἡ ⌉	ἡμέρα	κυρίου
akribōs	*oidate*	*hoti*	*hē*	*hēmera*	*kuriou*
accurately	you know	that	the	day	of Lord

5453.1 conj	2785.1 noun nom sing masc	1706.1 prep	3433.3 noun dat sing fem	3643.1 adv	2048.34 verb 3sing indic pres mid	3615.1 conj
ὡς	κλέπτης	ἐν	νυκτὶ	οὕτως	ἔρχεται·	3. ὅταν
hōs	*kleptēs*	*en*	*nukti*	*houtōs*	*erchetai*	*hotan*
as	a thief	by	night	so	comes.	When

3.a.Txt: 018K,020L
025P,byz.
Var: 01א-org,02A,33
Gries,Treg,Alf,Tisc
We/Ho,UBS/☆

1056.1 conj	2978.10 verb 3pl subj pres act	1503.1 noun nom sing fem	2504.1 conj	797.1 noun nom sing fem	4966.1 adv
⌈a γὰρ ⌉	λέγωσιν,	Εἰρήνη	καὶ	ἀσφάλεια,	τότε
gar	*legōsin*	*Eirēnē*	*kai*	*asphaleia*	*tote*
for	they may say,	Peace	and	security,	then

158.1 adj nom sing	840.2 prs- pron dat pl	2168.11 verb 3sing indic pres mid	3502.1 noun nom sing masc	5450.1 conj
αἰφνίδιος	αὐτοῖς	ἐφίσταται	ὄλεθρος,	ὥσπερ
aiphnidios	*autois*	*ephistatai*	*olethros*	*hōsper*
sudden	upon them	comes	destruction,	as

3450.9 art nom sing fem	5438.1 noun nom sing fem	3450.11 art dat sing fem	1706.1 prep	1057.1 noun dat sing fem	2174.24 verb dat sing fem part pres act
ἡ	ὠδὶν	τῇ	ἐν	γαστρὶ	ἐχούσῃ,
hē	*ōdin*	*tē*	*en*	*gastri*	*echousē*
the	labor pain	to the	in	womb	having;

2504.1 conj	3620.3 partic	3231.1 partic	1614.2 verb 3pl subj aor act	5050.1 prs- pron nom 2pl	1156.2 conj
καὶ	οὐ	μὴ	ἐκφύγωσιν.	4. ὑμεῖς	δέ,
kai	*ou*	*mē*	*ekphugōsin*	*humeis*	*de*
and	not	not	shall they escape.	You	but,

79.6 noun nom pl masc	3620.2 partic	1498.6 verb 2pl indic pres act	1706.1 prep	4510.4 noun dat sing neu	2419.1 conj	3450.9 art nom sing fem
ἀδελφοί,	οὐκ	ἐστὲ	ἐν	σκότει,	ἵνα	ἡ
adelphoi	*ouk*	*este*	*en*	*skotei*	*hina*	*hē*
brothers,	not	are	in	darkness,	that	the

2232.2 noun nom sing fem	5050.4 prs- pron acc 2pl	5453.1 conj	2785.1 noun nom sing masc	2608.3 verb 3sing subj aor act	3820.7 adj nom pl masc
ἡμέρα	ὑμᾶς	ὡς	κλέπτης	καταλάβῃ·	5. πάντες
hēmera	*humas*	*hōs*	*kleptēs*	*katalabē*	*pantes*
day	you	as	a thief	should overtake:	all

5.a.Var: 01א,02A,03B
06D,020L,025P,it.bo.
Gries,Lach,Treg,Alf
Word,Tisc,We/Ho,Weis
Sod,UBS/☆

1056.1 conj	5050.1 prs- pron nom 2pl	5048.6 noun nom pl masc	5295.2 noun gen sing neu	1498.6 verb 2pl indic pres act	2504.1 conj
[a☆+ γὰρ]	ὑμεῖς	υἱοὶ	φωτός	ἐστε	καὶ
gar	*humeis*	*huioi*	*phōtos*	*este*	*kai*
[for]	you	sons	of light	are	and

5048.6 noun nom pl masc	2232.1 noun fem	3620.2 partic	1498.5 verb 1pl indic pres act	3433.2 noun gen sing fem	3624.1 conj	4510.3 noun gen sing neu
υἱοὶ	ἡμέρας·	οὐκ	ἐσμὲν	νυκτὸς	οὐδὲ	σκότους.
huioi	*hēmeras*	*ouk*	*esmen*	*nuktos*	*oude*	*skotous*
sons	of day;	not	we are	of night	nor	of darkness.

soon the Lord would come. Paul did not need to add to what Jesus had said (Acts 1:7).

5:2. The believers knew perfectly well that the Day of the Lord will come as a thief in the night. The sudden, unexpected coming of the Day of the Lord had been explained to them. The present tense here means that it is sure to come. In other places Paul refers to signs which will indicate the time is approaching, but there will be no immediate warning so there will be time to get ready.

5:3. At the very time when the Lord returns, unbelievers will be rejecting the warnings of the Bible and crying, "Peace and safety" (security). But in the midst of their declarations that people do not need God to have peace (including health, well-being, and spiritual peace of heart and mind) or security (including the gaining of all that is certain and true), sudden destruction (ruin, death) will come upon them. (See Jeremiah 6:14.) Just as women have no way of stopping birth pangs once they start, even so once the Day of the Lord comes it will carry through to its conclusion. The words *ou mē* indicate strong negation and can be translated "by no means." There will be *no* possibility of escape.

5:4. What Paul said about the Day of the Lord with its judgments catching men by surprise applies only to the wicked, the careless, the unbelieving, the spiritually unprepared. This verse makes a strong contrast between believers and unbelievers. Paul was confident in the reality of the believers' faith and their dedication to the Lord. The Day of the Lord will not overtake Christians to seize them and carry them into the vortex of judgment. It will, however, not be because they know when it is coming. The day and the hour will be hid from them the same as it will be from everyone else.

5:5. But they will not be caught unprepared because they are not in darkness. Amos rebuked the people of his day who were talking about the Day of the Lord but doing nothing to prepare for it (Amos 5:18). For them, it would be a day of darkness and not light. This was because they were already walking in moral and spiritual darkness. God is light, and He has made provision for Christians to walk in the light (1 John 1:5-7).

Believers are not only walking in the light, they are "children of light." They are characterized by and share the nature and character of light. (See Luke 1:78,79; 2:32; John 1:9; 8:12 where Jesus is the light.)

Believers are also "children of the day." Some take this to mean the Day of the Lord. But the context shows Christians are children characterized by "day." Thieves come in the night. True believers are always in the day, spiritually speaking. Light is their way of life. They do not belong to darkness (Ephesians 5:8-11).

ye have no need that I write unto you: . . . there is no need for writing to you, *Fenton.*

2. For yourselves know perfectly: . . . for you are yourselves keenly aware, *Berkeley* . . . because you surely know, *Klingensmith* . . . For you well know, *Norlie.*

that the day of the Lord so cometh as a thief in the night:

3. For when they shall say, Peace and safety: Just at the moment when men are saying, *Lilly* . . . Things are peaceful and safe, *SEB* . . . Peace and security, *Klingensmith, Fenton* . . . All is quiet and safe, *TCNT.*

then sudden destruction cometh upon them: . . . destruction will strike them suddenly, *Norlie* . . . unforeseen is on them, *Berkeley* . . . then extermination is standing by them unawares, *Concordant* . . . seizes them, *Fenton.*

as travail upon a woman with child: . . . as the agony of, *Fenton* . . . like birth pains, *Williams* . . . like the birthpangs of a pregnant woman, *Berkeley* . . . as birth pangs upon, *Confraternity* . . . on an expectant mother, *Norlie.*

and they shall not escape:

4. But ye, brethren, are not in darkness, that that day should overtake you as a thief: . . . you are not in the dark, *SEB* . . . that the day falls on you, *Klingensmith* . . . take you by surprise, *Lilly* . . . to surprise you like a thief, *RSV* . . . That day will not surprise you as a robber would, *NLT* . . . take you by surprise as if you were thieves, *TCNT.*

5. Ye are all the children of light, and the children of the day:
we are not of the night, nor of darkness: We do not belong to, *Williams.*

331

1 Thess. 5:6

6.a.Txt: 01א-corr,06D
018K,020L,025P,byz.
Var: 01א-org,02A,03B
33,bo.Lach,Treg,Tisc
We/Ho,Weis,Sod
UBS/✷

679.1 partic	3631.1 partic	3231.1 partic	2490.6 verb 1pl subj pres act	5453.1 conj	2504.1 conj	3450.7 art nom pl masc
6. ἄρα	οὖν	μὴ	καθεύδωμεν	ὡς	ʽᵃ καὶ ʼ	οἱ
ara	oun	mē	katheudōmen	hōs	kai	hoi
So	then	not	we should sleep	as	also	the

3036.3 adj nom pl masc	233.2 conj	1121.2 verb 1pl subj pres act	2504.1 conj	3387.1 verb 1pl subj pres act
λοιποί,	ἀλλὰ	γρηγορῶμεν	καὶ	νήφωμεν.
loipoi	alla	grēgorōmen	kai	nēphōmen
rest,	but	we should watch	and	we should be sober;

3450.7 art nom pl masc	1056.1 conj	2490.8 verb nom pl masc part pres act	3433.2 noun gen sing fem	2490.4 verb 3pl indic pres act	2504.1 conj
7. οἱ	γὰρ	καθεύδοντες	νυκτὸς	καθεύδουσιν,	καὶ
hoi	gar	katheudontes	nuktos	katheudousin	kai
the	for	sleeping	by night	sleep,	and

3450.7 art nom pl masc	3153.2 verb nom pl masc part pres mid	3433.2 noun gen sing fem	3155.2 verb 3pl indic pres act	2231.1 prs-pron nom 1pl
οἱ	μεθυσκόμενοι	νυκτὸς	μεθύουσιν·	8. ἡμεῖς
hoi	methuskomenoi	nuktos	methuousin	hēmeis
the	being drunken	by night	get drunk;	we

1156.2 conj	2232.1 noun fem	1498.23 verb nom pl masc part pres act	3387.1 verb 1pl subj pres act	1730.10 verb nom pl masc part aor mid
δὲ	ἡμέρας	ὄντες	νήφωμεν,	ἐνδυσάμενοι
de	hēmeras	ontes	nēphōmen	endusamenoi
but	of day	being	should be sober,	having put on

2359.1 noun acc sing masc	3963.2 noun gen sing fem	2504.1 conj	26.2 noun gen sing fem	2504.1 conj	3893.1 noun acc sing fem
θώρακα	πίστεως	καὶ	ἀγάπης,	καὶ	περικεφαλαίαν
thōraka	pisteōs	kai	agapēs	kai	perikephalaian
breastplate	of faith	and	love,	and	helmet

1667.4 noun acc sing fem	4843.2 noun gen sing fem	3617.1 conj	3620.2 partic	4935.30 verb 3sing indic aor mid	2231.4 prs-pron acc 1pl
ἐλπίδα	σωτηρίας·	9. ὅτι	οὐκ	ἔθετο	ἡμᾶς
elpida	sōtērias	hoti	ouk	etheto	hēmas
hope	salvation's;	because	not	has set	us

3450.5 art nom sing masc	2296.1 noun nom sing masc	1519.1 prep	3572.4 noun acc sing fem	233.1 conj	233.2 conj
ὁ	θεὸς	εἰς	ὀργὴν,	ʽ ἀλλʼ	[✷ ἀλλὰ]
ho	theos	eis	orgēn	all'	alla
	God	for	wrath,	but	[idem]

1519.1 prep	3910.2 noun acc sing fem	4843.2 noun gen sing fem	1217.2 prep	3450.2 art gen sing	2935.2 noun gen sing masc
εἰς	περιποίησιν	σωτηρίας	διὰ	τοῦ	κυρίου
eis	peripoiēsin	sōtērias	dia	tou	kuriou
for	obtaining	salvation	through	the	Lord

2231.2 prs-pron gen 1pl	2400.2 name masc gen masc	5382.2 name gen masc		3450.2 art gen sing	594.16 verb gen sing masc part aor act
ἡμῶν	Ἰησοῦ	Χριστοῦ,	10. τοῦ		ἀποθανόντος
hēmōn	Iēsou	Christou	tou		apothanontos
our	Jesus	Christ,	the		having died

10.a.Txt: 01א-corr,02A
06D,018K,020L,025P
etc.byz.Sod
Var: 01א-org,03B,33
Treg,Tisc,We/Ho,Weis
UBS/✷

5065.1 prep	3875.1 prep	2231.2 prs-pron gen 1pl	2419.1 conj	1521.1 conj	1121.2 verb 1pl subj pres act
ʽ ὑπὲρ	[ᵃ περὶ]	ἡμῶν,	ἵνα	εἴτε	γρηγορῶμεν
huper	peri	hēmōn	hina	eite	grēgorōmen
for	[concerning]	us,	that	whether	you may watch

5:6. Since Christians are "day" people, Paul exhorts them not to keep on sleeping as do others. They must watch, be alert, be vigilant. They must also be sober in the sense of exercising self-control, well-balanced and avoiding excesses and extremes.

5:7. The world is like a drunken man whose liquor has deadened his sensibilities until he has fallen asleep and is unconscious of his true condition. Warnings against sin pass over him and bring no response. Those who are drunk become drunk in the night because they hope the darkness will cover their condition. But those who are of the day are willing to let the light of the Holy Spirit search their lives.

5:8. The command to watch suggests the vigilance of a sentry on duty and facing danger. First, Christians must be light. They are of the day. They must be sober (self-controlled, well-balanced) and make the proper preparations. They must put on their armor.

They are to put on over their hearts the "breastplate of faith and love" to guard their emotions. For a helmet to guard their thoughts, plans, and aspirations, they need the "hope of salvation" (cf. Ephesians 6:10-17; 2 Corinthians 10:4). The breastplate is very significant. Faith needs to work by love if it is to be effective (Galatians 5:6). Plans and ideas also need to be focused in the right direction by the hope of salvation. Salvation here speaks of the believers' future inheritance, including everything that will be theirs when Jesus comes again (cf. 1 Peter 1:3-5).

5:9. There is further assurance of the hope of salvation in that God has not appointed believers to wrath. Some take this to mean that they will not share the wrath that shall engulf the sinful world during the "Great Tribulation" because the Church will be taken out in the Rapture. God's *protection* of Noah during the flood and of Lot at the destruction of Sodom and Gomorrah illustrates how His people are sheltered from His wrath against sinners. The judgments indicated in Revelation are clearly stated to be wrath (Revelation 6:16,17; 11:18; 14:10,19; 15:1,7; 16:1,19; 19:15). This is the wrath Paul was referring to here.

5:10. Believers gain salvation, not by what they do, but by what Christ has already done. He died for all; but only those who accept His sacrifice will live together with Him. Here Paul gives the Thessalonian believers great comfort and encouragement, reinforcing what he wrote in 4:14-18. Not only is there great hope in knowing that believers will not suffer the wrath of God, but even death ("sleep") cannot separate them from being united with Christ for all eternity.

6. Therefore let us not sleep, as [do] others: So then, *Adams* . . . Consequently, then, we may not be drowsing, *Concordant* . . . like the rest, *Berkeley* . . . as do the rest, *Montgomery* . . . the rest of mankind, *Norlie*.

but let us watch and be sober: . . . let us keep alert, *Klingensmith* . . . alert and level-headed, *Adams* . . . but to be vigilant and alert, *Lilly* . . . be on our guard and composed, *Berkeley* . . . we should be awake and alert, *SEB* . . . but we keep guard and are sober, *Fenton* . . . watchful and self-controlled, *Montgomery*.

7. For they that sleep sleep in the night: . . . the sleepers, *Fenton*.

and they that be drunken are drunken in the night: . . . the drunkards, *Fenton* . . . get drunk at night, *Adams*.

8. But let us, who are of the day, be sober: . . . since we are of the day, *Adams* . . . let us keep our minds awake, *NLT* . . . be self-controlled, *Montgomery*.

putting on the breastplate of faith and love: . . . clothed in, *Fenton* . . . outfitted with faith, *Berkeley*.

and for an helmet, the hope of salvation: . . . the expectation of salvation, *Concordant*.

9. For God hath not appointed us to wrath: For God's intention is not to punish us, *Norlie* . . . has not destined us, *Confraternity* . . . for indignation, *Berkeley* . . . did not plan for us to be punished, *SEB* . . . to reap His wrath, *Williams*.

but to obtain salvation by our Lord Jesus Christ: . . . for the acquisition of, *Fenton* . . . to secure salvation through, *Adams* . . . but to win salvation through, *Montgomery*.

10. Who died for us:
that, whether we wake or sleep: . . . whether we remain alive or have fallen asleep, *TCNT*.

1521.1 conj	2490.6 verb 1pl subj pres act	258.1 adv	4713.1 prep	840.4 prs-pron dat sing	2180.24 verb 1pl subj aor act
εἴτε	καθεύδωμεν,	ἅμα	σὺν	αὐτῷ	ζήσωμεν.
eite	katheudōmen	hama	sun	autō	zēsōmen
or	we may sleep,	together	with	him	we may live.

	1346.1 conj	3731.6 verb 2pl impr pres act	238.3 prs-pron acc pl masc	2504.1 conj	3481.2 verb 2pl pres act
11.	Διὸ	παρακαλεῖτε	ἀλλήλους,	καὶ	οἰκοδομεῖτε
	Dio	parakaleite	allēlous	kai	oikodomeite
	Wherefore	encourage	one another,	and	build up

1518.3 num card nom masc	3450.6 art acc sing masc	1518.4 num card acc masc	2503.1 conj	2504.1 conj	4020.2 verb 2pl pres act
εἷς	τὸν	ἕνα,	καθὼς	καὶ	ποιεῖτε.
heis	ton	hena	kathōs	kai	poieite
one	the	one,	even as	also	you are doing.

	2049.3 verb 1pl indic pres act	1156.2 conj	5050.4 prs-pron acc 2pl	79.6 noun nom pl masc	3471.25 verb inf perf act
12.	Ἐρωτῶμεν	δὲ	ὑμᾶς,	ἀδελφοί,	εἰδέναι
	Erōtōmen	de	humas	adelphoi	eidenai
	We beseech	but	you,	brothers,	to know

3450.8 art acc pl masc	2844.8 verb acc pl masc part pres act	1706.1 prep	5050.3 prs-pron dat 2pl	2504.1 conj	4150.6 verb acc pl masc part pres mid
τοὺς	κοπιῶντας	ἐν	ὑμῖν,	καὶ	προϊσταμένους
tous	kopiōntas	en	humin	kai	proistamenous
the	laboring	among	you,	and	taking the lead

5050.2 prs-pron gen 2pl	1706.1 prep	2935.3 noun dat sing masc	2504.1 conj	3423.5 verb acc pl masc part pres act	5050.4 prs-pron acc 2pl
ὑμῶν	ἐν	κυρίῳ,	καὶ	νουθετοῦντας	ὑμᾶς,
humōn	en	kuriō	kai	nouthetountas	humas
of you	in	Lord,	and	admonish	you,

	2504.1 conj	2216.11 verb inf pres mid	840.8 prs-pron acc pl masc	5065.1 prep	1586.1 adv
13.	καὶ	ἡγεῖσθαι	αὐτοὺς	(ὑπὲρ	ἐκπερισσοῦ
	kai	hēgeisthai	autous	huper	ekperissou
	and	to esteem	them	above	exceedingly

5076.1 adv	1706.1 prep	26.3 noun dat sing fem	1217.2 prep	3450.16 art sing neu
[a✶ ὑπερεκπερισσοῦ]	ἐν	ἀγάπῃ	διὰ	τὸ
huperekperissou	en	agapē	dia	to
[idem]	in	love	on account of	in

13.a.**Txt:** 01ℵ,02A 06D-corr,018K,020L 025P,byz.
Var: 03B,06D-org,Lach Treg,Alf,Tisc,Weis UBS/✶

13.b.**Txt:** 02A,03B 06D-corr2,018K,020L 33,365,630,1175,1241 1739
Var: p30,01ℵ,06D-org 010F,012G,025P,044 81,104,2464

2024.1 noun sing neu	840.1 prs-pron gen pl	1502.1 verb 2pl impr pres act	1706.1 prep	1431.7 prs-pron dat pl masc	1431.18 prs-pron dat pl masc
ἔργον	αὐτῶν.	εἰρηνεύετε	ἐν	(✶ ἑαυτοῖς.	[b αὐτοῖς.]
ergon	autōn	eirēneuete	en	heautois	hautois
work	their.	Be at peace	among	yourselves.	[them.]

	3731.2 verb 1pl indic pres act	1156.2 conj	5050.4 prs-pron acc 2pl	79.6 noun nom pl masc	3423.2 verb 2pl impr pres act
14.	παρακαλοῦμεν	δὲ	ὑμᾶς,	ἀδελφοί,	νουθετεῖτε
	parakaloumen	de	humas	adelphoi	noutheteite
	We exhort	but	you,	brothers,	admonish

3450.8 art acc pl masc	807.1 adj acc pl masc	3749.1 verb 2pl impr pres mid	3450.8 art acc pl masc	3505.1 adj acc pl masc
τοὺς	ἀτάκτους,	παραμυθεῖσθε	τοὺς	ὀλιγοψύχους,
tous	ataktous	paramutheisthe	tous	oligopsuchous
the	disorderly,	console	the	fainthearted,

5:11. With this in mind Paul urged Christians to comfort one another, to edify or build up each other. This is parallel to the exhortation of 4:18. Paul is either making a continuing reference to what he had just explained concerning the second coming of Christ, or else he is still attempting to renew the hope of those who were mourning the death of fellow believers.

5:12. Paul concluded this letter with a series of loving exhortations. Someone has called these a chain of pearls of practical wisdom.

Though it is the Christian's responsibility to edify others, he needs additional encouragement and guidance. Therefore God has called and chosen leaders, equipped by gifts of the Spirit, to work among them. They are over believers in the Lord. That is, they are concerned about believers, care for them, and give them aid. This includes elders, pastors, and deacons, as well as teachers who instruct. Paul asked his brothers (and sisters) to know (and appreciate) these teachers and leaders.

5:13. Christians should esteem these leaders very highly, recognizing their worth, and giving them thoughtful consideration and superabundant respect. This is not a matter of exalting an office or of conferring personal prestige, however. It is a matter of giving honor where honor is due, not merely as a duty, but in love "for their work's sake." This implies that these spiritual leaders are really working hard as servants of the Body, not as lords over them (cf. Matthew 20:25-28).

The next exhortation might seem to be a complete change of subject. Actually, it is not. There is no greater way for Christians to encourage spiritual leaders and teachers than to live at peace among themselves. Nothing is more frustrating than an atmosphere of dissension, quarreling, and murmuring (criticism that is said under your breath). God is able to give leaders grace in spite of any lack of peace and unity among their people. But so much more can be done when the people are in one accord.

5:14. The remaining exhortations are directed to all the church. Paul never puts all the responsibility for good order, growth, and development of the church on the leaders. Love, courtesy, and respect for the ministry of the Spirit will bring order. (Compare 1 Corinthians 14:40 where Paul calls for moderation or self-control, not a moderator.)

All Christians have a responsibility to warn the unruly (including the idle or lazy). "Warn" here means more than rebuke or point a finger. It includes the idea of instructing. Believers must help the "unruly" to see they are going in the wrong direction and show them how to get back on the right path (Galatians 6:1).

we should live together with him: . . . we may find life in union with him, *Lilly* . . . we will be with Him, *NLT*.

11. Wherefore comfort yourselves together: Continue building each other up, *SEB* . . . encourage one another, *RSV*.
and edify one another, even as also ye do: . . . and strengthening one another, *Norlie* . . . as in fact you are doing, *Berkeley*.

12. And we beseech you, brethren:
to know them which labour among you: . . . to appreciate those who toil, *Lilly* . . . to respect those who work, *NLT* . . . to show regard for those who toil among you, *TCNT*.
and are over you in the Lord, and admonish you: . . . and your advisers, *Berkeley* . . . and presiding over you, *Concordant* . . . and teach you the way, *Norlie*.

13. And to esteem them very highly in love for their work's sake: . . . treat them with the greatest honor in love, *SEB* . . . lovingly in highest regard, *Berkeley*.
[And] be at peace among yourselves:

14. Now we exhort you, brethren:
warn them that are unruly: . . . warn the disorderly, *TCNT* . . . warn those who are lazy, *SEB* . . . reprove the idle, *Lilly* . . . reprove the irregular, *Confraternity*.
comfort the feebleminded: . . . cheer up the fainthearted, *Berkeley* . . . comfort the fainthearted, *Confraternity* . . . encourage the timid, *Norlie*.

1 Thess. 5:15

| 469.1 verb 2pl
impr pres mid
ἀντέχεσθε
antechesthe
sustain | 3450.1
art gen pl
τῶν
tōn
the | 766.5 adj
gen pl masc
ἀσθενῶν,
asthenōn
weak, | 3086.2 verb 2pl
impr pres act
μακροθυμεῖτε
makrothumeite
be patient | 4242.1
prep
πρὸς
pros
towards |

| 3820.8 adj
acc pl masc
πάντας.
pantas
all. | 3571.1 verb
2pl pres act
15. ὁρᾶτε
horate
See that | 3231.1
partic
μὴ
mē
not | 4948.3 indef-
pron nom sing
τις
tis
anyone | 2527.7 adj
sing neu
κακὸν
kakon
evil | 470.2
prep
ἀντὶ
anti
for |

| 2527.8 adj
gen sing neu
κακοῦ
kakou
evil | 4948.2 indef-
pron dat sing
τινι
tini
to anyone | 586.9 verb 3sing
subj aor act
ἀποδῷ·
apodō
render, | 233.2
conj
ἀλλὰ
alla
but | 3704.1
adv
πάντοτε
pantote
always | 3450.16 art
sing neu
τὸ
to
the |

| 18.3
adj sing
ἀγαθὸν
agathon
good | 1371.6 verb 2pl
impr pres act
διώκετε
diōkete
pursue | 2504.1
conj
⌐a καὶ ⌐
kai
both | 1519.1
prep
εἰς
eis
towards | 238.3 prs-pron
acc pl masc
ἀλλήλους
allēlous
one another | 2504.1
conj
καὶ
kai
and |

15.a.**Txt**: 01ℵ-corr,03B 018K,020L,025P,byz. Weis,Sod
Var: 01ℵ-org,02A,06D 33,bo.Lach,Treg,Tisc We/Ho,UBS/✶

| 1519.1
prep
εἰς
eis
towards | 3820.8 adj
acc pl masc
πάντας.
pantas
all; | 3704.1
adv
16. Πάντοτε
Pantote
always | 5299.7 verb 2pl
impr pres act
χαίρετε,
chairete
rejoice; | 88.1
adv
17. ἀδιαλείπτως
adialeiptōs
unceasingly |

| 4195.1 verb
2pl pres mid
προσεύχεσθε.
proseuchesthe
pray; | 1706.1
prep
18. ἐν
en
in | 3820.3 adj
dat sing
παντὶ
panti
everything | 2149.5 verb 2pl
impr pres act
εὐχαριστεῖτε·
eucharisteite
give thanks, | 3642.17 dem-
pron sing neu
τοῦτο
touto
this |

| 1056.1
conj
γὰρ
gar
for | 2284.1 noun
sing neu
θέλημα
thelēma
will | 2296.2 noun
gen sing masc
θεοῦ
theou
of God | 1706.1
prep
ἐν
en
in | 5382.3 name
dat masc
Χριστῷ
Christō
Christ | 2400.2
name masc
Ἰησοῦ
Iēsou
Jesus | 1519.1
prep
εἰς
eis
towards |

| 5050.4 prs-
pron acc 2pl
ὑμᾶς.
humas
you; | 3450.16 art
sing neu
19. τὸ
to
the | 4011.1 noun
sing neu
πνεῦμα
pneuma
Spirit | 3231.1
partic
μὴ
mē
not | 4426.1 verb 2pl
impr pres act
σβέννυτε.
sbennute
do quench; | 4252.1
noun fem
20. προφητείας
prophēteias
prophecies |

21.a.**Var**: 01ℵ-corr,03B 06D,018K,020L,025P byz.it.sa.Gries,Lach Treg,Alf,Word,Tisc We/Ho,Weis,Sod UBS/✶

| 3231.1
partic
μὴ
mē
not | 1832.3 verb 2pl
impr pres act
ἐξουθενεῖτε.
exoutheneite
do set ignore; | 3820.1
adj
21. πάντα
panta
all things | 1156.2
conj
[a✶+ δὲ]
de
[but] | 1375.1 verb
2pl pres act
δοκιμάζετε,
dokimazete
test, |

| 3450.16 art
sing neu
τὸ
to
the | 2541.1
adj sing
καλὸν
kalon
good | 2692.1 verb
2pl pres act
κατέχετε,
katechete
hold fast; | 570.3
prep
22. ἀπὸ
apo
from | 3820.2 adj
gen sing
παντὸς
pantos
every | 1482.2 noun
gen sing neu
εἴδους
eidous
form |

| 4050.2 adj
gen sing
πονηροῦ
ponērou
of wickedness | 563.8 verb 2pl
impr pres mid
ἀπέχεσθε.
apechesthe
abstain. | 840.5 prs-pron
nom sing masc
23. Αὐτὸς
Autos
Himself | 1156.2
conj
δὲ
de
now | 3450.5 art
nom sing masc
ὁ
ho
the | 2296.1 noun
nom sing masc
θεὸς
theos
God |

"Comfort the feeble-minded" in King James' day meant to encourage those who were irresolute, vacillating, too weak to have any real purpose or to overcome discouragements. It included those who were so despondent they were tempted to give up.

Supporting the weak implies holding on tightly or firmly to them to keep them from drifting away and to keep them in fellowship with the Church, never criticizing them for their weakness but helping them to feel they have the support of the Lord as well as of their fellow Christians. This means being patient and long-suffering with all believers (1 Corinthians 13:4; Ephesians 4:2; Colossians 3:13).

5:15. This kind of loving patience will keep believers from holding grudges. The command is that no one takes revenge or tries to pay back evil with evil. (Compare Romans 12:9-21.) Christians can best do this by always pursuing the good, not only toward other believers but toward all (including those who oppose them).

5:16-18. The remaining commands are all in a plural form so they apply to the whole church both as individuals and as a body. These things are to mark collective worship. Even more important, they are to mark the believer's daily life. There is no alternative but to rejoice always and to keep on rejoicing at all times in obedience to God.

Very closely related to this joy is the fellowship Christians have with the Lord as they engage in constant, unceasing prayer. At every opportunity their hearts go out to God. The channel of communication is always open. They may express themselves in a variety of ways (1 Corinthians 14:13-15).

It is also the will of God for believers in Christ to give thanks in everything. Because of who God is and what He has done, He is worthy of praise whether the believer feels like praising Him or not. Often the Holy Spirit will envelope those who praise Him with the joy of the Lord, regardless of the circumstances. (See Acts 16:25.)

5:19. Believers must also be careful not to quench (suppress, extinguish) the fire of the Spirit. The form of the Greek verb actually means "to stop putting out" the Spirit's fire. Fear, carelessness, and sin can all dampen our response to the Spirit.

5:20-22. Of all the gifts, the one which most often brings edification is the gift of prophecy (1 Corinthians 14:1,3). It brings spiritual strengthening, encouragement, challenge, and solace. Because it is so important Christians must not despise or treat it with contempt. There are counterfeits, however, so Christians must test everything and hold fast to what is good (noble, edifying). At the same time, believers are to "abstain from all appearance of evil."

support the weak: . . . uphold the infirm, *Concordant.*
be patient toward all [men]:

15. See that none render evil for evil unto any [man]; but ever follow that which is good:
both among yourselves, and to all [men]: . . . and to everybody, *Lilly.*

16. Rejoice evermore: Always be joyful, *Williams.*

17. Pray without ceasing: . . . pray constantly, *RSV.*

18. In every thing give thanks: Always be grateful, *Lilly* . . . give thanks in all circumstances, *RSV.*
for this is the will of God in Christ Jesus concerning you: . . . regarding you all, *Confraternity.*

19. Quench not the Spirit: Do not extinguish, *Lilly, Confraternity* . . . the Spirit's fire, *Berkeley* . . . Dampen, *Klingensmith.*

20. Despise not prophesyings: Scorn not, *Concordant* . . . prophetic utterance, *Berkeley.*

21. Prove all things: But test all things, *Confraternity.*
hold fast that which is good: . . . and retain what is good, *Berkeley* . . . retaining the ideal, *Concordant.*

22. Abstain from all appearance of evil: Keep away from evil in every form, *Berkeley.*

3450.10 art gen sing fem	1503.2 noun gen sing fem	37.7 verb 3sing opt aor act	5050.4 prs-pron acc 2pl	3514.1 adj acc pl masc	2504.1 conj
τῆς	εἰρήνης	ἁγιάσαι	ὑμᾶς	ὁλοτελεῖς·	καὶ
tēs	eirēnēs	hagiasai	humas	holoteleis	kai
of the	peace	may sanctify	you	wholly;	and

3511.2 adj sing neu	5050.2 prs-pron gen 2pl	3450.16 art sing neu	4011.1 noun sing neu	2504.1 conj	3450.9 art nom sing fem
ὁλόκληρον	ὑμῶν	τὸ	πνεῦμα	καὶ	ἡ
holoklēron	humōn	to	pneuma	kai	hē
entire	your	to the	spirit	and	the

5425.1 noun nom sing fem	2504.1 conj	3450.16 art sing neu	4835.1 noun sing neu	272.1 adv	1706.1 prep	3450.11 art dat sing fem
ψυχὴ	καὶ	τὸ	σῶμα	ἀμέμπτως	ἐν	τῇ
psuchē	kai	to	sōma	amemptōs	en	tē
soul	and	to the	body	blameless	at	the

3814.3 noun dat sing fem	3450.2 art gen sing	2935.2 noun gen sing masc	2231.2 prs-pron gen 1pl	2400.2 name masc	5382.2 name gen masc
παρουσίᾳ	τοῦ	κυρίου	ἡμῶν	Ἰησοῦ	Χριστοῦ
parousia	tou	kuriou	hēmōn	Iēsou	Christou
coming	of the	Lord	our	Jesus	Christ

4931.32 verb 3sing opt aor pass		3964.2 adj nom sing masc	3450.5 art nom sing masc	2535.4 verb nom sing masc part pres act	5050.4 prs-pron acc 2pl
τηρηθείη.	**24.** πιστὸς		ὁ	καλῶν	ὑμᾶς,
tērētheiē	pistos		ho	kalōn	humas
may be preserved.	Faithful		the	calling	you,

3614.5 rel-pron nom sing masc	2504.1 conj	4020.52 verb 3sing indic fut act		79.6 noun nom pl masc	4195.1 verb 2pl pres mid
ὃς	καὶ	ποιήσει.	**25.** Ἀδελφοί,		προσεύχεσθε
hos	kai	poiēsei	Adelphoi		proseuchesthe
who	also	will perform.	Brothers,		pray

25.a.**Var:** p30,03B 06D-org,33,sa.Lach We/Ho,Weis,Sod UBS/☆

2504.1 conj	3875.1 prep	2231.2 prs-pron gen 1pl		776.9 verb 2pl impr aor mid	3450.8 art acc pl masc
[a☆+ καὶ]	περὶ	ἡμῶν.	**26.** Ἀσπάσασθε		τοὺς
kai	peri	hēmōn	Aspasasthe		tous
[also]	for	us.	Greet		the

79.9 noun acc pl masc	3820.8 adj acc pl masc	1706.1 prep	5207.1 noun dat sing neu	39.3 adj dat sing	3589.1 verb 1sing indic pres act
ἀδελφοὺς	πάντας	ἐν	φιλήματι	ἁγίῳ.	**27.** (Ὁρκίζω
adelphous	pantas	en	philēmati	hagiō	Horkizō
brothers	all	with	a kiss	holy.	I adjure

27.a.**Txt:** 01א,06D-corr 018K,020L,025P,byz. **Var:** 02A,03B,06D-org 33,Lach,Treg,Alf,Word Tisc,We/Ho,Weis,Sod UBS/☆

1758.1 verb 1sing indic pres act	5050.4 prs-pron acc 2pl	3450.6 art acc sing masc	2935.4 noun acc sing masc	312.18 verb inf aor pass
[a☆ Ἐνορκίζω]	ὑμᾶς	τὸν	κύριον	ἀναγνωσθῆναι
Enorkizō	humas	ton	kurion	anagnōsthēnai
[idem]	you	the	Lord	to be read

27.b.**Txt:** 01א-corr,02A 018K,020L,025P,33,byz. bo.Weis,Sod **Var:** 01א-org,03B,06D sa.Lach,Treg,Alf,Tisc We/Ho,UBS/☆

3450.12 art acc sing fem	1976.4 noun acc sing fem	3820.5 adj dat pl	3450.4 art dat pl	39.8 adj dat pl masc
τὴν	ἐπιστολὴν	πᾶσιν	τοῖς	(b ἁγίοις)
tēn	epistolēn	pasin	tois	hagiois
the	epistle	to all	the	holy

79.8 noun dat pl masc	3450.9 art nom sing fem	5322.1 noun nom sing fem	3450.2 art gen sing	2935.2 noun gen sing masc	2231.2 prs-pron gen 1pl
ἀδελφοῖς.	**28.** Ἡ	χάρις	τοῦ	κυρίου	ἡμῶν
adelphois	Hē	charis	tou	kuriou	hēmōn
brothers.	The	grace	of the	Lord	our

5:23. In conclusion Paul commended the Thessalonians to God with a prayer. They could not fulfill all these exhortations in and by themselves. They needed help from God, who is the true Author of the Christian's peace (including spiritual health and well-being). He must come on the scene and sanctify (consecrate, dedicate) them completely (through and through). Paul prayed also that this sanctification would keep them blameless until the coming of our Lord Jesus.

5:24. Because God is faithful believers can depend on Him to do what He has promised and to act in carrying out His great plan and purpose of redemption. Thus Paul's prayer will be answered for all who respond in faith and heed the warnings he has given in this passage.

In writing to the Corinthians, Paul indicated he served a faithful God and he wanted to be just as faithful and trustworthy. So his word was not yes and at the same time no (2 Corinthians 1:18-20). That would be impossible, for in Christ there is only yes. In other words, Paul preached a positive gospel. He did not proclaim Christ as Saviour and say perhaps He would save them and perhaps He would not. He did not proclaim Him as Baptizer in the Holy Spirit and say perhaps He would fill believers with the Spirit and perhaps He would not. In Jesus Christ there is only "yes" to all the promises of God.

It is very important for Christians to recognize this positive nature of apostolic preaching. They spoke of positive proofs. They declared that what God was doing was according to the Scriptures. They constantly emphasized the fact that *gospel* means "good news" and is backed by the power, love, and faithfulness of the God who created this universe and who is determined to carry out His plan to its final consummation.

5:25-27. Paul brought this letter to an end by more brief exhortations followed by a benediction. First Paul asked them to pray for him and his fellow workers. Never did he suppose that the work of God could be done by his own faith, labor, or prayers alone. He was always conscious that the work of God must be done through a united body of believers with each contributing the gifts which the Holy Spirit distributes as He wills (1 Corinthians 12:11).

Next Paul asked that his love for them and their love for each other be expressed by the token of a "holy kiss" (probably on the cheek). This was acceptable in the culture of that day. It is still practiced by many Christians throughout the world. In other cultures a handshake or possibly a hug can be a holy greeting. "Holy" is the key word here.

Then Paul gave strict orders that this letter be read to all the "holy brethren," that is, to all the consecrated, dedicated Christians, both men and women. He did not want any of them to miss the message the Spirit had given him for them. The Early Church recognized that these letters were also needed by all the churches.

23. And the very God of peace sanctify you wholly: . . . sanctify you completely, *Confraternity, Adams* . . . consecrate you wholly, *Montgomery* . . . consecrate your whole being, *Williams* . . . will make you completely holy, *SEB* . . . make you entirely holy, *Klingensmith* . . . make you perfect in holiness, *Lilly* . . . purify you perfectly, *Fenton.*

and [I pray God] your whole spirit and soul and body be preserved blameless: . . . may your entire being, *Adams* . . . may your whole person, *Campbell* . . . be without a flaw, *Berkeley* . . . be kept sound, *RSV* . . . be kept perfect and faultless, *TCNT* . . . be kept altogether faultless, *Montgomery.*

unto the coming of our Lord Jesus Christ: . . . for the coming, *Adams.*

24. Faithful [is] he that calleth you: He who calls you can be trusted, *Norlie* . . . may be trusted, *TCNT* . . . is reliable, *Berkeley.*

who also will do [it]: . . . and He will accomplish it, *Berkeley, Adams* . . . he will fulfil my prayer, *Montgomery* . . . and He will effect it, *Fenton.*

25. Brethren, pray for us: Brothers, keep us in mind in your prayers, *BB.*

26. Greet all the brethren with an holy kiss: Give regards to, *Fenton* . . . Say hello to all the Christians with a kiss of holy love, *NLT* . . . a sacred kiss, *Berkeley, Williams.*

27. I charge you by the Lord: I solemnly charge you, *Campbell* . . . I adjure you, *TCNT, Montgomery* . . . I order you, *SEB* . . . I urge you, *Klingensmith.*

that this epistle be read unto all the holy brethren: . . . to have this letter read to all, *Montgomery* . . . to read this letter to all, *Adams.*

1 Thess. 5:28

28.a.**Txt:** 01ℵ,02A
06D-corr,018K,020L
025P,byz.it.bo.Sod
Var: 03B,06D-org,33,sa.
Gries,Lach,Treg,Alf
Word,Tisc,We/Ho,Weis
UBS/✻

28.b.**Txt:** 018K,Steph
Var: Gries,Lach,Word
Tisc,We/Ho,Weis,Sod
UBS/✻

2400.2 name masc	5382.2 name gen masc	3196.1 prep	5050.2 prs-pron gen 2pl	279.1 intrj	4242.1 prep
Ἰησοῦ	Χριστοῦ	μεθ'	ὑμῶν.	⌐ᵃ ἀμήν. ⌐	⌐ᵇ Πρὸς
Iēsou	Christou	meth'	humōn	amēn	Pros
Jesus	Christ	with	you.	Amen.	To

2309.4 name dat fem	4272.9 num ord nom sing fem	1119.21 verb 3sing indic aor pass	570.3 prep	116.1 name gen fem
Θεσσαλονικεῖς	πρώτη	ἐγράφη	ἀπὸ	Ἀθηνῶν. ⌐
Thessalonikeis	prōtē	egraphē	apo	Athēnōn
Thessalonians	first	written	from	Athens.

5:28. Paul's closing benediction called for the grace, the unmerited favor, of our Lord Jesus Christ to be with the believers in Thessalonica. This is the way he ended most of his letters.

28. The grace of our Lord Jesus Christ [be] with you. Amen: The love of our Lord, *Beck* ... The spiritual blessing of, *Williams* ... The favour of, *Rotherham* ... our Lord Jesus the Messiah, *Murdock* ... May the Grace, *NAB* ... The gracious care of, *Blackwelder* ... May the blessings of, *Hoerber*.

THE SECOND EPISTLE
OF PAUL TO THE
THESSALONIANS

Expanded Interlinear
Textual Critical Apparatus
Verse-by-Verse Commentary
Various Versions

Πρὸς Θεσσαλονικεῖς ἐπιστολὴ Παύλου δευτερα

4242.1 prep	2309.4 name dat fem	1976.1 noun nom sing fem	3834.2 name gen masc	1202.4 num ord nom sing fem
Πρὸς	**Θεσσαλονικεῖς**	**ἐπιστολὴ**	**Παύλου**	**δευτερα**
Pros	Thessalonikeis	epistolē	Paulou	deutera
To	Thessalonians	letter	of Paul	second

Textual Apparatus

3834.1 name nom masc	2504.1 conj	4465.1 name nom masc	2504.1 conj	4943.1 name nom masc	3450.11 art dat sing fem
1:1. Παῦλος	**καὶ**	**Σιλουανὸς**	**καὶ**	**Τιμόθεος,**	**τῇ**
Paulos	kai	Silouanos	kai	Timotheos	tē
Paul	and	Silvanus	and	Timothy,	to the

1564.3 noun dat sing fem	2308.2 name-adj gen pl masc	1706.1 prep	2296.3 noun dat sing masc	3824.3 noun dat sing masc	2231.2 prs-pron gen 1pl
ἐκκλησίᾳ	**Θεσσαλονικέων**	**ἐν**	**θεῷ**	**πατρὶ**	**ἡμῶν**
ekklēsia	Thessalonikeōn	en	theō	patri	hēmōn
assembly	of Thessalonians	in	God	Father	our

2504.1 conj	2935.3 noun dat sing masc	2400.2 name masc	5382.3 name dat masc	5322.1 noun nom sing fem	5050.3 prs-pron dat 2pl
καὶ	**κυρίῳ**	**Ἰησοῦ**	**Χριστῷ·**	**2. χάρις**	**ὑμῖν**
kai	kuriō	Iēsou	Christō	charis	humin
and	Lord	Jesus	Christ.	Grace	to you

2504.1 conj	1503.1 noun nom sing fem	570.3 prep	2296.2 noun gen sing masc	3824.2 noun gen sing masc	2231.2 prs-pron gen 1pl	2504.1 conj
καὶ	**εἰρήνη**	**ἀπὸ**	**θεοῦ**	**πατρὸς**	`ᵃ` **ἡμῶν** `⟩`	**καὶ**
kai	eirēnē	apo	theou	patros	hēmōn	kai
and	peace	from	God	Father	our	and

2935.2 noun gen sing masc	2400.2 name masc	5382.2 name gen masc	2149.8 verb inf pres act	3648.4 verb 1pl indic pres act
κυρίου	**Ἰησοῦ**	**Χριστοῦ.**	**3. Εὐχαριστεῖν**	**ὀφείλομεν**
kuriou	Iēsou	Christou	Eucharistein	opheilomen
Lord	Jesus	Christ.	To thank	we ought

3450.3 art dat sing	2296.3 noun dat sing masc	3704.1 adv	3875.1 prep	5050.2 prs-pron gen 2pl	79.6 noun nom pl masc
τῷ	**θεῷ**	**πάντοτε**	**περὶ**	**ὑμῶν,**	**ἀδελφοί,**
tō	theō	pantote	peri	humōn	adelphoi
	God	always	concerning	you,	brothers,

2503.1 conj	510.1 adj sing	1498.4 verb 3sing indic pres act	3617.1 conj	5069.1 verb 3sing indic pres act
καθὼς	**ἄξιόν**	**ἐστιν,**	**ὅτι**	**ὑπεραυξάνει**
kathōs	axion	estin	hoti	huperauxanei
even as	fitting	it is,	because	increases exceedingly

3450.9 art nom sing fem	3963.1 noun nom sing fem	5050.2 prs-pron gen 2pl	2504.1 conj	3981.1 verb 3sing indic pres act	3450.9 art nom sing fem	26.1 noun nom sing fem
ἡ	**πίστις**	**ὑμῶν,**	**καὶ**	**πλεονάζει**	**ἡ**	**ἀγάπη**
hē	pistis	humōn	kai	pleonazei	hē	agapē
the	faith	your,	and	abounds	the	love

1518.1 num card gen	1524.2 adj gen sing	3820.4 adj gen pl	5050.2 prs-pron gen 2pl	1519.1 prep	238.3 prs-pron acc pl masc
ἑνὸς	**ἑκάστου**	**πάντων**	**ὑμῶν**	**εἰς**	**ἀλλήλους·**
henos	hekastou	pantōn	humōn	eis	allēlous
of one	each	of all	you	to	one another;

2.a.**Txt:** 01ℵ,02A,018K 020L,byz.it.sa.Tisc
Var: 03B,06D,025P,33 Alf,We/Ho,Weis,Sod UBS/✱

THE SECOND EPISTLE OF PAUL TO THE
THESSALONIANS

1:1. Paul's first letter to the Thessalonians was intended to encourage them to remain faithful and to give them practical exhortations for Christian living in the light of Christ's return. Every chapter contains some reference to the Second Coming. After delivering the epistle, Timothy returned to Paul with the report that the believers now had even more questions about the Lord's return. Paul then wrote to deal with these questions.

The greeting shows that Silas (called by his full name Silvanus) and Timothy were still with Paul and were cosenders of the letter.

Paul recognized the Thessalonian church as being in a right relationship with God the Father and the Lord Jesus Christ, who is the very source and sphere of the believer's life. Notice that Christ is presented as equal with the Father. Because of the Son's deity the Church can be said to be in God the Father, also in Christ.

1:2. On this verse Marshall remarks, "Whereas grace is particularly associated with Christ (2 Corinthians 13:14) and peace with God (Romans 15:33; Philippians 4:7) here God the Father and the Lord Jesus Christ are named together as the one source of both grace and peace" (*New Century Bible*, 43:168).

1:3. Even though there were problems, Paul first drew attention to what was good about their situation. He (along with Silas) felt under obligation to give thanks to God at all times concerning them, as was fitting and proper. Paul felt very strongly that what God had done for the Thessalonian believers deserved his thanks to God. But that was not all; the believers had proved worthy of this. They did not need to feel ashamed or belittle themselves in any way. Clearly, the report Timothy brought back showed they were a healthy church.

Growth is always the sign of life and health. Their faith was growing wonderfully, like a luxuriant, spreading tree. The faithful, Calvary love of each one of them was abounding, becoming greater and richer, increasing and spreading like a flood toward each other. The "faith," of course, was a faith in Christ which was deepened and strengthened through obedience to His Word. Their love was a self-giving love that reached out to others, even to people they did not like, especially to people who might not deserve love. It was shown in service, in humility, in courtesy, and in consideration for one another. Above all, it was shown without restrictions.

Various Versions

1. Paul, and Silvanus, and Timotheus:
unto the church of the Thessalonians: To the congregation of, *SEB* . . . to the ecclesia, *Concordant* . . . in the city of Thessalonica, *NLT*.
in God our Father and the Lord Jesus Christ: . . . in union with, *TCNT*.

2. Grace unto you, and peace, from God our Father and the Lord Jesus Christ:

3. We are bound to thank God always for you, brethren, as it is meet: It is our duty, *Norlie*, *TCNT* . . . We must give thanks, *NLT* . . . We have a sense of personal obligation to be constantly thanking God, *Wuest* . . . It is fitting that we should, *Confraternity* . . . We ought always to thank God for you, brothers, as is appropriate, *Adams* . . . because it is right, *Klingensmith* . . . and rightly so, *NIV*.
because that your faith groweth exceedingly: . . . because of the abundant growth of, *Montgomery* . . . your faith is flourishing, *Concordant* . . . is growing wonderfully, *Wuest* . . . is growing so splendidly, *Berkeley* . . . is growing so well, *Adams* . . . is growing fast, *SEB*.
and the charity of every one of you all toward each other aboundeth: . . . and of the overflowing love with which every one of you is filled toward one another, *Montgomery* . . . and the love that every one of you has for one another is increasing so much, *Adams* . . . for each other is increasing, *NIV* . . . is also on the increase, *Norlie* . . . is stronger all the time, *NLT* . . . is continually increasing, *TCNT* . . . exists in great abundance, *Wuest*.

2 Thess. 1:4

4. ὥστε ἡμᾶς αὐτοὺς [✶ αὐτοὺς ἡμᾶς] ἐν
hōste hēmas autous autous hēmas en
so as for us ourselves [ourselves us] in

4.a.Txt: 06D,018K,020L
byz.
Var: 01א,02A,03B,025P
33,Lach,Treg,Alf,Sod
UBS/✶

ὑμῖν ʽ καυχᾶσθαι [ᵃ✶ ἐγκαυχᾶσθαι] ἐν ταῖς
humin kauchasthai enkauchasthai en tais
you to boast [idem] in the

ἐκκλησίαις τοῦ θεοῦ ὑπὲρ τῆς ὑπομονῆς
ekklēsiais tou theou huper tēs hupomonēs
assemblies of God for the endurance

ὑμῶν καὶ πίστεως ἐν πᾶσιν τοῖς διωγμοῖς
humōn kai pisteōs en pasin tois diōgmois
your and faith in all the persecutions

ὑμῶν καὶ ταῖς θλίψεσιν αἷς ἀνέχεσθε,
humōn kai tais thlipsesin hais anechesthe,
your and the tribulations which you are bearing;

5. ἔνδειγμα τῆς δικαίας κρίσεως τοῦ θεοῦ,
endeigma tēs dikaias kriseōs tou theou,
evidence of the righteous judgment of God,

εἰς τὸ καταξιωθῆναι ὑμᾶς τῆς
eis to kataxiōthēnai humas tēs
for the to be accounted worthy you of the

βασιλείας τοῦ θεοῦ, ὑπὲρ ἧς καὶ πάσχετε
basileias tou theou, huper hēs kai paschete
kingdom of God, for which also you suffer;

6. εἴπερ δίκαιον παρὰ θεῷ ἀνταποδοῦναι τοῖς
eiper dikaion para theō antapodounai tois
if at least righteous with God to repay to the

θλίβουσιν ὑμᾶς θλῖψιν, **7.** καὶ ὑμῖν τοῖς
thlibousin humas thlipsin, kai humin tois
oppressing you tribulation, and to you the

θλιβομένοις ἄνεσιν μεθ᾽ ἡμῶν, ἐν τῇ
thlibomenois anesin meth᾽ hēmōn, en tē
being oppressed rest with us, at the

346

1:4. As a result, Paul and his company gloried in them (boasted of them, spoke of them in the highest terms among all the churches). They especially rejoiced to tell other believers of the Thessalonians' patience (steadfast endurance, fortitude, perseverance) and their faith in the midst of their persecutions and the tribulations, pressures, oppression, affliction, and trouble which they continued to endure. In fact, they put up with all these troubles willingly. What a powerful faith this was! Unbelieving Jews assaulted them because of their Christian testimony. Unbelieving Gentiles joined in with persistent persecution. But faith and love kept the Christians triumphant!

1:5. Paul saw the patience and faith of the Thessalonians under persecution as a clear evidence of the righteous judgment of God. The very fact that God upheld them in the midst of all this suffering and testing was proof of His faithfulness. He could be counted on to reward them and to "recompense" their enemies as well (verse 6).

Their faith and brave endurance were also indications that they would be counted worthy of the future kingdom or rule of God. This was all the more true because it was on behalf of the Kingdom and in view of the Kingdom that they suffered and endured hardship.

Paul said he endured all things for the elect's sake, for the sake of those who had elected or chosen to follow Jesus. He wrote to Timothy, "That they may also obtain the salvation which is in Christ Jesus with eternal glory." Then he added, "It is a faithful saying: For if we be dead with him, we shall also live with him: if we suffer (endure), we shall also reign with him" (2 Timothy 2:10-12). Thus, whether Christians suffer physically or not, the important thing is to endure. This means that believers are to stand their ground when others are fleeing, to hold out when others are giving in, to remain steadfast to the end whatever others do.

1:6. To encourage the Thessalonians further in their brave endurance of persecution and trouble, Paul pointed out that it was also a "righteous thing with God to recompense (repay) tribulation" (including affliction and trouble) to those who troubled (afflicted) them. This is still a moral universe. God will see to it that what troublemakers have sown, they will also reap.

1:7. The present participle *thlibomenois* indicates that the Thessalonians were even then in the midst of suffering. To these who were "being oppressed," the promise of rest must have been most welcome. Eadie says, "This *anesis* is the immediate aspect of heaven to the suffering, rest to the weary and worn-out, release from all the disquiet, pain, and sorrow of the earth" (*Greek Text Commentaries*, 5:238).

4. So that we ourselves glory in you in the churches of God: We are proud of you, *NLT* . . . boast of you, *Confraternity* . . . mention you with pride, *Berkeley* . . . So that I myself am boasting about you among, *Montgomery* . . . in the assemblies of God, *Fenton*.

for your patience and faith in all your persecutions and tribulations that ye endure: . . . we boast about your perseverance, *NIV* . . . regarding your obedience and fidelity, *Fenton* . . . concerning your endurance and faith, *Klingensmith* . . . in spite of your persecutions and crushing sorrows, *Williams* . . . which you are displaying in all the troubles, *Montgomery* . . . that ye bear, *Young* . . . which you are bearing, *Concordant*.

5. [Which is] a manifest token of the righteous judgment of God: They are evidence of God's fair verdict, *Berkeley* . . . This is a clear proof, *Norlie* . . . a proof of, *Campbell* . . . These persecutions will vindicate God's justice as a judge, *TCNT* . . . the right decision of God, *Fenton*.

that ye may be counted worthy of the kingdom of God, for which ye also suffer: . . . shows that you are fit for the Kingdom, *Klingensmith* . . . in behalf of which you are even now suffering, *Montgomery*.

6. Seeing [it is] a righteous thing with God to recompense tribulation to them that trouble you: He will pay back trouble, *NIV* . . . to repay with trouble, *Norlie* . . . to repay affliction to those afflicting you, *Concordant* . . . to repay your afflictors with affliction, *Fenton* . . . those who afflict you, *Confraternity*.

7. And to you who are troubled rest with us: . . . you, the afflicted, *Campbell, Fenton* . . . rest, along with me, *Montgomery*.

2 Thess. 1:8

597.3 noun dat sing fem	3450.2 art gen sing	2935.2 noun gen sing masc	2400.2 name masc	570.2 prep	3636.2 noun gen sing masc
ἀποκαλύψει	τοῦ	κυρίου	Ἰησοῦ	ἀπ'	οὐρανοῦ
apokalupsei	tou	kuriou	Iēsou	ap'	ouranou
revelation	of the	Lord	Jesus	from	heaven

3196.2 prep	32.6 noun gen pl masc	1405.2 noun gen sing fem	840.3 prs-pron gen sing	1706.1 prep	4300.3 noun dat sing neu
μετ'	ἀγγέλων	δυνάμεως	αὐτοῦ,	8. [☆ ἐν	πυρὶ
met'	angelōn	dunameōs	autou,	en	puri
with	angels	of power	his,	in	a fire

8.a.Txt: 01ℵ,02A,0111 byz.
Var: 03B,06D,010F 012G,044,2464

5232.2 noun gen sing fem	1706.1 prep	5232.3 noun dat sing fem	4300.2 noun gen sing neu	1319.6 verb gen sing masc part pres act	1544.3 noun acc sing fem
φλογός,	[a ἐν	φλογὶ	πυρὸς,]	διδόντος	ἐκδίκησιν
phlogos	en	phlogi	puros,	didontos	ekdikēsin
of flame,	[in	a flame	of fire,]	awarding	vengeance

3450.4 art dat pl	3231.1 partic	3471.21 verb dat pl masc part perf act	2296.4 noun acc sing masc	2504.1 conj	3450.4 art dat pl	3231.1 partic
τοῖς	μὴ	εἰδόσιν	θεὸν,	καὶ	τοῖς	μὴ
tois	mē	eidosin	theon,	kai	tois	mē
on the	not	knowing	God,	and	to the	not

5057.2 verb dat pl masc part pres act	3450.3 art dat sing	2077.3 noun dat sing neu	3450.2 art gen sing	2935.2 noun gen sing masc	2231.2 prs-pron gen 1pl
ὑπακούουσιν	τῷ	εὐαγγελίῳ	τοῦ	κυρίου	ἡμῶν
hupakouousin	tō	euangeliō	tou	kuriou	hēmōn
obeying	the	good news	of the	Lord	our

8.b.Txt: 01ℵ,02A,byz.
Var: 03B,06D,018K 020L,025P,33,bo.Treg Alf,Tisc,We/Ho,Weis Sod,UBS/☆

2400.2 name masc	5382.2 name gen masc	3610.2 rel-pron nom pl masc	1343.2 noun acc sing fem	4947.1 verb 3pl indic fut act
Ἰησοῦ	[b Χριστοῦ]	9. οἵτινες	δίκην	τίσουσιν,
Iēsou	Christou	hoitines	dikēn	tisousin,
Jesus	Christ,	who	penalty	shall suffer,

3502.2 noun acc sing masc	164.1 adj sing	570.3 prep	4241.2 noun gen sing neu	3450.2 art gen sing	2935.2 noun gen sing masc
ὄλεθρον	αἰώνιον,	ἀπὸ	προσώπου	τοῦ	κυρίου,
olethron	aiōnion,	apo	prosōpou	tou	kuriou,
destruction	eternal,	from	face	of the	Lord,

2504.1 conj	570.3 prep	3450.10 art gen sing fem	1385.2 noun gen sing fem	3450.10 art gen sing fem	2452.2 noun gen sing	840.3 prs-pron gen sing
καὶ	ἀπὸ	τῆς	δόξης	τῆς	ἰσχύος	αὐτοῦ,
kai	apo	tēs	doxēs	tēs	ischuos	autou,
and	from	the	glory	of the	strength	his,

3615.1 conj	2048.8 verb 3sing subj aor act	1724.2 verb inf aor pass	1706.1 prep	3450.4 art dat pl
10. ὅταν	ἔλθῃ	ἐνδοξασθῆναι	ἐν	τοῖς
hotan	elthē	endoxasthēnai	en	tois
when	he shall have come	to be glorified	in	

39.8 adj dat pl masc	840.3 prs-pron gen sing	2504.1 conj	2273.19 verb inf aor pass	1706.1 prep	3820.5 adj dat pl	3450.4 art dat pl
ἁγίοις	αὐτοῦ	καὶ	θαυμασθῆναι	ἐν	πᾶσιν	τοῖς
hagiois	autou	kai	thaumasthēnai	en	pasin	tois
saints	his	and	to be wondered at	in	all	the

10.a.Txt: Steph
Var: 01ℵ,02A,03B,06D 018K,020L,025P,byz. Gries,Lach,Treg,Alf Word,Tisc,We/Ho,Weis Sod,UBS/☆

3961.3 verb dat pl masc part pres act	3961.33 verb dat pl masc part aor act	3617.1 conj	3961.58 verb 3sing indic aor pass
[πιστεύουσιν,	[a☆ πιστεύσασιν,]	ὅτι	ἐπιστεύθη
pisteuousin,	pisteusasin,	hoti	episteuthē
believing,	[having believed,]	because	was believed

This will take place in the revelation (unveiling, disclosure, revealing) of the Lord Jesus from heaven with the angels (messengers) of God's mighty power. This *unveiling* is a term used also of Christ's coming to destroy the present world system and set up His kingdom on earth (Daniel 2:35,45). Then those now troubled (oppressed, distressed, and persecuted) will be free from toil and conflict.

1:8. While the coming of Christ brings blessing to believers, it will be a time of judgment upon those who have been enemies of the gospel. Jesus will suddenly appear in "flaming fire" to take vengeance (in the sense of rendering justice) on those who know not God, those who "obey not the gospel of our Lord Jesus Christ."

Those who "know not God" include those who have willfully rejected knowledge that was available to them. (Compare Hosea 4:6; 8:12.) Paul also pointed out that the world once knew God, but men exalted themselves and began worshiping the created thing rather than the Creator (Romans 1:19-25).

Those who obey not the gospel are those who heard it but actively rejected it and took a course of disobedience. They are a specific group within the group that knows not God. They are even more guilty, for they know what they are doing.

1:9. Those who know not God and obey not the gospel will receive just judgment when Jesus appears in flaming fire and speaks the word that will destroy the Antichrist and his armies (Revelation 19:11-15). They will pay the full penalty, which will be eternal destruction, everlasting ruin, and eternal loss away from the presence of the Lord. They will be separated forever from fellowship with God, shut out from the visible glory of His power.

This banishment from the manifest presence of God will be the vindication of God's holy, righteous nature. The sinner imagines he can escape, but this is totally impossible by the very nature of things. It will be evident then that God has indeed created a moral universe. (See Luke 13:27; Matthew 8:12; 22:13; 25:30.)

1:10. The chief purpose of Christ's coming in glory is not simply to judge the wicked, however. They will be judged, for they failed to fulfill the very purpose for which they were created, and by their persecutions they attempted to hinder God. However, the real purpose of Christ's return and revelation is that He may be "glorified in his saints"; that is, in all the believers, including the Thessalonians to whom Paul was writing.

The emphasis may be that Jesus will be glorified and honored *among* His saints. As He returns in this revelation of flaming fire, He will be accompanied not only by the angels, but also by all the saints, by all true believers, all whose righteousness is in Christ. All who believe will be filled with awe as they see His supernatural power and glory revealed in His glorious appearing and in the just judgment of His enemies.

when the Lord Jesus shall be revealed from heaven with his mighty angels: . . . at the Appearing of, *TCNT* . . . comes down from heaven, *NLT* . . . with his powerful angels, *SEB*.

8. In flaming fire taking vengeance on them that know not God: He will punish those, *NIV* . . . in a blaze of fire...shall mete out retribution, *Berkeley* . . . to inflict punishment, *Confraternity* . . . handing out vengeance, *Klingensmith* . . . inflicting a just retribution on, *Campbell* . . . giving judgment to those not perceiving God, *Fenton* . . . to those who are not acquainted with, *Concordant* . . . who do not acknowledge God, *SEB*.

and that obey not the gospel of our Lord Jesus Christ: . . . who will not accept the Gospel, *Norlie* . . . who do not listen to the good news, *Klingensmith, Williams* . . . upon those who turn a deaf ear to the Good News, *TCNT*.

9. Who shall be punished: . . . who shall suffer justice, *Young* . . . They will pay the penalty of everlasting ruin, *Berkeley*.

with everlasting destruction from the presence of the Lord: . . . by being shut out forever from, *Klingensmith* . . . of eonian extermination, *Concordant* . . . and exclusion from the Lord's presence, *Norlie* . . . and shut out from, *NIV* . . . with eternal ruin, *Confraternity* . . . an enduring death, *TCNT*.

and from the glory of his power: . . . from the shining greatness of, *NLT* . . . from the glory of his strength, *SEB* . . . and His glorious might, *Williams*.

10. When he shall come to be glorified in his saints: . . . to be honoured in his People, *TCNT* . . . with his consecrated ones, *Williams*.

and to be admired in all them that believe: . . . and to be marveled at in, *Confraternity*.

2 Thess. 1:11

| 3450.16 art
sing neu
τὸ
to
the | 3115.1 noun
sing neu
μαρτύριον
marturion
testimony | 2231.2 prs-
pron gen 1pl
ἡμῶν
hēmōn
our | 1894.1
prep
ἐφ'
eph'
to | 5050.4 prs-
pron acc 2pl
ὑμᾶς,
humas
you, | 1706.1
prep
ἐν
en
in | 3450.11 art
dat sing fem
τῇ
tē
the |

| 2232.3 noun
dat sing fem
ἡμέρα
hēmera
day | 1552.11 dem-
pron dat sing fem
ἐκείνῃ.
ekeinē
that. | 1519.1
prep
11. εἰς
eis
For | 3614.16 rel-
pron sing neu
ὃ
ho
which | 2504.1
conj
καὶ
kai
also | 4195.4 verb 1pl
indic pres mid
προσευχόμεθα
proseuchometha
we pray |

| 3704.1
adv
πάντοτε
pantote
always | 3875.1
prep
περὶ
peri
for | 5050.2 prs-
pron gen 2pl
ὑμῶν,
humōn
you, | 2419.1
conj
ἵνα
hina
that | 5050.4 prs-
pron acc 2pl
ὑμᾶς
humas
you | 511.3 verb 3sing
subj aor act
ἀξιώσῃ
axiōsē
may count worthy |

| 3450.10 art
gen sing fem
τῆς
tēs
of the | 2794.2 noun
gen sing fem
κλήσεως
klēseōs
calling | 3450.5 art
nom sing masc
ὁ
ho | 2296.1 noun
nom sing masc
θεὸς
theos
God | 2231.2 prs-
pron gen 1pl
ἡμῶν,
hēmōn
our, | 2504.1
conj
καὶ
kai
and | 3997.5 verb 3sing
subj aor act
πληρώσῃ
plērōsē
may fulfill |

| 3820.12 adj
acc sing fem
πᾶσαν
pasan
every | 2086.3 noun
acc sing fem
εὐδοκίαν
eudokian
good pleasure | 19.2 noun
gen sing fem
ἀγαθωσύνης
agathōsunēs
of goodness | 2504.1
conj
καὶ
kai
and | 2024.1 noun
sing neu
ἔργον
ergon
work | 3963.2 noun
gen sing fem
πίστεως
pisteōs
of faith |

| 1706.1
prep
ἐν
en
with | 1405.3 noun
dat sing fem
δυνάμει·
dunamei
power, | 3567.1
conj
12. ὅπως
hopōs
so that | 1724.1 verb 3sing
subj aor pass
ἐνδοξασθῇ
endoxasthē
may be glorified | 3450.16 art
sing neu
τὸ
to
the | 3549.2 noun
sing neu
ὄνομα
onoma
name |

| 3450.2 art
gen sing
τοῦ
tou
of the | 2935.2 noun
gen sing masc
κυρίου
kuriou
Lord | 2231.2 prs-
pron gen 1pl
ἡμῶν
hēmōn
our | 2400.2
name masc
Ἰησοῦ
Iēsou
Jesus | 5382.2 name
gen masc
⌜a⌝ Χριστοῦ ⌝
Christou
Christ | 1706.1
prep
ἐν
en
in |

12.a.**Txt**: 02A,025P,33
Steph
Var: 01א,03B,06D
018K,020L,bo.Treg,Alf
Word,Tisc,We/Ho,Weis
Sod,UBS/⋆

| 5050.3 prs-
pron dat 2pl
ὑμῖν,
humin
you, | 2504.1
conj
καὶ
kai
and | 5050.1 prs-
pron nom 2pl
ὑμεῖς
humeis
you | 1706.1
prep
ἐν
en
in | 840.4 prs-
pron dat sing
αὐτῷ,
autō
him, | 2567.3
prep
κατὰ
kata
according to | 3450.12 art
acc sing fem
τὴν
tēn
the |

| 5322.4 noun
acc sing fem
χάριν
charin
grace | 3450.2 art
gen sing
τοῦ
tou | 2296.2 noun
gen sing masc
θεοῦ
theou
of God | 2231.2 prs-
pron gen 1pl
ἡμῶν
hēmōn
our | 2504.1
conj
καὶ
kai
and | 2935.2 noun
gen sing masc
κυρίου
kuriou
of Lord | 2400.2
name masc
Ἰησοῦ
Iēsou
Jesus |

| 5382.2 name
gen masc
Χριστοῦ.
Christou
Christ. | 2049.3 verb 1pl
indic pres act
2:1. Ἐρωτῶμεν
Erōtōmen
We urge | 1156.2
conj
δὲ
de
now | 5050.4 prs-
pron acc 2pl
ὑμᾶς,
humas
you, | 79.6 noun
nom pl masc
ἀδελφοί,
adelphoi
brothers, | 5065.1
prep
ὑπὲρ
huper
by |

1.a.**Var**: 03B,044,33

| 3450.10 art
gen sing fem
τῆς
tēs
the | 3814.2 noun
gen sing fem
παρουσίας
parousias
coming | 3450.2 art
gen sing
τοῦ
tou
of the | 2935.2 noun
gen sing masc
κυρίου
kuriou
Lord | 2231.2 prs-
pron gen 1pl
⌜a⌝ ἡμῶν ⌝
hēmōn
our | 2400.2
name masc
Ἰησοῦ
Iēsou
Jesus |

It is possible also to take this to mean that His marvelous character and glory will be reflected in the believers. Since this means, in either case, all believers, all who accept and obey the gospel, it will include the Thessalonians; they believed the testimony of Paul and his company when it was brought to them.

1:11. In view of all their suffering and faithfulness, and in view of Christ's return and the divine rest believers will enjoy with Him at that time, Paul prayed always and at all times for the Thessalonian believers.

His first request was that God would count (or make) them worthy of the call to which they were already responding.

Second, he asked that God would fulfill (perfect and complete) all the good pleasure, purpose, and delight of His goodness. God wants to bring believers to the place where, if they will let Him, their whole purpose and joy is to do what is good in His eyes.

Third, Paul asked that God would fulfill or perfect the work (activity) of faith, making it effective with power.

1:12. Only in connection with acts of faith could Paul's final petition in this prayer be fulfilled. Then, through the believers' worthy response to His call, their delight in goodness, and their activity of faith, the name of our Lord Jesus Christ will be glorified in them and they in Him.

"The name of our Lord" includes His whole person, character, and nature. "His name shall be called Wonderful (a supernatural wonder; He himself will be a miracle), Counselor, The mighty God, The everlasting Father, The Prince of Peace" (Isaiah 9:6). His name also speaks of His royal dignity and His supernatural power and majesty. (See Hebrews 1:4; Philippians 2:8-11; Acts 3:12-16.) It refers to all that God is.

The true and holy nature of Jesus is thus to be glorified in believers and they in Him (in close, personal union with Him, as in John 17:1,10,21-26). But Christians cannot do this in themselves or of themselves. There is no way Christians can bring glory to God apart from His grace. This grace was made manifest at Calvary.

2:1. It is important to take note of the events which will take place at the second coming of Christ. There will be a rapture of the Church. There will be a Great Tribulation. There will be the return of Christ in judgment to judge His enemies.

The sequence of events is a matter of controversy, which often finds good people on opposite sides. Some believe Christ will come in the Rapture before the Tribulation, others in the middle of the Tribulation, and others at the close. A large segment of evangelical believers concur in the pre-Tribulation view.

(because our testimony among you was believed) in that day: . . . for you also believed our testimony, *Montgomery* . . . has been confidently accepted among you, *Williams.*

11. Wherefore also we pray always for you: With this in mind, *NIV* . . . With this in view, *Williams* . . . To this end I am making my constant prayer for you, *Montgomery* . . . we always pray this about you, *Adams.*

that our God would count you worthy of [this] calling: . . . may consider you, *Adams* . . . beseeching God to make you worthy of your calling, *Montgomery.*

and fulfil all the good pleasure of [his] goodness: . . . and by His power fully satisfy your every desire for goodness, *Williams* . . . also accomplish in a powerful way all of the good you want to do, *SEB* . . . fill you with all the benevolence of goodness, *Campbell* . . . and to fulfil mightily every desire of goodness, *Montgomery* . . . fulfill every good intention, *Adams.*

and the work of faith with power: . . . and complete every activity of your faith, *Williams* . . . and effort of faith, *Montgomery* . . . every faith-inspired effort, *Berkeley* . . . and every faithful deed of yours by His power, *Adams.*

12. That the name of our Lord Jesus Christ may be glorified in you: . . . will be honored by you, *NLT.*

and ye in him, according to the grace of our God and the Lord Jesus Christ: . . . and you be glorified in him, *Montgomery* . . . and you by Him, in keeping with, *Adams* . . . and you through union with Him, in accordance with the favor of, *Williams* . . . through the mercy of, *Norlie.*

1. Now we beseech you, brethren, by the coming of our Lord Jesus Christ: We have a request to make of you, *Norlie* . . . we are asking you, *Concordant* . . . we request you, *NASB* . . . I entreat you...concerning the coming of our Lord, *Montgomery* . . . relative to the coming of, *Berkeley.*

2 Thess. 2:2

5382.2 name gen masc	2504.1 conj	2231.2 prs-pron gen 1pl	1981.1 noun gen sing fem	1894.2 prep	840.6 prs-pron acc sing masc
Χριστοῦ	καὶ	ἡμῶν	ἐπισυναγωγῆς	ἐπ'	αὐτόν,
Christou	kai	hēmōn	episunagōgēs	ep'	auton
Christ	and	our	gathering together	to	him,

1519.1 prep	3450.16 art sing neu	3231.1 partic	4878.1 adv	4388.9 verb inf aor pass	5050.4 prs-pron acc 2pl	570.3 prep
2. εἰς	τὸ	μὴ	ταχέως	σαλευθῆναι	ὑμᾶς	ἀπὸ
eis	to	mē	tacheōs	saleuthēnai	humas	apo
for	to	the	not	quickly	to be shaken	you	in

2.a.Txt: 06D-corr,018K 020L,025P,byz.
Var: 01ℵ,02A,03B 06D-org,Lach,Treg,Alf Word,Tisc,We/Ho,Weis Sod,UBS/✱

3450.2 art gen sing	3426.2 noun gen sing masc	3250.1 conj	3234.1 adv	2337.2 verb inf pres mid	3250.1 conj
τοῦ	νοὸς,	⸂ μήτε	[a✱ μηδὲ]	θροεῖσθαι,	μήτε
tou	noos	mēte	mēde	throeisthai	mēte
the	mind,	nor	[idem]	to be troubled,	neither

1217.2 prep	4011.2 noun gen sing neu	3250.1 conj	1217.2 prep	3030.2 noun gen sing masc	3250.1 conj	1217.1 prep
διὰ	πνεύματος,	μήτε	διὰ	λόγου,	μήτε	δι'
dia	pneumatos	mēte	dia	logou	mēte	di'
by	spirit,	nor	by	word,	nor	by

1976.2 noun gen sing fem	5453.1 conj	1217.1 prep	2231.2 prs-pron gen 1pl	5453.1 conj	3617.1 conj	1748.1 verb 3sing indic perf act
ἐπιστολῆς	ὡς	δι'	ἡμῶν,	ὡς	ὅτι	ἐνέστηκεν
epistolēs	hōs	di'	hēmōn	hōs	hoti	enestēken
epistle,	as if	by	us,	as	that	is present

3450.9 art nom sing fem	2232.2 noun nom sing fem	3450.2 art gen sing	5382.2 name gen masc	2935.2 noun gen sing masc
ἡ	ἡμέρα	τοῦ	⸂ Χριστοῦ.	[b✱ κυρίου.]
hē	hēmera	tou	Christou	kuriou
the	day	of the	Christ.	[Lord.]

2.b.Txt: 06D-corr,018K byz.
Var: 01ℵ,02A,03B 06D-org,020L,025P,33 Gries,Lach,Treg,Alf Word,Tisc,We/Ho,Weis Sod,UBS/✱

3231.1 partic	4948.3 indef-pron nom sing	5050.4 prs-pron acc 2pl	1802.4 verb 3sing subj aor act	2567.3 prep	3235.4 num card acc masc
3. Μή	τις	ὑμᾶς	ἐξαπατήσῃ	κατὰ	μηδένα
Mē	tis	humas	exapatēsē	kata	mēdena
Not	anyone	you	should deceive	in	not any

4999.3 noun acc sing masc	3617.1 conj	1430.1 partic	3231.1 partic	2048.8 verb 3sing subj aor act	3450.9 art nom sing fem
τρόπον·	ὅτι	ἐὰν	μὴ	ἔλθῃ	ἡ
tropon	hoti	ean	mē	elthē	hē
way,	because	if	not	shall have come	the

640.1 noun nom sing fem	4270.1 adv	2504.1 conj	596.8 verb 3sing subj aor pass	3450.5 art nom sing masc
ἀποστασία	πρῶτον	καὶ	ἀποκαλυφθῇ	ὁ
apostasia	prōton	kai	apokaluphthē	ho
apostasy	first,	and	shall have been revealed	the

3.a.Txt: 02A,06D,018K 020L,025P,byz.it.Weis Sod
Var: 01ℵ,03B,sa.bo. Treg,Tisc,We/Ho UBS/✱

442.1 noun nom sing masc	3450.10 art gen sing fem	264.1 noun fem	455.2 noun gen sing fem	3450.5 art nom sing masc
ἄνθρωπος	τῆς	⸂ ἁμαρτίας,	[a✱ ἀνομίας,]	ὁ
anthrōpos	tēs	hamartias	anomias	ho
man	of the	sin,	[lawlessness,]	the

5048.1 noun nom sing masc	3450.10 art gen sing fem	677.2 noun gen sing fem	3450.5 art nom sing masc	477.2 verb nom sing masc part pres mid	2504.1 conj
υἱὸς	τῆς	ἀπωλείας,	4. ὁ	ἀντικείμενος	καὶ
huios	tēs	apōleias	ho	antikeimenos	kai
son	of the	perdition,	the	opposing	and

When Paul speaks of the "coming of our Lord Jesus Christ," he is referring to the entire scope of the Second Coming. It is the reason for his advice in the following verses.

2:2. Instead of acting like intelligent people with sound judgment, the Thessalonian Christians were departing from their senses like a ship blown from its moorings. Thus they were disturbed (frightened, agitated) and filled with feverish anxieties.

The cause of all this confusion was the false teaching spread by people who claimed to have authority both from the Holy Spirit and from Paul. They seem to have produced forged letters purporting to come from Paul upholding their new teaching, which was that the Day of Christ (the period of time in which Christ will bring His judgments) had already come. Thus they taught that the persecutions and tribulations the Thessalonians were then experiencing were part of the Day of Christ, and they could not therefore be encouraged by the prospect of a literal rapture of believers. It is possible also that these false teachers taught that Christ had already returned spiritually, thus ignoring the plain statement of Acts 1:11.

Some of the older manuscripts have "the day of the *Lord*"instead of *Christ*. This then refers to the Old Testament use of this expression as a period of divine judgment at the end time.

2:3. No matter how logical the false teachers might have seemed, they were still wrong. The Day of the Lord could not have come because there must be a falling away first, and the "man of sin," the "son of perdition," must be revealed. Some take "first" in the sense of "prior," that is, before the Day of Christ. A more common meaning of "first," however, is first in sequence. That is, the first thing after the Day of the Lord begins will be the falling away and the revealing of the man of sin. Since these had not happened, the Day of Christ had not yet begun, and the Thessalonians could still expect the Rapture.

Some take the falling away to mean religious apostasy, a great abandonment of spiritual religion that will give the Antichrist opportunity to take over. Others take it to be a rebellion against truth and justice, a defiance of God's authority among all nations.

Dr. E. Schuler English suggests another possibility: that the word *apostasia* has a secondary meaning of "take away" and might point to the rapture of the Church. (See *Overview*, p.558 and the word study at *apostasia*, number 640.)

Some ancient manuscripts have "man of lawlessness" instead of "man of sin." This person will put himself above the law and make his will supreme as an absolute dictator. His reign will be short however. He is also the son of perdition, that is, he is doomed to eternal loss just as Judas was (John 17:12). This does not mean Judas will come back as the Antichrist. (See *Overview*, pp. 558-560.)

and [by] our gathering together unto him: . . . and our assembling to Him, *Concordant* . . . to meet him, *Montgomery* . . . and our final muster before Him, *Williams.*

2. That ye be not soon shaken in mind, or be troubled: Do not be alarmed, *Norlie* . . . to be readily unsettled or disturbed, *Berkeley* . . . not to allow your minds to be alarmed or quickly upset, *SEB* . . . you may not be quickly shaken, *KJII* . . . not to be hastily shaken, *Confraternity* . . . not to be quickly shaken out of your wits, *Montgomery* . . . be not suddenly shaken in mind, *Campbell* . . . shaken from your composure, *NASB* . . . not lightly to let your minds become unsettled, *TCNT* . . . or worried, *NLT* . . . nor even be excited, *Williams* . . . nor excited, *Klingensmith.*

neither by spirit, nor by word, nor by letter as from us: . . . by the talk you hear, *NLT* . . . or by a message, *Montgomery* . . . or by letter attributed to us, *Confraternity* . . . or by a letter allegedly from us, *Berkeley.*

as that the day of Christ is at hand: . . . the Day of the Lord is here now, *Klingensmith* . . . has already come, *Norlie, SEB* . . . is already here, *Williams.*

3. Let no man deceive you by any means: Do not let anyone fool you, *NLT* . . . lead you into a mistake, *Campbell* . . . by any method, *Concordant.*

for [that day shall not come], except there come a falling away first: . . . for the apostasy is to come, *Berkeley* . . . unless the apostasy comes first, *Confraternity* . . . because the apostasy must first appear, *Campbell* . . . there will be a falling away from the faith, *Norlie* . . . until after the Great Apostasy, *Montgomery* . . . until the great revolt occurs, *Williams* . . . departing, *Tyndale* (1526), *Coverdale, Geneva* (1557), *Beza.*

and that man of sin be revealed, the son of perdition: . . . the son of destruction, *SEB, Klingensmith* . . . and the appearing of that Incarnation of Wickedness, *TCNT.*

5066.2 verb nom sing masc part pres mid
ὑπεραιρόμενος
huperairomenos
exalting himself

1894.3 prep
ἐπὶ
epi
above

3820.1 adj
πάντα
panta
all

2978.29 verb sing part pres mid
λεγόμενον
legomenon
being called

2296.4 noun acc sing masc
θεὸν
theon
God

2211.1 conj
ἢ
ē
or

4429.1 noun sing neu
σέβασμα,
sebasma
object of veneration:

5452.1 conj
ὥστε
hōste
so as

840.6 prs-pron acc sing masc
αὐτὸν
auton
for him

1519.1 prep
εἰς
eis
in

3450.6 art acc sing masc
τὸν
ton
the

3348.4 noun acc sing masc
ναὸν
naon
temple

3450.2 art gen sing
τοῦ
tou

2296.2 noun gen sing masc
θεοῦ
theou
of God

5453.1 conj
(a ὡς
hōs
as

2296.4 noun acc sing masc
Θεὸν ᵕ
Theon
God

2495.12 verb inf aor act
καθίσαι,
kathisai
to sit down,

579.1 verb acc sing masc part pres act
ἀποδεικνύντα
apodeiknunta
setting forth

1431.6 prs-pron acc sing masc
ἑαυτὸν
heauton
himself

3617.1 conj
ὅτι
hoti
that

1498.4 verb 3sing indic pres act
ἔστιν
estin
he is

2296.1 noun nom sing masc
θεός.
theos
God.

3620.3 partic
5. Οὐ
Ou
Not

3285.1 verb 2pl pres act
μνημονεύετε
mnēmoneuete
do you remember

3617.1 conj
ὅτι
hoti
that,

2068.1 adv
ἔτι
eti
yet

1498.21 verb nom sing masc part pres act
ὢν
ōn
being

4242.1 prep
πρὸς
pros
with

5050.4 prs-pron acc 2pl
ὑμᾶς
humas
you,

3642.18 dem-pron pl neu
ταῦτα
tauta
these things

2978.25 verb indic imperf act
ἔλεγον
elegon
I was saying

5050.3 prs-pron dat 2pl
ὑμῖν;
humin
to you?

2504.1 conj
6. καὶ
kai
And

3431.1 adv
νῦν
nun
now

3450.16 art sing neu
τὸ
to
the

2692.7 verb sing neu part pres act
κατέχον
katechon
restraining

3471.6 verb 2pl indic perf act
οἴδατε,
oidate
you know,

1519.1 prep
εἰς
eis
for

3450.16 art sing neu
τὸ
to
the

596.10 verb inf aor pass
ἀποκαλυφθῆναι
apokaluphthēnai
to be revealed

840.6 prs-pron acc sing masc
αὐτὸν
auton
him

1706.1 prep
ἐν
en
in

3450.3 art dat sing
τῷ
tō
the

1431.4 prs-pron gen sing
(ἑαυτοῦ
heautou
his own

840.3 prs-pron gen sing
[a αὐτοῦ]
autou
[his]

2511.3 noun dat sing masc
καιρῷ.
kairō
time.

3450.16 art sing neu
7. τὸ
to
The

1056.1 conj
γὰρ
gar
for

3328.1 noun sing neu
μυστήριον
mustērion
mystery

2218.1 adv
ἤδη
ēdē
already

1738.8 verb 3sing indic pres mid
ἐνεργεῖται
energeitai
is working

3450.10 art gen sing fem
τῆς
tēs
of the

455.2 noun gen sing fem
ἀνομίας,
anomias
lawlessness;

3303.1 adv
μόνον
monon
only

3450.5 art nom sing masc
ὁ
ho
the

2692.4 verb nom sing masc part pres act
κατέχων
katechōn
restraining

732.1 adv
ἄρτι
arti
at present

2175.1 conj
ἕως
heōs
until

1523.2 prep gen
ἐκ
ek
out of

3189.4 adj gen sing neu
μέσου
mesou
midst

1090.40 verb 3sing subj aor mid
γένηται·
genētai
he be,

2504.1 conj
8. καὶ
kai
and

4966.1 adv
τότε
tote
then

596.11 verb 3sing indic fut pass
ἀποκαλυφθήσεται
apokaluphthēsetai
will be revealed

2:4. Paul wrote that the man of sin will continue long enough to set himself up against "all that is called God" (everything divine) and against every object of worship. He will tear down all the established religions of the world and all the minor religions and cults as well. He will claim to be God and will sit personally in the temple of God, claiming it as his possession. "Temple" (sanctuary) is used by Paul elsewhere of the Church or the Christians. Thus, some think the Antichrist's temple will be the apostate church. However, the sanctuary here is the Holy Place, and it is better to take it as a literal temple.

2:5. Paul had already explained this in his preaching at Thessalonica, but his explanation is not given here.

2:6. "What withholdeth" (or, "holds back") is neuter gender. Many commentators (both ancient and modern) take this to refer to the Roman Empire. Some ancient writers took it to be the preaching of the apostles. But since Paul uses the neuter to refer to the Holy Spirit (because the word *spirit* is neuter), many take it that the power that holds back the revelation of the Antichrist is the Holy Spirit. Having examined the structure of the Greek in this verse, Ellingsworth and Nida offer this translation: "You are experiencing the power which holds the Wicked One back now, so that he will be revealed at the proper time, and not before" (*Helps for Translators*, 17:169). However, they are not dogmatic about the precise interpretation of the verse. They agree with Best who states, "No theory can be held to be satisfactory and as Augustine realized long ago (*The City of God*, 20:19) we must acknowledge our ignorance" (*Black's New Testament Commentaries*, 10:301).

2:7. The many contradictory views on this verse emphasize how little any know. Some interpreters of the "historic school" have held that the masculine "he" refers to the Roman emperor, others the apostle Paul, and still others the popes who stepped into the gap after the fall of Rome. Modern post-Tribulationists may think the withholding power is "law and order." Most pre-Tribulationists hold that the neuter form of verse 6 and the masculine form of verse 7, the power and character which "withholdeth" the Antichrist, is the Holy Spirit.

Some pre-Tribulationists believe the power is the Christian Church. During this age the Holy Spirit works through believers, whose bodies are His temples. As a unit believers comprise a temple of the Spirit (1 Corinthians 3:16; 6:19). Thus the masculine words of verse 7 are thought to refer to the "gathered" believers who are caught up in the Rapture.

At least this is clear: this passage speaks of a power and/or a person strong enough to withhold Satanic influences, so the man of sin cannot be revealed as long as this power is at work in the world.

4. Who opposeth and exalteth himself above all that is called God, or that is worshipped: He will lift himself above all of these things, *SEB.*

so that he as God sitteth in the temple of God, showing himself that he is God: He will go into the temple of God and take his seat there, *Norlie* ... in the house of God, *NLT* ... he places himself in the temple of God, openly exhibiting himself, *Campbell* ... he takes his seat...displaying himself as being God, *NASB* ... setting himself out to be, *KJII* ... with the acclaim that he himself is God, *Berkeley* ... displays himself as actually being God! *TCNT* ... proclaiming himself to be, *Williams* ... claiming that he is God, *SEB.*

5. Remember ye not, that, when I was yet with you, I told you these things?:

6. And now ye know what withholdeth that he might be revealed in his time: ... you know now what the restraining influence is which prevents, *TCNT* ... there is a power that is now holding him back, *Norlie* ... You know the power that is keeping the man of sin back now, *NLT* ... you know the power that is holding him back, *Williams* ... what impedes his being revealed, *Berkeley* ... what restrains him from being revealed, *NASB* ... in his proper time, *Confraternity.*

7. For the mystery of iniquity doth already work: The secret of lawlessness, *SEB* ... is already operating, *Concordant* ... secretly works, *Campbell.*

only he who now letteth [will let], until he be taken out of the way: ... provided only that the who is at present restraining it, *Confraternity* ... only till he who now restrains, *Campbell* ... Someone is holding it back, *SEB* ... now must first be gotten out of the way, *Berkeley.*

2 Thess. 2:9

8.a.Var: 01א,02A
06D-org,020L-corr,025P
33,it.sa.bo.Gries,Lach
Treg,Alf,Word,Tisc
We/Ho,Sod,UBS/☆

8.b.Txt: 06D-corr,018K
020L,byz.
Var: 01א,02A,03B,025P
Lach,Treg,Alf,Tisc
We/Ho,Weis,Sod
UBS/☆

3450.5 art nom sing masc	456.2 adj nom sing masc	3614.6 rel-pron acc sing masc	3450.5 art nom sing masc	2935.1 noun nom sing masc	2400.1 name nom masc
ὁ	ἄνομος,	ὃν	ὁ	κύριος	[ᵃ☆+ Ἰησοῦς]
ho	anomos	hon	ho	kurios	Iēsous
the	lawless,	whom	the	Lord	[Jesus]

353.2 verb 3sing indic fut act	335.17 verb 3sing indic fut act	3450.3 art dat sing	4011.3 noun dat sing neu	3450.2 art gen sing
ἀναλώσει	[ᵇ☆ ἀνελεῖ]	τῷ	πνεύματι	τοῦ
analōsei	anelei	tō	pneumati	tou
will consume	[will destroy]	with the	breath	of the

4601.2 noun gen sing neu	840.3 prs-pron gen sing	2504.1 conj	2643.8 verb 3sing indic fut act	3450.11 art dat sing fem	1999.2 noun dat sing fem
στόματος	αὐτοῦ,	καὶ	καταργήσει	τῇ	ἐπιφανείᾳ
stomatos	autou	kai	katargēsei	tē	epiphaneia
mouth	his,	and	will abolish	by the	appearing

3450.10 art gen sing fem	3814.2 noun gen sing fem	840.3 prs-pron gen sing	3614.2 rel-pron gen sing	1498.4 verb 3sing indic pres act	3450.9 art nom sing fem
τῆς	παρουσίας	αὐτοῦ·	9. οὗ	ἐστιν	ἡ
tēs	parousias	autou	hou	estin	hē
of the	coming	his;	whose	is	the

3814.1 noun nom sing fem	2567.1 prep	1737.2 noun acc sing fem	3450.2 art gen sing	4423.2 noun sing masc
παρουσία	κατ'	ἐνέργειαν	τοῦ	Σατανᾶ
parousia	kat'	energeian	tou	Satana
coming	according to	working		of Satan

1706.1 prep	3820.11 adj dat sing fem	1405.3 noun dat sing fem	2504.1 conj	4447.4 noun dat pl neu	2504.1 conj	4907.3 noun dat pl neu
ἐν	πάσῃ	δυνάμει	καὶ	σημείοις	καὶ	τέρασιν
en	pasē	dunamei	kai	sēmeiois	kai	terasin
in	every	power	and	signs	and	wonders

10.a.Txt: 01א-corr,06D
018K,020L,025P,byz.
Var: 01א-org,02A,03B
33,Lach,Treg,Alf,Word
Tisc,We/Ho,Weis,Sod
UBS/☆

5414.2 noun gen sing neu	2504.1 conj	1706.1 prep	3820.11 adj dat sing fem	535.3 noun dat sing fem	3450.10 art gen sing fem
ψεύδους,	10. καὶ	ἐν	πάσῃ	ἀπάτῃ	[ᵃ τῆς]
pseudous	kai	en	pasē	apatē	tēs
of falsehood,	and	in	every	deceit	of the

10.b.Txt: 01א-corr
06D-corr,018K,020L
byz.
Var: 01א-org,02A,03B
06D-org,33,it.bo.Lach
Treg,Alf,Word,Tisc
We/Ho,Weis,Sod
UBS/☆

92.2 noun gen sing fem	1706.1 prep	3450.4 art dat pl	616.19 verb dat pl masc part pres mid	470.1 prep
ἀδικίας	[ᵇ ἐν]	τοῖς	ἀπολλυμένοις,	ἀνθ'
adikias	en	tois	apollumenois	anth'
unrighteousness	in	the	perishing,	on account of

3614.1 rel-pron gen pl	3450.12 art acc sing fem	26.4 noun acc sing fem	3450.10 art gen sing fem	223.2 noun gen sing fem	3620.2 partic
ὧν	τὴν	ἀγάπην	τῆς	ἀληθείας	οὐκ
hōn	tēn	agapēn	tēs	alētheias	ouk
whom	the	love	of the	truth	not

1203.8 verb 3pl indic aor mid	1519.1 prep	3450.16 art sing neu	4834.28 verb inf aor pass	840.8 prs-pron acc pl masc	2504.1 conj
ἐδέξαντο	εἰς	τὸ	σωθῆναι	αὐτούς·	11. καὶ
edexanto	eis	to	sōthēnai	autous	kai
they received	for	to	to be saved	them.	And

11.a.Txt: 01א-corr
06D-corr,018K,020L
025P,byz.bo.
Var: 01א-org,02A,03B
06D-org,33,Lach,Treg
Alf,Word,Tisc,We/Ho
Weis,Sod,UBS/☆

1217.2 prep	3642.17 dem-pron sing neu	3854.18 verb 3sing indic fut act	3854.23 verb 3sing indic pres act	840.2 prs-pron dat pl
διὰ	τοῦτο	πέμψει	[ᵃ☆ πέμπει]	αὐτοῖς
dia	touto	pempsei	pempei	autois
on account of	this	will send	[is sending]	to them

2:8. When this restraining influence is removed, the Antichrist, that wicked or lawless one, will immediately be revealed. But even at that very time his doom will already be sealed. When He comes in flaming fire (1:7,8), Jesus will consume (destroy) him with the spirit (breath) of His mouth. The way Jesus will destroy the Wicked One parallels the actions of the Lord Jehovah in Isaiah 11:4: "He shall smite the earth with the rod of his mouth, and with the breath of his lips shall he slay the wicked." (See also Revelation 19:15.) One word from the Lord is all it will take.

Two closely related words are used to describe the coming of Christ, *epiphaneia* ("appearing") and *parousia* ("coming"). Marshall points out that *epiphaneia* was used in the Septuagint to describe an epiphany or revelation of God (2 Samuel 7:23; 2 Maccabees 2:21; 3:24). He further states that it was used in Hellenistic Greek to describe visits from emperors and other dignitaries (*New Century Bible*, 43:200). It was also applied to the Christ's first coming (see 2 Timothy 1:10). *Parousia* is the common term used to describe the second coming of Christ.

The very brightness of Christ's coming, a glory which blesses the believers, will help bring violent destruction to the Antichrist and his armies.

2:9. To the people who do not know the Antichrist is doomed, his coming will seem supernatural. It is also called a "coming" (*parousia*, presence). It will be according to the working or energizing of Satan in all sorts of deeds of power, miraculous signs, and amazing wonders. But all these will be lies. ("Lying" applies to all three. See John 8:44.) Satan will use these signs and lying wonders to get the attention of the people of the world.

2:10. These false signs and wonders will entice those who make pleasure or money their god. The Antichrist will tempt them with every kind of wicked deception. The connotation of this ties it in with the seduction that comes from wealth (Matthew 13:22), sin (Hebrews 3:13), reveling in deceptive pleasures (2 Peter 2:13), and every kind of deceitful lust (Ephesians 4:22).

This seductive deception will be effective in those who are *already* perishing, lost, gone astray, already on the broad road leading to destruction (Matthew 7:13).

Satan's false signs will also deceive those who did not welcome the love of the truth that they might be saved. That is, they did not become real disciples of Jesus but continued to follow their own ways. (Compare John 8:31,32.)

"Saved" here does not refer to conversion, however, but to the salvation and inheritance which will be believers' when they are changed into Christ's likeness.

2:11. Because they have no love for the truth God will send them a strong, deluding influence. Bruce says that "a power is set in

8. And then shall that Wicked be revealed: ... the representative of lawlessness, *Williams* ... the lawless one, *Klingensmith, Montgomery.*

whom the Lord shall consume with the spirit of his mouth: ... will despatch with, *Concordant* ... will destroy him with, *Williams* ... with the breath of, *Berkeley, Montgomery* ... of his lips, *TCNT.*

and shall destroy with the brightness of his coming: ... and rub him out, *Klingensmith* ... and put a stop to his operations by, *Williams* ... by the appearance of, *NASB* ... the brightness of his appearing, *Montgomery.*

9. [Even him],' whose coming is after the working of Satan: Satan will use this man of sin, *NLT* ... whose coming is according to the energy of Satan, *Montgomery.*

with all power and signs and lying wonders: He will use all kinds of false powers, proofs, and miracles, *SEB* ... in the shape of all kinds of deceptive miracles, *TCNT* ... with his plenitude of power and pretended signs and wonders, *Williams* ... with pretended signs and miracles, *Norlie* ... many powerful works that will be false, *NLT* ... all of them false, *Berkeley.*

10. And with all deceivableness of unrighteousness in them that perish: ... with all the deception of wickedness, *NASB* ... with every seduction of injustice, *Concordant.*

because they received not the love of the truth, that they might be saved: ... because they did not welcome, *Berkeley* ... because they did not receive the love of the truth for their salvation, *Montgomery.*

11. And for this cause God shall send them strong delusion: It is because of this refusal, *Norlie* ... a working of error, *KJII* ... a deluding influence, *NASB* ... a deceiving power, *SEB.*

3450.5 art nom sing masc ὁ ho	2296.1 noun nom sing masc θεὸς theos God	1737.2 noun acc sing fem ἐνέργειαν energeian a working	3967.2 noun gen sing fem πλάνης, planēs of error,	1519.1 prep εἰς eis for	3450.16 art sing neu τὸ to the

3961.36 verb inf aor act πιστεῦσαι pisteusai to believe	840.8 prs-pron acc pl masc αὐτοὺς autous them	3450.3 art dat sing τῷ tō the	5414.3 noun dat sing neu ψεύδει· pseudei lie,	**12.** 2419.1 conj ἵνα hina that	2892.36 verb 3pl subj aor pass κριθῶσιν krithōsin may be judged

12.a.Txt: 03B,06D,044 byz.
Var: 01ℵ,02A,010F 012G,33,81,104,1739

3820.7 adj nom pl masc ✶ πάντες pantes all	533.4 adj nom pl masc [a ἅπαντες] hapantes [idem]	3450.7 art nom pl masc οἱ hoi the	3231.1 partic μὴ mē not	3961.31 verb nom pl masc part aor act πιστεύσαντες pisteusantes having believed

12.b.Txt: 01ℵ-corr,02A 06D-corr,018K,020L 025P,byz.
Var: 01ℵ-org,03B 06D-org,33,Treg,Tisc We/Ho,Weis,Sod UBS/✶

3450.11 art dat sing fem τῇ tē the	223.3 noun dat sing fem ἀληθείᾳ, alētheia truth,	233.1 conj ἀλλ' all' but	233.2 conj [✶ ἀλλὰ] alla [idem]	2085.10 verb nom pl masc part aor act εὐδοκήσαντες eudokēsantes having delighted	1706.1 prep [b ἐν] en in

3450.11 art dat sing fem τῇ tē the	92.3 noun dat sing fem ἀδικίᾳ. adikia unrighteousness.	**13.** 2231.1 prs-pron nom 1pl Ἡμεῖς Hēmeis We	1156.2 conj δὲ de but	3648.4 verb 1pl indic pres act ὀφείλομεν opheilomen ought	

2149.8 verb inf pres act εὐχαριστεῖν eucharistein to give thanks	3450.3 art dat sing τῷ tō	2296.3 noun dat sing masc θεῷ theō to God	3704.1 adv πάντοτε pantote always	3875.1 prep περὶ peri concerning	5050.2 prs-pron gen 2pl ὑμῶν, humōn you,

79.6 noun nom pl masc ἀδελφοὶ adelphoi brothers	25.30 verb nom pl masc part perf mid ἠγαπημένοι ēgapēmenoi having been loved	5097.3 prep ὑπὸ hupo by	2935.2 noun gen sing masc κυρίου, kuriou Lord,	3617.1 conj ὅτι hoti that	141.1 verb 3sing indic aor mid εἵλετο heileto chose

13.a.Txt: 018K,byz.
Var: 01ℵ,02A,03B,06D 020L,025P,33,Gries Lach,Treg,Alf,Word Tisc,We/Ho,Weis,Sod UBS/✶

141.4 verb 3sing indic aor mid [a✶ εἵλατο] heilato [idem]	5050.4 prs-pron acc 2pl ὑμᾶς humas you	3450.5 art nom sing masc ὁ ho	2296.1 noun nom sing masc θεὸς theos God	570.2 prep ἀπ' ap' from	741.2 noun gen sing fem ἀρχῆς archēs beginning

13.b.Txt: 01ℵ,06D,018K 020L,byz.Tisc,We/Ho
Var: 03B,025P,33,Lach Weis,Sod,UBS/✶

532.2 noun acc sing fem [b✶ ἀπαρχὴν] aparchēn [firstfruit]	1519.1 prep εἰς eis to	4843.3 noun acc sing fem σωτηρίαν sōtērian salvation	1706.1 prep ἐν en in	38.2 noun dat sing masc ἁγιασμῷ hagiasmō sanctification	

4011.2 noun gen sing neu πνεύματος pneumatos of Spirit	2504.1 conj καὶ kai and	3963.3 noun dat sing fem πίστει pistei belief	223.2 noun gen sing fem ἀληθείας, alētheias of truth;	**14.** 1519.1 prep εἰς eis to	3614.16 rel-pron sing neu ὃ ho which

14.a.Var: 01ℵ,025P,Tisc Weis,Sod,UBS/✶

2504.1 conj [a+ καὶ] kai [also]	2535.9 verb 3sing indic aor act ἐκάλεσεν ekalesen he called	5050.4 prs-pron acc 2pl ὑμᾶς humas you	1217.2 prep διὰ dia by	3450.2 art gen sing τοῦ tou the	2077.2 noun gen sing neu εὐαγγελίου euangeliou good news

operation within them which makes them prone to embrace error" (*Word Biblical Commentary*, 45:174). This will lead them to "believe a lie" (literally *the lie*, not any lie that happens to come along, but the big lie, the false claims and pretensions of the Antichrist).

2:12. The result will be that all who have not welcomed the love of the truth will "be damned" (judged, called to account, and condemned). The first and most important ground for their judgment will be the fact that they did not believe (and obey) the truth. Second, they took "pleasure in unrighteousness." They approved, considered good, took delight in, and sought satisfaction in wrong-doing, injustice, wickedness, and evil. In other words, they kept going along with sin, considered it normal, and promoted it as desirable. Strong delusion is already making many believe that those who practice the works of the flesh can still be acceptable to God. But the Bible clearly warns that "they which do such things shall not inherit the kingdom of God" (Galatians 5:19-21). God expects believers to cultivate the fruit of the Spirit and crucify the flesh with its affections and lusts or desires (Galatians 5:22-24). Those who do not do so will be well prepared to accept the Antichrist's false claims.

12. That they all might be damned: . . . that all may be, *Adams* . . . they all should be condemned, *Montgomery* . . . might be judged, *Wuest*.
who believed not the truth: . . . who do not trust to, *Fenton* . . . who are faithless to the truth, *Montgomery*.
but had pleasure in unrighteousness: . . . but delight in evil, *Norlie* . . . They enjoyed sin, *SEB* . . . but take pleasure in injustice, *Klingensmith* . . . in wickedness, *Wuest*.

2:13. Paul did not dwell long on the deceptions of the Antichrist. He quickly went on to say in a positive way how he felt bound (under obligation) to keep giving thanks at all times for his brothers (and sisters). They had received the love of the truth. They were loved not merely by Paul, but also by the Lord. In contrast to those who will be deceived by the Antichrist, they will be brought into salvation. God has chosen them for this end. God's purpose for believers is not only that they enjoy salvation but also reach Christian maturity.

God has not only chosen that believers be brought into ultimate salvation where they will be changed into Christ's likeness (1 John 3:2), He has also chosen the means to bring them to this goal. They only reach the goal through a continued sanctification by the Spirit and a steadfast belief of the truth. The Holy Spirit consecrates believers and separates them from sin, and at the same time He separates them to God and to obedience to His will. He also gives help and power to live a holy (dedicated) life. The believer's part is a continued faith in the truth, a faithful, obedient acceptance and practice of the truth.

13. But we are bound to give thanks alway to God for you: I ought to give thanks to God continually, *Montgomery* . . . we have a sense of moral obligation to be giving thanks to God, *Wuest*.
brethren beloved of the Lord: . . . brothers dear to the Lord, *Adams* . . . whom the Lord loves, *Montgomery*.
because God hath from the beginning chosen you to salvation: . . . from the rest of mankind, *Wuest* . . . planned for you to be saved, *SEB* . . . for salvation, *Adams*.
through sanctification of the Spirit and belief of the truth: . . . in consecration of, *Montgomery* . . . and by faith in the truth, *Adams*.

2:14. The means by which God called the Thessalonians to this salvation was Paul's preaching of the one true gospel ("good news"). It was the same gospel preached by the other apostles (Galatians 1:16,17; 2:2). Any other "gospel" can only bring a curse (Galatians 1:7-9).

2231.2 prs-pron gen 1pl	1519.1 prep	3910.2 noun acc sing fem	1385.2 noun gen sing fem	3450.2 art gen sing	2935.2 noun gen sing masc
ἡμῶν,	εἰς	περιποίησιν	δόξης	τοῦ	κυρίου
hēmōn	eis	peripoiēsin	doxēs	tou	kuriou
our,	to	obtaining	of glory	of the	Lord

2231.2 prs-pron gen 1pl	2400.2 name masc gen masc	5382.2 name gen masc		679.1 partic	3631.1 partic	79.6 noun nom pl masc
ἡμῶν	Ἰησοῦ	Χριστοῦ.	**15.** ἄρα	οὖν,	ἀδελφοί,
hēmōn	Iēsou	Christou.	ara	oun,	adelphoi,
our	Jesus	Christ.	So	then,	brothers,

4590.1 verb 2pl pres act	2504.1 conj	2875.1 verb 2pl pres act	3450.15 art acc pl fem	3724.4 noun acc pl fem	3614.15 rel-pron acc pl fem
στήκετε,	καὶ	κρατεῖτε	τὰς	παραδόσεις	ἃς
stēkete	kai	krateite	tas	paradoseis	has
stand firm,	and	hold fast	the	traditions	which

1315.23 verb 2pl indic aor pass	1521.1 conj	1217.2 prep	3030.2 noun gen sing masc	1521.1 conj	1217.1 prep
ἐδιδάχθητε,	εἴτε	διὰ	λόγου	εἴτε	δι'
edidachthēte	eite	dia	logou	eite	di'
you were taught,	whether	by	word	or	by

1976.2 noun gen sing fem	2231.2 prs-pron gen 1pl	840.5 prs-pron nom sing masc	1156.2 conj	3450.5 art nom sing masc	2935.1 noun nom sing masc
ἐπιστολῆς	ἡμῶν.	**16.** Αὐτὸς	δὲ	ὁ	κύριος
epistolēs	hēmōn.	Autos	de	ho	kurios
epistle	our.	Himself	but	the	Lord

2231.2 prs-pron gen 1pl	2400.1 name nom masc	5382.1 name nom masc	2504.1 conj	3450.5 art nom sing masc	2296.1 noun nom sing masc	2504.1 conj
ἡμῶν	Ἰησοῦς	Χριστὸς,	καὶ	ὁ	θεὸς	ʿ καὶ
hēmōn	Iēsous	Christos	kai	ho	theos	kai
our	Jesus	Christ,	and	the	God	and

3450.5 art nom sing masc	3824.1 noun nom sing masc	2231.2 prs-pron gen 1pl	3450.5 art nom sing masc	25.20 verb nom sing masc part aor act	2231.4 prs-pron acc 1pl
[ᵃ✦ ὁ]	πατὴρ	ἡμῶν,	ὁ	ἀγαπήσας	ἡμᾶς
ho	patēr	hēmōn,	ho	agapēsas	hēmas
[the]	Father	our,	the	having loved	us,

2504.1 conj	1319.28 verb nom sing masc part aor act	3735.4 noun acc sing fem	164.6 adj acc sing fem	2504.1 conj	1667.4 noun acc sing fem
καὶ	δοὺς	παράκλησιν	αἰωνίαν	καὶ	ἐλπίδα
kai	dous	paraklēsin	aiōnian	kai	elpida
and	having given	encouragement	eternal	and	hope

18.12 adj acc sing fem	1706.1 prep	5322.3 noun dat sing fem	3731.15 verb 3sing opt aor act	5050.2 prs-pron gen 2pl
ἀγαθὴν	ἐν	χάριτι,	**17.** παρακαλέσαι	ὑμῶν
agathēn	en	chariti,	parakalesai	humōn
good	by	grace,	may he encourage	your

3450.15 art acc pl fem	2559.1 noun fem	2504.1 conj	4592.2 verb 3sing opt aor act	5050.4 prs-pron acc 2pl	1706.1 prep
τὰς	καρδίας,	καὶ	στηρίξαι	ʿᵃ ὑμᾶς ʾ	ἐν
tas	kardias,	kai	stērixai	humas	en
the	hearts,	and	may he establish	you	in

3820.3 adj dat sing	3030.3 noun dat sing masc	2504.1 conj	2024.3 noun dat sing neu	2024.3 noun dat sing neu	2504.1 conj	3030.3 noun dat sing masc
παντὶ	ʿ λόγῳ	καὶ	ἔργῳ	[✦ ἔργῳ	καὶ	λόγῳ]
panti	logō	kai	ergō	ergō	kai	logō
every	word	and	work	[work	and	word]

The fulfillment of this salvation will be when Christians enter into the full possession of the glory of our Lord Jesus Christ. All who keep believing will enter the glory (Ephesians 1:4-10). Also implied here is the truth clearly expressed at Philippians 3:21 which says that Christ "shall change our vile body, that it may be fashioned like unto his glorious body."

2:15. In view of the glory to come, Paul challenged the Thessalonians to stand fast and keep holding on to the traditions (teachings) taught them by the Word (in his preaching) and in his epistles. Human traditions are not meant here. The word "traditions" in this case speaks of teachings handed down from God through Jesus. Paul was emphasizing that his teachings did not come from his own mind. He was simply passing along the message handed down by the Lord. Like the Old Testament prophets who spoke for God, he was not free to change it or mix in any of his own ideas. (See 2 Peter 1:20,21.)

For believers, this means taking a stand on and being true to the entire Bible. Careful examination of the Book of Acts and the Epistles shows that Paul and all the apostles preached the truths recorded in the four Gospels, truths Jesus repeated again and again in the many places where He preached and taught. They also preached the gospel from the Old Testament which was the only written Bible they had.

2:16. To his exhortation to stand firm, Paul added a prayer. In the final analysis, Christians cannot stand in their own strength or hold to the Scriptures through their own understanding. Believers need Jesus Christ himself and God the Father to help them. They can expect God to do this because of His love. He demonstrated and proved His love by giving His Son to die on Calvary (John 3:16). He pours that love into the believer's heart when He gives him the Spirit (Romans 5:5).

Believers have further assurance that God will always encourage and strengthen them because He has already given them everlasting consolation (eternal, unfailing, inexhaustible comfort and encouragement) and a "good hope" by His grace (His unmerited, undeserved favor).

2:17. As Christians stand firm, holding on to the teachings of God's Word, they can expect God and Christ to comfort (encourage) their hearts and to strengthen and confirm or firmly fix them, not merely in their minds, but in every good word and work. (Here some important ancient manuscripts place "work" before "word." This is the correct order for the Christian witness. The believer's works must be established in the grace of God before his words can mean very much.)

to the obtaining of the glory of our Lord Jesus Christ: . . . that you might secure for yourselves, *Adams* . . . resulting in your acquisition of, *Wuest.*

15. Therefore, brethren, stand fast: Consequently, then, *Concordant* . . . So then...be constantly standing firmly, *Wuest* . . . stand steady, *Klingensmith.*

and hold the traditions which ye have been taught: . . . and hold fast the teachings, *Montgomery* . . . and hold on to that which we have taught you, *Klingensmith* . . . hold on to the instructions you learned, *Berkeley* . . . and keep a tight grip on the teachings, *Williams* . . . that you were taught by us, *Adams* . . . which you were taught either orally or through our letter, *Wuest.*

whether by word, or our epistle: . . . by word of mouth, *Montgomery* . . . or letter, *Campbell.*

16. Now our Lord Jesus Christ himself, and God, even our Father, which hath loved us:

and hath given [us] everlasting consolation: . . . and has graciously given us, *Williams* . . . gave us unfailing comfort, *TCNT* . . . and gives us ageless encouragement, *Klingensmith* . . . eternal encouragement, *Montgomery* . . . everlasting encouragement, *Wuest.*

and good hope through grace: . . . and well-grounded hope, *Berkeley* . . . this gift having been given us in [His] grace, *Wuest.*

17. Comfort your hearts: . . . encourage your hearts, *Adams, Wuest.*

and stablish you in every good word and work: . . . and stabilize them in the sphere of, *Wuest* . . . and support you, *Adams* . . . will make you strong in, *SEB* . . . strengthen you in every good thing you do or say, *Williams.*

2 Thess. 3:1

18.4 adj dat sing	3450.16 art sing neu	3036.8 adj sing neu	4195.1 verb 2pl pres mid	79.6 noun nom pl masc
ἀγαθῷ. agathō good.	3:1. Τὸ To The	λοιπὸν, loipon rest,	προσεύχεσθε, proseuchesthe pray,	ἀδελφοί, adelphoi brothers,

3875.1 prep	2231.2 prs- pron gen 1pl	2419.1 conj	3450.5 art nom sing masc	3030.1 noun nom sing masc	3450.2 art gen sing	2935.2 noun gen sing masc
περὶ peri for	ἡμῶν, hēmōn us,	ἵνα hina that	ὁ ho the	λόγος logos word	τοῦ tou of the	κυρίου kuriou Lord

4983.4 verb 3sing subj pres act	2504.1 conj	1386.20 verb 3sing subj pres mid	2503.1 conj	2504.1 conj	4242.1 prep	5050.4 prs- pron acc 2pl
τρέχῃ trechē may run	καὶ kai and	δοξάζηται, doxazētai may be glorified,	καθὼς kathōs even as	καὶ kai also	πρὸς pros with	ὑμᾶς, humas you;

2504.1 conj	2419.1 conj	4363.8 verb 1pl subj aor pass	570.3 prep	3450.1 art gen pl	818.1 adj gen pl masc
2. καὶ kai and	ἵνα hina that	ῥυσθῶμεν rhusthōmen we may be delivered	ἀπὸ apo from	τῶν tōn the	ἀτόπων atopōn perverse

2504.1 conj	4050.4 adj gen pl	442.7 noun gen pl masc	3620.3 partic	1056.1 conj	3820.4 adj gen pl	3450.9 art nom sing fem
καὶ kai and	πονηρῶν ponērōn wicked	ἀνθρώπων· anthrōpōn men,	οὐ ou not	γὰρ gar for	πάντων pantōn of all	ἡ hē the

3963.1 noun nom sing fem	3964.2 adj nom sing masc	1156.2 conj	1498.4 verb 3sing indic pres act	3450.5 art nom sing masc	2935.1 noun nom sing masc
πίστις. pistis faith.	3. πιστὸς pistos Faithful	δέ de but	ἐστιν estin is	ὁ ho the	κύριος, kurios Lord,

3614.5 rel-pron nom sing masc	4592.5 verb 3sing indic fut act	5050.4 prs- pron acc 2pl	2504.1 conj	5278.14 verb 3sing indic fut act	570.3 prep
ὃς hos who	στηρίξει stērixei will establish	ὑμᾶς humas you	καὶ kai and	φυλάξει phulaxei will guard	ἀπὸ apo from

3450.2 art gen sing	4050.2 adj gen sing	3844.11 verb 1pl indic perf act	1156.2 conj	1706.1 prep	2935.3 noun dat sing masc
τοῦ tou the	πονηροῦ. ponērou evil.	4. πεποίθαμεν pepoithamen We have trusted	δὲ de but	ἐν en in	κυρίῳ kuriō Lord

1894.1 prep	5050.4 prs- pron acc 2pl	3617.1 conj	3614.17 rel- pron pl neu	3715.3 verb 1pl indic pres act	5050.3 prs- pron dat 2pl
ἐφ' eph' as to	ὑμᾶς, humas you,	ὅτι hoti that	ἃ ha which	παραγγέλλομεν parangellomen we charge	[a ὑμῖν,] humin you,

2504.1 conj	4020.2 verb 2pl pres act	2504.1 conj	4020.54 verb 2pl indic fut act	3450.5 art nom sing masc	1156.2 conj
καὶ kai both	ποιεῖτε poieite you are doing	καὶ kai and	ποιήσετε. poiēsete will do.	5. Ὁ Ho The	δὲ de but

2935.1 noun nom sing masc	2690.1 verb 3sing opt aor act	5050.2 prs- pron gen 2pl	3450.15 art acc pl fem	2559.1 noun acc pl fem	1519.1 prep
κύριος kurios Lord	κατευθύναι kateuthunai may direct	ὑμῶν humōn your	τὰς tas the	καρδίας kardias hearts	εἰς eis into

4.a.Txt: 01ℵ,06D-corr
018K,020L,025P,byz.
Var: 01ℵ,03B,06D-org
33,Treg,Alf,Tisc,We/Ho
Weis,Sod,UBS/✶

3:1. "Finally" indicates Paul was changing the subject and bringing this letter to an end with a variety of concluding exhortations.

First, he requested prayer for his situation. Paul and his evangelistic party were having difficulties in Corinth. Opposition was growing. But Paul's chief concern was not for himself, but that the Word of the Lord (the gospel) might have free course. He wanted to see it continue to spread rapidly and without hindrance. He wanted it to advance and be glorified (honored or received with honor). More than anything he wanted to see the gospel triumph. He knew the Thessalonians wanted this too.

3:2. Paul was not blind to the opposition. He knew he was surrounded by unreasonable (perverse, twisted) and wicked (evil, malicious) men. He wanted prayer that he might be delivered (preserved or rescued) from them. This prayer was urgent, "for all men have not faith" (literally, "the faith is not of all"); that is, the gospel had not been received by all. Thus, even in requesting deliverance, his chief concern was not mere self-preservation. He wanted more to hear and believe.

3:3. In spite of the dangers, the evil men, and the difficult circumstances, Paul declared that "the Lord is faithful." He is worthy of trust. Believers can depend on Him and His promises. He will establish (support, confirm, and strengthen) believers. He will keep (guard, defend, protect, and preserve) them from evil (from the Evil One or from that which is evil). "Keep" is really a military term used of one who stands guard. "Evil" most likely means the Evil One, Satan, who instigates evil men to assault believers. What a picture this is: God standing guard for us against the devil, at the same time strengthening us for the battle and putting us on firm footing.

3:4. Paul had no doubts about the faith of the Thessalonian believers. He had full "confidence in the Lord" for (toward) them. Their relation to the Lord as well as his own relationship to them made him confident that they were doing and would continue to do what he had commanded (instructed, directed) them to do. This command or instruction undoubtedly included the request to keep praying for him. But it also anticipates what he was about to command or instruct them to do.

3:5. Paul further prayed that the Lord would direct their "hearts into the love of God" and "into the patient waiting for Christ"; that is, into the patient endurance that Christ showed, or into Christlike

1. Finally, brethren, pray for us, that the word of the Lord may have [free] course: Furthermore, *Concordant* . . . My last words to you, *NLT* . . . In conclusion, *Confraternity* . . . pray on...that God's word may run swiftly, *Montgomery* . . . may make progress, *NAB* . . . may rapidly spread, *Campbell* . . . may spread quickly, and be received with honour, *JB*.

and be glorified, even as [it is] with you: . . . as in your own case, *Montgomery*.

2. And that we may be delivered from unreasonable and wicked men: Pray that we will be rescued from unfair, evil men, *SEB* . . . that we may be kept free from the snares of, *Norlie* . . . from confused and evil men, *NAB* . . . from troublesome and evil men, *Confraternity* . . . from those unbalanced and malicious people, *Berkeley*.

for all [men] have not faith: . . . do not hold the faith, *Montgomery*.

3. But the Lord is faithful:
who shall stablish you, and keep [you] from evil: . . . and guard you from, *Montgomery* . . . He will protect you from the evil one, *SEB*.

4. And we have confidence in the Lord touching you: . . . as regards you, *Confraternity* . . . fully fixed our faith on you, *Montgomery*.

that ye both do and will do the things which we command you: . . . and will continue to do, *Montgomery* . . . what we direct you, *TCNT* . . . whatever we enjoin, *NAB* . . . what we suggested, *Berkeley*.

5. And the Lord direct your hearts into the love of God: May the Lord guide your hearts, *SEB* . . . incline, *Montgomery* . . . lead you to a heartfelt love for God, *TCNT*.

2 Thess. 3:6

5.a.Var: 01ℵ,03B,06D
018K,020L,025P,byz.
Gries,Lach,Treg,Alf
Word,Tisc,We/Ho,Weis
Sod,UBS/✸

3450.12 art acc sing fem	26.4 noun acc sing fem	3450.2 art gen sing	2296.2 noun gen sing masc	2504.1 conj	1519.1 prep	3450.12 art acc sing fem
τὴν tēn the	ἀγάπην agapēn love	τοῦ tou	θεοῦ, theou of God,	καὶ kai and	εἰς eis into	[a✸+ τὴν] tēn [the]

5119.4 noun acc sing fem	3450.2 art gen sing	5382.2 name gen sing	3715.3 verb 1pl indic pres act	1156.2 conj
ὑπομονὴν hupomonēn endurance	τοῦ tou of the	Χριστοῦ. Christou Christ.	6. Παραγγέλλομεν Parangellomen We charge	δὲ de now

5050.3 prs- pron dat 2pl	79.6 noun nom pl masc	1706.1 prep	3549.4 noun dat sing neu	3450.2 art gen sing	2935.2 noun gen sing masc
ὑμῖν, humin you,	ἀδελφοί, adelphoi brothers,	ἐν en in	ὀνόματι onomati name	τοῦ tou of the	κυρίου kuriou Lord

6.a.Txt: 01ℵ,02A
06D-corr,018K,020L
025P,byz.bo.Tisc,Sod
Var: 03B,06D-org,Alf
We/Ho,Weis,UBS/✸

2231.2 prs- pron gen 1pl	2400.2 name masc	5382.2 name gen masc	4575.2 verb inf pres mid	5050.4 prs- pron acc 2pl
(a ἡμῶν) hēmōn our	Ἰησοῦ Iēsou Jesus	Χριστοῦ, Christou Christ,	στέλλεσθαι stellesthai to shun	ὑμᾶς humas you

570.3 prep	3820.2 adj gen sing	79.2 noun gen sing masc	808.1 adv	3906.13 verb gen sing masc part pres act
ἀπὸ apo from	παντὸς pantos every	ἀδελφοῦ adelphou brother	ἀτάκτως ataktōs disorderly	περιπατοῦντος, peripatountos walking,

2504.1 conj	3231.1 partic	2567.3 prep	3450.12 art acc sing fem	3724.2 noun acc sing fem	3614.12 rel- pron acc sing fem
καὶ kai and	μὴ mē not	κατὰ kata according to	τὴν tēn the	παράδοσιν paradosin tradition	ἣν hēn which

6.b.Txt: Steph
Var1: 01ℵ-org,02A
06D-org,33,Gries,Alf
Word,Tisc,Sod
Var2: 03B,Lach,Treg
We/Ho,Weis,UBS/✸

3741.6 verb 3sing indic aor act	3741.16 verb 3pl indic aor act	3741.7 verb 2pl indic aor act	3706.1 prep
(παρέλαβεν parelaben he received	[1b✸ παρελάβοσαν parelabosan [they received	2 παρελάβετε] parelabete you received]	παρ' par' from

2231.2 prs- pron gen 1pl	840.7 prs-pron nom pl masc	1056.1 conj	3471.6 verb 2pl indic perf act	4316.1 adv	1158.1 verb 3sing indic pres act
ἡμῶν. hēmōn us.	7. αὐτοὶ autoi Yourselves	γὰρ gar for	οἴδατε oidate you know	πῶς pōs how	δεῖ dei it is necessary

3265.3 verb inf pres mid	2231.4 prs- pron acc 1pl	3617.1 conj	3620.2 partic	806.1 verb 1pl indic aor act	1706.1 prep
μιμεῖσθαι mimeisthai to imitate	ἡμᾶς· hēmas us,	ὅτι hoti because	οὐκ ouk not	ἠτακτήσαμεν ētaktēsamen we behaved disorderly	ἐν en among

5050.3 prs- pron dat 2pl	3624.1 conj	1425.1 adv	735.4 noun acc sing masc	2052.29 verb 1pl indic aor act	3706.2 prep
ὑμῖν, humin you;	8. οὐδὲ oude nor	δωρεὰν dōrean for donation	ἄρτον arton bread	ἐφάγομεν ephagomen did we eat	παρά para from

4948.1 indef- pron gen sing	233.1 conj	1706.1 prep	2845.3 noun dat sing masc	2504.1 conj	3313.1 noun dat sing masc	3433.4 noun acc sing fem	2504.1 conj
τινος, tinos anyone;	ἀλλ' all' but	ἐν en in	κόπῳ kopō labor	καὶ kai and	μόχθῳ, mochthō toil,	(νύκτα nukta night	καὶ kai and

fortitude and steadfastness. This direction would make their way straight and remove the obstacles which Satan had used to obscure their path (see Rienecker, p.596, on the word *kateuthunai*).

3:6. First Thessalonians 5:14 urged the believers to warn the unruly (the indisciplined, the lazy, the idle, the truants from work and duty). Now it seems that Timothy's report had indicated that a considerable number were pious idlers, too "spiritual" to dirty their hands with manual labor. Instead of working they were busybodies, disorderly, and meddling. This cannot be tolerated in the life of Christians. With utmost seriousness and severity Paul commanded the rest of the Christians in the name of the Lord Jesus Christ not to associate with any who lived without working. Ellingsworth and Nida suggest that the phrase "in the name of the Lord Jesus Christ" is equivalent to saying "as representing our Lord Jesus Christ" or perhaps "on the authority of the Lord Jesus Christ." They state, "In this context, Paul is obviously asserting that he is speaking on behalf of the Lord Jesus Christ" (17:200). The very fact that they were Christians meant the rest of the believers could not ignore the lazy way they were living. The name (person, nature, and character) of Jesus is dishonored by such dereliction of duty. The name (authority) of Jesus as Lord and as Christ (God's Anointed) backed up Paul's command. They were living contrary to the tradition (teaching handed down from Jesus) which Paul had already given them.

and into the patient waiting for Christ: . . . and to a stedfastness like that of, *TCNT* . . . and into a patient endurance like Christ's, *Williams* . . . and the fortitude of Christ, *JB.*

6. Now we command you, brethren, in the name of our Lord Jesus Christ: I summon you, brothers, *Montgomery* . . . we are giving you strict orders, *Norlie* . . . by the authority of, *SEB* . . . on the authority, *Williams.*

that ye withdraw yourselves from every brother that walketh disorderly: . . . to keep away from, *JB* . . . to shun any brother who leads an idle and disorderly life, *Montgomery* . . . stay away from every brother, *Klingensmith* . . . who lives irregularly, *Confraternity* . . . any Christian who is lazy, *NLT* . . . who is a lazy person, a troublemaker, *SEB* . . . who is living as a shirker, *Williams.*

and not after the tradition which he received of us: . . . which is not according to the rule you received from me, *Montgomery.*

3:7. Paul had also set an example which the Thessalonians knew they ought to follow, even imitate. Paul could make this bold command because he was "imitating" Jesus (see 1 Corinthians 11:1, "Be ye followers [i.e., 'imitators'] of me, even as I also am of Christ"). There was nothing lazy about Paul's way of life when he was among them. He never played truant when there was work to do. Neither did he sit around idly and let others do the work when he could help. Even when he was shipwrecked he was concerned about the needs of others and was the first one out to collect more wood for the fire (Acts 28:3).

7. For yourselves know how ye ought to follow us: . . . you know well how you must imitate me, *Montgomery* . . . copy our example, *TCNT.*

for we behaved not ourselves disorderly among you: I did not lead an idle or disorderly life, *Montgomery.*

3:8. When Paul came to Thessalonica to preach the gospel, he did not accept any free meals. He paid room and board, not only for himself, but for his entire evangelistic party. He did this by laboring with constant exertion and hardship day and night. His trade of tentmaking was not an easy one. The purpose of all this toil and struggle to earn a living was that he and his fellow workers for the Lord might not be chargeable or be a burden to any of the believers. Actually, the love of Christ flooded his own heart and flowed out to them.

8. Neither did we eat any man's bread for nought: We were not indebted to anyone, *Norlie* . . . neither did we eat bread gratuitously from anyone, *Concordant* . . . without paying for it, *NLT* . . . without pay, *Berkeley* . . . unless we paid for it! *SEB.*

but wrought with labour and travail night and day: . . . instead, we did hard and heavy work, *Berkeley* . . . laboring to the point of exhaustion, *NAB.*

8.a.**Txt:** 02A,06D,018K
020L,025P,byz.Sod
Var: 01א,03B,33,Lach
Treg,Tisc,We/Ho,Weis
UBS/⋆

2232.4 noun acc sing fem	3433.2 noun gen sing fem	2504.1 conj	2232.1 noun fem	2021.10 verb nom pl masc part pres mid	4242.1 prep
ἡμέραν	[ᵃ⋆ νυκτὸς	καὶ	ἡμέρας]	ἐργαζόμενοι,	πρὸς
hēmeran	nuktos	kai	hēmeras	ergazomenoi	pros
day	[night	and	day]	working,	for

3450.16 art sing neu	3231.1 partic	1897.2 verb inf aor act	4948.5 indef-pron	5050.2 prs-pron gen 2pl	3620.1 partic
τὸ	μὴ	ἐπιβαρῆσαί	τινα	ὑμῶν·	**9.** οὐχ
to	mē	epibarēsai	tina	humōn	ouch
the	not	to be burdensome to	anyone	of you.	Not

3617.1 conj	3620.2 partic	2174.5 verb 1pl indic pres act	1833.4 noun acc sing fem	233.1 conj	2419.1 conj	1431.8 prs-pron acc pl masc
ὅτι	οὐκ	ἔχομεν	ἐξουσίαν,	ἀλλ'	ἵνα	ἑαυτοὺς
hoti	ouk	echomen	exousian	all'	hina	heautous
that	not	we have	authority,	but	that	ourselves

5020.2 noun acc sing masc	1319.21 verb 1pl subj aor act	5050.3 prs-pron dat 2pl	1519.1 prep	3450.16 art sing neu	3265.3 verb inf pres mid
τύπον	δῶμεν	ὑμῖν	εἰς	τὸ	μιμεῖσθαι
tupon	dōmen	humin	eis	to	mimeisthai
a pattern	we might give	to you	for	the	to imitate

2231.4 prs-pron acc 1pl	2504.1 conj	1056.1 conj	3616.1 conj	1498.36 verb 1pl indic imperf act	4242.1 prep	5050.4 prs-pron acc 2pl
ἡμᾶς.	**10.** καὶ	γὰρ	ὅτε	ἦμεν	πρὸς	ὑμᾶς
hēmas	kai	gar	hote	ēmen	pros	humas
us.	Also	for	when	we were	with	you

3642.17 dem-pron sing neu	3715.14 verb 1pl indic imperf act	5050.3 prs-pron dat 2pl	3617.1 conj	1479.1 conj	4948.3 indef-pron nom sing	3620.3 partic
τοῦτο	παρηγγέλλομεν	ὑμῖν,	ὅτι	εἴ	τις	οὐ
touto	parēngellomen	humin	hoti	ei	tis	ou
this	we were charging	you,	that	if	anyone	not

2286.3 verb 3sing indic pres act	2021.12 verb inf pres mid	3234.1 adv	2052.7 verb 3sing impr pres act	189.6 verb 1pl indic pres act
θέλει	ἐργάζεσθαι,	μηδὲ	ἐσθιέτω.	**11.** ἀκούομεν
thelei	ergazesthai	mēde	esthietō	akouomen
does wish	to work,	neither	let him eat.	We hear

1056.1 conj	4948.9 indef-pron acc pl masc	3906.16 verb acc pl masc part pres act	1706.1 prep	5050.3 prs-pron dat 2pl	808.1 adv
γὰρ	τινας	περιπατοῦντας	ἐν	ὑμῖν	ἀτάκτως,
gar	tinas	peripatountas	en	humin	ataktōs
for	some	walking	among	you	disorderly,

3235.6 num card neu	2021.11 verb acc pl masc part pres mid	233.2 conj	3883.1 verb acc pl masc part pres mid
μηδὲν	ἐργαζομένους,	ἀλλὰ	περιεργαζομένους.
mēden	ergazomenous	alla	periergazomenous
not at all	working,	but	being busy bodies.

3450.4 art dat pl	1156.2 conj	4955.3 dem-pron dat pl	3715.3 verb 1pl indic pres act	2504.1 conj
12. τοῖς	δὲ	τοιούτοις	παραγγέλλομεν	καὶ
tois	de	toioutois	parangellomen	kai
To the	now	such	we charge	and

3731.2 verb 1pl indic pres act	1217.2 prep	3450.2 art gen sing	2935.2 noun gen sing masc	2231.2 prs-pron gen 1pl
παρακαλοῦμεν	διὰ	τοῦ	κυρίου	ἡμῶν
parakaloumen	dia	tou	kuriou	hēmōn
exhort	by	the	Lord	our

3:9. By saying that he did not want to be a burden to them, Paul did not mean to give the impression that the work of the ministry should not be supported financially. He had the power (the authority and the right) to ask them to give him all the support he needed. But he waived that right for the sake of a greater spreading of the gospel in new areas. (See 1 Corinthians 9:3-18 where Paul deals with the same subject and shows his concern for the gospel.) In Thessalonica he waived that right also in order to provide believers with an example to follow or imitate. No doubt, there were Thessalonians who would have been glad to contribute to the support of Paul and his fellow laborers, as the believers in Philippi actually did (Philippians 4:15,16). But he knew some would use his example as a pretext for not working. He refused to give them that kind of excuse.

3:10. In addition to setting an example, Paul had repeatedly commanded the Thessalonians that if anyone was not willing to work, neither should he eat. This work ethic was suggested by the fact that Adam was given work to do in the Garden of Eden and by the judgment on Adam that, "In the sweat of thy face shalt thou eat bread" (Genesis 3:19). The Book of Proverbs has many warnings against laziness and characterizes the wise both as fearing the Lord and as industrious. Rabbis in New Testament times insisted that every young rabbi learn a trade, just as Paul had.

3:11. Again and again Paul had heard reports that there were those among the Thessalonian believers who were walking disorderly; that is, living in idleness, accepting no responsibility. Instead of being workers, they were meddlers. Instead of taking care of their own business, they were busybodies, poking their noses into everyone else's business.

Paul used the same word of young widows in writing to Timothy (1 Timothy 5:13). In those days it was practically impossible for widows to get jobs. The law of Moses made provision for them by commanding that gleanings of the harvest be left for them to gather (Deuteronomy 24:19-21). But among the heathen, widows often died of starvation. Thus, from the first, the Church accepted an obligation to support widows (Acts 6:1).

Paul found, however, that this kind of charity was not good for the younger widows. They learned to be idle (lazy, useless, and careless). With time on their hands they visited around and became tattlers or gossipers, spreading foolish chatter and nonsense, and sometimes malicious stories. They also became busybodies. They gave attention to things that were no concern of theirs and became meddlers. For this reason Paul encouraged them to marry again and accept the responsibilities of their own homes.

3:12. Jesus himself did not encourage idleness among His followers. His parables often call men to work in the harvest field.

that we might not be chargeable to any of you: . . . that we might not burden any of you, *Confraternity* . . . so that we would not be a load on any of you, *Klingensmith*.

9. Not because we have not power: Not that we had no claim on you, *NAB* . . . Not that I have no right to be supported, *Williams* . . . we had not a right to receive support, *TCNT* . . . Not that I have no right to such support, *Montgomery*.

but to make ourselves an ensample unto you to follow us: . . . it was simply to give you an example for you to imitate, *Montgomery* . . . but to give you a pattern to imitate us, *Klingensmith* . . . to give you in our conduct a pattern for you to imitate, *Norlie*.

10. For even when we were with you, this we commanded you: I used to charge you, *Montgomery* . . . I gave you this direction, *Williams*.

that if any would not work, neither should he eat: . . . if he refused to do any work, *JB* . . . If a person refuses to work, *SEB, Williams*.

11. For we hear that there are some which walk among you disorderly: But we are informed, *Williams* . . . there are those of your number who are leading idle and disorderly lives, *Montgomery* . . . some of you are wandering dead beats, *Klingensmith*.

working not at all, but are busybodies: . . . loafers, nosey about other people's affairs, *Klingensmith* . . . busy in other folks' affairs, *Berkeley* . . . but are meddling, *Concordant* . . . but prying into other people's affairs, *Campbell*.

12. Now them that are such we command and exhort by our Lord Jesus Christ: . . . and entreat, by the authority, *Montgomery*.

2 Thess. 3:13

12.a.**Txt:** 01ℵ-corr
06D-corr,018K,020L
byz.
Var: 01ℵ-org,02A,03B
06D-org,33,bo.Lach
Treg,Alf,Tisc,We/Ho
Weis,Sod,UBS/✶

2400.2 name masc	5382.2 name gen masc	1706.1 prep	2935.3 noun dat sing masc	2400.2 name masc	5382.3 name dat masc
Ἰησοῦ	Χριστοῦ,	[ᵃ✶ ἐν	κυρίῳ	Ἰησοῦ	Χριστῷ]
Iēsou	Christou	en	kuriō	Iēsou	Christō
Jesus	Christ,	[by	Lord	Jesus	Christ,]

2419.1 conj	3196.3 prep	2249.1 noun gen sing fem	2021.10 verb nom pl masc part pres mid	3450.6 art acc sing masc	1431.2 prs-pron gen pl
ἵνα	μετὰ	ἡσυχίας	ἐργαζόμενοι,	τὸν	ἑαυτῶν
hina	meta	hēsuchias	ergazomenoi	ton	heautōn
that	with	quietness	working,	the	their own

735.4 noun acc sing masc	2052.6 verb 3pl subj pres act		5050.1 prs-pron nom 2pl	1156.2 conj	79.6 noun nom pl masc	3231.1 partic
ἄρτον	ἐσθίωσιν.	**13.**	Ὑμεῖς	δέ,	ἀδελφοί,	μὴ
arton	esthiōsin		Humeis	de	adelphoi	mē
bread	they may eat.		You	but,	brothers,	not

13.a.**Txt:** 06D-corr,018K
020L,025P,byz.Sod
Var: 01ℵ,02A,Lach
Treg,Alf,Word,Tisc
Weis,UBS/✶

	1560.4 verb 2pl subj aor act	1450.4 verb 2pl subj aor act	2540.1 verb nom pl masc part pres act	1479.1 conj
	(ἐκκακήσητε	[ᵃ✶ ἐγκακήσητε]	καλοποιοῦντες.	**14.** εἰ
	ekkakēsēte	enkakēsēte	kalopoiountes	ei
	do lose heart	[idem]	doing well.	If

1156.2 conj	4948.3 indef-pron nom sing	3620.1 partic	5057.3 verb 3sing indic pres act	3450.3 art dat sing	3030.3 noun dat sing masc	2231.2 prs-pron gen 1pl
δέ	τις	οὐχ	ὑπακούει	τῷ	λόγῳ	ἡμῶν
de	tis	ouch	hupakouei	tō	logō	hēmōn
but	anyone	not	obeys	the	word	our

14.a.**Txt:** 06D-org,018K
020L,025P,byz.Sod
Var: 01ℵ,02A,03B
06D-corr,33,Lach,Treg
Alf,Tisc,We/Ho,Weis
UBS/✶

1217.2 prep	3450.10 art gen sing fem	1976.2 noun gen sing fem	3642.6 dem-pron acc sing masc	4448.1 verb 2pl impr pres mid	2504.1 conj
διὰ	τῆς	ἐπιστολῆς,	τοῦτον	σημειοῦσθε	(ᵃ καὶ)
dia	tēs	epistolēs	touton	sēmeiousthe	kai
by	the	epistle,	that	mark	and

14.b.**Txt:** 06D-corr,018K
020L,025P,byz.Tisc,Sod
Var: 01ℵ,02A,03B,33
Lach,Treg,Alf,We/Ho
Weis,UBS/✶

3231.1 partic	4725.2 verb 2pl pres mid		4725.1 verb inf pres mid		840.4 prs-pron dat sing
μὴ	(συναναμίγνυσθε		[ᵇ✶ συναναμίγνυσθαι]		αὐτῷ,
mē	sunanamignusthe		sunanamignusthai		autō
not	associate with		[to associate with]		him,

2419.1 conj	1772.4 verb 3sing subj aor pass		2504.1 conj	3231.1 partic	5453.1 conj	2172.3 adj acc sing masc
ἵνα	ἐντραπῇ˙	**15.**	καὶ	μὴ	ὡς	ἐχθρὸν
hina	entrapē		kai	mē	hōs	echthron
that	he may be ashamed;		and	not	as	an enemy

2216.3 verb 2pl impr pres mid	233.2 conj	3423.2 verb 2pl impr pres act	5453.1 conj	79.4 noun acc sing masc	840.5 prs-pron nom sing masc
ἡγεῖσθε,	ἀλλὰ	νουθετεῖτε	ὡς	ἀδελφόν.	**16.** Αὐτὸς
hēgeisthe	alla	noutheteite	hōs	adelphon	Autos
esteem,	but	admonish	as	a brother.	Himself

1156.2 conj	3450.5 art nom sing masc	2935.1 noun nom sing masc	3450.10 art gen sing fem	1503.2 noun gen sing fem	1319.24 verb 3sing opt aor act
δὲ	ὁ	κύριος	τῆς	εἰρήνης	δῴη
de	ho	kurios	tēs	eirēnēs	dōē
but	the	Lord	of the	peace	may give

5050.3 prs-pron dat 2pl	3450.12 art acc sing fem	1503.4 noun acc sing fem	1217.2 prep	3820.2 adj gen sing	1706.1 prep	3820.3 adj dat sing
ὑμῖν	τὴν	εἰρήνην	διὰ	παντὸς	ἐν	παντὶ
humin	tēn	eirēnēn	dia	pantos	en	panti
you	the	peace	through	all	in	every

Paul therefore commanded and exhorted (challenged, encouraged) by the Lord Jesus Christ, that any who were idle or busybodies should go to work. Instead of going around imposing on the hospitality and good nature of other Christians, they were to work in quietness; that is, with a quiet restful spirit and with an inner tranquility.

3:13. Paul recognized that the majority of the believers in Thessalonica were honest, hardworking people. The danger was that those who were neglecting their responsibilities might cause the rest to grow weary or lose heart. But whatever others do, Christians must never grow tired of doing what is right, honorable, noble, excellent, and fair to everyone concerned.

3:14. For the most part, these lazy loafers would not recognize themselves as guilty of the kind of idleness and interference in the affairs of others Paul was talking about. So Paul told the church to note them with disapproval and to cease to associate with them, with the intention of bringing them to their senses and making them ashamed of their idleness and meddling. The Greek implies also a hope of bringing them to the place where they would respect the Word given in this epistle.

3:15. In withdrawing their fellowship, the believers must not withdraw their love. The disobedient person who persisted in habits of laziness and gossip was still a brother (or sister). The warnings must be given in a gentle loving way, not as scathing denunciations. The warnings should bring the sin home to the person in such a tender way that the lazy ones would be ashamed. Thus, the call was for a withdrawal of close fellowship, not a complete shunning or avoidance of the person. As members together of the local Body, Christians should gently try to bring the idler to a place where he will not only be ashamed of laziness, but will go to work in obedience to Paul's command. Then the rest of the believers will be able to give him fellowship again without being afraid that he will meddle, spread gossip, or stir up trouble in the church.

3:16. Paul brought this epistle to a conclusion with a prayer that "the Lord of peace" would give them peace at all times and by all means; that is, in every way possible and in all places. In other words, what they really needed was Jesus himself. He is the One who gives peace, a peace the world knows nothing about (John 14:27). Without Him believers are nothing. Without Him they have nothing that is really worthwhile or of eternal value. Thus, when

that with quietness they work, and eat their own bread: ... to work in quietness, *Montgomery* . . . and so earn, *TCNT* . . . earn their own living, *Norlie, Klingensmith.*

13. But ye, brethren, be not weary in well doing: . . . never grow tired of doing what is right, *JB* . . . don't become weary, *Adams* . . . should not be despondent in, *Concordant* . . . never get tired of doing good, *SEB.*

14. And if any man obey not our word by this epistle: If any man does not give heed to what I have said in this letter, *Montgomery* . . . whoever doesn't obey what we say in this letter, *Adams.*
note that man: . . . mark that man, *Montgomery* . . . mark that person, *Williams* . . . remember who he is, *NLT* . . . single him out, *NAB* . . . give him notice, *SEB.*
and have no company with him: Don't associate with him! *SEB* . . . and avoid his company, *TCNT* . . . don't mix with him, *Adams* . . . do not get mixed up with him, *Berkeley* . . . stop having anything to do with him, *Williams* . . . to be ostracized, *NAB.*
that he may be ashamed: . . . so that he may become ashamed of himself, *Adams* . . . so as to make him feel, *Montgomery* . . . that he may be abashed, *Concordant.*

15. Yet count [him] not as an enemy: . . . do not regard him, *Confraternity.*
but admonish [him] as a brother: . . . but warn him, *Berkeley* . . . but caution him, *TCNT* . . . counsel him, *Adams.*

16. Now the Lord of peace himself give you peace: . . . who gives us peace, *Williams* . . . give you His peace, *Adams.*
always by all means: . . . everlasting...in every place, *Confraternity* . . . all the time and in every way, *JB* . . . always, in every thing, *Murdock* . . . in every way about everything, *Klingensmith* . . . in every possible way, *NAB* . . . in every event, *Campbell* . . . in whatever circumstances you may be, *Williams* . . . in every form,

2 Thess. 3:17

16.a.**Txt:** 01ℵ,02A-corr2
03B,06D-corr2,018K
025P,044,81,614,1739
byz.
Var: 02A-org,06D-org
010F,012G,33,76

18.a.**Txt:** 01ℵ-corr,02A
06D,018K,020L,025P
byz.it.bo.
Var: 01ℵ-org,03B,33,sa.
Treg,Alf,Tisc,We/Ho
Weis,Sod,UBS/☆

18.b.**Txt:** 02A,03B-corr
018K,020L,025P,Steph
Var: Gries,Lach,Word
Tisc,We/Ho,Weis,Sod
UBS/☆

4999.2 noun dat sing masc ⟨☆ τρόπῳ. tropō way.	4964.3 noun dat sing masc [ᵃ τόπῳ.] topō [idem]	3450.5 art nom sing masc ὁ ho The	2935.1 noun nom sing masc κύριος kurios Lord	3196.3 prep μετὰ meta with	3820.4 adj gen pl πάντων pantōn all
5050.2 prs-pron gen 2pl ὑμῶν. humōn you.	3450.5 art nom sing masc 17. Ὁ Ho The	777.1 noun nom sing masc ἀσπασμὸς aspasmos greeting	3450.11 art dat sing fem τῇ tē by the	1684.8 adj dat sing fem ἐμῇ emē my	5331.3 noun dat sing fem χειρὶ cheiri hand
3834.2 name gen masc Παύλου, Paulou of Paul,	3614.16 rel-pron sing neu ὅ ho which	1498.4 verb 3sing indic pres act ἐστιν estin is	4447.1 noun sing neu σημεῖον sēmeion sign	1706.1 prep ἐν en in	3820.11 adj dat sing fem πάσῃ pasē every
1976.3 noun dat sing fem ἐπιστολῇ· epistolē epistle;	3643.1 adv οὕτως houtōs so	1119.1 verb 1sing indic pres act γράφω. graphō I write.	3450.9 art nom sing fem 18. ἡ hē The	5322.1 noun nom sing fem χάρις charis grace	3450.2 art gen sing τοῦ tou of the
2935.2 noun gen sing masc κυρίου kuriou Lord	2231.2 prs-pron gen 1pl ἡμῶν hēmōn our	2400.2 name masc Ἰησοῦ Iēsou Jesus	5382.2 name gen masc Χριστοῦ Christou Christ	3196.3 prep μετὰ meta with	3820.4 adj gen pl πάντων pantōn all
5050.2 prs-pron gen 2pl ὑμῶν. humōn you.	279.1 intrj ⟨ᵃ ἀμήν. ⟩ amēn Amen.	4242.1 prep ⟨ᵇ Πρὸς Pros To	2309.4 name dat fem Θεσσαλονικεῖς Thessalonikeis Thessalonians		1202.4 num ord nom sing fem δευτέρα deutera second
1119.21 verb 3sing indic aor pass ἐγράφη egraphē written	570.3 prep ἀπὸ apo from	116.1 name gen fem Ἀθηνῶν. ⟩ Athēnōn Athens.			

370

Paul said, "The Lord be with you all," including those who were still disobedient to the commands of this letter, Paul expressed a fact, not a mere desire. The Lord was with them. He would continue to be with them. Paul had no doubt about this.

It was good that the Thessalonians were excited about the prospect of Christ's second coming. But Paul saw that what they needed was not greater expectation but better habits of life. They needed less talk about the time of His return and more living in the light of His coming. He had given them work to do. When He comes He expects to find Christians busy doing His will and seeking to please Him.

3:17. At this point, Paul took the pen from the scribe and wrote the concluding benediction in his own handwriting. The Thessalonians could have assurance that this letter was no forgery but was indeed one of his. The mention of "every epistle" implies he wrote often. Some of those letters may have been very brief notes or exhortations, however. Not all of his letters were preserved. But we have the assurance that those which we do have were not only inspired by the Holy Spirit, but used by the Spirit to bless all the churches where they were circulated and read.

3:18. Through this and the other epistles that have been preserved in God's divine providence, the "grace of our Lord Jesus Christ" that Paul wanted for the Thessalonians is still being ministered to Christians today.

Fenton ... continually, *PNT* ... at all times, *Clementson*.
The Lord [be] with you all:

17. The salutation of Paul with mine own hand, which is the token in every epistle: I append this signature to every letter I write, *NAB* ... I, Paul, add this farewell, *TCNT* ... write this greeting with my own hand, and this is the indication in every letter, *Adams* ... add this greeting in my own handwriting, which is my token in every letter, *Montgomery* ... This is the mark, *Confraternity* ... Paul's handwriting; which is a sign in, *Berkeley* ... which [circumstance, namely, that I wrote it personally, whereas the rest of the letter was dictated to a secretary] is the mark of genuineness in every letter, *Wuest* ... It is the way I finish all my letters, *NLT* ... This is the sign of all letters, *Klingensmith* ... It is my signature on every letter, *SEB* ... this a distinguishing mark in every letter, *NASB* ... the mark in every letter of mine, *Williams* ... my sign in every letter, *Fenton* ... which is the mark of genuineness, *JB*.
so I write: Thus, *Montgomery* ... that I have written it, *Adams* ... In this manner am I in the habit of writing, *Wuest* ... This is my handwriting, *Beck, Williams* ... am extending greetings, *Hoeber*.

18. The grace of our Lord Jesus Christ [be] with you all. Amen: The love of our Lord, *Beck* ... The favour of, *Rotherham* ... The spiritual blessing of our Lord, *Williams* ... of Jesus the Messiah, *Murdock*.

THE FIRST EPISTLE
OF PAUL TO
TIMOTHY

Expanded Interlinear

Textual Critical Apparatus

Verse-by-Verse Commentary

Various Versions

4242.1 prep	4943.4 name acc masc	1976.1 noun nom sing fem	3834.2 name gen masc	4272.9 num ord nom sing fem
Πρὸς	Τιμόθεον	ἐπιστολὴ	Παύλου	πρωτη
Pros	*Timotheon*	*epistolē*	*Paulou*	*prōtē*
To	Timothy	letter	of Paul	first

3834.1 name nom masc	646.1 noun nom sing masc	2400.2 name masc	5382.2 name gen masc	5382.2 name gen masc
1:1. Παῦλος	ἀπόστολος	ʽ Ἰησοῦ	Χριστοῦ	[✶ Χριστοῦ
Paulos	*apostolos*	*Iēsou*	*Christou*	*Christou*
Paul,	apostle	of Jesus	Christ	[of Christ

2400.2 name masc	2567.1 prep	1987.2 noun acc sing fem	2296.2 noun gen sing masc	4842.2 noun gen sing masc	2231.2 prs-pron gen 1pl
Ἰησοῦ]	κατ'	ἐπιταγὴν	θεοῦ	σωτῆρος	ἡμῶν,
Iēsou	*kat'*	*epitagēn*	*theou*	*sōtēros*	*hēmōn,*
Jesus]	according to	command	of God	Saviour	our,

2504.1 conj	2935.2 noun gen sing masc	2400.2 name masc	5382.2 name gen masc	5382.2 name gen masc	2400.2 name masc
καὶ	ʽᵃ Κυρίου ʼ	ʽ Ἰησοῦ	Χριστοῦ	[✶ Χριστοῦ	Ἰησοῦ
kai	*Kuriou*	*Iēsou*	*Christou*	*Christou*	*Iēsou*
and	of Lord	Jesus	Christ	[Christ	Jesus]

3450.10 art gen sing fem	1667.2 noun gen sing fem	2231.2 prs-pron gen 1pl	4943.3 name dat masc	1097.2 adj dat sing neu	4891.3 noun dat sing neu
τῆς	ἐλπίδος	ἡμῶν,	**2.** Τιμοθέῳ	γνησίῳ	τέκνῳ
tēs	*elpidos*	*hēmōn*	*Timotheō*	*gnēsiō*	*teknō*
the	hope	our,	to Timothy,	genuine	child

1706.1 prep	3963.3 noun dat sing fem	5322.1 noun nom sing fem	1643.2 noun sing neu	1503.1 noun nom sing fem	570.3 prep
ἐν	πίστει·	χάρις,	ἔλεος,	εἰρήνη	ἀπὸ
en	*pistei*	*charis,*	*eleos,*	*eirēnē*	*apo*
in	faith;	grace,	mercy,	peace,	from

2296.2 noun gen sing masc	3824.2 noun gen sing masc	2231.2 prs-pron gen 1pl	2504.1 conj	5382.2 name gen masc	2400.2 name masc
θεοῦ	πατρὸς	ʽᵃ ἡμῶν ʼ	καὶ	Χριστοῦ	Ἰησοῦ
theou	*patros*	*hēmōn*	*kai*	*Christou*	*Iēsou*
God	Father	our	and	Christ	Jesus

3450.2 art gen sing	2935.2 noun gen sing masc	2231.2 prs-pron gen 1pl	2503.1 conj	3731.11 verb 1sing indic aor act
τοῦ	κυρίου	ἡμῶν.	**3.** Καθὼς	παρεκάλεσά
tou	*kuriou*	*hēmōn.*	*Kathōs*	*parekalesa*
the	Lord	our.	Even as	I urged

4622.4 prs-pron acc 2sing	4215.5 verb inf aor act	1706.1 prep	2163.2 name dat fem	4057.7 verb nom sing masc part pres mid
σε	προσμεῖναι	ἐν	Ἐφέσῳ,	πορευόμενος
se	*prosmeinai*	*en*	*Ephesō,*	*poreuomenos*
you	to remain	in	Ephesus,	going

1519.1 prep	3081.4 name acc fem	2419.1 conj	3715.10 verb 2sing subj aor act	4948.8 indef-pron dat pl masc
εἰς	Μακεδονίαν,	ἵνα	παραγγείλῃς	τισὶν
eis	*Makedonian*	*hina*	*parangeilēs*	*tisin*
to	Macedonia,	that	you might command	some

THE FIRST EPISTLE OF PAUL TO
TIMOTHY

1:1. Paul began his letter to Timothy in the usual formal style of many of his epistles. He named himself and identified his relationship to God and Christ. Though this was a personal letter to Timothy, Paul made certain it was understood that his authority was equal to that of any of the original apostles Jesus appointed (2 Corinthians 11:5). After all, it was Jesus who had appointed him to his ministry (see Acts 9:15). Timothy would not doubt the authority of Paul, but some in Ephesus might.

The idea of authority is underscored by the phrase "by the commandment of God." From his conversion on the road to Damascus till the end of his earthly life, Paul understood he was under orders from God. His claim of authority was based on his call and divine commission as "an apostle of Jesus Christ."

"God our Saviour" is a title used by Paul in only six places (1 Timothy 1:1; 2:3; 4:10; Titus 1:3; 2:10; 3:4). The other New Testament writers who used it are Luke (Luke 1:47) and Jude (Jude 25). Its roots are in the Old Testament (see Deuteronomy 32:15; Psalms 24:5; 106:21; Isaiah 43:3; 45:15,21; 63:8). The word *Saviour* appears 24 times in the New Testament, 10 of which are in the Pastoral Epistles.

1:2. Paul addressed Timothy as "my own son in the faith." By this personal and intimate identification, the apostle might have been suggesting two things: (1) Timothy was converted under Paul's ministry, and (2) Paul "adopted" Timothy as a spiritual son. In Philippians 2:19-22 Paul gave Timothy high commendation, ending with these words: "As a son with the father, he hath served with me in the gospel."

To the usual salutation of "Grace . . . and peace," Paul added the word "mercy." Grace contains two concepts in the New Testament: undeserved generosity and God-ordained universality (God doesn't play favorites). "Peace" is the usual greeting in Eastern countries. By adding "mercy," Paul reminded Timothy of the Old Testament concept of God's loving-kindness and steadfast love.

1:3. The purpose for Timothy's presence in Ephesus, and a key to the purpose of this letter, is found in the words, "That thou mightest charge some that they teach no other doctrine." The word "doctrine" is a key word of the Pastoral Epistles. Of the 50 occurrences in the New Testament, 17 are in the Pastorals.

Various Versions

1. Paul, an apostle of Jesus Christ: Missionary, *Klingensmith* . . . an ambassador of, *Wuest*.

by the commandment of God our Saviour: . . . by order of, *Adams* . . . by the appointment, *Fenton* . . . according to the injunction of God, *Concordant*.

and Lord Jesus Christ, [which is] our hope:

2. Unto Timothy, [my] own son in the faith: . . . my genuine child, *Wuest, Williams* . . . my true son, *Montgomery* . . . his true Child in the Faith, *TCNT*.

Grace, mercy, [and] peace: . . . spiritual blessing, *Williams* . . . help, *Adams* . . . give you gracious love, *SEB* . . . loving favor and loving-kindness, *NLT*.

from God our Father and Jesus Christ our Lord: . . . by the appointment of, *TCNT*.

3. As I besought thee to abide still at Ephesus: As I begged you, *Montgomery* . . . I requested you, *Fenton* . . . As I urged you, *Adams* . . . As I entreated you to continue, *Campbell* . . . I still beg you to stay on in, *Williams*.

when I went into Macedonia: . . . was setting out for, *Montgomery* . . . While I was traveling to the Macedonian area, *SEB*.

that thou mightest charge some: . . . and instruct certain individuals there, *Montgomery* . . . so that you may give orders to certain persons, *Adams* . . . to warn certain teachers, *Williams*.

that they teach no other doctrine: . . . to stop teaching, *Adams* . . . some not to teach novel doctrines, *Confraternity* . . . not to teach any different doctrine, *RSV* . . . not to be teaching things contrary to sound doctrine, *Wuest* . . . not to be teaching heterodoxy, *Montgomery*.

3231.1 partic	2064.2 verb inf pres act		3234.1 adv	4196.5 verb inf pres act	3316.1 noun dat pl masc
μὴ	ἑτεροδιδασκαλεῖν,		**4.** μηδὲ	προσέχειν	μύθοις
mē	heterodidaskalein		mēde	prosechein	muthois
not	to teach other doctrines,		nor	to give heed	to myths

2504.1 conj	1069.1 noun dat pl fem	559.1 adj dat pl fem	3610.4 rel-pron nom pl fem	2197.3 noun acc pl fem
καὶ	γενεαλογίαις	ἀπεράντοις,	αἵτινες	‛ ζητήσεις
kai	genealogiais	aperantois	haitines	zētēseis
and	genealogies	endless,	which	questionings

4.a.Txt: 06D,018K,020L 025P,byz.
Var: 01א,02A,33,Treg Tisc,We/Ho,Weis,Sod UBS/✶

1554.1 noun pl fem	3792.2 verb 3pl indic pres act	3095.1 adv comp	2211.1 conj	3484.2 noun acc sing fem
[ᵃ✶ ἐκζητήσεις]	παρέχουσιν	μᾶλλον	ἢ	οἰκονομίαν
ekzētēseis	parechousin	mallon	ē	oikonomian
[idem]	bring	rather	than	administration

2296.2 noun gen sing masc	3450.12 art acc sing fem	1706.1 prep	3963.3 noun dat sing fem	3450.16 art sing neu	1156.2 conj	4904.1 noun sing neu
θεοῦ	τὴν	ἐν	πίστει	**5.** τὸ	δὲ	τέλος
theou	tēn	en	pistei	to	de	telos
God's	the	in	faith.	The	but	goal

3450.10 art gen sing fem	3714.1 noun fem	1498.4 verb 3sing indic pres act	26.1 noun nom sing fem	1523.2 prep gen	2485.7 adj gen sing fem
τῆς	παραγγελίας	ἐστὶν	ἀγάπη	ἐκ	καθαρᾶς
tēs	parangelias	estin	agapē	ek	katharas
of the	command	is	love	out of	clean

2559.1 noun fem	2504.1 conj	4743.2 noun gen sing fem	18.10 adj gen sing fem	2504.1 conj	3963.2 noun gen sing fem
καρδίας	καὶ	συνειδήσεως	ἀγαθῆς	καὶ	πίστεως
kardias	kai	suneidēseōs	agathēs	kai	pisteōs
a heart	and	a conscience	good	and	faith

502.2 adj gen sing fem	3614.1 rel-pron gen pl	4948.7 indef-pron nom pl masc	789.2 verb nom pl masc part aor act
ἀνυποκρίτου‧	**6.** ὧν	τινες	ἀστοχήσαντες
anupokritou	hōn	tines	astochēsantes
not insincere;	from which	some	having missed the mark,

1610.2 verb 3pl indic aor pass	1519.1 prep	3122.1 noun acc sing fem	2286.16 verb nom pl masc part pres act	1498.32 verb inf pres act
ἐξετράπησαν	εἰς	ματαιολογίαν,	**7.** θέλοντες	εἶναι
exetrapēsan	eis	mataiologian	thelontes	einai
turned aside	to	vain talking,	wishing	to be

3410.2 noun nom pl masc	3231.1 partic	3401.5 verb nom pl masc part pres act	3250.1 conj	3614.17 rel-pron pl neu
νομοδιδάσκαλοι,	μὴ	νοοῦντες	μήτε	ἃ
nomodidaskaloi	mē	noountes	mēte	ha
teachers of the law,	not	understanding	neither	what

2978.3 verb 3pl indic pres act	3250.1 conj	3875.1 prep	4949.5 intr-pron gen pl	1220.1 verb 3pl indic pres mid
λέγουσιν,	μήτε	περὶ	τίνων	διαβεβαιοῦνται.
legousin	mēte	peri	tinōn	diabebaiountai
they say,	nor	concerning	what	they strongly affirm.

3471.5 verb 1pl indic perf act	1156.2 conj	3617.1 conj	2541.3 adj nom sing masc	3450.5 art nom sing masc	3414.1 noun nom sing masc	1430.1 partic
8. Οἴδαμεν	δὲ	ὅτι	καλὸς	ὁ	νόμος,	ἐάν
Oidamen	de	hoti	kalos	ho	nomos	ean
We know	now	that	good	the	law,	if

1:4. False doctrine was endangering the Church, and Paul wanted Timothy to speak out against it. This heresy was known by two distinct characteristics: "fables" ("myths, idle tales") and "endless genealogies." False teachers used these to promote controversies among believers. Timothy was told to take a strong stand against these false teachers and command them to cease.

Some commentators see a reference here to the heresy of gnosticism. But it seems these false teachers were Judaizers, not Gnostics. Fables and genealogies were a favorite pastime of certain Jews who delighted in embellishing the text of the Old Testament and bringing others under condemnation with fabricated laws.

4. Neither give heed to fables and endless genealogies: . . . to invented stories and interminable genealogies, *Berkeley* . . . or endless lists of ancestors, *SEB* . . . to myths and endless pedigrees, *Norlie.*

which minister questions: Such studies promote controversies, *Lilly* . . . which beget controversies, *Confraternity.*

rather than godly edifying which is in faith: [so do]:

1:5. This verse introduces a basic precept of the gospel—love (translated "charity" here). The "end" or purpose of the "commandment" is love (see Romans 13:8-10). This *agapē* is to come from (1) a pure heart, (2) a good conscience, and (3) sincere faith.

"Pure heart" is *katharas kardias.* Originally, *katharos* meant "clean" as opposed to "soiled" or "dirty." Later it was used of something void of debasing admixture. A pure heart has motives that are absolutely pure and unmixed.

The word "conscience" appears 22 times in the New Testament. Paul wrote about consciences that are "good" (1 Timothy 1:5,19); "pure" (1 Timothy 3:9; 2 Timothy 1:3); "seared" (1 Timothy 4:2); and "defiled" (Titus 1:15).

5. Now the end of the commandment is charity: . . . whereas the aim of our charge is love, *RSV* . . . Love is the real reason, *SEB* . . . The aim of all your instruction, *TCNT* . . . Now the purpose of this charge is, *Confraternity* . . . The purpose of our instruction, *Berkeley.*

out of a pure heart, and [of] a good conscience, and [of] faith unfeigned: . . . a sincere faith, *Norlie.*

1:6,7. Note the verbs in this threefold description of "some": they had "swerved, . . . turned aside"; they were "desiring to be" but "(not) understanding." The "some" here are the same ones mentioned in verse 3, the false teachers. Paul said they had "turned aside unto vain jangling."

This is an interesting term. The context seems to show "vain jangling" to be the primary characteristic and activity of these false teachers. Paul pointed out that fables and endless genealogies were their stock in trade. It was all meaningless discussion, empty argument, and purposeless talk. He also said they had turned aside from the truth and were so ignorant they could not even understand their own words.

6. From which some having swerved: Some people have failed to hit the mark, *Lilly* . . . Some going astray from, *Confraternity* . . . have wandered away, *SEB.*

have turned aside unto vain jangling: They are lost in empty talk, *SEB* . . . turned off into empty talk, *Berkeley* . . . diverted to frivolous subjects, *TCNT* . . . to nonsensical discussions, *Norlie.*

7. Desiring to be teachers of the law; understanding neither what they say:

nor whereof they affirm: . . . or the things about which they make assertions, *RSV* . . . or that concerning which they are insisting, *Concordant.*

1:8. Verse 8 begins an extended sentence that does not end until verse 11. The initial verse is introductory; verse 11 is a bridge from "the law" to "the glorious gospel of the blessed God." In writing about God's law, Paul made two important points: (1) God's law is good if it is used properly, and (2) laws are not made for righteous men but for unrighteous people. The point he wanted Timothy to grasp was that the Law had a primary purpose—to restrain wickedness and evil behavior.

8. But we know that the law [is] good: . . . is admirable, *Berkeley.*

4948.3 indef-pron nom sing	840.4 prs-pron dat sing	3408.1 adv	5366.2 verb 3sing subj pres mid	3471.18 verb nom sing masc part perf act	3642.17 dem-pron sing neu
τις	αὐτῷ	νομίμως	χρῆται,	**9.** εἰδὼς	τοῦτο,
tis	*autō*	*nomimōs*	*chrētai,*	*eidōs*	*touto*
anyone	it	lawfully	use,	knowing	this,

3617.1 conj	1337.4 adj dat sing masc	3414.1 noun nom sing masc	3620.3 partic	2719.2 verb 3sing indic pres mid	456.1 adj dat pl
ὅτι	δικαίῳ	νόμος	οὐ	κεῖται,	ἀνόμοις
hoti	*dikaiō*	*nomos*	*ou*	*keitai,*	*anomois*
that	for a righteous	law	not	is enacting,	for lawless

1156.2 conj	2504.1 conj	503.2 adj dat pl masc	759.5 adj dat pl masc	2504.1 conj	266.6 adj dat pl masc
δὲ	καὶ	ἀνυποτάκτοις,	ἀσεβέσιν	καὶ	ἁμαρτωλοῖς,
de	*kai*	*anupotaktois,*	*asebesin*	*kai*	*hamartōlois*
but	and	insubordinate,	for ungodly	and	sinful,

459.2 adj dat pl masc	2504.1 conj	945.3 adj dat pl masc	3826.1 noun dat pl masc	2504.1 conj
ἀνοσίοις	καὶ	βεβήλοις,	πατραλῴαις	καὶ
anosiois	*kai*	*bebēlois,*	*patralōais*	*kai*
for unholy	and	profane,	for murderers of fathers	and

3254.1 noun dat pl masc	3255.1 noun dat pl masc	407.1 noun dat pl masc
ʼ μητραλῴαις,	[☆ μητρολῴαις,]	ἀνδροφόνοις,
mētralōais,	*mētrolōais*	*androphonois*
murderers of mothers;	[idem]	for slayers of man,

4064.3 noun dat pl masc	727.2 noun dat pl masc	403.1 noun dat pl masc	5418.4 noun dat pl masc
10. πόρνοις,	ἀρσενοκοίταις,	ἀνδραποδισταῖς,	ψεύσταις,
pornois	*arsenokoitais,*	*andrapodistais*	*pseustais,*
fornicators,	homosexuals,	kidnappers,	liars,

1950.1 adj dat pl masc	2504.1 conj	1479.1 conj	4948.10 indef-pron sing neu	2066.1 adj sing	3450.11 art dat sing fem
ἐπιόρκοις,	καὶ	εἴ	τι	ἕτερον	τῇ
epiorkois,	*kai*	*ei*	*ti*	*heteron*	*tē*
perjurers,	and	if	any thing	other	the

5039.8 verb dat sing fem part pres act	1313.3 noun dat sing fem	477.1 verb 3sing indic pres mid	2567.3 prep	3450.16 art sing neu
ὑγιαινούσῃ	διδασκαλίᾳ	ἀντίκειται,	**11.** κατὰ	τὸ
hugiainousē	*didaskalia*	*antikeitai,*	*kata*	*to*
being sound	teaching	opposes,	according to	to the

2077.1 noun sing neu	3450.10 art gen sing fem	1385.2 noun gen sing fem	3450.2 art gen sing	3079.3 adj gen sing masc	2296.2 noun gen sing masc
εὐαγγέλιον	τῆς	δόξης	τοῦ	μακαρίου	θεοῦ,
euangelion	*tēs*	*doxēs*	*tou*	*makariou*	*theou,*
good news	of the	glory	of the	blessed	God,

3614.16 rel-pron sing neu	3961.57 verb 1sing indic aor pass	1466.1 prs-pron nom 1sing	2504.1 conj	5322.4 noun acc sing fem
ὃ	ἐπιστεύθην	ἐγώ.	**12.** ⟨a Καὶ ⟩	χάριν
ho	*episteuthēn*	*egō*	*Kai*	*charin*
which	was entrusted with	I.	And	thank

2174.1 verb 1sing pres act	3450.3 art dat sing	1727.3 verb dat sing masc part aor act	1466.6 prs-pron acc 1sing	5382.3 name dat masc
ἔχω	τῷ	ἐνδυναμώσαντί	με	Χριστῷ
echō	*tō*	*endunamōsanti*	*me*	*Christō*
I	the	having strengthened	me,	Christ

1:9. Paul gave a long list of lawbreakers in verses 9 and 10. This list greatly resembles the Ten Commandments found in Exodus 20:1-17. Perhaps because Paul had just referred to the Law, the Holy Spirit directed him to list those people who correspond to and flagrantly break the "thou shalt nots" of the Old Testament.

The "lawless" deliberately break the law to satisfy their own desires and ambitions. The "disobedient" refuse to obey any authority; they are a law unto themselves. The "ungodly" have no reverence for God, and they defiantly withhold the praise and glory due Him. "Sinners" describes the character of those who miss the mark of God's law.

Note that all these descriptions are in pairs. "Unholy and profane" (*anosioi* and *bebēloi*) are precise and ugly words. The person who is *anosios* is worse than a mere lawbreaker. He violates the very decencies of life. The man who is *bebēlos* desecrates everything that is holy and dirties everything he touches.

1:10. This verse continues the list of lawbreakers that begins in verse 9. Two groups are similar in nature and conduct: the *pornoi* and *arsenokoitai*. "Whoremongers" are fornicators. "Them that defile themselves with mankind" are homosexuals. The culture of the First Century was replete with sexual sins. It was common practice in pagan religions to condone sexual immorality as behavior pleasing to the gods. At Corinth, the temple of Aphrodite, goddess of love, had 1,000 sacred prostitutes who plied their trade every day. "Liars" and "perjured persons" twist the truth to serve their own ends. They break the ninth commandment.

Finally, Paul concluded the list with the words "any other thing that is contrary to sound doctrine." The word "sound" here literally means "health-giving" and denotes the wholesomeness of true Christian teaching. This word occurs frequently in the Pastoral Epistles, but nowhere else.

1:11. The word "glorious" is appended to "gospel." Here and elsewhere it is in the genitive form and connotes content rather than quality. God's glory is revealed to men in the gospel that witnesses to Christ. (Compare John 1:14,18; 2 Corinthians 4:4,6.)

"Blessed" here describes God as experiencing within himself the perfection of bliss (Guthrie, *Tyndale New Testament Commentaries*, 14:62). Timothy was told to focus on the doctrine that is wholesome and the gospel that reveals God's glory. This gospel was committed to Paul's trust. The inference is that the same gospel was committed to Timothy's trust as well.

1:12. Beginning with verse 12 the tone changes. From verse 12 to verse 17, Paul bursts forth in praise and thanksgiving for the grace of Christ and the mercy of God. Paul thanked Christ for three things: strength, trust, and a call to service. No doubt Paul was seeking to encourage Timothy by recounting his own reception

if a man use it lawfully: . . . uses it rightly, *Confraternity* . . . if legitimately used, *TCNT* . . . in the right way, *Norlie*.

9. Knowing this:
that the law is not made for a righteous man: . . . is not laid down for an honest person, *Berkeley* . . . not for the person who is right with God, *NLT.*
but for the lawless and disobedient: . . . for the unjust and rebellious, *Confraternity* . . . for the immoral and profane, *Norlie* . . . and insubordinate, *Concordant* . . . rebels, *SEB.*
for the ungodly and for sinners: . . . for irreligious and wicked people, *TCNT.*
for unholy and profane, for murderers of fathers and murderers of mothers, for manslayers:

10. For whoremongers, for them that defile themselves with mankind: . . . for sexual perverts, *Berkeley* . . . homosexuals, *Lilly, SEB* . . . for people guilty of sodomy, *TCNT* . . . for sodomites, *Confraternity.*
for menstealers, for liars, for perjured persons: . . . slave traders, *SEB* . . . falsifiers, *Berkeley.*
and if there be any other thing that is contrary to sound doctrine: . . . and against any other crime contrary to, *Lilly* . . . against right teaching, *NLT* . . . against the healthy teaching, *SEB.*

11. According to the glorious gospel of the blessed God, which was committed to my trust:

12. And I thank Christ Jesus our Lord, who hath enabled me: I am deeply grateful to, *TCNT* . . . has strengthened me, *Confraternity* . . . who has qualified me, *Campbell* . . . Who invigorates men, *Concordant.*

1 Timothy 1:13

2400.2 name masc	3450.3 art dat sing	2935.3 noun dat sing masc	2231.2 prs-pron gen 1pl	3617.1 conj	3964.1 adj sing
Ἰησοῦ	τῷ	κυρίῳ	ἡμῶν,	ὅτι	πιστόν
Iēsou	tō	kuriō	hēmōn	hoti	piston
Jesus	the	Lord	our,	that	faithful

1466.6 prs-pron acc 1sing	2216.13 verb 3sing indic aor mid	4935.37 verb nom sing masc part aor mid	1519.1 prep	1242.4 noun acc sing fem
με	ἡγήσατο,	θέμενος	εἰς	διακονίαν,
me	hēgēsato	themenos	eis	diakonian
me	he esteemed,	having appointed	to	service,

13.a.Txt: 06D-corr,018K 020L,byz.
Var: 01א,02A,06D-org 025P,33,Lach,Treg,Alf Tisc,We/Ho,Weis,Sod UBS/☆

13.

3450.6 art acc sing masc	3450.16 art sing neu	4245.2 adj comp sing neu	1498.18 verb part pres act	982.1 adj acc sing
ʿ τὸν	[a☆ τὸ]	πρότερον	ὄντα	βλάσφημον
ton	to	proteron	onta	blasphēmon
the	[idem]	previously	being	a blasphemer

2504.1 conj	1370.1 noun acc sing masc	2504.1 conj	5037.1 noun acc sing masc	233.1 conj	233.2 conj
καὶ	διώκτην	καὶ	ὑβριστήν·	ʿ ἀλλ᾽	[☆ ἀλλὰ]
kai	diōktēn	kai	hubristēn	all'	alla
and	persecutor	and	violent person;	but	[idem]

1640.12 verb 1sing indic aor pass	3617.1 conj	49.7 verb nom sing masc part pres act	4020.22 verb 1sing indic aor act	1706.1 prep
ἠλεήθην,	ὅτι	ἀγνοῶν	ἐποίησα	ἐν
eleēthēn	hoti	agnoōn	epoiēsa	en
I was shown mercy,	because	being ignorant	I did	in

565.3 noun dat sing fem	5088.1 verb 3sing indic aor act	1156.2 conj	3450.9 art nom sing fem	5322.1 noun nom sing fem
ἀπιστίᾳ·	**14.** ὑπερεπλεόνασεν	δὲ	ἡ	χάρις
apistia	huperepleonasen	de	hē	charis
unbelief.	Superabounded	but	the	grace

3450.2 art gen sing	2935.2 noun gen sing masc	2231.2 prs-pron gen 1pl	3196.3 prep	3963.2 noun gen sing fem	2504.1 conj	26.2 noun gen sing fem
τοῦ	κυρίου	ἡμῶν	μετὰ	πίστεως	καὶ	ἀγάπης
tou	kuriou	hēmōn	meta	pisteōs	kai	agapēs
of the	Lord	our	with	faith	and	love

3450.10 art gen sing fem	1706.1 prep	5382.3 name dat masc	2400.2 name masc	3964.2 adj nom sing masc	3450.5 art nom sing masc
τῆς	ἐν	Χριστῷ	Ἰησοῦ.	**15.** πιστὸς	ὁ
tēs	en	Christō	Iēsou	pistos	ho
the	in	Christ	Jesus.	Faithful	the

3030.1 noun nom sing masc	2504.1 conj	3820.10 adj gen sing fem	589.1 noun gen sing fem	510.2 adj nom sing masc	3617.1 conj
λόγος	καὶ	πάσης	ἀποδοχῆς	ἄξιος,	ὅτι
logos	kai	pasēs	apodochēs	axios	hoti
word,	and	of all	acceptation	worthy,	that

5382.1 name masc	2400.1 name nom masc	2048.3 verb 3sing indic aor act	1519.1 prep	3450.6 art acc sing masc	2862.4 noun acc sing masc
Χριστὸς	Ἰησοῦς	ἦλθεν	εἰς	τὸν	κόσμον
Christos	Iēsous	ēlthen	eis	ton	kosmon
Christ	Jesus	came	into	the	world

266.7 adj acc pl masc	4834.10 verb inf aor act	3614.1 rel-pron gen pl	4272.5 num ord nom sing masc	1498.2 verb 1sing indic pres act
ἁμαρτωλοὺς	σῶσαι,	ὧν	πρῶτός	εἰμι
hamartōlous	sōsai	hōn	prōtos	eimi
sinners	to save,	of whom	first	am

of grace. The verbs in this and the following verses are in the aorist (past) tense. But Paul could not recount what Christ had done for him without breaking into thanksgiving and worship (see verses 12,17).

1:13. Paul said he had been a "blasphemer." Blasphemy is the opposite of "blessing" the name of God. Three Hebrew words are translated "blaspheme": *gādhaph*—"cut, wound, revile, blaspheme"; *chāraph*—"speak sharply against, reproach"; and *bārakh*—"utter a curse against." *Blasphēmeō*, used in the New Testament, means "speak harmfully against." Paul used the noun form to describe his blasphemy and could very well have had the Old Testament's meanings in mind.

The word "injurious" is a strong, descriptive term. It refers to a violent, insolent man—a doer of outrage and injury to others. It could include the idea of *sadist*—one who inflicts pain on another for the sheer joy it brings.

Though Paul was all this, he said, "But I obtained mercy (see verse 16), because I did it ignorantly in unbelief." Paul did not excuse his sinful past, he exalted God's mercy!

1:14. The phrase "and the grace . . . " is connected to and extends the previous verse where Paul said he was given "mercy." (Compare the greeting in verse 2.) For Paul, the "grace of our Lord" was not just an abstract concept but an active force dominating both his thoughts and actions. He wrote to the Corinthians, "By the grace of God I am what I am" (1 Corinthians 15:10; compare Romans 5:8,10,20,21). Paul then defined this grace with the words "exceeding abundant" (*huperepleonasen*). The prefix *huper* expresses the superabundance of divine grace given to Paul.

The words "faith" and "love" provide a strong contrast to the sinful life of unbelief and hatred that Paul had just mentioned. Someone has said of verse 14 that Paul saw "grace" as providing for his salvation, "faith" appropriating it, and "love" applying it.

1:15. The Pastoral Epistles have four "faithful sayings." They appear nowhere else. In two of them (1:15 and 4:9) Paul added the words "and worthy of all acceptation." (See 1:15; 3:1; 4:8,9; 2 Timothy 2:11.) Most commentators see the words here as a "current, primitive creedal statement." That Christ came into the world to save sinners is the very heart of the gospel. Jesus said of himself, "The Son of man is come to seek and to save that which was lost" (Luke 19:10). No greater truth exists. Jesus came to save sinners! And Paul said he was "chief" (*prōtos*). Paul used superlatives to refer to himself, whether it was the least of the apostles (1 Corinthians 15:9), or less than the least of all saints (Ephesians 3:8), or the "chief" of sinners.

for that he counted me faithful: . . . because he counted me trustworthy, *Confraternity* . . . for thinking me trustworthy, *Williams* . . . He deemed me worthy, *Berkeley* . . . considered me reliable, *Norlie*.

putting me into the ministry: . . . he appointed me for this work, *SEB*.

13. Who was before a blasphemer, and a persecutor, and injurious: Before He chose me, *NLT* . . . although formerly I defamed, *Lilly* . . . and a bitter adversary, *Confraternity* . . . and an oppressor, *Berkeley* . . . and a man of violence, *SEB*.

but I obtained mercy: . . . was shown me, *Williams*.

because I did [it] ignorantly in unbelief: I didn't know what I was doing, *SEB*.

14. And the grace of our Lord was exceeding abundant: . . . and the spiritual blessing of, *Williams* . . . was lavished superabundantly, *Lilly* . . . has abounded beyond measure, *Confraternity* . . . has superabounded, *Campbell* . . . There was no limit, *TCNT* . . . was overflowing, *Klingensmith*.

with faith and love which is in Christ Jesus: . . . inspired by union with, *Williams*.

15. This [is] a faithful saying: Reliable is the message, *Berkeley* . . . This statement is something you can trust, *SEB*.

and worthy of all acceptation: . . . and deserving of wholehearted acceptance, *Berkeley* . . . of all reception, *Campbell*.

that Christ Jesus came into the world to save sinners:

of whom I am chief: I am at the head of the list, *Lilly* . . . I am foremost, *Berkeley* . . . And I was the worst, *Norlie* . . . I myself am first! *Klingensmith* . . . and I am the worst sinner, *NLT* . . . the worst one, *SEB*.

1 Timothy 1:16

16. ἐγώ, — 1466.1 prs-pron nom 1sing — egō — I.

ἀλλὰ — 233.2 conj — alla — But

διὰ — 1217.2 prep — dia — because of

τοῦτο — 3642.17 dem-pron sing neu — touto — this

ἠλεήθην, — 1640.12 verb 1sing indic aor pass — eleēthēn — I was shown mercy,

ἵνα — 2419.1 conj — hina — that

ἐν — 1706.1 prep — en — in

ἐμοὶ — 1466.5 prs-pron dat 1sing — emoi — me,

πρώτῳ — 4272.6 num ord dat sing masc — prōtō — first,

ἐνδείξηται — 1715.7 verb 3sing subj aor mid — endeixētai — might show forth

Ἰησοῦς — 2400.1 name nom masc — Iēsous — Jesus

16.a.Txt: 01‭א‬,06D-corr2 015H,025P,byz. **Var:** 02A,06D-org,33 104,326,365,629,1175

Χριστὸς — 5382.1 name nom masc — Christos — Christ

[a☆ Χριστὸς — 5382.1 name nom masc — Christos — [Christ

Ἰησοῦς] — 2400.1 name nom masc — Iēsous — Jesus]

τὴν — 3450.12 art acc sing fem — tēn — the

πᾶσαν — 3820.12 adj acc sing fem — pasan — whole

16.b.Txt: 06D,018K 020L,025P,byz. **Var:** 01‭א‬,02A,33,Lach Treg,Alf,Word,Tisc We/Ho,Weis,Sod UBS/☆

[b☆ ἅπασαν] — 533.6 adj acc sing fem — hapasan — [idem]

μακροθυμίαν, — 3087.4 noun acc sing fem — makrothumian — longsuffering,

πρὸς — 4242.1 prep — pros — for

ὑποτύπωσιν — 5134.1 noun acc sing fem — hupotupōsin — a type

τῶν — 3450.1 art gen pl — tōn — of the

μελλόντων — 3165.11 verb gen pl part pres act — mellontōn — being about

πιστεύειν — 3961.16 verb inf pres act — pisteuein — to believe

ἐπ' — 1894.2 prep — ep' — on

αὐτῷ — 840.4 prs-pron dat sing — autō — him

εἰς — 1519.1 prep — eis — to

ζωὴν — 2205.4 noun acc sing fem — zōēn — life

αἰώνιον. — 164.1 adj sing — aiōnion — eternal.

17. τῷ — 3450.3 art dat sing — tō — To the

δὲ — 1156.2 conj — de — now

βασιλεῖ — 928.3 noun dat sing masc — basilei — King

τῶν — 3450.1 art gen pl — tōn — of the

αἰώνων, — 163.4 noun gen pl masc — aiōnōn — ages,

17.a.Txt: 01‭א‬-corr 06D-corr,018K,020L 025P,byz. **Var:** 01‭א‬-org,02A 06D-org,015H-org,33,sa. bo.Gries,Lach,Treg,Alf Word,Tisc,We/Ho,Weis Sod,UBS/☆

ἀφθάρτῳ, — 855.3 adj dat sing masc — aphthartō — incorruptible,

ἀοράτῳ, — 513.2 adj dat sing masc — aoratō — invisible,

μόνῳ — 3304.4 adj dat sing masc — monō — only

[a σοφῷ ⟩ — 4533.2 adj dat sing masc — sophō — wise

θεῷ, — 2296.3 noun dat sing masc — theō — God,

τιμὴ — 4940.1 noun nom sing fem — timē — honor

καὶ — 2504.1 conj — kai — and

δόξα — 1385.1 noun nom sing fem — doxa — glory

εἰς — 1519.1 prep — eis — to

τοὺς — 3450.8 art acc pl masc — tous — the

αἰῶνας — 163.6 noun acc pl masc — aiōnas — ages

τῶν — 3450.1 art gen pl — tōn — of the

αἰώνων. — 163.4 noun gen pl masc — aiōnōn — ages.

ἀμήν. — 279.1 intrj — amēn — Amen.

18. Ταύτην — 3642.12 dem-pron acc sing fem — Tautēn — This

τὴν — 3450.12 art acc sing fem — tēn — the

παραγγελίαν — 3714.3 noun acc sing fem — parangelian — charge

παρατίθεμαί, — 3769.7 verb 1sing indic pres mid — paratithemai — I commit

σοι, — 4622.3 prs-pron dat 2sing — soi — to you,

τέκνον — 4891.1 noun sing neu — teknon — child

Τιμόθεε, — 4943.5 name voc masc — Timothee — Timothy,

κατὰ — 2567.3 prep — kata — according to

τὰς — 3450.15 art acc pl fem — tas — the

προαγούσας — 4113.7 verb acc pl fem part pres act — proagousas — going before

ἐπὶ — 1894.3 prep — epi — upon

σὲ — 4622.4 prs-pron acc 2sing — se — you

προφητείας, — 4252.1 noun fem — prophēteias — prophecies,

ἵνα — 2419.1 conj — hina — that

1:16. The first part of this verse repeats the statement regarding Paul's reception of mercy. But here the purpose is revealed: "But for that very reason I was shown mercy so that in me, the worst of sinners, Christ Jesus might display his unlimited patience as an example for those who would believe on him and receive eternal life" (NIV). Paul saw his former life and his present life as an illustration, pattern, example, and exhibit for all who "should hereafter believe."

"The Greek word rendered *pattern* (*hupotupōsis*) may be understood either as an outline sketch of an artist, or as a word-illustration expressing an author's burning purpose . . . . The construction (*epi* with the dative) after the verb *believe* indicates that Christ is the firm basis of faith. Such unshakable assurance serves not only in this life but in eternity" (Guthrie, *Tyndale New Testament Commentaries*, 14:66). Paul's life—both his former life as a zealous persecutor of Christians and his present life as an incarcerated apostle of Christ—was to be a "pattern" for others. What God did for and with Paul, He could do for others. There was no shame for Paul. God's grace had been abundant for him (verse 14); it could be the same for others.

The "first" here does not reflect preference or superiority. It connects with the concept of "pattern." Paul had been saved 30 or so years before, and God's mercy shown in Paul illustrated, exhibited, and patterned what is available for all who believe in Jesus Christ. Those who followed Paul's example of belief were also candidates for the superabundant grace of the Lord Jesus Christ.

1:17. Paul began this section (verse 12) with thanksgiving; he closed it with praise. It is properly called a doxology (from *doxa*—"glory, brightness, majesty," and *logos*—"word, declaration"). This doxology burst forth as Paul remembered the mercy of God and the grace and patience of Christ. It contains five parts: God as (1) King, (2) eternal, (3) immortal, (4) invisible, and (5) the only God.

"King eternal" is literally "king of the ages." This is the only place where Paul used this term. Very likely he had the Jewish concept of two ages in mind: the age that is and the age to come. "Immortal" has the meaning of "not subject to death." "Invisible" means "unable to be seen." But the eye of faith sees God (compare Hebrews 11:27; John 14:9). Paul praised the "only wise God" (perhaps better read "only God") who is worthy of "honor and glory for ever and ever. Amen." (So be it!)

1:18. In this final paragraph of chapter 1, Paul picked up the "charge" he began at 1:3. He instructed "son Timothy" with two military metaphors. He charged (commanded) Timothy to "war a good warfare." As this first chapter has revealed, this warfare was on at least two fronts: doctrinal and moral. The situation in Ephesus was critical. If the church was to advance, a fight against false teaching and moral sins must be waged.

"The prophecies which went before on thee" probably refers to

16. Howbeit for this cause I obtained mercy: Yet for this very cause, *Montgomery* . . . for this reason, *Lilly* . . . for the express purpose, *TCNT*.

that in me first: . . . that in my case, *Williams* . . . so that in me, the chief of sinners, *Montgomery*.

Jesus Christ might show forth all longsuffering: . . . might display His unlimited patience, *Berkeley* . . . might display his perfect patience, *RSV* . . . might display all his boundless patience, *Montgomery* . . . to demonstrate how vast is His patience, *Norlie*.

for a pattern to them: . . . as an illustration for those, *Montgomery* . . . as an example to those, *Confraternity*.

which should hereafter believe on him to life everlasting: . . . who should later believe in him, and so gain life eternal, *Montgomery* . . . to obtain eternal life, *Williams*.

17. Now unto the King eternal, immortal, invisible, the only wise God: . . . to the King Who lives forever...He is the One Who never dies, *NLT* . . . the King of the ages, *Lilly, Klingensmith* . . . who cannot die or be seen, *SEB*.

[be] honour and glory for ever and ever. Amen: . . . throughout the endless ages! *Norlie* . . . Let it be so, *NLT*.

18. This charge I commit unto thee, son Timothy: This is the instruction, *Williams* . . . I am laying upon you, *Montgomery*.

according to the prophecies which went before on thee: It is in harmony with prophecies, *Norlie* . . . according to the predictions formerly made, *Montgomery* . . . in agreement with the previous prophecies, *Berkeley* . . . according to the inspired utterances which pointed to you, *Lilly* . . . the prophetic utterances, *RSV, Williams* . . . once made concerning thee, *Confraternity*.

18.a.**Txt:** 01ℵ-corr2,02A
06D-corr2,010F,012G
015H,byz.
Var: 01ℵ-org,06D-org
044,1175

4605.4 verb 2sing
subj pres mid
⸀ στρατεύῃ
strateuē
you might fight

4605.8 verb 2sing
indic fut act
[ᵃ στρατεύσῃ]
strateusē
[you will fight]

1706.1
prep
ἐν
en
by

840.14 prs-
pron dat pl fem
αὐταῖς
autais
them

3450.12 art
acc sing fem
τὴν
tēn
the

2541.8 adj
acc sing fem
καλὴν
kalēn
good

4603.2 noun
acc sing fem
στρατείαν,
strateian
fight,

2174.17 verb nom sing
masc part pres act
19. ἔχων
echōn
holding

3963.4 noun
acc sing fem
πίστιν
pistin
faith

2504.1
conj
καὶ
kai
and

18.12 adj
acc sing fem
ἀγαθὴν
agathēn
good

4743.4 noun
acc sing fem
συνείδησιν,
suneidēsin
a conscience;

3614.12 rel-
pron acc sing fem
ἥν
hēn
which

4948.7 indef-
pron nom pl masc
τινες
tines
some,

676.4 verb nom pl
masc part aor mid
ἀπωσάμενοι,
apōsamenoi
having cast away,

3875.1
prep
περὶ
peri
concerning

3450.12 art
acc sing fem
τὴν
tēn
the

3963.4 noun
acc sing fem
πίστιν
pistin
faith

3352.2 verb 3pl
indic aor act
ἐναυάγησαν·
enauagēsan
made shipwreck;

3614.1 rel-
pron gen pl
20. ὧν
hōn
of whom

1498.4 verb 3sing
indic pres act
ἐστιν
estin
are

5051.1 name
nom masc
Ὑμέναιος
Humenaios
Hymeneus

2504.1
conj
καὶ
kai
and

221.1 name
nom masc
Ἀλέξανδρος,
Alexandros
Alexander,

3614.8 rel-
pron acc pl masc
οὓς
hous
whom

3722.8 verb 1sing
indic aor act
παρέδωκα
paredōka
I delivered up

3450.3 art
dat sing
τῷ
tō

4423.3 noun
dat sing masc
Σατανᾷ,
Satana
to Satan,

2419.1
conj
ἵνα
hina
that

3674.10 verb 3pl
subj aor pass
παιδευθῶσιν
paideuthōsin
they may be disciplined

3231.1
partic
μὴ
mē
not

980.7 verb
inf pres act
βλασφημεῖν.
blasphēmein
to blaspheme.

3731.1 verb 1sing
indic pres act
2:1. Παρακαλῶ
Parakalō
I exhort

3631.1
partic
οὖν
oun
therefore,

4270.1
adv
πρῶτον
prōton
first

3820.4
adj gen pl
πάντων
pantōn
of all,

4020.66 verb
inf pres mid
ποιεῖσθαι
poieisthai
to be made

1157.6 noun
acc pl fem
δεήσεις,
deēseis
supplications,

4194.8 noun
acc pl fem
προσευχάς,
proseuchas
prayers,

1767.2 noun
acc pl fem
ἐντεύξεις,
enteuxeis
intercessions,

2150.1
noun fem
εὐχαριστίας,
eucharistias
thanksgivings,

5065.1
prep
ὑπὲρ
huper
for

3820.4
adj gen pl
πάντων
pantōn
all

442.7 noun
gen pl masc
ἀνθρώπων,
anthrōpōn
men;

5065.1
prep
2. ὑπὲρ
huper
for

928.7 noun
gen pl masc
βασιλέων
basileōn
kings

2504.1
conj
καὶ
kai
and

3820.4
adj gen pl
πάντων
pantōn
all

3450.1
art gen pl
τῶν
tōn
the

1706.1
prep
ἐν
en
in

5085.1 noun
dat sing fem
ὑπεροχῇ
huperochē
dignity

1498.20 verb gen
pl part pres act
ὄντων,
ontōn
being,

2419.1
conj
ἵνα
hina
that

2241.1 adj
acc sing masc
ἤρεμον
ēremon
a tranquil

2504.1
conj
καὶ
kai
and

2250.1 adj
acc sing masc
ἡσύχιον
hēsuchion
quiet

972.2 noun
acc sing masc
βίον
bion
life

Timothy's ordination into the ministry and his induction into mission-ary work (cf. 1 Timothy 4:14 and 2 Timothy 1:6).

1:19. Timothy was to fight the good fight with two offensive weapons: "faith, and a good conscience" (see verse 5). The Biblical word *conscience* is a compound and literally means "coperception." It is that within which enables a person to distinguish between right and wrong.

"Put away" (*apōtheomai*) implies a violent and deliberate rejection of one's personal conscience; the end result is shipwrecked faith. With the word "shipwreck" the metaphor turns from military to nautical.

1:20. Paul mentioned two men who had turned from the truth and were blaspheming God by their words and conduct. Little is known of these two. Hymeneus was a false teacher and is mentioned in 2 Timothy 2:17,18. Two Alexanders had connections with the city of Ephesus. One was a Jew (Acts 19:33,34) and the other was a coppersmith who did a great deal of harm to Paul (2 Timothy 4:14). Perhaps the second Alexander is indicated in verse 20. These two men were spiritually bound over to Satan (see Job 2:6; Matthew 16:19; 1 Corinthians 5:3-5) as a disciplinary measure to teach them not to blaspheme. This very likely means they were excommunicated from Christian fellowship. The purpose was intended to be remedial, not punitive.

2:1. Chapter 2 contains two topics: instructions concerning public prayer (1-8) and women in the church (9-15).

The words "first of all" stress the priority of prayer. The four words that follow describe prayer in its various aspects. (1) "Supplications" (*deēseis*) has the basic meaning of "requests." It is not exclusively a religious word; it means a request made either to a fellowman or to God. But it does connote need. (2) "Prayers" (*proseuchas*) differs from the first. Supplications may be addressed either to man or God, but prayer is always and only addressed to God. (3) "Intercessions" (*enteuxeis*) has the sense of "petitions." It is the noun form of *entunchanō*, a word that had acquired a special meaning in Paul's day: "to enter into a king's presence and to submit a petition to him." God is the King of kings. (4) "Giving of thanks" (*eucharistias*) brings in a beautiful balance. Prayer is not only asking God for things, it also means thanking God for who He is and what He does.

2:2. As Paul continued his exhortation regarding prayer, he designated "kings, and . . . all that are in authority." Paul made no distinction as to whether or not governmental leadership is hostile to Christianity. Christians are to pray for civil leaders so "we may lead a quiet and peaceable life." The Greek adjective *ēremon* trans-

that thou by them mightest war a good warfare: Use them to fight the good fight, *SEB* . . . continue to fight the good fight, *Williams* . . . that you might carry out a good campaign, *Klingensmith* . . . in the spirit of these predictions, *Montgomery*.

19. Holding faith, and a good conscience: . . . keeping fast hold of faith, *Montgomery*.
which some having put away: . . . they have discarded this, *TCNT* . . . have cast aside, *Montgomery*.
concerning faith have made shipwreck: . . . made shipwreck of their faith, *Montgomery*.

20. Of whom is Hymenaeus and Alexander: Among them are, *Montgomery*.
whom I have delivered unto Satan: . . . whom I have surrendered, *Berkeley* . . . whom I handed over to, *TCNT* . . . whom I have given over, *Montgomery*.
that they may learn not to blaspheme: . . . so that they could be corrected, *SEB* . . . as a punishment for blaspheming, *Norlie* . . . to teach them not to speak against God, *NLT* . . . to be so disciplined that they will stop their abusive speech, *Williams* . . . so that they may be taught not to blaspheme, *Montgomery*.

1. I exhort therefore, that, first of all: I am urging, *Montgomery*.
supplications, prayers, intercessions, [and] giving of thanks:
be made for all men: . . . be offered regularly, *Montgomery*.

2. For kings, and [for] all that are in authority: . . . for all in high positions, *Confraternity* . . . and all those being in a superior station, *Concordant* . . . all those in prominent places, *Klingensmith*.
that we may lead a quiet and peaceable life: . . . that with all reverence and dignity, *Berkeley* . . . live quiet God-like lives, *NLT*.

1 Timothy 2:3

1230.1 verb 1pl
subj pres act
διάγωμεν
diagōmen
we may lead

1706.1 prep
ἐν
en
in

3820.11 adj
dat sing fem
πάσῃ
pasē
all

2131.3 noun
dat sing fem
εὐσεβείᾳ
eusebeia
godliness

2504.1 conj
καὶ
kai
and

4442.2 noun
dat sing fem
σεμνότητι·
semnotēti
seriousness;

3642.17 dem-
pron sing neu
3. τοῦτο
touto
this

ᶠᵃ **1056.1** conj
γὰρ ᵊ
gar
for

2541.1 adj sing
καλὸν
kalon
good

2504.1 conj
καὶ
kai
and

582.1 adj
sing neu
ἀπόδεκτον
apodekton
acceptable

1783.1 prep
ἐνώπιον
enōpion
before

3450.2 art
gen sing
τοῦ
tou
the

4842.2 noun
gen sing masc
σωτῆρος
sōtēros
Saviour

2231.2 prs-
pron gen 1pl
ἡμῶν
hēmōn
our

2296.2 noun
gen sing masc
θεοῦ,
theou
God,

3614.5 rel-pron
nom sing masc
4. ὃς
hos
who

3820.8 adj
acc pl masc
πάντας
pantas
all

442.9 noun
acc pl masc
ἀνθρώπους
anthrōpous
men

2286.3 verb 3sing
indic pres act
θέλει
thelei
wishes

4834.28 verb
inf aor pass
σωθῆναι
sōthēnai
to be saved

2504.1 conj
καὶ
kai
and

1519.1 prep
εἰς
eis
to

1907.4 noun
acc sing fem
ἐπίγνωσιν
epignōsin
knowledge

223.2 noun
gen sing fem
ἀληθείας
alētheias
of truth

2048.23 verb
inf aor act
ἐλθεῖν.
elthein
to come.

1518.3 num
card nom masc
5. εἷς
heis
One

1056.1 conj
γὰρ
gar
for

2296.1 noun
nom sing masc
θεός,
theos
God,

1518.3 num
card nom masc
εἷς
heis
one

2504.1 conj
καὶ
kai
and

3186.1 noun
nom sing masc
μεσίτης
mesitēs
mediator

2296.2 noun
gen sing masc
θεοῦ
theou
of God

2504.1 conj
καὶ
kai
and

442.7 noun
gen pl masc
ἀνθρώπων,
anthrōpōn
men,

442.1 noun
nom sing masc
ἄνθρωπος
anthrōpos
man

5382.1 name
nom masc
Χριστὸς
Christos
Christ

2400.1 name
nom masc
Ἰησοῦς,
Iēsous
Jesus,

3450.5 art
nom sing masc
6. ὁ
ho
the

1319.28 verb nom
sing masc part aor act
δοὺς
dous
having given

1431.6 prs-pron
acc sing masc
ἑαυτὸν
heauton
himself

484.1 noun
sing neu
ἀντίλυτρον
antilutron
a ransom

5065.1 prep
ὑπὲρ
huper
for

3820.4 adj gen pl
πάντων,
pantōn
all,

3450.16 art
sing neu
τὸ
to
the

3115.1 noun
sing neu
μαρτύριον
marturion
testimony

2511.7 noun
dat pl masc
καιροῖς
kairois
in times

2375.5 adj dat pl
ἰδίοις,
idiois
its own,

1519.1 prep
7. εἰς
eis
to

3614.16 rel-
pron sing neu
ὃ
ho
which

4935.27 verb 1sing
indic aor pass
ἐτέθην
etethēn
was appointed

1466.1 prs-
pron nom 1sing
ἐγὼ
egō
I

2755.1 noun
nom sing masc
κῆρυξ
kērux
a herald

2504.1 conj
καὶ
kai
and

646.1 noun
nom sing masc
ἀπόστολος·
apostolos
apostle,

223.4 noun
acc sing fem
ἀλήθειαν
alētheian
truth

2978.1 verb
1sing pres act
λέγω
legō
I speak

ᶠᵃ **1706.1** prep
ἐν
en
in

5382.3 name
dat masc
Χριστῷ, ᵊ
Christō
Christ,

3620.3 partic
οὐ
ou
not

5409.1 verb 1sing
indic pres mid
ψεύδομαι·
pseudomai
I do lie,

1314.1 noun
nom sing masc
διδάσκαλος
didaskalos
a teacher

1477.5 noun
gen pl neu
ἐθνῶν,
ethnōn
of Gentiles,

1706.1 prep
ἐν
en
in

3963.3 noun
dat sing fem
πίστει
pistei
faith

3.a.Txt: 01ℵ-corr,06D
018K,020L,025P,byz.
Var: 01ℵ-org,02A,33,sa.
bo.Lach,Treg,Tisc
We/Ho,Weis,Sod
UBS/✶

7.a.Txt: 01ℵ-org
06D-corr,015H,018K
020L,33,byz.
Var: 01ℵ-corr,02A
06D-org,025P,it.sa.bo.
Gries,Lach,Treg,Alf
Word,Tisc,We/Ho,Weis
Sod,UBS/✶

lated "quiet" occurs only here in the New Testament. The basic meaning is that of "restfulness unmarred by disturbance."

"Godliness" contains the dual meaning of reverence for God and respect for man. The Greek word translated "honesty" (*semnotēs*) contains the varied meanings of "reverence, dignity, seriousness, respectfulness, holiness." Perhaps the meaning here is "a proper sense of the seriousness of life."

2:3. The placement of "for" and its meaning is uncertain. Most commentators think what follows refers back to the universal prayer of verse 1. Prayer for all is "good and acceptable in the sight of God our Saviour." Beginning with the title "God our Saviour" the emphasis shifts from the theme of prayer to that of salvation. This new theme extends through verse 7.

2:4. Much controversy has revolved around the meaning of this verse. Does God save all? Or does God *want* all to be saved. Peter's second epistle tells us God is "not willing that any should perish, but that all should come to repentance" (2 Peter 3:9). We know from other Scriptures that not everyone will believe the good news of God's provision for their salvation. Salvation has been provided for all, but only those who accept it are saved.

2:5. First Timothy 2:5 makes two exclusive declarations: "There is one God, and one mediator between God and men" (see Romans 3:29,30; 10:12). "Mediator" means "someone who stands between." In order for Jesus to be a true representative of mankind, He became a man. The One who existed with God in eternity came to live with man in time and understands both sides (see Hebrews 4:14-16).

2:6. The word "ransom" (*antilutron*) means "payment." In the First Century the word *lutron* was used for the ransom price paid to free a slave. The preposition *anti* ("instead of") suggests substitution (cf. Mark 8:37; 10:45).

"To be testified in due time" means "to be declared at the appointed time." God's appointed time for all men to be saved is "now" (2 Corinthians 6:2).

2:7. Paul's threefold ministry seems a strange insertion at this juncture. But it is a logical summary of what he has just said about God and Christ. Paul was "ordained" ("by God" is understood) a preacher, apostle, and teacher of the Gentiles (see 2 Timothy 1:11). No doubt the semiprivate nature of this epistle prompted Paul to establish his authority. Paul's authority would have relevance for Timothy's authority. The churches in Ephesus would view Timothy as Paul's envoy.

in all godliness and honesty: . . . in all piety and gravity, *Young* . . . in all piety and worthy behavior, *Confraternity* . . . in perfect piety and soberness, *Norlie* . . . and seriousness, *Williams* . . . in a truly religious and earnest spirit, *TCNT* . . . and holiness, *NIV* . . . and dignity, *Klingensmith.*

3. For this [is] good and acceptable in the sight of God our Saviour: This is the right thing to do, *Williams* . . . for this is ideal and welcome, *Concordant.*

4. Who will have all men to be saved: . . . who is ever willing, *Williams* . . . who wants all men, *NIV.*

and to come unto the knowledge of the truth: . . . and come into a realization of the truth, *Concordant* . . . to begin understanding the truth, *SEB* . . . to an increasing knowledge of, *Williams.*

5. For [there is] one God:
and one mediator between God and men, the man Christ Jesus: . . . and one go-between, *Berkeley* . . . and one intermediary, *Williams.*

6. Who gave himself a ransom for all: . . . a purchase price, *Klingensmith.*

to be testified in due time: . . . of which the testimony is in its proper season, *Campbell* . . . in its proper time, *NIV* . . . at the proper time, *Williams.*

7. Whereunto I am ordained a preacher, and an apostle: . . . for which purpose, *Williams* . . . that I was myself appointed a Herald, *TCNT.*
(I speak the truth in Christ, [and] lie not;):
a teacher of the Gentiles in faith and verity: . . . of the heathen in the realm of, *Williams.*

2504.1 conj
καὶ
kai
and

223.3 noun dat sing fem
ἀληθείᾳ.
alētheia
truth.

1007.1 verb 1sing indic pres mid
8. Βούλομαι
Boulomai
I wish

3631.1 partic
οὖν
oun
therefore

4195.15 verb inf pres mid
προσεύχεσθαι
proseuchesthai
to pray

3450.8 art acc pl masc
τοὺς
tous
the

433.9 noun acc pl masc
ἄνδρας
andras
men

1706.1 prep
ἐν
en
in

3820.3 adj dat sing
παντὶ
panti
every

4964.3 noun dat sing masc
τόπῳ,
topō
place,

1854.1 verb acc pl masc part pres act
ἐπαίροντας
epairontas
lifting up

3603.3 adj acc pl fem
ὁσίους
hosious
holy

5331.8 noun acc pl fem
χεῖρας
cheiras
hands

5400.1 prep
χωρὶς
chōris
without

3572.2 noun gen sing fem
ὀργῆς
orgēs
anger

2504.1 conj
καὶ
kai
and

1255.2 noun gen sing masc
διαλογισμοῦ·
dialogismou
dispute.

5447.1 adv
9. ὡσαύτως
hōsautōs
In like manner

2504.1 conj
⌐a καὶ ⌐
kai
also

3450.15 art acc pl fem
⌐b τὰς ⌐
tas
the

1129.9 noun acc pl fem
γυναῖκας
gunaikas
women

1706.1 prep
ἐν
en
in

2659.1 noun dat sing fem
καταστολῇ
katastolē
bearing

2860.2 adj dat sing fem
κοσμίῳ
kosmiō
seemly

3196.3 prep
μετὰ
meta
with

127.1 noun gen sing fem
αἰδοῦς
aidous
modesty

2504.1 conj
καὶ
kai
and

4849.1 noun gen sing fem
σωφροσύνης
sōphrosunēs
discreetness

2858.3 verb inf pres act
κοσμεῖν
kosmein
to adorn

1431.13 prs-pron acc pl fem
ἑαυτάς,
heautas
themselves,

3231.1 partic
μὴ
mē
not

1706.1 prep
ἐν
en
with

3977.1 noun dat pl neu
πλέγμασιν,
plegmasin
platings,

2211.1 conj
⌐ ἢ
ē
or

2504.1 conj
[c☆ καὶ]
kai
[and]

5392.3 noun dat sing masc
⌐ χρυσῷ,
chrusō
gold,

5388.3 noun dat sing neu
[d☆ χρυσίῳ]
chrusiō
[idem]

2211.1 conj
ἢ
ē
or

3107.4 noun dat pl masc
μαργαρίταις,
margaritais
pearls,

2211.1 conj
ἢ
ē
or

2417.3 noun dat sing masc
ἱματισμῷ
himatismō
clothing

4045.1 adj dat sing masc
πολυτελεῖ,
polutelei
costly,

233.1 conj
10. ἀλλ'
all'
but

3614.16 rel-pron sing neu
ὃ
ho
what

4100.1 verb 3sing indic pres act
πρέπει
prepei
is fitting

1129.8 noun dat pl fem
γυναιξὶν
gunaixin
to women

1846.2 verb dat pl fem part pres mid
ἐπαγγελλομέναις
epangellomenais
professing

2293.1 noun acc sing fem
θεοσέβειαν,
theosebeian
fear of God,

1217.1 prep
δι'
di'
by

2024.5 noun gen pl neu
ἔργων
ergōn
works

18.1 adj gen pl
ἀγαθῶν.
agathōn
good.

1129.1 noun nom sing fem
11. Γυνὴ
Gunē
A woman

1706.1 prep
ἐν
en
in

2249.2 noun dat sing fem
ἡσυχίᾳ
hēsuchia
quietness

3101.3 verb 3sing impr pres act
μανθανέτω
manthanetō
let learn

1706.1 prep
ἐν
en
in

3820.11 adj dat sing fem
πάσῃ
pasē
all

5130.1 noun dat sing fem
ὑποταγῇ·
hupotagē
subjection;

1129.3 noun dat sing fem
12. ⌐ γυναικὶ
gunaiki
a woman

1156.2 conj
δὲ
de
but

1315.10 verb inf pres act
διδάσκειν
didaskein
to teach

9.a.Txt: 01א-corr,06D 018K,020L,byz.sa.bo. Tisc
Var: 01א-org,02A,025P 33,Lach,We/Ho,Weis Sod,UBS/☆

9.b.Txt: 06D-corr,018K 020L,byz.
Var: 01א,02A,06D-org 025P,33,Lach,Treg,Alf Word,Tisc,We/Ho,Weis Sod,UBS/☆

9.c.Txt: 06D-corr,018K 020L,byz.sa.
Var: 01א,02A,06D-org bo.Lach,Treg,Alf,Tisc We/Ho,Weis,Sod UBS/☆

9.d.Txt: 01א,06D,018K 020L,byz.Tisc
Var: 02A,025P,33,Lach We/Ho,Weis,Sod UBS/☆

2:8. "I will" is a strong expression, meaning more than "I wish." It has the sense of "I command." This is a transitional verse. It refers back to the first verse and becomes a bridge to the next verse. Believers are to pray in all circumstances. "Every where" might be understood as "in every place"; that is, wherever Christians meet for worship.

Prayer was to be accompanied by "lifting up holy hands" (see 1 Kings 8:22; Psalms 28:2; 141:2; 143:6). These uplifted hands were to show the personal purity and freedom from improper motives of the worshiper. The word "doubting" is better rendered "disputing" or "dissension."

2:9,10. Verses 9 and 10 address a woman's appearance in public; verses 11 and 12 teach about women's place in the Church. Eve is used as an illustration of man's priority in creation and the woman's deception in the temptation (verses 13,14). Verse 15 tells of a woman's salvation in childbearing.

A careful reading of verses 9 and 10 shows three positives and three negatives concerning women's dress. The three positives are (1) modest apparel, (2) decency, and (3) sobriety. In general, what Paul was saying is that women are to give a silent witness by their modest dress and active good works. The word "modest" means "orderly, decent." It reflects a correct attitude toward propriety. "Shamefacedness" carries the meaning of "modesty, decency, godly fear." "Sobriety" means "self-control." It connotes a balanced and discreet self-restraint.

The negatives are more explicit. They are (1) braided hair, (2) gold and pearls, and (3) expensive clothes. All three of these relate to the customs of the first-century church. Some women spent hours preparing their long hair in highly fashionable styles, fastening their plaits with ribbons and brightly colored bows. Rich women would interweave gold, silver, and pearls in their hairstyles. It is very likely that expensive clothes were outlandish in style and color, drawing undue attention to the wearer.

Paul wrote to Timothy that immodest or inappropriate dress distracts from the witness of a Christian woman. It may distract others from seeing her "good works" which are to be the true adornment of those who profess godliness.

2:11,12. Paul next discussed how a woman ought to behave in the church. His instructions here are nearly identical to those found in his first letter to the church at Corinth: "Let your women keep silence in the churches: for it is not permitted unto them to speak" (14:34; see also 14:35). (In 1 Corinthians the context was the public worship service.) Note that in this passage the subject "women" has changed to the singular "woman," which may indicate Paul was speaking of "woman" in the generic sense.

In verse 11 Paul exhorted women to learn and to be in full submission. This parallels the prohibitions recorded in verse 12, i.e., not to teach and not to have authority over the man (see

8. I will therefore: So I want, *Williams.*

that men pray every where: . . . to offer prayer, *Williams.*

lifting up holy hands, without wrath and doubting: . . . with hands reverently uplifted, *TCNT* . . . which are kept unstained by anger and dissensions, *Williams* . . . and contention, *Confraternity* . . . without anger and disputing they lift up dedicated hands, *Berkeley* . . . without anger or argument, *Norlie.* . . . They should not be angry or argue, *NLT* . . . No anger. No arguing, *SEB.*

9. In like manner also:

that women adorn themselves in modest apparel: . . . that women should make themselves attractive by their discreet, quiet, and modest dress, *TCNT* . . . to be decently dressed, *Confraternity* . . . to dress modestly, *NIV.*

with shamefacedness and sobriety: . . . should use good sense and be proper, *SEB* . . . decorously, with modesty and sanity, *Concordant.*

not with broided hair, or gold: . . . avoiding fancy hairdos, *SEB.*

or pearls, or costly array: . . . or expensive clothing, *Confraternity.*

10. But (which becometh women professing godliness): . . . as is appropriate for women, *Berkeley* . . . they should make themselves attractive, *TCNT.*

with good works: . . . by their good actions, *TCNT.*

11. Let the woman learn in silence with all subjection: . . . should be quiet when they learn, *NLT* . . . learn quietly and be under authority, *Norlie* . . . should listen quietly to their teachers, *TCNT* . . . put herself completely under authority, *SEB.*

1 Timothy 2:13

1315.10 verb inf pres act	**1156.2** conj	**1129.3** noun dat sing fem	**3620.2** partic	**1994.1** verb 1sing indic pres act	**3624.1** conj
[✶ διδάσκειν	δὲ	γυναικὶ]	οὐκ	ἐπιτρέπω,	οὐδὲ
didaskein	*de*	*gunaiki*	*ouk*	*epitrepō*	*oude*
[to teach	but	a woman]	not	I do allow,	nor

825.1 verb inf pres act	**433.2** noun gen sing masc	**233.1** conj	**1498.32** verb inf pres act	**1706.1** prep
αὐθεντεῖν	ἀνδρός,	ἀλλ'	εἶναι	ἐν
authentein	*andros*	*all'*	*einai*	*en*
to exercise authority over	man,	but	to be	in

2249.2 noun dat sing fem	**75.1** name masc	**1056.1** conj	**4272.5** num ord nom sing masc	**3972.2** verb 3sing indic aor pass	**1520.1** adv
ἡσυχίᾳ.	**13.** Ἀδὰμ	γὰρ	πρῶτος	ἐπλάσθη,	εἶτα
hēsuchia	*Adam*	*gar*	*prōtos*	*eplasthē*	*eita*
quietness;	Adam	for	first	was formed,	then

2075.1 name nom fem	**2504.1** conj	**75.1** name masc	**3620.2** partic	**534.3** verb 3sing indic aor pass	**3450.9** art nom sing fem
Εὕα·	**14.** καὶ	Ἀδὰμ	οὐκ	ἠπατήθη·	ἡ
Eua	*kai*	*Adam*	*ouk*	*ēpatēthē*	*hē*
Eve:	and	Adam	not	was deceived;	the

14.a.**Txt:** 01ℵ-corr
06D-corr,018K,020L
byz.
Var: 01ℵ-org,02A
06D-org,025P,33,Lach
Treg,Alf,Word,Tisc
We/Ho,Weis,Sod
UBS/✶

1156.2 conj	**1129.1** noun nom sing fem	**534.4** verb nom sing fem part aor pass	**1802.5** verb nom sing fem part aor pass	**1706.1** prep
δὲ	γυνὴ	ʼ ἀπατηθεῖσα	[ᵃ✶ ἐξαπατηθεῖσα]	ἐν
de	*gunē*	*apatētheisa*	*exapatētheisa*	*en*
but	woman,	having been deceived,	[idem]	in

3709.3 noun dat sing fem	**1090.3** verb 3sing indic perf act	**4834.33** verb 3sing indic fut pass	**1156.2** conj	**1217.2** prep
παραβάσει	γέγονεν·	**15.** σωθήσεται	δὲ	διὰ
parabasei	*gegonen*	*sōthēsetai*	*de*	*dia*
transgression	has become.	She shall be saved	but	through

3450.10 art gen sing fem	**4890.1** noun gen sing fem	**1430.1** partic	**3176.21** verb 3pl subj aor act	**1706.1** prep	**3963.3** noun dat sing fem	**2504.1** conj
τῆς	τεκνογονίας,	ἐὰν	μείνωσιν	ἐν	πίστει	καὶ
tēs	*teknogonias*	*ean*	*meinōsin*	*en*	*pistei*	*kai*
the	childbearing,	if	they abide	in	faith	and

26.3 noun dat sing fem	**2504.1** conj	**38.2** noun dat sing masc	**3196.3** prep	**4849.1** noun gen sing fem	**3964.2** adj nom sing masc
ἀγάπῃ	καὶ	ἁγιασμῷ	μετὰ	σωφροσύνης.	**3:1.** Πιστὸς
agapē	*kai*	*hagiasmō*	*meta*	*sōphrosunēs*	*Pistos*
love	and	sanctification	with	discreetness.	Faithful

3450.5 art nom sing masc	**3030.1** noun nom sing masc	**1479.1** conj	**4948.3** indef-pron nom sing	**1968.1** noun gen sing fem	**3576.1** verb 3sing indic pres mid
ὁ	λόγος·	εἴ	τις	ἐπισκοπῆς	ὀρέγεται,
ho	*logos*	*ei*	*tis*	*episkopēs*	*oregetai*
the	word:	if	any	overseership	aspires to

2541.9 adj gen sing neu	**2024.2** noun gen sing neu	**1922.1** verb 3sing indic pres act	**1158.1** verb 3sing indic pres act	**3631.1** partic	**3450.6** art acc sing masc
καλοῦ	ἔργου	ἐπιθυμεῖ.	**2.** δεῖ	οὖν	τὸν
kalou	*ergou*	*epithumei*	*dei*	*oun*	*ton*
of good	a work	he is desirous.	It is necessary	then	the

1969.1 noun acc sing masc	**421.1** adj acc sing	**421.3** adj acc sing	**1498.32** verb inf pres act
ἐπίσκοπον	ʼ ἀνεπίληπτον	[✶ ἀνεπίλημπτον]	εἶναι,
episkopon	*anepilēpton*	*anepilēmpton*	*einai*
overseer	irreproachable	[idem]	to be,

"authenteō," number 825, in the *Greek-English Dictionary*). There may have been some very specific local problems Paul was addressing; however, if this is the case they are not identified in his Epistle. It appears that Paul was simply repeating instructions for rules of conduct. In verses 13 and 14 he appeals to principles put in place by God and His created order (cf. 1 Corinthians 11:9).

It is suggested that since Christianity had brought new freedom to women who had lived within an extremely male-dominated society, there may have been some localized abuses of this freedom by women who began to assert themselves more forcefully. Such conduct would have brought shame to the new churches and would have created a stumbling block to the people of that culture.

2:13,14. Paul supported his teaching with an allusion to Genesis. He recounted God's purpose in creation and Eve's part in the first sin. In these verses Paul was not basing what he said on the social position of women in his time but on the universal principle of priority seen in the creation of man and woman (compare 1 Corinthians 11:2-16). Paul was not putting the total blame for the Fall on Eve. In other places the apostle clearly shows that Adam was to blame (see Romans 5:12-21).

2:15. Most commentators agree this is the most difficult text in the Pastoral Epistles. Who is the "she" and does becoming a mother save a woman? Some view the woman here as referring to Eve because of the context. Her "deliverance" would come through the pain of childbirth (Genesis 3:15,16) because eventually the "seed of the woman" would come to bring salvation. Others see "she shall be saved in childbearing" as a reference to Mary's giving birth to the One who is the Saviour.

Still others take the statement "she shall be saved in childbearing" literally. The Greek word translated "saved" here has a wide variety of meanings. The primary rendering is "preserve or rescue from natural dangers and afflictions" (*BAGD*, "sōzō"). Paul followed that statement by mentioning the qualifications for claiming the promise: continuing in "faith and charity and holiness with sobriety." Many Christian women have claimed this promise when facing childbirth and have found special help.

3:1. The first seven verses of chapter 3 list the qualifications of a "bishop." A bishop in the First Century was an overseer or spiritual leader of a local church. *Pastor*, *bishop*, and *elder* are interchangeable terms. Acts 20:17 and 28 use three Greek terms that show these words to be synonymous.

3:2. Verses 2-6 list 15 qualifications for the "bishop" (overseer, elder, pastor). Ten are positive and five are negative. A 16th in the list (verse 7) addresses the overseer's reputation as it relates to the

12. But I suffer not a woman to teach, nor to usurp authority over the man: I do not consent to women becoming teachers, *TCNT* . . . or to exercise authority, *Confraternity* . . . nor to rule a husband, *Young* . . . neither to domineer over, *Berkeley* . . . or be leaders over men, *NLT*.
but to be in silence:

13. For Adam was first formed, then Eve: . . . was first molded, *Concordant*.

14. And Adam was not deceived: Adam was not fooled, *NLT* . . . was not seduced, *SEB*.
but the woman being deceived was in the transgression: . . . deluded, *Concordant* . . . and became a sinner, *NIV* . . . fell into sin, *SEB*.

15. Notwithstanding she shall be saved in childbearing: And yet, through her child-bearing, salvation has come, *Norlie* . . . through motherhood, *SEB*.
if they continue in faith and charity and holiness: . . . never abandon faith, *TCNT* . . . and sanctification, *Young*.
with sobriety: . . . sanity, *Concordant* . . . good sense, *SEB*.

1. This [is] a true saying: It is a trustworthy statement, *NASB* . . . This is something you can trust, *SEB* . . . Faithful is the saying, *Concordant*.
If a man desire the office of a bishop: If anyone is craving the supervision, *Concordant* . . . Anyone who aspires to be a Presiding-Officer, *TCNT* . . . wants to be a church leader, *NLT* . . . is eager for, *Confraternity* . . . aspires to, *Berkeley*.
he desireth a good work:

2. A bishop then must be blameless: . . . a man of irreproachable character, *Norlie* . . . must be a good man, *NLT* . . . must be above suspicion, *SEB*.

391

1518.6 num card gen fem	1129.2 noun gen sing fem	433.4 noun acc sing masc	3386.4 adj acc sing masc	3386.2 adj acc sing masc
μιᾶς *mias* of one	γυναικὸς *gunaikos* wife	ἄνδρα, *andra* husband,	ʻ νηφάλεον, *nēphaleon* sober,	[✶ νηφάλιον,] *nēphalion* [idem]

4850.2 adj acc sing masc	2860.1 adj acc sing masc	5219.1 adj acc sing masc	1311.1 adj acc sing masc	3231.1 partic
σώφρονα, *sōphrona* serious,	κόσμιον, *kosmion* well-behaved,	φιλόξενον, *philoxenon* hospitable,	διδακτικόν, *didaktikon* apt to teach;	3. μὴ *mē* not

3805.1 adj acc sing masc	3231.1 partic	3991.1 noun acc sing masc	3231.1 partic	146.1 adj acc sing masc
πάροινον, *paroinon* given to wine,	μὴ *mē* not	πλήκτην, *plēktēn* a striker,	ʻᵃ μὴ *mē* not	αἰσχροκερδῆ, ˎ *aischrokerdē* greedy of disgraceful gain,

233.1 conj	233.2 conj	1918.1 adj acc sing masc	267.1 adj acc sing masc	859.2 adj acc sing masc
ʻ ἀλλ᾽ *all'* but	[✶ ἀλλὰ] *alla* [idem]	ἐπιεικῆ, *epieikē* gentle,	ἄμαχον, *amachon* not contentious,	ἀφιλάργυρον˙ *aphilarguron* not loving money;

3450.2 art gen sing	2375.2 adj gen sing	3486.2 noun gen sing masc	2544.1 adv	4150.4 verb acc sing masc part pres mid
4. τοῦ *tou* the	ἰδίου *idiou* his own	οἴκου *oikou* house	καλῶς *kalōs* well	προϊστάμενον, *proistamenon* ruling,

4891.4 noun pl neu	2174.15 verb part pres act	1706.1 prep	5130.1 noun dat sing fem	3196.3 prep	3820.10 adj gen sing fem
τέκνα *tekna* children	ἔχοντα *echonta* having	ἐν *en* in	ὑποταγῇ *hupotagē* subjection	μετὰ *meta* with	πάσης *pasēs* all

4442.1 noun gen sing fem	1479.1 conj	1156.2 conj	4948.3 indef- pron nom sing	3450.2 art gen sing	2375.2 adj gen sing
σεμνότητος˙ *semnotētos* dignity;	5. εἰ *ei* if	δέ *de* but	τις *tis* a certain one	τοῦ *tou* the	ἰδίου *idiou* his own

3486.2 noun gen sing masc	4150.1 verb inf aor act	3620.2 partic	3471.4 verb 3sing indic perf act	4316.1 adv	1564.1 noun fem
οἴκου *oikou* house	προστῆναι *prostēnai* to rule	οὐκ *ouk* not	οἶδεν, *oiden* knows,	πῶς *pōs* how	ἐκκλησίας *ekklēsias* assembly

2296.2 noun gen sing masc	1944.3 verb 3sing indic fut pass	3231.1 partic	3367.1 adj acc sing masc	2419.1 conj
θεοῦ *theou* of God	ἐπιμελήσεται; *epimelēsetai* shall he take care of?	6. μὴ *mē* not	νεόφυτον, *neophuton* a novice,	ἵνα *hina* so that

3231.1 partic	5028.1 verb nom sing masc part aor pass	1519.1 prep	2890.1 noun sing neu	1690.2 verb 3sing subj aor act
μὴ *mē* not	τυφωθεὶς *tuphōtheis* having been puffed up,	εἰς *eis* into	κρίμα *krima* condemnation	ἐμπέσῃ *empesē* he may fall

3450.2 art gen sing	1222.2 adj gen sing masc	1158.1 verb 3sing indic pres act	1156.2 conj	840.6 prs-pron acc sing masc	2504.1 conj
τοῦ *tou* of the	διαβόλου. *diabolou* devil.	7. δεῖ *dei* It is necessary for	δὲ *de* but	ʻᵃ αὐτὸν ˎ *auton* him	καὶ *kai* also

world. Verse 2 sets forth seven positive characteristics. "Blameless" literally means "not to be laid hold of." Other translations are "above reproach" and "without fault." In 6:14 the same Greek term is translated "unrebukable."

"Husband of one wife" reflects the social and cultural situation of the First Century. Polygamy, easy divorce, and remarriage were prevalent. Paul taught that monogamy is God's requirement for a pastor. The spiritual leader must be a "one-wife man." Marital entanglements beyond the "one" can bring discredit to his position and reproach on the Church. (See Genesis 2:18-25; Matthew 19:3-9; Mark 10:2-12.)

"Sober" in general means "temperate" and specifically "free from excess, well-balanced, self-controlled." "Of good behavior" refers to conduct that is "orderly, respectable, honorable." "Apt to teach" means "able or competent to teach."

the husband of one wife: ... married but once, *Confraternity.*

vigilant, sober, of good behaviour: ... temperate, *KJII, Williams* ... respectable, *NASB.*

given to hospitality:
apt to teach: ... skillful in teaching, *Williams.*

3:3. Scholars disagree as to whether *oinos* ("wine") in this verse, verse 8, and 5:23 refers to grape juice or a fermented drink, and therefore, whether the apostle is advocating temperance or abstinence. Other Scriptures give guidance for believers and especially leaders. They take a strong stand against drunkenness (see Leviticus 10:8,9; Proverbs 20:1; 23:19-21,29-35). The awful consequences of traffic fatalities and ruined homes force a thinking believer to make his decision on the basis of the great principle stated in Romans 14:21, "It is good neither to eat flesh, nor to drink wine, nor any thing whereby thy brother stumbleth, or is offended." "Not greedy of filthy lucre" is "not a lover of money" in the New International Version. Money becomes dirty when it is viewed with greed or obtained dishonestly (cf. 6:10).

The only positive characteristic in this verse is the term "patient." Its basic meaning is "gentle, peaceable." This contrasts the following negative, "not a brawler." The literal meaning is "abstinence from fighting" and describes someone who is "disinclined to fight."

3. Not given to wine, no striker, not greedy of filthy lucre: ... not addicted to strong drink, *Williams* ... nor a fist-fighter, *Berkeley* ... not quarrelsome, *Concordant* ... not greedy of ill profit, *KJII* ... or pugnacious, *NASB* ... not after money, *Berkeley.*

but patient, not a brawler, not covetous: ... conciliatory, *Berkeley.*

3:4,5. Verses 4 and 5 deal with the family relationships of the spiritual leader. He is to be "one that ruleth well his own house." The Bible views the father as the head of the marriage and the family (see Ephesians 5:22-33; 6:1-4). The parenthetic question in verse 5 is a strong argument for this qualification. "With all gravity" (verse 4) does not mean with strict reserve or somber sternness. The sense here is "with complete dignity" and in a manner that fosters respect.

4. One that ruleth well his own house: ... controlling his own household ideally, *Concordant* ... presiding beautifully over his own home, *Berkeley.*

having his children in subjection with all gravity: ... keeping his children, *Williams* ... under control, *NASB* ... and perfectly respectful, *Confraternity.*

5. (For if a man know not how to rule his own house: ... to manage, *Berkeley.*

how shall he take care of the church of God?):

3:6. Being a leader demands experience and wisdom for making decisions. The new convert or inexperienced Christian faces many pitfalls. The Greek word for "novice" is the root of the modern term *neophyte.* "Lifted up with pride" literally means "to wrap up in smoke."

6. Not a novice:
lest being lifted up with pride: ... or else becoming conceited, *Williams* ... being conceited, *Concordant.*

he fall into the condemnation of the devil: ... he may incur the doom, *Williams* ... and incur the condemnation passed on the devil, *Confraternity* ... incurred by the devil, *NASB.*

3114.3 noun acc sing fem	2541.8 adj acc sing fem	2174.29 verb inf pres act	570.3 prep	3450.1 art gen pl	1839.1 prep
μαρτυρίαν	καλὴν	ἔχειν	ἀπὸ	τῶν	ἔξωθεν,
marturian	kalēn	echein	apo	tōn	exōthen
a testimony	good	to have	from	the	outside,

2419.1 conj	3231.1 partic	1519.1 prep	3543.1 noun acc sing masc	1690.2 verb 3sing subj aor act	2504.1 conj
ἵνα	μὴ	εἰς	ὀνειδισμὸν	ἐμπέσῃ	καὶ
hina	mē	eis	oneidismon	empesē	kai
so that	not	into	reproach	he may fall	and

3666.3 noun acc sing fem	3450.2 art gen sing	1222.2 adj gen sing masc	1243.5 noun acc pl masc		5447.1 adv
παγίδα	τοῦ	διαβόλου.	8. Διακόνους		ὡσαύτως
pagida	tou	diabolou	Diakonous		hōsautōs
snare	of the	devil.	Deacons,		in like manner,

4441.1 adj acc pl masc	3231.1 partic	1345.1 adj acc pl masc	3231.1 partic	3494.3 noun dat sing masc	4044.3 adj dat sing
σεμνούς,	μὴ	διλόγους,	μὴ	οἴνῳ	πολλῷ
semnous	mē	dilogous	mē	oinō	pollō
having integrity,	not	double tongued,	not	to wine	much

4196.4 verb acc pl masc part pres act	3231.1 partic	146.2 adj acc pl masc		2174.21 verb acc pl masc part pres act
προσέχοντας,	μὴ	αἰσχροκερδεῖς,		9. ἔχοντας
prosechontas	mē	aischrokerdeis		echontas
being given,	not	greedy of disgraceful gain,		holding

3450.16 art sing neu	3328.1 noun sing neu	3450.10 art gen sing fem	3963.2 noun gen sing fem	1706.1 prep	2485.8 adj dat sing fem
τὸ	μυστήριον	τῆς	πίστεως	ἐν	καθαρᾷ
to	mustērion	tēs	pisteōs	en	kathara
the	mystery	of the	faith	in	clean

4743.3 noun dat sing fem	2504.1 conj	3642.7 dem-pron nom pl masc	1156.2 conj	1375.14 verb 3pl impr pres mid
συνειδήσει.	10. καὶ	οὗτοι	δὲ	δοκιμαζέσθωσαν
suneidēsei	kai	houtoi	de	dokimazesthōsan
conscience.	And	these	also	let them be proved

4270.1 adv	1520.1 adv	1241.3 verb 3pl impr pres act	408.3 adj nom pl masc	1498.23 verb nom pl masc part pres act
πρῶτον,	εἶτα	διακονείτωσαν,	ἀνέγκλητοι	ὄντες.
prōton	eita	diakoneitōsan	anenklētoi	ontes
first,	then	let them serve,	without reproach	being.

1129.9 noun acc pl fem	5447.1 adv	4441.2 adj acc pl fem	3231.1 partic	1222.6 adj acc pl fem
11. γυναῖκας	ὡσαύτως	σεμνάς,	μὴ	διαβόλους,
gunaikas	hōsautōs	semnas	mē	diabolous
Women	in like manner	serious,	not	slanderers,

3386.3 adj acc pl masc	3386.1 adj acc pl	3964.13 adj acc pl fem	1706.1 prep	3820.5 adj dat pl
ʼ νηφαλέους,	[☆ νηφαλίους,]	πιστὰς	ἐν	πᾶσιν.
nēphaleous	nēphalious	pistas	en	pasin
sober,	[idem]	faithful	in	all things.

1243.3 noun nom pl masc	1498.33 verb 3pl impr pres act	1518.6 num card gen fem	1129.2 noun gen sing fem	433.6 noun nom pl masc
12. διάκονοι	ἔστωσαν	μιᾶς	γυναικὸς	ἄνδρες,
diakonoi	estōsan	mias	gunaikos	andres
Deacons	let be	of one	wife	husbands,

3:7. The spiritual leader (overseer, elder, pastor) "must have a good report of them . . . without." Non-Christians in Timothy's locale should have been able to look at the churches, and especially the leaders, and find nothing wrong or even suspect. A good reputation brings an effective witness.

3:8. This section (verses 8-13) lists the qualifications for the office of deacon. Several of those given for bishops (elders, pastors, overseers) are repeated. *Deacon, servant,* and *minister* all come from the Greek word *diakonos.* The collective term "deacons" is a special word for a class of helpers who were subordinate to bishops or elders (see Philippians 1:1). Acts 6 gives us a picture of the first deacons.

Deacons must first be "grave." The basic meaning here is "serious" or "worthy of honor and respect." Deacons are not to be "double-tongued" (*dilogos*). Two meanings are possible: (1) "saying different things to different people to suit the occasion" or (2) "given to repetition," i.e., a "talebearer." Either could be applied to the qualifications for this office. The words of a deacon are to be truthful and sincere. They are not to betray confidences or talk about others in derogatory terms.

3:9. In the New Testament the word *mystery* refers to a secret unknown to the masses but revealed to a believer or believers. For a parallel reading and an expansion of Paul's use of *mystery,* see Romans 16:25,26. Connected with "faith" it means the truths of the gospel revealed in Jesus Christ. Deacons, knowing the tenets of faith (the truth found in the gospel), should hold these with a "pure (clear, clean) conscience" (see 1:5,19).

3:10. The qualification here is similar to that for a bishop given in verse 6: "not a novice." The word "proved" (from *dokimazō*) means "to test in the hope of being successful," thus giving a positive result to the period or manner of proving. The idea is that of "careful scrutiny" (compare Acts 6:3). "Being found blameless" (*anenklētos*) carries the sense of "that which cannot be called to account, irreproachable."

3:11. Because the Greek word *gunē* is used for "woman" and "wife," it is uncertain whether Paul was writing about the wives of deacons or the office of deaconess. Since the context focuses on deacons, it is quite possible Paul extends their ministry as shared by their wives. Four qualifications are given. Two repeat those given to deacons. The other two involve discretion, self-control, and industry. "Not slanderers" (*diaboloi*) is translated "malicious talkers" in the New International Version. Gossip, out of control, can turn to slander. "Faithful in all things" may be translated "absolutely trustworthy."

7. Moreover he must have a good report of them which are without: . . . enjoy a favorable reputation, *Berkeley* . . . an ideal testimony, *Concordant* . . . with outsiders, *Williams.*

lest he fall into reproach and the snare of the devil: . . . not fall into disgrace, *Confraternity* . . . fall into the devil's trap, *Williams.*

8. Likewise [must] the deacons [be] grave: In the same way, *KJII* . . . be men of dignity, *NASB.*

not doubletongued, not given to much wine: . . . addicted to strong drink, *Williams.*

not greedy of filthy lucre: . . . fond of sordid gain, *NASB* . . . for base gain, *Confraternity* . . . for ill-gotten gains, *Berkeley* . . . dishonest gain, *Williams.*

9. Holding the mystery of the faith in a pure conscience: . . . the open secret of faith, *Williams.*

10. And let these also first be proved: . . . be put on probation, *Berkeley.*

then let them use the office of a deacon, being [found] blameless: . . . if they are beyond reproach, *NASB* . . . and then, if irreproachable, they may serve as deacons, *Berkeley* . . . being unimpeachable, *Concordant.*

11. Even so [must their] wives [be] grave: . . . let the women be honorable, *Confraternity.*

not slanderers, sober, faithful in all things: . . . not gossips...and perfectly trustworthy, *Williams.*

12. Let the deacons be the husbands of one wife: . . . should be men who have been married but once, *Confraternity.*

4891.5 noun gen pl neu	2544.1 adv	4150.5 verb nom pl masc part pres mid	2504.1 conj	3450.1 art gen pl	2375.1 adj gen pl
τέκνων	καλῶς	προϊστάμενοι	καὶ	τῶν	ἰδίων
teknōn	kalōs	proistamenoi	kai	tōn	idiōn
children	well	presiding over	and	the	their own

3486.5 noun gen pl masc	3450.7 art nom pl masc	1056.1 conj	2544.1 adv	1241.12 verb nom pl masc part aor act	892.1 noun acc sing masc
οἴκων.	**13.** οἱ	γὰρ	καλῶς	διακονήσαντες,	βαθμὸν
oikōn	hoi	gar	kalōs	diakonēsantes	bathmon
houses.	The	for	well	having served,	a degree

	1431.7 prs- pron dat pl masc	2541.1 adj sing	3909.1 verb 3pl indic pres mid	2504.1 conj	4044.12 adj acc sing fem
	ἑαυτοῖς	καλὸν	περιποιοῦνται,	καὶ	πολλὴν
	heautois	kalon	peripoiountai	kai	pollēn
	for themselves	good	acquire,	and	much

3816.4 noun acc sing fem	1706.1 prep	3963.3 noun dat sing fem	3450.11 art dat sing fem	1706.1 prep	5382.3 name dat masc	2400.2 name masc
παρρησίαν	ἐν	πίστει	τῇ	ἐν	Χριστῷ	Ἰησοῦ.
parrhēsian	en	pistei	tē	en	Christō	Iēsou
boldness	in	faith	the	in	Christ	Jesus.

3642.18 dem- pron pl neu	4622.3 prs- pron dat 2sing	1119.1 verb 1sing indic pres act	1666.5 verb nom sing masc part pres act	2048.23 verb inf aor act
14. Ταῦτά	σοι	γράφω,	ἐλπίζων	ἐλθεῖν
Tauta	soi	graphō	elpizōn	elthein
These things	to you	I write,	hoping	to come

14.a.**Txt:** 01ℵ,06D-corr2
010F,012G,byz.
Var: 02A,04C,06D-org
025P,044,33,81

4242.1 prep	4622.4 prs- pron acc 2sing	4880.1 adv comp	1706.1 prep	4882.1 noun dat sing neu	1430.1 partic
πρὸς	σὲ	′ τάχιον·	[ᵃ ἐν	τάχει·]	**15.** ἐὰν
pros	se	tachion	en	tachei	ean
to	you	more quickly;	[in	swiftness;]	if

1156.2 conj	1012.2 verb 1sing subj pres act	2419.1 conj	3471.15 verb 2sing subj perf act	4316.1 adv	1158.1 verb 3sing indic pres act	1706.1 prep
δὲ	βραδύνω,	ἵνα	εἰδῇς	πῶς	δεῖ	ἐν
de	bradunō	hina	eidēs	pōs	dei	en
but	I should delay,	that	you may know	how	must	in

3486.3 noun dat sing masc	2296.2 noun gen sing masc	388.6 verb inf pres mid	3610.3 rel-pron nom sing fem	1498.4 verb 3sing indic pres act
οἴκῳ	θεοῦ	ἀναστρέφεσθαι,	ἥτις	ἐστὶν
oikō	theou	anastrephesthai	hētis	estin
house	of God	to conduct oneself,	which	is

1564.2 noun nom sing fem	2296.2 noun gen sing masc	2180.11 verb gen sing part pres act	4620.1 noun nom sing masc	2504.1 conj	1470.1 noun sing neu
ἐκκλησία	θεοῦ	ζῶντος,	στῦλος	καὶ	ἑδραίωμα
ekklēsia	theou	zōntos	stulos	kai	hedraiōma
assembly	of God	living,	pillar	and	foundation

3450.10 art gen sing fem	223.2 noun gen sing fem	2504.1 conj	3535.1 adv	3144.16 adj sing neu
τῆς	ἀληθείας.	**16.** καὶ	ὁμολογουμένως	μέγα
tēs	alētheias	kai	homologoumenōs	mega
of the	truth.	And	confessedly	great

1498.4 verb 3sing indic pres act	3450.16 art sing neu	3450.10 art gen sing fem	2131.2 noun gen sing fem	3328.1 noun sing neu	2296.1 noun nom sing masc
ἐστὶν	τὸ	τῆς	εὐσεβείας	μυστήριον·	′ Θεὸς
estin	to	tēs	eusebeias	mustērion	Theos
is	the	of the	godliness	mystery:	God

3:12. As Paul returned to deacons, he repeated the qualifications he set forth for bishops (see verses 2,4). Marital fidelity and parental control are as important for deacons as for pastors.

3:13. Verse 13 ends Paul's instructions regarding deacons. It commends those who serve well. They gain the esteem and respect of those whom they serve and find boldness or assurance in their relationship with Jesus Christ. The words "good degree" are best understood as "reputation." The "great boldness" deacons demonstrate is first toward man; it could, however, be toward God just as well (compare Hebrews 10:19).

3:14. In the final paragraph of this chapter (verses 14-16) Paul gave the central focus and theme of the entire epistle. This key passage records Paul's purpose for writing and gives a creedlike statement that summarizes the gospel.

As discovered earlier (1:3), Paul left Timothy in Ephesus. Paul had probably given Timothy oral instructions and now was detailing them with written confirmation. The apostle hoped to come to Ephesus and see Timothy. It is unknown whether he did or not. Even at this writing Paul had serious doubts; note the words in the following verse, "But if I tarry long."

3:15. Many see in the words "that thou mayest know how thou oughtest to behave thyself in the house of God" the central purpose for this letter. Though addressed primarily to Timothy, it certainly would be read in a much wider circle (very possibly in the local congregations in and around Ephesus). So Paul's teaching in this entire epistle would guide many individual Christians in proper behavior. "To behave" is translated from the Greek verb *anastrephō*, "to conduct oneself," and includes both the walk and conversation of a Christian.

"In the house (*oikos*) of God" means "in God's household, in God's family." The next clause contains an expanded meaning in the words "the church (*ekklēsia*) of the living God." *Ekklēsia* means "a company of people who have been called out" and refers to a local congregation as a part of the Church.

This *ekklēsia* is "the pillar (*stulos*) and ground (*hedraiōma*) of the truth." The word "pillar" was sometimes used for the decorative column that often supported statues of famous citizens. "Ground" is the "support, bulwark, buttress" that supports the building. And "truth" refers to the gospel.

3:16. "Truth" carries over from verse 15 as the focus of the great creedal hymn of verse 16. This hymn begins with the preexistent Christ and ends with His glorious ascension. The phrase "mystery of godliness" occurs only here. (For comments on "mystery" see verse 9.)

ruling their children and their own houses well: ... and good managers of, *NASB* ... controlling children, *Concordant* ... and well-ordered households, *Norlie*.

13. For they that have used the office of a deacon well: ... those who render good service, *Williams*.

purchase to themselves a good degree: ... win a good standing for themselves, *Williams* ... a very good position, *SEB*.

and great boldness in the faith which is in Christ Jesus:

14. These things write I unto thee, hoping to come unto thee shortly:

15. But if I tarry long, that thou mayest know: ... yet, if I should be tardy, *Concordant* ... but in case I should be, *TCNT* ... In case I am delayed, *Norlie* ... if I am detained, *Williams* ... if I am delayed, *Confraternity*.

how thou oughtest to behave thyself in the house of God: ... how we must live in God's family, *SEB* ... how one ought to conduct himself, *NASB* ... how you should act among people in the church, *NLT* ... in the Household of God, *TCNT*.

which is the church of the living God:

the pillar and ground of the truth: ... and base of the truth, *Concordant* ... and support of the truth, *Campbell*.

16. And without controversy great is the mystery of godliness: And without doubt, *KJII* ... by common confession, *NASB* ... Very important indeed is the hidden truth of godliness, *Norlie* ... We must agree that the secret of our faith is great, *SEB*.

16.a.**Txt:** 01א-corr
02A-corr,04C-corr
06D-corr,018K,020L
025P,byz.
Var: 01א-org,02A-org
04C-org,33,Gries,Lach
Treg,Alf,Word,Tisc
We/Ho,Weis,Sod
UBS/✩

3614.5 rel-pron nom sing masc	**5157.10** verb 3sing indic aor pass	**1706.1** prep	**4418.3** noun dat sing fem	**1338.13** verb 3sing indic aor pass	**1706.1** prep
[a✩ Ὅς]	ἐφανερώθη	ἐν	σαρκί,	ἐδικαιώθη	ἐν
Hos	ephanerōthē	en	sarki	edikaiōthē	en
[who]	was manifested	in	flesh,	was justified	in

4011.3 noun dat sing neu	**3571.21** verb 3sing indic aor pass	**32.7** noun dat pl masc	**2756.23** verb 3sing indic aor pass	**1706.1** prep
πνεύματι,	ὤφθη	ἀγγέλοις,	ἐκηρύχθη	ἐν
pneumati	ōphthē	angelois	ekēruchthē	en
Spirit,	was seen	by angels,	was proclaimed	among

1477.6 noun dat pl neu	**3961.58** verb 3sing indic aor pass	**1706.1** prep	**2862.3** noun dat sing masc	**351.6** verb 3sing indic aor pass
ἔθνεσιν,	ἐπιστεύθη	ἐν	κόσμῳ,	ʹ ἀνελήφθη
ethnesin	episteuthē	en	kosmō	anelēphthē
nations,	was believed on	in	world,	was received up

351.8 verb 3sing indic aor pass	**1706.1** prep	**1374.19** verb 3sing subj aor act	**3450.16** art sing neu	**1156.2** conj	**4011.1** noun sing neu
[✩ ἀνελήμφθη]	ἐν	δόξῃ.	**4:1.** Τὸ	δὲ	πνεῦμα
anelēmphthē	en	doxē	To	de	pneuma
[idem]	in	glory.	The	but	Spirit

4346.1 adv	**2978.5** verb 3sing indic pres act	**3617.1** conj	**1706.1** prep	**5143.1** adj comp dat pl masc	**2511.7** noun dat pl masc
ῥητῶς	λέγει,	ὅτι	ἐν	ὑστέροις	καιροῖς
rhētōs	legei	hoti	en	husterois	kairois
expressly	says,	that	in	latter	times

861.12 verb 3pl indic fut mid	**4948.7** indef-pron nom pl masc	**3450.10** art gen sing fem	**3963.2** noun gen sing fem	**4196.3** verb nom pl masc part pres act
ἀποστήσονταί	τινες	τῆς	πίστεως,	προσέχοντες
apostēsontai	tines	tēs	pisteōs	prosechontes
shall depart from	some	the	faith,	paying attention

4011.7 noun dat pl neu	**3969.3** adj dat pl neu	**2504.1** conj	**1313.5** noun dat pl fem	**1134.4** noun gen pl neu
πνεύμασιν	πλάνοις	καὶ	διδασκαλίαις	δαιμονίων
pneumasin	planois	kai	didaskaliais	daimoniōn
to spirits	deceiving	and	teachings	of demons

1706.1 prep	**5110.3** noun dat sing fem	**5408.1** adj gen pl masc	**2722.1** verb gen pl masc part perf mid
2. ἐν	ὑποκρίσει	ψευδολόγων,	ʹ κεκαυτηριασμένων
en	hupokrisei	pseudologōn	kekautēriasmenōn
in	hypocrisy	of speakers of lies,	having been cauterized

2722.2 verb gen pl masc part perf mid	**3450.12** art acc sing fem	**2375.11** adj acc sing fem	**4743.4** noun acc sing fem
[✩ κεκαυστηριασμένων]	τὴν	ἰδίαν	συνείδησιν,
kekaustēriasmenōn	tēn	idian	suneidēsin
[idem]	the	their own	conscience,

2940.4 verb gen pl masc part pres act	**1053.5** verb inf pres act	**563.9** verb inf pres mid	**1026.5** noun gen pl neu	**3614.17** rel-pron pl neu
3. κωλυόντων	γαμεῖν,	ἀπέχεσθαι	βρωμάτων,	ἃ
kōluontōn	gamein	apechesthai	brōmatōn	ha
forbidding	to marry,	to abstain	from meats,	which

3450.5 art nom sing masc	**2296.1** noun nom sing masc	**2908.2** verb 3sing indic aor act	**1519.1** prep	**3206.1** noun acc sing fem
ὁ	θεὸς	ἔκτισεν	εἰς	ʹ μετάληψιν
ho	theos	ektisen	eis	metalēpsin
	God	created	for	partaking

In the hymn the first three statements are understood only by divine revelation. The last three are attested by historical records in the Gospel and Acts.

"God (He who = Christ) was manifest in the flesh (emphasizes the humanity of Christ), justified in (vindicated by) the Spirit (cf. Romans 1:3), seen of angels (cf. Ephesians 3:10; 1 Peter 1:12), preached unto the Gentiles (the nations), believed on in the world, received up into glory (the Ascension)."

4:1. Chapter 4 continues the explicit instructions Paul gave Timothy in this pastoral letter. The first five verses predict an imminent apostasy and give a solemn warning regarding false teaching. "The Spirit speaketh expressly" ("in specific terms") indicates God was giving "directions" through prophets in the Church (compare Acts 20:23; 21:11).

"In the latter times" refers to the time following this letter, not "last days" as in 2 Timothy 3:1. It is quite possible this apostasy and false teaching was being given at the very time this epistle was being read. The "some (who) depart from the faith" are apostates. *Apostasy* is "renunciation, abandonment, defection, departure, withdrawal," and "a falling away." An apostate is someone who does these things with regard to his religious beliefs. To "depart from the faith" means to willfully abandon belief in "the faith" ("the body of revealed truth") (compare Titus 1:13; Jude 3). "Faith" is an important word in 1 Timothy; it appears 19 times.

What these apostates do after abandoning "the faith" is incredible: they give heed to "seducing (misleading) spirits" and doctrines taught by demons. Having thrown off belief in the true God, they embrace and espouse the "doctrines" of supernatural evil beings (compare Ephesians 6:11ff.).

4:2. The human agents of these demons are found "speaking lies in hypocrisy." False teachers were foretold by Jesus (see Matthew 24:11; Mark 13:22). These hypocritical liars mentioned by Paul were probably early Gnostics who taught that *spirit* is altogether good and *matter* is totally evil (see verse 3). The word "seared" (*kautēriazō*) is the root for the word *cauterize*. "Conscience" is another important word in this first letter to Timothy; this is the fourth time it has appeared: 1:5,19; 3:9; 4:2. The idea of a seared conscience may mean their consciences have been branded with a hot iron to indicate ownership by Satan (Guthrie, *Tyndale New Testament Commentaries*, 14:92).

4:3. Two of these false teachings are given in verse 3: "They forbid people to marry and order them to abstain from certain foods" (NIV). This asceticism reflected the early evidence of gnosticism. The Gnostics taught that all matter is evil and only that which is spirit is good. One's abstinence from marriage and meat, they said, would make him holy and acceptable to God. Paul did

God was manifest in the flesh: Christ appeared in a human body, *SEB* . . . Christ came to earth as a Man, *NLT* . . . He was revealed in our nature, *TCNT*.

justified in the Spirit: . . . vindicated in, *NASB* . . . pure in His Spirit, *NLT* . . . He was shown to be right by the Spirit, *SEB*.

seen of angels: Appeared to angels, *Confraternity*.

preached unto the Gentiles: Proclaimed among, *NASB* . . . heralded among, *Berkeley* . . . The nations heard about Him, *NLT*.

believed on in the world: Men everywhere put their trust in Him, *NLT*.

received up into glory: He was taken up into heaven, *NLT*.

1. Now the Spirit speaketh expressly: . . . distinctly says, *NAB* . . . has explicitly said, *JB* . . . is saying explicitly, *Concordant* . . . The Holy Spirit tells us in plain words, *NLT*.

that in the latter times some shall depart from the faith: . . . that in subsequent eras, *Concordant* . . . in future times some will apostatize, *Campbell* . . . there will be some who will desert, *JB*.

giving heed to seducing spirits, and doctrines of devils: . . . deluding spirits and demonic teachings, *Berkeley*.

2. Speaking lies in hypocrisy: Like hypocrites they will tell lies, *SEB*.

having their conscience seared with a hot iron: . . . having their conscience branded, *Confraternity* . . . whose own consciences are burned out, *Norlie* . . . having been cauterized, *Concordant*.

3. Forbidding to marry, [and commanding] to abstain from meats: They prohibit marriage, *Berkeley* . . . and they discourage marriage, *TCNT* . . . to stay away from certian foods, *SEB*.

which God hath created to be received with thanksgiving:

3206.2 noun acc sing fem	3196.3 prep	2150.1 noun fem	3450.4 art dat pl	3964.8 adj dat pl masc
[✶ μετάλημψιν] metalēmpsin [idem]	μετὰ meta with	εὐχαριστίας eucharistias thanksgiving	τοῖς tois for the	πιστοῖς pistois faithful

2504.1 conj	1906.15 verb dat pl masc part perf act	3450.12 art acc sing fem	223.4 noun acc sing fem	3617.1 conj	3820.17 adj sing neu
καὶ kai and	ἐπεγνωκόσιν epegnōkosin having known	τὴν tēn the	ἀλήθειαν. alētheian truth.	4. ὅτι hoti Because	πᾶν pan every

2910.1 noun sing neu	2296.2 noun gen sing masc	2541.1 adj sing	2504.1 conj	3625.6 num card neu	574.1 adj sing neu
κτίσμα ktisma creature	θεοῦ theou of God	καλόν, kalon, good,	καὶ kai and	οὐδὲν ouden nothing	ἀπόβλητον, apoblēton to be rejected,

3196.3 prep	2150.1 noun fem	2956.38 verb sing neu part pres mid	37.10 verb 3sing indic pres mid
μετὰ meta with	εὐχαριστίας eucharistias thanksgiving	λαμβανόμενον· lambanomenon being received;	5. ἁγιάζεται hagiazetai it is being sanctified

1056.1 conj	1217.2 prep	3030.2 noun gen sing masc	2296.2 noun gen sing masc	2504.1 conj	1767.1 noun gen sing fem
γὰρ gar for	διὰ dia by	λόγου logou word	θεοῦ theou God's	καὶ kai and	ἐντεύξεως. enteuxeōs prayer.

3642.18 dem- pron pl neu	5132.2 verb nom sing masc part pres mid	3450.4 art dat pl	79.8 noun dat pl masc	2541.3 adj nom sing masc
6. Ταῦτα Tauta These things	ὑποτιθέμενος hupotithemenos laying before	τοῖς tois the	ἀδελφοῖς, adelphois, brothers,	καλὸς kalos good

1498.39 verb 2sing indic fut mid	1243.1 noun nom sing masc	2400.2 name masc	5382.2 name gen masc	5382.2 name gen masc
ἔσῃ esē you will be	διάκονος diakonos a servant	Ἰησοῦ Iēsou of Jesus	Χριστοῦ, Christou Christ,	[✶ Χριστοῦ Christou [of Christ

2400.2 name masc	1773.1 verb nom sing masc part pres mid	3450.4 art dat pl	3030.7 noun dat pl masc	3450.10 art gen sing fem
Ἰησοῦ,] Iēsou Jesus,]	ἐντρεφόμενος entrephomenos being nourished	τοῖς tois with the	λόγοις logois words	τῆς tēs of the

3963.2 noun gen sing fem	2504.1 conj	3450.10 art gen sing fem	2541.6 adj gen sing fem	1313.1 noun fem	3614.11 rel- pron dat sing fem
πίστεως, pisteōs, faith,	καὶ kai and	τῆς tēs of the	καλῆς kalēs good	διδασκαλίας didaskalias teaching	ᾗ hē which

3738.1 verb 2sing indic perf act	3450.8 art acc pl masc	1156.2 conj	945.1 adj acc pl	2504.1 conj
παρηκολούθηκας. parēkolouthēkas you have closely followed.	7. Τοὺς Tous The	δὲ de but	βεβήλους bebēlous profane	καὶ kai and

1120.1 adj acc pl masc	3316.2 noun acc pl masc	3729.2 verb 2sing impr pres mid	1122.1 verb 2sing impr pres act	1156.2 conj
γραώδεις graōdeis old wives'	μύθους muthous tales	παραιτοῦ· paraitou refuse,	γύμναζε gumnaze train	δὲ de but

not comment on the first teaching (Scripture deals with that, Genesis 2:18), but he did the second.

4:4. Regarding abstinence from certain foods, Paul repeated a principle of Scripture: "God saw every thing that he had made, and, behold, it was very good" (Genesis 1:31). In the second clause, "nothing to be refused" (*apobletos*, "to be thrown away"), Paul was perhaps referring to God's command to Noah (Genesis 9:3). He added "if it be received with thanksgiving" to give the correct context in eating any kind of food (compare Romans 14:6). The words "received with thanksgiving" are repeated from verse 3.

4:5. This verse presents some difficulty in interpretation. Connected with "if it be received with thanksgiving" (verse 4), the "it" of verse 5 must refer to "every creature" used for food. The primary meaning is the need for having a thankful attitude toward the food God has provided.

Another significance is related to the phrase "by the word of God." The "word of God" is "divinely inspired utterance" and primarily refers to the Scriptures. Genesis 1:31 states that everything God made "was very good." Genesis 9:3 points out that God has given mankind both meat and plant life for sustenance.

4:6. The first verses define a problem; verses 6-16 give the solution. "Put . . . in remembrance" (*hupotithēmi*) literally means "to point out or make known"; the term is a gentle, humble word. It is not "command" but "suggest, advise." Timothy was not to issue orders but to gently suggest the brothers consider "these things" (what Paul had just said in verses 4 and 5).

The words in the next clause, "a good minister of Jesus Christ," could be the title of this entire section (verses 6-16). A good minister is "nourished" by "words of faith" and "good doctrine." The NIV reads: " . . . brought up in the truths of the faith and of the good teaching that you have followed." "Attained" (*parakoloutheō*) can either be "which you have closely investigated" or "which you have followed as a standard" (see 2 Timothy 3:10).

4:7. First, Timothy was to "refuse profane and old wives' fables." "Refuse" carries the idea of strong rejection (compare 2 Timothy 2:23; Titus 3:10). "Profane" (*bebēlos*) was used in 1:9 to describe a certain type of sinner. "Old wives' fables" (*muthoi*, "silly myths") were stories old women told to children.

of them which believe and know the truth: . . . and have a clear knowledge of the truth, *Montgomery.*

4. For every creature of God [is] good: . . . everything that God has created, *Montgomery.*

and nothing to be refused: . . . and no food is to be rejected, *JB* . . . and nothing is to be rejected, *Confraternity, Montgomery.*

if it be received with thanksgiving: . . . provided it is accepted with, *Williams* . . . when gratefully received, *Berkeley.*

5. For it is sanctified by the word of God and prayer: For it is made clean by, *Norlie* . . . It is made holy, *SEB* . . . it is hallowed through the word, *Concordant.*

6. If thou put the brethren in remembrance of these things: As you lay all these things before the brothers, *Montgomery* . . . before the brotherhood, *NAB.*

thou shalt be a good minister of Jesus Christ: . . . a noble minister, *Montgomery.*

nourished up in the words of faith and of good doctrine: . . . in the precepts of the faith and that noble teaching, *Montgomery* . . . the fine teaching, *Williams.*

whereunto thou hast attained: . . . to which you have been conforming your life, *Berkeley* . . . which you have so faithfully practiced, *Norlie* . . . which you have followed, *Montgomery, Williams.*

7. But refuse profane and old wives' fables: But avoid, *Confraternity* . . . But make it your habit to let worldly and old women's stories alone, *Williams* . . . Have nothing to do with godless myths, *JB* . . . Stay away from unholy stories, *SEB* . . . old womanish myths, *Montgomery.*

4427.4 prs-pron acc sing masc	4242.1 prep	2131.4 noun acc sing fem	3450.9 art nom sing fem	1056.1 conj	4836.1 adj nom sing fem
σεαυτὸν	πρὸς	εὐσέβειαν·	**8.** ἡ	γὰρ	σωματικὴ
seauton	pros	eusebeian	hē	gar	sōmatikē
yourself	to	godliness;	the	for	bodily

1123.1 noun nom sing fem	4242.1 prep	3504.1 adj sing	1498.4 verb 3sing indic pres act	5457.1 adj nom sing fem	3450.9 art nom sing fem
γυμνασία	πρὸς	ὀλίγον	ἐστὶν	ὠφέλιμος·	ἡ
gumnasia	pros	oligon	estin	ōphelimos	hē
exercise	for	a little	is	profitable,	the

1156.2 conj	2131.1 noun nom sing fem	4242.1 prep	3820.1 adj nom sing fem	5457.1 adj nom sing fem	1498.4 verb 3sing indic pres act
δὲ	εὐσέβεια	πρὸς	πάντα	ὠφέλιμός	ἐστιν,
de	eusebeia	pros	panta	ōphelimos	estin
but	godliness	for	everything	profitable	is,

1845.4 noun acc sing fem	2174.22 verb nom sing fem part pres act	2205.2 noun gen sing fem	3450.10 art gen sing fem	3431.1 adv	2504.1 conj	3450.10 art gen sing fem
ἐπαγγελίαν	ἔχουσα	ζωῆς	τῆς	νῦν	καὶ	τῆς
epangelian	echousa	zōēs	tēs	nun	kai	tēs
promise	having	of life,	of the	now	and	of the

3165.15 verb gen sing fem part pres act	3964.2 adj nom sing masc	3450.5 art nom sing masc	3030.1 noun nom sing masc	2504.1 conj	3820.10 adj gen sing fem
μελλούσης.	**9.** πιστὸς	ὁ	λόγος	καὶ	πάσης
mellousēs	pistos	ho	logos	kai	pasēs
coming.	Faithful	the	word	and	of all

589.1 noun gen sing fem	510.2 adj nom sing masc	1519.1 prep	3642.17 dem-pron sing neu	1056.1 conj	2504.1 conj
ἀποδοχῆς	ἄξιος.	**10.** εἰς	τοῦτο	γὰρ	⌜a καὶ ⌝
apodochēs	axios	eis	touto	gar	kai
acceptance	worthy;	for,	this	for	both

2844.3 verb 1pl indic pres act	2504.1 conj	3542.7 verb 1pl indic pres mid	74.6 verb 1pl indic pres mid
κοπιῶμεν	καὶ	⌜ ὀνειδιζόμεθα,	[b☆ ἀγωνιζόμεθα,]
kopiōmen	kai	oneidizometha	agōnizometha
we labor	and	are being reproached,	[are contending,]

3617.1 conj	1666.10 verb 1pl indic perf act	1894.3 prep	2296.3 noun dat sing masc	2180.12 verb dat sing masc part pres act	3614.5 rel-pron nom sing masc
ὅτι	ἠλπίκαμεν	ἐπὶ	θεῷ	ζῶντι,	ὅς
hoti	ēlpikamen	epi	theō	zōnti	hos
because	we have hoped	in	a God	living,	who

1498.4 verb 3sing indic pres act	4842.1 noun nom sing masc	3820.4 adj gen pl	442.7 noun gen pl masc	3094.1 adv sup
ἐστιν	σωτὴρ	πάντων	ἀνθρώπων,	μάλιστα
estin	sōtēr	pantōn	anthrōpōn	malista
is	Saviour	of all	men,	especially

3964.7 adj gen pl masc	3715.4 verb 2sing impr pres act	3642.18 dem-pron pl neu	2504.1 conj	1315.5 verb 2sing impr pres act
πιστῶν.	**11.** Παράγγελλε	ταῦτα	καὶ	δίδασκε.
pistōn	Parangelle	tauta	kai	didaske
of believers.	Charge	these things	and	teach.

3235.3 num card nom masc	4622.2 prs-pron gen 2sing	3450.10 art gen sing fem	3366.1 noun gen sing fem	2675.3 verb 3sing impr pres act
12. μηδείς	σου	τῆς	νεότητος	καταφρονείτω,
mēdeis	sou	tēs	neotētos	kataphroneitō
No one	your	the	youth	let despise,

10.a.**Txt:** 018K,020L,byz.
Var: 01ℵ,02A,04C,06D
025P,33,Lach,Treg,Tisc
We/Ho,Weis,Sod
UBS/☆

10.b.**Txt:** 01ℵ-corr,06D
020L,025P,byz.it.sa.bo.
Weis,Sod
Var: 01ℵ-org,02A,04C
018K,33,Lach,Treg,Tisc
We/Ho,UBS/☆

Second, Timothy was to "exercise . . . unto godliness." The figure of athletics is introduced here and developed in the next verse (compare 1 Corinthians 9:25-27).

4:8. Some have misread Paul's statement here. He did not say physical exercise is unprofitable. He said it is of some profit or value. But spiritual exercise ("godliness") brings value or profit to all things. Godliness brings "promise" of blessings in this life and in the next life too. The godly person has the best of both worlds.

4:9. In this verse there is another one of Paul's "faithful sayings" (cf. 1:15; 3:1), but a puzzle confronts our attempt at understanding. Does the "faithful saying" go with verse 8 or verse 10? Most commentators are divided because the Greek construction can be understood either way. Here are the main arguments:

The contrast of verse 8 seems to be a "faithful saying." It reads like a proverbial statement—something that would likely be repeated and possibly taught to others.

Those who contend the "faithful saying" is found in verse 10 point out the evident theological content of this verse. It follows the pattern of two previous statements (1 Timothy 1:15; 3:1) and another found in 2 Timothy 2:11. In all these instances the content follows the word "saying."

4:10. This appears to be the first time Paul resorted to the plural "we" in this letter. In this verse Paul wrote that he was giving the ministry his best efforts. The word for "labor" is *kopiōmen* and suggests vigorous work; it also continues the metaphor of "exercise" in verses 7 and 8. The other word Paul used is *oneidizō*. Matthew 27:44 uses the same term, stating, "The robbers who were crucified with him also heaped insults on him" (NIV). Paul understood as well as anyone what it means to know the fellowship of the sufferings of Christ. The word "trust" signifies "hope," and the perfect tense shows a continuous state of hope in the "living God."

4:11. Beginning with verse 11 Paul gave Timothy practical advice concerning his public ministry. It related to Timothy's sound teaching and behavior. Timothy's earliest training had been in Judaism. As a young person he was converted to Christianity (very possibly by Paul himself). Timothy gained his spiritual strength and stature from the truths he absorbed and the sound teaching or doctrine he followed. These were to be the starting point of his ministry toward others.

4:12. Though others might be older than Timothy, he was to allow no one to despise him because of his age. (It is very possible Timothy was about 30 at this time.)

and exercise thyself [rather] unto godliness: Train yourself spiritually, *JB* . . . Train yourself to lead a religious life, *TCNT* . . . Train yourself to be godly, *SEB*.

8. For bodily exercise profiteth little: For bodily training, *Confraternity* . . . Physical exercise is profitable to some extent, *Norlie* . . . Physical training has some importance, *SEB* . . . is beneficial, *Concordant*.
but godliness is profitable unto all things:
having promise of the life that now is, and of that which is to come: . . . of the future life as well, *JB* . . . and that which is impending, *Concordant*.

9. This [is] a faithful saying and worthy of all acceptation: You can depend on this as worthy of complete acceptance, *NAB* . . . This teaching is reliable, *TCNT* . . . is true and absolutely trustworthy, *Norlie* . . . it is worth complete acceptance, *SEB* . . . and they can be trusted, *NLT* . . . worthy of all welcome, *Concordant* . . . of entire acceptance, *Confraternitiy*.

10. For therefore we both labour and suffer reproach: For this purpose, *Berkeley*.
because we trust in the living God:
who is the Saviour of all men: . . . of the whole human race, *JB*.
specially of those that believe: . . . particularly of believers, *Berkeley*.

11. These things command and teach: Continue to give these orders and to teach these truths, *Williams*.

12. Let no man despise thy youth: Let no one look down on you, *NAB* . . . because you are young, *NLT*.

1 Timothy 4:13

233.2 conj	5020.1 noun nom sing masc	1090.29 verb 2sing impr pres mid	3450.1 art gen pl	3964.7 adj gen pl masc	1706.1 prep	3030.3 noun dat sing masc
ἀλλὰ	τύπος	γίνου	τῶν	πιστῶν	ἐν	λόγῳ,
alla	tupos	ginou	tōn	pistōn	en	logō
but	a pattern	be	of the	believers	in	word,

12.a.Txt: 018K,020L 025P,byz. Var: 01ℵ,02A,04C,06D 33,sa.bo.Gries,Lach Treg,Alf,Word,Tisc We/Ho,Weis,Sod UBS/✱

1706.1 prep	389.2 noun dat sing fem	1706.1 prep	26.3 noun dat sing fem	1706.1 prep	4011.3 noun dat sing neu
ἐν	ἀναστροφῇ,	ἐν	ἀγάπῃ,	⌐a ἐν	πνεύματι, ⌐
en	anastrophē	en	agapē	en	pneumati
in	conduct,	in	love,	in	Spirit,

1706.1 prep	3963.3 noun dat sing fem	1706.1 prep	46.1 noun dat sing fem	2175.1 conj	2048.32 verb 1sing indic pres mid
ἐν	πίστει,	ἐν	ἁγνείᾳ.	13. ἕως	ἔρχομαι,
en	pistei	en	hagneia	heōs	erchomai
in	faith,	in	purity.	Till	I come,

4196.1 verb 2sing impr pres act	3450.11 art dat sing fem	318.1 noun dat sing fem	3450.11 art dat sing fem	3735.3 noun dat sing fem
πρόσεχε	τῇ	ἀναγνώσει,	τῇ	παρακλήσει,
proseche	tē	anagnōsei	tē	paraklēsei
give heed	to the	reading,	to the	exhortation,

3450.11 art dat sing fem	1313.3 noun dat sing fem	3231.1 partic	270.1 verb 2sing impr pres act	3450.2 art gen sing	1706.1 prep
τῇ	διδασκαλίᾳ.	14. μὴ	ἀμέλει	τοῦ	ἐν
tē	didaskalia	mē	amelei	tou	en
to the	teaching.	Not	do neglect	of the	in

4622.3 prs-pron dat 2sing	5321.2 noun gen sing neu	3614.16 rel-pron sing neu	1319.44 verb 3sing indic aor pass	4622.3 prs-pron dat 2sing	1217.2 prep
σοὶ	χαρίσματος,	ὃ	ἐδόθη	σοι	διὰ
soi	charismatos	ho	edothē	soi	dia
you	gift,	which	was given	to you	through

4252.1 noun fem	3196.3 prep	1921.1 noun gen sing fem	3450.1 art gen pl	5331.6 noun gen pl fem	3450.2 art gen sing
προφητείας	μετὰ	ἐπιθέσεως	τῶν	χειρῶν	τοῦ
prophēteias	meta	epitheseōs	tōn	cheirōn	tou
prophecy	with	laying on	of the	hands	of the

4103.2 noun gen sing neu	3642.18 dem-pron pl neu	3161.1 verb 2sing impr pres act	1706.1 prep	3642.3 dem-pron dat pl
πρεσβυτερίου.	15. ταῦτα	μελέτα,	ἐν	τούτοις
presbuteriou	tauta	meleta	en	toutois
elderhood.	These things	meditate on,	in	them

1498.15 verb 2sing impr pres act	2419.1 conj	4622.2 prs-pron gen 2sing	3450.9 art nom sing fem	4156.1 noun nom sing fem	5156.4 adj
ἴσθι·	ἵνα	σου	ἡ	προκοπὴ	φανερὰ
isthi	hina	sou	hē	prokopē	phanera
be,	that	your	the	advancement	apparent

15.a.Txt: 06D-corr,018K 020L,025P,byz. Var: 01ℵ,02A,04C 06D-org,33,bo.Lach Treg,Alf,Word,Tisc We/Ho,Weis,Sod UBS/✱

1498.10 verb 3sing subj pres act	1706.1 prep	3820.5 adj dat pl	1892.1 verb 2sing impr pres act	4427.2 prs-pron dat sing masc
ᾖ	⌐a ἐν ⌐	πᾶσιν.	16. ἔπεχε	σεαυτῷ
ē	en	pasin	epeche	seautō
may be	among	all.	Give heed	to yourself

2504.1 conj	3450.11 art dat sing fem	1313.3 noun dat sing fem	1946.2 verb 2sing impr pres act	840.2 prs-pron dat pl
καὶ	τῇ	διδασκαλίᾳ·	ἐπίμενε	αὐτοῖς·
kai	tē	didaskalia	epimene	autois
and	to the	teaching;	continue	in them;

Timothy was to become an example to other believers; he was to show exemplary characteristics and conduct. The first two in this list relate to his public life: "in word" = teaching, speech; "in conversation" = conduct, life-style. The final characteristics are inner qualities that motivate outward action.

4:13. Here is another reference to Paul's hope of coming to Ephesus in the near future (compare 1:3; 3:14). Till that time Timothy was to give priority to a threefold public ministry.

"Reading" probably refers to the public reading of Scripture (the Old Testament). "Exhortation" refers to public proclamation of the gospel ("preaching"). "Doctrine" means Timothy was to have a teaching ministry that presented the basic tenets of the Faith.

4:14. Paul reminded Timothy of the gift (*charisma*) that had come to him. The gift was very possibly the spiritual abilities Timothy needed for the ministry. The Lord bestowed these when the elders ordained Timothy for the ministry. "No difficulty need be entertained over the fact that in 2 Timothy 1:6 Paul speaks exclusively of his own part in such a ceremony, for there are two possible solutions: either the elders were associated with Paul in the ceremony, ... or else the two references to laying on of hands may refer to different occasions. The former, on the whole, seems the more likely explanation" (Guthrie, *Tyndale New Testament Commentaries*, 14:98).

4:15. This summary verse refers to what Paul had just written in verses 13 and 14. The initial word translated "meditate" is the verb *meletaō* which can also mean "practice, attend to." This sense is given in the NIV: "Be diligent in these matters." The next clause, "give thyself wholly to them," is literally "be in them." "Profiting" (*prokopē*) may be translated "progress" or "advance." The purpose for Timothy's diligent and wholehearted involvement was to be an effective witness to everyone, thus giving no one grounds for "despising" or looking down upon him because of his youth.

4:16. Here is a twofold challenge: "Take heed unto thyself, and unto the doctrine." The Greek for this clause is literally: "Give attention to yourself and to the teaching." No matter how correct Timothy's doctrine might be, if there was a flaw in his life, his ministry would be ineffective.

Donald Guthrie comments: "The danger of neglecting one's own salvation is greater in the Christian minister than in others, and even the apostle Paul himself could fear lest he became a castaway after preaching to others (1 Corinthians 9:27). Calvin suggestively comments that although salvation is God's gift alone, yet human

but be thou an example of the believers: ... but always set an example for, *Williams*.

in word, in conversation, in charity, in spirit, in faith, in purity: ... in behavior, *Berkeley, Concordant* ... in chastity, *Confraternity*.

13. Till I come, give attendance to: Till I arrive, *Berkeley* ... devote yourself, *NAB, Williams* ... be diligent, *Confraternity* ... Make use of the time, *JB* ... spend time, *SEB*.

reading, to exhortation, to doctrine: ... the public reading of, *Williams*.

14. Neglect not the gift that is in thee: Make good use of this gift, *Norlie* ... that was prophetically granted you, *Berkeley* ... you received, *Williams*.

which was given thee by prophecy: ... in fulfilment of the predictions, *TCNT*.

with the laying on of the hands of the presbytery: ... when the elders laid their hands upon you, *Williams* ... with the imposition of the hands of the eldership, *Campbell*.

15. Meditate upon these things; give thyself wholly to them: Care about these things, *SEB* ... Think about all this, *NLT* ... Attend to your duties, *NAB* ... Practise these things, *TCNT* ... Continue cultivating these things; be devoted to them, *Williams*.

that thy profiting may appear to all: ... so that everybody will see your progress, *Williams* ... your progress may be apparent to all, *Concordant* ... may be obvious to every one, *TCNT*.

16. Take heed unto thyself, and unto the doctrine: Take great care about what you do, *JB* ... Paying special attention always to your conduct, *Norlie*.

3642.17 dem-pron sing neu	1056.1 conj	4020.15 verb nom sing masc part pres act	2504.1 conj	4427.4 prs-pron acc sing masc	4834.12 verb 2sing indic fut act
τοῦτο	γὰρ	ποιῶν,	καὶ	σεαυτὸν	σώσεις
touto	gar	poiōn	kai	seauton	sōseis
this	for	doing,	both	yourself	you shall save

2504.1 conj	3450.8 art acc pl masc	189.16 verb acc pl masc part pres act	4622.2 prs-pron gen 2sing		4104.4 adj comp dat sing masc
καὶ	τοὺς	ἀκούοντάς	σου.	5:1.	Πρεσβυτέρῳ
kai	tous	akouontas	sou		Presbuterō
and	the	hearing	you.		An elder man

3231.1 partic	1954.1 verb 2sing subj aor act	233.2 conj	3731.5 verb 2sing impr pres act	5453.1 conj	3824.4 noun acc sing masc
μὴ	ἐπιπλήξῃς,	ἀλλὰ	παρακάλει	ὡς	πατέρα·
mē	epiplēxēs	alla	parakalei	hōs	patera
not	do sharply rebuke,	but	exhort	as	a father;

3365.6 adj comp acc pl masc	5453.1 conj	79.9 noun acc pl masc		4104.8 adj comp acc pl fem	5453.1 conj
νεωτέρους	ὡς	ἀδελφούς·	2.	πρεσβυτέρας	ὡς
neōterous	hōs	adelphous		presbuteras	hōs
younger men	as	brothers;		elder women	as

3251.5 noun acc pl fem	3365.7 adj comp acc pl fem	5453.1 conj	78.6 noun acc pl fem	1706.1 prep	3820.11 adj dat sing fem
μητέρας·	νεωτέρας	ὡς	ἀδελφὰς	ἐν	πάσῃ
mēteras	neōteras	hōs	adelphas	en	pasē
mothers;	younger women	as	sisters,	with	all

46.1 noun dat sing fem		5339.6 noun acc pl fem	4939.4 verb 2sing impr pres act	3450.15 art acc pl fem	3552.1 adv	5339.6 noun acc pl fem
ἁγνείᾳ.	3.	Χήρας	τίμα	τὰς	ὄντως	χήρας.
hagneia		Chēras	tima	tas	ontōs	chēras
purity.		Widows	honor	the	indeed	widows;

1479.1 conj	1156.2 conj	4948.3 indef-pron nom sing	5339.1 noun nom sing fem	4891.4 noun pl neu	2211.1 conj	1536.1 adj pl neu
4. εἰ	δέ	τις	χήρα	τέκνα	ἢ	ἔκγονα
ei	de	tis	chēra	tekna	ē	ekgona
if	but	any	widow	children	or	grandchildren

2174.4 verb 3sing indic pres act	3101.4 verb 3pl impr pres act	4270.1 adv	3450.6 art acc sing masc	2375.4 adj sing
ἔχει,	μανθανέτωσαν	πρῶτον	τὸν	ἴδιον
echei	manthanetōsan	prōton	ton	idion
has,	let them learn	first	the	their own

3486.4 noun acc sing masc	2132.2 verb inf pres act	2504.1 conj	285.1 noun acc pl fem	586.6 verb inf pres act
οἶκον	εὐσεβεῖν,	καὶ	ἀμοιβὰς	ἀποδιδόναι
oikon	eusebein	kai	amoibas	apodidonai
house	to practice godliness,	and	recompense	to render

3450.4 art dat pl	4128.2 adj dat pl masc	3642.17 dem-pron sing neu	1056.1 conj	1498.4 verb 3sing indic pres act	2541.1 adj sing
τοῖς	προγόνοις·	τοῦτο	γὰρ	ἐστιν	⌐ᵃ καλὸν
tois	progonois	touto	gar	estin	kalon
to the	parents;	this	for	is	good

2504.1 conj	582.1 adj sing neu	1783.1 prep	3450.2 art gen sing	2296.2 noun gen sing masc	3450.9 art nom sing fem
καὶ ⌐	ἀπόδεκτον	ἐνώπιον	τοῦ	θεοῦ.	5. ἡ
kai	apodekton	enōpion	tou	theou	hē
and	acceptable	before	the	God.	The

4.a.Txt: bo.Steph
Var: 01ℵ,02A,04C,06D
018K,020L,025P,byz.
Gries,Lach,Treg,Alf
Word,Tisc,We/Ho,Weis
Sod,UBS/✱

ministry is needed, as is here implied" (*Tyndale New Testament Commentaries*, 14:99). Too often the minister expends all his energies toward others and neglects his own pursuit of spiritual vitality and daily communion with God.

If Timothy did this he would save himself and his hearers. This is not a proof text for salvation by works. What Paul was writing here correlates with his Spirit-inspired challenge to the Philippians: "Work out your own salvation with fear and trembling" (Philippians 2:12; cf. verse 13).

A.M. Stibbs supplies this comment: "Note how the minister not only fulfils his ministry by what he says (those he serves are described as *your hearers*), but also necessarily completes it, or spoils its effectiveness, by how he himself lives" (p.1173). Often our character and conduct shout so loudly those listening cannot hear a thing we say. A godly character is a more important possession than great abilities or special talent.

5:1,2. Chapter 5 begins a new section. Paul now addressed the subject of relationships. These are contained in 5:1 to 6:2.

First are age relationships (verses 1,2). The word "elder" does not refer to church officials (as in 5:17) but to older men. Timothy was not to "rebuke" (a strong term meaning "censure severely") an older man. If correction was necessary, Timothy was to "entreat" ("exhort," a softer term) him as if he were Timothy's own father.

Younger men were to be treated as brothers. Timothy was to treat older women as he would his mother and younger women as his own sisters. Paul's instructions show a spirit of family relationships within the congregations. An added caution was to be observed with younger women: "with all purity." Timothy was to avoid impropriety or intimacy in ministering to young women. His relationship with women was to be above reproach.

5:3. This verse begins a section devoted to widows (3-16). Four classes of widows are mentioned: real widows (verses 3,5,9,10), widows with relatives (verses 4,8,16), widows living in pleasure (verses 6,7), and young widows (verses 11-15). The "widows indeed" ("real widows" who were without means or relatives and thus were truly destitute) were to be given "honor." This included proper recognition, value, and reverence. This "honor" might include material assistance, compensation, and care.

5:4. Then there were widows with relatives who were able to support them. These relatives were instructed to "requite" ("repay, make return"). They were to support and provide for them. The word "nephews" (*ekgona*) means "descendants" and is better translated "grandchildren." The care of a female parent or grandparent "is good and acceptable before God" (see Exodus 20:12).

continue in them: Stay true to what is right, *NLT* . . . Persevere in these things, *Montgomery, Williams.*

for in doing this:
thou shalt both save thyself, and them that hear thee: . . . and your hearers, *Montgomery* . . . those who listen to you, *Williams.*

1. Rebuke not an elder: Do not chide, *Berkeley* . . . Do not rebuke sharply, *Norlie* . . . Do not reprimand, *TCNT* . . . Don't criticize an older man, *SEB* . . . sharply rebuke an old person, *Klingensmith.*

but intreat him as a father: . . . but always appeal to him, *Williams* . . . but exhort him, *Confraternity.*

and the younger men as brethren:

2. The elder women as mothers:

the younger as sisters, with all purity: . . . with perfect chastity, *Lilly* . . . with absolute purity, *Berkeley.*

3. Honour widows that are widows indeed: Always care for, *Williams* . . . who are really widows, *Campbell.*

4. But if any widow have children or nephews: . . . or grandchildren, *NLT, Montgomery* . . . or descendants, *Klingensmith.*

let them learn first to shew piety at home: . . . toward their own household, *Montgomery* . . . in the treatment of their own families, *Williams.*

and to requite their parents: . . . to pay the debt they owe their parents, *Williams* . . . should repay what they owe to their grandparents, *SEB* . . . and to make some return to their parents, *Montgomery.*

for that is good and acceptable before God: . . . since this is pleasing to God, *Lilly* . . . pleasing in God's sight, *Montgomery.*

1 Timothy 5:6

5.a.Txt: 01ℵ-corr,02A
06D,018K,020L,byz.
We/Ho,Sod
Var: 01ℵ-org,04C,025P
Tisc,Weis,UBS/✶

8.a.Txt: 04C,06D-corr
018K,020L,025P,etc.byz.
Var: 01ℵ,02A,06D-org
Lach,Treg,Tisc,We/Ho
Weis,Sod,UBS/✶

8.b.Txt: 01ℵ-corr2,02A
04C,06D-corr1,044,byz.
Var: 01ℵ-org,06D-org
010F,012G,016I,104
1881

1156.2 conj	3552.1 adv	5339.1 noun nom sing fem	2504.1 conj	3306.1 verb nom sing fem part perf mid
δὲ	ὄντως	χήρα	καὶ	μεμονωμένη
de	ontōs	chēra	kai	memonōmenē
now	indeed	a widow,	and	having been left alone,

1666.9 verb 3sing indic perf act	1894.3 prep	3450.6 art acc sing masc	2296.4 noun acc sing masc	2504.1 conj	4215.1 verb 3sing indic pres act
ἤλπικεν	ἐπὶ	⌐a τὸν ⌐	θεὸν,	καὶ	προσμένει
ēlpiken	epi	ton	theon,	kai	prosmenei
has hope	in		God,	and	continues

3450.14 art dat pl fem	1157.5 noun dat pl fem	2504.1 conj	3450.14 art dat pl fem	4194.7 noun dat pl fem	3433.2 noun gen sing fem
ταῖς	δεήσεσιν	καὶ	ταῖς	προσευχαῖς	νυκτὸς
tais	deēsesin	kai	tais	proseuchais	nuktos
in the	supplications	and	in the	prayers	night

2504.1 conj	2232.1 noun fem	3450.9 art nom sing fem	1156.2 conj	4537.1 verb nom sing fem part pres act
καὶ	ἡμέρας·	**6.** ἡ	δὲ	σπαταλῶσα,
kai	hēmeras	hē	de	spatalōsa
and	day.	The	but	living in self gratification,

2180.16 verb nom sing fem part pres act	2325.1 verb 3sing indic perf act	2504.1 conj	3642.18 dem-pron pl neu	3715.4 verb 2sing impr pres act
ζῶσα	τέθνηκεν.	**7.** καὶ	ταῦτα	παράγγελλε,
zōsa	tethnēken	kai	tauta	parangelle
living	is dead.	And	these things	command,

2419.1 conj	421.2 adj nom pl masc	421.4 adj nom pl masc	1498.12 verb 3pl subj pres act	1479.1 conj
ἵνα	⌐ ἀνεπίληπτοι	[✶ ἀνεπίλημπτοι]	ὦσιν.	**8.** εἰ
hina	anepilēptoi	anepilēmptoi	ōsin	ei
that	irreproachable	[idem]	they may be.	If

1156.2 conj	4948.3 indef-pron nom sing	3450.1 art gen pl	2375.1 adj gen pl	2504.1 conj	3094.1 adv sup	3450.1 art gen pl
δέ	τις	τῶν	ἰδίων	καὶ	μάλιστα	⌐a τῶν ⌐
de	tis	tōn	idiōn	kai	malista	tōn
but	anyone	the	his own	and	especially	the

3472.2 adj gen sing masc	3620.3 partic	4165.1 verb 3sing indic pres act	4165.4 verb 3sing indic pres mid	3450.12 art acc sing fem
οἰκείων	οὐ	⌐✶ προνοεῖ,	[b προνοεῖται,]	τὴν
oikeiōn	ou	pronoei	pronoeitai	tēn
household	not	does provide for,	[is being provided for,]	the

3963.4 noun acc sing fem	714.14 verb 3sing indic perf mid	2504.1 conj	1498.4 verb 3sing indic pres act	566.3 adj gen sing masc
πίστιν	ἤρνηται,	καὶ	ἔστιν	ἀπίστου
pistin	ērnētai	kai	estin	apistou
faith	he has denied,	and	is	than an unbeliever

5337.1 adj comp nom sing	5339.1 noun nom sing fem	2609.1 verb 3sing impr pres mid	3231.1 partic	1629.3 adj comp sing neu
χείρων.	**9.** Χήρα	καταλεγέσθω	μὴ	ἔλαττον
cheirōn	Chēra	katalegesthō	mē	elatton
worse.	A widow	let be put on the list	not	less

2073.4 noun gen pl neu	1818.1 num card	1090.10 verb nom sing fem part perf act	1518.1 num card gen	433.2 noun gen sing masc
ἐτῶν	ἑξήκοντα	γεγονυῖα,	ἑνὸς	ἀνδρὸς
etōn	hexēkonta	gegonuia	henos	andros
of years	sixty	having been,	of one	man

5:5. The "widow indeed" (identified as the one "who is really in need" in the NIV text of verses 3 and 5) was the most destitute and desolate of persons. She had no children and no relatives to care for and support her. So the Church was to be her family. Though this kind of widow was desolate (*memonōmenē* = "left entirely alone") she maintained a strong faith in God as her Provider. The Greek verb translated "continueth" indicates this is an attitude rather than continuous action.

5:6. A unique class of widows was those living in pleasure. The verb here is *spatalaō* and literally means "live wantonly, live riotously." In Ephesus and elsewhere in the First Century, many single women resorted to immoral living as a means of support. Paul might have had this kind of widow in mind when he said, "But she that liveth in pleasure is dead while she liveth." Because these widows had chosen to support themselves in this unchristian manner, they were outside the sphere of the Church's responsibility and care. The phrase "is dead while she liveth" indicates a condition when though the body's physical life is maintained, its spiritual life is dead.

5:7. As Paul often did in this pastoral letter, he reminded Timothy of the "charge" ("command") he was to give (compare 1:3,18; 4:11). The purpose was "that they may be blameless." But the "they" is somewhat obscure. Are "they" the widows who lived in pleasure (verse 6) or the relatives of destitute widows (verse 8)? Some think verse 7 refers back to the widows living in pleasure. If Timothy commanded them to stop "living wontonly," then they would be blameless. But Guthrie says it "must refer to the responsibility of children to support their forbears (verse 4), and the responsibility of widows to fulfil the requirements mentioned in verse 5" (*Tyndale New Testament Commentaries*, 14:101).

5:8. Though the primary application is to widows in the Ephesian churches, the principle of caring for those in a person's immediate family applies universally. Christian families are obligated to provide for members of the family. "Worse than an infidel" suggests that even the unbeliever has this sense of family responsibility.

5:9. Having clearly defined who a real widow is, Paul now gave instructions regarding the local church's relationship to her. Because she was destitute and in need of care, she was eligible to be put on an official list ("taken into the number") of widows. But there were certain qualifications beyond need.

The second qualification, "having been the wife of one man," literally means "a one-man wife." It does not have to restrict the sense to "married only once." The main idea in "wife of one man" is monogamous fidelity.

5. Now she that is a widow indeed, and desolate: ... who is really a widow, *Williams* ... and left solitary, *Confraternity* ... and is left all alone, *RSV*.

trusteth in God: ... has fixed her hope on God, *Williams* ... relies on God, *Concordant*.

and continueth in supplications and prayers night and day: ... devotes herself to prayers and entreaties, *Williams*.

6. But she that liveth in pleasure: ... she who is self-indulgent, *RSV* ... who lives voluptuously, *Berkeley* ... who gives herself up to luxury, *Williams* ... only for the joy she can receive from this world, *NLT* ... who is devoted to pleasure, *TCNT*.

is dead while she liveth: ... she is spiritually dead, *Norlie* ... is a living death, *TCNT*.

7. And these things give in charge: Drive home these suggestions, *Berkeley*.

that they may be blameless: ... be without reproach, *Williams*.

8. But if any provide not for his own: ... for his own family, *RSV* ... for his own relations, *TCNT* ... does not support his relatives, *SEB*.

and specially for those of his own house: ... of his immediate family, *Lilly*.

he hath denied the faith: ... he has disowned, *Concordant* ... he shows that he does not believe, *SEB*.

and is worse than an infidel: ... than an unbeliever, *Berkeley*.

9. Let not a widow be taken into the number under threescore years old:

having been the wife of one man: ... having been married but once, *Confraternity*.

1129.1 noun nom sing fem	1706.1 prep	2024.6 noun dat pl neu	2541.2 adj dat pl	3113.35 verb nom sing fem part pres mid
γυνή,	10. ἐν	ἔργοις	καλοῖς	μαρτυρουμένη,
gunē	en	ergois	kalois	marturoumenē
wife,	in	works	good	being borne witness to,

1479.1 conj	4892.1 verb 3sing indic aor act	1479.1 conj	3442.1 verb 3sing indic aor act
εἰ	ἐτεκνοτρόφησεν,	εἰ	ἐξενοδόχησεν,
ei	eteknotrophēsen	ei	exenodochēsen
if	she brought up children,	if	she entertained strangers,

1479.1 conj	39.4 adj gen pl	4087.7 noun acc pl masc	3400.4 verb 3sing indic aor act	1479.1 conj	2323.5 verb dat pl masc part pres mid
εἰ	ἁγίων	πόδας	ἔνιψεν,	εἰ	θλιβομένοις
ei	hagiōn	podas	enipsen	ei	thlibomenois
if	saints'	feet	she washed,	if	being oppressed

1869.2 verb 3sing indic aor act	1479.1 conj	3820.3 adj dat sing neu	2024.3 noun dat sing neu	18.4 adj dat sing
ἐπήρκεσεν,	εἰ	παντὶ	ἔργῳ	ἀγαθῷ
epērkesen	ei	panti	ergō	agathō
she imparted relief,	if	every	work	good

1857.3 verb 3sing indic aor act	3365.7 adj comp acc pl fem	1156.2 conj	5339.6 noun acc pl fem	3729.2 verb 2sing impr pres mid
ἐπηκολούθησεν.	11. Νεωτέρας	δὲ	χήρας	παραιτοῦ·
epēkolouthēsen	Neōteras	de	chēras	paraitou
she followed after.	Younger	but	widows	refuse;

3615.1 conj	1056.1 conj	2661.1 verb 3pl subj aor act	3450.2 art gen sing	5382.2 name gen masc
ὅταν	γὰρ	καταστρηνιάσωσιν	τοῦ	Χριστοῦ,
hotan	gar	katastrēniasōsin	tou	Christou
when	for	sensuality turns them against	the	Christ,

1053.5 verb inf pres act	2286.6 verb 3pl indic pres act	2174.26 verb nom pl fem part pres act	2890.1 noun sing neu	3617.1 conj
γαμεῖν	θέλουσιν,	12. ἔχουσαι	κρίμα	ὅτι
gamein	thelousin	echousai	krima	hoti
to marry	they wish,	having	condemnation	because

3450.12 art acc sing fem	4272.12 num ord acc sing fem	3963.4 noun acc sing fem	114.6 verb 3pl indic aor act	258.1 adv
τὴν	πρώτην	πίστιν	ἠθέτησαν.	13. ἅμα
tēn	prōtēn	pistin	ēthetēsan	hama
the	first	faith	they cast off.	At the same time

1156.2 conj	2504.1 conj	686.3 adj nom pl fem	3101.1 verb 3pl indic pres act	3885.4 verb nom pl fem part pres mid	3450.15 art acc pl fem
δὲ	καὶ	ἀργαὶ	μανθάνουσιν,	περιερχόμεναι	τὰς
de	kai	argai	manthanousin	perierchomenai	tas
and	also	idle	they learn,	going about to	the

3477.1 noun fem	3620.3 partic	3303.1 adv	1156.2 conj	686.3 adj nom pl fem	233.2 conj	2504.1 conj
οἰκίας·	οὐ	μόνον	δὲ	ἀργαί,	ἀλλὰ	καὶ
oikias	ou	monon	de	argai	alla	kai
houses;	not	only	and	idle,	but	also

5234.1 adj nom pl fem	2504.1 conj	3884.1 adj nom pl fem	2953.22 verb nom pl fem part pres act	3450.17 art pl neu	3231.1 partic
φλύαροι	καὶ	περίεργοι,	λαλοῦσαι	τὰ	μὴ
phluaroi	kai	periergoi	lalousai	ta	mē
gossips	and	busy bodies,	speaking	the things	not

5:10. The qualifications for "official widows" (those recognized and supported by the churches) are listed. "Good works" begin and end this verse. The words "well reported" refer to the reputation of a Christian widow. She earns a good reputation by her good works which are: (1) child care, (2) hospitality, (3) humble service, and (4) benevolence. In the matter of child care she must have brought up her own children well (compare 3:4,5 for the elder) and have taken in and cared for orphans. Historians tell us it was very common for children in ancient times to be orphaned because of their parents' divorce or death. Widows who took these children in were showing compassion.

"Washed the saints' feet" may be literal foot washing. But it can also be representative of any menial task. The general meaning is the widow's willingness to accept the humblest job.

Some see in these verses the earliest reference to an "order" of widows who were set apart by the local church for special duties. There was such an order in the Third Century, but whether it existed in A.D. 64 when Paul wrote to Timothy is uncertain. The Greek verb standing behind "taken into the number" (verse 9) is *katalegō* which can mean "reckon." If this is the case, real widows (see verses 3,5) would be reckoned at the age of 60.

5:11,12. Beginning with verse 11 Paul gave instructions concerning a group called "younger widows." He dealt with them somewhat severely. The word "refuse" suggests younger widows were not to be put on the register as the others were. There was a special danger for them that might lead them into sin because of a desire to remarry. They were not being told they must not remarry at all. This would contradict Paul's teaching of verse 14 and 1 Corinthians 7:9. The danger Paul was warning against was that these widows might "wax wanton," that is, turn away from Christ and marry an unbeliever. This would be leaving their "first faith" and their pledge to serve Christ wholeheartedly. Also, younger widows might lack the spiritual maturity to devote themselves to prayer and good works and thus become lax in their devotion to the Lord.

5:13. Paul continued to list the characteristics of younger widows. They would "learn" to become idle busybodies who were social gadabouts and vicious gossips. William Barclay comments: "Because a woman had not enough to do, she might become one of those creatures who drift from house to house in an empty social round. It was almost inevitable that such a woman would become a *gossip*; because she had nothing important to talk about, she would tend to talk scandal, repeating tales from house to house, each time with a little more embroidery and a little more malice . . . . She would be very apt to be over-interested and over-interfering in the affairs of others" (*The Daily Study Bible, The Letters to Timothy, Titus, and Philemon*, p.114). A *busybody* pays attention to affairs of others and is meddlesome. A *tattler* ("tale-bearer") betrays private confidences.

10. Well reported of for good works: She should have a reputation for good deeds, *Lilly*.
if she have brought up children: . . . bringing up, *Williams*.
if she have lodged strangers: . . . being hospitable, *Williams*.
if she have washed the saints' feet: . . . the feet of God's people, *Williams*.
if she have relieved the afflicted: . . . helping people in distress, *Williams*.
if she have diligently followed every good work: . . . and for showing kindness, *NLT* . . . in carefully pursuing, *Confraternity* . . . devoting herself to any sort of doing good, *Williams* . . . to every charitable cause, *Norlie*.

11. But the younger widows refuse: Keep...off this roll, *Williams*.
for when they have begun to wax wanton against Christ: . . . become impatient of the restraint of Christ, *Campbell* . . . when they grow restive under the yoke of the Christ, *TCNT* . . . after their sexual desires become strong again, *SEB*.
they will marry:

12. Having damnation: . . . and so deserve censure, *Williams*.
because they have cast off their first faith: . . . because they reject, *SEB* . . . they become guilty of breaking their first promise, *Norlie* . . . for breaking their previous pledge, *Williams* . . . violated, *RSV*.

13. And withal they learn to be idle: Presently they acquire habits of idleness, *Berkeley* . . . they learn to be lazy, *SEB*.
wandering about from house to house:
and not only idle, but tattlers also and busybodies: . . . but gossipers as well, *Confraternity*.
speaking things which they ought not:

1158.4 verb pl neu part pres act	1007.1 verb 1sing indic pres mid	3631.1 partic	3365.7 adj comp acc pl fem	1053.5 verb inf pres act
δέοντα.	14. βούλομαι	οὖν	νεωτέρας	γαμεῖν,
deonta	boulomai	oun	neōteras	gamein
being proper.	I wish	therefore	younger	to marry,

4889.1 verb inf pres act	3479.1 verb inf pres act	3235.5 num card acc acc fem	867.1 noun acc sing fem	1319.10 verb inf pres act
τεκνογονεῖν,	οἰκοδεσποτεῖν,	μηδεμίαν	ἀφορμὴν	διδόναι
teknogonein	oikodespotein	mēdemian	aphormēn	didonai
to bear children,	to rule the house,	no	occasion	to give

3450.3 art dat sing	477.3 verb dat sing masc part pres mid	3033.1 noun gen sing fem	5320.1 prep	2218.1 adv
τῷ	ἀντικειμένῳ	λοιδορίας	χάριν.	15. ἤδη
tō	antikeimenō	loidorias	charin	ēdē
to the	opposing	reproach	on account of.	Already

1056.1 conj	4948.7 indef- pron nom pl masc	1610.2 verb 3pl indic aor pass	3557.1 prep gen	3450.2 art gen sing	4423.2 noun sing masc
γὰρ	τινες	ἐξετράπησαν	ὀπίσω	τοῦ	Σατανᾶ.
gar	tines	exetrapēsan	opisō	tou	Satana
for	some	were turned aside	after		Satan.

1479.1 conj	4948.3 indef- pron nom sing	3964.2 adj nom sing masc	2211.1 conj	3964.10 adj nom sing fem
16. Εἴ	τις	[a πιστὸς	ἢ]	πιστὴ
Ei	tis	pistos	ē	pistē
If	any	believing man	or	believing woman

2174.4 verb 3sing indic pres act	5339.6 noun acc pl fem	1869.1 verb 3sing impr pres act	1869.4 verb 3pl subj aor act
ἔχει	χήρας,	[✱ ἐπαρκείτω	[b ἐπαρκείσθω]
echei	chēras	eparkeitō	eparkeisthō
have	widows,	let him impart relief	[let them impart relief]

840.14 prs- pron dat pl fem	2504.1 conj	3231.1 partic	911.1 verb 3sing impr pres mid	3450.9 art nom sing fem	1564.2 noun nom sing fem
αὐταῖς.	καὶ	μὴ	βαρείσθω	ἡ	ἐκκλησία,
autais	kai	mē	bareisthō	hē	ekklēsia
to them,	and	not	let be burdened	the	assembly,

2419.1 conj	3450.14 art dat pl fem	3552.1 adv	5339.5 noun dat pl fem	1869.3 verb 3sing subj aor act	3450.7 art nom pl masc
ἵνα	ταῖς	ὄντως	χήραις	ἐπαρκέσῃ.	17. Οἱ
hina	tais	ontōs	chērais	eparkesē	Hoi
that	to the	being	widows	it may impart relief.	The

2544.1 adv	4150.2 verb nom pl masc part perf act	4104.5 adj comp nom pl masc	1356.1 adj gen sing fem	4940.2 noun gen sing fem
καλῶς	προεστῶτες	πρεσβύτεροι	διπλῆς	τιμῆς
kalōs	proestōtes	presbuteroi	diplēs	timēs
well	having taken the lead	elders	of double	honor

511.5 verb 3pl impr pres mid	3094.1 adv sup	3450.7 art nom pl masc	2844.7 verb nom pl masc part pres act	1706.1 prep
ἀξιούσθωσαν,	μάλιστα	οἱ	κοπιῶντες	ἐν
axiousthōsan	malista	hoi	kopiōntes	en
let be counted worthy,	especially	the	laboring	in

3030.3 noun dat sing masc	2504.1 conj	1313.3 noun dat sing fem	2978.5 verb 3sing indic pres act	1056.1 conj	3450.9 art nom sing fem
λόγῳ	καὶ	διδασκαλίᾳ.	18. λέγει	γὰρ	ἡ
logō	kai	didaskalia	legei	gar	hē
word	and	teaching;	says	for	the

5:14. Paul, still addressing the topic of younger widows which he began in verse 11, expressed his "will" concerning them. (He used this same expression in 2:8 when he instructed men to pray everywhere.) He wrote to Timothy, "I will therefore that the younger women marry." Paul then listed the specific duties of the married woman: (1) she was to bear children, (2) guide or "rule" the house ("household"), and (3) by occupying her time and effort in these pursuits keep slander from her doorstep.

The word "occasion" is a military term and means "a base of operations" (compare Paul's use of this term in such passages as Romans 7:8,11; 2 Corinthians 11:12; Galatians 5:13). The "adversary" here is not the devil but any human opponent who might take advantage of or bring an accusation against a young widow.

5:15. The instructions in verse 14 are all the more imperative when Paul reminded Timothy that "some are already turned aside after Satan." It seems some young widows were appointed in the recent past to serve the churches in practical and benevolent ministry (see verse 10). Because they lacked the wisdom of age and experience, they fell prey to their own sexual desires (verse 11) and gave themselves over to immoral conduct. In doing so they removed themselves from the protection of the church and entered the domain of Satan.

5:16. Before moving on to a new set of relationships, Paul summarized his instructions concerning widows. J.B. Phillips paraphrases it this way: "As a general rule it should be taken for granted that any Christians who have widows in the family circle should do everything possible for them and not allow them to become the church's responsibility. The church will then be free to look after those widows who are alone in the world" (Phillips).

5:17. Spiritual leaders are the second major group treated in chapter 5. In verses 17-20 Paul covered several items: how much a pastor should be paid, how he should be protected from slander, and how he should be rebuked publicly if he has sinned.

The text uses the word "elders." This is different from its use in verse 1. Here it means the officials set over local churches, i.e., "pastors." The term "rule" (literally, "superintend") indicates general oversight. "Well" seems to be the condition laid down for special consideration regarding payment. These pastors are worthy of "double honor." No doubt this refers to remuneration, especially in the context of verse 18. "Double" may not mean "twice" in the strictest sense. "Ample" or "generous" is probably Paul's intent.

Paul singled out a special class of spiritual leaders in the last clause of verse 17. "They who labor in the word and doctrine" are the preachers and teachers of the Word and tenets of the Christian faith.

14. I will therefore that the younger women marry: My advice is, *Norlie* . . . I think it is best for, *NLT* . . . young widows marry again...manage a home, *Berkeley* . . . and govern their house, *Klingensmith.*

give none occasion to the adversary to speak reproachfully: This will not give the enemy a chance to say bad things about us, *SEB* . . . and avoid giving our opponents an opportunity for scandal, *TCNT* . . . to criticize them, *Lilly* . . . for abusing us, *Confraternity.*

15. For some are already turned aside after Satan: . . . to follow, *Williams.*

16. If any man or woman that believeth have widows: . . . has widowed relatives, *Lilly, Confraternity.*

let them relieve them: . . . she should help them, *Williams* . . . let her take care of them, *Berkeley* . . . let him come to their aid, *Norlie* . . . you must care for them, *NLT.*

and let not the church be charged: . . . be free from the burden, *Williams* . . . be burdened, *Confraternity.*

that it may relieve them that are widows indeed: . . . so that it can help the widows who are really dependent, *Williams* . . . real widows who have no support, *Norlie.*

17. Let the elders that rule well: . . . who preside well, *Campbell.*

be counted worthy of double honour: . . . should be given twice as much pay, *NLT* . . . should be held deserving of especial esteem, *TCNT* . . . as deserving twice the salary they get, *Williams* . . . deserve double the pay, *SEB.*

especially they who labour in the word and doctrine: . . . work hard at preaching, *SEB* . . . in preaching and teaching, *RSV.*

1 Timothy 5:19

1118.1 noun nom sing fem	1009.2 noun acc sing masc	246.2 verb acc sing masc part pres act	3620.3 partic	5229.3 verb 2sing indic fut act
γραφή, graphē scripture,	Βοῦν Boun An ox	ἀλοῶντα aloōnta treading wage	οὐ ou not	φιμώσεις· phimōseis you shall muzzle,

2504.1 conj	510.2 adj nom sing masc	3450.5 art nom sing masc	2023.1 noun nom sing masc	3450.2 art gen sing	3272.2 noun gen sing masc
καί, kai and,	Ἄξιος Axios Worthy	ὁ ho the	ἐργάτης ergatēs workman	τοῦ tou of the	μισθοῦ misthou hire

840.3 prs-pron gen sing	2567.3 prep	4104.1 adj comp gen sing masc	2694.2 noun acc sing fem	3231.1 partic
αὐτοῦ. autou his.	**19.** Κατὰ Kata Against	πρεσβυτέρου presbuterou an elder	κατηγορίαν katēgorian an accusation	μὴ mē not

3720.3 verb 2sing impr pres mid	1609.1 prep	1479.1 conj	3231.1 partic	1894.3 prep	1411.3 num card	2211.1 conj
παραδέχου, paradechou receive,	ἐκτὸς ektos except	εἰ ei if	μὴ mē not	ἐπὶ epi on	δύο duo two	ἢ ē or

4980.2 num card gen	3116.5 noun gen pl masc	3450.8 art acc pl masc	262.9 verb acc pl masc part pres act	1783.1 prep
τριῶν triōn three	μαρτύρων. marturōn witnesses.	**20.** Τοὺς Tous The	ἁμαρτάνοντας hamartanontas sinning	ἐνώπιον enōpion before

3820.4 adj gen pl	1638.3 verb 2sing impr pres act	2419.1 conj	2504.1 conj	3450.7 art nom pl masc	3036.3 adj nom pl masc	5238.4 noun acc sing masc
πάντων pantōn all	ἔλεγχε, elenche expose,	ἵνα hina that	καὶ kai also	οἱ hoi the	λοιποὶ loipoi rest	φόβον phobon fear

2174.10 verb 3pl subj pres act	1257.1 verb 1sing indic pres mid	1783.1 prep	3450.2 art gen sing	2296.2 noun gen sing masc
ἔχωσιν. echōsin may have.	**21.** Διαμαρτύρομαι Diamarturomai I earnestly testify	ἐνώπιον enōpion before	τοῦ tou	θεοῦ theou God

21.a.**Txt:** 06D-corr,018K 020L,025P,byz.Sod **Var:** 01א,02A,06D-org 33,Lach,Treg,Alf,Word Tisc,We/Ho,Weis UBS/✲

2504.1 conj	2935.2 noun gen sing masc	2400.2 name masc	5382.2 name gen masc	5382.2 name gen masc	2400.2 name masc
καὶ kai and	ʼ κυρίου kuriou Lord	Ἰησοῦ Iēsou Jesus	Χριστοῦ Christou Christ	[a✲ Χριστοῦ Christou [Christ	Ἰησοῦ] Iēsou Jesus]

2504.1 conj	3450.1 art gen pl	1575.4 adj gen pl masc	32.6 noun gen pl masc	2419.1 conj	3642.18 dem-pron pl neu
καὶ kai and	τῶν tōn the	ἐκλεκτῶν eklektōn elect	ἀγγέλων, angelōn angels,	ἵνα hina that	ταῦτα tauta these things

5278.10 verb 2sing subj aor act	5400.1 prep	4158.1 noun gen sing neu	3235.6 num card neu	4020.15 verb nom sing masc part pres act
φυλάξῃς phulaxēs you should keep,	χωρὶς chōris apart from	προκρίματος, prokrimatos prejudice,	μηδὲν mēden nothing	ποιῶν poiōn doing

21.b.**Txt:** 01א,010F 012G,018K,81,630 1881 **Var:** 02A,06D,044,byz.

2567.3 prep	4204.1 noun acc sing fem	4203.1 noun acc sing fem	5331.8 noun acc pl fem
κατὰ kata by	ʼ✲ πρόσκλισιν. prosklisin partiality.	[b πρόσκλησιν.] prosklēsin [idem]	**22.** Χεῖρας Cheiras Hands

5:18. To give strength to his instruction in verse 17, Paul quoted Deuteronomy 25:4 which says: "Thou shalt not muzzle the ox when he treadeth out the corn" (compare 1 Corinthians 9:9). The slight difference in the Deuteronomy passage and here is the words "when he." This is found in the Greek present participle here in verse 18; the meaning is "while it is treading." The idea is the ox may be muzzled at other times but not while it is working at the threshing floor. Paul probably quoted this to appeal to the moral principle behind the illustration rather than the letter of the Law.

Paul's second quotation from Scripture is from Jesus (Matthew 10:10 and Luke 10:7). Luke had already written his Gospel before he wrote Acts (Acts 1:1), was a close coworker with Paul during much of his ministry, and was with him when this epistle was written. Very likely Paul had read Luke's Gospel and here was quoting from it. It is noteworthy that Paul recognized Luke's writings as Scripture, as Peter did Paul's (2 Peter 3:15,16).

The meaning is clear. Applied to "the elders that rule well" (verse 17), they are "worthy of double honor" and "worthy of . . . reward." If the first is questionable as meaning remuneration, the second certainly cannot be taken any other way.

5:19. The Law was very clear that no man was to be condemned on the testimony of a single witness: "One witness shall not rise up against a man for any iniquity, or for any sin, in any sin that he sinneth: at the mouth of two witnesses, or at the mouth of three witnesses, shall the matter be established" (Deuteronomy 19:15).

Paul applied this principle to any accusation against an elder. This practice would protect spiritual leaders from unwarranted slander. Later on the rule was amended to require that the two witnesses should be Christians. This was to prevent untrue accusations from those who sought to slander church leaders.

5:20. Paul told Timothy that if a leader was found to be guilty of sin, he was to be rebuked ("reproved, corrected") before all. Whether the "all" means before all the elders or before the entire church is not clear. But the reason for this public rebuke is plain: it would deter others from falling into the same sin.

These instructions have direct reference to spiritual leaders. It would be improper to apply them to Christians in general with the exception of the principle regarding witnesses (see verse 19; compare Matthew 18:16).

5:21. Although verses 21-25 continue the instructions regarding elders, they contain personal counsel to Timothy. In verse 21 Paul laid an especially strong "charge" ("I solemnly protest") on Timothy before three witnesses: God, the Lord Jesus Christ, and the elect angels (compare 2 Timothy 4:1). Paul told Timothy he was to "observe" ("guard, keep") and to apply all the rules without prejudice or partiality.

18. For the scripture saith: Thou shalt not muzzle the ox that treadeth out the corn: . . . when he is treading out the grain, *Williams.*

And, The labourer is worthy of his reward: A person who works should be paid, *NLT* . . . is entitled to his support, *Lilly* . . . deserves his wage, *Berkeley* . . . deserves to get his pay, *Norlie* . . . is worth his wages, *TCNT* . . . of his wages, *Confraternity.*

19. Against an elder receive not an accusation: Do not entertain a charge against an elder, *Berkeley* . . . Make it a rule not to consider a charge preferred against, *Williams* . . . do not assent to an accusation, *Concordant* . . . against a presbyter, *Lilly.*

but before two or three witnesses: . . . unless it is supported by, *Lilly, Confraternity, Berkeley.*

20. Them that sin rebuke before all: Rebuke habitual sinners, *Lilly* . . . Rebuke offenders publicly, *TCNT* . . . Prove them wrong publicly, *SEB.*

that others also may fear: Then the others will show respect, *SEB* . . . that the rest may be awed, *Berkeley.*

21. I charge thee before God, and the Lord Jesus Christ, and the elect angels:

that thou observe these things without preferring one before another: . . . carry out these directions uninfluenced by prejudice, *TCNT* . . . without discrimination, *Norlie.*

doing nothing by partiality: Don't pre-judge or give any special favors to anyone, *SEB* . . . in no way favoring either side, *Lilly, Confraternity* . . . that you act with no favoritism, *Berkeley* . . . Show favors to no one, *NLT* . . . doing nothing from bias, *Concordant.*

1 Timothy 5:23

4878.1 adv	3235.2 num card dat	1991.5 verb 2sing impr pres act	3234.1 adv	2814.3 verb 2sing impr pres act	264.7 noun dat pl fem
ταχέως	μηδενὶ	ἐπιτίθει,	μηδὲ	κοινώνει	ἁμαρτίαις
tacheōs	mēdeni	epitithei	mēde	koinōnei	hamartiais
quickly	on no one	lay,	nor	share	in sins

243.7 adj dat pl fem	4427.4 prs-pron acc sing masc	52.2 adj acc sing masc	4931.6 verb 2sing impr pres act	3239.1 adv
ἀλλοτρίαις.	σεαυτὸν	ἁγνὸν	τήρει.	23. Μηκέτι
allotriais	seauton	hagnon	tērei	Mēketi
of others.	Yourself	pure	keep.	No longer

5043.1 verb 2sing impr pres act	233.1 conj	233.2 conj	3494.3 noun dat sing masc	3504.2 adj dat sing	5366.3 verb 2sing impr pres mid
ὑδροπότει,	ʼ ἀλλʼ	[☆ ἀλλὰ]	οἴνῳ	ὀλίγῳ	χρῶ
hudropotei	all'	alla	oinō	oligō	chrō
drink water,	but	[idem]	wine	a little	use

23.a.Txt: 06D-corr,018K 020L,byz.sa.bo. Var: 01א,02A,06D-org 025P,33,Lach,Treg,Alf Tisc,We/Ho,Weis,Sod UBS/☆

1217.2 prep	3450.6 art acc sing masc	4602.1 noun acc sing masc	4622.2 prs-pron gen 2sing	2504.1 conj	3450.15 art acc pl fem
διὰ	τὸν	στόμαχον	ʼa σου ʻ	καὶ	τὰς
dia	ton	stomachon	sou	kai	tas
on account of	the	stomach	your	and	the

4295.1 adj acc pl fem	4622.2 prs-pron gen 2sing	763.1 noun fem	4948.4 indef-pron gen pl	442.7 noun gen pl masc
πυκνάς	σου	ἀσθενείας.	24. Τινῶν	ἀνθρώπων
puknas	sou	astheneias	Tinōn	anthrōpōn
frequent	your	infirmities.	Of some	men

3450.13 art nom pl fem	264.5 noun nom pl fem	4130.1 adj nom pl fem	1498.7 verb 3pl indic pres act	4113.6 verb nom pl fem part pres act
αἱ	ἁμαρτίαι	πρόδηλοί	εἰσιν,	προάγουσαι
hai	hamartiai	prodēloi	eisin	proagousai
the	sins	evident	are,	going before

1519.1 prep	2893.4 noun acc sing fem	4948.8 indef-pron dat pl masc	1156.2 conj	2504.1 conj	1857.1 verb 3pl indic pres act
εἰς	κρίσιν·	τισὶν	δὲ	καὶ	ἐπακολουθοῦσιν.
eis	krisin	tisin	de	kai	epakolouthousin
to	judgment;	some	and	also	they follow after.

5447.1 adv	2504.1 conj	3450.17 art pl neu	2541.11 adj pl neu	2024.4 noun pl neu
25. ὡσαύτως	καὶ	τὰ	ʼ καλὰ	ἔργα
hōsautōs	kai	ta	kala	erga
In like manner	also	the	good	works

25.a.Txt: 018K,020L,byz. Var: 01א,02A,06D 025P,33,Lach,Treg,Alf Word,Tisc,We/Ho,Weis Sod,UBS/☆

2024.4 noun pl neu	3450.17 art pl neu	2541.11 adj pl neu	4130.3 adj pl neu	1498.4 verb 3sing indic pres act	2504.1 conj
[a☆ ἔργα	τὰ	καλὰ]	πρόδηλα	ʼb ἐστιν ʻ	καὶ
erga	ta	kala	prodēla	estin	kai
[works	the	good]	clear	are,	and

25.b.Txt: 018K,020L,byz. Var: 01א,02A,Lach Treg,Alf,Tisc,We/Ho Weis,Sod,UBS/☆

3450.17 art pl neu	245.1 adv	2174.15 verb part pres act	2900.6 verb inf aor pass	3620.3 partic	1404.4 verb 3sing indic pres mid
τὰ	ἄλλως	ἔχοντα,	κρυβῆναι	οὐ	ʼ δύναται.
ta	allōs	echonta	krubēnai	ou	dunatai
the	otherwise	having,	to be hidden	not	is able.

25.c.Txt: 01א,018K 020L,byz.Weis Var: 02A,06D,025P,33 Lach,Treg,Alf,Word Tisc,We/Ho,Sod,UBS/☆

1404.7 verb 3pl indic pres mid	3607.2 rel-pron nom pl masc	1498.7 verb 3pl indic pres act	5097.3 prep	2201.3 noun acc sing masc
[c☆ δύνανται.]	6:1. Ὅσοι	εἰσὶν	ὑπὸ	ζυγὸν
dunantai	Hosoi	eisin	hupo	zugon
[are able.]	As many as	are	under	yoke

5:22. "Lay hands suddenly on no man" has been seen by some as referring to the discipline of an impenitent wrongdoer (a Christian). But it is better to conclude the reference is to ordaining elders. The treatment of elders is the immediate context and "laying on of hands" was used by Paul to mean the rite of ordination (1 Timothy 4:14; 2 Timothy 1:6). The meaning here is "ordain no one with undue haste" and connects with "partiality" in verse 21. If there is bias in the selection of elders, the ordination process may be hasty and regrettable.

Some believe that in the reference to "other men's sins" Paul was cautioning Timothy that ordaining others placed him as surety for their characters. Timothy might be implicated in any sins a newly ordained elder committed. At any rate it is wise to avoid involvement in other's misconduct. "Pure" here has the sense of honorable and upright conduct, though it also can mean "holy, chaste."

5:23. This verse is a personal parenthesis. Paul was concerned for Timothy's health and gave him a prescription for his infirmity. It may connect with "keep thyself pure" in verse 22.

Timothy evidently was a total abstainer. Possibly his abstinence was based on the Nazarite vow (see Numbers 6:3,4). His mother was a Jewess (Acts 16:1), so he may have received this teaching from her (2 Timothy 1:5; 3:15). "Drink no longer water" suggests Timothy was drinking water exclusively. Water in that day and throughout the eastern countries was polluted and unsafe. (For discussion about *oinos* see the commentary on 3:3.) Paul prescribed a "little wine" as medicine for Timothy's "often infirmities." Timothy had a weak stomach and the polluted water was aggravating his condition. So Paul suggested a remedy.

5:24,25. Verses 24 and 25 present a contrast of sins and good works and enlarge on Paul's caution, "Neither be partaker of other men's sins" (5:22). "Open beforehand" refers to sins that are "conspicuous, clearly evident, immediately obvious." The words "going before" mean "pointing, leading the way." "Judgment" refers to God's judgment of men.

The meaning of these contrasts is clear. Obvious sins lead the way to judgment. Hidden sins follow men to judgment. Obvious good works are noticed, applauded, and appreciated. Hidden good works are known to God and will be rewarded. God will deal with men in a fair and equitable manner.

"These parallel observations, viewing human potentialities both negatively and positively, bring out forcibly the complexities involved in selecting suitable candidates for God's work. Hasty action relies on first impressions, but these impressions are often deceptive. Unworthy men might be chosen, whose moral culpability lies deeper than the surface; and worthy men, whose good actions are not in the limelight, might easily be overlooked. The whole situation demands extreme caution" (Guthrie, *Tyndale New Testament Commentaries*, 14:109).

22. Lay hands suddenly on no man: Impose hands hastily on one, *Campbell* . . . hands of ordination on no one hastily, *Berkeley* . . . Never ordain any one hastily, *TCNT* . . . Do not be in a hurry about choosing a church leader, *NLT*.

neither be partaker of other men's sins: . . . nor participate in, *RSV* . . . Don't share in the sins of others, *SEB* . . . not to be responsible for the sins of others, *Williams*.

keep thyself pure: Keep your life untarnished, *TCNT*.

23. Drink no longer water: Do not drink water only, *NLT*.

but use a little wine: . . . but be using a sip of wine, *Concordant* . . . take a little wine, *Williams*.

for thy stomach's sake and thine often infirmities: You are often sick, *SEB* . . . to strengthen your stomach and relieve its frequent attacks, *Williams* . . . and your recurring illness, *Berkeley* . . . and your frequent illnesses, *Klingensmith*.

24. Some men's sins are open beforehand: The sins of some men can be seen, *NLT* . . . before investigation, *Lilly, Confraternity* . . . are very evident, *Williams* . . . are conspicuous, *RSV, TCNT*.

going before to judgment: . . . clearly lead them on to, *Williams* . . . and pave the way for their judgment, *TCNT*.

and some men they follow after: . . . their sins show up later, *Norlie* . . . The sins of others appear later, *SEB* . . . the sins of others lag behind, *Williams*.

25. Likewise also the good works of some are manifest beforehand: . . . usually very evident, *Williams*.

and they that are otherwise cannot be hid:

1395.6 noun nom pl masc	3450.8 art acc pl masc	2375.8 adj acc pl masc	1197.6 noun acc pl masc	3820.10 adj gen sing fem	4940.2 noun gen sing fem
δοῦλοι,	τοὺς	ἰδίους	δεσπότας	πάσης	τιμῆς
douloi	tous	idious	despotas	pasēs	timēs
slaves,	the	their own	masters	of all	honor

510.4 adj acc pl masc	2216.4 verb 3pl impr pres mid	2419.1 conj	3231.1 partic	3450.16 art sing neu	3549.2 noun sing neu
ἀξίους	ἡγείσθωσαν,	ἵνα	μὴ	τὸ	ὄνομα
axious	hēgeisthōsan	hina	mē	to	onoma
worthy	let them esteem,	that	not	the	name

3450.2 art gen sing	2296.2 noun gen sing masc	2504.1 conj	3450.9 art nom sing fem	1313.2 noun	980.19 verb 3sing subj pres mid
τοῦ	θεοῦ	καὶ	ἡ	διδασκαλία	βλασφημῆται.
tou	theou	kai	hē	didaskalia	blasphēmētai
	of God	and	the	teaching	be blasphemed.

3450.7 art nom pl masc	1156.2 conj	3964.9 adj acc pl masc	2174.19 verb nom pl masc part pres act	1197.6 noun acc pl masc	3231.1 partic
2. οἱ	δὲ	πιστοὺς	ἔχοντες	δεσπότας,	μὴ
hoi	de	pistous	echontes	despotas	mē
The	and	believing	having	masters,	not

2675.4 verb 3pl impr pres act	3617.1 conj	79.6 noun nom pl masc	1498.7 verb 3pl indic pres act	233.2 conj
καταφρονείτωσαν,	ὅτι	ἀδελφοί	εἰσιν·	ἀλλὰ
kataphroneitōsan	hoti	adelphoi	eisin	alla
let them despise,	because	brothers	they are;	but

3095.1 adv comp	1392.5 verb 3pl impr pres act	3617.1 conj	3964.6 adj nom pl masc	1498.7 verb 3pl indic pres act	2504.1 conj
μᾶλλον	δουλευέτωσαν,	ὅτι	πιστοί	εἰσιν	καὶ
mallon	douleuetōsan	hoti	pistoi	eisin	kai
rather	let them serve,	because	believing	they are	and

27.6 adj pl masc	3450.7 art nom pl masc	3450.10 art gen sing fem	2087.1 noun gen sing fem	479.1 verb nom pl masc part pres mid
ἀγαπητοὶ	οἱ	τῆς	εὐεργεσίας	ἀντιλαμβανόμενοι.
agapētoi	hoi	tēs	euergesias	antilambanomenoi
beloved	the	the	good service	being helped by.

3642.18 dem- pron pl neu	1315.5 verb 2sing impr pres act	2504.1 conj	3731.5 verb 2sing impr pres act	1479.1 conj
Ταῦτα	δίδασκε	καὶ	παρακάλει.	3. Εἴ
Tauta	didaske	kai	parakalei	Ei
These things	teach	and	exhort.	If

4948.3 indef- pron nom sing	2064.1 verb 3sing indic pres act	2504.1 conj	3231.1 partic	4193.10 verb 3sing indic pres mid
τις	ἑτεροδιδασκαλεῖ	καὶ	μὴ	προσέρχεται
tis	heterodidaskalei	kai	mē	proserchetai
anyone	teaches other doctrine,	and	not	draws near

5039.5 verb dat pl masc part pres act	3030.7 noun dat pl masc	3450.4 art dat pl	3450.2 art gen sing	2935.2 noun gen sing masc	2231.2 prs- pron gen 1pl
ὑγιαίνουσιν	λόγοις,	τοῖς	τοῦ	κυρίου	ἡμῶν
hugiainousin	logois	tois	tou	kuriou	hēmōn
being sound	to words,	the	of the	Lord	our

2400.2 name masc	5382.2 name gen masc	2504.1 conj	3450.11 art dat sing fem	2567.1 prep	2131.4 noun acc sing fem
Ἰησοῦ	Χριστοῦ,	καὶ	τῇ	κατ'	εὐσέβειαν
Iēsou	Christou	kai	tē	kat'	eusebeian
Jesus	Christ,	and	the	according to	godliness

6:1. Chapter 6 continues the topic of relationships but introduces a new group: slaves. Verse 1 was addressed to Christian slaves with non-Christian masters. Christian slaves found equality in the Church but were still considered inferior in society. The words "under the yoke" reflect the attitude of non-Christian masters. They regarded slaves in the same category as cattle. If a Christian slave considered himself as an heir of salvation and his master as a son of perdition, a feeling of pious superiority on the part of the slave could result. This would put strain on the master-slave relationship and seriously hinder the slave's service to his master and witness for Christ. So a new attitude is needed. Paul says Christian slaves are to give full respect to these masters. This would bring glory to God and would not bring reproach on His name or the gospel.

6:2. Paul now addressed Christian slaves who were owned by "believing masters." Both were members of the same local church; a dilemma existed: equality in the spiritual realm but masters and slaves in the natural realm. Slaves with Christian masters were advised "not to show less respect for them because they are brothers" (NIV). Because a slave and his master were equal in the Church and brothers in Christ the tendency on the part of the slave would be to treat his master on an equal basis at home. The slave would forget his place and tend to show less respect to his master when he should "do them service," that is, serve them well.

Why did not the Church fight slavery by requiring Christian slave owners to free their slaves? When we consider that possibly half the population of the Roman Empire in the First Century was composed of slaves, we then understand what social and political havoc this would have brought. The spiritual fellowship and equality within the Christian church was the seed whose maturation, in the course of time, did away with slavery (see Galatians 3:26-28). The gospel brought to men a freedom which a revolutionary rebellion could never have accomplished.

"Partakers of the benefit" may refer to masters or slaves. If the master, he would receive benefit from the conscientious and joyful work of the slave. If the slave, he would benefit from the kindness and brotherly love of the master. So the benefit was mutual. "These things teach and exhort" introduces what follows.

6:3. Verses 3-10 is a new section and contains further warnings to Timothy. False teachers is the subject of verses 3-5. The teaching here is similar to that found in 1:3-7.

These false teachers "consent not to wholesome words." The word "consent" (*proserchomai*) means "approach," with a derived sense of "attaching oneself to." "The words of our Lord Jesus Christ" could mean the sayings of Jesus or words about Jesus, i.e., the gospel. The latter is better suited to the context since "doctrine" ("teaching") immediately follows. Paul made "doctrine" one of the major themes of this letter to Timothy (see 1:3,10; 4:6,13,16; 5:17; 6:1).

1. Let as many servants as are under the yoke: ... who are owned by someone, *NLT.*

count their own masters worthy of all honour: ... esteem their masters as, *Montgomery* ... deserving of, *Confraternity* ... of all respect, *Berkeley* ... worthy of full respect, *NIV* ... of the highest respect, *Williams.*

that the name of God and his doctrine be not blasphemed: ... and the teachings, *Montgomery* ... may not be dishonored, *Norlie* ... may not be maligned, *TCNT* ... is not slandered, *Klingensmith* ... may not be abused, *Williams.*

2. And they that have believing masters: ... if they have Christian masters, *Norlie* ... whose masters are Christian believers, *Montgomery.*

let them not despise them, because they are brethren: ... let them not slight them, *Young* ... must not treat them with disrespect, *Montgomery* ... should not look down on their masters, *SEB.*

but rather do them service: ... to serve them even better, *NIV* ... rather slave for them the better, *Montgomery.*

because they are faithful and beloved partakers of the benefit: ... because those who get the benefit of their services are believing and beloved, *Montgomery.*

These teach and exhort: Continue to teach and preach this, *Montgomery* ... the things to teach and insist on, *TCNT.*

3. If any man teach otherwise: ... teaches heterodoxy, *Montgomery* ... different doctrines, *Williams.*

and consent not to wholesome words: ... and refuses to consent, *Montgomery* ... to agree with, *Williams.*

even the words of our Lord Jesus Christ: ... the wholesome messages of, *Williams.*

and to the doctrine which is according to godliness: ... to the teaching that fosters godliness, *Berkeley* ... and to the teachings of religion, *Montgomery* ... and godly teaching, *SEB.*

1 Timothy 6:4

1313.3 noun dat sing fem	5028.2 verb 3sing indic perf mid	3235.6 num card neu	1971.5 verb nom sing masc part pres mid	233.2 conj
διδασκαλία,	**4.** τετύφωται,	μηδὲν	ἐπιστάμενος,	ἀλλὰ
didaskalia	*tetuphōtai*	*mēden*	*epistamenos*	*alla*
teaching,	he is puffed up,	nothing	knowing,	but

3415.1 verb nom sing masc part pres act	3875.1 prep	2197.3 noun acc pl fem	2504.1 conj	3029.1 noun acc pl fem
νοσῶν	περὶ	ζητήσεις	καὶ	λογομαχίας,
noson	*peri*	*zētēseis*	*kai*	*logomachias*
being sick	about	questions	and	disputes of words,

1523.1 prep gen	3614.1 rel-pron gen pl	1090.14 verb 3sing indic pres mid	5192.1 noun nom sing masc	2038.1 noun nom sing fem	2038.5 noun nom pl fem
ἐξ	ὧν	γίνεται	φθόνος,	⸂✶ ἔρις,	[ᵃ ἔρεις,]
ex	*hōn*	*ginetai*	*phthonos*	*eris*	*ereis*
out of	which	comes	envy,	strife,	[strifes,]

981.4 noun nom pl fem	5121.1 noun nom pl fem	4050.13 adj nom pl fem	3721.1 noun nom pl fem
βλασφημίαι,	ὑπόνοιαι	πονηραί,	**5.** ⸀ παραδιατριβαὶ
blasphēmiai	*huponoiai*	*ponērai*	*paradiatribai*
blasphemies,	suspicions	wicked,	vain argumentations

1269.1 noun nom pl fem	1305.6 verb gen pl masc part perf mid	442.7 noun gen pl masc
[ᵃ✶ διαπαρατριβαὶ]	διεφθαρμένων	ἀνθρώπων
diaparatribai	*diephtharmenon*	*anthrōpon*
[constant quarrellings]	having been corrupted	of men

3450.6 art acc sing masc	3426.4 noun acc sing masc	2504.1 conj	644.5 verb gen pl masc part perf mid	3450.10 art gen sing fem
τὸν	νοῦν,	καὶ	ἀπεστερημένων	τῆς
ton	*noun*	*kai*	*apesterēmenōn*	*tēs*
the	mind,	and	having been destitute	of the

223.2 noun gen sing fem	3406.4 verb gen pl masc part pres act	4059.2 noun acc sing masc	1498.32 verb inf pres act	3450.12 art acc sing fem
ἀληθείας,	νομιζόντων	πορισμὸν	εἶναι	τὴν
alētheias	*nomizontōn*	*porismon*	*einai*	*tēn*
truth,	holding	gain	to be	the

2131.4 noun acc sing fem	861.11 verb 2sing impr pres mid	570.3 prep	3450.1 art gen pl	4955.1 dem-pron gen pl
εὐσέβειαν·	⸀ᵇ ἀφίστασο	ἀπὸ	τῶν	τοιούτων. ⸃
eusebeian	*aphistaso*	*apo*	*tōn*	*toioutōn*
piety;	withdraw	from	the	such.

1498.4 verb 3sing indic pres act	1156.2 conj	4059.1 noun nom sing masc	3144.2 adj nom sing masc	3450.9 art nom sing fem	2131.1 noun nom sing fem
6. Ἔστιν	δὲ	πορισμὸς	μέγας	ἡ	εὐσέβεια
Estin	*de*	*porismos*	*megas*	*hē*	*eusebeia*
Is	but	gain	great	the	godliness

3196.3 prep	835.1 noun gen sing fem	3625.6 num card neu	1056.1 conj	1517.2 verb 1pl indic aor act	1519.1 prep
μετὰ	αὐταρκείας.	**7.** οὐδὲν	γὰρ	εἰσηνέγκαμεν	εἰς
meta	*autarkeias*	*ouden*	*gar*	*eisēnenkamen*	*eis*
with	contentment.	Nothing	for	we brought	into

3450.6 art acc sing masc	2862.4 noun acc sing masc	1206.1 adj sing	3617.1 conj	3624.1 conj	1613.5 verb inf aor act
τὸν	κόσμον,	⸀ᵃ δῆλον ⸃	ὅτι	οὐδὲ	ἐξενεγκεῖν
ton	*kosmon*	*dēlon*	*hoti*	*oude*	*exenenkein*
the	world,	clear	that	neither	to carry out

6:4. Verses 4 and 5 describe the characteristics of a false teacher. "Proud" means "conceited, puffed up." "Knowing nothing" means "ignorant." "Doting" is a strange and unique word and possibly can be translated "being sick (mentally)" and by extension, "having a morbid craving for." "Questions" means "controversies," and "strifes of words" is "arguments." In a few words Paul said a false teacher is (1) conceited, (2) ignorant, (3) sick, and (4) argumentative.

Four negative results (a fifth is listed in verse 5) of this argumentative nature are: (1) "envy," (2) "strife" ("dissension, quarreling"), (3) "railings" ("blasphemies, slander, malicious talk"), (4) "evil surmisings" ("suspicions"). All of this is evil and disruptive and has no place in the company of believers.

6:5. "Disputings" are "constant frictions" or "incessant quarrelings." These are the stock-in-trade of "men of corrupt minds." This term means these men were incapable of moral judgment and therefore were "destitute of the truth." The false teacher believed the lies he spouted in foolish and perverse arguments. This had brought him to intellectual and moral deprivation.

Donald Guthrie questions the reading "supposing that gain is godliness." He says in his commentary: "The concluding clause should read 'supposing that godliness is a way of gain,' or as Moffatt translates it, 'they imagine religion is a paying concern' " (*Tyndale New Testament Commentaries*, 14:112). The Greek construction supports this, as does the context. The idea of using religion for profit is what Paul addressed next.

6:6. Paul repeated what he had just written in verse 5 but with one significant difference, he added the word "contentment." "Contentment" is an inward sufficiency that comes from a full acceptance of and appreciation for God's provisions. This contentment is an inner possession and is unaffected by outward circumstances.

The word "gain" is *porismos* and means "good business, profit." Here in verse 6 it connotes more than material wealth. The possession of things is not the only measure of "gain."

6:7. Godliness with contentment is great gain because "we brought (absolutely) nothing into this world (when we were born), and it is certain we can carry (absolutely) nothing out (when we die)." This proverbial statement was not new with Paul. God inspired both Job and Solomon to speak and write this same truth (see Job 1:21; Ecclesiastes 5:15). Paul was saying that material possessions are of fleeting, secondary importance. They are not part of the true self which will abide. The words "carry nothing out" refer to a person's "exit" from this life.

Possessions are external; contentment is internal. Money is material; godliness is spiritual. Godliness and contentment will go with us when we depart. All the other things will be left behind.

4. He is proud, knowing nothing: Such a man is nothing but a conceited ignoramus, *Norlie* . . . he is boastful, *SEB* . . . he is puffed up, *Klingensmith* . . . though really he is utterly ignorant, *TCNT*.

but doting about questions and strifes of words: . . . has an unhealthy interest in controversies, *NIV* . . . about controversies and disputes, *Confraternity* . . . and verbal contentions, *Campbell* . . . with a morbid appetite for, *Williams*.

whereof cometh envy, strife, railings, evil surmisings: . . . which lead to, *Williams* . . . bad suspicions, *Berkeley* . . . wicked suspicions, *Concordant* . . . unjust suspicions, *Campbell*.

5. Perverse disputings of men of corrupt minds: . . . and incessant wrangling, *TCNT* . . . empty arguments from men of poisoned minds, *Klingensmith* . . . perpetual contention between people of depraved minds, *Berkeley* . . . who have polluted minds, *SEB*.

and destitute of the truth: They do not have the truth, *NLT* . . . who have lost all hold on the Truth, *TCNT*.

supposing that gain is godliness: They think religion is a way to get much for themselves, *NLT* . . . They think that religion is a way of making money, *SEB* . . . that godliness is a means to financial gain, *NIV*.

from such withdraw thyself: Keep aloof from such, *Norlie* . . . Keep away from such, *Klingensmith*.

6. But godliness with contentment is great gain: . . . is great prosperity, *Klingensmith*.

7. For we brought nothing into this world:
and it is certain we can carry nothing out: . . . and, obviously, *Berkeley* . . . it is manifest, *Young* . . . it is evident, *Concordant*.

1 Timothy 6:8

4948.10 indef-pron sing neu	1404.5 verb 1pl indic pres mid	2174.19 verb nom pl masc part pres act	1156.2 conj	1299.1 noun acc pl fem	2504.1 conj
τι	δυνάμεθα·	8. ἔχοντες	δὲ	διατροφὰς	καὶ
ti	*dunametha*	*echontes*	*de*	*diatrophas*	*kai*
anything	are we able.	Having	but	sustenance	and

4484.1 noun pl neu	3642.3 dem-pron dat pl	708.7 verb 1pl indic fut pass	3450.7 art nom pl masc	1156.2 conj
σκεπάσματα,	τούτοις	ἀρκεσθησόμεθα.	9. Οἱ	δὲ
skepasmata	*toutois*	*arkesthēsometha*	*Hoi*	*de*
coverings,	with these	we shall be satisfied.	The	but

1007.10 verb nom pl masc part pres mid	4007.3 verb inf pres act	1690.1 verb 3pl indic pres act	1519.1 prep	3848.4 noun acc sing masc
βουλόμενοι	πλουτεῖν,	ἐμπίπτουσιν	εἰς	πειρασμὸν
boulomenoi	*ploutein*	*empiptousin*	*eis*	*peirasmon*
desiring	to be rich,	fall	into	temptation

2504.1 conj	3666.3 noun acc sing fem	2504.1 conj	1924.1 noun fem	4044.15 adj acc pl fem	451.3 adj acc pl fem	2504.1 conj
καὶ	παγίδα	καὶ	ἐπιθυμίας	πολλὰς	ἀνοήτους	καὶ
kai	*pagida*	*kai*	*epithumias*	*pollas*	*anoētous*	*kai*
and	a snare	and	desires	many	unwise	and

976.1 adj acc pl fem	3610.4 rel-pron nom pl fem	1029.1 verb 3pl indic pres act	3450.8 art acc pl masc	442.9 noun acc pl masc
βλαβερὰς,	αἵτινες	βυθίζουσιν	τοὺς	ἀνθρώπους
blaberas	*haitines*	*buthizousin*	*tous*	*anthrōpous*
harmful,	which	sink	the	men

1519.1 prep	3502.2 noun acc sing masc	2504.1 conj	677.3 noun acc sing fem	4347.1 noun nom sing fem	1056.1 conj
εἰς	ὄλεθρον	καὶ	ἀπώλειαν.	10. ῥίζα	γὰρ
eis	*olethron*	*kai*	*apōleian*	*rhiza*	*gar*
into	destruction	and	perdition.	A root	for

3820.4 adj gen pl	3450.1 art gen pl	2527.1 adj gen pl	1498.4 verb 3sing indic pres act	3450.9 art nom sing fem	5202.1 noun nom sing fem
πάντων	τῶν	κακῶν	ἐστιν	ἡ	φιλαργυρία·
panton	*tōn*	*kakōn*	*estin*	*hē*	*philarguria*
of all	the	evils	is	the	love of money;

3614.10 rel-pron gen sing fem	4948.7 indef-pron nom pl masc	3576.3 verb nom pl masc part pres mid	629.2 verb 3pl indic aor pass
ἧς	τινες	ὀρεγόμενοι	ἀπεπλανήθησαν
hēs	*tines*	*oregomenoi*	*apeplanēthēsan*
which	some	aspiring after	were seduced

570.3 prep	3450.10 art gen sing fem	3963.2 noun gen sing fem	2504.1 conj	1431.8 prs-pron acc pl masc	3907.1 verb 3pl indic aor act
ἀπὸ	τῆς	πίστεως,	καὶ	ἑαυτοὺς	περιέπειραν
apo	*tēs*	*pisteōs*	*kai*	*heautous*	*periepeiran*
from	the	faith,	and	themselves	pierced

3464.2 noun dat pl fem	4044.14 adj dat pl fem	4622.1 prs-pron nom 2sing	1156.2 conj	5434.1 intrj	442.5 noun voc sing masc
ὀδύναις	πολλαῖς.	11. Σὺ	δέ,	ὦ	ἄνθρωπε
odunais	*pollais*	*Su*	*de*	*ō*	*anthrōpe*
with sorrows	many.	You	but,	O	man

11.a.**Txt**: 01ℵ-corr,06D 018K,020L,025P,byz. **Var**: 01ℵ-org,02A,33 Lach,Treg,Tisc,We/Ho Weis,Sod,UBS/✱

3450.2 art gen sing	2296.2 noun gen sing masc	3642.18 dem-pron pl neu	5180.2 verb 2sing impr pres act	1371.5 verb 2sing impr pres act	1156.2 conj
ᶜᵃ τοῦ ᵕ	θεοῦ,	ταῦτα	φεῦγε·	δίωκε	δὲ
tou	*theou*	*tauta*	*pheuge*	*diōke*	*de*
	of God,	these things	flee,	pursue	and

6:8. "Having food and raiment" reminds us of Jesus' words in Matthew 6:25-34. "Food" ("nourishments, sustenance" [plural]) suggests a full supply for each day. "Raiment" (also in the plural, "coverings") includes both clothing and shelter. So Paul was certainly aware he was repeating what Jesus said. "Be therewith content" is in the future indicative tense and is not so much an exhortation to be content but an assertion that this is the path to real contentment.

6:9. The opposite of godliness with contentment is greed. This greed takes one in an ever-downward spiral. Verses 9 and 10 are not addressed to the already rich but to those who want to become rich. These people "fall," then "drown." The language vividly describes the destiny of the greedy: "temptation and a snare" (usually refers to the devil's snare), "foolish and hurtful lusts" (sensual desires), "destruction and perdition" (eternal loss, utter ruin).

6:10. Paul concluded his instructions regarding those who are greedy with the now oft-quoted phrase, "For the love of money is the root of all evil." Many, however, misquote it. They think it to be, "Money is the root of all evil." If this were so, only the rich would be capable of wrongdoing; the poor would not be bothered by evil. Actually, the reading is "*a* root of all evil," not the only root, for that would be an exaggeration. Rather, it is a root from which every kind of evil can grow.

The results of this greed are disillusionment, backsliding, grief, and heartbreaking remorse. The literal Greek for the word "erred" (passive form) is "were led astray." This suggests those who covet after money are victims in the grip of an unrelenting deception. "Pierced themselves through" means the "many sorrows" ("pains") were self-inflicted.

6:11. Verse 11 begins the final section of this first letter to Timothy. It contains a personal charge that repeats and summarizes much of what Paul has already written.

The title "man of God" was given to Old Testament greats like Moses, Samuel, and many of the prophets (see Deuteronomy 33:1; 1 Samuel 9:6). Paul paid tribute to Timothy by addressing him with this lofty title. In his second letter, Paul used the same term to refer to every mature Christian (2 Timothy 3:17).

Timothy was told to "flee" and "follow" (cf. 2 Timothy 2:22). The "these things" are all Paul has just enumerated from verse 4 to the present point. Timothy was to focus his attention on six virtues. "Righteousness" means "giving God and men their due," i.e., "what is right." "Godliness" means "piety" (cf. Titus 2:12). This is godly faith, the devout and practical expression of Christianity.

"Faith" connotes "fidelity, faithfulness." "Love" (*agapē*) in this frame of reference means a high, holy love that seeks the best for others. "Patience" means "endurance, steadfastness" that perse-

8. And having food and raiment let us be therewith content: . . . and sufficient clothing, *Confraternity* . . . we will be satisfied with these things, *SEB*.

9. But they that will be rich: But men who want lots of money, *NLT* . . . men who keep planning to get rich, *Williams*.
fall into temptation and a snare: . . . are tempted . . . They are trapped into, *NLT*.
and into many foolish and hurtful lusts: . . . and hurtful cravings, *Berkeley* . . . and harmful ambitions, *TCNT* . . . hurtful desires, *Williams*.
which drowned men in destruction and perdition: . . . which plunge men, *Campbell* . . . plunge people, *Berkeley* . . . that sink men into ruin, *Young* . . . These things drag them into sin and will destroy them, *NLT* . . . into destruction and ruin, *Williams*.

10. For the love of money is the root of all evil: For covetousness, *Confraternity* . . . Loving money is the root of all kinds of, *SEB* . . . of all kinds of evil, *NIV* . . . of every kind of evil, *Norlie* . . . of all sorts of evil, *Williams*.
which while some coveted after: . . . and in their eager desire to be rich, *Montgomery* . . . reaching after riches, *Williams*.
they have erred from the faith: . . . have been seduced from, *Norlie* . . . have turned from the faith, *NLT* . . . have wandered from the faith, *Williams*.
and pierced themselves through with many sorrows: . . . and have been pierced to the heart by many a regret, *TCNT* . . . a pang, *Williams*.

11. But thou, O man of God, flee these things: . . . as a man of God, *Williams* . . . must avoid all this, *TCNT* . . . run away from, *SEB*.
and follow after: Hunt, *Klingensmith*.

1 Timothy 6:12

1336.4 noun acc sing fem	2131.4 noun acc sing fem	3963.4 noun acc sing fem	26.4 noun acc sing fem	5119.4 noun acc sing fem
δικαιοσύνην, dikaiosunēn righteousness,	εὐσέβειαν, eusebeian godliness,	πίστιν, pistin faith,	ἀγάπην, agapēn love,	ὑπομονήν, hupomonēn endurance,

11.b.Txt: 06D-corr,018K 020L,byz.
Var: 01א-org,02A,025P Tisc,We/Ho,Weis,Sod UBS/✳

4095.4 noun acc sing fem		4097.1 noun acc sing fem	74.1 verb 2sing impr pres mid	3450.6 art acc sing masc
ʹ πραότητα· praotēta meekness.	[b✳	πραϋπαθίαν.] praupathian [idem]	**12.** ἀγωνίζου agōnizou Contest	τὸν ton the

2541.1 adj sing	72.2 noun acc sing masc	3450.10 art gen sing fem	3963.2 noun gen sing fem	1934.4 verb 2sing impr aor mid	3450.10 art gen sing fem
καλὸν kalon good	ἀγῶνα agōna contest	τῆς tēs of the	πίστεως· pisteōs faith.	ἐπιλαβοῦ epilabou Lay hold	τῆς tēs of the

12.a.Txt: Steph
Var: 01א,02A,06D 018K,020L,025P,byz.sa. bo.Gries,Lach,Treg,Alf Word,Tisc,We/Ho,Weis Sod,UBS/✳

164.2 adj gen sing	2205.2 noun gen sing fem	1519.1 prep	3614.12 rel- pron acc sing fem	2504.1 conj	2535.36 verb 2sing indic aor pass
αἰωνίου aiōniou eternal	ζωῆς, zōēs life,	εἰς eis to	ἣν hēn which	ʹa καὶ ʹ kai also	ἐκλήθης, eklēthēs you were called,

2504.1 conj	3533.7 verb 2sing indic aor act	3450.12 art acc sing fem	2541.8 adj acc sing fem	3534.2 noun acc sing fem
καὶ kai and	ὡμολόγησας hōmologēsas did confess	τὴν tēn the	καλὴν kalēn good	ὁμολογίαν homologian confession

13.a.Txt: 01א-corr,02A 06D,018K,020L,025P byz.We/Ho
Var: 01א-org,33,Tisc Weis,Sod,UBS/✳

13.b.Var: 01א

1783.1 prep	4044.1 adj gen pl	3116.5 noun gen pl masc	3715.1 verb 1sing indic pres act	4622.3 prs- pron dat 2sing
ἐνώπιον enōpion before	πολλῶν pollōn many	μαρτύρων. marturōn witnesses.	**13.** Παραγγέλλω Parangellō I charge	ʹa σοι ʹ soi you

1783.1 prep	3450.2 art gen sing	2296.2 noun gen sing masc	3450.2 art gen sing	2210.2 verb gen sing masc part pres act
ἐνώπιον enōpion before	ʹb τοῦ ʹ tou	θεοῦ theou God	τοῦ tou the	ʹ ζωοποιοῦντος zōopoiountos making alive

13.c.Txt: 01א,018K 020L,byz.
Var: 02A,06D,025P,33 Lach,Treg,Alf,Tisc We/Ho,Weis,Sod UBS/✳

2208.3 verb gen sing masc part pres act	3450.17 art pl neu	3820.1 adj	2504.1 conj	5382.2 name gen masc
[c✳ ζωογονοῦντος] zōogonountos [preserving alive]	τὰ ta the	πάντα, panta all things,	καὶ kai and	Χριστοῦ Christou Christ

2400.2 name masc	3450.2 art gen sing	3113.23 verb gen sing masc part aor act	1894.3 prep	4053.2 name gen masc
Ἰησοῦ Iēsou Jesus	τοῦ tou the	μαρτυρήσαντος marturēsantos having witnessed	ἐπὶ epi before	Ποντίου Pontiou Pontius

3952.2 name gen masc	3450.12 art acc sing fem	2541.8 adj acc sing fem	3534.2 noun acc sing fem	4931.21 verb inf aor act
Πιλάτου Pilatou Pilate	τὴν tēn the	καλὴν kalēn good	ὁμολογίαν, homologian confession,	**14.** τηρῆσαί tērēsai to keep

4622.4 prs- pron acc 2sing	3450.12 art acc sing fem	1769.3 noun acc sing fem	778.1 adj acc sing	421.1 adj acc sing
σε se you	τὴν tēn the	ἐντολὴν entolēn commandment	ἄσπιλον, aspilon spotless,	ʹ ἀνεπίληπτον, anepilēpton irreproachable,

veres in the worst of circumstances. "Meekness" is a "gentleness" that is the opposite of the argumentative, divisive, envious spirit of those who run after riches.

6:12. "Fight the good fight of faith" reflects the figure taken from the Olympic games where the contestant keeps on until the prize is won. The difference in the Greek tenses of the verbs here suggests "fight" as an ongoing process and "lay hold on" as a decisive act. The word "fight" (*agōnizomai*) means "contend for a prize." The prize or goal here is eternal life. This is not just unending life in the future, but eternal life that has its source in God. It is a present possession as well as a future promise.

The latter part of this verse probably refers to Timothy's baptism where he "professed (confessed) a good profession (confession)" (compare verse 13). This was "before many witnesses"; it was a "public" confession of his faith in Jesus Christ.

6:13. "I give thee charge in the sight of God . . . and before Christ Jesus" indicates the solemnity and authority of Paul's words. This was not just a casual correspondence letter; it was a communication of the very words of God. Beginning with this verse Paul, inspired by the Spirit, wrote one of those long sentences for which he is famous. It extends to the end of verse 16 and is 92 words in the King James Version. Much of this section is taken up with a praise doxology.

The words "who quickeneth all things" refer to God as Lifegiver, Creator. They imply His eternality and sovereignty, a theme repeated in the following verses. The references to "Christ Jesus" and His "confession" before Pilate are a reminder to Timothy that just as Christ made a good confession, so Timothy should also (compare verse 12). John records Jesus' "confession" in John 18:37: "Pilate therefore said unto him, Art thou a king then? Jesus answered, Thou sayest that I am a king. To this end was I born, and for this cause came I into the world, that I should bear witness unto the truth. Every one that is of the truth heareth my voice."

6:14. The word "commandment" in this verse possibly refers to Timothy's baptismal commission. There he would have received directions to fulfill all the obligations and duties of the ministry. Then again it may refer to the charge Paul had just given him in verses 11 and 12. The "thou" here is emphatic. "Keep" means "guard, hold, reserve, preserve." This commandment was to be kept "without spot" and "unrebukable" ("without blame, irreproachable").

In the last clause of this verse Paul made reference to Christ's "appearing" (*epiphaneia*; "manifestation, showing"). The coming of Christ is constantly in focus in Paul's letters. (Compare 1 Corinthians 1:8; Philippians 2:15,16; 1 Thessalonians 3:13; 5:23 for the concept of blamelessness at the coming of Christ.)

---

righteousness, godliness, faith, love, patience, meekness: . . . uprightness...steadfastness, gentleness, *Williams* . . . integrity, piety, *Montgomery* . . . endurance, *Adams* . . . justice, *Klingensmith* . . . mildness, *Confraternity.*

12. Fight the good fight of faith: Keep contending in the noble contest of, *Montgomery* . . . Keep up the good fight of, *Williams.*
lay hold on eternal life: . . . seize hold, *Montgomery* . . . hold firmly on everlasting life, *Klingensmith.*
whereunto thou art also called: . . . to which you were called *Montgomery.*
and hast professed a good profession before many witnesses: . . . you made the good confession, *Adams* . . . when you confessed the good confession in the presence of, *Montgomery.*

13. I give thee charge in the sight of God: I urge you, *TCNT* . . . I tell you this in front of God, *NLT* . . . In the presence of, *Montgomery* . . . I instruct you with authority, *Adams.*
who quickeneth all things: . . . gives life to everything, *NIV, SEB* . . . gives life to all, *Montgomery* . . . who preserves the life of all His creatures, *Williams.*
and before Christ Jesus:
who before Pontius Pilate witnessed a good confession: Who made the good confession, *Adams* . . . in testifying before, *Williams* . . . who bore witness to the good confession, *Montgomery.*

14. That thou keep this commandment without spot, unrebukable: I solemnly charge you, *Williams* . . . I charge you, keep your commission spotless, *Montgomery* . . . and free from suspicion, *Adams* . . . keep the principles stainless and irreproachable, *Berkeley.*

1 Timothy 6:15

421.3 adj acc sing	3230.1 prep	3450.10 art gen sing fem	1999.1 noun gen sing fem	3450.2 art gen sing
[✶ ἀνεπίλημπτον] anepilēmpton [idem]	μέχρι mechri until	τῆς tēs the	ἐπιφανείας epiphaneias appearing	τοῦ tou of the

2935.2 noun gen sing masc	2231.2 prs- pron gen 1pl	2400.2 name masc	5382.2 name	3614.12 rel- pron acc sing fem	2511.7 noun dat pl masc
κυρίου kuriou Lord	ἡμῶν hēmōn our	Ἰησοῦ Iēsou Jesus	Χριστοῦ, Christou Christ;	**15.** ἣν hēn which	καιροῖς kairois in times

2375.5 adj dat pl	1161.12 verb 3sing indic fut act	3450.5 art nom sing masc	3079.2 adj nom sing masc	2504.1 conj	3304.2 adj nom sing masc
ἰδίοις idiois its own	δείξει deixei shall show	ὁ ho the	μακάριος makarios blessed	καὶ kai and	μόνος monos only

1407.1 noun nom sing masc	3450.5 art nom sing masc	928.1 noun nom sing masc	3450.1 art gen pl	929.3 verb gen pl masc part pres act
δυνάστης, dunastēs Power,	ὁ ho the	βασιλεὺς basileus King	τῶν tōn of the	βασιλευόντων basileuontōn being kings

2504.1 conj	2935.1 noun nom sing masc	3450.1 art gen pl	2934.4 verb gen pl masc part pres act	3450.5 art nom sing masc
καὶ kai and	κύριος kurios Lord	τῶν tōn of the	κυριευόντων, kurieuontōn being lords;	**16.** ὁ ho the

3304.2 adj nom sing masc	2174.17 verb nom sing masc part pres act	110.1 noun acc sing fem	5295.1 noun sing neu	3474.2 verb nom sing masc part pres act
μόνος monos alone	ἔχων echōn having	ἀθανασίαν, athanasian immortality,	φῶς phōs in light	οἰκῶν oikōn dwelling

670.1 adj sing neu	3614.6 rel-pron acc sing masc	1481.3 verb 3sing indic aor act	3625.2 num card nom masc	442.7 noun gen pl masc
ἀπρόσιτον, aprositon unapproachable,	ὃν hon whom	εἶδεν eiden did see	οὐδεὶς oudeis no one	ἀνθρώπων anthrōpōn of men

3624.1 conj	1481.19 verb inf aor act	1404.4 verb 3sing indic pres mid	3614.3 rel- pron dat sing	4940.1 noun nom sing fem	2504.1 conj	2877.1 noun sing neu
οὐδὲ oude nor	ἰδεῖν idein to see	δύναται, dunatai is able;	ᾧ hō to whom	τιμὴ timē honor,	καὶ kai and	κράτος kratos might

164.1 adj sing	279.1 intrj	3450.4 art dat pl	4004.5 adj dat pl masc	1706.1 prep	3450.3 art dat sing
αἰώνιον· aiōnion eternal.	ἀμήν. amēn Amen.	**17.** Τοῖς Tois To the	πλουσίοις plousiois rich	ἐν en in	τῷ tō the

3431.1 adv	163.2 noun dat sing masc	3715.4 verb 2sing impr pres act	3231.1 partic	5147.2 verb inf pres act	3234.1 adv
νῦν nun now	αἰῶνι aiōni age	παράγγελλε, parangelle command,	μὴ mē not	ὑψηλοφρονεῖν, hupsēlophronein to be high minded,	μηδὲ mēde nor

17.a.**Txt:** 06D-corr,018K
020L,byz.Weis,Sod
Var: 01א,02A,06D-org
025P,33,Lach,Treg,Tisc
We/Ho,UBS/✶

1666.13 verb inf perf act	1894.3 prep	4009.2 noun gen sing masc	82.1 noun dat sing fem	233.1 conj	1706.1 prep	1894.3 prep
ἠλπικέναι ēlpikenai to have hope	ἐπὶ epi in	πλούτου ploutou of riches	ἀδηλότητι, adēlotēti uncertainty;	ἀλλ' all' but	' ἐν en in	[a✶ ἐπὶ] epi [on]

426

6:15. Verses 15 and 16 contain a doxology of praise. Some commentators see this as a doxology used in the synagogue worship because of its Jewish-sounding structure and words. Very possibly when Paul focused his attention on God's sovereignty, the Spirit brought these words to mind. The words "which in his times" reflects God's sovereignty: He holds the time in His own hands. "Potentate" (*dunastēs*) signifies "prince, chieftain, ruler, sovereign" (compare Acts 8:27). The word "only" preceding "Potentate" suggests power was not delegated but resident in God alone; this power is unique to God.

The title "King of kings, and Lord of lords" is found only here in all the writings of Paul. There are parallels of this title in the Old Testament—see Deuteronomy 10:17; Psalm 136:2,3; compare Daniel 4:34—that may have prompted Paul to praise God using these words. John the Revelator is the only other New Testament writer to use this title (Revelation 17:14; 19:16).

6:16. Paul praised God for His "immortality." The word "only" signifies a unique kind of immortality: that which is "unending life" from beginning to end. The Christian will experience immortality (see 1 Corinthians 15:53,54), but his will be the kind that extends a life that had a beginning. God had no beginning and will have no ending; He is the "immortal . . . God" (1:17).

Paul then praised two attributes of God: first, His transcendence: "dwelling in the light which no man can approach unto" (literally, "unapproachable light"); second, His invisibility: "whom no man hath seen nor can see" (compare Exodus 33:17-23). The repetition of the word "see" may be of some significance. God can see men but men cannot see God. God is aware of all that men are doing but men are unaware of what God is doing. This brings the thought back to God's sovereignty just expressed in verse 15.

Finally, Paul ended this doxology with the words, "To whom be honor and power everlasting. Amen." The word "power" means "might, rule" and focuses again on the sovereignty of God. In Ephesians 1:19, 6:10, and Colossians 1:11 Paul wrote about God's power as it relates to Christians.

6:17. If verses 11-16 are considered as parenthetic, the link can be seen between those who wish to be rich (verses 9,10) and those who are rich (verses 17-19). Paul instructed Timothy to command the rich to avoid arrogance and a false trust ("hope") in perishable wealth. The words "in this world" contrast with "the time to come" in verse 19.

The rich are "to put their hope in God, who richly provides us with everything for our enjoyment" (NIV). In an age of rampant materialism (Paul's day and the present), the reminder of the uncertainty of riches may fall on deaf ears. But those who are wise will put their hope in God; those who are foolish will trust in this world's "uncertain riches."

until the appearing of our Lord Jesus Christ: . . . till the manifestation of, *Young* . . . unto the advent of, *Concordant.*

15. Which in his times he shall shew: At the right time, we will be shown, *NLT* . . . For in his own good time this will be brought about by, *Montgomery.*

who is the blessed and only Potentate: . . . that God is the One Who has all power, *NLT* . . . Sovereign, *Berkeley, Williams* . . . and only Ruler, *Norlie, Klingensmith.*

the King of kings, and Lord of lords:

16. Who only hath immortality: Only God never dies, *SEB* . . . who alone possesses immortality, *Montgomery, Williams* . . . He only has everlasting life, *Klingensmith.*

dwelling in the light which no man can approach unto: . . . and dwells in light inaccessible, *Confraternity* . . . in unapproachable light, *Berkeley, Williams.*

whom no man hath seen nor can see:

to whom be honour and power everlasting. Amen: . . . and everlasting dominion! *Norlie* . . . and eternal dominion, *Williams.*

17. Charge them that are rich in this world: Command those, *NIV* . . . Continue charging, *Williams* . . . the rich of this world, *Montgomery.*

that they be not highminded: . . . not to brag, *SEB* . . . not to be elated in mind, *Campbell* . . . not to be haughty, *Norlie* . . . not to be supercilious, *Montgomery.*

nor trust in uncertain riches: They shouldn't place their hope upon wealth, *SEB* . . . to rely on the dubiousness of riches, *Concordant* . . . and not to fix their hope on, *Williams* . . . on such an uncertain thing as wealth, *TCNT.*

1 Timothy 6:18

17.b.**Txt:** 02A,06D-corr
018K,020L,025P,byz.
Sod
Var: 01ℵ,06D-org,Treg
Tisc,We/Ho,Weis
UBS/✶

17.c.**Txt:** 06D,018K
020L,byz.
Var: 01ℵ,02A,025P,33
sa.bo.Lach,Treg,Alf,Tisc
We/Ho,Weis,Sod
UBS/✶

3450.3 art dat sing	2296.3 noun dat sing masc	3450.3 art dat sing	2180.12 verb dat sing masc part pres act	3450.3 art dat sing	3792.5 verb dat sing masc part pres act
[b τῷ	θεῷ	[c τῷ	ζῶντι,	τῷ	παρέχοντι
tō	theō	tō	zōnti	tō	parechonti
to	God	the	living,	the	giving

2231.3 prs-pron dat 1pl	4005.1 adv	3820.1 adj	3820.1 adj	4005.1 adv
ἡμῖν	πλουσίως	πάντα	[✶ πάντα	πλουσίως]
hēmin	plousiōs	panta	panta	plousiōs
us	richly	all things	[all things	richly]

1519.1 prep	613.1 noun acc sing fem	14.1 verb inf pres act	4007.3 verb inf pres act	1706.1 prep
εἰς	ἀπόλαυσιν·	**18.** ἀγαθοεργεῖν,	πλουτεῖν	ἐν
eis	apolausin	agathoergein	ploutein	en
for	enjoyment;	to do good,	to be rich	in

2024.6 noun dat pl neu	2541.2 adj dat pl	2111.1 adj acc pl masc	1498.32 verb inf pres act	2816.1 adj acc pl masc
ἔργοις	καλοῖς,	εὐμεταδότους	εἶναι,	κοινωνικούς,
ergois	kalois	eumetadotous	einai	koinōnikous
works	good,	liberal in distributing	to be,	ready to share,

592.1 verb acc pl masc part pres act	1431.7 prs-pron dat pl masc	2287.4 noun acc sing masc	2541.1 adj sing
19. ἀποθησαυρίζοντας	ἑαυτοῖς	θεμέλιον	καλὸν
apothēsaurizontas	heautois	themelion	kalon
treasuring up	for themselves	a foundation	good

1519.1 prep	3450.16 art sing neu	3165.17 verb sing neu part pres act	2419.1 conj	1934.3 verb 3pl subj aor mid	3450.10 art gen sing fem
εἰς	τὸ	μέλλον,	ἵνα	ἐπιλάβωνται	τῆς
eis	to	mellon	hina	epilabōntai	tēs
for	the	future,	that	they may lay hold	of the

19.a.**Txt:** 06D-corr,018K
020L,025P,byz.
Var: 01ℵ,02A,06D-org
it.sa.bo.Gries,Lach,Treg
Alf,Word,Tisc,We/Ho
Weis,Sod,UBS/✶

20.a.**Txt:** Steph
Var: 01ℵ,02A,06D
018K,020L,025P,byz.sa.
bo.Gries,Lach,Treg,Alf
Word,Tisc,We/Ho,Weis
Sod,UBS/✶

164.2 adj gen sing	3552.1 adv	2205.2 noun gen sing fem	5434.1 intrj	4943.5 name voc masc
[αἰωνίου	[a✶ ὄντως]	ζωῆς.	**20.** Ὦ	Τιμόθεε,
aiōniou	ontōs	zōēs	Ō	Timothee
eternal	[really]	life.	O	Timothy,

3450.12 art acc sing fem	3733.1 noun acc sing fem	3727.1 noun acc sing fem	5278.11 verb 2sing impr aor act
τὴν	[παρακαταθήκην	[a✶ παραθήκην]	φύλαξον,
tēn	parakatathēkēn	parathēkēn	phulaxon
the	deposit committed	[deposit]	keep,

1610.1 verb nom sing masc part pres mid	3450.15 art acc pl fem	945.1 adj acc pl	2728.1 noun acc pl fem	2504.1 conj
ἐκτρεπόμενος	τὰς	βεβήλους	κενοφωνίας,	καὶ
ektrepomenos	tas	bebēlous	kenophōnias	kai
avoiding	the	godless	empty babblings,	and

474.1 noun acc pl fem	3450.10 art gen sing fem	5416.1 adj gen sing fem	1102.2 noun gen sing fem	3614.12 rel-pron acc sing fem
ἀντιθέσεις	τῆς	ψευδωνύμου	γνώσεως·	**21.** ἣν
antitheseis	tēs	pseudōnumou	gnōseōs	hēn
oppositions	of the	falsely named	knowledge,	which

4948.7 indef-pron nom pl masc	1846.1 verb nom pl masc part pres mid	3875.1 prep	3450.12 art acc sing fem	3963.4 noun acc sing fem
τινες	ἐπαγγελλόμενοι,	περὶ	τὴν	πίστιν
tines	epangellomenoi	peri	tēn	pistin
some	professing,	in reference to	the	faith

428

6:18. In this verse Paul gave Timothy several positive and practical demands for the rich to consider. Primarily, these are goodness and generosity. The words "be rich" mean "liberal." "Ready to distribute" means "generous." "Willing to communicate" means "willing to share."

So the charge to the rich involves at least three demands: (1) acquiring a sensitivity to the needs of others; (2) doing good works toward others; and (3) being generous and willing to share. This is difficult for many wealthy persons to follow. The danger of riches is that they blind the owner to the realities of life. The rich person is often unaware of those who are poor and destitute. He must be "charged" to do these things (verse 17).

6:19. When the rich do the good works of verse 18, they are "laying up in store for themselves a good foundation against the time to come." This is not salvation by works. The rich who are addressed in verses 17-19 are Christians—they are already saved. So their good works provide treasure in heaven (compare Matthew 6:20). The words "time to come" refer to the future world; see the contrast of verse 17, "in this world." The words "eternal life" (*tēs aiōniou zōēs*) may be translated "life which is life indeed." The same expression is found in verse 12. This underscores the contrast of true life to an uncertain life wholly supported by earthly riches.

So Paul's instructions to Timothy regarding those who are rich are clear: they are to avoid the attitudes of arrogance and selfishness and to do good works and share their wealth with others. By doing these things the rich will be laying a foundation for the future and an assurance for the life to come. They do not do these things to buy their way into heaven, however. They demonstrate their love for the Lord and their fellow human beings by using their wealth in ministry to others (compare Luke 12:15; 1 John 3:17).

6:20,21. In Paul's final words to Timothy in this first letter, no new note is struck. He repeated a challenge and a caution that have already filled the letter. But the words selected by the Spirit are significant. First, Paul called Timothy by name. *Timothy* is from two words: *timaō* = "to honor," and *theos* = "God." Literally this means "he who honors God."

Second, Timothy was to keep ("guard," see verse 14) what has been committed ("entrusted") to his trust (*parakatathēkē*, literally "deposit"). *Deposit* is the word for money deposited with a banker or a friend. When demanded, the entire sum is to be returned. The word *parakatathēkē* is used only here and in 2 Timothy 1:12,14. A free translation of this clause might be, "Guard the deposit of the gospel that is committed to you."

Third, Timothy was to avoid "profane and vain babblings" ("godless, empty talk," cf. 1 Timothy 1:4; 4:7; 2 Timothy 2:16), "oppositions" ("objections, contradictions, word battles"), and "science

but in the living God, who giveth us richly all things to enjoy: . . . who richly and ceaselessly provides us with everything for our enjoyment, *Williams* . . . who provides all things in abundance, *Confraternity* . . . richly for our use, *Montgomery*.

18. That they do good, that they be rich in good works: Charge them to practise benevolence, *Montgomery*.

ready to distribute, willing to communicate: . . . to be openhanded, *TCNT* . . . and generous-hearted, *Williams* . . . to give generously, *Norlie* . . . to be generous givers, *Berkeley* . . . They must be generous and want to share, *SEB* . . . and willing to share, *NIV* . . . to be liberal in giving, glad for fellowship, *Klingensmith*.

19. Laying up in store for themselves: . . . laying up a reserve, *Klingensmith*.

a good foundation against the time to come: . . . a sound foundation for the future, *Berkeley*.

that they may lay hold on eternal life: Then they will have the only true life! *NLT*.

20. O Timothy, keep that which is committed to thy trust: . . . guard what you were given! *SEB* . . . guard the deposit in your trust, *Klingensmith*.

avoiding profane and vain babblings: Shun, *Montgomery* . . . Turn your back on, *TCNT* . . . from the irreligious and empty discussions, *Berkeley*.

and oppositions of science falsely so called: . . . futile phrases and contradictions of, *Williams* . . . and the contradictions of so-called knowledge, *Confraternity* . . . of falsely named knowledge, *Klingensmith*.

21. Which some professing: have erred concerning the faith: Have erred from, *Murdock* . . . have missed the mark, *Roth-*

1 Timothy 6:21

21.a.**Txt:** 06D,018K
020L,byz.it.Sod
Var: 01ℵ,02A,025P,33
bo.Lach,Treg,Tisc
We/Ho,Weis,UBS/✶

21.b.**Txt:** 01ℵ-corr
06D-corr,018K,020L
025P,byz.bo.Sod
Var: 01ℵ-org,02A
06D-org,33,sa.Gries
Lach,Treg,Alf,Word
Tisc,We/Ho,Weis
UBS/✶

21.c.**Txt:** 018K,020L
Steph
Var: Gries,Lach,Word
Tisc,We/Ho,Weis,Sod
UBS/✶

789.1 verb 3pl indic aor act	3450.9 art nom sing fem	5322.1 noun nom sing fem	3196.3 prep	4622.2 prs-pron gen 2sing	3196.1 prep
ἠστόχησαν.	Ἡ	χάρις	⸀ μετὰ	σοῦ.	[ᵃ✶ μεθ'
ēstochēsan	Hē	charis	meta	sou	meth'
missed the mark.	The	grace	with	you.	[with

5050.2 prs-pron gen 2pl	279.1 intrj	4242.1 prep	4943.4 name acc masc	4272.9 num ord nom sing fem
ὑμῶν.]	⸀ᵇ ἀμήν. ⸂	⸀ᶜ Πρὸς	Τιμόθεον	πρώτη
humōn	amēn	Pros	Timotheon	prōtē
you.]	Amen.	To	Timothy	first

1119.21 verb 3sing indic aor pass	570.3 prep	2965.1 name gen fem	3610.3 rel-pron nom sing fem	1498.4 verb 3sing indic pres act
ἐγράφη	ἀπὸ	Λαοδικείας,	ἥτις	ἐστιν
egraphē	apo	Laodikeias	hētis	estin
written	from	Laodicea,	which	is

3255.1 noun nom sing fem	5271.1 name gen fem	3450.10 art gen sing fem	3681.1 name-adj gen sing fem
μητρόπολις	Φρυγίας	τῆς	Πακατιανῆς. ⸂
mētropolis	Phrugias	tēs	Pakatianēs
the chief city	of Phrygia	the	Pacatiania.

falsely so called" ("science" here is the word *gnōsis* which means "knowledge"). Very likely this is a reference to an early form of gnosticism, a heresy of the Second Century that taught salvation through knowledge. The word translated "oppositions" is *antithesis*. Two possible meanings have been offered: (1) "controversies" and (2) "rival theses, opposing tenets," i.e., opposite views of an argument.

Those who have adhered to the above have "erred" ("missed the mark, wandered away," translated "swerved" in 1:6) from the Faith.

The Greek for "with thee" is singular. However, it is likely that Paul expected Timothy to share this letter and that it would be read to the entire Ephesian congregation, which could have been several churches.

erham ... as regards the faith, *Norlie* ... Have gone astray from, *PNT* ... Have deviated from, *Panin* ... gone altogether astray, *TCNT* ... have fallen away from, *Confraternity* ... but they have strayed away from the faith, *SEB* ... have missed the target of the faith, *Adams* ... and have lost their faith, *Beck* ... have failed in the faith, *Williams*.

Grace be with thee. Amen: May you have God's loving favor, *NLT* ... Favour with you, *Rotherham* ... God's love be with you all! *Beck* ... Spiritual blessing be with you all, *Williams*.

THE SECOND EPISTLE OF PAUL TO
TIMOTHY

Expanded Interlinear

Textual Critical Apparatus

Verse-by-Verse Commentary

Various Versions

4242.1
prep
Πρὸς
Pros
To

4943.4 name
acc masc
Τιμόθεον
Timotheon
Timothy

1976.1 noun
nom sing fem
ἐπιστολὴ
epistolē
letter

3834.2 name
gen masc
Παύλου
Paulou
of Paul

1202.4 num ord
nom sing fem
δευτερα
deutera
second

Textual Apparatus

3834.1 name
nom masc
1:1. Παῦλος
Paulos
Paul,

646.1 noun
nom sing masc
ἀπόστολος
apostolos
apostle

2400.2 name masc
᾿Ιησοῦ
Iēsou
of Jesus

5382.2 name
gen masc
Χριστοῦ
Christou
Christ

5382.2 name
gen masc
[✶ Χριστοῦ
Christou
[of Christ

2400.2 name masc
᾿Ιησοῦ]
Iēsou
Jesus]

1217.2 prep
διὰ
dia
by

2284.2 noun
gen sing neu
θελήματος
thelēmatos
will

2296.2 noun
gen sing masc
θεοῦ
theou
of God

2567.1 prep
κατ'
kat'
according to

1845.4 noun
acc sing fem
ἐπαγγελίαν
epangelian
promise

2205.2 noun
gen sing fem
ζωῆς
zōēs
of life

3450.10 art
gen sing fem
τῆς
tēs
the

1706.1 prep
ἐν
en
in

5382.3 name
dat masc
Χριστῷ
Christō
Christ

2400.2 name masc
᾿Ιησοῦ,
Iēsou
Jesus,

4943.3 name
dat masc
2. Τιμοθέῳ
Timotheō
to Timothy

27.2 adj
dat sing
ἀγαπητῷ
agapētō
beloved

4891.3 noun
dat sing neu
τέκνῳ·
teknō
child:

5322.1 noun
nom sing fem
χάρις,
charis
Grace,

1643.2 noun
sing neu
ἔλεος,
eleos
mercy,

1503.1 noun
nom sing fem
εἰρήνη
eirēnē
peace

570.3 prep
ἀπὸ
apo
from

2296.2 noun
gen sing masc
θεοῦ
theou
God

3824.2 noun
gen sing masc
πατρὸς
patros
Father

2504.1 conj
καὶ
kai
and

5382.2 name
gen masc
Χριστοῦ
Christou
Christ

2400.2 name masc
᾿Ιησοῦ
Iēsou
Jesus

3450.2 art
gen sing
τοῦ
tou
the

2935.2 noun
gen sing masc
κυρίου
kuriou
Lord

2231.2 prs-
pron gen 1pl
ἡμῶν.
hēmōn
our.

5322.4 noun
acc sing fem
3. Χάριν
Charin
Thanks

2174.1 verb
1sing pres act
ἔχω
echō
I have

3450.3 art
dat sing
τῷ
tō

2296.3 noun
dat sing masc
θεῷ,
theō
to God,

3614.3 rel-
pron dat sing
ᾧ
hō
whom

2973.1 verb 1sing
indic pres act
λατρεύω
latreuō
I serve

570.3 prep
ἀπὸ
apo
from

4128.1 adj
gen pl masc
προγόνων
progonōn
ancestors

1706.1 prep
ἐν
en
with

2485.8 adj
dat sing fem
καθαρᾷ
kathara
pure

4743.3 noun
dat sing fem
συνειδήσει,
suneidēsei
conscience,

5453.1 conj
ὡς
hōs
how

87.2 adj
acc sing fem
ἀδιάλειπτον
adialeipton
unceasingly

2174.1 verb
1sing pres act
ἔχω
echō
I have

3450.12 art
acc sing fem
τὴν
tēn
the

3875.1 prep
περὶ
peri
of

4622.2 prs-
pron gen 2sing
σοῦ
sou
you

3281.2 noun
acc sing fem
μνείαν
mneian
remembrance

1706.1 prep
ἐν
en
in

3450.14 art
dat pl fem
ταῖς
tais
the

1157.5 noun
dat pl fem
δεήσεσίν
deēsesin
supplications

1466.2 prs-
pron gen 1sing
μου
mou
my

434

THE SECOND EPISTLE OF PAUL TO
TIMOTHY

1:1. Paul's greeting in this second letter is similar to that of his first epistle to Timothy. Here it is abbreviated and changed slightly (compare 1 Timothy 1:1,2). It is accepted by most that 2 Timothy was Paul's final epistle, written about A.D. 67. Many see it as Paul's "last will and testament," written from a Roman prison shortly before his death (see the tone in 4:6-8).

As in most of his letters, Paul identified himself as "an apostle of Jesus Christ." "Apostle" means "one sent on a mission, a messenger, envoy." (See comments on 1 Timothy 1:1.) The words "by the will of God" indicate Paul was aware of the divine purpose in his life and ministry. He wrote in a similar manner in several other letters (cf. the first verses of 1 and 2 Corinthians, Ephesians, Colossians; see also Galatians 1:1,15,16). "The promise of life" in Jesus is eternal life that comes through faith in Him (cf. Titus 1:1-3).

1:2. Paul's fatherly affection for Timothy is indicated in the words "Timothy, my dearly beloved son" (see comments on 1 Timothy 1:2, compare 1 Corinthians 4:17). *Timothy* means literally "he who honors God." The word "son" is literally "child." Paul and Timothy had a very special relationship.

The greeting of "grace . . . and peace" is very common in Paul's letters. Here he added "mercy" as he did in 1 Timothy; these are the only two times this word is appended to a greeting. "Peace" is a common Hebrew greeting (Hebrew, *shalōm*). But those who used it in the Christian context meant more than a common greeting like "hello." When Jesus used this term in John 14:27 He meant the total well-being and inner rest of spirit that comes from fellowship with God.

1:3. As in many of his letters, Paul began by thanking God. Then he wrote that he served God "as my forefathers did" (NIV). Paul cherished his Jewish heritage and later reminded Timothy of his own (1:5; 3:15).

Paul served God "with (a) pure (clear) conscience" (compare 1 Timothy 1:5). He had no ulterior motives; his mind and heart were untainted. The words "without ceasing" connect with "remembrance of thee in my prayers" but not with "night and day." The meaning is: "Whenever (or 'as often as') I remember you in my prayers, I give thanks." For similar wordings, see Romans 1:9; Philippians 1:3; Colossians 1:3.

3433.2 noun gen sing fem	2504.1 conj	2232.1 noun fem	1955.3 verb nom sing masc part pres act	4622.4 prs- pron acc 2sing	1481.19 verb inf aor act
νυκτὸς	καὶ	ἡμέρας,	4. ἐπιποθῶν	σε	ἰδεῖν,
nuktos	kai	hēmeras,	epipothōn	se	idein
night	and	day,	longing	you	to see,

	3279.11 verb nom sing masc part perf mid	4622.2 prs- pron gen 2sing	3450.1 art gen pl	1139.2 noun gen pl neu	2419.1 conj	5315.2 noun gen sing fem
	μεμνημένος	σου	τῶν	δακρύων,	ἵνα	χαρᾶς
	memnēmenos	sou	tōn	dakruōn,	hina	charas
	having remembered	your	the	tears,	that	with joy

	3997.21 verb 1sing subj aor pass		5118.2 noun acc sing fem	2956.8 verb nom sing masc part pres act	2956.25 verb nom sing masc part aor act
	πληρωθῶ·	5. ὑπόμνησιν		⸆ λαμβάνων	[a☆ λαβὼν]
	plērōthō	hupomnēsin		lambanōn	labōn
	I may be filled;	remembrance		taking	[having taken]

3450.10 art gen sing fem	1706.1 prep	4622.3 prs- pron dat 2sing	502.2 adj gen sing fem	3963.2 noun gen sing fem	3610.3 rel-pron nom sing fem
τῆς	ἐν	σοὶ	ἀνυποκρίτου	πίστεως,	ἥτις
tēs	en	soi	anupokritou	pisteōs,	hētis
of the	in	you	not insincere	faith,	which

1758.4 verb 3sing indic aor act	4270.1 adv	1706.1 prep	3450.11 art dat sing fem	3097.1 noun dat sing fem	4622.2 prs- pron gen 2sing
ἐνῴκησεν	πρῶτον	ἐν	τῇ	μάμμῃ	σου
enōkēsen	prōton	en	tē	mammē	sou
dwelt	first	in	the	grandmother	your

3062.1 name dat fem	2504.1 conj	3450.11 art dat sing fem	3251.3 noun dat sing fem	4622.2 prs- pron gen 2sing	2112.1 name dat fem
Λωιδι	καὶ	τῇ	μητρί	σου	⸆ Εὐνείκῃ,
Lōidi	kai	tē	mētri	sou	Euneikē,
Lois	and	in	mother	your	Eunice,

2112.2 name dat fem	3844.28 verb 1sing indic perf mid	1156.2 conj	3617.1 conj	2504.1 conj	1706.1 prep	4622.3 prs- pron dat 2sing
[☆ Εὐνίκη,]	πέπεισμαι	δὲ	ὅτι	καὶ	ἐν	σοί.
Eunikē	pepeismai	de	hoti	kai	en	soi
[idem]	I am persuaded	and	that	also	in	you.

1217.1 prep	3614.12 rel- pron acc sing fem	155.3 noun acc sing fem	362.1 verb 1sing indic pres act	4622.4 prs- pron acc 2sing
6. Δι'	ἣν	αἰτίαν	ἀναμιμνήσκω	σε
Di'	hēn	aitian	anamimnēskō	se
For	which	cause	I remind	you

327.1 verb inf pres act	3450.16 art sing neu	5321.1 noun sing neu	3450.2 art gen sing	2296.2 noun gen sing masc	3614.16 rel- pron sing neu
ἀναζωπυρεῖν	τὸ	χάρισμα	τοῦ	θεοῦ,	ὃ
anazōpurein	to	charisma	tou	theou,	ho
to fan into flame	the	gift	of God	of God	which

1498.4 verb 3sing indic pres act	1706.1 prep	4622.3 prs- pron dat 2sing	1217.2 prep	3450.10 art gen sing fem	1921.1 noun gen sing fem
ἐστιν	ἐν	σοὶ	διὰ	τῆς	ἐπιθέσεως
estin	en	soi	dia	tēs	epitheseōs
is	in	you	by	the	laying on

3450.1 art gen pl	5331.6 noun gen pl fem	1466.2 prs- pron gen 1sing	3620.3 partic	1056.1 conj	1319.14 verb 3sing indic aor act	2231.3 prs- pron dat 1pl
τῶν	χειρῶν	μου·	7. οὐ	γὰρ	ἔδωκεν	ἡμῖν
tōn	cheirōn	mou	ou	gar	edōken	hēmin
of the	hands	my.	Not	for	gave	us

1:4. Many commentators and a few translations connect "night and day" with "greatly desiring to see thee." This seems to be the sense of what Paul was expressing (see 4:9,21). Note the contrast between "tears" and "joy." Paul remembered the tears Timothy shed at their last parting (possibly when Paul left for Macedonia, 1 Timothy 1:3). But he knew that when they met again his heart would be "filled with joy."

In these expressions—and in this entire letter—we see the personal emotions of the aged apostle Paul. He knew his time on this earth was short. He wrote in affectionate terms with great intensity. In his first letter he addressed Timothy as "my own son in the faith." This reflected the spiritual relationship they had. In this second letter Paul called Timothy "my dearly beloved son." This set the tone for the warmth and affectionate reminiscence that fills the epistle. No other letter of Paul (with perhaps the exception of Philemon) is so personal as 2 Timothy.

1:5. The thought of verse 4 continues but turns to a new "remembrance" (this term is used three times in verses 3, 5, and 6). The Greek for "call to remembrance" is *hupomnēsin lambanōn*. It literally means "having received a reminder" and suggests that Paul had just received news regarding Timothy.

Paul commended Timothy for his sincere faith (compare 1 Timothy 1:5). According to Guthrie, "Scott supposes that 'faith' here means no more than religious feeling, since no question of sincerity could arise over the inner relation of the soul to God. Yet a profession of such faith could certainly be unreal, and where the sincerity of faith is transparent there is good reason for its special mention. It may be, as White suggests, that Timothy was deficient in other aspects of his conduct, but 'his unfeigned faith made up for much' " (Guthrie, *Tyndale New Testament Commentaries*, 14:124).

This same faith "dwelt" ("lived") in his mother and grandmother. The word "first" (*prōton*) could mean Lois was the first to believe, then her daughter Eunice, then Timothy. Acts 16:1 refers to Timothy's mother as a Jewess who "believed." Timothy's father is called a "Greek," a term used by Jews at that time to mean non-Jew. Nothing is said of his faith. Very possibly he was not a believer. It is clear that Timothy's faith was modeled by his maternal parent and grandparent.

1:6. The word "wherefore" refers back to "unfeigned faith." Paul's use of the term "remembrance" in this verse is similar to that of 1 Corinthians 4:17. The New International Version gives this sense: "I remind you to fan into flame the gift of God, which is in you through the laying on of my hands." What was the "gift of God" in Timothy? This *charisma* was more than natural ability; it was a special empowering of the Holy Spirit, received at the time of Timothy's ordination (compare 1 Timothy 4:14). Timothy was urged to develop this gift through regular use. He did not need a new gift but was to "rekindle" the gift he already had.

4. Greatly desiring to see thee, being mindful of thy tears: I yearn to see you, *Berkeley, SEB* . . . longing to see you, even as I recall your tears, *NASB* . . . When I remember, *Adams*.

that I may be filled with joy: . . . that I might be perfectly happy, *Berkeley* . . . that my happiness may be complete, *Montgomery* . . . that I may feel the fullest joy, *Williams*.

5. When I call to remembrance the unfeigned faith that is in thee: I have been reminded of that sincere faith which is in your heart, *Montgomery* . . . your genuine faith, *KJII* . . . your unalloyed faith, *Berkeley* . . . your sincere faith, *Adams*.

which dwelt first in thy grandmother Lois, and thy mother Eunice: . . . a faith that first found a home in the heart of, *Williams*.

and I am persuaded that in thee also: I am convinced, *TCNT* . . . I am fully persuaded, *Montgomery* . . . and am sure is in you, *Klingensmith* . . . and I am sure that it is in you as well, *NASB* . . . and dwells, I am certain, *Confraternity* . . . dwells in you too, *Adams*.

6. Wherefore I put thee in remembrance: I am reminding you, *SEB, TCNT* . . . For this reason let me remind you, *Montgomery*.

that thou stir up the gift of God: I remind you to kindle afresh, *NASB* . . . to stir into flame, *TCNT* . . . I ask you to keep using, *NLT* . . . to rekindle the inner fire which God gave you, *Norlie* . . . to keep ever blazing that gift of God, *Montgomery* . . . to rekindle into a flame God's gift, *Adams* . . . the fire of the divine gift, *Williams* . . . to keep the fire of God's spiritual gift burning, *SEB*.

which is in thee by the putting on of my hands: . . . which came upon you, *Williams* . . . when I ordained you, *Norlie* . . . through the laying on of my hands, *Montgomery*.

3450.5 art nom sing masc	2296.1 noun nom sing masc	4011.1 noun sing neu	1162.1 noun gen sing fem	233.2 conj	1405.2 noun gen sing fem
ὁ	θεὸς	πνεῦμα	δειλίας,	ἀλλὰ	δυνάμεως
ho	*theos*	*pneuma*	*deilias*	*alla*	*dunameōs*
	God	a spirit	of cowardice,	but	of power,

2504.1 conj	26.2 noun gen sing fem	2504.1 conj	4847.1 noun gen sing fem	3231.1 partic	3631.1 partic
καὶ	ἀγάπης	καὶ	σωφρονισμοῦ.	**8.** μὴ	οὖν
kai	*agapēs*	*kai*	*sōphronismou*	*mē*	*oun*
and	of love,	and	of sound mindedness.	Not	therefore

	1855.5 verb 2sing subj aor pass		3450.16 art sing neu	3115.1 noun sing neu	3450.2 art gen sing	2935.2 noun gen sing masc
	ἐπαισχυνθῇς		τὸ	μαρτύριον	τοῦ	κυρίου
	epaischunthēs		*to*	*marturion*	*tou*	*kuriou*
	you should be ashamed of		the	testimony	of the	Lord

2231.2 prs- pron gen 1pl	3234.1 adv	1466.7 prs- pron acc 1sing	3450.6 art acc sing masc	1192.2 noun acc sing masc	840.3 prs- pron gen sing
ἡμῶν,	μηδὲ	ἐμὲ	τὸν	δέσμιον	αὐτοῦ·
hēmōn	*mēde*	*eme*	*ton*	*desmion*	*autou*
our,	nor	me	the	prisoner	his;

233.2 conj	4628.1 verb 2sing impr aor act	3450.3 art dat sing	2077.3 noun dat sing neu	2567.3 prep
ἀλλὰ	συγκακοπάθησον	τῷ	εὐαγγελίῳ	κατὰ
alla	*sunkakopathēson*	*tō*	*euangeliō*	*kata*
but	join with in suffering	for the	gospel	according to

1405.4 noun acc sing fem	2296.2 noun gen sing masc	3450.2 art gen sing	4834.9 verb gen sing masc part aor act	2231.4 prs- pron acc 1pl	2504.1 conj
δύναμιν	θεοῦ,	**9.** τοῦ	σώσαντος	ἡμᾶς	καὶ
dunamin	*theou*	*tou*	*sōsantos*	*hēmas*	*kai*
power	God's;	the	having saved	us	and

2535.15 verb gen sing masc part aor act	2794.3 noun dat sing fem	39.12 adj dat sing fem	3620.3 partic	2567.3 prep
καλέσαντος	κλήσει	ἁγίᾳ,	οὐ	κατὰ
kalesantos	*klēsei*	*hagia*	*ou*	*kata*
having called	with a calling	holy,	not	according to

3450.17 art pl neu	2024.4 noun pl neu	2231.2 prs- pron gen 1pl	233.2 conj	2567.1 prep	2567.3 prep
τὰ	ἔργα	ἡμῶν,	ἀλλὰ	ʹ κατʹ	[✶ κατὰ]
ta	*erga*	*hēmōn*	*alla*	*kat'*	*kata*
the	works	our,	but	according to	[idem]

2375.11 adj acc sing fem	4145.4 noun acc sing fem	2504.1 conj	5322.4 noun acc sing fem	3450.12 art acc sing fem	1319.51 verb acc sing fem part aor pass
ἰδίαν	πρόθεσιν	καὶ	χάριν·	τὴν	δοθεῖσαν
idian	*prothesin*	*kai*	*charin*	*tēn*	*dotheisan*
his own	purpose	and	grace,	the	having been given

2231.3 prs- pron dat 1pl	1706.1 prep	5382.3 name dat masc	2400.2 name masc	4112.1 prep	5385.5 noun gen pl masc
ἡμῖν	ἐν	Χριστῷ	Ἰησοῦ	πρὸ	χρόνων
hēmin	*en*	*Christō*	*Iēsou*	*pro*	*chronōn*
us	in	Christ	Jesus	before	of times

164.4 adj gen pl masc	5157.16 verb acc sing fem part aor pass	1156.2 conj	3431.1 adv	1217.2 prep
αἰωνίων,	**10.** φανερωθεῖσαν	δὲ	νῦν	διὰ
aiōniōn	*phanerōtheisan*	*de*	*nun*	*dia*
ages,	having been made manifest	but	now	by

438

1:7. "For" connects this verse with verse 6 and extends the idea of God's gift. The Greek aorist of "hath not given" refers to a specific point in the past. God has not ever given "the spirit of fear" (*deilias*, used only here and meaning "timidity, cowardice"). The general idea could be "lack of confidence" (see 1 Corinthians 16:10,11). When Paul used the plural "us" he was probably wanting to soften what Timothy could have felt was a personal criticism.

Following this negative reminder, Paul emphasized three qualities for effective service: power, love, and self-control. "Power" can be understood as authority and boldness that come from strength of character. "Love" is the *agapēs* that reaches out toward others in caring and effective ministry. The servant of God must be of "sound mind" ("self-disciplined, self-controlled") to be effective. This is a divinely given self-control. A person must rule himself first, then he will be able and worthy to rule others.

1:8. Although it had not happened yet, Timothy's timidity could have made him ashamed enough to stop testifying for the Lord. Paul added that Timothy might be tempted to be ashamed of Paul as a prisoner. Natural timidity could produce inaction that would be misunderstood as shame. Continued timidity would bring shame. Paul encouraged Timothy to be a "partaker of the afflictions of the gospel." This denoted a readiness to share in the sufferings the gospel might bring (compare 2:3). "According to the power of God" means that sharing in suffering is not done in human strength alone; God's power is always present to encourage and edify.

1:9. The last word in verse 8, "God," is the subject of the next 22 English words. The word "grace" in verse 9 then becomes the subject for the following 22 words. Then "Jesus Christ" (verse 10) becomes the subject for the next 15 words. The final clause of 15 words (verse 11) has Paul ("I") as its subject. Those 110 words from verse 8 through verse 11 are all one sentence in the King James Version. (The Greek text goes on through verse 12 before the thought is concluded.)

The progression of verses 9 and 10 gives the essence of the gospel: believers are saved and called to holiness according to God's purpose and grace given and revealed in Jesus Christ who abolished death and brought life and immortality to light. Some commentators have suggested these verses form the basis of an early liturgical hymn much like that in 1 Timothy 3:16 (compare 2 Timothy 2:11-13).

The Christian's calling is to holiness. First Peter 1:15,16 also says this same thing. Paul reiterated that "our works" do not save us (see Titus 3:5 where he emphatically stated this truth; compare Ephesians 2:8-10). Salvation and a call to holiness are purely at God's initiative; they are His "purpose and grace . . . given us in Christ Jesus" (see Romans 8:28; 9:11; Ephesians 1:11). This was "before the world began" (literally "before times eternal," compare Titus 1:2).

7. For God hath not given us the spirit of fear: I say this because, *Adams* . . . the Spirit that God has given us does not impart, *Williams* . . . a cowardly attitude, *SEB* . . . of fearfulness, *KJII* . . . of timidity, *NASB, Concordant* . . . of being afraid, *Klingensmith.*

but of power, and of love, and of a sound mind: . . . and discipline, *NASB* . . . and self-control, *Berkeley, Klingensmith, Williams* . . . and of self-government, *Campbell* . . . and of self-restraint, *Adams* . . . and wise discretion, *Norlie.*

8. Be not thou therefore ashamed of the testimony of our Lord: So then, don't be, *Adams* . . . So you must never be ashamed of, *Williams* . . . to bear witness for our Lord, *Montgomery.*

nor of me his prisoner:

but be thou partaker of the afflictions of the gospel: Nay, join with me in suffering for, *Montgomery* . . . but suffer for the good news in fellowship with me, *Williams* . . . but rather share with me my suffering for the good news, *Adams.*

according to the power of God: . . . as far as God enables you, *TCNT.*

9. Who hath saved us:

and called [us] with an holy calling: . . . the One Who chose us to do His work, *NLT.*

not according to our works: This was not by our efforts, *SEB* . . . not because of our deeds, *Adams* . . . not dealing with us according to our works, *Montgomery.*

but according to his own purpose and grace: . . . on account of, *Campbell* . . . because of His own design, *Norlie* . . . unmerited favor, *Williams.*

which was given us in Christ Jesus before the world began: . . . from all eternity, *NASB* . . . before this world existed, *Confraternity* . . . before the beginning of time, *Montgomery.*

3450.10 art gen sing fem	1999.1 noun gen sing fem	3450.2 art gen sing	4842.2 noun gen sing masc	2231.2 prs-pron gen 1pl	2400.2 name masc
τῆς	ἐπιφανείας	τοῦ	σωτῆρος	ἡμῶν	ʼ Ἰησοῦ
tēs	epiphaneias	tou	sōtēros	hēmōn	Iēsou
the	appearing	of the	Saviour	our	Jesus

5382.2 name gen masc	5382.2 name gen masc	2400.2 name masc	2643.5 verb gen sing masc part aor act	3173.1 conj
Χριστοῦ,	[✶ Χριστοῦ	Ἰησοῦ,]	καταργήσαντος	μὲν
Christou	Christou	Iēsou	katargēsantos	men
Christ,	[Christ	Jesus,]	having abolished	men

3450.6 art acc sing masc	2265.4 noun acc sing masc	5297.4 verb gen sing masc part aor act	1156.2 conj	2205.4 noun acc sing fem	2504.1 conj
τὸν	θάνατον,	φωτίσαντος	δὲ	ζωὴν	καὶ
ton	thanaton,	phōtisantos	de	zōēn	kai
the	death,	having brought to light	and	life	and

854.2 noun acc sing fem	1217.2 prep	3450.2 art gen sing	2077.2 noun gen sing neu	1519.1 prep	3614.16 rel-pron sing neu
ἀφθαρσίαν	διὰ	τοῦ	εὐαγγελίου,	**11.** εἰς	ὃ
aphtharsian	dia	tou	euangeliou,	eis	ho
incorruptibility	by	the	good news;	to	which

4935.27 verb 1sing indic aor pass	1466.1 prs-pron nom 1sing	2755.1 noun nom sing masc	2504.1 conj	646.1 noun nom sing masc	2504.1 conj
ἐτέθην	ἐγὼ	κῆρυξ	καὶ	ἀπόστολος	καὶ
etethēn	egō	kērux	kai	apostolos	kai
was appointed	I	a herald	and	apostle	and

1314.1 noun nom sing masc	1477.5 noun gen pl neu	1217.1 prep	3614.12 rel-pron acc sing fem	155.3 noun acc sing fem	2504.1 conj
διδάσκαλος	⌜a ἐθνῶν ⌝	**12.** δι᾽	ἣν	αἰτίαν	καὶ
didaskalos	ethnōn	di᾽	hēn	aitian	kai
teacher	of Gentiles.	For	which	cause	also

3642.18 dem-pron pl neu	3819.1 verb 1sing indic pres act	233.1 conj	3620.2 partic	1855.1 verb 1sing indic pres mid	3471.2 verb 1sing indic perf act
ταῦτα	πάσχω᾿	ἀλλ᾽	οὐκ	ἐπαισχύνομαι,	οἶδα
tauta	paschō	all᾽	ouk	epaischunomai,	oida
these things	I suffer;	but	not	I am ashamed;	I know

1056.1 conj	3614.3 rel-pron dat sing	3961.37 verb 1sing indic perf act	2504.1 conj	3844.28 verb 1sing indic perf mid	3617.1 conj
γὰρ	ᾧ	πεπίστευκα,	καὶ	πέπεισμαι	ὅτι
gar	hō	pepisteuka,	kai	pepeismai	hoti
for	whom	I have believed,	and	have been persuaded	that

1409.1 adj nom sing masc	1498.4 verb 3sing indic pres act	3450.12 art acc sing fem	3727.1 noun acc sing fem	1466.2 prs-pron gen 1sing
δυνατός	ἐστιν	τὴν	παραθήκην	μου
dunatos	estin	tēn	parathēkēn	mou
able	he is	the	deposit committed	my

5278.13 verb inf aor act	1519.1 prep	1552.12 dem-pron acc sing fem	3450.12 art acc sing fem	2232.4 noun acc sing fem	5134.1 noun acc sing fem
φυλάξαι	εἰς	ἐκείνην	τὴν	ἡμέραν.	**13.** ὑποτύπωσιν
phulaxai	eis	ekeinēn	tēn	hēmeran.	hupotupōsin
to keep	for	that	the	day.	An example

2174.13 verb 2sing impr pres act	5039.4 verb gen pl masc part pres act	3030.6 noun gen pl masc	3614.1 rel-pron gen pl	3706.1 prep	1466.3 prs-pron gen 1sing
ἔχε	ὑγιαινόντων	λόγων,	ὧν	παρ᾽	ἐμοῦ
eche	hugiainontōn	logōn,	hōn	par᾽	emou
have	of being sound	words,	which	from	me

11.a.**Txt:** 01א-corr,04C 06D,018K,020L,025P byz.it.sa.bo. **Var:** 01א-org,02A,33 Tisc,We/Ho,Weis,Sod UBS/✶

1:10. Paul next moved from the idea of eternity back to time with the words "now made manifest" ("revealed"). The "appearing" (*epiphaneias*) of Christ refers to His first advent. The same word is used in Titus 2:11-13 of His second advent. The Jews used the word *epiphaneias* of God's saving acts during the Maccabean struggles. The Greeks used this word to refer to the coming of the emperor to his throne.

The word "abolished" is from the Greek *katargēsantos* which means "render inoperative." The aorist tense shows a completed action in the past (compare 1 Corinthians 15:26 which refers to a future event). The sense here is that in a onetime act Christ "abolished" death. He "rendered inoperative" the power that had previously held men in its grasp.

Christ "brought" (again the aorist tense) "life and immortality to light." The idea here is that life and immortality had been obscured, hidden. Christ, through His life, death, and resurrection, brought them out where they could be seen. The word "gospel" includes the full revelation of God in Christ.

1:11. The words in this verse are very similar to those in 1 Timothy 2:7 (see comments there). "Preacher" is *kērux*, "herald," and denotes "one, with authority, who makes a public proclamation." "Apostle" is *apostolos*, "one who is sent; envoy, ambassador." Paul did not speak for himself but for the One who sent him. Paul's authority was not his own. He was a preacher and teacher sent by God.

1:12. Paul was suffering imprisonment, privation, loneliness (and whatever else is included in "these things") for the sake of the gospel and his commitment to proclaim and teach its truths. He wrote, "I am not ashamed; for I know whom I have believed, and am persuaded." These verbs are significant. The Greek perfect tense of "I have believed" implies a continuing attitude of belief and trust. The present tense of "I am not ashamed" and "am persuaded" ("convinced") agree with "I have committed" to show Paul's present attitude and continuing action.

The Greek word behind "that which I have committed" is *paratheken* and equals "my deposit" (so also in verse 14, compare 1 Timothy 6:20). "That day" is the Day of Judgment at Christ's coming (so also in verse 18).

1:13. Verses 13 and 14 comprise a charge to Timothy and extend the thought of Paul's personal commitment (verse 12). Timothy was told to "hold fast" and "keep." He was to hold fast the "form of sound words." "Form" (*hupotupōsin*) can mean "example" ("pattern" in 1 Timothy 1:16). Paul not only preached the gospel, he also lived it so others might follow him. "Sound" means "health-giving." "Words" means "teaching, doctrine" (compare Titus 1:9) and refers to the gospel in particular.

10. But is now made manifest by the appearing of our Saviour Jesus Christ: . . . but has only recently been made known through, *Williams.*

who hath abolished death: . . . who truly made death of no effect, *KJII* . . . He has destroyed death, *Confraternity* . . . who has, indeed, vanquished death, *Campbell* . . . He has made an end of Death, *TCNT* . . . has put a stop to the power of death, *Williams.*

and hath brought life and immortality to light: . . . yet illuminates life, *Concordant* . . . and incorruption, *Confraternity.*

through the gospel:

11. Whereunto I am appointed a preacher, and an apostle, and a teacher of the Gentiles: . . . of which I am appointed a herald, *Campbell.*

12. For the which cause I also suffer these things: On this account, too, *Berkeley* . . . This is why, *Williams.*

nevertheless I am not ashamed: for I know whom I have believed: . . . in Whom I have put my trust, *NLT* . . . whom I have put my faith, *TCNT.*

and am persuaded that he is able to keep: I am convinced that He is able to guard, *NASB* . . . I am absolutely sure, *Williams* . . . has the power to guard, *Klingensmith.*

that which I have committed unto him against that day: . . . what I have trusted to Him, *SEB* . . . that which he has put in my care, *Klingensmith* . . . entrusted to Him, *Berkeley* . . . my work which I have given back into His care, *Norlie* . . . until the day He comes again, *NLT.*

13. Hold fast the form of sound words: Retain the standard of, *NASB* . . . Continue to be an example in wholesome instructions, *Williams.*

189.20 verb 2sing indic aor act	1706.1 prep	3963.3 noun dat sing fem	2504.1 conj	26.3 noun dat sing fem	3450.11 art dat sing fem	1706.1 prep
ἤκουσας,	ἐν	πίστει	καὶ	ἀγάπῃ	τῇ	ἐν
ēkousas	en	pistei	kai	agapē	tē	en
you did hear,	in	faith	and	love	the	in

5382.3 name dat masc	2400.2 name masc	3450.12 art acc sing fem	2541.8 adj acc sing fem	3733.1 noun acc sing fem
Χριστῷ	Ἰησοῦ.	**14.** τὴν	καλὴν	⸂ παρακαταθήκην
Christō	Iēsou	tēn	kalēn	parakatathēkēn
Christ	Jesus.	The	good	deposit committed

14.a.**Txt:** Steph
Var: 01ℵ,02A,04C,06D
018K,020L,025P,byz.
Gries,Lach,Treg,Alf
Word,Tisc,We/Ho,Weis
Sod,UBS/☆

3727.1 noun acc sing fem	5278.11 verb 2sing impr aor act	1217.2 prep	4011.2 noun gen sing neu	39.2 adj gen sing
[ª☆ παραθήκην]	φύλαξον	διὰ	πνεύματος	ἁγίου
parathēkēn	phulaxon	dia	pneumatos	hagiou
[idem]	guard	by	Spirit	Holy

3450.2 art gen sing	1758.2 verb gen sing neu part pres act	1706.1 prep	2231.3 prs-pron dat 1pl	3471.3 verb 2sing indic perf act
τοῦ	ἐνοικοῦντος	ἐν	ἡμῖν.	**15.** Οἶδας
tou	enoikountos	en	hēmin	Oidas
the	dwelling	in	us.	You know

3642.17 dem-pron sing neu	3617.1 conj	648.9 verb 3pl indic aor pass	1466.6 prs-pron acc 1sing	3820.7 adj nom pl masc	3450.7 art nom pl masc
τοῦτο,	ὅτι	ἀπεστράφησάν	με	πάντες	οἱ
touto	hoti	apestraphēsan	me	pantes	hoi
this,	that	turned away from	me	all	the

1706.1 prep	3450.11 art dat fem	767.3 name dat fem	3614.1 rel-pron gen pl	1498.4 verb 3sing indic pres act	5272.1 name nom masc
ἐν	τῇ	Ἀσίᾳ,	ὧν	ἐστιν	⸂ Φύγελλος
en	tē	Asia	hōn	estin	Phugellos
in		Asia,	of whom	is	Phygellus

5272.2 name nom masc	2504.1 conj	2045.1 name nom masc	1319.24 verb 3sing opt aor act	1643.2 noun sing neu
[☆ Φύγελος]	καὶ	Ἑρμογένης.	**16.** Δῴη	ἔλεος
Phugelos	kai	Hermogenēs	Dōē	eleos
[idem]	and	Hermogenes.	May grant	mercy

3450.5 art nom sing masc	2935.1 noun nom sing masc	3450.3 art dat sing	3546.1 name gen masc	3486.3 noun dat sing masc
ὁ	κύριος	τῷ	Ὀνησιφόρου	οἴκῳ·
ho	kurios	tō	Onēsiphorou	oikō
the	Lord	to the	of Onesiphorus	house,

3617.1 conj	4038.1 adv	1466.6 prs-pron acc 1sing	402.1 verb 3sing indic aor act	2504.1 conj	3450.12 art acc sing fem
ὅτι	πολλάκις	με	ἀνέψυξεν,	καὶ	τὴν
hoti	pollakis	me	anepsuxen	kai	tēn
because	often	me	he refreshed,	and	the

16.a.**Txt:** 01ℵ-org,018K
byz.
Var: 01ℵ-corr,02A,04C
06D,020L,025P,33
Lach,Treg,Alf,Tisc
We/Ho,Weis,Sod
UBS/☆

252.2 noun acc sing fem	1466.2 prs-pron gen 1sing	3620.2 partic	1855.4 verb 3sing indic aor pass	1855.8 verb 3sing indic aor pass
ἅλυσίν	μου	οὐκ	⸂ ἐπῃσχύνθη,	[ª☆ ἐπαισχύνθη,]
halusin	mou	ouk	epēschunthē	epaischunthē
chain	my	not	was ashamed of;	[idem]

233.2 conj	1090.53 verb nom sing masc part aor mid	1706.1 prep	4373.2 name dat fem	4559.1 adj comp sing
17. ἀλλὰ	γενόμενος	ἐν	Ῥώμῃ,	⸂ σπουδαιότερον
alla	genomenos	en	Rhōmē	spoudaioteron
but	having been	in	Rome,	more diligently

Timothy was to temper his teaching with "faith and love." It is also possible these words relate to the verb "hold fast"; he was to show a spirit and manner that reflected pure faith and love.

"Faith" includes the ideas of fidelity and hope. "Love" is the Greek *agapē*, a Godlike love that desires the best for others. The words "in Christ Jesus" emphasize union with Christ as needful for the above. Faith and love are not possible apart from Christ. These virtues issue from Him.

1:14. "That good thing" means the gospel (compare 1 Timothy 6:20). Timothy was to "keep" ("guard") what had been "committed" (*parakatathēkēn*, again see verse 12) to him. "Keep by the Holy Ghost" implies that without the help of the Holy Spirit it would be impossible for Timothy to guard the deposit of the gospel.

Stanley Horton comments: "We must have a twofold commitment: to Christ and to the gospel. In Paul's commitment to Christ, he put his life and ministry in Christ's hands as a deposit for Christ to guard and keep.... The other side of our Christian commitment is the accepting of the gospel as a deposit which we must keep and guard. The very form of the words in which the gospel was originally given is important."

1:15. Paul used hyperbole (a deliberate exaggeration) when he said "all" had deserted him. Not all had turned away, but there was a mass exodus and widespread desertion, perhaps led by Phygellus and Hermogenes. Nothing else is known of these two; that they are named suggests they were the leaders of this defection. The "all" may refer to all those who had been asked by the Roman authorities to vouch for Paul and failed to do so. "Asia" refers especially to the Roman province in western Asia Minor comprising Mysia, Lydia, Caria, most of Phrygia, and the islands off the coast.

1:16. There was one who stood by Paul: Onesiphorus ("profitable, help-bringer"). He "oft refreshed" Paul by making personal visits and possibly giving material assistance. He also "was not ashamed" of Paul's imprisonment. Paul prayed that God would give mercy to the household of Onesiphorus (see 1:18).

1:17. Onesiphorus was commended for specific spiritual and practical ministry to Paul. A native of Ephesus, Onesiphorus traveled to Rome and "sought ... out (Paul) very diligently." The circumstances of imprisonment in the First Century made it very difficult to locate and provide assistance to political prisoners. Onesiphorus no doubt had to risk his own safety in order to find Paul.

which thou hast heard of me: ... you have heard from me, *Montgomery* ... learned from me, *Williams.*

in faith and love which is in Christ Jesus: ... that come from union with, *Williams.*

14. That good thing which was committed unto thee keep: Guard what you were trusted with, *SEB* ... guard the good deposit, *Adams* ... Guard the glorious trust, *Montgomery* ... that precious entrusted deposit, *Berkeley* ... this fine deposit of truth, *Williams* ... that has been entrusted to you, *Norlie.*

by the Holy Ghost which dwelleth in us: ... by the help of, *Berkeley* ... by the aid...who has His home in our hearts, *Williams* ... that lives in us, *Klingensmith* ... who makes his home in us, *Montgomery.*

15. This thou knowest: You are aware of the fact that, *NASB* ... You already know that, *Montgomery.*

that all they which are in Asia be turned away from me: ... who are in the province of, *Adams* ... abandoned me, *SEB* ... forsook me, *Montgomery.*

of whom are Phygellus and Hermogenes: ... among them, *Montgomery* ... including, *Adams.*

16. The Lord give mercy unto the house of Onesiphorus:

for he oft refreshed me: ... for many a time, *Montgomery* ... He came often to comfort me, *NLT.*

and was not ashamed of my chain: ... of my being a prisoner, *Berkeley.*

17. But, when he was in Rome: Indeed, when he arrived at Rome, *Adams* ... when he came to Rome, *Montgomery.*

2 Timothy 1:18

17.a.Txt: 06D-corr,018K
020L,byz.
Var: 01א,04C,06D-org
025P,33,Lach,Treg,Tisc
We/Ho,Sod,UBS/✶

[a✶ σπουδαίως]
spoudaiōs
[diligently]
4560.1 adv

ἐζήτησέν
ezētēsen
he sought out
2195.14 verb 3sing indic aor act

με
me
me
1466.6 prs-pron acc 1sing

καὶ
kai
and
2504.1 conj

εὗρεν·
heuren
found,
2128.8 verb 3sing indic aor act

18. δῴη
dōē
may grant
1319.24 verb 3sing opt aor act

αὐτῷ
autō
to him
840.4 prs-pron dat sing

ὁ
ho
the
3450.5 art nom sing masc

κύριος
kurios
Lord
2935.1 noun nom sing masc

εὑρεῖν
heurein
to find
2128.21 verb inf aor act

ἔλεος
eleos
mercy
1643.2 noun sing neu

παρὰ
para
from
3706.2 prep

κυρίου
kuriou
Lord
2935.2 noun gen sing masc

ἐν
en
in
1706.1 prep

ἐκείνῃ
ekeinē
that
1552.11 dem-pron dat sing fem

τῇ
tē
the
3450.11 art dat sing fem

ἡμέρᾳ·
hēmera
day,
2232.3 noun dat sing fem

καὶ
kai
and
2504.1 conj

ὅσα
hosa
how much
3607.8 rel-pron pl neu

ἐν
en
in
1706.1 prep

Ἐφέσῳ
Ephesō
Ephesus
2163.2 name dat fem

διηκόνησεν
diēkonēsen
he served
1241.10 verb 3sing indic aor act

βέλτιον
beltion
better
950.1 adj comp sing neu

σὺ
su
you
4622.1 prs-pron nom 2sing

γινώσκεις.
ginōskeis
know.
1091.2 verb 2sing indic pres act

2:1. Σὺ
Su
You
4622.1 prs-pron nom 2sing

οὖν,
oun
therefore,
3631.1 partic

τέκνον
teknon
child
4891.1 noun sing neu

μου,
mou
my,
1466.2 prs-pron gen 1sing

ἐνδυναμοῦ
endunamou
be strong
1727.4 verb 2sing impr pres mid

ἐν
en
in
1706.1 prep

τῇ
tē
the
3450.11 art dat sing fem

χάριτι
chariti
grace
5322.3 noun dat sing fem

τῇ
tē
the
3450.11 art dat sing fem

ἐν
en
in
1706.1 prep

Χριστῷ
Christō
Christ
5382.3 name dat masc

Ἰησοῦ·
Iēsou
Jesus.
2400.2 name masc

2. καὶ
kai
And
2504.1 conj

ἃ
ha
which things
3614.17 rel-pron pl neu

ἤκουσας
ēkousas
you did hear
189.20 verb 2sing indic aor act

παρ'
par'
of
3706.1 prep

ἐμοῦ
emou
me
1466.3 prs-pron gen 1sing

διὰ
dia
with
1217.2 prep

πολλῶν
pollōn
many
4044.1 adj gen pl

μαρτύρων,
marturōn
witnesses,
3116.5 noun gen pl masc

ταῦτα
tauta
these
3642.18 dem-pron pl neu

παράθου
parathou
commit
3769.13 verb 2sing impr aor mid

πιστοῖς
pistois
to faithful
3964.8 adj dat pl masc

ἀνθρώποις,
anthrōpois
men,
442.8 noun dat pl masc

οἵτινες
hoitines
such as
3610.2 rel-pron nom pl masc

ἱκανοὶ
hikanoi
competent
2401.6 adj nom pl masc

ἔσονται
esontai
shall be
1498.43 verb 3pl indic fut mid

καὶ
kai
also
2504.1 conj

ἑτέρους
heterous
others
2066.8 adj acc pl masc

διδάξαι.
didaxai
to teach.
1315.18 verb inf aor act

3. ⌜ σὺ
su
You
4622.1 prs-pron nom 2sing

3.a.Txt: 04C-corr
06D-corr,018K,020L
byz.
Var: 01א,02A,04C-org
06D-org,025P,Lach
Treg,Alf,Word,Sod
UBS/✶

οὖν
oun
therefore
3631.1 partic

κακοπάθησον
kakopathēson
suffer hardship
2524.3 verb 2sing impr aor act

[a✶ συγκακοπάθησον]
sunkakopathēson
[suffer hardship with]
4628.1 verb 2sing impr aor act

ὡς
hōs
as
5453.1 conj

Then, to visit him on several occasions would put Onesiphorus' life in jeopardy. But Paul said this Ephesian layman "searched hard for me until he found me" (NIV).

1:18. The commendation of Onesiphorus is continued in the context of a brief prayer. This verse repeats verse 16 with an important addition and a significant change. In verse 16 Paul mentioned "the house (household) of Onesiphorus." In verse 18 Paul used the personal pronoun and did not mention the household. Then Paul referred to the Day of Judgment ("in that day"). Comparing the two requests, it seems Paul was concerned with the household in verse 16 and the man in verse 18. Some commentators speculate that Onesiphorus was dead and cite 4:19 as further evidence. They then question whether Paul was praying for the dead in verse 18. There is no evidence at all to support the speculation that Onesiphorus was dead. Verse 18 could very possibly be understood as a spoken desire that Onesiphorus would find God's mercy in the day when all men will need that mercy. It is unwise to build a doctrine of prayer for the dead from a verse that needs 20th Century speculation about the demise of an individual.

Timothy was well aware of the ministry of Onesiphorus at Ephesus. This would have taken place either in Paul's third missionary journey (Acts chapter 19) or his fourth journey that ended with his imprisonment in Rome (1 Timothy 1:3).

2:1. The second chapter opens a new topic that involves personal encouragement to Timothy. He was encourged to be a good soldier of Christ and to endure hardship (verses 1-13). He was to be an approved workman who correctly handled the Word of God (verses 14-26). "Thou" is emphatic. "Therefore" contrasts Timothy with the "all" (see 1:15) who took part in the defection from Paul. Paul called Timothy "my son," a very personal, affectionate term.

"Be strong" (*endunamou*) is in the present tense and passive voice. These project the meaning "be continually strengthened." "Grace" is qualified by "in Christ Jesus." This grace is divine help freely given to those who do not deserve it. But it is only available in and from Jesus Christ.

2:2. Paul's instruction in this verse was for Timothy to be faithful as a teacher. He was to take the words heard from Paul and "commit" ("entrust") them to "faithful" ("reliable, trustworthy") men. These men were to be true believers who cherished the Christian faith and were full of faith themselves. They would not only be loyal to the gospel but would also become competent teachers who would pass the truth on to others.

2:3. In verses 3-6 Paul used three illustrations from life to show Timothy the scope of his Christian calling. The first is that of a

he sought me out very diligently, and found [me]: But he hunted carefully for me, *Klingensmith* ... he sought for me, *Montgomery* ... he searched and searched until he found me, *SEB* ... and finally found me, *Williams.*

18. The Lord grant unto him that he may find mercy of the Lord in that day:

and in how many things he ministered unto me at Ephesus: ... how great were the services, *Williams* ... how many services, *Montgomery* ... he rendered to me, *Campbell.*

thou knowest very well: ... you very well know, *Williams* ... you know best, *KJII* ... you know better than I, *Montgomery.*

1. Thou therefore, my son, be strong: Do you then, my son, strengthen your heart, *Montgomery* ... Accept the strength, my dear son, that comes from, *JB* ... be strengthened in, *Confraternity* ... be invigorated, *Concordant.*

in the grace that is in Christ Jesus: ... in the favor, *Klingensmith.*

2. And the things that thou hast heard of me: The teachings which you, *Montgomery.*

among many witnesses: ... attested by many witnesses, *Montgomery* ... in the presence of many listeners, *TCNT.*

the same commit thou to faithful men: Pass these things on, *SEB* ... commend to trustworthy men, *Confraternity* ... to reliable men, *Berkeley* ... reliable people, *JB.*

who shall be able to teach others also: ... who shall be competent to teach, *Concordant.*

3. Thou therefore endure hardness: Conduct thyself in work as, *Confraternity* ... Put up with your share of difficulties, *JB* ... take your share of hard sufferings, *Norlie.*

2541.3 adj nom sing masc καλὸς *kalos* good	4608.1 noun nom sing masc στρατιώτης *stratiōtēs* a soldier	2400.2 name masc ᾽ Ἰησοῦ *Iēsou* of Jesus	5382.2 name gen masc Χριστοῦ. *Christou* Christ.	5382.2 name gen masc [✩ Χριστοῦ *Christou* [of Christ

2400.2 name masc Ἰησοῦ.] *Iēsou* Jesus.]	3625.2 num card nom masc **4.** οὐδεὶς *oudeis* No one	4605.5 verb nom sing masc part pres mid στρατευόμενος *strateuomenos* serving as a soldier	1691.1 verb 3sing indic pres mid ἐμπλέκεται *empleketai* entangles himself

3450.14 art dat pl fem ταῖς *tais* with the	3450.2 art gen sing τοῦ *tou* of the	972.1 noun gen sing masc βίου *biou* life	4089.1 noun dat pl fem πραγματείαις, *pragmateiais* affairs,	2419.1 conj ἵνα *hina* that

3450.3 art
dat sing
τῷ
tō
the

4609.1 verb dat sing masc part aor act στρατολογήσαντι *stratologēsanti* having enrolled him as a soldier	694.7 verb 3sing subj aor act ἀρέσῃ. *aresē* he may please.	1430.1 partic **5.** ἐὰν *ean* If	1156.2 conj δὲ *de* and

2504.1 conj καὶ *kai* also	118.1 verb 3sing subj pres act ἀθλῇ *athlē* contend	4948.3 indef- pron nom sing τις, *tis* anyone,	3620.3 partic οὐ *ou* not	4588.2 verb 3sing indic pres mid στεφανοῦται *stephanoutai* he is being crowned	1430.1 partic ἐὰν *ean* if

3231.1 partic μὴ *mē* not	3408.1 adv νομίμως *nomimōs* lawfully	118.2 verb 3sing subj aor act ἀθλήσῃ. *athlēsē* he shall have contended.	3450.6 art acc sing masc **6.** τὸν *ton* The	2844.6 verb acc sing masc part pres act κοπιῶντα *kopiōnta* laboring

1086.2 noun acc sing masc γεωργὸν *geōrgon* farmer	1158.1 verb 3sing indic pres act δεῖ *dei* must	4270.1 adv πρῶτον *prōton* before	3450.1 art gen pl τῶν *tōn* of the	2561.4 noun gen pl masc καρπῶν *karpōn* fruits

3205.2 verb inf pres act μεταλαμβάνειν. *metalambanein* to partake.	3401.3 verb 2sing impr pres act **7.** Νόει *Noei* Consider	3614.17 rel- pron pl neu ᾽ ἃ *ha* what things	3614.16 rel- pron sing neu [ᵃ✩ ὃ] *ho* [what]	2978.1 verb 1sing pres act λέγω· *legō* I say,

7.a.**Txt**: 01‭‬-corr,06D
018K,020L,byz.bo.
Var: 01‭‬-org,02A,04C
025P,33,Lach,Treg,Alf
Word,Tisc,We/Ho,Weis
Sod,UBS/✩

7.b.**Txt**: 04C-corr,018K
020L,025P,byz.
Var: 01‭‬,02A,04C-org
06D,33,bo.Lach,Treg
Alf,Word,Tisc,We/Ho
Weis,Sod,UBS/✩

1319.24 verb 3sing opt aor act ᾽ δώῃ *dōē* may give	1319.38 verb 3sing indic fut act [ᵇ✩ δώσει] *dōsei* [will give]	1056.1 conj γὰρ *gar* for	4622.3 prs- pron dat 2sing σοι *soi* you	3450.5 art nom sing masc ὁ *ho* the

2935.1 noun
nom sing masc
κύριος
kurios
Lord

4757.3 noun acc sing fem σύνεσιν *sunesin* understanding	1706.1 prep ἐν *en* in	3820.5 adj dat pl πᾶσιν. *pasin* all things.	3285.5 verb 2sing impr pres act **8.** Μνημόνευε *Mnēmoneue* Remember	2400.3 name acc masc Ἰησοῦν *Iēsoun* Jesus

5382.4 name acc masc Χριστὸν *Christon* Christ	1446.30 verb acc sing masc part perf mid ἐγηγερμένον *egēgermenon* having been raised	1523.2 prep gen ἐκ *ek* from among	3361.2 adj gen pl νεκρῶν, *nekrōn* dead,	1523.2 prep gen ἐκ *ek* of

soldier. The word "hardness" means "hardship." The adjective "good" means "noble, excellent." A soldier is called upon to endure the hardship and rigors of battle. As a good soldier of Jesus Christ, Timothy would suffer hardship—which includes persecutions, misunderstanding, and opposition.

2:4. The New International Version renders this verse: "No one serving as a soldier gets involved in civilian affairs—he wants to please his commanding officer." The emphasis here is not a renunciation of family, friends, home, business, etc., but a caution against preoccupation with things that entangle. The Greek is *empleketai* (middle voice, "become entangled, involved"), used only here and in 2 Peter 2:20. The caution does not mean the affairs of this life are wrong; they are wrong when they entangle and keep believers from the priority of pleasing God (compare Mark 4:18,19). Being a soldier demands sacrifice, discipline, obedience, and an uncompromising loyalty.

2:5. The second illustration is that of an athlete. "Strive for masteries" means "competes as an athlete" (NIV) and reflects what Paul wrote in 1 Corinthians 9:24-27. "Except he strive lawfully" is "unless he competes according to the rules" (NASB). The Greek *nomimōs athlēsē* refers to the professional athlete, not the amateur. Probably Paul was referring to the athlete who participated in the Olympic Games.

In Paul's time the Olympic Games were well known. Athletes trained long and hard. Winners of the various contests became national heroes. If a contestant cheated to gain advantage and was discovered, he was publicly shamed and barred from the games. Each athlete was to adhere strictly to the rules.

2:6. The third illustration is that of a hardworking farmer. "Laboreth" is the Greek verb *kopiōnta* which denotes hard, diligent toil. The farmer works hard because he expects to partake of his crops. He must plant, cultivate, water, weed, and wait. Then, in the time of harvest, he must toil long and hard. But his dedicated effort will be rewarded.

2:7. Paul summarized his three illustrations with a charge to Timothy. "Consider" means "put your mind on" and implies Timothy should grasp the meaning of what has just been said and how it applied to his own ministry. As Timothy did this the Lord would add "understanding" ("insight," i.e., the ability to make right judgments) that was beyond Timothy's human ability.

2:8. This verse begins a new thought that focuses on Jesus Christ. "Of the seed of David" points to the humanity of Christ and would

as a good soldier of Jesus Christ: As a noble soldier, *Berkeley* . . . A soldier on active service, *TCNT*.

4. No man that warreth: No enlisted recruit, *Berkeley* . . . No soldier, *SEB*.

entangleth himself with the affairs of [this] life: . . . is involved in, *Concordant* . . . gets mixed up with the world of business, *SEB* . . . gets himself mixed up in civilian life, *JB* . . . with the occupations of this life, *Campbell*.

that he may please him who hath chosen him to be a soldier: . . . to please his commanding officer, *NAB*.

5. And if a man also strive for masteries: If someone competes as an athlete, *SEB*.

[yet] is he not crowned, except he strive lawfully: . . . unless he has competed according to the rules, *Confraternity* . . . unless he competes fairly, *Berkeley* . . . unless he has kept all the rules, *JB*.

6. The husbandman that laboureth: The toiling farmer, *Concordant*.

must be first partaker of the fruits: . . . must have first share of the produce, *Berkeley*.

7. Consider what I say: Reflect on what, *NAB* . . . Think over what I say, *Norlie*.

and the Lord give thee understanding in all things:

8. Remember that Jesus Christ: of the seed of David was raised from the dead: Who was born from the early family of David, *NLT* . . . with David as a human ancestor, *Norlie*.

4543.2 noun gen sing neu	1132.1 name masc	2567.3 prep	3450.16 art sing neu	2077.1 noun sing neu
σπέρματος	Δαβίδ,	κατὰ	τὸ	εὐαγγέλιόν
spermatos	Dabid	kata	to	euangelion
seed	of David,	according to	the	good news

1466.2 prs- pron gen 1sing	1706.1 prep	3614.3 rel- pron dat sing	2524.1 verb 1sing indic pres act	3230.1 prep	1193.4 noun gen pl
μου·	**9.** ἐν	ᾧ	κακοπαθῶ	μέχρι	δεσμῶν
mou	en	hō	kakopathō	mechri	desmōn
my,	in	which	I suffer hardship	unto	bonds

5453.1 conj	2528.1 adj nom sing masc	233.1 conj	233.2 conj	3450.5 art nom sing masc	3030.1 noun nom sing masc
ὡς	κακοῦργος·	ʽ ἀλλ'	[☆ ἀλλὰ]	ὁ	λόγος
hōs	kakourgos	all'	alla	ho	logos
as	an evil doer:	but	[idem]	the	word

3450.2 art gen sing	2296.2 noun gen sing masc	3620.3 partic	1204.15 verb 3sing indic perf mid	1217.2 prep	3642.17 dem- pron sing neu
τοῦ	θεοῦ	οὐ	δέδεται.	**10.** διὰ	τοῦτο
tou	theou	ou	dedetai	dia	touto
	of God	not	has been bound.	Because of	this

3820.1 adj	5116.2 verb 1sing indic pres act	1217.2 prep	3450.8 art acc pl masc	1575.6 adj acc pl masc	2419.1 conj
πάντα	ὑπομένω	διὰ	τοὺς	ἐκλεκτούς,	ἵνα
panta	hupomenō	dia	tous	eklektous	hina
all things	I endure	for sake of	the	elect,	that

2504.1 conj	840.7 prs-pron nom pl masc	4843.2 noun gen sing fem	5018.3 verb 3pl subj aor act	3450.10 art gen sing fem	1706.1 prep
καὶ	αὐτοὶ	σωτηρίας	τύχωσιν	τῆς	ἐν
kai	autoi	sōtērias	tuchōsin	tēs	en
also	they	salvation	may obtain	the	in

5382.3 name dat masc	2400.2 name masc	3196.3 prep	1385.2 noun gen sing fem	164.2 adj gen sing	3964.2 adj nom sing masc
Χριστῷ	Ἰησοῦ	μετὰ	δόξης	αἰωνίου.	**11.** πιστὸς
Christō	Iēsou	meta	doxēs	aiōniou	pistos
Christ	Jesus	with	glory	eternal.	Faithful

3450.5 art nom sing masc	3030.1 noun nom sing masc	1479.1 conj	1056.1 conj	4731.1 verb 1pl indic aor act
ὁ	λόγος·	εἰ	γὰρ	συναπεθάνομεν,
ho	logos	ei	gar	sunapethanomen
the	word;	if	for	we died together with,

2504.1 conj	4651.2 verb 1pl indic fut act	1479.1 conj	5116.4 verb 1pl indic pres act	2504.1 conj
καὶ	συζήσομεν·	**12.** εἰ	ὑπομένομεν,	καὶ
kai	suzēsomen	ei	hupomenomen	kai
also	we shall live together;	if	we endure,	also

4672.2 verb 1pl indic fut act	1479.1 conj	714.1 verb 1pl indic pres mid	714.22 verb 1pl indic fut mid
συμβασιλεύσομεν·	εἰ	ʽ ἀρνούμεθα,	[a☆ ἀρνησόμεθα,]
sumbasileusomen	ei	arnoumetha	arnēsometha
we shall reign together;	if	we deny,	[we will deny]

12.a.Txt: 01א-corr,06D
018K,020L,025P,byz.
Var: 01א-org,02A,04C
33,Lach,Treg,Alf,Tisc
We/Ho,Weis,Sod
UBS/☆

2519.6 dem-pron nom sing masc	714.17 verb 3sing indic fut mid	2231.4 prs- pron acc 1pl	1479.1 conj	564.1 verb 1pl indic pres act
κἀκεῖνος	ἀρνήσεται	ἡμᾶς·	**13.** εἰ	ἀπιστοῦμεν,
kakeinos	arnēsetai	hēmas	ei	apistoumen
that also	will deny	us;	if	we are unfaithful,

thus encourage Timothy to "remember" that Jesus was a man tempted like everyone else (Hebrews 4:15). "Raised from the dead" focuses attention on the deity of Christ and God's power shown in the Resurrection (compare Romans 1:1-4). To Paul the Resurrection is the premier truth of the gospel which he called "my gospel" (compare Romans 2:16; 16:25; 1 Corinthians 15:1).

2:9. The word "wherein" refers to the last word in verse 8: "gospel." Paul was in trouble and chains for preaching the gospel. "Evildoer" means a common criminal. The only other New Testament use of this word is in reference to the two criminals crucified with Jesus (Luke 23:32,39). There it is translated "malefactors." "Bonds" means "fetters, chains." From his own present suffering and bondage, Paul could exclaim, "But the word of God is not bound!" The sense here is that Paul could still preach in prison, and the gospel was being proclaimed by many others.

2:10. "Therefore" means "on this account," i.e., "for the sake of the gospel and its proclamation." Paul endured (compare verse 3) everything "for the elect's sake." "Elect" means "chosen" or "choice." It does not refer to an elite group, but to all those who will yet believe on Christ, i.e., all Christians. The following phrases verify this. Note how the word "salvation" is connected with "in Christ Jesus." He added here the words "with eternal glory." This refers to the final state of salvation.

2:11. Verses 11-13 comprise a "faithful saying" that is considered by most scholars to be lines from an early Christian hymn. Of the five "faithful sayings" in the Pastorals (1 Timothy 1:15; 3:1; 4:9; here; Titus 3:8), this is the longest.

"If we be dead" is the Greek aorist tense that refers to a specific act in the past and could be rendered "if we died with him." These words could refer either to Christ's death on the cross (we were crucified with Him) or the act of Christian baptism where believers spiritually identify with Christ (see Romans 6:3,4,8). Some see in this reference to death and eternal life Paul's expression of his coming martyrdom. This may be possible.

2:12. "If we suffer" is better rendered "if we endure." The same Greek word is translated "endure" in verse 10. Here the verb is in the Greek present tense which indicates a sustained activity. Suffering is important, but endurance is more important. Endurance contains the idea of remaining steadfast and faithful when others are giving up.

"If we deny (disown) him" in the Greek suggests a remote possibility rather than a certainty. If we repudiate or disown Christ, He will disown us in the Day of Judgment. These words are reminiscent of Jesus' statement in Matthew 10:32,33.

according to my gospel: This is the Good News I tell, *SEB* . . . to the gospel I proclaim, *Montgomery.*

9. Wherein I suffer trouble: I suffer punishment, *Berkeley.*

as an evil doer, [even] unto bonds: . . . as a criminal, *Confraternity* . . . as a malefactor, *Campbell, Montgomery* . . . even to the extent of wearing chains, *Williams* . . . even to shackles, *Berkeley.*

but the word of God is not bound: But God's message is no prisoner, *Montgomery* . . . but they cannot chain up God's news, *JB* . . . But, God's message has not been confined, *SEB* . . . is not chained, *NLT.*

10. Therefore I endure all things: That is why, *Montgomery.*

for the elect's sakes: . . . for the sake of the chosen, *Montgomery.*

that they may also obtain the salvation which is in Christ Jesus with eternal glory:

11. [It is] a faithful saying: You can depend on this, *NAB* . . . It is a trustworthy message, *Berkeley* . . . that you can rely on, *JB.*

For if we be dead with [him], we shall also live with [him]: As we have shared his death, we shall also share his life, *TCNT.*

12. If we suffer, we shall also reign with [him]: If we hold out to the end, *NAB* . . . If we hold firm, *JB.*

if we deny [him], he also will deny us: If we say we do not know Him, *NLT* . . . If we say no to him, *SEB* . . . He will also personally go back on us, *Berkeley* . . . he, too, will disown us, *TCNT.*

13.a.**Var:** 01א-org,02A
04C,06D,020L,025P,33
bo.Lach,Treg,Alf,Word
Tisc,We/Ho,Weis,Sod
UBS/✠

1552.3 dem-pron nom sing masc	3964.2 adj nom sing masc	3176.1 verb 3sing indic pres act	714.13 verb inf aor mid	1056.1 conj
ἐκεῖνος	πιστὸς	μένει·	ἀρνήσασθαι	[ᵃ✠+ γὰρ]
ekeinos	pistos	menei	arnēsasthai	gar
that	faithful	abides;	to deny	[for]

1431.6 prs-pron acc sing masc	3620.3 partic	1404.4 verb 3sing indic pres mid	3642.18 dem-pron pl neu	5117.1 verb 2sing impr pres act
ἑαυτὸν	οὐ	δύναται.	**14.** Ταῦτα	ὑπομίμνησκε,
heauton	ou	dunatai	Tauta	hupomimnēske
himself	not	he is able.	These things	put in remembrance of,

14.a.**Txt:** 02A,06D,018K
020L,025P,048,byz.
Weis,Sod
Var: 01א,04C,016I,it.sa.
bo.Treg,Tisc,We/Ho
UBS/✠

1257.4 verb nom sing masc part pres mid	1783.1 prep	3450.2 art gen sing	2935.2 noun gen sing masc	3450.2 art gen sing
διαμαρτυρόμενος	ἐνώπιον	ꞌ τοῦ	κυρίου	[ᵃ✠ τοῦ
diamarturomenos	enōpion	tou	kuriou	tou
testifying earnestly	before	the	Lord	

14.b.**Txt:** 01א-corr,06D
018K,020L,byz.
Var: 01א-org,02A,04C
025P,33,Lach,Treg,Alf
Tisc,We/Ho,Weis,Sod
UBS/✠

2296.2 noun gen sing masc	3231.1 partic	3028.1 verb inf pres act	1519.1 prep	1894.2 prep
θεοῦ]	μὴ	λογομαχεῖν	ꞌ εἰς	[ᵇ✠ ἐπ']
theou	mē	logomachein	eis	ep'
[God]	not	to dispute about words	for	[idem]

3625.6 num card neu	5374.1 adj sing neu	1894.3 prep	2662.1 noun dat sing fem	3450.1 art gen pl	189.15 verb gen pl masc part pres act
οὐδὲν	χρήσιμον,	ἐπὶ	καταστροφῇ	τῶν	ἀκουόντων.
ouden	chrēsimon	epi	katastrophē	tōn	akouontōn
nothing	profitable,	to	subversion	of the	hearing.

4557.5 verb 2sing impr aor act	4427.4 prs-pron acc sing masc	1378.2 adj acc sing masc	3798.12 verb inf aor act	3450.3 art dat sing
15. σπούδασον	σεαυτὸν	δόκιμον	παραστῆσαι	τῷ
spoudason	seauton	dokimon	parastēsai	tō
Be diligent	yourself	approved	to present	

2296.3 noun dat sing masc	2023.2 noun acc sing masc	420.1 adj acc sing masc	3581.1 verb acc sing masc part pres act	3450.6 art acc sing masc
θεῷ,	ἐργάτην	ἀνεπαίσχυντον,	ὀρθοτομοῦντα	τὸν
theō	ergatēn	anepaischunton	orthotomounta	ton
to God,	a workman	not ashamed,	straightly cutting	the

3030.4 noun acc sing masc	3450.10 art gen sing fem	223.2 noun gen sing fem	3450.15 art acc pl fem	1156.2 conj	945.1 adj acc pl
λόγον	τῆς	ἀληθείας·	**16.** τὰς	δὲ	βεβήλους
logon	tēs	alētheias	tas	de	bebēlous
word	of the	truth;	the	but	godless

2728.1 noun acc pl fem	3889.3 verb 2sing impr pres mid	1894.3 prep	3979.8 adj comp sing neu	1056.1 conj
κενοφωνίας	περιΐστασο·	ἐπὶ	πλεῖον	γὰρ
kenophōnias	periistaso	epi	pleion	gar
empty babblings	stand aloof from,	to	more	for

4157.2 verb 3pl indic fut act	757.1 noun fem	2504.1 conj	3450.5 art nom sing masc	3030.1 noun nom sing masc
προκόψουσιν	ἀσεβείας,	**17.** καὶ	ὁ	λόγος
prokopsousin	asebeias	kai	ho	logos
they will advance of	ungodliness,	and	the	word

840.1 prs-pron gen pl	5453.1 conj	1037.1 noun nom sing fem	3405.1 noun acc sing fem	2174.39 verb 3sing indic fut act	3614.1 rel-pron gen pl
αὐτῶν	ὡς	γάγγραινα	νομὴν	ἕξει·	ὧν
autōn	hōs	gangraina	nomēn	hexei	hōn
their	as	a gangrene	pasture	will have;	of whom

2:13. The idea of unfaithfulness underscores the first clause. It could be rendered "if we are faithless." This contrasts with God's utter faithfulness. He is trustworthy. He, because of His perfect nature, cannot deny himself.

2:14. This verse opens a new topic that might be titled "An Approved Workman." It extends to the end of chapter 2. Paul entrusted Timothy to remind and charge others. He was saying, "Don't engage in word fights!" They result in "no profit" and "subverting" ("ruin"; Greek, *katastrophē*, literally, "turning upside down") of the hearers. This is similar to Paul's charge in 1 Timothy 1:3-7 and his description in 1 Timothy 6:4,5.

2:15. "Study" here is much broader than the meaning of the word as it relates to book learning. It means "be eager, be zealous, be diligent, make every effort, do your utmost." Timothy was to do his best to "show" (*parastēsai*, "present oneself for service") himself "approved" (*dokimon*, "accepted after testing") unto God.

This presentation to God involves two aspects: (1) a worker who is not ashamed (the Greek word used here has a passive force: "not to be put to shame," cf. Philippians 1:20) and (2) a worker who can rightly divide or correctly handle the truth. "Rightly dividing" (*orthotomounta*) is literally "straight cutting." The possible metaphor behind this phrase is the farmer who plows a straight furrow or the road builder who cuts a road across country in a straight direction. Timothy was to be a person who goes straight ahead, not veering to the right or to the left.

Another meaning is "correctly handling" and refers to Timothy's call to the correct exegesis of God's Word. He must not twist or change the truth. "The word of truth" refers to the "gospel." Paul also used this phrase in Ephesians 1:13 and Colossians 1:5.

2:16. Paul warned Timothy to shun godless chatter and empty sounds. Walter Lock paraphrases this first clause: "But to all these irreligious and frivolous hairsplittings give a wide berth" (*International Critical Commentary, Commentary on the Pastoral Epistles*, p.97). "Vain babblings" is talk that is void of value and irreverent in substance and spirit.

The "they" in the second clause could have two meanings. It could refer to the profane and vain babblings that lead to increased ungodliness. "They" could also refer to false teachers who go on and on toward ungodliness. The next two verses refer to specific false teachers.

2:17. "Their word (the false teachers' words) will eat (Greek, 'find pasture') as doth a canker (gangrene)." The Greek word *gangraina* was a medical term in Paul's day that described a malignant sore that eats away healthy tissue.

13. If we believe not, [yet] he abideth faithful: We may be unfaithful, *JB* . . . If we are not faithful, *SEB*.

he cannot deny himself: . . . for he cannot disown himself, *Confraternity* . . . He cannot play false to Himself, *Berkeley* . . . He cannot go against what He is, *NLT* . . . he must remain true to himself, *SEB*.

14. Of these things put [them] in remembrance: Remind them of this, *JB* . . . Recall these things to their minds, *Confraternity*.

charging [them] before the Lord:

that they strive not about words to no profit: . . . about words for nothing useful, *Campbell* . . . words that are not important, *NLT*.

[but] to the subverting of the hearers: . . . leading to the ruin of the listeners, *Confraternity*.

15. Study to show thyself approved unto God: . . . as one who has passed the test, *SEB*.

a workman that needeth not to be ashamed:

rightly dividing the word of truth: . . . correctly analyzing, *Berkeley* . . . as one who is correct in his analysis of, *Norlie* . . . accurate in delivering the Message, *TCNT*.

16. But shun profane [and] vain babblings: Avoid worldly, idle talk, *NAB* . . . Have nothing to do with pointless philosophical discussions, *JB* . . . Stay away from unholy stories and empty talk, *SEB*.

for they will increase unto more ungodliness: . . . for they contribute much to, *Confraternity*.

17. And their word will eat as doth a canker: . . . the influence of their talk will spread like the plague, *NAB* . . . like cancer, *SEB*.

1498.4 verb 3sing indic pres act
ἐστιν
estin
is

5051.1 name nom masc
Ὑμέναιος
Humenaios
Hymeneus

2504.1 conj
καὶ
kai
and

5209.1 name nom masc
Φίλητος,
Philetos
Philetus;

3610.2 rel-pron nom pl masc
18. οἵτινες
hoitines
who

3875.1 prep
περὶ
peri
concerning

3450.12 art acc sing fem
τὴν
ten
the

223.4 noun acc sing fem
ἀλήθειαν
aletheian
truth

789.1 verb 3pl indic aor act
ἠστόχησαν,
estochesan
missed the mark,

2978.16 verb nom pl masc part pres act
λέγοντες
legontes
asserting

18.a.**Txt:** 02A,04C,06D 018K,020L,025P,etc.byz. Weis
Var: 01ℵ,048,33,Treg Tisc,We/Ho,Sod,UBS/✢

3450.12 art acc sing fem
⌐ᵃ τὴν ⌐
ten
the

384.4 noun acc sing fem
ἀνάστασιν
anastasin
resurrection

2218.1 adv
ἤδη
ede
already

1090.13 verb inf perf act
γεγονέναι,
gegonenai
to have taken place;

2504.1 conj
καὶ
kai
and

394.1 verb 3pl indic pres act
ἀνατρέπουσιν
anatrepousin
are overthrowing

3450.12 art acc sing fem
τὴν
ten
the

4948.4 indef-pron gen pl
τινων
tinon
of some

3963.4 noun acc sing fem
πίστιν.
pistin
faith.

3450.5 art nom sing masc
19. ὁ
ho
The

3175.1 partic
μέντοι
mentoi
nevertheless

4582.1 adj nom sing masc
στερεὸς
stereos
firm

2287.3 noun nom sing masc
θεμέλιος
themelios
foundation

3450.2 art gen sing
τοῦ
tou

2296.2 noun gen sing masc
θεοῦ
theou
God's

2449.18 verb 3sing indic perf act
ἕστηκεν,
hesteken
has stood,

2174.17 verb nom sing masc part pres act
ἔχων
echon
having

3450.12 art acc sing fem
τὴν
ten
the

4825.2 noun acc sing fem
σφραγῖδα
sphragida
seal

3642.12 dem-pron acc sing fem
ταύτην,
tauten
this,

1091.17 verb 3sing indic aor act
Ἔγνω
Egno
Knows

2935.1 noun nom sing masc
κύριος
kurios
Lord

3450.8 art acc pl masc
τοὺς
tous
the

1498.25 verb acc pl masc part pres act
ὄντας
ontas
being

840.3 prs-pron gen sing
αὐτοῦ,
autou
his,

2504.1 conj
καί,
kai
and

861.5 verb 3sing impr aor act
Ἀποστήτω
Aposteto
Let depart

570.3 prep
ἀπὸ
apo
from

92.2 noun gen sing fem
ἀδικίας
adikias
unrighteousness

3820.6 adj nom sing masc
πᾶς
pas
everyone

3450.5 art nom sing masc
ὁ
ho
the

3550.1 verb nom sing masc part pres act
ὀνομάζων
onomazon
naming

3450.16 art sing neu
τὸ
to
to the

3549.2 noun sing neu
ὄνομα
onoma
name

5382.2 name gen masc
⌐ Χριστοῦ.
Christou
of Christ.

2935.2 noun gen sing masc
[ᵃ✢ κυρίου.]
kuriou
[of Lord.]

1706.1 prep
20. Ἐν
En
In

3144.11 adj dat sing fem
μεγάλῃ
megale
great

1156.2 conj
δὲ
de
but

19.a.**Txt:** Steph
Var: 01ℵ,02A,04C,06D 018K,020L,025P,sa.bo. Gries,Lach,Treg,Alf Word,Tisc,We/Ho,Weis Sod,UBS/✢

3477.3 noun dat sing fem
οἰκίᾳ
oikia
a house

3620.2 partic
οὐκ
ouk
not

1498.4 verb 3sing indic pres act
ἔστιν
estin
there are

3303.1 adv
μόνον
monon
only

4487.3 noun pl neu
σκεύη
skeue
vessels

5387.8 adj pl neu
χρυσᾶ
chrusa
golden

2504.1 conj
καὶ
kai
and

687.2 adj pl neu
ἀργυρᾶ,
argura
silver,

233.2 conj
ἀλλὰ
alla
but

2504.1 conj
καὶ
kai
also

3447.1 adj pl neu
ξύλινα
xulina
wooden

2504.1 conj
καὶ
kai
and

3611.1 adj pl neu
ὀστράκινα,
ostrakina
earthen,

2504.1 conj
καὶ
kai
and

Twice Paul named Hymeneus as one who had departed from the truth (see 1 Timothy 1:20; 2 Timothy 2:18). Philetus was also named as a cohort of Hymeneus. Both their names occur separately among those of Caesar's household whose relics have been found in the Columbaria (vaults) at Rome.

2:18. "Erred" is *ēstochēsan*, "wandered away" (see 1 Timothy 1:6; 6:21). Hymeneus and Philetus were probably teaching that there was no bodily resurrection, but only the spiritual resurrection, which Paul described in Romans 6:1-11. This "spiritualizing" destroyed the faith of some believers because the resurrection is one of the central truths of the gospel. The word "overthrow" can be rendered "overturn, upset, ruin, destroy."

2:19. The word "nevertheless" (*mentoi*, a particle of contrast) is a traditional term. Paul moved from a negative tone in the preceding verses to one of encouragement in the next few verses. "Foundation" (*themelios*, variously translated "foundation stone, treasure, reserve") could refer to several things: Christ, the apostles, the Church, or the truth. Because of its clear use in Ephesians 2:20 (see verses 19-22 there), the Church seems the best choice (compare 1 Timothy 3:15).

"Seal" is *sphragida*, a term meaning "inscription." It carries the idea of ownership (compare Ephesians 1:13). The presence of God's seal identifies the true Christian. Two quotations from the Old Testament make up this "seal"; the first reflects God's ownership, the second speaks of man's responsibility. "The Lord knoweth them that are his" is a paraphrase of Numbers 16:5. That text comes from the narrative of Korah's rebellion. Moses told the people God would show them who was His and who was not. "Knoweth" means "is intimately acquainted with."

The second quotation, "Let every one that nameth the name of Christ ('the Lord' is found in all the uncials and versions) depart from iniquity," is a reflection of Moses' words in Numbers 16:26—again from the Korah narrative.

Both of these concepts were taught by Jesus (Matthew 7:22,23; Luke 13:27). They present two principles regarding the Church. First, the Church consists of those who belong to God. Second, the Church consists of those who have departed from unrighteousness.

2:20. In verses 20 and 21 Paul introduced an illustration to show the different functions of people in the Church. The "great house" is the Church and the "vessels of gold and silver" and "of wood and of earth ('clay, earthenware')" are the different kinds of people in the Church. Contrast is a secondary idea here; variety is the primary meaning.

of whom is Hymenaeus and Philetus:

18. Who concerning the truth have erred: . . . missed out on the truth, *Berkeley*.

saying that the resurrection is past already: . . . has already occurred, *Concordant* . . . already happened, *Campbell* . . . has already taken place, *TCNT*.

and overthrow the faith of some: . . . in consequence, they are upsetting, *Norlie* . . . and are subverging the faith, *Concordant* . . . are undermining some people's faith, *Williams* . . . This upsets the faith of some, *Klingensmith*.

19. Nevertheless the foundation of God standeth sure: God's solid foundation stone is still in position, *JB* . . . God's solid foundation stands firm, *SEB* . . . the truth of God cannot be changed, *NLT* . . . still stands unmoved, *TCNT* . . . stands unshaken, *Williams*.

having this seal: . . . bearing this seal, *Confraternity* . . . with these inscriptions, *Williams* . . . and this is the inscription on it, *JB*.

The Lord knoweth them that are his: . . . knows who belongs to him, *SEB*.

And, Let every one that nameth the name of Christ depart from iniquity: . . . who professes the name of, *NAB* . . . who bears the name of the Lord must abstain from evil, *Williams* . . . stand aloof from wickedness, *Berkeley* . . . quit sinning! *Norlie* . . . must turn away from sin! *NLT* . . . let him step aside from injustice, *Klingensmith*.

20. But in a great house there are not only vessels of gold and of silver: . . . there are different bowls, *SEB* . . . articles, *Williams*.

but also of wood and of earth: . . . and clay, *NAB, Confraternity* . . . and pottery, *Klingensmith*.

3614.17 rel-pron pl neu	3173.1 conj	1519.1 prep	4940.4 noun acc sing fem	3614.17 rel-pron pl neu	1156.2 conj	1519.1 prep
ἅ	μὲν	εἰς	τιμὴν,	ἃ	δὲ	εἰς
ha	men	eis	timēn,	ha	de	eis
which things		to	honor,	which things		to

813.4 noun acc sing fem	1430.1 partic	3631.1 partic	4948.3 indef-pron nom sing	1558.1 verb 3sing subj aor act
ἀτιμίαν·	**21.** ἐὰν	οὖν	τις	ἐκκαθάρῃ
atimian	ean	oun	tis	ekkatharē
dishonor.	If	therefore	a certain one	shall have purged

1431.6 prs-pron acc sing masc	570.3 prep	3642.2 dem-pron gen pl	1498.40 verb 3sing indic fut mid	4487.1 noun sing neu	1519.1 prep
ἑαυτὸν	ἀπὸ	τούτων,	ἔσται	σκεῦος	εἰς
heauton	apo	toutōn	estai	skeuos	eis
himself	from	these,	he shall be	a vessel	to

4940.4 noun acc sing fem	37.20 verb sing neu part perf mid	2504.1 conj	2154.1 adj sing	3450.3 art dat sing
τιμήν,	ἡγιασμένον,	⌐a καὶ ⌐	εὔχρηστον	τῷ
timēn,	hēgiasmenon,	kai	euchrēston	tō
honor,	having been sanctified,	and	serviceable	to the

1197.2 noun dat sing masc	1519.1 prep	3820.17 adj sing neu	2024.1 noun sing neu	18.3 adj sing	2069.14 verb sing neu part perf mid
δεσπότῃ,	εἰς	πᾶν	ἔργον	ἀγαθὸν	ἡτοιμασμένον.
despotē,	eis	pan	ergon	agathon	hētoimasmenon.
master,	for	every	work	good	having been prepared.

3450.15 art acc pl fem	1156.2 conj	3374.1 adj acc pl fem	1924.1 noun fem	5180.2 verb 2sing impr pres act	1371.5 verb 2sing impr pres act
22. τὰς	δὲ	νεωτερικὰς	ἐπιθυμίας	φεῦγε·	δίωκε
tas	de	neōterikas	epithumias	pheuge	diōke
The	but	youthful	lusts	flee,	pursue

1156.2 conj	1336.4 noun acc sing fem	3963.4 noun acc sing fem	26.4 noun acc sing fem	1503.4 noun acc sing fem	3196.3 prep
δὲ	δικαιοσύνην,	πίστιν,	ἀγάπην,	εἰρήνην	μετὰ
de	dikaiosunēn,	pistin,	agapēn,	eirēnēn	meta
but	righteousness,	faith,	love,	peace	with

3450.1 art gen pl	1926.7 verb gen pl masc part pres mid	3450.6 art acc sing masc	2935.4 noun acc sing masc	1523.2 prep gen	2485.7 adj gen sing fem
τῶν	ἐπικαλουμένων	τὸν	κύριον	ἐκ	καθαρᾶς
tōn	epikaloumenōn	ton	kurion	ek	katharas
the	calling on	the	Lord	out of	clean

2559.1 noun fem	3450.15 art acc pl fem	1156.2 conj	3336.6 adj acc pl fem	2504.1 conj	517.1 adj acc pl fem
καρδίας.	**23.** τὰς	δὲ	μωρὰς	καὶ	ἀπαιδεύτους
kardias	tas	de	mōras	kai	apaideutous
a heart.	The	but	foolish	and	undisciplined

2197.3 noun acc pl fem	3729.2 verb 2sing impr pres mid	3471.18 verb nom sing masc part perf act	3617.1 conj	1074.1 verb 3pl indic pres act
ζητήσεις	παραιτοῦ,	εἰδὼς	ὅτι	γεννῶσιν
zētēseis	paraitou,	eidōs	hoti	gennōsin
questionings	refuse,	knowing	that	they beget

3135.2 noun acc pl fem	1395.4 noun acc sing masc	1156.2 conj	2935.2 noun gen sing masc	3620.3 partic	1158.1 verb 3sing indic pres act
μάχας·	**24.** δοῦλον	δὲ	κυρίου	οὐ	δεῖ
machas	doulon	de	kuriou	ou	dei
contentions.	A slave	and	of Lord	not	it is necessary

21.a.**Txt:** 01א-corr
04C-org,06D-corr,018K
020L,025P,byz.sa.Sod
Var: 01א-org,02A
04C-corr,06D-org,33,bo.
Lach,Treg,Alf,Tisc
We/Ho,Weis,UBS/✻

"Some to honor" ("for noble purposes") and "some to dishonor" ("for ignoble purposes") should not be considered parallel to "gold and silver" and "wood and . . . earth." The idea of contrast is primary here and very possibly refers back to the false teachers mentioned above. The focus in this verse is on the cleanliness of each "vessel" (person).

2:21. "If a man therefore purge (*ekkatharē*, used only here and in 1 Corinthians 5:7) himself from these (probably the false teachings mentioned earlier), he shall be a vessel unto honor ('for noble purposes')." The obvious reference is to Timothy and the false teachers. The application is for all Christians.

Three results are clear: (1) he is "sanctified" ("set apart for a holy purpose"); (2) he is "meet (*euchrēston* ['useful, profitable'], cf. 2 Timothy 4:11; Philemon 11) for the master's use"; and (3) he is "prepared unto every good work" ("ready to do any and every good work"). Readiness is the emphasis in this last clause.

2:22. Here Paul began a direct address to Timothy. To the end of chapter 2, this text includes at least three imperatives: (1) flee youthful lusts (verse 22), (2) avoid arguments (verse 23), and (3) be gentle and teach (verse 24). Warnings as well as exhortations are found in verses 22-26.

"Flee" is *pheuge* ("flee from, avoid, shun"). "Youthful lusts" is variously translated "evil desires of youth" (NIV), "youthful passions" (RSV), or "turbulent desires of youth" (Phillips). Timothy is told to run away from these.

Then Paul commanded Timothy to "follow" (*diōke*, "to pursue without hostility, to follow after") four positive virtues: "righteousness, faith, charity, peace." This repeats what Paul wrote in his first letter (1 Timothy 6:11) with the exception of "peace." "Faith" includes the ideas of integrity, loyalty, reliability, faithfulness, and obedience. "Charity" is the kind of love that seeks the highest good for others. "Peace" denotes a right relationship with God and men. (See 1:2.)

2:23. Paul cautioned Timothy: "Don't have anything to do with foolish and stupid arguments, because you know they produce quarrels" (NIV). Again, this was not a new instruction (see 1 Timothy 1:4; 4:7; 6:20; 2 Timothy 2:16). Timothy was told to make a conscious effort to sidestep the divisive, unprofitable, foolish, and ignorant questions that "gender (produce, breed) strifes" (*machas*, "quarrels," cf. Titus 3:9 where it refers to legal contentions).

2:24. Here Timothy is called "the servant of the Lord" ("the Lord's bondservant"). This term could apply to any Christian (compare 1 Corinthians 7:22), but in this case it specifically refers to Timothy as one called to a special ministry. God's servant (1) "must

and some to honour, and some to dishonour: . . . some are kept for special occasions, *JB* . . . some for noble, some for ignoble uses, *Montgomery* . . . some for lowly uses, *Williams*.

21. If a man therefore purge himself from these: . . . will cleanse himself, *Williams*.

he shall be a vessel unto honour: . . . a distinguished vessel, *NAB* . . . for honorable uses, *Williams*.

sanctified, and meet for the master's use: He is special and useful for, *SEB* . . . consecrated, *Montgomery* . . . and useful to the Lord, *Confraternity* . . . an article serviceable to its owner, *TCNT* . . . made holy and pleasing to the big boss, *Klingensmith*.

[and] prepared unto every good work: . . . and kept ready for any good work, *JB* . . . fit for any good purpose, *Norlie* . . . ready for any good service, *Williams*.

22. Flee also youthful lusts: Run away from the evil desires, *SEB* . . . Flee from the passions of youth, *Montgomery* . . . from the evil impulses of youth, *Williams*.

but follow righteousness, faith, charity, peace: Go in pursuit of, *Berkeley* . . . run after, *Montgomery* . . . fasten your attention on, *JB* . . . ever strive for uprightness, *Williams* . . . and pursue integrity, *NAB*.

with them that call on the Lord out of a pure heart: . . . in company with, *Montgomery*.

23. But foolish and unlearned questions avoid: Avoid these futile and silly speculations, *JB* . . . Stay away from brainless arguments, *Klingensmith* . . . and ignorant controversies, *Confraternity*.

knowing that they do gender strifes: . . . they breed quarrels, *Confraternity* . . . they beget contentions, *Campbell* . . . It can only lead to trouble, *NLT*.

24. And the servant of the Lord must not strive: . . . a slave of the Lord must not quarrel, *Williams*.

3136.3 verb inf pres mid
μάχεσθαι,
machesthai
to contend,

233.1 conj
' ἀλλ'
all'
but

233.2 conj
[✶ ἀλλὰ]
alla
[idem]

2239.1 adj acc sing masc
ἤπιον
ēpion
gentle

1498.32 verb inf pres act
εἶναι
einai
to be

4242.1 prep
πρὸς
pros
towards

3820.8 adj acc pl masc
πάντας,
pantas
all;

1311.1 adj acc sing masc
διδακτικόν,
didaktikon
apt to teach;

418.1 adj acc sing masc
ἀνεξίκακον,
anexikakon
forbearing;

25. **1706.1** prep
ἐν
en
in

4095.3 noun dat sing fem
' πραότητι
praotēti
meekness

4095.6 noun dat sing fem
[✶ πραΰτητι]
prautēti
[idem]

3674.3 verb acc sing masc part pres act
παιδεύοντα
paideuonta
disciplining

3450.8 art acc pl masc
τοὺς
tous
the

472.1 verb acc pl masc part pres mid
ἀντιδιατιθεμένους,
antidiatithemenous
opposing,

3246.1 partic
μήποτε
mēpote
if perhaps

1319.19 verb 3sing subj aor act
' δῷ
dō
may give

1319.62 verb 3sing subj aor act
[ª✶ δώῃ]
dōē
[idem]

840.2 prs-pron dat pl
αὐτοῖς
autois
them

3450.5 art nom sing masc
ὁ
ho
the

2296.1 noun nom sing masc
θεὸς
theos
God

25.a.Txt: 01ℵ-corr
06D-corr,018K,020L
025P,byz.Sod
Var: 01ℵ-org,02A,04C
06D-org,Lach,Treg,Alf
Word,Tisc,We/Ho,Weis
UBS/✶

3211.2 noun acc sing fem
μετάνοιαν
metanoian
repentance

1519.1 prep
εἰς
eis
to

1907.4 noun acc sing fem
ἐπίγνωσιν
epignōsin
acknowledgment

223.2 noun gen sing fem
ἀληθείας,
alētheias
of truth,

26. **2504.1** conj
καὶ
kai
and

365.1 verb 3pl subj aor act
ἀνανήψωσιν
ananēpsōsin
they may awake up

1523.2 prep gen
ἐκ
ek
out of

3450.10 art gen sing fem
τῆς
tēs
the

3450.2 art gen sing
τοῦ
tou
of the

1222.2 adj gen sing masc
διαβόλου
diabolou
devil

3666.2 noun gen sing fem
παγίδος,
pagidos
snare,

2204.2 verb nom pl masc part perf mid
ἐζωγρημένοι
ezōgrēmenoi
having been taken

5097.2 prep
ὑπ'
hup'
by

840.3 prs-pron gen sing
αὐτοῦ
autou
him

1519.1 prep
εἰς
eis
for

3450.16 art sing neu
τὸ
to
the

1552.2 dem-pron gen sing
ἐκείνου
ekeinou
that

2284.1 noun sing neu
θέλημα.
thelēma
will.

3:1. **3642.17** dem-pron sing neu
Τοῦτο
Touto
This

1156.2 conj
δὲ
de
but

1091.9 verb 2sing impr pres act
γίνωσκε,
ginōske
know you,

3617.1 conj
ὅτι
hoti
that

1706.1 prep
ἐν
en
in

2057.10 adj dat pl fem
ἐσχάταις
eschatais
last

2232.7 noun dat pl fem
ἡμέραις
hēmerais
days

1748.6 verb 3pl indic fut mid
ἐνστήσονται
enstēsontai
will be present

2511.5 noun nom pl masc
καιροὶ
kairoi
times

5303.1 adj nom pl masc
χαλεποί.
chalepoi
difficult;

2. **1498.43** verb 3pl indic fut mid
ἔσονται
esontai
will be

1056.1 conj
γὰρ
gar
for

3450.7 art nom pl masc
οἱ
hoi
the

442.6 noun nom pl masc
ἄνθρωποι
anthrōpoi
men

5204.1 adj nom pl masc
φίλαυτοι,
philautoi
lovers of self,

5203.1 adj nom pl masc
φιλάργυροι,
philarguroi
lovers of money,

211.1 noun nom pl masc
ἀλαζόνες,
alazones
boasters,

5082.1 adj nom pl masc
ὑπερήφανοι,
huperēphanoi
proud,

982.2 adj nom pl masc
βλάσφημοι,
blasphēmoi
evil speakers,

1112.3 noun dat pl masc
γονεῦσιν
goneusin
to parents

541.2 adj pl masc
ἀπειθεῖς,
apeitheis
disobedient,

877.1 adj nom pl masc
ἀχάριστοι,
acharistoi
unthankful,

not strive"—he doesn't get embroiled in quarrels or word battles; (2) must "be gentle" (*ēpion einai*, "kind")—even when he has to point out a fault in another; (3) must be "apt ('able') to teach"—he is skillful in the important position of Christian teacher; (4) must be "patient" (*anexikakon*, "forbearing, bearing evil without resentment," used only here)—he possesses an attitude of patient forbearance toward those who oppose him.

2:25. God's servant (5) must in "meekness" instruct "those that oppose themselves"—the meaning here is a gentleness that corrects others with kindness, self-control, and a humility that is willing to forgive. "Those that oppose themselves" are people who set themselves up as opponents to God's servant by their false teachings and immoral conduct.

2:26. The purpose of God's gift of repentance (verse 25) is seen in the words "that they may recover (*ananēpsōsin*, literally, 'that they may return to soberness') themselves out of the snare ('trap') of the devil" (compare 1 Timothy 3:7; 6:9). These people had been "taken captive" (*ezōgrēmenoi*, "to catch alive," used only here and in Luke 5:10) by the devil "to do his will" (NIV, RSV).

3:1. The character of men in the last days is the theme of the first nine verses of chapter 3. "The last days" refers not only to the end of the Messianic Age, but to the times in which Paul was living as well. "Perilous" (*chalepoi*, "difficult, terrible, grievous, hard to live in") times were coming.

3:2. Verses 2-5 comprise one sentence. Eighteen evil characteristics of men in the last days are listed.

"Lovers of their own selves" (*philautoi*, "self-loving") and "covetous" (*philarguroi*, "lovers of money") are the twin sins from which flow all the others cataloged. The "boasters" and "proud" have similar traits. A boaster (*alazones*) is a braggart. *Alazones* was originally a "quack doctor" who wandered about with medicines and spells, boasting he could cure people. "Proud" is *huperēphanoi*, "to show oneself above," and denotes a person who is haughty, arrogant, and prone to swagger.

"Blasphemers" (*blasphēmoi*) are "evil-speaking, slanderous, abusive" people. They speak disrespectfully of God and their fellowmen. The "disobedient to parents" break the civil and moral laws. To strike one's father was as bad as murder in Roman law. Abusing a parent in the Greek culture caused disinheritance. Jews honored their parents because this is one of the Ten Commandments. The "unthankful" (*acharistoi*, "ungrateful") and the "unholy" (*anosioi*, "offenders of all that is holy") seem to be a pair. The sin of ingratitude often comes from the secular person who is out of fellowship with God.

but be gentle unto all [men]: ... on the contrary, to be courteous to every one, *TCNT*.

apt to teach, patient: ... skilled in teaching, *Berkeley*.

25. In meekness instructing those that oppose themselves: He must gently correct people, *SEB*.

if God peradventure will give them repentance: God might grant them, *Williams*.

to the acknowledging of the truth: ... that would lead them to a full knowledge of the truth, *Williams*.

26. And [that] they may recover themselves: ... they may come to their senses, *Berkeley* ... Then they will wake up and get away from, *SEB*.

out of the snare of the devil: who are taken captive by him at his will: ... in which they have been caught by him to do his will, *Williams*.

1. This know also: But understand this, *RSV* ... You must understand that, *NLT*.

that in the last days perilous times shall come: ... dangerous times, *Lilly* ... there are troublesome times impending, *Berkeley* ... the times will be dangerous, *Norlie* ... There will be hard times during, *SEB*.

2. For men shall be lovers of their own selves: ... selfish, *TCNT*.

covetous, boasters, proud, blasphemers: ... mercenary, *TCNT* ... arrogant, abusive, *RSV*.

disobedient to parents, unthankful, unholy: ... ungrateful, *Lilly, Confraternity* ... irreverent, *Norlie*.

459.1 adj
nom pl masc
ἀνόσιοι,
anosioi
unholy,

788.1 adj
nom pl masc
3. ἄστοργοι,
astorgoi
without natural affection,

780.2 adj
nom pl masc
ἄσπονδοι,
aspondoi
implacable,

1222.5 adj
nom pl masc
διάβολοι,
diaboloi
slanderers,

191.1 adj
nom pl masc
ἀκρατεῖς,
akrateis
not master of one's self,

432.1 adj
nom pl masc
ἀνήμεροι,
anēmeroi
savage,

858.1 adj
nom pl masc
ἀφιλάγαθοι,
aphilagathoi
not lovers of good,

4132.2 noun
nom pl masc
4. προδόται,
prodotai
betrayers,

4171.1 adj
nom pl masc
προπετεῖς,
propeteis
rash,

5028.3 verb nom pl
masc part perf mid
τετυφωμένοι,
tetuphōmenoi
having been puffed up,

5206.1 adj
nom pl masc
φιλήδονοι
philēdonoi
lovers of pleasure

3095.1
adv comp
μᾶλλον
mallon
rather

2211.1
conj
ἢ
ē
than

5214.1 adj
nom pl masc
φιλόθεοι,
philotheoi
lovers of God;

2174.19 verb nom pl
masc part pres act
5. ἔχοντες
echontes
having

3309.1 noun
acc sing fem
μόρφωσιν
morphōsin
a form

2131.2 noun
gen sing fem
εὐσεβείας,
eusebeias
of godliness,

3450.12 art
acc sing fem
τὴν
tēn
the

1156.2
conj
δὲ
de
but

1405.4 noun
acc sing fem
δύναμιν
dunamin
power

840.10 prs-pron
gen sing fem
αὐτῆς
autēs
of it

714.15 verb nom pl
masc part perf mid
ἠρνημένοι.
ērnēmenoi
having denied:

2504.1
conj
καὶ
kai
and

3642.8 dem-
pron acc pl masc
τούτους
toutous
these

659.1 verb 2sing
impr pres mid
ἀποτρέπου.
apotrepou
turn away from.

1523.2
prep gen
6. ἐκ
ek
Of

3642.2 dem-
pron gen pl
τούτων
toutōn
these

1056.1
conj
γάρ
gar
for

6.a.**Txt:** 06D-corr,018K
020L,byz.Sod
Var: 01ℵ,02A,04C
06D-org,025P,Gries
Lach,Treg,Alf,Word
Tisc,We/Ho,Weis
UBS/⋆

6.b.**Txt:** Steph
Var: 01ℵ,02A,04C,06D
018K,020L,025P,byz.
Gries,Lach,Treg,Alf
Word,Tisc,We/Ho,Weis
Sod,UBS/⋆

1498.7 verb 3pl
indic pres act
εἰσιν
eisin
are

3450.7 art
nom pl masc
οἱ
hoi
the

1728.1 verb nom pl
masc part pres act
ἐνδύνοντες
endunontes
entering

1519.1
prep
εἰς
eis
into

3450.15 art
acc pl fem
τὰς
tas
the

3477.1
noun fem
οἰκίας
oikias
houses

2504.1
conj
καὶ
kai
and

160.1 verb nom pl
masc part pres act
⸂ αἰχμαλωτεύοντες
aichmalōteuontes
leading captive

161.2 verb nom pl
masc part pres act
[ᵃ⋆ αἰχμαλωτίζοντες]
aichmalōtizontes
[idem]

3450.17
art pl neu
⸃ᵇ τὰ ⸄
ta
the

1127.1
noun pl neu
γυναικάρια
gunaikaria
silly women

4839.2 verb pl
neu part perf mid
σεσωρευμένα
sesōreumena
having been laden

264.7 noun
dat pl fem
ἁμαρτίαις,
hamartiais
with sins,

70.23 verb pl
neu part pres mid
ἀγόμενα
agomena
being led away

1924.7 noun
dat pl fem
ἐπιθυμίαις
epithumiais
by lusts

4024.3 adj
dat pl fem
ποικίλαις,
poikilais
various,

3704.1
adv
7. πάντοτε
pantote
always

3101.5 verb pl
neu part pres act
μανθάνοντα
manthanonta
learning

2504.1
conj
καὶ
kai
and

3236.1
adv
μηδέποτε
mēdepote
never

1519.1
prep
εἰς
eis
to

1907.4 noun
acc sing fem
ἐπίγνωσιν
epignōsin
knowledge

223.2 noun
gen sing fem
ἀληθείας
alētheias
of truth

2048.23 verb
inf aor act
ἐλθεῖν
elthein
to come

1404.21 verb pl
neu part pres mid
δυνάμενα.
dunamena
being able.

3:3. The six sins listed in this verse are those (1) "without natural affection" (*astorgoi*, from *storgē*, "family love"); (2) "trucebreakers" (*aspondoi*, from *spondai*, "truce, agreement"); (3) "false accusers" (*diaboloi*, "slanderers"); (4) "incontinent" (*akrateis*, "without self-control"); (5) "fierce" (*anēmeroi*, "brutal, savage"—describes wild beasts); (6) "despisers of those that are good" (*aphilagathoi*, "haters of good"—i.e., all that is good, whether in people or things).

3:4. The final four in Paul's catalog of godlessness are (1)"traitors" (*prodotai*, "treacherous"—those in Paul's day who, because of hatred, turned Christians in to the Roman authorities); (2) the "heady" (*propeteis*, "rash, reckless, hasty"); (3) the "high-minded" (*tetuphōmenoi*, "conceited"); and (4) "lovers of pleasures more than lovers of God" (*philēdonoi mallon ē philotheoi*).

3:5. All these people have a "form" (*morphōsin*, "outline, semblance") of godliness, but they deny the power. They go through the motions and maintain all the external forms, but they know nothing of true Christianity as a dynamic power to change lives. Timothy was told to "turn away" from such people.

3:6. After describing their character, Paul next warned Timothy about the actions of the "men" just mentioned. "For of this sort" refers to these men. They "creep" (*endunontes*, "worm one's way"—implies devious methods of entry) into houses described in terms of the female occupants. They are described as silly, sinful, and sensual. "Silly women" (*gunaikaria*) means literally "little women" and is a diminutive expressing contempt. It could be translated "weak-willed women, gullible women, foolish women."

These silly women are (1) led "captive" (the same Greek word used to describe prisoners of war), (2) "laden with sins" (the idea here is an acute state of guilt consciousness), and (3) "led away with divers lusts" ("swayed and led away by various evil desires and seductive impulses," *The Amplified Bible*).

3:7. A fourth description of these "silly women" is that they are "ever learning, and never able to come to the knowledge of the truth." "Ever learning" does not mean they assimilate what they hear. It might better be translated: "Always listening, but never able to learn or know the truth." This suggests that they only hear the sensational and not the serious or sacred. Possibly they wish to pose as enlightened, learned females. But in truth they are ignorant of the truth.

3. Without natural affection, trucebreakers, false accusers: ... implacable, *RSV* ... pledge-breakers, *Lilly* ... lacking in love for kinsmen, irreconcilable, *Williams*.

incontinent, fierce, despisers of those that are good: ... profligates, *RSV* ... brutal, *Berkeley*.

4. Traitors, heady, high-minded: ... treacherous, *Confraternity* ... swollen with pride, *Lilly* ... swollen with conceit, *RSV* ... conceited, *Berkeley*.

lovers of pleasures more than lovers of God: ... pleasure-loving, *Berkeley*.

5. Having a form of godliness: They will have a semblance of religion, *Lilly* ... keeping up the forms of, *Williams* ... holding the form of religion, *RSV*.

but denying the power thereof: ... but disowning its power, *Confraternity* ... they are strangers to its power, *Berkeley*.

from such turn away: These, also, shun, *Concordant* ... Avoid such people, *Williams*.

6. For of this sort are they which creep into houses:

and lead captive silly women: ... captivate weak-natured women, *Berkeley*.

laden with sins:

led away with divers lusts: ... controlled by all sorts of impulses, *Berkeley* ... swayed by various impulses, *RSV* ... by various lusts and gratifications, *Concordant*.

7. Ever learning, and never able to come to the knowledge of the truth:

2 Timothy 3:8

3614.6 rel-pron acc sing masc	4999.3 noun acc sing masc	1156.2 conj	2366.1 name nom masc	2504.1 conj	2364.1 name nom masc
8. ὃν	τρόπον	δὲ	Ἰάννης	καὶ	Ἰαμβρῆς
hon	*tropon*	*de*	*Iannēs*	*kai*	*Iambrēs*
Which	way	now	Jannes	and	Jambres

434.2 verb 3pl indic aor act	3338.3 name dat masc	3643.1 adv	2504.1 conj	3642.7 dem-pron nom pl masc	434.7 verb 3pl indic pres mid
ἀντέστησαν	Μωϋσεῖ,	οὕτως	καὶ	οὗτοι	ἀνθίστανται
antestēsan	*Mōusei*	*houtōs*	*kai*	*houtoi*	*anthistantai*
withstood	Moses,	thus	also	these	withstand

3450.11 art dat sing fem	223.3 noun dat sing fem	442.6 noun nom pl masc	2673.1 verb nom pl masc part perf mid
τῇ	ἀληθείᾳ,	ἄνθρωποι	κατεφθαρμένοι
tē	*alētheia*	*anthrōpoi*	*katephtharmenoi*
the	truth,	men	having been utterly corrupted

3450.6 art acc sing masc	3426.4 noun acc sing masc	95.3 adj nom pl masc	3875.1 prep	3450.12 art acc sing fem	3963.4 noun acc sing fem
τὸν	νοῦν,	ἀδόκιμοι	περὶ	τὴν	πίστιν.
ton	*noun*	*adokimoi*	*peri*	*tēn*	*pistin*
the	mind,	reprobate	as regards	the	faith.

233.1 conj	3620.3 partic	4157.2 verb 3pl indic fut act	1894.3 prep	3979.8 adj comp sing neu	3450.9 art nom sing fem
9. ἀλλ'	οὐ	προκόψουσιν	ἐπὶ	πλεῖον·	ἡ
all'	*ou*	*prokopsousin*	*epi*	*pleion*	*hē*
But	not	they shall advance	to	more,	the

1056.1 conj	452.1 noun nom sing fem	840.1 prs-pron gen pl	1539.1 adj nom sing fem	1498.40 verb 3sing indic fut mid	3820.5 adj dat pl
γὰρ	ἄνοια	αὐτῶν	ἔκδηλος	ἔσται	πᾶσιν,
gar	*anoia*	*autōn*	*ekdēlos*	*estai*	*pasin*
for	folly	their	fully manifest	shall be	to all,

5453.1 conj	2504.1 conj	3450.9 art nom sing fem	1552.1 dem-pron gen pl	1090.33 verb 3sing indic aor mid	4622.1 prs-pron nom 2sing
ὡς	καὶ	ἡ	ἐκείνων	ἐγένετο.	**10.** Σὺ
hōs	*kai*	*hē*	*ekeinōn*	*egeneto*	*Su*
as	also	the	of those	became.	You

1156.2 conj	3738.1 verb 2sing indic perf act	3738.4 verb 2sing indic aor act		1466.2 prs-pron gen 1sing
δὲ	ʿ παρηκολούθηκάς	[ᵃ☆ παρηκολούθησάς]		μου
de	*parēkolouthēkas*	*parēkolouthēsas*		*mou*
but	have closely followed	[closely followed]		my

10.a.**Txt:** 06D,018K 020L,025P,byz. **Var:** 01ℵ,02A,04C,33 Lach,Treg,Alf,Tisc We/Ho,Weis,Sod UBS/☆

3450.11 art dat sing fem	1313.3 noun dat sing fem	3450.11 art dat sing fem	71.1 noun dat sing fem	3450.11 art dat sing fem	4145.3 noun dat sing fem
τῇ	διδασκαλίᾳ,	τῇ	ἀγωγῇ,	τῇ	προθέσει,
tē	*didaskalia*	*tē*	*agōgē*	*tē*	*prothesei*
the	teaching,	the	conduct,	the	purpose,

3450.11 art dat sing fem	3963.3 noun dat sing fem	3450.11 art dat sing fem	3087.3 noun dat sing fem	3450.11 art dat sing fem	26.3 noun dat sing fem
τῇ	πίστει,	τῇ	μακροθυμίᾳ,	τῇ	ἀγάπῃ,
tē	*pistei*	*tē*	*makrothumia*	*tē*	*agapē*
the	faith,	the	patience,	the	love,

3450.11 art dat sing fem	5119.3 noun dat sing fem	3450.4 art dat pl	1369.5 noun dat pl masc	3450.4 art dat pl	3667.4 noun dat pl neu
τῇ	ὑπομονῇ,	**11.** τοῖς	διωγμοῖς,	τοῖς	παθήμασιν,
tē	*hupomonē*	*tois*	*diōgmois*	*tois*	*pathēmasin*
the	endurance,	the	persecutions,	the	sufferings:

3:8. Jannes and Jambres are not mentioned in the Old Testament. But Jewish tradition (Targum of Jonathan) says they were two of the Egyptian magicians who withstood Moses and Aaron when they came to Pharaoh (Exodus 7:10-13). Paul had three things to say about these false teachers who were like Jannes and Jambres: (1) They "resist the truth" (stronger than passive resistance, the Greek means "oppose"). "The truth" is the gospel.

(2) The phrase "men of corrupt minds" indicates depravity and utter corruption, describing those who can no longer understand the truth (compare Romans 1:21,22; Ephesians 4:17,18; 1 Timothy 6:5). (3) "Reprobate (*adokimoi*) concerning the faith" means "not standing the test, worthless, base, rejected." The RSV renders these two descriptions as "men of corrupt mind and counterfeit faith."

3:9. The NIV translates this verse, "But they will not get very far because, as in the case of those men, their folly will be clear to everyone." Paul used the Old Testament contrast of truth and folly (see especially in Proverbs). Because these men oppose "the truth" and reject "the faith" (verse 8), their end is utter folly which will be evident to everyone. The word "manifest" is *ekdēlos*, "clearly evident, clear, plain." The words "as theirs also was" refer back to Jannes and Jambres (verse 8). Timothy was assured that truth will triumph in the end. The cover-up of sin is unwise. Those who profess to love and serve God but seek to hide their evil desires and sinful actions will suffer shame in the end. If their sin is not exposed in this life, they will face it in the next.

3:10. Verse 10 begins a new section that might be titled "Paul's Final Advice to Timothy." It begins with the example of Paul's own experiences. His testimony would be an encouragement to Timothy who had an inclination toward timidity.

The "but thou" is emphatic and shows the contrast between Timothy and the men Paul had just been writing about. "Thou hast fully known" is the Greek word *parēkolouthēkas* which means literally "to follow alongside." Here it could be translated "have observed, investigated" (compare Luke 1:3). Paul commended Timothy for his responsive discipleship (compare 1 Timothy 4:6).

Paul then enumerated nine qualities that showed his own experiences. "Doctrine" ("teaching") is first. This is a major theme of both letters to Timothy. "Manner of life" (*agōgē*, "conduct, way of life") denotes Paul's general behavior. "Purpose" is *prothesei* and means "chief aim." "Faith" (*pistei*) is the body of truth that constitutes the gospel. "Long-suffering" is *makrothumia* and denotes "patience," especially patience with people. "Charity" is *agapē*, a love that seeks the best for others. "Patience" is *hupomonē* and is better translated "endurance" or "steadfastness." This is not passive patience but active mastery of the ups and downs of life.

8. Now as Jannes and Jambres withstood Moses: . . . set themselves against, *Wuest* . . . opposed Moses, *TCNT*.

so do these also resist the truth: . . . so also these people oppose the truth, *Adams* . . . withstand, *Montgomery* . . . set themselves against the truth, *Wuest*.

men of corrupt minds: . . . they are persons with corrupted minds, *Adams* . . . men of a depraved mind, *Concordant*.

reprobate concerning the faith: . . . and worthless in all that concerns the faith, *Montgomery* . . . disapproved concerning the Faith, *Wuest* . . . rejects when it comes to the faith, *Adams* . . . and counterfeits, *Berkeley* . . . They have failed the faith, *SEB*.

9. But they shall proceed no further: They will not, however, make very much progress, *TCNT* . . . But they will not get on, *Montgomery* . . . they shall make no further progress, *Wuest*.

for their folly shall be manifest unto all [men]: . . . their insane folly shall become evident to all, *Wuest* . . . will be as plain to everyone, *Adams* . . . will be obvious to all, *Lilly, Confraternity* . . . will be made as openly manifest to all, *Montgomery*.

as theirs also was: . . . as was that of, *Montgomery*.

10. But thou hast fully known: You, in contrast, *Adams* . . . But as for you, you were attracted as a disciple to me because of, *Wuest* . . . closely followed, *Confraternity* . . . have followed, *Montgomery*.

my doctrine, manner of life, purpose, faith: . . . motive, *Concordant* . . . my teaching, my conduct, my aims, *Montgomery*.

longsuffering, charity, patience: . . . my great concern, *Klingensmith* . . . patience, love, endurance, *Montgomery*.

3497.7 rel-pron pl neu	1466.4 prs-pron dat 1sing	1090.33 verb 3sing indic aor mid	1706.1 prep	487.2 name dat fem	1706.1 prep
οἷά	μοι	ἐγένετο	ἐν	Ἀντιοχείᾳ,	ἐν
hoia	moi	egeneto	en	Antiocheia	en
such as	to me	happened	in	Antioch,	in

2406.2 name dat neu	1706.1 prep	3054.2 name dat pl neu	3497.4 rel-pron acc pl masc	1369.6 noun acc pl masc
Ἰκονίῳ,	ἐν	Λύστροις,	οἵους	διωγμοὺς
Ikoniō	en	Lustrois	hoious	diōgmous
Iconium,	in	Lystra;	what manner of	persecutions

5135.2 verb 1sing indic aor act	2504.1 conj	1523.2 prep gen	3820.4 adj gen pl	1466.6 prs-pron acc 1sing	4363.6 verb 3sing indic aor mid
ὑπήνεγκα,	καὶ	ἐκ	πάντων	με	ἐρρύσατο
hupēnenka	kai	ek	pantōn	me	errhusato
I endured;	and	out of	all	me	delivered

3450.5 art nom sing masc	2935.1 noun nom sing masc		2504.1 conj	3820.7 adj nom pl masc	1156.2 conj	3450.7 art nom pl masc
ὁ	κύριος.	**12.** καὶ		πάντες	δὲ	οἱ
ho	kurios	kai		pantes	de	hoi
the	Lord.	And		all	indeed	the

2286.16 verb nom pl masc part pres act	2134.1 adv	2180.19 verb inf pres act	2180.19 verb inf pres act	2134.1 adv	1706.1 prep
θέλοντες	⸀ εὐσεβῶς	ζῆν	[ζῆν	εὐσεβῶς]	ἐν
thelontes	eusebōs	zēn	zēn	eusebōs	en
wishing	godly	to live	[to live	godly]	in

5382.3 name dat masc	2400.2 name dat masc	1371.26 verb 3pl indic fut pass		4050.8 adj nom pl masc	1156.2 conj
Χριστῷ	Ἰησοῦ	διωχθήσονται·	**13.** πονηροὶ		δὲ
Christō	Iēsou	diōchthēsontai	ponēroi		de
Christ	Jesus	will be persecuted.	Wicked		but

442.6 noun nom pl masc	2504.1 conj	1108.1 noun nom pl masc	4157.2 verb 3pl indic fut act	1894.3 prep	3450.16 art sing neu
ἄνθρωποι	καὶ	γόητες	προκόψουσιν	ἐπὶ	τὸ
anthrōpoi	kai	goētes	prokopsousin	epi	to
men	and	impostors	shall advance	to	the

5337.3 adj comp sing neu	3966.5 verb nom pl masc part pres act	2504.1 conj	3966.13 verb nom pl masc part pres mid	4622.1 prs-pron nom 2sing
χεῖρον,	πλανῶντες	καὶ	πλανώμενοι.	**14.** σὺ
cheiron	planōntes	kai	planōmenoi	su
worse,	misleading	and	being misled.	You

1156.2 conj	3176.8 verb 2sing impr pres act	1706.1 prep	3614.4 rel-pron dat pl	3101.7 verb 2sing indic aor act	2504.1 conj
δὲ	μένε	ἐν	οἷς	ἔμαθες	καὶ
de	mene	en	hois	emathes	kai
but	abide	in	which things	you did learn,	and

14.a.**Txt:** 04C-corr,06D 018K,020L,byz.bo. **Var:** 01ℵ,02A,04C-org 025P,33,Lach,Treg,Alf Tisc,We/Ho,Weis,Sod UBS/☆

3965.1 verb 2sing indic aor pass	3471.18 verb nom sing masc part perf act	3706.2 prep	4949.4 intr-pron gen sing	4949.5 intr-pron gen pl
ἐπιστώθης,	εἰδὼς	παρὰ	⸀ τίνος	[ᵃ☆ τίνων]
epistōthēs	eidōs	para	tinos	tinōn
were assured of,	having known	from	whom	[idem]

15.a.**Txt:** 02A,04C-org 06D-corr,018K,020L 025P,byz.Sod **Var:** 01ℵ,04C-corr 06D-org,33,Tisc,We/Ho Weis,UBS/☆

3101.7 verb 2sing indic aor act		2504.1 conj	3617.1 conj	570.3 prep	1018.2 noun gen sing neu	3450.17 art pl neu
ἔμαθες,	**15.** καὶ		ὅτι	ἀπὸ	βρέφους	⸀ τὰ ⸀
emathes	kai		hoti	apo	brephous	ta
you did learn;	and		that	from	a babe	the

3:11. The list continues with "persecutions" and "afflictions" Paul received in his missionary work in Antioch (Acts 13:50), Iconium (Acts 14:5,6), and Lystra (Acts 14:19,20). These three cities in Galatia were visited on Paul's first and second missionary journeys. Lystra was Timothy's hometown (Acts 16:1).

Paul then declared, "But out of them all the Lord delivered (rescued) me." This deliverance included a premature death by stoning (Acts 14:19,20). These triumphant words reflect the Psalmist's words in Psalm 34:17. Though in prison when he wrote, Paul was constantly aware of the hand of God in his life.

3:12. Paul now moved from his own experiences to encourage Timothy and all who would read this letter. Paul wrote, "In fact, everyone who wants to live a godly life in Christ Jesus will be persecuted" (NIV). This Biblical principle is found throughout the New Testament (see Matthew 10:22; Acts 14:22; Philippians 1:29; 1 Peter 4:12,13).

The "all that will" in the King James Version means "all who desire to, all who are so minded or determined." The idea of volitional choice is inherent in the Greek behind this phrase. The words "in Christ Jesus" mean more than "Christian." They stress the mystical union of the believer and Christ.

William Barclay comments: "It is Paul's conviction that the real follower of Christ cannot escape persecution .... If anyone proposes to accept a set of standards quite different from the world's, he is bound to encounter trouble. If anyone proposes to introduce into his life a loyalty which surpasses all earthly loyalties, there are bound to be clashes. And that is precisely what Christianity demands that a man should do" (*The Daily Study Bible Series, Letters to Timothy, Titus, and Philemon*, pp.197,198).

3:13. Some commentators see verse 13 as the start of a new section. But it seems more of a transitional sentence, linking Paul's experiences with his charge to Timothy that begins in verse 14. The "seducers" (*goetes*, "wizards, wailers") are "imposters" who "wax worse and worse" (*prokopsousin . . . cheiron*, "go from bad to worse"). The literal meaning of "wailers" refers to incantation by howling and implies these seducers/imposters were using black magic. While deceiving others, they deceived themselves.

3:14. In Paul's charge to Timothy, the apostle reminded his son "in the faith" (see 1 Timothy 1:2) of the basics of the Christian faith. These verses (14-17) are key texts of the letter. They could be titled "The Value of the Scriptures." Timothy was told to "continue" ("abide, stay") in what he had learned and had been "assured" ("convinced") of. He knew those who had taught him. The final clause is no doubt a reference not only to Paul as Timothy's spiritual "father," but to Timothy's mother and grandmother as well.

11. Persecutions, afflictions, which came unto me at Antioch, at Iconium, at Lystra: . . . as well as the persecutions and sufferings which befell me, *Montgomery* . . . the hurts, *Klingensmith* . . . and the sufferings that I underwent, *Adams.*

what persecutions I endured: You know all the persecutions, *Montgomery* . . . what persecutions I went through, *TCNT* . . . I bore, *Adams.*

but out of [them] all the Lord delivered me: . . . rescued me, *Berkeley.*

12. Yea, and all that will live godly in Christ Jesus shall suffer persecution: Yes indeed, *Williams* . . . In fact, all who want to, *Adams* . . . all who purpose to live a godly life, *Montgomery* . . . will be persecuted, *SEB* . . . will have plenty of trouble, *Klingensmith.*

13. But evil men and seducers shall wax worse and worse: . . . wicked men, *Berkeley* . . . and swindlers, *Concordant* . . . and pretenders, *Norlie* . . . and impostors will go from bad to worse, *Confraternity, TCNT* . . . will go on to their worst, *Adams.*

deceiving, and being deceived: . . . deceiving others, and being themselves deceived, *Montgomery* . . . misleading others and misled themselves, *Williams.*

14. But continue thou in the things which thou hast learned: . . . do you hold fast what you have learned, *Montgomery.*

and hast been assured of: . . . and are convinced of, *Adams* . . . and have held to be true, *Montgomery* . . . and been led to rely upon, *Williams.*

knowing of whom thou hast learned [them]: You know those from whom you have learned it, *Montgomery.*

2393.1 adj pl neu	1115.4 noun pl neu	3471.3 verb 2sing indic perf act	3450.17 art pl neu	1404.21 verb pl neu part pres mid
ἱερὰ	γράμματα	οἶδας,	τὰ	δυνάμενά
hiera	*grammata*	*oidas*	*ta*	*dunamena*
sacred	letters	you have known,	the	being able

4622.4 prs-pron acc 2sing	4532.1 verb inf aor act	1519.1 prep	4843.3 noun acc sing fem	1217.2 prep	3963.2 noun gen sing fem
σε	σοφίσαι	εἰς	σωτηρίαν	διὰ	πίστεως
se	*sophisai*	*eis*	*sōtērian*	*dia*	*pisteōs*
you	to make wise	to	salvation,	through	faith

3450.10 art gen sing fem	1706.1 prep	5382.3 name dat masc	2400.2 name masc	3820.9 adj nom sing fem	1118.1 noun nom sing fem
τῆς	ἐν	Χριστῷ	Ἰησοῦ.	**16.** πᾶσα	γραφὴ
tēs	*en*	*Christō*	*Iēsou*	*pasa*	*graphē*
the	in	Christ	Jesus.	Every	scripture

2292.1 adj sing fem	2504.1 conj	5457.1 adj nom sing fem	4242.1 prep	1313.4 noun acc sing fem
θεόπνευστος	καὶ	ὠφέλιμος	πρὸς	διδασκαλίαν,
theopneustos	*kai*	*ōphelimos*	*pros*	*didaskalian*
God breathed	and	profitable	for	teaching,

16.a.**Txt**: 06D,018K 020L,025P,byz.
Var: 01ℵ,02A,04C,Lach Treg,Alf,Tisc,We/Ho Weis,Sod,UBS/★

4242.1 prep	1637.2 noun acc sing masc	1635.1 noun acc sing masc	4242.1 prep	1867.1 noun acc sing fem
πρὸς	⸂ ἐλεγχόν,	[ª★ ἐλεγμόν,]	πρὸς	ἐπανόρθωσιν,
pros	*elenchon*	*elegmon*	*pros*	*epanorthōsin*
for	conviction,	[reproof,]	for	correction,

4242.1 prep	3672.4 noun acc sing fem	3450.12 art acc sing fem	1706.1 prep	1336.3 noun dat sing fem	2419.1 conj
πρὸς	παιδείαν	τὴν	ἐν	δικαιοσύνῃ·	**17.** ἵνα
pros	*paideian*	*tēn*	*en*	*dikaiosunē*	*hina*
for	discipline	the	in	righteousness;	that

734.1 adj nom sing masc	1498.10 verb 3sing subj pres act	3450.5 art nom sing masc	3450.2 art gen sing	2296.2 noun gen sing masc	442.1 noun nom sing masc
ἄρτιος	ᾖ	ὁ	τοῦ	θεοῦ	ἄνθρωπος,
artios	*ē*	*ho*	*tou*	*theou*	*anthrōpos*
complete	may be	the		of God	man,

4242.1 prep	3820.17 adj sing neu	2024.1 noun sing neu	18.3 adj sing neu	1806.2 verb nom sing masc part perf mid
πρὸς	πᾶν	ἔργον	ἀγαθὸν	ἐξηρτισμένος.
pros	*pan*	*ergon*	*agathon*	*exērtismenos*
to	every	work	good	having been fully fitted.

1.a.**Txt**: 06D-corr,018K 020L,byz.Sod
Var: 01ℵ,02A,04C 06D-org,025P,33,Gries Lach,Treg,Alf,Word Tisc,We/Ho,Weis UBS/★

1257.1 verb 1sing indic pres mid	3631.1 partic	1466.1 prs-pron nom 1sing	1783.1 prep	3450.2 art gen sing
4:1. Διαμαρτύρομαι	⸂ª οὖν	ἐγὼ ⸃	ἐνώπιον	τοῦ
Diamarturomai	*oun*	*egō*	*enōpion*	*tou*
Earnestly testify	therefore	I	before	

2296.2 noun gen sing masc	2504.1 conj	3450.2 art gen sing	2935.2 noun gen sing masc	2400.2 name masc	5382.2 name gen masc
θεοῦ	καὶ	⸂ᵇ τοῦ	κυρίου ⸃	⸂ Ἰησοῦ	Χριστοῦ,
theou	*kai*	*tou*	*kuriou*	*Iēsou*	*Christou*
God	and	the	Lord	Jesus	Christ.

1.b.**Txt**: 06D-corr,018K 020L,byz.
Var: 01ℵ,02A,04C 06D-org,025P,bo.Gries Lach,Treg,Alf,Word Tisc,We/Ho,Weis,Sod UBS/★

5382.2 name gen masc	2400.2 name masc	3450.2 art gen sing	3165.9 verb gen sing part pres act	2892.12 verb inf pres act
[★ Χριστοῦ	Ἰησοῦ,]	τοῦ	μέλλοντος	κρίνειν
Christou	*Iēsou*	*tou*	*mellontos*	*krinein*
[Christ	Jesus,]	the	being about	to judge

3:15. "From a child" means "from infancy, from a babe." "The holy Scriptures" refers to the Old Testament and can also be translated "the Sacred Writings." A Jewish boy began to study the Old Testament at the age of 5. Timothy was even younger when his mother Eunice and his grandmother Lois taught him at home (see 1:5). They taught him the Old Testament discipline of obedience to God and pointed him to the coming Messiah. As he responded in faith, Timothy received the salvation God had promised in the Old Testament and provided in the person of His Son Jesus Christ.

The words "able to make thee wise unto salvation" carry the idea of giving the ability to make the choice that results in salvation. "Able" is the present participle that means a permanent, enduring quality.

3:16. This verse is the "Golden Text" on the inspiration of the Word. "All Scripture" in this context (see verse 15) refers primarily to the Old Testament since much of the New Testament had not been written. Of course, the New Testament also has adequate support for believing it was divinely inspired. The phrase "given by inspiration of God" is one word in the Greek, *theopneustos*, which means "God-breathed." Inspiration was the process used to produce "all Scripture." By the inbreathing of the Holy Spirit, men spoke or wrote the actual words of God (see 2 Peter 1:21).

This inspiration applies only to the original documents we call autographs. Archaeological discoveries have not produced a single autograph. All we have today are copies of those originals. Though there are minor differences in these copies, they are in perfect agreement concerning the major doctrines of the Christian faith.

The second half of verse 16 lists four profitable uses of Scripture. (1) "Doctrine" ("teaching") is important to a correct understanding of the truth and the reception of salvation. (2) "Reproof" ("rebuking" or "conviction of sin") from reading or hearing the Word of God is important to conviction, repentance, and confession. (3) "Correction" ("restoration to an upright position or a right state") brings man back to a proper relationship with God. (4) "Instruction ('training, discipline') in righteousness" is profitable because it gives God's view of life's priorities.

3:17. All these uses of Scripture have a purpose: "that the man of God may be perfect, thoroughly furnished unto all good works." The word "perfect" means "fit, capable, complete." "Furnished" means "equipped." The result is "all good works."

4:1. The central theme of Paul's final charge to Timothy comes into sharp focus at the beginning of chapter 4. Verses 1-5 are a key passage of the entire letter. Though Paul had written some very important words, his "charge" here is direct, brief, and emphatic. "Before God" means "in the presence of God."

15. And that from a child thou hast known the holy scriptures: . . . from childhood, *Adams* . . . from thy infancy, *Confraternity* . . . you are acquainted, *Concordant* . . . the Sacred Writings, *TCNT*.
which are able to make thee wise unto salvation: . . . which are able to instruct you, *RSV* . . . to make you wise about salvation, *Adams*.
through faith which is in Christ Jesus:

16. All scripture [is] given by inspiration of God, and [is] profitable: Every Scripture, seeing that it is God-breathed, *Montgomery* . . . is breathed out by, *Adams* . . . is inspired by, *Norlie* . . . and useful, *SEB* . . . is valuable for, *Klingensmith*.
for doctrine, for reproof, for correction: . . . for teaching, *SEB* . . . for conviction, *Adams* . . . for refuting error, for giving guidance, *TCNT*.
for instruction in righteousness: . . . for disciplined training, *Adams* . . . for training in doing what is right, *Norlie* . . . for training others in the path of duty, *TCNT*.

17. That the man of God may be perfect: . . . may himself be complete, *Montgomery* . . . will be right, *SEB*.
thoroughly furnished unto all good works: . . . well-fitted and adequately equipped for, *Berkeley* . . . up to date, *Klingensmith* . . . completely fitted for, *Campbell* . . . fully equipped for, *Norlie* . . . completely equipped for every good work, *Montgomery* . . . fitted out for every good act, *Concordant* . . . and perfectly equipped for every good action, *TCNT* . . . for every good task, *Adams*.

1. I charge [thee] therefore before God, and the Lord Jesus Christ: I solemnly call on you, *Adams* . . . I adjure you in the presence of God, *Montgomery*.

2 Timothy 4:2

1.c.Txt: 01א-corr
06D-corr,018K,020L
025P,byz.sa.
Var: 01א-org,02A,04C
06D-org,33,it.bo.Gries
Lach,Treg,Alf,Word
Tisc,We/Ho,Weis,Sod
UBS/✶

2180.15 verb acc pl masc part pres act	2504.1 conj	3361.7 adj acc pl masc	2567.3 prep	2504.1 conj	3450.12 art acc sing fem
ζῶντας	καὶ	νεκρούς,	ʿ κατὰ	[ᶜ✶ καὶ]	τὴν
zōntas	kai	nekrous	kata	kai	tēn
living	and	dead	according to	[and]	the

1999.3 noun acc sing fem	840.3 prs-pron gen sing	2504.1 conj	3450.12 art acc sing fem	926.4 noun acc sing fem	840.3 prs-pron gen sing
ἐπιφάνειαν	αὐτοῦ	καὶ	τὴν	βασιλείαν	αὐτοῦ,
epiphaneian	autou	kai	tēn	basileian	autou
appearing	his	and	the	kingdom	his,

2756.15 verb 2sing impr aor act	3450.6 art acc sing masc	3030.4 noun acc sing masc	2168.4 verb 2sing impr aor act	2103.1 adv
2. κήρυξον	τὸν	λόγον,	ἐπίστηθι	εὐκαίρως
kēruxon	ton	logon	epistēthi	eukairōs
proclaim	the	word;	be urgent	in season,

169.1 adv	1638.6 verb 2sing impr aor act	1992.6 verb 2sing impr aor act	3731.16 verb 2sing impr aor act	1706.1 prep
ἀκαίρως,	ἔλεγξον,	ἐπιτίμησον,	παρακάλεσον,	ἐν
akairōs	elenxon	epitimēson	parakaleson	en
out of season,	convict,	rebuke,	encourage,	with

3820.11 adj dat sing fem	3087.3 noun dat sing fem	2504.1 conj	1316.3 noun dat sing fem	1498.40 verb 3sing indic fut act	1056.1 conj
πάσῃ	μακροθυμίᾳ	καὶ	διδαχῇ.	3. ἔσται	γὰρ
pasē	makrothumia	kai	didachē	estai	gar
all	patience	and	teaching.	There will be	for

2511.1 noun nom sing masc	3616.1 conj	3450.10 art gen sing fem	5039.7 verb gen sing fem part pres act	1313.1 noun fem	3620.2 partic
καιρὸς	ὅτε	τῆς	ὑγιαινούσης	διδασκαλίας	οὐκ
kairos	hote	tēs	hugiainousēs	didaskalias	ouk
a time	when	the	being sound	teaching	not

428.6 verb 3pl indic fut mid	233.2 conj	2567.3 prep	3450.15 art acc pl fem	1924.1 noun fem
ἀνέξονται,	ἀλλὰ	κατὰ	τὰς	ʿ ἐπιθυμίας
anexontai	alla	kata	tas	epithumias
they will bear;	but	according to	the	lusts

3.a.Txt: 018K,020L,byz.
Sod
Var: 01א,02A,04C,06D
025P,Gries,Lach,Treg
Alf,Word,Tisc,We/Ho
Weis,UBS/✶

3450.15 art acc pl fem	2375.9 adj fem	2375.9 adj fem	1924.1 noun fem	1431.7 prs-pron dat pl masc
τὰς	ἰδίας	[ᵃ✶ ἰδίας	ἐπιθυμίας]	ἑαυτοῖς
tas	idias	idias	epithumias	heautois
the	their own	[their own	desires]	to themselves

1986.1 verb 3pl indic fut act	1314.6 noun acc pl masc	2806.1 verb nom pl masc part pres mid	3450.12 art acc sing fem
ἐπισωρεύσουσιν	διδασκάλους,	κνηθόμενοι	τὴν
episōreusousin	didaskalous	knēthomenoi	tēn
will heap up	teachers,	tickling	the

187.4 noun acc sing fem	2504.1 conj	570.3 prep	3173.1 conj	3450.10 art gen sing fem	223.2 noun gen sing fem	3450.12 art acc sing fem
ἀκοήν·	4. καὶ	ἀπὸ	μὲν	τῆς	ἀληθείας	τὴν
akoēn	kai	apo	men	tēs	alētheias	tēn
ear;	and	from	men	the	truth	the

187.4 noun acc sing fem	648.5 verb 3pl indic fut act	1894.3 prep	1156.2 conj	3450.8 art acc pl masc	3316.2 noun acc pl masc
ἀκοὴν	ἀποστρέψουσιν,	ἐπὶ	δὲ	τοὺς	μύθους
akoēn	apostrepsousin	epi	de	tous	muthous
ear	they will turn away,	to	and	the	myths

When Paul referred to "the Lord Jesus Christ" he added "who shall judge the quick (living) and the dead." This idea of judgment is a primary theme of Paul's preaching and writing (see Acts 17:31; Romans 2:16; 1 Corinthians 4:5). Jesus Christ is the One to whom this judgment is given by the Father. It will happen "at his appearing and (the coming of) his kingdom." "Appearing" is *epiphaneian*, a Greek term used to refer to the Roman emperor's (1) ascension to the throne and (2) visit to a province or town. In this application, both concepts fit Christ's appearing and kingdom.

4:2. Five exhortations in this verse comprise the focus of Paul's charge to Timothy. The aorist tense adds solemnity to the imperatives. Timothy was commanded to "preach the word"; this reference is to the gospel he heard from Paul.

"Be instant in season, out of season" is rendered in the *Amplified Bible*, "Keep your sense of urgency . . . , be at hand and ready, whether the opportunity seems to be favorable or unfavorable, whether it is convenient or inconvenient, whether it be welcome or unwelcome." "Instant" is the verb *ephistēthi*, "to stand by, be at hand," i.e., "prepared, ready, urgent."

"Reprove" is the Greek *elenxon*, "correct, convince." Compare 1 Timothy 5:20; Titus 1:13; 2:15 for Paul's other uses of this term. "Rebuke" is *epitimēson*, a term denoting censure. "Exhort" is *parakaleson*, a term that may be translated "exhort" or "encourage" depending on the context. Either meaning may be used here. "Reprove" and "rebuke" are negative terms that denote correction and discipline. "Exhort/encourage" means to bring comfort and edification.

All of these imperatives are to be accompanied by "great patience and careful instruction" (NIV). Here are both the manner ("patience") and the method ("careful instruction") Timothy should use.

4:3. Paul warned Timothy of a future time when opposition to the gospel would be flagrant. Men would not "endure (*anexontai*, 'bear with, put up with, have the mind or patience to receive') sound doctrine ('teaching')." Instead, they would "heap" (*episōreusousin*, "heap together, accumulate") teachers who would say things that would tickle their ears. The idea behind "itching ears" is that of entertainment. Such people want their ears tickled with sensational, stimulating oratory. So, opportunistic teachers take advantage of them and tell them what they want to hear.

4:4. Because some would not put up with sound doctrine, they would "turn away their ears from the truth." This suggests a deliberate refusal to hear the truth of the gospel. When they did this, then they would "be turned unto fables." "Turned unto" is from *ektrapēsontai*, a Greek verb that suggests a wandering from the true path without knowing it. "Fables" is *muthoi*, "myths."

who shall judge the quick and the dead: . . . the living, *Williams*.
at his appearing and his kingdom:

2. Preach the word: Herald the message, *Berkeley*.
be instant in season, out of season: . . . be prepared, *NIV* . . . be earnest, *Young* . . . stay at it, *Williams* . . . Preach it when it is easy and people want to listen and when it is hard and people do not want to listen, *NLT* . . . in good times and bad times, *Klingensmith*.
reprove, rebuke, exhort: . . . convince, *TCNT*.
with all longsuffering and doctrine:

3. For the time will come: For the era will be when, *Concordant* . . . for there shall be a season, *Young*.
when they will not endure sound doctrine: . . . when men will not put up with, *NIV* . . . they will not listen to, *Williams* . . . when they will not tolerate wholesome instruction, *Berkeley* . . . will not put up with healthy teaching, *SEB* . . . wholesome doctrine, *Campbell* . . . sound teaching, *TCNT*.
but after their own lusts: . . . to gratify their own evil desires, *Williams*.
shall they heap to themselves teachers: . . . will surround themselves with, *Williams* . . . many teachers, *SEB*.
having itching ears: . . . to say what they want to hear, *SEB* . . . that will tickle their ears, *Berkeley* . . . tickle their itching fancies, *Norlie*.

4. And they shall turn away [their] ears from the truth: They will not listen, *NLT*.
and shall be turned unto fables: . . . to hear myths, *Berkeley* . . . to fairy stories, *Klingensmith*.

1610.4 verb 3pl indic fut pass	4622.1 prs-pron nom 2sing	1156.2 conj	3387.2 verb 2sing impr pres act	1706.1 prep	3820.5 adj dat pl
ἐκτραπήσονται.	5. σὺ	δὲ	νῆφε	ἐν	πᾶσιν,
ektrapēsontai	su	de	nēphe	en	pasin
will be turned aside.	You	but,	be sober	in	all things,

5.a.Var: 01ℵ-org

5.b.Var: 02A

2524.3 verb 2sing impr aor act		5453.1 conj	2541.3 adj nom sing masc	4608.1 noun nom sing masc
[ᵃ κακοπάθησον,		[ᵇ+ ὡς	καλὸς	στρατιωτης
kakopathēson		hōs	kalos	stratiōtēs
suffer hardships,		[as	good	a soldier

5382.2 name gen masc	2400.2 name masc	2024.1 noun sing neu	4020.34 verb 2sing impr aor act	2078.1 noun gen sing masc
Χριστοῦ	Ἰησοῦ,]	ἔργον	ποίησον	εὐαγγελιστοῦ,
Christou	Iēsou	ergon	poiēson	euangelistou
of Christ	Jesus,]	work	do	of an evangelist,

3450.12 art acc sing fem	1242.4 noun acc sing fem	4622.2 prs-pron gen 2sing	3995.1 verb 2sing impr aor act	1466.1 prs-pron nom 1sing
τὴν	διακονίαν	σου	πληροφόρησον.	6. Ἐγὼ
tēn	diakonian	sou	plērophorēson	Egō
the	service	your	fully carry out.	I

1056.1 conj	2218.1 adv	4542.1 verb 1sing indic pres mid	2504.1 conj	3450.5 art nom sing masc	2511.1 noun nom sing masc
γὰρ	ἤδη	σπένδομαι,	καὶ	ὁ	καιρὸς
gar	ēdē	spendomai	kai	ho	kairos
for	already	am being poured out,	and	the	time

6.a.Txt: 06D,018K,020L byz.
Var: 01ℵ,02A,04C,025P 33,Lach,Treg,Tisc We/Ho,Weis,Sod UBS/✮

7.a.Txt: 06D,018K,020L 025P,byz.Sod
Var: 01ℵ,02A,04C,33 Lach,Treg,Tisc,We/Ho Weis,UBS/✮

3450.10 art gen sing fem	1684.7 adj gen sing fem	357.1 noun gen sing fem	357.1 noun gen sing fem	1466.2 prs-pron gen 1sing
τῆς	ἐμῆς	ἀναλύσεώς	[ᵃ✮ ἀναλύσεώς	μου]
tēs	emēs	analuseōs	analuseōs	mou
of the	my	release	[release	my]

2168.8 verb 3sing indic perf act	3450.6 art acc sing masc	72.2 noun acc sing masc	3450.6 art acc sing masc	2541.1 adj sing	2541.1 adj sing
ἐφέστηκεν.	7. τὸν	ἀγῶνα	τὸν	καλὸν	[ᵃ✮ καλὸν
ephestēken	ton	agōna	ton	kalon	kalon
is come.	The	contest	the	good	[good

72.2 noun acc sing masc	74.4 verb 1sing indic perf mid	3450.6 art acc sing masc	1402.1 noun acc sing masc	4903.8 verb 1sing indic perf act
ἀγῶνα]	ἠγώνισμαι,	τὸν	δρόμον	τετέλεκα,
agōna	ēgōnismai	ton	dromon	teteleka
combat]	I have contested,	the	course	I have finished,

3450.12 art acc sing fem	3963.4 noun acc sing fem	4931.22 verb 1sing indic perf act	3036.8 adj sing neu	601.1 verb 3sing indic pres mid
τὴν	πίστιν	τετήρηκα·	8. λοιπὸν	ἀπόκειταί
tēn	pistin	tetērēka	loipon	apokeitai
the	faith	I have kept.	Henceforth	is being laid up

1466.4 prs-pron dat 1sing	3450.5 art nom sing masc	3450.10 art gen sing fem	1336.2 noun gen sing fem	4586.1 noun nom sing masc	3614.6 rel-pron acc sing masc
μοι	ὁ	τῆς	δικαιοσύνης	στέφανος,	ὃν
moi	ho	tēs	dikaiosunēs	stephanos	hon
for me	the	of the	righteousness	crown,	which

586.17 verb 3sing indic fut act	1466.4 prs-pron dat 1sing	3450.5 art nom sing masc	2935.1 noun nom sing masc	1706.1 prep	1552.11 dem-pron dat sing fem
ἀποδώσει	μοι	ὁ	κύριος	ἐν	ἐκείνῃ
apodōsei	moi	ho	kurios	en	ekeinē
will reward	to me	the	Lord	in	that

4:5. Here are found four brief imperatives directed exclusively to Timothy. "Watch" (*nēphe*, "be sober") suggests moral alertness (compare 1 Thessalonians 5:6,8). The meaning here is that of self-control and self-possession. "Endure afflictions" is similar to Paul's charge in 2:3. "Afflictions" may be translated "hardship, suffering." It is the same word used in 2:3; there it is translated "endure hardness."

"Evangelist" (*euangelistou*, literally, "a messenger of good") denotes a preacher of the gospel. It is used three times in the New Testament: here, Acts 21:8, and Ephesians 4:11. Though Timothy had important administrative duties in Ephesus, he was not to neglect bold, public declaration of the gospel.

"Make full proof (*plērophorēson*) of thy ministry (*diakonian*)" contains the idea of fulfillment. The *Amplified Bible* renders it: "Fully perform all the duties of your ministry."

4:6. Verses 6-8 contain very personal remarks about Paul's view of his "departure" and beyond. Two illustrations show Paul's triumphant view of death. The first is the Old Testament "drink offering" (wine poured around the base of the altar, Numbers 15:1-10). Paul said, "I am now ready to be offered" ("poured out as a libation"). The verb tense indicates the action is already in process.

The second illustration is found in the word "departure." It is the Greek *analuseōs* which literally means "loosing" (as a ship from its moorings or an animal from its yoke) or "dismantling" (as of a tent). The loosing connotes freedom. The dismantling of a tent is reminiscent of the words in 2 Peter 1:14,15.

4:7. The three illustrations in this verse relate to the Olympic Games. "I have fought a good fight" (*agōna*, "contest, struggle"). "I have finished my course" (*dromon*, "race"). Notice Paul did not say, "I have won my race." Rather, he said "finished."

Two meanings are possible in the phrase "I have kept the faith." The first is from the games: "I have kept the rules" (compare 2:5). The second is from the business world: "I have kept the conditions of the contract." Paul had "guarded the deposit of Christian truth" (compare 1:14). See *Various Versions* for a fuller meaning.

4:8. "Henceforth (*loipon*, 'already') there is laid up (*apokeitai*, 'reserved, set aside') for me a crown of righteousness ('laurel wreath of honor')." Paul knew he would receive this crown "at that day" (the Day, when Christ will come again). Then he added that "the Lord, the righteous judge," will award a crown to everyone who loves His appearing. The perfect tense suggests they have loved and will continue to love His appearing.

5. But watch thou in all things, endure afflictions: Use self-control in everything, *SEB* . . . keep your head in all situations, *NIV* . . . be always self-controlled, *Montgomery* . . . Face hardships, *TCNT*.

do the work of an evangelist: . . . do the work of a Missionary, *TCNT, Montgomery.*

make full proof of thy ministry: Finish your ministry, *SEB* . . . discharge all the duties of your ministry, *NIV, Montgomery* . . . fully perform your ministry, *Campbell* . . . of your Office, *TCNT.*

6. For I am now ready to be offered: I for my part am a libation, *Montgomery* . . . I am already being poured out in sacrifice, *Confraternity.*

and the time of my departure is at hand: . . . the time of my release hath arrived, *Young* . . . and the time of my unmooring is at hand, *Montgomery.*

7. I have fought a good fight: . . . fought in the glorious contest, *Montgomery* . . . the grand fight, *Berkeley.*

I have finished [my] course: I have finished my career, *Concordant* . . . I have finished the work I was to do, *NLT* . . . I have finished the race, *SEB* . . . I have run the race, *Montgomery.*

I have kept the faith: I have continued faithful, *Campbell* . . . I have preserved, *TCNT.*

8. Henceforth there is laid up for me a crown of righteousness: At last, *SEB* . . . there is in store for me, *NIV* . . . there is reserved, *Klingensmith* . . . There is a prize, *NLT* . . . the garland of righteousness, *Montgomery.*

which the Lord, the righteous judge, shall give me at that day: . . . will award to me, *Montgomery.*

3450.11 art dat sing fem	2232.3 noun dat sing fem	3450.5 art nom sing masc	1337.3 adj nom sing masc	2896.1 noun nom sing masc	3620.3 partic	3303.1 adv
τῇ	ἡμέρᾳ,	ὁ	δίκαιος	κριτής·	οὐ	μόνον
tē	hēmera	ho	dikaios	kritēs	ou	monon
the	day	the	righteous	judge;	not	only

1156.2 conj	1466.5 prs- pron dat 1sing	233.2 conj	2504.1 conj	3820.5 adj dat pl	3450.4 art dat pl	25.37 verb dat pl masc part perf act
δὲ	ἐμοὶ,	ἀλλὰ	καὶ	πᾶσιν	τοῖς	ἠγαπηκόσιν
de	emoi	alla	kai	pasin	tois	ēgapēkosin
and	to me,	but	also	to all	the	having loved

3450.12 art acc sing fem	1999.3 noun acc sing fem	840.3 prs- pron gen sing		4557.5 verb 2sing impr aor act	2048.23 verb inf aor act
τὴν	ἐπιφάνειαν	αὐτοῦ.	**9.** Σπούδασον		ἐλθεῖν
tēn	epiphaneian	autou	Spoudason		elthein
the	appearing	his.	Be diligent		to come

4242.1 prep	1466.6 prs- pron acc 1sing	4878.1 adv		1208.1 name nom masc	1056.1 conj	1466.6 prs- pron acc 1sing
πρός	με	ταχέως.	**10.** Δημᾶς		γὰρ	με
pros	me	tacheōs	Dēmas		gar	me
to	me	quickly;	Demas		for	me

	1452.3 verb 3sing indic aor act		1452.10 verb 3sing act	25.20 verb nom sing masc part aor act	3450.6 art acc sing masc
	⟨☆ ἐγκατέλιπεν,	[ᵃ	ἐγκατέλειπεν,]	ἀγαπήσας	τὸν
	enkatelipen		enkateleipen	agapēsas	ton
	deserted,		[was deserting,]	having loved	the

10.a.**Txt:** 01א,044,byz.
Var: 02A,04C,06D-corr2
010F,012G,020L,025P
33,81,1175,1881

3431.1 adv	163.3 noun acc sing masc	2504.1 conj	4057.16 verb 3sing indic aor pass	1519.1 prep	2309.3 name acc fem
νῦν	αἰῶνα,	καὶ	ἐπορεύθη	εἰς	Θεσσαλονίκην·
nun	aiōna	kai	eporeuthē	eis	Thessalonikēn
now	age,	and	is gone	to	Thessalonica;

10.b.**Var:** 01א,04C,81
104,326

2885.1 name nom masc	1519.1 prep	1046.2 name acc fem	1051.4 name acc masc	4951.1 name nom masc
Κρήσκης	εἰς	⟨☆ Γαλατίαν,	[ᵇ Γαλλιαν,]	Τίτος
Krēskēs	eis	Galatian	Gallian	Titos
Crescens	to	Galatia,	[Gallia,]	Titus

1519.1 prep	1144.1 name acc fem		3037.1 name nom masc	1498.4 verb 3sing indic pres act	3304.2 adj nom sing masc	3196.2 prep
εἰς	Δαλματίαν·	**11.** Λουκᾶς		ἐστιν	μόνος	μετ'
eis	Dalmatian	Loukas		estin	monos	met'
to	Dalmatia.	Luke		is	alone	with

1466.3 prs- pron gen 1sing	3111.3 name acc masc	351.4 verb nom sing masc part aor act	70.5 verb 2sing impr pres act	3196.3 prep	4427.1 prs-pron gen sing masc
ἐμοῦ.	Μᾶρκον	ἀναλαβὼν	ἄγε	μετὰ	σεαυτοῦ·
emou	Markon	analabōn	age	meta	seautou
me.	Mark	having taken	bring	with	yourself,

1498.4 verb 3sing indic pres act	1056.1 conj	1466.4 prs- pron dat 1sing	2154.2 adj nom sing masc	1519.1 prep	1242.4 noun acc sing fem
ἔστιν	γάρ	μοι	εὔχρηστος	εἰς	διακονίαν.
estin	gar	moi	euchrēstos	eis	diakonian
he is	for	to me	useful	for	service.

	5031.3 name acc masc	1156.2 conj	643.6 verb 1sing indic aor act	1519.1 prep	2163.3 name acc fem	3450.6 art acc sing masc
12. Τυχικὸν		δὲ	ἀπέστειλα	εἰς	Ἔφεσον.	**13.** Τὸν
	Tuchikon	de	apesteila	eis	Epheson	Ton
	Tychicus	but	I sent	to	Ephesus.	The

4:9. Verse 9 begins a new section that includes personal instructions, greetings, and a final testimony. Paul wanted to see Timothy before he died so he wrote, "Do thy diligence (do your best) to come shortly (quickly) unto me." He repeated this request a little later, implying that inclement weather might prevent Timothy from coming if he did not "come before winter" (verse 21).

4:10. As Paul began his list of coworkers, a blight appears. "Demas hath forsaken (deserted) me, having loved this present world" (aiōna, "age, era, life"). Paul had mentioned Demas twice before. In Philemon 24 Paul called him a "fellow laborer." In Colossians 4:14 Paul merely mentioned Demas' name. And now the apostle called him a deserter. The charge was not that Demas had deserted the Faith or the Church; he had deserted Paul. This suggests Demas left Paul when Paul needed him most.

Crescens had departed to Galatia. Nothing else is mentioned in Scripture regarding Crescens. Galatia was either the northern area of Asia Minor (Gaul) or a Roman province in what is now central Turkey. Titus had been sent to Dalmatia. Titus had earlier been sent as an emissary to Corinth (2 Corinthians 8:16ff.), then was left on the island of Crete (Titus 1:4,5).

4:11. This verse includes information and instructions concerning two other coworkers. First, Paul wrote, "Only Luke is with me." Paul called Luke "the beloved physician" in Colossians 4:14 and listed Luke among the "fellow laborers" in Philemon 24. (Note that these references are the same as those mentioning Demas.) Possibly Luke stayed with Paul to care for the physical needs of the aged apostle.

"Take Mark, and bring him with thee: for he is profitable (eu-chrēstos, 'helpful, useful') to me for the ministry (diakonian, a term meaning general 'service')." This service could either be in the gospel or to Paul's personal needs. John Mark had earlier deserted Paul and Barnabas (Acts 13:13), but later he proved himself and attended Paul in his first Roman imprisonment (Colossians 4:10; Philemon 24). Now Paul said Mark was useful in service.

4:12. Tychicus was a trusted emissary who carried at least two other epistles to their destinations. The Epistle to the Ephesians came via Tychicus from an earlier imprisonment of Paul in Rome (see Ephesians 6:21,22). From that same imprisonment, the Epistle to the Colossians was delivered by Tychicus (see Colossians 4:7,8). In addition, Tychicus may have brought this letter to Timothy since Paul was sending him to Ephesus. It is also possible that Tychicus delivered Paul's letter to Titus (see Titus 3:12).

This reference to Tychicus' departure for Ephesus may give reason for Paul's request that Mark be brought to Rome. Paul needed Mark to take Tychicus' place. Too, Tychicus could have been sent to replace Timothy in Ephesus.

and not to me only: . . . me alone, Adams.

but unto all them also that love his appearing: . . . who love His advent, Concordant . . . who have longed for, SEB . . . to all who desire His appearing, Fenton.

9. Do thy diligence to come shortly unto me: Do your best to come to me soon, Adams, Williams . . . Try to come to me soon, Fenton . . . Make haste to visit me soon, Berkeley . . . to come to me speedily, Montgomery.

10. For Demas hath forsaken me: . . . has deserted me, TCNT, Montgomery . . . abandoned me, SEB . . . has left me, Fenton.

having loved this present world: . . . for love of, Montgomery . . . loving the present age, Fenton.

and is departed unto Thessalonica: . . . and is gone to, Montgomery . . . and went off to, Adams.

Crescens to Galatia, Titus unto Dalmatia:

11. Only Luke is with me: Luke alone is, Adams . . . There is no one but Luke with me, TCNT . . . is the only one who is now with me, Williams.

Take Mark, and bring him with thee: Taking up Mark, Fenton . . . Bring Mark when you come, NLT . . . Pick up Mark, Montgomery, Williams . . . Get Mark, Adams.

for he is profitable to me for the ministry: . . . for he is useful to me, Confraternity . . . he is useful for the work, SEB . . . for he can be of great help to me, Norlie . . . He is a great help, Klingensmith . . . he is useful to me in my ministry, Montgomery . . . useful in serving me, Adams.

12. And Tychicus have I sent to Ephesus: I dispatch to, Concordant.

2 Timothy 4:14

13.a.Txt: 01א,06D,044 byz.
Var: 02A,04C,010F 012G,020L,025P,33 104,326,1175,1881

5153.1 noun acc sing masc	3614.6 rel-pron acc sing masc	614.1 verb 1sing indic aor act	614.4 verb 1sing act	1706.1 prep
φαιλόνην	ὃν	ʼ☆ ἀπέλιπον	[ᵃ ἀπέλειπον]	ἐν
phailonēn	hon	apelipon	apeleipon	en
cloak	which	I left	[I was leaving]	in

5015.2 name dat fem	3706.2 prep	2562.1 name dat masc	2048.44 verb nom sing masc part pres mid	5179.6 verb 2sing impr pres act	2504.1 conj
Τρῳάδι	παρὰ	Κάρπῳ	ἐρχόμενος	φέρε,	καὶ
Trōadi	para	Karpō	erchomenos	phere	kai
Troas	with	Carpus,	coming	bring,	and

3450.17 art pl neu	968.4 noun pl neu	3094.1 adv sup	3450.15 art acc pl fem	3170.1 noun acc pl fem
τὰ	βιβλία,	μάλιστα	τὰς	μεμβράνας.
ta	biblia,	malista	tas	membranas.
the	books,	especially	the	parchments.

221.1 name nom masc	3450.5 art nom sing masc	5307.1 noun nom sing masc	4044.17 adj pl neu	1466.4 prs-pron dat 1sing
14. Ἀλέξανδρος	ὁ	χαλκεὺς	πολλὰ	μοι
Alexandros	ho	chalkeus	polla	moi
Alexander	the	smith	many	against me

14.a.Txt: 06D-corr,018K 020L,byz.
Var: 01א,02A,04C 06D-org,33,bo.Lach Treg,Alf,Word,Tisc We/Ho,Weis,Sod UBS/☆

2527.9 adj pl neu	1715.4 verb 3sing indic aor mid	586.10 verb 3sing opt aor act	586.17 verb 3sing indic fut act	840.4 prs-pron dat sing
κακὰ	ἐνεδείξατο·	ʼ ἀποδῴη	[ᵃ☆ ἀποδώσει]	αὐτῷ
kaka	enedeixato	apodōē	apodōsei	autō
evil things	did.	May repay	[will repay]	to him

3450.5 art nom sing masc	2935.1 noun nom sing masc	2567.3 prep	3450.17 art pl neu	2024.4 noun pl neu	840.3 prs-pron gen sing
ὁ	κύριος	κατὰ	τὰ	ἔργα	αὐτοῦ·
ho	kurios	kata	ta	erga	autou
the	Lord	according to	the	works	his.

3614.6 rel-pron acc sing masc	2504.1 conj	4622.1 prs-pron nom 2sing	5278.15 verb 2sing impr pres mid	3003.1 adv	1056.1 conj
15. ὃν	καὶ	σὺ	φυλάσσου,	λίαν	γὰρ
hon	kai	su	phulassou,	lian	gar
Whom	also	you	guard against,	exceedingly	for

15.a.Txt: 01א-corr 06D-corr,018K,020L 025P,byz.Sod
Var: 01א-org,02A,04C 06D-org,33,Lach,Treg Alf,Word,Tisc,We/Ho Weis,UBS/☆

434.5 verb 3sing indic perf act	434.9 verb 3sing indic aor act	3450.4 art dat pl	2233.3 adj dat 1pl masc	3030.7 noun dat pl masc
ʼ ἀνθέστηκεν	[ᵃ☆ ἀντέστη]	τοῖς	ἡμετέροις	λόγοις.
anthestēken	antestē	tois	hēmeterois	logois.
he has withstood	[he opposed]	the	our	words.

1706.1 prep	3450.11 art dat sing fem	4272.11 num ord dat sing fem	1466.2 prs-pron gen 1sing	621.3 noun dat sing fem	3625.2 num card nom masc
16. Ἐν	τῇ	πρώτῃ	μου	ἀπολογίᾳ	οὐδείς
En	tē	prōtē	mou	apologia	oudeis
In	the	first	my	defense	no one

16.a.Txt: 01א-corr,06D 018K,020L,025P,byz. Sod
Var: 01א-org,02A,04C 33,Lach,Treg,Tisc We/Ho,Weis,UBS/☆

1466.4 prs-pron dat 1sing	4687.1 verb 3sing indic aor mid	3716.3 verb 3sing indic aor mid	233.2 conj
μοι	ʼ συμπαρεγένετο,	[ᵃ☆ παρεγένετο,]	ἀλλὰ
moi	sumparegeneto,	paregeneto,	alla
me	stood with,	[stood beside,]	but

16.b.Txt: 01א,06D-org 044,byz.
Var: 02A,04C,06D-corr1 010F,012G,020L,025P 33,104,326,1175

3820.7 adj nom pl masc	1466.6 prs-pron acc 1sing	1452.4 verb 3pl indic aor act	1452.11 verb 3pl act
πάντες	με	ʼ☆ ἐγκατέλιπον·	[ᵇ ἐγκατέλειπον·]
pantes	me	enkatelipon	enkateleipon
all	me	forsook.	[were forsaking.]

472

4:13. In this verse Paul referred to personal belongings: his cloak, books, and parchments. The "cloak" (*phailonēn*) was a large outer garment that was sleeveless and circular in shape with a hole in the middle for the head. It resembled a poncho and extended to the ground. This cloak would help Paul cope with the cold, damp atmosphere of his prison cell.

The "books" (*biblia*, "scrolls") were of papyrus, an inexpensive writing material. The "parchments" (*membranas*) were made from animal skins (vellum). Some commentators speculate that the parchments were Paul's official papers such as his certificate of Roman citizenship. These same commentators also say the parchments could have been copied portions of the Old Testament and that Paul would want the Scriptures with him during the coming winter (verse 21).

Donald Guthrie comments: "It is impossible to say what either the books or the parchments (*membranai*) were, but the latter word suggests documents of some value, since vellum was too expensive to replace the common papyrus for general purposes . . . . But though there can be no more than speculation about their identity, the desire to receive them throws interesting light on Paul's literary pursuits, even while on missionary journeys. It is not impossible, at least, that Paul had in his possession some written account of the Lord's doings and sayings and that he wished to have them to hand (sic) in his present critical situation" (*Tyndale New Testament Commentaries*, 14:173).

4:14,15. Very little is known of the Alexander mentioned here. The name is given in two other references (Acts 19:33; 1 Timothy 1:20). It is uncertain whether these are the same individual. It is not stated what Alexander did to Paul. The only clue is in the words "did me much evil" and "greatly withstood our words." This might mean Alexander had argued with Paul when he sought to teach other Christians. Or it may mean Alexander had testified against Paul at his trial.

Paul said the Lord would "reward" ("repay") Alexander for what he had done. This reflects the Bible's teaching of divine "payment" in passages like Psalm 62:12, Proverbs 24:12, and Romans 12:19. Timothy was told to "be thou ware." The literal meaning is "be on your guard against" or "keep yourself away from" this "copper-smith" ("metalworker") named Alexander.

4:16. "At my first answer" (*apologia*, "defense") probably refers to Paul's preliminary hearing prior to the formal trial. It may have been early in his stay in Rome (Acts 28:30,31). That "no man stood with" him could be explained by the fact that Roman Christians were not acquainted with Paul's ministry, hence they could not appear as witnesses for the defense. Though "all men forsook" Paul, he did not hold it against them but forgave them. He asked for God's mercy on those who had deserted him. (For further discussion see *Overview*, pp.574-76.)

13. The cloak that I left at Troas with Carpus: I left a heavy coat with, *SEB*.

when thou comest, bring [with thee]:

and the books, [but] especially the parchments: . . . and the scrolls, especially the vellums, *Concordant* . . . especially the leather scrolls, *SEB*.

14. Alexander the copper-smith did me much evil: . . . the metalworker, *Berkeley* . . . did me a great deal of harm, *NIV* . . . showed much ill-feeling towards me, *TCNT* . . . hurt me very much, *SEB*.

the Lord reward him according to his works:

15. Of whom be thou ware also: Do thou also avoid him, *Confraternity* . . . You, also, must be on your guard against him, *TCNT*.

for he hath greatly withstood our words: . . . for he has vehemently opposed, *Confraternity* . . . he is violent in his attacks on our teaching, *Norlie* . . . He fought against every word we preached, *NLT* . . . He was very much against our teachings, *SEB*.

16. At my first answer no man stood with me: At my first trial no one helped me, *NLT* . . . no one supported me, *Berkeley*.

but all [men] forsook me: . . . but everyone deserted me, *NIV*.

[I pray God] that it may not be laid to their charge: May it not be reckoned against them! *Concordant* . . . May the Lord not hold this against them! *SEB*.

3231.1 partic μὴ mē Not	840.2 prs- pron dat pl αὐτοῖς autois to them	3023.14 verb 3sing opt aor pass λογισθείη· logistheiē may it be reckoned.	3450.5 art nom sing masc **17.** ὁ ho The	1156.2 conj δὲ de but	2935.1 noun nom sing masc κύριός kurios Lord

1466.4 prs- pron dat 1sing μοι moi me	3798.3 verb 3sing indic aor act παρέστη, parestē stood by,	2504.1 conj καὶ kai and	1727.2 verb 3sing indic aor act ἐνεδυνάμωσέν enedunamōsen strengthened	1466.6 prs- pron acc 1sing με, me me,	2419.1 conj ἵνα hina that

1217.1 prep δι’ di’ through	1466.3 prs- pron gen 1sing ἐμοῦ emou me	3450.16 art sing neu τὸ to the	2754.1 noun sing neu κήρυγμα kērugma proclamation	3995.3 verb 3sing subj aor pass πληροφορηθῇ, plērophorēthē might be fully made,

17.a.**Txt:** 018K,020L,byz.
Var: 01א,02A,04C,06D
025P,33,Lach,Treg,Alf
Word,Tisc,We/Ho,Weis
Sod,UBS/✮

2504.1 conj καὶ kai and	189.18 verb sing act ⸂ ἀκούσῃ akousē should hear	189.27 verb 3pl subj aor act [ᵃ✮ ἀκούσωσιν] akousōsin [might hear]	3820.1 adj πάντα panta all	3450.17 art pl neu τὰ ta the

1477.4 noun pl neu ἔθνη· ethnē Gentiles;	2504.1 conj καὶ kai and	4363.5 verb 1sing indic aor pass ἐρρύσθην errhusthēn I was delivered	1523.2 prep gen ἐκ ek out of	4601.2 noun gen sing neu στόματος stomatos mouth	2997.2 noun gen sing masc λέοντος. leontos lion's.

18.a.**Txt:** 06D-corr,018K
020L,025P,byz.
Var: 01א,02A,04C
06D-org,33,Lach,Treg
Alf,Tisc,We/Ho,Weis
Sod,UBS/✮

2504.1 conj **18.** ⸀ καὶ ⸀ kai And	4363.12 verb 3sing indic fut mid ῥύσεταί rhusetai will deliver	1466.6 prs- pron acc 1sing με me me	3450.5 art nom sing masc ὁ ho the	2935.1 noun nom sing masc κύριος kurios Lord	570.3 prep ἀπὸ apo from

3820.2 adj gen sing παντὸς pantos every	2024.2 noun gen sing neu ἔργου ergou work	4050.2 adj gen sing πονηροῦ, ponērou wicked,	2504.1 conj καὶ kai and	4834.13 verb 3sing indic fut act σώσει sōsei will preserve	1519.1 prep εἰς eis for	3450.12 art acc sing fem τὴν tēn the

926.4 noun acc sing fem βασιλείαν basileian kingdom	840.3 prs- pron gen sing αὐτοῦ autou his	3450.12 art acc sing fem τὴν tēn the	2016.6 adj acc sing fem ἐπουράνιον· epouranion heavenly;	3614.3 rel- pron dat sing ᾧ hō to whom	3450.9 art nom sing fem ἡ hē the

1385.1 noun nom sing fem δόξα doxa glory	1519.1 prep εἰς eis unto	3450.8 art acc pl masc τοὺς tous the	163.6 noun acc pl masc αἰῶνας aiōnas ages	3450.1 art gen pl τῶν tōn of the	163.4 noun gen pl masc αἰώνων· aiōnōn ages.	279.1 intrj ἀμήν. amēn Amen.

776.8 verb 2sing impr aor mid **19.** Ἄσπασαι Aspasai Salute	4110.1 name acc fem Πρίσκαν Priskan Prisca	2504.1 conj καὶ kai and	205.2 name acc masc Ἀκύλαν, Akulan Aquila,	2504.1 conj καὶ kai and	3450.6 art acc sing masc τὸν ton the

3546.1 name gen masc Ὀνησιφόρου Onēsiphorou of Onesiphorus	3486.4 noun acc sing masc οἶκον. oikon house.	2020.1 name nom masc **20.** Ἔραστος Erastos Erastus	3176.16 verb 3sing indic aor act ἔμεινεν emeinen remained	1706.1 prep ἐν en in

4:17. The translation "notwithstanding" may be too strong for the Greek *de*. The normal "but" is probably more accurate: "But the Lord stood with me." "Stood" is from the verb *paristēmi*, "to stand by for help." The Greek verb *enedunamōsen* translated "strengthened" implies the giving of moral courage—in this case to proclaim the gospel in Rome.

Paul expressed his single objective in the words "that by me the preaching might be fully known." The verb *plērophorēthē* means "fully performed." "All the Gentiles" is *panta ta ethnē*, a phrase used in Romans to describe the scope of Paul's apostleship (Romans 1:15) and the extent of the revelation of the mystery of the gospel (Romans 16:26).

"I was delivered" is in the aorist tense which suggests Paul was reflecting on a past event. "Out of the mouth of the lion" adds an expression which was commonly used in Paul's day to express deliverance from extreme danger. Several interpretations have been proposed: (1) Paul was delivered from actual lions in the amphitheater; (2) this may be a metaphoric way for Paul to say his first hearing (verse 16) did not bring a guilty verdict or sentence of death; (3) the "lion" was Nero who could not convict Paul because of lack of evidence; (4) the "lion" was the devil (see 1 Peter 5:8). The first or second explanations seem most plausible.

4:18. The future tense of "and the Lord shall deliver me" contrasts with the aorist of verse 17. Whether this future deliverance refers to a physical or spiritual deliverance is uncertain. However, it is probably better to see it as spiritual because of the words that follow. The verb translated "preserve" is *sōsei*, "save." Here it means "keep safe." "Unto" is the Greek *eis*, "into, for." This meaning makes more sense when used with "heavenly kingdom" than a physical meaning would. Paul's salvation would be completed when Christ brought Paul *into* the heavenly kingdom. Deliverance was not to be *from* death but *through* death.

4:19. Paul's final greetings begin here and extend to the end of the letter. He names nine coworkers; some were in Ephesus with Timothy, some were in Rome, and two were elsewhere. First in the list are Prisca (Priscilla) and Aquila. This couple had assisted Paul in Corinth and accompanied him to Ephesus (Acts 18:2,3,18,19). They had instructed Apollos (Acts 18:26) and had risked their lives for Paul (Romans 16:3,4).

Onesiphorus had found Paul in Rome and "refreshed" him (see comments on 1:16,17). It is possible that Onesiphorus may have lost his life for his loyalty and service to Paul. Note the greeting was to Onesiphorus' household, not to the man personally.

4:20. Acts 19:22 tells of an Erastus who was sent as an emissary of Paul to Macedonia. Romans 16:23 refers to a church member named Erastus who was city treasurer or director of public works.

17. Notwithstanding the Lord stood with me, and strengthened me: . . . the Lord stood at my side, *NIV*.

that by me the preaching might be fully known: . . . the proclamation, *TCNT*.

and [that] all the Gentiles might hear:

and I was delivered out of the mouth of the lion: And I was drawn to His side, *Wuest* . . . was freed out of, *Young* . . . rescued from the lion's jaws, *Montgomery, Williams* . . . from the lion's jaw, *Berkeley* . . . from a lion's mouth, *Fenton*.

18. And the Lord shall deliver me from every evil work: . . . will keep me from every sinful plan they have, *NLT* . . . will rescue me from every wicked act, *Adams* . . . The Lord will draw me to himself away from every pernicious work actively opposed to that which is good, *Wuest* . . . from all the evil that is done, *Beck* . . . from all the attempts of the wicked, *Fenton* . . . from every evil attack, *NIV* . . . from every wicked scheme, *Norlie* . . . from every wicked work, *Williams* . . . from every evil assault, *Montgomery* . . . from every evil deed, *NASB*.

and will preserve [me] unto his heavenly kingdom: . . . and will keep me safe to, *Wuest* . . . and save me to, *Williams* . . . and will save me and take me to, *Beck* . . . will continue to rescue me from all attempts to do me harm, *NAB* . . . for His celestial kingdom, *Concordant* . . . for His heavenly empire, *Adams*.

to whom [be] glory for ever and ever. Amen: To him be, *Montgomery* . . . be honor, *Fenton* . . . forever and forever, *Wuest* . . . for the ages of the ages, *Wilson*.

19. Salute Prisca and Aquila, and the household of Onesiphorus: Greet, *Adams, Wuest* . . . Give my love to, *Norlie* . . . Give my good wishes, *TCNT* . . . Give my greetings to, *Montgomery* . . . Remember me to, *Williams* . . . Regards to, *Fenton* . . . and the family of, *Campbell, Beck*.

2855.1 name dat fem	5002.2 name acc masc	1156.2 conj	614.1 verb 1sing indic aor act	1706.1 prep	3263.2 name dat fem
Κορίνθῳ·	Τρόφιμον	δὲ	ἀπέλιπον	ἐν	Μιλήτῳ
Korinthō	Trophimon	de	apelipon	en	Milētō
Corinth,	Trophimus	but	I left	in	Miletus

764.7 verb acc sing masc part pres act		4557.5 verb 2sing impr aor act	4112.1 prep	5330.2 noun gen sing masc	2048.23 verb inf aor act
ἀσθενοῦντα.	21.	Σπούδασον	πρὸ	χειμῶνος	ἐλθεῖν.
asthenounta		Spoudason	pro	cheimōnos	elthein
being sick.		Be diligent	before	winter	to come.

776.2 verb 3sing indic pres mid	4622.4 prs- pron acc 2sing	2082.1 name nom masc	2504.1 conj	4086.1 name nom masc	2504.1 conj
Ἀσπάζεταί	σε	Εὔβουλος,	καὶ	Πούδης,	καὶ
Aspazetai	se	Euboulos	kai	Poudēs	kai
Greets	you	Eubulus,	and	Pudens,	and

3018.1 name nom masc	2504.1 conj	2776.1 name nom fem	2504.1 conj	3450.7 art nom pl masc	79.6 noun nom pl masc
Λίνος,	καὶ	Κλαυδία,	καὶ	οἱ	ἀδελφοὶ
Linos	kai	Klaudia	kai	hoi	adelphoi
Linus	and	Claudia,	and	the	brothers

3820.7 adj nom pl masc	3450.5 art nom sing masc	2935.1 noun nom sing masc	2400.1 name nom masc	5382.1 name nom masc
πάντες.	22. Ὁ	κύριος	⸂ Ἰησοῦς ⸃[a]	⸂ Χριστὸς ⸃[b]
pantes	Ho	kurios	Iēsous	Christos
all.	The	Lord	Jesus	Christ

3196.3 prep	3450.2 art gen sing	4011.2 noun gen sing neu	4622.2 prs- pron gen 2sing	3450.9 art nom sing fem	5322.1 noun nom sing fem
μετὰ	τοῦ	πνεύματός	σου.	ἡ	χάρις
meta	tou	pneumatos	sou	hē	charis
with	the	spirit	your.	The	grace

3196.1 prep	5050.2 prs- pron gen 2pl	279.1 intrj	4242.1 prep	4943.4 name acc masc
μεθ'	ὑμῶν.	⸂ ἀμήν. ⸃[c]	⸂[d] Πρὸς	Τιμόθεον
meth'	humōn	amēn	Pros	Timotheon
with	you.	Amen.	To	Timothy

1202.4 num ord nom sing fem	3450.10 art gen sing fem	2162.1 name- adj gen pl masc	1564.1 noun fem	4270.1 adv
δευτέρα,	τῆς	Ἐφεσίων	ἐκκλησίας	πρῶτον
deutera	tēs	Ephesiōn	ekklēsias	prōton
second,	of the	of Ephesians	assembly	first

1969.1 noun acc sing masc	5336.3 verb acc sing masc part aor pass	1119.21 verb 3sing indic aor pass	570.3 prep	4373.1 name gen fem
ἐπίσκοπον	χειροτονηθέντα,	ἐγράφη	ἀπὸ	Ῥώμης,
episkopon	cheirotonēthenta	egraphē	apo	Rhōmēs
overseer	having been chosen,	written	from	Rome,

3616.1 conj	1523.2 prep gen	1202.1 num ord gen sing	3798.3 verb 3sing indic aor act	3834.1 name nom masc
ὅτε	ἐκ	δευτέρου	παρέστη	Παῦλος
hote	ek	deuterou	parestē	Paulos
when	from	second time	was placed before	Paul

3450.3 art dat sing	2512.2 name dat masc	3367.1 name dat masc
τῷ	Καίσαρι	Νέρωνι. ⸃
tō	Kaisari	Nerōni
	Caesar	Nero.

22.a.**Txt:** 01‫א‬-corr,02A 04C,06D,018K,020L 025P,byz.sa.bo.Sod **Var:** 01‫א‬-org,33,Treg Tisc,We/Ho,Weis UBS/✻

22.b.**Txt:** 01‫א‬-corr,04C 06D,018K,020L,025P byz.sa.bo. **Var:** 01‫א‬-org,02A,33 Lach,Treg,Tisc,We/Ho Weis,Sod,UBS/✻

22.c.**Txt:** 01‫א‬-corr,06D 018K,020L,025P,byz. **Var:** 01‫א‬-org,02A,04C 33,Gries,Lach,Treg,Alf Word,Tisc,We/Ho,Weis Sod,UBS/✻

22.d.**Txt:** 018K,020L Steph **Var:** Gries,Lach,Word Tisc,We/Ho,Weis,Sod UBS/✻

Although we cannot be certain of the identity of the man named here, Timothy knew him and would be interested in his whereabouts. Trophimus is mentioned in Acts 20:4 and 21:29. Miletus is a seaport on the coast of Asia Minor about 50 miles south of Ephesus.

20. Erastus abode at Corinth: Erastus hath stopped at, *Murdock* . . . remained at, *Montgomery* . . . stayed in the city of, *SEB*.
but Trophimus have I left at Miletum sick: I left behind me, *Montgomery* . . . I left in Miletus infirm, *Young* . . . being infirm, *Concordant* . . . being ill, I left behind, *Wuest*.

4:21. "Do thy diligence (best) to come before winter" is the second time Paul expressed his desire to see Timothy. The apostle said essentially the same thing in verse 9.

"Before winter" expresses Paul's urgency. Navigation on the Adriatic Sea would cease during the winter months. This fact suggests that Paul may not have expected to live until spring. Paul desperately wanted to see his "dearly beloved son" (1:2); whether he did or not is uncertain.

Paul sent greetings to Timothy from four unknown Christians: Eubulus, Pudens, Linus, and Claudia. Nothing else is known of these four except from tradition.

The name *Eubulus* means "good in counsel." *Pudens* is the Greek name from Latin that means "modest, bashful." He is commemorated in the Byzantine (Greek Orthodox) Church on April 14 and in the Roman Catholic Church on May 19. He has a fanciful and probably fictional connection with Claudia. Irenaeus and Eusebius, Ancient Church fathers, reported that Linus was the first bishop of Rome (Kelly, p.6).

Claudia is the feminine form of *Claudius.* "By some she is thought to have been the daughter of the British King Cogidunus, and the wife of Pudens (mentioned in the same verse), and sent to Rome to be educated; that there she was the protegee of Pomponia (wife of the late commander in Britain, Aulus Plautius) and became a convert to Christianity. On the other hand, it may be said that this attempt at identification rests on no other foundation than the identity of the names of the parties, which, in the case of names so common as Pudens and Claudia, may be nothing more than a mere accidental coincidence" (*Unger's Bible Dictionary*, "Claudia").

"And all the brethren" shows that Paul held no grudge against any who might have "deserted" him at the time of his first trial. A few sentences earlier he had said, "All men forsook me" (see comments on verse 16). Now he sends their greetings to Timothy.

21. Do thy diligence to come before winter: If possible, *Klingensmith* . . . Exert yourselves, *Murdock* . . . Do your best to get here, *NIV, Williams* . . . Do your best to come, *SEB, Wuest* . . . Try to come before, *NLT, Montgomery, Fenton* . . . Hurry to arrive, *Berkeley* . . . Endeavor to come, *Concordant* . . . Hasten to come, *Confraternity* . . . Make haste to come, *Campbell*.
Eubulus greeteth thee, and Pudens, and Linus, and Claudia: There greet you, *Wuest* . . . greets you along with, *Adams* . . . say hello to you, *NLT* . . . wishes to be remembered to you, *Williams* . . . send regards to you, *Fenton*.
and all the brethren: . . . all the brotherhood, *Montgomery* . . . and all the fellow Christians, *Beck* . . . and all the friends, *Fenton*.

22. The Lord Jesus Christ [be] with thy spirit:
Grace [be] with you. Amen: God's love be with you all! *Beck* . . . Spiritual blessing be with you all, *Williams* . . . Blessing be with you, *Fenton* . . . Favour [be] with you, *Rotherham*.

4:22. The benediction of verse 22 is in two parts. "The Lord Jesus Christ be with thy spirit" was directed personally to Timothy. The word "thy" is singular (compare Philemon 25). But the second part, "Grace be with you," is for all Christians. The word "you" is plural (similar endings are found in Paul's first letter to Timothy and his letter to Titus). This shows the present letter to Timothy was intended for public reading (compare Paul's closing in 2 Thessalonians 3:17,18).

As Paul began this letter (and all his letters) with the salutation of grace, so he ended this final letter with, "Grace be with you (all). Amen."

THE EPISTLE
OF PAUL TO
TITUS

Expanded Interlinear
Textual Critical Apparatus
Verse-by-Verse Commentary
Various Versions

4242.1 prep	4951.4 name acc masc	1976.1 noun nom sing fem	3834.2 name gen masc
Πρὸς	Τίτον	ἐπιστολὴ	Παύλου
Pros	Titon	epistolē	Paulou
To	Titus	letter	of Paul

Textual Apparatus

3834.1 name nom masc	1395.1 noun nom sing masc	2296.2 noun gen sing masc	646.1 noun nom sing masc	1156.2 conj	2400.2 name masc
1:1. Παῦλος	δοῦλος	θεοῦ,	ἀπόστολος	δὲ	Ἰησοῦ
Paulos	doulos	theou	apostolos	de	Iēsou
Paul	slave	of God,	apostle	and	of Jesus

5382.2 name gen masc	2567.3 prep	3963.4 noun acc sing fem	1575.4 adj gen pl masc	2296.2 noun gen sing masc	2504.1 conj
Χριστοῦ	κατὰ	πίστιν	ἐκλεκτῶν	θεοῦ	καὶ
Christou	kata	pistin	eklektōn	theou	kai
Christ	according to	faith	chosen	of God's	and

1907.4 noun acc sing fem	223.2 noun gen sing fem	3450.10 art gen sing fem	2567.1 prep	2131.4 noun acc sing fem
ἐπίγνωσιν	ἀληθείας	τῆς	κατ'	εὐσέβειαν,
epignōsin	alētheias	tēs	kat'	eusebeian
knowledge	of truth	the	according to	godliness;

1894.2 prep	1667.3 noun dat sing fem	2205.2 noun gen sing fem	164.2 adj gen sing	3614.12 rel-pron acc sing fem	1846.3 verb 3sing indic aor mid
2. ἐπ'	ἐλπίδι	ζωῆς	αἰωνίου,	ἣν	ἐπηγγείλατο
ep'	elpidi	zōēs	aiōniou	hēn	epēngeilato
in	hope	of life	eternal,	which	promised

3450.5 art nom sing masc	886.1 adj nom sing masc	2296.1 noun nom sing masc	4112.1 prep	5385.5 noun gen pl masc	164.4 adj gen pl masc
ὁ	ἀψευδὴς	θεὸς	πρὸ	χρόνων	αἰωνίων,
ho	apseudēs	theos	pro	chronōn	aiōniōn
the	who cannot lie	God	before	of times	the ages,

5157.3 verb 3sing indic aor act	1156.2 conj	2511.7 noun dat pl masc	2375.5 adj dat pl	3450.6 art acc sing masc	3030.4 noun acc sing masc
3. ἐφανέρωσεν	δὲ	καιροῖς	ἰδίοις	τὸν	λόγον
ephanerōsen	de	kairois	idiois	ton	logon
manifested	but	in seasons	its own	the	word

840.3 prs-pron gen sing	1706.1 prep	2754.3 noun dat sing neu	3614.16 rel-pron sing neu	3961.57 verb 1sing indic aor pass
αὐτοῦ,	ἐν	κηρύγματι	ὃ	ἐπιστεύθην
autou	en	kērugmati	ho	episteuthēn
his	in	proclamation	which	was entrusted with

1466.1 prs-pron nom 1sing	2567.1 prep	1987.2 noun acc sing fem	3450.2 art gen sing	4842.2 noun gen sing masc
ἐγὼ	κατ'	ἐπιταγὴν	τοῦ	σωτῆρος
egō	kat'	epitagēn	tou	sōtēros
I	according to	commandment	of the	Saviour

2231.2 prs-pron gen 1pl	2296.2 noun gen sing masc	4951.3 name dat masc	1097.2 adj dat sing neu	4891.3 noun dat sing neu	2567.3 prep
ἡμῶν	θεοῦ,	4. Τίτῳ	γνησίῳ	τέκνῳ	κατὰ
hēmōn	theou	Titō	gnēsiō	teknō	kata
our	God;	to Titus	true	child	according to

THE EPISTLE OF PAUL TO
TITUS

1:1. The formal salutation of the letter to Titus is longer than those in the other Pastorals. Beside length, additional significant differences are: (1) Paul called himself a "servant of God"—used only here and not in any of his other letters. (2) The content of this greeting is replete with doctrinal terms. The salutation is contained in the first four verses.

"Servant" is *doulos*, "slave" or "servant." The Greek means (1) "slave"—one who completely belongs to his master with no freedom of his own; or (2) "servant"—one who willingly chooses to serve his master (compare Exodus 21:1-6). Paul was both a "servant of God" and an "apostle of Jesus Christ." The claim to apostleship adds weight to the letter, since an apostle was especially commissioned by Christ.

Three important terms—faith, knowledge, godliness—focus on three practical truths. "Faith" in Scripture means absolute trust in God. Paul wrote of "the faith of God's elect." The elect are believers who make up the Church (compare Romans 8:33; Colossians 3:12). Added to faith is "acknowledging (*epignōsin*, 'knowledge') of the truth." "Godliness" is active reverence toward God. Clearly, faith in God and knowledge of the truth lead to godliness.

1:2. Another virtue is "hope" (*elpidi*). In the Bible it is firm assurance and expectation, not wishful thinking. Here it is anchored in eternal life promised by God who "cannot lie" (*apseudēs*) (Numbers 23:19; Hebrews 6:18). He stands in strong contrast to the Cretans who were habitual liars (Titus 1:12). "Before the world began" is literally "before time eternal."

1:3. "Due times" contrasts with "before the world began" in the previous verse. The plural *kairois idiois* could refer to various times or as a collective singular to a particular time (Galatians 4:4). The NIV has "his appointed season."

"His word" is God's authoritative message that centers in Jesus Christ, i.e., the gospel. "Manifested" means "brought to light" and emphasizes the clear proclamation ("preaching") of the gospel. This ministry was "committed" (*episteuthēn*, "to be entrusted with") to Paul (compare Galatians 1:1; 2:7; 1 Timothy 1:11; 2 Timothy 1:11).

Three times in Titus Paul used the phrase "God our Saviour" (here; Titus 2:10; and 3:4; compare 1 Timothy 1:1; 2:3; 4:10).

Various Versions

1. Paul, a servant of God: . . . a slave of, *Montgomery* . . . a bondservant of God, *NASB*.

and an apostle of Jesus Christ: . . . but missionary of, *Klingensmith*.

according to the faith of God's elect: . . . appointed to strengthen the faith of God's Chosen People, *TCNT* . . . to stimulate faith in God's chosen people, *Williams* . . . to promote the faith of God's chosen people, *Adams*.

and the acknowledging of the truth which is after godliness: . . . and the full knowledge of the truth that brings about godliness, *Adams* . . . to lead them on to a full knowledge of religious truth, *Williams* . . . which goes with piety, *Montgomery*.

2. In hope of eternal life: I write in hope of, *Montgomery* . . . in expectation of life eonian, *Concordant* . . . of everlasting life, *Klingensmith*.

which God, that cannot lie, promised before the world began: . . . who never lies, promised before times eternal, *Montgomery* . . . long ages ago, *NASB* . . . before the ages began, *Confraternity* . . . before time began, *Berkeley, SEB*.

3. But hath in due times manifested his word: At the proper time, *Norlie, Williams* . . . it is revealed in its own time, *KJII* . . . at the proper season, *Campbell*.

through preaching, which is committed unto me: . . . in proclaiming which I have been entrusted, *Montgomery* . . . through the message that I preach, *Williams*.

according to the commandment of God our Saviour: . . . by order of, *SEB* . . . according to the injunction of, *Concordant*.

481

Titus 1:5

4.a.**Txt:** 02A,04C-corr
018K,020L,byz.
Var: 01ℵ,04C-org,06D
025P,088,33,it.bo.Treg
Alf,Word,Tisc,We/Ho
Weis,Sod,UBS/✡

2812.4 adj acc sing fem	3963.4 noun acc sing fem	5322.1 noun nom sing fem	1643.2 noun sing neu	2504.1 conj	1503.1 noun nom sing fem
κοινὴν	πίστιν,	χάρις,	ʿ ἔλεος,	[ᵃ✡ καὶ]	εἰρήνη
koinēn	pistin,	charis,	eleos,	kai	eirēnē
common	faith:	Grace,	mercy	[and]	peace

570.3 prep	2296.2 noun gen sing masc	3824.2 noun gen sing masc	2504.1 conj	2935.2 noun gen sing masc	2400.2 name masc
ἀπὸ	θεοῦ	πατρὸς,	καὶ	ʿ κυρίου	Ἰησοῦ
apo	theou	patros	kai	kuriou	Iēsou
from	God	Father,	and	Lord	Jesus

4.b.**Txt:** 06D-corr,018K
020L,025P,byz.
Var: 01ℵ,02A,04C
06D-org,088,33,bo.Lach
Treg,Alf,Tisc,We/Ho
Weis,Sod,UBS/✡

5382.2 name gen masc	5382.2 name gen masc	2400.2 name masc	3450.2 art gen sing	4842.2 noun gen sing masc
Χριστοῦ	[ᵇ✡ Χριστοῦ	Ἰησοῦ]	τοῦ	σωτῆρος
Christou	Christou	Iēsou	tou	sōtēros
Christ	[Christ	Jesus]	the	Saviour

5.a.**Txt:** 01ℵ-corr
06D-corr,018K,020L
025P,byz.Sod
Var1: 01ℵ-org,06D-org
088,33,Lach,Treg,Alf
Word,Tisc,Weis,UBS/✡
Var2: 02A,04C,010F
012G,088,0240,33,1175

2231.2 prs-pron gen 1pl	3642.1 dem-pron gen sing	5320.1 prep	2611.2 verb indic aor act	614.1 verb 1sing indic aor act
ἡμῶν.	5. Τούτου	χάριν	ʿ κατέλιπόν	[¹ᵃ✡ ἀπέλιπόν
hēmōn.	Toutou	charin	katelipon	apelipon
our.	For this	cause	I left	[idem

614.4 verb 1sing act	4622.4 prs-pron acc 2sing	1706.1 prep	2887.2 name dat fem	2419.1 conj	3450.17 art pl neu
² ἀπέλειπόν]	σε	ἐν	Κρήτῃ,	ἵνα	τὰ
apeleipon	se	en	Krētē,	hina	ta
I was leaving]	you	in	Crete,	that	the

2981.3 verb pl neu part pres act	1915.1 verb 2sing subj aor mid	1915.2 verb 2sing subj aor pres
λείποντα	ʿ✡ ἐπιδιορθώσῃ	[ᵇ ἐπιδιορθώσῃς]
leiponta	epidiorthōsē	epidiorthōsēs
lacking	you might go on to set right,	[idem]

2504.1 conj	2497.5 verb 2sing subj aor act	2567.3 prep	4032.4 noun acc sing fem	4104.2 adj comp acc pl masc
καὶ	καταστήσῃς	κατὰ	πόλιν	πρεσβυτέρους,
kai	katastēsēs	kata	polin	presbuterous,
and	might appoint	in every	city	elders,

5453.1 conj	1466.1 prs-pron nom 1sing	4622.3 prs-pron dat 2sing	1293.6 verb 1sing indic aor mid	1479.1 conj	4949.3 intr-pron nom sing
ὡς	ἐγώ	σοι	διεταξάμην·	6. εἴ	τίς
hōs	egō	soi	dietaxamēn	ei	tis
as	I	you	ordered:	if	anyone

1498.4 verb 3sing indic pres act	408.1 adj nom sing masc	1518.6 num card gen fem	1129.2 noun gen sing fem	433.1 noun nom sing masc
ἐστιν	ἀνέγκλητος,	μιᾶς	γυναικὸς	ἀνήρ,
estin	anenklētos,	mias	gunaikos	anēr,
is	irreproachable,	of one	wife	husband,

4891.4 noun pl neu	2174.17 verb nom sing masc part pres act	3964.14 adj pl neu	3231.1 partic	1706.1 prep	2694.1 noun dat sing fem
τέκνα	ἔχων	πιστά,	μὴ	ἐν	κατηγορίᾳ
tekna	echōn	pista,	mē	en	katēgoria
children	having	believing,	not	under	accusation

804.2 noun gen sing fem	2211.1 conj	503.4 adj pl neu	1158.1 verb 3sing indic pres act	1056.1 conj
ἀσωτίας	ἢ	ἀνυπότακτα.	7. δεῖ	γὰρ
asōtias	ē	anupotakta.	dei	gar
of debauchery	or	insubordinate.	It is necessary for	for

482

1:4. Titus was a Greek and a valuable coworker of Paul (see 2 Corinthians 2:12,13; 7:5,6; 8:6,23; 12:18; Galatians 2:1-5). Paul called him his "own" (*gnēsiō*, "genuine, true") son. This word, used also of Timothy (1 Timothy 1:2), suggests Titus was converted under Paul's ministry. "The common faith" is the faith shared by all believers.

1:5. Paul gave Titus a twofold assignment for his work in Crete. The two had ministered together on the island, then Paul left Titus behind to (1) "set in order the things that are wanting" and (2) "ordain elders in every city."

Crete is a mountainous island southeast of Greece, approximately 160 miles long and 35 miles wide. An immoral, savage people populated numerous coastal cities. The Cretans had a bad reputation throughout the entire Mediterranean world.

The two objectives follow Paul's usual pattern for establishing churches. Perhaps because Paul's visit was brief he had not had time to "set in order (straighten out) the things that are wanting (unfinished, defective)." So Titus was to do what Paul had left undone. Second, Titus was to "ordain (appoint) elders (*presbuterous*) in every city." The term *elder* suggests maturity and experience. It is synonymous with "bishop" (verse 7). Appointing elders was Paul's usual procedure (see Acts 14:23).

1:6. Verses 6-9 contain a list of qualifications for elders. It is similar to the list given in 1 Timothy 3:1-7. An elder must be *anenklētos* ("blameless, irreproachable"). (Note this is repeated for the "bishop" in verse 7.) Emphasis is placed on the family life of an elder. This seems to be a prerequisite to becoming a spiritual leader ("overseer") of the church.

"Husband of one wife" (1) assumes the elder is an older man who is married but does not categorically exclude a single man; (2) does not restrict marriage to a second wife if a previous wife is deceased; (3) has the primary meaning of a faithful, monogamous marriage (compare comments on 1 Timothy 3:2).

"Faithful" should be understood as "believing"; i.e., "having believing children." The two negatives here are meaningful because of the life-style of Cretans. An elder's children must not be accused of *asōtias* ("debauchery, dissipation, profligacy, wild extravagance"). This term is used in Luke 15:13 of the Prodigal Son. The elder's children must not be *anupotakta* ("unruly, undisciplined, disobedient, rebellious, insubordinate").

1:7. The term "bishop" (synonymous with "elders," verse 5) can be translated "overseer" and suggests responsibility. "Steward of God" conveys the idea of a manager of a household or estate. The

4. To Titus, [mine] own son after the common faith: . . . his true Child in their one Faith, *TCNT* . . . You are my true son, *NLT* . . . genuine child, *Williams* . . . my genuine son, *Campbell* . . . my true son in a common faith, *Montgomery* . . . by the faith we share, *SEB*.

Grace, mercy, [and] peace: . . . be spiritual blessing, *Williams*.

from God the Father and the Lord Jesus Christ our Saviour:

5. For this cause left I thee in Crete: . . . for this reason, *Montgomery* . . . for this express purpose, *Williams* . . . The reason why I left you behind, *Norlie*.

that thou shouldest set in order the things that are wanting: . . . that you might straighten out unfinished business, *Berkeley* . . . to finish up the thing left undone, *Klingensmith* . . . to straighten out things that still needed to be done, *SEB* . . . anything that is defective, *Confraternity* . . . the things left unfinished, *Campbell*.

and ordain elders in every city: . . . and constitute elders city by city, *Concordant* . . . and appoint presbyters, *Montgomery* . . . and appoint Officers of the Church in the various towns, *TCNT*.

as I had appointed thee: . . . as I had instructed you, *Montgomery* . . . as I gave you directions, *Berkeley*.

6. If any be blameless: . . . must be above suspicion, *SEB* . . . of irreproachable character, *TCNT*.

the husband of one wife:

having faithful children: . . . having believing children, *Klingensmith*.

not accused of riot or unruly: . . . not charged with being incorrigible or unruly, *Berkeley* . . . and have never been charged with dissolute or unruly conduct, *TCNT* . . . of being wild or disobedient, *SEB* . . . of dissipation or rebellion, *NASB* . . . or insubordination, *Montgomery*.

3450.6 art acc sing masc	**1969.1** noun acc sing masc	**408.2** adj acc sing masc	**1498.32** verb inf pres act	**5453.1** conj	**2296.2** noun gen sing masc
τὸν	ἐπίσκοπον	ἀνέγκλητον	εἶναι,	ὡς	θεοῦ
ton	*episkopon*	*anenklēton*	*einai*	*hōs*	*theou*
the	overseer	without reproach	to be,	as	God's

3485.2 noun acc sing masc	**3231.1** partic	**823.1** adj acc sing masc	**3231.1** partic	**3574.1** adj acc sing masc	**3231.1** partic
οἰκονόμον·	μὴ	αὐθάδη,	μὴ	ὀργίλον,	μὴ
oikonomon	*mē*	*authadē*	*mē*	*orgilon*	*mē*
steward;	not	self-willed,	not	passionate,	not

3805.1 adj acc sing masc	**3231.1** partic	**3991.1** noun acc sing masc	**3231.1** partic	**146.1** adj acc sing masc
πάροινον,	μὴ	πλήκτην,	μὴ	αἰσχροκερδῆ,
paroinon	*mē*	*plēktēn*	*mē*	*aischrokerdē*
given to wine,	not	a striker,	not	greedy of shameful gain,

233.2 conj	**5219.1** adj acc sing masc	**5195.1** adj acc sing masc	**4850.2** adj acc sing masc	**1337.1** adj sing
8. ἀλλὰ	φιλόξενον,	φιλάγαθον,	σώφρονα,	δίκαιον,
alla	*philoxenon*	*philagathon*	*sōphrona*	*dikaion*
but	hospitable,	a lover of good,	sound-minded,	just,

3603.2 adj acc sing masc	**1461.1** adj acc sing masc	**469.2** verb acc sing masc part pres mid	**3450.2** art gen sing	**2567.3** prep
ὅσιον,	ἐγκρατῆ,	**9.** ἀντεχόμενον	τοῦ	κατὰ
hosion	*enkratē*	*antechomenon*	*tou*	*kata*
holy,	self-controlled,	holding to	the	according to

3450.12 art acc sing fem	**1316.4** noun acc sing fem	**3964.3** adj gen sing masc	**3030.2** noun gen sing masc	**2419.1** conj	**1409.1** adj nom sing masc
τὴν	διδαχὴν	πιστοῦ	λόγου,	ἵνα	δυνατὸς
tēn	*didachēn*	*pistou*	*logou*	*hina*	*dunatos*
the	teaching	faithful	word,	that	able

1498.10 verb 3sing subj pres act	**2504.1** conj	**3731.10** verb inf pres act	**1706.1** prep	**3450.11** art dat sing fem	**1313.3** noun dat sing fem
ᾖ	καὶ	παρακαλεῖν	ἐν	τῇ	διδασκαλίᾳ
ē	*kai*	*parakalein*	*en*	*tē*	*didaskalia*
he may be	both	to encourage	with	the	teaching

3450.11 art dat sing fem	**5039.8** verb dat sing fem part pres act	**2504.1** conj	**3450.8** art acc pl masc	**480.5** verb acc pl masc part pres act	**1638.5** verb inf pres act
τῇ	ὑγιαινούσῃ	καὶ	τοὺς	ἀντιλέγοντας	ἐλέγχειν.
tē	*hugiainousē*	*kai*	*tous*	*antilegontas*	*elenchein*
the	sound,	and	the	contradicting	to convict.

10.a.**Txt:** 06D,016I 018K,020L,byz.
Var: 01א,02A,04C,025P 088,33,sa.bo.Lach,Treg Tisc,We/Ho,Weis,Sod UBS/☆

1498.7 verb 3pl indic pres act	**1056.1** conj	**4044.7** adj nom pl masc	**2504.1** conj	**503.1** adj nom pl masc	**3123.1** adj nom pl masc
10. Εἰσὶν	γὰρ	πολλοὶ	⸂[a] καὶ ⸃	ἀνυπότακτοι,	ματαιολόγοι
Eisin	*gar*	*polloi*	*kai*	*anupotaktoi*	*mataiologoi*
There are	for	many	and	insubordinate	vain talkers

10.b.**Var:** 01א,04C 06D-org,088,33,Treg Tisc,We/Ho,Weis,Sod UBS/☆

2504.1 conj	**5259.1** noun nom pl masc	**3094.1** adv sup	**3450.7** art nom pl masc	**1523.2** prep gen	**3450.10** art gen sing fem
καὶ	φρεναπάται,	μάλιστα	οἱ	ἐκ	[b☆+ τῆς]
kai	*phrenapatai*	*malista*	*hoi*	*ek*	*tēs*
and	mind deceivers,	especially	the	of	[the]

3921.2 noun gen sing fem	**3614.8** rel-pron acc pl masc	**1158.1** verb 3sing indic pres act	**1977.1** verb inf pres act
περιτομῆς,	**11.** οὓς	δεῖ	ἐπιστομίζειν·
peritomēs	*hous*	*dei*	*epistomizein*
circumcision,	whom	it is necessary	to stop the mouths of,

overseer or steward of God's "household" (the local church) must not be (1) *authadē* ("overbearing, arrogant"), the idea here is a man of conceit, intolerance, arrogance, stubbornness, and contemptuousness; (2) *orgilon* ("quick-tempered, inclined to anger"); (3) *paroinon* (literally, "given to overindulgence in wine"); (4) *plēktēn* ("not violent, no striker"), not ready to come to blows. (5) *Aischrokerdē* ("fond of dishonest gain") denotes a man who does not care how he gets money so long as he gets it.

1:8. Next Paul lists positive requirements. First, he is to be *philoxenon* (literally, "a lover of strangers," in other words, "hospitable"). Next, he is to be *philagathon* ("a lover of good things" or "a lover of good people"). The Greek word is used only here in the New Testament. Probably the sense is "good things" or "goodness" more than "good men." An elder is to be *sōphrona* ("prudent, thoughtful, self-controlled, sober"). The sense here is the wise control of every thought and instinct.

As to the elder's spiritual requirements, he is to be *dikaion* ("upright, just, righteous"), giving respect to man and reverence to God, as well as *hosion* ("pious, devout, holy").

"Temperate" (*enkratē*) means "disciplined, in full control of oneself." It is similar to "sober" but has the added meaning of possessing inner strength to control one's desires and actions.

1:9. The leader (elder, overseer) must hold the "faithful (reliable, sure, trustworthy) word" he has been taught. By "sound doctrine" (occuring eight times in the Pastoral Epistles, it means "correct teaching") he will be able to "exhort" (encourage, edify) and "convince" (refute, convict, point out, rebuke in a convincing way) the "gainsayers" (those who oppose sound doctrine).

1:10. Verses 10-16 describe false teachers whose character is totally opposite to that of the elder just described. False teachers were (1) *anupotaktoi* ("unruly, rebellious, insubordinate"). This rebelliousness is against God's Word and God's messengers, specifically those who were troubling Paul and Titus. They were (2) *mataiologoi*—"vain talkers, empty-headed babblers" (compare 1 Timothy 1:6). They were (3) *phrenapatai* ("deceivers, misleaders") who taught things without substance.

Paul then identified them as "of the circumcision." These Judaizers (Galatians 2:12ff.) believed circumcision and the keeping of Jewish ceremonial laws were necessary for salvation. They held to unscriptural Jewish myths (verse 14) and genealogies (Titus 3:9; see 1 Timothy 1:4). They were ascetics with scruples against things God considered good (Titus 1:14,15; see 1 Timothy 4:3-5).

1:11. Paul wrote Titus that these Judaizers' "mouths must be stopped" (muzzled, silenced, bridled) because they were subverting

7. For a bishop must be blameless, as the steward of God: . . . a pastor must be above reproach, *Williams* . . . must be unimpeachable, *Concordant*.

not selfwilled, not soon angry: . . . not irritable, *Concordant* . . . nor full of passion, *KJII* . . . not quick-tempered, *NASB*.

not given to wine, no striker, not given to filthy lucre:

8. But a lover of hospitality, a lover of good men:

sober, just, holy, temperate: . . . sensible, *NASB, Williams* . . . continent, *Confraternity* . . . self-controlled, *Concordant*.

9. Holding fast the faithful word as he hath been taught: . . . who continues to cling to the trustworthy message, *Williams* . . . clinging to, *KJII*.

that he may be able by sound doctrine both to exhort: . . . able to entreat with sound teaching as well as to expose those who contradict, *Concordant*.

and to convince the gainsayers: . . . to refute those who contradict, *NASB* . . . and to confute opponents, *Confraternity* . . . the ones who speak against the truth, *KJII* . . . those who oppose him, *Williams*.

10. For there are many unruly: . . . insubordinate people, *Williams*.

and vain talkers and deceivers: . . . senseless talkers, *Berkeley*.

specially they of the circumcision:

11. Whose mouths must be stopped: These ought to be silenced, *Berkeley* . . . who must be gagged, *Concordant*.

Titus 1:12

3610.2 rel- pron nom pl masc	3513.5 adj acc pl masc	3486.7 noun acc pl masc	394.1 verb 3pl indic pres act	1315.9 verb nom pl masc part pres act
οἵτινες hoitines who	ὅλους holous whole	οἴκους oikous houses	ἀνατρέπουσιν, anatrepousin overthrow,	διδάσκοντες didaskontes teaching

3614.17 rel- pron pl neu	3231.1 partic	1158.1 verb 3sing indic pres act	149.2 adj gen sing neu	2742.2 noun gen sing neu
ἃ ha things which	μὴ mē not	δεῖ, dei ought,	αἰσχροῦ aischrou disgraceful	κέρδους kerdous gain

12.a.Var: 01א-org,010F 012G,81

5320.1 prep	1500.5 verb 3sing indic aor act	1156.2 conj	4948.3 indef- pron nom sing	1523.1 prep gen	840.1 prs- pron gen pl
χάριν· charin for sake of.	12. εἶπέν eipen Said	[a+ δὲ] de [but]	τις tis one	ἐξ ex of	αὐτῶν autōn themselves

2375.6 adj nom sing masc	840.1 prs- pron gen pl	4254.1 noun nom sing masc	2886.1 name nom pl masc	103.1 adv	5418.3 noun nom pl masc
ἴδιος idios of own	αὐτῶν autōn their	προφήτης, prophētēs a prophet,	Κρῆτες Krētes Cretans	ἀεὶ aei always	ψεῦσται, pseustai liars,

2527.9 adj pl neu	2319.4 noun pl neu	1057.2 noun nom pl fem	686.3 adj nom pl fem	3450.9 art nom sing fem	3114.1 noun nom sing fem
κακὰ kaka evil	θηρία, thēria wild beasts,	γαστέρες gasteres gluttons	ἀργαί. argai lazy.	13. ἡ hē The	μαρτυρία marturia testimony

3642.9 dem-pron nom sing fem	1498.4 verb 3sing indic pres act	225.2 adj nom sing	1217.1 prep	3614.12 rel- pron acc sing fem	155.3 noun acc sing fem
αὕτη hautē this	ἐστὶν estin is	ἀληθής· alēthēs true;	δι' di' for	ἣν hēn which	αἰτίαν aitian cause

1638.3 verb 2sing impr pres act	840.8 prs-pron acc pl masc	658.1 adv	2419.1 conj	5039.1 verb 3pl subj pres act
ἔλεγχε elenche reprove	αὐτοὺς autous them	ἀποτόμως, apotomōs severely,	ἵνα hina that	ὑγιαίνωσιν hugiainōsin they may be sound

1706.1 prep	3450.11 art dat sing fem	3963.3 noun dat sing fem	3231.1 partic	4196.3 verb nom pl masc part pres act
ἐν en in	τῇ tē the	πίστει, pistei faith,	14. μὴ mē not	προσέχοντες prosechontes paying attention

2426.1 name- adj dat pl masc	3316.1 noun dat pl masc	2504.1 conj	1769.6 noun dat pl fem	442.7 noun gen pl masc
Ἰουδαϊκοῖς Ioudaikois to Jewish	μύθοις muthois myths	καὶ kai and	ἐντολαῖς entolais commandments	ἀνθρώπων anthrōpōn of men,

15.a.Txt: 01א-corr
06D-corr,018K,020L
byz.
Var: 01א-org,02A,04C
06D-org,025P,33,Lach
Treg,Alf,Word,Tisc
We/Ho,Weis,Sod
UBS/*

648.8 verb gen pl masc part pres mid	3450.12 art acc sing fem	223.4 noun acc sing fem	3820.1 adj	3173.1 conj
ἀποστρεφομένων apostrephomenōn turning away from	τὴν tēn the	ἀλήθειαν. alētheian truth.	15. πάντα panta All things	(a μὲν) men

2485.6 adj	3450.4 art dat pl	2485.5 adj dat pl masc	3450.4 art dat pl	1156.2 conj	3256.6 verb dat pl masc part perf mid
καθαρὰ kathara pure	τοῖς tois to the	καθαροῖς· katharois pure;	τοῖς tois to the	δὲ de but	(μεμιασμένοις memiasmenois having been defiled

(ruining, upsetting, overturning) "whole houses" (households, families). They were teaching what was wrong "for filthy lucre's sake"; that is, "for dishonest gain."

1:12. Paul quoted Epimenides, a 6th-century, B.C., native of Knossos, Crete, and a philosopher held in high esteem. In Greek literature "to Cretanize" meant to lie and cheat. "Evil beasts" (brutes) suggests the maliciousness attributed to animals. The words "slow bellies" can be translated "lazy gluttons." This describes the Cretan's uncontrolled greed.

1:13. With the words "this witness (testimony) is true," Paul gave credence to the words of Epimenides (verse 12). Because Cretans were liars and lazy gluttons, Titus was to "rebuke them sharply." "Rebuke" is from the Greek verb *elenche* which has three basic meanings in the Pastorals: (1) "bring to light, expose, set forth" (Titus 2:15); (2) "convict, convince, point out" (Titus 1:9); and (3) "reprove, correct" (see 1 Timothy 5:20). The second meaning is the sense in this verse.

"Sharply" is the Greek adverb *apotomōs* ("severely, rigorously"). It occurs only here and in 2 Corinthians 13:10. "That they may be sound in the faith" is the purpose and objective of this sharp rebuke. Correction and restoration are the goals Paul set before Titus. "The faith" refers to the doctrine (accepted tenets of faith among the early Christians).

1:14. This verse describes what the Cretan Christians were already doing. It shows the Judaistic influence, first toward fables, then toward asceticism. The Cretans were giving heed to "Jewish fables" (myths). (Compare Titus 3:9; see 1 Timothy 1:4 and comments there.) They were being turned from the truth of the gospel by the "commandments of men." This is reminiscent of the Colossian heresy that Paul addressed in Colossians 2:20-22 and is further delineated in Titus 1:15. The New International Version translates this last clause: "the commands of those who reject the truth." Compare Isaiah's words in Isaiah 29:13 and Jesus' teaching in Mark 7:6-9.

1:15. "The pure" (*katharois*, "clean," both ceremonially and morally) refers to believers who are a contrast to the next clause and the term "unbelieving." "Things" does not include actions; Paul was not saying, "Unto the pure all actions are pure." Jesus said, "Behold, all things are clean unto you" (Luke 11:41). Paul repeated this in similar words in Romans 14:20 and taught that God made everything good (1 Timothy 4:4).

who subvert whole houses: . . . who subvert whole families, *Campbell* . . . They are upsetting entire families, *SEB.*

teaching things which they ought not: . . . not to think, *Williams.*

for filthy lucre's sake: . . . on behalf of sordid gain, *Concordant* . . . for the sake of dishonest gain, *Williams* . . . to make money, *NLT.*

12. One of themselves, [even] a prophet of their own, said: By one of their own number, *Montgomery* . . . their own countrymen, *Williams.*

The Cretians [are] alway liars, evil beasts, slow bellies: . . . bad actors, lazy fatties, *Klingensmith* . . . idle gluttons, *Montgomery* . . . lazy gluttons, *NASB, Confraternity* . . . but they love to eat, *SEB.*

13. This witness is true: This testimony, *Montgomery* . . . this opinion of them is true enough, *Norlie* . . . this tendency is true, *Williams.*

Wherefore rebuke them sharply: . . . correct them sternly, *Berkeley* . . . be exposing them severely, *Concordant.*

that they may be sound in the faith: . . . that they may be healthy, *Campbell.*

14. Not giving heed to Jewish fables: . . . and may pay no attention to Jewish legends, *TCNT* . . . must not hold onto Jewish legends, *SEB* . . . and not hang on to Jewish fairy tales, *Klingensmith.*

and commandments of men, that turn from the truth: . . . and to injunctions of people who turn their backs on the truth, *Berkeley.*

15. Unto the pure all things [are] pure: . . . all meats are pure, *Campbell.*

15.b.**Txt:** 06D-corr,byz.
Var: 01א,02A,04C,020L
33,Lach,Treg,Tisc
We/Ho,Weis,Sod
UBS/✶

3256.5 verb dat pl masc part perf mid	2504.1 conj	566.6 adj dat pl masc	3625.6 num card neu	2485.1 adj sing
[b✶ μεμιαμμένοις]	καὶ	ἀπίστοις	οὐδὲν	καθαρόν,
memiammenois	kai	apistois	ouden	katharon
[idem]	and	unbelieving	nothing	pure;

233.2 conj	3256.3 verb 3sing indic perf mid	840.1 prs-pron gen pl	2504.1 conj	3450.5 art nom sing masc	3426.1 noun nom sing masc	2504.1 conj
ἀλλὰ	μεμίανται	αὐτῶν	καὶ	ὁ	νοῦς	καὶ
alla	memiantai	autōn	kai	ho	nous	kai
but	are defiled	their	both	the	mind	and

3450.9 art nom sing fem	4743.1 noun nom sing fem	2296.4 noun acc sing masc	3533.3 verb 3pl indic pres act	3471.25 verb inf perf act
ἡ	συνείδησις.	16. θεὸν	ὁμολογοῦσιν	εἰδέναι,
hē	suneidēsis	theon	homologousin	eidenai
the	conscience.	God	they confess	to know,

3450.4 art dat pl neu	1156.2 conj	2024.6 noun dat pl neu	714.2 verb 3pl indic pres mid	940.1 adj nom pl masc	1498.23 verb nom pl masc part pres act
τοῖς	δὲ	ἔργοις	ἀρνοῦνται,	βδελυκτοὶ	ὄντες
tois	de	ergois	arnountai	bdeluktoi	ontes
in the	but	works	deny,	abominable	being

2504.1 conj	541.2 adj pl masc	2504.1 conj	4242.1 prep	3820.17 adj sing neu	2024.1 noun sing neu
καὶ	ἀπειθεῖς,	καὶ	πρὸς	πᾶν	ἔργον
kai	apeitheis	kai	pros	pan	ergon
and	disobedient,	and	as to	every	work

18.3 adj sing	95.3 adj nom pl masc	4622.1 prs-pron nom 2sing	1156.2 conj	2953.8 verb 2sing impr pres act
ἀγαθὸν	ἀδόκιμοι.	2:1. Σὺ	δὲ	λάλει
agathon	adokimoi	Su	de	lalei
good	found worthless.	You	but	speak

3614.17 rel-pron pl neu	4100.1 verb 3sing indic pres act	3450.11 art dat sing fem	5039.8 verb dat sing fem part pres act	1313.3 noun dat sing fem
ἃ	πρέπει	τῇ	ὑγιαινούσῃ	διδασκαλίᾳ·
ha	prepei	tē	hugiainousē	didaskalia
things that	are fitting	the	being sound	teaching:

4105.2 noun acc pl masc	3386.1 adj acc pl	1498.32 verb inf pres act	4441.1 adj acc pl masc	4850.1 adj acc pl
2. πρεσβύτας	νηφαλίους	εἶναι,	σεμνούς,	σώφρονας,
presbutas	nēphalious	einai	semnous	sōphronas
elderly men	sober	to be,	dignified,	self-controlled,

5039.6 verb acc pl masc part pres act	3450.11 art dat sing fem	3963.3 noun dat sing fem	3450.11 art dat sing fem	26.3 noun dat sing fem	3450.11 art dat sing fem
ὑγιαίνοντας	τῇ	πίστει,	τῇ	ἀγάπῃ,	τῇ
hugiainontas	tē	pistei	tē	agapē	tē
being sound	in the	faith,	in the	love,	in the

5119.3 noun dat sing fem	4106.1 noun acc pl fem	5447.1 adv	1706.1 prep	2658.1 noun dat sing neu
ὑπομονῇ·	3. πρεσβύτιδας	ὡσαύτως	ἐν	καταστήματι
hupomonē	presbutidas	hōsautōs	en	katastēmati
endurance;	aged women	in like manner	in	bearing

3.a.**Txt:** 01א-corr,06D
018K,020L,025P,byz.
Tisc
Var: 01א-org,02A,04C
Treg,Alf,We/Ho,Weis
Sod,UBS/✶

2388.1 adj acc pl fem	3231.1 partic	1222.6 adj acc pl fem	3231.1 partic	3234.1 adv
ἱεροπρεπεῖς,	μὴ	διαβόλους,	ʹ μὴ	[a✶ μηδὲ]
hieroprepeis	mē	diabolous	mē	mēde
as becomes sacred ones,	not	slanderers,	not	[nor]

But the "defiled and unbelieving" (*apistois*, "faithless") find nothing *katharon* ("pure"). The "unbelieving" could possibly refer to weak Jewish Christians who did not believe Christ abolished the ceremonial law (compare Romans 10:4; Ephesians 2:15; Colossians 2:14). Paul said their minds and consciences were defiled. Defilement begins in the mind and conscience (see Jesus' teaching in Matthew 15:10,11,16-20; Mark 7:14-23). The *Living Bible* renders this final clause: "for his dirty mind and rebellious heart color all he sees and hears." The word "defiled" (both places) means "corrupted."

1:16. A strong contrast exists between the first two clauses: "They profess (claim) . . . but in works they deny (disown)." False teachers stood condemned by their own conduct. Paul said they were (1) *bdeluktoi* ("abominable, detestable, repulsive"); (2) *apeitheis* ("disobedient"); and (3) *adokimoi* ("reprobate, unfit, unqualified, worthless, useless, rejected after testing"). The mention of "every good work" introduces a key emphasis in Titus (see 2:7,14; 3:1,8,14).

2:1. Chapter 2 opens with a shift in content. Paul addressed Titus with "But . . . thou." This is an emphatic pronoun contrasting Titus' work with that of the false teachers which Paul denounced in 1:10-16.

The word "speak" is also in contrast to the speech and conduct of the Cretan false teachers (see 1:10,11). Titus was to speak about the things that "become (*prepei*, 'to be suitable, fitting') sound doctrine" (compare 1:9). Other translations for "become" are "in accord with, befits." The Greek word *prepei* was used by Paul in several different contexts: see 1 Corinthians 11:13; Ephesians 5:3; 1 Timothy 2:10.

2:2. In his instructions to Titus, Paul indicated how behavior must line up with belief and illustrated how this applies to various age groups and sexes. In this verse Paul wrote about what the "aged men" must be. He listed six traits.

(1) They were to be *nēphalious* ("sober, temperate, practicing restraint"). This denotes refraining from wine and having moderation in general. (2) They were to be *semnous* ("grave, serious, worthy of respect, responsible"; compare 1 Timothy 3:8,11). (3) They were to be *sōphronas* ("temperate, sensible, prudent, self-controlled, thoughtful, sober-minded"; compare verse 8).

(4) Older men must be "sound" (*hugiainontas*), healthy in faith, love (*agapē*), and patience (*hupomonē* ["endurance, steadfastness, fortitude"]). Years should add strength to a man's faith, increase tolerance of others, and produce ability to endure whatever comes.

2:3. "Likewise" (*hōsautōs*) stresses that the aged women should have the same moral fiber as older men. They must be reverent in

but unto them that are defiled and unbelieving [is] nothing pure: . . . but nothing is clean to those, *SEB*.

but even their mind and conscience is defiled: . . . are polluted, *Campbell* . . . are alike filthy, *TCNT*.

16. They profess that they know God: They claim, *KJII, SEB* . . . They are avowing an acquaintance with, *Concordant*.

but in works they deny [him]: . . . they disown him, *TCNT*.

being abominable, and disobedient: . . . being detestable, *NASB* . . . They are rotten, *SEB*.

and unto every good work reprobate: . . . and are found worthless in every good task, *Norlie* . . . they are utterly unsatisfactory, *TCNT*.

1. But speak thou the things which become sound doctrine: . . . let your speech be consistent with, *NAB* . . . what falls in line with wholesome doctrine, *Berkeley*.

2. That the aged men be sober, grave, temperate: . . . be reserved, *Confraternity* . . . venerable, sensible, *Berkeley* . . . be vigilant...prudent, *Campbell* . . . worthy of respect, self-controlled, *SEB* . . . and discreet, *TCNT*.

sound in faith, in charity, in patience: . . . and constancy, *JB* . . . and enduring, *SEB*.

3. The aged women likewise: . . . that elderly women, *Confraternity* . . . in like manner, *Campbell*.

that [they be] in behaviour as becometh holiness: . . . should be reverent in their behavior, *Norlie* . . . be reverent in their demeanour, *TCNT* . . . be in deportment, *Campbell* . . . in demeanor, *Concordant* . . . behave in ways that befit those who belong to God, *NAB*.

Titus 2:4

3494.3 noun dat sing masc	4044.3 adj dat sing	1396.7 verb acc pl fem part perf mid	2538.1 adj acc pl fem
οἴνῳ	πολλῷ	δεδουλωμένας,	καλοδιδασκάλους,
oinō	pollō	dedoulōmenas	kalodidaskalous
to wine	much	having been enslaved,	teachers of what is right;

4.a.Txt: 01א-corr2,04C 06D,044,byz.
Var: 02A,010F,012G 015H,025P,104,326,365 1241

	2419.1 conj	4846.1 verb 3pl subj pres act	4846.2 verb 3pl indic pres act
	4. ἵνα	(✶ σωφρονίζωσιν	[ᵃ σωφρονίζουσιν]
	hina	sōphronizōsin	sōphronizousin
	that	might train in self-control	[train in self-control]

3450.15 art acc pl fem	3365.3 adj fem	5199.1 adj acc pl fem	1498.32 verb inf pres act	5225.1 adj acc pl fem
τὰς	νέας	φιλάνδρους	εἶναι,	φιλοτέκνους,
tas	neas	philandrous	einai	philoteknous
the	young	lovers of husbands	to be,	lovers of children,

5.a.Txt: 01א-corr 06D-corr,015H,018K 020L,025P,byz.Sod
Var: 01א-org,02A,04C 06D-org,Lach,Treg,Alf Tisc,We/Ho,Weis UBS/✶

4850.1 adj acc pl	52.6 adj acc pl fem	3488.1 adj acc pl fem	3487.1 adj acc pl fem
5. σώφρονας,	ἁγνάς,	(οἰκουρούς,	[ᵃ✶ οἰκουργούς,]
sōphronas	hagnas	oikourous	oikourgous
self-controlled,	chaste,	keepers at home,	[idem]

18.13 adj acc pl fem	5131.14 verb acc pl fem part pres mid	3450.4 art dat pl	2375.5 adj dat pl	433.8 noun dat pl masc
ἀγαθάς,	ὑποτασσομένας	τοῖς	ἰδίοις	ἀνδράσιν,
agathas	hupotassomenas	tois	idiois	andrasin
good,	being subject	to the	their own	husbands,

2419.1 conj	3231.1 partic	3450.5 art nom sing masc	3030.1 noun nom sing masc	3450.2 art gen sing	2296.2 noun gen sing masc
ἵνα	μὴ	ὁ	λόγος	τοῦ	θεοῦ
hina	mē	ho	logos	tou	theou
that	not	the	word		of God

980.19 verb 3sing subj pres mid	3450.8 art acc pl masc	3365.6 adj comp acc pl masc	5447.1 adv
βλασφημῆται.	6. τοὺς	νεωτέρους	ὡσαύτως
blasphēmētai	tous	neōterous	hōsautōs
may be evil spoken of.	The	younger	in like manner

3731.5 verb 2sing impr pres act	4845.3 verb inf pres act	3875.1 prep	3820.1 adj	4427.4 prs-pron acc sing masc
παρακάλει	σωφρονεῖν,	7. περὶ	πάντα	σεαυτὸν
parakalei	sōphronein	peri	panta	seauton
exhort	to be sensible;	in	all things	yourself

3792.13 verb nom sing masc part pres mid	5020.2 noun acc sing masc	2541.12 adj gen pl neu	2024.5 noun gen pl neu	1706.1 prep	3450.11 art dat sing fem
παρεχόμενος	τύπον	καλῶν	ἔργων,	ἐν	τῇ
parechomenos	tupon	kalōn	ergōn	en	tē
holding forth	an example	of good	works;	in	the

7.a.Txt: 01א-corr 06D-corr,byz.
Var: 01א-org,02A,04C 06D-org,018K,025P,33 Lach,Treg,Alf,Word Tisc,We/Ho,Weis,Sod UBS/✶

1313.3 noun dat sing fem	89.1 noun acc sing fem	855.1 noun acc sing fem	4442.3 noun acc sing fem
διδασκαλίᾳ	(ἀδιαφθορίαν,	[ᵃ✶ ἀφθορίαν,]	σεμνότητα,
didaskalia	adiaphthorian	aphthorian	semnotēta
teaching	sincerity,	[soundness,]	respectability,

7.b.Txt: 06D-corr,018K 020L,Steph
Var: 01א,02A,04C 06D-org,025P,Elzev Gries,Lach,Treg,Alf Word,Tisc,We/Ho,Weis Sod,UBS/✶

854.2 noun acc sing fem	3030.4 noun acc sing masc	5040.2 adj acc sing masc	174.1 adj acc sing masc
(ᵇ ἀφθαρσίαν,)	8. λόγον	ὑγιῆ,	ἀκατάγνωστον,
aphtharsian	logon	hugiē	akatagnōston
incorruption,	speech	sound,	not to be condemned;

behavior. The Greek behind "as becometh holiness" means "as befits a holy person." Slander and drunkenness are two vices that were common practices among Cretan women. Christian women are to resist these actions and conduct and instead be "teachers of good things." The Greek word is *kalodidaskalous* and may be translated "teach what is good." This teaching would take place primarily in the home and among the younger women, not in the church (compare 1 Timothy 2:11,12).

2:4,5. Older women were to teach the young women *philandrous* ("to love their husbands") and *philoteknous* ("to love their children"). Both Greek terms occur only here in the New Testament. The base word is *phileō* ("to love, have affection for, like").

Five important teachings follow: (1) "to be discreet," *sōphronas* ("sensible, self-controlled, prudent"); (2) "chaste," *hagnas* ("pure"); (3) "keepers at home," *oikourous* (possibly "workers at home, busy at home, domestics"); (4) "good," *agathas* ("kind," i.e., not hard or mean in their management of the home); (5) "obedient (subject, submissive) to their own husbands." The purpose for all this was "that the word of God be not blasphemed" (maligned, discredited).

2:6. Titus was to address the young men with one message: "Be soberminded!" He was to "exhort" (encourage, urge) them to this one objective. *Sōphronein* ("soberminded, self-controlled, prudent") is a word often found in this letter to Titus (see 1:8; 2:2,4). It stresses the need for self-mastery.

2:7. Having given instructions regarding young men, Paul now charged Titus (who may be considered a "young man") to proclaim the gospel by his life. The word "pattern" is *tupon* ("example, model"). Literally it means "an impress of a die." The same charge was given to Timothy (1 Timothy 4:12). But here Titus was commanded to be an example of "good works" (a key term in this epistle). His life should show what the gospel is and can do.

But his talk was important too. His "doctrine" (teaching) was to show "uncorruptness" (untaintedness, integrity). This underscores the need for purity of motive. Titus' teaching was to show "gravity" (seriousness, reverence, dignity). This points out the need for dignity of manner. As a teacher, Titus should demonstrate both purity of motive and dignity of manner.

2:8. "Sound speech" (soundness of speech or wholesome speech) that "cannot be condemned" (censured, reproached) would put his opponents to shame. If Titus was an example in the words he spoke,

not false accusers, not given to much wine: ... with no scandal-mongering, *JB* ... not enslaved to much wine, *Campbell.*

teachers of good things: ... teachers of the right behavior, *JB.*

4. That they may teach the young women to be sober: ... that they may train, *Confraternity* ... teachers of what is noble, *Berkeley.*

to love their husbands, to love their children: ... to be affectionate wives and mothers, *Williams.*

5. [To be] discreet, chaste, keepers at home, good: ... to control themselves, *SEB* ... domestic, *Confraternity* ... pure-minded, *TCNT* ... good housekeepers, *Berkeley.*

obedient to their own husbands: ... submissive to, *Berkeley* ... subordinate to, *Williams.*

that the word of God be not blasphemed: ... will not fall into disrepute, *NAB* ... be not reviled, *Confraternity* ... so that the message of God is never disgraced, *JB* ... may not be maligned, *TCNT* ... suffer reproach, *Williams.*

6. Young men likewise exhort to be sober minded: ... exhort to govern their passions, *Campbell* ... to control themselves, *SEB* ... to behave prudently, *Berkeley* ... to be sensible, *Norlie.*

7. In all things showing thyself a pattern of good works: ... a model of ideal acts, *Concordant.*

in doctrine [showing] uncorruptness, gravity, sincerity: ... be serious and be sincere, *SEB.*

8. Sound speech, that cannot be condemned: Offer a healthy message that cannot be criticized, *SEB* ... so wholesome that nobody can make objections to it, *JB.*

Titus 2:9

2419.1 conj	3450.5 art nom sing masc	1523.1 prep gen	1711.4 adj gen sing fem	1772.4 verb 3sing subj aor pass	3235.6 num card neu
ἵνα	ὁ	ἐξ	ἐναντίας	ἐντραπῇ,	μηδὲν
hina	ho	ex	enantias	entrapē	mēden
that	the	of	contrary	may be ashamed,	nothing

8.a.Txt: Steph
Var: 01ℵ,02A,04C,06D
025P,Lach,Treg,Alf
Tisc,We/Ho,Weis,Sod
UBS/☆

2174.17 verb nom sing masc part pres act	3875.1 prep	5050.2 prs-pron gen 2pl	2978.24 verb inf pres act	2978.24 verb inf pres act
ἔχων	(περὶ	ὑμῶν	λέγειν	[a☆ λέγειν
echōn	peri	humōn	legein	legein
having	concerning	you	to say	[to say

3875.1 prep	2231.2 prs-pron gen 1pl	5175.1 adj sing neu	1395.9 noun acc pl masc	2375.5 adj dat pl
περὶ	ἡμῶν]	φαῦλον.	9. Δούλους	ἰδίοις
peri	hēmōn	phaulon	Doulous	idiois
concerning	you]	evil.	Slaves	to their own

1197.5 noun dat pl masc	5131.15 verb inf pres mid	1706.1 prep	3820.5 adj dat pl	2080.3 adj acc pl masc
δεσπόταις	ὑποτάσσεσθαι,	ἐν	πᾶσιν	εὐαρέστους
despotais	hupotassesthai	en	pasin	euarestous
masters	to be subject,	in	everything	well pleasing

1498.32 verb inf pres act	3231.1 partic	480.5 verb acc pl masc part pres act	3231.1 partic	3420.1 verb acc pl masc part pres mid	233.2 conj
εἶναι,	μὴ	ἀντιλέγοντας,	10. μὴ	νοσφιζομένους,	ἀλλὰ
einai	mē	antilegontas	mē	nosphizomenous	alla
to be,	not	contradicting;	not	theiving,	but

3963.4 noun acc sing fem	3820.12 adj acc sing fem	3820.12 adj acc sing fem	3963.4 noun acc sing fem	1715.2 verb acc pl masc part pres mid
(πίστιν	πᾶσαν	[☆ πᾶσαν	πίστιν]	ἐνδεικνυμένους
pistin	pasan	pasan	pistin	endeiknumenous
faithfulness	all	[all	faithfulness]	showing

10.a.Var: 01ℵ,02A,04C
06D,33,Lach,Treg,Alf
Word,Tisc,We/Ho,Weis
Sod,UBS/☆

18.12 adj acc sing fem	2419.1 conj	3450.12 art acc sing fem	1313.4 noun acc sing fem	3450.12 art acc sing fem	3450.2 art gen sing
ἀγαθήν·	ἵνα	τὴν	διδασκαλίαν	[a☆+ τὴν]	τοῦ
agathēn	hina	tēn	didaskalian	tēn	tou
good,	that	the	teaching	[the]	of the

10.b.Txt: Steph
Var: 01ℵ,02A,04C,06D
018K,020L,025P,byz.
Elzev,Gries,Lach,Treg
Alf,Word,Tisc,We/Ho
Weis,Sod,UBS/☆

4842.2 noun gen sing masc	5050.2 prs-pron gen 2pl	2231.2 prs-pron gen 1pl	2296.2 noun gen sing masc	2858.2 verb 3pl subj pres act
σωτῆρος	(ὑμῶν	[b☆ ἡμῶν]	θεοῦ	κοσμῶσιν
sōtēros	humōn	hēmōn	theou	kosmōsin
Saviour	your	[our]	God	they may adorn

1706.1 prep	3820.5 adj dat pl	1998.3 verb 3sing indic aor pass	1056.1 conj	3450.9 art nom sing fem	5322.1 noun nom sing fem
ἐν	πᾶσιν.	11. Ἐπεφάνη	γὰρ	ἡ	χάρις
en	pasin	Epephanē	gar	hē	charis
in	all things.	Appeared	for	the	grace

11.a.Txt: 04C-corr
06D-corr,018K,020L
025P,byz.Sod
Var: 01ℵ,02A,04C-org
06D-org,Lach,Treg,Alf
Tisc,We/Ho,Weis
UBS/☆

3450.2 art gen sing	2296.2 noun gen sing masc	3450.9 art nom sing fem	4844.1 adj nom sing fem	3820.5 adj dat pl	442.8 noun dat pl masc
τοῦ	θεοῦ	(a ἡ)	σωτήριος	πᾶσιν	ἀνθρώποις,
tou	theou	hē	sōtērios	pasin	anthrōpois
	of God	the	saving	for all	men,

3674.4 verb nom sing fem part pres act	2231.4 prs-pron acc 1pl	2419.1 conj	714.12 verb nom pl masc part aor mid	3450.12 art acc sing fem
12. παιδεύουσα	ἡμᾶς	ἵνα	ἀρνησάμενοι	τὴν
paideuousa	hēmas	hina	arnēsamenoi	tēn
instructing	us	that,	having denied	the

those who opposed him ("he that is of the contrary part") would find nothing they could gainsay. The final clause of this verse, "having no evil thing to say of you," carries the idea that Titus was to present no opportunity for his opponents to use an evil report against him. His "sound speech" was to be truthful, wholesome, and absolutely irreproachable. Anything his opponents might say would then be seen as false, fabricated, empty, and evil.

2:9. Next Paul addressed the subject of slavery as he did in 1 Timothy 6:1,2. Titus was to "exhort" (teach, urge, bid) Christian slaves to be "obedient" (subject, submissive) to their masters. The Greek for "masters" is the root for the English word *despot* and shows the absolute authority the master had over his slave. Roman slaves had no legal rights whatsoever.

Slaves were to "please them well in all things," that is, give satisfaction in every respect. The verb translated "not answering again" is literally "to contradict" and can mean "to oppose, to show active enmity against."

2:10. "Purloining" is literally "put on one side for themselves" and connotes petty stealing. This was easily done by household slaves. On the positive side, slaves were to show they could be trusted. In so doing they would "adorn" the gospel. *Kosmōsin* ("adorn, do credit to") is literally "put in proper order." The Greek verb can be used of the setting of a jewel to show its best features and full beauty. Christian slaves could testify of the gospel by their willing obedience to their masters.

2:11. Verses 11-14 constitute one of the two doctrinal sections of this epistle (the other is 3:4-7). Paul here described God's grace and its effect on believers. It brings salvation and results in rejection of ungodliness and demonstration of holy living.

The word "for" introduces this new paragraph and the doctrinal basis for the ethical demands just given (verses 2-10). "Grace" is God's undeserved love (compare Romans 5:6-10) shown in Christ and independent from any human effort (see Titus 3:5; Ephesians 2:8,9). "Hath appeared" is in the aorist tense which points to one definite act. In this case it is the Incarnation that brought Christ to us (compare 3:4).

2:12. "Teaching" here is more than instruction. The word in the Greek means the whole process of educating a child—instruction, encouragement, and discipline. The grace of God teaches that Christians should live differently. First, negatively, they deny or

that he that is of the contrary part may be ashamed: . . . that will shame the opponent, *Berkeley* . . . may be put to shame, *Williams.*

having no evil thing to say of you: . . . having nothing bad to say concerning us, *Concordant* . . . and not open to criticism, *Norlie* . . . against us, *SEB.*

9. [Exhort] servants to be obedient unto their own masters: Continue urging slaves to practice perfect submission, *Williams* . . . to be submissive, *TCNT.*

[and] to please [them] well in all [things]: . . . to give them perfect satisfaction, *Williams.*

not answering again: Tell them not to contradict, *TCNT* . . . not contradicting them, *NAB* . . . not to talk back, *Berkeley* . . . without argument, *Norlie* . . . They must not argue, *NLT.*

10. Not purloining: . . . or pilfer, *TCNT* . . . not pilfering, *Confraternity* . . . no petty thieving, *JB* . . . not embezzling, *Concordant* . . . not secretly stealing, *Campbell.*

but showing all good fidelity: . . . but showing faithfulness, *Confraternity* . . . but prove they can be trusted in every way, *NLT.*

that they may adorn the doctrine of God our Saviour in all things: . . . they are in every way a credit to the teaching, *JB* . . . they shall beautify the teaching of, *Berkeley.*

11. For the grace of God that bringeth salvation hath appeared to all men: . . . the saving grace of God made its advent to all humanity, *Concordant* . . . with its offer of salvation to all mankind, *Williams* . . . for all people, *Berkeley* . . . to save all mankind, *SEB.*

12. Teaching us that: . . . instructing us, *Confraternity.*

757.2 noun
acc sing fem
ἀσέβειαν
asebeian
ungodliness

2504.1 conj
καὶ
kai
and

3450.15 art
acc pl fem
τὰς
tas
the

2859.1 adj
acc pl fem
κοσμικὰς
kosmikas
wordly

1924.1 noun fem
ἐπιθυμίας,
epithumias
desires,

4848.1 adv
σωφρόνως
sōphronōs
sensibly

2504.1 conj
καὶ
kai
and

1341.1 adv
δικαίως
dikaiōs
righteously

2504.1 conj
καὶ
kai
and

2134.1 adv
εὐσεβῶς
eusebōs
piously

2180.24 verb
1pl subj aor act
ζήσωμεν
zēsōmen
we should live

1706.1 prep
ἐν
en
in

3450.3 art
dat sing
τῷ
tō
the

3431.1 adv
νῦν
nun
now

163.2 noun
dat sing masc
αἰῶνι,
aiōni
age,

13. 4185.5 verb nom pl
masc part pres mid
προσδεχόμενοι
prosdechomenoi
awaiting

3450.12 art
acc sing fem
τὴν
tēn
the

3079.6 adj
acc sing fem
μακαρίαν
makarian
blessed

1667.4 noun
acc sing fem
ἐλπίδα
elpida
hope

2504.1 conj
καὶ
kai
and

1999.3 noun
acc sing fem
ἐπιφάνειαν
epiphaneian
appearing

3450.10 art
gen sing fem
τῆς
tēs
of the

1385.2 noun
gen sing fem
δόξης
doxēs
glory

3450.2 art
gen sing
τοῦ
tou
of the

3144.3 adj
gen sing masc
μεγάλου
megalou
great

2296.2 noun
gen sing masc
θεοῦ
theou
God

2504.1 conj
καὶ
kai
and

4842.2 noun
gen sing masc
σωτῆρος
sōtēros
Saviour

2231.2 prs-
pron gen 1pl
ἡμῶν
hēmōn
of our

2400.2 name masc
Ἰησοῦ
Iēsou
Jesus

5382.2 name
gen masc
Χριστοῦ,
Christou
Christ;

2400.2 name masc
[✻ Ἰησοῦ
Iēsou
[Jesus

5382.2 name
gen masc
Χριστοῦ,]
Christou
Christ;]

14. 3614.5 rel-pron
nom sing masc
ὃς
hos
who

1319.14 verb 3sing
indic aor act
ἔδωκεν
edōken
gave

1431.6 prs-pron
acc sing masc
ἑαυτὸν
heauton
himself

5065.1 prep
ὑπὲρ
huper
for

2231.2 prs-
pron gen 1pl
ἡμῶν,
hēmōn
us,

2419.1 conj
ἵνα
hina
that

3056.3 verb 3sing
subj aor mid
λυτρώσηται
lutrōsētai
he might redeem

2231.4 prs-
pron acc 1pl
ἡμᾶς
hēmas
us

570.3 prep
ἀπὸ
apo
from

3820.10 adj
gen sing fem
πάσης
pasēs
all

455.2 noun
gen sing fem
ἀνομίας,
anomias
lawlessness,

2504.1 conj
καὶ
kai
and

2483.5 verb 3sing
subj aor act
καθαρίσῃ
katharisē
might purify

1431.5 prs-pron
dat sing masc
ἑαυτῷ
heautō
to himself

2967.4 noun
acc sing masc
λαὸν
laon
a people

3904.1 adj
acc sing masc
περιούσιον,
periousion
special,

2190.2 noun
acc sing masc
ζηλωτὴν
zēlōtēn
zealous

2541.12 adj
gen pl neu
καλῶν
kalōn
of good

2024.5 noun
gen pl neu
ἔργων.
ergōn
works.

15. 3642.18 dem-
pron pl neu
Ταῦτα
Tauta
These things

2953.8 verb 2sing
impr pres act
λάλει,
lalei
speak,

2504.1 conj
καὶ
kai
and

3731.5 verb 2sing
impr pres act
παρακάλει,
parakalei
exhort,

2504.1 conj
καὶ
kai
and

1638.3 verb 2sing
impr pres act
ἔλεγχε
elenche
reprove

3196.3 prep
μετὰ
meta
with

3820.10 adj
gen sing fem
πάσης
pasēs
all

1987.1 noun
gen sing fem
ἐπιταγῆς.
epitagēs
command.

3235.3 num
card nom masc
μηδείς
mēdeis
No one

4622.2 prs-
pron gen 2sing
σου
sou
you

3925.1 verb 3sing
impr pres act
περιφρονείτω.
periphroneitō
let despise.

3:1. 5117.1 verb 2sing
impr pres act
Ὑπομίμνησκε
Hupomimnēske
Put in remembrance

renounce "ungodliness" (lack of reverence for God, godlessness). Second, they give up "worldly lusts" (passions, desires).

Positively, Christians live "soberly" (self-controlled, prudently), "righteously" (upright, justly), and "godly" (reverently). A triad of relationships may be seen in these adverbs. A Christian lives right in relation to himself (self-controlled), to others (justly), and to God (reverently). He does this "in this present world" (age).

2:13. The doctrinal emphasis now moves from the Incarnation to the Second Advent. Paul calls it "that blessed hope." It is not just a wish but divine assurance for life beyond this life. Paul referred to this event in his other pastoral letters (see 1 Timothy 6:14; 2 Timothy 4:1). Here he wrote of the "glorious appearing" (*epiphaneian*) of Jesus Christ. His first coming was with fullness of grace (Titus 2:11, compare John 1:14). His second coming will be in the fullness of glory.

The phrase "the great God and our Saviour Jesus Christ" can refer to both Father and Son. It can also be translated "our great God and Saviour Jesus Christ" and focus on the Son's deity. No matter which translation is accepted, the primary sense is that Jesus is coming again, and He will be seen in His true glory and majesty. This is our blessed hope!

2:14. The doctrinal emphasis now focuses on Christ's atonement. He "gave himself for us" in order to "redeem" (*lutrōsētai*, literally, "to release on receipt of a ransom") us from all "iniquity" (wickedness, lawlessness) and "purify" (compare Ephesians 5:25,26) us. Redemption and purification are the two great works involved in salvation.

"Peculiar" means "special, chosen, one's own possession" (1 Peter 2:9). Such people are "zealous" (eager, devoted) to do good work.

2:15. As a summary, verse 15 is transitional to 3:1 where Titus was to speak, exhort, and rebuke. "Speak" (teach) involves proclamation.

The command "exhort" involves encouragement (compare 2 Timothy 4:2). Titus was to encourage the Cretan Christians with positive and edifying words, but with the balance of the next command. "Rebuke" (reprove) involves the ministry of conviction. Titus was to convince wrongdoers of their sins so that they might repent and seek God's forgiveness and cleansing.

Titus was to do all this "with all authority" (*epitagēs*). This Greek term is used only by Paul and always in the sense of a divine command. Titus was to recognize that his authority came from God. He then must not allow anyone to "despise" (disregard) him (compare 1 Timothy 4:12).

denying ungodliness and worldly lusts: . . . to renounce impiety and evil passions, *Montgomery* . . . to give up godless ways and worldly cravings, *Williams* . . . and all our worldly ambitions, *JB*.

we should live soberly, righteously, and godly: . . . and live temperately, *NAB* . . . to live self-controlled, *SEB* . . . we should live wisely, *Klingensmith* . . . serious, upright, *Williams*.

in this present world: . . . in this present age, *Montgomery*.

13. Looking for that blessed hope, and the glorious appearing: While we look for, *Montgomery* . . . with expectation of, *Berkeley* . . . while we are waiting for the realization of, *Williams* . . . expecting the blessed hope, *Campbell* . . . as we await our blessed hope, *NAB*.

of the great God and our Saviour Jesus Christ:

14. Who gave himself for us:
that he might redeem us from all iniquity: . . . to buy us back from all lawlessness, *Klingensmith* . . . to ransom us from, *Williams* . . . from every kind of sin, *SEB*.

and purify unto himself a peculiar people: . . . to cleanse for himself, *NAB* . . . a nation, *SEB*.

zealous of good works: . . . eager to do good deeds, *SEB* . . . eager to do good works, *Berkeley* . . . good deeds, *Norlie*.

15. These things speak, and exhort, and rebuke: . . . and expose with every injunction, *Concordant* . . . use them to refute opponents, *TCNT*.

with all authority: . . . with absolute authority, *TCNT*.

Let no man despise thee: . . . and no one is to question it, *JB* . . . Let no one slight you, *Concordant* . . . Let no one disregard you, *Norlie* . . . Don't let anyone look down on you! *SEB* . . . Let no one belittle you, *Williams*.

Titus 3:2

1.a.Txt: 06D-corr,018K 020L,025P,byz.it.sa.bo. Weis
Var: 01ℵ,02A,04C 06D-org,33,Lach,Treg Alf,Tisc,We/Ho,Sod UBS/✶

840.8 prs-pron acc pl masc	741.6 noun dat pl fem	2504.1 conj	1833.7 noun dat pl fem	5131.15 verb inf pres mid
αὐτοὺς	ἀρχαῖς	⌐a καὶ ⌐	ἐξουσίαις	ὑποτάσσεσθαι,
autous them	archais to rulers	kai and	exousiais to authorities	hupotassesthai, to subject themselves,

3842.2 verb inf pres act	4242.1 prep	3820.17 adj sing neu	2024.1 noun sing neu	18.3 adj sing	2071.3 adj acc pl masc
πειθαρχεῖν,	πρὸς	πᾶν	ἔργον	ἀγαθὸν	ἑτοίμους
peitharchein, to be obedient,	pros to	pan every	ergon work	agathon good	hetoimous ready

1498.32 verb inf pres act	3235.4 num card acc masc	980.7 verb inf pres act	267.2 adj acc pl masc
εἶναι,	**2.** μηδένα	βλασφημεῖν,	ἀμάχους
einai to be,	mēdena no one	blasphēmein, to speak evil of,	amachous not contentious

1498.32 verb inf pres act	1918.3 adj acc pl masc	3820.12 adj acc sing fem	1715.2 verb acc pl masc part pres mid	4095.4 noun acc sing fem
εἶναι,	ἐπιεικεῖς,	πᾶσαν	ἐνδεικνυμένους	⌐ πραότητα
einai to be,	epieikeis gentle,	pasan all	endeiknumenous demonstrating	praotēta meekness

4095.5 noun acc sing fem	4242.1 prep	3820.8 adj acc pl masc	442.9 noun acc pl masc	1498.36 verb 1pl indic imperf act
[✶ πραυ˙τητα]	πρὸς	πάντας	ἀνθρώπους.	**3.** Ἦμεν
prautēta [idem]	pros towards	pantas all	anthrōpous men.	Ēmen Were

1056.1 conj	4077.1 adv	2504.1 conj	2231.1 prs-pron nom 1pl	451.1 adj nom pl masc	541.2 adj pl masc
γὰρ	ποτε	καὶ	ἡμεῖς	ἀνόητοι,	ἀπειθεῖς,
gar for	pote then	kai also	hēmeis we	anoētoi senseless,	apeitheis disobedient,

3966.13 verb nom pl masc part pres mid	1392.7 verb nom pl masc part pres act	1924.7 noun dat pl fem	2504.1 conj	2220.3 noun dat pl fem
πλανώμενοι,	δουλεύοντες	ἐπιθυμίαις	καὶ	ἡδοναῖς
planōmenoi being led astray,	douleuontes serving	epithumiais lusts	kai and	hēdonais pleasures

4024.3 adj dat pl fem	1706.1 prep	2520.3 noun dat sing fem	2504.1 conj	5192.3 noun dat sing masc	1230.2 verb nom pl masc part pres act
ποικίλαις,	ἐν	κακία	καὶ	φθόνῳ	διάγοντες,
poikilais various,	en in	kakia malice	kai and	phthonō envy	diagontes living,

4618.1 adj nom pl masc	3268.6 verb nom pl masc part pres act	238.3 prs-pron acc pl masc	3616.1 conj	1156.2 conj	3450.9 art nom sing fem
στυγητοί,	μισοῦντες	ἀλλήλους·	**4.** ὅτε	δὲ	ἡ
stugētoi hateful,	misountes hating	allēlous one another.	hote When	de but	hē the

5379.1 noun nom sing fem	2504.1 conj	3450.9 art nom sing fem	5200.1 noun nom sing fem	1998.3 verb 3sing indic aor pass	3450.2 art gen sing
χρηστότης	καὶ	ἡ	φιλανθρωπία	ἐπεφάνη	τοῦ
chrēstotēs kindness	kai and	hē the	philanthrōpia love to man	epephanē appeared	tou of the

4842.2 noun gen sing masc	2231.2 prs-pron gen 1pl	2296.2 noun gen sing masc	3620.2 partic	1523.1 prep gen	2024.5 noun gen pl neu	3450.1 art gen pl
σωτῆρος	ἡμῶν	θεοῦ,	**5.** οὐκ	ἐξ	ἔργων	τῶν
sōtēros Saviour	hēmōn our	theou, God,	ouk not	ex by	ergōn works	tōn the

3:1. Verses 1 and 2 open a new topic that might be titled "Practical Christian Living." The first verse addresses the Christian's obligation to earthly government. Verse 2 deals with the Christian's obligations to his fellowman. Both Paul (Romans 13:1-7) and Peter (1 Peter 2:13-17) addressed the issue of duty to civil government.

Christians are to be "subject" (submissive) to "principalities and powers" (rulers and authorities). These terms are meant to be inclusive; they refer to all levels of government. "To obey magistrates" is one part of this submission. "To be ready (for) every good work" is the other part. Good works is a major theme of this epistle (see 1:16; 2:7,14; 3:1,8,14).

1. Put them in mind: Constantly remind people, *Williams*.
to be subject to principalities and powers, to obey magistrates: . . . to obey the leaders of their country, *NLT* . . . to respect government authorities, *Klingensmith*.
to be ready to every good work: . . . for any honest work, *RSV* . . . for any good enterprise, *Williams*.

3:2. Outlined here are the Christian's obligations to his fellowman, whether or not he is a Christian. Four duties are listed; the first two are negative, the last two are positive. The Christian is not to "speak evil of" (slander) anyone. This was an especially favorite pastime of the beastly Cretans (1:12). The Christian is not to be a "brawler" (*amachous*, "not a fighter"). The English word *macho* came from this root through the Latin and Spanish languages.

The positive duties are gentleness (considerateness, kindness) and meekness (*praoteta*—which describes the person whose temper is always under control and who bears wrongs done to him, showing humility and perfect courtesy).

2. To speak evil of no man, to be no brawlers: . . . not to slander anyone, *Berkeley* . . . to avoid quarreling, *Lilly, TCNT* . . . stop abusing anyone, *Williams* . . . not quarrelsome, *Confraternity* . . . to be peaceable, *SEB*.
[but] gentle, showing all meekness unto all men: . . . to be considerate, *SEB* . . . but moderate, *Confraternity* . . . but equitable, *Campbell*.

3:3. This verse provides a general description of unregenerate human nature. Paul expressed this in the past tense, and the list shows how great the grace of God really is. "Foolish" is *anoētoi*, literally, "senseless, without spiritual understanding." Disobedience is directed toward God and deception is related to man. A metaphor of slavery describes man's bondage to his passions and pursuit of pleasures. Malice and envy have but one result: being hated by others and "hating one another."

3. For we ourselves also were sometimes: . . . once we too were, *Williams*.
foolish, disobedient, deceived: . . . were thoughtless, *Berkeley* . . . and deluded, *Norlie* . . . misled, *TCNT*.
serving divers lusts and pleasures: . . . habitual slaves, *Williams* . . . slavishly serving divers inordinate desires, *Campbell* . . . slaves to various lusts, *Confraternity* . . . to passion and all sorts of pleasures, *Klingensmith*.
living in malice and envy: . . . spending our lives, *Williams* . . . wasting our time in, *Berkeley*.
hateful, [and] hating one another: People hated us and we hated them, *SEB*.

3:4. The "but" that begins this verse provides a strong contrast to that which has gone before. Man's degenerate human nature—the worst—is contrasted with God's kindness and love—the best. Verses 4-7 form the second doctrinal section of this letter (2:11-14 is the first).

Paul wrote to Titus that two wonderful characteristics of God have "appeared" (*epephanē*, compare 2:11). God's *chrēstotēs* ("kindness, goodness, generosity") has come to man. *Chrēstotēs* is not just a warm feeling on God's part, but His generous action toward man that is a part of His nature (and in contrast to man's nature described in verse 3). God's *philanthrōpia* ("love for mankind," the root of the English word *philanthropy*) means His love for all mankind (compare John 3:16). Paul built on these two characteristics in the next verses with such words as "mercy" and "grace." God's kindness and love are the beginning point of God's salvation of man.

4. But after that the kindness and love of God our Saviour toward man appeared: . . . then there dawned on us the, *Norlie* . . . and philanthropy of God, *Campbell*.

Titus 3:6

5.a.Txt: 04C-corr
06D-corr,018K,020L
025P,byz.
Var: 01‭‮-org,02A,04C-org
06D-org,33,Lach,Treg
Alf,Tisc,We/Ho,Weis
Sod,UBS/*

5.b.Txt: 06D-corr,018K
020L,byz.
Var: 01‭‮,02A,025P,33
Lach,Treg,Alf,Word
Tisc,We/Ho,Weis,Sod
UBS/*

1706.1 prep	1336.3 noun dat sing fem	3614.1 rel-pron gen pl	3614.17 rel-pron pl neu	4020.25 verb 1pl indic aor act	2231.1 prs-pron nom 1pl
ἐν	δικαιοσύνῃ	ʽ ὧν	[ᵃ☆ ἃ]	ἐποιήσαμεν	ἡμεῖς,
en	*dikaiosunē*	*hōn*	*ha*	*epoiēsamen*	*hēmeis*
in	righteousness	which	[idem]	practiced	we,

233.2 conj	2567.3 prep	3450.6 art acc sing masc	840.3 prs-pron gen sing	1643.1 noun acc sing masc	3450.16 art sing neu
ἀλλὰ	κατὰ	ʽ τὸν	αὐτοῦ	ἔλεον	[ᵇ☆ τὸ
alla	*kata*	*ton*	*autou*	*eleon*	*to*
but	according to	the	his	mercy	[the

840.3 prs-pron gen sing	1643.2 noun sing neu	4834.5 verb 3sing indic aor act	2231.4 prs-pron acc 1pl	1217.2 prep	3039.1 noun gen sing neu
αὐτοῦ	ἔλεος]	ἔσωσεν	ἡμᾶς,	διὰ	λουτροῦ
autou	*eleos*	*esōsen*	*hēmas*	*dia*	*loutrou*
his	mercy]	he saved	us,	through	washing

3686.1 noun gen sing fem	2504.1 conj	340.1 noun gen sing fem	4011.2 noun gen sing neu	39.2 adj gen sing
παλιγγενεσίας	καὶ	ἀνακαινώσεως	πνεύματος	ἁγίου,
palingenesias	*kai*	*anakainōseōs*	*pneumatos*	*hagiou*
of regeneration	and	renewing	of Spirit	Holy,

3614.2 rel-pron gen sing	1618.1 verb 3sing indic aor act	1894.1 prep	2231.4 prs-pron acc 1pl	4005.1 adv	1217.2 prep
6. οὗ	ἐξέχεεν	ἐφ᾽	ἡμᾶς	πλουσίως	διὰ
hou	*execheen*	*eph'*	*hēmas*	*plousiōs*	*dia*
which	he poured out	on	us	richly	through

2400.2 name masc	5382.2 name gen masc	3450.2 art gen sing	4842.2 noun gen sing masc	2231.2 prs-pron gen 1pl	2419.1 conj
Ἰησοῦ	Χριστοῦ	τοῦ	σωτῆρος	ἡμῶν,	**7.** ἵνα
Iēsou	*Christou*	*tou*	*sōtēros*	*hēmōn*	*hina*
Jesus	Christ	the	Saviour	our;	that

1338.17 verb nom pl masc part aor pass	3450.11 art dat sing fem	1552.2 dem-pron gen sing	5322.3 noun dat sing fem	2791.3 noun nom pl masc
δικαιωθέντες	τῇ	ἐκείνου	χάριτι,	κληρονόμοι
dikaiōthentes	*tē*	*ekeinou*	*chariti*	*klēronomoi*
having been justified	by the	that	grace,	heirs

7.a.Txt: 01‭‮-corr
06D-corr,018K,020L
byz.
Var: 01‭‮-org,02A,04C
06D-org,025P,33,Lach
Treg,Alf,Word,Tisc
We/Ho,Weis,Sod,UBS/*

1090.41 verb 1pl subj aor mid	1090.79 verb 1pl subj aor pass	2567.1 prep	1667.4 noun acc sing fem
ʽ γενώμεθα	[ᵃ☆ γενηθῶμεν]	κατ᾽	ἐλπίδα
genōmetha	*genēthōmen*	*kat'*	*elpida*
we should become	[idem]	according to	hope

2205.2 noun gen sing fem	164.2 adj gen sing	3964.2 adj nom sing masc	3450.5 art nom sing masc	3030.1 noun nom sing masc	2504.1 conj
ζωῆς	αἰωνίου.	**8.** Πιστὸς	ὁ	λόγος,	καὶ
zōēs	*aiōniou*	*Pistos*	*ho*	*logos*	*kai*
of life	eternal.	Faithful	the	word,	and

3875.1 prep	3642.2 dem-pron gen pl	1007.1 verb 1sing indic pres mid	4622.4 prs-pron acc 2sing
περὶ	τούτων	βούλομαί	σε
peri	*toutōn*	*boulomai*	*se*
concerning	these things	I desire	you

1220.2 verb inf pres mid	2419.1 conj	5267.1 verb 3pl subj pres act	2541.12 adj gen pl neu	2024.5 noun gen pl neu
διαβεβαιοῦσθαι,	ἵνα	φροντίζωσιν	καλῶν	ἔργων
diabebaiousthai	*hina*	*phrontizōsin*	*kalōn*	*ergōn*
to affirm strongly,	that	may take care	good	works

The title "God our Saviour" has been used in this epistle twice before (1:3; 2:10; compare 1:4; 2:13; 3:6).

3:5. Salvation is God's work. Paul said it is "*not* by works of righteousness (deeds prescribed by the law of Moses) which we have done, but according to *his* mercy he saved *us*" (italics supplied to show the emphasis in the Greek). Man cannot earn his salvation by good deeds.

Then Paul added the means of this salvation: "By the washing of regeneration (rebirth), and renewing (renewal) of the Holy Ghost." This is what Jesus taught Nicodemus (compare the wording in John 3:5). "Washing" is seen by most commentators as a reference to water baptism which is an outward seal and sign of regeneration. "Renewing" is that inner work of the Spirit Jesus was talking about in John chapter 3.

5. Not by works of righteousness which we have done: . . . not for upright deeds, *Williams* . . . not in consequence of any righteous actions, *TCNT* . . . not because of any deeds that we had done in righteousness, *Montgomery.*

but according to his mercy he saved us: . . . but in agreement with His mercy, *Berkeley* . . . in virtue of his own mercy, *RSV* . . . because of his own pity for us, *Montgomery.*

by the washing of regeneration: . . . through the bath, *Confraternity, Williams* . . . by the renovating power of, *TCNT.*

and renewing of the Holy Ghost: . . . renewal, that come from, *Adams.*

3:6. Verse 6 says God "shed" (*execheen*, "poured out"—the verb here is in the aorist tense and therefore looks back to a specific event, i.e., the Day of Pentecost) His Holy Spirit "abundantly" (generously, richly; compare Acts 2:33). "On us" refers to Paul and his associates' personal experience of being filled with the Holy Spirit. The mediator of this wonderful outpouring is "Jesus Christ our Saviour."

6. Which he shed on us abundantly: . . . which he poured out on us richly, *Campbell* . . . who was given to us freely, *Norlie* . . . God generously poured out, *SEB* . . . He poured out effusively, *Adams.*

through Jesus Christ our Saviour:

3:7. Paul moved from the doctrines of salvation and the Holy Spirit to those of justification and adoption. The past, present, and future can be seen in this verse. God's grace brings justification—past sins are forgiven. Then He adopts those who believe on Christ (Galatians 3:4,5), and their present life is hid with Christ in God (Colossians 3:3). The hope of eternal life is yet future (compare Titus 1:2; Romans 8:11,15-17).

The word "heirs" contains tremendous significance. Imagine a similar situation in the natural, of an urchin on the streets—homeless, unloved, with a bleak future. Then a rich man adopts him, gives him his name, and makes him his heir. That, in a small way, describes what God has done for believers. Heirs of all He has! Only eternity will reveal what that means.

7. That being justified by his grace: In order that, *Montgomery* . . . so that we might come into right standing with God, *Williams.*

we should be made heirs according to the hope of eternal life: . . . become possessors of enduring Life, *TCNT.*

3:8. This verse is transitional. "This is a faithful saying" refers to the doctrinal statement of verses 4-7. Titus was to keep on affirming "these things" (compare 2:15). The purpose is given in the next clause. Carefulness to "maintain" (*proistasthai*, literally, "to be forward in, to devote themselves before all else to") good works is good and profitable for everyone.

8. [This is] a faithful saying: What I have just said is trustworthy, *Lilly* . . . This saying is trustworthy, *Montgomery* . . . It is a message to be trusted, *Williams* . . . This word is dependable, *Klingensmith.*

and these things I will that thou affirm constantly: Now, I want you to insist on these things with assurance *Adams* . . . I want you to be emphatic about these things, *Williams* . . . on these subjects that I desire you to lay especial stress, *TCNT* . . . On this I want you to firmly insist, *Montgomery.*

8.a.**Txt:** Steph
Var: 01א,02A,04C,06D
018K,020L,025P,Lach
Treg,Alf,Word,Tisc
We/Ho,Weis,Sod
UBS/✶

8.b.**Txt:** 06D-corr,018K
020L,byz.
Var: 01א,02A,04C
06D-org,Treg,Alf
Word,Tisc,We/Ho,Weis
Sod,UBS/✶

9.a.**Txt:** 01א-corr,02A
04C,018K,020L,025P
byz.bo.Sod
Var: 01א-org,06D,Tisc
We/Ho,Weis,UBS/✶

4150.7 verb inf pres mid	3450.7 art nom pl masc	3961.45 verb nom pl masc part perf act	3450.3 art dat sing	2296.3 noun dat sing masc
προι ʿστασθαι	οἱ	πεπιστευκότες	ʿa τῷ ʾ	θεῷ.
proistasthai	hoi	pepisteukotes	tō	theō
to be devoted to	the	having believed		God.

3642.18 dem-pron pl neu	1498.4 verb 3sing indic pres act	3450.17 art pl neu	2541.11 adj pl neu	2504.1 conj	5457.2 adj pl neu
ταῦτά	ἐστιν	ʿb τὰ ʾ	καλὰ	καὶ	ὠφέλιμα
tauta	estin	ta	kala	kai	ōphelima
These things	are	the	good	and	profitable

3450.4 art dat pl	442.8 noun dat pl masc		3336.6 adj acc pl fem	1156.2 conj	2197.3 noun acc pl fem	2504.1 conj
τοῖς	ἀνθρώποις·	**9.** μωρὰς		δὲ	ζητήσεις	καὶ
tois	anthrōpois	mōras		de	zētēseis	kai
to the	men;	foolish		but	questions	and

1069.2 noun acc pl fem	2504.1 conj	2038.5 noun pl fem	2038.4 noun acc sing fem	2504.1 conj	3135.2 noun acc pl fem
γενεαλογίας	καὶ	ʿ ἔρεις	[ªʾ✶ ἔριν]	καὶ	μάχας
genealogias	kai	ereis	erin	kai	machas
genealogies	and	strifes	[strife]	and	contentions

3407.7 adj acc pl fem	3889.3 verb 2sing impr pres mid	1498.7 verb 3pl indic pres act	1056.1 conj	508.1 adj nom pl fem
νομικὰς	περι ʿστασο·	εἰσὶν	γὰρ	ἀνωφελεῖς
nomikas	periistaso	eisin	gar	anōpheleis
about law	stand aloof from;	they are	for	unprofitable

2504.1 conj	3124.1 adj nom pl	140.1 adj acc sing masc	442.4 noun acc sing masc	3196.3 prep	1518.8 num card acc fem
καὶ	μάταιοι.	**10.** Αἱρετικὸν	ἄνθρωπον	μετὰ	μιαν
kai	mataioi	Hairetikon	anthrōpon	meta	mian
and	vain.	A factious	man	after	one

2504.1 conj	1202.7 num ord acc sing fem	3422.2 noun acc sing fem	3729.2 verb 2sing impr pres mid	3471.18 verb nom sing masc part perf act
καὶ	δευτέραν	νουθεσίαν	παραιτοῦ,	**11.** εἰδὼς
kai	deuteran	nouthesian	paraitou	eidōs
and	a second	admonition	reject,	knowing

3617.1 conj	1599.1 verb 3sing indic perf mid	3450.5 art nom sing masc	4955.4 dem-pron nom sing masc	2504.1 conj	262.2 verb 3sing indic pres act
ὅτι	ἐξέστραπται	ὁ	τοιοῦτος,	καὶ	ἁμαρτάνει,
hoti	exestraptai	ho	toioutos	kai	hamartanei
that	is perverted	the	such a one,	and	sins,

1498.21 verb nom sing masc part pres act	837.1 adj nom sing masc		3615.1 conj	3854.4 verb 1sing act
ὢν	αὐτοκατάκριτος.	**12.** Ὅταν		πέμψω
ōn	autokatakritos	Hotan		pempsō
being	self-condemned.	When		I shall send

729.1 name acc masc	4242.1 prep	4622.4 prs-pron acc 2sing	2211.1 conj	5031.3 name acc masc	4557.5 verb 2sing impr aor act
Ἀρτεμᾶν	πρὸς	σὲ	ἢ	Τυχικόν,	σπούδασον
Arteman	pros	se	ē	Tuchikon	spoudason
Artemas	to	you,	or	Tychicus,	be diligent

2048.23 verb inf aor act	4242.1 prep	1466.6 prs-pron acc 1sing	1519.1 prep	3395.2 name acc fem	1550.1 adv	1056.1 conj
ἐλθεῖν	πρός	με	εἰς	Νικόπολιν·	ἐκεῖ	γὰρ
elthein	pros	me	eis	Nikopolin	ekei	gar
to come	to	me	to	Nicopolis;	there	for

3:9. Paul closed this letter with a summary instruction to Titus. What he wrote he also wrote to Timothy (1 Timothy 1:4; 6:4,20) and would do so again (2 Timothy 2:23). From all this we know the situation in Ephesus and that on Crete were similar. Paul was greatly concerned about false teachers who were challenging sound doctrine and the practice of Christian good works.

Titus was told to avoid four things. "Avoid" is *periistaso*, literally, "to turn oneself about so as to face the other way." (1) "Questions" may be translated "controversies, speculations." (2) "Genealogies" refers to Old Testament genealogical lists. Jewish false teachers would insert stories and myths between the names, attributing fictitious exploits to people in the lists. (3) "Contentions" may be translated "arguments, dissensions." (4) "Strivings (quarrels) about the law" refers to "legalistic battles" centered on the Mosaic law. This phrase summarizes what Paul wrote in Titus 1:10-16 (cf. 1 Timothy 1:3-7). These are unprofitable and "vain" (useless, futile).

3:10. "Heretic" (*hairetikon*, "contentious man, factious man") describes a divisive person. Originally this term described someone who took legitimate doctrine to the extreme. Not until later did it mean "holding false doctrine." Titus was to admonish (warn) such a person once, admonish him the second time, and have nothing to do with him on the third occasion. "Reject" is *paraitou* ("to leave out of account," different from "avoid," verse 9). Admonition, not argument, is called for. Rejection severs fellowship.

3:11. "He that is such" refers to the one in verse 10 who will not listen and stubbornly refuses any correction. He is (1) "subverted" (warped, perverted), (2) sinful, and (3) self-condemned. The idea of this last description is that Titus need not spend time either in contention or condemnation. The heretic is self-condemned by his perverted mind and sinful actions.

3:12. This verse begins the final personal instructions and greetings so characteristic of Paul's letters. Nothing is known of Artemas. Tychicus was a trusted coworker who traveled with Paul and on occasion was Paul's emissary who carried letters to certain churches (see Acts 20:4; Ephesians 6:21,22; Colossians 4:7,8; 2 Timothy 4:12). Either one or the other of these men would probably take over the work in Crete so Titus could meet Paul in Nicopolis. There were three cities of this name (which means "city of victory"): one in Cilicia, one in Thrace, and one in Epirus. The Nicopolis Paul referred to here is probably the last one and was on the western shore of Greece in the Roman province of Dalmatia.

Paul wrote he had "determined" (decided) to winter there. By his use of "there" instead of "here" Paul showed he was not yet in Nicopolis when he wrote this epistle. Further, he was still free to travel. This places the time of writing between Paul's first and second imprisonments in Rome.

that they which have believed in God:

might be careful to maintain good works: . . . may be anxious to excel in good deeds, *Lilly* . . . to devote themselves to doing good deeds, *SEB* . . . may be careful to take the lead in doing good, *Williams*.

These things are good and profitable unto men: . . . which is excellent and beneficial for all people, *Berkeley* . . . and render service to mankind, *Williams*.

9. But avoid foolish questions, and genealogies: . . . from foolish issues, *SEB* . . . controversies, *Williams* . . . pedigrees, *Berkeley*.

and contentions, and strivings about the law: . . . strife, and wranglings about, *Berkeley*.

for they are unprofitable and vain: . . . they are useless and futile, *Lilly, Confraternity* . . . for they are futile and purposeless, *Berkeley* . . . These are useless and without purpose, *SEB* . . . and unsatisfactory, *TCNT*.

10. A man that is an heretic: . . . who is factious, *RSV, Williams* . . . A sectarian man, *Concordant*.

after the first and second admonition reject: . . . stop having anything to do with him, *Williams*.

11. Knowing that he that is such is subverted: . . . you may be sure that such a man is crooked, *Williams*.

and sinneth, being condemned of himself: He is sinning and he knows it, *NLT* . . . he knows he's wrong, *SEB*.

12. When I shall send Artemas unto thee, or Tychicus, be diligent to come unto me to Nicopolis:

for I have determined there to winter: . . . for I have arranged, *TCNT*.

2892.21 verb 1sing indic perf act	3775.1 verb inf aor act		2194.1 name acc masc	3450.6 art acc sing masc	3407.2 adj acc sing masc
κέκρικα	παραχειμάσαι.	**13.**	Ζηνᾶν	τὸν	νομικὸν
kekrika	paracheimasai		Zēnan	ton	nomikon
I have decided	to winter.		Zenas	the	lawyer

2504.1 conj	619.2 name acc masc	619.3 name acc masc	4560.1 adv	4170.3 verb 2sing impr aor act
καὶ	⸂ Ἀπολλῶ	[a☆ Ἀπολλῶν]	σπουδαίως	πρόπεμψον,
kai	Apollō	Apollōn	spoudaiōs	propempson
and	Apollos	[idem]	diligently	set forward,

2419.1 conj	3235.6 num card neu	840.2 prs-pron dat pl	2981.2 verb 3sing subj pres act	3101.4 verb 3pl impr pres act
ἵνα	μηδὲν	αὐτοῖς	λείπῃ.	**14.** μανθανέτωσαν
hina	mēden	autois	leipē	manthanetōsan
that	nothing	to them	may be lacking;	let learn

1156.2 conj	2504.1 conj	3450.7 art nom pl masc	2233.2 adj nom 1pl masc	2541.12 adj gen pl neu	2024.5 noun gen pl neu
δὲ	καὶ	οἱ	ἡμέτεροι	καλῶν	ἔργων
de	kai	hoi	hēmeteroi	kalōn	ergōn
and	also	the	ours	good	works

4150.7 verb inf pres mid	1519.1 prep	3450.15 art acc pl fem	314.2 adj acc pl fem	5367.1 noun fem	2419.1 conj
προΐστασθαι	εἰς	τὰς	ἀναγκαίας	χρείας,	ἵνα
proistasthai	eis	tas	anankaias	chreias	hina
to be devoted to	for	the	necessary	wants,	that

3231.1 partic	1498.12 verb 3pl subj pres act	173.2 adj nom pl masc	776.3 verb 3pl indic pres mid	4622.4 prs-pron acc 2sing
μὴ	ὦσιν	ἄκαρποι.	**15.** Ἀσπάζονταί	σε
mē	ōsin	akarpoi	Aspazontai	se
not	they may be	unfruitful.	Greet	you

3450.7 art nom pl masc	3196.2 prep	1466.3 prs-pron gen 1sing	3820.7 adj nom pl masc	776.8 verb 2sing impr aor mid	3450.8 art acc pl masc
οἱ	μετ'	ἐμοῦ	πάντες.	Ἄσπασαι	τοὺς
hoi	met'	emou	pantes	Aspasai	tous
the	with	me	all.	Salute	the

5205.7 verb acc pl masc part pres act	2231.4 prs-pron acc 1pl	1706.1 prep	3963.3 noun dat sing fem	3450.9 art nom sing fem	5322.1 noun nom sing fem	3196.3 prep
φιλοῦντας	ἡμᾶς	ἐν	πίστει.	ἡ	χάρις	μετὰ
philountas	hēmas	en	pistei	hē	charis	meta
loving	us	in	faith.	The	grace	with

3820.4 adj gen pl	5050.2 prs-pron gen 2pl	279.1 intrj	4242.1 prep	4951.4 name acc masc	3450.10 art gen sing fem
πάντων	ὑμῶν.	⸂a ἀμήν. ⸃	⸂b Πρὸς	Τίτον,	τῆς
pantōn	humōn	amēn	Pros	Titon	tēs
all	you.	Amen.	To	Titus	of the

2886.2 name gen pl masc	1564.1 noun fem	4272.2 num ord sing	1969.1 noun acc sing masc	5336.3 verb acc sing masc part aor pass
Κρητῶν	ἐκκλησίας	πρῶτον	ἐπίσκοπον	χειροτονηθέντα,
Krētōn	ekklēsias	prōton	episkopon	cheirotonēthenta
of Cretans	assembly	first	overseer	having been chosen,

1119.21 verb 3sing indic aor pass	570.3 prep	3395.1 name gen fem	3450.10 art gen sing fem	3081.2 name gen fem
ἐγράφη	ἀπὸ	Νικοπόλεως	τῆς	Μακεδονίας. ⸃
egraphē	apo	Nikopoleōs	tēs	Makedonias
written	from	Nicopolis		of Macedonia.

13.a.Txt: 04C,06D-org 015H-corr,018K,020L 025P,byz.Sod
Var: 01א,06D-corr 025P-org,Tisc,We/Ho Weis,UBS/☆

15.a.Txt: 01א-corr 06D-corr,015H,018K 020L,025P,byz.it.bo.
Var: 01א-org,02A,04C 06D-org,048,33,sa.Gries Treg,Alf,Word,Tisc We/Ho,Weis,Sod UBS/☆

15.b.Txt: 015H,018K 020L,Steph
Var: Gries,Lach,Word Tisc,We/Ho,Weis,Sod UBS/☆

3:13. Titus was asked to bring two men with him to Nicopolis. Zenas the lawyer (*nomikon*—the Greek word does not indicate nationality) is mentioned only here. If he was a Jewish convert, "lawyer" could mean he was an expert in the Mosaic law, i.e., a scribe. If he was a Gentile convert, it could mean he was a Roman lawyer. It is quite possible Paul wanted Zenas to come for some legal reason. Did Paul know he would soon be imprisoned again? Was he wanting legal advice concerning his rights as a Roman citizen? These questions are only speculative, but the historical situation makes them probable.

Apollos was a Jew, a native of Alexandria, and a well-known coworker (see Acts 18:24-28; 1 Corinthians 1:12; 3:4-6,22; 16:12). In his early ministry he was counseled by Aquila and Priscilla who taught him "the way of God more perfectly" (Acts 18:26). Acts 18:28 says that after this "he mightily convinced the Jews, and that publicly, showing by the Scriptures that Jesus was Christ."

"Bring . . . on their journey diligently" could mean Zenas and Apollos were in Crete or they would be picked up by Titus on his way to Nicopolis. The last phrase may be translated "see that they have everything they need." Titus was to provide material assistance to Zenas and Apollos. This suggests the practice of Christian hospitality in which itinerant workers such as evangelists and missionaries were given room and board plus traveling expenses (compare Romans 15:24; 1 Corinthians 16:6; 3 John 5–8).

3:14. In this verse Paul gave a general exhortation. "And let ours (our people) also learn to maintain (the idea of this Greek verb is priority, i.e., devoting oneself before all else to) good works" (a main theme of this epistle, see 1:16; 2:7,14; 3:1,8).

Paul added the phrase "for necessary uses." This is the practical side of good works. Two concepts are inherent in these words: (1) The Cretan Christians were to "maintain good works" so they might be independent and provide for their own needs. (2) They were to give priority to good works so they would be able to help those who were in need.

3:15. The closing benediction is very similar to most in Paul's epistles. "All" refers either to those in Paul's traveling party or possibly to those seen on his trip whom Titus knew.

"Love" in this greeting is *philountas* and denotes Christian love, not natural love. It is this uniquely Christian love that unites believers. The Greek behind "in the faith" has no article. *En pistei* could mean "faithfully," i.e., "those who love us faithfully as Christians."

The closing blessing is similar to the other Pastorals (see 1 Timothy 6:21; 2 Timothy 4:22). "All" begins and ends this verse. As in Paul's letters to Timothy, the plural closing indicated this letter was to be read to the churches.

13. Bring Zenas the lawyer and Apollos on their journey diligently: Equip Zenas, the jurist and Apollos carefully for their journey, *Berkeley* . . . the Teacher of the Law, *TCNT* . . . diligently set forward on their journey, *Wuest*.

that nothing be wanting unto them: Let them want nothing, *Montgomery* . . . Do your best to supply everything that Zenas...and Apollos need for their trip; be sure they lack nothing, *Adams* . . . in order that not even one thing be lacking to them, *Wuest* . . . see that they lack nothing, *RSV*.

14. And let ours also learn to maintain good works: . . . let our people learn to devote themselves to honest work, *Montgomery* . . . to engage in good deeds, *Adams* . . . learn...at good works, *Klingensmith* . . . learn to busy themselves constantly in good works, *Wuest*.

for necessary uses: . . . to supply the necessities of their teachers, *Montgomery* . . . to meet pressing needs, *Adams* . . . the right use of their hands, *Klingensmith* . . . for necessary needs, *Wuest*.

that they be not unfruitful: In this way they will not be destitute of good deeds, *Lilly* . . . in order that, *Wuest* . . . so that their lives may not be barren of results, *TCNT* . . . may not be unproductive, *Berkeley* . . . Then they will not be useless, *Klingensmith* . . . They must learn to be productive, providing for real needs, *SEB*.

15. All that are with me salute thee: All my companions greet you, *Lilly* . . . All those with me send greetings to you, *Wuest*.

Greet them that love us in the faith: . . . greet our affectionate friends in the faith, *Adams* . . . those who are fond of us in the Faith, *Wuest*.

Grace [be] with you all. Amen: The grace, *Wuest* . . . Favor be with you, *Campbell* . . . Help be with all of you, *Adams*.

THE EPISTLE
OF PAUL TO
PHILEMON

Expanded Interlinear

Textual Critical Apparatus

Verse-by-Verse Commentary

Various Versions

Πρὸς Φιλήμονα ἐπιστολὴ Παύλου

4242.1 prep	5208.2 name acc masc	1976.1 noun nom sing fem	3834.2 name gen masc
Πρὸς	Φιλήμονα	ἐπιστολὴ	Παύλου
Pros	Philēmona	epistolē	Paulou
To	Philemon	letter	of Paul

1:1.

3834.1 name nom masc	1192.1 noun nom sing masc	5382.2 name gen masc	2400.2 name masc	2504.1 conj	4943.1 name nom masc
Παῦλος	δέσμιος	Χριστοῦ	Ἰησοῦ,	καὶ	Τιμόθεος
Paulos	desmios	Christou	Iēsou	kai	Timotheos
Paul,	prisoner	of Christ	Jesus,	and	Timothy

3450.5 art nom sing masc	79.1 noun nom sing masc	5208.1 name dat masc	3450.3 art dat sing	27.2 adj dat sing	2504.1 conj
ὁ	ἀδελφὸς,	Φιλήμονι	τῷ	ἀγαπητῷ	καὶ
ho	adelphos	Philēmoni	tō	agapētō	kai
the	brother,	to Philemon	the	beloved	and

4754.2 adj dat sing masc	2231.2 prs-pron gen 1pl	2504.1 conj	675.1 name dat fem	3450.11 art dat sing fem	27.8 adj dat sing fem
συνεργῷ	ἡμῶν,	**2.** καὶ	Ἀπφίᾳ	τῇ	ʹ ἀγαπητῇ,
sunergō	hēmōn	kai	Apphia	tē	agapētē
fellow worker	our,	and	to Apphia	the	beloved,

78.3 noun dat sing fem	2504.1 conj	746.1 name dat masc	3450.3 art dat sing	4813.1 noun dat sing masc
[ᵃ⋆ ἀδελφῇ]	καὶ	Ἀρχίππῳ	τῷ	συστρατιώτῃ
adelphē	kai	Archippō	tō	sustratiōtē
[sister]	and	to Archippus	the	fellow soldier

2231.2 prs-pron gen 1pl	2504.1 conj	3450.11 art dat sing fem	2567.1 prep	3486.4 noun acc sing masc	4622.2 prs-pron gen 2sing	1564.3 noun dat sing fem
ἡμῶν,	καὶ	τῇ	κατ'	οἶκόν	σου	ἐκκλησίᾳ·
hēmōn	kai	tē	kat'	oikon	sou	ekklēsia
our,	and	to the	in	house	your	assembly:

5322.1 noun nom sing fem	5050.3 prs-pron dat 2pl	2504.1 conj	1503.1 noun nom sing fem	570.3 prep	2296.2 noun gen sing masc	3824.2 noun gen sing masc
3. χάρις	ὑμῖν	καὶ	εἰρήνη	ἀπὸ	θεοῦ	πατρὸς
charis	humin	kai	eirēnē	apo	theou	patros
Grace	to you	and	peace	from	God	Father

2231.2 prs-pron gen 1pl	2504.1 conj	2935.2 noun gen sing masc	2400.2 name masc	5382.2 name gen masc	2149.1 verb 1sing indic pres act
ἡμῶν	καὶ	κυρίου	Ἰησοῦ	Χριστοῦ.	**4.** Εὐχαριστῶ
hēmōn	kai	kuriou	Iēsou	Christou	Eucharistō
our	and	Lord	Jesus	Christ.	I thank

3450.3 art dat sing	2296.3 noun dat sing masc	1466.2 prs-pron gen 1sing	3704.1 adv	3281.2 noun acc sing fem	4622.2 prs-pron gen 2sing
τῷ	θεῷ	μου,	πάντοτε	μνείαν	σου
tō	theō	mou	pantote	mneian	sou
to	God	my,	always	mention	of you

4020.64 verb nom sing masc part pres mid	1894.3 prep	3450.1 art gen pl	4194.6 noun gen pl fem	1466.2 prs-pron gen 1sing
ποιούμενος	ἐπὶ	τῶν	προσευχῶν	μου,
poioumenos	epi	tōn	proseuchōn	mou
making	at	the	prayers	my,

THE EPISTLE OF PAUL TO
PHILEMON

1. Rather than identify himself as an apostle since he wrote to a friend, Paul called himself a "prisoner of Jesus Christ," not of Nero. He named Timothy as an associate. The definite article (*ho*) specified him as *the* brother. The addressee is Philemon whom the apostle called "dearly beloved" and "fellow laborer."

2. The address continues with the mention of Apphia and Archippus, possibly the other members of the family to which Paul wrote the epistle. Archippus is called a "fellow soldier." The title suggests he was a church leader, perhaps interim pastor in Epaphras' absence. The address closes with a reference to the assembly that met in the house of Philemon. He opened his home to believers as a place for worship and study.

3. Paul's greeting concludes with the normal combination of the Greek idea of "grace" and the Hebrew concept of "peace." Since "grace" (*charis*) occupies the emphatic position in Paul's statement, it definitely points to the necessity of depending upon it in our Christian lives. "Peace," or inner tranquility that does not depend upon external circumstances, naturally follows the reception of God's grace by a human being. This grace and peace come from "God our Father and the Lord Jesus Christ" (compare Romans 1:7; 1 Corinthians 1:3; 2 Corinthians 1:2; Galatians 1:3; Ephesians 1:2; and all of Paul's letters; note he adds "mercy" to the greetings in the Pastoral Epistles).

4. In the Greek the verb translated "I thank" occupies the first position, the position of emphasis, and comes from the term (*eucharistō*) from which we get *eucharist*, one of the outstanding terms describing the communion service which the Scriptures teach should be a time of thanksgiving. God never intended for the Lord's Supper to become a ceremony full of empty formality and devoid of His presence. Neither did He intend for people to think He automatically conveys His grace to them just because they keep this ceremony religiously. As usual, Paul allowed his inner being to express itself in praise before he took his petitions to God. Commentators disagree as to whether the term "always" (*pantote*) should go with the thanksgiving expressed in this verse or with the prayer request he was about to express to God.

Various Versions

1. Paul, a prisoner of Jesus Christ: . . . for Jesus, *Williams, Fenton.*

and Timothy [our] brother: . . . brother Timothy, *Montgomery* . . . my fellow worker, *Beck.*

unto Philemon our dearly beloved, and fellowlabourer: . . . to our dear friend, *Adams* . . . our dear fellow worker, *Beck* . . . To my beloved friend and coworker, *Montgomery.*

2. And to [our] beloved Apphia: . . . the dear Apphia, *Fenton* . . . to my sister Apphia, *Montgomery.*

and Archippus our fellow-soldier: . . . our fellow Christian, *Beck.*

and to the church in thy house: . . . the group that meets, *SET* . . . and to the ecclesia, *Concordant* . . . the [local] assembly, *Wuest* . . . to the congregation, *Fenton* . . . that meets at your home, *Berkeley.*

3. Grace to you, and peace: . . . spiritual blessing be with you, *Williams* . . . help and peace, *Adams* . . . [Sanctifying] grace to you and [tranquilzing] peace, *Wuest* . . . love you and give you peace, *Beck.*

from God our Father and the Lord Jesus Christ: May God, *Beck.*

4. I thank my God: I always thank, *Adams, Williams* . . . and giving thanks to God, *Montgomery.*

making mention of thee always in my prayers: I am ever mentioning you, *Montgomery* . . . every time I mention you, *Williams* . . . remembering you on the occasions of my seasons of prayer, *Wuest.*

189.11 verb nom sing masc part pres act	4622.2 prs-pron gen 2sing	3450.12 art acc sing fem	26.4 noun acc sing fem	2504.1 conj	3450.12 art acc sing fem
5. ἀκούων	σου	τὴν	ἀγάπην	καὶ	τὴν
akouōn	sou	tēn	agapēn	kai	tēn
hearing	of your	the	love	and	the

3963.4 noun acc sing fem	3614.12 rel-pron acc sing fem	2174.3 verb 2sing indic pres act	4242.1 prep	1519.1 prep	3450.6 art acc sing masc
πίστιν	ἣν	ἔχεις	⌜☆πρὸς	[a εἰς]	τὸν
pistin	hēn	echeis	pros	eis	ton
faith	which	you have	towards	[idem]	the

2935.4 noun acc sing masc	2400.3 name acc masc	2504.1 conj	1519.1 prep	3820.8 adj acc pl masc	3450.8 art acc pl masc	39.9 adj acc pl masc
κύριον	Ἰησοῦν	καὶ	εἰς	πάντας	τοὺς	ἁγίους,
kurion	Iēsoun	kai	eis	pantas	tous	hagious
Lord	Jesus,	and	towards	all	the	saints,

3567.1 conj	3450.9 art nom sing fem	2815.1 noun nom sing fem	3450.10 art gen sing fem	3963.2 noun gen sing fem	4622.2 prs-pron gen 2sing
6. ὅπως	ἡ	κοινωνία	τῆς	πίστεώς	σου
hopōs	hē	koinōnia	tēs	pisteōs	sou
so that	the	fellowship	of the	faith	your

1740.1 adj nom sing	1090.40 verb 3sing subj aor mid	1706.1 prep	1907.3 noun dat sing fem	3820.2 adj gen sing
ἐνεργὴς	γένηται	ἐν	ἐπιγνώσει	παντὸς
energēs	genētai	en	epignōsei	pantos
efficient	may become	in	acknowledgment	of every

18.2 adj gen sing	3450.2 art gen sing	1706.1 prep	5050.3 prs-pron dat 2pl	2231.3 prs-pron dat 1pl	1519.1 prep
ἀγαθοῦ	⌜a☆ τοῦ ⌝	ἐν	ὑμῖν	[b☆ ἡμῖν]	εἰς
agathou	tou	en	humin	hēmin	eis
good	the	in	you	[us]	towards

5382.4 name acc masc	2400.3 name acc masc	5322.4 noun acc sing fem	5315.4 noun acc sing fem	1056.1 conj
Χριστόν	⌜c Ἰησοῦν. ⌝	**7.** ⌜ χάριν	[a☆ χαρὰν]	γὰρ
Christon	Iēsoun	charin	charan	gar
Christ	Jesus.	Thankfulness	[Joy]	for

2174.5 verb 1pl indic pres act	4044.12 adj acc sing fem	4044.12 adj acc sing fem	2174.30 verb indic aor act	2504.1 conj
⌜ ἔχομεν	πολλὴν	[b☆ πολλὴν	ἔσχον]	καὶ
echomen	pollēn	pollēn	eschon	kai
we have	great	[great	I had]	and

3735.4 noun acc sing fem	1894.3 prep	3450.11 art dat sing fem	26.3 noun dat sing fem	4622.2 prs-pron gen 2sing	3617.1 conj	3450.17 art pl neu
παράκλησιν	ἐπὶ	τῇ	ἀγάπῃ	σου,	ὅτι	τὰ
paraklēsin	epi	tē	agapē	sou	hoti	ta
encouragement	over	the	love	your,	because	the

4551.1 noun pl neu	3450.1 art gen pl	39.4 adj gen pl	372.8 verb 3sing indic perf mid	1217.2 prep	4622.2 prs-pron gen 2sing
σπλάγχνα	τῶν	ἁγίων	ἀναπέπαυται	διὰ	σοῦ,
splanchna	tōn	hagiōn	anapepautai	dia	sou
bowels	of the	saints	have been refreshed	by	you,

79.5 noun voc sing masc	1346.1 conj	4044.12 adj acc sing fem	1706.1 prep	5382.3 name dat masc	3816.4 noun acc sing fem
ἀδελφέ.	**8.** Διό,	πολλὴν	ἐν	Χριστῷ	παρρησίαν
adelphe	Dio	pollēn	en	Christō	parrhēsian
brother.	Wherefore	much	in	Christ	boldness

5.a.Txt: 01ℵ,06D-corr2 010F,012G,044,byz. Var: 02A,04C,06D-org 048,33

6.a.Txt: 01ℵ,06D,010F 012G,044,byz. Var: p61,02A,04C,048 33,629

6.b.Txt: p61,01ℵ,025P 33,byz.sa.bo.Tisc,Sod Var: 02A,04C,06D 018K,020L,Gries,Lach Treg,Alf,Word,We/Ho Weis,UBS/☆

6.c.Txt: 01ℵ-corr,06D 018K,020L,025P,byz. Var: 01ℵ-org,02A,04C 33,bo.Lach,Treg,Tisc We/Ho,Weis,Sod UBS/☆

7.a.Txt: 018K,020L 025P,byz.Steph Var: 01ℵ,02A,04C,06D 33,bo.Elzev,Gries,Lach Treg,Alf,Word,Tisc We/Ho,Weis,Sod UBS/☆

7.b.Txt: (06D-corr),018K 020L,byz. Var: 01ℵ,02A,04C,025P 33,bo.Lach,Treg,Alf Word,Tisc,We/Ho,Weis Sod,UBS/☆

5. Now we begin to see why Paul always thanked God and always prayed for Philemon. This believer certainly enjoyed a good balance between his relationship with God and man. Paul expressed this proper balance he detected in Philemon by referring to his "love and faith" which he had toward the Lord Jesus and the saints. It is very possible that Paul was thanking God for the love and faith that Philemon had "toward" (*pros*) the Lord Jesus and for the love and faithfulness he expressed "to" (*eis*) all the saints. The horizontal expression should stem from the vertical relationship.

6. After thanking God for what he saw in his friend Philemon, Paul prayed that this man always would be active in sharing his faith with other people. "Communication" comes from the Greek noun (*koinōnia*) from which we get the English word *fellowship*. The word, however, carries the idea of participating with someone or participating in some kind of ministry. Verse 7 makes clear that in Philemon's case "fellowship" included sharing with brethren who were in need. The apostle knew that as Philemon would share his faith with other people in this practical way, it in turn would help him to become more and more effectual in his witness for Christ. "Become" indicates something that definitely is progressive in nature. Paul believed in the possibility of improving in one's witness for the Lord. This fact becomes even more evident by the Greek word (*epignōsei*) that the NIV translators rendered "full understanding." Therefore, as a person shares his faith in the Lord Jesus Christ, the person who receives the message not only benefits from it, but the person who gives the message also comes to a more complete understanding of all the good things that God has promised to His people. All these benefits, of course, come to us only "in Christ Jesus" or "through Christ" because we belong to Him.

7. Not only did Philemon's expression of love (*agapē*) help him to gain a more complete understanding of what he possessed in Christ, but it also brought "joy and consolation" to Paul. Philemon literally "refreshed the bowels (*splanchna*) of the saints" by his activities. This interesting phrase expresses the way people of that day spoke of the innermost being of a person. Because the bowels, or intestines, of a person occupy a position of depth in the human body, this type of terminology speaks very fittingly of the deepest emotions a person can express. Often translators use the word *heart* to try to capture the idea expressed in the term. Therefore, Philemon obviously practiced a ministry of Christian relationships in which he allowed the Holy Spirit to make him a definite encouragement to people.

8. The heart of the epistle, of course, consists of a passionate appeal for Philemon to accept Onesimus back into his household. The appeal was based upon several matters that are expressed in the next few verses. First, instead of using bold authority, Paul

5. Hearing of thy love and faith, which thou hast: . . . because I hear of...faithfulness that you show, *Adams* . . . you practice, *Berkeley* . . . which you hold, *Montgomery*.

toward the Lord Jesus, and toward all saints: . . . and for all the Christians, *Norlie* . . . and all His people, *Williams*.

6. That the communication of thy faith: I pray that the generosity which springs from your faith, *Lilly* . . . praying that this sharing of your faith, *Adams* . . . that your participation, *Montgomery* . . . that you will actively share your faith, *SEB* . . . in sharing, *NIV*.

may become effectual by the acknowledging of: . . . that you may be active, *NIV* . . . may result in their recognition in us, *Williams* . . . may become operative in the realization of, *Concordant* . . . may have the effect of bringing about a full knowledge of, *Adams* . . . as you come to acknowledge, *Montgomery*.

every good thing which is in you in Christ Jesus: . . . all the good things that we have, *Adams* . . . everything that is right with reference to Christ, *Williams*.

7. For we have great joy and consolation in thy love: I have enjoyed much happiness and encouragement from, *Adams* . . . and comfort, *Montgomery*.

because the bowels of the saints: The hearts of the Christians, *NLT*.

are refreshed by thee, brother: . . . have refreshed the hearts of, *NIV* . . . you have revived the hearts of, *Adams* . . . and you have likewise cheered the hearts of, *Norlie*.

8. Wherefore, though I might be much bold in Christ: Christ gives me full liberty, *TCNT* . . . I have plenty of freedom, *SEB* . . . So then, although I am quite free, *Adams*.

2174.17 verb nom sing masc part pres act	1988.3 verb inf pres act	4622.3 prs-pron dat 2sing	3450.16 art sing neu	431.1 verb sing neu part pres act
ἔχων	ἐπιτάσσειν	σοι	τὸ	ἀνῆκον,
echōn	epitassein	soi	to	anēkon
having	to order	you	to	becoming,

1217.2 prep	3450.12 art acc sing fem	26.4 noun acc sing fem	3095.1 adv comp	3731.1 verb 1sing indic pres act
9. διὰ	τὴν	ἀγάπην	μᾶλλον	παρακαλῶ·
dia	tēn	agapēn	mallon	parakalō
for the sake of	the	love	rather	I exhort,

4955.4 dem-pron nom sing masc	1498.21 verb nom sing masc part pres act	5453.1 conj	3834.1 name nom masc	4105.1 noun nom sing masc	3432.1 adv
τοιοῦτος	ὢν	ὡς	Παῦλος	πρεσβύτης,	νυνὶ
toioutos	ōn	hōs	Paulos	presbutēs	nuni
such a one	being	as	Paul	aged,	now

1156.2 conj	2504.1 conj	1192.1 noun nom sing masc	2400.2 name masc	5382.2 name gen masc	5382.2 name gen masc
δὲ	καὶ	δέσμιος	(Ἰησοῦ	Χριστοῦ·	[✶ Χριστοῦ
de	kai	desmios	Iēsou	Christou	Christou
and	also	prisoner	of Jesus	Christ.	[of Christ

2400.2 name masc	3731.1 verb 1sing indic pres act	4622.4 prs-pron acc 2sing	3875.1 prep	3450.2 art gen sing	1466.3 prs-pron gen 1sing
Ἰησοῦ·]	**10.** παρακαλῶ	σε	περὶ	τοῦ	ἐμοῦ
Iēsou	parakalō	se	peri	tou	emou
Jesus.]	I exhort	you	for	the	my

4891.2 noun gen sing neu	3614.6 rel-pron acc sing masc	1074.3 verb 1sing indic aor act	1706.1 prep	3450.4 art dat pl	1193.5 noun dat pl	1466.2 prs-pron gen 1sing
τέκνου,	ὃν	ἐγέννησα	ἐν	τοῖς	δεσμοῖς	(ᵃ μου,)
teknou	hon	egennēsa	en	tois	desmois	mou
child,	whom	I begot	in	the	bonds	my,

3545.3 name acc masc	3450.6 art acc sing masc	4077.1 adv	4622.3 prs-pron dat 2sing	883.1 adj acc sing masc	3432.1 adv
Ὀνήσιμον,	**11.** τόν	ποτέ	σοι	ἄχρηστον.	νυνὶ
Onēsimon	ton	pote	soi	achrēston	nuni
Onesimus,	the	once	to you	useless,	now

1156.2 conj	2504.1 conj	4622.3 prs-pron dat 2sing	2504.1 conj	1466.5 prs-pron dat 1sing	2154.1 adj sing
δὲ	[ᵃ✶+ καὶ]	σοὶ	καὶ	ἐμοὶ	εὔχρηστον,
de	kai	soi	kai	emoi	euchrēston
but	[both]	to you	and	to me	useful:

3614.6 rel-pron acc sing masc	374.1 verb 1sing indic aor act	4622.3 prs-pron dat 2sing	4622.1 prs-pron nom 2sing	1156.2 conj
ὃν	ἀνέπεμψα·	[ᵇ+ σοι]	**12.** (ᵃ σὺ	δὲ)
hon	anepempsa	soi	su	de
whom	I sent back:	[to you:]	you	but

840.6 prs-pron acc sing masc	4969.1 verb	3642.16 dem-pron sing neu	1498.4 verb 3sing indic pres act	3450.17 art pl neu
αὐτόν,	(τουτέστιν	[✶ τοῦτ'	ἔστιν]	τὰ
auton	toutestin	tout'	estin	ta
him,	that is,	[that	is]	the

1684.12 adj pl neu	4551.1 noun pl neu	4213.5 verb 2sing impr aor mid	3614.6 rel-pron acc sing masc	1466.1 prs-pron nom 1sing
ἐμὰ	σπλάγχνα	(ᵇ προσλαβοῦ·)	**13.** ὃν	ἐγὼ
ema	splanchna	proslabou	hon	egō
my	bowels,	receive:	whom	I

appealed to the mutual love shared by him and his friend. Church leaders today would do well to follow Paul's example.

9. Instead of using boldness to command Philemon to acquiesce to the apostle's wishes, he appealed to his friend on the basis of love. The Greek word for "beseech" (*parakalō*) is a very strong word, so the use of this verb shows even more the humility and tact of the person who used it. Again Paul reminded his friend that he was a prisoner of Christ Jesus, another way of affirming that he had been incarcerated in accordance with God's will, not just at the whim of the evil Nero. More importantly, Paul added the fact he was an aged man at the time of making this passionate appeal. The Greek noun (*presbutēs*) Paul used here also is translated a number of times in the New Testament as "elder" or "presbyter." However, here it obviously refers to an aged man.

10. Furthermore, Paul attested that Onesimus had experienced a true conversion to Jesus Christ, so he appealed to Philemon on the basis of this important bond they enjoyed. "My son" literally comes from a phrase meaning "my child" (*tou emou teknou*). It would be difficult to mistake this terminology to mean anything but the fact God had permitted Paul to lead Onesimus to an experience of true regeneration. It must have occurred during Paul's 2-year imprisonment in Rome (Acts 28:30,31).

11. In fact, Onesimus' life had so changed that now he was "profitable" whereas he previously had been "unprofitable." This is a very vivid description of the results of true salvation. Paul used a form of the Greek word *chrēstos* twice. First, by adding an alpha to the term (*achrēston*), he negated the word. Then, he added *eu*, or the adverb "well." It expresses the dramatic change Christ can make in a person's life. "Onesimus" means "profitable." He had not lived up to his name before. Now he could.

12. As he continued his letter it is clear Paul believed in making restitution whenever it was possible to do so; he knew Onesimus owed a definite obligation to Philemon. Again Paul used the Greek term for "bowels" to express the emotional connection that being able to lead Onesimus to the Lord had knit between them. It was not easy to send back this man who meant so much to him. Can you picture the emotional response Philemon must have experienced as he read these words? The fact Paul manifested his sincere respect for Philemon must have elicited an even greater respect from the heart of Philemon for the apostle. People in leadership positions should always realize that respect does not come because it is demanded. It is generated by actions such as the one exhibited by the famous apostle on this occasion. He is a good example to follow.

to enjoin thee that which is convenient: . . . to order you to do what you should do, *SEB* . . . that I might charge thee, *Confraternity* . . . to give you directions as to your duty, *Berkeley* . . . to lay down the course you should adopt, *TCNT* . . . as to what is proper, *Concordant.*

9. Yet for love's sake I rather beseech [thee]: I prefer in the interests of love, *Lilly* . . . I prefer to make my appeal on the basis of love, *Berkeley* . . . I prefer that you do it for love's sake, *Norlie.*
being such an one as Paul the aged: . . . an old man, *Campbell.*
and now also a prisoner of Jesus Christ:

10. I beseech thee for my son Onesimus: I plead with thee, *Confraternity* . . . I appeal to you, *Williams* . . . for my child, *SEB.*
whom I have begotten in my bonds: . . . for I have become his spiritual father here, *Norlie* . . . during my imprisonment, *Lilly* . . . I have given Life, *TCNT.*

11. Which in time past was to thee unprofitable: He once was useless to thee, *Confraternity* . . . Formerly he was useless to you, *NIV.*
but now profitable to thee and to me: . . . now he is useful, *Williams.*

12. Whom I have sent again: thou therefore receive him: . . . whom I have sent back, *Campbell* . . . I sent him...back to you, *SEB.*
that is, mine own bowels: . . . as though he were my very heart, *Confraternity* . . . as an object of my tenderest affection, *Campbell* . . . though it is like tearing out my very heart, *TCNT.*

1007.16 verb 1sing indic imperf mid	4242.1 prep	1670.3 prs-pron acc 1sing masc	2692.8 verb inf pres act	2419.1 conj	5065.1 prep
ἐβουλόμην	πρὸς	ἐμαυτὸν	κατέχειν,	ἵνα	ὑπὲρ
eboulomēn	pros	emauton	katechein,	hina	huper
was desiring	with	myself	to keep,	that	for

4622.2 prs-pron gen 2sing	1241.2 verb 3sing subj pres act	1466.4 prs-pron dat 1sing	1466.4 prs-pron dat 1sing	1241.2 verb 3sing subj pres act
σοῦ	ʹ διακονῇ	μοι	[☆ μοι	διακονῇ]
sou	diakonē	moi	moi	diakonē
you	he might serve	me	[me	he might serve]

1706.1 prep	3450.4 art dat pl	1193.5 noun dat pl	3450.2 art gen sing neu	2077.2 noun gen sing neu	5400.1 prep
ἐν	τοῖς	δεσμοῖς	τοῦ	εὐαγγελίου·	**14.** χωρὶς
en	tois	desmois	tou	euangeliou	chōris
in	the	bonds	of the	good news;	apart from

1156.2 conj	3450.10 art gen sing fem	4528.5 adj gen 2sing fem	1100.2 noun gen sing fem	3625.6 num card neu	2286.20 verb 1sing indic aor act
δὲ	τῆς	σῆς	γνώμης	οὐδὲν	ἠθέλησα
de	tēs	sēs	gnōmēs	ouden	ēthelēsa
but	the	your	opinion	nothing	I wished

4020.41 verb inf aor act	2419.1 conj	3231.1 partic	5453.1 conj	2567.3 prep	316.4 noun acc sing fem	3450.16 art sing neu
ποιῆσαι,	ἵνα	μὴ	ὡς	κατὰ	ἀνάγκην	τὸ
poiēsai,	hina	mē	hōs	kata	anankēn	to
to do,	that	not	as	of	necessity	the

18.3 adj sing	4622.2 prs-pron gen 2sing	1498.10 verb 3sing subj pres act	233.2 conj	2567.3 prep	1582.1 adj sing neu
ἀγαθόν	σου	ᾖ,	ἀλλὰ	κατὰ	ἑκούσιον.
agathon	sou	ē	alla	kata	hekousion
good	your	might be,	but	of	willingness:

4877.1 adv	1056.1 conj	1217.2 prep	3642.17 dem-pron sing neu	5398.7 verb 3sing indic aor pass
15. τάχα	γὰρ	διὰ	τοῦτο	ἐχωρίσθη
tacha	gar	dia	touto	echōristhē
perhaps	for	because of	this	he was separated

4242.1 prep	5443.4 noun acc sing fem	2419.1 conj	164.1 adj sing	840.6 prs-pron acc sing masc	563.7 verb 2sing subj aor act
πρὸς	ὥραν,	ἵνα	αἰώνιον	αὐτὸν	ἀπέχῃς·
pros	hōran,	hina	aiōnion	auton	apechēs
for	a time,	that	eternally	him	you might possess;

3629.1 adv	5453.1 conj	1395.4 noun acc sing masc	233.1 conj	233.2 conj	5065.1 prep
16. οὐκέτι	ὡς	δοῦλον,	ʹ ἀλλ'	[☆ ἀλλὰ]	ὑπὲρ
ouketi	hōs	doulon,	all'	alla	huper
no longer	as	a slave,	but	[idem]	more than

1395.4 noun acc sing masc	79.4 noun acc sing masc	27.1 adj sing	3094.1 adv sup	1466.5 prs-pron dat 1sing	4073.9 intr-pron dat sing neu
δοῦλον,	ἀδελφὸν	ἀγαπητόν,	μάλιστα	ἐμοί,	πόσῳ
doulon,	adelphon	agapēton,	malista	emoi,	posō
a slave,	a brother	beloved,	specially	to me,	how much

1156.2 conj	3095.1 adv comp	4622.3 prs-pron dat 2sing	2504.1 conj	1706.1 prep	4418.3 noun dat sing fem	2504.1 conj	1706.1 prep
δὲ	μᾶλλον	σοὶ	καὶ	ἐν	σαρκὶ	καὶ	ἐν
de	mallon	soi	kai	en	sarki	kai	en
and	rather	to you	both	in	flesh	and	in

13. Paul had every right to request Onesimus' assistance in gospel ministry, but the apostle respected his friend Philemon too much to take advantage of the circumstances. What did Paul mean by "in thy stead"? In verse 19 the apostle reminded Philemon that the latter owed the former his very life. This no doubt refers to Philemon's spiritual life, although we cannot be positive about all Paul meant by the statement. Onesimus had ministered to Paul as Philemon would have done if he had been present. He had been Philemon's substitute.

It was not easy for Paul to send Onesimus back to his master Philemon. Paul used a very descriptive phrase here: "the bonds of the gospel." Paul was a prisoner at the time, enduring hardship for the sake of the gospel. Onesimus had been a great blessing to the aged prisoner. Now he would no longer have the comfort and assistance of the one he had led to the Lord.

14. Paul would not take the liberty to assume Philemon would go along with Paul's desire to keep Onesimus as his assistant. He did not want to act without his friend's consent, even though he probably had the authority to do so. Then Paul gave the main reason for his approach relative to this matter. He did not believe in manipulating people into positions so they would have to do him favors—what he called "of necessity" (*kata anankēn*). Paul preferred for people to act "willingly" (*kata hekousion*).

15. This verse seems a little puzzling when one realizes that God certainly did not will for Onesimus to desert his master. However, God did permit it to happen. He made an evil circumstance "work together for good." As a result, Onesimus heard the message of salvation, gave his life to the Lord Jesus Christ, and became a new creature in the Lord. "Season" literally refers to "an hour" (*hōran*), that is, for a short time; and the phrase "for ever" means for eternity (*aiōnion*).

16. There is a definite relationship between the thought expressed in verse 15 and the one in verse 16. But there is a slight shift from the previous basis of Paul's sincere respect for his friend Philemon to an emphasis upon the spiritual relationship they both had shared for some time and that now Onesimus also shared with them. Did Paul mean by the words "not now as a servant" that he expected Philemon to free Onesimus and grant him a completely different social status from what he previously had? Although we cannot be sure about the apostle's intentions, it sounds as if he was not in favor of slavery for Onesimus. There is at least a hint that Philemon should consider the possibility of changing Onesimus' status as a slave.

13. Whom I would have retained with me: I would have liked to, *NIV* . . . I would have preferred to keep him with me, *Lilly* . . . I should like to retain him for myself, *Berkeley*.

that in thy stead he might have ministered unto me: . . . so that in your place, *Klingensmith* . . . to serve me on your behalf, *Norlie* . . . to wait on me, *Williams*.

in the bonds of the gospel: . . . while I wear these chains for the good news, *Williams*.

14. But without thy mind would I do nothing: . . . without your consent, *ET* . . . unless you knew about it, *SEB* . . . I would not do a single thing about it, *Williams*.

that thy benefit should not be as it were of necessity: . . . your kind action may not be compulsory, *Berkeley* . . . Then your goodness would not be forced, *SEB* . . . not be as of compulsion, *Concordant* . . . and not forced, *NIV*.

but willingly: . . . but voluntary, *Confraternity, Concordant, Williams* . . . will be spontaneous, *NIV* . . . because you wanted to, *NLT*.

15. For perhaps he therefore departed for a season: Perhaps this is why he was briefly separated from you, *Lilly*.

that thou shouldest receive him for ever: . . . that you might get him back permanently, *Norlie*.

16. Not now as a servant: . . . for he is not only your property, *Norlie* . . . not as a slave any longer, *Williams*.

but above a servant, a brother beloved: . . . but better than, *Berkeley*.

specially to me, but how much more unto thee:

both in the flesh, and in the Lord?: . . . both as a man and as a Christian, *Lilly, TCNT*.

17.a.**Txt:** 018K,byz.
Var: 01א,02A,04C,06D
020L,025P,Gries,Lach
Treg,Alf,Word,Tisc
We/Ho,Weis,Sod
UBS/✱

2935.3 noun dat sing masc	1479.1 conj	3631.1 partic	1466.7 prs-pron acc 1sing	1466.6 prs-pron acc 1sing	2174.3 verb 2sing indic pres act
κυρίῳ;	**17.** Εἰ	οὖν	⸀ ἐμὲ	[ᵃ✱ με]	ἔχεις
kuriō	Ei	oun	eme	me	echeis
Lord?	If	therefore	me	[idem]	you hold

2817.2 noun acc sing masc	4213.5 verb 2sing impr aor mid	840.6 prs-pron acc sing masc	5453.1 conj	1466.7 prs-pron acc 1sing	1479.1 conj
κοινωνόν,	προσλαβοῦ	αὐτὸν	ὡς	ἐμέ.	**18.** εἰ
koinōnon	proslabou	auton	hōs	eme	ei
a partner,	receive	him	as	me;	if

1156.2 conj	4948.10 indef-pron sing neu	90.6 verb 3sing indic aor act	4622.4 prs-pron acc 2sing	2211.1 conj	3648.3 verb 3sing indic pres act
δέ	τι	ἠδίκησέν	σε	ἢ	ὀφείλει,
de	ti	ēdikēsen	se	ē	opheilei
but	anything	he wronged	you,	or	owes,

18.a.**Txt:** (01א-corr),06D
018K,020L,byz.Sod
Var: 01א-org,02A,04C
025P,33,Lach,Treg,Alf
Tisc,We/Ho,Weis
UBS/✱

3642.17 dem-pron sing neu	1466.5 prs-pron dat 1sing	1664.1 verb 2sing impr pres act	1664.3 verb 2sing impr pres act	1466.1 prs-pron nom 1sing	
τοῦτο	ἐμοὶ	⸀ ἐλλόγει.	[ᵃ✱ ἐλλόγα·]	**19.** ἐγὼ	
touto	emoi	ellogei	elloga	egō	
this	my	put to account.	[reckon.]	I	

3834.1 name nom masc	1119.7 verb 1sing indic aor act	3450.11 art dat sing fem	1684.8 adj dat sing fem	5331.3 noun dat sing fem	1466.1 prs-pron nom 1sing
Παῦλος	ἔγραψα	τῇ	ἐμῇ	χειρί,	ἐγὼ
Paulos	egrapsa	tē	emē	cheiri	egō
Paul	wrote	with the	my	hand;	I

655.1 verb 1sing indic fut act	2419.1 conj	3231.1 partic	2978.1 verb 1sing pres act	4622.3 prs-pron dat 2sing	3617.1 conj	2504.1 conj
ἀποτίσω·	ἵνα	μὴ	λέγω	σοι	ὅτι	καὶ
apotisō	hina	mē	legō	soi	hoti	kai
will repay;	that	not	I am saying	to you	that	even

4427.4 prs-pron acc sing masc	1466.4 prs-pron dat 1sing	4217.1 verb 2sing indic pres act	3346.1 intrj	79.5 noun voc sing masc
σεαυτόν	μοι	προσοφείλεις.	**20.** Ναί,	ἀδελφέ,
seauton	moi	prosopheileis	Nai	adelphe
yourself	to me	you owe also.	Yes,	brother,

1466.1 prs-pron nom 1sing	4622.2 prs-pron gen 2sing	3548.1 verb 1sing opt aor mid	1706.1 prep	2935.3 noun dat sing masc
ἐγώ	σου	ὀναίμην	ἐν	κυρίῳ·
egō	sou	onaimēn	en	kuriō
I	of you	may have profit	in	Lord:

372.2 verb 2sing impr aor act	1466.2 prs-pron gen 1sing	3450.17 art pl neu	4551.1 noun pl neu	1706.1 prep	2935.3 noun dat sing masc
ἀνάπαυσόν	μου	τὰ	σπλάγχνα	ἐν	⸀ κυρίῳ.
anapauson	mou	ta	splanchna	en	kuriō
refresh	my	the	bowels	in	Lord.

20.a.**Txt:** 06D-corr,018K
byz.
Var: 01א,02A,04C
06D-org,020L,025P,bo.
Gries,Lach,Treg,Alf
Word,Tisc,We/Ho,Weis
Sod,UBS/✱

5382.3 name dat masc	3844.13 verb nom sing masc part perf act	3450.11 art dat sing fem	5056.3 noun dat sing fem
[ᵃ✱ Χριστῷ.]	**21.** Πεποιθὼς	τῇ	ὑπακοῇ
Christō	Pepoithōs	tē	hupakoē
[Christ.]	Having been persuaded of	the	obedience

4622.2 prs-pron gen 2sing	1119.7 verb 1sing indic aor act	4622.3 prs-pron dat 2sing	3471.18 verb nom sing masc part perf act	3617.1 conj	2504.1 conj
σου	ἔγραψά	σοι,	εἰδὼς	ὅτι	καὶ
sou	egrapsa	soi	eidōs	hoti	kai
your	I wrote	to you,	knowing	that	even

17. As a result of the spiritual bond among the three now, the apostle knew he could depend upon his "partner" (*koinōnon*) to accept Onesimus as he would Paul himself. Obviously, God had not called Philemon to fulfill the same function in the New Testament church that He had called Paul to fulfill, nor had He given to Philemon the same responsibility He had placed upon Paul. Still, they were "partners."

18. Here we come to the heart of the matter of restitution in Paul's letter to Philemon. This fifth basis for Paul's appeal to his friend to accept Onesimus stands in stark contrast to the fourth one, showing that the spiritual should not be separated from the practical. Paul's promise to make any necessary restitution certainly would have been a meaningless offer unless he had the funds to back up his statement. We do know that he lived in his own rented house (Acts 28:30), so he must have had some material means. In a spiritual sense the apostle's example here gives us a beautiful picture of what Christ did for humans when He took the penalty for our sins upon himself. We owed a debt that we never could have paid to God, but Jesus took the debt upon himself and paid a debt He really did not owe.

19. If the apostle indeed dictated the epistle to an amanuensis as was his normal custom (Romans 16:22), he must have taken the writing instrument suddenly from the writer and with his own hand wrote, "I will repay it." Just as suddenly, though, he reminded the recipient of the letter of the reciprocal debt Philemon owed him. As was noted previously, this reminder must have referred to the spiritual debt Philemon owed to the apostle because he probably heard the gospel message through Paul's ministry, either during the time the apostle spent in Ephesus (Acts 19) or on some other occasion, or by some indirect means. Possibly Epaphras, or someone else who received training under Paul in Ephesus, preached the gospel of salvation to Philemon, resulting in his conversion to Christianity. The statement, though, may mean even more than that.

20. The sixth and final basis for Paul's appeal was his confidence in his friend Philemon. Paul was not above asking other people for help when special needs existed. Besides, his request was not for himself, but for a friend whom God had blessed in a special way by bringing him into the family of God. For the third time in this short letter Paul used the Greek neuter term (*ta splanchna*) that expresses the deepest emotions possible for a person to feel.

21. The apostle was sure Philemon would do even more than he asked. Paul must have known Philemon well enough to realize he would respond positively to such a request. How could anyone turn

17. If thou count me therefore a partner: . . . if you consider me a comrade, *Williams* . . . as a true friend, *NLT*.

receive him as myself: . . . accept Onesimus as you would accept me, *SEB* . . . welcome him as me, *Klingensmith* . . . take him to your bosom as you would me, *Williams*.

18. If he hath wronged thee, or oweth [thee] ought: . . . if he cheated you at all, *Berkeley* . . . if he have injured you, *Campbell*.

put that on mine account: . . . charge it to me, *Confraternity*, *TCNT* . . . put it on my bill, *Klingensmith*.

19. I Paul have written [it] with mine own hand:

I will repay [it]: I will refund it, *Concordant* . . . I will pay it in full, *Williams*.

albeit I do not say to thee: . . . not to mention, *Williams*.

how thou owest unto me even thine own self besides: . . . you, yourself, are indebted to me, *Norlie* . . . you owe me your life, *NLT* . . . your very life, *SEB* . . . your very soul, *TCNT*.

20. Yea, brother, let me have joy of thee in the Lord: I would like some return myself from you, *Williams*.

refresh my bowels in the Lord: Comfort my heart, *Lilly* . . . Console my heart, *Confraternity* . . . Refresh my inmost being, *Klingensmith* . . . you will lift up my heart in Christ, *SEB* . . . buoy up my deepest feelings in Christ, *Berkeley*.

21. Having confidence in thy obedience I wrote unto thee: Confident of your compliance, *Lilly* . . . Trusting in thy compliance, *Confraternity*.

21.a.**Txt:** 06D,018K
020L,byz.
Var: 01‭א‬,02A,04C,025P
33,bo.Lach,Treg,Alf
Tisc,We/Ho,Weis,Sod
UBS/✱

5065.1 prep	3450.5 art nom sing masc	3614.17 rel-pron pl neu	2978.1 verb 1sing pres act	4020.51 verb 2sing indic fut act	258.1 adv
ὑπὲρ	ʼ ὃ	[ᵃ✱ ἃ]	λέγω	ποιήσεις.	**22.** Ἅμα
huper	ho	ha	legō	poiēseis	Hama
above	what	[idem]	I may say	you will do.	At the same time

1156.2 conj	2504.1 conj	2069.1 verb 2sing impr pres act	1466.4 prs-pron dat 1sing	3440.1 noun acc sing fem	1666.1 verb 1sing indic pres act	1056.1 conj
δὲ	καὶ	ἑτοίμαζέ	μοι	ξενίαν·	ἐλπίζω	γὰρ
de	kai	hetoimaze	moi	xenian	elpizō	gar
but	also	prepare	me	a lodging;	I hope	for

3617.1 conj	1217.2 prep	3450.1 art gen pl	4194.6 noun gen pl fem	5050.2 prs-pron gen 2pl	5319.13 verb 1sing indic fut pass
ὅτι	διὰ	τῶν	προσευχῶν	ὑμῶν	χαρισθήσομαι
hoti	dia	tōn	proseuchōn	humōn	charisthēsomai
that	through	the	prayers	your	I shall be granted

23.a.**Txt:** 06D-corr,018K
020L,byz.
Var: 01‭א‬,02A,04C
06D-org,025P,bo.Gries
Lach,Treg,Alf,Word
Tisc,We/Ho,Weis,Sod
UBS/✱

5050.3 prs-pron dat 2pl		776.3 verb 3pl indic pres mid	776.2 verb 3sing indic pres mid		4622.4 prs-pron acc 2sing
ὑμῖν.	**23.** ʼ Ἀσπάζονταί		[ᵃ ἀσπάζεταί]		σε
humin	Aspazontai		aspazetai		se
to you.	Greet		[Greets]		you

1874.1 name nom masc	3450.5 art nom sing masc	4720.1 noun nom sing masc	1466.2 prs-pron gen 1sing	1706.1 prep
Ἐπαφρᾶς	ὁ	συναιχμάλωτός	μου	ἐν
Epaphras	ho	sunaichmalōtos	mou	en
Epaphras	the	fellow prisoner	my	in

5382.3 name dat masc	2400.2 name masc	3111.1 name nom masc	702.1 name nom masc	1208.1 name nom masc
Χριστῷ	Ἰησοῦ,	**24.** Μᾶρκος,	Ἀρίσταρχος,	Δημᾶς,
Christō	Iēsou	Markos	Aristarchos	Dēmas
Christ	Jesus;	Mark,	Aristarchus,	Demas,

25.a.**Txt:** 02A,04C,06D
018K,020L,byz.it.sa.bo.
Weis
Var: 01‭א‬,025P,33,Tisc
We/Ho,Sod,UBS/✱

25.b.**Txt:** 01‭א‬,04C
06D-corr,018K,020L
025P,byz.it.bo.Sod
Var: 02A,06D-org,048
33,sa.Gries,Lach,Treg
Alf,Word,Tisc,We/Ho
Weis,UBS/✱

25.c.**Txt:** 018K,Steph
Var: Gries,Lach,Word
Tisc,We/Ho,Weis,Sod
UBS/✱

3037.1 name nom masc	3450.7 art nom pl masc	4754.4 adj nom pl masc	1466.2 prs-pron gen 1sing	3450.9 art nom sing fem
Λουκᾶς,	οἱ	συνεργοί	μου.	**25.** Ἡ
Loukas	hoi	sunergoi	mou	Hē
Luke,	the	fellow workers	my.	The

5322.1 noun nom sing fem	3450.2 art gen sing	2935.2 noun gen sing masc	2231.2 prs-pron gen 1pl	2400.2 name masc	5382.2 name gen masc
χάρις	τοῦ	κυρίου	ʼᵃ ἡμῶν ʼ	Ἰησοῦ	Χριστοῦ
charis	tou	kuriou	hēmōn	Iēsou	Christou
grace	of the	Lord	our	Jesus	Christ

3196.3 prep	3450.2 art gen sing	4011.2 noun gen sing neu	5050.2 prs-pron gen 2pl	279.1 intrj	4242.1 prep
μετὰ	τοῦ	πνεύματος	ὑμῶν.	ʼᵇ ἀμήν. ʼ	ʼᶜ Πρὸς
meta	tou	pneumatos	humōn	amēn	Pros
with	the	spirit	your.	Amen.	To

5208.2 name acc masc	1119.21 verb 3sing indic aor pass	570.3 prep	4373.1 name gen fem	1217.2 prep	3545.1 name gen masc
Φιλήμονα	ἐγράφη	ἀπὸ	Ῥώμης,	διὰ	Ὀνησίμου
Philēmona	egraphē	apo	Rhōmēs	dia	Onēsimou
Philemon	written	from	Rome,	by	Onesimus

3473.2 noun gen sing masc
οἰκέτου. ʼ
oiketou
a servant.

down a request couched in the terms of this passage? It would be interesting to know exactly what Philemon's response was. It would not be too difficult, though, for a spiritually minded individual to conclude that the recipient of the letter must have acquiesced to Paul's request without any hesitation. All of us need to make serious requests at times. If we would allow it to do so at such times, Paul's pattern in making his crucial request of Philemon could be a great help to us.

22. As in the other Prison Epistles, here again Paul indicates an expectation of imminent release from his first Roman imprisonment. His request of Philemon to prepare a guest room for him makes it clear. It also shows early believers provided for traveling ministers. But even while making this request, showing tact once more, Paul commended his future host for his prayers for him.

23. The Colossian correspondence contains added information about Epaphras, and the reference in this verse no doubt concerns the same person. What did Paul mean by calling Epaphras "my fellow prisoner in Christ Jesus"? Was he using the phrase metaphorically to mean Epaphras also had become a bondslave of Jesus Christ, or had this man actually been placed in prison for some reason? Maybe Epaphras became a prisoner voluntarily in order to assist Paul.

24. The reader should notice that the same five people are mentioned in this passage as in Colossians 4:10,12,14. This fact helps lend credence to the belief of many commentators that Paul wrote Colossians and Philemon at approximately the same time. Mark was a relative of Barnabas, a very close friend and associate of the apostle Paul. Fortunately, Barnabas had shown more patience than Paul, and it seems that Barnabas was right, and that Paul realized this fact at a later time. Mark not only became an associate of Paul and a definite help to him, but he also assisted the apostle Peter in his ministry (1 Peter 5:13), as well as being privileged to write the Gospel that bears his name. Aristarchus also became one of Paul's trusted associates and traveled with him many times (Acts 19:29; 20:4), even on his journey as a captive to Rome (Acts 27:2). At this time even Demas served as a trusted assistant of Paul. Luke, a Gentile physician who dedicated his life to the Lord Jesus Christ, completed the entourage of people with Paul at that time, people that Paul honored by calling them "fellow laborers."

25. Paul's closing statement serves as another excellent reminder of his dependence upon God's grace and his consuming desire that other people do the same. "The grace of our Lord Jesus Christ" is that operating principle which caused Christ to sacrifice himself on the cross for the sins of mankind.

knowing that thou wilt also do more than I say: I am sure that, *Williams* . . . knowing that thou wilt do even beyond, *Confraternity* . . . knowing full well that you will do by me what I am asking, *Montgomery* . . . I know you'll do even more than I ask, *Beck* . . . do even more than I have suggested, *Adams* . . . even beyond the things I say, *Wuest* . . . more than I request, *Berkeley*.

22. But withal prepare me also a lodging: One thing more, *Beck* . . . Please also prepare for me, *Montgomery* . . . At the same time get a room ready for me, *Adams* . . . be putting in readiness a guest room for me, *Wuest* . . . get the guest room ready, *Klingensmith* . . . have a guest-room ready for me, too, *Williams*.

for I trust that through your prayers: . . . for I am expecting, *Wuest* . . . for I am hoping by your prayers, *Montgomery* . . . through your prayers, *Adams*.

I shall be given unto you: I shall have the gracious privilege of coming to you, *Williams* . . . being restored to you, *Lilly* . . . to be given back to, *Beck* . . . granted to you, *Wuest*.

23. There salute thee Epaphras: . . . sends you his best regards, *Norlie* . . . sends you greetings, *Montgomery* . . . greets you, *Adams* . . . wishes to be remembered to you, *Williams*.

my fellowprisoner in Christ Jesus: . . . my cellmate, *SEB* . . . my fellow captive, *Concordant* . . . in the cause of, *Williams*.

24. Marcus, Aristarchus, Demas, Lucas, my fellowlabourers: . . . along with, *Adams* . . . so do...my fellow workers, *Montgomery, Williams*.

25. The grace of our Lord Jesus Christ [be] with your spirit. Amen: The help of, *Adams* . . . The love of the Lord, *Beck*.

The *Overview* is a significant section of the *Study Bible*. It offers important background information concerning each book. It usually provides a comprehensive outline of the book, then presents in-depth studies on themes which relate to the subject matter. Since it serves as a background, it does not necessarily cover every chapter or section. It provides material for which there would not be enough space in the *Verse-by-Verse Commentary*.

BACKGROUND
The Recipients of the Epistle

The ethnic term *Galatian* comes from the same root as the word *Gaul*. It refers to some Celtic tribes that had for many centuries lived in the territory now known as Turkey (Asia Minor), near where Ankara, the capital of Turkey, is situated. Shortly before the birth of Christ the territory of the Galatians had come under the control of the Roman Empire. It was made a Roman province, together with other countries in Asia Minor, among them Pisidia (Acts 13:14) and Lycaonia (Acts 14:6).

The Activity of Paul Among the Galatians

Paul's first visit to Galatia must then have taken place during his second missionary journey. He was warmly received by the Galatians in spite of his "infirmity of the flesh" (4:13,14) which did not hinder them from assisting him in every way. The apostle visited the Galatians a second time with the intent of securing and building up that which had been won during his first visit. However, a short time (cf. 1:6) after this second visit Paul received word that a serious heterodoxy was threatening the Galatian church. In order to counteract this heresy Paul wrote the Epistle to the Galatians. It was written perhaps during Paul's ministry in Ephesus (Acts 19), but it is also possible that it was written earlier from Corinth, perhaps almost at the same time as the Epistle to the Romans. Some scholars believe it was written from Antioch, just prior to the Jerusalem conference recorded in Acts 15.

The Purpose of the Epistle

The epistle was written to refute the dangerous teaching the Judaizers were seeking to promote. Their teaching had already caused problems in the church at Jerusalem (Acts 15:1-5), but it had been unanimously rejected by the apostles (Acts 15:6-12). However, the heresy was emerging in other places where there were Jews who would nourish it.

The Galatians had evidently been quick to listen to the arguments of the Judaizers who were seeking to convince the new Christians they must keep the Mosaic law concerning circumcision and observance of the Jewish feasts (5:2-6). Paul maintained that it is impossible to mix faith in Christ as the way of salvation and the Law as a means of salvation (2:16; 5:2). He insisted that circumcision inevitably involved an obligation to keep the entire Law (5:3).

The Judaizers were also seeking to undermine Paul's authority in the very churches he had founded. They sought to give the impression that Paul was a second class apostle, that he ranked far below the apostles in Jerusalem. Paul met this kind of attack everywhere even though he insisted there was the best possible relationship between him and the other apostles (Galatians 2:7,9; Acts 15:1-29). He continually maintained that he had been called to be an apostle by the resurrected Lord Jesus, not through any action of the other apostles (1:1,15-17).

Paul's refutation of the Judaizers' heretical teaching is the main issue of the epistle, but there are references to some of the effects false doctrine has on the daily lives of those who are led astray by it. The epistle mentions some indication of a backsliding into paganism (4:8,9), to mutual disagreement (5:15), and an indecent life-style (5:17-21).

The Distinctive Characteristics of the Epistle

Paul had no cowriter when he wrote the Epistle to the Galatians. Unlike some of his other epistles, it contains no personal greetings, nor does it give any indication of where it was written. Paul often dictated his epistles, adding his own personal greetings at the end, but the conclusion of Galatians is much longer than usual (6:11-18). However, there are three distinctive characteristics.

From its beginning this epistle is unusual. First, it is remarkable that there is no thanksgiving or intercession for the recipients of the letter. First Timothy and Titus do not have these distinctives either, but in the Epistle to the Galatians it almost seems sinister since they are replaced by the ill-boding words, "I marvel that ye are so soon removed from him that called you into the grace of Christ unto another gospel" (1:6).

The second distinctive mark is that the epistle is unusually impassioned in its language. In 10 places at least Paul used very sharp and blunt expressions: 1:8,9; 2:11,13; 3:1,3; 4:11; 5:10,12; 6:13. In addition, Paul interrupted his discussion of the main theme of the epistle by referring to the personal response of the Galatian believers to the heresy being taught by the Judaizers: 3:1-4; 4:8-20; 5:7-12. We see this kind of interruption in 2 Corinthians but with this difference: the spontaneous interruptions to the teaching being given in that epistle were due to joy and comfort, whereas the interruptions in Galatians were due to Paul's anger because of the heresy being promulgated by the Judaizers and his sorrow because the Galatian Christians had been enticed to forsake the doctrine of faith in Christ alone for their salvation.

The third distinctive mark of the epistle is that it contains the longest connected account of Paul's life in any of the Epistles: 1:15 through 2:15. Here we are given Paul's view of his life as recorded by Luke in Acts 7:58; 8:3; portions of chapters 9 and 11, and chapters 12–15. Paul's account in Galatians verifies his apostolic authority which the Judaizers were challenging.

It must be emphasized that in spite of Paul's wrath which is directed toward the heretics, the epistle testifies strongly of his love for the Ga-

latian Christians. Many times he used the expression "brethren" (1:11; 3:15; 4:12,28,31; 6:1,18). He spoke of the Galatians as "sons" (4:6,7) in whom he wanted to have confidence (5:10), and he gave directions to those who were "spiritual" (6:1). He wrote of the good memories he had of his visits with them (4:12,14,15; 5:7), and he called them "my little children" (4:19). The epistle closes with Paul's desire that peace and mercy be upon those who accept his "rule" (6:16).

OUTLINE OF GALATIANS
I. INTRODUCTION (1:1-14)

This section contains Paul's greeting (verses 1-5), his reason for writing the epistle (verses 6-9), and his testimony that the gospel he preached was from God and had been given him by "the revelation of Jesus Christ" (verses 10-12), a gospel that was contrary to his earlier, self-chosen manner of life (verses 13,14).

II. PAUL'S EARLIER LIFE (1:15–2:15)

Paul had been predestined to preach the gospel and called to be an apostle not by man, not even the original apostles or the Early Church. His calling and training came to him directly from the Lord Jesus Christ, and the apostles in Jerusalem were at last persuaded that he had been called by Christ to take the gospel to the Gentiles.

III. PAUL'S TEACHING (2:16–5:12)

Paul's main theme in the epistle is that justification comes through faith in Christ alone, not by works of the Law. The Law was given to unveil sin. It was the "schoolmaster to bring us unto Christ, that we might be justified by faith. But after that faith is come, we are no longer under a schoolmaster" (3:24,25).

IV. ADMONITIONS (5:13–6:10)

Paul was careful to stress that the liberty which believers have in Christ is not to be used as an excuse for resorting to the works of the flesh. Rather, the true effect of Christian liberty which comes through justification by faith leads to a life of faith and good works which are motivated by love.

V. CONCLUSION (6:11-18)

The epistle ends with a short summary of the main contents of the letter which Paul had written with his "own hand." He gave further testimony to the power of the Cross, refusing any additional means for salvation. The basic premise of the epistle is Jesus only, not Jesus plus anything else.

ATTACK ON THE HERETICS

After his initial greeting to the Galatians, Paul began immediately to deal with the heresy which was causing so much division and confusion. He marveled that the Galatian Christians had "so soon" turned away from the true gospel he had preached to them. He declared that the Judaizers were distorting the gospel. He felt it was necessary to vindicate his apostolic authority, since the Judaizers were seeking to discredit that authority.

Paul had once been a persecutor of the Church. He had been more zealous for the Jewish religion than any other person. But the day came when God revealed His Son and called him to preach the gospel to the Gentiles. Three years after his conversion Paul went to Jerusalem to see Peter, with whom he stayed for 2 weeks. It was at this time he met James, the brother of the Lord.

Fourteen years later he went to Jerusalem again, accompanied by Barnabas and Titus. The purpose of this visit was to present the Law-free gospel to them "of reputation" (2:2). The apostles to whom he referred enjoined nothing of importance on Paul and accepted his call to preach the gospel to the Gentiles. They gave him and Barnabas "the right hands of fellowship" as colaborers in the gospel.

Paul next related to the Galatians an incident when he had to withstand Peter to his face. In Antioch Peter had eaten with the Gentile Christians, thus expressing his emancipation from the Jewish manner of eating. However, when some Jewish Christians came in, Peter withdrew. Since Peter had agreed with the Law-free gospel Paul preached, Paul considered his actions hypocritical. It is interesting to note that in his epistle to the Galatians, written many years later, Paul did not hesitate to unveil Peter's weakness in Antioch. Nor did he spare Barnabas who "also was carried away with their dissimulation" (2:13). In chapter 1 Paul wrote, "But though we, or an angel from heaven, preach any other gospel unto you, than that which we have preached unto you, let him be accursed" (verse 8). These words indicate how serious Paul was in his desire that the gospel be kept clean. He spared neither himself nor any fellow apostle or close friend if there should be any deviation from the truth.

Christ had broken down, by His death on the cross, the division between Jew and Gentile (Ephesians 2:11-13). Peter had a practical part in breaking down the division by entering the house of Cornelius and preaching the gospel (Acts 10:28), and by maintaining in the circle of the apostles the truth that God had poured out upon the Gentiles the same Holy Spirit the Jewish believers had received (Acts 11:1-18; 15:7-11). By his action at Antioch, he rebuilt the wall which he himself had had a hand in breaking down.

When Paul did not retreat from attacking a fellow apostle who had shown weakness when he should have stood firmly, it is easy to understand that he did not show the real heretics any mercy. The so-called Judaizers whom Paul was opposing did not really deny the gospel, but they wanted to add something to the gospel. This distorted the gospel of Christ into "another gospel," a false gospel. The delusion of the Judaizers was that they mixed the Law and gospel together. They maintained that salvation is partly by faith, partly by works. With flaming zeal, Paul opposed this falsification of the gospel: "But though we, or an angel from heaven, preach any other gospel unto you than that which we have preached unto you, let him be accursed" (1:8).

Paul's argument was that this false gospel robbed God of the honor that belongs to Him because it implies that His grace is not great enough to forgive sin until the sinner deserves it. The argument continues: If faith is not enough for salvation, then it can only be because the redemptive work of Christ is not sufficient. If salvation can be obtained in whole or in part by works it disparages the work of Christ and maligns the character of God by doubting His free grace.

Such an attitude is a demonstration of unbelief. Therefore, Paul wrote to those who believed they could be justified by their works that they had fallen out of grace and that the work of Christ on their behalf would profit them nothing (2:21; 3:1-4; 5:2-4). The heterodoxy which they had accepted had robbed them of their salvation. That is why Paul opposed the heretics so strongly. They led men astray. Paul wrote, "Christ is become of no effect unto you, whosoever of you are justified by the law; ye are fallen from grace" (5:4). Paul feared that all the Galatian believers had experienced had been in vain (3:4). His only hope was that in their confusion they had not become real Judaists, that they did not understand the real issues, and that they had kept their faith in Christ (3:26; 5:10).

The Judaism which penetrated the early Christian churches and which Paul opposed so strongly was the same distorted view of Jewish religion that Jesus fought against during His entire earthly ministry, that is, Pharisaism. Some Jews had joined the first Christian churches without being loosed from their Pharisaic attitude (Acts 15:5). Paul, who had been a Pharisee, knew how totally impossible it was to combine Christianity and Pharisaism. Paul's struggle against it wherever he found it was a continuation of the battle which Jesus had faced.

In addition to the Christianized form of Pharisaism which had its origin in the backslidden Jewish religion, another spiritual current which had its origin in paganism threatened to infiltrate the churches. The Gnostic mystery religions mixed myths of the Orient with Greek philosophy. The "Christian" forms of gnosticism mixed the gospel of Jesus Christ with so-called "wisdom," the worship of angels and an explanation of "man and the physical universe as resulting from a series of emanations from the supreme godhead," as well as an ascetic element with a strong emphasis upon mortification of the body (Colossians 2:23).

Paul warned that after his departure these forces would gain power in the churches which would cause a great backsliding and precede the revelation of the Antichrist. History shows that this was so. The main delusion was seeking to add something to the work of Christ in order to gain salvation. From this root all other delusions have grown up.

The Reformation is the great historical testimony to the doctrine of justification by faith alone in Christ's redemptive work. Forgiveness of sin comes only through faith in His atoning death. This expresses the Biblical doctrine of salvation: "Therefore we conclude that a man is justified by faith without the deeds of the law" (Romans 3:28). "It is God that justifieth" (Romans 8:33). "But to him that worketh not, but believeth on him that justifieth the ungodly, his faith is counted for righteousness" (Romans 4:5). "But for us also, to whom it shall be imputed, if we believe on him that raised up Jesus our Lord from the dead; who was delivered for our offenses, and was raised again for our justification" (Romans 4:24,25).

The question could be asked, "What was the motive and intent of these Judaizers? What did they really want?" Perhaps their first and most important supposition was that the work, death, and resurrection of Jesus Christ could be incorporated into the Jewish religion. In the Gospels we find the disciples had the same line of thought. In Acts we see that in spite of repeated signs and events it was almost impossible for the first pure Jewish church in Jerusalem to understand that they had entered into a totally new covenant into which all nations are welcomed and who do not have to come through the Law.

Paul met their activity everywhere he went. They taught, "Except ye be circumcised after the manner of Moses, ye cannot be saved" (Acts 15:1). "There rose up certain of the sect of the Pharisees which believed, saying, That it was needful to circumcise them, and to command them to keep the law of Moses" (Acts 15:5). We can have some sympathy for these men who valued the old covenant so highly that they did not spare any effort in order to make the Gentiles join it. But we can also understand that the Spirit of God did signs and wonders in order to open their eyes to the truth. It is perhaps more difficult to understand that only a few of them received the truth.

Paul revealed the pride which lay behind their activities. Fallen, sinful man, "the flesh," would not give up its own honor, admit its total fall, and accept the preaching of the Cross as the only way to salvation. Paul recognized the deadly danger of adding anything to the gospel. Delusions of later periods have often consisted of the same kind of false doctrine: that of seeking to add something else to the work of Jesus on the cross. Regardless of what this other thing or things may be, it has always led to heterodoxy, and also has often led to a reprobate and sinful life with all kinds of excesses.

SURVEY COMMENT

The genuineness of the Epistle to the Galatians has been almost undisputed. In it the apostle spoke of his Damascus experience. He spoke with authority, fully aware of the One who had sent him (1:1). He was confident that the same God who raised up Jesus from the dead had called him for His service, separating him from his mother's womb to preach the gospel to the Gentiles (1:15,16). That God-given authority to go to the Gentiles meant also that he was bound. If he made any attempt to change the contents of the message, he himself would be accursed (1:8).

It is remarkable that in the opening section of the epistle, Paul did not present the contents of the gospel but rather its immutability. If it is altered, it is no longer the gospel (1:7). The gospel is not a work of man which can be presented today but becomes out of fashion tomorrow. It stands firm eternally because it came from God and was revealed by His Son. It is constantly called "the gospel of Christ" (1:7). This expression can be understood as the gospel which belongs to and descends from Christ (subjective genitive) as well as the gospel which concerns Christ and reveals Him as the central figure (objective genitive).

In 1:4 Jesus is presented as the One who gave himself in order to deliver us from our sins. This truth is referred to again in 4:3-5. Jesus is the deliverer from the powers of wickedness. The believer is plainly "called unto liberty" (5:13). Those who pervert the gospel are characterized as those who spy on the liberty believers have in Christ Jesus.

In 2:16 to 3:24 Paul dealt with the theme of justification by faith. What is meant by this expression? To justify means to pass a sentence of acquittal. This takes place when an individual gives his life to Jesus Christ. Jesus took upon himself our sins and gives us instead His righteousness. This involves a deep union with Christ which can best be expressed by Paul's words "I am crucified with Christ" (2:20). The result is the "I" lives no longer. Christ lives within the believer: He is formed within the Christian (4:19). That is why the phrase "in Christ" is used so often. It is a word which God speaks and man hears, and receiving involves faith, trusting that when God says it, it happens. Therefore, believing is a main point in the Epistle to the Galatians. Paul illustrated this by referring to a child's relationship with his father (5:4-6). The believer's faith is like the trust of a child and results in obedience (6:16).

This "obedience to the faith" (Romans 1:5) is not to be confused with keeping the Law. They are as different as night and day as the Epistle to the Galatians shows. When an individual seeks to be "justified by the works of the law" (2:16), he is relying on his own works, but this is a great illusion. If one prefers to follow the way of the Law and one's own righteousness, he must keep the entire Law without exception (5:3). No man can do this (3:10). "No man is justified by the law in the sight of God" (3:11).

These two terms, justification by the Law and salvation by grace are diametrically opposed. Where one is the other must give way; they are contradictory propositions. The delusion which the Galatians were facing was that they wanted it both ways. Paul said those who were seeking to make the Law the way of salvation were under a curse, a curse which Christ died to free us from (3:10,13).

What is the Law then? "It was added because of transgressions," Paul said (3:19). There are different opinions as to what this means. Some feel that the works of the Law produce transgression. It is more likely that he meant the Law illuminates the transgressions which have already taken place, the transgressions which can no longer be hidden. Thus the Law works not only as a judge but as a protector.

Paul used the illustration of the pedagogue (schoolmaster, 3:24) and the tutor or governor (4:2). Their important work for the child lasted only "until the time appointed of the father" (4:2). Then the child became free. The holy commandment of the Law was fulfilled by God himself in Jesus Christ. His innocent suffering and punishment became an atonement for all our sins. The Law can no longer judge the believer. Its work was to conclude all under sin (3:22), so that grace is given by faith. Thus justification does not come through the works of the Law, but through "the obedience of faith." The believer receives the Spirit not by works of the Law but by "the hearing of faith" (3:2). He can only be taught to call God "Father" by the Holy Spirit (4:6). No one on his own can understand that he is a child of God. This understanding is a gift of the Spirit.

The doctrine of justification by faith is foretold in the Old Testament: "The scripture, foreseeing that God would justify the heathen through faith, preached before the gospel unto Abraham" (3:8). Jesus himself on the walk to Emmaus spoke to the two disciples of all that the Old Testament said "concerning himself" (Luke 24:25-27). The view that the Old Testament is totally irrelevant for Christians is completely foreign to the teaching of the Bible.

Paul used examples from the Old Testament in different ways. Abraham was an example of faith (3:6-9). Paul explained the expression concerning the offspring of Abraham as referring directly to Christ, who was of the family of Abraham (3:16). Paul used Sarah and Hagar as "types" of two different kinds of life. The son of the bondwoman was begotten "after the flesh" (4:23). Sarah's son was begotten by virtue of the "promise," corresponding exactly with the story in the Old Testament. Paul was certain that the story of these two women tells something which is of the greatest importance to the entire salvation history. Paul declared that the promise given to Abraham cannot be annulled by the Law which was given much later. The Law was never intended as a way of salvation. The Law could never justify, it could only judge (3:21).

The doctrine of justification by faith leads us to consider the liberty which believers have in Christ. Paul wrote of the believers' release from the curse of the Law (3:13; 4:5). Another important release which Paul mentioned is from "the elements" and from the gods "which by nature are no gods" (4:3,8-10). Opinions differ among interpreters, but the most natural interpretation is to think of this as a reference to Gentile idols. Behind these the evil spirits of Satan hide (cf. 1 Corinthians 10:19,20).

The Galatians who wanted to make the Law a way of salvation had a tendency to return to some of the paganism from which they had been delivered. This resulted in their turning away from Christ to something else. The result was bondage. They turned to the ways of "the flesh" (3:3). They flattered the old, evil man and nourished his pride. They provided for man's honor, not God's. This has been observed on many mission fields. Paganism is a dark spiritual power of great strength. If this spiritual power has the slightest opportunity, it will reenter an individual from whom it has been driven by Christ. There is a good reason why Paul used the expression "in vain" (4:11). We do not know the extent of the Galatians' backsliding into paganism, but Paul considered his short remark sufficient.

We now reach a new main theme in the epistle: the description of the work of the Holy Spirit in the Church and in the life of each individual. In matters great and small the apostles wanted to be guided by the Spirit, not only in those matters which concerned eternal things but also in temporal, for example, the agreement Paul wrote of in 2:7-10. It concerned a temporary matter, but the small word "saw" in verse 7 discloses that the Spirit influences and guides believers to the truth in temporary situations. Paul also called attention to the miracles which the Spirit works in the lives of believers (3:5). The Book of Acts witnesses to these miraculous acts of the Holy Spirit. But whether the Spirit works in miraculous ways or in quiet everyday ministry to the believers, it is still the Spirit who is at work.

The Epistle to the Galatians calls attention to what Paul called the "walk in the Spirit" (5:16), being "led by the Spirit" (5:18), bearing "the fruit of the Spirit" (5:22). All of these encompass the work of the Spirit in the life of the individual believer and in the life of the Church collectively.

To "walk in the Spirit" seems to indicate the initiative of each individual while on the contrary to "be led by the Spirit" reminds one of an irresistible force which comes from above. In this case, the individual does not himself decide the direction he will walk. Because of the work of the Holy Spirit, each believer can reach his full potential so that he can take the initiative, work, and live, but at the same time realize that he is no longer his own master. It is the Spirit that drives him. This becomes clear when one considers the Christian life as a child- or son-connection to God the Father by Jesus Christ (4:5,6). This new dependence as a child of God leads to true liberty.

The expression "fruit" which Paul used to describe the work of the Spirit in the life of the Christian was used by Jesus himself in John 15:4,5. It is difficult to find any better picture. The fruit is totally dependent on the tree and is typical for this special tree. The believer is united with the Father and the Son. Therefore the fruit the believer bears is of a certain kind (5:22,23). Love is mentioned first. It is the meaning and fulfillment of the Law (5:13,14). It is the secret behind all of God's work because He is love. The other fruit mentioned are included in the love that is the fruit of the Spirit.

The fruit of the Spirit is contrary to the works of the flesh (5:19-21). The words "the flesh" can indicate many different things. In 4:13,14 it indicates the body in a totally neutral meaning. In other places it refers to man, or more definitely fallen, sinful man. When this word is used, the translator as well as the interpreter must be very careful. In the Epistle to the Galatians the word is used in the sense of that which is contrary to the Spirit (3:3; 4:29; 5:16f.; 6:8), the natural man in his sinfulness. The work of the Holy Spirit in each individual is exercised in the spirit of the individual, in the heart as Jesus said (Mark 7:19).

There is a distinct contrast between the works of the flesh and the fruit of the Spirit which Paul mentions by name. This is seen clearly when a comparison is made:

Adultery, uncleanness—love

Lasciviousness—joy

Idolatry, witchcraft—peace (that which God
gives, Ephesians 2:14)

Hatred—longsuffering

Variance, emulations, wrath—gentleness

Strife—goodness

Seditions, heresies—faithfulness

Envyings—meekness

Murders, drunkenness, revelings—temperance

Individuals respond to persons, events, and problems according to whether or not they are following Christ. The non-Christian exhibits one type of behavior because he is doing the works of the flesh. The Christian who is bearing the fruit of the Spirit exhibits another type of behavior. It is not a matter of psychological difference which causes the two types of behavior. Flesh is flesh and can only produce the works of the flesh, although they can be embellished differently according to breeding and temperament. But behavior changes when Christ is Lord of the life. He and He alone can produce the fruit of the Spirit in the life of the individual who is born again.

Thus we see once more that it is the Holy Spirit in the life of the Church and the individual that creates this great difference. It is the difference between light and darkness, salvation and perdition. That is why Paul fought so strongly against those who were contending that salvation comes through doing the works of the Law. The Law is holy and good, and it will be fulfilled (5:14), but the "flesh" cannot fulfill it. The natural man cannot justify himself. It is arrogant to try to do so. Such individuals are seeking to "make a fair show in the flesh" (6:12). They are living in self-delusion (6:3).

Those who were telling the Galatians they must be circumcised according to the Mosaic law, saying that not until then could they consider themselves true Christians, were perverting the gospel. That is why Paul stood so strongly against them. It was a matter of eternal life or eternal death (1:6,7).

But even though Paul stood firmly against the heresy of salvation through works, it does not mean that the gospel approves the works of the flesh. Christian liberty is not a "liberty for an occasion to the flesh" (5:13). In his epistles Paul gave many instructions which were taken directly from the Old Testament (5:14; 6:7,8). The Lutheran fathers called this "the third use of the law." Just as the Holy Spirit throws light on the salvation history of the Old Testament, showing that it points to Christ, so He can throw light on the admonitions of the Law to be used in the Christian life. But never does He indicate that salvation can be built upon the works of the Law.

Galatians 5:5 is a short summary of all that the gospel gives to the believer: "We through the Spirit wait for the hope of righteousness by faith." "We wait" is the attitude of the Christian as he daily turns to God and when he looks forward to the return of the Lord Jesus. "Through the Spirit" involves a negative response to all the "works of the flesh." "By faith" indicates there can be no attempt to make oneself deserving of salvation, no compromise with the "works of the law." "The hope of righteousness" is the sentence of acquittal which God has pronounced because of the Cross and which will on that great Day free us from perdition and lead us into glory.

Overview—Ephesians

Ephesians is the main epistle of the New Testament concerning Christ and the Church. The closely related Epistle to the Colossians has as its main theme the cosmic Christ. It declares His preexistence, His coming in the flesh, and His inherent glory. The theme of the Epistle to the Ephesians is the universal Church which gathers together all the people of God, Jew as well as Gentile (2:11-19). The major feature of the epistle, however, is that it presents the most complete picture of the theology of the New Testament.

OUTLINE OF THE EPISTLE

I. PRAISE AND PRAYER (1:1-23)
  A. Authorship and Greeting (1:1,2)
  B. Praise for Salvation (1:3-14)
    1. Introduction: What was lost in Fall is regained in Christ (1:3).
    2. God has chosen us in Christ before the foundation of the world (1:4-6).
    3. In the crucified Christ we have redemption from guilt and death (1:7).
    4. In Christ all are united (1:8-10).
    5. In Christ both Jew and Gentile are united unto one Body (1:11-14).
  C. Prayer (1:15-23)
    1. Thanks to God that all believers are united in faith and love (1:15,16).
    2. Petition that God by His Spirit will give believers hope and strength (1:17-19).
    3. Praise that the resurrected and ascended Christ is Lord and Head of His church (1:19-23).

II. THE PREACHING OF THE GOSPEL (2:1—3:21)
  A. It is by the grace of God that believers are saved from death and given new life (2:1-10).
  B. Though Israel has a special place in salvation history, there is now no division between Jew and Gentile. Both are saved by grace and are each part of the Body, the Church (2:11-22).
  C. Paul is the apostle to the Gentiles (3:1-13).
  D. Believers must be strengthened in the Faith and in their fellowship with other believers in their life in Christ, rooted in His love and kept in His hope until the day of completion (3:14-21).

III. THE FRUIT OF THE GOSPEL (4:1—6:18)
  A. In the life of the Church the gospel produces the fruit of unity (4:3-6).
  B. Each new believer receives his special gifts with which he is to serve others (4:7-16).
  C. The new life in Christ must be lived out in the particulars of every day (4:17—6:9).
  D. In the home man and wife are both under the dominion of the love of Christ, parents and children are under the education of Christ, and slaves and masters are both subject to the same Lord (5:21—6:9).
  E. The new life in Christ is portrayed as a struggle against evil powers. However, in this struggle believers are to put on the whole armor of God, fight with His weapons, and in all situations support one another through prayer and supplication (6:10-18).

IV. CONCLUSION (6:19-23)
  A. Paul asked the church at Ephesus to remember his work in prayer (6:19,20).
  B. Paul recommends Tychicus who brought the epistle (6:21,22).
  C. Benediction (6:23,24)

AUTHORSHIP OF THE EPISTLE

Paul himself claimed to be the writer of the epistle (1:1; 3:1). The writer is obviously of Jewish descent (1:11; 2:3). He belonged to "the holy apostles" (1:1; 3:3,5). He had been entrusted with the secret of God, His plan of salvation for the entire world through Christ, and he had been called to preach that good news (3:7), but he was aware that his calling was by grace, that indeed he was "less than the least of all saints" (3:8). All this points to Paul as the author.

Early Church history supports this fact. Irenaeus, Tertullian, and Clement of Alexandria were convinced Paul was the author of the epistle. Most of the apostolic fathers referred to the epistle or quoted from it directly. In his first epistle to the Corinthians (46:6), Clement of Rome referred to Ephesians 4:4-6. In a letter to Polycarp (chapter 5), Ignatius made reference to Ephesians 5:25. Polycarp himself alluded several times to the Epistle to the Ephesians (*Epistle to the Philippians* 1:3; 10:2; 12:1). It seems that it is the best attested of all Paul's letters.

PLACE AND DATE OF AUTHORSHIP

When and where did Paul write this epistle? Though not directly stated, there are several indications. In 3:1 the author presented himself as "the prisoner of Jesus Christ for you Gentiles." In 3:13, he wrote of the tribulations he suffered "for you." In 4:1 he again characterized himself as "the prisoner of the Lord," and in 6:20 as "an ambassador in bonds." These words are most probably to be interpreted as from a prisoner in an actual prison. There are three possibilities to consider.

(1) In the beginning of this century some scholars felt these words of Paul referred to an imprisonment in Ephesus. One mentioned Paul's reference to his missionary sufferings in Ephesus (1 Corinthians 15:32; 2 Corinthians 1:8) which, according to the wording, could very well have referred to an arrest and a threatening sentence of death. Paul wrote that in the year 54 he had already been "in prison more frequent" (2 Corinthians 11:23). Clement of Rome mentioned in his letter to the church in Corinth (5:6) that Paul had a total of seven imprisonments. However, there is no direct knowledge of any imprisonment in Ephesus, even though archeology has unearthed a building in Ephesus which is shown as "the prison of Paul." Although Luke did not include all of the details of Paul's ministry, it is unlikely he would have failed to mention such an imprisonment of the apostle. If there was such an event it was more likely that it was of only a few days' duration.

(2) Another possibility is that the Epistle to the Ephesians was written during the 2-year-long period when Paul was in custody in Caesarea, from the summer of 55 to the fall of 57 (Acts 24 to 26). The only real argument for this hypothesis is that Paul was apprehended not many weeks after his farewell to the Ephesian elders at Miletus (Acts 20:17f.). Paul's words concerning his opportunities for ministry (6:19f.; Colossians 4:3) speak directly against the Caesarean hypothesis. So does his mention of the many friends and coworkers who surrounded him (Colossians 4:7f.).

(3) The nearly unanimous church tradition is that the Epistle to the Ephesians was written by Paul during his imprisonment in Rome from the spring of 58 to 60. Paul's mention (6:21f.) of Tychicus, "a beloved brother and faithful minister," as the bearer of the epistle speaks also for this point of view. Tychicus is mentioned also in the same way in Paul's epistle to the Colossians (4:7f.). Although he was in bonds (3:1; 4:1; 6:20; Colossians 4:18; Philippians 1:12f.), Paul was given liberty to receive guests, to preach, and teach those who came to him (Acts 28:30,31). He could also write letters!

THE READERS

The epistle is obviously directed toward Gentile Christians (1:13; 2:1,11f.; 3:1) who had recently entered the Christian community (1:13,18; 2:5; 4:1,4,20; 5:14). Because of their recent past, there was a risk of backsliding. They must be strengthened and matured in the life of the Christian community (3:14; 4:13) and be admonished to live separated lives (4:17f.).

Where did these people live? The epistle indicates at Ephesus (1:1). Another hint is given in 6:21 where Tychicus is mentioned as the one who delivered the epistle. According to Colossians 4:7ff., he was also the one who carried Paul's letter to the church at Colossae which had a strong spiritual and geographic connection with the churches in Laodicea and Hierapolis (Colossians 2:1; 4:13f.). These three churches lay in the southeast part of Phrygia (Acts 16:6; 18:23). Politically they belonged to the Roman province of Asia as did Ephesus in the western section. In these territories the readers of the Epistle to the Colossians as well as the Epistle to the Ephesians lived.

THE GENUINENESS OF THE EPISTLE

As has been mentioned, Ephesians is among the best confirmed letters of Paul as far as "outward" testimony is concerned. But during the end of the 17th Century certain questions arose concerning its authenticity because of "internal" problems.

(1) The first concerned the language and style of the epistle. This question arose because there are about 50 words which are not found in the generally undisputedly genuine epistles of Paul. Some of those words are used only once in the New Testament. Also, there are long, involved sentences, and participle and genitive constructions which indicate a richness of language not usually found in Paul's writings.

However, this argument does not hold up. For instance, in the indisputable Epistle to the Galatians, of the same length as the Epistle to the Ephesians, there occur a similar number of "special" words which indicate Paul knew and used these words. There is absolutely nothing in the epistle which does not find a natural explanation in the purpose Paul had in writing.

(2) The second objection was that the doctrinal content of the epistle belonged to a later period. Especially mentioned was Christ's pre-existence, His activity in the creation, and His dominion over the visible as well as the invisible world. Also attacked was the fully developed idea of the Church as well as the choice of words used to describe justification by faith and the Parousia. But, with no exception, all of these doctrinal teachings are found in the generally accepted epistles of Paul. Paul wrote of Christ the universal Lord especially in Romans 8:28f.; 1 Corinthians 8:5f.; and Philippians 2:6-11. It was the resurrected, glorified Lord who met Paul on the road to Damascus. The Church is something more than a series of individual churches. It is a literal, organic unity. First Corinthians 12:22f., as well as Romans 12:4f., characterize it as the body of Christ.

In the Epistle to the Ephesians we must allow Paul to use new expressions for indisputable truths of the Christian faith. The crucified and resurrected Christ is referred to as "our peace" (2:14). The return of Christ in the clouds, the resurrection of the dead, and the catching away of those still alive are described as our "hope" (1:18) "in the ages to come" (2:7) and "the day of redemption" (4:30). We find all of these ideas mentioned in the Epistle to the Colossians.

(3) The most important argument against the Pauline authorship of the Epistle to the Ephesians is that although Ephesians and Colossians are almost parallel epistles, Ephesians contains entire sections which do not appear in Colossians. Examples are the doxology (1:3-14), the development of the unity of Jews and Gentiles in Christ in the Church (2:11-22), the section concerning the unity of the Church and the multitude of gifts (4:3-16), and the wonderful words concerning the Church as the bride of Christ (5:22-33). Colossians contains a distinct argument against a particular heterodoxy being promulgated in Colossae, while the corresponding theme in the Epistle to the Ephesians is addressed by preaching and instruction rather than direct argument.

The Epistle to the Colossians contains a series of named persons who either sent greetings or who were greeted personally (4:9-17). It seems that the author of the Ephesian letter was not on close personal terms with most of his readers. This does not necessarily mean that the readers were total strangers to the author. (Some years had passed since Paul had visited them. He had spent 3 years ministering to the Christians at Ephesus and was on personal terms with them.) The twice repeated "heard of" (1:15; 3:2) and the fact that the epistle lacks personal greetings led to the argument concerning the authorship of the epistle.

The words "at Ephesus" (1:1) are not found in two of the oldest manuscripts (Sinaiticus and Vaticanus). Neither Origenes in Alexandria nor Basilius in Caesarea in Asia Minor found these words in any of the manuscripts placed before them. However, there must have been a place named. One cannot read the first sentence of the epistle without it.

The most probable explanation is as follows: Paul is a prisoner in Rome. He receives a visitor from the Colossian church and learns of problems there. Paul dictates his letter to the Colossians, dealing with the heterodoxy of which he has been informed. That is why this epistle has such a personal and polemic character. Tychicus is to take the epistle to Colossae, and the thought occurs to Paul that he could make a circular trip with epistles to all the churches in the province. So Paul writes another epistle. It is broader and clearer and less polemic. It expresses some of the matters discussed in his letter to the Colossians, but it is in a form which can meet the situation in all the churches in the province. Copies are made for the different churches. The name of each church is added in the opening of the letter along with Paul's blessing in his own handwriting.

It is not puzzling that the copy of the letter which was given to the church in Ephesus has been "kept" and has found its place in the New Testament. The original church grew until there was not enough space for it under one roof. Thus there were quite a few churches in the great city. Each church would naturally want a copy of Paul's letter for continual reading. When Ephesus became one of the leading centers of Christianity, the epistle spread from place to place and was best known as "The Epistle of Paul to the Ephesians." But originally it was "the circular of Paul, the apostle, to the church in the province of Asia."

The connection between the actual, personal, and polemic epistle to the church at Colossae and the circular letter to a larger group of churches (the Epistle to the Ephesians) can be compared to the connection between the Epistle to the Galatians and the Epistle to the Romans. The Epistle to the Galatians is the actual "real" epistle, written to correct a situation. The Epistle to the Romans is a systematized, precise theological explanation of the same gospel and its "problems."

AN "EPISTLE"

No matter how many personal greetings and actual problems were dealt with in the New Testament epistles, none of them are a "once only" epistle, still less a private epistle. They are all "official" letters intended for reuse, for continued reading in the churches (Colossians 4:16; 1 Thessalonians 5:27). Gradually they were given to an even larger group of churches and finally to the whole of Christianity.

But the Epistle to the Ephesians is, to a larger extent than any other, to be read in the church service. This is evident not only from 3:4, where Paul assumed such a reading (*anaginōskontes*, meaning to read with a loud voice), but also from the tone and disposition of the entire epistle.

Attention has been drawn to the fact that the Epistle to the Ephesians is a church service via an epistle! There is the greeting (1:2), the opening hymn (1:3-14), and thanksgiving and prayer (1:15-23). The sermon falls in two parts— preaching (2:1 to 3:21) and admonition (4:1 to 6:18). There are "announcements" (6:19-22), and finally there is the blessing (6:23).

Although this goes too far, there is no doubt about the liturgical tone and design of the epistle. This is evident not only in the preaching which is Christ-centered, but we listen also to the oldest Christian hymn. There is no doubt that 1:3-14 is a complete hymn. There are also well-known doxologies as quotations (1:20f.; 2:14-18; 5:14). Water baptism and the Lord's Supper have their place, and 5:28-30 speaks of Christ as the One who gives His church nourishment for their new life. The joyful "gloria" is sounded in 3:20, and the epistle ends with an "amen" and inheritance from the synagogue service. Intercession (1:15f.) has the same liturgical tone as the preceding hymn.

PROBLEMS ADDRESSED IN THE EPISTLE

The fact that because of its universality the Epistle to the Ephesians differs from the Epistle to the Colossians does not mean there are no problems addressed in its admonitions. One cannot think of the Epistle to the Ephesians so universally edifying that it floats in the air!

(1) Chapter 2 deals with the old problem of the Law versus grace. Certain Jewish Christians felt the death and resurrection of Jesus Christ were not sufficient for salvation. They insisted that circumcision and the commandments of the Law must be added to the preaching of salvation by grace.

(2) The well-known question concerning Paul's apostleship was also inescapable. Paul addressed this matter in 3:1-13.

(3) Backsliding into the old ways of paganism was such a threatening problem that it drove the apostle to his knees in prayer that God would keep, strengthen, and mature the believers so that they would not be "carried away with every wind of doctrine" (3:14f.; 4:13f.).

(4) Paul did not hesitate to deal with moral problems (4:17f.; 5:23-13).

(5) Paul had dealt strongly with the problem of gnosticism which was making inroads into the Christian community of Colossae. The apostle addressed the subject again in the Epistle to the Ephesians, but this time from a positive angle, presenting Christ as Lord of all. All in heaven and on earth are subject to Him (1:10,20f.; 2:2,7; 3:10,21; 4:10; 6:12).

PAUL'S MINISTRY IN EPHESUS

At the beginning of his second missionary journey, Paul intended to go to the Roman province of Asia. It seemed to the apostle that Ephesus was geographically and strategically the next place to establish a church. But the Holy Spirit led otherwise, and the fruitful ministry in Europe was the result. On the return journey, however, the apostle visited Ephesus (Acts 18:18-21). On the Sabbath Day he went to the synagogue and "reasoned with the Jews" who invited him to remain for a longer time with them. The apostle realized that the time had come for a rich ministry in Ephesus. It would be the bridgehead for the gospel in the province of Asia. Because of this, Paul left Aquila and Priscilla, a married couple of his working group, to arrange for the future work in Ephesus.

After a "stay at home" during the winter of 51–52, Paul began his third missionary journey. On his way to Ephesus, he visited the young churches in Galatia and Phrygia and arrived in Ephesus in the spring of 52. From the "upper coasts" (Acts 19:1), the apostle overlooked the city which would become his place of ministry for the next 3 years, a city which would become one of the centers of the Christian church during the next centuries.

The City of Ephesus

Down in the broad valley where the river

Kaystros flowed out into the Aegean Sea, the city lay before Paul's eyes. It was large and beautiful with its white houses and long streets, the great harbor, and the multitude of people, over 300,000 inhabitants. There were other cities too in this corner of the Roman Empire. The province was the richest of all the provinces. The seaport towns were Smyrna and Miletus. Pergamum was the residence of the governor of the province. Thyatira, Sardis, Philadelphia, Hierapolis, Laodicea, and Colossae were there, but Ephesus was the greatest and most important city.

In Paul's time Ephesus was already an old city. It was founded about 900 B.C. by Greek emigrants. By the time a Christian church was founded there, Ephesus had become the fourth largest city of the Roman Empire with a mixed population. Besides the descendants of the original Greek population there were people from Asia Minor, the Orient, and the Jews who had established a synagogue.

Ephesus was an important commercial city and shipping center. It was the transit trade route between Rome and the province of Asia. It was also a great tourist city. The great attraction which drew visitors from all parts of the then known world was the temple of Artemis. Artemis was originally a Greek goddess of the hunters. She became a symbol of fertility, a sex goddess, encircled and served by 1,000 temple prostitutes. Her temple, Artemision, was built about 700 B.C. It was burned in 356 B.C. by Herostrat. Fifty years later it was rebuilt by Deinokrates, the architect, and it was described as one of the seven wonders of the ancient world. This temple stood for 500 to 600 years until it was destroyed by the Goths in the migration period of A.D. 262. The Goths destroyed the city so totally that the English archeologist J.T. Wood took 7 years to confirm its location and recover artifacts. That it disappeared so completely is due to the fact that parts of the city were used for other construction purposes, for example, the church of Sophia in Bysants about A.D. 500.

The destruction and subsequent disappearance of the temple and the city changed the level of the land, filling the great harbor with sand. Not until recent decades have archeologists been able to uncover the streets and houses, squares and temples, the mighty amphitheater and other public buildings of the once prosperous city.

The Epistle to the Ephesians describes Gentile life in a city given over to paganism—its fascinating power (2:1-3), its emptiness and licentiousness (4:17-19), its lewdness, drinking, lust, and other darkness (5:3f.). Sex in Ephesus, as well as religion, had become big business. Among the buildings which have been uncovered is the great and distinguished bordello of the city. It was difficult for Christians to maintain a Christian life-style in such surroundings, and Paul warned of the danger of compromise.

The Revival in Ephesus and the Province of Asia

According to Acts 19:1-7, Paul's first experience in Ephesus was his meeting with some of the disciples of John the Baptist. The revival which came as a result of John's preaching bore fruit not only among Jews in Palestine but also in the Diaspora, notably in the province of Asia and in Alexandria in Egypt (Acts 18:24f.). Paul preached the gospel to these disciples of John in Ephesus, baptizing them in the name of Jesus. And when Paul laid his hands upon these men, they received the baptism of the Spirit.

Paul also went to the synagogue and shared with the Jews the good news of the gospel of Christ. With frankness and persuasion he spoke concerning "the kingdom of God." For 3 months the apostle presented the gospel to the Jews. But division came. "(Many) were hardened, and believed not, but spake evil of that way before the multitude" (Acts 19:9). It had been Paul's experience everywhere (Acts 13:14f.; 14:1f.; 17:1f.; 18:4f.). Paul now had to separate himself and organize an independent Christian church. The meeting place at first was in the school of Tyrannus where lectures and conversations took place during the early hours of the forenoon before the noonday heat came. Ordinarily Tyrannus could rent his rooms to other similar purposes. Codex D adds in Acts 19:9 that Paul used the rooms "from the 5th until the 10th hour." In the morning Paul worked at his trade of tentmaking, along with his coworkers Aquila and Priscilla (Acts 20:33-35).

That Paul indulged in "disputing" ("dialogue," *dialegomenos*, Acts 19:9) does not mean that he tried to find a religious denominator. Paul preached Christ without any compromise, not as a way but as *the* Way (Acts 19:9,23). In the Epistle to the Ephesians the same distinct testimony to Christ is given. Only through Him is there access to God (2:18; 3:12). Thus, the

"dialogue" refers only to the Greek form of public speaking. Believers met for fellowship and worship in the largest Christian homes (Acts 20:20), for example, the home of Aquila and Priscilla (1 Corinthians 16:19). This type of ministry lasted without interruption for 2 years "so that all they which dwelt in Asia heard the word of the Lord Jesus, both Jews and Greeks" (Acts 19:10).

Epenetus was the first convert in Asia. Paul spoke highly of him (Romans 16:5). An extensive revival followed. Jews as well as Greeks heard the word of the Lord. The revival spread to all the towns of the province. Sick ones were healed and evil spirits cast out of those who were possessed (Acts 19:10-20). One of the distinguishing marks of the revival was joy. An outcome of this joy was obedience. The Christians burned the things connected with their pagan rituals. Their release from the evil spiritual powers was expressed in visible actions (1:21; 2:2; 6:12).

Opposition and Departure

Paul now decided to leave Ephesus in order to visit some of the churches he had begun on his second missionary journey. The apostle was zealous in his service to the Lord and to those who had been won to Christ. He was already planning his fourth journey which he hoped would bring him to Rome, the capital of the world. However, something took place which caused Paul to send Timothy and Erastus ahead, while he himself remained in Asia "for a season."

The silversmiths in Ephesus had a lucrative business making small silver shrines to Artemis (Diana), but since so many in the city had become Christians their business was seriously affected. Something had to be done. Demetrius, a silversmith, summoned the workmen to discuss the matter. Income had diminished, unemployment threatened, and the honor of the goddess had been violated! Tempers began to boil. A great shout used at all the feasts of Artemis sounded: "Great is Diana of the Ephesians."

A demonstration march followed. The workers went to the greatest rallying place in the city, the theater. The inhabitants of the city, hearing the tumult, joined in the march. Two of Paul's coworkers were dragged along. Paul wanted to interfere, but he was stopped by members of the church and friends in the city council. The disturbance in the theater lasted

for 2 hours. Finally the town clerk was able to speak to the people, warning them that unless they dispersed the Roman authorities would become involved, and they would have to account for their actions.

When the uproar ceased, Paul called the Christians together, bade them farewell, and departed for Macedonia.

Retrospect and Anxiety

How did Paul himself judge his years of activity in Ephesus? We can ascertain some of his feelings from the epistles he wrote. In spite of the great results of his ministry, there were problems. In 1 Corinthians 15:32 we read Paul's words, "I have fought with beasts at Ephesus." The struggle was so difficult that it was only his faith in the Resurrection which upheld him. The apostle also wrote to the Corinthians about the trouble he and his coworkers had to endure in the province of Asia: "We were pressed out of measure, above strength, insomuch that we despaired even of life" (2 Corinthians 1:8). Paul could not have meant the Demetrius demonstration, since this took place after the Corinthian epistle was written. But his words unveil some of the tense and perilous conditions under which Paul labored in Ephesus.

In addition, Paul was concerned about the work in Ephesus. He longed for an opportunity to speak to the leaders of the Ephesian church. That opportunity came half a year later (Acts 20:15 to 21:1). In the spring of 55, after visiting Greece, Paul set sail for Syria. The ship harbored in Miletus. The apostle's friends in Ephesus were only a day's journey away, so he sent for them to come to him. Paul felt he would never again visit Ephesus, that "bonds and afflictions" awaited him. So his sermon to the Ephesian elders was full of admonition concerning their role as overseers in the church. He reminded them of certain facts concerning his ministry among them. He warned them that even in the midst of the church some would arise speaking perverse things which would draw some believers after them. Their motive would be gain. Paul exhorted the leaders of the church to be watchful, to remember the apostle's warning to the church when he was ministering to them. He reminded the leaders that during his 3 years among them he had not taken any remuneration from the church but had earned his own living by his craft. After praying with the leaders, the elders accompanied Paul to the ship and bade him farewell with tears.

MAJOR THEMES OF THE EPISTLE

The Epistle to the Ephesians has been called the deepest book of the New Testament, where the "vision of the purpose of God stretches from eternity to eternity" (Hiebert, p.269). It has been called "the most divine composition of man which includes each Christian doctrine" (Coleridge as cited by Bruce, *New International Commentary on the New Testament, Colossians, Philemon, and Ephesians*, p.230). In a few short chapters the fundamental truths of the gospel are concentrated.

Citing Peake who calls it "the quintessence of Paulinism," Bruce goes on to conclude that it sums up the leading themes of Paul's epistles (*New International Commentary on the New Testament, Colossians, Philemon, and Ephesians*, p.229). The doctrines preached by the great apostle have been brought together in a completed unity. Harpur states that doctrines which in other places are presented in sentences are here placed together in a harmonious connection with the Christian faith as an entirety, each thing in its own place and context. The doctrine of the Epistle to the Romans concerning salvation by grace through faith, the appeal for Christian unity in the First Epistle to the Corinthians, the claim for apostolic authority in the Second Epistle to the Corinthians, matters concerning the Law and the gospel in the Epistle to the Galatians, the Christology of the Epistle to the Colossians, the eschatology of the First Epistle to the Thessalonians are all presented in the Epistle to the Ephesians. However, instead of the argumentative and polemic style of some of the other epistles, these doctrines are presented in a clarified style in the Epistle to the Ephesians.

The main themes of the epistle are not presented in a systematic or dogmatic form. The epistle is not a theological essay. The main contents are presented in a stream of inspiration. New thoughts come from the preceding ones in a network of sentences and subsidiary clauses, often connected by the small word *in*, (Greek, *en*) which is used not less than 120 times in the Greek text. N.B. Harrison calls the theme of oneness in Christ "the loftiest truth of the Bible" (p.135). The continual theme is what Christians have and are in Christ. In a style which is at the same time plain and exalted, Paul describes the riches of salvation. Doctrine is lifted to praise, theology becomes worship. The epistle is a hymn concerning Christ and His holy bride (Schaff, *History of the Christian Church*, 1:780).

However, the apostle does not lose contact with the world of everyday realities. Along with the doctrinal teaching of the epistle, there is admonition and instruction for the daily life of Christians in the home and in the church.

Christology

The Christology of the Epistle to the Ephesians (as well as that of the Epistle to the Colossians) is one of the most exalted in the New Testament. It includes:

(1) Christ's Humility

"Now that he ascended, what is it but that he also descended first into the lower parts of the earth? He that descended is the same also that ascended up far above all heavens, that he might fill all things" (4:9,10). This passage corresponds with the section concerning the humiliation and exaltation of Christ recorded in Philippians 2:5-11. What does the expression "the lower parts of the earth" mean? Does it refer to the earth itself (which is lower than the heavens) or the kingdom of death (which is lower than the earth)? John 3:13 speaks of the admission of the Son of Man into heaven, and it is contrasted to His coming to the earth, which strengthens the first interpretation. In Romans 10:6f. (cf. Deuteronomy 30:12f.) the ascension of Christ is contrasted with His descent to the kingdom of death. Both interpretations are thus possible.

(2) Christ's Death on the Cross

It was through His bodily death on the cross that Christ won our redemption through His blood (2:7). The cross is the symbol of the substitutional death of Christ on our behalf, a death which was under the curse of God (Galatians 3:13). That is why the Cross expresses the totality of the gospel (1 Corinthians 1:18; cf. Romans 1:16). On the cross Christ received in our stead the sentence of God's wrath upon sin (Romans 3:24,25; cf. 1 John 2:2).

(3) Christ's Resurrection

In 1 Corinthians 15:5f., Paul gave the historical proof of the resurrection of Christ. In Ephesians Paul spoke of the resurrection of Christ as a demonstration of the power of God and a testimony that this power is "to us-ward who believe" (1:19,20). As in the other epistles, as well as the whole of the New Testament, the resurrection of Christ has a central place in the

Epistle to the Ephesians (see Acts 2:24; Romans 1:4; 4:25; 14:9; 1 Corinthians 15; 1 Peter 1:3; Revelation 1:18).

(4) Christ's Exaltation

Christ's exaltation is a leading theme in the Epistle to the Ephesians. Christ was not only resurrected, He is seated at the right hand of God in heaven, elevated above every power and authority in this world and the one to come. All has been placed under His feet, and He has been made the Head of all things (1:20,23). He ascended up above all heavens in order to fill all things (4:8-10). The Epistle to the Ephesians maintains a Christology which can be traced throughout the New Testament, from the earliest Christian preaching (Acts 3:20,21) to the last book of the Bible (Revelation 1:13-18).

Soteriology

The doctrine of salvation is presented in the Epistle to the Ephesians. Paul declared that salvation is in Christ. It is called "redemption through his blood" (1:7), and it is presented through the words of the gospel (1:13). Salvation consists of the forgiveness of sins (1:7), and believers are made partakers of His eternal life (2:1-5). Salvation is not of works (2:9). It is given by grace and must be received through faith (2:8) and brings about a new manner of life which results in good deeds (2:10).

Forgiveness of sin is called justification in Romans 4:5,6, and it consists in the fact that sin is not imputed to us. Salvation makes us new creatures in Christ (2 Corinthians 5:17). It is "by grace through faith" (2:8), and the antithesis "not of works" and "unto good works" (2:9,10) expresses the main principle in the doctrine of salvation in the New Testament.

Ecclesiology

The doctrine concerning the Church is one of the most important themes in the Epistle to the Ephesians. Paul used the word *church* (*ekklēsia*) to refer to local churches and to the Church universal (1 Corinthians 12:28; 15:9; Galatians 1:13; Philippians 3:6; Colossians 1:18-24). In the Epistle to the Ephesians Paul wrote mainly of the Church universal, but when particular matters needed attention Paul wrote to the local churches.

The Church is the body of Christ. Christ himself is the Head (4:15,16), and Christians are the members of that Body (4:25; cf. 1 Corin-

thians 12:12f.). The Church is also the temple of God, built on the foundations which the apostles and prophets laid, and Jesus Christ is the Cornerstone (2:20-22; cf. 1 Corinthians 3:9-17). Paul called the Church of the New Testament a "secret, a mystery." According to its usage in the New Testament, this word means a divine plan which has been made known through revelation. It was Paul's privilege as the apostle to the Gentiles to make known the mystery that Jesus Christ, the Messiah of Israel and the Son of God, now resides in the Church which consists of Gentiles as well as Jews (3:1-12). Gentiles are no longer strangers and foreigners, excluded from the household of God. Through faith they are now a part of the family of God and share in the promise in Christ.

Paul defined precisely the universality of the Church and its unity. The division between Jew and Gentile has been broken down forever: "He is our peace, who hath made both one, and hath broken down the middle wall of partition between us, having abolished in his flesh the enmity" (2:14,15). The expression "middle wall" is probably a reference to the wall in the temple beyond which Gentiles could not pass. In Christ the barriers have fallen. Jews and Gentiles alike are made nigh by the blood of Christ, with access by one Spirit to the Father. The picture of the Church drawn by Paul in 3:10-12 has cosmic dimensions and opens up perspectives whose depths we do not fully understand at the present time. The future of the Church, that which God has prepared for those who love Him, exceeds all that the eye can see, the ear hear, or that which has entered into the heart of man. Even though it has been revealed, it still remains a mystery (1 Corinthians 2:9,10).

Eschatology

Ecclesiology now becomes eschatology. The glory which the Church now has will be exceeded by the glory of the world to come (Hebrews 6:5). The Church which is pictured as sitting "together in heavenly places in Christ Jesus" (2:6) is said now to be in battle with the devil and all his powers (6:12). But that Church is waiting for the return of Christ (4:30). The earnest of our inheritance is the Spirit He has given us (1:14). The Church has received the firstfruits of the Spirit (Romans 8:23) and awaits the new day which shall break with the return of Christ.

Overview—Philippians

PAUL'S MINISTRY IN PHILIPPI

At the beginning of Paul's second missionary journey (Acts 15:36 to 18:21) the apostle, accompanied by Silas, traveled from Antioch in Syria throughout Asia Minor. Timothy joined them in Lystra. The three men then journeyed to Philippi via Troas. They arrived probably in the year 49/50 (cf. Acts 16:9f.). Their stay at this time was short and quite dramatic. They were subjected to rough treatment from some of the citizens of Philippi and as a result were thrown into prison. However, they were delivered by direct intervention from God (Acts 16:25-28), and as a result of Paul's ministry a vigorous church was born, consisting mostly of Gentile converts.

Paul often mentioned the churches of Macedonia (Romans 15:26; 2 Corinthians 8:1-5; 11:9). He received economic assistance from the church at Philippi (4:10-16), even though normally he was reluctant to receive support from anyone (1 Corinthians 9:15f.). Even though the church at Philippi was not rich, the people participated willingly in the collection for the poor in Jerusalem (Romans 15:26; 2 Corinthians 8:1-5). Paul visited the church at Philippi whenever possible and again toward the end of his third missionary journey (Acts 20:3-6).

THE CITY OF PHILIPPI

The city of Philippi, which originally was called Krenides, was conquered in 360 B.C. by Philip II of Macedonia. He fortified the city, utilized its minerals, and renamed it Philippi. It was incorporated into the Roman Empire in 167 B.C. In 42 B.C., the territory around the city became the scene of the battle between the victorious armies of the emperor and the forces which were commanded by Brutus and Cassius, the murderers of Julius Caesar. After the battle quite a few of the veteran soldiers settled in the city. In 31 B.C., it became a Roman colony (Acts 16:12). The total name of the city became "Colonia Julia Augusta Philippensis."

Often a Roman colony was exempted from taxes and duties to the emperor. A Roman settlement was ruled according to the same laws which were in force in Italy. Because of this Roman citizens felt they were on "Italian soil" even though their city might be far removed from the native country. Roman patriotism was no doubt strong in Philippi. Notice the words of the accusation against Paul and his companions as recorded in Acts 16:21, "(They) teach customs, which are not lawful for us to receive, neither to observe, being Romans."

CONTENT OF THE EPISTLE

Paul's letter to the Philippians was written at a time when he was in captivity in Rome (1:7,13,14,16). The church at Philippi had heard of the apostle's imprisonment, and the believers were anxious to know how things were going with him. They had sent him economic assistance by their messenger Epaphroditus (2:30; 4:10,14,18).

In the first main section (1:12-26), Paul described his situation. It was his joy to tell the Philippians that his captivity had been a means of strengthening the gospel rather than repressing it. His bodyguards were convinced that he had been imprisoned because he was a Christian, not because he was guilty of any crime.

His imprisonment had given confidence to many of his "brethren in the Lord," so that they were preaching the gospel without fear. Paul even rejoiced that though some were preaching Christ out of envy and strife, at least Christ was being preached.

From the very beginning of the epistle, the keynote was joy—joy in spite of external tribulation and adversity (1:4,18; 2:2,17; 4:4). Paul was not certain as to the outcome of his imprisonment, whether he would be set free or be condemned and executed. Of vital importance to him was that Christ should be glorified whether by his life or by his death (1:20). From the introductory section, Paul moved into a series of exhortations concerning Christian conduct (1:27 to 2:18).

After speaking about his own situation, the apostle began to speak to the Philippians about theirs. He exhorted the believers to be of one mind, to show mutual humility and love. This admonition may have been in reference to an incipient schism in the church (4:2f.). It cannot be overlooked that this situation may have been the main reason for his writing the epistle. Paul often used the expression *all*. He constantly emphasized that he prayed for them all and that he longed for them all with the love of Christ (1:4,7,8,25).

The section of admonition contains the famous Christ hymn which describes the humiliation of Christ, His obedience to death, and His subsequent resurrection and victory over the powers of evil.

In 2:19-30 Paul wrote of his plans for the

future. He promised to send Timothy to Philippi as soon as possible to learn the exact situation there. In the meantime he had decided to send Epaphroditus immediately. It is possible also that he was the one who delivered Paul's letter to the Philippians. Paul often used Timothy as his special and trusted messenger (cf. 1 Thessalonians 3:2 and 1 Corinthians 4:17). In addition to correcting any possible disagreement, Timothy could add verbally to what Paul had written (see 1 Corinthians 4:17). First Corinthians 11:34 shows that Paul did not mention all matters in his epistles, that he sometimes preferred oral instruction. However, in 3:1 Paul wrote, "To write the same things to you, to me indeed is not grievous." The expression "the same things" may refer to what Timothy would tell them.

But suddenly Paul launched into a violent and vehement attack on the heretics who represented a great danger to the Philippian church. After this digression, Paul returned once more to a discussion of conditions in the church at Philippi and especially to the strife between Euodias and Syntyche. His exhortation to them was accompanied by an appeal to others to help these women who had labored with him in the gospel.

Not until the close of the epistle did Paul mention directly the economic assistance he had received from the church (4:10-20). His words in this passage bear testimony to the close and warm fellowship which existed between the apostle and this church. More than any other, the Epistle to the Philippians is characterized by personal warmth and love between the writer and the church.

OUTLINE

THE AUTHOR OF THE EPISTLE

That Paul is the author of Philippians is generally accepted. However, there are some who do not agree that the epistle in its present form is from Paul's hand. It is the abrupt change of subject from 3:1 to 3:2 that is questioned. In 3:2 the theme and tone of the epistle changed radically when Paul made his sharp attack upon the heretics.

Quite a few investigators are inclined to believe this is an interpolation from an earlier or later epistle of Paul. It is not denied that chapter 3 was written by Paul. The question is whether it belongs to the present Epistle to the Philippians. Opinions differ also as to the length of the insertion. Either it begins with 3:2 and ends with 4:1 or 4:3, or that it continues to 4:9 or 4:20. Some investigators think 4:10-20 is the original letter of thanks to the Philippians.

As an argument that the Epistle to the Philippians consists of excerpts from a number of epistles of Paul there are those who cite the letters of Polycarp, bishop of Smyrna in the first part of the Second Century. Polycarp said that Paul wrote many letters to the Philippians. In regard to the radical change of tone and theme in 3:2, it is well to remember similar digressions in other epistles of Paul (see 2 Corinthians chapters 10 through 13).

If the Epistle to the Philippians was dictated (cf. Romans 16:22), it is possible that new information concerning the Judaistic heretics was received during a pause in the dictation. This would cause Paul to repeat either what he had previously written or to add to the instructions which he had asked Timothy and Epaphroditus to give the church orally. This would explain the sudden change of tone in 3:2.

As an argument that 4:10-20 originally

formed an independent epistle, the following can be stated: (1) It seems strange that Paul would wait until the end of the epistle to mention his thanks for the assistance he had received from the Philippians. (2) The greatest problem is caused by the long interval between the receipt of the Philippians' gift and the sending of the epistle. Chapter 2:25-27 assumes that word was sent to the Philippians concerning the sickness of Epaphroditus during his stay with Paul and that the apostle had been told of the anxiety of the church. If the epistle was written from Rome, this could have been a period of up to 4 months.

It can generally be said that this discussion does not solve any of the matters of exegesis of the epistle. It is possible to link the different sections and give plausible explanations of the differences. It is best not to take these theories seriously until we face an exegetical difficulty that can be solved only by rethinking the possibility of fragments.

THE CHRIST HYMN

There can be no doubt that this hymn (2:5-11) is an integral part of the epistle even though it differs distinctly from the other text. It is a one-piece, poetic composition, characterized by many participle constructions, parallel expressions, and short, condensed sentences. The hymn consists of two main sections which are built up in parallel style. One section describes the debasement of Christ and the other emphasizes His exaltation. There is a natural pause between verses 8 and 9 ("Wherefore") where there is a distinct change of theme.

The traditional view of the hymn expresses the true humility and pure, devoted love of Christ. In this He is a model for believers. "Let this mind be in you, which was also in Christ Jesus" (2:5). The hymn describes how God's own being was manifested in Jesus. The borders of this world have burst because God revealed himself as a Man.

This redemptive wonder is described by the antithetical words, He who was "in the form of God . . . took upon him the form of a servant." The fact that Christ is described as a servant is because He totally accepted the conditions of man's existence in order to redeem man (cf. Galatians 4:3,9; Colossians 2:8,20).

But the hymn indicates further that though Christ became a man, that identification did not express His entire being. The Greek word *homoiōmati* contains, as in Romans 8:1, a contrasting element. This appears, among other things, in the subsequent description of His obedience. The obedience of Christ is contrasted to the disobedience of Adam. Christ, in contrast to Adam, accomplished something vital by His obedience (Romans 5:12-17; 1 Corinthians 15:20-49).

The obedience of Christ is often described in the New Testament as the final act of salvation (Romans 5:12; Hebrews 5:8). He took upon himself the body of a servant and as such became subject to the conditions of death. Thus the Incarnation and death are linked together. By humbling himself and entering the human situation He became subject to death (Hebrews 2:15,16). The obedience of Christ indicates His humility and His deep union with man. But at the same time when He became obedient unto death He also became the Lord of death.

In verse 9 there is a change of subject. The word "Wherefore" indicates that that which follows is a direct result of that which precedes. The New Testament teaches that God exalts the one who humbles himself (Matthew 23:12; Luke 14:11). But the exaltation of Christ is not to be understood as a result of His humility but as a consequence of His obedience and death.

The obedience of Christ was something more than an ethical performance. It was His final act that made our salvation possible. That is why God exalted Him. The power of death was broken. He was not destroyed by death but gained the victory over it (Colossians 2:15; 1 Peter 3:22).

Jesus Christ is the Lord. The title of God in the Old Testament is thus ascribed to Jesus. Verse 10 quotes Isaiah 45:23 where the *Kurios* (Lord) title is ascribed to God. When the *Kurios* title which originally belongs to God is ascribed to Jesus we have a strong testimony to the deity of Christ. Jesus is the representative of God, and God acts through Jesus. The way to God is through Jesus. The hidden God has revealed himself through Jesus. To place oneself under the dominion of Christ is tantamount to the experience of true liberty.

TIME AND PLACE OF WRITING

The epistle contains no exact information concerning the time or place of its writing. However, it is evident that Paul was a prisoner when he wrote the epistle (1:7,13,14,16; 2:17). It is also clear that his captivity was one that could result in condemnation and execution (1:20; 2:17). The major possibilities are Rome,

Caesarea, or Ephesus. According to Acts 23:11,12 Paul was imprisoned in Jerusalem, in Caesarea (23:23f.), and in Rome (28:16f.). The imprisonment in Jerusalem was very short. The Epistle to the Philippians indicates a longer time of captivity. Second Corinthians, which was written at the end of the third missionary journey, indicates that Paul had been in prison many times (2 Corinthians 6:4-10; 11:23,24).

Rome

The traditional viewpoint is that the Epistle to the Philippians was written in Rome. The strongest evidences in favor of this viewpoint are as follows: (1) Paul's imprisonment in Rome (Acts 28:16f.) lasted for 2 years. He was transferred to Rome from Caesarea when he appealed his case to the emperor (Acts 25:11). In that case the epistle was written toward the end of this period, about A.D. 60. The epistle presupposes an extensive, preceding correspondence between Paul and the church in Philippi. (2) The mention of "all the palace" (1:13) and "they that are of Caesar's household" (4:22) point to Rome.

(3) The picture Paul painted of the rivaling groups, where some preached Christ out of envy and strife, intending to cause Paul pain and grief (1:14-18) also points to Rome. Such a situation is almost unimaginable in Ephesus where Paul ministered for so many years. (4) The Epistle to the Philippians indicates a serious captivity where the possiblity of appealing an unfavorable sentence was available to the prisoner. This points to Rome and the court of the emperor where Paul (Acts 25:11) had just pleaded his case.

(5) Paul wrote concerning the economic support he had received from the church in Philippi as he admitted his "affliction" (4:14). There would probably not have been any need of such support if he had been in captivity in Ephesus. Neither would the need for support have been so great in Caesarea. The believers in Jerusalem would not have forsaken the one who had brought the church the collected gifts of money.

Other Views

Although there are many reasons to support the view that the Epistle to the Philippians was written in Rome, there are other points of view which can be mentioned. (1) Before the Epistle to the Philippians was sent, there had evidently been an extensive period of travel and correspondence between Paul and the church at Phi-lippi. They had been informed of Paul's arrest and imprisonment. A collection for him had been undertaken and the money had been sent with Epaphroditus who became ill while he was with Paul. The Philippians had learned of this serious illness, and their anxiety concerning Epaphroditus had been conveyed to the apostle. Paul had then decided to send Epaphroditus back to Philippi so that the church could see he was fully recovered (2:25-28). Thus it must be supposed that word was sent between Philippi and Rome four times before the Epistle to the Philippians was sent.

This extensive traveling seems to indicate that the writing place must have been near Philippi with possibilities for frequent and fast contact. If one accepts that Paul wrote the epistle from Rome, this traveling activity during the conditions of the time must have taken place within a period of about 10 months.

(2) Mention of "the palace" in 1:13 does not necessarily point to Rome. The palace was in fact the normal designation of the residence of a governor of the province with appurtenant adminstration premises for the soldiers who would be stationed there. The expression in 4:22 does not point absolutely to Rome. Civil employees might well be designated as employees of the emperor.

(3) It appears from the epistle that Paul expected to return to the church in Philippi and to spend some time there (2:24; 1:24-27). This could indicate that the epistle was written at a time when Paul was still ministering in these territories. However, these arguments against Rome as the place where Paul wrote the epistle are not conclusive. First, Paul's conditions as a prisoner had no doubt changed radically during the 5 years he had been in prison. Years of captivity can change a person so that he no longer has the strength to begin another work.

Caesarea

Those who maintain that Caesarea was the place from which the epistle was written argue: (1) The mention of "bonds" in 1:13 is best understood in connection with the conditions under which Paul lived as a captive in Caesarea. He was under military guard and without liberty to preach (Acts 23:35). The captivity mentioned in Acts 28 is described as a type of house custody where Paul was free to receive visitors and to preach the gospel.

(2) The Jews who made the charges against Paul (Acts 21:27) are the ones about whom Paul

wrote in Philippians 3. However, the conditions of Paul's captivity cannot be conclusive as an argument against Rome or as an argument for Caesarea. This could not have been a real possibility if Paul was able to make an appeal. Paul did indeed make an appeal to the emperor (Acts 25:11). We know that Felix was willing to free Paul in Caesarea (Acts 24:26). In addition, Paul had a strong desire to go to Rome (Acts 23:11). There is no indication of this in the Epistle to the Philippians. Finally, Acts 24:26 indicates Paul had sufficient funds in Caesarea, while Philippians 4:12 shows he had suffered economic need.

Ephesus

When Ephesus is proposed as the place where the Epistle to the Philippians was written, the following reasons are given: (1) Paul's words in 2 Corinthians 1:8,9 and 1 Corinthians 15:31,32 correspond with the description he gave in the Epistle to the Philippians. The expression Paul used in 1 Corinthians 15:32 should no doubt be understood figuratively. It is probable that as a Roman citizen Paul could not have been sentenced to fight against wild beasts. But it is obvious that he had some experiences in Asia which endangered his life. This also corresponds with the description in the Epistle to the Philippians.

(2) Many of the difficulties which appear if Rome is taken as the writing place of the epistle are solved immediately if we suppose that Ephesus was the writing place. The short distance between Ephesus and Philippi makes the various journeys possible. The plans which are explained in Philippians 2:19f. correspond with the information given in Acts 19:22 (cf. 1 Corinthians 4:17; 16:10). Paul's desire to meet the Philippians once more (Philippians 1:26; 2:24) is also fulfilled (Acts 20:1; cf. 19:1).

(3) Acts 19:22 confirms that Timothy was with Paul in Ephesus. On the contrary there is no indication Timothy was in Rome. (4) The similarity of the contents of the Epistle to the Philippians on the one hand and the epistles to the Galatians, Romans, and 1 and 2 Corinthians points to Ephesus as the writing place. However, content similarity does not necessarily indicate the same period of writing. It must also be asked why Paul did not appeal his case if he was in Ephesus. The possibility for appeal was present in Ephesus just as it was in Caesarea. It is also strange that Paul did not receive assistance from the church if he was in Ephesus. It is also difficult to imagine men in Ephesus who preached the gospel with the intent to hurt Paul. There is also need to prove that Paul's captivity in Ephesus lasted for at least 3 months. During this period the traveling activity mentioned before could have taken place. There is another question: Was Paul at liberty to write and work as a missionary during his captivity in Ephesus? We know that he had this liberty during his captivity in Rome.

THE HERETICS OF CHAPTER 3

In 1:13-18 Paul wrote the Philippians about some of his "brethren in Christ" who were preaching Christ out of "envy and strife," hoping to cause Paul more grief. But Paul was filled with joy because Christ was being preached. But in chapter 3, when Paul wrote about those who were spreading error, the tone is quite different. Evidently these men had not yet penetrated the church but were a distinct danger.

The description Paul gave seems to indicate these men were the Judaizers he had written about in the Epistle to the Galatians. However, it is questionable if these were the same as those referred to in verse 18f. It appears that the men described in the first part of the chapter were men who thought they had received a special revelation. Perhaps they were Gnostics who boasted of their special revelation which they believed gave them a share of the heavenly glory in this life. That is why they did not expect a resurrection of the dead (cf. verse 11 and 1 Corinthians 15:12; Timothy 2:18). They were enemies of the cross of Christ (verse 18; cf. 1 Corinthians 1:23; 2:2). The glory of which they boasted (verse 19; 2 Corinthians 3:7 to 4:17) was in reality their shame.

The expression "whose god is their belly" indicates these men thought only of themselves. The word "belly" in this context could refer to their selfish ego (cf. Job 15:35). Paul rejected their view of perfection (3:12f.). He himself did not feel he had reached such a state. His determination was to press on. Christian living involves faith in the righteousness of Christ which has been imputed to the believer. It implies community with Christ in His suffering and death (Romans 6:1-11). For the Christian the power of the Resurrection is a reality. By it a believer can overcome sin. His final resurrection is ahead when his true perfection will be completed (3:10-21).

Overview—Colossians

The city of Colossae, with its neighboring cities Hierapolis and Laodicea, was situated in the Lycus Valley in the south of Phrygia. During the time of the apostles this territory belonged to the Roman province of Asia. Colossae was the oldest of the three. Though it had once been a great city, now it was overshadowed by its sister cities.

Paul had not visited the churches in the Lycus Valley, but evidently many of the members of the Colossae church knew him personally from his ministry in Ephesus which was situated in the same province (see Acts 19:10). Epaphras, a native of Colossae and one of Paul's coworkers, founded the church in Colossae and perhaps others in neighboring cities as well.

What prompted Paul to write this epistle? First, Epaphras had visited the apostle while he was in prison and told him of problems the church was experiencing. Second, Paul was moved by the Holy Spirit to write a letter addressing these problems and the issue of false teachers in the church. (See the section below titled "The Colossian Heresy.")

According to the tradition of the Ancient Church, Paul wrote this epistle from Rome, as he did the letters to Philemon and the Ephesians. The close connection with these two epistles is obvious. In the Epistle to Philemon many names are repeated. And more than one-fourth of the Epistle to the Colossians' content is found in the Epistle to the Ephesians.

Apart from its opening and close, Colossians contains three main sections: teaching on the person of Christ in the second half of chapter 1; a polemic on freedom in Christ from human regulations in chapter 2; and admonition toward practical Christian living in chapter 3 and the early part of chapter 4. One main theme pervades the Epistle to the Colossians: Christ is presented as the supreme image and Head of all things—in the natural world and the spiritual realm. Christians, united with Him, are freed from sin and live out that freedom in holy behavior and loving relationships.

OUTLINE OF THE EPISTLE
I. GREETING AND PRAYER (1:1-14)
II. TEACHING (1:15-29)
    A. The Person of Christ (1:15-19)
    B. The Work of Christ (1:20-23)
    C. The Tool of Christ (1:24-29)
III. POLEMIC (2:1-23)
    A. The Mystery of God (2:1-5)
    B. The Wisdom of the World (2:6-8)
    C. The Complete Salvation (2:9-15)
    D. The Rudiments of the World (2:16-23)
IV. ADMONITION (3:1–4:6)
    A. Seek That Which Is Above (3:1-4)
    B. Mortify the Earthly Members (3:5-11)
    C. A New Life (3:12-17)
    D. Rules for Households (3:18–4:1)
    E. Prayer and Supplication (4:2-4)
    F. Those Who Are Without (4:5,6)
V. CLOSING AND PERSONAL GREETINGS (4:7-18)

THE COLOSSIAN HERESY

Colossians was written as a polemic, and this is important to understanding it fully. Like Galatians, Colossians was sent to combat heresy that threatened to disrupt and possibly destroy the church. But Colossians is much milder than Galatians as a polemic. This is due, in part, to the Colossians' resistance to the heresy they faced, whereas the Galatian church had allowed the false teachers an entrance and were already being deceived. Paul could give thanks for the Colossians and praise them for their faith, hope, and love (1:3ff.). He commended them for their orderliness and firm faith (2:5). Yet the apostle was very concerned that the Colossian believers were in great danger of being taken captive by vain philosophy (2:8). So he wrote to instruct and encourage them.

Paul does not name or explain in any detail the heresy in the Colossian church. This suggests that we do not have to understand a delusion or heresy to know and believe the truth. The Christology of this epistle belongs to the highest form of polemics and preaching in the New Testament. It rises far above its polemic intent, however, and exalts Christ in a unique way. Paul combats the Colossian heresy in an edifying manner. He presents the "cosmic Christ" as the source and goal of creation and redemption. He opens perspectives far beyond the issue of correcting some heretics in a small church in Phrygia. And he gives to the believers in Colossae, and us, a view of Christ that no other book does.

It is wrong, however, to view the epistle without considering the heresy Paul addressed. Though the content does focus on the person of Christ, modern readers must understand the controversy to fully appreciate that focus. The "Colossian delusion," like the Galatian heresy, is alive and among us today. Though it may be disguised in different wrappings, the dogma of syncretism never changes. An admixture of religious beliefs threatened the church in Colossae; this is what the epistle addressed.

Heresies Facing the Early Church

Two basic aberrations of Christian doctrine faced the Early Church. One came from the Jewish religion and consisted of a mixture of Law and gospel. In Galatians, written much earlier, Paul strongly opposed this delusion. He called it "another gospel" which was no gospel at all but a distortion of the true gospel of Christ. The second attack came from Gentile philosophy, the so-called "wisdom" of men. In First Corinthians Paul wrote that the infiltration of Gentile thoughts and ideas would oppose the power of the gospel. Faith and "wisdom" are just as incompatible as faith and works of the Law.

The church in Corinth was threatened by infiltration from Greek philosophy—the "wisdom of men." The Galatian churches had been invaded by Jewish legalists teaching salvation by "works of the Law." Here in Colossae the church was under attack by a form of heterodoxy that included both Greek philosophy and Jewish legalism. This is clear from Paul's description of the heresy—it consisted of a mixture of Jewish and Gentile elements.

The specific content of the Colossian heresy is difficult to determine. Judging from the content of the messages to the churches in Revelation 2 and 3, various heresies gradually penetrated the churches in Asia Minor before the end of the First Century. In Ephesus there were some who said they were Jews but really were the synagogue of Satan (Revelation 2:9). In Thyatira the woman Jezebel, who called herself a "prophetess," taught and seduced believers to "commit fornication, and to eat things sacrificed unto idols" (Revelation 2:20). In Pergamos, some held to "the doctrine of Balaam" and "the doctrine of the Nicolaitans" (Revelation 2:14,15). Long before this Paul had warned the elders in Ephesus that after his departure false teachers would appear. Some of these would come from outside, but others would arise from within the Church (Acts 20:29,30).

Among the Jewish religious forms existing at this time in Asia Minor was a group of John's disciples. These imitators of John the Baptist can be traced far into the Christian Era. Paul met this group during his visit to Ephesus (Acts 19:1-3).

The First Century experienced a tremendous variety of religious transition and upheaval. Christianity was affected by many "voices." Some aided the Church's growth, while others threatened its existence as the true expression of Christ's body. Though there are distinct differences in the heresies in Corinth, the churches in Galatia, and that in Colossae, there are common elements as well. For example, the "delusion in Colossae" and the "delusion in Galatia" contain Judaistic elements that are similar. Greek philosophy found in the Corinthian "wisdom" parallels the "philosophy" that sought to invade the church in Colossae.

The form of Judaism which had become Christian and had penetrated the Galatian churches had its origin in Jerusalem (Galatians 2:4; compare Acts 15:24). But the Judaistic tendencies in Colossae had another source because they were not the same as the original Palestinian doctrine. They may have come from the immediate local situation. The Jewish colony in Colossae was old. Two centuries earlier Antiochus the Great had deported 2,000 Jewish families to Phrygia (Josephus, *Antiquities of the Jews*, 12:3:4). During the long exile these Jews had adopted some of the practices and doctrine of the Gentiles, and their orthodox Jewish brethren were displeased with this. The Talmud (*Shabbath*, 147b.) has sometimes been quoted to substantiate this orthodox dissatisfaction: "The wine of Perugitha and the water of Diomsith cut off the Ten Tribes from Israel!" The name Perugitha is understood as Phrygia, and if this is correct, the Phrygian Jews were considered as belonging to the 10 tribes.

The Jewish Diaspora was often influenced by the philosophies and beliefs of their environment. One example is the Jewish philosopher Philo from Alexander (circa 30 B.C. to A.D. 50). He attempted to form a synthesis of Hebrew faith in God and Greek philosophy. His disciples spread his ideas widely.

Lightfoot poses an interesting theory in his commentary (pp.81-113). He suggests the Colossian heresy can be traced to the sect of the Essenes. Lightfoot says there are pre-Gnostic features found in the Essenes' beliefs, and that they displayed a Gnostic Judaism. He believes this special form of Judaism secured a foothold in this part of Asia Minor during the time of the apostle.

These theories have some support in the Qumran texts. W.D. Davies lists the similarities as: linguistic peculiarities, calendar correspondences, Sabbath rules, and decisions concerning food and asceticism. Also, there is a strong emphasis on wisdom and knowledge which includes a special worldview and angel doctrine. But we do not find in the Epistle to the Colossians any mention of the ritual bath of the Essenes. F.F. Bruce thinks the Qumran texts do not support a connection between the sect of the Essenes or the Qumran community and the Colossian heresy. He instead adopts Matthew Black's formulation of a nonconformist Judaism (*New International Commentary on the New Testament, Colossians, Philemon, and Ephesians*, p.23).

It is evident there had existed a great variety of groups and beliefs in the Jewish religion, and not the least in the Diaspora. We discover in Acts traces of Judaism mixed with occultism. Acts 13:4-12 tells of a Jewish sorcerer and false prophet who opposed Paul's preaching of the gospel. Acts 19:13-16 describes Jewish conjurers who tried to use the name of Jesus as Paul had done (compare Matthew 7:22). Luke says these exorcists were sons of a Jewish high priest. When they were overcome by the evil spirit of a possessed man, many in Ephesus became Christians and confessed they had been occupied with the same practice of "curious arts." They brought their books of sorcery and burned them, disassociating themselves from all such things.

Occultism had gained admittance into certain Jewish groups and could also easily infiltrate the new and possibly naive Christian congregations. Magic was perceived as the ability to force evil beings to submit or flee by the use of superior means. Often that means was superior spiritual beings who had authority over the lower beings that roamed the earth and tormented or possessed men. This kind of necromancy was forbidden in Israel but was common in paganism. It was this heresy that seemed to be threatening the church in Colossae. Paul speaks of the "principalities and powers" and warns against the worship of angels (2:15,18).

Here is an important feature of the possible heresy in Colossae. As already noted, there was probably an admixture of Jewish legalism and Gentile philosophy as the basis for the Colossian heresy. But each of these had unique characteristics. The Judaism that appeared in Colossae was not the Pharisaic orthodoxy that Jesus confronted in the Gospels. Likewise, the Gentile "wisdom" preached in Colossae was not the same as the rational, intellectual, Greek wisdom which appeared in Corinth. In the Colossian heresy we discern an element of mysticism that later became a dominant characteristic of gnosticism in the Second Century.

Such a fusion of different religious and philosophical elements had already taken place in some forms of Judaism and Gentile systems of thought. The First Century was characterized by syncretism. This mixture of religions was a product of the new age brought about by the removal of the East-West barrier. Alexander the Great marched his armies to the East. Later on the Roman Empire united the Occident and the Orient. When the old Greek and Roman gods lost their appeal, the time was ripe for a fusion of the East's religions and the West's philosophy. Mystery religions of the Orient made their entry into the religious life and thinking of the West. Because Colossae was situated on a commercial route between East and West, it was susceptible to "new" and "different" patterns of thought.

Angel Worship and the Colossian Church

The new age had the distinctive stamp of an idolatry that had been "spiritualized." It was more insidious than the idolatry that worshiped graven images of stone or precious metals. This worship of spiritual powers replaced tangible idols with "principalities and powers" that were conjured in the mind. Many such "worshipers" shunned pictures and monuments of their gods. They sought to contact the "powers" directly.

This "worshipping of angels" threatened to penetrate and destroy the true worship of the church in Colossae (2:18). Paul wrote his polemic against this because it concerned a form of religion which was disguised by its spirituality. The old idolatry was clearly discerned by its use of tangible idols. The new idolatry was aimed toward spiritual beings and therefore appeared more legitimate.

Even the Jews, who turned away from image worship with disgust, could give the angels such an elevated position that it would be considered worship. Philo maintained that the angels participated in creation. Justin Martyr wrote of Jewish teachers who preached that man's outward form had been prepared by angels. These teachers maintained that when God said, "Let us make man," He spoke to angels (Genesis 1:26). Among the Nag Hammadi texts has been found a saying that some of the Jewish sects taught that God has created all which exists, while others said that "the multitude of the angels stood by him and they received from the powers the seven substances . . . in order to create" (*The Apocryphon of John*, 2:1:15).

It was a frightful and dangerous thought that man could see an angel as his creator. Such a view was no less dangerous when fitted into a Gentile philosophical train of thought in the First Century. It was an old Greek view that material substance was so unholy that God could have nothing to do with it. The false teachers in Colossae were saying the angels or "powers" created the material world, and man could only be delivered from his bodily imprisonment by these same powers (H.M. Carson, *Tyndale New Testament Commentaries*, 12:16).

One view held that these powers (angels) controlled the connection links between heaven and earth (Bruce, *New International Commentary on the New Testament, Colossians, Philemon, and Ephesians*, p.26). Angels became the mediators for man, bringing men divine revelation and carrying their prayers to God. There was even an extreme view that Christ himself had to submit to the authority of the prince of angels on His way from heaven to earth. By extension, this same view would put Christ under the authority of this "power" when He returned to heaven.

A strong objection must be registered against this artificial product of fantasy. It is a doctrine that reduces the person and work of Christ. Instead of being the one and unique Son, Christ becomes one of the many. He who is the Creator is placed on a level with the creature.

Many of those who had listened with interest to the heretics in Colossae had very little understanding of the consequences which the new doctrine produced. But Paul was aware of them. He understood that the primary thing in jeopardy was their salvation; someone was about to "beguile" them of the "reward" (2:18). This was a serious matter. So when Paul wrote his epistle, he did not explain any details of the preaching of the heretics. His readers had a good understanding of it, but Paul did oppose the heresy in several particulars. He did this polemically by rejecting the heresy. But first and more importantly he addressed the heresy by teaching the supremacy of Christ.

This heresy confronting the Colossians, both in its contents and its consequences, was one of the most dangerous heterodoxies that ever attacked the Church. Though the heresy was first found in a special form and unique to Colossae, it represented something much more than a local phenomenon. First, it was a mixture of the Gentile doctrine of wisdom that threatened to infiltrate many of the Gentile churches. Second, this delusion contained the germ of the later Gnostic heresy which in the Second Century caused such havoc in the Church.

The characteristic feature of so many delusions is that they offer believers something more than that which they already have in Christ. They imply that what Christ has done is not enough and needs something additional. That was the teaching of the Judaistic seducers in Galatia. The heretics in Colossae seem to have presented the same falsehood that what Christ gives is not enough. The fullness of life in God could not, in their opinion, be achieved through Jesus Christ only. It must be sought through works of the Law, asceticism, worshiping of angels, and a special, secret knowledge. The Colossian heresy represented an attempt to achieve a higher level of spirituality than other believers had attained. Implied was the need for a total change of attitude concerning Christianity.

This was exactly what early gnosticism taught. The idea was that one could "improve" on Christianity. This later developed into a bitter controversy. But even in its early form, gnosticism was no less dangerous, though perhaps more disguised. During the First Century gnosticism was more of a religious-philosophical attitude than a system of belief in a finished form. That is why it could easily adapt to Gentile or Jewish groups and find admittance to Christian churches. Thus the "wisdom" in Corinth showed a face different from that seen in Colossae. Yet Corinth was not without certain features of the early Gnostic heresy. One example was the Greek idea of indifference to the body, which led to sexual immorality. The Gnostics taught that since the body was evil, what was done with the body was inconsequential. In Colossae the false teachers went to the opposite extreme and demanded asceticism and ill-treatment of the body.

In these two extremes the Gnostics attempted to solve the problem of physical embodiment: either they ignored the body as insignificant and consigned to licentiousness, or they tried to suppress the body with rigid asceticism. The Christian churches troubled by this heresy were in a twin danger; the extremes of the heresy were very confusing. Paul warned the church against both extremes. First he attacked the tendencies of the Colossian church to succumb to adding works of the Law and the wisdom of men to salvation. Then he listed in the admonition section of the Colossian epistle a comprehensive "vice-catalog" and warned the believers against the sins which bring God's wrath on the children of disobedience. But he made it clear that the Colossian Christians no longer lived in such practices. So there is no real indication of moral sin or ethical problems in the church at Colossae.

But this infiltration of Gentile "wisdom" and Jewish "law-keeping" was a matter of great concern. In the Colossian church there was significant evidence of these problems, and Paul addressed these with apostolic earnestness.

"The Rudiments of the World"

It is obvious that Jewish teachers of the Law had gained access to the Colossian church. These legalists agitated for strict adherence to certain rules of the Mosaic law (2:16). They may have attempted to introduce the separation of clean and unclean animals (compare Leviticus 11). They sought to obligate others to keep the calendar of Jewish feasts (compare Leviticus 23) and the day of the new moon (see Numbers 10:10; 28:11). They taught that Gentile Christians should keep the Jewish Sabbath (compare Exodus 20:8-11; 31:14-16). Paul opposed all of this and showed that it was but a shadow of that which should come (compare Hebrews 8:5; 10:1). It belonged to the tradition of men (2:8), and Christ died to deliver believers from all this. Christians are no longer subject to "rudiments of the world" because they are "dead with Christ" (2:20). Paul asks, "Why, as though living in the world, are ye subject to ordinances, (touch not; taste not; handle not; which all are to perish with the using;) after the commandments and doctrines of men?" (2:20).

The Greek term behind "rudiments" is *stoicheion* which means "an element" or "first principle" and was used, for example, of the letters of the alphabet as basic elements of speech. As is usually the case, the meaning of *stoicheion* is controlled by its context. In Hebrews 5:12 *stoicheion* is used to mean the first principles or ABCs found in the Word of God.

Opinions differ as to what Paul meant when he used the expression "the rudiments of the world." The two most widely accepted positions which have surfaced in the discussion are: (1) that Paul used it in reference to the Law (Ga-

latians 4:3,9) or worldly philosophy (Colossians 2:8,20). Adam Clarke suggests that Paul, in Galatians 4:3, is adapting a Jewish phrase concerning the Jewish teachers' explanation of the Law (*Clarke's Commentary*, 6:403). When this is called the "tradition of men" (2:8), Clarke thinks it must be understood against the background of the Hebrew expression *haolam hazzeh* which is translated literally by the Greek expression *tou kosmon toutou* (ibid., 6:523). This is often used to signify the Jewish system of rites and ceremonies. In Hebrews 7:16-18 the Law is characterized as "the law of a carnal commandment" which has "weakness and unprofitableness." Paul also refers to the "weak and beggarly elements" in Galatians 4:9.

Furthermore, some interpreters who promote this first position believe *stoicheion* stands for the Gnostic or proto-Gnostic philosophers' teaching. This view is found among other writers in antiquity. Tertullian (A.D. 145–220) wrote that Paul warned the Colossians they must beware of the seducing philosophy or *stoicheion* of this world "not understanding thereby the mundane fabric of sky and earth but worldly learning, and 'the traditions of men,' subtle in their speech and their philosophy" (*Against Marcion*, 5:19). Those commentators who understand *stoicheion* to be the rudimentary teachings of the Law or heathen philosophy, which would enslave believers and nullify the freedom of the gospel would include: A.T. Robertson (p.117); J.B. Lightfoot (p.180); C.F.D. Moule (p.91); and W. Hendriksen (*New Testament Commentary, Colossians and Philemon*, pp.109f.).

(2) In more recent times a second position has arisen which views *stoicheion* in the Epistle to the Galatians and the Epistle to the Colossians to mean "spiritual powers" which, according to the astrological views of that time, ruled over the heavenly bodies and the elements of earth, fire, air, and water. Such a view makes a connection between these "spiritual powers" and the angels which were worshiped in the church at Colossae. However, it is impossible to know for certain how much of this was included in the Gentile philosophical teaching that was attacking the first-century Christian churches. It is true, however, that not one instance can be found of *stoicheion* being used to refer to demons or spiritual powers at this time. The silence of Clement of Alexandria and Tertullian on this point suggests they were unaware of this interpretation. Those scholars who

hold to this view include: F.W. Beare (p.101) and E.F. Scott (*Moffatt's New Testament Commentary, Colossians, Philemon, and Ephesians*, p.43). As F.F. Bruce states, regardless of the precise nature of this heretical teaching, for the Colossian Christians to accept it would be a sign of "spiritual retrogression" (*New International Commentary on the New Testament, Colossians, Philemon, and Ephesians*, p.99).

Although opinions differ as to the meaning of this special Greek term, all agree that the Colossian heresy involved worship of angels. This is one of the things Paul strongly argued against in this epistle. It is puzzling that he connected the worship of angels with humility. What relationship is found in the two? Perhaps it was because the false teachers said man was too insignificant and unworthy to appear before God directly. Any approach or appeal to God must be mediated through angels. This assumes the angels that were worshiped were good angels. But the practice was not more acceptable because of this.

Hendriksen calls on several witnesses to testify to the actual practice of angel worship in these times and territories. First, the church father Theodoret said in his commentary on Colossians 2:18: "The disease which Paul denounces, continued for a long time in Phrygia and Pisidia." Second, Irenaeus stated that the true church opposed this practice. In his work titled *Against Heresies*, Irenaeus assured his readers that one does not call on angels or use other evil tricks, but he directs his prayer to the Lord who has made all things. Third, in the year A.D. 363 the Synod in Laodicea, a neighboring city of Colossae, declared: "It is not right for Christians to abandon the church of God and go away to invoke angels." Fourth, according to W.M. Ramsey, the archangel Michael was worshiped widely in Asia Minor, and this went on for centuries. As late as A.D. 739 the victory over the Saracens was ascribed to the assistance of Michael. He was also given credit for miraculous healings (Hendriksen, *New Testament Commentary, Colossians and Philemon*, p.126).

In occult circles there were many different concepts concerning spiritual powers worthy of worship. They were sometimes considered benevolent assistants, some kind of "fellow-redeemers" who made the work of Christ perfect. Others considered these spiritual powers as mighty opposers who had to be placated so they

did not hinder men from reaching God. This was all done through "gnosis." Within "gnosis" is something far more than intellectual knowledge. It involves a secret insight that is won through mysterious and mystical experiences. In effect, this "gnosis" is the only way men can reach God and perfection. And it is aided by spiritual powers that guard admittance to God.

Paul wielded his full apostolic authority and spiritual power against this idea. His message was: There are no secret paths to God prepared for a select few. There is just one way, and it is open to all. The primary weapon Paul used against occult syncretism was the mighty preaching of Christ. Paul sets a convincing argument and positive teaching against the delusion that threatens the Colossian church.

Each age has its domineering form of occultism, whether it is the mystery religions of ancient time, the sorcery of the middle ages, or the pseudo-religious witchcraft of the present. Each age boasts its own intellectualism or science or philosophy. But during the changing epochs of time the Epistle to the Colossians has stood in sharp contrast with its unchangeable message focused on Christ, God's key to the secrets of the universe. Christ is the Creator and Sustainer of all things. He is Lord of and far above all powers in heaven and on earth. In Him are all the treasures of wisdom and knowledge.

THE CHRISTOLOGY OF THE EPISTLE TO THE COLOSSIANS

In its purest essence the Epistle to the Colossians is a Christological discussion of cosmic dimensions. Inspired by the Spirit, Paul discussed the relationship between Christ and God, Christ's connection with creation, and Christ's headship of the Church. It must be said here that the expression "the cosmic Christ," a designation used by some, must not be misunderstood. Paul is not presenting a "Christ of the Philosophers." As he does in all his other epistles, the apostle presents the crucified Christ as the focus of God's plan for the universe.

The Christology of the epistle refutes the syncretistic delusion that had infiltrated the church at Colossae. This shows once more that Christian doctrine is often formed in the struggle against heresy. It was not just on a theoretical or theological basis that Paul wrote about these great themes in this letter. What kindled the inspired presentation was a real need in a small and vulnerable church, in danger of being seduced by clever propagandists. The preaching of Christ as the mystery of God—the center of creation and redemption—was the apostle's reply to the present need of the church. The church itself was stretching to see Christ as supreme. That such a tremendous presentation of the person and work of Christ could be made in a few short chapters is a wonder of inspiration.

Christ's Deity

The Preexistent Christ

Paul named Christ as the mystery of God and began his Christology by discussing Christ's relationship with God. What he presented had not even entered the heart and thought of man. Paul received it by revelation from the Holy Spirit who searches and knows the deep things of God (1 Corinthians 2:6-10). The eternal, Triune God unveiled the secrets of His being to His creation. The mystery is not that there is something hidden in God. What is most amazing is that we have such a clear knowledge of this Triune God! This knowledge, though far from perfect because of our limited human understanding, is revealed to us in Holy Scripture.

Paul reveals inter-Trinitarian relationship when he writes of Christ's place in the Godhead. Christ is the Son of God and the beloved of God (1:13). He is "the image of the invisible God," the perfect and completely valid expression of what God is (Colossians 1:15; compare Hebrews 1:3). He is the firstborn of all creation (1:15); He has no genesis; yet He is before all things (1:17). This echoes God's proclamation of His name to Moses, "I AM" (Exodus 3:14; compare John 1:1).

The allusion to the wisdom in Proverbs 8 and 9 is unmistakable. Here and elsewhere in the Wisdom literature wisdom is personified. It is more than a divine qualification. It is a divine Person. The wisdom of God has existed as long as God has existed—for all eternity. The Hebrew term *qānāh* has many shades of meaning. It can mean to buy or win something for oneself. It can mean create or take possession of something through a symbolic action. But *qānāh* can also mean to own, to have something in one's possession. It is obvious this is how the term should be understood in Proverbs 8:22. The Lord neither created nor bought this wisdom. He possessed it from the beginning, from eternity.

The Incarnated Christ

The Son existed before He entered His human existence. All thought of Incarnation without preexistence is first without meaning and second without Biblical support. Incarnation did not mean that a new individual of mankind had arisen but that an eternal, divine Person had entered the sphere of human life. John 1:14 says, "The Word was made flesh." The Incarnation means God was revealed in flesh (see 1 Timothy 3:16).

Paul emphasized to the Colossians that God's fullness resides in Jesus Christ (1:19; 2:9). This is a mystery, and because of this Christ is called the "mystery of God" (2:2). Jesus Christ is all that God is. Secondly, Paul emphasized the true humanity of Jesus. Though the fullness of God dwells bodily in Him (2:9), reconciliation took place "in the body of his flesh" (1:22). The reference here is not to a body that seems to be or looks like a body; it is an actual physical body. The Incarnation involved the deity of Christ (the fullness of the Godhead) and the humanity of Christ (His entering the human race through natural birth). This is the true God (1 John 5:20), found in the body and nature of a man.

The Glorified Christ

The preexistent and incarnated Christ is now the glorified Christ (3:1-4). Paul emphasized three things: (1) Christ is risen from the dead (3:1). (2) Christ is "above," He "sitteth on the right hand of God" (3:1). (3) At His return Christ will be revealed in glory (3:4). Christ includes His people in all this. They are dead with Him (3:3), risen with Him (3:1), hid with Him (3:3), and will be revealed with Him when He returns (3:4).

Christ in Creation

Paul explained Christ's connection with creation by saying He is the firstborn of every creature (1:15). He is before everything in time and above all in authority. He created that which is visible as well as that which is invisible. This includes the principalities and powers which the heretics in Colossae wanted to place on an equal or even higher level than Christ. Paul used three phrases to describe the creation work of Christ.

By Him Were All Things Created (1:16)

When speaking of Christ's connection with creation in Romans 11:36, Paul said, "For of him, and through him, and to him, are all things." Here in 1:16 it is changed to "by him" which is stronger yet. It is the same expression Paul used in his sermon at Athens: "In him we live, and move, and have our being" (Acts 17:28). Christ is the One who creates and sustains the creation. In the beginning He spoke everything into existence. Now He upholds everything by the power of His word (compare Hebrews 1:3). As Creator and Sustainer, Christ is the fountain of our existence.

All Things Were Created by Him (1:16)

Christ is the mediator of creation. God said, "Let us make man." And Christ is the One who executed the command of God. John tells us: "All things were made by him; and without him was not any thing made that was made" (John 1:3). The word translated "by" in John 1:3 and Colossians 1:16 is *dia* and means "by, through, by means of." Creation was brought into existence through the action of Christ.

All Things Were Created for Him (1:16)

He who is the beginning is also the end. Christ did not create to give the creation to someone else. It will be His eternal possession. He will never abandon it. When His creation was lost because of sin, He came to earth to win it back. One day the sacrificed Lamb will be handed the deed to the redeemed creation (Revelation 5:1-10; compare Jeremiah 32:11). Creation exists because of Christ. It is His by the first act of creation and His by the final act of redemption.

Christ in Redemption

The third major point in this Christology of the Epistle to the Colossians is the place of Christ in redemption. This doctrine of soteriology is remarkably complete.

The Means of Redemption

Redemption was effected by "the blood of his cross" (1:20) and "in the body of his flesh" (1:22). Through this the demand of God's righteousness is satisfied and the handwriting of ordinances is blotted out because Christ nailed it to the cross (2:14). Because of this, we have redemption, the forgiveness of sins (Colossians 1:14; compare Ephesians 1:7). This redemption and forgiveness is received by faith and demonstrated in water baptism (2:12). Everyone who continues in the Faith will achieve the goal the gospel gives: to be presented "holy and unblamable and unreprovable in his sight" (1:22,23).

The Victory of Christ over the Enemy

The victory of Christ over spiritual powers stands as a triumphant contrast to that which the heretics in Colossae obviously taught. It seems these heretics maintained that Christ had to give up part of His authority to rulers or powers in the heavens on His way from heaven to earth (at the time of the Incarnation). Later on these same powers forced the suffering of Christ on the cross. This argument was used as a proof that certain spiritual powers stood above Christ in authority and power. But Paul says that the opposite is the case. It was not the evil powers that were triumphant when Christ suffered and died on the cross. It was Christ who conquered the powers and authorities and made a show of them openly in their defeat (2:15).

Christ in You

By the work of Christ the believer is delivered from the power of darkness and translated into the kingdom of the beloved Son of God (1:13). This means that Christ is now among and in believers (2:17). This life-changing experience has its origin in our union with Christ who is Saviour and Lord (2:19). As Paul moves into the admonition segment of the epistle, he has as its starting point that believers are dead and risen with Christ (3:1ff.).

Rather than giving a higher revelation of the truth or shedding light on the apostolic preaching, the heresy of the false teachers consisted of a worthless mixture of religious substitutes. It is but an apparent wisdom, something which may gain a reputation for wisdom, but which does not contain true values.

In Jesus Christ are hid all the treasures of wisdom and knowledge (2:3).

Overview—1 Thessalonians

The epistles of Paul can be separated into four groups: (1) *Eschatological*, epistles which deal with last things. (2) *Soteriological*, epistles which deal with the doctrine of salvation. (3) *Ecclesiastical*, epistles which deal with matters concerning the Church. (4) *Pastoral*, epistles which contain direction for the coworkers of Paul, the men who were shepherding local bodies of believers.

The two epistles to the Thessalonians belong to the first of these groups. The first epistle gives one of the most complete presentations of the return of Christ and the events connected with it which we have in the New Testament. The second epistle contains one of the principal prophecies concerning the man of sin, the Antichrist. Paul did not give this teaching in the form of an essay. As was his custom, he wove it together with encouragement and admonition.

It is possible to consider the epistles to the Thessalonians only from a strict, eschatological point of view. The exhortation sections were then directed to those who had misunderstood some of Paul's teaching concerning the Lord's return. In 1 Thessalonians the apostle replied to the questions which had arisen concerning believers who had died. Second Thessalonians deals primarily with questions concerning the return of the Lord and the Day of the Lord. It is no doubt correct to say that eschatological matters are the dominant theme of these two epistles, but there are other elements, especially in the First Epistle to the Thessalonians.

First Thessalonians is strongly related to 2 Corinthians where Paul defended his apostolic ministry. It seems that during this entire period of Paul's ministry he was persecuted continually by Jewish opponents who slandered him and used every opportunity to undermine his authority. They attacked not only his doctrine and preaching but his character and manner of living. This forced Paul to defend his ministry. This is evident both in 2 Corinthians and 1 Thessalonians as well as other places in his epistles.

The accusations against the apostle in Thessalonica seem, at least partly, to be the same as those he faced in Corinth. He was obviously accused of intending to take advantage of the church economically. His opponents tried to make the church he had founded suspicious of his motives. The future of the church depended on whether or not these personal attacks were rejected. Paul was the first Christian they had met. He represented the Christian faith (Moffatt, *Expositor's Greek Testament*, 4:6,7). If their trust in him personally was undermined, it would quite naturally have a destructive influence on their faith in the message he had brought them. Paul defended himself not for his own sake but for the good of the church. The first half of this epistle deals with his defense.

In addition to the personal and eschatological themes, Paul also dealt with ethical and ecclesiastical matters. When we consider these insertions, 1 Thessalonians falls into six different parts including the Opening and Closing. Thus the following outline:

I. OPENING (1:1-4)
II. HISTORICAL MATTERS (1:5–2:16)
III. PERSONAL MATTERS (2:17–3:13)
IV. ETHICAL MATTERS (4:1-12)
V. ESCHATOLOGICAL TEACHING (4:13–5:11)
VI. CLOSING (5:23-28)

Paul reminded the Thessalonians of his ministry among them. He rejected all the accusations of his opponents by reminding the Thessalonians of the good results from the preaching of the gospel among them. He called their attention to the holy and blameless lives he and his coworkers had lived among them. He called God himself as a witness to this (2:5,10), but he appealed also to the believers themselves (2:1,5,9,10,11). The Christians should not be affected by the accusations which had been brought against Paul and his fellow workers when they themselves had witnessed the clean and unselfish lives the missionaries lived. Paul reminded the church that those who now opposed the apostles had earlier killed the prophets and the Lord Jesus.

In 2:17 through 3:13 the apostle continued his defense by assuring the Thessalonians of his deep, personal affection for them. He wrote of his keen desire to visit them again and of the hindrance of Satan to the many attempts he had made to come to them (2:18). The Thessalonians were not to believe that indifference had caused Paul to delay his visit to them. On the contrary, he prayed night and day that God would make it possible for him to visit his friends again (3:10,11). In the meantime the apostle had sent Timothy to them and rejoiced because of the good news Timothy had brought back (3:2-7).

PAUL'S MINISTRY IN THESSALONICA

Paul first came to the city of Thessalonica with Silas during his first missionary journey (Acts 17:1f.). Thessalonica, which corresponds to the present-day Salonika, was a large and important seaport town. It was one of the most important cities in the Roman province of Macedonia. It was named after the half sister of Alexander the Great. When the Romans divided the conquered Macedonia into four republics, Thessalonica became the capital of one of these. When the province was once more united, Thessalonica became the capital and residence of the Roman governor.

The majority of the population was Greek, with an infusion of Romans and Orientals. There was a large Jewish colony in the city. As was his custom, Paul began his ministry in the synagogue where he spoke to the Jews on 3 Sabbath days. Paul lived and worked with a man named Jason, probably a Jew who had the same trade.

Paul's ministry in Thessalonica did not last long, but it had results. Some Jews and "of the devout Greeks a great multitude, and of the chief women not a few" were won for the gospel. This made the Jews jealous, and they stirred up a tumult. Jason's house was stormed with the intent of bringing Paul and Silas out to the people so they could be accused on some political matter. But Paul and Silas had slipped away, and in order not to cause further difficulty for the church, they traveled on.

During their stay in Thessalonica, which perhaps lasted 2 or 3 months, or perhaps up to half a year, Paul received gifts of money from the church in Philippi (Philippians 4:15,16).

From the account in Acts it appears that Paul and Silas first went to Beroea where they had a successful work. When the aggressive Jews from Thessalonica heard this, they went to Beroea and "stirred up the people" there (Acts 17:13). In order to avoid further trouble, the believers sent Paul and his traveling companions to Athens. Timothy and Silas remained in Beroea. After a short stay in Athens, Paul went on to Corinth where he ministered for quite some time.

Paul had sent Timothy back to Thessalonica, and it was through him that Paul later learned of developments in the church in that city. The church had shown remarkable progress. Word of their faith in God had spread. Paul wrote that they had become a model for all the believers in Macedonia and Achaia.

However, the church at Thessalonica was not without problems. It seems that some were not showing proper respect for their leaders (5:12f.). Some of the members had become idle (4:11f., 5:14). It is possible the reason for this was that they did not understand the eschatological preaching of the apostles. Their misunderstanding of these matters possibly caused them to feel there was no reason to be concerned unduly with earthly matters when the coming of the Lord was so close at hand.

One matter which caused uneasiness in the church was the thought of "those which are asleep," the dead in Christ. Paul answered their questions in 4:13f. It must be remembered that this was still early in the history of the Church. It is generally accepted that Paul's letters to the Thessalonians are the earliest of his epistles, with the possible exception of the Epistle to the Galatians. Paul was ministering in Corinth when Timothy brought him the report of the church in Thessalonica (Acts 18:5). This was during the time when Gallio was the deputy of Achaia (Acts 18:12f.). On the basis of Roman records this was the year A.D. 51. It was during this year that both epistles to the Thessalonians were written.

There have never been any serious objections to the genuineness of the First Epistle to the Thessalonians. It is accepted as a genuine writing of Paul. Internal as well as external evidences confirm this. With some justification it has been said that the epistle itself is its strongest testimony. The epistle fits exactly into the historical context where it is placed. The external evidences are also distinct. It is included in Marcion's as well as in Muratori's canon. It can be found in ancient Syrian as well as in Latin translations. Irenaeus mentioned it in his great work *Against Heresies.* Tertullian quoted it as written by the apostle. Clement of Alexandria as well as other leading men of the Early Church ascribed it to Paul.

ESCHATOLOGICAL TEACHING

The distinctive mark of 1 Thessalonians is Paul's teaching on eschatological matters (4:13 through 5:11). This teaching falls naturally into three parts: (1) Anticipation of Christ's return; (2) The Second Coming; (3) Times and seasons.

ANTICIPATION OF CHRIST'S RETURN

"And to wait for his Son from heaven, whom he raised from the dead, even Jesus, which delivered us from the wrath to come" (1:10). In a few compressed words this verse gives us a picture of the early return of Christ as viewed by the Early Church. The Thessalonians did not wait for an event but for a Person. This Person is identified in several ways: He is the Son of God. He is "the man Christ Jesus" (cf. 1 Timothy 2:5). He is the deliverer from the wrath to come. He is "Jesus of Nazareth, which was crucified" (Mark 16:6), now risen from the dead. He is the One who by His resurrection from the dead proved He is the mighty Son of God (Romans 1:4). He is "this same Jesus" (Acts 1:11) for whom the Thessalonians were waiting.

However, this event which represented hope and deliverance will also be a time of God's judgment upon sin. Therefore, the message concerning the return of Christ is a paradox. Christ's return will deliver believers from "the wrath to come," the wrath which His coming precedes. His return is therefore a consoling as well as a fear-inspiring event.

This judgment of wrath must by no means be understood as an impersonal process of nature, a product of cause and effect. On the contrary, the coming wrath is God's holy reaction against all unrighteousness and evil. It is not blind causation which brings judgment upon sin, but a God who sees everything. God has not given judgment upon sin to the dead laws of nature but to His only begotten Son. The wrath which will come upon sinners is the wrath of the Lamb (Revelation 6:16).

The Word gives examples of those who were saved from God's wrath in the past: Noah and his family in the ark; Lot from wicked Sodom; Israel from Egypt's bondage, having first been delivered from judgment by the blood placed upon the houses. In like manner the people of God will be delivered from God's judgment of wrath when Christ returns. That deliverance will come as a result of the grace that "is to be brought unto you at the revelation of Jesus Christ" (1 Peter 1:13).

God has called believers "unto his kingdom and glory" (2:12). The kingdom of God, which is now hidden in those who believe (Romans 14:17; 1 Corinthians 4:20; Colossians 1:13), will be manifested visibly (Matthew 25:31; Luke 1:32,33; Revelation 2:26,27; 20:4). Believers enter into the kingdom of God through many tribulations (Acts 14:22; 2 Thessalonians 1:4,5), but those who suffer with Christ will be glorified with Him (Romans 8:17; 1 Peter 4:13).

Paul wrote (2:19,20) that those whom he had won for Christ were his joy and honor. He considered the Thessalonian believers as his wreath of victory. To see them at Christ's coming would be reward indeed.

The hope of the return of Christ is the supreme motive for holy living (1 Thessalonians 3:13; cf. 1 John 3:3). However, Paul was not speaking here of sanctification as a process but of the complete and perfect holiness of believers at the return of Christ: "unblamable in holiness before God, even our Father, at the coming of our Lord Jesus Christ with all his saints." The Greek word which is used for *holiness* (*hagiōsunē*) here is used only one other time in the New Testament (Romans 1:4), and in the Septuagint it is used only concerning the holiness of God himself. This holiness was Paul's highest aim for his fellow believers. It is the holiness which God himself will produce in His own. Thus the return of Christ means not only that believers will be glorified, but that they will be perfectly sanctified.

THE COMING OF THE LORD

Although Paul had given the Thessalonian church a thorough introduction to the doctrine of latter things, evidently his oral teaching had not touched upon the questions the believers had concerning those who were dead in Christ. This matter had caused unrest in the church. These newly converted believers had a vivid expectation of the Lord's return. Their entire manner of life was adjusted to waiting for the Son of God from the heavens (1:10). Therefore, it took them totally by surprise when some of the members of the church died. These Christians were waiting not for death but for the return of Christ. Had the believers who died lost that which was the real aim and completion of their salvation? And, if they had not lost salvation itself, had they lost the opportunity to participate in the glorious climax of salvation history which His return represents?

Paul replied to this question, and he did so in a context which gives the most complete presentation of the return of Christ in the New Testament. His explanation is short and terse, but it presents a detailed picture of the different phases of the second coming of Christ. Paul spoke with apostolic authority. He had received many revelations from the Lord ever since the beginning of his ministry (cf. Acts 9:5,6; 22:17-21; 1 Corinthians 11:23; Galatians 1:12; 2:2). In 1 Corinthians 15:51-54 Paul spoke of a "mystery" revealed to him concerning the transformation of believers at the return of the Lord. It is reasonable to believe that in the same revelation the Lord had given him information concerning those who are "dead in Christ."

The "dead in Christ" (4:16) are referred to as "them which are asleep" (4:13). Sleep as a picture of death among the Jews, as well as the Gentiles, spoke especially of the inactivity and cessation of the mind. For the Christian the picture of death as sleep has a much deeper and stronger meaning. By His death and resurrection Christ has changed death for the believer. To die in Christ is to expire and awake. It must not be understood as any kind of soul sleep. It is the body that sleeps in the grave (cf. Daniel 12:2). The spirit, the conscious personality, is separated from the body by death (James 2:26) and goes to be with the Lord (2 Corinthians 5:8). Paul declared that whether believers wake or sleep, they are together with the Lord. That this means a fully conscious condition appears from Philippians 1:23 where Paul declared that to be with the Lord is "far better" than the life on earth.

Paul thus sets the church at Thessalonica at rest concerning their fear and sorrow for the dead in Christ. This does not mean Paul praised death. He still considered death an enemy, even though it has lost its sting for the Christian (1 Corinthians 15:26,55). The apostle wished to be "clothed upon with our house which is from heaven" (2 Corinthians 5:2). This transformation will occur at the coming of Christ. But if the coming of the Lord should be delayed, Paul said he would rather "be absent from the body, and to be present with the Lord," that is, by death to be moved from life on earth to heavenly life (2 Corinthians 5:8).

It was important for Paul to convince the Thessalonians that the believers who had died would not suffer any loss. First, they were already with the Lord. Second, they would by no means lose the triumphant glory of the Lord's return. When the believers who live at the return of Christ are transformed, the dead in Christ will rise incorruptible (1 Corinthians 15:22). They who are alive will not go ahead of those who sleep. The dead in Christ will rise first (4:15,16). In this connection, although Paul gave a survey of the events at the return of Christ, he did not mention any time interval because 1 Corinthians 15:52 tells us all will take place in a moment, in the twinkling of an eye. But even though from a human point of view it seems it will all take place simultaneously, it has its divine order of occurrence.

Before Paul explained the succession of the events, he referred to that which is the basis of the Christian hope for the future: ". . . if we believe that Jesus died and rose again" (4:14). Christian belief and hope have a historical anchorage. Christians do not build on philosophical speculations but on divine revelation. The resurrection of Christ is a model and guarantee of the resurrection of His people. He himself is the firstfruits of those who are asleep (1 Corinthians 15:20). In Him the resurrection of believers is a reality already. That which will take place with them has been demonstrated in Christ's resurrection (cf. Ephesians 1:19,20).

Paul began this section with the words, "I would not have you to be ignorant, brethren, concerning them which are asleep" (4:13). Paul used this expression many times when he wanted to draw attention to an important matter or to introduce a new theme (Romans 1:13; 11:25; 1 Corinthians 10:1; 12:1; 2 Corinthians 1:8). The negative form is positive in meaning: "But I would have you know" (1 Corinthians 11:3; Colossians 2:1). It does not imply an accusation, as for instance the words, "Do ye not know?" (1 Corinthians 6:2,3; 9:13) which refer to things they should have known.

Thus the apostle did not reproach the believers in Thessalonica for the unrest they were feeling because of the believers who had died. He exhorted them not to sorrow "as others which have no hope." Paul was not talking about natural, human sorrow because of the death of a believer. Jesus himself wept at the tomb of Lazarus and He understands human feelings. But when a believer goes to be with Christ, the church should not sorrow as those who have no hope. The apostle encouraged Christians to remember two things: First, the dead in Christ are now with Him; second, the dead in Christ will be together with Christ when He returns.

In a series of concise, short statements Paul drew a rough draft of the events which would take place at the parousia of Christ. This Greek word, the *parousia*, which also can mean "presence," is one of the principal words of the New Testament used in connection with Christ's return.

The first thing Paul mentioned is that Christ personally will return. He will not send a deputation of angels to take His people from the earth. The Lord himself will come down from the heavens. It will be an official, royal arrival.

It will be accompanied by a commanding shout, with the voice of the archangel and the trumpet of God. The people of the world will probably hear but not understand the shout and the sound in a similar manner as men heard the voice from heaven when God spoke to Jesus (John 12:28,29) or when the companions of Saul on the road to Damascus heard the heavenly voice (Acts 9:7; 22:9). But those who believe in Christ will understand immediately when they hear the Lord's shout and the sound of the trumpet.

The dead in Christ will arise and they, together with those who are alive in Christ, will receive their resurrection bodies, similar to the glorious body of Christ himself. Without any process of death those who "are alive and remain" will be clothed upon with their new house from heaven.

The two groups of believers, the dead and they who are alive, will be caught up in the clouds to meet the Lord in the air. The new bodies which believers will receive will make it possible for them to move about in space without difficulty, just as Jesus himself. But the air is only the meeting place, not a permanent residence. Opinions differ as to what happens next. Paul gives no details. He simply says, "And so shall we ever be with the Lord. Wherefore comfort one another with these words" (4:17,18).

THE TIMES AND THE SEASONS

In the preceding section Paul dealt with matters concerning the return of the Lord of which the Thessalonians were "ignorant" (4:13). But it seems the believers at Thessalonica, like the apostles (Acts 1:6,7), wanted further information concerning the "times and the seasons."

In this new section (5:1-11) Paul appealed to the knowledge which the Thessalonians had received from his oral teaching during his time of ministry among them. The apostle used two words for "times" and "seasons." Times (*kronon*) speaks of chronological order. Seasons (*kairon*), while synonymous, speaks of the quality of the times rather than the chronology (cf. 1 Peter 1:11). The expression "day of the Lord" has an Old Testament background. "Lord" as well as "day" is without the article, so the designation almost always must be considered as a proper name (Morris, *New International Commentary on the New Testament, 1&2 Thessalonians*, p.151 note 5). The Day of the Lord is the judgment day when God will punish sin. It is just as inevitable as the travail which comes upon a woman with child. Paul discussed the Day of the Lord further in his second epistle to the Thessalonians.

Next, Paul contrasted the attitudes of two different groups concerning "that day." Sudden and inevitable perdition will come to the children of darkness, but deliverance will come to the children of light. "For God hath not appointed us to wrath, but to obtain salvation through our Lord Jesus Christ" (5:9). The basis for this deliverance is that Christ "died for us, that, whether we wake or sleep, we should live together with him" (5:10). Here the apostle refers again to the preceding section where he has assured believers that the dead in Christ and those who are alive and remain will be caught away together. But judgment will come to the children of darkness who have lived in self-deceit. Their false security, when they say "Peace and safety," will only bring upon them "sudden destruction" (5:3).

The overview to 1 Thessalonians gives the background for both epistles. At the end of the Second Century 2 Thessalonians was commonly accepted as written by Paul. It was included in Marcion's canon and in the fragment of Muratoris.

Besides the general comparison of teaching and exhortation, a common pattern in Paul's epistles, 2 Thessalonians follows these chapter divisions:

I. OPENING (1:1,2)
II. TRIBULATION AND WARNING (1:3-12)
III. THE DAY OF THE LORD AND THE LAWLESS ONE (2:1-17)
IV. ADMONITIONS (3:1-15)
V. CLOSING (3:16-18)

THE DAY OF THE LORD AND THE LAWLESS ONE

The main part of the epistle (chapter 2) is an eschatological section concerning the man of sin. It is one of the most detailed prophecies in the Bible concerning Antichrist. No other prophetic passages totally cover the divine revelation Paul provided in this chapter. It is therefore of vital importance to the understanding of latter-time prophecies. Eschatological interpretation systems that do not take chapter 2 into account are suspect no matter how extensive or detailed they might be otherwise. Second Thessalonians chapter 2 stands as a test and corrective for any popular teaching concerning the return of Christ (Erdman, p.85).

Even though this chapter gives information concerning the events of which we would have no knowledge otherwise, it also raises certain questions. It must be admitted this is no doubt one of the most difficult passages in the entire New Testament. It may be one of the passages which Peter wrote was "hard to be understood" (2 Peter 3:15,16). This is partly because what Paul wrote was a supplement to the oral teaching he had given the Thessalonian church (2:5,6). It is possible that, like us, even the Thessalonians did not fully understand all the apostle wrote in this chapter.

Paul's second letter to the Thessalonians was in response to certain questions which had arisen concerning "the coming of our Lord Jesus Christ, and by our gathering together unto him" (2:1). Some think the questions were a result of a misunderstanding of what Paul had written in his first letter to them. But such an interpretation is contradicted by the apostle's own words. It appears from what Paul wrote (2:2,3) that false teachers had caused the Thessalonians to be "shaken in mind." It is obvious that those who were seeking to deceive the believers were accusing Paul of false doctrine, an accusation which the apostle rejected without hesitation (2:2).

Paul did not say definitely that a false epistle, supposedly to have come from him, was being circulated, but he did reckon with such a possibility. The troublemakers seem to have indicated that such a document existed. The first Christian churches had to take into account the possibility of false epistles and to learn how to differentiate between the false and the authentic (W.A. Stevens, *American Commentary on the New Testament*, 5:82).

What was the false doctrine and the misconception of the Thessalonians? The false assertion was that the Day of the Lord had already come. Paul did not deny that the Day of the Lord was at hand (Romans 13:12; Philippians 2:16); he did deny that it had come to pass already. Other New Testament passages maintain the same view (Hebrews 10:37; James 5:8; Revelation 1:1; 22:20). Could the Thessalonians really have thought the coming of Christ had taken place, that deceased believers were risen, and that they themselves had been left behind? If this had been the case, would not the apostle simply have rejected such a position by reminding the Thessalonians that he, as well as they and believers in other places, had not experienced the Rapture?

Instead of doing so, Paul wrote about two facts: The Day of the Lord would be preceded by "a falling away" and the revealing of Antichrist, "the son of perdition" (2:3). Many Bible scholars offer the explanation that the Day of the Lord with its mighty acts of judgment is something essentially different from the Parousia, the second coming of Christ. Even Bible interpreters who disagree with this explanation admit that the Day of the Lord represents a complex idea which includes many different events (Morris, *New International Commentary on the New Testament, 1&2 Thessalonians*, p.217). But can one separate the Day of the Lord from the Parousia since Paul's opening statement binds the two events together? In 1:7-10 the apostle declared that the Day of the Lord would be for salvation and judgment.

Some interpreters have indicated there should be a contrast between the eschatological section in 1 Thessalonians 5:1-5, which speaks of the immediate coming of Christ, and 2 Thessalonians 2:1f., which indicates that certain events must precede the Day of the Lord. In this connection some say that the same tension between that which nobody knows and that which we all ought to know can also be found in the eschatological sermons of Jesus (Matthew 24:32-36) (Bruce, *Word Biblical Commentary*, 45:116). Others say Paul is speaking of two different events in the two epistles: In 1 Thessalonians, the Parousia, the coming of the Lord for His church; in 2 Thessalonians, the *apokalupsei*, the revelation of Christ to the world (Walvoord, pp.108f.; Hiebert, p.65). Opposing theological views will interpret this section from their own eschatological general viewpoint, and each of them will find support and face the difficulties which are rather evenly distributed.

THE APOSTASY

Before the Day of the Lord the apostasy must take place. Jesus warned of this *hē apostasia* which will be characteristic of the latter days (Matthew 24:11,12,24; Luke 18:8). Paul foretold it and described it in detail (1 Timothy 4:1-3; 2 Timothy 3:1-5; cf. James 5:1-8; 2 Peter 2:1-22; 3:3-6; Jude 18). The apostasy made itself known in the days of the apostles. It has grown steadily worse during the intervening centuries, but it will reach its culmination in the latter days.

Paul defined this apostasy as a rejection of sound doctrine accompanied by ethical and moral decay. But this apostasy seems in fact to be combined with a false piety (2 Timothy 3:5). In classical Greek the word is used to indicate military or political revolt. In the Septuagint it is used in connection with revolt against God (Joshua 22:22). The apostasy of the latter days will not be limited to the Christian church, although Matthew 24:24 says that even some of the elect will be led astray. The apostasy of which Paul wrote will be a revolt against all divine law and authority and a general rejection of the truth of the gospel.

This last great revolt against God will have its origin in that part of the world that is called Christian. The nations that have had the light of the gospel for centuries will turn to the lie. This apostasy will be expressed in an active and aggressive hatred of all Christianity, and it will culminate in anti-Christian persecution (Matthew 24:9; Revelation 13:15). But this universal revolt against God will have its root within the nominal Christian church. It is when the salt loses its power and the light becomes darkness that cruelty is given unlimited power in the world (Matthew 5:13f.).

In passing it may be mentioned that some scholars have suggested that the word *apostasia* can be translated "snatching away." Liddell and Scott give a secondary meaning of the word as "departure, disappearance" (*LSJ*, "apostasia"). If this were the correct translation, it could mean the rapture of the Church. However, there is not strong support for this view.

THE MAN OF SIN

As a consequence of the apostasy, the man of sin will appear. Although Paul did not use the name *Antichrist*, there is no doubt that he was describing this last great opponent of God and the people of God. This section of the Scripture (2:1-12) is one of the three major prophecies concerning this puzzling person (cf. Daniel 7 and Revelation 13).

Paul wrote that the man of sin will be "revealed," which emphasizes the supernatural aspect of his coming (Morris, *New International Commentary on the New Testament, 1&2 Thessalonians*, p.221). The word is used three times (2:3,6,8). It stands as an antithesis to the revelation of Christ (1:7). It is not the existence, birth, or presence of Antichrist which marks the beginning of the anti-Christian period, but his revelation, the fact that he makes himself known and is revealed as he really is. His public appearance in the arena of history will unveil his identity. He will no doubt have lived many years on earth before his manifestation as Antichrist (Ryrie, p.105). He will be revealed "in his time" (2:6), that is, when the time for his appearance has come, and the world is ripe for receiving its despot.

The appearance of Antichrist is also called his coming (*parousia*, 2:9) and is once more an antithesis to the coming of Christ (*parousia*) mentioned in 2:8. Paul wrote that the coming of Antichrist "is after the working of Satan with all power and signs and lying wonders" (2:9). The term "lying wonders" does not mean tricks or deceptions. These wonders will be genuine miracles that will support the preaching of lies. They will be the means of making men believe the lies (2:11). These wonders of the lie will be characterized by three words which are used to describe the miracles of Jesus (Acts 2:22) and the miracles which confirmed the ministry of the apostles (Hebrews 2:4). The term *dunamei*, "power" (here in the singular), refers to the supernatural power which will produce the works. The word *semeiois*, "sign," does not mean empty, aimless demonstrations of power, but rather supernatural events which will signify authority and confirm a message. The word *terasin*, "wonders," refers to the surprise and attention which these works will create in the spectators.

The power of God was behind the miracles which Jesus and the apostles performed, and they were signs of Jesus' deity and the truth of His message. Conversely, the wonders of the lie caused by satanic powers will give a false authority to the message of the lie, forming an integral part of the system of seduction. This system, this "mystery of iniquity" (2:7), which in due time will bring "that Wicked" (2:8) into power, that is, the Antichrist, was active in the time of the apostles. There had been many antichrists already (1 John 2:18), but the great Antichrist could not arise yet because there was a Power which kept him back.

Paul gave a distinct picture of the character of Antichrist. First, he called him the "man of sin" (2:3). Some manuscripts have "the man of lawlessness." This is accepted by UBS, which admits it is an uncertain translation. *Textus Receptus* follows the majority of texts and uses "the man of sin." These words express the evil character of Antichrist. He will be the embodiment of sin itself. He will be the contrast of Jesus Christ who did not know sin (2 Corinthians 5:21), who did no sin (1 Peter 2:22), and had no sin (1 John 3:5).

Paul also called Antichrist "the son of perdition" (2:3). The expression is a Hebrew idiom. It refers to the nature as well as to the destiny of Antichrist (cf. Revelation 17:8). Jesus used the same term for Judas Iscariot (John 17:12). This has caused some to think that Judas will come from the abyss as Antichrist in the latter days, a thought which is totally foreign to the New Testament. The mere fact that Judas committed suicide (Matthew 27:5), while Antichrist will receive his deadly wound from a sword (Revelation 13:14), makes the idea impossible.

The third term Paul used of Antichrist is the "Wicked" one (2:8). He will be the embodiment of the secret of lawlessness that has been active down through the ages. The word *lawlessness* in this instance stands for something more than anarchy in a social or political sense. Anarchy will not be a distinguishing mark of Antichrist's rule. When Antichrist gathers humanity under his dominion, it will be, among other things, because he will offer an alternative to anarchy and terrorism. The lawless one will become the absolute emperor, exponent of a totally unlimited willfulness (Daniel 7:25). Antichrist is called the "Wicked" one because he will oppose the law of God and introduce his own godless, lawless system founded on principles which are diametrically opposed to the law and will of God.

Paul mentioned two other characteristics of Antichrist. He will be the opponent of God and the people of God. The Hebrew word for *Satan* means the opponent or the enemy. Thus we see that Antichrist is mentioned here by the same name as his master. Antichrist will also be the one who exalts himself (2 Thessalonians 2:4), while Christ is the One who subjected himself (Philippians 2:5f.).

Paul did not say much about the career of Antichrist. Immediately after the apostle wrote about the revelation of the "Wicked" one, he spoke of Antichrist's destruction at the coming of the Lord (2:8). In an earlier part of the chapter (2:4) Paul wrote that the man of sin will sit down in the temple of God "showing himself that he is God." This will be a demonstration of the innermost characteristic of anti-Christianity, that of deifying man.

Does the expression "the temple of God" refer to a literal temple of God in Jerusalem, or must it be understood figuratively to refer to the Church as the temple of God? There might be a strong case for both views. One view does not necessarily exclude the other. Many interpreters throughout the ages have understood the temple metaphorically. The reformers believed the expression referred to the power of the pope. Modern interpreters maintain that it means the Antichrist will seek to dethrone God in men's hearts.

Those who maintain a literal understanding point to the close relationship with the words of Jesus concerning the abomination of desolation that shall stand in the holy place (Matthew 24:15f.). Jesus' words were distinctly connected with things that will take place in the future in Jerusalem and Judea and were literally understood by those who heard Him. The connection between the sermon of Jesus and that which Paul wrote is further strengthened because of the fact that the words of Jesus in Mark 13:14 concerning the abomination of desolation are rendered in a grammatical form which shows they refer to a person who then could be none other than the Antichrist.

As long as the temple in Jerusalem remained, it was natural to understand Paul's words literally. Later on, it was usual for the Early Church to suppose a rebuilt Jewish temple and a literal fulfillment of that which Jesus and Paul said. This view was maintained by many Early Church fathers, among others by Irenaeus in his work *Against Heresies* (5:30:4). If the Jews do rebuild their temple it will reinforce such a view. Whether or not these words refer to a literal fulfillment, it is evident that Antichrist will proclaim his deity and demand public worship (cf. Revelation 13:8,12,15).

THE RESTRAINING POWER

In chapter 2 Paul gave an important account of the succession of eschatological events. Preceding the Day of the Lord, the apostasy must come and the "Wicked" one must be revealed (2:2,3). But before Antichrist can be revealed, that which "letteth" his revelation must be taken away (2:6,7). This power which withholds cruelty and prevents the revelation of Antichrist is spoken of as a person (2:6) as well as a thing (2:7) and can then be understood as a person and the effect of this person. The Thessalonians knew who and what this power was (2:5,6). This power must be something and someone stronger than Satan, because it prevents the devil from revealing the Antichrist. It must also be a power and a person who has been active during the entire Christian period and who continually restrains Antichrist.

The church in Thessalonica knew what Paul was referring to, but even the Early Church fathers had lost this knowledge. Among the interpreters of the Bible there have been a number of conjectures:

(1) The Roman Empire, embodied in the Emperor Nero. But that empire perished without any appearance of Antichrist.

(2) The authority at the time of Paul represented by the emperor. But although authorities can keep human cruelty in check to some extent, they cannot restrain Satan. Besides, the realm of Antichrist will not be without authority. On the contrary, it will be a totalitarian government. Those who accept this conjecture state that Paul used a veiled and mysterious language in order to hide the fact that he was speaking of the downfall of the empire.

(3) The Holy Spirit in the Church. The argument for this view is that God alone is stronger than Satan and can thus restrain him from revealing Antichrist. Those who maintain this view believe that when the Church is caught away and the Holy Spirit has completed His work in and through the Church the hindrance to the revelation of Antichrist will be removed.

As we have stated, the question is a puzzling and difficult matter. It is hard to understand how a matter which was distinctly understood by the early Christians has been a problem for all later generations. Perhaps God wanted to keep it secret.

TWO GROUPS OF MEN

The last part of chapter 2 concerns two groups of men of a quite different situation and destination. At first, Paul spoke of those to whom God will send strong delusions so they will believe the lie and receive His sentence of judgment (2:10-12). Next Paul addressed those whom God had chosen "from the beginning" to receive "salvation through sanctification of the Spirit and belief of the truth" (2:13-17). Only those who will not receive the love of the truth will believe the lie (cf. Romans 1:24-28).

God did not harden the heart of Pharaoh until he had hardened himself (Exodus 8:32; 9:12). In like manner, those who will not believe the truth but who delight in unrighteousness will be sentenced and lost. But those who believe in the truth and in the saving message of the gospel will win "the glory of our Lord Jesus Christ" (2:13f.).

Overview–1 Timothy

STRUCTURE

The letter is the first of the so-called Pastoral Epistles, which also include 2 Timothy and Titus (see commentary). Timothy, the recipient of the letter, was the younger friend and co-worker of Paul. He is mentioned in Acts and several of the other Pauline letters. One can presume that 1 Timothy was written sometime between A.D. 61 and 64, after Paul's first Roman imprisonment and prior to the Neronian persecutions.

Some have attempted to identify the structural outline of the letter; however, usually these constructions become somewhat artificial. Nonetheless, there are some interesting models. W.B. Wallis discerns a pattern of themes centering on task and poetic doxology: in the opening doxology (1:17), in the main body of the letter (3:16, the hymn), and in the closing doxology (6:15,16). J. Sidlow Baxter finds two main sections, chapters 2 and 3, which concern the Church and the local assembly, and chapters 4 through 6, which addresses pastors (pp.371-380). The structure of most other interpretations is either too rigid or too flexible.

The absence of agreement on structure may indicate that structure is limited in the letter; after all, it is a letter, not a treatise. The author's thought flows evenly and naturally from theme to theme, with pauses and interruptions much like those in a conversation. Obviously, little insight is gained by trying to force the letter's contents into some rigid or dogmatic framework. Actually, the chapter divisions in the epistle seem as useful as any other structural arrangement.

As with most of Paul's other letters, 1 Timothy has a theoretical teaching element and section which contains admonitions. There is one difference. Whereas normally the two elements are distinct, in 1 Timothy the material is subdivided into several subsections, which may contain both practical and theoretical parts.

The teaching section is of a polemic and dogmatic nature in which Paul discussed faith and the proclamation of the Church. It occurs in three smaller sections, chapters 1, 4, and 6. The practical admonition section, which addresses worship and conduct in the local church, appears in two subsections in chapters 2, 3, and 5.

If one accepts this kind of arrangement, the following structure reflects the contents of 1 Timothy:

I. TEACHING SECTION (1:1-20; 4:1-16; 6:1-21)

- A. The Law and the Gospel (1:1-20)
  1. Deceivers and False Teachers of the Law (1:3-11)
  2. Paul's Testimony and Gospel (1:12-17)
  3. Timothy's Task (1:18-20)
- B. False and True Doctrine (4:1-16)
  1. The Falling Away (4:1-3)
  2. Sound Teaching (4:4-11)
  3. Personal Admonition (4:12-16)
- C. False Teaching and the Profit Motive (6:1-21)

II. PRACTICAL ADMONITION (2:1-15; 3:1-16; 5:1-25)

- A. The Worship Service (2:1-15)
  1. Prayer and Intercession (2:1-7)
  2. The Conduct of Men (2:8)
  3. The Conduct of Women (2:9-15)
- B. Elders and Deacons (3:1-16)
  1. Elders (Overseers) (3:1-7)
  2. Deacons (3:8-13)
  3. The Church and Its Message (3:14-16)
- C. Support and Service (5:1-25)
  1. The Ministry of Admonition (5:1,2)
  2. The Support of Widows (5:3-16)
  3. The Treatment of Elders (5:17-25)

I. TEACHING SECTION (1:1-20; 4:1-16; 6:1-21)

Paul opened this section with a reminder that he was an apostle of Jesus Christ. Although Paul was writing to one of his close friends, a fellow laborer in the gospel, the letter is something more than mere personal correspondence. The letter would be received as Holy Scripture and read in the church. The letter thus authorized Timothy to perform the charge given to him to oversee the church in Ephesus. Wielding apostolic authority, Paul reminded Timothy of the charge given to him on a former occasion. His words are instructive for the Church throughout all generations.

A central theme in this letter is "sound doctrine." Apostolic teachings, as reflected by the New Testament writings, were already fairly well defined by this time. All preaching and teaching were tested against the standard of the apostolic testimony. Paul's understanding of "sound" should be seen in light of this. The sense is probably not too far removed from the expressions "sound, healthy, whole" in our language. The sound teaching of the gospel is "whole, true, and correct." It brings restoration and healing, two essential ingredients of salvation. The term "sound," *hugiainō*, occurs in the New Testament only in the Pastoral Epistles. "Sound doctrine" (1 Timothy 1:10; 2 Timothy 4:3; Titus 1:9; 2:1) is evidently synonymous with "the 'healthy' words" of the gospel (1 Timothy 6:3), which Timothy heard from Paul (2 Timothy 1:13). Such "sound, healthy" teaching results in a "sound, healthy" faith (Titus 1:13; 2:2) and encourages "sound speech that cannot be condemned" (Titus 2:8).

In contrast to the sound teaching of the gospel stand the "unhealthy" doctrines of the false teachers (cf. 1 Timothy 6:4; 2 Timothy 2:17). It is Timothy's task to resist these false teachers and their useless and harmful teachings. False teachers do not create true faith in God, but make people "reprobate concerning the faith" (2 Timothy 3:8).

It appears that Paul left Timothy in Ephesus with the responsibility to "charge some that they teach no other doctrine (than the gospel)" (1:3). Timothy was to do the work of an evangelist (2 Timothy 4:5); and from the esteem Paul had for this rather young man, it appears that he was one of the most effective workers on Paul's team of ministers. Paul and Timothy saw the gospel spreading at an almost unbelievable rate during this time. But, while the gospel had the potential to spread as never before, it also came under attack by heretical doctrines that threatened to force their way into the churches and destroy the progress that had been made. That Paul would devote a letter to this problem speaks of the kind of leader he was. It shows how seriously the apostles took the task of keeping the gospel pure and unadulterated.

From what Paul wrote to Timothy, we have only partial knowledge of the nature of the heresy Timothy was to combat. The heresy in Ephesus apparently had some of the syncretistic features (i.e., a "mixed" conglomeration of religio-cultural ideas) found in the Colossian heresy (see commentary on Colossians), but it was probably not identical to this. Actually, Paul may have been attacking several kinds of deceptive teachings in his letters to Timothy. In some cases the problems had not yet occurred, while in others they had only begun. Some forms of the aberration involved useless "word-battles" (see 2 Timothy 2:14ff.) over foolish and trivial questions (2 Timothy 2:23). Other distortions of the principal teachings of the Christian faith, such as the resurrection, also were taking place (2 Timothy 2:18; cf. 1 Timothy 1:20).

Paul warned against "false knowledge" (6:20). This perhaps suggests some teaching similar to gnosticism had infiltrated the church, as it had in Corinth and especially Colossae. Paul advised that in the last days, false teachers would preach seductive doctrines that would deceive many. Part of their message would include a false asceticism and the forbidding of marriage (4:1f.).

A. The Law and the Gospel (1:1-20)
1. Deceivers and False Teachers of the Law (1:3-11)

One major aspect of the heresy in Ephesus seems to have been Jewish in origin. Paul referred to those who desired "to be teachers of the law" (1:7). This suggests they were not qualified, legitimate teachers of Jewish law, but wanted to appear to be so as to gain the respect this knowledge would bring to them. Paul spoke with bitter irony of their ignorance and lack of perception. These so-called teachers did not even understand what they themselves were saying, not to mention their lack of understanding what they were talking about so confidently (1:7). They were focusing their attention on tales, endless genealogies, and myths, in much the same manner as ancient rabbis. Evidently they had created imaginative additions to the Old Testament genealogies, added fanciful stories about the characters, and then created wild, allegorical interpretations. Paul said their "genealogies" were "endless" (1:4) (Hiebert, p.30).

Paul's description of these deceivers as teaching "false doctrines" (NIV; Greek, *heterodidaskalein*) is very striking. It suggests they were teaching something "other" than the gospel. It probably included material outside of the scope of the divine revelation of the Word of God. Indeed, much of what they were engaged in was entirely speculation and was even outside the realm of common sense. Latent in its "stupidity," therefore, was a kind of impenetrable nature. Fighting against speculation with common sense and logic is often useless; the very premise of reason is foreign to those obligated to their own speculations. Both Greek and Hebrew thought agree: one argues in vain with stupidity (see Proverbs 27:22). Any cogent response to speculations such as these is only wasted; thus, the very system supporting them must be rejected. Some false teaching deserves no other acknowledgment than dismissal without discussion.

Paul addressed the problem of those who were presuming to integrate the Law and the gospel. Over against the false teachers' prideful ignorance, he places a statement elementary and common to Christian teaching: "But we know that the law is good, if a man use it lawfully" (1 Timothy 1:8; cf. Romans 7:12). But this is precisely what the false teachers fail to do. They did not know or understand the proper use of the Law, so they perverted it and used it in ways neither intended nor appropriate. Paul exposed their error in both negative and positive terms.

First, the Law is *not* for the sake of the righteous, who do not violate it, but for the lawbreakers who break the commands not to steal or to murder. Neither did Paul view the Law as a restriction or a threat to Christian freedom. The judgments and penalties of the Law are irrelevant to the righteous man because he keeps the Law. The false teachers, therefore, were totally unjustified in using the Law to put the righteous under the slavery and fear of the Law. A motive much higher than fear keeps the Christian from sinning. "The goal of this command is love" (1:5, NIV); the motive of love is the fulfillment of the Law (cf. Romans 13:8-10).

Second, Paul showed who the Law *is* for by giving a list of sins which he considered as among the worst the ungodly can commit. The Law stands against all this. Moreover, at this point the Law is in complete agreement with the "sound doctrine; according to the glorious gospel" (1:10,11). Whatever is condemned by the Law is condemned by the gospel too. Faith in the gospel does not abolish the Law; it confirms and fulfills it (cf. Romans 3:31).

2. Paul's Testimony and Gospel (1:12-17)

Unlike the heretics in Ephesus who wanted to be teachers (1:7), Paul had been entrusted with something greater than the Law—the "glorious gospel of the blessed God" (1:11). This was not something Paul deserved, or earned; on the contrary, he was himself formerly a "persecutor," "blasphemer," and a "violent man." He regarded himself as among the "worst" of sinners. However, he received God's grace, thereby becoming the very proof of the gospel that he was called to preach. Paul included both his being entrusted with the gospel and his experience of salvation in the powerful words, "This is a faithful saying, and worthy of all acceptation, that Christ Jesus came into the world to save sinners" (1:15). The words of Jesus (Matthew 9:13) are echoed in Paul's comments.

This is the first of the sayings in the Pastoral Epistles marked by the introductory words, "this is a faithful saying." On two occasions "and worthy of all acceptation" are added (1:15; 4:9). Its shorter form appears in 1 Timothy 3:1; 2 Timothy 2:11; and Titus 2:11.

3. Timothy's Task (1:18-20)

The gospel, which meant everything to Paul, must be preached to others. He must defend it and confirm it (Philippians 1:7), and he could not remain silent when it was under attack or in danger of perversion, for that would be treason. In this "good struggle" he also included his spiritual son, Timothy.

Paul, now an elderly servant of the Lord, began transferring the responsibility for the gospel to his younger coworker. This explains why he asked—or rather commanded—that Timothy remain in Ephesus. Timothy was essentially there to defend the gospel and the local church from the heretics who threatened to take it over.

Paul passed on to Timothy a commandment, an order (*parangelian*; 1:18). The term fits nicely with Paul's military imagery: the higher ranking officer was passing on a command to the younger soldier of the Cross. The command or the task to which Timothy was entrusted was first and foremost to guard the truth of the gospel against the false teachers (1:3). But this involved supervising the conduct of believers in the house of God (3:15). Doctrinal instruction and practical teaching thus are joined in the Pastoral Epistles as integral components of successful pastoral work.

Next, with a series of personal encouragements and admonitions aimed at Timothy, Paul wove the practical and theological together. In 1:19 the apostle mentioned the two qualities that are necessary and inseparable: faith and a good conscience. Christian faith can never be divorced from Christian life-style. Hymeneus and Alexander forgot this and consequently made a "shipwreck" of their faith (1:20). The secret of faith can only be kept by a clean conscience (3:9).

B. False and True Doctrine (4:1-16)

Whereas in chapters 2 and 3 Paul introduced

a large section on worship in the church and the practical concerns associated with it, he resumed his discussion of doctrinal issues in chapter 4. The concluding statement of chapter 3, with its mighty declaration that summarizes the Christian proclamation, "God was manifest in the flesh," is the bridge to the doctrinal section. Paul continued to forewarn that in the coming times the church of Christ and its followers would be rejected and persecuted. The Church represents the essence of the truth. For this reason, all the powers of delusion and falsehood will come against it.

1. The Falling Away (4:1-3)

Throughout the New Testament there is the warning that in the last days there will be a great falling away. Jesus himself spoke of this (Matthew 24:11,12; Luke 18:8), and the apostles Peter (2 Peter 2:1ff.) and John (1 John 2:18f.) described the coming apostasy in strong language. The apostle Paul often discussed the theme (see 2 Thessalonians 2:3f. and 2 Timothy 3:1f.). Paul appealed to a special revelation: "Now the Spirit speaketh expressly" (4:1-3). This is not some vague symbolic warning or sign. The Holy Spirit says expressly that apostasy will occur. It is essential that the Church be prepared to meet the challenge apostasy brings.

In the original language there is an interesting, subtle difference between the "coming" or "latter times" (1 Timothy 4:1) and the "last days" (2 Timothy 3:1). The first expression almost certainly includes the backsliding of the end times, but it is not restricted to the apostasy of the last days. The Church of the New Testament as an eschatological body actually lived in the circumstances of the last days (1 Corinthians 10:11). Throughout history, the church has had to combat apostasy, for its development seems to parallel the spread of the gospel.

Paul's comments in 1 Timothy 4:1f. strongly resemble those in 2 Thessalonians 2:3f. where apostasy takes on a concrete form. It is described as if the first recipients of the letter were familiar with it. It also seems to point to a larger, more extensive apostasy that is expressed in a variety of heresies and which climaxes at the coming of the Antichrist. It is obvious that this apostasy originated and had its source in the heretical teachings that confronted the Early Church. But the apostasy described in the New Testament also extends beyond the scope of those early heresies.

The kind of apostasy Paul envisioned in this epistle was characterized by a willing turning away of some from the revealed truths of the gospel. Paul recognized that full knowledge of the secrets of the Faith belongs to the future; the Church is only on the way to such knowledge (Ephesians 4:13). Even though he recognized the believer's understanding is only partial (1 Corinthians 13:9), he nevertheless maintained that he preached the whole counsel of God (Acts 20:27). Heralds of the gospel must hold this dual aspect of knowledge in tension. However, there is a substantial difference between possessing an incomplete knowledge of the divine plan and rejecting the fundamental truths of the Word of God. The latter is heresy, whether it adds to or subtracts from what is written (Revelation 22:18).

Paul suggested that the falling away from the Faith has a demonic as well as a human origin. The heresy he opposed is the "doctrines of devils" (4:1). But it is also "the tradition of men" (Colossians 2:8), championed and propagated by men. Paul described these false teachers as "hypocrites" whose consciences were "seared" or "cauterized" (4:2).

In describing the nature of the false teachings, Paul mentioned two things which were forbidden: (1) marriage, and (2) eating of certain foods (4:3). This is a remarkable as well as startling example of how seriously the apostle regarded false teaching. The false asceticism propagated by the false teachers was in no way viewed as some harmless by-product of religious zeal. Paul condemned the teachings as demonic and those endorsing them as false.

2, 3. Sound Teaching and Personal Admonition (4:4-16)

The opposite of the "other teachings" is the "good doctrine" (4:6). Timothy was to nourish himself and others with it. Paul joined warnings against succumbing to the false teachings with personal instructions to Timothy concerning his responsibility to preach the truth: "Take heed unto thyself, and unto the doctrine . . . for in doing this thou shalt both save thyself, and them that hear thee" (4:16).

C. False Teaching and the Profit Motive (6:1-21)

The final chapter of this letter contains a warning to slaves and to the rich who were members of the church. For the most part, however, it continues to reflect Paul's concern about false teaching. In chapter 5 Paul had already admonished his readers about practical matters in the life of the church.

A characteristic feature of this last section is that Paul attacked not only the false teaching per se, but also the false teachers. Paul did not draw a distinction between the person and the problem, nor did Jesus (cf. Matthew 23:1-33; cf. 2 Corinthians 11:13-15; Philippians 3:2). The teaching and the teacher were judged together. A tree is known by its fruit (Matthew 7:15-20). From his evil treasure an evil man brings forth evil things (cf. Matthew 12:33-35).

Paul was not interested in having dialogue with every kind of false teaching under the sun. To take them seriously would in effect be dignifying them with a response they did not deserve (Hiebert). But he did characterize the false teaching. He called it "fables" (1:4), "vain jangling" (1:6), "the doctrines of devils" (4:1), and "old wives fables" (4:7). He described the false teachers too. He exposed them as arrogant and ignorant (1:7), moral reprobates, having their consciences seared with a hot iron (4:2). They were conceited and foolish, with a sick craving for conflict (6:4). Their minds were corrupt.

At the climax of his condemnation, Paul used familiar language to indict his opponents: They were preachers of the gospel for the sake of making a living. They were shysters who enslaved others and devoured the churches (2 Corinthians 11:20). They nullified the Word of God for their own profit (2 Corinthians 2:17). They served not the Lord but their stomachs! (See Romans 16:18.) Their stomach was their god (Philippians 3:18,19). Paul had said this earlier, and Timothy had certainly heard it before, but the inspired apostle seemed to think it should be repeated: the false teachers thought that godliness was to be used as a means to financial gain (6:10). Unclean motives defile one's life and teaching. But Paul addressed Timothy: "But thou, O man of God, flee these things" (6:11).

He concluded the letter with a sincere personal appeal. First, he gave an admonition to keep the commandment pure (6:13-16). After adding a warning to the rich, he made another personal appeal to avoid all false teaching: "O Timothy, keep that which is committed to thy trust, avoiding profane and vain babblings, and oppositions of science falsely so called" (6:20,21).

II. PRACTICAL ADMONITION (2:1-15; 3:1-16; 5:1-25)

The section of practical admonition is composed of two sections, chapters 2 and 3 and chapter 5; however, the topic itself falls into three parts. The first gives guidelines for conducting the worship service (chapter 2). The second outlines requirements for elders and deacons (chapter 3). The third discusses how the church is to support some of its members and the responsibilities of those it serves (chapter 5). Woven throughout this material is a series of principles and personal admonitions to Timothy.

Actually, this practical section is why these letters came to be called the Pastoral Epistles. One of their characteristic features is that they contain guidelines for worship and leadership structure in the church. Jointly the Pastoral Epistles provide a practical resource for teachers. But it would be a total misunderstanding of the nature of the worship service as described in the New Testament to think that the letters are not relevant to the Church as a whole. It is fundamental to ministry that the Church is to insure that worship and proclamation take place properly and in accordance with the Scriptures (1 Peter 2:9). Leaders of the church are not to dominate over their "flock" (1 Peter 5:3). They are shepherds who lead the flock by their example.

A. The Worship Service (2:1-15)

The believer's life of devotion is expressed in two ways. The Christian can seek fellowship with God in quiet and solitude, but he or she can also worship God in fellowship with those who share the same faith. This joining together around the Word and prayer has always been a trademark of genuine Christianity.

The apostle Paul offered guidelines (chapter 2) for the worship gatherings, just as he had done elsewhere. For example, 1 Corinthians chapters 11 through 14 are devoted to the worship service. Rules are given for men and women on how to conduct themselves during gatherings for prayer, and instructions are given concerning proper behavior at the love feasts and Lord's Supper. Further, Paul outlined how the gifts of the Spirit are to be used in the church services. The section falls into three parts: an admonition to pray, a warning to men about their behavior, and a word to women about their conduct in the worship service.

1. Prayer and Intercession (2:1-7)

The apostle underscored the importance of prayer: "I exhort therefore, that, first of all. . . ." He appealed to their love and conscience. Four words are used to denote the nature of public prayer. *Prayers*: this is the normal word for a "request." It comes from a verb meaning "to lack something"; it thus denotes prayer on the basis of need. *Supplications*: this is a decidedly religious term that is only used in connection with prayer to God. It emphasizes the reverence that must be shown during prayer. *Intercessions*: the Greek term denotes prayer for others, especially prayer for a leader or superior. It connotes trust and expectation. *Thanks*: this is the proper response in prayer. One is to be thankful for what has already been received and grateful for the answer to prayer that is forthcoming.

The Church is to pray for all men, since God wants all men to be saved. The intercession of the Church especially on behalf of those in high positions in society affects the life and circumstances of the Church, and consequently its impact upon society.

2. The Conduct of Men (2:8)

At issue here is not liturgical prayers offered by ministers, but the prayers of the entire congregation. The one who leads the entire Body to the throne of God must himself be fit for this. There is to be no wrath, strife, or quarrels among believers. Such conditions are an impediment to prayer.

3. The Conduct of Women (2:9-15)

Women played an active role in prayer in the Early Church (1 Corinthians 11:5). When they participated in the worship service, they were to dress modestly. Related to their role in the church Paul said the women must not exert authority over or teach a man (2:12). As a basis of this prohibition he appealed to the arrangement of creation and to the sentence of God upon the woman because she was deceived at the Fall (1 Timothy 2:13,14; cf. Genesis 3:6). Nevertheless, it appears from 1 Corinthians 11:5 (cf. 1 Corinthians 14:3) that Paul acknowledged the right of women to prophesy and pray. From Titus 2:3,4 and Acts 18:26 (cf. Philippians 4:2,3), it seems that Paul was not excluding women from all kinds of teaching in the congregation.

B. Elders and Deacons (3:1-16)

After Paul gave some rules for the kind of behavior expected in the worship service, it is natural that he should then discuss spiritual leadership. In chapter 3 he particularly spoke of overseers (elders) and deacons. He concluded this section by a further reminder of the role of the Church and the greatness of its message.

1. Elders (Overseers) (3:1-7)

Paul wrote (Ephesians 4:11) that it is God who gives pastors and teachers to the Church. But God does not give these gifts to disinterested parties. Paul suggested that those aspiring to the "office" of overseer "desire a good work." The Greek term used here for "aspire" denotes "seeking," "reaching for." There is no sense that such "yearning" is improper; on the contrary, it is viewed as commendable, provided one is qualified. The ability to be an elder does not depend on the opinion of the one seeking the position, but whether other believers find his character in keeping with the demands of the position of overseer and teacher.

Related to this accountability, the Scriptures provide certain requirements which must be met if one is going to serve as a leader in the Church. Paul lists 15 qualifications demanded of the candidate. There are certain expectations as to moral blamelessness, an ability to control one's temper, and spiritual maturity.

2. Deacons (3:8-13)

The same qualifications apply to those wanting to serve as deacons. If they meet the requirements, they may serve (3:10). Paul did not outline their duties. Most likely the elders had a position of spiritual oversight, while the deacons took care of the practical affairs of the church. Hard and fast distinctions cannot be drawn between the two ministries. Some might not have regarded the practical aspect of ministry as valuable as the more "spiritual" role of oversight. This may explain why Paul mentioned that the good deacon can acquire a "respected position."

Verse 11 could suggest that Paul also envisioned women in the role of deaconess. Romans 16:1 indicates that women did serve as deacons—whether the "office" was present or not—in the early churches. Without question there was a need for the ministry of women; their qualifications correspond, for the most part, with the requirements upon deacons.

3. The Church and Its Message (3:14-16)

Besides what Paul said about the nature of worship and leadership roles, Paul added some personal words to Timothy about the greatness of the Church and its message. The Church is God's house; it undergirds the presence of the truth in this world.

The truth and the message proclaimed and supported by the Church are united in what many regard as an ancient Christian hymn. In six brief sentences Paul summarized the life story of Christ, from His incarnation to His ascension. It is a magnificent proclamation of "God manifest in the flesh" (3:16).

C. Support and Service (5:1-25)

Having discussed the question of false and genuine doctrine (chapter 4), Paul once again picked up the theme (from chapters 2 and 3) about the divine ministry of the Church and some unique ministries for which some are chosen. The apostle offered further instruction in practical local church life matters, using his personal instructions to Timothy as the means.

1. The Ministry of Admonition (5:1,2)

First the apostle advised regarding each member's role of spiritual leadership. He listed the various groups according to sex and age. The young man Timothy was to show respect and honor to the older person, even when as the leader he must admonish them (cf. Leviticus 19:32). He was not to speak harshly or disrespectfully. Timothy was to treat younger men as brothers. Thus he was not to patronize them or lord it over them as a superior, even though he is the leader of God's people in Ephesus. To older women he was to speak with gentleness and respect worthy of his own mother.

The final group Paul mentioned were the young women. They were to be treated as sisters. Here the apostle added: "with all purity." Paul was fully aware of the temptations associated with being a pastor. Care must be taken when restoring an erring brother and even more so a sister. That Paul should caution one of his most trusted coworkers (Philippians 2:19-22) and close personal friends about this brings out Paul's understanding of basic human nature. Paul realized that one falling prey to sexual temptation will find it difficult to be restored in the eyes of men (Proverbs 6:33). How many scandals could have been avoided had young men and elders alike applied the warn-

ing "in all purity" to every thought, word, look, and deed (cf. Matthew 5:28).

2. The Support of Widows (5:3-16)

The first Jerusalem church took care of widows (Acts 6:1f.). Later, all Christian churches were taught to show such care. When Paul wrote that widows were to be respected (5:3), the same idea is conveyed as when Jesus quoted the fourth commandment to the Pharisees (Matthew 15:3-6). To honor and respect one's father and mother includes—as far as Jesus is concerned—providing for their basic needs.

It should be noted here, however, that Paul asked the recipients of such support to return the favor by serving the body of believers. It was the church's responsibility to see to it that poor churches were not exploited by shysters and undeserving needy. Paul has no pity for the lazy: "If any would not work, neither should he eat!" (2 Thessalonians 3:10).

The widows to be enrolled to receive support from the church must be over 60 years old (5:9). During their lifetime they must have demonstrated their fear of God in a variety of ways. They must be genuine widows—truly alone, without family. If they had children or grandchildren, it was their responsibility to care for their parents. There is no excuse for trying to pass this responsibility on to the church.

Younger widows were not to be included in the group to receive support. Of course this did not prevent them from receiving temporary assistance if necessary, but they were not exempt from the responsibility of caring for themselves. Paul did not want them to learn idleness by wandering from house to house spreading foolish talk (5:13). The support provided by the church was not to encourage laziness. Paul advised the younger women to marry and run their own house (5:14). This resembles his advice in 1 Corinthians 7:9 where he stated that those who do not have the gift of remaining unmarried should get married.

The word used here is *pistin*, the word usually translated "faith" in the New Testament. Apparently, Paul was referring here to the sad possibility that some younger women, who had become widows, had strayed from a path of righteousness and had married nonbelievers.

Paul was certainly not saying they must remain in celibacy, i.e., could not marry again, for in the next verse he recommends that the younger women marry. Since the elders and deacons of the church and the apostles themselves were married, it could not be said that these women sinned if they remarried. Earlier in this epistle Paul had written that forbidding to marry was heretical (4:3).

Some of the older widows were perhaps deaconesses. Possibly if their health allowed, they were assigned certain duties and tasks in exchange for assistance. Early fathers of the Church allude to "widows of the church" who were chosen to take care of administering charity, caring for orphans, and so on.

3. The Treatment of Elders (5:17-25)

Paul used the term "honor" ("double honor") in describing what is due the elders of the church. Here *time* refers to financial support, as the context makes plain, which contains a saying of Jesus found in Luke's Gospel: "The laborer is worthy of his reward" (1 Timothy 5:18; cf. Luke 10:7). The Church is obligated to support its elders, especially those who "labor in the word and teaching." A church must support those who devote all their time to its service.

Paul concluded this section by giving some principles for dealing with an elder who has sinned (5:19,20). He warned against hastily installing someone in this spiritual position (5:22). Related to this, time must be allowed to prove or disprove the true nature of the man's character (5:24,25). All of this, however, must be done without partiality or prejudice (5:21).

Overview–2 Timothy

Imprisoned in Rome for the second time, the apostle Paul wrote a second epistle to Timothy, his friend and coworker. It is the most personal of all of Paul's letters. Despite its warm personal nature, the letter is also an apostolic "handing over" of the gospel into the care and supervision of Timothy, Paul's spiritual son and successor.

STRUCTURE

Some of Paul's letters reflect a highly organized structure. This is most clear in Paul's letter to the Romans, which has a very systematic arrangement. Other letters also have a distinct separation between theological teaching and more practical advice. In the Pastoral Epistles (1 and 2 Timothy and Titus) it is difficult to differentiate between the didactic and practical portions of the letters. Doctrine, advice, warnings, and instruction all course in and out of the work. The Pastoral Epistles are furthermore not treatises of some kind, but are genuine letters, characterized by the open sharing of feelings and thoughts.

Nevertheless, they reflect a common theme. Aspects of teaching and revelation are integrated with a logical and orderly presentation. In spite of any digressions or parenthetic statements, the chief lines of thought are clearly traceable.

Second Timothy falls into three sections. The first consists mainly of practical advice and encouragement to Timothy as he carried out his spiritual ministry. The second part addresses Timothy's problem with false teachers. The third contains Paul's words of farewell, the final testimony of that great apostle.

The following outline surveys the letter's general contents:

I. THE SOLDIER OF JESUS CHRIST (1:3–2:15)

Paul primarily wrote 2 Timothy to encourage his younger friend and coworker to labor fruitfully for the gospel. The epistle repeatedly encourages and challenges to action. This especially characterizes the first part of the letter, which is more personal and pertains to Timothy's ministry and role in the community.

A. The Completion of the Former Covenant (1:3-5)

It is most remarkable that when Paul encouraged Timothy in his work, he began by reminding him of his spiritual ancestry and heritage. Because of his pious Jewish mother, Timothy shared in the sincere faith of his mother and grandmother (verse 5; cf. Acts 16:1ff.). Paul's, as well as Timothy's, ancestors were among those who in faith awaited the fulfillment of the messianic promises and prophecies (Hebrews 11:13,39). Thus, Paul could claim that like his "forefathers" before him, he had served God with a clear conscience. He participated in a chain of servants offering holy service to God just as others had before him. This recalls what Jesus said His disciples would do. They would enter into the work of others and reap what others had sown (John 4:36-38). If those living in the time of promise served God faithfully, how much more should those who live in the time of fulfillment be faithful. Timothy was urged to prove himself worthy of the heritage of faith that had been in his family for generations.

B. The Fulfillment of the New Covenant (1:6–2:13)

The heritage of faith of the old covenant carried over into the new. Gentiles can be "grafted" (Romans 11:17) into the family of God (Ephesians 2:19). There is a transmission of revealed truth, sacred knowledge, and gifts of grace. Timothy had shared in this chain. Through the laying on of the apostle's hands, the "good deposit" (NIV) of the revealed word had been committed to him (1:13,14). It was his responsibility to hand over that truth to faithful men who would, in turn, instruct others (2:2).

What Timothy received from Paul was heard in the presence of many witnesses. Thus, it was not secret or esoteric knowledge intended for some special group. Christianity knows no special knowledge reserved for some elite few. Neither Jesus (John 18:20,21) nor His apostles passed on anything other than what they proclaimed in public. It was this "good deposit" (NIV) Timothy was to "guard" (1:14). He was not to bury it (cf. Matthew 25:18). The gospel is not to be hidden, inaccessible, or unusable. As an influential force in the world it must be continually passed on from generation to generation until the end of time. "This is true, apostolic succession" (Lenski).

Timothy was vital to the transmission and administration of the gospel at this point in time. Therefore, he was to "fan into flame" (NIV) his gift of grace (1:6). He was to be strong in the grace that is in Christ (2:1), and he must endure hardship as a good soldier of Jesus Christ (2:3).

II. THE APOSTASY (2:14–4:5)

The second section, which is perhaps the heart of the epistle's message, concerns the struggle against heresy, a problem that Paul continually dealt with in his letters. He had written earlier to Timothy warning him of the problem. Now he again broached the topic. First, he mentioned those deceivers who had already assaulted the Church (2:14-26). Second, he warned of future false teachings (3:13), and third, he noted that Scripture and the proclamation of the Word are the two weapons the Church has against such deception (3:14 to 4:5).

A. The False Teachings of the Present Age (2:14-26)

The Church has battled false teaching and heresy since its inception. If the "profane and vain babblings" are not resisted by the leadership of the church, they will "eat as doth a canker" and pollute the entire Body (2:16,17). Timothy was to have nothing to do with false teaching (2:16,23); he was to give it no place whatsoever.

The second section opens with a solemn charge to Timothy to warn those who are "quarreling about words" (NIV). Such arguments do not benefit anyone and, in fact, only lead to further ungodliness (2:14). The apostle

was not forbidding doctrinal discussions; neither was he ordering Timothy not to denounce false teaching. On the contrary, Paul was urging him to take action, to warn the false teachers to cease their useless "fighting over words" (*logomachein*). The prohibition is applied to those who encourage and propagate error. This is clear in light of 1 Timothy 6:3-5, which uses the same Greek word for "quarreling about words" (cf. verse 4). Timothy was to avoid disputes over fanciful Jewish legends, genealogical records, and philosophy. Such debate serves no purpose except to promote controversy and strife. A servant of the Lord is not to wage warfare in this manner (2:23,24). And even when he defends the truth, he is to remain gentle. With humility and gentleness, he is to instruct his opponents. Only in this way will he have a chance to convert his challengers to Christ (2:25,26).

Timothy was told to warn and instruct those flirting with false teaching, but only to a point. If he had warned them twice before and they still refused to listen, he was to sever any ties with them so as to keep himself from being defiled (2 Timothy 2:21; cf. Titus 3:10,11). He was not to continue arguing with such men or attempt to disprove their silly contrivances (2:23). His duty was to preach "the word of truth" (2:15).

B. The Apostasy of the End Times (3:1-13)

In spite of the fact that Paul lived during the greatest time of growth the Church has ever known, the Holy Spirit made him aware of the dangers of erroneous doctrines already present. He knew that the heretical inclinations he saw in his own day would only worsen. False teachings would always continue (2:16). The lure of the present age would evolve into the falling away of the last days (cf. 1 Timothy 4:1-3). Enemies of the truth would increase, while morality in general would decline at an alarming rate. The relationship between false doctrine and ethical/moral standards was repeatedly emphasized by Paul. Now he drew a frightening picture of some who would live in the last days. There are striking similarities between the vices listed in 2 Timothy 3:1-5 and the ones in Romans 1:21-32. The difference, however, is alarming and tragic: Whereas in the letter to the Romans Paul referred to the unenlightened ignorance of paganism, he referred here to the logical end of apostasy. This involves persons who sin knowingly against the light.

Even though Paul was confident that the particular false teachers against whom Timothy was struggling would not grow any stronger (3:9), he nevertheless realized that such false doctrines would flourish in the future (3:13). He warned Timothy of a time when people would not endure sound teaching, when they would turn away from what is true to what is false (4:3,4). If Timothy was to face opposition and persecution, he must realize that everyone wishing to live a godly life in Christ Jesus will be persecuted (3:12). Whatever form enemies of the gospel take, the true Church must always endure their opposition.

C. The Scripture and Proclamation (3:14—4:5)

Paul warned Timothy not to be carried away by all these false allurements. He was encouraged to stand fast in what he had been taught and in what he was convinced was true, because he knew from whom it had come: the pious and holy men and women whose moral uprightness far exceeded that of the false teachers. And most importantly, he was to remain faithful because of the "holy Scriptures," which he had learned from his childhood, which have the power to make one wise unto salvation through faith in Jesus Christ. All the Holy Scriptures (plural, verse 15), and the entire Scripture (singular, verse 16), was given by the inspiration of God and are "profitable" in the Church.

Timothy was to hold fast to the truth of Scripture for his own sake. But it was also to be his message: "Preach the word," commanded Paul (4:2). While people are still willing to listen, the truth must be proclaimed, because the time is coming when they will turn their ears away (verses 3,4). Timothy labored under the constraint of time, as the Church has throughout the centuries. The very stubbornness of people to receive the Word will bring the day of grace to its close. The night will come when no one can work (John 9:4). Then the Lord will call His servants home from the harvest fields.

III. PAUL'S FAREWELL WORDS (4:6-18)

Up to this point the letter has focused on Timothy. The first section encouraged him to be a good soldier of Jesus Christ. The second centered around the struggle Timothy had with the false teachers. But in this third section Paul moved to his own situation. His farewell words gave the letter as a whole a heightened sense of dignity, and they possess the kind of distinctive forcefulness the final words of a remarkable and noble person always have. The farewell words thus became Paul's "last will and testament," not only for Timothy but for the Church throughout the ages. For the final time the apostle to the Gentiles speaks to us.

A. A Completed Course (4:6-8)

These verses contain one of the most poignant testimonies ever given in the face of death and the grave. Paul realized that his "departure" was drawing near. The Greek term for "departure" originally meant "a release." It was used of "loosening" tent cords when a military troop prepared to move on, or it referred to "hoisting" (i.e., "freeing") the anchor of a ship to get under way.

1. Retrospect (4:7)

Facing death, Paul reviewed his service. The unbelief and sin of his past were forgotten, hidden in the immeasurable grace and forgiveness of God. He summarized his pilgrimage as a Christian in three concise statements.

a. "I have fought a good fight." Paul's entire life and apostolic ministry were a struggle against the devil and the forces of evil, against blatant enemies and treacherous brethren. But he regarded it as the "good fight," the supreme and most noble struggle a person can undertake. He struggled for the sake of the gospel and for the salvation of men and women everywhere.

b. "I have finished the course." Throughout his ministry, in an effort to attain "perfection" and to secure the prize of victory, Paul had pressed toward the goal (Philippians 3:12-14). Now he was about to cross the finish line. He did not slow his pace as he neared the end; neither did he waver at the prospects of entering the judgment hall and the site of sentencing. He was not deterred from finishing the race by any of these (Acts 20:24). From his perspective the race was finished!

c. "I have kept the faith." Paul had maintained his personal faith and could joyfully affirm, "I know whom I have believed" (1:12). "Faith" here denotes more than personal faith, however. "Faith" is the essence of the truth of the gospel, the valuable "deposit" which had been entrusted to him and which he had passed on to Timothy in its purest form. This is the same faith once entrusted to the saints (Jude 3).

2. A Glimpse of the Goal (4:8)

The Lord, the just Judge, would give the crown of righteousness to His servant. Paul had stood before many judges, and he knew that an unjust judge would now pass the sentence of death on his physical life. But this was not the final word. Paul knew the judgment seat of Christ awaited him; he did not fear the judgment of men (1 Corinthians 4:3-5; 2 Corinthians 5:10). The judgment of Christ held no fear for Paul, for throughout his earthly pilgrimage he had kept the Faith. He was assured of reward; there would be no injustice in the Lord's judgment. But Paul knew others would share in the reward: "Not to me only," he wrote, "but unto all them also that love his appearing."

B. Paul's Loneliness (4:9-13)

Despite the triumph of faith and the confidence of hope expressed by Paul, he was nonetheless tired and lonely. Just as he had spoken openly about his faith and confidence, so now he spoke frankly about his loneliness and hardship. He reflected no "otherworldly" attitude where his circumstances were concerned; unlike the fanatic, his feet were firmly planted on the ground. Thus, he was deeply grieved that so many had deserted him in his time of need. So many stalwarts of the Faith have shared in similar circumstances.

Paul had sent some of his coworkers on new missions. Others left for their own reasons. Perhaps most troubling was that Demas deserted him for the sake of the world which he loved. Luke alone remained. Now, one final time before he died, Paul wanted to see his spiritual son in the Faith. "Timothy, come soon," he pleaded. "Come before winter." Mark, once rejected by Paul as a coworker, was now welcome, having regained Paul's confidence (Colossians 4:10). Paul needed his scrolls and a cloak which he had left at Troas, the scrolls perhaps for his trial and his cloak for winter. This request places a stamp of authenticity on the letter. What pseudepigrapher would have thought of mentioning something so ordinary in a letter he hoped to pass off as sacred?

C. The First Defense (4:14-18)

Paul had already faced trial when he wrote this last letter. He was at this point neither condemned nor acquitted. The trial had been postponed indefinitely, but there was every reason to believe it would continue. Paul did not doubt the outcome.

The New Testament's records of Paul (Acts 28) close with him being under house arrest at Rome, waiting for his case to be heard by the emperor, which was his right as a Roman citizen. After this there is no completely reliable information as to what happened. Many answers are offered, each having some degree of possibility, some more than others. There seem to be four basic possibilities: (1) Paul was condemned and executed after being imprisoned in Rome for 2 years. This is perhaps the first impression one receives from comparing Acts with the Pauline letters. Against this argument is that such a scenario does not allow for any other visits to Asia Minor or Crete as the Pastoral Epistles imply took place. However, a question should be raised here: Can the brief records of the journeys of Paul recorded in Acts positively exclude an earlier dating of the Pastorals? The letters to the Corinthians contain evidence of travels not mentioned in Acts; why shouldn't the Pastoral Epistles reflect a similar condition? This possibility is not as easily dismissed as some would contend.

Related to this, the farewell address of the apostle to the elders in Ephesus (Acts 20:16-38) should be mentioned. Paul stated here, not as idle conjecture but with the confidence of a divine revelation, that he would not see them again (Acts 20:25; cf. Acts 20:38). He also described what would take place after his death (Acts 20:29), and his words implied again that this was more than idle speculation; it was revealed prophetic knowledge. Paul showed no intention of returning to Ephesus or of taking up any work in the eastern part of the Roman Empire (cf. Romans 15:23). He planned to go to Jerusalem (Acts 20:22), then to Rome and Spain (Romans 15:25,28).

(2) The second possibility of Paul's situation in Rome is that after 2 years of relatively relaxed custody (house arrest), he was transferred to harsher conditions. After a time he was then sentenced to be executed (P.N. Harrison). From 2 Timothy 1:16-18 it appears that Paul no longer enjoyed the privilege of house arrest that Acts 28:16 reflects.

(3) A third possibility is that Paul was exiled from Rome. This view finds support in 1 Clement which mentions that Paul endured exile among other hardships (1 Clement 5:6). This theory opens some attractive prospects. Just as

Paul's desire to visit Rome was fulfilled when he was sent there as a prisoner, it is possible that his plans to visit the south of Spain were realized when he was sent there in exile (J.J. Gunther). Such an outcome of his trial is not impossible. Apollonius of Tyana, for example, was exiled to Spain. The emperor's court may have found it expedient to forbid Paul from returning to his former labors in Jerusalem, where his presence often resulted in disturbances. Thus, they sent him to Spain where he would not be such a threat to "law and order."

(4) The most common view held is that Paul was released from his first imprisonment in Rome, perhaps after a sentence of acquittal or perhaps because his Jewish accusers did not appear within the length of time prescribed by Roman law. Paul may have then voluntarily fulfilled his desire to preach the gospel in Spain. This follows Ancient Church tradition, which claims that after his acquittal Paul visited other regions of the empire.

Numerous Scriptures can be appealed to as supporting this view. For example, Philippians, which was written while Paul was imprisoned in Rome, indicates that he was expecting to be released soon and to go to Philippi (Philippians 2:24). To Philemon he wrote: "But withal prepare me also a lodging: for I trust that through your prayers I shall be given unto you" (Philemon 22). Other facts imply that Paul traveled later to Rome, shortly before writing 2 Timothy. For example, in 4:20, Paul wrote, "Erastus abode at Corinth." This cannot refer to Paul's having left Erastus while he traveled to Jerusalem, for on that journey Timothy accompanied him and would have already known this (cf. Acts 20:4,5). The same reasoning applies to the comment, "Trophimus have I left at Miletus sick." When Paul was sent as a prisoner to Rome, the ship did not stop at either Corinth or Miletus. If Paul did not make a later trip to Rome, he was telling Timothy something he already knew, which happened before his journey to Jerusalem. Another factor favoring a later imprisonment is that among others, Mark and Timothy were with Paul in Rome when he wrote Colossians (Colossians 1:1; 4:10). Now in 4:11, Paul asked Timothy to come to him and bring Mark along. Jointly these references are strong evidence that Paul was released from his first imprisonment and was in a second imprisonment in Rome when he wrote 2 Timothy.

Whether Paul was exiled or whether he was released after his first imprisonment, it is clear that later he was put in prison again. When he wrote the final letter to Timothy he was under strict confinement and knew the outcome of his case would be death. The "first defense" had occurred, but we are not told who his accusers were. Silence up to this point concerning their identity may be telling. If Jews from Jerusalem had traveled to Rome to testify against Paul, their presence would almost certainly have been noted; but it was not. However, in the immediate context, one "Alexander the coppersmith" is mentioned, which perhaps indicates that he was Paul's accuser and principal opponent. If this is true, it is very easy to see why Paul cautioned Timothy against him.

The charge against Paul appears to have been related to his activity in Asia Minor. He might have been trying to summon witnesses from that region to Rome in order to testify on his behalf. His coworkers could not be witnesses; they would only be considered accomplices. But, testimonies from respected individuals from the churches of Asia Minor might have some effect. But fearing consequences, none of those he called upon came to his defense. They might also have felt Paul's case was so prominent that their testimony would be useless. Paul states: "At my first answer no man stood with me, but all men forsook me" (4:16).

The statement in 1:15 that "all they which are in Asia be turned away from me" may be an allusion that at least some lacked sympathy for Paul's case. Some may have viewed his aggressive evangelistic activity as causing unnecessary hostility from opponents. Some may have leveled unjust charges against him, which further undermined his confidence in others. Paul was pained when his friends deserted him, but he forgave them just the same! "I pray God that it may not be laid to their charge" (4:16). He was naturally fully aware of the personal risk they would have had to take to be a witness for his defense.

From Paul's perspective, however, much more was at stake than his personal defense. He viewed his testimony at the trial as *kerygma*, i.e., preaching, proclamation of the gospel (4:17). This testimony thus completed Paul's "course" in this life as far as he was concerned. Death was now welcomed as a benefit and relief (Acts 20:24; Philippians 2:21-24). "The Lord shall deliver me from every evil work, and will preserve me into his heavenly kingdom" (4:18) was his final summation. He ended the letter with salutations similar to those in the other Pastoral Epistles.

The city of Rome contains many reminders of the life and ministry of the apostle Paul. In some ways he left his stamp upon the city at least as much as Peter did.

Near the site of the Roman Forum is a church which covers the traditional location of the Mamertine Prison where Paul was imprisoned before his death. It contains a plaque and a door which pay tribute to the great apostle.

The plaque asserts that both Paul and Peter were incarcerated here and makes an interesting claim. It names 2 guards of the prison, and 47 others who were won to Jesus Christ through the witness of these 2 men. Whether apocryphal or not, we can be sure that these early leaders of the Church improved every opportunity to win men to the cause of the Son of God, whom they loved supremely.

On the other side of the small prison cell is a huge iron door. It is claimed that behind it is a tunnel which terminates at the River Tiber. When prisoners died of natural causes or execution, their bodies were dragged through the tunnel and dumped in the river. If this was indeed the place of Paul's imprisonment, his comment in this epistle carries unusual significance: "God hath not given us the spirit of fear; but of power, and of love, and of a sound mind" (1:7).

The Ostian Gate is the traditional site of Paul's execution. Nearby is one of Rome's seven basilicas, St. Paul Outside the Walls. At the entrance to the church stands a statue of the apostle. Like most of the other statues of him in the city, if not all, he is shown with an upraised sword in one hand, and a scroll under the other arm. Undoubtedly the sculptor meant this to signify Paul's position as the human author of much of the New Testament and to honor him as a champion of the gospel.

Paul has been described as a "Christ-drunk agitator" who, wherever he went, had either a riot or a revival—and sometimes both. It appears accurate to say that aside from Jesus Christ he did more to shape the course of Christianity than any other man.

The Epistle to Titus, together with 1 and 2 Timothy, form the group of letters known since the middle of the 18th Century as the Pastoral Epistles. The name points to the idea that these letters provided detailed guidance for structuring and organizing church leadership. The letters are very closely related both in terms of historical circumstance and literary style.

AUTHORSHIP

Like the other two Pastoral Epistles, the letter to Titus claims quite explicitly to have been written by Paul the apostle. This appears expressly in the author's opening salutation (1:1) and finds further support in the personal elements within the letter. No one in the Early Church ever questioned Pauline authorship. It rightfully claims apostolic authority and validity for the entire Church.

The external witnesses to the Pauline authorship of Titus are quite strong. Many writers during the early Christian Era directly or indirectly confirmed its authenticity; for example, 1 Clement (ca. A.D. 96), Justin Martyr (ca. A.D. 155–161), Theophilus from Antioch (ca. A.D. 150–180), and Irenaeus (ca. A.D. 180). In addition, the Muratorian Canon (ca. A.D. 200) confirms the genuineness of the letter and its authority in the Church. That the heretic Marcion did not include any of the three Pastoral Epistles in his collection should not be afforded too much weight. His theology stands in direct opposition to many of the main points of these letters. He, therefore, had reason to reject the Pastorals (he also rejected three of the Gospels).

Serious objections against the letters' claim of authenticity only appeared in modern times. Since the middle of the 19th Century increasingly numerous interpreters reject Pauline authorship. It should be noted here there is agreement the letters stem from the same source. Thus it is impossible to say one epistle is genuine and another not, or vice versa.

The arguments most often used to question the authenticity of the Pastoral Epistles include:

Personal Data

The letters contain certain personal data (e.g., travels, companions, circumstances) about Paul which do not fit with what is known about Paul from other sources, especially Acts. With respect to Titus, one especially thinks of the missionary efforts on Crete, which the letter presumes Paul and Titus undertook jointly (1:5).

To maintain the authenticity of the letter, therefore, it must be assumed that Paul was released from his incarceration in Rome mentioned in Acts 28. But this is not held to be very likely.

The counterargument: It must be admitted that Paul's personal circumstances described in the Pastorals demand that Paul be free from prison and on some type of journey. Evidence strongly suggests that this is precisely the case. Paul expected the trial of Acts 28 to end in his justification (Philippians 2:24, Philemon 22). Further, it is clear that neither Festus nor Herod Agrippa found any fault in Paul. In their eyes he should have been released. The account of Paul's imprisonment does not leave the reader feeling uncertain about Paul's fate; rather, it gives the impression that there was no real danger at the time. If Paul's trial had resulted in his death, we could expect a report to that effect. In addition, according to the most logical understanding of 1 Clement, Paul did indeed travel to Spain as he had planned (Romans 15:28). Later historical sources testify to this as well.

Stylistic Reasons

A rather extensive analysis of the language and style of the Pastoral Epistles has been done which uncovers some noteworthy facts: An unusually high number of words not otherwise appearing in the New Testament occur in the Pastorals. Similarly, a significantly high percentage of words occur in the Pastorals which do not appear in the other Pauline writings. Moreover, some of the more characteristic features of Paul are absent in the Pastorals, and there is a remarkable similarity between the writings of the second-century "apostolic fathers" and that of the Pastoral Epistles.

Counterarguments assert that the linguistic analysis of the letters is less than reliable for settling the authorship question. Many factors could explain satisfactorily the linguistic and stylistic differences. Paul certainly was capable of adjusting or altering his style and vocabulary, and the occurrence of atypical Pauline themes could explain the presence of new vocabulary and the absence of old. The similarity between themes in the Pastorals could explain the similarity in language between the apostolic fathers of the early Second Century and the Pastorals. A significant number of the terms otherwise not found in the New Testament do occur in the Septuagint, which Paul used and with which he was certainly familiar. Furthermore, it is noteworthy that many of the linguistic arguments used to reject the Pastorals as authentic could also "prove" inauthentic those Pauline epistles whose authorship is not disputed! If authenticity depended on a percentage of "non-Pauline" words, then Romans could be rejected as Pauline. Also, within the remaining 10 Pauline letters there is an extraordinary number of fundamental Pauline words which are absent in part or in whole.

Official View and Organization

Another argument against the authenticity of the Pastorals is the alleged presence of the so-called monarchial episcopate, i.e., church government by a single bishop. If this were true, it would suggest a kind of church structure that belongs to a later period. In addition, it is curious that Paul, who is otherwise so flexible on such matters, should be discussing church polity at all.

Counterarguments to this position concede that the monarchial episcopate does appear for the first time in the Second Century. Such a rigid structure first occurs in the writings of Ignatius. But such a later church structure does not necessarily occur in the Pastoral Epistles. Titus 1:5-9 shows clearly there is no precise distinction between an elder (*presbuteros*) (1:5), and a bishop (*episkopos*) (1:7). The terms are freely applied to the same persons. Earlier letters by Paul reflect a similar kind of church structure to that found in the Pastorals. For example, Philippians 1:1 mentions bishops (*episkopois*) as well as deacons (*diakonois*) and suggests Paul's interest in such matters (cf. 1 Corinthians 12 and Acts 14:23). That Christianity should develop in the direction of a leading elder or overseer should not seem strange. After all, James assumed a similar position in the Early Church in Jerusalem (Galatians 2:12). From Revelation 2 and 3, where almost certainly the leader of the church is called an "angel" of the church, the leader represents a special envoy to the church (cf. 1 Timothy 5:17). Thus, it is reasonable to assume that church structure developed rapidly in Paul's lifetime. In fact, even the Qumran writings show that an organized society with structured leadership was extant prior to Paul.

Heresy Reflects Later Struggles

This position maintains that the heresy of the Pastoral Epistles reflects the more developed,

emerging Gnostic systems of the Second Century. Some point especially to the "genealogies" and "myths" (cf. Titus 3:9; 1 Timothy 1:4).

Counterarguments to this position contend that "genealogies" should be understood as a reference to Jewish speculations concerning genealogies of the Old Testament (cf. 1:10). The term *genealogias* (Titus 3:9; cf. 1 Timothy 1:4) never occurs in Gnostic writings in reference to the Gnostic technical term "aeon." Myths (1:14) are distinctly identified as Jewish myths; neither are these to be regarded as Gnostic speculations of the Second Century.

Conclusion: In spite of the intensive study of the problem regarding authenticity of the Pastorals, no one has proved that Paul could not have written them. The authority of Holy Scripture itself assures us that this will not take place in the future either.

DATE

The letter to Titus was written in the last year of Paul's life, in the period between his release from his 2-year imprisonment in Rome and his final martyrdom in Rome, which Paul himself anticipates in 2 Timothy. His release from prison must have occurred before the fire of Rome (A.D. 64, July 19–27), since after the fire it would have been unlikely that he would be freed. The first confinement took place either in 60–62 or 61–63. It is not clear whether Paul was martyred during the persecution of the fall of A.D. 64, or whether he—as Ancient Church tradition claims—was executed during the last year of Emperor Nero's reign (A.D. 67–68). The best date for the letter, therefore, is probably around A.D. 62 and 67.

PURPOSE

The purpose of the letter is to offer guidance for organizing the church and for answering ethical questions. In addition, it serves to exhort Titus to come to Paul in Nicopolis as soon as possible (3:12) and to insure that Zenas and Apollos have what they need for their journey (3:13).

OUTLINE
I. SALUTATION (1:1-4)
II. DIRECTIVES FOR ELDERS OF THE CHURCH (1:5-9)
    A. Personal Qualifications (1:6-8)
    B. Spiritual Qualifications (1:9)
III. INSTRUCTIONS FOR DEALING WITH FALSE TEACHERS (1:10-16)

I. SALUTATION (1:1-4)

The salutation sheds light on Paul's ministry and affords some insight into what Paul's apostleship involved. Paul introduced himself as the "servant of God, and an apostle of Jesus Christ." He used the expression "servant (literally 'slave,' *doulos*) of God" only this one time. In using this epithet he was aligning himself with the prophets and patriarchs of old. In contrast to the false Jewish teachers who have infiltrated the church and who dismiss the truth of the gospel as having nothing to do with the old covenant, Paul considered himself as the final link in the chain of authoritative revelation extending from the Old Testament to the apostles of the Lord in the new covenant.

The goal of ministry (service) is faith and knowledge. Paul's entire efforts aimed toward this goal. He did not merely want to awaken faith in those who had not heard the gospel, he also wanted to strengthen the faith of God's elect.

II. DIRECTIVES FOR ELDERS OF THE CHURCH (1:5-9)

The evidence suggests that there is no difference between "elders" (verse 5, *presbuterous*) and "bishops" (verse 7, *episkopon*). When Titus appoints elders, he must realize that not everybody is suited for such a task. Therefore, some guidelines for choosing elders are given.

A. Personal Qualifications (1:6-8)

The qualifications for eldership take into consideration one's life-style. The home life of an aspiring elder is first to be examined. He must be the husband of one wife; his children are to exhibit proper behavior. The Christian home is a reflection of the church. The head of a household is responsible for directing the home and rearing the children. Similarly, those

in charge of the church should manifest an exemplary home life before they are even considered fit to be church leaders.

The qualities not proper for a bishop are listed (1:7); such features are not to be part of Christian character. Such characteristics would render a professing Christian's testimony null and void. Titus 1:8 addresses those positive qualities a church leader *is* to have. A spiritual leader must not only impose certain requirements on others, he or she must exemplify proper behavior. First and foremost he must have pledged himself to God.

B. Spiritual Qualifications (1:9)

Great emphasis is laid upon the fact that leaders hold fast to apostolic teaching. This is the last, and perhaps most important, requirement of a leader. Only when apostolic teaching is rigidly followed can genuine proclamation be assured. By living this way, the leader will be able to carry out two other functions of the bishop role. First, he will be able to bring the Word of God in comfort and admonition in every circumstance of life. Second, he will be able to dispute those who doubt or argue. At stake here is not only human talent, such as eloquence; rather, the ultimate issue is insight that is anchored in the Word of God, the foundation of the church.

III. INSTRUCTIONS FOR DEALING WITH THE FALSE TEACHERS (1:10-16)

No one preaching the gospel should be surprised when opposition arises. It is a natural consequence, because the Word of God challenges the thoughts of the natural person (cf. 2 Corinthians 10:4,5). It happens in Crete, though, that the opposition stems directly from the false teaching. Verse 10 reveals that Jewish Christians are involved, and verse 14 suggests that some have been swayed by certain Jews who directly oppose Christ. In the latter case the opponents are not Jewish Christians, but blatant enemies of the gospel who have turned away from the Faith. They revelled in Jewish legends (verse 14), i.e., legends based in part upon the Bible and in part on imaginative speculation. The result was non-Biblical teachings. From verse 15 we learn that included in these teachings was asceticism (cf. 1 Timothy 4:3). Jewish Christians were affected by such teachings and tried to incorporate them in the church at Crete.

Paul characterizes the teaching of the opponents as "vain talk" (verse 10). Nothing of what they say originates in God. Titus is advised to take two steps: (1) to silence the harmful, destructive talk of the false teachers, for it is more than absurd, it is dangerous. False teaching caused homes to split (cf. Matthew 12:25; contrary to the model in verse 6). (2) The opponents, whose faith was "diseased, sick," were to be "rebuke(d) sharply" (NIV) in an effort to turn them from their error (verse 13).

IV. ETHICAL INSTRUCTIONS (2:1-10)

Various groups within the church are given ethical guidelines. Five groups are mentioned in this passage. Paul gives admonitions that will preserve and strengthen the family unit and which will assist it in functioning according to the creative power of God. The admonitions are related to sound doctrine (verse 1) and to the instructive grace of God (verse 10). The dynamic Word of God is active. Paul admonishes his readers to make room for the spiritual power intrinsic in the sound teaching of the gospel.

V. THE POWER OF GOD'S GRACE TO TEACH (2:11-15)

This section is grammatically linked to the preceding. It reiterates that Paul's admonitions are founded upon and sustained by the Word of God. Christian conduct and Christian doctrine are inseparable, just as fruit cannot exist apart from a tree. This relationship between behavior and doctrine permeates the entire letter.

The grace of God which brings salvation to all men is the same grace that teaches us to reject ungodliness (verses 11,12; cf. Colossians 1:6). It saves not on the basis of our works or on the condition that we satisfy some demand. (1) Grace is a continuous process. Our sanctification is not complete, and neither is salvation totally realized in this life. (2) Grace allows us to say *no* to ungodliness and *yes* to godliness. That grace teaches us to say no to the world's values does not imply some kind of ascetic attitude toward life. Instead, it means believers say no to anything that encourages worshiping the creature more than the Creator. (3) A perspective that recognizes the reality of eternal life is part of the process of the sanctified life and it constantly governs one's motives.

VI. THE BELIEVER'S RELATIONSHIP WITH AUTHORITIES (3:1,2)

Even though believers are people of hope who live their lives looking to the coming of Christ, they must not neglect their responsibilities in this life. Such an eschatological perspective should, on the contrary, help believers to be faithful to carry out the responsibilities God gives them in this life.

Paul does not particularize the relationship believers are to have with authorities, but he admonishes Titus to warn the church to be subject, i.e., obey the laws of the land, and to be prepared to do any good work.

The advice is more general in verse 2. The important thing is to refrain from a critical and disruptive attitude, and to show instead an attitude of respect, gentleness, and meekness towards all men. The extent to which one yields is without measure ("all gentleness," "all men").

VII. SALVATION AND REGENERATION PRESUPPOSED IN THE NEW LIFE (3:3-8)

This passage reflects the basis and the relevance of the admonition given in verses 1 and 2. The ideas of "formerly" and "now" as well as the inclusive term "we" are typically Pauline (cf. Ephesians 2:3; 5:8). In contrast with the seven attitudes in verses 1 and 2 to which we are now called, verse 3 reminds us of seven conditions under which we were once enslaved. Verses 4-8 contain another aspect of the basis for this caution. God's work of salvation is being disclosed. The ethical implications of that salvation are now made plain.

VIII. FURTHER GUIDANCE FOR HANDLING THE FALSE TEACHERS (3:9-11)

Time and authority must be used wisely. Paul warns Titus not to enter into a disruptive, time-consuming debate over the arguments of the false teachers. He is to use his authority to rebuke and reject them, having first thoroughly warned them of the consequences of their actions.

IX. PERSONAL REMARKS AND GREETINGS (3:12-15)

Obviously Paul needs Titus. But the situation at Crete is so unstable and critical that Titus cannot leave the island now. He must wait until he finds a replacement.

Overview–Philemon

THE AUTHENTICITY OF THE LETTER

The Pauline authorship of the letter to Philemon is virtually undisputed. Since it was first known it has been included in the letters of the apostle Paul. Only a few maintain that it is a "Christian social treatise" on the master-slave relationship placed on the lips of Paul for effect. If that were the case, however, the argument for social equity would have appeared much more vividly.

A PRIVATE CONCERN OR A LETTER FOR THE WHOLE CHURCH?

It may seem that Philemon is only a private correspondence to a specific individual about a particular, confidential matter. Were that the case, why was it included in the canon of the New Testament? Everything indicates that it is an apostolic letter to a church; only formally does it appear as a private correspondence. The more one examines the letter, the more obvious its relevance for the Church of all times becomes.

The circumstances pointing in this direction are as follows:

(1) It is true that the personal term "you" (singular) recurs in the main body of the letter. These instances are referring to Philemon, but not only him. A woman, Apphia, is also mentioned, who may be Philemon's wife (cf. 1 Corinthians 9:5) or a female servant of the church (cf. Romans 16:1). The letter is also addressed to Archippus who, according to Colossians 4:17, was also entrusted with a ministry in the Lord. But primarily, as mentioned in its opening words, the letter is aimed at the church in the house of Philemon (verse 2). Thus, it is a letter for the church, but because of a unique problem it is addressed to the host of the church (cf. Romans 16:23).

(2) Timothy is a cosender. He regularly accompanied the apostle Paul in his duties, not the least in the Asian province where Colossae was located.

(3) Paul does not describe himself as an apostle as he usually does; nevertheless, his apostolic call and authority shine through. Paul's authority as apostle would allow him to give Philemon specific commands concerning the present problem (verse 8); however he does not. Neither does he doubt that Philemon would respond to such commands (verse 21).

PHILEMON—HOST OF THE CHURCH

The name Philemon does not appear anywhere else in the New Testament. Almost certainly he is from Colossae in Phyrgia. The generally acknowledged relationship between this letter and the letter to the Colossians is obvious. Onesimus is mentioned in both letters (Colossians 4:9; Philemon 10), and those named in verses 23,24 also send their greetings in Colossians 4:10-15.

Philemon is called "our dearly beloved" (*agapētō*) (verse 1). Whether this means a dear friend or one beloved by God is not clear. Paul and Philemon are apparently good friends (verse 17). The description of Philemon as a coworker (verse 1) shows that he was involved in Christian ministry. He opened his home for worship services (verse 2), and he invited guests like Paul and his coworkers to attend (verse 22). Philemon demonstrated his Christian faith in acts of charity. He also helped the poor in the church (verses 5-7). From verse 19 we note that Paul was the instrument through whom Philemon became a Christian. How or when this occurred is not recorded.

ONESIMUS AND HIS CONFESSION

Philemon was a "master" (*kurios*), in other words a "slave-owner." Slavery was seen during that time period as an inevitable by-product of the structure of society. Slaves often received humane treatment. Some, however, worked in chains, as in the silver mines, while others were "household slaves" in the houses of the well-to-do. The latter were entrusted with a great deal of responsibility in caring for the children.

There were slaves in Christian households as well. The issue here is not that slavery existed, but how the slaves were treated. Among the earliest Christians many were slaves, but in the relationship between God and the individual, there was no difference between a slave and a master (1 Corinthians 12:13; Galatians 3:28; Colossians 3:11). At the Lord's table they sat side by side.

Onesimus means "one who benefits another"; that is, "profitable." Paul made a play on words with this in verses 11 and 20. It is stated expressly that Onesimus was a slave (verse 16), and Colossians 4:9 describes him as faithful, dear, a brother, one of their own, and thus a member of the church.

Verse 10 indicates that Onesimus became a Christian when he met Paul. Onesimus was associated with Paul in a unique way during the latter's confinement. It is virtually certain that the imprisonment spoken of was Paul's confinement in Rome. Ephesus would be too close to Colossae, and Caesarea too small for the runaway slave to hide. Rome, though, would be well suited.

PAUL AS A SPONSOR

We are not told all the circumstances, but Onesimus had deserted his master Philemon, stealing some money while doing so. There is much missing in the story as it is recorded in the Scriptures. We are not told the sum of the money, how he was able to reach Rome, how he happened to contact Paul, and the steps by which Paul was able to lead Onesimus to salvation. It is sufficient to learn all this occurred.

Now Onesimus faced a difficult problem. He had wronged his master, he must confess. His restitution required that he return to Philemon putting himself back into slavery. Wishing to help in the reconciliation, Paul wrote this letter, interceding for Onesimus who had become like a "son" to him.

The apostle asked Philemon to receive Onesimus as if he were Paul himself (verse 17). The stolen funds were lost, but Paul requested that they be charged to his account. Paul tried to open Philemon's eyes to the fact that something good could come from all this misfortune.

WHAT "MORE" DID PAUL EXPECT?

What did the apostle mean when he stated he was sure Philemon would "do more than I say" (verse 21)? It could have been just a general expression of confidence, but some students give a greater significance to the term. (1) He was asking for Onesimus' release from being a slave. But this could cause a problem if Philemon's other slaves were kept in servitude. (2) He was asking Philemon to send Onesimus back to him to minister to him in his own bondage. But if this were so, why did Paul request lodging be prepared for him in a soon-coming visit (verse 21)? At any rate, it is apparent from verse 16 that Paul expected Philemon to receive Onesimus in a special relationship: "Not now as a servant, but above a servant, a brother beloved."

THE DOUBLE CITIZENSHIP OF BELIEVERS

Paul did not claim Onesimus must be freed. The abolition of slavery was not an issue of that time. It is obvious that for Paul Christians were to be obedient to civil law as far as was possible. They lived in a world with masters and slaves,

but they were not of this world. Christ was their real Master.

Life in this dual existence meant that Christian slaves served their masters from a willing heart. They served sincerely and were obedient as if their service to their master was service to Christ. For Christian slave owners, the dual citizenship of Christian slaves meant they were not harshly treated or overworked (Ephesians 6:9). Slaves were to be treated reasonably and with justice (Colossians 4:1).

Joined with every other loyal citizen group throughout history and within various social structures, Christians have worked to improve social conditions, even in the employer/employee relationship. The Christian must carefully discriminate between the private and political consequences of his actions as a believer. He or she must realize that though the "more" cannot always be explicitly identified, it is nevertheless always present.

CHRISTIAN LOVE—ALWAYS IN PROCESS

As we have seen, the letter to Philemon is not a Christian social treatise with a specific answer for a specific social problem. Rather, it is an apostle's teaching of faith and trust in Christ and an apostolic admonition to a Christian and his church to discern the proper response of love. On this occasion the issue concerned a slave/master relationship; today it could be the employee/employer— the essence is the same. The response is the same: love has no limit; it is always in the process of realization.

If the letter to Philemon were only intended for private consumption, it would have never made the canon or the body of Pauline letters. It has been read throughout the churches of the ancient world as an "epistle" to be read in the worship service, just as the other letters of Paul.

LATER TRADITIONS AND THEIR SIGNIFICANCE

The young Church took this letter to heart. The multiplicity of traditions associated with the characters of the letter attest to this. A great deal could be said about any of them. Philemon became the bishop in his town, and his entire family was martyred under Nero's reign. Onesimus became a prominent member of the church at Colossae. When the martyr and bishop Ignatius wrote around A.D. 110 to the church in Ephesus, he gave thanks because he had received encouragement from a delegation of elders from Ephesus, led by the bishop named Onesimus. There is good reason to accept these traditions. This is almost certainly the Onesimus from the Book of Philemon.

Some, however, think that Onesimus became the bishop of Beroea of Macedonia. Others think he followed Paul on a missionary journey to Spain. Finally, some contend that he was martyred in Italy. Whatever the case, all of this reflects how highly the Early Church regarded the letter to Philemon.

Manuscripts

Egyptian Papyri

Note: (a) designates the section of the New Testament on which the manuscript is based; (b) designates the century in which it is believed the manuscript was written (using the Roman numerals); (c) provides information on the present location of the manuscript.

p1 (a) Gospels; (b) III; (c) Philadelphia, University of Pennsylvania Museum, no. E2746.

p2 (a) Gospels; (b) VI; (c) Florence, Museo Archeologico, Inv. no. 7134.

p3 (a) Gospels; (b) VI, VII; (c) Vienna, Österreichische Nationalbibliothek, Sammlung Papyrus Erzherzog Rainer, no. G2323.

p4 (a) Gospels; (b) III; (c) Paris, Bibliothèque Nationale, no. Gr. 1120, suppl. 2⁰.

p5 (a) Gospels; (b) III; (c) London, British Museum, P. 782 and P. 2484.

p6 (a) Gospels; (b) IV; (c) Strasbourg, Bibliothèque de la Université, 351^r, 335^v, 379, 381, 383, 384 copt.

p7 (a) Gospels; (b) V; (c) now lost, was in Kiev, library of the Ukrainian Academy of Sciences.

p8 (a) Acts; (b) IV; (c) now lost; was in Berlin, Staatliche Museen, P. 8683.

p9 (a) General Epistles; (b) III; (c) Cambridge, Massachusetts, Harvard University, Semitic Museum, no. 3736.

p10 (a) Paul's Epistles; (b) IV; (c) Cambridge, Massachusetts, Harvard University, Semitic Museum, no. 2218.

p11 (a) Paul's Epistles; (b) VII; (c) Leningrad, State Public Library.

p12 (a) General Epistles; (b) late III; (c) New York, Pierpont Morgan Library, no. G. 3.

p13 (a) General Epistles; (b) III, IV; (c) London, British Museum, P. 1532 (verso), and Florence, Biblioteca Medicea Laurenziana.

p14 (a) Paul's Epistles; (b) V (?); (c) Mount Sinai, St. Catharine's Monastery, no. 14.

p15 (a) Paul's Epistles; (b) III; (c) Cairo, Museum of Antiquities, no. 47423.

p16 (a) Paul's Epistles; (b) III, IV; (c) Cairo, Museum of Antiquities, no. 47424.

p17 (a) General Epistles; (b) IV; (c) Cambridge, England, University Library, gr. theol. f. 13 (P), Add. 5893.

p18 (a) Revelation; (b) III, IV; (c) London, British Museum, P. 2053 (verso).

p19 (a) Gospels; (b) IV, V; (c) Oxford, Bodleian Library, MS. Gr. bibl. d. 6 (P.).

p20 (a) General Epistles; (b) III; (c) Princeton, New Jersey, University Library, Classical Seminary AM 4117 (15).

p21 (a) Gospels; (b) IV, V; (c) Allentown, Pennsylvania, Library of Muhlenberg College, Theol. Pap. 3.

p22 (a) Gospels; (b) III; (c) Glasgow, University Library, MS. 2-x. 1.

p23 (a) General Epistles; (b) early III; (c) Urbana, Illinois, University of Illinois, Classical Archaeological and Art Museum, G. P. 1229.

p24 (a) Revelation; (b) IV; (c) Newton Center, Massachusetts, Library of Andover Newton Theological School.

p25 (a) Gospels; (b) late IV; (c) now lost, was in Berlin, Staatliche Museen, P. 16388.

p26 (a) Paul's Epistles; (b) c. 600; (c) Dallas, Texas, Southern Methodist University, Lane Museum.

p27 (a) Paul's Epistles; (b) III; (c) Cambridge, England, University Library, Add. MS. 7211.

p28 (a) Gospels; (b) III; (c) Berkeley, California, Library of Pacific School of Religion, Pap. 2.

p29 (a) Acts; (b) III; (c) Oxford, Bodleian Library, MS. Gr. bibl. g. 4 (P.).

p30 (a) Paul's Epistles; (b) III; (c) Ghent, University Library, U. Lib. P. 61.

p31 (a) Paul's Epistles; (b) VII; (c) Manchester, England, John Rylands Library, P. Ryl. 4.

p32 (a) Paul's Epistles; (b) c. 200; (c) Manchester England, John Rylands Library, P. Ryl. 5.

p33 (a) Acts; (b) VI; (c) Vienna, Österreichische Nationalbibliothek, no. 190.

p34 (a) Paul's Epistles; (b) VII; (c) Vienna, Österreichische Nationalbibliothek, no. 191.

p35 (a) Gospels; (b) IV (?); (c) Florence, Biblioteca Medicea Laurenziana.

p36 (a) Gospels; (b) VI; (c) Florence, Biblioteca Medicea Laurenziana.

p37 (a) Gospels; (b) III, IV; (c) Ann Arbor, Michigan, University of Michigan Library, Invent. no. 1570.

p38 (a) Acts; (b) c. 300; (c) Ann Arbor, Michigan, University of Michigan Library, Invent. no. 1571.

p39 (a) Gospels; (b) III; (c) Chester, Pennsylvania, Crozer Theological Seminary Library, no. 8864.

p40 (a) Paul's Epistles; (b) III; (c) Heidelberg, Universitätsbibliothek, Inv. Pap. graec. 45.

p41 (a) Acts; (b) VIII; (c) Vienna, Österreichische Nationalbibliothek, Pap. K.7541-8.

p42 (a) Gospels; (b)VII, VIII; (c) Vienna, Österreichische Nationalbibliothek, KG 8706.

p43 (a) Revelation; (b) VI, VII; (c) London, British Museum, Pap. 2241.

p44 (a) Gospels; (b) VI, VII; (c) New York, Metropolitan Museum of Art, Inv. 14-1-527.

p45 (a) Gospels, Acts; (b) III; (c) Dublin, Chester Beatty Museum; and Vienna, Osterreichische Nationalbibliothek, P. Gr. Vind. 31974.

p46 (a) Paul's Epistles; (b) c. 200; (c) Dublin, Chester Beatty Museum, and Ann Arbor, Michigan, University of Michigan Library, Invent. no. 6238.

p47 (a) Revelation; (b) late III; (c) Dublin, Chester Beatty Museum.

p48 (a) Acts; (b) late III; (c) Florence, Museo Medicea Laurenziana.

p49 (a) Paul's Epistles; (b) late III; (c) New Haven, Connecticut, Yale University Library, P. 415.

p50 (a) Acts; (b) IV, V; (c) New Haven, Connecticut, Yale University Library, P. 1543.

p51 (a) Paul's Epistles; (b) c. 400; (c) London British Museum.

p52 (a) Gospels; (b) early II; (c) Manchester, John Rylands Library, P. Ryl. Gr. 457.

p53 (a) Gospels, Acts; (b) III; (c) Ann Arbor, Michigan, University of Michigan Library, Invent. no. 6652.

p54 (a) General Epistles; (b) V, VI; (c) Princeton, New Jersey, Princeton University Library, Garrett Depos. 7742.

p55 (a) Gospels; (b) VI, VII; (c) Vienna, Österreichische Nationalbibliothek, P. Gr. Vind. 26214.

p56 (a) Acts; (b) V, VI; (c) Vienna, Österreichische Nationalbibliothek, P. Gr. Vind. 19918.

p57 (a) Acts; (b) IV, V; (c) Vienna, Österreichische Nationalbibliothek, P. Gr. Vind. 26020.

p58 (a) Acts; (b) VI; (c) Vienna, Österreichische Nationalbibliothek, P. Gr. Vind. 17973, 36133[54], and 35831.

p59 (a) Gospels; (b) VII; (c) New York, New York University, Washington Square College of Arts and Sciences, Department of Classics, P. Colt. 3.

p60 (a) Gospels; (b) VII; (c) New York, New York University, Washington Square College of Arts and Sciences, Department of Classics, P. Colt. 4.

p61 (a) Paul's Epistles; (b) c. 700; (c) New York, New York University, Washington Square College of Arts and Sciences, Department of Classics, P. Colt. 5.

p62 (a) Gospels; (b) IV; (c) Oslo, University Library.

p63 (a) Gospels; (b) c. 500; (c) Berlin, Staatliche Museen.

p64 (a) Gospels; (b) c. 200; (c) Oxford, Magdalen College Library.

p65 (a) Paul's Epistles; (b) III; (c) Florence, Biblioteca Medicea Laurenziana.

p66 (a) Gospels; (b) c. 200; (c) Cologny/Genève, Bibliothèque Bodmer.

p67 (a) Gospels; (b) c. 200; (c) Barcelona, Fundación San Lucas Evangelista, P. Barc. 1.

p68 (a) Paul's Epistles; (b) VII (?); (c) Leningrad, State Public Library, Gr. 258.

p69 (a) Gospels; (b) III; (c) place (?)

p70 (a) Gospels; (b) III; (c) place (?)

p71 (a) Gospels; (b) IV; (c) place (?)

p72 (a) General Epistles; (b) III, IV; (c) Cologny/Genève, Bibliothèque Bodmer.

p73 (a) Gospels; (b)—; (c) Cologny/Genève, Bibliothèque Bodmer.

p74 (a) Acts, General Epistles; (b) VII; (c) Cologny/Genève, Bibliothèque Bodmer.

p75 (a) Gospels; (b) early III; (c) Cologny/Genève, Bibliothèque Bodmer.

p76 (a) Gospels; (b) VI; (c) Vienna, Österreichische Nationalbibliothek, P. Gr. Vind. 36102.

Major Codices

01, aleph:	Sinaiticus
02, A:	Alexandrinus
03, B:	Vaticanus
04, C:	Ephraemi Rescriptus
05, D:	Bezae Cantabrigiensis
06, E:	Claromontanus

Majuscules

No.	Contents	Century
01, *aleph*	Total New Testament	4th
02, A	Total New Testament	5th
03, B	New Testament, Revelation	4th
04, C	Total New Testament	5th
05, D	Gospels, Acts	6th
06, D	Paul's Epistles	6th
07, E	Gospels	8th
08, E	Acts	6th
09, F	Gospels	9th
010, F	Paul's Epistles	9th
011, G	Gospels	9th
012, G	Paul's Epistles	9th
013, H	Gospels	9th
015, H	Paul's Epistles	6th
016, I	Paul's Epistles	5th
017, K	Gospels	9th
018, K	Acts, Paul's Epistles	9th
019, L	Gospels	8th
020, L	Acts, Paul's Epistles	9th
021, M	Gospels	9th
022, N	Gospels	6th
023, O	Gospels	6th
024, P	Gospels	6th
025, P	Acts, Paul's Epistles, Revelation	9th
026, Q	Gospels	5th
028, S	Gospels	10th
029, T	Gospels	9th
030, U	Gospels	9th
031, V	Gospels	9th
032, W	Gospels	5th
033, X	Gospels	10th
034, Y	Gospels	9th
036,	Gospels	10th
037,	Gospels	9th
038,	Gospels	9th
039,	Gospels	9th
040,	Gospels	6th-8th
041,	Gospels	9th
042,	Gospels	6th
043,	Gospels	6th
044,	Gospels, Acts, Paul's Epistles	8th-9th

In addition to these manuscripts identified by a letter (letter uncials), there are 200 other numbered majuscule manuscripts. Even though most of these manuscripts are very valuable, there is not enough room to list them all. Our apparatus gives the official numbers, 046, 047 etc.

Minuscules

There are about 2800 of these. A total classification of these is only possible in specialized literature dealing with textual criticism.

Early Versions

it	Itala, early Latin	II-IV
vul	Vulgate	IV-V
old syr	Old Syrian	II-III
syr pesh	"peshitta"	V
got	Gothic	IV
arm	Armenian	IV-V
geo	Georgian	V
cop	Coptic	VI
nub	Nubian	VI
eth	Ethiopian	VI

Early Church Fathers

Ambrosius, deacon of Alexandria, and intimate friend of Origen, died 250.

Athanasius, was bishop of Alexandria, 326; died in 373.

Athenagoras, a Christian philosopher of Athens, flourished in 178.

Augustine, 354-430.

Basil the Great, bishop of Caesarea, born in Cappadocia, 329; died 379.

Bede, the Venerable, born 673.

Chrysostom, bishop of Constantinople, born 344; died 407.

Clemens Alexandrinus, Clement of Alexandria, the preceptor of Origen, died 212.

Clemens Romanus, Clement of Rome, *supposed* to have been fellow laborer with Peter and Paul, and bishop of Rome, 91.

Cyprian, bishop of Carthage, in 248; was martyred, 258.

Cyrillus Alexandrinus, this Cyril was patriarch of Alexandria 412; died 444.

Cyrillus Hierosolymitanus, Cyril, bishop of Jerusalem, was born 315; died 386.

Ephraim Syrus, Ephraim the Syrian, was deacon of Edessa; and died 373.

Eusebius of Caesarea, c.260-340.

Gregory the Great, bishop of Rome, flourished in 590.

Gregory Thaumaturgus, was a disciple of Origen, and bishop of Neocaesarea in 240.

Hippolytus, a Christian bishop, flourished 230; died 235.

Ignatius, bishop of Antioch, was martyred about 110.

Irenaeus, disciple of Polycarp; born in Greece about 140; martyred 202.

Jerome, also called Hieronymus, one of the most eminent of the Latin fathers; author of the translation of the Scriptures called the Vulgate; born about 342, died in 420.

Justin Martyr, a Christian philosopher, martyred 165.

Origen, one of the most eminent of the Greek fathers, 185-254.

Tertullian, a most eminent Latin father, died about 220.

Books of the New and Old Testament and the Apocrypha

New Testament Books

Matthew
Mark
Luke
John
Acts
Romans
1 Corinthians
2 Corinthians
Galatians
Ephesians
Philippians
Colossians
1 Thessalonians
2 Thessalonians
1 Timothy
2 Timothy
Titus
Philemon
Hebrews
James
1 Peter
2 Peter
1 John
2 John
3 John
Jude
Revelation

Old Testament Books

Genesis
Exodus
Leviticus
Numbers
Deuteronomy
Joshua
Judges
Ruth
1 Samuel
2 Samuel
1 Kings
2 Kings
1 Chronicles
2 Chronicles
Ezra
Nehemiah
Esther
Job
Psalms
Proverbs
Ecclesiates
Song of Solomon
Isaiah
Jeremiah
Lamentations
Ezekiel
Daniel

Hosea
Joel
Amos
Obadiah
Jonah
Micah
Nahum
Habakkuk
Zephaniah
Haggai
Zechariah
Malachi

Books of the Apocrypha

1 & 2 Esdras
Tobit
Judith
Additions to Esther
Wisdom of Solomon
Ecclesiasticus or the
   Wisdom of Jesus
   Son of Sirach
Baruch
Prayer of Azariah and
   the Song of the Three
   Holy Children
Susanna
Bel and the Dragon
The Prayer of Manasses
1–4 Maccabees

Bibliography

Modern Greek Texts

Aland, K. et al. in cooperation with the Institute for New Testament Textual Research. *The Greek New Testament*. 2nd ed. London: United Bible Societies. 1968.

Aland, K. et al. in cooperation with the Institute for New Testament Textual Research. *The Greek New Testament*. 3rd ed. New York: United Bible Societies. 1975.

Nestle, E. and K. Aland. *Novum Testamentum Graece.* 25th ed. Stuttgart: Deutsche Bibelstiftung. 1963.

Nestle, E. and K. Aland. et al. *Novum Testamentum Graece.* 26th ed. Stuttgart: Deutsche Bibelstiftung. 1979.

General Reference Sources with Abbreviations

BAGD
Bauer, W., W.F. Arndt and F.W. Gingrich. *A Greek-English Lexicon of the New Testament and Other Early Christian Literature.* 2nd ed. Revised and augmented by F.W. Gingrich and F.W. Danker. Chicago: University of Chicago Press. 1958.

NIDNTT
Brown, Colin. ed. *The New International Dictionary of New Testament Theology.* 4 vols. Grand Rapids: Zondervan. 1975.

TDNT
Kittel, G. and G. Friedrich. *Theological Dictionary of the New Testament.* Trans. by G.W. Bromiley. 10 vols. Grand Rapids: Wm.B. Eerdmans. 1964-72.

LSJ
Liddell, H.G. and R. Scott. *A Greek-English Lexicon.* 9th ed., Ed. by H. Stuart Jones and R. McKenzie. Oxford: Clarendon. 1940.

M-M
Moulton, J.H. and G. Milligan. *The Vocabulary of the Greek Testament Illustrated from the Papyri and Other Non-Literary Sources.* London: Hodder and Stoughton. 1914-30. Reprint. Grand Rapids: Wm. B. Eerdmans. 1985.

General Bibliography

Abbott, T. K. *A Critical and Exegetical Commentary on the Epistles to the Ephesians and to the Colossians. The International Critical Commentary.* Ed. by S. R. Driver, A. Plummer, and C. A. Briggs. Edinburgh: T. & T. Clark. 1968.

The Apocryphon of John. In *The Nag Hammadi Library in English.* Trans. by Frederik Wisse. New York: Harper & Row, Publishers. 1977.

The Babylonian Talmud. Trans. by I. Epstein. London: The Soncino Press. 1952.

Barclay, William. *The Letters to the Galatians and Ephesians. The Daily Study Bible.* Rev. ed. Philadelphia: The Westminster Press. 1976.

Barclay, William. *The Letters to Timothy, Titus, and Philemon. The Daily Study Bible.* Rev. ed. Philadelphia: The Westminster Press. 1975.

Barrett, C. K. *Freedom and Obligation: A Study of the Epistle to the Galatians.* Philadelphia: The Westminster Press. 1985.

Barth, Markus. *Ephesians.* Vol. 24 of *The Anchor Bible.* Ed. by William Foxwell Albright and David Noel Freedman. Garden City, NY: Doubleday & Company, Inc. 1974.

Baxter, J. Sidlow. *The Strategic Grasp of the Bible.* Grand Rapids: Zondervan Publishing House. 1970.

Beare, Frank W. *St. Paul and His Letters.* Nashville: Abingdon Press. 1971.

Best, Ernest. *A Commentary on the 1st and 2nd Epistles to the Thessalonians.* Vol. 10 of *Black's New Testament Commentaries.* London: Adam and Charles Black. 1972.

Betz, H. D. *A Commentary on Paul's Letter to the Churches in Galatia. Hermeneia.* Ed. by Helmut Koester, et al. Philadelphia: Fortress Press. 1979.

Bruce, F. F. *The Epistle to the Galatians. New International Greek Testament Commentary.* Ed. by I. Howard Marshall and W. Ward Gasque. Grand Rapids: William B. Eerdmans Publishing Co. 1982.

Bruce, F. F. *The Epistles to the Colossians, to Philemon, and to the Ephesians. The New International Commentary on the New Testament.* Ed. by F. F. Bruce. Grand Rapids: William B. Eerdmans Publishing Co. 1984.

Bruce, F. F. *1 and 2 Thessalonians.* Vol. 45 of *Word Biblical Commentary.* Ed. by David A. Hubbard, et al. Waco, TX: Word Books. 1982.

Burton, E. D. *A Critical and Exegetical Commentary on the Epistle to the Galatians. The International Critical Commentary.* Ed. by S. R. Driver, A. Plummer, and C. A. Briggs. Edinburgh: T. & T. Clark. 1975.

Carson, Herbert M. *The Epistles of Paul to the Colossians and Philemon.* Vol. 12 of *Tyndale New Testament Commentaries.* Ed. by R. V. G. Tasker. Grand Rapids: William B. Eerdmans Publishing Co. 1960.

Chrysostom, John. *Homilies on Thessalonians.* In *Chrysostom.* Vol. 13 of *The Nicene and Post-Nicene Fathers.* Ed. by Philip Schaff. Edinburgh, 1867. Reprint. Grand Rapids: William B. Eerdmans Publishing Co. 1969.

Clarke, Adam. *Romans to the Revelation.* Vol. 6 of *Clarke's Commentary.* Nashville: Abingdon Press. N.d.

Clement of Rome. *Epistle to the Corinthians.* In *The Apostolic Fathers.* Vol. 1 of *The Ante-Nicene Fathers.* Ed. by Alexander Roberts and James Donaldson. Edinburgh. 1867. Reprint. Grand Rapids: William B. Eerdmans Publishing Co. 1973.

Bibliography Continued

Coleridge, H. N., ed. *Specimens of the Table Talk of the Late Samuel Taylor Coleridge*. London, 1835.

Conybeare, W. J., and J. S. Howson. *The Life and Epistles of St. Paul*. Grand Rapids: William B. Eerdmans Publishing Co. 1978.

Craddock, Fred B. *Philippians*. *Interpretation*. Ed. by J. L. Mays, et al. Atlanta: John Knox Press. 1985.

Davies, W. D. *Paul and Rabbinic Judaism*. London: S.P.C.K. 1955.

Dibelius, Martin, and Hans Conzelmann. *A Commentary on the Pastoral Epistles*. Trans. by P. Buttolph and A. Yarbro. *Hermenia*. Ed. by Helmut Koester, et al. Philadelphia: Fortress Press. 1972.

Eadie, John. *Commentary on the Greek Text of the Epistles of Paul to the Thessalonians*. Vol. 5 of *The John Eadie Greek Text Commentaries*. Ed. by William Young. Macmillan and Company. 1877. Reprint. Grand Rapids: Baker Book House. 1979.

Eerdman, Charles R. *The Epistles of Paul to the Thessalonians*. Philadelphia: The Westminster Press. 1935.

Ellingsworth, Paul, and Eugene Nida. *A Translator's Handbook on Paul's Letters to the Thessalonians*. Vol. 17 of *Helps for Translators*. Stuttgart: United Bible Societies. 1975.

Fee, Gordon D. *1 and 2 Timothy, Titus. A Good News Commentary*. Ed. by W. Ward Gasque. San Francisco: Harper & Row. 1984.

Foulkes, Francis. *The Epistle of Paul to the Ephesians*. Vol. 10 of *Tyndale New Testament Commentaries*. Ed. by R. V. G. Tasker. Grand Rapids: William B. Eerdmans Publishing Co. 1961.

Frame, James Everett. *A Critical and Exegetical Commentary on the Epistles of St. Paul to the Thessalonians*. *The International Critical Commentary*. Ed. by S. R. Driver, A. Plummer, and C. A. Briggs. Edinburgh: T. & T. Clark. 1970.

Fung, Ronald Y. *The Epistle to the Galatians*. *The New International Commentary on the New Testament*. Ed. by F. F. Bruce. Grand Rapids: William B. Eerdmans Publishing Co. 1988.

Gaebelein, Frank E., ed. *The Expositor's Bible Commentary*. Vol. 11, *Ephesians—Philemon*. Grand Rapids: Zondervan Publishing House. 1978.

Goodspeed, E. J. *The Meaning of Ephesians*. Chicago: The University of Chicago Press. 1933.

Gunther, John J. *St. Paul's Opponents and Their Backgrounds: A Study of Apocalyptic and Jewish Sectarian Teachings*. Vol. 35 of *Supplements Novum Testamentum*. Leiden: E. J. Brill. 1973.

Guthrie, Donald. *Galatians. New Century Bible*. Ed. by Ronald E. Clements and Matthew Black. Greenwood, SC: The Attic Press. 1977. Guthrie, Donald. *The Pastoral Epistles*. Vol. 14 of *Tyndale New Testament Commentaries*. Ed. by R. V. G. Tasker. Grand Rapids: William B. Eerdmans Publishing Co. 1957.

Harrison, Norman B. *Living: A Book of Christian Culture for All Ages*. Minneapolis: The Harrison Service. 1944.

Harrison, Percy Neale. *The Problem of the Pastoral Epistles*. Oxford: Oxford University Press. 1921.

Hawthorne, Gerald F. *Philippians*. Vol. 43 of *Word Biblical Commentary*. Ed. by David A. Hubbard, et al. Waco, TX: Word Books. 1983.

Hendriksen, William. *Exposition of Colossians and Philemon*. New Testament Commentary. Grand Rapids: Baker Book House. 1975.

Hiebert, D. Edmond. *An Introduction to the Pauline Epistles*. Chicago: Moody Press. 1972.

Hiebert, D. Edmond. *First Timothy*. Chicago: Moody Press. 1957.

Horton, Stanley M. *Adult Teacher, 1971*. Vol. 7 of *Adult Teacher Commentary*. Springfield, MO: Gospel Publishing House. 1970.

Ignatius. *Epistle to Polycarp*. In *The Apostolic Fathers*. Vol. 1 of *The Ante-Nicene Fathers*. Ed. by Alexander Roberts and James Donaldson. Edinburgh. 1867. Reprint. Grand Rapids: William B. Eerdmans Publishing Co. 1973.

Irenaeus. *Against Heresies*. In *The Apostolic Fathers*. Vol. 1 of *The Ante-Nicene Fathers*. Ed. by Alexander Roberts and James Donaldson. Edinburgh. 1867. Reprint. Grand Rapids: William B. Eerdmans Publishing Co. 1973.

Josephus, F. *The Complete Works of Flavius Josephus*. Trans. by William Whiston. Grand Rapids: Kregel Publications. 1960.

Kelly, J. N. D. *The Oxford Dictionary of Popes*. Oxford: Oxford University Press. 1986.

Lenski, R. C. H. *The Interpretation of St. Paul's Epistles to the Colossians, to the Thessalonians, to Timothy, to Titus, and to Philemon*. Minneapolis: Augsburg Publishing House. 1961.

Lightfoot, J. B. *St. Paul's Epistles to the Colossians and to Philemon*. Rev. ed. New York: Macmillan and Company. 1829. Reprint. Grand Rapids: Zondervan Publishing House. 1959.

Lock, Walter. *A Critical and Exegetical Commentary on the Pastoral Epistles*. The International Critical Commentary. Ed. by S. R. Driver, A. Plummer, and C. A. Briggs. Edinburgh: T. & T. Clark. 1966.

Lohse, Eduard. *A Commentary on the Epistles to the Colossians and Philemon*. Trans. by W. R. Poehlmann and R. J. Karris. *Hermeneia*. Ed. by Helmut Koester, et al. Philadelphia: Fortress Press. 1971.

Louw, Johannes P. and Eugene A. Nida, eds. *Greek-English Lexicon of the New Testament Based on Semantic Domains*. 2 vols. New York: United Bible Societies. 1988.

Marshall, I. Howard. *1 and 2 Thessalonians*. *New Century Bible*. Ed. by Donald E. Clements and Matthew Black. Grand Rapids: William B. Eerdmans Publishing Co. 1983.

Martin, Ralph P. *Carmen Christi*. Rev. ed. Grand Rapids: William B. Eerdmans Publishing Co. 1983.

Martin, Ralph P. *The Epistle of Paul to the Philippians*. Vol. 11 of *Tyndale New Testament Commentaries*. Rev. ed. by Leon Morris. Grand Rapids: William B. Eerdmans Publishing Co. 1988.

Meyer, H. A. W. *Critical and Exegetical Hand-Book to the Epistle to the Ephesians*. Trans. by M. J. Evans. Rev. ed. by W. P. Dickson. New York: Funk and Wagnalls, Publishers. 1884. Reprint. Alpha Publications. 1979.

Michael, J. Hugh. *The Epistle of Paul to the Philippians*. The Moffatt New Testament Commentary. London: Hodder and Stoughton. 1964.

Mitton, C. Leslie. *Ephesians*. New Century Bible. Ed. by Donald E. Clements and Matthew Black. London: Oliphants. 1976.

Mitton, C. Leslie. *The Epistle to the Ephesians: Its Authorship, Origin and Purpose*. Oxford: Oxford University Press. 1951.

Moffatt, James. *1 Thessalonians—James*. Vol. 4 of *The Expositor's Greek Testament*. Ed. by W. Robertson Nicoll. Grand Rapids: William B. Eerdmans Publishing Co. 1951.

Morris, Leon. *The First and Second Epistles to the Thessalonians*. The New International Commentary on the New Testament. Ed. by F. F. Bruce. Grand Rapids: William B. Eerdmans Publishing Co. 1959.

Moule, C. F. D. *The Epistles of Paul the Apostle to the Colossians and to Philemon.* Cambridge: Cambridge University Press. 1968.

Peake, A. S. "The Quintessence of Paulinism." *Bulletin of the John Rylands Library* 4(1917-1918): 285-211.

Polycarp. *Epistle to the Philippians.* In *The Apostolic Fathers.* Vol. 1 of *The Ante-Nicene Fathers.* Ed. by Alexander Roberts and James Donaldson. Edinburgh. 1867. Reprint. Grand Rapids: William B. Eerdmans Publishing Co. 1973.

Ramsay, William M. *A Historical Commentary on St. Paul's Epistle to the Galatians.* G. P. Putnam's Sons. 1900. Reprint. Minneapolis: Klock & Klock Christian Publishers. 1978.

Ridderbos, H. N. *The Epistle of Paul to the Churches of Galatia. The New International Commentary on the New Testament.* Ed. F. F. Bruce. Grand Rapids: William B. Eerdmans Publishing Co. 1953.

Robertson, Archibald Thomas. *Paul and the Intellectuals: The Epistle to the Colossians.* New York: Doubleday, Doran and Company. 1928.

Ryrie, Charles Caldwell. *First and Second Thessalonians.* Chicago: Moody Press. 1959.

Schaff, Philip. *Apostolic Christianity.* Vol. 1 of *History of the Christian Church.* Charles Scribner's Sons. 1910. Reprint. Grand Rapids: William B. Eerdmans Publishing Co. 1971.

Scott, E. F. *The Epistles of Paul to the Colossians, to Philemon and to the Ephesians. The Moffatt New Testament Commentary.* London: Hodder and Stoughton. 1930.

Stevens, William Arnold. *Commentary on the Epistles to the Thessalonians.* In *Corinthians to Thessalonians.* Vol. 5 of *An American Commentary on the New Testament.* Ed. by Alvah Hovey. Valley Forge, PA: The Judson Press. N.d.

Stibbs, A. M. *The Pastoral Epistles.* In *The New Bible Commentary: Revised.* 3rd ed. Ed. by Donald Guthrie, et al. Grand Rapids: William B. Eerdmans Publishing Co. 1970.

Stott, John R. W. *The Message of Galatians.* Downers Grove, Ill.: Inter-Varsity Press. 1968.

Summers, Ray. *Essentials of New Testament Greek.* Nashville: Broadman Press. 1950.

Tertullian. *Against Marcion.* In *Latin Christianity: Its Founder Tertullian.* Vol. 3 of *The Ante-Nicene Fathers.* Ed. by Alexander Roberts and James Donaldson. Edinburgh. 1867. Reprint. Grand Rapids: William B. Eerdmans Publishing Co. 1973.

Unger, Merrill F. *Unger's Bible Dictionary.* Chicago: Moody Press. 1972.

Walvoord, John F. *The Thessalonian Epistles.* Grand Rapids: Zondervan Publishing House. 1967.

Wright, N. T. *The Epistles of Paul to the Colossians and to Philemon.* Vol. 12 of *Tyndale New Testament Commentaries.* Rev. ed. Ed. by Leon Morris. Grand Rapids: William B. Eerdmans Publishing Co. 1986.

Wuest, Kenneth S. *Galatians in the Greek New Testament.* Grand Rapids: William B. Eerdmans Publishing Co. 1944.

Various Versions Acknowledgments

Scripture quotations found in Various Versions were taken from the following sources with special permission as indicated. The sources listed may be found in one or all of the volumes of THE COMPLETE BIBLICAL LIBRARY.

AB
Fitzmyer, Joseph A., S.J., trans. *The Gospel According to Luke I- IX; (Anchor Bible).* New York: Doubleday & Company, Inc. 1985. Reprinted with permission. ©1981, 1985.

ADAMS
Adams, Jay E. *The Christian Counselor's New Testament: a New Translation in Everyday English with Notations, Marginal References, and Supplemental Helps.* Grand Rapids, MI: Baker Book House. 1977. Reprinted with permission. ©1977.

ALBA
Condon, Kevin. *The Alba House New Testament.* Staten Island, NY: Alba House, Society of St. Paul copublished with The Mercier Press Ltd. 1972. Reprinted with permission. *The Mercier New Testament.* 4 Bridge Street. Cork, Ireland: The Mercier Press Ltd. ©1970.

ALFORD
Alford, Henry. *The New Testament of Our Lord and Saviour Jesus Christ: After the Authorized Version.* Newly compared with the original Greek, and revised. London: Daldy, Isbister. 1875.

AMPB
The Amplified Bible. Grand Rapids, MI: Zondervan Publishing House. 1958. Reprinted with permission from the *Amplified New Testament.* © The Lockman Foundation. 1954, 1958.

ASV
(American Standard Version) The Holy Bible Containing the Old and New Testaments: Translated out of the original tongues; being the version set forth A.D. 1611, compared with the most ancient authorities and rev. A.D. 1881-1885. New York: Thomas Nelson Inc., Publishers. 1901, 1929.

BARCLAY
Barclay, William. *The New Testament: A New Translation.* Vol. 1, *The Gospels and the Acts of the Apostles.* London: William Collins Sons & Co. Ltd. 1968. Reprinted with permission. ©1968.

BB
The Basic Bible: Containing the Old and New Testaments in Basic English. New York: Dutton. 1950. Reprinted with permission. *The Bible In Basic English.* © Cambridge University Press. 1982.

BECK
Beck, William F. *The New Testament in the Language of Today.* St. Louis, MO: Concordia Publishing House. 1963. Reprinted with permission. © Mrs. William Beck, *An American Translation.* Leader Publishing Company: New Haven, MO.

BERKELEY
The Holy Bible: the Berkeley Version in Modern English Containing the Old and New Testaments. Grand Rapids: Zondervan Publishing House. 1959. Used by permission. ©1945, 1959, 1969.

BEZA
Iesv Christi, D.N. Novum Testamentum. Geneva: Henricus Stephanus. 1565.

BLACKWELDER
Blackwelder, Boyce W. *The Four Gospels: An Exegetical Translation.* Anderson, IN: Warner Press, Inc. 1980.

BLACKWELL
Blackwell, Boyce W. *Letters from Paul: An Exegetical Translation.* Anderson, IN: Warner Press, 1971.

598

BRUCE

Bruce, F.F. *The Letters of Paul: An Expanded Paraphrase Printed in Parallel with the RV*. Grand Rapids: William B. Eerdmans Publishing Co. 1965. Reprinted with permission. F.F. Bruce. *An Expanded Paraphrase of the Epistles of Paul*. The Paternoster Press: Exeter, England. ©1965, 1981.

CAMPBELL

Campbell, Alexander. *The Sacred Writings of the Apostles and Evangelists of Jesus Christ commonly styled the New Testament*: Translated from the original Greek by Drs. G. Campbell, J. Macknight & P. Doddridge with prefaces, various emendations and an appendix by A. Campbell. Grand Rapids: Baker Book House. 1951 reprint of the 1826 edition.

CKJB

The Children's 'King James' Bible: New Testament. Translated by Jay Green. Evansville, IN: Modern Bible Translations, Inc. 1960.

CLEMENTSON

Clementson, Edgar Lewis. *The New Testament: a Translation*. Pittsburg, PA: Evangelization Society of Pittsburgh Bible Institute. 1938.

CONCORDANT

Concordant Version: The Sacred Scriptures: Designed to put the Englished reader in possession of all the vital facts of divine revelation without a former knowledge of Greek by means of a restored Greek text. Los Angeles: Concordant Publishing Concern. 1931. Reprinted with permission. *Concordant Literal New Testament*. Concordant Publishing Concern. 15570 Knochaven Road, Canyon Country, CA 91351. ©1931.

CONFRATERNITY

The New Testament of Our Lord and Savior Jesus Christ: Translated from the Latin Vulgate, a revision of the Challoner-Rheims Version edited by Catholic scholars under the patronage of the Episcopal Committee of the Confraternity Christian Doctrine. Paterson, NJ: St. Anthony Guild Press. 1941. Reprinted with permission by the Confraternity of Christian Doctrine, Washington, DC. ©1941.

CONYBEARE

Conybeare, W.J. and Rev. J.S. Howson D.D. *The Life and Epistles of St. Paul*. Rev. ed. 2 vols. London: Longman, Green, Longman, and Roberts. 1862.

COVERDALE

The New Testament: The Coverdale Version. N.p. 1535(?), 1557.

CRANMER

Cranmer or Great Bible. *The Byble in Englyshe, . . .* translated after the veryte of the Hebrue and Greke text, by ye dilygent studye of dyverse excellent learned men, expert in the forsayde tonges. Prynted by Richard Grafton & Edward Whitchurch. Cum privilegio ad Imprimendum solum. 1539.

DARBY

Darby, J.N. *The Holy Scriptures A New Translation from the Original Languages*. Lansing, Sussex, England: Kingston Bible Trust. 1975 reprint of the 1890 edition.

DOUAY

The Holy Bible containing the Old and New Testaments: Translated from the Latin Vulgate . . . and with the other translations diligently compared, with annotations, references and an historical and chronological index. New York: Kennedy & Sons. N.d.

ET

Editor's Translation. Gerard J. Flokstra, Jr., D.Min.

EVERYDAY

The Everyday Bible: New Century Version. Fort Worth: Worthy Publishing. 1987. Reprinted with permission. World Wide Publications. *The Everyday Study Bible: Special New Testament Study Edition*. Minneapolis: World Wide Publications. 1988.

FENTON

Fenton, Farrar. *The Holy Bible in Modern English*. London: A. & C. Black. 1944 reprint of the 1910 edition.

GENEVA

The Geneva Bible: a facsimile of the 1560 edition. Madison, WI: University of Wisconsin Press. 1969.

GENEVA (1557)

The Nevve Testament of Ovr Lord Iesus Christ. Printed by Conrad Badius. 1557.

GOODSPEED

The Bible: An American Translation. Translated by Edgar J. Goodspeed. Chicago: The University of Chicago Press. 1935.

HANSEN

Hansen, J.W. The New Covenant. 2nd. ed. 2 vols. Boston: Universalist Publishing House. 1888.

HBIE

The Holy Bible containing the Old and New Testaments: an improved edition (based in part on the Bible Union Version). Philadelphia: American Baptist Publication Society 1913.

HISTNT

The Historical New Testament: Being the literature of the New Testament arranged in the order of its literary growth and according to the dates of the documents: a new translation by James Moffatt. Edinburgh: T & T Clark. 1901.

HOERBER

Hoerber, Robert G. *Saint Paul's Shorter Letters.* Fulton, MO: Robert G. Hoerber. 1954.

JB

The Jerusalem Bible. Garden City, NY: Darton, Longman & Todd, Ltd. and Doubleday and Co, Inc. 1966. Reprinted by permission of the publisher. ©1966.

KJII

King James II New Testament. Grand Rapids: Associated Publishers and Authors, Inc. ©Jay P. Green. 1970.

KLEIST

The New Testament Rendered from the Original Greek with Explanatory Notes. Translated by James A. Kleist and Joseph L. Lilly. Milwaukee: The Bruce Publishing Company. 1954.

KLINGENSMITH

Klingensmith, Don J. *Today's English New Testament.* New York: Vantage Press. 1972. Reprinted by permission of author. ©Don J. Klingensmith, 1972.

KNOX

Knox, R.A. *The New Testament of our Lord and Saviour Jesus Christ: A New Translation.* New York: Sheen and Ward. 1946. Reprinted by permission of The Liturgy Commission.

LAMSA

Lamsa, George M. *The Holy Bible From Ancient Eastern Text.* Translated from original Aramaic sources. Philadelphia: Holman. 1957. From *The Holy Bible From Ancient Eastern Text* by George Lamsa. ©1933 by Nina Shabaz; renewed 1961 by Nina Shabaz. ©1939 by Nina Shabaz; renewed 1967 by Nina Shabaz. ©1940 by Nina Shabaz; renewed 1968 by Nina Shabaz. ©1957 by Nina Shabaz. Reprinted by permission of Harper & Row, Publishers, Inc.

LATTIMORE

Lattimore, Richmond. *Four Gospels and The Revelation:* Newly translated from the Greek. New York: Farrar, Straus, Giroux, Inc. 1979. Reprinted by permission of the publisher. © Richard Lattimore, 1962, 1979.

LAUBACH

Laubach, Frank C. *The Inspired Letters in Clearest English.* Nashville: Thomas Nelson Publishers. 1956.

LIVB

The Living Bible: Paraphrased. Wheaton, IL: Tyndale House Publishers. 1973. Used by permission of the publisher. © Tyndale House Publishers. 1971.

LOCKE

Locke, John. *A Paraphrase and Notes on the Epistles of St. Paul to the Galatians, First and Second Corinthians, Romans, and Ephesians:* To which is prefixed an essay for the understanding of St. Paul's Epistles. Campbridge, England: Brown, Shattuck; Boston: Hilliard, Gray, and Co. 1832.

MACKNIGHT

Macknight, James. *New Literal Translation:* From the original Greek, of all the Apostolical Epistles, with a commentary, and notes, philological, critical, explanatory, and practical. Philadelphia: Wardkem. 1841.

MACKNIGHT

Macknight, James. *Harmony of the Four Gospels:* 2 vols. in which the natural order of each is preserved, with a paraphrase and notes. London: Longman, Hurst, Rees, Orme and Brown. 1819.

MJV

English Messianic Jewish Version. May Your Name Be Inscribed in the Book of Life. Introduction and footnotes by The Messianic Vision. Washington, D.C.: ©1981. Bible text by Thomas Nelson, Inc. Nashville: Thomas Nelson Publishing Company. ©1979.

MOFFATT

The New Testament: A New Translation. New York: Harper and Row Publishers, Inc.; Kent, England: Hodder and Stoughton Ltd. c.1912. Reprinted with permission.

MONTGOMERY

Montgomery, Helen Barrett. *The Centenary Translation of the New Testament:* Published to signalize the completion of the first hundred years of work of the American Baptist Publication Society. Philadelphia: American Baptist Publishing Society. 1924. Used by permission of Judson Press. *The New Testament in Modern English* by Helen Barrett Montgomery. Valley Forge: Judson Press. 1924, 1952.

MURDOCK

Murdock, James. *The New Testament: The Book of the Holy Gospel of our Lord and Our God, Jesus the Messiah:* A literal translation from the Syriac Peshito version. New York: Stanford and Swords. 1851.

NAB

The New American Bible. Translated from the original languages with critical use for all the ancient sources by members of the Catholic Biblical Association of America. Encino, California: Benzinger. 1970.

NASB

The New American Standard Bible. Anaheim, CA: Lockman Foundation. 1960. Reprinted with permission. © The Lockman Foundation 1960, 1962, 1963, 1968, 1971, 1972, 1973, 1975, 1977.

NCV

The Word: New Century Version New Testament. Fort Worth, TX: Sweet Publishing. 1984.

NEB

The New English Bible: New Testament. Cambridge, England: Cambridge University Press. 1970. Reprinted by permission. ©The Delegates of the Oxford University Press and The Syndics of the Cambridge University Press 1961, 1970.

NIV

The Holy Bible: New International Version. Grand Rapids: Zondervan Publishing House. 1978. Used by permission of Zondervan Bible Publishers. ©1973, 1978, International Bible Society.

NKJB

The New King James Bible, New Testament. Nashville, TN: Royal Pub. 1979. Reprinted from *The New King James Bible-New Testament.* ©1979, 1982, Thomas Nelson, Inc., Publishers.

NLT

The New Life Testament. Translated by Gleason H. Ledyard. Canby, Oregon: Christian Literature Foundation. 1969.

NOLI

Noli, S. *The New Testament of Our Lord and Savior Jesus Christ: Translated into English from the Approved Greek Text of the Church of Constantinople and the Church of Greece.* Boston: Albanian Orthodox Church in America. 1961.

NORLIE

Norlie, Olaf M. *Simplified New Testament: In plain English for today's reader: A new translation from the Greek.* Grand Rapids: Zondervan Publishing House. 1961. Used by permission. ©1961.

NORTON

Norton, Andrews. *A Translation of the Gospels with Notes.* Boston: Little, Brown. 1856.

NOYES

Noyes, George R. *The New Testament:* Translated from the Greek text of Tischendorf. Boston: American Unitarian Association. 1873.

NTPE

The New Testament: A New Translation in Plain English. Translated by Charles Kingsley Williams. Grand Rapids: Wm. B. Eerdmans Publishing Company. 1963.

PANIN

Panin, Ivan., ed. *The New Testament from the Greek Text as Established by Bible Numerics.* Toronto, Canada: Clarke, Irwin. 1935.

PHILLIPS

Phillips, J.B., trans. *The New Testament in Modern English.* Rev. ed. New York: Macmillan Publishing Company, Inc. 1958. Reprinted with permission. ©J.B. Phillips 1958, 1960, 1972.

PNT

A Plain Translation of the New Testament by a Student. Melbourne, Australia: McCarron, Bird. 1921.

RHEIMS

The Nevv Testament of Iesus Christ. Translated faithfully into English, out of the authentical Latin, . . . In the English College of Rhemes. Printed at Rhemes by Iohn Fogny. Cum privilegio. 1582.

RIEU

Rieu, E.V. *The Four Gospels.* London: Penguin Books Ltd. 1952. Reprinted with permission. ©E.V. Rieu, 1952.

ROTHERHAM

Rotherham, Joseph B. *The New Testament:* Newly translated (from the Greek text of Tregelles) and critically emphasized, with an introduction and occasional notes. London: Samual Bagster. 1890.

RPNT
>Johnson, Ben Cambell. *The Heart of Paul: A Relational Paraphrase of the New Testament.* Vol. 1. Waco: Word Books. 1976.

RSV
>*Revised Standard Version;* The New Covenant commonly called the New Testament of our Lord and Saviour Jesus Christ: Translated from the Greek being the version set forth A.D. 1611, revised A.D. 1881, A.D. 1901. New York: Thomas Nelson Inc. Publishers. 1953. Used by permission. ©1946, 1952, 1971, 1973 by the Division of Christian Education of the National Council of the Churches of Christ in the U.S.A.

RV
>*The New Testament of our Lord and Savior Jesus Christ:* Translated out of the Greek . . . being the new version revised 1881. St. Louis, MO: Scammell. 1881.

SAWYER
>Sawyer, Leicester Ambrose. *The New Testament: Translated from the original Greek,* with chronological arrangement of the sacred books, and improved divisions of chapters and verses. Boston: Walker, Wise. 1861.

SCARLETT
>Scarlett, Nathaniel. *A translation of the New Testament from the original Greek:* humbly attempted. London: T. Gillett. 1798.

SEB
>*The Simple English® Bible, New Testament:* American edition. New York: International Bible Translators, Inc. 1981. Used by permission from International Bible Translators, Inc.

SWANN
>Swann, George. *New Testament of our Lord and Saviour Jesus Christ.* 4th. ed. Robards, KY: George Swann Company. 1947.

TCNT
>*The Twentieth Century New Testament: a Translation into Modern English Made from the Original Greek:* (Westcott & Hort's text). New York: Revell. 1900.

TEV
>*The Good News Bible, Today's English Version.* New York: American Bible Society. 1976. Used by permission. © American Bible Society, 1966, 1971, 1976.

TNT
>*The Translator's New Testament.* London: The British and Foreign Bible Society. 1973.

TORREY
>Torrey, Charles Cutler. *The Four Gospels: A New Translation.* New York: Harper and Row Publishers Inc. 1933. Reprinted by permission. ©1933.

TYNDALE
>Tyndale, William. *The Newe Testament dylygently corrected and compared with the Greke.* and fynesshed in the yere of oure Lorde God anno M.D. and XXXIIII in the month of Nouember. London: Reeves and Turner. 1888.

TYNDALE (1526)
>*The First New Testament in the English Language (1525 or 1526).* Reprint. Bristol. 1862. Or Clevland: Barton. N.d.

WADE
>Wade, G. W. *The Documents of the New Testament: Translated & Historically Arranged with Critical Introductions.* N.p., n.d.

WAY

Way, Arthur S., trans. *Letters of St. Paul: To seven churches and three friends with the letter to the Hebrews.* 8th ed. Chicago: Moody. 1950 reprint of the 1901 edition.

WESLEY

Wesley, John. *Explanatory notes upon the New Testament.* London: Wesleyan-Methodist Book-room. N.d.

WEYMOUTH

Weymouth, Richard Francis. *The New Testament in Modern Speech:* An idiomatic translation into everyday English from the text of the "Resultant Greek Testament." Revised by J. A. Robertson. London: James Clarke and Co. Ltd. and Harper and Row Publishers Inc. 1908. Reprinted by permission.

WILLIAMS

Williams, Charles B. *The New Testament: A Translation in the Language of the People.* Chicago: Moody Bible Institute of Chicago. 1957. Used by permission of Moody Press. Moody Bible Institute of Chicago. ©1937, 1966 by Mrs. Edith S. Williams.

WILLIAMS C. K.

Williams, Charles Kingsley. *The New Testament: A New Translation in Plain English.* Grand Rapids: William B. Eerdmans Publishing Co. 1963.

WILSON

Wilson, Benjamin. *The Emphatic Diaglott containing the original Greek Text of what is commonly styled the New Testament* (according to the recension of Dr. F.F. Griesback) with interlineary word for word English translation. New York: Fowler & Wells. 1902 reprint edition of the 1864 edition.

WORRELL

Worrell, A.S. *The New Testament: Revised and Translated:* With notes and instructions; designed to aid the earnest reader in obtaining a clear understanding of the doctrines, ordinances, and primitive assemblies as revealed. Louisville, KY: A.S. Worrell. 1904.

WUEST

Wuest, Kenneth S. *The New Testament: An Expanded Translation.* Grand Rapids: Wm. B. Eerdmans Publishing Company. 1961. Used by permission of the publisher. ©1961.

WYCLIF

Wyclif(fe), John. *The Holy Bible containing the Old and New Testaments with the Apocryphal Books:* in the earliest English version made from the Latin Vulgate by John Wycliffe and his followers. London: Reeves and Turner. 1888.

YOUNG

Young, Robert. *Young's Literal Translation of the Holy Bible.* Grand Rapids: Baker Book House. 1953 reprint of the 1898 3rd edition.